D0922984

Economics: New Ways of Thinking

Annotated Teacher's Edition

Roger A. Arnold
California State University San Marcos

St. Paul, Minnesota

Editors: Lance Cooper, Laura Cooper, Cheryl Drivdahl, Ashley Kuehl, Nichola Torbett
Proofreaders: Amy Hanson, Sharon O'Donnell

Electronic Design and Production Manager: Shelley Clubb
Cover Designer: Leslie Anderson
Interior Designer: Hespenheide Design
Production Specialists: Lisa Beller, Matthias Frasch, Petrina Nyhan, Erica Tava

ISBN 0-8219-3402-3

875 Montreal Way
St. Paul, MN 55102
E-mail: educate@emcp.com
Web site: www.emcp.com

Printed in the United States of America

16 15 14 13 12 11 10 09 08 07 XXX 1 2 3 4 5 6 7 8 9 10

PROGRAM OVERVIEW

Surprise Your Students... *Energize* Your Teaching!

Why didn't Chris Rock go to college?

Would you hear hip-hop in a barter economy?

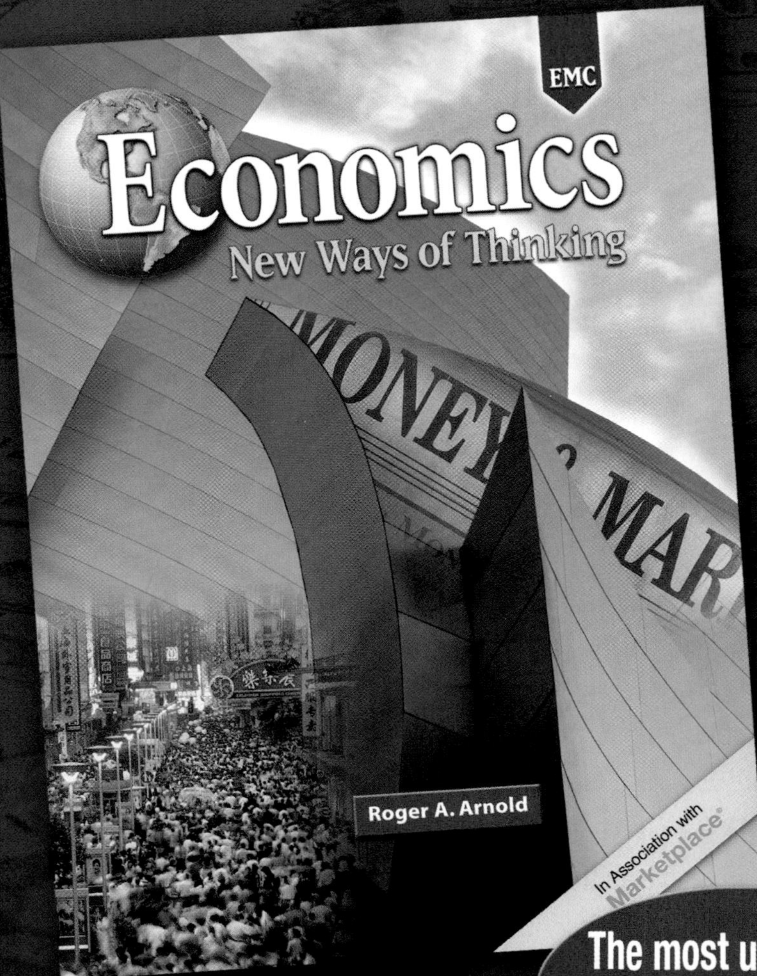

Do seatbelts cause accidents?

Why is the iPod scrollwheel so slick?

The most up-to-date economics textbook available! © 2007

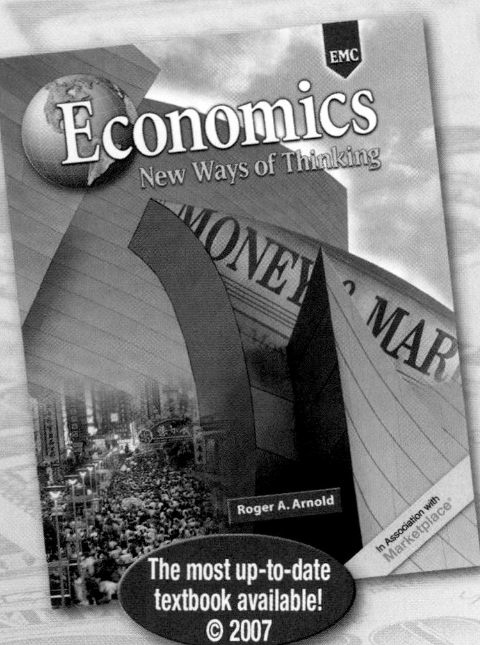

Economics
New Ways of Thinking

Economics: New Ways of Thinking shows students how to find economics in unusual and surprising places. It grabs their attention with **real-world examples** – the NFL draft, rock concert ticket prices, NASCAR – and then provides clear explanations and hundreds of supporting **graphs and charts** to teach students solid economic principles. Students learn these basic principles in the context of **globalization** – the process by which the nations of our world are becoming increasingly integrated.

The unique features of the Student Text *include these:*

- ***Why It Matters*** – Each chapter opens with an explanation of what the subject of that chapter means to economics, society, and students.
- ***Economics Around the Clock*** – Each chapter also opens with short descriptions of daily events that involve economics – accompanied by pertinent questions to help get students thinking.
- ***Economics in the Real World*** – Engaging questions such as "Are you nicer to nice people?" "Why didn't Chris Rock go to college?" and "Why did British troops wear bright red uniforms?" prompt students to learn to think like economists.
- ***A Student Asks*** – Throughout the text, the author anticipates questions students will have as they read, and answers them in friendly, conversational language.
- ***The Global Impact*** – Vignettes in every chapter aim to heighten students' understanding of globalization.
- ***Economics on the Web*** – Links to Web addresses help students find the most current economics data.
- ***By the Numbers*** – Pertinent statistics relate economic concepts to real-world measures.
- ***Quotes*** – Insightful words from economists and economic thinkers provide food for thought and discussion.
- ***Your Personal Economics*** – Topics like the increasing value of education in a global economy, the psychology of credit cards, and how to avoid scams and economic bubbles connect students with economics on a personal level.
- ***Debating the Issues*** – In imaginary conversations, people debate today's economic issues, providing students with a kickoff for class discussion and activities.
- ***Photos and Exhibits*** – Photos and exhibits throughout the text highlight key concepts and pose thought-provoking questions to engage students.
- ***Examples! Examples! Examples!*** – Hundreds of interesting, relevant examples immediately follow the introduction of new concepts.

Use the Complete Program!

- ***Annotated Teacher's Edition*** – chapter planning guides, full teacher support including discussion starters and background information, and assessment materials
- ***Assessment Book*** – two separate tests for every chapter, plus section quizzes
- ***Applying the Principles Workbook*** – multiple activities and exercises for the major economic concepts, with an emphasis on creating and interpreting graphs and charts
- ***Guided Reading and Study Guide*** – outlining activities, and textbook lessons rewritten for students who read below grade level
- ***Lesson Plans*** – detailed lesson plans for every section of the textbook
- ***Daily Lectures: Overheads and Notes*** – full-color transparencies with notes for classroom lectures
- ***Finding Economics*** – fictional short stories embedded with economic principles for students to discover; accompanied by a *Teacher's Edition* that contains suggestions and discussion questions

Energize with Technology!

- ***Test Generator CD*** – test bank and capability to add and edit questions
- ***Spanish Audio Summaries CD*** – summaries, in Spanish, of key points from each section
- ***Marketplace® Audio Lessons CD*** – high-interest segments from national broadcasts of the popular radio program, accompanied by teaching suggestions and tied to chapter content
- ***Economic Principles Lectures on Videocassette and DVD*** – lectures on key economic principles presented by author Roger Arnold for classroom use
- ***Internet Resource Center***
  - ***Current Event Lectures/Lessons*** – new economics lessons based on current events posted throughout the school year by the author and award-winning high school economics teachers
  - ***Study Guide and Practice Tests*** – self-grading review questions to help students prepare for formal assessment
  - ***Lesson Plans*** – lesson plans that teachers can easily edit and print

Economics New Ways of Thinking

Breaks new ground in the teaching of economic principles!

Makes Economics Fun and Exciting for Students

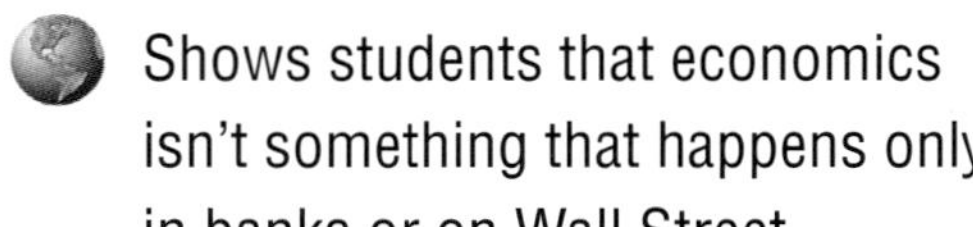

- Shows students that economics isn't something that happens only in banks or on Wall Street.
- Shows students how to think in a new way – to see and use economics in their everyday lives.

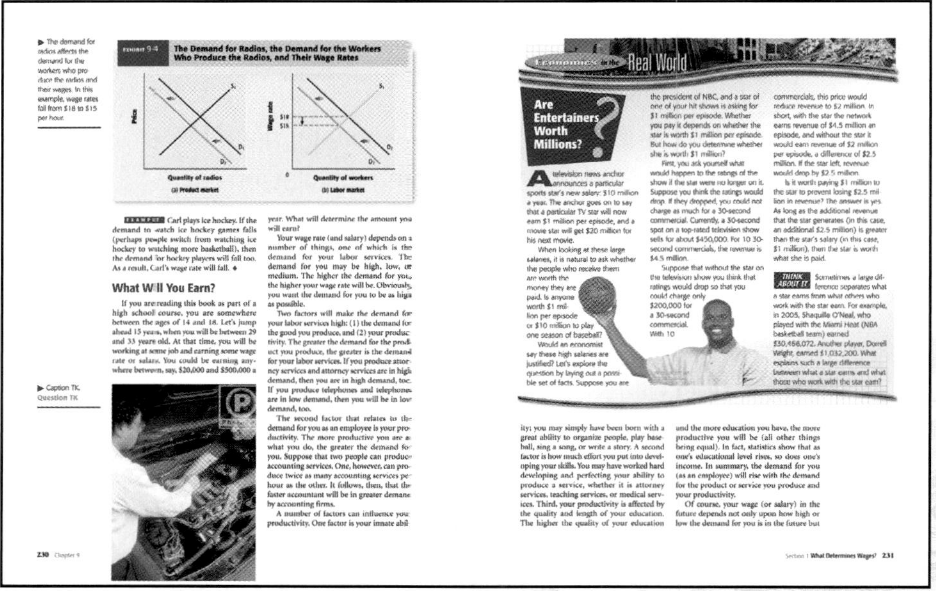

▶ The demand for radios affects the demand for the workers who produce the radios and their wages. In this example, wage rates fall from $18 to $15 per hour.

EXHIBIT 9-4 The Demand for Radios, the Demand for the Workers Who Produce the Radios, and Their Wage Rates

EXAMPLE Carl plays ice hockey. If the demand to watch ice hockey games falls (perhaps people switch from watching ice hockey to watching more basketball), then the demand for hockey players will fall too. As a result, Carl's wage rate will fall. ◆

What Will You Earn?

If you are reading this book as part of a high school course, you are somewhere between the ages of 14 and 18. Let's jump ahead 15 years, when you will be between 29 and 33 years old. At that time, you will be working at some job and earning some wage rate or salary. You could be earning anywhere between, say, $20,000 and $500,000 a year. What will determine the amount you will earn?

Your wage rate (and salary) depends on a number of things, one of which is the demand for your labor services. The demand for you may be high, low, or medium. The higher the demand for you, the higher your wage rate will be. Obviously, you want the demand for you to be as high as possible.

Two factors will make the demand for your labor services high: (1) the demand for the good you produce, and (2) your productivity. The greater the demand for the product you produce, the greater is the demand for your labor services. If you produce attorney services and attorney services are in high demand, then you are in high demand, too. If you produce telephones and telephones are in low demand, then you will be in low demand, too.

The second factor that relates to the demand for you as an employee is your productivity. The more productive you are at what you do, the greater the demand for you. Suppose that two people can produce accounting services. One, however, can produce twice as many accounting services per hour as the other. It follows, then, that the faster accountant will be in greater demand by accounting firms.

A number of factors can influence your productivity. One factor is your innate ability; you may simply have been born with a great ability to organize people, play baseball, sing a song, or write a story. A second factor is how much effort you put into developing your skills. You may have worked hard developing and perfecting your ability to produce a service, whether it is attorney services, teaching services, or medical services. Third, your productivity is affected by the quality and length of your education. The higher the quality of your education and the more education you have, the more productive you will be (all other things being equal). In fact, statistics show that as one's educational level rises, so does one's income. In summary, the demand for you (as an employee) will rise with the demand for the product or service you produce and your productivity.

Of course, your wage (or salary) in the future depends not only upon how high or low the demand for you is in the future but

▶ Caption TK. Question TK

230 Chapter 9

Economics in the Real World

Are Entertainers Worth Millions?

A television news anchor announces a particular sports star's new salary: $10 million a year. The anchor goes on to say that a particular TV star will now earn $1 million per episode, and a movie star will get $20 million for his next movie.

When looking at these large salaries, it is natural to ask whether the people who receive them are worth the money they are paid. Is anyone worth $1 million per episode or $10 million to play one season of baseball?

Would an economist say these high salaries are justified? Let's explore the question by laying out a possible set of facts. Suppose you are the president of NBC, and a star of one of your hit shows is asking for $1 million per episode. Whether you pay it depends on whether the star is worth $1 million per episode. But how do you determine whether she is worth $1 million?

First, you ask yourself what would happen to the ratings of the show if the star were no longer on it. Suppose you think the ratings would drop. If they dropped, you could not charge as much for a 30-second commercial. Currently, a 30-second spot on a top-rated television show sells for about $450,000. For 10 30-second commercials, the revenue is $4.5 million.

Suppose that without the star on the television show you think that ratings would drop so that you could charge only $200,000 for a 30-second commercial. With 10 commercials, this price would reduce revenue to $2 million. In short, with the star the network earns revenue of $4.5 million an episode, and without the star it would earn revenue of $2 million per episode, a difference of $2.5 million. If the star left, revenue would drop by $2.5 million.

Is it worth paying $1 million to the star to prevent losing $2.5 million in revenue? The answer is yes. As long as the additional revenue that the star generates (in this case, an additional $2.5 million) is greater than the star's salary (in this case, $1 million), then the star is worth what she is paid.

THINK ABOUT IT Sometimes a large difference separates what a star earns from what others who work with the star earn. For example, in 2005, Shaquille O'Neal, who played with the Miami Heat (NBA basketball team) earned $30,456,072. Another player, Dorrell Wright, earned $1,032,200. What explains such a large difference between what a star earns and what those who work with the star earn?

Section 1 What Determines Wages? 231

Opens Students' Eyes to the Impact of Globalization

- Charts and graphs bring economics alive and help students think like economists.
- A chapter dedicated to global economics combines a discussion of economic systems and an introduction to the causes, benefits, and costs of globalization.

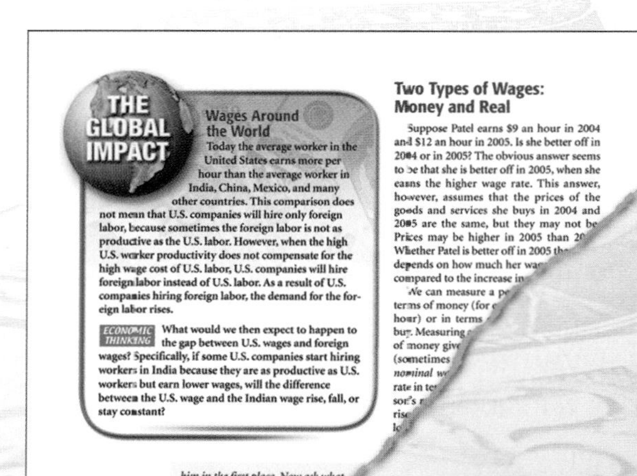

THE GLOBAL IMPACT

Wages Around the World

Today the average worker in the United States earns more per hour than the average worker in India, China, Mexico, and many other countries. This comparison does not mean that U.S. companies will hire only foreign labor, because sometimes the foreign labor is not as productive as the U.S. labor. However, when the high U.S. worker productivity does not compensate for the high wage cost of U.S. labor, U.S. companies will hire foreign labor instead of U.S. labor. As a result of U.S. companies hiring foreign labor, the demand for the foreign labor rises.

ECONOMIC THINKING What would we then expect to happen to the gap between U.S. wages and foreign wages? Specifically, if some U.S. companies start hiring workers in India because they are as productive as U.S. workers but earn lower wages, will the difference between the U.S. wage and the Indian wage rise, fall, or stay constant?

Two Types of Wages: Money and Real

Suppose Patel earns $9 an hour in 2004 and $12 an hour in 2005. Is she better off in 2004 or in 2005? The obvious answer seems to be that she is better off in 2005, when she earns the higher wage rate. This answer, however, assumes that the prices of the goods and services she buys in 2004 and 2005 are the same, but they may not be. Prices may be higher in 2005 than 20 Whether Patel is better off in 2005 th depends on how much her wa compared to the increase in

We can measure a p terms of money (for hour) or in terms buy. Measuring of money giv (sometimes nominal w rate in te son's rise lo

him in the first place. Now ask what happens if the minimum wage is scrapped. Do the 100 people wh earning $5.15 find themsel only $2 an hour? Not hired when the wa at $5.15, then th $5.15 an hour them $2 to wo th

- Global Impact features in every chapter relate globalization to wages, employment, productivity, and trade.

Other economics textbooks talk about isolated economic activities in countries around the globe. Only EMC's economics textbook teaches about globalization – the ways in which world economies are becoming more and more interrelated.

CORRELATION

of the Voluntary National Content Standards in Economics

to *Economics: New Ways of Thinking*

Several organizations involved with economics education worked together to produce the Voluntary National Content Standards in Economics as a guide to economics instruction in American schools. These groups included the National Council on Economic Education and its network of councils and centers, the Foundation for Teaching Economics, the National Association of Economic Educators, and the American Economic Association's Committee on Economic Education. The table on pages ATE8–ATE11 shows the chapters, sections, and special features in *Economics: New Ways of Thinking* that support the teaching of the 20 Voluntary National Content Standards in Economics.

Content Standards	Chapter and Section Coverage	Special Feature Coverage
Standard 1 **Scarcity** Productive resources are limited. Therefore, people cannot have all the goods and services they want; as a result, they must choose some things and give up others.	Chapter 1, Section 1 Chapter 1, Section 3 Chapter 2, Section 1 Chapter 3, Section 4 Chapter 12, Section 3 Chapter 15, Section 1	▸ Why Didn't Chris Rock Go to College? 9 ▸ Why Did British Troops Wear Bright Red Uniforms? 26 ▸ Working After School: What Are the Trade-Offs? 84 ▸ Will You Sleep Less if You Earn More? 241 ▸ Can Economic Growth Eliminate Politics? 333
Standard 2 **Marginal Cost/Benefit** Effective decision making requires comparing the additional costs of alternatives with the additional benefits. Most choices involve doing a little more or a little less of something; few choices are "all or nothing" decisions.	Chapter 1, Section 2 Chapter 7, Section 3 Chapter 8, Section 1	▸ Why Is It So Easy to Put on Weight? 174 ▸ How Much Time Should You Study? 182 ▸ Will You Sleep Less if You Earn More? 241
Standard 3 **Allocation of Goods and Services** Different methods can be used to allocate goods and services. People, acting individually or collectively through government, must choose which methods to use to allocate different kinds of goods and services.	Chapter 2, Section 1 Chapter 3, Section 1 Chapter 3, Section 2 Chapter 15, Section 4	▸ Do People Around the World Work the Same Number of Hours? 34 ▸ What Should I Tip? 38 ▸ Where Do TiVo, Podcasts, and Blogs Come From? 118
Standard 4 **Role of Incentives** People respond predictably to positive and negative incentives.	Chapter 1, Section 2 Chapter 3, Section 1 Chapter 3, Section 2 Chapter 3, Section 3 Chapter 3, Section 4 Chapter 5, Section 1	▸ What Saved the Pilgrims? 64 ▸ Did the Airlines Overlook the Overbooking Problem? 69 ▸ Why Is the iPod Scrollwheel So Slick? 72
Standard 5 **Gain from Trade** Voluntary exchange occurs only when all participating parties expect to gain. This is true for trade among individuals or organizations within a nation, and usually among individuals or organizations in different nations.	Chapter 1, Section 2 Chapter 2, Section 2 Chapter 3, Section 1 Chapter 4, Section 1 Chapter 6, Section 1 Chapter 10, Section 1 Chapter 15, Section 1 Chapter 15, Section 3	▸ Would You Hear Hip-Hop in a Barter Economy? 259 ▸ What Is Money in a Prisoner of War Camp? 266 ▸ Might Someone in India Grade Your Homework? 410 ▸ Is Free Trade the Best Policy for the United States? 458
Standard 6 **Specialization and Trade** When individuals, regions, and nations specialize in what they can produce at the lowest cost and then trade with others, both production and consumption increase.	Chapter 2, Section 2 Chapter 10, Section 1 Chapter 15, Section 1	▸ To Mow, or Clean, or Both? 399 ▸ Might Someone in India Grade Your Homework? 410

Content Standards	Chapter and Section Coverage	Special Feature Coverage
Standard 7 **Markets—Price and Quantity Determination** Markets exist when buyers and sellers interact. This interaction determines market prices and thereby allocates scarce goods and services.	Chapter 1, Section 2 Chapter 4, Section 1 Chapter 5, Section 1 Chapter 6, Section 1 Chapter 6, Section 2	► Are the Prices at Disneyland Goofy? 92 ► New Coke, Classic Coke, or Pepsi? 98 ► How Much Would You Pay for an Ocean View? 133
Standard 8 **Role of Price in Market System** Prices send signals and provide incentives to buyers and sellers. When supply or demand changes, market prices adjust, affecting incentives.	Chapter 2, Section 1 Chapter 4, Section 1 Chapter 4, Section 2 Chapter 5, Section 1 Chapter 5, Section 2 Chapter 6, Section 1 Chapter 6, Section 2	► The Price Gap Between Brains and Brawn: Is It Increasing? 48 ► Are You Nicer to Nice People? 113 ► Why All the Reality TV Shows? 114 ► How Much Would You Pay for an Ocean View? 133 ► Who Feeds Cleveland? 144
Standard 9 **Role of Competition** Competition among sellers lowers costs and prices, and encourages producers to produce more of what consumers are willing and able to buy. Competition among buyers increases prices and allocates goods and services to those people who are willing and able to pay the most for them.	Chapter 2, Section 2 Chapter 3, Section 1 Chapter 3, Section 4 Chapter 7, Section 1 Chapter 8, Section 1 Chapter 8, Section 2	► The Price Gap Between Brains and Brawn: Is It Increasing? 48 ► Should NASCAR Be Required for an MBA? 161
Standard 10 **Role of Economic Institutions** Institutions evolve in market economies to help individuals and groups accomplish their goals. Banks, labor unions, corporations, legal systems, and not-for-profit organizations are examples of important institutions. A different kind of institution, clearly defined and enforced property rights, is essential to a market economy.	Chapter 3, Section 1 Chapter 3, Section 5 Chapter 7, Section 1 Chapter 8, Section 3 Chapter 9, Section 2 Chapter 10, Section 2 Chapter 10, Section 4	► What Saved the Pilgrims? 64 ► Why Does McDonald's Put Hash Browns In Half-Sized Bags? 80 ► What Is Money in a Prisoner of War Camp? 266
Standard 11 **Role of Money** Money makes it easier to trade, borrow, save, invest, and compare the value of goods and services.	Chapter 10, Section 1 Chapter 10, Section 2 Chapter 10, Section 3 Chapter 10, Section 4 Chapter 10, Section 5	► Spend a Little Now, or a Lot More Later? 22 ► Investing in Yourself 124 ► Would You Hear Hip-Hop in a Barter Economy? 259 ► What Is Money in a Prisoner of War Camp? 266 ► How Is the English Language Like Money? 278
Standard 12 **Role of Interest Rates** Interest rates, adjusted for inflation, rise and fall to balance the amount saved with the amount borrowed, which affects the allocation of scarce resources between present and future uses.	Chapter 10, Section 1 Chapter 12, Section 1 Chapter 13, Section 2 Chapter 16, Section 2	► Spend a Little Now, or a Lot More Later? 22 ► Investing in Yourself 124 ► The Psychology of Credit Cards 268 ► Can Monetary Policy Determine Eye Color? 352

Content Standards	Chapter and Section Coverage	Special Feature Coverage
Standard 13 **Role of Resources in Determining Income** Income for most people is determined by the market value of the productive resources they sell. What workers earn depends, primarily, on the market value of what they produce and how productive they are.	Chapter 2, Section 1 Chapter 9, Section 1 Chapter 9, Section 2 Chapter 11, Section 4	► Are Entertainers Worth Millions? 231 ► Education—It's Like Multiplying Yourself 236 ► Will You Sleep Less if You Earn More? 241 ► Your Goal: Generic, Not Specific, Human Capital 336
Standard 14 **Profit and the Entrepreneur** Entrepreneurs are people who take the risks of organizing productive resources to make goods and services. Profit is an important incentive that leads entrepreneurs to accept the risks of business failure.	Chapter 1, Section 2 Chapter 3, Section 1 Chapter 3, Section 4 Chapter 7, Section 2 Chapter 14, Section 1	► The Price Gap Between Brains and Brawn: Is It Increasing? 48 ► Why Is the iPod Scrollwheel So Slick? 72
Standard 15 **Growth** Investment in factories, machinery, new technology, and in the health, education, and training of people can raise future standards of living.	Chapter 2, Section 1 Chapter 3, Section 3 Chapter 12, Section 3 Chapter 16, Section 1 Chapter 16, Section 2	► Spend a Little Now, or a Lot More Later? 22 ► Investing in Yourself 124 ► Your Goal: Generic, Not Specific, Human Capital 336
Standard 16 **Role of Government** There is an economic role for government in a market economy whenever the benefits of a government policy outweigh its costs. Governments often provide for national defense, address environmental concerns, define and protect property rights, and attempt to make markets more competitive. Most government policies also redistribute income.	Chapter 3, Section 5 Chapter 9, Section 2 Chapter 14, Section 1 Chapter 14, Section 2	► Should There Be Price Controls on Some Goods at Certain Times? 152 ► Should There Be a Minimum Wage? 250 ► Why Does the Public Know So Little About Economic Policy? 358 ► What Is Government's Role When It Comes to the Economy? 388
Standard 17 **Using Cost/Benefit Analysis to Evaluate Government Programs** Costs of government policies sometimes exceed benefits. This may occur because of incentives facing voters, government officials, and government employees, because of actions by special interest groups that can impose costs on the general public, or because social goals other than economic efficiency are being pursued.	Chapter 14, Section 1 Chapter 14, Section 2 Chapter 15, Section 2	► Why Does the Public Know So Little About Economic Policy? 358 ► Are You Paying Someone Else's Taxes? 368 ► What Is Government's Role When It Comes to the Economy? 388 ► Is Free Trade the Best Policy for the United States? 458

Content Standards	Chapter and Section Coverage	Special Feature Coverage
Standard 18 **Macroeconomy—Income/Employment, Prices** A nation's overall levels of income, employment, and prices are determined by the interaction of spending and production decisions made by all households, firms, government agencies, and others in the economy.	Chapter 3, Section 1 Chapter 11, Section 1 Chapter 11, Section 2 Chapter 11, Section 3 Chapter 11, Section 4	► Is There Real GDP Growth in Your Future? 299 ► Did President Kennedy Earn More than Today's President? 304 ► What Is the All-Time Top-Grossing Movie? 306
Standard 19 **Unemployment and Inflation** Unemployment imposes costs on individuals and nations. Unexpected inflation imposes costs on many people and benefits some others because it arbitrarily redistributes purchasing power. Inflation can reduce the rate of growth of national living standards because individuals and organizations use resources to protect themselves against the uncertainty of future prices.	Chapter 11, Section 4 Chapter 12, Section 1 Chapter 12, Section 2	► Grade Inflation: When Is a B+ No Better than a C? 318 ► Can You Have "Too Much Money"? 321 ► Did the Great Depression Change the Country? 327
Standard 20 **Monetary and Fiscal Policy** Federal government budgetary policy and the Federal Reserve System's monetary policy influence the overall levels of employment, output, and prices.	Chapter 10, Section 3 Chapter 13, Section 1 Chapter 13, Section 2 Chapter 13, Section 3 Chapter 14, Section 1	► Can Monetary Policy Determine Eye Color? 352 ► What Is *The Wizard of Oz* Really About? 354 ► Do Tax Rates Affect Athletic Performance? 371 ► Are You Paying Someone Else's Taxes? 368

Economics

New Ways of Thinking

Roger A. Arnold
California State University San Marcos

St. Paul, Minnesota

Cover Photographs: The Walt Disney Concert Hall © Ted Soqui/Corbis, Shanghai © Bob Krist/Corbis
Cover Design: Leslie Anderson
Copyeditor: Cheryl Wilms
Proofreader: Michele Gitlin

Interior Design and Production: Hespenheide Design
Production: Patti Zeman, Christine Rocha, Robert Alexander
Illustration: Randy Miyake, Bruce Miyake
Photo Research: Natalie Richmond
Proofreader: Bridget Neumayr

ISBN 0-8219-3401-5

875 Montreal Way
St. Paul, MN 55102
E-mail: educate@emcp.com
Web site: www.emcp.com

Printed in the United States of America

16 15 14 13 12 11 10 09 08 07 XXX 1 2 3 4 5 6 7 8 9 10

About the Author

Professor Roger Arnold is first and foremost an economics educator, having taught a variety of economics courses at several major universities. He has also served for many years as Director for a Center for Economic Education. He currently teaches at California State University in San Marcos, California.

Professor Arnold received his Bachelor of Social Science degree from the University of Birmingham, England, and his Master's and Doctorate degrees from Virginia Polytechnic Institute and State University. He completed his Ph.D. dissertation under Nobel Laureate James M. Buchanan.

Professor Arnold is an experienced teacher, researcher, and writer. He has written numerous successful textbooks, as well as articles and columns for the *Wall Street Journal* and other respected publications.

Dedication

To Sheila, Daniel, and David

Content Reviewers and Program Contributors

Michael Eggers
Sunnyside High School
Fresno, California

Lars Johannson
McClane High School
Fresno, California

Ken Karrer
LBJ High School
Austin, Texas

Jeanne Leslie
Avon Grove High School
West Grove, Pennsylvania

Donna McCreadie
Temple City High School
Temple City, California

Jeanne McNamara
Foundation for Teaching Economics
Davis, California

Tara O'Brien
EconomicsPennsylvania
Pittsburg, Pennsylvania

Stephen E. Reilly, PhD
Haverford High School
Havertown, Pennsylvania

Larry Robinette
Broken Arrow High School
Broken Arrow, Oklahoma

Brad Siegel
Scotch Plains-Fanwood School District
Scotch Plains, New Jersey

Scott Wolla
Hibbing High School
Hibbing, Minnesota

vi

Contents in Brief

vii

Contents

UNIT I

Introduction to Economics 2

UNIT II

The Basics 86

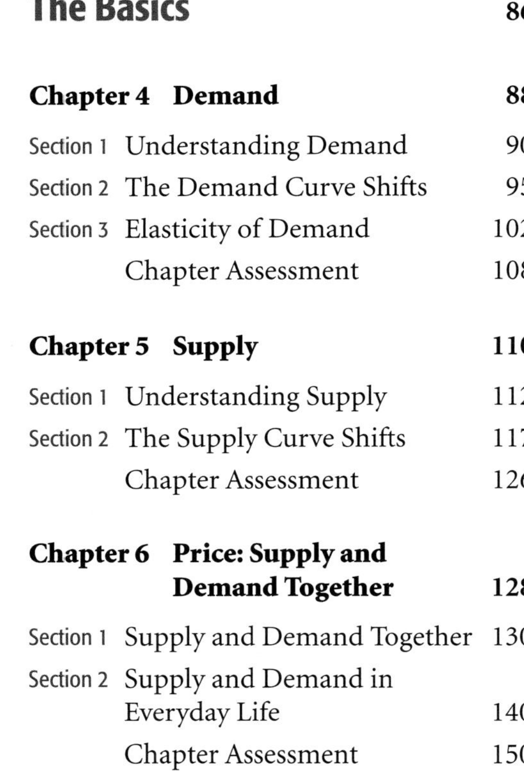

UNIT III

Microeconomics 154

UNIT IV

Macroeconomics 252

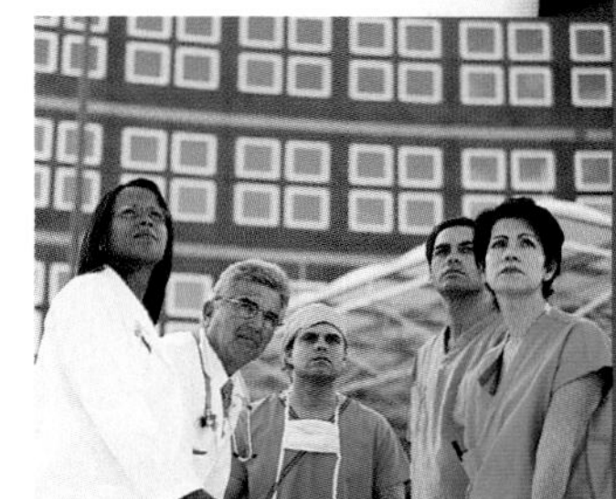

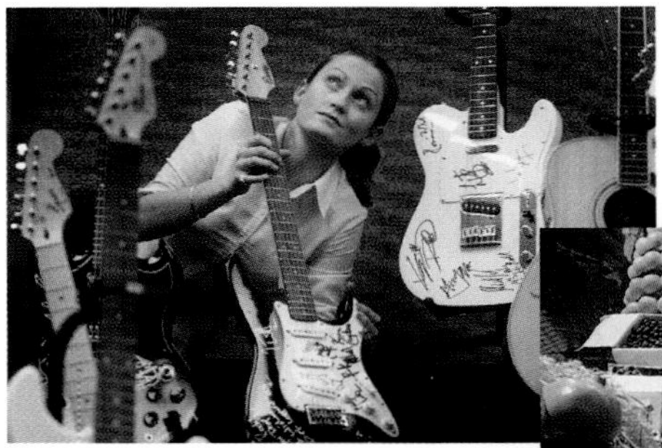

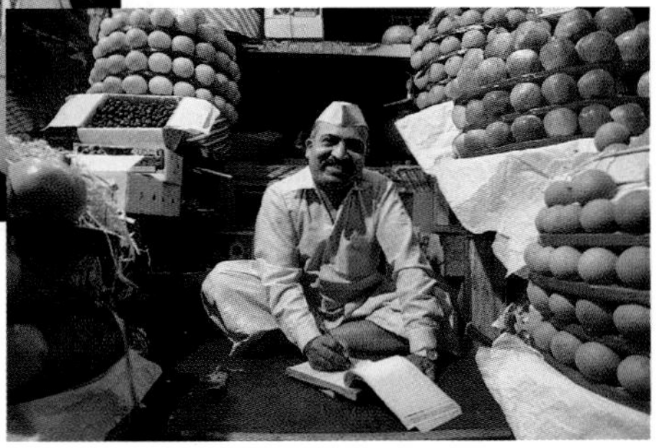

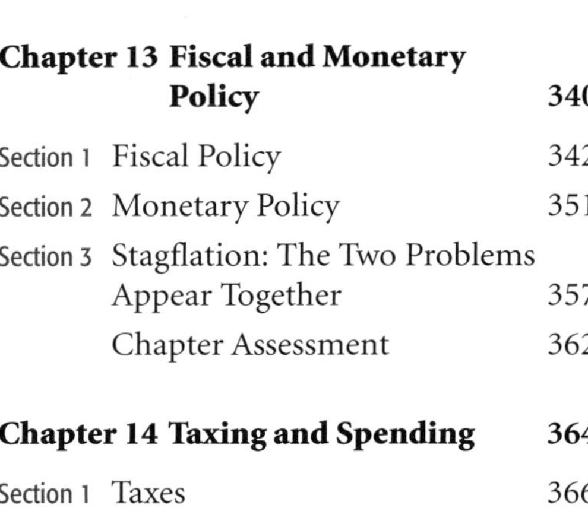

Trade and Investment 390

Resource Center

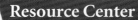

Economics in the Real World

Your Personal Economics

The Global Impact

Debating the Issues

Exhibits

xiii

Introduction

Economics can be either boring or exciting, depending on *how* it is presented. Increasingly, I have come to believe that the right way to present economics is to *surprise* students and readers.

Perhaps you come to the study of economics with low expectations; perhaps you think that economics will be a dull and dry subject. If so, you will be surprised when you see that

- economics often occurs in the unlikeliest places;
- what happens on the other side of the world is linked to you through economic channels; and
- economics can answer your questions.

Economics Often Occurs in the Unlikeliest Places

Most people think that economics occurs only on Wall Street; in Washington, D.C.; on the factory floor; in a bank; or in a conference room at a major corporation. Economics is in all these places, but it is in many other places too.

Economics is in the classroom, at the beach, at a NASCAR race, and at a basketball game. You can find economics on a trip to Disneyland, on a television show, on a freeway, and even in your sleep. Economics pops up almost everywhere.

A major best seller in 2005 was *Freakonomics,* by Steven Levitt and Stephen Dubner. It isn't your ordinary economics book. It isn't about economic growth, exchange rates, or inflation. It isn't about interest rates, unemployment, or free trade. It is about things like sumo wrestlers and drug dealers and parents who have children in day care. Levitt and Dubner get people excited about economics because they show their readers all the unlikely places that economics can and does pop up. No doubt, readers go away from the book saying, "I didn't know economics had so many interesting things to say about the everyday world that I live in."

In this book—*Economics: New Ways of Thinking*—we want not only to present good, solid economics to you, but to show you how powerfully economic analysis explains many of the things that you encounter in your life. If you take a quick look at the features in this book, you will realize that this isn't your father's or grandfather's economics book. Those books didn't apply economic analysis to surfing or senioritis—but this one does. Those books didn't apply economic analysis to football picks, iPods, friendship, and hundreds of other things—but this one does. What is our objective in using economics to talk about everyday things? Is it simply to get your attention? Not at all. It is to show you just how important economic thinking is to your everyday life. It is to show you just how important learning economics can be to your understanding of the world you inhabit.

What Happens on the Other Side of the World Is Linked to You Through Economic Channels

You don't live in the same economy that people lived in during the 1920s, or 1950s, or even 1980s. You live in a different kind of economy; you live in a global economy. You live in an economy in which what happens in China or India or Russia can touch your economic life in a matter of seconds. Any current economics textbook that doesn't discuss economic globalization and the global economy is not worth its price. To overlook globalization in an economics course today is to miss out on what makes today different from yesterday.

No doubt about it: *globalization* has become a buzzword. People talk about "globalizing" this and that, and say the "global economy" is moving this way and that way. Sometimes, you get the feeling that globalization and the global economy are fads, and will go away soon enough.

But they are not fads. And even though *globalization* has become a buzzword, it describes an economic process of which students today should be aware. In this book, we discuss globalization and the global economy in a deep and meaningful way: a way that shows you just how globalization affects you.

Economics Can Answer Your Questions

You walk into a store and pay $14 for a CD. Would you like to know why you didn't pay a lower or a higher price? Economics has the answer.

You read that a movie star earns $20 million a film and that a secretary at a real estate firm earns $22,000 a year. Do you want to know why the movie star earns so much more than the secretary? Economics has the answer.

You discover that housing prices are higher in San Francisco, California, than in Louisville, Kentucky. Do you want to know why? Economics has the answer.

Even though wages are lower in Mexico than in the United States, thousands of U.S. firms hire workers in the United States instead of hiring workers in Mexico. Do you want to know why? Economics has the answer.

There are literally hundreds of such questions that economics can answer for you.

Paul Samuelson (b. 1915) was the first American economist to win the Nobel Prize in Economic Sciences. He once said that setting out to explore the exciting world of economics for the first time is a unique thrill. You are about to set out to explore the world of economics, perhaps for the first time. You may not know what awaits you, but those of us who have passed this way before know. We know that you are in for a very special time. You are likely to be surprised at how much you learn about your world in just a few months. And you know something else? You're likely to be pleasantly surprised at how much fun you have along the way.

Economics

New Ways of Thinking

CHAPTER 1
What Is Economics?

CHAPTER 2
Economic Systems and the Global Economy

CHAPTER 3
Free Enterprise

Foundations for the Unit

Unit 1 begins your students' journey into the world of economics. In this unit, your students will learn some of the basic concepts on which the study of economics is built. Among those concepts are scarcity, opportunity cost, supply, demand, and price. It is hoped that as your students work through Unit 1, they will also begin to understand how the study of economics can broaden their appreciation of the world around them by helping them engage in the economic way of thinking.

UNIT I

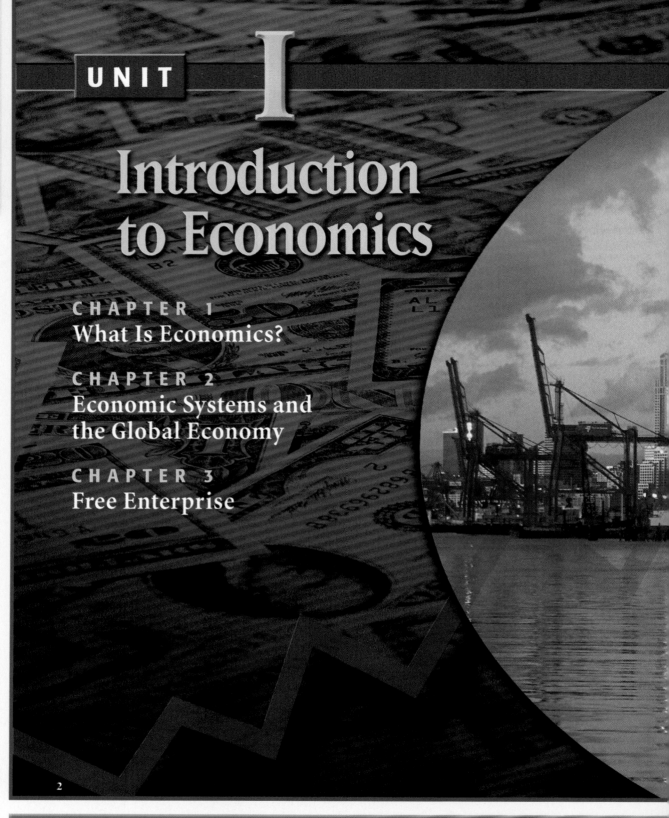

Introduction to Economics

CHAPTER 1
What Is Economics?

CHAPTER 2
Economic Systems and the Global Economy

CHAPTER 3
Free Enterprise

2

Resources for the Unit

Books

Buchholz, Todd G. *New Ideas from Dead Economists.* New York: Penguin Books, 1989.

Smith, Adam. *An Inquiry into the Nature and Causes of the Wealth of Nations.* Chicago: University of Chicago Press, 1976.

Articles

Scahill, Edward M. "Did Babe Ruth Have a Comparative Advantage As a Pitcher?" *The Journal of Economic Education,* Fall 1990, vol. 21(4), pp. 402–410.

Tinari, Frank D., and Kailash Khandke. "From Rhythm 'n' Blues to Broadway: Using Music to Teach Economics," *Journal of Economic Education*, Summer 2000, vol. 31(3).

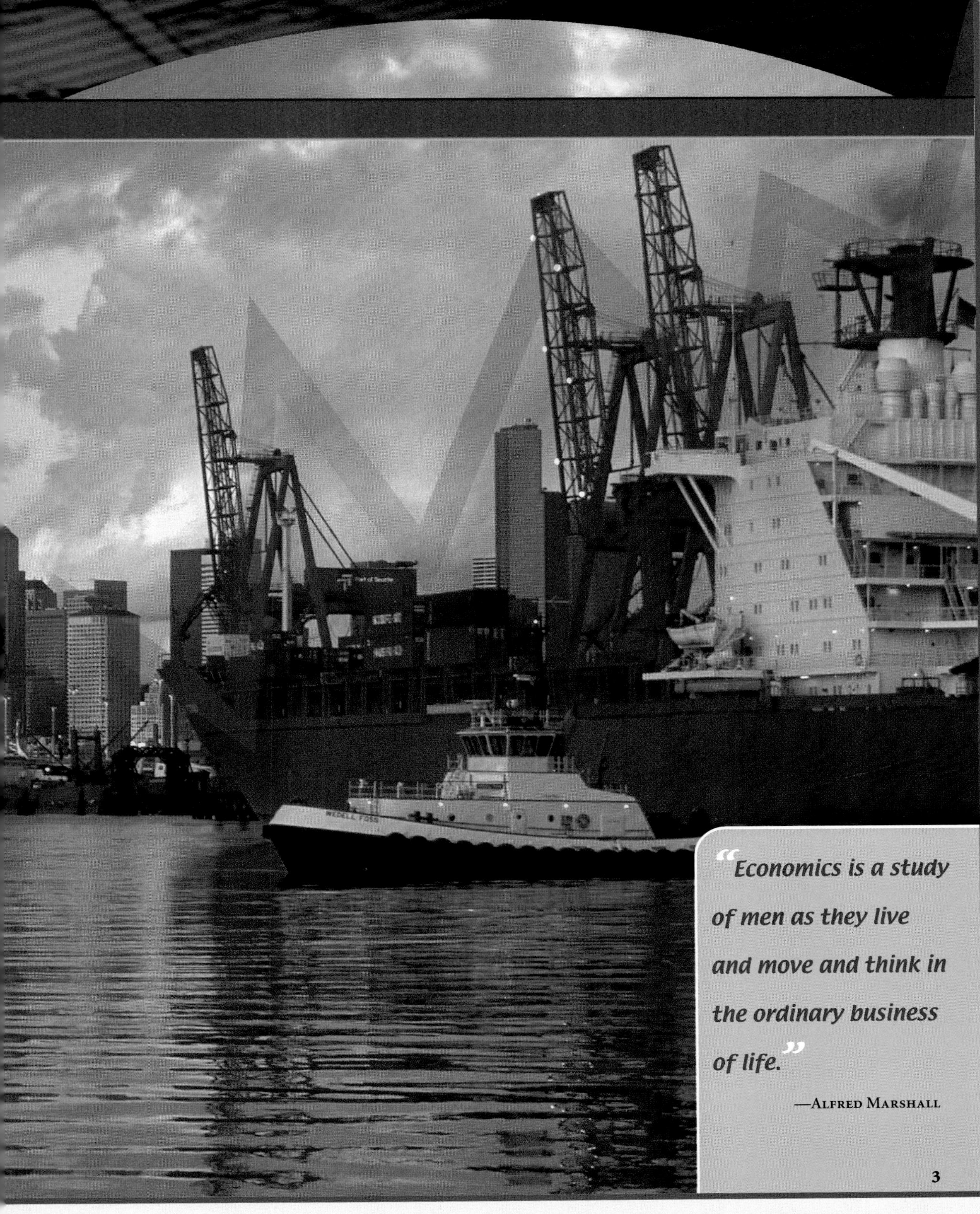

"Economics is a study of men as they live and move and think in the ordinary business of life."

—Alfred Marshall

3

Introducing the Unit

You might want to introduce Unit 1 by writing the word *economics* on the chalkboard. Ask the students to list the first 10 words that come to their minds when they look at the word *economics*. After they have had a few minutes to compose their lists, ask students to share their lists. You might have a volunteer keep a running list for the class, noting each time a particular word, such as *money*, is mentioned. No matter which words your students name, those terms are likely to be related to economics, since economics is a field of study that relates to much of our lives.

Performance Task

All students should keep running journals of any purchases they make during the time they study Unit 1. As each chapter is completed, students should write a brief essay examining one of those purchases, using their newly acquired understanding of economics. For example, after studying Chapter 1, each student should examine how the choice of a particular purchase was influenced by the condition of scarcity and should describe his or her opportunity cost in making that purchasing choice.

Encourage students to refer to as many economic topics as possible in their essays. You might particularly stress that students should use the skills and concepts acquired through the study of the special features found in this unit.

Multimedia

The Art of a Balanced Budget. In *Understanding Free Market Economics: Lessons Learned in the Former Soviet Union.* VHS. Films for the Humanities and Sciences.

Economics at Work. Videos, videodiscs, and simulation software. National Council on Economics Education.

Introductory Economics. 17-part series. Hosted by Ellen Roseman and John Palmer of the University of Western Ontario. Films for the Humanities and Sciences.

Thinking Economics. CDs, simulation software, and study guide. National Council on Economic Education.

Chapter 1 Planning Guide

SECTION ORGANIZER

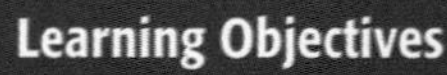

Section	Learning Objectives	Reproducible Worksheets and Handouts	Assessment
 **The Foundation of Economics** (pages 6–12)	► Explain how choice is related to scarcity. ► Provide examples of opportunity costs. ► Understand a production possibilities frontier. ► Describe how competition determines the way rationing devices are distributed.	 Section 1 Activity, *Applying the Principles Workbook*  Outlining Activity, *Guided Reading and Study Guide* Just the Facts Handout, *Guided Reading and Study Guide*	Section Assessment, *Student Text,* page 12 Quick Quiz, *Annotated Teacher's Edition,* page 11 Section Quiz, *Assessment Book*
 **The Economic Way of Thinking** (pages 13–21)	► Explain how costs and benefits affect decisions. ► Identify incentives. ► Distinguish between microeconomics and macroeconomics. ► Explain why economists develop theories.	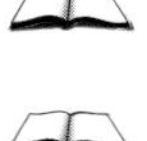 Section 2 Activity, *Applying the Principles Workbook* Outlining Activity, *Guided Reading and Study Guide* Just the Facts Handout, *Guided Reading and Study Guide*	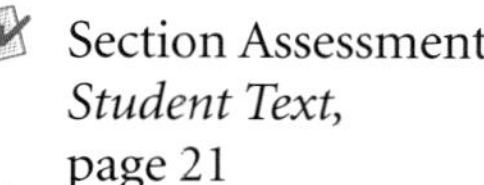 Section Assessment, *Student Text,* page 21 Quick Quiz, *Annotated Teacher's Edition,* page 21 Section Quiz, *Assessment Book*
 **Basic Economic Language** (pages 24–27)	► Describe the different ways economists talk about goods. ► Identify services. ► List the four types of resources. ► Explain why labor and entrepreneurship are different categories of resources.	 Section 3 Activity, *Applying the Principles Workbook* Outlining Activity, *Guided Reading and Study Guide* 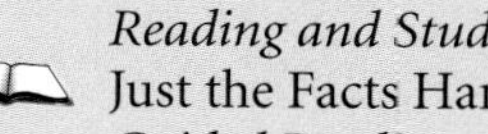 Just the Facts Handout, *Guided Reading and Study Guide*	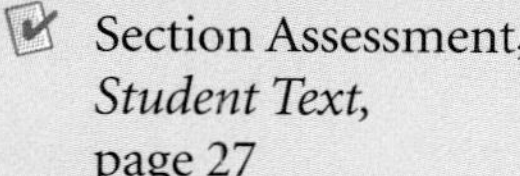 Section Assessment, *Student Text,* page 27 Quick Quiz, *Annotated Teacher's Edition,* page 27 Section Quiz, *Assessment Book*

CHAPTER AND PROGRAM RESOURCES

Reproducible Chapter Resources and Assessment Materials

- Graphic Organizer Activity, *Guided Reading and Study Guide*
- Vocabulary Activity, *Guided Reading and Study Guide*

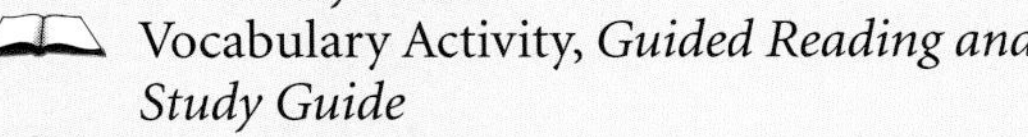

- Working with Graphs and Charts, *Guided Reading and Study Guide*
- Practice Test, *Guided Reading and Study Guide*
- Critical Thinking Activity, *Finding Economics*

- Chapter Test A, *Assessment Book*
- Chapter Test B, *Assessment Book*

Technology Resources

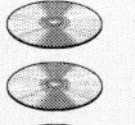

- *Test Generator CD*
- *Spanish Audio Summaries CD*
- *Marketplace® Audio Lessons CD*
- *Economic Principles Lectures, Videocassette or DVD*

Lesson Planning and Teaching Resources

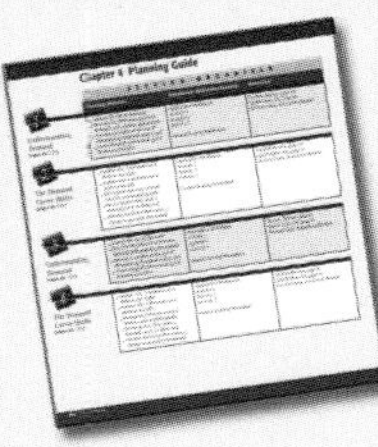

The *Economics: New Ways of Thinking* Teacher Resources include detailed lesson plans for each section in this chapter; the lesson plans are available in print form *(Lesson Plans)* and electronic form. The Teacher Resources also include *Daily Lectures: Overheads and Notes,* which provides prepared overheads and discussion notes covering the key concepts in each section of this chapter.

EMC Publishing Economics Online

Go to Economics Online, at www.emcp.com, for a variety of Internet resources to help you keep your course current and relevant. At Economics Online you will find these items:

- Economics in the News Lessons
- Study Guide Questions
- Practice Tests
- Lesson Plans

Internet Resources

Economics: New Ways of Thinking encourages students to use the Internet to find out more about economics. With the wealth of current, valid information available on Web sites, using the Internet as a research tool is likely to increase your students' interest in and understanding of economics principles and topics. In addition, doing Internet research can help your students form the habit of accessing and using economics information, as well as help them develop investigative skills they will use throughout their educational and professional careers.

To aid your students in achieving these ends, each chapter of *Economics: New Ways of Thinking* includes the addresses of several Web sites at which students will find engaging, relevant information. When students type in the addresses provided, they will immediately arrive at the intended sites. The addresses have been modified so that EMC Publishing can monitor and maintain the proper links—for example, the government site http://stats.bls.gov/ has been changed to www.emcp.net/prices. In the event that the address or content of a site changes or is discontinued, EMC's Internet editors will create a link that redirects students to an address with similar information.

Activities in the *Annotated Teacher's Edition* often suggest that students search the Internet for information. For some activities, you might want to find reputable sites beforehand, and steer students to those sites. For other activities, you might want students to do their own searching, and then check out the sites they have found and discuss why they might be reliable or unreliable.

CHAPTER 1 Overview

This chapter introduces a few of the most important concepts that form the foundation of economics. This is the first of three chapters in which students learn about the basics of economics, economic systems, and free enterprise. The following statements provide brief descriptions of the major concepts covered in each section of this chapter.

The Foundation of Economics

Section 1 deals with the backbone of all economic thinking, scarcity and choice. Students learn how scarcity of resources creates the need for making choices, and how those choices lead to opportunity costs.

The Economic Way of Thinking

Section 2 explores cost-benefit decisions and the differences between microeconomics and macroeconomics. Students also learn why economists develop theories, and what purposes those theories serve.

Basic Economic Language

Section 3 introduces the four types of economic resources: land, labor, capital, and entrepreneurship.

CHAPTER 1 What Is Economics?

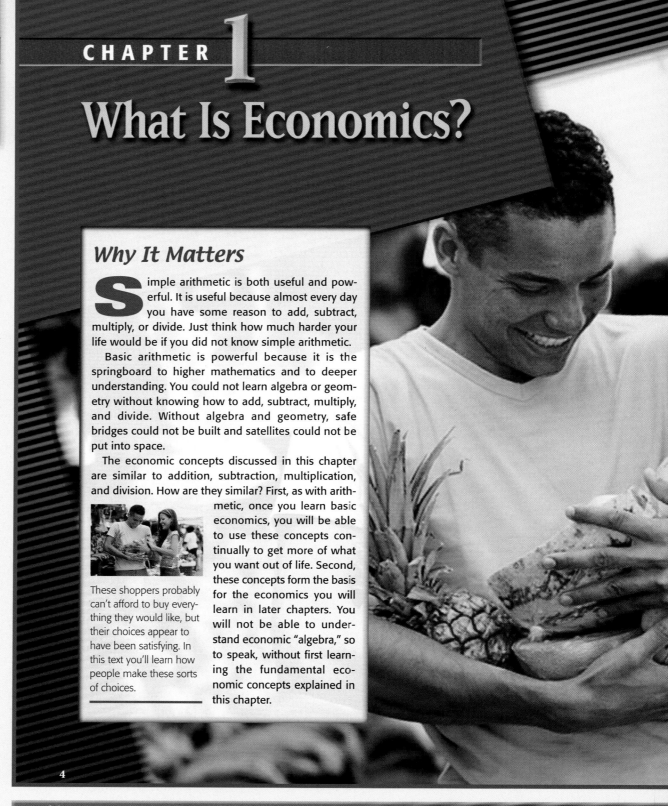

Why It Matters

Simple arithmetic is both useful and powerful. It is useful because almost every day you have some reason to add, subtract, multiply, or divide. Just think how much harder your life would be if you did not know simple arithmetic.

Basic arithmetic is powerful because it is the springboard to higher mathematics and to deeper understanding. You could not learn algebra or geometry without knowing how to add, subtract, multiply, and divide. Without algebra and geometry, safe bridges could not be built and satellites could not be put into space.

The economic concepts discussed in this chapter are similar to addition, subtraction, multiplication, and division. How are they similar? First, as with arithmetic, once you learn basic economics, you will be able to use these concepts continually to get more of what you want out of life. Second, these concepts form the basis for the economics you will learn in later chapters. You will not be able to understand economic "algebra," so to speak, without first learning the fundamental economic concepts explained in this chapter.

These shoppers probably can't afford to buy everything they would like, but their choices appear to have been satisfying. In this text you'll learn how people make these sorts of choices.

Teaching Suggestions from the Author

Students come to the study of economics not fully knowing what economics is. They think that economics is a list of topics—unemployment, inflation, deflation, economic growth, interest rates, costs, revenues, and so on. Certainly economics deals with all these topics and more, however, the essence of economics is not the list of topics, but *how* the topics are discussed. After all, everyone can talk about unemployment, inflation, and so on, but not everyone talks about these topics the way an economist does.

At the heart of economics is a *way of thinking.* Economists think in terms of scarcity, choices, costs and benefits, unintended effects, supply and demand, building and testing theories, and much more. In this

Economics Around the Clock

The following events occurred one day in November.

8:12 A.M. Jessica is a senior in high school; next year she hopes to enroll in a college that is very selective. Currently she is at home filling out one of the many college applications on her desk. The acceptance rate at this particular college is 14 percent. Jessica whispers under her breath, "Why such a low acceptance rate?"

- **Why is it so hard to get into certain colleges?**

8:33 A.M. Each morning on his way to work, George, 30 years old, drives through a senior citizen community. It usually takes him longer to go one-half mile in the senior citizen community than to go one-half mile anywhere else along his commute. George is currently going 15 mph in a 25 mph zone because the person driving in front of him is driving 15 mph. George is frustrated because he has no way to get around this slow driver.

- **What economic reason might explain why, on average, senior citizens drive slower than 30-year-old drivers?**

7:43 P.M. José, a junior in high school, is at home studying. José's mother is surprised that he is home studying on a Saturday night. Usually he is out with his friends. She asks, "What are you doing home tonight? Do you have a big test next week?" José answers, "No, it's just that Jimmy is sick and Tom is out of town."

- **What do José's friends either being sick or out of town have to do with his studying on a Saturday night?**

8:45 P.M. David and Elaine Anderson are at home watching television. They are thinking of buying a new car, so after the last Volvo commercial Elaine says, "I wonder if we should buy a new Volvo, maybe an S80 [starting price, $36,365]." As he gets up to get something to drink, David says, "There goes the vacation to Maui."

- **What does buying a car have to do with taking a vacation?**

5

chapter, I introduce the student to the economic way of thinking.

It is a good idea at the beginning of this chapter to tell students to forget about memorizing definitions and to forget about outlining topics in a detailed way. Instead, they should concentrate on how economists approach the study of the world. What do economists focus on? What is important to them? What are the types of questions they ask and seek to answer? By approaching the chapter in this way, students will more quickly understand that economics is essentially a way of thinking about the world.

Introducing the Chapter

Ask students to write a short answer to the following question: What do economists do? Allow students to share their answers. Then explain that economists study markets, prices, costs, production, inflation, unemployment, interest rates, business cycles, budget deficits, trade deficits, exchange rates, and so on. These subjects and others are discussed in this textbook. This chapter covers some basic elements of economics, including scarcity and opportunity cost. Tell students that although the concepts may sound foreign, we all deal with them every day without even thinking about them. Students should now begin to examine things from an economic viewpoint, in the same distinctive way economists view, interpret, and analyze the world.

Teaching with Visuals

Students will learn about the basics of economics in this chapter. Have them look at the photo on this spread and ask them to think about what the buying and selling of goods has to do with economics.

SECTION 1

Teacher Support

Focus and Motivate

Section Objectives

After completing this section, students will be able to

- explain how choice is related to scarcity;
- provide examples of opportunity costs;
- understand a production possibilities frontier; and
- describe how competition determines the way rationing devices are distributed.

Economics Around the Clock

Kickoff Activity

Instruct students to respond in writing to the 8:12 A.M. scenario in Economics Around the Clock (page 5).

Invite students to share their answers with the class. They should come up with several reasons why certain colleges can be more selective than others.

Activating Prior Knowledge

Have students each describe one thing they did last week—such as "Studied history for one hour" or "Talked to my friend for 20 minutes." Then ask students to identify what they would have done during the same period of time, had they not done what they did. In other words, if they had not studied history for one hour, what would they have done during that hour?

SECTION 1

The Foundation of Economics

Focus Questions

- What is scarcity?
- How is choice related to scarcity?
- How is opportunity cost related to choice?
- Why are rationing devices needed?
- What is the purpose of a production possibilities frontier?
- What activity determines the way in which rationing devices are distributed?

Key Terms

want
resource
scarcity
opportunity cost
trade-off
production possibilities frontier
rationing device
economics

Scarcity Exists

People have **wants**—things they desire to have. They do not want just anything, however. They want the things they think will make them happy and satisfied. Most people want cars, houses, haircuts, clothes, entertainment, better health, and countless other things. Few people are completely satisfied, even after getting their initial wants satisfied. Then they want a *bigger* house, a *newer* car, and *more* CDs. All the wants of all the people in the world make the list of wants unlimited.

want
A thing that we desire to have.

resource
Anything that is used to produce goods or services. For example, a person's labor may be used to produce computers, TV sets, and much more, and therefore a person's labor is a resource.

scarcity
The condition in which our wants are greater than the resources available to satisfy those wants.

Resources Are Needed

How do people satisfy their wants? As you probably know, in most cases you cannot get something by just wishing for it. The things we want do not simply appear on our doorsteps because we desire them. Instead, **resources** are needed to produce the goods and services that satisfy our wants. If you want a new desk for your room, it takes wood, tools, and labor (all of which are resources) to produce that desk. Nanette may want a computer, but she is not going to get one by simply wishing for it. It takes many resources to produce it. (You will learn more about how economists define *resources*, *goods*, and *services* later in this chapter.)

Resources Are Limited

Unfortunately the world's supply of resources is limited. So, when you want a new desk or Nanette wants a computer, you and Nanette face an ongoing problem in life that we all face, an economic problem. Our wants are unlimited, but the resources available to satisfy these wants are limited. Stated in another way, people's wants are greater than the limited resources available to satisfy all the wants.

This condition in which our wants are greater than the resources available to satisfy them is called **scarcity**. Scarcity is an economic fact of life, much as the law of gravity is a fact of life. In fact, scarcity is such an important, fundamental economic concept that some economists have said that the science of economics wouldn't exist were it not for scarcity.

Differentiating Instruction

Kinesthetic Learners

Help students understand the concept of scarcity by playing musical chairs. Divide the class into three groups. Have each group circle a set of chairs numbering one fewer than the students. Play music briefly, and then stop it while everyone tries to sit in a chair. Anyone left standing is eliminated owing to the scarcity of chairs, and one chair is removed from each set of chairs. Continue until only two students are left in each group. Combine the final six contestants so that they circle five chairs. Continue until there is a final winner. Point out that the desire of the contestants (sitting) is always higher than the amount of resources (chairs).

A Student Asks

QUESTION: *I know that I must deal with scarcity, but do wealthy people, people like Bill Gates, the multibillionaire, face scarcity too? Bill Gates may have unlimited wants, but doesn't he also have unlimited resources?*

ANSWER: *No, both you and Bill Gates have to deal with scarcity. The fact that he can buy more "things" than you can doesn't mean that his resources are unlimited. Keep in mind that Gates wants more than just goods, such as cars, houses, and vacations; he also wants more friendship, more time to spend with his kids, more time to do some leisurely reading. In addition, he has tried to help solve many of the world's problems by donating millions of dollars to charities, but not even his vast fortune can provide everyone in the world with everything they want.*

Scarcity Means Making Choices

Wants are unlimited, and resources are limited. Therefore, scarcity exists, and people must make choices. After all, without enough resources to satisfy all our wants (yours, mine, and everybody else's), we have to choose which wants (of the unlimited number we have) we will satisfy.

EXAMPLE: Maria earns $1,000 a month. She wants a new outfit, 10 new books, a trip to Hawaii, a new car, and many other things. The problem is that she can't have everything she wants, given her income. She has to *choose* between the new outfit or the 10 new books. She also has to choose between the trip to Hawaii and a down payment on a new car. ♦

Consider the choices a society makes because scarcity exists. Some groups of people want more health care for the poor, some want more police protection, some want more schools, and some a cleaner environment. As we know, wants are not satisfied simply by the asking. It takes resources to bring these things about. The problem, though, is that even if we could satisfy all the wants listed here, there would be more later. Even if we provided more health care to the poor, hired more police officers, built more schools, and cleaned up the environment, we would still discover other things to do—always more wants and never enough resources to satisfy those unlimited wants. Therefore, we must choose how we are going to use our limited resources. We must choose which wants we will try to satisfy and which wants will be left unsatisfied.

> ***"The first lesson of economics is scarcity: There is never enough of anything to satisfy all those who want it."***
> —Thomas Sowell, economist

Making Choices Means Incurring Opportunity Costs

Every time you make a choice, such as choosing to buy a sweater instead of two

▲ In a world of scarcity, we must make choices. **Would you choose the most expensive or the least expensive shoes? How would this decision affect other decisions?**

Teach

Discussion Starter

Some people have suggested that one way of eliminating scarcity is to have fewer wants. Ask students if they think this is possible. Which wants would they be willing to give up?

A Student Asks

Make sure students understand that not all wants focus on tangible things that can be purchased.

Cause and Effect

The relationship between wants and scarcity is clear. The more people who want a particular item, the scarcer the item. In history, many groups have stated that if you eliminate wants, you gain a sense of understanding and peace. Others have said that someday, far into the future, all wants will be fulfilled. Ask students to think about the following questions: Is it possible that someday all wants could be fulfilled? Is it possible to eliminate all of your wants? What would happen if all wants were fulfilled or eliminated?

Teaching with Visuals

Answers will vary. They should be expressed in terms of limited resources and the costs of choosing either the least expensive or the most expensive shoes.

Background Information: Scarcity Example

To give students a sense of scarcity, share this information with them: In Cebu, in the Philippines, Canadian bird experts captured on video, for the first time, the rarest bird in the world, the Cebu Flowerpecker. This bird was believed to be extinct in the 19th century, but a single specimen was spotted on the island in 1992. Since then, experts have determined that there are four living specimens of this rare bird. Encourage students to imagine what it would be like if the Cebu Flowerpecker were the greatest pet bird in the world. If everyone wanted a Cebu Flowerpecker as a pet, how would its incredibly rare nature affect its scarcity and the amount of resources needed to acquire one?

Teaching with Visuals

Direct students to make a list of their opportunity costs for one day. Invite them to share their lists, and the choices that caused them, in a class discussion.

Students sometimes think that scarcity exists only in poor countries. On the contrary, scarcity is a fact of life—no matter where a person lives. There is scarcity in India, Argentina, Brazil, Russia, the United States, and every other nation. Scarcity "goes around the world" because people's wants (no matter where they live) are always greater than the resources available to satisfy those wants.

Discussion Starter

Scarcity affects everything, even land, air, and water. It may be hard for students to understand that although Earth is more than 70% water, water is scarce in many parts of the world. What choices might have to be made if water were scarce in your area?

EXHIBIT 1-1 Opportunity Cost

What to do	What you would have done	Opportunity cost
Watch television	Read a book	The opportunity cost of watching television is reading a book.
Buy a computer	Take a vacation in France	The opportunity cost of buying a computer is taking a vacation in France.
Go to sleep at 9:00 p.m. instead of 11:00 p.m.	Watch a two-hour video	The opportunity cost of sleeping from 9:00 to 11:00 p.m. is watching a two-hour video.

▲ The most valued opportunity or alternative you give up to do something—the next best choice—is that something's opportunity cost.

CDs, you incur an **opportunity cost**. The most valued opportunity or alternative you give up (or forfeit) to do something is that something's opportunity cost. Thus, the opportunity cost of your choosing to buy a sweater is two compact discs. (See Exhibit 1-1 for more examples.)

Economists often say that life is full of **trade-offs**. What do they mean by this statement? The nature of a trade-off is that you can get more of one good, but only by getting less of another good. Speaking about trade-offs is just another way of speaking about opportunity cost. In other words, saying that "life is full of trade-offs" is really no different from saying that "every time we choose one thing over another, we incur an opportunity cost." (You will read more about trade-offs in the next section.)

opportunity cost
The most highly valued opportunity or alternative forfeited when a choice is made.

trade-off
A situation in which more of one thing necessarily means less of something else.

A Student Asks

QUESTION: *Suppose I decide to spend $50 to buy some used car stereo speakers from a friend. If I hadn't spent the money on the speakers, I could have purchased $50 worth of new clothes, or spent $50 on a present for my girlfriend, or given $50 to my mom's favorite charity. Because I could have done any of these things, aren't all of them the opportunity cost of buying the speakers?*

ANSWER: *No. It is necessary to differentiate between what you could have done and what you would have done. Opportunity cost refers to what you would have done if you had not bought the speakers. It's your next best choice, and only that choice. If you would have spent the $50 on your girlfriend's present, then the present—and only the present—is what you actually gave up to buy the speakers. Your opportunity cost in this case can only be $50 worth of opportunity, not $100, $150, or $200 worth.*

Opportunity costs affect people's decisions every day. In fact, a change in opportunity cost can, and often does, change a person's behavior. Suppose Sunil has a part-time job at a local grocery store. Each day he goes to work at 2 p.m. and leaves at 6 p.m. Does he incur any opportunity costs when he chooses to work each day between 2 and 6 p.m.? He certainly does; whatever he would be doing if he weren't working is the opportunity cost of his working.

Now let's increase the opportunity cost of Sunil's going to work. Suppose one day Sunil is on his way to work when someone stops him and offers to pay him $300 for doing an easy task, but doing the task means that Sunil will not be able to go to work that day. What will Sunil do? Will he continue on his way to work or take the $300 and not go to work? An economist would predict that as the opportunity cost of working at his part-time job increases, compared to the benefits of working, Sunil is less likely to go to work. According to how economists think about behavior, whether it is Sunil's or your own behavior, the higher the cost of doing something, the less likely it will be done.

EXAMPLE: An economics professor at a California college noticed that more students are absent from class when the surf is good than when it isn't. What might explain these absences? Well, it turned out that quite a few of the professor's students were surfers. When the surf is not good, the

Cross-Curricular Activity

Tell students to list several major activities in which they have been involved over the last year, such as traveling or buying a large-ticket item. Then have them create a table for the activities, list the opportunity cost of each activity, and write in the approximate monetary cost for each activity. How does the monetary cost of the activity compare with the monetary cost of the opportunity not taken? Are monetary issues the only concerns when determining what actions are taken? What other concerns need to be considered when weighing opportunity costs?

Why Didn't Chris Rock Go to College?

Chris Rock was born on February 7, 1966, in Andrews, South Carolina. Many of his early years were spent in the neighborhood of Bedford-Stuyvesant in Brooklyn, New York. He had two idols: one was boxer Sugar Ray Leonard and the other was comedian Eddie Murphy. Realizing that he wasn't much of a boxer, Chris decided to become a comedian, like Murphy.

One night, Eddie Murphy caught Chris Rock's act at a club. He was so impressed with Rock that he cast him in his 1987 movie, *Beverly Hills Cop 2*. In the early 1990s, Rock became a regular on television's *Saturday Night Live*. He went on to become one of America's funniest comedians—doing movies, HBO specials, and more. Chris's hard work and talent began paying off for him financially, with his earnings far exceeding that of the average 21-year-old.

While Chris Rock was pursuing his comedy career, many people the same age were attending college. Why didn't Rock go to college? He certainly could have afforded the tuition, and he would have been accepted had he applied. Could it be that the opportunity costs of attending college were just too high for Chris Rock?

> *"We were so poor my daddy unplugged the clocks when we went to bed."*
> —Chris Rock

To understand, think what it will cost you to attend college. Let's say that room, board, tuition, books, fees, and living expenses add up to $20,000 a year. Multiplied by 4 years that comes to $80,000. Is $80,000 really the full cost of your attending college? What would you be doing if you didn't go to college? Chances are that you'd be earning income working at a job. For example, perhaps you could be working at a full-time job earning $25,000 annually. Multiplied by 4 years that's $100,000. Certainly this forfeited $100,000 is part of the cost of your attending college. Even if you earn some money working part-time while in school, you will be giving up some earnings.

How do the earnings you would give up compare to the earnings that someone like Chris Rock would have to give up? Even though the tuition, room, board, and other costs of attending college are roughly the same for everyone who attends your college, the *opportunity costs* will not be. Some people have higher opportunity costs of attending college than others do. Can you see how it was simply too "costly" for Chris Rock to attend college?

THINK ABOUT IT You may not be making hundreds of thousands of dollars shortly after graduating from high school, but if you decide to go to college, you will have opportunity costs. What will be your opportunity costs for going to college?

opportunity cost (for the surfer students) is low and they are more likely to come to class. After all, they're not giving up any good waves. But when the surf is good, the opportunity cost for these students is high, and they are less likely to come to class. In other words, the more the students have to give up (in terms of good waves), the higher their opportunity cost of attending class, and the less likely they will attend class. The less students have to give up (in terms of good waves), the lower their opportunity cost of attending class, and the more likely they will attend class. ♦

Economics in the Real World

Instruct students to read the feature, then tell them to compare the opportunity cost of college for Chris Rock with the opportunity cost they face by going to college. Ask, How might these costs differ?

ANSWERS TO THINK ABOUT IT Answers will vary. Invite students to share with the class their ideas of what their opportunity costs for going to college might be.

Background Information: Scarcity in Different Cultures

The value of any good, service, or activity may vary over time and across cultures. For instance, in the 18th century, a group of colonists offered to "properly educate" some Native American young men at the College of William and Mary, in Williamsburg, VA. The Native American elders refused the offer. They had heard that other young men who had been "educated" at colonial schools had returned to their people "neither fit [to be] hunters, warriors, nor councellors [*sic*]; they were totally good for nothing." Remind students that scarcity is related to the value of a good or service for a particular person.

Economics Around the Clock

After reading and discussing "Making Choices Means Incurring Opportunity Costs" (pages 7–10), you may want to remind students of the 7:43 P.M. scenario in Economics Around the Clock (page 5) and discuss their answers to its question.

Help students understand that when José's friends are unavailable, he has to give up less to study than when his friends are available—in other words, José's opportunity cost for studying is lower when his friends aren't available. We would expect him to study more the lower his opportunity cost for studying happens to be.

Teaching with Visuals

To ensure that students understand Exhibit 1-2, pick three unlabeled points—perhaps 30,000 snowboards, 15,000 skis, and 25,000 skis—and ask what amounts of snowboards and skis would be produced in these combinations.

EXAMPLE: High school teachers have observed that seniors, in their last semester in school, cut classes more often than any other time of the year. Does this behavior have a "surfer explanation," which is really an opportunity cost explanation?

Yes, the opportunity cost explanation says that by the time their last semester at high school rolls around, many seniors have already been admitted to college. In their minds, missing a class here or there will not do much harm to their chances of getting into college. Let's put it the way an economist would: the opportunity cost of going to class is less after a senior has been admitted to college than before he or she has been admitted to college; therefore, we would expect a higher absentee rate (among seniors) when the opportunity cost of attending class is lower.

(Be aware: Some colleges will grant admission, but on the condition that a student maintain his or her GPA. In this case, then the opportunity cost of attending class is the same before and after the senior is admitted to college.) ♦

production possibilities frontier
A graphic representation of all possible combinations of two goods that an economy can produce.

EXHIBIT 1-2 Production Possibilities Frontier

Combination	Snowboards	and	Skis
A	50,000	and	0
B	40,000	and	20,000
C	25,000	and	40,000
D	0	and	60,000

(a)

(b)

▲ The economy can produce any of the four combinations of snowboards and skis in part (a); these combinations are plotted in part (b).

One Diagram, Three Economic Concepts

You have probably heard the saying, "A picture is worth a thousand words." With that saying in mind, let's look at a diagram that can be used to illustrate the three economic concepts we have discussed: scarcity, choice, and opportunity cost.

The diagram is called a production possibilities frontier (or PPF, for short). A **production possibilities frontier** shows all possible combinations of two goods that an economy can produce in a certain period of time (see Exhibit 1-2). To keep things simple, we have assumed that only two goods, snowboards and skis, can be produced in an economy. In Exhibit 1-2(a) you see the four different combinations (A–D) of these two goods that an economy can produce. For example, it can produce 50,000 snowboards and 0 sets of skis, or 40,000 snowboards and 20,000 sets of skis, and so on.

We then take each of the four combinations and plot them in Exhibit 1-2(b). If we simply connect these four points, A–D, we have a production possibilities frontier. In other words, the curve you see in Exhibit 1-2(b) is a production possibilities frontier (PPF).

Scarcity and the PPF

Now let's think about scarcity in terms of the PPF. Scarcity, as you know, is the condition in which our wants are greater than the resources available to satisfy them. The PPF itself, the actual curve in Exhibit 1-2(b), illustrates this concept. The PPF tells us that certain things are available to us and certain things are not. We can't have everything we

Internet Research

Tell students to go to a few commercial Web sites, such as the sites for their favorite stores or sites that sell CDs, and choose products they would like to purchase. Ask students to list the products next to their prices. Then have students list the opportunity cost for each item. What are the most valued opportunities or alternatives they would give up if they bought these items? Are they willing to give up these opportunities for the enjoyment of the products?

want. Any point on the PPF itself, such as points A–D, is available to us. For example, we can have point B, which represents 40,000 snowboards and 20,000 sets of skis. We can also have the combination of goods represented by any point below the PPF, such as point E. What we can't have—what is unavailable to us because we don't have enough resources to produce it—is the combination of goods represented by point F, which lies beyond the PPF.

Can you see then that the PPF itself (the actual curve) illustrates scarcity by creating two regions for us? One region—consisting of points on the PPF and below it—represents what is available to us. Another region (the points beyond the PPF) represents what is unavailable to us. Scarcity told us we couldn't have everything we want, and the PPF makes this point visually clear.

Choices and the PPF

Now consider the concept of choice. We stated earlier that because of scarcity we must make choices. Looking again at Exhibit 1-2(b), we know we cannot be at points A–D at the same time. We must make a choice. Is it going to be A or B or C or D? Once we make a choice, opportunity cost "pops up." For example, suppose we narrowed our choices down to points B and C, and in the end chose point C. What is the opportunity cost of a set of skis over this range? Well, we know that we produce 20,000 more sets of skis by choosing point C over B, but at the opportunity cost of producing 15,000 fewer snowboards. In other words, the opportunity cost of 20,000 more sets of skis is 15,000 snowboards.

A Consequence of Scarcity: The Need for a Rationing Device

Because scarcity exists, we need a **rationing device**, some way to decide who gets what portion of all the resources and goods available. What is the most common way in our society to determine who gets which goods, and how much each person gets? If you guessed "money," you were on the right track. Price (a certain number of dollars) is the most widely used rationing device in our society. If you are willing and able to pay the price for something, it is yours. If you are either unwilling or unable to pay the price, it won't be yours. In this way, by using price, all products are rationed out to the people who are willing and able to pay.

"There's no such thing as a free lunch."
—MILTON FRIEDMAN, ECONOMIST

If scarcity did not exist, a rationing device would not be necessary. Everyone would get everything he or she wanted.

Another Consequence of Scarcity: Competition

Today's world is very competitive. People compete for jobs, companies compete for profits, and students compete for grades. Economists believe that competition exists because of scarcity. If enough resources were available to satisfy all of our wants, people would not have to compete for the limited resources.

Economists also believe that competition takes the form of people trying to get more of the rationing device. If (money or dollar) price is the rationing device, people will compete to earn dollars. People compete to earn dollars every day. Say three people are up for the same promotion at their business firm. Why do they want the promotion? Certainly added prestige and responsibility may be part of the answer, but still people are more likely to seek and accept promotions that come with more money.

Suppose something other than price—muscular strength, for example—were used as the rationing device. People with more muscular strength would receive more resources and goods than people with less muscular strength. In this situation, an economist would predict that people would compete for muscular strength and would lift weights each day. The lesson is simple: whatever the rationing device, people will compete for it. See Exhibit 1-3 for a summary of the concepts described in this section.

rationing device A means for deciding who gets what portion of the available resources and goods.

Reinforcement Activity

To reinforce understanding of the concepts of choice and opportunity cost, have each student write at the top of one sheet of paper "Buying Choice" and at the top of a second sheet "Opportunity Cost." On the sheet labeled "Buying Choice," students should either draw a picture or paste an advertisement of an item that they recently purchased. On the sheet labeled "Opportunity Cost," students should place a picture or advertisement of what they could have purchased with the same money.

Prediction Activity

Ask students to suppose that the U.S. Congress makes it illegal to use money (price) as a rationing device. Ask, Does some other rationing device arise to take its place?

The answer is yes. Congress can outlaw the use of money (price) as a rationing device, but it cannot eliminate scarcity. It is because of scarcity that there is a need for a rationing device. If price is outlawed as a rationing device, something else will have to arise to ration resources and goods, because scarcity will still exist.

Application Activity

After reading and discussing Section 1, you may want to assign the Section Activity in the *Applying the Principles Workbook*.

Assess

Quick Quiz

The following true-or-false quiz will help you assess student understanding of the material covered in this section.

1. People have wants—things they desire to obtain. (True)
2. Deep friendship is a tangible good. (False)
3. The three concepts scarcity, choice, and competition are linked together. (False)
4. Price is a rationing device. (True)
5. Economics is the science that studies the choices of people trying to satisfy their wants in a world of scarcity. (True)

Assessment Book

You will find a quiz for this section in the *Assessment Book*.

Reteaching Activity

Guide students in examining choices that they have recently made. For each choice, help students name the scarcity conditions that prompted the choice, the choice made, and the opportunity cost incurred.

Guided Reading

For further reteaching of the key concepts in this section, assign the Outlining Activity and the Just the Facts Handout from the *Guided Reading and Study Guide.*

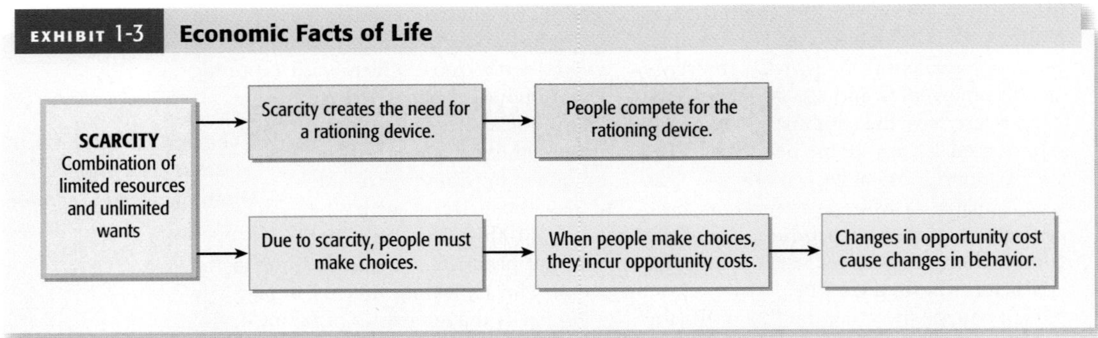

▲ The science of economics probably would not exist were it not for scarcity—an economic fact of life.

A Definition of Economics

economics
The science that studies the choices of people trying to satisfy their wants in a world of scarcity.

In this section, you learned about three important and closely related economic concepts: scarcity, choice, and opportunity costs. You also learned something about the way economists think about the world (and you will learn more in the next section). So, now it's time for a formal definition of the term. **Economics** is the science that studies the choices people make as they try to satisfy their wants in a world of scarcity. Put another way, you could say that economics is the study of how people use their limited resources to satisfy their unlimited wants.

SECTION 1 ASSESSMENT

Defining Terms

1. Define the following terms:
   a. scarcity
   b. opportunity cost
   c. economics
   d. want
   e. resource
   f. production possibilities frontier
   g. rationing device

Reviewing Facts and Concepts

2. Because scarcity exists, people must make choices. Explain why.
3. Give an example to illustrate how a person may incur an opportunity cost without paying anyone any money.
4. Is the opportunity cost of attending high school the same for all high school students? Explain why or why not.

Critical Thinking

5. If price were not used as a rationing device, would something else have to be used? If so, what might it be? Suppose that a local movie theatre decided to use something other than price to determine who got to see the latest movies. Devise a rationing device that would be fair to both moviegoers and theater owners.

Applying Economic Concepts

6. Gallagher is planning on going to college in a few months. The tuition is $10,000 a year. Assuming that Gallagher goes to college for four years, is the opportunity cost of his attending college $40,000? Why or why not?
7. Explain how a PPF can be used to illustrate both choice and opportunity cost.

SECTION 1 ASSESSMENT ANSWERS

Defining Terms

1. a. scarcity: the condition in which our wants are greater than the resources available to satisfy those wants; **b. opportunity cost:** the most highly valued opportunity or alternative forfeited, or given up, when a choice is made; **c. economics:** the science that studies the choices of people trying to satisfy their wants in a world of scarcity; **d. want:** something we desire to have; **e. resource:** anything used to produce goods or services; **f. production possibilities frontier:** a diagram that shows all possible combinations of two goods that an economy can produce in a certain period of time; **g. rationing device:** a means for deciding who gets what portion of the available resources and goods.

Reviewing Facts and Concepts

2. Scarcity means our wants are greater than the resources available to satisfy them. Because we can't satisfy all our wants, we must choose which ones to satisfy.
3. Answers will vary.
4. No, not all students are giving up the same opportunities to attend high school.

Critical Thinking

5. As long as scarcity exists, there is a need for a rationing device—if not price, then something else. The rationing device could be almost anything—for instance, first come, first served; brute force; or physical appearance.

Applying Economic Concepts

6. The opportunity cost of attending college is what a person gives up to attend college. Suppose that if he didn't attend college, Gallagher would work full-time, earning $23,000 a year. The opportunity cost of his attending college would then be $92,000 ($23,000 × 4 years). The $40,000 referred to in the question is simply the out-of-pocket expense Gallagher would incur to attend college. His opportunity cost would be much higher.
7. A PPF illustrates scarcity. The choice that must be made because of scarcity reveals the opportunity cost of choosing to produce more of one item than another.

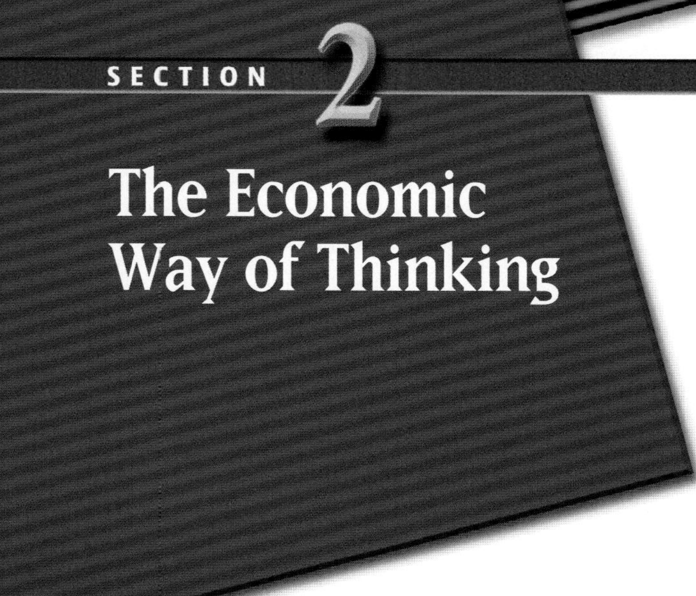

SECTION 2

The Economic Way of Thinking

Focus Questions

- How do costs and benefits affect decisions?
- What are incentives and why are they important?
- What is the difference between microeconomics and macroeconomics?
- Why do economists develop theories?

Key Terms

marginal
incentive
microeconomics
macroeconomics
theory

Economic Thinking

Economists have a particular way of looking at the world. Just as a pair of sunglasses can change how you view your surroundings (things look darker), so can the economic way of thinking.

When economists put on their "glasses," they see choices and opportunity costs, as you learned in the last section. You will recall, the economist saw the surfer student being absent from class because, on the day the waves were high, the opportunity cost of attending class was higher than on other days. In other words, besides seeing a student, a surfer, the surfboard, the beach and the waves, the economist "saw" (in his mind's eye) opportunity cost too.

One of the objectives of this book is to get you to understand and use the economist's way of thinking. It is not the only way to look at the world. It is, however, one way of looking at the world that often does help you understand the world you live in. This new way of thinking will also, in many cases, help you get more of what you want in life.

Thinking in Terms of Costs and Benefits

According to an economist, almost everything we do involves costs (negatives, disadvantages) and benefits (positives, advantages). There are costs and benefits to learning economics, eating a hamburger, driving a car, asking a person out on a date, sleeping an extra hour, taking a vacation, or talking on the telephone.

Making Cost-Benefit Decisions

According to the economist, a person will want to do a particular activity only if the benefits are greater than the costs. A person will buy a computer only if the benefits of buying the computer are expected to be greater than the costs of buying it. If the costs are perceived to be greater than the benefits, then the person will not purchase the computer.

Suppose a student graduates from high school and decides to go on to college. At college, she decides to major in psychology. What do we know about her choice of a

SECTION 2

Teacher Support

Focus and Motivate

Section Objectives

After completing this section, students will be able to

- explain how costs and benefits affect decisions;
- identify incentives;
- distinguish between microeconomics and macroeconomics; and
- explain why economists develop theories.

Economics Around the Clock

Kickoff Activity

Direct students to reread the 8:33 A.M. scenario in Economics Around the Clock (page 5) and write their answers to the question that accompanies it. Have them share their responses with the class.

Look for students to mention that some older people have a lower opportunity cost of time. Point out that older people may take their time on the road because they aren't racing to work or other activities.

Activating Prior Knowledge

Tell students to write and share a few sentences describing costs and benefits that they encounter each day. Encourage students to share their sentences with the class.

Teach

Discussion Starter

Tell students to think about decisions that they made recently. Ask if they considered the costs and benefits of the decisions before making them. Invite volunteers to share their decisions and the costs and benefits that they have identified. Urge the class to suggest other costs and benefits for those decisions. Finally, ask whether the volunteers would make the same decisions, after considering the additional costs and benefits.

Answers will vary. Students should realize that, in economic terms and for most people, the benefits of attending college are greater than the costs.

Analyzing

After students have read this feature, have them investigate a college, university, or other postsecondary institution that interests them. Tell students to list the costs and benefits of attending this school and then give an oral presentation about why they chose this school. Presentations must include five benefits and five costs related to attending this particular institution.

Reinforcement Activity

Marginal cost is an important concept in economics. Tell students that when they hear or read the word *marginal,* they should think of the word *additional.* In economics, *additional* is a synonym for *marginal.* Suggest that students reread the definition of *marginal cost.*

Economists think in terms of both benefits and costs. For example, attending college has both benefits and costs. Usually, the benefits far exceed the costs. To learn more about colleges, go to the following Web site: www.emcp.net/college.

Once at the site, click on "College Directory" and then "United States." The next screen you see will list the 50 states and Washington, D.C. Click on the state in which you think you may want to attend college. From there, click on the names of a few colleges, and read about them. After spending some time looking at different colleges, identify what you think are the benefits and costs of attending college. Finally, do you think the benefits are greater than, less than, or equal to the costs?

major? According to the economist, we know that when she made the decision to major in psychology, she thought that the benefits to her of majoring in psychology would be greater than the costs. When economists study a problem, weighing the costs and the benefits, they refer to this process as a *cost-benefit analysis.*

EXAMPLE: John has been studying four hours for his English test tomorrow. It's now 10:30 at night. John considers studying one more hour. The benefits to studying another hour might be a higher grade on the test. The cost of studying another hour is one less hour of sleep, which could adversely affect his ability to concentrate during the test (which, in turn, could adversely affect his grade). He thinks the costs of studying an additional hour are greater than the benefits, so he goes to bed. ♦

Thinking at the Margin

marginal
In economics, marginal means additional.

incentive
Something that encourages or motivates a person to take action.

An important economic term will come up throughout this text when discussing costs and benefits. That word is **marginal**, which means "additional."

Why is the term *marginal* so important? It is because economists believe that when people make decisions, they do not think of the *total* costs and benefits involved in the decision. Instead, they think about the *additional,* or *marginal,* costs and benefits.

EXAMPLE: You have just eaten two chicken tacos for lunch and are trying to decide whether or not to go back for a third. You are still hungry, but if you get another taco now, you will have no money left for a soda after school. Are you really that hungry? ♦

In making the decision described above, you are comparing the marginal benefits of one more (an additional) taco against the marginal costs of one more taco. If you decide that the marginal benefits are greater than the marginal costs, you will buy the additional taco. If, on the other hand, you decide that the marginal costs are greater than the marginal benefits, you will keep your money and go without the additional taco. An economist would say that you were "making decisions at the margin," a process that you will encounter in several of the following chapters.

Thinking in Terms of Incentives

Economists often speak of incentives in reference to actions. An **incentive** is something that encourages or motivates a person to take an action. For example, suppose that Amy lives in a country where every dollar she earns is taxed (by government) at 100 percent. With a tax rate of 100 percent, an economist might argue that Amy does not have an incentive to produce anything for sale. Why work all day to produce a good that is sold for, say $100, when you will have to turn over the full $100 to the government in taxes?

Now let's lower the tax rate in Amy's country from 100 percent to 20 percent. In your mind, has the lower tax rate provided Amy with an incentive to work and produce? An economist would say it has. The lower tax rate encourages or motivates Amy toward a particular action—working and producing—because now Amy can keep 80 cents out of every dollar she earns.

Differentiating Instruction

English Language Learners

To help ELL students, the following resources are provided as part of the *Economics: New Ways of Thinking* program:

- a Spanish glossary in the *Student Text*
- Spanish versions of the Chapter Summaries on an audio CD

EXAMPLE: Kenneth, who is 15 years old, and lives with his parents, does not have an incentive to mow the lawn. There is absolutely nothing that encourages or motivates him toward mowing the lawn. Then one day Kenneth's father offers him $10 to mow the lawn. The $10—the money—is an incentive for Kenneth to mow the lawn. It encourages or motivates him toward mowing the lawn. ♦

EXAMPLE: Jimmy lives in country A, where people are not permitted to own property, so Jimmy rents a house from the government. Adam lives in country B, where people are permitted to own property, so Adam owns his house. Who is more likely to take care of the house he lives in? The answer is Adam. The reasoning is simple: Adam can sell the house he lives in (because he owns it); Jimmy cannot sell the house he lives in. Any damage Adam does to his house lowers the selling price of the house. The moral of the story? Private property ownership acts as an incentive to taking care of things. ♦

Thinking in Terms of Trade-Offs

As you learned in Section 1, trade-offs involve opportunity costs. When more of one thing necessarily means less of something else, we have a trade-off. For example, when we drive our cars, we pollute the air. One way to cut down on the amount of pollution is to drive less. In other words, more driving means less clean air, and less driving means more clean air. More of one thing (driving) necessarily means less of something else (clean air). We have a trade-off between driving and clean air.

> ***"Most of economics can be summarized in four words: People respond to incentives."***
> —Steven Landsburg, economist

Individuals Face Trade-Offs

You might notice that when trade-offs arise in life, you sometimes have to stop and think what course of action you want to take.

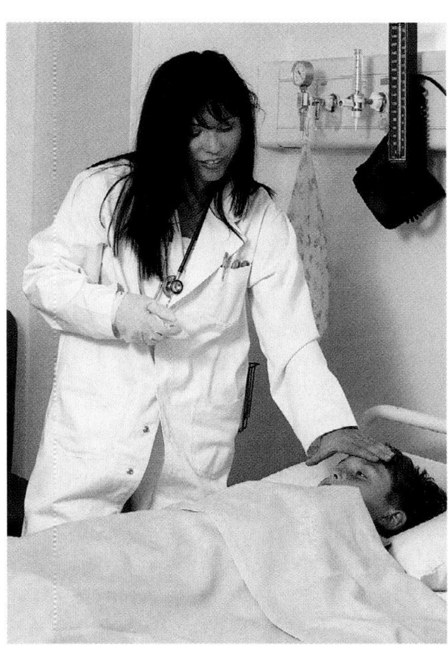

▲ Like individuals, societies face trade-offs. **What trade-off is represented by these two photographs?**

Cause and Effect

To fully understand economics, students need to understand scarcity. To reinforce the concepts of scarcity and trade-offs, tell students to imagine that they have a big economics test tomorrow and their friends want them to go to a movie tonight. They are busy with other activities until 7:00 tonight, and they need to get up by 7:00 tomorrow morning. Going to the movie would take about four hours. Students need to study at least three hours for the test. They also need to sleep eight hours. Have each student make trade-offs with his or her time tonight: what does the student give up—studying, going out with friends, or sleep? What are the effects of his or her trade-offs?

Economics Around the Clock

You may want to remind students of the 8:45 P.M. scenario in Economics Around the Clock (page 5) and discuss their answers to the question it poses.

Point out that buying a car may make it impossible to take a vacation (especially a vacation in some faraway place). Life is full of trade-offs. More of one thing (a car) often means less of something else (a vacation).

Teaching with Visuals

These images represent the trade-off between government spending for health care and for the military.

Cooperative Learning

Divide students into groups of four or five and assign each group to develop one question about something that happens at school—questions could be as simple as Why do students bring their lunches when food is available at school? or Why do students bring cell phones (or pagers) to school? Each group should then come up with one theory about its question that can be tested in class, develop a way of testing the theory, predict an outcome for the test, and conduct the test. When groups have finished testing their theories, give them class time to compile the results and to prepare graphs showing their findings. Then have each group share its work with the class.

Reinforcement Activity

Instruct students to each select one extracurricular activity or hobby in which they participate and have them prepare a two-column chart that lists the benefits and costs of this activity or hobby. Invite students to share their charts with the class, and encourage the class to suggest other benefits and costs that could be added to each chart.

Thinking Like an Economist

There are really two lessons in the story about the baker's window, each of which relates to the other: (1) Money that is spent to purchase one thing cannot be used to purchase something else. For example, money that goes to purchase a new window cannot now go to purchase a new suit. (2) To understand things fully, we need to be aware of not only what is, but also of what would have been.

EXAMPLE: Suppose Mary Ann loves to eat, but she has recently put on (what she considers to be) a few too many pounds. She wants to lose some weight for two reasons: (1) to feel more comfortable in her clothes and (2) to reduce the risk of heart disease, which is linked to being overweight. So Mary Ann goes on a diet and cuts her calorie intake from 2,500 to 1,800 calories a day.

Does Mary Ann face a trade-off? Sure she does. On the one hand, if she doesn't go on a diet, she gets to continue eating what she wants to eat (that's good), but she won't feel as comfortable in her clothes and she increases her risk of heart disease (that's bad). Of course, on the other hand, if she does go on the diet, she will likely feel more comfortable in her clothes and be healthier (that's good), but she will have to avoid some of her favorite foods and feel hungry much of the day (that's bad).

No matter what Mary Ann decides, Mary Ann gets something she likes and something she doesn't like. She gets more of one thing (comfort and health) and less of something else (enjoyment from eating what she wants) if she chooses to diet. If she chooses not to diet, she still gets more of one thing (enjoyment from eating what she wants) and less of something else (less comfort and health). ◆

Societies Face Trade-Offs

Just as individuals face trade-offs, so do societies. At any one point in time, the federal government has only so much money from tax revenues. If more tax dollars go for, say, education, it means fewer tax dollars to spend on roads and highways. If more tax dollars go for national defense, then fewer dollars can be spent on health and welfare.

Trade-offs sometimes lead to conflicts in society. One group may think it better to spend more money on national defense and less on health and welfare. Another group might prefer the opposite. A conflict arises. In a household, some members of the family might prefer to spend more of the family budget on boats, plasma TV sets, and computers. Other members might prefer to spend more of the family budget on education, vacations, and furniture. A conflict arises.

Thinking in Terms of What Would Have Been

Economists often think in terms of "what would have been." It is important to be able to think in terms of what would have been, because only then do we know the opportunity costs for "what is."

The Story of the Broken Window

A famous economist-journalist once wrote a book in which he told the story of a boy who threw a rock through a baker's shop window. In the story the townspeople gather around the baker's shop and complain about the actions of today's youth. Then one person has a quite different perspective. He says that because the boy broke the window, the baker now has to buy a window, which means the window maker will now have more business. And because the window maker has more business, he will earn more money. And because he has more money, he will spend more money. And because he spends more money, someone else in the town will sell more goods, and on and on. So, says the person with the different perspective, what the boy has done is a good thing: he has generated economic activity for the town. After listening to this different view of the situation, the townspeople are happy. What had at first seemed like a tragedy (a boy breaking a window), now clearly appears to be the beginning of an economic boom for the town.

What do you think? Did the boy set off a chain reaction that will create work, income, and profits for many people in the town? And if so, should the townspeople hope that more boys throw more rocks through windows?

Before you begin encouraging people to throw rocks in your town, stop and ask, as the economist did, this simple question: If the baker didn't have to buy a new window, what would he have purchased with the money he would have spent on the window? Suppose that he would have spent the money for a new suit. But, now that the window is broken, the baker will have no

Background Information: The United States and the World Market

In recent years, the United States has dominated the world market so strongly that trade embargoes from the United States alone have caused some countries to suffer economically. The United States is so powerful economically that recent crashes in other world markets have barely affected its economic market. In an effort to combine their economic power, some nations of Europe banded together in the European Union. Direct students to research the European Union and write a one-page report on its policies, focusing on how those policies lead to trade-offs in the world market.

money for the suit, so the suit maker will earn less money (than otherwise). Without that money, the suit maker will be able to make fewer purchases, which will translate into fewer sales for others, and so on and so on.

Simply put, the economist urges us to see "what would have been" if the boy had not broken the window. The economist urges us to see more than "what will be" because the boy broke the window.

It is easy for all of us to see "what will be": we will actually see with our eyes the window maker selling a window and getting paid for it. It is not so easy, though, to see "what would have been." We can't see with our eyes the suit maker not selling the suit.

Seeing with Your Mind

It takes a certain kind of vision to see "what would have been." It takes your mind (and not your eyes) to see what would have been. You have to think your way to understanding that one new window means one fewer suit.

EXAMPLE: Suppose the federal government sets aside funds for a new interstate highway system. Thousands of people are hired to work on the project. Local newspapers in the towns along the highway write lots of stories on all the increased job activity, and soon there are more and better highways in the area. It is easy to see the "what will be" benefits of more jobs and better roads. ♦

We need to remind ourselves, however, that someone—namely, the taxpayers—had to pay for the new highway system. What did these taxpayers give up by paying the taxes to fund the new highway? They gave up the opportunity to buy goods for themselves, such as clothes, computers, and books. We now begin to think in terms of all the products that "would have been" produced and consumed had the highway not been built. If, say, more clothes would have been produced instead of highways, more people would have worked in the clothing industry and fewer would have worked in highway construction.

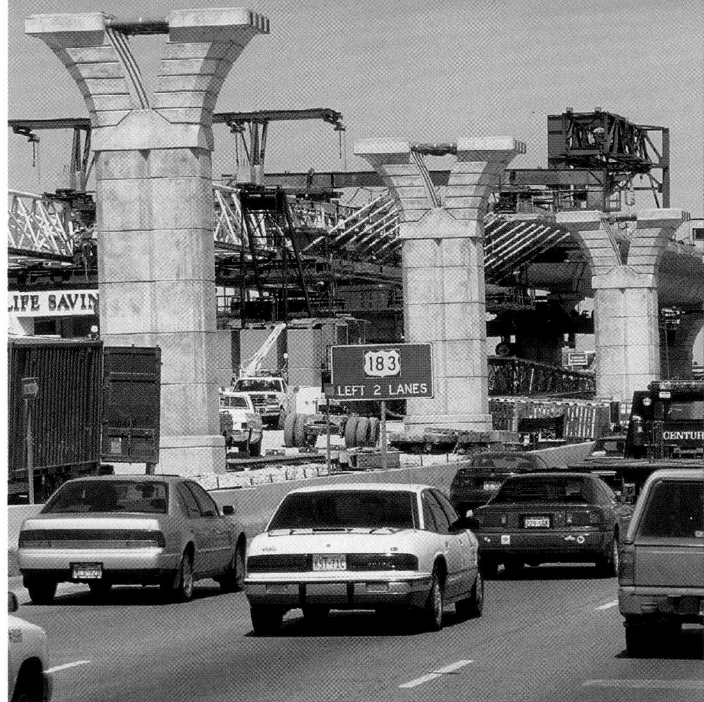

▲ Building and improving highways is expensive. **What sorts of things might not exist as a result of this highway being built?**

Thinking in Terms of Unintended Effects

Economists often look for the "unintended effects" of actions that people take. Has anything ever turned out differently from what you intended?

EXAMPLE: On an average day a shoe store sells 100 pairs of shoes at an average price of $40 a pair, thereby earning $4,000. One day the store owner decides to raise the price of shoes from an average of $40 to $50. What do you think he expects the effect of his action to be? He probably expects to increase his earnings from $4,000 a day to some greater amount, perhaps to $5,000 (100 pairs of shoes × $50 = $5,000). The store owner might be surprised by the results. At a higher price, it is likely that he will sell fewer pairs of shoes. Suppose that at a price of $50 a pair, the owner sells an average of 70 pairs of shoes a day. What are his

Teaching with Visuals

Answers will vary.

In the United Kingdom, a regulation specifies that noncitizens with a work visa cannot stay in the country beyond a certain period of time. The intended effect of the regulation is to keep the supply of labor in the country lower than it would be if noncitizens were allowed to work in the country indefinitely. An unintended effect of the regulation is that it has created a market for bogus marriages. Now a "fixer" will arrange a marriage between a noncitizen and a citizen, because if married to a citizen, the noncitizen can stay in the country. Soon after the marriage, husband and wife go their separate ways.

Cross-Curricular Activity

Team with a history teacher to discuss the concept of unintended effects as it relates to the mobilization of women in the U.S. workforce during World War II. During the war, the government supported a campaign of domestic propaganda to make working women appear patriotic. Participation in the workforce by women during the war established a precedent.

The history teacher can discuss the intended effects of the government's efforts to increase female participation in the workplace, allowing you to lead an analysis of some of the unintended effects (increased economic power of women, increased political involvement, the Equal Rights Amendment movement, etc.).

ANSWERS TO THINK ABOUT IT Answers will vary. Students might suggest that safety caps have made it difficult for some people to open medications.

Clarifying Terms

Check student understanding of the following term by asking them to use it in a sentence: *unintended effects.* Ensure that students show an understanding that this term means "the result of action that was neither the original intent nor an anticipated consequence."

Do Seatbelts Cause Accidents?

Most states have mandatory seatbelt laws for drivers. Seatbelt legislation was passed to save lives. That was its intent.

Soon after states started adopting mandatory seatbelt laws, an economist undertook a study. He wanted to find out if seatbelt laws really did save lives. His study showed that the number of car deaths before seatbelt laws was the same as the number of car deaths after seatbelt laws. This finding perplexed him because common sense tells us that if you are in an accident you have a better chance of surviving if you are wearing your seatbelt. So, what explained the economist's finding? The answer is this simple equation:

Number of car deaths = Number of accidents × Probability of being killed in a car accident

What seatbelt laws did was lower the "probability of being killed in a car accident." Yet, if they lowered this probability, and the number of car deaths was still the same (before and after the seatbelt law), then the only thing that could

explain this finding was that the "number of accidents" had to rise. This change is exactly what the economist found. In other words, one *unintended effect* of the seatbelt law was that the number of accidents increased. (Economists are interested in *unintended effects.*)

Why did the number of accidents increase? Some have suggested that drivers feel safer wearing a seatbelt and that drivers who feel safe are more likely to take risks on the road than drivers who do not feel safe. (Might drivers in large Hummers take more risks than drivers in Honda Civics?) Obviously, the way to be safe while driving a car is to wear your seatbelt and drive as carefully as you would if you weren't wearing your seatbelt. In other words, don't let wearing the seatbelt lull you into driving recklessly.

THINK ABOUT IT The intended effect of placing a safety cap on medications is so that children don't get into the medicine and eat it because they mistakenly think it is candy. Can you think of an unintended effect of placing safety caps on medications?

average daily earnings now? ($3,500 = 70 pairs of shoes × $50) The owner did not intend for things to turn out this way; he intended to increase his earnings by raising the price of shoes. The decrease in his earnings is an unintended effect of his actions. ♦

EXAMPLE: Suppose that U.S. citizens are buying some Japanese goods (such as Japanese cars), and that Japanese citizens are buying some goods produced in the United States (such as U.S. computers). Then things change: the Japanese government decides to place a $200 tax on every U.S. computer sold in Japan. People in Japan who buy U.S. computers will have to pay $200 more than they would have paid without the tax. Why might the Japanese government impose this tax? It may want Japanese computers to outsell U.S. computers; it may want to generate higher profits and greater employment in the Japanese computer industry. To accomplish these goals, the government deliberately makes U.S. computers more expensive than Japanese computers by placing the tax on U.S. computers. This action ends up hurting U.S. computer companies, because they sell fewer computers.

Internet Research

Tell students to browse the Web site for Project Vote Smart to learn about the spending choices that the federal government has to make each year. Ask them to write paragraphs answering these questions: What types of spending decisions does the federal government have to make, and how do those decisions relate to the concept of scarcity? What types of things do you think the government should spend its limited resources on?

The United States could decide to retaliate by placing a tax on Japanese cars sold in the United States. Japanese cars will be more expensive, and fewer will be sold. This action will hurt Japanese car companies.

Do you see what has happened? Japan initially takes an action—placing a tax on U.S. computers sold in Japan—hoping that the Japanese people will buy more Japanese computers and fewer U.S. computers (the intended effect of the action). The intended effect is realized: the Japanese people actually do buy more Japanese computers and fewer U.S. computers. But there is an unintended effect too: the United States places a tax on Japanese cars, which ends up hurting Japanese car companies. When the Japanese placed a tax on U.S. computers, they did not intend to do harm to Japanese car companies. ♦

Do unintended effects matter? The answer is yes, they matter a great deal. That is why, for any action, economists think in terms of both intended and unintended effects. Can you see the advantage of being able to think about and anticipate unintended effects when making decisions?

Thinking in Terms of the Small and the Big

Economics is divided into two branches, **microeconomics** and **macroeconomics**. In microeconomics, economists look at the small picture. They study the behavior and choices of relatively small economic units, such as an individual or a single business firm. Economists who deal with macroeconomics look at the big picture, studying behavior and choices as they relate to the entire economy (see Exhibit 1-4). For example, in microeconomics, an economist would study and discuss the unemployment that exists in a particular industry, such as the car industry; in macroeconomics, an economist would investigate the unemployment that exists in the nation. In microeconomics, an economist would look at the buying behavior of consumers in regard to a single product, such as computers; an economist dealing in macroeconomics would study the buying behavior of consumers in regard to all goods. We might say that the tools of macroeconomics are telescopes, while the tools of microeconomics are microscopes. Macroeconomics stands back from the trees to see the forest. Microeconomics gets up close and examines the tree itself, including its bark, its branches, and the soil in which it grows. In this book you will learn to look at the world from both "micro" and "macro" perspectives.

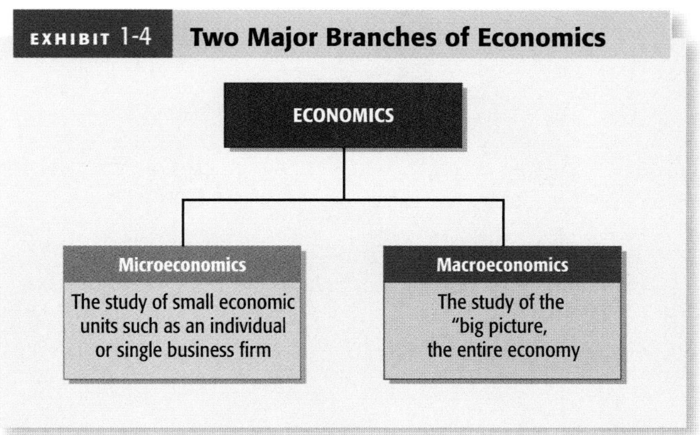
EXHIBIT 1-4 Two Major Branches of Economics
ECONOMICS
Microeconomics
The study of small economic units such as an individual or single business firm
Macroeconomics
The study of the "big picture, the entire economy

▲ Economists divide economics into two major branches: microeconomics and macroeconomics.

Thinking in Terms of Theories

Some questions have obvious answers, and others do not. For example, if you hold a ball in your right hand and ask someone what will happen if you let go of it, the person will likely say that the ball will drop to the ground. Right answer. If the classroom clock reads 10:12 and you ask someone in the class what time it is, that person will say 10:12. Again, right answer.

Now suppose you ask someone any of the following questions:

- Why is the crime rate higher in some countries than in other countries?
- What causes the stock market to rise or fall?
- What causes some nations to be rich and others to be poor?

microeconomics
The branch of economics that deals with human behavior and choices as they relate to relatively small units—an individual, a business firm, or a single market.

macroeconomics
The branch of economics that deals with human behavior and choices as they relate to the entire economy.

Reinforcement Activity

Point out to students that although the word *micro* means "small," microeconomics often deals with very large players in the economy. The activities of a huge corporation such as General Motors are considered a topic of microeconomics even though the company's output exceeds that of some nations.

Discussion Starter

Discuss with students their understanding of the word *theory.* Some students will know the word from science classes. How are the definitions of theory for economists and scientists similar? How are they different?

Background Information: Microeconomics and Macroeconomics

Microeconomics is the study of small economic units, and macroeconomics is the study of the way in which choices and behavior relate to far larger economic units, such as the entire U.S. economy. Microeconomics examines how a tax change might affect a single firm's output, and macroeconomics examines how that tax change might affect the entire economy's output. Microeconomics studies the individual, the household, the company. Macroeconomics studies whole economic systems and how different sectors interact. National economic policies are part of the study of macroeconomics.

Teaching with Visuals

Answers will vary. Students might suggest that political leaders use economic theories to support or oppose particular issues.

Reinforcement Activity

Ask students to pose questions for which they have no answers. Then ask how they would go about creating a proper theory to gain answers to those questions. Also create some questions about situations like those presented in the text (e.g., Why do people get sick after operations?), and ask students to propose theories based on those situations. Remind students that theories should be judged by how well they predict the outcome.

Teaching with Visuals

Answers will vary. For example, economists may wonder whether unemployment is tied to tax breaks offered for particular industries or products, to a cultural attitude toward spending versus saving, or to natural disasters.

Application Activity

After reading and discussing Section 2, you may want to assign the Section Activity in the *Applying the Principles Workbook.*

▲ U.S. Representative James Sensenbrenner Jr. (left) and Senator Charles Grassley (right) meet with President Bush to discuss economic policy. **Do you think these men make use of economic theories? If so, how?**

You probably would agree that these questions have no obvious, easy answers.

Because some economic questions do not have obvious answers, economists build theories. Think of a **theory** as a mechanism that an economist uses to answer a question that has no obvious, easy answer. Here are only five of hundreds of questions for which economists have built theories:

1. What causes inflation?
2. What causes the unemployment rate to rise or fall?
3. How do business firms operate?
4. What causes the prices of goods and services to rise, fall, or remain stable?
5. Why do countries experience good economic times in some years and bad economic times in other years?

theory
An explanation of how something works, designed to answer a question for which there is no obvious answer.

EXAMPLE: Suppose you are living in the days before anyone has heard the word *calorie.* Over a period of three years, you notice that your weight changes. At one time you weigh 140 pounds, then 145 pounds, then 155 pounds. You wonder why you are gaining weight.

Along comes a person who gives you a simplified explanation of what is happening. She says that there are things called "calories," and that we can measure food in terms of how many calories it has. Some foods have more calories than others. She then says that every day you use up, or burn, calories when you walk, run, and clean the house. You even burn them, she says, when you are sitting still on the couch watching television. Finally, she says that your weight depends on how many calories you take in compared to how many you burn. If you consume more calories than you burn, you will gain weight. ♦

This calorie theory is used to explain one's weight. You will notice that this theory explains how things work (how your body takes in and uses up calories) in order to answer a question. All theories have this structure. A theory always offers some explanation of how things work in order to answer a question that does not have an obvious answer.

A Student Asks

QUESTION: *I've always thought that theories were difficult to understand because they contain a lot of mathematics. Is this correct?*

ANSWER: *Some theories contain mathematics, but many do not. Your impression of a theory is the common one. Many people think that a theory has to be abstract, mathematical, and almost impossible to understand. But this is a misconception.*

To a large extent, a theory is simply a "best guess" offered to explain something. Anyone can build a theory; in fact, you may (unknowingly) do so.

Suppose your best friend always eats lunch with you. Then, one day he doesn't. You may wonder what explains his change in behavior.

Once you have a question in your mind—What led to the change in his behavior?—you are on your way to building a theory. Your "best guess" may be that he doesn't like you anymore, or that you said something to upset him, or something

Background Information: Economic Theories

Many advancements in technology and science started as theories. Assign students to research one familiar scientific or technological advancement and to present a report on who developed the theory that led to the discovery. Then present a couple of economic theories from Keynes, Locke, and others, to show students that theories are developed in various fields.

altogether different. Trying to answer your question by offering your "best guess" is really no different from an economist creating a theory about some aspect of economics. The economist puts forth his or her "best guess" as to what causes inflation, high interest rates, or economic growth.

Is It Reasonable?

Many people evaluate a theory based on whether it seems reasonable. However, many theories that at first seemed very unreasonable to people turned out to be correct. Think about how it might have sounded to you if you had lived before microscopes were invented and someone told you that people were getting sick because of tiny "things" (which today we call germs) that no one could see. You might have thought that sounded ridiculous. Or suppose you had lived during the days of the Roman Empire and someone proposed the round-earth theory to answer a question. You might have said, "There is no such thing as a round earth!"

Does It Predict Accurately?

Scientists believe that we should evaluate theories based not on how they sound to us, or whether they seem right, but on how well they predict. If they predict well, then we should accept them; if they predict poorly, then we should not. No doubt, as you read this text, you will come across an economic theory here or there that you think sounds wrong. You are urged to adopt the scientific attitude and hold off judging any economic theory until you learn how well it predicts.

▲ Many of these people are unemployed and looking for work. **Why do you think economists propose theories to explain unemployment?**

SECTION 2 ASSESSMENT

Defining Terms

1. Define:
   a. incentive
   b. microeconomics
   c. macroeconomics
   d. theory
2. Use *marginal costs* correctly in a sentence.

Reviewing Facts and Concepts

3. According to economists, almost everything we do has costs and benefits. Identify the costs and benefits of each of the following: going to the dentist for a checkup, doing your homework, and getting an extra hour of sleep.
4. Give an example of an unintended effect.
5. What is the difference between microeconomics and macroeconomics?

Critical Thinking

6. If there were zero opportunity cost to everything you did, would you ever face a trade-off? Explain your answer.

Applying Economic Concepts

7. Describe a recent situation in which you weighed marginal costs versus marginal benefits to make a decision.

Assess

Quick Quiz

The following true-or-false quiz will help you assess student understanding of the material covered in this section.

1. There are costs and benefits to almost everything we do. (True)
2. A theory does not explain anything. (False)
3. Economists must think of what would have been. (True)
4. In macroeconomics, economists look at the small picture. (False)
5. Theories should omit everything that is unnecessary. (True)

Assessment Book

You will find a quiz for this section in the *Assessment Book.*

Reteaching Activity

Use the Section Assessment to gauge which students may need reteaching on this section. Have these students reread the definition of *theory* and then think of a question with no obvious answer (e.g., Why is the sky blue? or Where does wind come from?) Then have them pose a theory to explain the phenomenon.

Guided Reading

For further reteaching of the key concepts in this section, assign the Outlining Activity and the Just the Facts Handout from the *Guided Reading and Study Guide.*

SECTION 2 ASSESSMENT ANSWERS

Defining Terms

1. a. incentive: something that encourages or motivates a person to take an action; **b. microeconomics:** the branch of economics in which economists look at the small picture; **c. macroeconomics:** the branch of economics in which economists study behavior and choices as they relate to the entire economy; **d. theory:** a mechanism that an economist uses to answer a question that has no obvious, easy answer.
2. Answers will vary.

Reviewing Facts and Concepts

3. Answers will vary.
4. Answers will vary. (*Sample answer:* Caroline takes an antibiotic to cure an infection. An unintended effect is that Caroline develops a rash and itching because she is allergic to the antibiotic.)
5. Microeconomics concerns the small picture; macroeconomics concerns the big picture. Microeconomics looks at some component of the economy; macroeconomics looks at the entire economy.

Critical Thinking

6. No. In a trade-off, you give up something to get more of something else. If there were zero opportunity cost to everything you did, you would never give up anything to get something else—hence, you would never encounter a trade-off.

Applying Economic Concepts

7. Answers will vary.

Your Personal Economics

Discussion Starter

Ask students if they have a savings account. Do students who have savings accounts know how much interest they are earning on their savings? Do they deposit money in their savings accounts on a regular basis? Do students who have not saved any money believe they could have saved some had they made doing so a priority?

Research Activity

After students have read the first savings scenario in the text, have them use a compound interest calculator to find out how much they will have if they save $2,000 at various interest rates from ages 22 to 65 (43 years), compounded quarterly. For example, at 4%, they will have $11,074.05; at 3%, $7,230.68; and at 2%, $4,716.20. Emphasize the importance of shopping for the best available interest rate.

Your Personal Economics

Spend a Little Now, or a Lot More Later?

Many people underestimate the power of saving. That's because they don't realize the large gains one can earn by saving—especially if they start saving when they are young.

Save Now, or Save Later?

You are probably 17 or 18 years old if you are reading this book. Suppose you go to college and when you are 22 you get your first full-time job, earning $45,000 a year. If, in that first year after graduating college—and only in that year—you save $2,000, at an annual interest rate of 5 percent, and your interest is compounded quarterly (which means you earn an interest payment every three months), how much money will you have when you retire at age 65? The answer is $16,942. In other words, a one-time savings of $2,000 when you are 22 will turn into $16,942 by the time you retire at 65.

It is likely, however, that if you are able to save money when you are 22, you will be able to save some when you are 23, 24, and so on. So, let's suppose that instead of saving $2,000 only once, when you are 22, you save $2,000 *every year* between the ages of 22 and 65. We will assume again that your annual interest rate of return is 5 percent and that interest is compounded quarterly. How much will money will you have at 65? The answer is $319,526.46.

▼ Saving now—even if you save only a small amount—will pay off later. **Have you opened a savings account yet?**

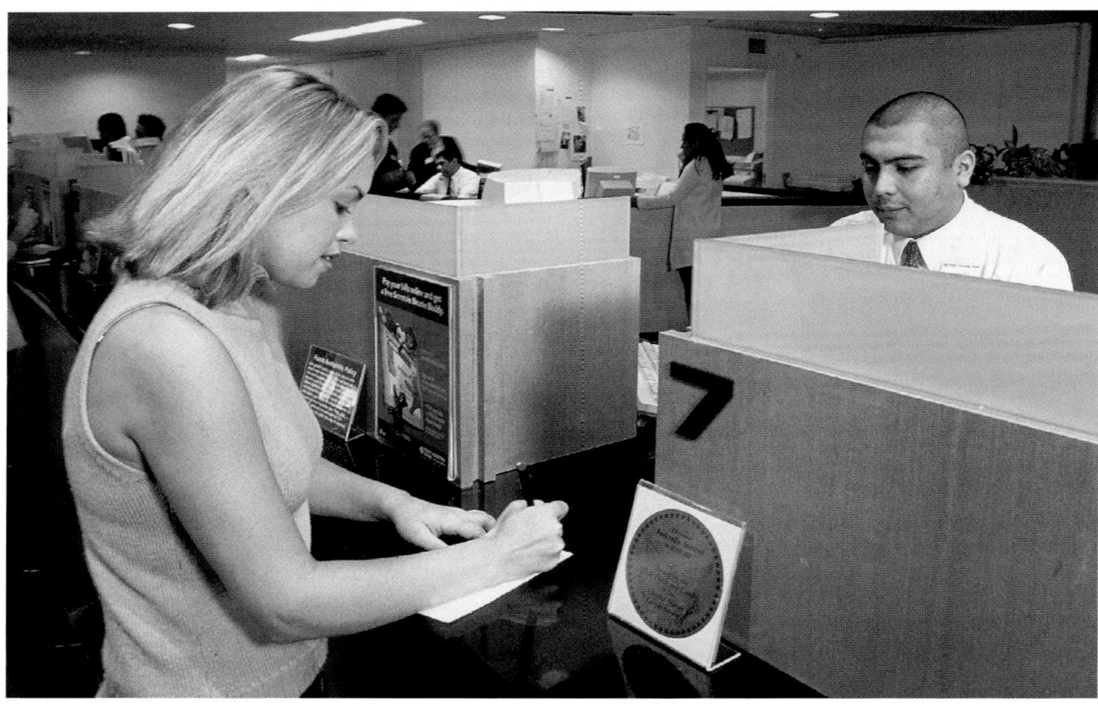

Cooperative Learning

After students have read "Smoking or Saving?" divide them into groups of three or four. Tell each group to brainstorm a list of items that they could give up entirely or reduce in number of purchases, and to estimate an amount of savings that would result. After 15 minutes, have the groups report their lists and totals to the class. Discuss realistic expectations for saving.

▲ Most of us spend small amounts of money every day that could become large amounts later in life. **What could you give up in favor of regular deposits to your savings account?**

Now, just to show you how much it matters to start saving when you are young, suppose that instead of beginning to save when you are 22, you wait until you are 40 to start saving. At 40 and each year after until you reach 65, you save $2,000. How much money would you have at 65? $106,694.68. So, how important is it to begin saving early? By setting aside just an additional $36,000 ($2,000 a year for each year between age 22 and age 40), you end up with an extra $212,831.78.

Smoking or Saving?

Now let's look at saving in a different way. Recently, a person who purchased a pack of cigarettes every other day ended up buying 182 packs a year at a cost of $4 a pack. That's a total of $728 per year spent on cigarettes. If that person had simply saved that $728 each year, instead of spending it on cigarettes, it would have ended up being $45,493.32 after 25 years (at an interest rate of 6 percent, compounded quarterly). What is the opportunity cost to smoking? Is smoking costly? It appears to be not only costly when it comes to your health, but also when it comes to your wallet.

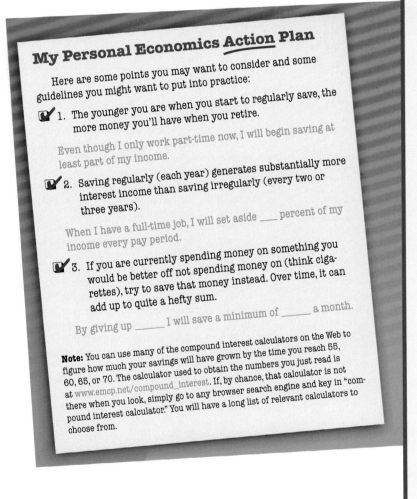

One Last Point

If you find it hard to save, then perhaps you need to know what saving really is. It is not, as some people think, the same as *not spending*. Instead, it is *postponed spending* or *future spending*. In other words, because you have saved today, you have more money to spend in the future. Your decision is not between spending and saving; your decision is between spending now and spending *more* later.

My Personal Economics Action Plan

Here are some points you may want to consider and some guidelines you might want to put into practice:

1. The younger you are when you start to regularly save, the more money you'll have when you retire.

   Even though I only work part-time now, I will begin saving at least part of my income.

2. Saving regularly (each year) generates substantially more interest income than saving irregularly (every two or three years).

   When I have a full-time job, I will set aside ___ percent of my income every pay period.

3. If you are currently spending money on something you would be better off not spending money on (think cigarettes), try to save that money instead. Over time, it can add up to quite a hefty sum.

   By giving up ______ I will save a minimum of ______ a month.

Note: You can use many of the compound interest calculators on the Web to figure how much your savings will have grown by the time you reach 55, 60, 65, or 70. The calculator used to obtain the numbers you just read is at www.emcp.net/compound_interest. If, by chance, that calculator is not there when you look, simply go to any browser search engine and key in "compound interest calculator." You will have a long list of relevant calculators to choose from.

Discussion Starter

To help students realize the power of compound interest and saving, ask them to list the things they might buy with the $106,694.68 that they will have at retirement if they begin saving $2,000 a year at the age of 40. Then ask them to list what they might buy if they begin saving $2,000 a year at age 22 and therefore have $319,526.46 at retirement. Make sure they realize that they will be able to purchase all the additional items as a result of setting aside just an additional $36,000.

My Personal Economics Action Plan Have students survey adults they know to determine how those people are saving money. If students find that the adults are not saving, they should ask whether the adults feel that they could save if they made doing so a priority. Students may want to prepare for the survey by developing a list of items that most people purchase but could do without, with the resulting possible savings. Students could ask the adults which of those items they use and which they might stop purchasing in order to save money. Ask students to report their survey findings to the class.

SECTION 3 Teacher Support

Focus and Motivate

Section Objectives

After completing this section, students will be able to

- describe the different ways economists talk about goods;
- identify services;
- list the four types of resources; and
- explain why labor and entrepreneurship are different categories of resources.

Kickoff Activity

Write the following statement on the board: "Write down two particular items in the classroom, and list the materials or resources that were used to produce these goods."

Activating Prior Knowledge

Encourage students to share their responses to the Kickoff Activity. Make sure they understand that the physical makeup of a good is not the only resource that goes into the production of that good. Explain that when we talk about goods, we should think about all the resources that went into producing them.

Teach

Discussion Starter

Have each student give two examples of each factor of production. Emphasize that in economics, the word *land* means more than just a "plowed field"; it also refers to all the resources found in nature, including water and minerals.

SECTION 3 Basic Economic Language

Focus Questions

- What are the different ways that economists talk about "goods"?
- What are services?
- What are the four types of resources or factors of production?
- Why are labor and entrepreneurship different categories of resources?

Key Terms

tangible	services
intangible	land
goods	labor
utility	capital
disutility	entrepreneurship

tangible
Able to be felt by touch. For example, a book is tangible: you can touch and feel it.

intangible
Not able to be felt by touch. For example, an economics lecture is intangible.

goods
Anything that satisfies a person's wants or brings satisfaction; also, tangible products.

utility
The quality of bringing satisfaction or happiness.

disutility
The quality of bringing dissatisfaction or unhappiness.

services
Tasks that people pay others to perform for them.

Goods and Services

If you look closely at all the things people want, you will notice that some are **tangible** and some are **intangible**. Something is tangible if it can be felt or touched. A computer is tangible; you can touch it. Something is intangible if it cannot be felt by touch. Friendship is intangible.

Economists use the term **goods** in different ways. On the most basic level a good is anything that satisfies a person's wants, that brings a person satisfaction, **utility**, or happiness. In this sense a good can be either tangible (such as a candy bar) or intangible (the feeling of being safe and secure). It might help you to think of these goods as anything that isn't a *bad*, which is something that brings a person dissatisfaction, **disutility**, or unhappiness.

Economists and others who talk about the economy use the term *goods* in another way, usually when they are talking about how our economy is performing. You have probably read in the newspaper or heard on the television news the phrase *goods and services*. In these cases, people are referring to goods as tangible items only, not both tangible and intangible. They are talking about all the tangible products that have been produced and are available for you to buy in our economy. Toothpaste, alarm clocks, cereal, clothes—all of these items are goods.

Services, on the other hand, are intangible. They are the tasks that you pay other people to perform for you. When people care for you at your doctor's office, wait on you at a local restaurant, or cut your hair at the beauty shop or barbershop, these people are performing services. You will read more about how "goods and services" are produced and measured in several later chapters.

Resources

Goods and services cannot be produced without resources. Because the world has limited resources (scarcity), and because the central economic questions deal with the ways people use these limited resources to satisfy their unlimited wants, economists have spent much time studying and classifying resources.

Internet Research

Tell students to search the Internet for sites discussing or promoting resources in land, labor, and capital for a particular industry. For example, they might find the official Web site of a national forest, a site for a union representing workers in the logging industry, and a site for a company that sells machinery used in the logging process. Ask them to explain, in writing, how each of these sites represents the land, labor, and capital resources for that industry. Then have them explain what they think a person would need to do to demonstrate entrepreneurship, the fourth economic resource, in this industry.

▲ Both the oil refinery on the left and the newly planted forest on the right represent resources, or factors of production, as economists often call resources. **Into which of the four major categories of resources would you place oil and wood ? In what way are these two resources different?**

In economics, a synonym for *resources* is *factors of production*. Resources, or factors of production, are what people use to produce goods and services. For example, corn, other natural substances, and many different machines are resources that were used to produce the cereal that you ate for breakfast this morning. Economists place resources in four broad categories: land, labor, capital, and entrepreneurship.

Sometimes economists differentiate between renewable and nonrenewable resources. A *renewable resource* is a resource that can be drawn on indefinitely if it is replaced. For example, wood, or timber, is a renewable resource because once trees have been cut down, new trees can be planted. In other words, timber can be "renewed" to maintain a certain supply of it.

A *non-renewable* (or exhaustible) *resource* is obviously a resource that cannot be replenished. For example, oil and natural gas are nonrenewable resources. There is no way to "plant" more oil the way you can plant more trees. Using a certain quantity of oil means just that much less oil is left.

Land

When the word **land** is mentioned, you may picture an acre of woods or a plowed field in your mind's eye. The resource *land* is more, however. It includes all the natural resources found in nature, such as water, minerals, animals, and forests.

Labor

Labor refers to the physical and mental talents that people contribute to the production of goods and services. For example, a person working in a factory is considered to be the resource *labor*. A TV weatherperson telling you what the weather will be like tomorrow is considered to be the resource *labor*. Your economics teacher is a resource —a labor resource.

Capital

In economics, **capital** refers to produced goods that can be used as resources for further production. Such things as machinery, tools, computers, trucks, buildings, and factories are all considered to be capital, or

land
All the natural resources found in nature. An acre of land, mineral deposits, and water in a stream are all considered land.

labor
The physical and mental talents that people contribute to the production of goods and services.

capital
Produced goods that can be used as resources for further production. Such things as factories, machines, and farm tractors are capital.

Teaching with Visuals

An economist would place wood and oil in the land category. Wood is renewable; oil is nonrenewable.

Thinking Like an Economist

Tell students that before the introduction of the steam engine, work could be performed only by humans, animals, wind, or moving water. To use wind or moving water, people had to go where these resources could be found. Thus, early factories had to be located in the countryside, where wind and water (streams) were most likely to be found. The goods produced in the factories were then carried to markets. By the time the goods were produced and transported to the cities, the price of the goods was so high that only the richest could afford to buy them.

In 1769, James Watt developed a steam engine that could run anywhere. Ask students how this might have affected producers' labor and transportation costs. How, in turn, would this have affected the price of the goods?

Cooperative Learning

Divide the class into four groups. Assign each group one of the four factors of production. Each group should complete the following assignments for its resource:

1. Develop a one-minute oral report describing the factor of production and its importance.

2. Using images clipped from magazines or newspapers, or original artwork, or both, create a collage depicting the resource. Have the groups take turns sharing their work with the rest of the class.

ANSWERS TO THINK ABOUT IT Answers will vary. David Friedman argues that a formation of neat rows made it easy to see any soldier who broke ranks and tried to desert.

Reinforcement Activity

The concept of dressing in distinctive clothing is not uncommon. Urge students to think of groups who dress distinctively in order to stand out from the general society. Ask: Should everyone have a distinctive set of clothing to show his or her cultural and personal designations? What would we lose if everyone had a prescribed set of clothing? What might we gain? Encourage students to include economics loses and gains in their answers.

Discussion Starter

Students may think that finding and taking advantage of new opportunities sounds imaginative, creative, and financially rewarding. However, not all entrepreneurs are successful. And even successful entrepreneurs are not successful all the time. Instruct students to each identify a different entrepreneur and research her or his efforts. Then discuss whether the various entrepreneurs have been successful in all their endeavors.

Application Activity

After reading and discussing Section 3, you may want to assign the Section Activity in the *Applying the Principles Workbook.*

Why Did British Troops Wear Bright Red Uniforms?

When George Washington and the colonists fought the British, the colonists were dressed in rags, while the British troops were clad in fine, bright red uniforms. Commenting on this difference, people often say, "The British were foolish to have worn bright red uniforms. You could see them coming for miles."

Economists would not be so quick to label the British as foolish. Instead they would ask why the British troops wore bright red. For instance, David Friedman, an economist, thinks it is odd that the British, who at the time were the greatest fighting force in the world, would make such a seemingly obvious mistake. He has an alternative explanation, an economic explanation.

Friedman reasons that the British generals did not want their men to break ranks and desert, because winning the war would be hard, if not impossible, if a lot of men deserted. Thus, the generals had to think up a way to make the opportunity cost of desertion high for their soldiers. The generals reasoned that the higher the cost of desertion, the fewer deserters there would be. The British generals effectively told their soldiers that if they deserted, they would have to forfeit their freedom or their lives.

Of course, the problem is that a stiff penalty is not effective if deserters cannot be found. Therefore, the generals had to make it easy to find deserters, which they did by dressing them in bright red uniforms. Certainly it was possible for a deserter to throw off his uniform and walk through the countryside in his underwear alone, but in the harsh winters of New England, doing so would guarantee death. He had almost no choice but to wear the bright red uniform.

THINK ABOUT IT In battle, the British soldiers marched toward their enemy in neat rows. Was this foolish, or was this formation perhaps done based on a sound economic reason? What economic explanations would you propose for this type of formation?

capital goods. Each capital good is used to produce some other good or service. Computers are used to produce books and magazines, trucks are used to carry groceries to your local supermarket, and factories produce most, if not all, of the items you see as you look around your classroom.

A Student Asks

QUESTION: *I thought "capital" referred to money. When my uncle said he needed more capital to invest in his business, wasn't he talking about needing more money?*

ANSWER: *Maybe your uncle did use the word "capital" as a synonym for "money." But capital to an economist refers to such things as machinery, tools, and so on—things that can be used as resources for further production. So, when an economist says a firm wants to buy more capital, he is saying that the firm wants to buy more machinery and tools.*

Entrepreneurship

If someone asked you to point to the resource *land*, you might point to a forest. For the resource *labor*, you might point to yourself as an example. To show capital, you might point to a computer. But what would you point to if someone asked you to give an example of **entrepreneurship**? This resource is not so easy to identify.

Entrepreneurship refers to the special talent that some people have for searching out and taking advantage of new business opportunities, as well as for developing new products and new ways of doing things. For example, Steve Jobs, one of the developers of the first personal computer, exhibited entrepreneurship. He saw a use for the personal computer and developed it, and hundreds of thousands of customers then purchased his product—the Apple computer. Of late, millions of dollars in revenue have been generated by a relatively new Apple product, the iPod.

A Student Asks

QUESTION: *Since only people can exhibit entrepreneurship, why isn't entrepreneurship considered a type of labor? In short, why aren't there only three resources—land, labor, and capital—instead of four?*

ANSWER: *Economists consider entrepreneurship sufficiently different from the ordinary talents of people to deserve its own category. Consider this explanation. Both the star player on your high school basketball team and LeBron James fall into the category "basketball player," just as entrepreneurs and laborers both fall into the category "people." But are they the same in terms of the impact they would have on the success of a team? Even if the star of your team is an outstanding player, it is unlikely that you would consider him to be "in the same category" as LeBron James. LeBron James is considered a superstar—he has extraordinary basketball talents. So it is with labor and entrepreneurship. The ordinary mental and physical talents of people are considered labor. The special talents that are directed toward searching out and taking advantage of new business opportunities, products, and methods are considered entrepreneurship.*

entrepreneurship
The special talent that some people have for searching out and taking advantage of new business opportunities and for developing new products and new ways of doing things.

Section 3 Assessment

Defining Terms

1. Define:
   a. tangible
   b. intangible
   c. goods
   d. utility
   e. services
   f. land
   g. labor
   h. capital
   i. entrepreneurship
2. The resource that involves goods used to produce other goods is ____________.

Reviewing Facts and Concepts

3. Identify the following resources. Write "Ld" for land, "Lb" for labor, "C" for capital, and "E" for entrepreneurship.
   a. Francis's work as a secretary
   b. iron ore
   c. a farm tractor
   d. a computer used to write a book
   e. a comedian telling jokes on a television show
   f. a singer singing at an outdoor concert
   g. your teacher teaching you economics
   h. someone inventing a new product
   i. crude oil
   j. oil-drilling equipment

Critical Thinking

4. Entrepreneurship is sometimes the "forgotten resource." Why do you think it is easier to forget entrepreneurship than, say, labor or capital?

Applying Economic Concepts

5. Some economists will talk about the resource *time*. Under what category of resource (land, labor, capital, or entrepreneurship) would you most likely place *time*? Explain your answer.

Defining Terms

1. a. tangible: something that can be felt or touched; **b. intangible:** something that cannot be felt by touch; **c. goods:** anything that satisfies a person's wants; **d. utility:** the quality of bringing satisfaction or happiness; **e. services:** tasks that people pay others to perform for them; **f. land:** all the natural resources found in nature; **g. labor:** the physical and mental talents that people contribute to the production of goods and services; **h. capital:** produced goods that can be used as resources for further production; **i. entrepreneurship:** the special talent that some people have for searching out and taking advantage of new business opportunities.
2. capital.

Reviewing Facts and Concepts

3. a. Lb; **b.** Ld; **c.** C; **d.** C; **e.** Lb; **f.** Lb; **g.** Lb; **h.** E; **i.** Ld; **j.** C.

Critical Thinking

4. Entrepreneurship is easier to forget because it is more difficult to identify.

Applying Economic Concepts

5. Answers will vary. Students might say land, because time is a natural resource that is used along with labor and capital to produce goods.

Assess

Quick Quiz

The following true-or-false quiz will help you assess student understanding of the material covered in this section.

1. A synonym for *resources* is *factors of enterprise.* (False)
2. The four categories of resources include labor. (True)
3. An intangible good is something that can be touched. (False)
4. A good is anything that satisfies a person's wants. (True)
5. Services are intangible. (True)

Assessment Book

You will find a quiz for this section in the *Assessment Book.*

Reteaching Activity

Assign students to work with partners to create a pictorial chart depicting the four types of resources.

Guided Reading

For further reteaching of the key concepts in this section, assign the Outlining Activity and the Just the Facts Handout from the *Guided Reading and Study Guide.*

CHAPTER 1

Assessment Answers

Economics Vocabulary

1. scarcity; **2.** wants; **3.** production possibilities frontier; **4.** Opportunity cost; **5.** Economics; **6.** microeconomics; **7.** theory; **8.** tangible; **9.** intangible; **10.** disutility; **11.** utility; **12.** incentive; **13.** capital; **14.** entrepreneurs.

Understanding the Main Ideas

1. Scarcity is the condition in which people's wants are greater than the resources available to satisfy those wants.
2. Because scarcity exists, people must *choose* which of their many wants they will satisfy.
3. By making a choice, people give up something; in other words, they incur an opportunity cost.
4. Scarcity implies the need for some rationing device. People will compete for the rationing device.
5. The opportunity cost of attending high school is what one would be doing if not attending high school. Opportunity costs exist even when tuition does not.
6. It is preferable to think in terms of costs and benefits rather than just benefits because most things in life (activities, purchases, and so on) have both costs and benefits connected with them.
7. The PPF illustrates scarcity by showing which items are available and which are not.
8. You cannot be at different points on the PPF at the same time; you must make a choice to be at only one point on the PPF.
9. Two lessons may be learned from the story about the baker's window: (1) Money that is spent to purchase one thing cannot be used to purchase something else. For example, money that goes to purchase a new window cannot now go to purchase a new suit. (2) To understand things fully, we need to be aware not only of what is, but also of what would have been.

CHAPTER 1 ASSESSMENT

Chapter Summary

Be sure you know and remember the following key points from the chapter sections.

Section 1

- People have unlimited wants, but resources are limited. The condition in which our wants are greater than the limited available resources is known as scarcity.
- Because of scarcity, people must make choices, which means they must incur opportunity costs.
- A production possibilities frontier shows all the possible combinations of two goods that an economy can produce.
- Rationing devices are needed to decide who gets what portion of the available goods. Because people compete for the rationing device, competition is a consequence of scarcity.

Section 2

- Economists often consider both the costs and benefits of an activity.
- Economists believe that people act as they do in response to incentives.
- Individuals and societies must deal with trade-offs.
- Economists try to see "what would have been" as well as "what will be."
- Decisions and actions often have important unintended effects.
- Economics is divided into two branches: microeconomics and macroeconomics.
- Economists construct theories to answer economic questions.

Section 3

- Utility means the same thing as satisfaction or happiness; disutility means the same thing as dissatisfaction or unhappiness.
- Goods are tangible items; services are tasks that people perform for others.
- The four categories of resources, or factors of production, are land, labor, capital, and entrepreneurship.

Economics Vocabulary

To reinforce your knowledge of the key terms in this chapter, fill in the following blanks on a separate piece of paper with the appropriate word or phrase.

1. The condition where wants are greater than the resources available to satisfy those wants is called ______.
2. Things that we desire to have are called ______.
3. A(n) ______ represents the possible combinations of two goods that can be produced in a certain time period.
4. ______ is the most highly valued, or next best, alternative that is forfeited when a choice is made.
5. ______ is the science that studies the choices of people trying to satisfy their wants in a world of scarcity.
6. The branch of economics that deals with human behavior and choices as they relate to relatively small units is called ______.
7. A(n) ______ is an explanation of how something works, designed to answer a question that has no obvious answer.
8. A good that can be touched is considered to be ______.
9. A service is not tangible, but ______.
10. Another word for dissatisfaction or unhappiness is ______.
11. To an economist, another word for satisfaction or happiness is ______.
12. A(n) ______ encourages a person to take action.
13. Produced goods used for further production are referred to as ______.
14. People who have a special talent for taking advantage of new business opportunities are called ______.

Understanding the Main Ideas

Write answers to the following questions to review the main ideas in this chapter.

1. What is scarcity?
2. Explain this statement: Because scarcity exists, choices must be made.

10. Economists believe that in making decisions, people think in terms not of total costs, but of marginal costs and benefits.
11. No. The benefits of building (and using) the schools may outweigh the costs. Even though the costs will be high, the benefits may be higher.
12. An unintended effect of this law might be that a typical apple seller's income actually falls. People might buy fewer apples at 75 cents or more apiece than they did at 50 cents. As a result, a seller's income might be lower at 75 or more cents an apple than at 50 cents an apple.
13. When we evaluate a theory according to whether it sounds right or reasonable, we are prejudging the theory before we even test it to see if it is a "good" or "bad" theory. The problem with this approach is that often what sounds right or reasonable may turn out to be wrong, and what

3. Describe the connection between choices and opportunity costs.
4. Explain the link between scarcity and competition.
5. If you attend a public high school, you are not charged admission fees or tuition. Does it follow, then, that you face no opportunity cost in attending school? Explain your answer.
6. Why is it preferable to think in terms of costs and benefits rather than in terms of benefits only?
7. Explain how scarcity is illustrated by a production possibilities frontier.
8. Why do the points on a production possibilities frontier represent choices?
9. What lesson is to be learned from the story in this chapter about the boy and the broken window?
10. What does it mean to think "at the margin"?
11. Suppose it is costly to build more schools in your city or town. Does it necessarily follow that the schools should not be built? Explain your answer.
12. Suppose apples are currently selling for 50 cents each. Someone says that apple sellers can't make a decent living if they sell their apples so cheaply. He says there should be a law stating that no one can sell an apple, and no one can buy an apple, for less than 75 cents. He intends for the law to raise the income of apple sellers. What might be an unintended effect of this law? Explain your answer.
13. Why is it better to judge theories by how well they predict than by whether they sound right or reasonable to us?
14. Identify some trade-off that you face.
15. How does entrepreneurship differ from labor?

Doing the Math

Do the calculations necessary to solve the following problems.

1. Bill decided to buy six books on history instead of four books on politics. It follows, then, that the opportunity cost of each history book was ______ books on politics.
2. The owner of a movie theater decides to raise ticket prices from $10 to $12 a ticket. Since he sells an average of 789 tickets a day, he might expect to collect ____ more per day in ticket sales. Why might he be disappointed?

Solving Economic Problems

Use your thinking skills and the information you learned in this chapter to find solutions to the following problems.

1. **Application.** The person who developed Music Television (MTV) said that today's younger generation particularly enjoys two things: (1) television and (2) music, especially rock music. His idea was to combine the two, and MTV was born. Would you say that he was exhibiting entrepreneurship? Explain your answer.
2. **Application.** Think like an entrepreneur. Identify a new product or service that you believe many people will want to buy. List the land, labor, and capital that will be needed to produce this new product or service, and explain why you think people will want to buy it.
3. **Analysis.** Explain how scarcity is related to each of the following: (1) choice, (2) opportunity cost, and (3) a rationing device.
4. **Cause and Effect.** "Because we have to make choices, there is scarcity." What is wrong with this statement?
5. **Writing.** Write a one-page paper explaining how the world would be different if scarcity did not exist.
6. **Economics in the Media.** Find an example in your local newspaper of one effect of scarcity. Your example may come from an article, editorial, or advertisement.
7. **Analysis.** What does a classroom full of college students have to do with scarcity?

Practice Tests and Study Guide

Go to www.emcp.net/economics and choose *Economics: New Ways of Thinking*, Chapter 1, if you need more help in preparing for the chapter test.

sounds wrong or unreasonable may turn out to be right. Knowing this, we can see that it is better to judge theories by how well they perform (how well they predict) and not to prejudge them.
14. Answers will vary.
15. *Labor* refers to the physical and mental talents that people contribute to the production of goods and services. *Entrepreneurship* refers to a special talent (that not everyone has) for searching out and taking advantage of new business opportunities, developing new products, and so on.

Doing the Math

1. For every history book Bill purchased, he could have purchased two-thirds of a book on politics (*calculation:* Cost of 6 history books = cost of 4 politics books; Cost of $\frac{6}{6}$ history books = cost of $\frac{4}{6}$ politics books; Cost of 1 history book = $\frac{4}{6}$ politics books; Cost of 1 history book = $\frac{2}{3}$ politics books).
2. $1,578 (*calculation:* Average daily increase in ticket sales = daily increase in price per ticket × average number of tickets sold per day = ($12 – $10) × 789 = $2 × 789 = $1,578). He might be disappointed because demand might fall as the price goes up.

Solving Economic Problems

1. Yes. Part of the definition of entrepreneurship refers to "searching out and taking advantage of new business opportunities."
2. Answers will vary. Keep in mind that the reason for the question is to get students to realize just how hard it is to think up a new and good product.
3. (1) Scarcity is the condition in which our wants outstrip the resources available to satisfy those wants. Because we want more things than we can possibly have, we must choose which of our wants will be satisfied and which will not be, or which will be satisfied to a greater degree. (2) Scarcity implies choice, and choice implies opportunity cost. In short, once we make choices, we incur opportunity costs. To choose X, for example, is to not choose Y, so Y is the opportunity cost of X. (3) People need resources to satisfy their wants, so there needs to be a way of deciding who gets what resources and in what quantities. Hence, there is a need for a rationing device.
4. Cause and effect are reversed. The statement says that because we make choices, scarcity exists. In fact, it is the other way around: because scarcity exists, we have to make choices.
5. Student essays should describe the role of scarcity.
6. Answers will vary.
7. Because of scarcity, the students have incurred an opportunity cost by attending college. In other words, they have given up something to attend college.

Chapter 2 Planning Guide

SECTION ORGANIZER

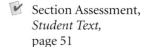

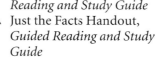

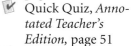

	Learning Objectives	Reproducible Worksheets and Handouts	Assessment
Section 1: Economic Systems (pages 32–40)	► List three economic questions every society must answer. ► Distinguish between free enterprise and socialism. ► Explain what an economic system is. ► Describe what Adam Smith said about self-interest. ► Define the labor theory of value.	Section 1 Activity on economic systems, *Applying the Principles Workbook* Section 1 Activity on the visions, *Applying the Principles Workbook* Outlining Activity, *Guided Reading and Study Guide* Just the Facts Handout, *Guided Reading and Study Guide*	Section Assessment, *Student Text,* page 40 Quick Quiz, *Annotated Teacher's Edition,* page 39–40 Section Quiz, *Assessment Book*
Section 2: Globalization (pages 41–51)	► Define globalization and explain its causes. ► Describe evidence that indicates that globalization is taking place. ► Describe the benefits and costs of globalization. ► Explain why the trend toward globalization is likely to continue.	Section 2 Activity, *Applying the Principles Workbook* Outlining Activity, *Guided Reading and Study Guide* Just the Facts Handout, *Guided Reading and Study Guide*	Section Assessment, *Student Text,* page 51 Quick Quiz, *Annotated Teacher's Edition,* page 51 Section Quiz, *Assessment Book*

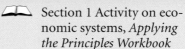

CHAPTER AND PROGRAM RESOURCES

Reproducible Chapter Resources and Assessment Materials

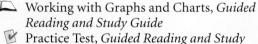

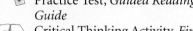

- Graphic Organizer Activity, *Guided Reading and Study Guide*
- Vocabulary Activity, *Guided Reading and Study Guide*
- Working with Graphs and Charts, *Guided Reading and Study Guide*
- Practice Test, *Guided Reading and Study Guide*
- Critical Thinking Activity, *Finding Economics*
- Chapter Test A, *Assessment Book*
- Chapter Test B, *Assessment Book*

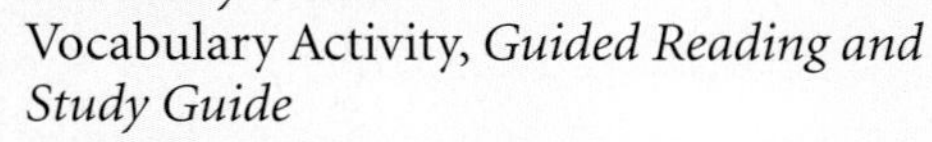

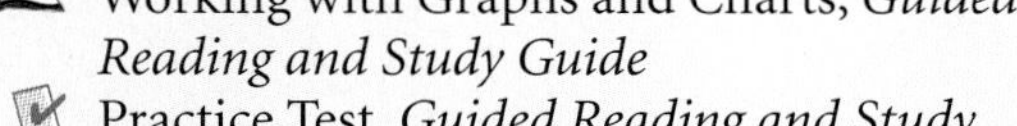

Technology Resources

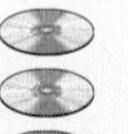

- *Test Generator CD*
- *Spanish Audio Summaries CD*
- *Marketplace® Audio Lessons CD*
- *Economic Principles Lectures, Videocassette or DVD*

Lesson Planning and Teaching Resources

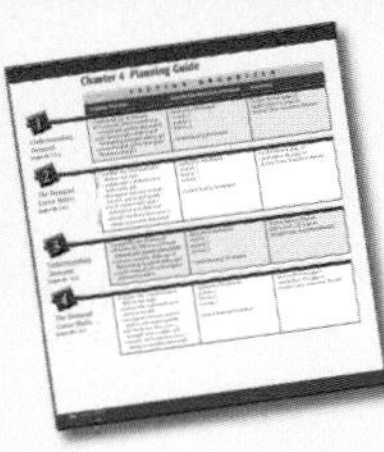

The *Economics: New Ways of Thinking* Teacher Resources include detailed lesson plans for each section in this chapter; the lesson plans are available in print form *(Lesson Plans)* and electronic form. The Teacher Resources also include *Daily Lectures: Overheads and Notes,* which provides prepared overheads and discussion notes covering the key concepts in each section of this chapter.

EMC Publishing Economics Online

Go to Economics Online, at www.emcp.com, for a variety of Internet resources to help you keep your course current and relevant. At Economics Online you will find these items:

- Economics in the News Lessons
- Study Guide Questions
- Practice Tests
- Lesson Plans

Internet Resources

Economics: New Ways of Thinking encourages students to use the Internet to find out more about economics. With the wealth of current, valid information available on Web sites, using the Internet as a research tool is likely to increase your students' interest in and understanding of economics principles and topics. In addition, doing Internet research can help your students form the habit of accessing and using economics information, as well as help them develop investigative skills they will use throughout their educational and professional careers.

To aid your students in achieving these ends, each chapter of *Economics: New Ways of Thinking* includes the addresses of several Web sites at which students will find engaging, relevant information. When students type in the addresses provided, they will immediately arrive at the intended sites. The addresses have been modified so that EMC Publishing can monitor and maintain the proper links—for example, the government site http://stats.bls.gov/ has been changed to www.emcp.net/prices. In the event that the address or content of a site changes or is discontinued, EMC's Internet editors will create a link that redirects students to an address with similar information.

Activities in the *Annotated Teacher's Edition* often suggest that students search the Internet for information. For some activities, you might want to find reputable sites beforehand, and steer students to those sites. For other activities, you might want students to do their own searching, and then check out the sites they have found and discuss why they might be reliable or unreliable.

CHAPTER 2 Overview

This chapter discusses the two major economic systems in the world: free enterprise and socialism. Students will also learn about globalization, something that has made the world a much smaller place. The following statements provide brief descriptions of the major concepts covered in each section of this chapter.

SECTION 1 Economic Systems

Section 1 explains what an economic system is, and describes the details of the free enterprise vision and the details of the socialist vision.

SECTION 2 Globalization

Section 2 covers globalization, including what it is, what caused it, and how people are affected by it.

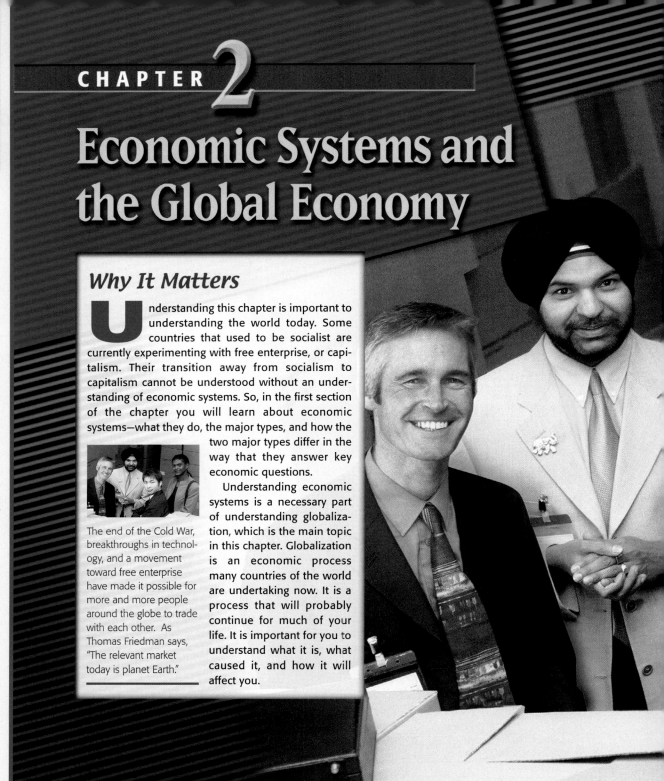

CHAPTER 2 Economic Systems and the Global Economy

Why It Matters

Understanding this chapter is important to understanding the world today. Some countries that used to be socialist are currently experimenting with free enterprise, or capitalism. Their transition away from socialism to capitalism cannot be understood without an understanding of economic systems. So, in the first section of the chapter you will learn about economic systems—what they do, the major types, and how the two major types differ in the way that they answer key economic questions.

Understanding economic systems is a necessary part of understanding globalization, which is the main topic in this chapter. Globalization is an economic process many countries of the world are undertaking now. It is a process that will probably continue for much of your life. It is important for you to understand what it is, what caused it, and how it will affect you.

The end of the Cold War, breakthroughs in technology, and a movement toward free enterprise have made it possible for more and more people around the globe to trade with each other. As Thomas Friedman says, "The relevant market today is planet Earth."

Teaching Suggestions from the Author

There are many countries in the world but principally only two economic systems—free enterprise (or capitalism) and socialism. Students are usually familiar with the terms *capitalism* and *socialism* and come to class with a bias in favor of one or the other. As suggested in other chapters, it is better if they can set aside their biases while they read and study this chapter.

One of the things we try to do in this chapter is to get students to realize that economic systems do not fall from the sky. They are created here on Earth. And here on Earth, people's ideas or visions (of how the world works) are the foundation stones upon which economic systems are built.

Economics Around the Clock

The following events occurred one day in September.

10:13 A.M. The leaders of some of the richest countries in the world were gathering for a meeting in a small town in Switzerland. The topic for discussion: economic globalization. Outside the meeting, hundreds of people from all over the world screamed slogans and held up signs. One of the most common signs read, "Globalization hurts the poor." One of the chants heard there was, "Hey, Hey, Ho, Ho, Globalization has got to go!"

- **What is globalization? Does it hurt the poor?**

6:14 P.M. Ken works as a software engineer for a large firm in New York City. He just walked into his house after a hard day at work. His wife, Alexis, who usually gets home about 7:00, is already at home. She says to Ken, "What's got you so down? You look as if you lost your job today." "I did," says Ken. "The company is sending my job out of the country."

- **Will globalization lead to some people losing jobs?**

7:45 P.M. Diane is watching a television news show. Here is what the TV news reporter is currently saying: "People are somewhat afraid that with globalization, their jobs and their livelihoods will be determined by forces outside of their control, perhaps by forces emanating from halfway around the world. This is the scary side of globalization. But on the other hand, some people look upon this new global economy with optimism. They say that with globalization come opportunities–opportunities to end poverty and to turn a turbulent and hostile world into a peaceful one. We'll just have to wait and see. For WTYX News, this is Tabitha Sherman."

- **Does everyone agree as to what the benefits and costs of globalization are?**

11:54 P.M. Elizabeth lives in Kentucky. Last week she bought a computer online from a U.S. company. She is having a little trouble with the computer so she calls the customer service number. In a matter of minutes, a voice on the other end of the line asks for her service tag number. She gives it to the person. The person she is speaking with is in India.

- **Why is the person in India?**

31

Introducing the Chapter

To introduce Chapter 2, you might write the word "socialism" on the board. Ask students, What do you think of when you see the word *socialism?* Allow students to share responses. It might be helpful for you to know what preconceived notions and predilections students bring to the study of economic systems and the discussion of globalization.

Tell students to read the chapter title—"Economic Systems and the Global Economy." To what do they think "Economic Systems" refers in this title? Explain that in this chapter, they will be looking at a different economic system, socialism, and comparing it with the system they live under, free enterprise.

Stress that this comparison is only part of the chapter. In addition, this chapter examines how individuals and businesses are affected by events in other parts of the world—that is, by globalization.

Teaching with Visuals

Ask students: Why, do you think, are many former socialist countries currently experimenting with free enterprise? How does this trend relate to globalization?

In other words, certain ideas form the basis of socialism and certain ideas form the basis of capitalism. In this chapter, we try to make this clear to students.

You may want to begin by asking students: What ideas or visions underlie capitalism? Is one foundation stone the idea that private property is sacred? the idea that people have the right to trade with others? What ideas underlie socialism? Is one basis the idea of equality? the idea that economic plans are efficient?

SECTION 1 Teacher Support

Focus and Motivate

Section Objectives

After completing this section, students will be able to

- list three economic questions every society must answer;
- distinguish between free enterprise and socialism;
- explain what an economic system is;
- describe what Adam Smith said about self-interest; and
- define the labor theory of value.

Kickoff Activity

Read the following quote from Aristotle: "What is common to many is taken least care of, for all men have greater regard for what is their own than for what they possess in common with others." Invite students to identify from their daily lives examples of the truth of this statement.

Activating Prior Knowledge

Instruct students to list the first four words that come to mind when you say the word *vision.* Encourage them to share their lists. Explain that in this section, the class will talk about the free enterprise, or capitalist, vision and the socialist vision. Mention that for the purposes of this discussion, a vision is a sense of how the world works.

Teach

Discussion Starter

Pose the following question: Who or what decides what goods should be produced by a society, and in what quantities? Mention that this question must be answered by every society. Some people might think that more artwork and houses need to be produced. Other people might think that more medical services should be produced. Somehow, a society as a whole must address such issues.

SECTION 1 Economic Systems

Focus Questions

- What are three economic questions every society must answer?
- What are the major differences between free enterprise and socialism?
- What is an economic system?
- What did Adam Smith say about self-interest?
- What is the labor theory of value?

Key Terms

economic system
free enterprise
socialism
economic plan
income distribution
mixed economy
traditional economy
vision
labor theory of value
surplus value

Three Economic Questions

All nations in the world share something fundamental: All must decide how to answer three economic questions about the production and distribution of goods.

- *What goods will be produced?* The first economic question every society has to answer concerns what goods to produce. Because of scarcity, no country can produce every good it wants in the quantity it would like. More of one good (say, television sets) leaves fewer resources to produce other goods (such as cars). No matter what nation we are talking about—the United States, China, Japan, India, Russia, Cuba, or Brazil—each must decide what goods will be produced.
- *How will the goods be produced?* The next question every society has to answer deals with the ways in which people produce the goods. Will farmers using modern tractors produce food, or will farmers using primitive tools produce it? Will the food be produced on private farms, where production decisions are made by individual farmers, or will it be produced on collective farms, where production decisions are made by people in the government?
- *For whom will the goods be produced?* This third question relates to who gets the goods. Will anyone who is able and willing to pay the prices for the goods be able to obtain them, or will government decide who will have the goods?

economic system
The way in which a society decides what goods to produce, how to produce them, and for whom goods will be produced.

free enterprise
An economic system in which individuals (not government) own most, if not all, the resources and control their use. Government plays only a small part in the economy.

socialism
An economic system in which government controls and may own many of the resources.

Two Major Economic Systems

How a society answers these three economic questions defines its **economic system**. The two major economic systems are free enterprise and socialism. **Free enterprise** is an economic system in which individuals own most, if not all, the resources and control their use. In **socialism**, government controls and may own many of the resources. Sometimes free enterprise is called *capitalism* or a *market economy*. This book will mainly use the term

Cooperative Learning

Divide students into groups of three or four. Ask each group to choose a country at random (pulling a name out of a hat or pinning a flag on a world map could be fun). Then have the groups research the goods that their selected countries produce and the goods that those countries trade (import and export) most often. Each group should give a short presentation about its country that answers the three economic questions:

- What goods are produced?
- How are the goods produced?
- For whom are the goods produced?

In addition, each group should describe the economic system that the country runs under—free enterprise, socialism, or mixed.

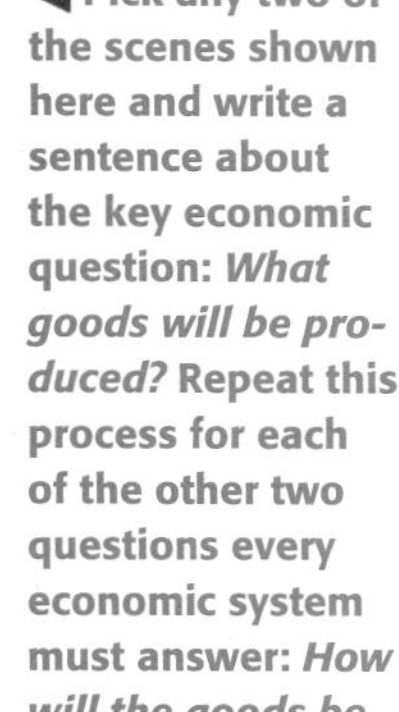

◀ **Pick any two of the scenes shown here and write a sentence about the key economic question: *What goods will be produced?* Repeat this process for each of the other two questions every economic system must answer: *How will the goods be produced?* and *For whom will they be produced?***

free enterprise, but occasionally it will speak of a capitalist economic system or a market economy. Socialism is sometimes loosely referred to as a *command economy*. To be more accurate, a command economy is a particular type of socialist economic system.

A Student Asks

QUESTION: *I thought there were more than two economic systems. For example, isn't communism an economic system?*

ANSWER: *Yes, communism is sometimes considered an economic system. So why are we talking essentially about two economic systems instead of three, four, or five? Essentially, all other systems are variations within one of the two major systems. Here is an analogy. Think of all people in the world: people with red hair, black hair, blue eyes, green eyes, brown eyes, people who are tall, people who are thin, and so on. If we were to ask how many different types of people in the world, one answer would be "many," but another way of looking at things says that people come in only two types, men and women. Instead of talking about all the various minor modifications in economic systems (for example, some with slightly more government control than others), we choose to talk about the two major, and distinctly different, economic systems: free enterprise and socialism. Communism, then, would go in the "socialism" category, in that it is a type of socialism, because it is a system with extensive government control over economic matters.*

Major Differences Between Free Enterprise and Socialism

Let's look at the major differences between free enterprise and socialism in a few areas.

Resources

Resources are used to produce goods and services. In a free enterprise economic system, these resources are owned and controlled by private individuals. In a socialist economic system, the government controls and may own many of the resources. For example, in the former Soviet Union, the central government owned many of the resources in the country. Today, in North Korea, the government owns almost all the resources in the country.

Teaching with Visuals

Answers will vary. Students should write about two of the scenes, and for each scene they should address each of the three economic questions.

A Student Asks

You may want to use this A Student Asks to make sure that students understand that *communism* is not limited to an economic sense, but also carries a political one.

Thinking Like an Economist

Some people look at countries and see differences. For example, they might note that citizens speak French in France and English in the United States, or that the crime rate is higher in the United States than in Belgium. Economists look at countries and see similarities. For example, they might note that the United States, China, Russia, Mexico, Egypt, and other countries all make different decisions about what goods will be produced, how those goods will be produced, and for whom the goods will be produced.

Have students each choose two or three countries, making sure that the class covers Canada, Sweden, Finland, Cuba, Vietnam, Australia, and India. Instruct students to search the Internet, current reference texts, or other sources to discover which economic system (free enterprise, socialism, or a mixed economy) is used in each of their selected countries. Display a chart with the column heads "Free Enterprise," "Socialism," and "Mixed Economy," and enter the results of the class's research in the chart. Discuss the class's findings and possible reasons for them. Make sure students can locate their countries on a world map.

Differentiating Instruction

Visual and English Language Learners

If students have difficulty understanding free enterprise and socialism ask them to create a collage for each system. Suggest that they include photos, graphs, headlines, quotes, and so on for each characteristic of the systems:

- free enterprise—small role of government in economic decisions, no economic plan, little attention to income distribution, economic incentives, competition, no price control, private property
- socialism—large role of government in economic decisions, government control of resources, economic plan, more attention to income distribution, price control, public (government-owned) property

Economics in the Real World

After students have read this feature, ask if they believe that workers in some countries have a stronger preference for leisure than do workers in other countries. Ask them to explain what information they might gather to support their position.

Teaching with Visuals

Answers will vary. Students might mention that for some people, spending relaxed time with family and friends is more important than making a lot of money, or that some business owners earn enough during the winter to suspend operations during the summer.

ANSWERS TO THINK ABOUT IT Answers will vary. Students might suggest that some cultures stress leisure activities and allow official time for them—for instance, in Europe, laws give workers a certain amount of vacation (usually four or five weeks) each year.

Economics in the Real World

Do People Around the World Work the Same Number of Hours?

Workers in different countries don't always work the same number of hours a year. For example, the following table shows the average hours worked by a worker in three countries in 2003.

Country	Hours worked
Australia	1,814
Japan	1,801
United States	1,792

In contrast, here are the average hours worked by a worker in three other countries.

Country	Hours worked
Sweden	1,564
France	1,453
Norway	1,337

It is also the case that the percentage of the workforce that works more than 40 hours a week varies from country to country. For example, in Japan, 75.9 percent of the workforce works more than 40 hours a week and in the United States it is 67.6 percent. In contrast, in France 21.4 percent of the workforce works more than 40 hours a week and in Norway it is 15.8 percent.

Do workers in some countries simply have a stronger preference for leisure (over work) than in other countries? For example, do the French and the Norwegians place a higher value on leisure time than the Americans and the Japanese? It is possible, but it could also be something else. Taxes, for example, are higher in some countries than in other countries. The difference between "what one earns" and "what one gets to keep" (after taxes) is the money reward for working. We would expect where the money reward from working is lower, people would want to work less, and where the money reward from working is higher, people would want to work more.

If we look at total tax receipts as a percentage of income earned, we find that percentage to be lower in Australia, Japan, and the United States—all countries where workers work relatively more hours. For example, in Australia this percentage was recently 31.5 percent, in Japan it was 27.1 percent, and in the United States it was 29.6 percent.

In contrast, in Sweden, France, and Norway, total tax receipts as a percentage of income earned was much higher. It was 54.2 percent in Sweden, 45.3 percent in France, and 40.3 percent in Norway.

Another explanation of why people work more or fewer hours has to do with how well one can do if he or she does not work. In some countries, the social assistance given to the unemployed is higher than in other countries. All other things being equal, we would expect that "not working" causes fewer problems in a country that provides relatively greater social benefits.

CERRADO
CERRADO por
VACACIONES
HASTA
SEPTIEMBRE

▲ This sign in Madrid, Spain, says the store will be closed until September. **What reasons might explain why workers would choose to take long vacations?**

Taxes and social spending may not explain all the difference between hours worked, however.

It is still possible that people in various countries are willing to make different trade-offs when it comes to labor and leisure. After all, some people, *within* a country, for whatever reason, seem to value leisure more than others. The same effect might occur, on average, between people in *different* countries.

THINK ABOUT IT Suppose that 60 percent of the difference between hours worked is explained by taxes and social spending, and 40 percent is explained by different trade-offs people in different countries make. What might make one person value leisure more than another person?

Background Information: Socialism

In 1848, two Germans, Karl Marx and Friedrich Engels, wrote a treatise called *The Communist Manifesto*. Marx and Engels were distressed at the extremely poor conditions of the working class in factories. They wrote that the cause of these deplorable conditions was the system of industrial capitalism and the ruling class that it created, the *bourgeoisie*. They proposed that the *proletariat*, or the working class, would someday violently overthrow the bourgeoisie and organize the means of production. From this socialist revolution would be developed a classless society, in which economic differences among people would be abolished.

Government's Role in the Economy

In a free enterprise economic system, government plays a small role in the economy. It does not make decisions on things like what goods and services will be produced or how they will be produced. Under socialism, government may make those decisions. For example, in the United States, the federal government doesn't make decisions on how many pairs of shoes will be produced in the country, or how many cars, television sets, or computers. These decisions are made by individuals in private firms. In contrast, in North Korea today the government sets production levels for almost all products.

Economists tell a story about the days of the Soviet Union when the Soviet official who was in charge of deciding what goods got produced came to the United States. When he arrived in the United States, his U.S. hosts asked him if he would like to meet anyone in particular. He told his hosts he wanted to meet his counterpart in the United States—the person who decided what goods would be produced. His hosts told him no such person existed in the United States. The Soviet official was shocked and couldn't understand how things got done in the United States if no one was issuing economic orders.

Economic Plans

Under socialism, government decision makers may write an **economic plan**, a plan that specifies the direction economic activities are to take. For example, a plan may state that over the next five years, the nation's economy will produce more manufactured goods (such as cars and trucks) and fewer agricultural goods (such as wheat and corn). A free enterprise economic system would have no such plan.

Income Distribution

Income distribution refers to how all the income earned in a country is divided among different groups of income earners. For example, the top 10 percent of income earners may earn 20 percent of the total income of the country, whereas the bottom 10 percent of income earners may earn 4 percent of the total income of the country. In a free enterprise economic system less attention is paid to the income distribution than in a socialist economic system. Government decision makers under socialism are more likely to use government's powers to redistribute income, usually directing it away from society's high earners.

economic plan
A government program specifying economic activities, such as what goods are to be produced and what prices will be charged.

income distribution
The way all the income earned in a country is divided among different groups of income earners.

◀ These North Korean workers are storing maize on a cooperative farm. **Who do you think determines the production levels that these workers are expected to achieve?**

35

Analyzing

Form pairs of students and direct each pair to find a financial news article on the Internet; one source of such articles is the CNN/Money Web site. Ask one partner to summarize the article from the perspective of a capitalist thinker (which is probably the perspective from which the article was written), and the other partner to summarize the article from the perspective of a socialist thinker. Then allow the pair to debate the issue. After the debate, ask the partners to write a brief summary answering this question: How do the two analyses differ?

Teaching with Visuals

The government of North Korea determines the production levels that these workers are expected to achieve.

Marxist thought dominated the world scene for most of the 20th century. Communism, the antithesis of capitalism, formed the basis for much of the hysteria that drove U. S. foreign policy during the Cold War. Communism contributed an ideological edge to the existing military threat of the Soviet Union after World War II. After the Revolution of 1917, the United States experienced no less than two Red Scares, in which constitutional freedoms were curtailed to protect the country from communism. Most Americans understood the fear, but had little understanding of what communism actually was.

Reinforcement Activity

Assign students to write a paragraph on how the three economic questions are answered in a free enterprise economy, in a socialist economy, and in a mixed economy. Ask them to also identify who decides how the four types of resources are allocated in each type of economic system.

Teaching with Visuals

Answers will vary. Students might say that employment tends to be less stable at factories owned by individuals or companies, because private owners might be more vulnerable to market fluctuations for the goods they produce.

Controlling Prices

In a free enterprise economic system, prices are allowed to fluctuate—that is, to go up and down. Government does not attempt to control prices. In a socialist economic system, government decision makers do control prices, although not all socialist systems control prices to the same extent. For example, government decision makers may say that no one can buy or sell bread for more than $1.50 a loaf. Or they may say wage rates for unskilled labor are too low at $4 an hour and order that no one be allowed to "buy" or "sell" unskilled labor for less than $6 an hour.

Private Property

Under free enterprise, private property is sacred. The proponents of free enterprise believe that if you own something yourself—if, say, your house is your private property—you are more likely to take care of it than if it were owned communally by you and others or owned by the government.

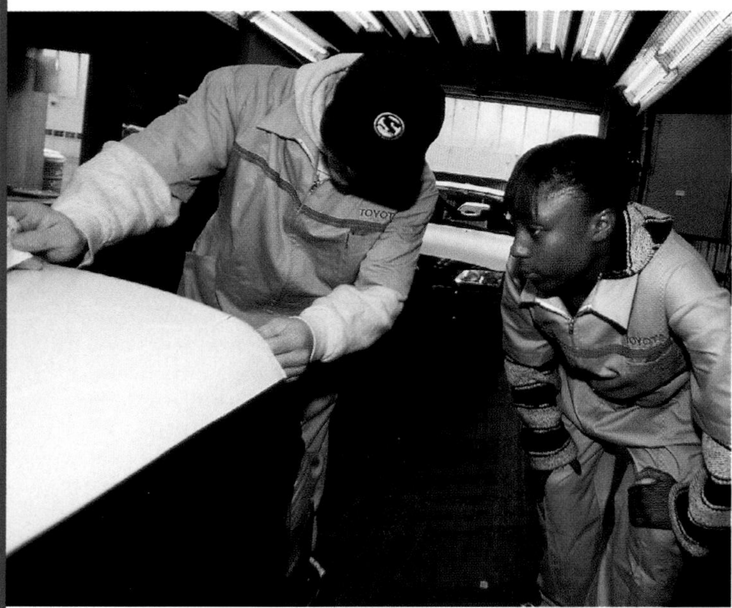

▲ These quality-control inspectors work at a Toyota plant in the United States. **What are the advantages and disadvantages of such factories being owned by individuals or companies, as opposed to being owned by a government?**

The proponents also believe that having private property encourages individuals to use their resources in a way that benefits others. For example, suppose Johnson owns a factory that is her private property. If Johnson wants to maximize her income, she will have to use her factory to produce goods that people are willing and able to buy. If she did otherwise and produced something that people were unwilling and unable to buy, she would not benefit the people nor earn an income.

The socialist view of things is different. Socialists believe that those who own property will end up having more political power than those who do not own it. Furthermore, they will use their greater political power to their advantage and to the disadvantage of others. According to socialists, it would be better for government to own most of the nonlabor property in the economy (such things as factories, raw materials, and machinery). Government would be more likely than private individuals to make sure this property was used to benefit the many instead of the few.

Mixed Economies

You might be wondering whether we can easily place each country's economy in either the free enterprise or socialism camp. The answer is no. In reality, a country's economic system may contain some ingredients of free enterprise and some ingredients of socialism too. For example, the United States is considered to have a free enterprise economic system. After all, most of the resources are owned by private individuals, and no overall economic plans determine the use of those resources. However, the U.S. government plays a larger role in the economy than it would play in a *pure* free enterprise system, and some prices are controlled. Thus, while the United States is considered a free enterprise nation, it has a few features of socialism.

A similar point can be made for other nations. For example, China is considered to be a communist country. However, since 1978, China has experimented with numerous market, or free enterprise, practices; so

Cooperative Learning

Divide the class into three groups and have each group research feudalism as it existed either in Europe, in medieval Japan, or in the 15th-century Aztec civilization. Each group should report on political, social, and economic developments as well as cultural achievements. Have each group prepare a presentation to share the information it has obtained, emphasizing economic developments. Students within each group should have individual as well as group responsibilities. After the presentations, you may want to lead a class discussion on the groups' findings, and compare similarities and differences, especially of the economic systems.

to say that China is 100 percent socialist would be incorrect.

Economies with features of both free enterprise and socialism are called **mixed economies**. If we were to adopt this terminology, we would have to say that both the U.S. and Chinese economies are mixed economies. However, to call them both mixed economies could be misleading. It makes them sound alike (even identical) when they are not. The United States has much more free enterprise than China, and China has much more socialism than the United States; the economies of these two nations are different. It is clearer to refer to the United States as a free enterprise nation and to China as principally a socialist nation, while noting some socialist practices occur in the United States and some free enterprise practices take place in China.

Each year the *Wall Street Journal* and the Heritage Foundation rank countries according to how much economic freedom and free enterprise exist in the country. In 2005, they scored 155 countries on a scale of 1 to 5. The closer a country's index of economic freedom number is to 1, the more economic freedom and free enterprise in the country; the closer a country's index of economic freedom number is to 5, the less economic freedom in the country.

Keep in mind that different organizations can sometimes rank countries differently as to how much economic freedom exists in the country. We show the rankings and index numbers for selective countries in Exhibit 2-1. (Hong Kong had the most economic freedom and North Korea the least.)

EXHIBIT 2-1 Index of Economic Freedom Scores

Rank	Country	Index of Economic Freedom Score
1	Hong Kong	1.35
5	Ireland	1.70
10	Australia	1.79
12	United States	1.85
16	Canada	1.91
26	Italy	2.28
39	Japan	2.46
44	France	2.63
45	South Korea	2.64
63	Mexico	2.89
71	Thailand	2.98
90	Brazil	3.25
103	Egypt	3.38
112	China	3.46
118	India	3.53
124	Russia	3.56
137	Vietnam	3.83
149	Cuba	4.29
155	North Korea	5.00

Source: 2005 Index of Economic Freedom, a joint publication of the *Wall Street Journal* and Heritage Foundation.

▲ Countries were scored according to economic freedom on a scale of 1.00 to 5.00. The lower the score, the more economic freedom in the country; the higher the score, the less economic freedom.

Economic Systems: Past, Present, and Future

Before economies were free enterprise or socialist, many were **traditional economies**. A traditional economy is an economic system in which the answers to the three economic questions are based on customs, skills, and cultural beliefs.

In a traditional economy, these customs, skills, and beliefs are passed on from one generation to the next. An example of a traditional economy is the old feudal system in Western Europe. Under the feudal system, all land was owned by a king. The king granted land to nobles, who in turn granted small plots of land to peasants to farm. The peasants kept part of what they produced; the remainder went to the nobles and, ultimately, to the king.

Few traditional economies exist today. Most economies today are mixed economies. Of course, the "mixture" of free enterprise and socialism often differs between nations' economies.

What does the future hold? Will most economies of the future be mixed economies (as they are today)? More importantly, will the mix between free enterprise and socialism in the future be the same as the mix that exists today? For instance, if we considered a representative mixed economy today, and noted that it is 65 percent free enterprise and 35 percent socialist, will this same 65/35 mix hold for the representative economy in 2015, or 2025? This question concerns much of what we will be discussing in the next section, when we talk about globalization.

mixed economy An economy that is neither purely capitalist nor purely socialist; an economy that has some elements of both capitalism and socialism. Most countries in the world have mixed economies.

traditional economy An economic system in which the answers to the three economic questions are based on customs, traditions, and cultural beliefs.

Teaching with Visuals

If students would like to learn more about the Index of Economic Freedom Scores, tell them to check out the description of this tool at the Heritage Foundation Web site.

Reinforcement Activity

Point out North Korea's score in Exhibit 2-1. Ask students to write a one-page paper summarizing the key features of North Korea's economy. Tell them to include some background information about how North Korea arrived at the economic system it has today.

Discussion Starter

Ask students if they would be willing to live in a traditional economic system. Would they be comfortable living off the land at a subsistence level, using their customs and beliefs to dictate the allocation of resources?

Reinforcement Activity

Lead a discussion of why some traditional economies still exist. Ask students to list advantages of living in a traditional economy. Then have them list disadvantages.

Application Activity

After reading and discussing "Economic Systems: Past, Present, and Future," you may want to assign the Section Activity on economic systems in the *Applying the Principles Workbook*.

Background Information: Traditional Economies

The Hadza of Tanzania are a nomadic hunting culture, without a fixed location or many material possessions. They live in a land of fierce and powerful predators where, while they hunt for their own food, they might be hunted as well. Fewer than 1,000 Hadza remain in the Tanzanian bush. They build no shelters, have no chieftains, and have no economic structures. What they do have is a traditional economy, based on thousands of years of life in the same region, hunting the same animals, with only the smallest introduction of outside goods like Western clothes.

Economics in the Real World

After students have read this feature, ask if they think the states that tried to ban tipping in the early 1900s were successful. Encourage them to name reasons why those laws might have been repealed.

ANSWERS TO THINK ABOUT IT **1.** Answers will vary. Students might mention that in the first practice, servers try to provide better service in an effort to earn higher tips. Or students might argue that if servers earn a good, stable wage, they will work harder and stay with their jobs longer, and thus the second practice might guarantee good service.

2. Answers will vary. Students might suggest that tipping does tend to reflect the values of the society. For example, where success and materialism are highly valued, tipping is more common.

What Should I Tip?

In the United States, tipping in restaurants amounts to $16 billion a year. Even though tipping in the United States is common today, 24 percent of the individuals in one study said that they thought tipping was unfair to customers. In the past, some states prohibited tipping. For example, in the early 1900s, Arkansas, Mississippi, Iowa, South Carolina, Tennessee, and Washington passed laws to prohibit tipping.

What about the rest of the world? Do people around the world have the same tipping practices as Americans do? Some do, but certainly not all. For example, it is increasingly more customary in European restaurants to have an automatic service charge added to a restaurant bill than to tip the server. Little tipping of any sort goes on in Argentina and Vietnam. Much less tipping occurs (fewer service providers expect tips) in Australia, New Zealand, and Italy than in the United States, and more tipping goes on in Mexico and Egypt than in the United States.

In several studies, researchers looked at the number of different service providers (out of a total of 33) for which tipping is customary in a given country. The more service providers it was customary to tip in a country, the higher the country's "prevalence of tipping." For example, if it was customary to tip 31 different service providers in country A but only 15 in country B, then country A would have a higher prevalence of tipping than country B.

The conclusion of these studies is that countries where success and materialism were highly valued had a higher prevalence to tip than countries where caring and personal relationships were highly valued. Also, the prevalence of tipping increased as the national need for achievement and recognition rose. In one study, tipping was more prevalent in countries with lower taxes than in countries with higher taxes.

If it becomes increasingly relevant to speak of a world economy instead of hundreds of national economies, will tipping practices around the world become more the same? If they do become more similar from country to country, will countries gravitate toward more or less tipping?

We do not know the answer to this question, so you might then wonder: Why ask? First, it gets us to thinking about what changes we are likely to see in our everyday lives as globalization continues. Second, it causes us to wonder whether those changes will affect economic issues only (we can buy more clothes from China), or spread into the social and cultural parts of life too. And third, asking such questions helps us see which practices are deeply embedded in the character of a people (and therefore unlikely to change) and which ones are superficial (and therefore more likely to change).

1. Compare two tipping practices. In the first, a customer at a restaurant decides whether to tip a server. In the second, a 15 percent service charge is added to the restaurant bill. Which practice, if either, is more likely to guarantee good service and why?

2. Do you think that a society's general tipping practices might reflect the values of that society? If so, give an example.

Cooperative Learning

Divide the class into small groups. Have each group research a country that has a primarily socialist economic system. (Students might use the Index of Economic Freedom scores to identify those countries.) Each group should present its findings, including especially information about resource ownership and allocation; the government's role in the economy; an economic plan, if there is one; income distribution policies; price controls; private versus public property; and trade policies and figures. The group should also provide a map of the country, recent news photos, and brief descriptions of current events, particularly those related to economics. Allow class time for the presentations.

The Visions Behind Free Enterprise and Socialism

Both free enterprise and socialism are the products of certain **visions**—ways of looking at, understanding, and explaining the world. Adam Smith, the eighteenth century economist, is a major thinker whose ideas are fundamental to free enterprise. For Smith, free enterprise is not only the economic system that produces the most economic wealth (the most goods and services), but it is the most ethical of the economic systems too.

In contrast, the ideas of Karl Marx, a nineteenth century economist, are at the heart of socialism (and communism). It was Marx who pointed out what he believed were many of the failures and injustices of free enterprise. In his major work, *Das Kapital,* he presents his vision for an alternative system.

How important are the ideas of these two men? As one example, in late 1999, *Life* magazine created a list of the 100 most important people of the second millennium (1000–1999). Both Smith and Marx were on the list. (See Exhibit 2-2 for more information about both Smith and Marx.)

To get a sense of how their visions differed, and therefore how the two major economic systems differ, let's take a closer look at one major idea from both Smith and Marx. For Smith, it is the idea that self-interest can lead to good things not only for the individual, but for others too.

Self-Interest

Smith said that from the minute we enter this world until the day we go to our graves, we feel a desire to make ourselves better off. Smith felt that self-interest is a major part of who we are. He believed that our self-interest prompts us to work hard, take risks, and in the end benefit others through our activities.

How can we benefit *others* through *our* self-interest? After all, doesn't a person's self-interest pit that person against the best interests of others? Smith believed that if people wanted to serve their own self-interest, they had to serve others first. In a passage from his major work, *The Wealth of Nations,* Smith says:

> It is not from the benevolence of the butcher, the brewer, or the baker, that we expect our dinner, but from their regard

vision
A sense of how the world works.

◀ The ideas of Adam Smith and Karl Marx have changed the world.

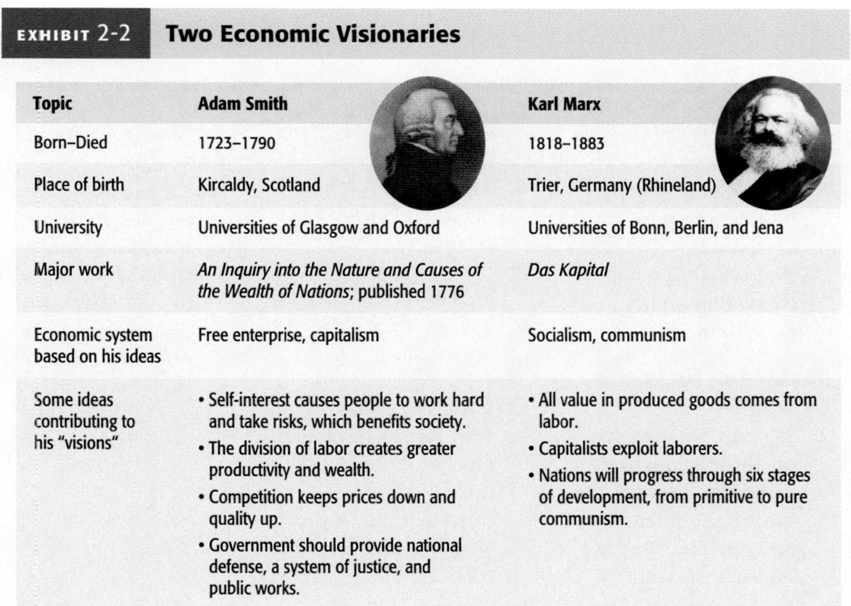

EXHIBIT 2-2 Two Economic Visionaries

Topic	Adam Smith	Karl Marx
Born–Died	1723–1790	1818–1883
Place of birth	Kircaldy, Scotland	Trier, Germany (Rhineland)
University	Universities of Glasgow and Oxford	Universities of Bonn, Berlin, and Jena
Major work	*An Inquiry into the Nature and Causes of the Wealth of Nations*; published 1776	*Das Kapital*
Economic system based on his ideas	Free enterprise, capitalism	Socialism, communism
Some ideas contributing to his "visions"	• Self-interest causes people to work hard and take risks, which benefits society. • The division of labor creates greater productivity and wealth. • Competition keeps prices down and quality up. • Government should provide national defense, a system of justice, and public works.	• All value in produced goods comes from labor. • Capitalists exploit laborers. • Nations will progress through six stages of development, from primitive to pure communism.

Reinforcement Activity

Explain that Adam Smith's philosophy is one of the economic supports of the capitalist system that allows people to own telephones, computers, and automobiles. Smith believed that competition among merchants could act as a regulator of the economic system. Ask students to explain what Smith meant by that thought. He also felt that private enterprise would stimulate fair distribution of wealth in a country. Ask: Have you noticed that to be true in the United States? Why or why not?

Reinforcement Activity

Consider reading to students the following passage translated from Karl Marx's *Das Kapital:* "The directing motive, the end and aim of capitalist production, is to extract the greatest possible amount of surplus-value, and consequently to exploit labour-power to the greatest possible extent" (Karl Marx, *Capital,* vol. 1, New York: International Publishers, 1975, p. 331). Ask for student volunteers who can answer the following question: What is the aim of capitalist production?

Here is another quote translated from *Das Kapital:* "As the number of cooperating labourers increases, so too does their resistance to the domination of capital, and with it, the necessity for capital to overcome this resistance by counter-pressure" (ibid.). Ask students, this: According to Marx, what happens as the number of laborers increases?

Application Activity

After reading and discussing "The Visions Behind Free Enterprise and Socialism," you may want to assign the Section Activity on the visions in the *Applying the Principles Workbook.*

Assess

Quick Quiz

The following true-or-false quiz will help you assess student understanding of the material covered in this section.

1. A traditional economic system uses customs, traditions, and beliefs to answer the three economic questions. (True)

Differentiating Instruction

Enrichment and Extension

Instruct students to prepare to role-play either Adam Smith or Karl Marx, and to review the chapter until they have a good understanding of that person's viewpoint. Also ask them to write a question they would like to ask the other economist. Gather students acting as Smith on one side of the room and students acting as Marx on the other side. Call on a Smith to read a question, and a Marx to answer it, and list the main points made by the respondent. Next, call on a Marx to read a question and a Smith to answer it. After everyone has had a chance to ask a question and respond to a question, encourage students to explain what they learned from this exercise.

Section 1 Economic Systems 39

2. The two dominant economic systems are traditional and free enterprise. (False)
3. Our economic vision is our sense of how the world works. (True)
4. A socialist thinks price should be set and controlled by the government. (True)
5. All nations must answer three basic economic questions. (True)

Assessment Book

You will find a quiz for this section in the *Assessment Book.*

Reteaching Activity

Write the words "free enterprise" and "socialism" at opposite ends of the board. Draw a line between the two terms. Make sure that students understand that all economies exist some where along this line (or spectrum).

Guided Reading

For further reteaching of the key concepts in this section, assign the Outlining Activity and the Just the Facts Handout from the *Guided Reading and Study Guide.*

to their own interest. We address ourselves, not to their humanity but to their self-love, and never talk to them of our own necessities but of their advantages.

In other words, the butcher, brewer, and baker do not give us our dinner because they love us or because they want to assist us. They give us our dinner because they cannot get what they want from us until they first give us what we want. According to Smith, we are led by an "invisible hand" to do good for others. In probably the most famous passage in *The Wealth of Nations,* he says:

> Every individual . . . neither intends to promote the public interest, nor knows how much he is promoting it . . . he intends only his own gain, and he is in this, as in many other cases, led by an invisible hand to promote an end which was no part of his intention.

labor theory of value The belief that all value in produced goods is derived from labor.

surplus value The difference between the total value of production and the subsistence wages paid to workers.

Labor Theory of Value

Karl Marx saw things very differently. He didn't see self-interest as leading to good things; instead, he saw it as hurting others. Marx believed that capitalists, in pursuing their self-interests, actually exploited the workers. How does this happen?

Marx argued in his **labor theory of value** that all value in produced goods comes from labor. The value of any item, he said, is determined by the necessary labor time needed to produce that item. For example, if it takes 5 hours of labor time to produce a chair and 10 hours to produce a table, then the table is twice as valuable as the chair.

Marx believed that the owners of factories and businesses exploited the workers by paying them far less than they were worth. For example, suppose a worker produced $100 a day worth of value for the factory owner but was only paid $20. The difference between the total value of production ($100) and the wages paid to the worker ($20) is what Marx called **surplus value** ($80). According to Marx this surplus should go to the worker, but instead is stolen by the capitalist for himself.

Ideas That Changed the World

The ideas of both Smith and Marx have been with us for many years. Smith's ideas compose much of the foundation upon which free enterprise rests, while Marx's ideas provide much of the foundation for socialism Their ideas have changed the world, and will probably continue to have a major impact on the world for years to come.

SECTION 1 ASSESSMENT

Defining Terms

1. Define:
   a. economic system
   b. free enterprise
   c. socialism
   d. traditional economy
   e. economic plan
   f. surplus value

Reviewing Facts and Concepts

2. What are the three economic questions every society must answer?
3. What is the difference between free enterprise (or capitalism) and socialism as each relates to private property?
4. Are all mixed economies the same? Explain your answer.
5. What is Smith's position on self-interest?
6. Explain Marx's labor theory of value.

Critical Thinking

7. Why do you think that most economies are mixed economies instead of purely capitalist or purely socialist economies?

Applying Economic Concepts

8. Choose a current economic issue or policy measure and then contrast the way a proponent of capitalism would discuss it versus how a proponent of socialism would discuss it.

SECTION 1 ASSESSMENT ANSWERS

Defining Terms

1. a. **economic system:** the way in which a society answers the three economic questions that all societies must answer; **b. free enterprise:** an economic system in which individuals own most, if not all, the resources and control their use; **c. socialism:** an economic system in which government controls and may own many of the resources; **d. traditional economy:** an economic system in which the answers to the three economic questions are based on customs, traditions, and cultural beliefs; **e. economic plan:** a government program that specifies the direction economic activities are to take; **f. surplus value:** the difference between the total value of production and wages paid to a worker.

Reviewing Facts and Concepts

2. What goods will be produced? How will the goods be produced? For whom will the goods be produced?
3. In a free enterprise system, property is owned by individuals. In a socialist system, the government owns much of the property.
4. No. Some have more aspects of capitalism, and others lean more toward socialism.
5. Smith believed that society benefited from self-interest; that in pursuing their own needs, people are guided by an "invisible hand" to act in ways that benefit society.
6. Marx argued that all value in produced goods comes from labor.

Critical Thinking

7. Answers will vary.

Applying Economic Concepts

8. Answers will vary.

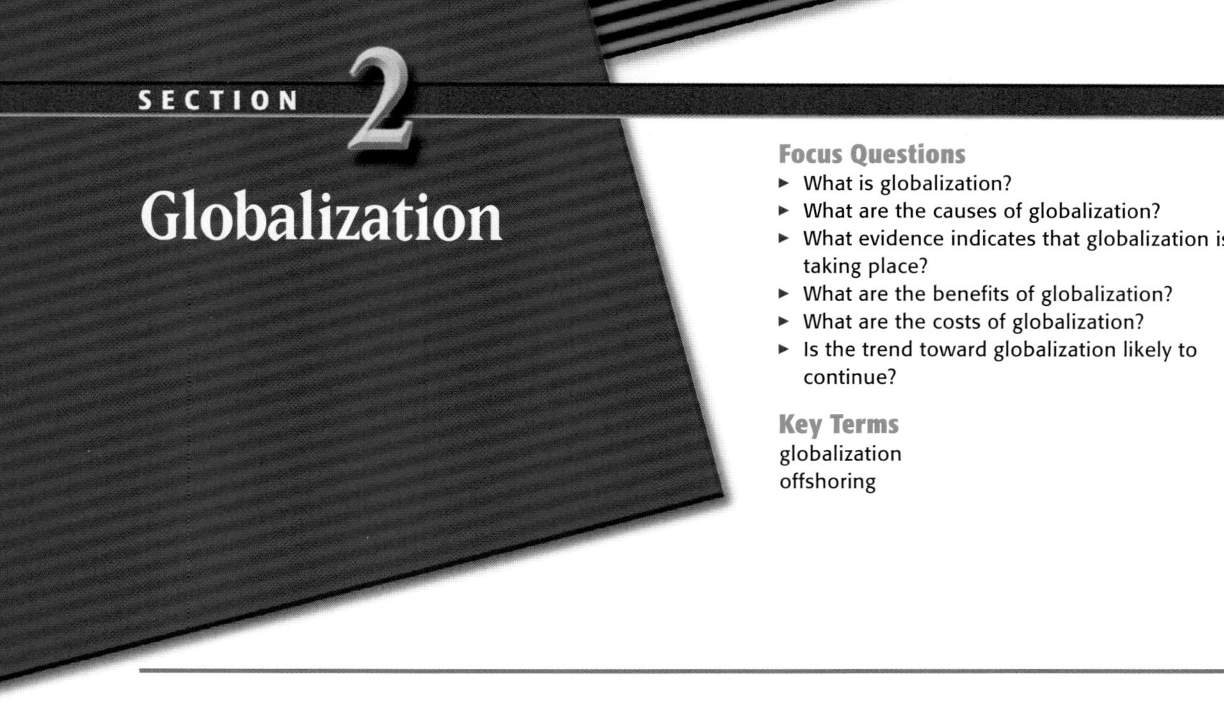

SECTION 2 Globalization

Focus Questions
- What is globalization?
- What are the causes of globalization?
- What evidence indicates that globalization is taking place?
- What are the benefits of globalization?
- What are the costs of globalization?
- Is the trend toward globalization likely to continue?

Key Terms
globalization
offshoring

What Is Globalization?

From the 1950s through the 1980s, it was common to hear people talk about a capitalist or free enterprise country, and about a socialist or communist country. It was as if each country in the world was definitely one or the other. It was also the case that for the most part these countries only associated (politically and economically) with their "own kind."

Things have changed. Few countries can be easily labeled "capitalist" or "socialist," and countries that never communicated have become major trading partners. Why? Well, according to many thinkers, it's because of *globalization*.

So what is this thing called **globalization**? Many economists define it as a process by which individuals and businesses in any part of the world are much more affected by events elsewhere in the world than they used to be. Globalization can also be defined as the growing integration of the national economies of the world. Some believe that this integration may eventually lead to the existence of a single worldwide economy. Let's take a closer look at some of the key features of globalization.

A Smaller World

The first definition of globalization emphasizes that economic agents (individuals, businesses, governments) in any given part of the world are affected by events elsewhere in the world. In other words, living in the United States, you are not only affected by what happens in the United States, but what happens in Brazil, Russia, and China.

EXAMPLE: In 2005, the Chinese government was taking much of the money it earned in trade with the United States and buying bonds issued by the U.S. government. As a result of Chinese purchases of U.S. bonds, interest rates in the United States ended up being lower than they would have been. Are you affected by interest rates? Sure you are whenever you buy a car, a house, or anything else you take out a loan to purchase. ♦

globalization A phenomenon by which economic agents in any given part of the world are affected by events elsewhere in the world; the growing integration of the national economies of the world to the degree that we may be witnessing the emergence and operation of a single worldwide economy.

Differentiating Instruction

Enrichment and Extension

Robert Burton, an English clergyman, wrote, "A dwarf standing on the shoulders of a giant may see farther than a giant himself." He meant that people who build on the ideas of earlier thinkers can often build better concepts.

Tell students to each research a capitalist or socialist thinker, and write down the person's name, dates, birthplace, education, economic vision (capitalist or socialist), and significant works, theories, and ideas. Post their summaries in chronological order. Give students time to view the resulting time line and jot notes about any trends or relationships that strike them. As a class, discuss what students found in their research and in their viewing of the time line.

SECTION 2 Teacher Support

Focus and Motivate

Section Objectives

After completing this section, students will be able to
- define globalization and explain its causes;
- describe evidence that indicates that globalization is taking place;
- describe the benefits and costs of globalization; and
- explain why the trend toward globalization is likely to continue.

Economics Around the Clock

Kickoff Activity

Direct students to read the 10:13 A.M. scenario in Economics Around the Clock (page 31) and then write their answers to the accompanying question.

Invite students to share their answers with the class. Draw attention to the ways their thoughts on globalization differ. Explain that globalization is a fairly recent phenomenon that students will explore in this chapter.

Activating Prior Knowledge

Have students read the definition of globalization on this page and then write a few sentences describing how free enterprise and socialist economies might react differently to globalization. Encourage volunteers to share their sentences with the class.

Teach

Teaching with Visuals

Answers will vary. If students have trouble responding to the question, you might ask what they would say if trading at the Tokyo Stock Exchange were less expensive than trading at the New York Stock Exchange; in that case, they might expect more people to trade at the Tokyo Stock Exchange.

Discussion Starter

Urge students to think about clothes and shoes that they have purchased recently. Do they know where the items were made? Do they usually pay more, less, or the same, for clothes or shoes that were made outside the United States? Ask students to consider how the trend toward globalization might have affected the costs of these items.

Reinforcement Activity

Have students reread the quote from Thomas Friedman. Note that Friedman believes that globalization represents the spread of free market capitalism. Ask students to think of reasons why globalization represents the spread of capitalism rather than socialism.

▶ These financial workers are making and recording trades at the Tokyo Stock Exchange. **Do you expect more or fewer Americans to buy and sell shares traded on this exchange in the years to come? Explain.**

Can you see how, in a sense, globalization makes the world smaller? China hasn't moved physically; it isn't any closer to the United States (in terms of distance) than it was 100 years ago. Still, what happens in China today, because of globalization, has the same effect on you as what might happen 10 or 100 miles away from you. For all practical purposes, we live in a "smaller world" today than people did 100 years ago.

A Free Enterprise World

Globalization is closely aligned with a movement toward more free enterprise, freer markets, more freedom of movement for people and goods. Thomas Friedman, author of several books on globalization, states that "globalization means the spread of free-market capitalism in the world." There is no doubt that many countries are moving toward greater free enterprise practices.

What does this trend mean for our study of economic systems? Speaking of various economic systems made sense when national economies were the most important economies. With globalization, however, the world is moving from hundreds of national economies toward *one large world economy*. In a world of one, it does not make sense to speak of *different* economic systems. It makes sense to speak of "the" economic system for that one world economy. And, the economic system that best describes what is happening in the world economy is free enterprise or capitalism.

A Student Asks

QUESTION: *What specifically is the difference between a national economy and a global economy?*

ANSWER: *Think of an invisible string as connecting you and everyone you have an economic relationship with. If you buy something from someone, a string connects the two of you; if you work for someone, a string connects you. Now, perhaps the best way to think of a national economy is to think of strings only linking those people who reside in the same country. In a world or global economy, however, strings link individuals with people in their own country and in other countries too. In other words, their economic relationships extend beyond the nation's borders. In the past, a few strings extended outside of country borders, but only a few, and for a long time the strings only went to certain countries. With globalization, more and more strings, a seemingly unlimited number of strings, are being connected across borders. And, these strings are being connected between people in more and more countries.*

Cooperative Learning

Direct students to each find a news articles about globalization and write a brief summary of the articles. Then divide the class into groups of three or four and pose the following questions for group discussions: In what ways do the articles relate to globalization? Do they cast globalization in a good or bad light? Ask each group to write a paragraph explaining how its articles reflect the trend away from thinking in terms of national economies to thinking in terms of one large world economy. As the groups share their summaries, list their main points on the board, focusing on evidence that supports or disputes the trend toward globalization, and evidence that casts globalization in a good or bad light.

Movement Toward Globalization

How did we come to live in a global economy? Did someone push a button years ago and start the process of globalization? No, things don't happen that way.

Early History

Globalization did not just occur on the world stage two decades ago. The world has gone through different globalization periods. For example, during the period from the mid-1800s to the late 1920s, globalization was occurring. Some people today refer to it as the First Era of globalization. In some ways, that world was a freer world when it came to the movement of people than the world today, as evidenced by the fact that many people moved from country to country without a passport, which was not required.

This early era of globalization was largely ended by the two world wars (World War I and World War II) and the Great Depression. Even though both the Great Depression and both world wars were over by 1945, globalization did not start anew. The Cold War essentially divided the world into different camps (free vs. unfree, capitalist vs. communist), which led to relatively high political and economic barriers. The visible symbol of these barriers—the Berlin Wall—separated not only East from West Germany but one group of countries living under one political and economic system from another group of countries living under a different political and economic system.

Recent Causes

Several factors have led to the more recent period of globalization. Let's look at a few of the most frequently mentioned factors.

The End of the Cold War The Cold War intensified after World War II and, most agree, ended with the visible fall of the Berlin Wall in 1989. This event occurred while the Soviet empire was beginning to crumble and many of the communist East European countries were breaking away from Soviet control.

As some explain it, the end of the Cold War resulted in turning two different worlds (the capitalist and communist worlds) into one world. It resulted in a thawing of not only political but economic relations between former enemies.

Why was this important economically? People are reluctant to trade with their enemies, but once that person or country is no longer your enemy, the barriers begin to fade away. The Cold War acted as a political barrier between certain groups of countries. Once it ended, one giant barrier standing in the way of trade was no longer there.

▼ In the past we traded exclusively with certain people, in certain countries. Today, with the movement toward globalization and worldwide free enterprise, we are more closely connected through trade with people all across the globe.

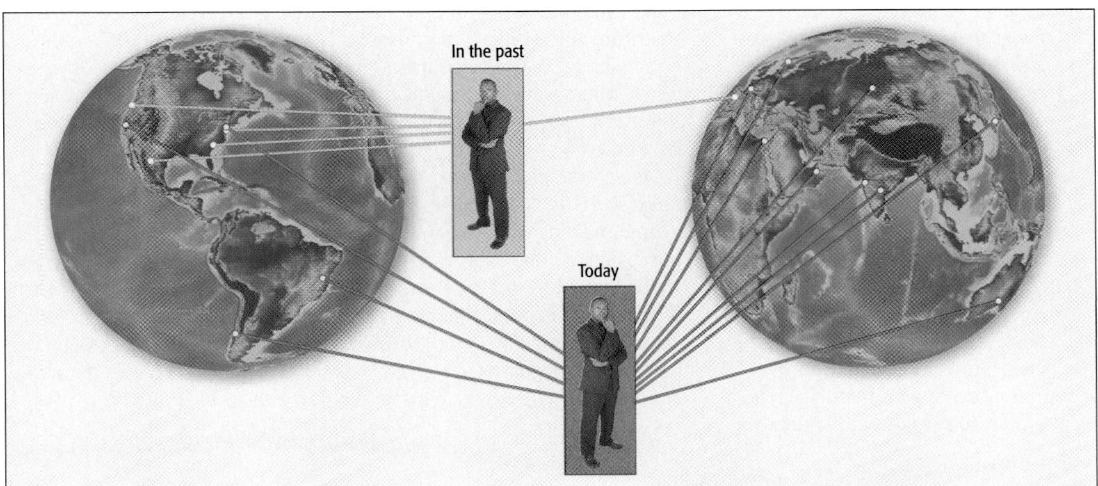

Reinforcement Activity

The fall of the Berlin Wall reflects the often close relationship between politics and economics. Assign students to write a one-page paper discussing how political differences limited trade between nations before the collapse of the Soviet Union. Tell students to also explain how the removal of those political barriers affected trade after the Soviet Union's collapse.

As an alternative, encourage students to work individually or in pairs to create a political cartoon illustrating the economic effects of removing one of those political barriers. Post their results, and instruct each student to choose a cartoon created by a classmate and to write a sentence or two summarizing its meaning.

Teaching with Visuals

The lower part of this visual represents the growing number of strings, or ties, that appear between people and nations as barriers to trade fall away.

Internet Research

Suggest that students each find an online news article about a formerly communist nation of Eastern Europe and how the fall of the Berlin Wall has affected that nation economically. Ask students to write a brief report describing what items were produced in the nation under communism. Then students should explain how the nation's economy has changed in recent years. Tell students to be sure to explain whether the economic changes resulted from globalization or from other forces.

Economics in the Real World

After students have read this feature, ask them to consider barriers that a musician might still face, even in a world of increased globalization.

ANSWERS TO THINK ABOUT IT Answers will vary. Students might suggest that the greater number of students in larger high schools likely means a wider variety of interests, which probably leads to a wider variety of clubs.

Discussion Starter

Ask students to think about types of businesses that are well positioned to benefit from globalization. Suggest that they consider businesses offering goods or services that appeal to people in a variety of countries.

Economics in the Real World

Will Globalization Change the Sound of Music?

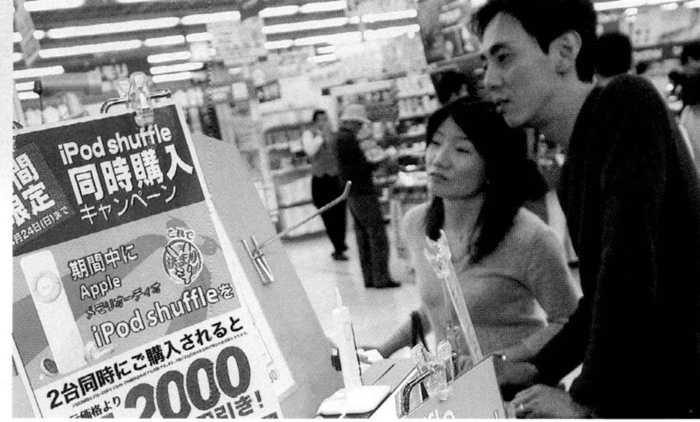

Suppose you had only 100 people to whom you could sell some good. Given this small number, if you want to sell something, you had better sell something that some of these 100 people want to buy. For example, if these 100 people don't like fruit salad, then you better not produce and offer to sell fruit salad; if some of these 100 people like bread, then perhaps you should produce and offer to sell bread.

Now increase the number of people from 100 to 1 million. Is it more or less likely that some people within a group of 1 million will like fruit salad, as compared to a group of 100 people? The answer is that as the size of the potential customer base increases, the number of things that you can sell increases too. In a world of 100 people, you can only sell bread; but in a world of 1 million people, you can sell fruit salad or bread.

Now suppose you are a musician. As a musician, you can play different styles of music: jazz, pop, classical, hard rock, metal, hip-hop, and so on. If you are limited to selling your music to the people of a single state of the United States, there would be fewer styles of music you could offer to sell than if you could sell your music to the people who reside in the United States.

The general point is a simple one: the larger the size of the potential customer base (simply put, the more people you can possibly sell to), the greater the variety of goods we are likely to see.

Globalization is, to a large degree, expanding everyone's ability to potentially sell to more people. American companies aren't limited to selling to only Americans; they can sell to others in the world too. Chinese firms aren't limited to selling to only the Chinese; they can sell to others in the world too.

As an example, consider some musician in the United States who is experimenting with a new style of music. With a population of only the United States as a potential customer base (the population of the U.S. is approximately 300 million), the musician might not yet have enough actual customers to make it worth producing and offering to sell this particular, unique, and narrowly defined music. However, if the musician can draw on the population of the world (population 6.4 billion), then the musician might be able to find enough people who are willing to buy this particular new type of music.

As we move toward a world economy, we see a greater variety within almost every category of goods you can think of: a greater variety of music to listen to, books to read, types of television shows to watch, and so on. Today, the greater variety of goods you see in your world is an effect of globalization.

THINK ABOUT IT A greater variety of clubs can usually be found in large high schools than in small high schools. Does this difference have anything to do with the issue of globalization we discussed in the feature? Explain.

Background Information: GATT

A number of international trade agreements have helped to bring about globalization. The most important one of the post–World War II era was the General Agreement on Tariffs and Trade (GATT) of 1947. Twenty-three nations signed this agreement. Several rounds of talks followed the signing. Over the next 40 years, tariffs were reduced to enhance free trade. Nations also worked to reduce other barriers to trade, such as quotas and licensing requirements. In 1995, GATT was superseded by the World Trade Organization (WTO).

Advancing Technology In the past, innovations such as the internal combustion engine, steamship, telephone, and telegraph led to increased trade between people in different countries. All of these inventions led to lower transportation or communication costs, and lower costs mean fewer barriers to trade.

EXAMPLE: The cost of a three-minute telephone call from New York to London in 1930 was $250. In 1960, it was $60.42; in 1980 it was $6.32; and in 2000 it was 40 cents. Today, it is even less. As the costs of communicating continue to fall, in some sense the obstacle of physical distance (to trade) is overcome. Businesspeople in the United States, for example, can more cheaply talk with businesspeople in China. ♦

EXAMPLE: What was the cost of a computer in 1960, one comparable to the desktop computer that many people today have on their desk at home? The answer is $1.8 *million*. (Yes, you read that right — $1.8 million.) That computer was $199,983 in 1970, $27,938 in 1980, $7,275 in 1990, and only $1,000 in 2000. People today not only use computers for their work, but to communicate with others via the Internet. This computer and Internet technology make it possible for people to communicate with others over long distances, thus increasing the probability that people will trade with each other. ♦

Policy Changes Governments have the power to slow down the process of globalization, if they want. Suppose that two countries, A and B, have free economic relations with each other. Neither country prevents its citizens from going to the other country to live and work. Neither country hampers its citizens from investing in the other country. Then, one day, for whatever reason, the government of country A decides to limit its citizens from traveling to and investing in country B. In other words, the government of country A decides to close its political and economic doors.

Just as the government of one country can close the door on another country, it can open that door too. It can open that door a little, more than a little, or a lot. In recent decades, governments of many countries have been opening their doors to other countries. China has opened its door; India has opened its door; Russia has opened its door. See Exhibit 2-3 for some selected facts showing the recent trend toward globalization.

▲ Policy changes in Vietnam have opened the door to more free enterprise. Nike employs close to 50,000 Vietnamese workers and exports over 22 million pairs of shoes annually.

▼ Here are some "Then" and "Now" facts that indicate a trend toward globalization.

EXHIBIT 2-3 Globalization Facts

Topic	Then	Now
U.S. tariff rates (tax on imported goods)	40% in 1946	2.6% in 2005
Foreign exchange trading (buying and selling of foreign currencies)	$820 million in 1998	$1.5 trillion in 2004
Foreign direct investment (companies from one country investing in companies from another country)	$23 billion in 1975	$644 billion in 1997
U.S. ownership of foreign stocks	2% of portfolios in 1980	14% of portfolios in 2005
Membership in World Trade Organization (WTO)	18 countries in 1948	148 countries in 2005
Americans working in the U.S. for foreign companies	4.9 million in 1991	6.5 million in 2001

Economics Around the Clock

You may want to remind students of the 11:54 P.M. scenario in Economics Around the Clock (page 31) and discuss their answers to its question. Students might say that the customer service representative is in India because the U.S. company found it cheaper to hire someone in India than to hire someone in the United States, the United Kingdom, or some other country.

Analyzing

Assign students to write a short essay describing how advances in communication technology have made international trade easier and multinational corporations more common in the world today.

Teaching with Visuals

Urge students to review Exhibit 2-3. Discuss with them which facts they find most surprising.

Cross-Curricular Activity

Invite a history teacher to speak to your class about the role innovation and technology have played in reducing barriers to trade. Ask the teacher to explain, for example, how the steamship or the telegraph affected trade between nations in the past. Following the teacher's presentation, ask students to point out other innovations that have lowered barriers to trade.

Background Information

The International Monetary Fund is an international organization that provides economic advice and temporary funds to nations with economic difficulties. If a nation requests assistance, the IMF might submit a list of economic reforms for the nation to follow in exchange for a loan from the IMF.

Discussion Starter

Stimulate a class discussion on the costs and benefits of a global economy, by asking students the following questions: What examples of international trade do you find in your everyday lives? What do the countries involved gain or lose in each exchange? You might want to supplement this discussion by bringing to class the business section from a newspaper and allowing students to find articles or statistics related to international trade.

Discussion Starter

In recent years, China has opened up its economy to globalization. Its communist government, however, maintains a tight grip on the nation. Urge students to consider how the increasing economic freedom in China might affect the nation's political structure in the future.

Teaching with Visuals

After students review Exhibit 2-4, ask them to consider what, if any, factors other than globalization might contribute to increased life expectancy.

The Costs and Benefits of Globalization

Some people believe that globalization is, in general, a good thing and that its benefits outweigh its costs. Other people take the opposite view—that the costs of globalization are greater than the benefits. Let's look at what those who favor globalization say are its benefits, and what those who oppose it say are its costs. As you read, you will probably begin to form your own opinion.

Benefits

Following are some of the major benefits of globalization.

Trade To say that the world is undergoing the process of globalization is really no more than saying that people are trading with more people, at greater distances, than they once did. They are trading different things: money for goods, their labor services for money, their savings for expected returns, and so on. In other words, expanding trade—which is what globalization is about—is no more than extending the benefits of trading to people one might not have traded with earlier.

Standard of Living As both India and China opened up their economies to globalization in recent decades, they experienced increases in income per person. For example, between 1980 and 2000, income per person doubled in India. Between 1940 and 2000, income per person increased by 400 percent in China, much of this increase coming in recent years. According to the International Monetary Fund, these dramatic increases in income per person accompanied the expansion of free international trade (which is a key component of globalization).

Also, according to the International Monetary Fund, in the last 30 years hunger and child labor have been cut in half and life expectancy has dramatically increased in developing countries. According to the World Bank, 200 million people in the world were raised up out of poverty in the past 20 years.

People in the United States have benefited as well. According to work done by two economists, globalization increases U.S. income by roughly $1 trillion a year, or $10,000 per household. In other words, without the United States globalizing, Americans would be poorer by $1 trillion a year.

Another benefit to globalization seems to be longer life expectancy. One study compared the globalization index (a rating based on how globalized a country is; the higher the number, the more globalized) with life expectancy as computed by the United Nations. The study found that generally the more globalized a country was, the greater the life expectancy. See Exhibit 2-4.

EXHIBIT 2-4 Globalization and Life Expectancy

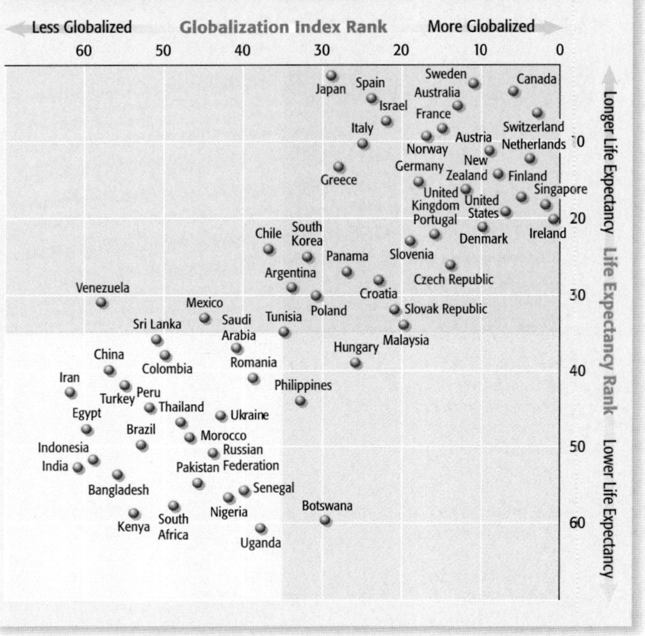

▲ The Globalization Index for various countries (prepared by *Foreign Policy* magazine at www.ForeignPolicy.com) was compared to life expectancy. A strong correlation appears between the degree to which a country has globalized and that country's life expectancy.

A Student Asks

QUESTION: *How do we know that the benefits you say are a result of globalization are, in fact, caused by globalization? Couldn't they be caused by something else?*

Internet Research

Tell students to search the Web for information about how India's economy has changed during the last two decades. Ask students to pay particular attention to the relationship between U.S. businesses and India. For example, they might look for answers to these questions: How has the availability of computer training in India affected the Indian economy? Why have many U.S. companies developed relationships with Indian companies and workers in recent years?

ANSWER: *Economists are fairly sure that globalization leads to an increased standard of living based on their comparisons of countries with similar characteristics. For example, take a look at Exhibit 2-5, which shows that the annual percentage change during the 1990s in output per person is positive in globalized developing countries but negative in less globalized countries.*

Or consider an extreme case, North and South Korea. The two countries share a people and a culture, but North Korea avoided the process of globalization during the period in which South Korea embraced it. What we observe is that South Koreans enjoy a much higher standard of living than North Koreans.

EXHIBIT 2-5 Annual Average Percentage Change in Output per Person in the 1990s

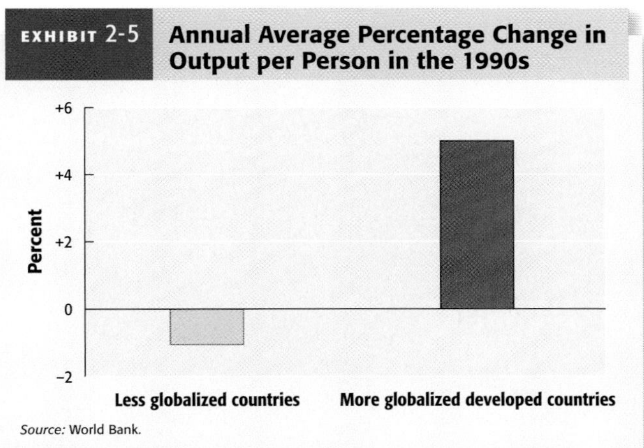

Source: World Bank.

▲ During the 1990s, the annual average percentage change in output per person was positive for the more globalized developing countries. The percentage was negative for the less globalized countries.

Costs

Described below are some of the costs associated with globalization.

Increased Income Inequality Globalization's critics often point out that globalization seems to go hand in hand with increased income inequality in the world. Has income inequality increased? Yes it has. For example, 100 years ago people in rich countries had about 10 times more income than people in poor countries. Today, they have about 75 times more income. Without a doubt, globalization and income inequality (between rich and poor countries) are strongly correlated. The question, though, is whether globalization causes the income inequality. The critics of globalization say it does; the supporters say it does not.

Losing American Jobs Many of the critics of globalization argue that globalization can result in Americans losing certain jobs. Suppose a U.S. company hires engineers in India to do jobs that once were done by

◀ East Indian American Express employees work at their computer in Delhi, India. **Name at least one possible cost and one possible benefit of American Express offshoring work to India.**

Teaching with Visuals

Have students review Exhibit 2-5. Ask them to think about why output per person increased in countries that embraced globalization and decreased in countries that did not.

Reinforcement Activity

Divide the class into two groups to debate whether the benefits of globalization outweigh the costs. Assign one group to present the benefits and the other group to emphasize the costs. Tell students to prepare for the debate by collecting evidence to support their assigned side of the issue. Also tell students that particular topics for the debate will be trade, standard of living, increased income inequality, loss of American jobs, and the power of corporations. As you conduct the debate, use a chart on the board to note the major points made by each side. At the end, attempt to reach a class consensus on the issue.

Teaching with Visuals

One cost of American Express's hiring people in India is that some American jobs are lost. One benefit may be that American Express reduces its expenses, which probably increases its profits.

Cross-Curricular Activity

Invite a government teacher to speak to your class about the political impact globalization has had in the United States. Ask the teacher to explain whether the loss of American jobs has been a major issue in political campaigns in the United States. Also suggest that the teacher discuss whether the issue resulted in laws designed to protect American jobs, and if so, what effects those laws have had.

Economics in the Real World

After students have read this feature, ask why higher education is increasingly valuable in a globalized economy. You might list their responses on the board, and then encourage students to choose one reason and create a billboard, public service announcement, jingle, or other creative advertising tool to convey that message.

ANSWERS TO THINK ABOUT IT Answers will vary. Students might suggest that competition will grow because more people will be competing for scarce resources.

Background Information

The Indian Institute of Technology dates to 1946 when a committee was created to explore the creation of institutions to help with postwar industrial development in India. The committee called for the creation of several campuses across India. The first Indian Institute of Technology opened in May 1950 in Hijli, Kharagpur, in the eastern part of India. Like the facilities in other parts of India, IIT Kharagpur has grown rapidly. Today it employs some 450 teachers and serves several thousand students.

The Price Gap Between Brains and Brawn: Is It Increasing?

The Indian Institute of Technology (in India) is one of the hardest universities in the world to be admitted to, largely because of its reputation. In an average year, about 178,000 high school seniors in India take the exam necessary to apply to the Indian Institute of Technology. Just over 3,500 students are admitted. In other words, only 1.96 percent of all applicants are admitted. In comparison, the admission rate of Harvard University is nearly 10 percent.

Like the Indian Institute of Technology, prestigious U.S. universities such as Princeton, Stanford, and Duke have very selective admission criteria. Each year, students who have the grade point average and standardized test scores to (potentially) be admitted to these universities are turned away. This has been occurring at the same time that college tuition has been increasing rapidly. For example, during the period from 1990 to 2003, college tuition went up by 130 percent, considerably more than medical care costs, housing, and food. Around the world at other prestigious schools we see the same theme: the admission rate is usually low and the cost is usually high.

As you know, grades (one admissions criterion) and money function as rationing devices. In the last chapter, you learned that because of scarcity, some mechanism has to ration the available resources, goods, and services. Still we have to ask: Why have both of these rationing devices—grades and money—become stiffer when it comes to being admitted to the top universities in the world? Why ever higher grades and ever more money? The answer is twofold.

First, the population of the world increased but the number of Harvards did not. Harvard cannot clone itself. To a large degree, the world has only one Harvard or Oxford (in the United Kingdom) or Indian Institute of Technology (in India). We can produce more computers, houses, and dining room chairs as the population of the world increases, but it seems much more difficult to produce more Harvards. So, what happens over time is an increasing scarcity of top-notch, one-of-a-kind educational institutions. As a result, the rationing devices for such institutions must do more work to ration, which essentially means that it will become harder and more expensive to get admitted to such places.

The second reason involves globalization. One of the things that pays a high dividend in a global economy is education. "Brains" seem to matter more than "brawn," which will increase the overall demand for a college education—not just at Harvard, but at all levels of high education.

So, will the premium being placed on education in a global economy cause the demand at the most prestigious schools to rise at a faster rate than at other colleges? The likely answer is yes. With a growing world population, and with the global economy paying a high premium to those who are educated, we can expect admission to the world's best institutions of higher learning to become even more difficult.

THINK ABOUT IT Some people suggest that the competition to be the best in a world economy will be much stiffer than the competition to be the best in a national economy. Do you think this assumption is true? Explain your answer.

Internet Research

Encourage students to look online for information about how other nations are preparing their young people for the global economy. Either assign students each a country to research, or let them pick one. Pose questions like these to guide their study: What steps is the country taking to prepare students for life after school? How will students' postgraduate experiences differ from their school experiences? Invite students to share their findings in brief oral reports. Then ask the class whether they themselves feel ready to compete in the global economy, or what steps might help them to prepare.

48 Chapter 2 Economic Systems and the Global Economy

Americans. This practice of hiring people in other countries is often called **offshoring**. (You will study *offshoring* and *outsourcing* in detail in Chapter 15).

It is true that some Americans may lose their jobs to workers in other countries due to globalization. It has already happened. Over the past few years a major New York securities firm replaced its team of 800 American software engineers, who earned about $150,000 per year, with an equally competent team in India earning an average of about $20,000 a year. Additionally, the number of radiologists in the United States is expected to fall significantly because it is now possible to send the data (that U.S. radiologists analyze) over the Internet to Asian radiologists who can analyze the data at a fraction of the cost.

Keep in mind, though, that offshoring is a two-way street. The United States might offshore certain jobs to, say, India or China, but foreign countries offshore jobs to the United States too. Also, while some Americans do lose jobs due to globalization, we must remember that jobs are always being lost (and found) in an economy responding to market changes. Even if the degree of offshoring in the United States were zero, people would still be losing old jobs and getting new jobs every day.

BY THE NUMBERS

One measure of globalization is the dollar amount of exports for a country. The greater the value of a country's exports, the more globalized it is. For example, in 1998, the United Kingdom had $271 billion in exports, and in 2003 it had $307 billion in exports. So, based on the value of exports, the United Kingdom was more globalized in 2003 than in 1998. Here are the export values for several countries in 1998 and 2003.

Country	Exports in 1998 (billions of dollars)	Exports in 2003 (billions of dollars)
Austria	$ 63	$ 89
Canada	220	285
China	183	438
France	303	361
India	34	59
Japan	374	449
Mexico	117	164
Norway	40	69
Russia	74	135
Sweden	85	102
Thailand	52	78
United States	672	716

A Student Asks

QUESTION: *I have heard of the word "outsourcing" but not "offshoring." Do these two words mean the same thing?*

ANSWER: *Yes and no. Offshoring is a particular kind of outsourcing.* Outsourcing *refers to any work done for a company by people other than the company's employees. More and more companies are outsourcing work to people who live in other countries. This special kind of outsourcing is called* offshoring. *Sometimes people use the word* outsourcing *when the correct word is* offshoring. *It is not uncommon to hear "Yes, many U.S. companies are outsourcing jobs to India and China." The correct word is* offshoring.

More Power to Big Corporations Many of the critics of globalization argue that the process will simply "turn over" the world (and especially the developing countries of the world) to large corporations headquartered in wealthier countries such as the United States, the United Kingdom, and France. In fact, in the minds of many people, globalization is not as we have defined it in this chapter; rather, it is the process of *corporatizing* the world. Instead of governments deciding what will and will not be done, large corporations will assume the responsibility.

The proponents of globalization often point out a major difference between a corporation and a government. First, a government can force people to do certain things (pay taxes, join the military). No corporation can do the same; instead, corporations can simply produce goods that they hope customers will buy. Additionally,

offshoring
The term used to describe work done for a company by persons other than the original company's employees in a country other than the one in which the company is located.

A Student Asks

You may want to use this A Student Asks to make sure that students understand the difference between *outsourcing* and *offshoring*.

Economics Around the Clock

You may want to remind students of the 6:14 P.M. scenario in Economics Around the Clock (page 31) and discuss their answers to the question posed there.

The answer is yes. Globalization is not a static process, in which everything stays the same from day to day. One result of globalization is that some people will lose jobs. However, even without globalization, some people will lose jobs. Even in a country that never trades with other countries, people's preferences for certain goods and services will change, and some people will lose their jobs as a consequence.

Cooperative Learning

Divide students into groups of three or four. Ask each group to look into whether globalization could be more accurately described as the *corporatizing* of the world. Ask students to find out why some people see globalization as the corporatization of the world. What evidence exists to support this point of view? What evidence supports the opposing view?

Reinforcement Activity

Remind students that the benefits of globalization are often less obvious than the costs. Ask students to think of some of the hard-to-see benefits of globalization. Work with the class to create a list of such benefits.

Economics Around the Clock

Instruct students to reread the 7:45 P.M. scenario in Economics Around the Clock (page 31). Call on students to name all the benefits of globalization mentioned in the scenario, listing their responses as they are offered. Do the same for all the costs mentioned in the scenario. Invite students to add to both lists from their own experience.

Teaching with Visuals

Answers to the photo question on this page will vary. Students might say that the presence of Japanese-made cameras in the American marketplace points to the greater choice available to American consumers because of globalization. They might also mention that competition from Japanese-made cameras pushes U.S. manufacturers to improve technology and lower prices, and that profits from sales of Japanese-made cameras in the United States help increase the standard of living in Japan.

Teaching with Visuals

Answers to the photo question on page 51 will vary. Students might mention the lowering of trade barriers, advances in communication and transportation, and policy changes.

Application Activity

After reading and discussing Section 2, you may want to assign the Section Activity in the *Applying the Principles Workbook.*

The Globalization Institute operates a blog at www.emcp.net/globalizationinstitute. If you go to the site, you will find numerous articles and essays on globalization. At the left of the page you will find categories such as agriculture, outsourcing, immigration, and more. Click on one of the categories and read a few of the articles and essays. For instance, you will see "Cobden," which stands for Richard Cobden (1804–1865), who was a prominent nineteenth century politician. Click on "Cobden" and read about his life. Cobden was a strong advocate of free trade. He believed that international trade was necessary between major powers if war was to be avoided. If he were alive today, no doubt he would strongly support economic globalization efforts.

▼ These U.S. consumers are shopping for cameras made by a Japanese company. **How might this scene represent the hidden benefits of globalization?**

the proponents of globalization often argue that the critics overestimate the influence and reach of large transnational companies. For example, in 2000, the top 100 transnational companies produced only 4.3 percent of the entire world's output, which is about as much as one country, the United Kingdom, produced in 2000.

The Continuing Globalization Debate

To a large degree, whether one supports or criticizes globalization seems to depend on where "one is sitting." Globalization doesn't affect everyone in the same way, and often *how* it affects *you* determines how you feel about it.

EXAMPLE: Suppose Sanders, an American worker residing in New York, loses his job to an Indian worker in New Delhi, India, who will do Sanders's job for less pay. In this case Sanders incurs real costs, but what about Sanders's company, and the company's customers? For the company, this change means lower costs and higher profits. For the company's customers, prices for the company's products may go down. So, in this case Sanders is probably a strong opponent of offshoring, while his company and its customers are probably supporters. ♦

When it comes to globalization, it is often much more difficult to see the benefits than it is to see the costs. For example, the supporters of globalization argue that it brings greater economic wealth, lower prices, more innovation, and less poverty. Yet, sometimes it is difficult for us to see all these benefits. When you buy cheaper goods or different goods because of globalization, you probably never say, "Wow, I can't believe all the benefits I get from globalization!" In fact, you might not even connect the lower-priced goods with globalization at all. The benefits of globalization tend to be difficult to see, partly because they are so widely dispersed.

The costs of globalization, in contrast, are more visible, often because they are so concentrated. A person who loses a job because of freer international trade in the world knows exactly what is to blame for the predicament he or she is in. This person surely could receive some benefits from globalization (in the role of a consumer), but this person also could, for a time, incur some rather high costs from globalization (as an unemployed worker). It is likely that this person will know of the costs but be unaware of the benefits.

Differentiating Instruction

To help ELL students, use the following resources, which are provided as part of the *Economics: New Ways of Thinking* program:

- a Spanish glossary in the *Student Text*
- Spanish versions of the Chapter Summaries on an audio CD

◀ This new IKEA store opened in Russia in September of 2005. **How does a Swedish retailer opening a store in Russia reflect the recent trend toward globalization?**

A Fad or Here to Stay?

Thomas Friedman states that "globalization is not just some economic fad, and it is not a passing trend." He also argues that the "relevant market today is planet Earth."

The basic globalization force that will probably not be overcome—no matter how strong the political forces may be against it—is the human inclination that the founder of modern economics, Adam Smith, noticed more than 200 years ago. Smith said that human beings want to trade with each other. In fact, it is the desire to trade that separates us from all other species, he says. In his words, "Man is an animal that makes bargains: no other animal does this—no dog exchanges bones with another."

In other words, we want to trade with people. We want to trade with our next-door neighbor, the person on the other side of town, the person in the next state, the person on the other side of the country, and finally, the person on the other side of the world. Some economists go on to suggest that this "trading" inclination we possess is a good thing, in that when we trade with people we not only will tolerate them, but have much less reason to fight with them.

> ***"The relevant market today is planet Earth."***
> —Thomas Friedman

SECTION 2

ASSESSMENT

Defining Terms

1. Define:
   a. globalization
   b. offshoring

Reviewing Facts and Concepts

2. Identify two costs and two benefits of globalization.
3. Why does it make less sense to speak of different economic systems in a global economy than in a world of national economies?
4. What does "changing technology" have to do with globalization?

Critical Thinking

5. Why might it be easier to recognize the costs of globalization than the benefits?

Applying Economic Concepts

6. If globalization continues over the next few decades, how might your life be different?

Assess

Quick Quiz

The following true-or-false quiz will help you assess student understanding of the material covered in this section.

1. In part because of globalization, few countries can be easily labeled "capitalist" or "socialist." (True)
2. The early era of globalization began during the two world wars. (False)
3. Innovations have helped to lower trade barriers. (True)
4. The practice of hiring people in other countries is often called offshoring. (True)
5. It is often easier to see globalization's benefits than to see its costs. (False)

Assessment Book

You will find a quiz for this section in the *Assessment Book.*

Reteaching Activity

Use the Section Assessment to gauge which students may need reteaching on this section. Have those students reread the first part of the section and then explain why the world is becoming both smaller and freer economically.

Guided Reading

For further reteaching of the key concepts in this section, assign the Outlining Activity and the Just the Facts Handout from the *Guided Reading and Study Guide.*

SECTION 2 ASSESSMENT ANSWERS

Defining Terms

1. a. globalization: a phenomenon by which individuals and businesses in any part of the world are affected by events elsewhere in the world, and the growing integration of national economies of the world; **b. offshoring:** the practice by which a company located in one country hires workers located in other countries.

Reviewing Facts and Concepts

2. Two costs of globalization are increased income inequality and loss of American jobs; two benefits are increased trade and improved standard of living.
3. With globalization, almost all economies are tied much more closely together and differences between them are less pronounced.
4. Changing technology can improve communication and lower trade barriers, thereby helping globalization.

Critical Thinking

5. The benefits of globalization tend to be widely dispersed and thus more difficult to see.

Applying Economic Concepts

6. Answers will vary. Look for mention of situations affected by the benefits of trade and increases in standard of living, and by the costs of income inequality, global movement of jobs, and corporatization.

CHAPTER 2 Assessment Answers

Economics Vocabulary

1. traditional economy; **2.** mixed economy; **3.** economic system; **4.** Free enterprise; **5.** Socialism; **6.** income distribution; **7.** economic plan; **8.** Globalization; **9.** vision; **10.** labor theory of value; **11.** offshoring.

Understanding the Main Ideas

1. An economics system is how a society answers the three basic economic questions. Free enterprise and socialism are the two major economic systems today.
2. Most of the resources are controlled by individuals and companies in free enterprise, by the government in socialism; socialist governments prepare economic plans; and prices are allowed to fluctuate in a free enterprise system.
3. Their self-interest in getting something from us motivates them to offer us dinner.
4. Marx saw self-interest as harmful to society. He believed that capitalists, in pursuing their self-interests, exploit workers.
5. The end of the Cold War eliminated many trade barriers that had previously existed. Advancing technology led to lower transportation or communication costs, and lower costs mean fewer barriers to trade. Governments of many nations have been changing policies to encourage globalization.
6. Globalization has increased U.S. income by roughly $1 trillion per year.
7. Yes. One hundred years ago, people in rich countries had about 10 times more income than people in poor countries. Today, they have about 75 times more income.
8. Yes. Some people might lose their jobs because of globalization.
9. The benefits of globalization tend to be more widely dispersed than the costs, so they can be more difficult to recognize.
10. People might be less inclined to attack a trading partner.

Working with Graphs and Tables

1. A.
2. B.

Solving Economic Problems

1. Answers will vary. Some students might say families are more like socialist economies because the parents (the government) own the property and decide how the three basic economic questions are answered.
2. Smith's words mean that people have an inherent desire to trade.

2 CHAPTER 2 ASSESSMENT

Chapter Summary

Be sure you know and remember the following key points from the chapter sections.

Section 1

- All nations must answer three economic questions:
  - What goods will be produced?
  - How will the goods be produced?
  - For whom will the goods be produced?
- The two main economic systems are free enterprise and socialism.
- Free enterprise, also known as capitalism or a market economy, is an economic system in which individuals own most, if not all, the resources and control their use.
- In socialism, government controls and may own many of the resources.
- The ideas of Adam Smith, an eighteenth century economist, provided the foundation for capitalism, or free enterprise.
- Karl Marx, a highly influential economic thinker, proposed an alternative to free enterprise, and helped formulate the vision for socialism and communism.

Section 2

- Globalization is a growing integration of the national economies of the world into a single worldwide economy and is closely aligned with free enterprise, freer markets, and greater movement of people and goods.
- The end of the Cold War, advancing technologies, and governments' policy changes all contributed to the growth of globalization.
- Benefits of globalization include greater trade, increases in standard of living, lower prices, and growing innovation.
- Costs of globalization include increased income inequality, greater corporate power, and lost jobs for some people.

Economics Vocabulary

To reinforce your knowledge of the key terms in this chapter, fill in the following blanks on a separate piece of paper with the appropriate word or phrase.

1. A(n) ______ is an economy based on customs and beliefs that have been handed down from one generation to the next.
2. A(n) ______ is an economy with a mixture of capitalist and socialist elements.
3. A(n) ______ is the way in which a society decides what goods to produce, how to produce them, and for whom they will be produced.
4. ______ is an economic system in which individuals (not government) own most, if not all, the resources and control their use.
5. ______ is an economic system in which government controls and may own many of the resources.
6. The ______ is the way all the income earned in a country is divided among different groups of income earners.
7. A(n) ______ is a government program specifying economic activities, such as what goods are to be produced and what prices will be charged.
8. ______ refers to the integration of economic activities across (national) borders; a phenomenon by which economic agents in any given part of the world are affected by events elsewhere in the world; the extension of the division of labor and specialization beyond national borders.
9. Karl Marx and Adam Smith each had a ______, or a certain way of looking at and explaining the world.
10. The ______ states that any value in produced goods comes from the labor used to produce those goods.
11. Work done for a company by people other than the company's employees is called ______ if the people doing the work live in a country other than the country in which the company is located.

UNDERSTANDING AND APPLICATION

Understanding the Main Ideas

Write answers to the following questions to review the main ideas in this chapter.

1. What is an economic system? What are the two major economic systems in the world today?
2. List three ways in which free enterprise (or capitalism) and socialism are different.
3. According to Adam Smith, why do the butcher, brewer, and baker provide us with our dinner?
4. How would Marx respond to Smith's claim that self-interest is vital to the workings of a productive economy?
5. Identify and explain each of the three causes of globalization.
6. By how much (per year) has globalization affected U.S. income?
7. Is there greater income inequality in the world today than, say, 100 years ago? Explain.
8. Might globalization benefit some residents of a country more than others? Explain your answer.
9. Why might it be easier for an individual to recognize the costs of globalization than the benefits?
10. Explain how increased globalization might lessen intolerance and conflict in the world.

Working with Graphs and Tables

1. Which bar (A or B) in Exhibit 2-6 represents the annual average percentage change in output per person in the 1990s in *less* globalized countries?
2. Which bar (A or B) in Exhibit 2-6 represents the annual average percentage change in output per person in the 1990s in *more* globalized countries?

EXHIBIT 2-6

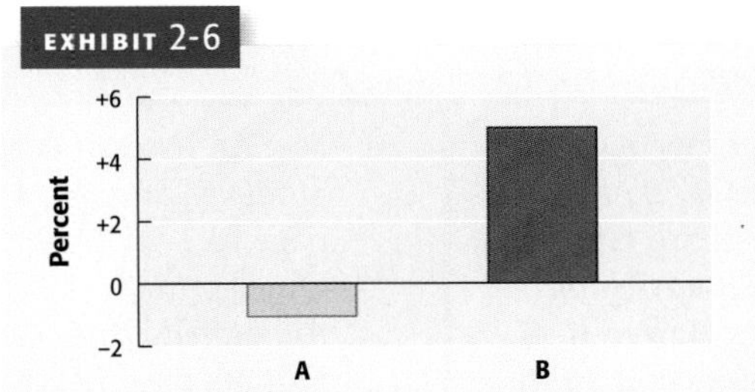

Solving Economic Problems

Use your thinking skills and the information you learned in this chapter to find solutions to the problems described below.

1. **Application.** Do you think that a typical family operates more like a free enterprise economy or like a socialist economy? Might different families operate differently? Explain your answers.
2. **Analysis.** What does the Adam Smith quotation "Man is an animal that makes bargains: no other animal does this—no dog exchanges bones with another" have to do with globalization?
3. **Cause and Effect.** In this chapter we identified three recent causes of globalization. Which of the three causes do you think played the biggest role in promoting globalization? Explain your answer.
4. **Writing.** Imagine two worlds. In the first, you live in a country that is open to other countries (when it comes to trade, movement of people, and so on). In the second world, the country is closed to all these things. Write a two-page essay explaining how your life would differ in the two worlds.
5. **Economics in the Media.** Find a recent newspaper or magazine article that addresses the issue of globalization in some way. Write a one-page essay summarizing the article.
6. **Economics in the Media.** Find a story on a television news show that addresses capitalism, socialism, private property, or global economic forces. Identify the major ideas of the story. Describe these ideas to your class in the form of a short televised news report.

ONLINE emcp.com **Practice Tests and Study Guide**

Go to www.emcp.net/economics and choose *Economics: New Ways of Thinking,* Chapter 2, if you need more help in preparing for the chapter test.

3. Answers will vary. Students might say that the end of the Cold War played the biggest role in promoting globalization because it not only removed political barriers to trade, but also opened up communication between nations and increased exposure to other economies and to the variety of goods and services available worldwide.
4. Student essays should describe differences between the two worlds.
5. Students should submit their articles along with their essays. Their essays should accurately summarize their articles.
6. Answers will vary.

Chapter 3 Planning Guide

SECTION ORGANIZER

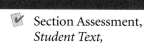

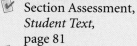

Section	Learning Objectives	Reproducible Worksheets and Handouts	Assessment
 SECTION 1 **Characteristics of Free Enterprise** 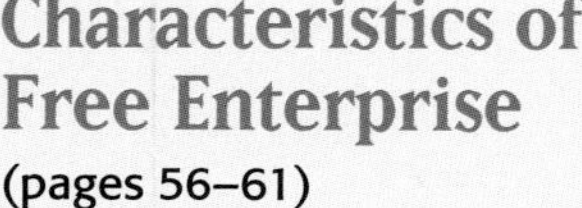 (pages 56–61)	▸ Explain what goods will be produced in a free enterprise economy. ▸ Tell who decides what goods will be produced in a free enterprise economy. ▸ Explain for whom goods will be produced in a free enterprise economy. ▸ List five major features of free enterprise. ▸ Describe the circular flow of economic activity.	Section 1 Activity, *Applying the Principles Workbook* Outlining Activity, *Guided Reading and Study Guide* Just the Facts Handout, *Guided Reading and Study Guide*	Section Assessment, *Student Text,* page 61 Quick Quiz, *Annotated Teacher's Edition,* page 60 Section Quiz, *Assessment Book*
 SECTION 2 **Profit and Loss in Free Enterprise** (pages 62–65)	▸ Describe the roles that profits and losses play in a free enterprise economy. ▸ Explain what profits, losses, and resources have to do with one another.	 Section 2 Activity, *Applying the Principles Workbook* Outlining Activity, *Guided Reading and Study Guide* 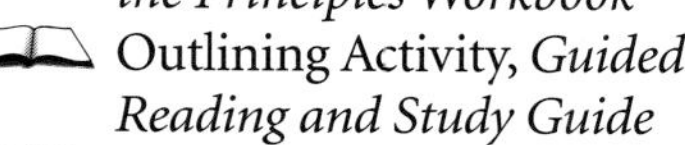 Just the Facts Handout, *Guided Reading and Study Guide*	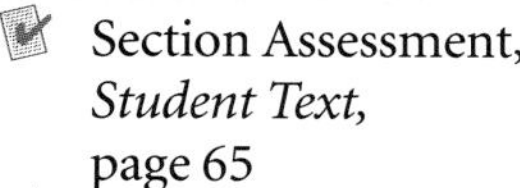 Section Assessment, *Student Text,* page 65 Quick Quiz, *Annotated Teacher's Edition,* pages 64–65 Section Quiz, *Assessment Book*
 SECTION 3 **The Ethics of the Free Enterprise System** (pages 66–70)	▸ Describe some of the qualities and characteristics of an ethical economic system. ▸ List some of the freedoms in free enterprise. ▸ Explain what economic principles are stated in the Bill of Rights, the Constitution, and the Declaration of Independence. ▸ Describe some of the responsibilities people have in a free enterprise system.	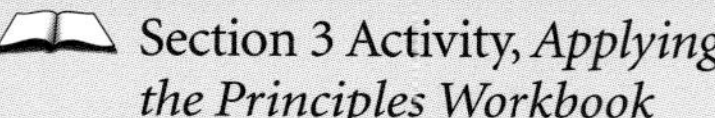 Section 3 Activity, *Applying the Principles Workbook* 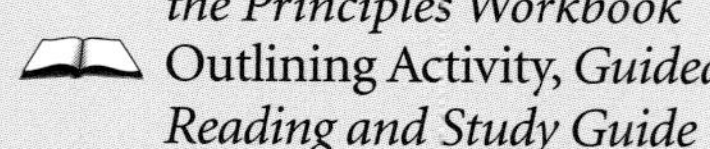 Outlining Activity, *Guided Reading and Study Guide* Just the Facts Handout, *Guided Reading and Study Guide*	Section Assessment, *Student Text,* page 70 Quick Quiz, *Annotated Teacher's Edition,* page 69 Section Quiz, *Assessment Book*
 SECTION 4 **Entrepreneurs**  (pages 71–73)	▸ Describe what an entrepreneur is. ▸ Explain how consumers benefit from the actions of entrepreneurs. ▸ Describe the effect that a law that limited profits would have on future entrepreneurs. ▸ Explain why entrepreneurs are willing to risk their time and money.	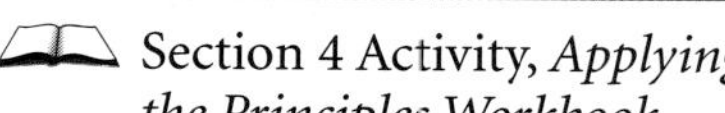 Section 4 Activity, *Applying the Principles Workbook* Outlining Activity, *Guided Reading and Study Guide* Just the Facts Handout, *Guided Reading and Study Guide*	Section Assessment, *Student Text,* page 73 Quick Quiz, *Annotated Teacher's Edition,* page 73 Section Quiz, *Assessment Book*
 SECTION 5 **The Role of Government in a Free Enterprise Economy** (pages 74–81)	▸ Describe what would happen if government did not enforce contracts. ▸ Describe a public good. ▸ Explain why, in a free enterprise economy, individuals will not produce nonexcludable public goods for sale. ▸ Define negative and positive externalities.	Section 5 Activity, *Applying the Principles Workbook* 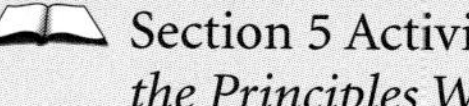 Outlining Activity, *Guided Reading and Study Guide* Just the Facts Handout, *Guided Reading and Study Guide*	Section Assessment, *Student Text,* page 81 Quick Quiz, *Annotated Teacher's Edition,* page 80 Section Quiz, *Assessment Book*

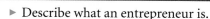

CHAPTER AND PROGRAM RESOURCES

Reproducible Chapter Resources and Assessment Materials

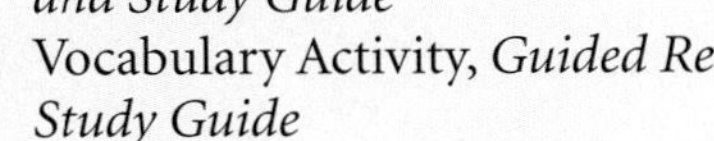

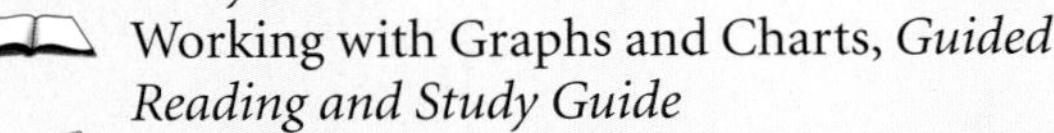

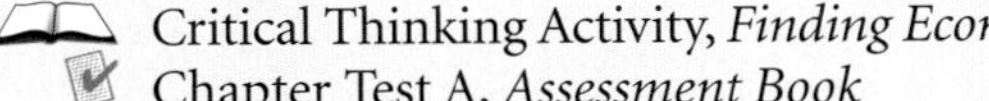

- Graphic Organizer Activity, *Guided Reading and Study Guide*
- Vocabulary Activity, *Guided Reading and Study Guide*
- Working with Graphs and Charts, *Guided Reading and Study Guide*
- Practice Test, *Guided Reading and Study Guide*
- Critical Thinking Activity, *Finding Economics*
- Chapter Test A, *Assessment Book*
- Chapter Test B, *Assessment Book*

Technology Resources

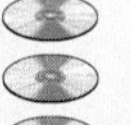

- *Test Generator CD*
- *Spanish Audio Summaries CD*
- *Marketplace® Audio Lessons CD*
- *Economic Principles Lectures, Videocassette or DVD*

Lesson Planning and Teaching Resources

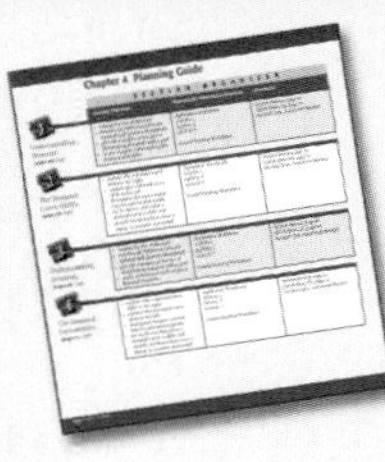

The *Economics: New Ways of Thinking* Teacher Resources include detailed lesson plans for each section in this chapter; the lesson plans are available in print form *(Lesson Plans)* and electronic form. The Teacher Resources also include *Daily Lectures: Overheads and Notes,* which provides prepared overheads and discussion notes covering the key concepts in each section of this chapter.

EMC Publishing Economics Online

Go to Economics Online, at www.emcp.com, for a variety of Internet resources to help you keep your course current and relevant. At Economics Online you will find these items:

- Economics in the News Lessons
- Study Guide Questions
- Practice Tests
- Lesson Plans

Internet Resources

Economics: New Ways of Thinking encourages students to use the Internet to find out more about economics. With the wealth of current, valid information available on Web sites, using the Internet as a research tool is likely to increase your students' interest in and understanding of economics principles and topics. In addition, doing Internet research can help your students form the habit of accessing and using economics information, as well as help them develop investigative skills they will use throughout their educational and professional careers.

To aid your students in achieving these ends, each chapter of *Economics: New Ways of Thinking* includes the addresses of several Web sites at which students will find engaging, relevant information. When students type in the addresses provided, they will immediately arrive at the intended sites. The addresses have been modified so that EMC Publishing can monitor and maintain the proper links—for example, the government site http://stats.bls.gov/ has been changed to www.emcp.net/prices. In the event that the address or content of a site changes or is discontinued, EMC's Internet editors will create a link that redirects students to an address with similar information.

Activities in the *Annotated Teacher's Edition* often suggest that students search the Internet for information. For some activities, you might want to find reputable sites beforehand, and steer students to those sites. For other activities, you might want students to do their own searching, and then check out the sites they have found and discuss why they might be reliable or unreliable.

CHAPTER 3 Overview

Today, many of us take life's conveniences for granted—washing machines to clean our clothes, radios to provide music in our cars, television sets to inform and to entertain us, and computers at school and on the job. These things and others that make our lives easier and more pleasant were developed mainly in free enterprise economies. This chapter considers what the free enterprise system is, how it operates, and its ethical basis. Students will also learn the roles that government and entrepreneurs play in a free enterprise system. The following statements provide brief descriptions of the major concepts covered in each section of this chapter.

Characteristics of Free Enterprise

Section 1 explains how a free enterprise economy answers the three economic questions. Students will learn the five major features of free enterprise and will be able to explain the circular flow of economic activity and how government actions affect this model.

Profit and Loss in Free Enterprise

Section 2 explains the role profits and losses play in a free enterprise economy. Students will learn how to calculate total revenue, total cost, and average costs for businesses.

The Ethics of the Free Enterprise System

Section 3 covers the characteristics of an ethical system. Students will also learn some of the freedoms that the free-enterprise system allows.

CHAPTER 3 Free Enterprise

Why It Matters

Free enterprise can be examined in two ways. One way looks at it much the way Winston Churchill, a former prime minister of Great Britain, looked at democracy. Churchill said it's not that democracy is so good, but that the other political systems are so bad. In other words, democracy is far from perfect, but it is the best system we have. Some people feel the same way about free enterprise: it's not that free enterprise is so good, but that it's the best system we have.

Others take a different view. To them, free enterprise is not only the best of a bad lot; it is good in an absolute sense. Free enterprise is not only an economic system that puts the "bacon on the table" but also a system that does so in an ethically desirable way.

These shop owners can own the property on which their business is built, make their own business decisions, and enjoy the profits of their hard work if their business is successful. The economic system that provides them with these opportunities is *free enterprise*.

No matter what you think of free enterprise, it is an economic system to reckon with. As you know from reading Chapter 2, in the late 1980s and early 1990s countries that had not yet adopted free enterprise ways began to do so. As an economic system, free enterprise has always played a major role in the development of economic wealth in the world. As globalization spreads, free enterprise promises to play an even bigger role in the twenty-first century.

Teaching Suggestions from the Author

If your car drives well, you rarely question how it does what it does. You just go on about your business happy that your car is doing what you want it to do.

It is much the same with economic systems. If the economic system under which you live does a good job of putting bread on the table and generally gives you a good life, rarely do you question how it works. This is the attitude of most of us with respect to the free enterprise system. It gets the job done, so what is there to discuss?

In this chapter, we take some time to examine free enterprise. What is it? Most people think they know what it is, but often they do not. They might say, "Free enterprise is about letting people do what they want to

Economics Around the Clock

The following events occurred one day in May.

7:38 A.M. Danielle is reading a story in her local newspaper about a billionaire who hired a major rock band for his son's 12th birthday party. It turns out that the total cost for the party is more than $7 million. Danielle thinks: *It is absolutely ridiculous to spend that much money on a kid's birthday party. I mean, people in the world are starving, and this guy spends $7 million on a birthday party*?

- **What does a $7 million party have to do with free enterprise?**

11:02 A.M. James wants to buy a new sports jacket for summer. He is currently looking at jackets at a clothing store in the mall. The jacket he is looking at is nice, and he'd like to buy it, but the price is a little high. A salesman walks over to James and asks if he can help him. James says that he is just looking. James thinks that he is going to look for a new jacket at another store.

- **What does deciding to go to another store have to do with free enterprise?**

2:33 P.M. Tory is in her economics class at Binghampton High School. Her teacher is talking about the role of the entrepreneur in the economy. He says, "The entrepreneur is one of the most important persons in the economy. Without the entrepreneur, we wouldn't have many of the goods and services we enjoy." As her teacher talks on, Tory wonders whether she should study economics in college if she wants to be an entrepreneur.

- **What do you study if you want to be an entrepreneur?**

6:42 P.M. Lisa is in her car delivering pizzas. Her radio is up loud and she is listening to a Gwen Stefani song. The windows of her car are rolled down as she is stopped at an intersection. Her head is going left and right as she sings along with the song. The gentleman in the car next to Lisa's looks over at her. He wishes she would turn the music down. Lisa doesn't notice him. She sings it again and she just keeps on singing. The light turns green and Lisa moves off.

- **What does listening to a Gwen Stefani song have to do with free enterprise?**

55

Entrepreneurs

Section 4 explains what an entrepreneur does and how an entrepreneur is affected by a free enterprise system.

The Role of Government in a Free Enterprise Economy

Section 5 explores the differences between a public good and a private good, between an excludable and a nonexcludable public good, and why individuals in a free enterprise economy will not produce a public good.

Introducing the Chapter

Ask students to list five words or phrases that come to mind when they hear the words *free enterprise.* Allow volunteers to share their answers.

Explain that the economic system of the United States is a free enterprise system. Tell students that the free enterprise system is something that many Americans hold dear because it is a part of the framework of this nation. Explain to students that in this chapter they will explore the nature of the free enterprise system, and they will discuss the ethics of this system.

Teaching with Visuals

One hallmark of free enterprise is choice—of stores, brands of products, and varying prices. Discuss with students how their lives might be different without the element of choice.

do," or "Free enterprise is about businesses producing the goods that consumers want to buy." Both these statements represent elements of the truth about free enterprise, but are woefully incomplete.

In this chapter we put the free enterprise system under the microscope and examine it carefully. One of the things students may be surprised to learn is that free enterprise is about more than buying and selling. It is about private property, ethics, entrepreneurs, and much more.

SECTION 1 Teacher Support

Focus and Motivate

Section Objectives

After completing this section, students will be able to

- explain what goods will be produced in a free enterprise economy;
- tell who decides what goods will be produced in a free enterprise economy;
- explain for whom goods will be produced in a free enterprise economy;
- list five major features of free enterprise; and
- describe the circular flow of economic activity.

Kickoff Activity

Ask students to reread and respond in writing to the 7:38 A.M. scenario in Economics Around the Clock (page 55). Students should specify how they think an expensive party relates to free enterprise.

Activating Prior Knowledge

Allow students to share their responses to the Kickoff Activity with the rest of the class. Tell them that the phrase *free enterprise* refers to the ability to act as you want in an economic system.

Teach

Discussion Starter

Tell students that dictionaries typically define *enterprise* as a project or undertaking that is difficult, complicated, or risky. What does this definition suggest about the nature of the free enterprise system?

SECTION 1 Characteristics of Free Enterprise

Focus Questions

- What goods will be produced in a free enterprise economy?
- Who decides what goods will be produced in a free enterprise economy?
- For whom will goods be produced in a free enterprise economy?
- What are five major features of free enterprise?
- What is the circular flow of economic activity?

Key Terms

private property
public property
household
circular flow of economic activity

How Does Free Enterprise Answer the Three Economic Questions?

You read about the three key economic questions that every economic system must answer in Chapter 2. Now let's look at how these questions are answered in a free enterprise economy.

What Goods Will Be Produced?

In a free enterprise economy, business firms will produce the goods that consumers want to buy. For example, suppose consumers are willing and able to buy goods A, B, and C at a price and quantity that will earn profits for business firms. Also suppose that consumers are either unwilling or unable to buy goods D, E, and F at a price and quantity that will result in profits for the businesses that produce the goods. Business firms will produce goods A, B, and C, but they will *not* produce D, E, or F.

EXAMPLE: In the United States, General Motors and Ford Motor Company decide what style and make of cars they will produce. Each company bases its production on what it thinks the car-buying public wants to buy. ♦

How Will These Goods Be Produced?

The individuals who own and manage the business firms decide how goods will be produced. For example, if the owners and managers of an automobile company want to use robots to produce cars, then they will purchase the robots and produce cars with them. If a company prefers that its secretaries use computers produced by Apple instead of computers produced by Hewlett-Packard, the secretaries will use computers produced by Apple.

For Whom Will the Goods Be Produced?

In a free enterprise economy, goods are produced for those people who are willing and able to buy them. Notice that it takes both *willingness* to buy and the *ability* to buy. A person has the ability to buy a

Differentiating Instruction

Visual Learners

Students might have difficulty understanding the characteristics of free enterprise just from reading the text. If students do have trouble, ask them to create a visual collage. Students must find or create visuals of each characteristic of the free enterprise system: private property, economic incentives, competition, voluntary exchange, and freedom to choose. By showing concrete, pictorial examples, both visual learners and those students who have difficulty with the English language will be able to better grasp the concepts within this section of the text.

$25,000 car if that person has $25,000 to spend, but if the same person is unwilling to spend $25,000 for the car, he or she will not purchase the car. Also, no purchase will occur if a person has the willingness to buy something but is unable to do so. For example, Shelly may be willing to spend $800 to buy a computer but may currently be unable to do so because she does not have the money.

A Student Asks

QUESTION: *Aren't some goods and services produced in a free enterprise economy that we would be better off not producing? Harmful products, such as pornography and drugs; and showy, unnecessary products like a $20,000 watch, or a $1 million diamond ring, or a solid gold faucet for the bathroom? Should these goods and services be produced?*

ANSWER: *Probably everyone can find some good or service produced, bought, and sold in a free enterprise economy that he or she thinks we would be better off without. Some people dislike hip-hop and think the country would be better without it; some people think that big Hummers on the road are something we would be better off without. The free enterprise economic system doesn't really make value judgments; it simply produces goods and services that individuals (maybe not all individuals) want to buy. Look at it this way. You might be in favor of free speech, but still not like everything that people say. Similarly, you might be in favor of free enterprise, but still not like everything that people produce, sell, and buy.*

Five Features of Free Enterprise

Five major features or characteristics define free enterprise: private property, choice, voluntary exchange, competition, and economic incentives. (See Exhibit 3-1.)

EXHIBIT 3-1 Characteristics of Free Enterprise

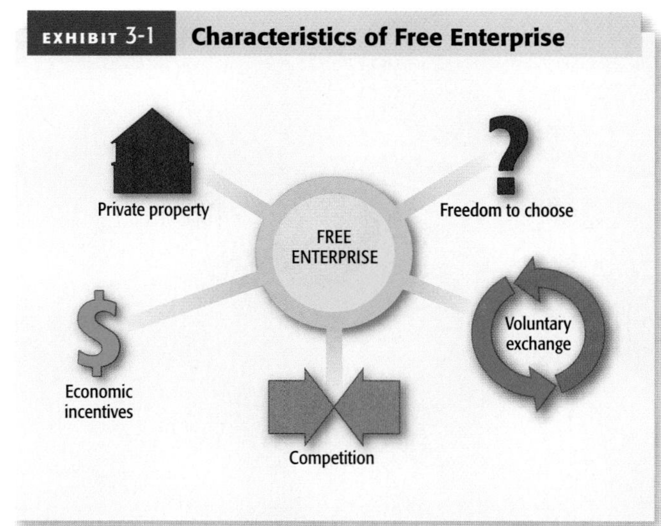

▲ Economic systems are often defined by their characteristics. Five characteristics that define free enterprise are private property, choice (or freedom to choose), voluntary exchange, competition, and economic incentives.

Private Property

Any good—such as a car, house, factory, or piece of machinery—that is owned by an individual or a business is referred to as **private property**. Any good that is owned by the government—such as the Statue of Liberty—is referred to as **public property**. Under free enterprise, individuals and businesses have the right to own property. Furthermore, they may own as much property as they are willing and able to purchase, and they may sell whatever property they own.

The right to own private property is not, however, absolute in all cases. Suppose the government wants to run a new road through the private property of some homeowners. The government offers to buy the property from the homeowners, but a few owners refuse to sell. What happens next? Generally, under the right of *eminent domain*, the government can take ownership of the land even without the consent of the owner. In such cases the government will compensate owners for the loss of their land.

private property Any good that is owned by an individual or a business.

public property Any good that is owned by the government.

A Student Asks

You may want to use this A Student Asks to emphasize that a free enterprise economic system does not make value judgments. Rather, the free enterprise system simply provides goods and services.

Reinforcement Activity

After students have read the subsection on free enterprise and the three economic questions, guide them in a discussion of the answers that the free enterprise system gives to the three economic questions.

Do students feel that the answers are reasonable or unreasonable? For example, students might believe the answer that the free enterprise system gives to the question, "What goods will be produced?" is unreasonable, because they believe that businesses don't really know what consumers want to buy.

Internet Research

Direct students to an online news source to find an article on a new or popular product and the company producing it. The product might be a new technological gadget or a new line of clothing by a popular fashion designer. Assign students to analyze the article to explain how it relates to each of the five features of free enterprise: private property, choice, voluntary exchange, competition, and economic incentives. Ask students how their selected products and companies fit into the free enterprise model.

Teaching with Visuals

Answers will vary. Possible answers include these: This car is probably being built because a similar model sold well. Automobile manufacturers decided how this car should be built, and they are building it for consumers who are willing and able to buy it.

Discussion Starter

Ask students to identify some areas of their city that are owned privately. Then have them identify publicly owned areas, such as parks and gardens. Ask which of these is better maintained, privately held land or publicly held land? Why, do they think, is this so?

Reinforcement Activity

The text refers to five features of free enterprise: private property, choice, voluntary exchange, competition, and economic incentives. Ask students to find newspaper articles that discuss any of these five features and to bring copies of the articles to class for discussion. You might also wish to make a bulletin board display of these for the classroom.

Clarifying Terms

You may want to provide students with the definition of the word *voluntary*—coming from a person's own will or consent.

▲ Why is this car, rather than a different model, being produced? Who decided how it should be built? For whom is it being built?

In 2005, a fairly controversial Supreme Court ruling (*Kelo v. New London*) touched on the issue of eminent domain. In a 5-to-4 ruling, the U.S. Supreme Court held that local governments may force property owners to sell to make way for private economic development if city officials decide that such a sale would benefit the public. The local officials can do this even if the new project's success is not guaranteed.

Opponents of this ruling argued that forcibly shifting land from one private owner to another, even with fair compensation, violated the Fifth Amendment of the U.S. Constitution, which prohibits the taking of property except for "public use."

Justice John Paul Stevens, of the Supreme Court, argued that "public use" could be interpreted to include not only traditional projects like highways or bridges, but also things such as slum clearance and land redistribution. He said that even such things as creating jobs in a depressed city could be interpreted as satisfying "public use."

Justice Sandra Day O'Connor, of the Supreme Court, disagreed with the ruling. She argued that the ruling favors the most powerful and influential in society and leaves small property owners with little recourse. She stated that the "specter of condemnation hangs over all property. Nothing is to prevent the State from replacing any Motel 6 with a Ritz-Carlton, any home with a shopping mall, or any farm with a factory."

Choice (or Freedom to Choose)

Choice is a key element of free enterprise. Workers have the right to choose what work they will do and for whom they will work. Businesses have the right to choose the products they will produce and offer for sale. Buyers have the right to choose the products they will buy.

EXAMPLE: Morgan, living in a free enterprise economy, wants to buy some vitamins, tofu, barbells, and a classic novel by William Faulkner. Ashley, also living in a free enterprise economy, wants to buy a CD by 50 Cent, a tattoo of an eagle, a book by Ayn Rand, and a motorcycle. Both Morgan and Ashley can buy what they want in a free enterprise economy. ♦

Voluntary Exchange

In free enterprise, individuals have the right to make exchanges or trades they believe will make them better off. For example, suppose Mei has $10, Michael has a book, and they trade. We conclude that Mei believes she is better off having the book than the $10, and Michael believes he is better off having the $10 than the book. Individuals make themselves better off by entering into exchanges—by trading what they value less for what they value more.

Competition

Under free enterprise, individuals are free to compete with others. Suppose you live in a town with five bakeries. You think you would like to open your own bakery and compete for customers with the other five bakeries. In a free enterprise system, no person or law stops you.

As a consumer living in a free enterprise system, you are likely to benefit from com-

Background Information: Socialist Nations

In the late 1980s and early 1990s, some formerly socialist countries turned toward free enterprise. People in these countries soon learned that profits are not guaranteed in a free enterprise economy. This means that jobs are not guaranteed either. If a company doesn't earn profits, it usually goes out of business—forcing the employees to look for other jobs. In a socialist country, people have secure jobs for life. Some of the people who were forced to look for work were unhappy with this aspect of a free enterprise system.

petition between sellers. You will probably have a bigger selection of products from which to choose, and sellers will compete with each other for your dollars by increasing the quality of the goods they sell, offering lower prices, providing better service, and so on. Although consumers in a free enterprise system may still have justified consumer complaints, the system usually provides major advantages. It may also have some disadvantages, which may or may not be present in other economic systems.

As a worker in a free enterprise economy, you may benefit from competition in another way. The competition between employers for your labor services will often result in your earning a higher wage or income than you would without competition. For example, suppose you are an accountant working for one of the five accountancy firms in town. A person opens up another accountancy firm and wants you to come to work for her. How might she get you to quit your present job and come to her firm? She may offer you a higher income than you are currently earning.

Economic Incentives

As we learned in Chapter 1, an incentive is something that encourages or motivates a person toward action. Under free enterprise, money acts as an incentive to produce. If you produce goods and services that people are willing and able to buy, you receive money in return. As you learned in Chapter 2, Adam Smith wrote about the usefulness of economic (or monetary) incentives in a free enterprise economy. He explained that business owners are interested in making themselves better off. This desire to earn an income strongly motivates them to produce for others.

Laws, Institutions, and Regulations

A free enterprise economy (such as the U.S. economy) does not operate in a vacuum. Free enterprise operates in countries, which have different systems of laws, institutions, and regulations. What a particular country's legal system permits and prohibits affects the "economic climate" of that country and determines, to a large degree, how free enterprise operates in that country.

"Some see private enterprise as a target to be shot, others as a cow to be milked, but few are those who see it as a sturdy horse pulling the wagon."

—Winston Churchill

Legal systems and institutions can either help or hinder free enterprise. For example, imagine a country in which the banking sector is somewhat undeveloped, and private property is *not* viewed as important. In this country the free enterprise system would have a difficult time operating (and doing what it does well). In a country such as the United States, however, laws have been developed to regulate banking and protect private property, which helps promote free enterprise.

As you read along in this text, you will learn how some of the institutions and laws in the United States influence the economy. For example, the last section of this chapter introduces you to government's role in free enterprise; Chapter 8 discusses antitrust laws; Chapter 9 describes certain business regulations; and Chapter 10 examines the banking system.

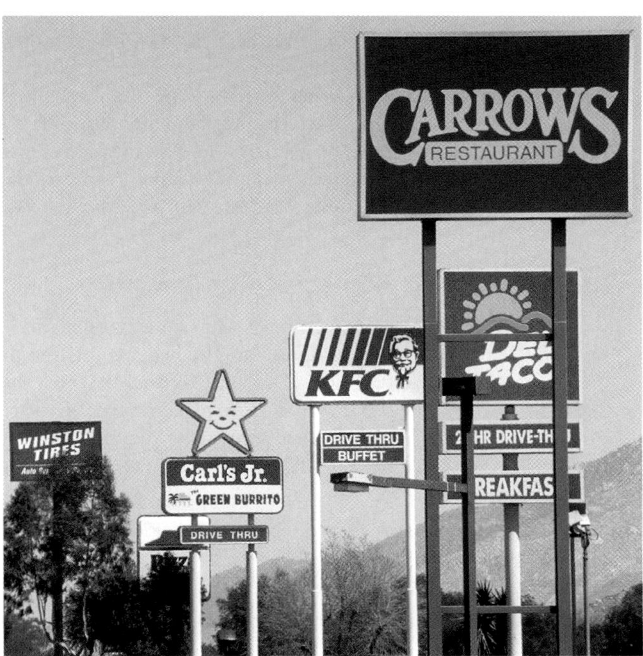

▼ The owner of a fast-food franchise might prefer fewer competitors nearby. **How might competition benefit you as a worker when you join the workforce?**

Reinforcement Activity

According to economist Adam Smith, even if a country had a lot of gold, that country wasn't necessarily rich. Instead, a country was rich according to "the achievement of an abundance of the necessities of life." In other words, a country was rich if it had the necessities—houses, clothes, food. Having necessities makes a country rich; money doesn't.

Activating Prior Knowledge

Share with students the fact that if a company offers its employees incentives, employees are likely to continue to work there. Discuss with students some common incentives at various jobs. (Examples include money, discounted food at a restaurant, social contacts, and health benefits.)

Free enterprise countries trade more with other countries than with socialist countries. In recent years, however, some formerly socialist countries have turned to free enterprise. We can expect the United States to enter into more trade with these countries.

Teaching with Visuals

When you are a worker, competition might benefit you by resulting in higher pay.

Differentiating Instruction

Enrichment and Extension

Allow selected students to present, either in oral report form or in a multimedia presentation, a discussion of Adam Smith and his views on free enterprise.

One student could prepare an oral report or poster describing economic conditions in England during Adam Smith's lifetime that led to his work *An Inquiry into the Nature and Causes of the Wealth of Nations* (1776). Another student, or a group of students, could create a slide or PowerPoint presentation describing how Smith's work was received in the years after its publication.

Teaching with Visuals

The circular flow diagram in Exhibit 3-2 represents the economic activity of the United States. Lead students in a discussion of how the diagram might be different when considering other countries.

Cause and Effect

Ask students if there is a connection between the arrows in Exhibit 3-2. What would happen if one of the arrows (and the good it represents) increased in size? (*Answer:* Another arrow would probably change size as well.) Encourage students to describe the relationships between the parts of the diagram.

Problem Solving

Tell your students to create new circular flow diagrams, this time increasing the amount of money, goods, or services flowing from one point to another point. They can choose which arrow to increase. Remind the class that as one arrow is increased, others will be affected. Allow volunteers to share their new diagrams with the class.

Application Activity

After reading and discussing Section 1, you may want to assign the Section Activity in the *Applying the Principles Workbook.*

Assess

Quick Quiz

The following true-or-false quiz will help you assess student understanding of the material covered in this section.

1. In a free enterprise system, businesses are free to choose which goods to produce. (True)
2. Any good owned by the government is referred to as a public good. (True)
3. Under free enterprise, only certain individuals are able to compete in certain markets. (False)
4. In a free enterprise system, there is competition for your labor. (True)
5. Under free enterprise, money is an incentive to produce. (True)

▶ The circular flow of economic activity shows the relationships between different economic groups. For example, in this circular flow diagram we see that households buy goods from businesses and sell resources to businesses. We see that both businesses and households pay taxes to government and receive benefits from government.

EXHIBIT 3-2 The Circular Flow of Economic Activity in the U.S. Economy

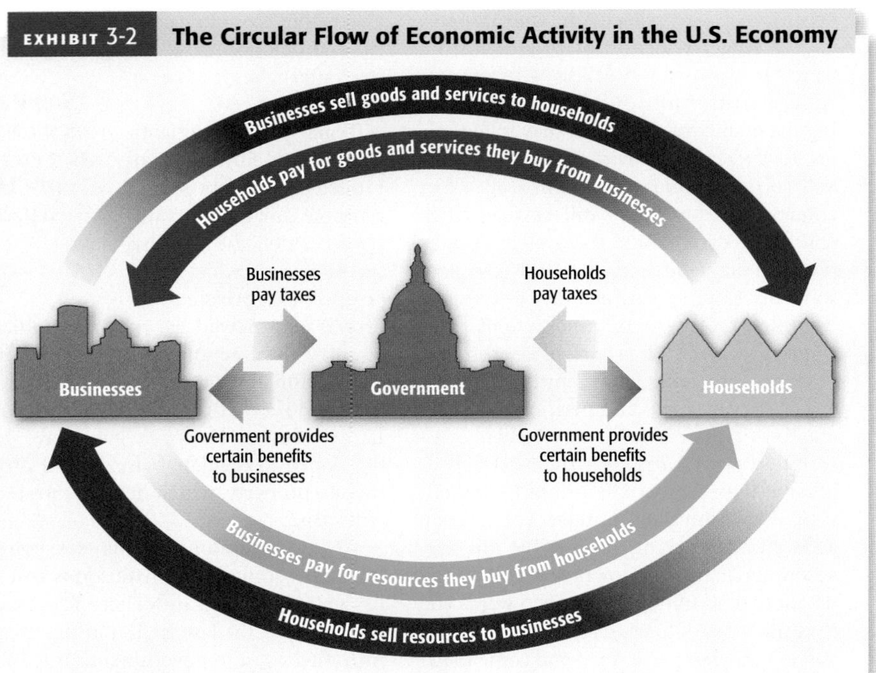
Businesses sell goods and services to households
Households pay for goods and services they buy from businesses
Businesses pay taxes
Households pay taxes
Businesses
Government
Households
Government provides certain benefits to businesses
Government provides certain benefits to households
Businesses pay for resources they buy from households
Households sell resources to businesses

The Circular Flow

Much of what characterizes a free enterprise economy has to do with how the key economic sectors—government, businesses, and **households**—deal with each other. Does government play a big role in the economy, or a small role? Are businesses free to produce what they want? What goods do businesses produce in order to sell to the household sector?

A Snapshot of an Economy

A picture of what an economy can look like in action might help us answer these questions. Look at Exhibit 3-2, which shows the **circular flow of economic activity** in the U.S. economy. The picture shows who the key players are in the economy, the relationships they have with each other, and the ways in which they interact. At first sight, it simply looks like a picture with lines going every which way, but those lines tell a story.

household
An economic unit of one person or more that sells resources and buys goods and services.

circular flow of economic activity
The economic relationships that exist between different economic groups in an economy.

1. As mentioned above, it is customary to think of an economy as composed of businesses, government, and households. In the exhibit, businesses, government, and households are visually represented in the center of the diagram.
2. An economic relationship exists between businesses and households. Businesses sell goods and services to households (purple arrow), for which households must make monetary payments (blue arrow). For example, a consumer decides to buy a sofa from a furniture company.
3. Businesses and households have another economic relationship: individuals in households sell resources (such as their labor services) to business firms (red arrow), and in return, businesses pay individuals for these resources (green arrow). For example, a business pays a worker a day's wage.
4. Both businesses and households have a certain economic relationship with the government. Households pay taxes to the government (yellow arrow) and in

Differentiating Instruction

Visual and English Language Learners

Either create a larger version of the circular flow diagram or show one on an overhead. Assign students to identify specific examples for each of the points and arrows on the diagram. This activity will show how the diagram is directly related to their lives.

Next instruct students to draw a circular flow diagram that includes specific examples in the arrows. For example, in the bottom right-pointing arrow might be "A cereal company pays workers to put cereal in boxes" and in the bottom left-pointing arrow might be "The Diaz family buys a box of cereal."

return receive certain goods and services (gray arrow). For example, the government provides individuals with roads, schools, and national defense. The same kind of relationship holds between businesses and the government: businesses pay taxes to the government (orange arrow), and the government provides certain goods and services to businesses (brown arrow).

Now look at Exhibit 3-2 as a whole rather than focusing on any of its parts. Notice in particular the relationships between different economic individuals, businesses, and institutions.

- *Businesses and households.* Households sell resources to businesses, and businesses pay for those resources. It is also the case that businesses sell goods and services to households, and then households pay for those goods and services.
- *Government and households.* Households pay taxes to the government, and the government provides goods and services to households.
- *Government and businesses.* Businesses pay taxes to the government, and the government provides goods and services to businesses.

Why Is the Circular Flow Diagram Useful?

Suppose you are watching the news one night on television. An economist who works for the president of the United States is stating that the president is seriously considering raising people's taxes. Look at Exhibit 3-2 and ask yourself which arrow will be affected by this action. It is the yellow arrow labeled "Households pay taxes," which goes from households to the government. If all other things remain the same, this arrow grows larger, because more tax dollars will flow through it.

Next, ask yourself this question: If more tax dollars flow through the yellow arrow from households to government, will fewer dollars flow through some other arrow? The answer is yes—through the blue arrow that moves from households to businesses. In other words, because households pay more of their income in taxes, they have less of their income to buy things such as television sets, cars, and computers. The circular flow diagram helps us see how a change in one economic activity (such as paying taxes) will lead to a change somewhere else in the economy (such as the amount households spend on goods and services produced by businesses).

SECTION 1 ASSESSMENT

Defining Terms

1. Define:
   a. private property
   b. public property
   c. households
   d. circular flow of economic activity
2. Use the word *incentive* correctly in a sentence.

Reviewing Facts and Concepts

3. According to the circular flow of economic activity, in what economic activities is the government engaged? (Look at Exhibit 3-2 to help you answer the question.)
4. In a free enterprise economy, how would you answer this question: *For whom are goods produced?*
5. Under free enterprise, everyone has the right to own property. Does it follow that everyone will own property? Why or why not?
6. How does voluntary exchange benefit a person?
7. What advantages do consumers get from the competition between sellers?

Critical Thinking

8. Would Adam Smith agree that the benefits of free enterprise are a consequence of the human desire to make life better for others? Explain.

Applying Economic Concepts

9. Teachers want students to do their homework completely, carefully, and on time. Identify an incentive that you think would increase student efforts toward reaching these objectives.

Assessment Book

You will find a quiz for this section in the *Assessment Book.*

Reteaching Activity

Guide the students in examining their favorite aspects of the free enterprise system. Is it competition between employers for a worker's labor service? Is it the fact that businesses will produce the goods that consumers want to buy? Ask volunteers to share the reasons that they prefer their favorites.

Guided Reading

For further reteaching of the key concepts in this section, assign the Outlining Activity and the Just the Facts Handout from the *Guided Reading and Study Guide.*

Defining Terms

1. a. private property: any good that is owned by an individual or a business; **b. public property:** any good that is owned by the government; **c. household:** an economic unit of one person or more that sells resources and buys goods and services; **d. circular flow of economic activity:** the economic relationships that exist between different economic groups in an economy.

2. Answers will vary. Students should write sentences that show that they clearly understand the economic use of the term.

Reviewing Facts and Concepts

3. The government is involved in the economic activity of receiving taxes and providing certain benefits to households and to businesses.

4. In a free enterprise economy, goods are produced for those people who are willing and able to buy them.

5. No. Some people will not have the money or necessary resources to buy property. Some people will have the money to buy property but choose not to.

6. When a person trades, she gives up something of less value to her in exchange for something she values more highly.

7. Consumers are likely to have a larger selection of products from which to choose. They are likely to have higher-quality goods, pay lower prices, and receive better service.

Critical Thinking

8. No. According to Adam Smith, good things happen under free enterprise because people can't make themselves better off unless they help others first.

Applying Economic Concepts

9. Answers will vary. You might wish to compile a list of student suggestions on the board and discuss them.

SECTION 2

Teacher Support

Focus and Motivate

Section Objectives

After completing this section, students will be able to

- describe the roles that profits and losses play in a free enterprise economy; and
- explain what profits, losses, and resources have to do with one another.

Economics Around the Clock

Kickoff Activity

Tell students to reread the 11:02 A.M. scenario in Economics Around the Clock (page 55) and respond in writing.

Allow volunteers to share their answers with the class. Students should explain how deciding to go to another store relates to free enterprise.

Activating Prior Knowledge

Profit pulls resources toward itself. To help students understand this concept clearly, draw an analogy between profit and a magnet. A magnet pulls things toward itself, too. Ask the students to describe what profit is pulling toward itself. (*Answer:* resources.)

Teach

Discussion Starter

Ask how many of your students have jobs in retail stores. Ask if those students are aware of the wholesale cost (average cost of a good) of each item that they sell in the stores.

SECTION 2

Profit and Loss in Free Enterprise

Focus Questions

- What roles do profits and losses play in a free enterprise economy?
- What do profits, losses, and resources have to do with one another?
- How do profit and loss operate as signals to business firms?

Key Terms

profit
loss

Profits and Losses

In a free enterprise economy there are no guarantees. A business can either succeed or fail. Whether a business is successful or not depends on whether it generates profits or losses.

Profits

Suppose that a computer company spends $800 to produce a computer, and then sells the computer for $1,200. In this case the company earns $400 in profit. **Profit** is the amount of money left over after all the costs of production have been paid.

Profit can also be described in terms of total revenue and total cost. *Total revenue* is the price of a good times the number of units of the good sold:

profit
The amount of money left over after all the costs of production have been paid. Profit exists whenever total revenue is greater than total cost.

loss
The amount of money by which total cost exceeds total revenue.

Total revenue =
Price of a good × Number of units sold

For example, suppose you sell radios at a price of $50 apiece. On Monday you sell five radios, so the total revenue for Monday is $250.

Total cost is the *average cost* of a good times the number of units of the good sold:

Total cost =
Average cost of a good × Number of units sold

Suppose the average cost of the five radios you sell is $30 per radio. The total cost is $150. For the five radios, the difference between total revenue ($250) and total cost ($150) is $100. This $100 is profit.

Losses

Notice that profit results any time total revenue is greater than total cost. When the opposite is true—when total cost is greater than total revenue—a **loss** occurs, stated in terms of the amount of money by which total cost exceeds total revenue. For example, suppose that in a given year, a clothing store has a total revenue of $150,000 and total costs of $200,000. If we subtract the store's costs from its revenues, we get –$50,000, a loss for the year.

Profit = Total revenue > Total cost
Loss = Total cost > Total revenue

Cross-Curricular Activity

Invite a history teacher to speak to your class about the role that the profit motive played in the American Revolution. Ask the history teacher, for example, to put the Boston Tea Party into an economic context. Many Patriots believed that Great Britain was infringing upon their economic rights as well as other rights and liberties. Ask students to think about how closely related economic rights can sometimes be to other rights, such as the right to freedom of speech.

62 Chapter 3 Free Enterprise

A Student Asks

QUESTION: *How many new businesses start up in the United States each year? How many business failures happen each year?*

ANSWER: *About 3.4 million new businesses start up each year (including businesses of all sizes, even one-person businesses) and about 3.2 million businesses fail each year. The source for these data is the Statistical Abstract of the United States which you can find online at www.emcp.net/businesses.*

▲ In a free enterprise economy there is no guarantee that a new business will succeed. **Why do you think more than 3 million businesses fail each year?**

Profit and Loss as "Signals"

At any time in a free enterprise economy, some business firms are earning profits, and some are taking losses. Profits and losses are (1) signals to the firms actually earning the profits or taking the losses and (2) signals to firms standing on the sidelines.

Suppose the NBC television network airs a comedy show on Thursday night that earns high ratings. Because companies will pay more to advertise on high-rated shows, the comedy show creates more profits for NBC. The CBS network airs a crime show on Thursday night that receives low ratings and losses. What are NBC and CBS likely to do now?

NBC will probably do nothing new; it will continue doing what it has been doing. The comedy show is earning high ratings, and the network is earning high profits. CBS, in contrast, will probably cancel its crime show, because the public does not like it. CBS might replace the crime show with a comedy, because NBC already showed that a comedy does better than a crime show.

So far the third major network, ABC, remained on the sidelines watching what was happening to NBC and CBS on Thursday night. ABC is thinking about developing a new program. Will what happened to NBC and CBS influence ABC's decision as to what type of program it will

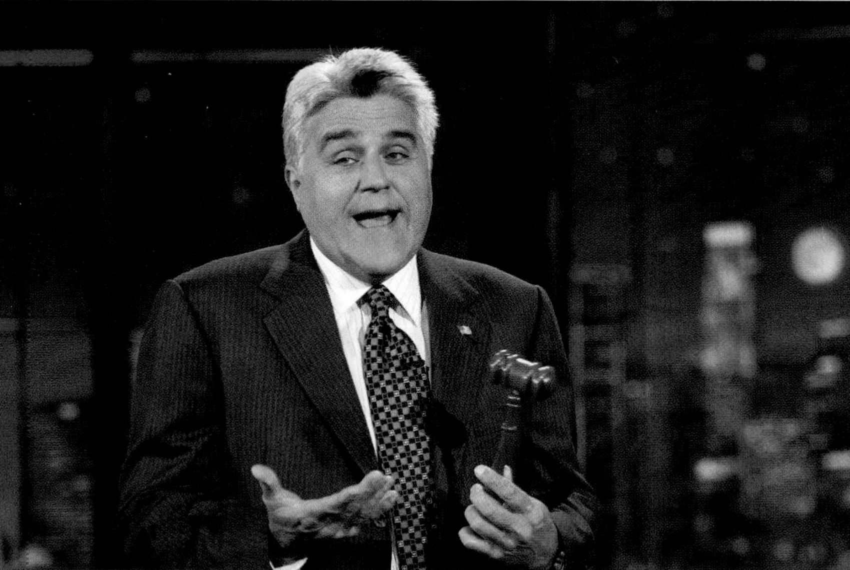

◀ *The Tonight Show with Jay Leno* is a profitable show for NBC. **How do one company's profits affect decisions made by its competitors?**

Teaching with Visuals

Businesses fail because they experience too many losses.

Activating Prior Knowledge

Instruct students to write one sentence in which they relate profit to total cost and total revenue. One example could be, "Profits exist whenever total revenue is greater than total cost."

Thinking Like an Economist

Some people believe that if you favor a free enterprise economy, you must be in favor of everything that businesspeople do. The economist thinks differently. She knows that businesspeople might want to hamper the free enterprise economy. For example, suppose a U.S. car company wants the government to restrict the number of new foreign cars that can be imported into the country to be sold. In doing so, the U.S. car company hopes to lessen the competition it faces from foreign car companies. This act is not consistent with free enterprise, which promotes competition. In other words, being pro-business is not the same as being pro-free enterprise. Being pro-free enterprise is usually more consistent with being pro-consumer and pro-competition. Invite students to name another instance in which a business wanted to stifle the free economy.

Teaching with Visuals

One company's profits signal to its competitors that perhaps they should copy what the successful company has done.

Cooperative Learning

Write the following sentences on the board: "Some people believe that profit benefits only those people who earn it. Others say that profit has a social function, too. This means that it provides some good to society."

Divide the class into two groups, one for each side of this issue. Ask the members of each group to work together to prepare presentations supporting their side. Tell students that they will need to be able to explain why their viewpoint is the better one.

After students have read this feature, ask them to compare personal experiences of owning private property with personal experiences of using common property. Which experience do they prefer?

ANSWERS TO THINK ABOUT IT Students' answers will vary. Let them share their ideas about which setting would lead them to take good care of the car.

Reinforcement Activity

The role of profits and losses in free enterprise can be defined in many relationships in an economic system. Instruct students to identify the role of profits and losses in various sectors of the economic world in which they live. To make sure they can see the impact of these economic factors on their daily lives, ask them to describe ways in which profit and loss affect them every day.

THE GLOBAL IMPACT

ANSWERS TO ECONOMIC THINKING

The answer to the question for this feature on page 65 is that if the trend toward economic globalization continues, a larger percentage of the world's population will experience freedom.

Application Activity

After reading and discussing Section 2, you may want to assign the Section Activity in the *Applying the Principles Workbook.*

Assess

Quick Quiz

The following true-or-false quiz will help you assess student understanding of the material covered in this section.

1. Total revenue is the average cost of a good divided by the number of units of the good sold. (False)

What Saved the Pilgrims?

Private property is one of the features of free enterprise. Many of the advocates of free enterprise argue that without private property, free enterprise could not produce as much wealth as it does.

Private property is not without its critics, though. Some people argue that private property breeds greed and selfishness. Common property—property held in common by the community—motivates people to be more civic minded, peaceful, and caring, they say. The advocates of private property retort that this notion of common property is idealistic and wrong. The truth is, they say, that common property often leads to poverty and unhappiness.

With this background, consider the Pilgrims in the early 1600s. When the Pilgrims left the Old World, they formed a partnership in a joint-stock company with some London merchants. When the Pilgrims landed off the coast of Massachusetts in 1620, they followed the advice of the company and declared that all pastures and produce would be common property. The result was chaos and starvation; after the first winter, half the colonists were dead.

Bad weather is often blamed for what happened to the Pilgrims, but the governor of the Plymouth colony, William Bradford, believed otherwise. He thought it had a lot to do with the fact that the Pilgrims held common property instead of private property. Bradford, therefore, assigned every family in the colony a private parcel of land, on which the family could produce food that it sold for profit. In his diary, Bradford wrote that privatizing the land "had very good success for it made all the hands very industrious, as much more corn was planted than otherwise would have been." He also remarked on how unsuccessful the common property scheme had turned out to be when he said, somewhat philosophically, that it had proved the "vanity of that conceit of Plato's . . . that the taking away of [private] property and bringing community into a commonwealth [of common property] would make them happy and flourishing." It seemed that common property, far from making people happy and flourishing, had instead made them poor and hungry.

Some historians now say that it was probably Bradford's decision to turn common property into private property, more than a change in the weather, that produced the first plentiful harvest in the Plymouth colony—a plentiful harvest that was subsequently celebrated as Thanksgiving.

THINK ABOUT IT To get an idea of how private property affects incentives, consider two settings. In the first setting, you and five of your friends share the ownership of a car. In the second setting, you are the only owner of the car. In which setting are you more likely to take care of the car (for example, to make sure it is clean and in good running order)? Explain your answer.

Differentiating Instruction

English Language Learners

To help ELL students, use the following resources, which are provided as part of the *Economics: New Ways of Thinking* program:

- a Spanish glossary in the *Student Text*
- Spanish versions of the Chapter Summaries on an audio CD

develop? Yes, ABC will be more likely to develop a comedy than a crime show.

Let's summarize what happened:

- The people at home decide what they want to watch on television.
- Many more people watch the NBC comedy show (giving it high ratings) than the CBS crime show (which gets low ratings).
- Companies pay more to advertise on high-rated shows than low-rated shows, so NBC earns profits on its Thursday show and CBS takes losses.
- NBC realizes it has a winning show, so it keeps the comedy show on the air. CBS realizes it has a losing show, so it takes the crime show off the air.
- ABC, on the sidelines, decides to copy NBC instead of CBS.

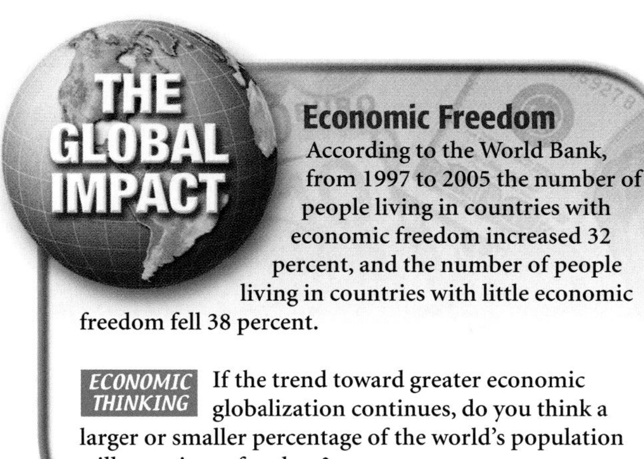

Economic Freedom

According to the World Bank, from 1997 to 2005 the number of people living in countries with economic freedom increased 32 percent, and the number of people living in countries with little economic freedom fell 38 percent.

ECONOMIC THINKING **If the trend toward greater economic globalization continues, do you think a larger or smaller percentage of the world's population will experience freedom?**

You recall that resources consist of land, labor, capital, and entrepreneurship. When CBS decides to take its crime show off the air and replace it with a comedy show, what happens to the resources that were previously used to produce the crime show? An economist would say the resources are being reallocated—moved from one place to another, or used differently. Some of the resources used to produce the crime show—the people who worked on the show, the cameras used to film the show, the accountants who kept the books—will probably be used to work on a comedy show instead of a crime show. Simply put, resources flow toward profit; resources flow away from losses. Profit is like a big magnet: it pulls resources toward it. Loss is like a big wind: it pushes resources away.

EXAMPLE: In the early days of the VCRs, DVD players, personal calculators, and personal computers, profits were relatively high for the relatively few companies that produced the new products. This "high profit" attracted competitors. It was as if the high profit were saying, "Look, I'm over here, come and get me." Soon, numerous companies were producing VCRs, DVD players, calculators, and personal computers, instead of only few. As a result, the prices of these goods came down, and with it, profit too. ◆

SECTION 2 ASSESSMENT

Defining Terms

1. Define:
   a. profit
   b. loss

Reviewing Facts and Concepts

2. Explain how profits and losses affect where resources will be used.
3. If a business is currently earning high profits producing lamps, what are other firms that observe this fact likely to do? Explain your answer.
4. If price is $40, number of units sold is 450, and average cost is $33, what is the profit?
5. If average cost is $423, price is $399, and the number of units sold is 23, what is the loss?

Critical Thinking

6. Many people think that profit benefits only the person who earns it; in other words, profit provides no social function. Do you agree or disagree? Explain your answer.

2. Resources flow toward losses. (False)
3. When total cost is greater than total revenue, there is a loss. (True)
4. Profit is the price of a good times the number of units of the good sold. (False)
5. Goods that earned profits in the past always earn profits in the future. (False)

Assessment Book

You will find a quiz for this section in the *Assessment Book.*

Reteaching Activity

Guide the students in examining profit. Write the following chart on the board and ask, What is the profit in each case?

	Total Cost	Total Revenue
A.	$100	$120
B.	$75	$100
C.	$1,250	$1,550

The answers are **A.** $20; **B.** $25; **C.** $300. Review these answers with students to ensure that they understand how profit is determined.

Guided Reading

For further reteaching of the key concepts in this section, assign the Outlining Activity and the Just the Facts Handout from the *Guided Reading and Study Guide.*

Defining Terms

1. a. profit: the amount of money left over after all the costs of production have been paid—in other words, profit is total revenue minus total costs; **b. loss:** the amount of money by which total cost exceeds total revenue.

Reviewing Facts and Concepts

2. Profits and losses significantly affect distribution of resources. Resources gravitate toward activities that generate profits. Resources move away from activities that generate losses.
3. Other firms are likely to start producing lamps. The reason for this is that they want to try to capture some of the profits that can be made in the lamp market.
4. $3,150.
5. $552.

Critical Thinking

6. Answers will vary, but economists would disagree with this statement. Profit does benefit the person who earns it, but it does more. It directs resources in ways that people want resources directed. To illustrate, suppose good X earns high profits on its production and sale. In a sense, what buyers are saying by rewarding the firm with profits is, "We want more Xs. Use resources to produce Xs." Some firms that currently are not producing good X will begin to produce it. In short, firms will respond by producing those goods for which profit can be earned.

SECTION 3

Teacher Support

Focus and Motivate

Section Objectives

After completing this section, students will be able to

- describe some of the qualities and characteristics of an ethical economic system;
- list some of the freedoms in free enterprise;
- explain what economic principles are stated in the Bill of Rights, the Constitution, and the Declaration of Independence; and
- describe some of the responsibilities people have in a free enterprise system.

Kickoff Activity

Write the following questions on the board for students to answer: "The word *ethics* is usually associated with people. Do you think that an economic system can be considered ethical? For example, do you think free enterprise is ethical?"

Activating Prior Knowledge

In the last section, students learned that there are no guarantees in a free enterprise economy. A business can either fail or succeed. Ask students to think about whether this might create pressure in some instances for people to act less than ethically, and ask them to cite examples. Discuss how these situations could be changed to encourage ethical behavior.

SECTION 3

The Ethics of the Free Enterprise System

Focus Questions

- What are some of the qualities or characteristics of an ethical economic system?
- What are some of the freedoms in free enterprise?
- What economic principles are stated in the Bill of Rights, the Constitution, and the Declaration of Independence?
- What are some of the responsibilities people have in a free enterprise system?

Key Term

ethics

Ethics and Free Enterprise

Ethics consists of the principles of conduct, such as right and wrong, morality and immorality, good and bad. We often evaluate a person as being ethical or not. Can we do the same thing for an economic system? For example, can we determine whether the free enterprise system is an ethical economic system? Another way of approaching this question is to ask what characteristics or qualities would the free enterprise system need to have to be an ethical system. What goals would it need to meet? (See Exhibit 3-3.)

ethics
The principles of conduct, such as right and wrong, morality and immorality, good and bad.

People Can Choose

First, the supporters of free enterprise state that an ethical economic system allows individuals to choose their own occupations or professions. An ethical system, they say, does not force people to do jobs or tasks that they would rather not do. On this count, the supporters of free enterprise argue that it is an ethical system, because no one is forced to work at a job he or she does not want. People are free to choose the type of work they want to do.

A Variety of Products

Second, an ethical economic system produces the goods and services preferred by both the majority and the minority. The supporters of free enterprise argue that under that economic system, if the majority of the people want to buy cars that are light colored and medium sized, with CD players, then manufacturers will produce that kind

EXHIBIT 3-3 An Ethical Economic System

1. Allows individuals to choose their own occupations or professions
2. Produces goods and services preferred by both the majority and the minority
3. Rewards or punishes producers based on how well or poorly they respond to the buying public
4. Supports the right of the individual to be free, including the freedom to acquire property, work where you choose, and start your own business

Cooperative Learning

The characteristics of an ethical free enterprise system are sometimes difficult to understand. To help students better understand these characteristics, divide the class into groups of three or four. Ask each group to choose a characteristic from Exhibit 3-3, then to research real-world examples for each characteristic. Ask the groups to present their findings to the class.

of car. (After all, they do not want to produce goods that consumers are not willing to buy.) If a few people want big cars instead of medium-sized cars, then it is likely that some big cars will be produced, too. If other people want small cars, some small cars will probably be produced.

Think of free enterprise at work in the restaurant business. In most U.S. cities of moderate size, many different types of restaurants serve a particular style of food: home cooking, fast food, and ethnic foods, for example. A wide variety of goods and services are available because free enterprise responds both to the majority and to minorities.

Rewards Depend on Performance

Third, an ethical economic system rewards (or punishes) producers according to how well (or poorly) they respond to the preferences of the buying public. Free enterprise fits this description. Sellers that continue to give consumers what they want to buy in terms of type of good, quality of good, and price of good will likely earn profits and stay in business. Those sellers that do not respond to public preferences end up taking losses and going out of business.

Numerous Freedoms

Fourth, the proponents of free enterprise argue that no economic system can be ethical if it limits people's freedom. In free enterprise, they say, people have numerous freedoms: the freedom to work where they want to work, the freedom to start their own businesses if they want, the freedom to acquire property, the freedom to buy and sell the goods they want to buy and sell, and even the freedom to fail.

EXAMPLE: Suppose Harris Jackson takes his entire savings and opens a shoe store. Six months later, Harris shuts down his business and declares bankruptcy. His problem was that few people wanted to buy shoes from him. ♦

Businesses close in the U.S. free enterprise system every day. Free enterprise gives us the freedom to spend our money as we choose, and sometimes this freedom results in business failures for other people. Individuals must accept the consequences of their decisions. Free enterprise does not offer any guaranteed outcomes; rather, it offers freedom.

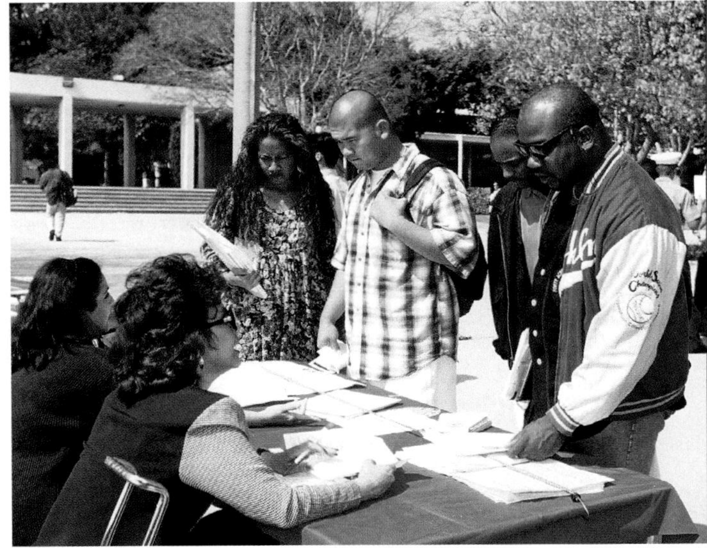

▲ These students are learning about career possibilities. **Why is this something they can do in a free enterprise economy, but not in some other economic systems?**

A Student Asks

QUESTION: *Having the freedom to do something is different from having the ability to do it. What use is the freedom to start your own business if you do not have the money to start the business? Without the ability, the freedom seems useless.*

ANSWER: *No economic system can provide people with the ability to do anything, such as write a great novel, run the four-minute mile, or be a successful entrepreneur. However, economic systems may or may not give individuals the opportunity to realize their potential.*

The supporters of free enterprise argue that free enterprise does provide

Teach

Teaching with Visuals

One of the freedoms that people living in a free enterprise economy enjoy is the freedom to choose a career.

Discussion Starter

Ethics may be a difficult concept for students to comprehend. Dictionaries commonly define ethics as a set of moral principles or values, a theory or system of moral values, and a guiding philosophy. Ask: Where do ethics come from? Do you have personal ethics? How would you apply your own values to an economic system?

Analyzing

Many people forget to mention that one of the freedoms in free enterprise is the freedom to fail. Explain to students that sometimes people fail in their business efforts in a free enterprise economy because other people have the freedom to spend their money as they choose. Ask students why the freedom to fail is considered a freedom.

Reinforcement Activity

Ask your students if they see the importance of ethics in a free enterprise economic system. Have them identify both examples of ethics in the free enterprise system and examples of what occurs when companies do not act ethically, such as monopolies and fixed pricing.

Cross-Curricular Activity

Invite a history teacher to speak to your class about "rags to riches" stories in U.S. history. Suggest to the teacher that he or she include stories that reflect the ethnic diversity of your school's community. Ask the history teacher what features of the U.S. economy made these successes possible. Consider asking students to prepare, individually or in groups, one-page papers about an economic success story from American history.

Reinforcement Activity

Urge students to tie rights to responsibilities; that is, if a person has the right to do something, then he or she should assume the responsibility that goes along with that right. Ask students to discuss what rights they have in today's society. They may mention the right to drive a car (after a person has reached a certain age) or the right to buy and sell goods and services. Once they have identified certain rights in their daily lives, ask them to develop a list of the responsibilities that go along with those particular rights. For example, if they have a right to drive a car, they may mention the responsibility of operating the car in a safe and sane manner.

Teaching with Visuals

The Bill of Rights and the Declaration of Independence helped solidify free enterprise as the economic system for the United States.

people with the opportunity, or freedom, to start a business. They also argue that free enterprise gives individuals the opportunity to strengthen and develop their abilities. Suppose a person does not currently have the money or the knowledge to open up her own business, and she is currently working at a low-wage job. Is she destined never to start her own business? Not necessarily.

She can begin today doing those things that are necessary to start her own business in the future. These steps may include working hard in her current job, saving some money, attending school to learn about the business she wants to start, and obtaining a business loan. The economic history of the United States, under free enterprise, is full of stories of people who were poor and uneducated (and, in many cases, did not know the English language), yet went on to start their own businesses and become economically successful.

Economic Principles in Key Documents

The Constitution, the Bill of Rights, and the Declaration of Independence hold a special place in the hearts and minds of most Americans. It can also be argued that these three documents have a special significance to free enterprise: each document has free enterprise economic principles contained within it.

Remember that private property, choice, and competition are important features of free enterprise and that the essence of free enterprise is freedom. It is not difficult to find evidence that the Constitution, the Bill of Rights, and the Declaration of Independence are also about private property, choice, competition, and freedom, among other things.

Bill of Rights

The Bill of Rights, for example, notes that "private property [shall not] be taken for public use, without just compensation." In other words, if the government wants some land you own in order to put in a road, it cannot simply take that land from you. It must justly compensate, or pay, you for that land. This fact shows the high regard for private property in the Bill of Rights.

Declaration of Independence

The signers of the Declaration of Independence listed many complaints against the king of Great Britain, George III. One complaint was that the king had prevented the 13 colonies from "trad[ing] with all parts of the world." Surely the signers of the Declaration of Independence were angry at King George III for not allowing them to practice free trade—an essential ingredient of free enterprise—with the rest of the world.

▶ The signing of the Constitution in Philadelphia, in 1787, helped establish the principles of free enterprise in the United States. **What other key documents helped solidify free enterprise as the economic system for the young nation?**

Background Information: Founding Documents

The political and economic ideals expressed in the Constitution of the United States are still important today. The Constitution still dictates the structure of American government. It also guarantees many of the economic freedoms we all enjoy.

The Constitution has affected not only the United States, but many other countries and world organizations as well. Other countries and world organizations have used the Constitution to assist in the development of their own political and economic rights.

Economics in the Real World

Did the Airlines Overlook the Overbooking Problem?

??????????????????

Suppose the jet for the flight from Atlanta, Georgia, to Chicago, Illinois, can hold 150 passengers. How many tickets will an airline sell? The answer is "more than 150," because the airlines know that some people will cancel their flight at the last moment or won't turn up at the airport. In other words, the airlines "overbook" flights—they sell more tickets than seats available.

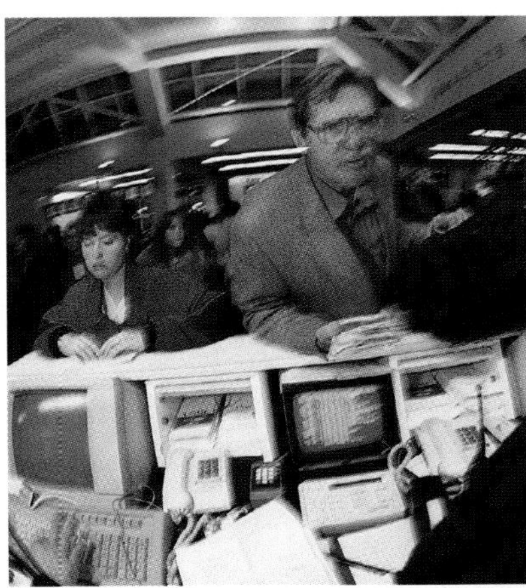

Because of overbooked flights, every now and then more people will turn up at the airport (to take a flight) than are seats available. For example, 155 people may turn up with reservations for 150 seats. In the past, airlines would often "bump" some passengers to the next flight. The bumped passengers were usually angry that they, and not someone else, had been bumped.

Today the airlines don't bump passengers. What they do is ask passengers if they would be willing to take an "upgrade" on a later flight (fly first class) or take a $200 voucher (or more) on any of their flights in exchange for taking a later flight. This new system of dealing with overbooked flights has resulted in much more satisfied flying customers.

Who came up with the system of offering overbooked passengers compensation (of one form or another) if they would take a later flight? Was it the president of an airline? Was it the airline ticket agents, the people who had to deal with the disgruntled bumped passengers? No, it was an economist, Julian Simon (1932–1998). In this regard, Simon behaved as an entrepreneur: he figured out a new and better way to do something.

Simon's plan to deal with overbooked flights came to him as he was shaving one day. He wrote the presidents of several airlines, and each told him that his was a good idea, but that they weren't going to implement it.

One day, Alfred Kahn, also an economist, was appointed chairman of the Civil Aeronautics Board. Simon wrote him about his plan for dealing with overbooked flights. Kahn liked the idea and strongly suggested that the airlines adopt it. They did. The rest, as they say, is history.

THINK ABOUT IT The Simon plan ended up being a plan that benefited the airlines and flying customers. Airline executives admitted that the Simon plan made it easier for them to overbook flights (and lower their costs because it is costly to fly an airplane half full) while at the same time maintaining a happy customer base. If the Simon plan was as good for the airlines as they now say, why didn't an airline executive come up with the plan?

The Constitution

Article 1, Section 8, of the U.S. Constitution says that "no tax or duty shall be laid on articles exported from any State." The Constitution favors preserving competition; if states had been allowed the right to impose a tax on each other's goods, competition within each state would have been lessened. To preserve competition—an important feature of free enterprise—it was important to deny states the right to tax each other's goods.

Ask students to imagine how their lives would be different if the colonists had not rebelled against British rule and if the Constitution had never been written. Ask student volunteers to express in their own words how knowing more about the Constitution helps in their understanding of the free enterprise system. Tell students to also think broadly about the Constitution's impact worldwide. How would the world be different without the U.S. Constitution?

Economics in the Real World

After students have read this feature, find out if any of them have ever accepted a voucher in exchange for taking a later flight. Ask: Did you mind taking the later flight? How would your opportunity cost of taking the flight compare with that of a businessperson who would miss an important meeting by flying later?

ANSWERS TO THINK ABOUT IT Answers will vary, but students might suggest that airline executives were too focused on the cost of upgrading passengers or offering them vouchers for later flights.

Reinforcement Activity

Currently the 50 states cannot tax each other's goods. For example, North Carolina cannot impose a special tax on a good that is produced in Virginia and sold in North Carolina. Divide the class into groups of four or five students and ask them to discuss how they think life would be different if states did have the right to tax each other's goods.

Application Activity

After reading and discussing Section 3, you may want to assign the Section Activity in the *Applying the Principles Workbook.*

Assess

Quick Quiz

The following true-or-false quiz will help you assess student understanding of the material covered in this section.

1. In an ethical system, people are free to choose whatever job they wish. (True)
2. An ethical system produces nothing for the minority. (False)
3. An ethical system does not punish producers. (False)
4. An ethical system gives producers the freedom to fail. (True)
5. Rights rarely come without responsibilities. (True)

Assessment Book

You will find a quiz for this section in the *Assessment Book.*

Reteaching Activity

Have students work in pairs to create charts that depict individual rights and responsibilities in a free enterprise system.

Guided Reading

For further reteaching of the key concepts in this section, assign the Outlining Activity and the Just the Facts Handout from the *Guided Reading and Study Guide.*

Economic Rights and Responsibilities in a Free Enterprise Economy

People have certain rights in a free enterprise economy, but rights rarely come without responsibilities. What are the responsibilities of persons in a free enterprise economy?

Open Disclosure

Many people argue that the right to voluntary exchange comes with the responsibility of giving the other person accurate information about what is being exchanged. Suppose Steve wants to exchange (sell) his 12-year-old house for the $270,000 that Roberto is willing and able to pay for it. In a free enterprise economic system, Steve and Roberto have the economic right to complete this exchange, but Steve also has the responsibility to tell Roberto the particulars about the house. For example, if the house has termites or faulty plumbing, Steve should tell Roberto this fact. In other words, Steve has the responsibility of truthfully relating to Roberto the facts about the product he is considering buying. This disclosure is a matter of simple fairness or justice.

"If you wish to prosper, let your customer prosper."
—Frederic Bastiat, economist

Obeying the Law

Consider another economic right in a free enterprise economy: the right to private property. The responsibility associated with this right is the responsibility of using one's property only for legal purposes; it is a responsibility to respect and abide by the law. Suppose Isabella owns a car. She certainly has the right to use that car to drive to and from work, go on vacations, pick up friends at school, and so on. It is also the case, however, that Isabella has some responsibilities. For example, she has the responsibility of obeying the speed limit, knowing and following all other traffic laws, and driving carefully.

Being Truthful

Finally, consider the economic right to compete in a free enterprise system. The responsibility attached to this right is to compete in a truthful, legitimate manner. If both Tushar and Yolanda own pizzerias in town and are thus in competition with each other, both have the responsibility to be truthful about the other's business. Tushar should not lie to his customers that Yolanda's pizzeria was cited by the government health examiner for having insects in the kitchen. Yolanda must not lie and say that Tushar uses less cheese in his pizzas than he actually does.

Assessment

Defining Terms

1. Define *ethics.*

Reviewing Facts and Concepts

2. "Under free enterprise, only the majority of people can buy the goods they prefer; the minority always end up buying those goods they would prefer not to buy." Do you agree or disagree with this statement? Explain your answer.
3. "Free enterprise guarantees economic success." Do you agree or disagree with this statement? Explain your answer.
4. Explain what responsibility goes with each of the following rights:
   a. the right to voluntary exchange
   b. the right to private property
   c. the right to compete

Critical Thinking

5. "In a free enterprise system, it is possible that more trashy novels will be published and sold than serious, soul-inspiring works of literature. Any system that produces this outcome can't be ethical." Do you agree or disagree with this statement? Explain your answer.

Assessment Answers

Defining Terms

1. ethics: the principles of conduct, such as right and wrong, morality and immorality, good and bad.

Reviewing Facts and Concepts

2. Disagree. If the minority is willing and able to buy certain goods, producers will find it in their best interest to produce those goods. Stated differently, if the minority is willing and able to pay a price for a good that will return a profit to the producer, the producer is very likely to produce that particular good.
3. Disagree. Free enterprise does not guarantee anyone success.
4. a. the responsibility of giving the other person involved in the exchange accurate information about what is being exchanged; **b.** the responsibility of using one's property only for legal purposes; **c.** the responsibility to compete in a truthful, legitimate manner.

Critical Thinking

5. Answers will vary. (*Sample answer:* Even if we agree that under free enterprise, more trashy novels will be published and sold than serious, soul-inspiring works of literature, it does not follow that free enterprise is unethical. Maybe more people are willing and able to buy trashy novels than serious literature. Free enterprise may simply reflect this fact. In short, it is responding to people's preferences. It is hard to see how doing this is unethical. If tomorrow people began to prefer serious literature to trashy novels, free enterprise would deliver more serious literature and fewer trashy novels. Free enterprise does not decide which preferences are right or wrong, or good or bad; its goal is to satisfy preferences.)

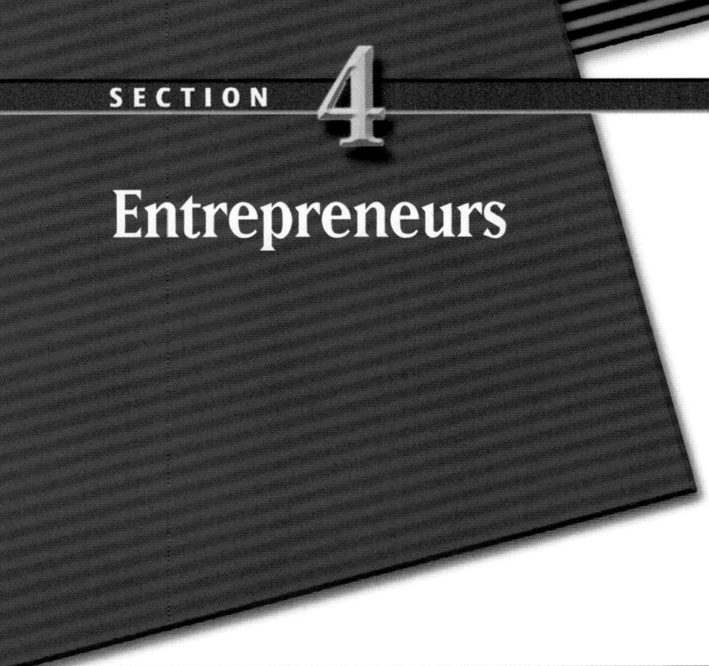

SECTION 4 Entrepreneurs

Focus Questions
- What is an entrepreneur?
- How might the actions of an entrepreneur benefit you?
- What impact would a law that limited profits have on future entrepreneurs?
- Why are entrepreneurs willing to risk their time and money?

Key Term
entrepreneur

Imagine Being an Entrepreneur

An **entrepreneur** is a person who has a special talent for searching out and taking advantage of new business opportunities, as well as developing new products and new ways of doing things. To get some idea of what being an entrepreneur is like, try to imagine you are one.

New Opportunities

How would you search out new business opportunities? No book in the library can give you a personalized answer. Even if such a book existed, by the time it was published and found its way into the library, the business opportunities listed in it would no longer be new. Most people, when confronted with the task of finding a new business opportunity, end up scratching their heads. Most people are not entrepreneurs; entrepreneurs are a tiny minority of the population.

New Products

Think about the second task of an entrepreneur: developing new products. What new product can you think of developing? Most of us are accustomed to thinking in

entrepreneur
A person who has a special talent for searching out and taking advantage of new business opportunities.

▲ Entrepreneurs feel that they have new and better ways of satisfying customers. **What sort of business might you want to start some day?**

Cooperative Learning

Divide the class into groups of no more than four. Tell each group that it is a group of entrepreneurs that will develop something for a new business opportunity. They need a rough sketch of the new product, and, if possible, a prototype of the product. One group member should write a description of the product, and then the group should list the benefits and risks that developing this product may bring forward.

SECTION 4 Teacher Support

Focus and Motivate

Section Objectives

After completing this section, students will be able to
- describe what an entrepreneur is;
- explain how consumers benefit from the actions of entrepreneurs;
- describe the effect that a law that limited profits would have on future entrepreneurs; and
- explain why entrepreneurs are willing to risk their time and money.

Kickoff Activity

Write the following instruction on the board for students to answer: "Make a list of five products that you believe make your life easier or more enjoyable."

Activating Prior Knowledge

Invite students to discuss their responses to the Kickoff Activity. Explain that entrepreneurs developed many of the goods that they have listed. For extra credit, students might research the products on their lists to find out who developed them and when.

Teach

Cause and Effect

Some people believe that only the entrepreneur benefits from a new product. The entrepreneur develops a new product, or a new process, and earns a profit based on that activity. Too often we forget that the activity has benefits for others. Point out these three products to students and let them discuss the benefits these new products had for others: the streetlight, plastic, and the telephone.

Teaching with Visuals

Answers will vary.

Economics in the Real World

After students have read this feature, ask them to consider why Apple chose an outside company to develop a better scroll wheel.

ANSWERS TO THINK ABOUT IT Answers will vary. Students should choose businesses that create or adapt new and unique products.

THE GLOBAL IMPACT Students need to remember that not only Americans can be entrepreneurs. In fact, entrepreneurs can come from any country. Even the word *entrepreneur* is from the French words *entre prendre,* which mean "to undertake." To give students a sense of the universal nature of the free enterprise system and the role of entrepreneurs within this global construct, have them research a list of foreign entrepreneurs and their contributions. Can they see the interconnection between all parts of a global free enterprise system?

Reinforcement Activity

Request that students think of a popular product from the past year. Their assignment is to research its creator, whether it be a person or company. Ask: What is the creator's entrepreneurial history? What background or training might one need to become this type of entrepreneur?

Economics Around the Clock

After discussing the section on entrepreneurs, remind students of the 2:33 P.M. scenario in Economics Around the Clock (page 55), and discuss their answers to the question that accompanies it.

Answers will vary. Students may suggest that they study economics, business, accounting, or current product trends.

Economics in the Real World

Why Is the iPod Scrollwheel So Slick?

iPod users will tell you that they like their iPods for many reasons. It's sleek looking, it holds thousands of songs, it's lightweight, and you can take it anywhere. For many iPod users, one of the features they like best is the scrollwheel. It's touch sensitive and has a rather slick, lightning fast feel about it.

> *"Buy it, use it, break it, fix it, trash it, change it, melt—upgrade it."*
>
> —FROM AN iPod COMMERCIAL ("TECHNOLOGIC" BY DAFT PUNK)

Interestingly enough, the first generation of iPods didn't come with the current touch-sensitive scrollwheel. The first scrollwheel on the iPod was developed by Apple. It physically rotated and was not touch sensitive.

Apple wanted a better scrollwheel, so it turned to a company called Synaptics. (Synaptics makes touchpads for laptop computers.) Synaptics came up with the touch-sensitive, slick, lightning fast scrollwheel that iPods use today. In this regard, Synaptics was acting as an entrepreneur: it was developing new ways of doing things.

The new scrollwheel came with four touch-sensitive buttons above it. These buttons were used for various playback functions. When Apple was in the process of designing the iPod Mini, it decided that those buttons had to go because there just wasn't enough room for them. Synaptic then came up with new scrollwheel with the former four buttons placed around the periphery of the scrollwheel. Now the scrollwheel could perform two functions: it could be used to scroll for songs and for playback control too.

THINK ABOUT IT We tend to think of an entrepreneur as a person; however, business firms can behave "entrepreneurially" as well. What business firms can you point to that act entrepreneurially?

terms of products that already exist, such as televisions, computers, or cars. Thinking of a new product is not easy, especially one with a high potential for sales.

New Processes

As for the third task of an entrepreneur—developing new ways of doing things—ask yourself what things people would want to do differently. Then ask how people could do these things differently. You'll probably find that these questions are difficult to answer. Indeed, entrepreneurs must overcome obstacles, solve problems, and answer challenging questions.

Who Benefits?

If an entrepreneur succeeds in coming up with an idea for a new product, develops and produces it, and then offers it for sale, how are we made better off? Think of entrepreneurs whose new products have helped you. For example, think about Steve Jobs, one of the developers of the personal computer and the iPod. Was your life affected positively or negatively as a result of his entrepreneurship? Most would say we benefited from the introduction of, say, the personal computer. Entrepreneurs, it would seem, play an important role in society by taking risks to develop new products or new ways of doing things that benefit the public. From a consumer's point of view, having more risk-taking entrepreneurs in a society likely means having more choices of goods and services in that society.

EXAMPLE: On August 1, 1981, MTV was launched. The originators of MTV were entrepreneurs: They were one of the first to see that a market existed for combining one product (music) with another product (television). The first music video shown on MTV was "Video Killed the Radio Star" by the Buggles. The first music video shown on MTV Europe was "Money for Nothing" by Dire Straits. Choosing "Money for Nothing" was done tongue-in-cheek by MTV executives because the song mentions MTV—"Now look at them yo-yos, that's the way you do it, you play the guitar on the MTV." ♦

The author W. Somerset Maugham wrote a short story titled "The Verger." It can be found online at www.emcp.net/verger. A verger is a man who takes care of the interior of a church. In the Maugham story, the vicar of a church fires the verger because he does not know how to read or write. The verger then sets out to find work. In the process, he becomes a successful entrepreneur. Read the story and find out just how the verger becomes an entrepreneur.

Entrepreneurs, Profit, and Risk

"You can't get something for nothing." This saying is certainly true for entrepreneurship. We can't get people to risk their own time and money, to try to develop new products, and to innovate unless they can potentially earn a profit. With this in mind, how would you respond to someone who says, "Look at that entrepreneur. He's a billionaire; he's earned high profits for years. We ought to pass a law that people can earn no more than 5 percent profit on anything they produce and sell"?

You may be inclined to agree, thinking that with a law that limited profits, you would be able to buy goods and services at lower prices. Less profit for the billionaire entrepreneur, in other words, would simply mean more money in your own pocket.

Things don't always work this way, however. If potential entrepreneurs knew that they could earn only a 5 percent profit at best, they might not be willing to take the risks necessary to become actual entrepreneurs. With fewer entrepreneurs, fewer new goods and services and fewer innovations would be available for your benefit. Not all entrepreneurs are successful, of course. In fact, many entrepreneurs risk their time and money and end up with nothing. A few do end up with millions or even billions of dollars. It is the prospect of millions or billions of dollars that motivates entrepreneurs to assume the risks inherent in entrepreneurship.

> ***"American prosperity and American free enterprise are both highly unusual in the world, and we should not overlook the possibility that the two are connected."***
> —Thomas Sowell, economist

Section 4 Assessment

Reviewing Facts and Concepts

1. What does an entrepreneur do?
2. How might an entrepreneur's risk-taking activities benefit society?

Critical Thinking

3. Economists speak of four categories of resources: land, labor, capital, and entrepreneurship. Suppose that country A has much more land, labor, and capital than country B, but it has no entrepreneurs. Country B, however, has many entrepreneurs. In which country would you prefer to live, and why?

Application Activity

After reading and discussing Section 4, you may want to assign the Section Activity in the *Applying the Principles Workbook.*

Assess

Quick Quiz

The following true-or-false quiz will help you assess student understanding of the material covered in this section.

1. An entrepreneur develops new products. (True)
2. No entrepreneur can make us better off. (False)
3. Less profit for entrepreneurs means more money in our pockets. (False)
4. Entrepreneurs develop new ways of doing things. (True)

Assessment Book

You will find a quiz for this section in the *Assessment Book.*

Reteaching Activity

Use the Section 4 Assessment to gauge which students may need reteaching. Ask students to list the three ways in which an individual might be an entrepreneur.

Guided Reading

For further reteaching of the key concepts in this section, assign the Outlining Activity and the Just the Facts Handout from the *Guided Reading and Study Guide.*

Section 4 Assessment Answers

Reviewing Facts and Concepts

1. An entrepreneur searches out and takes advantage of new business opportunities, develops new products, or develops new ways of doing things.
2. If an entrepreneur takes a risk, society may obtain a product that it didn't have before—a product that could make life more enjoyable, more interesting, or easier. (Ask students to think of products they have today that improve their lives and were developed by entrepreneurs.)

Critical Thinking

3. Answers will vary. We hope that students will be able to identify the critical role that entrepreneurship plays in their daily lives by imagining a world without it. Also, without entrepreneurs, land, labor, and capital are not as valuable. Entrepreneurs contribute significantly to the economy because entrepreneurs are the people who arrange the land, labor, and capital in ways that are new and innovative. A country that has a lot of land, labor, and capital is not guaranteed to be a rich country. Much depends on how these resources are used. For example, labor that is used to dig and fill up ditches is not as valuable as labor used to produce medicines, computers, telecommunications equipment, and so on.

SECTION 5

Teacher Support

Focus and Motivate

Section Objectives

After completing this section, students will be able to

- describe what would happen if government did not enforce contracts;
- describe a public good;
- explain why, in a free enterprise economy, individuals will not produce nonexcludable public goods for sale; and
- define negative and positive externalities.

Kickoff Activity

Write the following questions on the board for students to answer: "What do you think government's role should be in a free enterprise economy? Why do you think so?"

Activating Prior Knowledge

Allow students to discuss their responses to the Kickoff Activity. Explain that in this section they will discuss the role of government in a free enterprise economy.

Teach

Discussion Starter

Guide students in a discussion of times when they made a contract with someone. Ask whether they lived up to their side of the agreement and what the repercussions were if they did not fulfill their part of the contract. Ask whether the other party fulfilled her or his part of the agreement as well.

SECTION 5

The Role of Government in a Free Enterprise Economy

Focus Questions

- What would happen if government did not enforce contracts?
- What is a public good?
- In a free enterprise economy, why won't individuals produce nonexcludable public goods for sale?
- What is a negative externality? a positive externality?

Key Terms

contract
private good
public good
excludable public good
nonexcludable public good
free rider
negative externality
positive externality

contract
An agreement between two or more people to do something.

private good
A good of which one person's consumption takes away from another person's consumption.

public good
A good of which one person's consumption does not take away from another person's consumption.

excludable public good
A public good that individuals can be excluded (physically prohibited) from consuming.

nonexcludable public good
A public good that individuals cannot be excluded (physically prohibited) from consuming.

Government as Enforcer of Contracts

Think of what life would be like in a nation without government—no city government, no state government, no federal government. Suppose you own a construction company and regularly purchase supplies from people. On Tuesday, you enter into a **contract** with a person (an agreement between the two of you to do something). You agree to pay her $1,000 today if she delivers a shipment of wood to you on Friday. Friday comes, and no wood is delivered. Saturday, no wood. Sunday, no wood. On Monday you call the person to ask what happened. She says that she has no intention of delivering the wood to you. "But you took my $1,000. That is theft!" you say. She just laughs at you and hangs up the telephone.

What do you do now? You can't turn to the police, because police services are part of government, which doesn't exist. You can't take the person to court, because the court system also is a part of government.

You can see the need for some institution to enforce contracts. In our society today, government stands ready to punish persons who break their contracts.

Who is better off and who is worse off with government standing ready to enforce contracts? Just about everybody is better off. Only the contract breakers are worse off, because they can no longer break their contracts without at least the threat of punishment.

Could the free enterprise system function without a government to enforce contracts? Most economists believe that it could function, but not nearly as well as it does now. Instead, it would be severely crippled. Without government to enforce contracts, economists argue, the risk of going into business would be too great for many people. (Would you go into business if you knew people could break their contracts with you and not be punished?) Only a few people would assume the high risks of producing such items as television sets, houses, cars, and computers. The economy would be much smaller. Some economists believe that

Cross-Curricular Activity

To clarify the role government plays in a free enterprise system, invite a government or civics teacher to speak to the class. You might ask the teacher to discuss how the government's role in the economy has changed since World War II. While there are more connections between government and economics than those discussed in this chapter, the role of government *preferred* by free enterprise economists is a limited one.

a free enterprise system will be a large, thriving economy when government acts to enforce contracts and a small, sluggish economy when it does not.

Government as Provider of Nonexcludable Public Goods

Goods are categorized as two major types: private goods and public goods. A **private good** is a good in which one person's consumption takes away from another person's consumption. For example, an apple and a computer are both private goods. If Micala takes a bite of an apple, then much less of the apple is available for someone else to consume. If Bill is working on the computer, then Janey cannot also be on the computer; in other words, Bill's use of the computer takes away from Janey's use of the computer.

In contrast, a **public good** is a good in which one person's consumption does not take away from another person's consumption. A movie in a movie theater and a lecture in college are public goods. If the movie is showing in a theater, then the fact that Vernon is watching the movie does not detract from Xavier's watching the movie. Both men can view the same movie to the same degree. If a teacher in college is lecturing on biology to 30 students, one student's consumption of the lecture does not take away anything from any other student's consumption.

Not all public goods are alike, however. They might be **excludable public goods** or **nonexcludable public goods**. A public good is *excludable* if individuals can be excluded (physically prohibited) from consuming it. A public good is *nonexcludable* if individuals cannot be excluded from consuming it.

Excludable Public Goods

Again, consider the movie in the theater. It is an excludable public good, because movie theater owners can (and do) prevent people from watching the movie. If you go to the movie theater and choose not to pay the ticket price, then the theater owner will not

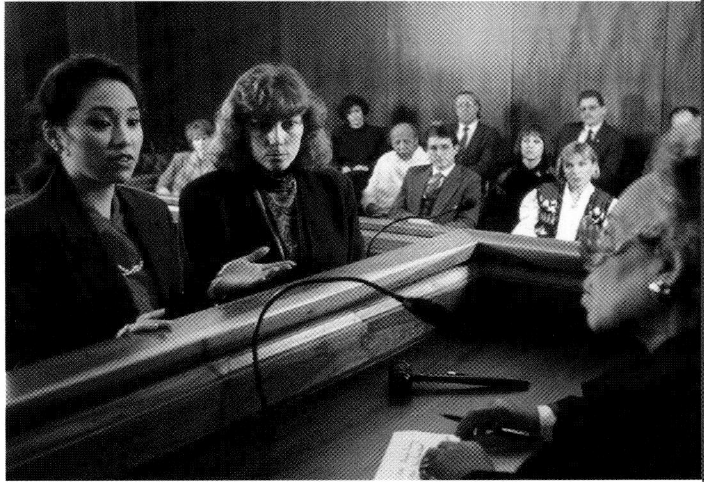

▲ Free enterprise would be less effective if there were no legal system to enforce contracts. **Can you describe a situation in which a trial would be necessary to prevent one business from dealing unfairly with another?**

▲ This college lecture is a public good. **Is it an excludable or nonexcludable public good?**

Teaching with Visuals

Answers will vary. Students might say that a trial would be necessary if one party to the contract refuses to live up to its part of the agreement.

Prediction Activity

Tell students that a country has decided to change its economic system from socialism to free enterprise. There is one problem, though: the country has a very poor institutional mechanism for enforcing contracts. Ask students to predict whether free enterprise will flourish in the country. Why or why not? (*Answer*: It will not flourish because people have to be sure that contracts will be enforced.)

Teaching with Visuals

A college lecture is an excludable public good.

Differentiating Instruction

Kinesthetic and Visual Learners

To reinforce an understanding of the concepts of public goods and private goods, you might assign half the class to find and copy photographs of public goods from a newspaper or magazine. The remainder of the class will find and copy photographs of private goods. Students should then work together to create a bulletin board display depicting public and private goods. Each picture in the display should be labeled appropriately.

Teaching with Visuals

A bridge is an excludable public good because people could be excluded from using it by the requirement of a toll.

Problem Solving

The problem of free riders in a free enterprise system can be an obstacle to some government activities. Assign students to create a scenario in which an individual acts as a free rider. Ask if they can think of any ways of solving the problem of free riders. Ask students how governments handle this problem.

Reinforcement Activity

Lead students in brainstorming a list of public goods. Then ask, Which of these public goods are excludable and which are nonexcludable? Make sure students can define the difference between excludable and nonexcludable public goods. For extra credit, some students might determine which level of government (local, state, or national) controls the public goods named by the class.

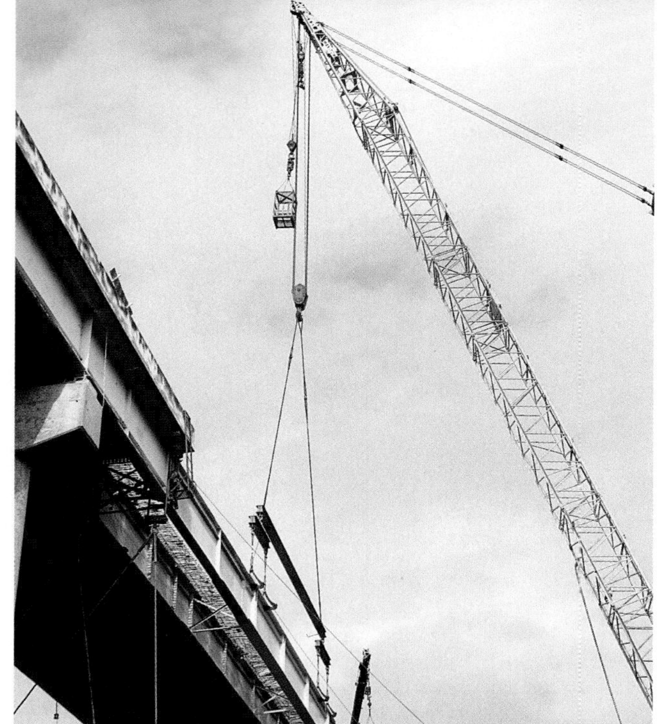

▲ **Is a bridge a private good, a nonexcludable public good, or an excludable public good?**

permit you to enter the theater. The owner will exclude you from viewing the movie.

What about a lecture in a college classroom? It is also an excludable public good. If you do not get admitted to the college or do not pay your tuition, the college can see to it that you do not sit in the college classroom and listen to the lecture.

Nonexcludable Public Goods

The classic example of a nonexcludable public good is national defense, which consists of missiles, soldiers, tanks, and so on. Suppose that the U.S. government produced a certain amount of national defense. National defense is definitely a public good, because one person's consumption of it does not detract from another person's consumption. In this way, national defense is like a movie or a lecture.

free rider
A person who receives the benefits of a good without paying for it.

In another way, however, national defense is not like a movie or a lecture. The seller of a movie and the seller of a lecture can each exclude people from consuming what they have to sell, but the producer of national defense cannot exclude people from consuming the good it produces. The U.S. government cannot exclude anyone in the United States from consuming its national defense because it is physically impossible, or prohibitively costly, to do so.

For example, suppose an enemy's missiles are headed for the United States. The U.S. government decides to take action and fire on the incoming missiles. When it fires and destroys the incoming missiles, it protects Yang, who lives in a rather large city, and it is also (automatically) protects many other people. It cannot be any other way.

To make the matter even more stark, suppose that one of the spies of the country that launched the attack against the United States lives in the same city as Yang. The U.S. government may not want to protect this spy from the incoming missile attack, but it is physically impossible to protect some people and not others.

Who Will Produce Nonexcludable Public Goods?

Economists contend that in a free enterprise economy, people will be willing to produce private goods and excludable public goods, but no one will want to produce nonexcludable public goods. Why not? Because once a nonexcludable public good is produced, no one will pay for it. People will not pay for something they cannot be excluded from consuming.

Suppose a company builds a dam to stop the flooding on people's lands. After the dam is built, representatives of the company ask the people if they want to buy the dam's services (flood prevention). Each person says, "The dam is already in place, I am benefiting from it, and there is no physical way you can exclude me from benefiting from it. So why should I pay?" Economists call persons who receive the benefits of a good without paying for it **free riders**.

Background Information: Public Bad

Although it is not discussed in the text, you may want to ask students if they believe there is anything such as a *public bad.* A *bad* in economics is defined as "something that gives someone disutility or dissatisfaction." This is in direct contrast to a good, which gives a person utility or satisfaction. Some economists have suggested that something like air pollution is a public bad. Once it is produced by a person's car, it negatively affects people nearby, giving them dissatisfaction or disutility. Ask students to think of a public bad and analyze its effect on other people. Does the government have any role in eliminating or reducing a public bad?

People know that they usually cannot get others to voluntarily pay for a nonexcludable public good, so they decide not to produce it. (Looking back, we can now see that the company that produced the dam in our example would probably never produce the dam in real life.) In contrast, though, people in a free enterprise economy will be quite willing to produce and offer to sell private goods and excludable public goods. First, all private goods are excludable. If you do not pay for an apple, computer, car, or book, then you do not get the good; you are excluded from it. If you do not pay for a movie or lecture, you do not get to consume these excludable public goods. In short, people in a free enterprise economy will produce those things that they can withhold from buyers if they do not get paid for producing them.

The Political Process

A free enterprise economy will produce private goods and excludable public goods, but it will not produce nonexcludable public goods. Suppose, though, that people still want nonexcludable public goods, such as national defense or flood protection. If the free enterprise economy will not produce these goods, who will?

The government will provide nonexcludable public goods and pay for them with taxes. Many economists argue that the government *should* provide nonexcludable public goods because no one else will. The framers of the Constitution recognized the legitimate role of government in providing nonexcludable public goods, such as national defense, in the Preamble:

> *We, the People of the United States, in Order to form a more perfect Union, establish Justice, insure domestic Tranquility,* provide for the common defence, *promote the general Welfare, and secure the Blessings of Liberty to ourselves and our Posterity, do establish this Constitution for the United States of America. (Emphasis added.)*

You might wonder how people communicate to their government what nonexcludable public goods, and how much of these goods, it should provide. In the U.S. system of government, one way people communicate what nonexcludable public goods, and how much of these goods, they want is through the political process.

U.S. citizens have the right to vote, and they can influence what government does through the ballot box. For example, suppose the majority of the people want the U.S. government to provide less instead of more national defense. They will likely vote for politicians who voice this same preference and vote against politicians who do not share their preference. U.S. citizens also have the right to lobby their elected representatives directly, by writing letters or talking to the representatives in person.

▲ As you know, scarcity prevents us from producing all the goods we want. **How can you voice your opinion as to which nonexcludable public goods the government should produce?**

Reinforcement Activity

Request that students write one sentence in which they list the two roles that advocates of free enterprise feel government should play in the economy.

Analyzing

Ask students to think about excludability in the context of unauthorized downloading of music and video games, and ask: How is excludability of these products affected when people can obtain them illegally? How might this affect musicians or video game developers?

Teaching with Visuals

People can voice their opinions about nonexcludable public goods by exercising the right to vote, lobbying, and talking to their representatives.

Cooperative Learning

Divide students into groups of three or four. Ask each group to find an example of a nonexcludable public good. They will work together to prepare an oral presentation about the political process that led to the creation or continued existence of that good, and think about whether people disagreed about the good. Ask students to present both sides of the issue. Suggest that students include visual aids in the presentation if they would make the issue clearer.

Discussion Starter

Give students the following assignment: "Using your own words, write a definition of the word *external* and use the word in a sentence." Allow volunteers to share their definitions and sentences with the rest of the class. Explain that one definition of *external* is "situated outside." This definition relates to the economic definition of *externality.*

Background Information

California banned smoking in most restaurants and bars in 1995. The law was passed in response to complaints from employees of the establishments. Their health was affected by the negative externality of the secondhand smoke. Since then, some establishments have reported significant losses in revenue, as smoking consumers stayed away. This action created a positive externality for some and a negative externality for others.

Teaching with Visuals

After students review By the Numbers, ask them to consider reasons why the degree of free enterprise in the United States did not change much from 1995 to 2005.

A Student Asks

QUESTION: *I am used to thinking that any good the government provides is a "public good," but that thought is wrong, isn't it?*

ANSWER: *Yes, it's wrong. Remember, we are talking here about three kinds of goods: (1) private goods, (2) excludable public goods, and (3) nonexcludable public goods. A free enterprise economy will produce both private goods (shirts, shoes, computers) and excludable public goods (movies in movie theaters, music at a rock concert). What a free enterprise economy will not produce is a nonexcludable public good. So, if nonexcludable public goods are going to be produced, they must be produced by government. However, it does not follow that government will necessarily restrict itself to producing only nonexcludable public goods. For example, the U.S. government is involved in delivering mail, building roads, collecting Social Security taxes and writing out checks to Social Security recipients, and much more. None of these things fall into the category of a nonexcludable public good.*

Externalities

Suppose it is 3 a.m., and you are fast asleep. Suddenly, you awaken to the sounds of a radio blasting away. You get up, open the window of your bedroom, and realize that the loud music is coming from your neighbor's house. Your neighbor is taking an action—playing the radio loudly—that has an adverse side effect on you. Economists call this adverse side effect a **negative externality**, or a negative third-party effect.

negative externality
An adverse side effect of an act that is felt by others.

positive externality
A beneficial side effect of an action that is felt by others.

EXAMPLE: The owners of a house rarely mow their lawn or cut their shrubbery. The people who live in the houses nearby complain that not only is this property not kept up and therefore unpleasant to look at, but the property also lowers the value of their own houses. One neighbor, who lives across the street, says, "I need to sell my house, but I'm going to have a hard time doing it because the people across the street don't keep up their property. No one wants to live across from an eyesore. I will probably have to lower the price of my house before anyone will start to think about buying it." Undoubtedly, the owners of the property that is not kept up are acting in a way that adversely affects their neighbors. The adverse side effect is a negative externality. ♦

Externalities are not always negative. For example, Erica Richards is a beekeeper, who lives near an apple orchard. Erica's bees occasionally fly over to the orchard and pollinate the blossoms of the apple trees, in the process making the orchard more productive. In this situation Erica takes an action—keeping bees—that benefits another person, the orchard owner. Because Erica's beekeeping activity results in an externality that benefits someone else, it is referred to as a **positive externality**, or a positive third-party effect.

BY THE NUMBERS

In the last chapter, we mentioned that the *Wall Street Journal* and the Heritage Foundation annually rank countries according to how much or how little economic freedom and free enterprise exists in a country. The rankings are on a scale of 1 to 5; the closer a country's score is to 1, the more free enterprise it has. Here are the scores for the United States in the years 1995–2005. As you can see, the degree of free enterprise in the United States has not changed much during this period.

Year	Score
1995	1.99
1996	1.94
1997	1.88
1998	1.89
1999	1.89
2000	1.84
2001	1.78
2002	1.84
2003	1.86
2004	1.85
2005	1.85

Internet Research

Although only less than 3% of the U.S. workforce is employed in agriculture, it has been one of the most regulated and assisted industries in the American economy. Direct students to visit the United States Department of Agriculture (USDA) Web site and research the services the USDA provides American farmers. Tell students to pretend they are farmers who need assistance. Their assignment is to write a one-page proposal outlining services they would like to request from the government, according to the types of economic assistance available for the agriculture industry.

EXAMPLE: Yolanda visits a physician and is inoculated against polio. Now she can be sure that she will not become sick with polio. Yolanda's actions also benefit other people: People who come into contact with Yolanda are protected from getting polio from her. As far as the community as a whole is concerned, Yolanda's inoculation against polio is a positive externality. ♦

Government and Positive Externalities

Some people argue that education generates positive externalities. They say that when you attend school, you not only learn things that will directly help you in life and in the workplace, but you also become a better citizen and a more informed voter. Becoming a better citizen and a more informed voter ends up benefiting more people than just yourself.

Let's analyze your own case. You are in high school taking this economics course. Because of the course, it is hoped, you will become more knowledgeable about economics issues than you would have been otherwise. One day, you are listening to two politicians running for the U.S. Senate from your state; they are debating some economics issues on television. One politician makes inaccurate statements on almost all the issues, while the other accurately portrays the economics issues. You decide to vote for the politician who is accurate on the issues, because you feel she will more likely end up promoting economic policies that are good for the United States.

Your informed vote increases (by a tiny percentage) the probability that the politician who understands economics will get elected. If she is elected, whom did you help? You helped yourself, no doubt, but you also helped all the other people who will now benefit by having a person knowledgeable about economics, instead of an uninformed person, shape government policy. In this case, your education produced a positive externality.

Some people argue that because your education can help other people, these other people ought to pay something for the benefits they derive from your education. One solution might be to have the members of society pay taxes to support the schools you attend. In other words, because the public benefits from your education and the education of other persons like you, it should pay toward that education. The public school system is a result of this thinking.

▲ Buses, classrooms, books, and teachers' salaries all contribute to the thousands of dollars required each year to provide you with an education. **Should other people have to pay for your education? Why?**

Persons who attend public schools do not directly pay for the education they receive (although they indirectly pay if their parents pay property taxes). Instead, their education is paid for with taxpayer money. That is, the education of public school students is subsidized. Some people argue that government should subsidize all of the activities that generate positive externalities for society at large.

Government and Negative Externalities

If you are on the receiving end of a negative externality—if you are awakened at 3 a.m. by loud music, or the smoke a factory is emitting is getting into your lungs—you will probably feel that negative externalities are bad. But what can be done? Some people argue that it is government's duty to minimize the "bad" in society—in other words, to reduce the negative externalities.

Teaching with Visuals

Answers will vary, but students might say that other people in addition to students benefit from public education.

Reinforcement Activity

List on the board half a dozen negative and positive externalities. Do not separate them into two groups—just jumble them together. One of the best ways for students to learn the difference between a negative and a positive externality is to identify them from a large group. The criteria are simple: if the action affects a third party in a positive way, it's a positive externality; if it affects someone in a negative way, it's a negative externality.

Discussion Starter

Ask students if they believe that their education generates a positive externality for others. If they do believe this is true, ask them to give examples of how others benefit from their education.

Economics Around the Clock

Now that students have a general grasp of free enterprise, ask them to reconsider the 6:42 P.M. scenario in Economics Around the Clock (page 55), and discuss their answers to the question it poses.

In this case, Lisa's choice of music has a negative externality on the driver next to her. There may be government-regulated noise restrictions in the neighborhood, which would force Lisa to lower the volume.

Cooperative Learning

Divide the class into groups of four or five. Each group should take a piece of paper and divide it down the middle. On one side of the paper, students will write "Positive Externalities," and on the other side "Negative Externalities." Then each group should make a list of the positive and the negative externalities that its members have experienced in the last three days. Remind students that externalities are the actions of people or groups that produce side effects that are felt by another. After they have finished this activity, instruct them to start a new piece of paper. Now they should list the positive and negative externalities they have caused to others in the last three days.

After students have read this feature, ask if any of them get stuck in traffic on a regular basis. As the feature explained, this is a common situation for many working people. Ask students to think of ideas for products that might make someone's commute more productive.

ANSWERS TO THINK ABOUT IT Answers will vary.

Problem Solving

Explain to students that one of the jobs of the court system is to deal with negative externality cases. In these cases, one person is usually claiming the right to do something that another person claims she or he does not have the right to do. In other words, the first person is negatively affecting the second person. Ask students to look through newspapers and magazines to find examples of the courts deciding on a negative externality case. Then, using the example on this page, have the students act as the court. What should be the outcome of the case?

Application Activity

After reading and discussing Section 5, you may want to assign the Section Activity in the *Applying the Principles Workbook.*

Assess

Quick Quiz

The following true-or-false quiz will help you assess student understanding of the material covered in this section.

1. A contract is a good shared by two or more people. (False)
2. A private good is a good of which one person's consumption takes away from another person's consumption. (True)
3. National defense is an excludable public good. (False)
4. Regulation and taxation are always positive externalities. (False)
5. Government actions on negative externalities can sometimes have unintended effects. (True)

Why Does McDonald's Put Hash Browns in Half-Sized Bags?

Almost half the population of the United States lives in 39 metropolitan areas. Most of the people who live in those metropolitan areas have fairly long commutes to work. Although 13 percent of all commuters spend 45 minutes or more in their cars each day, it is not uncommon for many commuters in major metropolitan areas to spend $1\frac{1}{2}$ to 3 hours in their cars each day commuting to and from work.

Try to think of people spending 45 minutes or more each day driving to work as a business opportunity. How could an entrepreneur—a person who has that special talent for searching out and taking advantage of new business opportunities—respond to these commuters?

Some entrepreneurs realized that people who spend at least 45 minutes each day in a car have plenty of time to listen to a book being read to them, so they started producing books on tape. Listening to a book on tape has become an important part of the way many commuters pass their time. Also, a satellite radio in the car gives drivers much of what they want on a long drive—music without the interruption of commercials.

McDonald's, the fast-food franchise, responded to long commutes by making sure that its food can be eaten in a car. For example, McDonald's places its hash browns in a half-sized paper bag with the top sticking out so that drivers can eat with one hand and drive with the other. McDonald's also offers super-sized sodas with containers that fit easily into traditional car cup holders. Other fast-food franchises have started offering sandwiches in bread pockets or tightly wrapped paper so that drivers can easily and comfortably eat and drive without any mess.

The rush to produce a cell phone may have been motivated partly by the desire of entrepreneurs to come up with a product that people with long commutes were likely to buy. Other entrepreneurs have been coming up with new uses for the cell phone. For example, you can now take photos with a cell phone, as well as play music, watch a music video, play a video game, and check your e-mail.

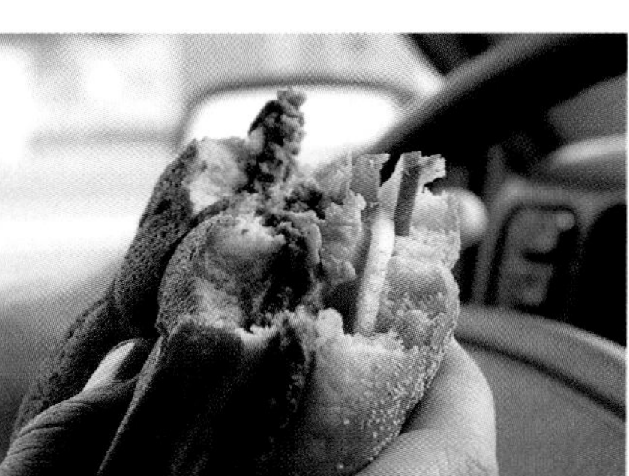

THINK ABOUT IT As wages and salaries rise in real terms, the value of time rises, too. A person who earns $100 an hour finds that his or her time is more valuable than a person who earns $30 an hour. Entrepreneurs realize that when the value of time rises people want to economize on time. Microwave ovens, computers, and cell telephones are all products that help people reduce the time it takes to complete a given task. Can you think of other relatively new products that help people economize on time?

Government can do so in three principal ways: through the court system, regulation, and taxation.

The Court System Suppose a firm near where you live is emitting smoke and pollutants into the air. As far as you are concerned, the polluted environment is a negative externality. You think you should be able to breathe unpolluted air, so you sue the firm. Obviously, the firm will hire a lawyer to counter your suit. In the end, a court will decide who has the right to do what. In other words, does the firm have the right to emit smoke and pollutants into the air, or do you have the right to breathe unpolluted air?

Regulation Sometimes government creates regulations to deal with negative externalities. For example, most states require car owners to meet pollution standards, and government often limits the amount of pollution that factories can emit into the air. Government may also deem it illegal to dump chemicals into rivers and lakes.

Taxation Suppose a business firm is producing steel. As a by-product, pollutants are discharged into the air through a smokestack. Instead of imposing an environmental regulation on the steel-producing firm to clean up the air, government decides to impose a tax. For every ton of steel produced, the firm has to pay $100 in taxes.

As a result of the tax, the business firm will find it costlier to produce steel. The firm is likely to produce less steel, which means fewer pollutants discharged into the air. In other words, the tax on steel indirectly reduced the amount of negative externality (pollutants in the air) by making the production of steel more costly.

We have to be careful in our analysis, though. Taxation, like regulation, sometimes comes with unintended consequences. For example, let's say that in year 1, the automobile industry pays no taxes. In year 2, government places a tax of $500 per car on the auto industry. In other words, for every new car a firm produces, it must pay the government $500 in taxes. Do you think the auto industry will produce more cars in year 1 or year 2? The correct answer is year 1, all other things remaining the same. Taxes of the sort described here raise the cost of producing and selling cars, and car firms react by producing fewer cars.

At this point, you might point out that fewer cars mean less pollution. This statement overlooks something important, though. Although fewer new cars are produced and purchased, people may simply drive their old cars longer, and old cars emit more pollution than new cars. Thus, the tax on the production of new cars reduces the number of new cars on the road compared to the number of old cars. In this case, if miles driven do not change, we can expect more, not less, pollution from cars. Taxation, like regulation, does not always have its intended effect.

▲ **What negative externality is represented in this photograph? How does the government attempt to minimize this negative externality?**

SECTION 5 ASSESSMENT

Defining Terms

1. Define:
   a. free rider
   b. contract
   c. private good
   d. public good
   e. excludable public good
   f. nonexcludable public good
   g. negative externality
   h. positive externality

Reviewing Facts and Concepts

2. Identify each of the following as a public or a private good: (a) a pair of shoes, (b) sunshine, (c) a pen, (d) a pizza, and (e) national defense.
3. Why won't a private business firm produce a nonexcludable public good?
4. How are nonexcludable public goods paid for?
5. Explain how taxes can be used to deal with negative externalities.

Applying Economic Concepts

6. Give an example of a setting in which a free rider is present.

Assessment Book

You will find a quiz for this section in the *Assessment Book.*

Reteaching Activity

Use the Section Assessment to gauge which students may need reteaching. Have a student read the definition of *externality* on page 78. Then ask students to list some negative and positive externalities.

Guided Reading

For further reteaching of the key concepts in this section, assign the Outlining Activity and the Just the Facts Handout from the *Guided Reading and Study Guide.*

SECTION 5 ASSESSMENT ANSWERS

Defining Terms

1. a. free rider: a person who receives the benefits of a good without paying for it; **b. contract:** an agreement between two or more people to do something; **c. private good:** a good of which one person's consumption takes away from another person's consumption; **d. public good:** a good of which one person's consumption does not take away from another person's consumption; **e. excludable public good:** a public good that individuals can be excluded (physically prohibited) from consuming; **f. nonexcludable public good:** a public good that individuals cannot be excluded (physically prohibited) from consuming; **g. negative externality:** an adverse side effect felt by others; **h. positive externality:** a beneficial side effect felt by others.

Reviewing Facts and Concepts

2. (a) private good; (b) public good; (c) private good; (d) private good; (e) public good.
3. A private business will not produce nonexcludable public goods because it cannot collect any payment for the good. To illustrate, once the nonexcludable public good is produced and provided to one person, it would be available to all other people as well. Because all these other people could have the benefits of the good without paying for it, many of them would choose not to pay for it.
4. Nonexcludable goods are paid for through taxes.
5. Taxes can be used to make an activity that generates negative externalities more costly. As a result, less of that activity will be performed.

Applying Economic Concepts

6. Answers will vary. (*Sample answer:* Ortiz lives across the street from Desai. Ortiz creates a beautifully landscaped lawn, which Desai enjoys but doesn't pay for. Desai is a free rider. *Another sample answer:* Peterson lives near a baseball field. When teams play on the field, he can watch the games with binoculars from the second story of his house. Peterson receives benefits from watching the games, but he doesn't pay for the benefits. Peterson is a free rider.)

CHAPTER 3 Assessment Answers

Economics Vocabulary

1. total revenue; **2.** incentive; **3.** Ethics; **4.** public property; **5.** entrepreneur; **6.** loss; **7.** free riders; **8.** contract; **9.** public good; **10.** private; **11.** positive externality.

Understanding the Main Ideas

1. The individuals who own and manage the business firms will decide how goods will be produced.
2. Consider two individuals, Muong and Sally. Muong has $1, and Sally has a pen. If they exchange—that is, trade $1 for the pen—we assume that each one has been made better off through the exchange, or he or she would not have made the exchange in the first place.
3. The five features of a free enterprise economy are private property, choice, voluntary exchange, competition, and economic incentives.
4. a. $78 (profit); **b.** $232 (loss); **c.** $314 (loss); **d.** $442,868 (profit).
5. The message is that company Z is using resources to produce a good that people do not want to buy at the price that Z is charging.
6. Profit attracts resources into the production of the good from which the business is earning a profit. For example, if company B is earning a profit on the production and sale of good X, then other companies currently not producing good X will shift resources into the production of good X.
7. Entrepreneurs search out and take advantage of new business opportunities, develop new products, and develop new ways of doing things.
8. Government should be limited to enforcing contracts and providing nonexcludable public goods. Contract enforcement provides security and ensures high levels of exchange and economic activity. Government should provide nonexcludable public goods because the private sector will not provide these goods. The private sector won't provide them because once they have been provided, there is no way to collect payment for them.
9. Exhibit 3-2 shows the economic relationships in an economy. It is useful because a change somewhere in the economy can be shown to have effects at other places in the economy.
10. Government can deal with a negative externality in three ways: the court system; regulation; and taxation. Court rulings and regulations can curtail negative externalities. Taxation can also be used to make certain activities more costly.
11. Public school students are not the only people who benefit from public education. Students will one day be voters. Because of their education, they will presumably cast votes for candidates and policies that will benefit all of society.

Chapter Summary

Be sure you know and remember the following key points from the chapter sections.

Section 1

- In a free enterprise economy, business firms will produce the goods that consumers want.
- Five major features define free enterprise: private property, choice, voluntary exchange, competition, and economic incentives.

Section 2

- Profit is the money left over after the costs of production are paid.
- Profits and losses are signals to business firms.

Section 3

- An ethical economic system allows individuals to choose their occupations, produces goods and services preferred by buyers, rewards (or punishes) producers according to how well (or poorly) they respond to buyer preferences, and does not limit individual freedom in making choices.

Section 4

- The prospect of great profit motivates entrepreneurs to assume the risks inherent in entrepreneurship.

Section 5

- One of government's roles in free enterprise is to enforce contracts.
- A public good is a good in which one person's consumption does not take away from another person's consumption.
- A free enterprise economy will not produce nonexcludable public goods because no one will pay for them.
- Many believe that government should provide nonexcludable public goods and adjust for externalities.

Economics Vocabulary

To reinforce your knowledge of the key terms in this chapter, fill in the following blanks on a separate piece of paper with the appropriate word or phrase.

1. The price of a good times the number of units of the good sold equals ______.
2. A(n) ______ is something that encourages or motivates a person toward an action.
3. ______ relates to principles of right and wrong, morality and immorality, good and bad.
4. Any good that is owned by the government is considered ______.
5. A(n) ______ is a person with a special talent for searching out and taking advantage of new business opportunities, as well as for developing new products and new ways of doing things.
6. If a product's total cost is greater than total revenue, the firm incurs a(n) ______.
7. One reason a private business firm will not supply a nonexcludable public good is because it cannot collect payment from ______.
8. A(n) ______ is an agreement between two or more people to do something.
9. A good of which one person's consumption does not take away from another person's consumption is called a(n) ______.
10. A computer is an example of a(n) ______ good.
11. A(n) ______ is a beneficial side effect of an action that is felt by others.

Understanding the Main Ideas

Write answers to the following questions to review the main ideas in this chapter.

1. How is the question "How will goods be produced?" answered in a free enterprise economy?
2. Explain how voluntary exchange can make individuals better off.
3. What are the five major features of a free enterprise economy?
4. Calculate the profit or loss in each of the following situations (TR stands for total revenue, and TC stands for total cost). Be sure to put a minus (–) in front of a loss figure.

82 Chapter 3 Free Enterprise

a. TR = $400; TC = $322
b. TR = $4,323; TC = $4,555
c. TR = $576; TC = $890
d. TR = $899,765; TC = $456,897

5. Company Z produces men's clothes. For the past 18 months, the company has been taking a loss. What is the loss "saying" to company Z? Stated differently, what message should be coming through loud and clear to company Z?
6. An economist would say that profit attracts resources. What does this statement mean? You may want to give an example to illustrate your point.
7. What do entrepreneurs do?
8. According to supporters of free enterprise, what should government do? Why should it do these things?
9. What does the circular flow diagram illustrated in Exhibit 3-2 show, and how is it useful?
10. Identify and explain the three ways government may deal with a negative externality.
11. Justify the public school system on positive externality grounds.

Doing the Math

Do the calculations necessary to solve the following problems.

1. For each letter (A through H) in Exhibit 3-4, provide the correct number or dollar amount.
2. A business firm earns $5,000 profit on 1,000 units of a good that it sells for $6.99 each. What is the average cost of the good?

EXHIBIT 3-4

Price	Quantity produced and sold	Average cost	Total cost	Profit
$10	100	$ 4	A	B
$15	C	$ 7	$ 700	$ 800
$12	10	$10	$ 100	D
E	F	$50	$1,000	$2,000
$ 4	G	$ 3	H	$ 100

Working with Graphs and Tables

1. Look back at the circular flow diagram in Exhibit 3-2 and answer the following questions.
   a. Where do households get the funds to pay for the goods and services they buy from businesses?
   b. Where do businesses get the funds to pay for the resources they purchase from households?
   c. Where does the government get the funds to provide benefits to businesses and households?
2. Look at the circular flow diagram in Exhibit 3-2. Suppose you are a member of the household sector, so you have to pay taxes to the government. Your total tax bill is $100. Now suppose you sign your name on a $100 bill and give it to the government. Can you determine any way that the same $100 bill could ever be back in your hands again? Explain.

Solving Economic Problems

Use your thinking skills and the information you learned in this chapter to find solutions to the following problems.

1. **Analysis.** "Some mechanism is necessary to decide where resources will be used in an economy. Free enterprise is such a mechanism." Explain.
2. **Analysis.** Five features of free enterprise were discussed in this chapter. If you had to pick the most important two features, which two would you pick? Explain your answer.
3. **Cause and Effect.** In an earlier chapter you read that "It is not from the benevolence of the butcher, the brewer, or the baker, that we expect our dinner, but from their regard to their own interest." What is the cause of our getting our dinner?

Practice Tests and Study Guide

Go to www.emcp.net/economics and choose *Economics: New Ways of Thinking*, Chapter 3, if you need more help in preparing for the chapter test.

Doing the Math

1. A. $400 (*calculation:* Total cost = quantity sold × average cost); **B.** $600 (*calculation:* Profit = (price × quantity sold) – total cost); **C.** 100 (*calculation:* Total cost ÷ average cost = quantity sold); **D.** $20 (*calculation:* Profit = (price × quantity sold) – total cost); **E.** $150 (*calculation:* Price = (total cost + profit) ÷ quantity); **F.** 20 (*calculation:* Quantity sold = total cost ÷ average cost); **G.** 100 (*calculation:* Quantity sold = profit ÷ (price – average cost); **H.** $300 (*calculation:* Total cost = quantity sold × average cost).
2. $1.99. Because total revenue minus total cost equals profit, we know that $6,990 – *x* = $5,000, so total cost = $1,990. If we divide $1,990 by the number of units (1,000), we see that the average cost is $1.99.

Working with Graphs and Tables

1. a. Households get the funds from selling resources to businesses. Also, you will notice (in Exhibit 3-2) that households receive certain benefits from the government. If these are money benefits, we conclude that households also get funds from the government. **b.** Businesses get their funds from the households that buy their goods and services. Also, you will notice that businesses receive certain benefits from the government. If these are money benefits, we conclude that businesses also get funds from the government. **c.** The government gets funds from businesses and households (that pay taxes).
2. Yes. You give the $100 bill to the government to pay your taxes. What does the government do with the money? The diagram shows that it provides benefits to households and businesses. One way for the $100 bill to get back in your hands would be for the government to provide you with $100 money benefits. (In other words, you give the $100 bill to the government via the yellow arrow in the exhibit, and the government gives it back to you via the purple arrow.) Alternatively, the government could provide a business with $100 money benefits (brown arrow), in which case business has the $100 bill. Business, in turn, buys some resources from you (say, your labor) and pays you with the $100 bill (green arrow).

Solving Economic Problems

1. No one doubts that under free enterprise there are both profits and losses. Resources are linked to profits and losses in the following way: resources move toward activities that are generating profits, and they move away from activities that are generating losses.
2. Answers will vary. This question should lead to a good classroom discussion.
3. The butcher, brewer, and baker provide us with our dinner not because they want us to be happy and full and not because they like us, but because they know that the only way they can get what they want from us is to give us what we want. They are motivated by self-interest to provide us with our dinner.

Debating ↔ the Issues

Discussion Starters

1. Ask how many students have or have had after-school jobs. Allow volunteers to share their personal experiences on how the after-school jobs affected their schoolwork, and also what they've learned from having jobs.

2. Ask students what outside factors might influence a student's decision to get an after-school job? (*Answer:* parents' opinions, peers' opinions, family financial situations.)

3. Ask whether any students feel that they have missed out because they have never had an after-school job. If so, discuss what they have missed, and how this lack has affected their lives. (*Examples:* They may not have had opportunities to learn life skills such as developing a good work ethic and managing a budget, and they may not have had extra money for personal items.) Ask students to brainstorm other examples of learning and experiencing things that young people miss out on by not working after school.

4. Ask whether any students who have had after-school jobs feel that they have missed out on anything. If so, what? Discuss how working has affected their lives. (*Examples:* They may have had less needed sleep and rest, a diminished social life, less time and energy for schoolwork, and less time to participate in school activities.) If necessary, students may rethink the trade-off and make a different decision about having an after-school job.

Debating ↔ the Issues

Working After School: What Are the Trade-Offs?

Through our study of economics, we learn that there are trade-offs in life. More of one thing often means less of something else. Spending more money on clothes means less money for entertainment. More time spent studying means less time to hang out with your friends.

One of the major trade-offs high school students face is whether or not to work after school. Some people argue that high school students should work after school; others argue against it, saying their time is better spent studying. Let's hear what five people have to say.

Rebecca Clark, a junior in high school

I work after school and on the weekends at a fast-food restaurant here in town. It may be hard to believe, but I actually like the work. I meet a lot of nice people, I earn some money, and I am developing a good work ethic. When I first went to work, I thought it was going to be easier than it turned out to be. I thought I was just going to have some fun and make some money. But I've learned that to do a job well you have to be conscientious, follow orders closely, and focus on what you are doing. These are qualities that I think will benefit me throughout my life. I think I am a better person because I work. My parents are concerned about how work takes time away from my studies, but I never was much of a student. If I weren't working, I might be just wasting my time. I might even get into some trouble.

Tommy Sanchez, a senior in high school

I know I could work after school, but I choose not to. Working after school would come at too high a price for me. If I worked after school, I wouldn't have as much time to study. I want to get into a really good college and to do that I need to have high grades. If I worked, I probably couldn't get the A's that I am currently getting in my courses. The way I look at it, I will have 40 or 50 years to work. I am young now and I like learning, and the more I learn, the brighter my future will be. I think I would be sacrificing my future if I worked after school now.

My older brother didn't work at a job when he was in high school. He spent most of his time studying. As a result, he got high grades and a good score on the SAT. What is even more important is that he got into Yale. He received a top-quality education at Yale and made many good future business contacts. In fact, he now works in a company owned by the father of one of his best friends at Yale.

Some of my friends talk about the money they make in their after-school jobs. They can buy a lot of things that I can't. They buy better clothes, and some of them have even bought a car. I'd like to have a car, too, but I don't want to take away from my studies right now to get a job just so I can buy a car.

Bob Neidelman, parent

I think it is important for teens to develop a sense of responsibility and that's why I have urged my daughter to get a job after school and on the weekends. I worked when

Differentiating Instruction

Enrichment and Extension

1. Form small groups, and assign each group to create a short skit demonstrating positive and negative aspects of having after-school jobs. Ideas include, but are not limited to, a workplace scenario, discussion with family about a job, and how a classroom might be affected by students' jobs.

2. Ask students to pretend that they are writing an article for the school newspaper, which is doing a feature on the pros and cons of after-school jobs. Students might interview other students, or a supervisor at a company that employs high school students.

I was her age, and I learned a lot from what I did. Mainly, I learned the value of a dollar. I know that people say teens should not work, that they should devote more time to their education, but the truth of the matter is there are different types of education. There is the book-learning type of education, where a person learns geometry, calculus, English literature, and history. And then there is the education that you receive from getting out in life and working. When you work, you learn how to get along with people. You learn to persevere in order to get a job done. These are important things to learn. In the long run they'll be more important to her than learning how to solve calculus problems.

Nancy Drummon, guidance counselor

I think working after school is good for some students and not for others. It really depends on the trade-offs the particular student faces. For instance, I often get students in my office who work but who are doing poorly in their courses. I tell them they would be better off if they didn't work, but instead spent their time after school studying and trying to get their grades up.

But I've got other students who are doing well in their courses and feel they can continue to do well even though they get jobs. I see working as a good idea. Not only will they learn some things in their work that they might not otherwise learn, but they will have a little extra spending money, too. There are things they want to do and buy, and working gives them the opportunity to do those things.

I think that whether or not a student should work depends on the individual student. Not all students face the same trade-offs. What is right for one student may not be right for another.

Amy Yoshii, college student

I worked all through high school, and I really regret it now. I worked for all the wrong reasons. I worked simply to get the money to buy the same things my friends were buying. My friends were spending a lot of money on clothes, so I thought I had to, too. I worked to get a down payment for a car. Once I bought the car, I had to continue to work so I could make the payments and keep it running. There were many weekends when I was dead tired from working. I'd come home Sunday night, after working all day Saturday and all day Sunday, and have to study for a biology or calculus test. I can't tell you how many times I just went to bed, telling myself I would get up early and study. The alarm clock would ring, and I'd shut it off. I paid the price in lower grades.

I got into college, and I am doing better now, but college hasn't been easy for me. I think if I had worked less in high school, and studied more, college would have been more enjoyable, and easier.

I've learned that it is extremely important to prioritize—a person just can't do too many things and do them well. The world we live in values education a lot. You can't cut corners when it comes to your education. Working just gets in the way. My advice to any high school student is if you don't have to work, don't. Study more, work less. You'll be glad you did in the long run.

What Do You Think?

1. Who do you most nearly agree with? Why?
2. Do you think there is a trade-off between education and work? Why or why not?

Activities for What Do You Think?

1. For a class survey, ask students to "vote with their feet," and physically move to labeled points at the front of the room. The group of students that meets at each point should spend 5 minutes listing their reasons for voting for that opinion, then each group can spend 1 minute presenting its reason to the class. Hold another class vote, and see if there is any change in the voting.
2. Tell students to make lists describing the positives and negatives of working after school. Assign a short persuasive essay, in which students take a position and defend it with examples from their lists.

Closure

Instruct students to write a paragraph summing up their current opinions on whether having an after-school job is right for them. If their opinions changed over the course of this discussion, they should include that information, along with what changed their minds.

Listed below are the chapters included in this unit.

CHAPTER 4
Demand

CHAPTER 5
Supply

CHAPTER 6
Price: Supply and Demand Together

Foundations for the Unit

Unit 2 focuses on two key concepts of economics: demand and supply. Students will see how supply and demand play out in markets. It is hoped that as your students work through this unit, they will also begin to understand the effect that markets have on their lives. Like everyone else, students are affected by prices. In this unit they will learn how prices arise from the interplay of supply and demand.

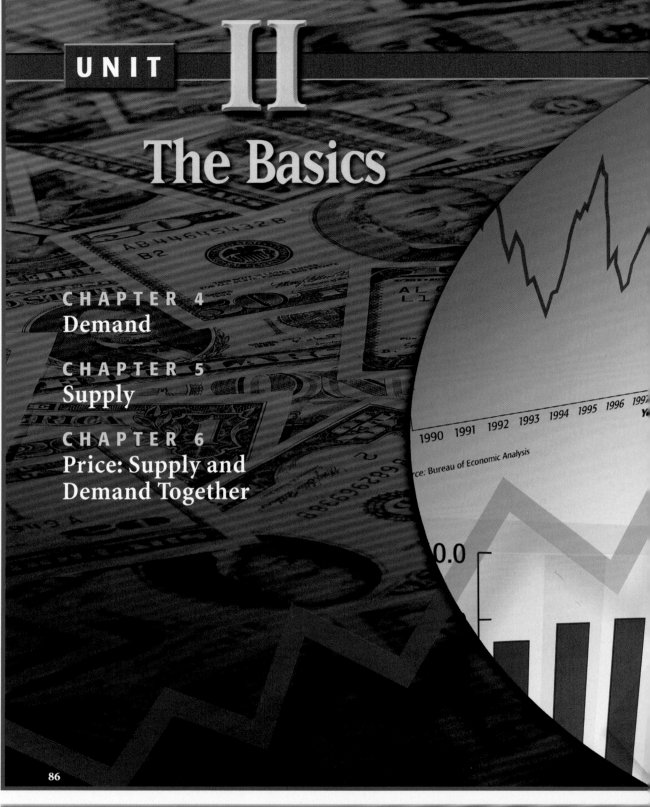

UNIT II

The Basics

CHAPTER 4
Demand

CHAPTER 5
Supply

CHAPTER 6
Price: Supply and Demand Together

Resources for the Unit

Books

Fischer, David Hackett. *The Great Wave: Price Revolutions and the Rhythm of History.* New York: Oxford University Press, 2000.

Heilbroner, Robert L. *The Worldly Philosophers: The Lives, Times, and Ideas of the Great Economic Thinkers.* New York: Touchstone Books, 1999.

Ott, Rick. *Creating Demand.* Symmetric Systems, 1999.

Thurow, Lester, and Robert Heilbroner. *Economics Explained.* New York: Touchstone Books, 1998.

Articles

Hailing, Zang. "Time Takes Its Toll: Getting in First Does Not Ensure Market Success," *Time International,* May 29, 2000, vol. 155(21).

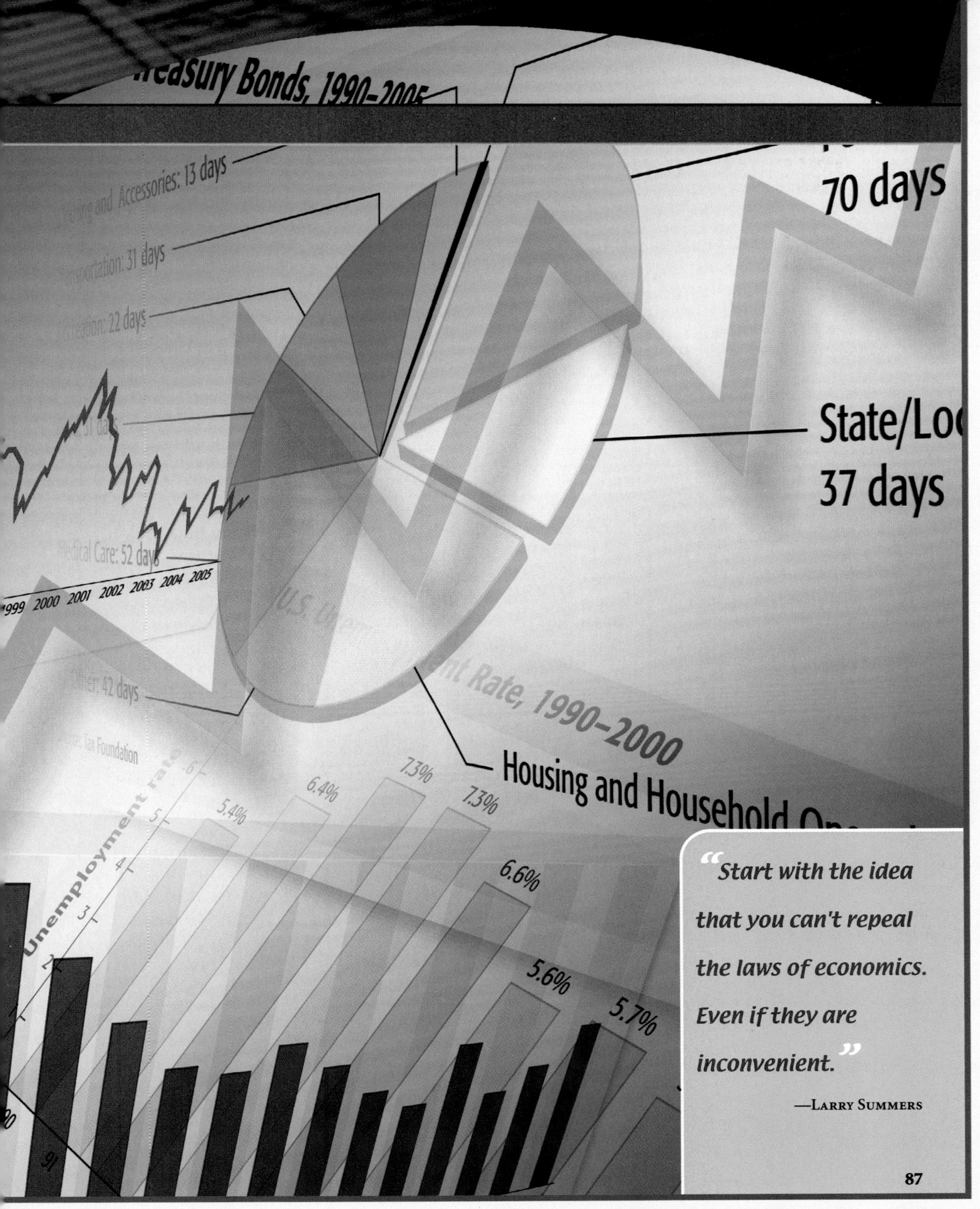

"Start with the idea that you can't repeal the laws of economics. Even if they are inconvenient."

—Larry Summers

87

Introducing the Unit

To introduce Unit 2, ask students if they have recently had a *willingness* to purchase a new CD, video game, or other item. Did they also have the *ability* to purchase the item? Tell students that willingness and ability to purchase are both necessary to create demand. Creating demand is a step in creating a price for a good or service. Ask for student volunteers to suggest what happens to price if demand increases. Also ask why students think this occurs.

Performance Task

Divide students into groups of three or four to learn about demand, supply, and prices. Have the students choose a good and research how demand for the product has affected its price. Ask the groups to consider the factors that affected demand for the good. For example: Did demand change seasonally? in response to a competitor's actions? Invite each group to present an oral report of its findings to the class.

Multimedia

Economics at Work. Videos, software, and print materials. National Council on Economics Education.

Exchanging. Videotape and teacher's guide. Films for the Humanities and Sciences.

Chapter 4 Planning Guide

SECTION ORGANIZER

Section	Learning Objectives	Reproducible Worksheets and Handouts	Assessment
 **Understanding Demand** (pages 90–94)	▸ Explain the law of demand. ▸ Describe the difference between demand and quantity demanded. ▸ Provide examples of the law of diminishing marginal utility. ▸ Create demand curves from given demand schedules.	 Section 1 Activity, *Applying the Principles Workbook* Outlining Activity, *Guided Reading and Study Guide* Just the Facts Handout, *Guided Reading and Study Guide* 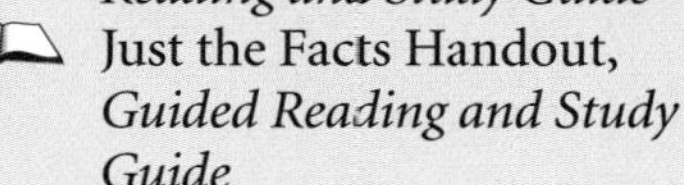	 Section Assessment, *Student Text,* page 94 Quick Quiz, *Annotated Teacher's Edition,* pages 93–94 Section Quiz, *Assessment Book*
 **The Demand Curve Shifts** (pages 95–99)	▸ Explain why a demand curve shifts to the right or the left. 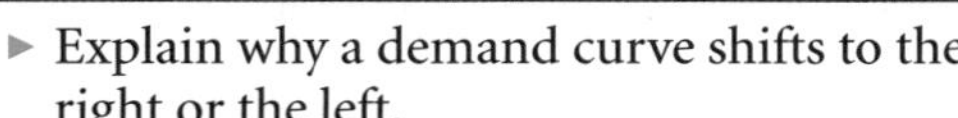 ▸ Distinguish between normal, inferior, and neutral goods. ▸ List the factors that cause a change in demand. ▸ Identify the factor that causes a change in quantity demanded.	 Section 2 Activity, *Applying the Principles Workbook* Outlining Activity, *Guided Reading and Study Guide* Just the Facts Handout, *Guided Reading and Study Guide*	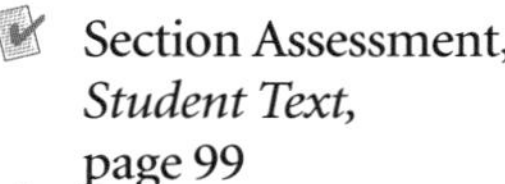 Section Assessment, *Student Text,* page 99 Quick Quiz, *Annotated Teacher's Edition,* page 98 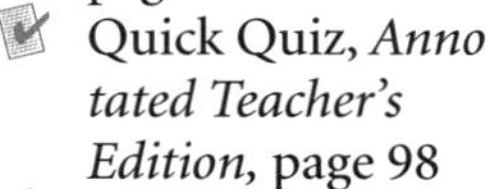 Section Quiz, *Assessment Book*
 **Elasticity of Demand** (pages 102–107)	▸ Describe elasticity of demand. ▸ Compute elasticity of demand. ▸ Distinguish between elastic, inelastic, and unit-elastic demand. ▸ List the factors that can change the elasticity of demand. ▸ Describe the relationship between an increase in price for a good, and higher total revenue.	 Section 3 Activity, *Applying the Principles Workbook* Demand Practice Activity, *Applying the Principles Workbook* 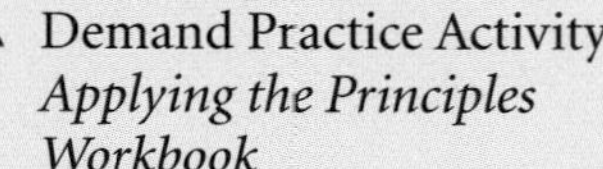  Outlining Activity, *Guided Reading and Study Guide* Just the Facts Handout, *Guided Reading and Study Guide* 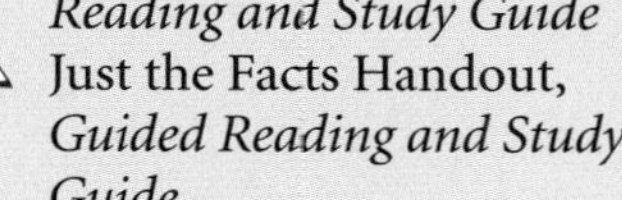	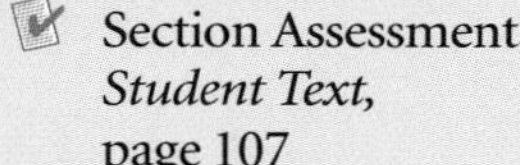 Section Assessment, *Student Text,* page 107 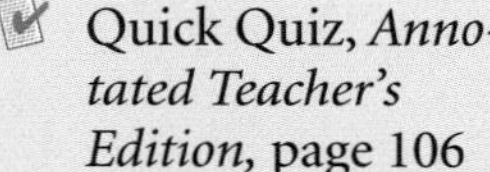 Quick Quiz, *Annotated Teacher's Edition,* page 106 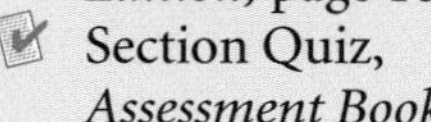 Section Quiz, *Assessment Book*

CHAPTER AND PROGRAM RESOURCES

Reproducible Chapter Resources and Assessment Materials

 Graphic Organizer Activity, *Guided Reading and Study Guide*
 Vocabulary Activity, *Guided Reading and Study Guide*
 Working with Graphs and Charts, *Guided Reading and Study Guide*
 Practice Test, *Guided Reading and Study Guide*
 Critical Thinking Activity, *Finding Economics*
 Chapter Test A, *Assessment Book*
Chapter Test B, *Assessment Book*

Technology Resources

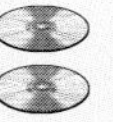 *Test Generator CD*
 *Spanish Audio Summaries CD*
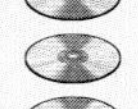 *Marketplace® Audio Lessons CD*
Economic Principles Lectures, Videocassette or DVD

Lesson Planning and Teaching Resources

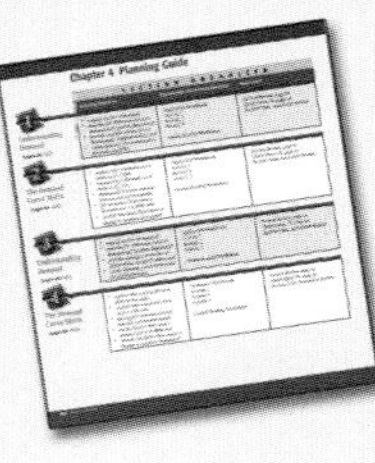

The *Economics: New Ways of Thinking* Teacher Resources include detailed lesson plans for each section in this chapter; the lesson plans are available in print form *(Lesson Plans)* and electronic form. The Teacher Resources also include *Daily Lectures: Overheads and Notes,* which provides prepared overheads and discussion notes covering the key concepts in each section of this chapter.

EMC Publishing Economics Online

Go to Economics Online, at www.emcp.com, for a variety of Internet resources to help you keep your course current and relevant. At Economics Online you will find these items:

- Economics in the News Lessons
- Study Guide Questions
- Practice Tests
- Lesson Plans

Internet Resources

Economics: New Ways of Thinking encourages students to use the Internet to find out more about economics. With the wealth of current, valid information available on Web sites, using the Internet as a research tool is likely to increase your students' interest in and understanding of economics principles and topics. In addition, doing Internet research can help your students form the habit of accessing and using economics information, as well as help them develop investigative skills they will use throughout their educational and professional careers.

To aid your students in achieving these ends, each chapter of *Economics: New Ways of Thinking* includes the addresses of several Web sites at which students will find engaging, relevant information. When students type in the addresses provided, they will immediately arrive at the intended sites. The addresses have been modified so that EMC Publishing can monitor and maintain the proper links—for example, the government site http://stats.bls.gov/ has been changed to www.emcp.net/prices. In the event that the address or content of a site changes or is discontinued, EMC's Internet editors will create a link that redirects students to an address with similar information.

Activities in the *Annotated Teacher's Edition* often suggest that students search the Internet for information. For some activities, you might want to find reputable sites beforehand, and steer students to those sites. For other activities, you might want students to do their own searching, and then check out the sites they have found and discuss why they might be reliable or unreliable.

CHAPTER 4 Overview

This chapter introduces and discusses a very important concept in economics: demand. This is the first of three chapters in which students learn about demand, supply, and the ways demand and supply work together in markets. The following statements provide brief descriptions of the major concepts covered in each section of this chapter.

Understanding Demand

Section 1 discusses the basic concepts of the law of demand. It also introduces the elements of the demand curve.

The Demand Curve Shifts

Section 2 explores the factors that cause the demand curve to shift. These factors include income, preferences, prices of related goods, number of buyers, and buyers' expectations of future price. Section 2 also explains the difference between a change in demand and a change in quantity demanded.

Elasticity of Demand

Section 3 covers the relationship between the percentage change in quantity demanded and the percentage change in price. This is the elasticity of demand.

CHAPTER 4 Demand

Why It Matters

Certain people and institutions play important roles in your life. For example, your parents, teachers, and friends are important. Government is an institution that also plays an important part in your life. It determines such things as when you can get a driver's license, the amount of taxes you must pay, and when you will be able to vote.

Markets also have a major impact on your life. A market is any place where people come together to buy and sell goods or services. Markets determine what prices you pay for computers, cars, television sets, books, and clothes. Markets also determine what people earn as teachers, truck drivers, television and movie stars, baseball players, and nurses. How much money you earn in the future will depend on markets.

If you are interested in the prices you pay for the goods and services you buy, or in why some people earn higher salaries than others, then you will be interested in learning how markets work. The first step is to learn about demand, the subject of this chapter.

Shopping for a more powerful computer and the latest software program can be fun. Whether or not these shoppers decide to make a purchase will depend on their willingness and ability to buy, conditions you will learn more about in this chapter.

88

Teaching Suggestions from the Author

This is the first chapter of the book that begins to use diagrams in a big way. Most students will be unaccustomed to translating what they know into diagrams. For example, in this chapter we discuss the law of demand and a demand schedule, and then translate each into a demand curve. Students seem to have little trouble understanding what the law of demand states, and they understand the numbers in a demand schedule, but when it comes to understanding what a demand curve says, they initially go blank.

I know of no better way of getting students to understand a diagram than to have them repeatedly put into their own words what the diagram says. What does a demand curve say? What does a movement

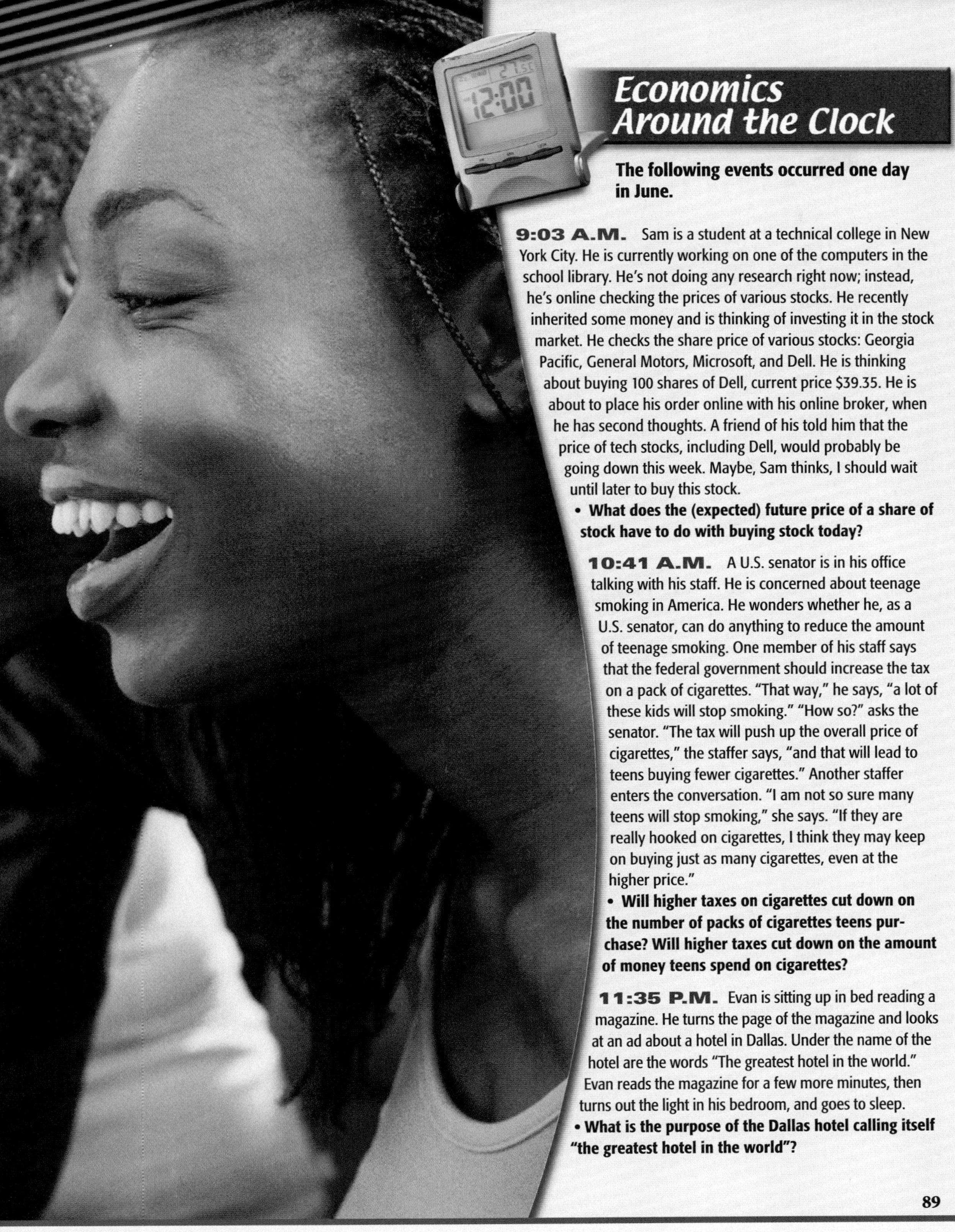

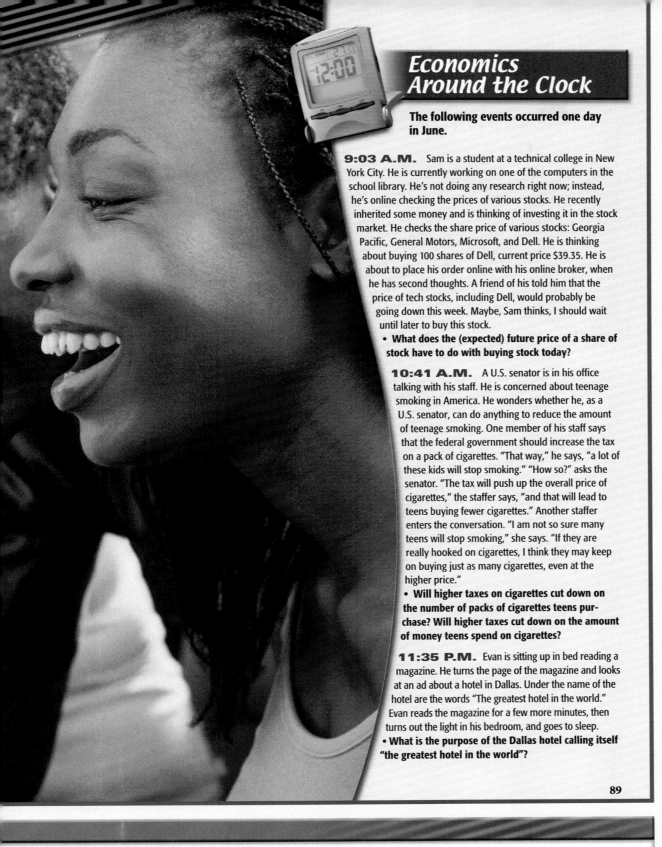

Economics Around the Clock

The following events occurred one day in June.

9:03 A.M. Sam is a student at a technical college in New York City. He is currently working on one of the computers in the school library. He's not doing any research right now; instead, he's online checking the prices of various stocks. He recently inherited some money and is thinking of investing it in the stock market. He checks the share price of various stocks: Georgia Pacific, General Motors, Microsoft, and Dell. He is thinking about buying 100 shares of Dell, current price $39.35. He is about to place his order online with his online broker, when he has second thoughts. A friend of his told him that the price of tech stocks, including Dell, would probably be going down this week. Maybe, Sam thinks, I should wait until later to buy this stock.

- **What does the (expected) future price of a share of stock have to do with buying stock today?**

10:41 A.M. A U.S. senator is in his office talking with his staff. He is concerned about teenage smoking in America. He wonders whether he, as a U.S. senator, can do anything to reduce the amount of teenage smoking. One member of his staff says that the federal government should increase the tax on a pack of cigarettes. "That way," he says, "a lot of these kids will stop smoking." "How so?" asks the senator. "The tax will push up the overall price of cigarettes," the staffer says, "and that will lead to teens buying fewer cigarettes." Another staffer enters the conversation. "I am not so sure many teens will stop smoking," she says. "If they are really hooked on cigarettes, I think they may keep on buying just as many cigarettes, even at the higher price."

- **Will higher taxes on cigarettes cut down on the number of packs of cigarettes teens purchase? Will higher taxes cut down on the amount of money teens spend on cigarettes?**

11:35 P.M. Evan is sitting up in bed reading a magazine. He turns the page of the magazine and looks at an ad about a hotel in Dallas. Under the name of the hotel are the words "The greatest hotel in the world." Evan reads the magazine for a few more minutes, then turns out the light in his bedroom, and goes to sleep.

- **What is the purpose of the Dallas hotel calling itself "the greatest hotel in the world"?**

Introducing the Chapter

You might want to open the chapter by telling students that many objects, such as buildings and computers, are composed of separate parts or building blocks. Ask them to provide examples of objects and their component parts. Then tell them that a subject like economics is like those objects, and that a major building block of economics is demand. You may also want to mention that another key component of economics is supply, which students will learn about in the next chapter. Write the definition of *demand* (see page 90) on the board, stressing the two parts of that definition—"willingness" and "ability."

Teaching with Visuals

Demand is a concept with which students are familiar, even though the term *demand* may be new to them. Have them look at the photo on this spread and explain how demand is at work in it. Students will probably say that the buyers want the goods they are buying. An economist would say that the buyers are expressing their demand for the goods—their willingness and ability to purchase the goods.

from one point on a demand curve to another point on the same demand curve say? What does a shift rightward in the demand curve say? What does a shift leftward say? Only by repeatedly going from the diagram to their own words, will students come to understand that a diagram is no more than a form of shorthand. For example, simply drawing a rightward shift in a demand curve says, "Buyers are willing and able to buy more units of the good or service at each and every price." One shift in a curve as opposed to 19 words. Must be that economists use diagrams because they like to economize.

SECTION 1 Teacher Support

Focus and Motivate

Section Objectives

After completing this section, students will be able to

- explain the law of demand;
- describe the difference between demand and quantity demanded;
- provide examples of the law of diminishing marginal utility; and
- create demand curves from given demand schedules.

Economics Around the Clock

Kickoff Activity

Tell students to reread the 9:03 A.M. scenario in Economics Around the Clock (page 89) and then write their answers to the accompanying question.

Invite students to share their answers with the class. Students should see that there is a direct relationship between price and quantity demanded.

Activating Prior Knowledge

Students often instinctively understand demand and the law of demand. They refer to the willingness to pay for a product and the understanding that as price increases, demand decreases. Ask students to identify situations in which the price of a good or service increased and their own demand for that good or service decreased, or vice versa.

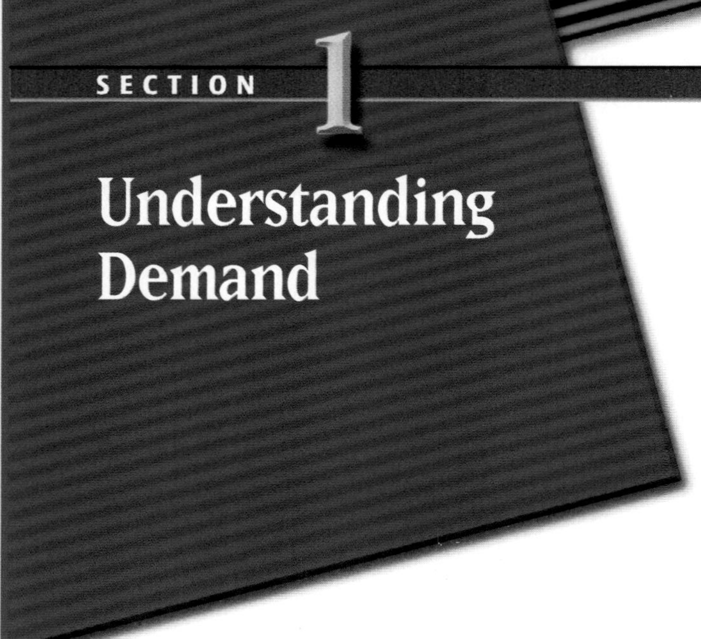

SECTION 1 Understanding Demand

Focus Questions

- What is demand?
- What is the difference between demand and quantity demanded?
- Why do price and quantity demanded move in opposite directions?
- What is the law of diminishing marginal utility?
- What is the difference between a demand schedule and a demand curve?

Key Terms

market
demand
law of demand
quantity demanded
law of diminishing marginal utility
demand schedule
demand curve

What Is Demand?

A **market** is any place where people come together to buy and sell goods or services. Economists often say a market has two sides: a buying side and a selling side. In economics, the buying side is referred to as *demand*, and the selling side is referred to as *supply*. In this chapter, you will learn about demand; in the next chapter, you will learn about supply.

The word **demand** has a specific meaning in economics. It refers to the willingness and ability of buyers to purchase different quantities of a good at different prices during a specific time period. *Willingness to purchase* a good refers to a person's want or desire for the good. Having the *ability to purchase* a good means having the money to pay for the good. Both willingness and ability to purchase must be present for demand to exist. It is important for you to remember that if either one of these conditions is absent, there is no demand.

market
Any place where people come together to buy and sell goods or services.

demand
The willingness and ability of buyers to purchase different quantities of a good at different prices during a specific time period.

law of demand
A law stating that as the price of a good increases, the quantity demanded of the good decreases, and that as the price of a good decreases, the quantity demanded of the good increases.

EXAMPLE: Cruz doesn't have the $34,000 needed to buy a particular car. If she did have the money, though, she says that she certainly would buy the car. Notice that Cruz has the willingness (she wants the car), but not the ability (not enough money) to buy the car. Under these circumstances (willingness, but not ability, to buy), Cruz does not have a demand for the car. ♦

EXAMPLE: Molly is shopping for a new cell phone. The one she likes is $129, which is within her price range. She was worried that she wouldn't have enough money, but she has set aside just enough for the new phone. Because Molly has the willingness and the ability to buy the cell phone, demand does exist. ♦

What Does the Law of Demand "Say"?

Suppose the average price of a compact disc rises from $10 to $15. Will customers want to buy more or fewer compact discs at the higher price? Most people would say that customers would buy fewer CDs.

Now suppose the average price of a compact disc falls from $10 to $5. Will customers want to buy more or fewer compact discs at the lower price? Most people would say more.

Differentiating Instruction

English Language Learners

This chapter contains a number of terms that are difficult for ELL students or others who have difficulty reading English. Assign these students to work in pairs, and have them make a list of the key terms. Students should define the terms both in English and in their native language, if appropriate, and then write new sentences on their own that show that they understand the meaning of the word and how to use the word correctly in English. You might also want to ask them to provide clear, concrete examples of the terms on their lists. Ask students to turn in their lists to you or make a copy for you so that you can individually quiz them on the terms at the end of the study of the chapter.

If you answered the questions the way most people would, you instinctively understand the **law of demand.** This law says that as the price of a good increases, the quantity demanded of the good decreases. The law of demand also says that as the price of a good decreases, the quantity demanded of the good increases. In other words, price and quantity demanded move in opposite directions. This relationship (you have probably heard it referred to as an *inverse relationship* in your math classes) can be shown in symbols:

Law of Demand

If P ↑ then Q_d ↓
If P↓ then Q_d ↑
(where P = price and Q_d = quantity demanded)

If you were reading closely, you probably noticed two words that sound alike: *demand* and *quantity demanded.* Don't make the mistake of thinking they mean the same thing. *Demand,* as you learned earlier, refers to both the willingness and ability of buyers to purchase a good or service. For example, if an economist said that Karen had a *demand* for popcorn, you would know that Karen has both the willingness and ability to purchase popcorn.

Quantity demanded is a new and different concept. It refers to the *number of units* of a good purchased at a specific price. For example, suppose the price of popcorn is $5 a bag, and Karen buys two bags. In this case two bags of popcorn is the *quantity demanded* of popcorn at $5 a bag. As you work your way through this chapter, you will see why it is important to know the difference between demand and quantity demanded.

Why Do Price and Quantity Demanded Move in Opposite Directions?

The law of demand says that as price rises, quantity demanded falls, and that as price falls, quantity demanded rises. Why? According to economists, it is because of the **law of diminishing marginal utility**, which states that as a person consumes additional units of a good, eventually the utility or satisfaction gained from each additional unit of the good decreases. For example, you may receive more utility (satisfaction) from eating your first hamburger at lunch than your second and, if you continue, more utility from your second hamburger than your third.

"The main reason economists believe so strongly in the law of demand is that it is so plausible, even to noneconomists."
— David R. Henderson

What does this have to do with the law of demand? Economists state that the more utility you receive from a unit of a good, the higher price you are willing to pay for it; and the less utility you receive from a unit of a good, the lower price you are willing to pay for it. According to the law of diminishing marginal utility, individuals eventually obtain less utility from additional units of a good (such as hamburgers), so it follows that they will buy larger quantities of a good only at lower prices. And this is what the law of demand states.

quantity demanded
The number of units of a good purchased at a specific price.

law of diminishing marginal utility
A law stating that as a person consumes additional units of a good, eventually the utility gained from each additional unit of the good decreases.

▲ *Harry Potter and the Order of the Phoenix* was in great demand hours after its release in Russia in early 2004. **Do these people have both willingness and ability to purchase?**

Teach

Clarifying Terms

Students might confuse the meanings of the words *want* and *demand,* which they might think of as synonymous. For example, a person who says "I want the television set" could be thought to be saying "I demand the television set." In economics, however, *want* and *demand* mean two different things. The person who demands something is expressing a willingness and ability to pay for something. The person who simply uses the word *want* is not expressing willingness and ability to pay. For example, a person may say "I want a car." That does not mean that the person has the ability to buy a car.

Thinking Like an Economist

Tell students that many people believe that the more money a person has, the more expensive version of a product the person will buy. Point out that those people are assuming that someone who has the ability to buy something also has the willingness to buy it. Economists do not think this way. The economist knows that most people try to find the best deal available to them.

Encourage students to survey family members and friends to find out whether they buy the most expensive items available when they can afford them, or look for the best buys even when they have more than enough money for the most expensive items. Tabulate the results of all the students. Discuss the findings, focusing on willingness as well as ability as elements of demand.

Teaching with Visuals

Answers will vary. It appears that the people pictured have both the willingness and the ability to purchase; they seem to be making an effort to obtain the book, and smiling while doing so.

Background Information: Diminishing Marginal Utility and Advertising

Students have probably not paid much attention to the concept and pricing associated with diminishing marginal utility, a key economic concept in this section. To emphasize this concept, instruct students to spend the next week keeping a log of goods and services that appear to have diminishing marginal utility in stores, advertisements, and other places. For example, a supermarket may offer 3 pounds of oranges for $2, and charge $1 per pound for any quantity less than 3 pounds. Ask students to create visuals to accompany their logs and to present both to the class. When the presentations are finished, guide students in a discussion of diminishing marginal utility and advertising practices.

Economics in the Real World

After students read this feature, invite them to describe personal experiences at amusement parks or other recreational sites. Ask if they enjoyed their visits more, the same, or less on each succeeding hour or day. Find out if they agree or disagree with the theory of diminishing marginal utility.

ANSWERS TO THINK ABOUT IT Answers will vary. Encourage students to share their personal experiences with the class. You might list their responses under the heading "Goods and Services with Diminishing Marginal Utility."

Reinforcement Activity

Direct students to create price change examples from their own everyday experiences that demonstrate the law of demand. Begin by urging them to imagine that the prices of movie tickets at local theaters have dropped from over $7 to below $5, and to decide whether they would be more likely to go to the movies. Now ask them to name several goods and services that they typically purchase, imagine specific price change situations for each of those goods and services, and describe how those changes would affect the quantities they would demand.

Economics in the Real World

Are the Prices at Disneyland Goofy?

The Walt Disney Company operates two major theme parks in the United States: Disneyland in Anaheim, California, and Walt Disney World in Orlando, Florida. Each year millions of people visit each park.

Regardless of which park you visit, the price you pay for your ticket will depend on how many days you want to spend at the park. For example, Disneyland's Web site lists prices for one- to five-day tickets. On the day we checked, the various ticket prices were as follows:

- One-day ticket, $63
- Two-day ticket, $85
- Three-day ticket, $109
- Four-day ticket, $129
- Five-day ticket, $139

Notice that the price of a one-day ticket ($63), when doubled, is $126. Disneyland does not charge visitors double its one-day ticket price for visiting two days; it charges $85. Similarly, triple the price of a one-day ticket would be $189, but Disneyland charges $109 for a three-day ticket.

Disneyland seems to be telling visitors that if they want to visit the theme park for one day, they have to pay $63, but a second day will cost only $22 more, not $63 more. Notice that the price Disneyland charges to stay a fifth day is only $10 more than staying four days. Do you wonder how much Disneyland would charge to stay, say, a tenth day? By the tenth day, it might be that you would only have to pay 25 cents more.

Why does Disneyland charge less for the second day than the first day? It's because of the law of diminishing marginal utility, which states that as a person consumes additional units of a good, eventually the utility (satisfaction or happiness) from each additional unit of the good decreases. Disneyland can't charge as high a price when utility is low as when it is high. If you have never been to Disneyland, or haven't been for five years, your first day is likely to be quite enjoyable. If you've already spent, say, two days at Disneyland, your third consecutive day isn't likely to give you as much utility as your first.

THINK ABOUT IT Can you think of a good or service that is priced the way visits to Disneyland are priced (for two units of the good or service, you pay less than double what you pay for one unit)?

The Law of Demand in Numbers and Pictures

demand schedule The numerical representation of the law of demand.

The law of demand can be represented both in numbers and pictures. Look at Exhibit 4-1(a), which has a "Price" column and a "Quantity demanded" column. Notice that as the prices fall (from $4 to $3 to $2 to $1), the quantity demanded rises (from 1 to 2 to 3 to 4). Do you see that price and quantity demanded are moving in opposite directions? The economic term for this type of numerical chart showing the law of demand is **demand schedule**.

Now let's see how you would illustrate the law of demand in picture form. The simple way is to plot the numbers from a demand schedule in a graph. Look at Exhibit 4-1(b), which shows how the combinations of price and quantity demanded

Differentiating Instruction

Kinesthetic Learners

The law of diminishing marginal utility is a fun economic concept to show students. Call on five student volunteers to come to the front of the class. Give each of them a breath mint and then offer each of them another mint. Continue to offer mints until one student has had enough. Ask your volunteers if they noticed any difference between their level of satisfaction from the first, to the second, on to the last mint. (You might post a chart with a 10-point enjoyment scale on the vertical axis and the number of mints on the horizontal axis, and ask each volunteer to plot his or her satisfaction level after each mint.) Explain that this is an example of the law of diminishing marginal utility.

in Exhibit 4-1(a) are plotted. The first combination (a price of $4 and a quantity demanded of 1) is labeled as point A. The second price and quantity demanded combination ($3 and a quantity demanded of 2) is labeled B. The same process continues for points C and D. If we connect all four points, from A to D, we have a line that slopes downward from left to right. This line, called a **demand curve**, is the graphic representation of the law of demand.

You might be wondering why we use the word *curve* when, as you can see in Exhibit 4-1(b), we ended up drawing a straight line to represent demand. The answer has to do with the standard practice in economics, which is to call the graphic representation of the relationship between price and quantity demanded a *demand curve*, whether it is a curve or a straight line.

A Student Asks

QUESTION: *I've seen a car, a radio, and a diamond ring in the real world, but I've never seen a demand curve in real life. (I have seen one in this textbook, though.) Do demand curves exist in the real world?*

ANSWER: *If you go outside and look up into the sky, you're not going to see a demand curve. If you look under your bed or in the school auditorium, you won't see a demand curve, which doesn't mean that demand curves don't exist in the real world. (You also can't see a virus with the naked eye, but that doesn't mean viruses don't exist.)*

The data (numbers) that make up a demand curve—combinations of price and quantity demanded—do exist in the real world. When people (in the real world) buy more of a good (such as a can of soda or a new pair of jeans) at a lower price than at a higher price, they are expressing the law of demand, which is graphically portrayed as a demand curve (in a textbook). So what do you think? Do demand curves exist in the real world?

EXHIBIT 4-1 Demand Schedule and Demand Curve

Price (in dollars)	Quantity demanded (in units)
$4	1
3	2
2	3
1	4

(a)

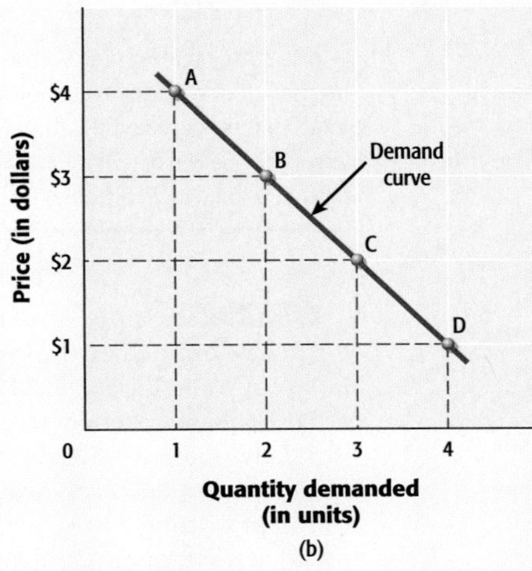

(b)

▲ (a) A demand schedule for a good. Notice that as price decreases, quantity demanded increases. (b) Plotting the four combinations of price and quantity demanded from part (a) and connecting the points gives us a demand curve. Price, on the vertical axis, represents price per unit of a good. Quantity demanded, on the horizontal axis, always applies to a specific time period (a week, a month, a year, and so on).

Individual Demand Curves and Market Demand Curves

An individual demand curve and a market demand curve are different. An individual demand curve is what it sounds like: the demand curve that represents an individual's demand. For example, Harry's demand curve represents Harry's (and only Harry's) demand for, say, DVDs. A market demand curve is simply the sum of all the different individual demand curves added together.

demand curve
The graphical representation of the law of demand.

Teaching with Visuals

The law of demand says that price and quantity demanded move in opposite directions. Exhibit 4-1(a) shows this in numbers and 4-1(b) shows this as a graph.

A Student Asks

You may want to expand this A Student Asks to make sure students are not confused by the fact that some demand "curves" are actually straight lines.

Some students think that the law of demand and the downward-sloping demand curve hold only in the United States, only in rich countries, or only in free enterprise countries. Not true. The law of demand and the downward-sloping demand curve are relevant all over the world. Whenever the price of a good rises, people will buy fewer units of the good. The law of demand is universal.

Teaching with Visuals

A market demand curve is the sum of different individual demand curves added together. To further illustrate the point in Exhibit 4-2 (page 94), have students work in groups of three or four to create individual and market demand curves for a similar good. Arrange for them to share their demand curves with the class.

Application Activity

After reading and discussing Section 1, you may want to assign the Section Activity in the *Applying the Principles Workbook.*

Assess

Quick Quiz

The following true-or-false quiz will help you assess student understanding of the material covered in this section.

1. Both willingness and ability to purchase must be present for demand to exist. (True)

Internet Research

Direct students to find an online news article, an online press release, or a corporate Web page describing a new technological product. Tell them to name two or three related products and services, and to explain how the advancement in technology will affect demand curves for those products and services. Ask, How will this product facilitate the production of other items or help people provide better services?

2. As price decreases, the quantity demanded decreases. (False)
3. The more utility you receive from a good, the higher the price you are willing to pay for that good. (True)

Assessment Book

You will find a quiz for this section in the *Assessment Book.*

Reteaching Activity

Guide students in examining the definitions of *demand, quantity demanded, law of demand,* and *law of diminishing marginal utility.* Then instruct students to create and share with the class their own sentences using these terms.

Guided Reading

For further reteaching of the key concepts in this section, assign the Outlining Activity and the Just the Facts Handout from the *Guided Reading and Study Guide.*

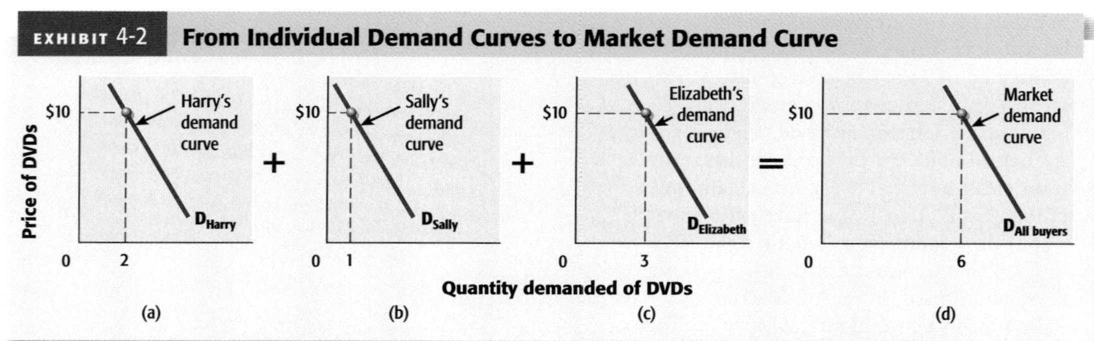

▲ In parts (a) through (c) you see the individual demand curve for Harry, Sally, and Elizabeth. The market demand curve, shown in part (d), is simply the sum of the individual demand curves. Stated differently, we know that at a price of $10 per DVD, the quantity demanded of DVDs is 2 for Harry, 1 for Sally, and 3 for Elizabeth. It follows that all three buyers together would like to buy 6 DVDs at a price of $10 per DVD. This point is identified on the market demand curve in part (d).

EXAMPLE: Suppose that the whole world has only three buyers of DVDs: Harry, Sally, and Elizabeth. At a price of $10 per DVD, quantity demanded is 2 for Harry, 1 for Sally, and 3 for Elizabeth. As a result, the *market demand curve* would include a point representing a price of $10 per DVD and a market quantity demanded of 6 DVDs (2 + 1 + 3).

To see this graphically, look at Exhibit 4-2. In panels (a) through (c) you see the *individual* demand curves for Harry, Sally, and Elizabeth, respectively. (To keep things simple, we identify only one point on the demand curve for each person.) Now look at panel (d). Here you can see the *market* demand curve (for all buyers—Harry, Sally and Elizabeth—of DVDs). Notice that the point we identify on the market demand curve simply represents the quantity demanded of all three buyers together if the price of a DVD is $10. ♦

SECTION 1 ASSESSMENT

Defining Terms

1. Define:
   a. demand
   b. quantity demanded
   c. market
   d. demand schedule
   e. demand curve
   f. law of demand
2. Use the terms *demand* and *quantity demanded* correctly in a sentence about concert tickets.

Reviewing Facts and Concepts

3. State the law of demand.
4. Give an example of a demand schedule.

Critical Thinking

5. Yesterday the price of a good was $10, and the quantity demanded was 100 units. Today the price of the good is $12, and the quantity demanded is 87 units. Did quantity demanded fall because the price increased, or did the price rise because quantity demanded fell?
6. What does the law of diminishing marginal utility have to do with the law of demand?

Applying Economic Concepts

7. Assume that the law of demand applies to criminal activity. What might community leaders do to reduce the number of crimes committed in the community?

SECTION 1 ASSESSMENT ANSWERS

Defining Terms

1. a. demand: the willingness and ability to purchase a good; **b. quantity demanded:** the number of units a person purchases at a certain price; **c. market:** any place where people come together to buy and sell goods or services; **d. demand schedule:** the numerical representation of the law of demand; **e. demand curve:** the graphical representation of the law of demand; **f. law of demand:** a law stating that as the price of a good increases, the quantity demanded of the good decreases, and that as the price of a good decreases, the quantity demanded of the good increases.
2. Answers will vary.

Reviewing Facts and Concepts

3. As the price of a good increases, the quantity demanded of the good decreases, and vice versa.
4. Answers will vary. Ensure that students provide a numerical representation.

Critical Thinking

5. The increase in price (from $10 to $12) is the cause, and the fall in quantity demanded (from 100 units to 87 units) is the effect.
6. The law of diminishing marginal utility states that individuals eventually obtain less utility from additional units of a good, so it follows that they will buy larger quantities of a good only at lower prices. The law of demand states that individuals will buy more of a good at lower prices.

Applying Economic Concepts

7. Answers will vary. Students might mention that increasing the punishment for a crime (price) is likely to decrease people's willingness to commit the crime (demand).

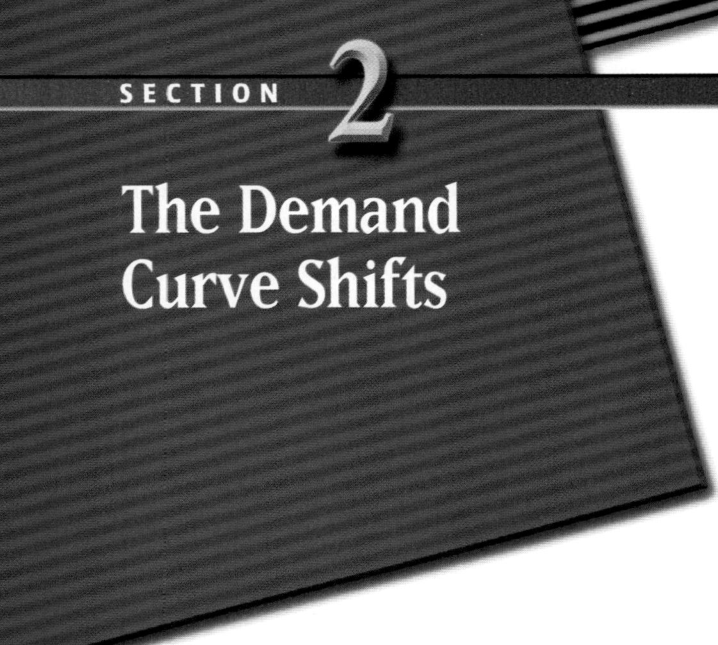

SECTION 2 The Demand Curve Shifts

Focus Questions

- What does it mean when a demand curve shifts to the right?
- What does it mean when a demand curve shifts to the left?
- What is a normal good? An inferior good? A neutral good?
- What factors can change demand?
- What factors can change quantity demanded?

Key Terms

normal good
inferior good
neutral good
substitute
complement

When Demand Changes, the Curve Shifts

Demand can go up, and it can go down. For example, the demand for orange juice can rise or fall. The demand for CDs can rise or fall. Every time the demand changes for a good, any good, the demand curve for that good shifts. By *shift* we mean that it moves; it moves either to the right or to the left.

For example, if the demand for orange juice increases, the demand curve for orange juice shifts to the right. If the demand for orange juice decreases, the demand curve for orange juice shifts to the left.

Demand increases → Demand curve shifts rightward
Demand decreases → Demand curve shifts leftward

We can understand shifts in demand curves better with the aid of Exhibit 4-3. Look at the curve labeled D_1 in Exhibit 4-3. Suppose this demand curve represents the original and current demand for orange juice. Notice that the quantity demanded at a price of $1 is 400 quarts of orange juice. Now suppose that the demand for orange juice increases. For whatever reason, people want to buy more orange juice. This increase in demand is shown by the demand curve D_1 shifting to the right and becoming D_2.

EXHIBIT 4-3 Shifts in a Demand Curve

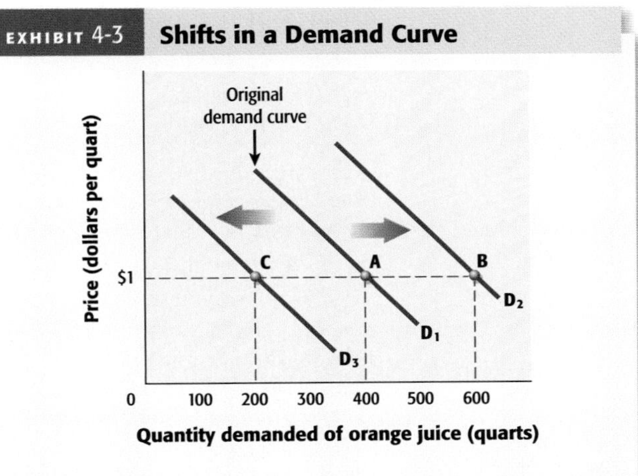

▲ Moving from D_1 (original demand curve) to D_2 represents a rightward shift in the demand curve. Demand has increased. Moving from D_1 to D_3 represents a leftward shift in the demand curve. Demand has decreased.

Differentiating Instruction

Kinesthetic Learners

To help kinesthetic learners understand the factors that create shifts in demand curves, you might prepare a felt or sticky board, and provide materials for students to use in creating demand curves and symbols representing the factors that would cause the curves to shift. Kinesthetic learners could manipulate these curves and factors to better understand their functions. You could put each factor on a scale to show it rising and falling, and encourage students to demonstrate the changes in the demand curve.

SECTION 2 Teacher Support

Focus and Motivate

Section Objectives

After completing this section, students will be able to

- explain why a demand curve shifts to the right or the left;
- distinguish between normal, inferior, and neutral goods;
- list the factors that cause a change in demand; and
- identify the factor that causes a change in quantity demanded.

Kickoff Activity

Before instructing students to open their books to this page, explain that economists often tell economic stories with graphs. For example, a demand curve tells a story about the relationship between the price of a good and the quantity demanded of that good. Ask students to draw a picture of a demand curve, and to illustrate what happens to that curve when demand increases and when demand decreases.

Activating Prior Knowledge

Tell students that to learn how to tell stories with graphs, as economists do, they can start by translating graphs in the text into their own words. Have them pick a graph from the preceding section and tell its story in their own words.

Teach

Teaching with Visuals

To make sure that students understand Exhibit 4-3, display a new graph—perhaps showing the demand curve for kayaks or bungee cords. Illustrate both a rightward shift and a leftward shift in the demand curve. Call on student volunteers to explain what is happening with demand as the curve shifts.

A Student Asks

You may want to use this A Student Asks to make sure students understand the difference between the *demand* changing and the *quantity demanded* changing.

Reinforcement Activity

Divide the class into groups of four or five students. Assign each student the task of finding out from at least three people in his or her group what they would consider a normal good, an inferior good, and a neutral good. When students have finished their questions, have volunteers read their lists to the class. You might chart the students' responses and note any trends.

Thinking Like an Economist

An economist believes that if the demand rises for a good, there must be a cause. Prompt students to identify the most popular holiday gifts last year. Ask: What are some of the reasons that the demand for these items was so high last year? Do you think the demand will be as high again this year? Why or why not?

What does it mean for a demand curve to shift to the right? The answer is easy if you again look at Exhibit 4-3, focusing on the horizontal axis and the numbers on it, along the bottom of the graph. What is the quantity demanded on curve D_2 at the price of $1? The answer is 600 quarts of orange juice. In other words, an increase in demand (or a shift righward in the demand curve) is the same thing as saying, "Buyers want to buy more of a good at each and every price." In our example, buyers want to buy more quarts of orange juice at $1.

How would we graphically represent a decrease in demand? In Exhibit 4-3, again let's suppose that D_1 is our original and current demand curve. A decrease in demand would then be represented as a shift leftward in the demand curve from D_1 to D_3. A decrease in demand means that buyers want to buy less of the good at each and every price. Specifically, if we look at the price $1, we see that buyers once wanted to buy 400 quarts of orange juice at $1 a quart, but now they want to buy only 200 quarts at $1 a quart.

A Student Asks

QUESTION: *Is saying that demand has increased for a good the same as saying that buyers are buying more of the good?*

ANSWER: *Yes, but with one important qualification. Buyers are buying more of the good* at the same price *at which they earlier bought less. For example, suppose that on Monday buyers bought 100 units of a good at $3 per unit. Then on Tuesday they bought 150 units of the same good at $3 per unit. An economist would say that demand for the good increased between Monday and Tuesday because the buyers bought more at the same price. If the good's price changed, the economist would describe the situation differently. The economist would say that the* quantity demanded *changed, rather than any change in* demand.

normal good
A good for which the demand rises as income rises and falls as income falls.

inferior good
A good for which the demand falls as income rises and rises as income falls.

neutral good
A good for which the demand remains unchanged as income rises or falls.

What Factors Cause Demand Curves to Shift?

Demand curves do not shift to the right or left without cause. They shift because of changes in demand, which can result from changes in several factors. These factors include income, buyer preferences, prices of related goods, number of buyers, and future price.

Income

As their income changes, people may buy more or less of a particular good. You might think that if income goes up, demand will go up, and if income goes down, demand will go down. This relationship is not necessarily the case, however. Much of what happens depends on what goods are involved.

If a person's income and demand change in the same direction (both go up, or both go down), then the good is called a **normal good**. For example, if Robert's income rises and he buys more CDs, then CDs are a normal good for Robert. If, however, income and demand go in different directions (one goes up, while the other goes down), the good is called an **inferior good**. If a person buys the same amount of the good when income changes, the good is called a **neutral good**.

EXAMPLE: On the average, each month Simon bought and consumed five hot dogs, one steak, and one tube of toothpaste when he was a college student earning $100 a week. Now that he has graduated from college, and is earning $700 a week, he buys two hot dogs, three steaks, and one tube of toothpaste a month. During this time, prices have been stable, meaning no changes in prices. So, for Simon, hot dogs are an inferior good (he buys *less* as his income *rises*), steak is a normal good (he buys *more* as his income *rises*), and toothpaste is a neutral good (he buys the same amount as his income rises). ◆

If you're wondering if a good can be a normal good for one person and an inferior good for another person, the answer is yes. People, not economists, decide whether a good is normal or inferior for them. If Bob's income goes up and he buys fewer potato chips, then potato chips are an inferior good

Cooperative Learning

Divide the class into groups, and tell each group to create an advertisement to increase the demand for a good of its choice. The advertisement should speak to the factors that cause demand curves to shift. For example, "Buy a tennis racket, and get a free tube of tennis balls!" reflects the connection between two goods as complements. The advertisement may take the form of a television or radio piece (either of which can be acted out in front of the class, or videotaped and played for the class), a print piece, a billboard, an Internet pop-up—anything that might catch the public's eye. Each group should provide a written copy or outline of its presentation for your evaluation.

for Bob. If Georgia's income goes up and she buyers more potato chips, then potato chips are a normal good for Georgia.

Preferences

People's preferences affect how much of a good they buy. A change in preferences in favor of a good shifts the demand curve to the right. A change in preferences away from a good shifts the demand curve to the left.

EXAMPLE: People begin to favor (prefer) small, gas-efficient cars more than they did in the past. As a result, the demand curve for small, gas-efficient cars shifts rightward. At the same time, people may begin to favor several new brands of computers and stop buying Dell computers, which had been the most popular computer for several years. As a result, the demand curve for Dell computers shifts leftward. ♦

Prices of Related Goods

Demand for goods is affected by the prices of related goods. The two types of related goods are substitutes and complements.

When two goods are **substitutes,** the demand for one good moves in the *same* direction as the price of the other good. In other words, if the price for a good, say peanuts, goes up, the demand for that good's substitutes, say pretzels, will also go up. For many people coffee is a substitute for tea. Thus, if the *price* of coffee increases, the *demand* for tea increases as people substitute tea for the higher-priced coffee.

EXAMPLE: Jessica is in the supermarket looking at the soft drinks. She usually buys a six-pack of Coke a week. She notices that the price of Coke has risen from what it was last week. So, instead of buying a six-pack of Coke, she buys a six-pack of Pepsi. For Jessica, Coke and Pepsi are substitutes, which means that as the price of Coke goes up, so does Jessica's demand for Pepsi. ♦

Two goods are **complements** if they are consumed together. For example, tennis rackets and tennis balls are used together to play tennis. With complementary goods, the demand for one moves in the *opposite* direction as the price of the other. As the price of tennis rackets rises, for example, the demand for tennis balls falls. Other examples of complements (or complementary goods) include cars and tires, lightbulbs and lamps, and golf clubs and golf balls.

▲ If Southwest Airlines expects the price of fuel to rise, and decides to buy fuel now instead of later, what will happen to the current demand for fuel?

Number of Buyers

The demand for a good in a particular market area is related to the number of buyers in the area. The more buyers, the higher the demand; the fewer buyers, the lower the demand. The number of buyers may increase because of a higher birthrate, increased immigration, or the migration of people from one region of the country to another. Factors such as a higher death rate or the migration of people can also cause the number of buyers to decrease.

Future Price

Buyers who expect the price of a good to be higher in the future may buy the good now, thus increasing the current demand for the good. Buyers who expect the price of a good to be lower in the future may wait until the future to buy the good, thus decreasing the current demand for the good.

Suppose Brandon is willing and able to buy a house (demand exists), but he thinks the price of houses on average will be lower next month. As a result, Brandon is likely to hold off on making a purchase, which has the effect of decreasing current demand.

substitute
A similar good. With substitutes, the price of one and the demand for the other move in the same direction.

complement
A good that is consumed jointly with another good. With complements, the price of one and the demand for the other move in opposite directions.

Teaching with Visuals

The demand for fuel will increase.

Discussion Starter

Brainstorm with students a list of goods that they would demand, and write their responses on the board. Help the class create a list of substitute goods for each item. Then guide the class in developing a list of complements. Discuss the differences to make sure students understand both categories.

Prediction Activity

Present students with a comparison between a local bricks-and-mortar bookstore (at the mall perhaps) and an online bookstore. Ask students to predict what will happen to the demand for books at the local bookstore if the online store offers the same titles at a lower price. (*Answer:* Demand will fall at the local store.)

A change in the price of a good produced and sold in a foreign country can change the demand for a related good produced and sold in the United States. To illustrate: Suppose X and Y are substitute goods, and X is produced and sold in Mexico and Y is produced and sold in the United States. Now suppose the price of X rises. Consequently, the demand for Y rises. It rises because people in Mexico are likely to switch from buying the higher-priced X to buying (importing) the lower-priced Y.

Application Activity

After reading and discussing "What Factors Cause Demand Curves to Shift?" (pages 96–97), you may want to assign the Section 2 Activity in the *Applying the Principles Workbook.*

Internet Research

Tell students that some products, such as books, are increasingly sold online. Have them visit two major online booksellers, Amazon.com and Barnesandnoble.com, and compare prices and offerings. They'll probably find the sites to be very similar. Ask them to discuss the factors that could contribute to a change in the demand curve for books sold online. What might make people buy more or fewer books on the Internet? What could these booksellers do to increase the demand for books on their sites?

Economics in the Real World

After students read this feature, ask them which of the two soft drinks—Coke and Pepsi—they prefer and why. Document their responses. Then administer your own taste test like the one Coca-Cola conducted, and poll students again. Compare your class's results with Coca-Cola's results.

ANSWERS TO THINK ABOUT IT Answers will vary. Students might say that Coca-Cola could have conducted a controlled study in which people tasted more than a few teaspoons of Coke.

Reinforcement Activity

The difference between a change in demand and a change in quantity demanded may be difficult for students to grasp. Have them cite particular situations that show a change in demand and others that show a change in quantity demanded. Ensure that they understand the difference and can articulate it.

Assess

Quick Quiz

The following true-or-false quiz will help you assess student understanding of the material covered in this section.

1. When a demand curve shifts to the right, demand has decreased. (False)
2. Demand has increased when the demand curve shifts to the right. (True)
3. The prices of related goods affect the demand curve. (True)
4. A change in the number of buyers creates a change in the quantity demanded. (True)

Economics in the Real World

New Coke, Classic Coke, or Pepsi?

In the early 1980s, the Pepsi company started asking people to take the "taste test." The taste test consisted of two small paper cups with a few teaspoons of Coke in one cup and a few teaspoons of Pepsi in the other. Members of the public didn't know which cup contained Pepsi and which cup contained Coke. It is important to note here that Pepsi is a slightly sweeter cola than Coke.

Members of the public were asked to drink the contents of both cups and then state which cola they preferred. Pepsi won the "taste test" more often than Coke. This news scared Coca-Cola, which, at the time, was holding on to a small lead in sales over Pepsi. Coca-Cola decided to undertake its own taste test. During its taste test, it experimented with the taste of Coke. One option consisted of sweetening the taste of Coke to lure more teenagers to its brand.

In its own taste tests, Coca-Cola learned that its new, sweeter Coke was beating Pepsi. In other words, Coca-Cola thought it had found the way to gain market share in the soft drink market. So, it undertook to replace its old, original Coke with what was called "New Coke."

On April 23, 1985, Coca-Cola launched New Coke. It was a disaster. Coke consumers across the country turned their backs on New Coke. One person said replacing the old Coke with New Coke was like "spitting on the flag." Another said, "At first I was numb. Then I was shocked. Then I started to yell and scream and run up and down."

Coca-Cola experienced a backlash from consumers. What had gone wrong? The company hadn't realized a fundamental problem with these taste tests. As it turns out, asking people to decide between a few teaspoons of different sodas is quite different from asking them to decide between entire bottles of soda. Often, when only a small amount of a cola is consumed, people choose the sweeter of the two colas. But when people have to drink larger amounts, they often find that the sweetness they liked in a teaspoon becomes "too sweet" before they finish the

hundreds of teaspoons contained in an entire bottle.

Coca-Cola obviously thought that its taste tests indicated a strong demand for New Coke. That interpretation was wrong. What the taste tests actually showed was a strong demand for a few teaspoons of New Coke, not a demand for a six-pack of New Coke, especially when it meant taking old Coke off the market. Coca-Cola made a mistake in thinking that buyers had a demand for New Coke when they didn't. On July 11, 1985, Coca-Cola brought old Coke back as Classic Coke. And over time it did away with New Coke.

THINK ABOUT IT What might Coca-Cola have done during its taste test to reduce the chances of making such a costly mistake?

What Factor Causes a Change in Quantity Demanded?

We identified the factors (income, preferences, etc.) that can cause *demand* to change, but what factor can cause a change in *quantity demanded*? Only one: price. For example, the only thing that can cause customers to change their quantity demanded of orange juice is a change in the price of orange juice; the only thing that can cause a change in the quantity demanded of pencils is a change in the price of pencils.

As we stated earlier, a change in demand is represented as a shift in the demand curve. The curve moves either right or left. See Exhibit 4-4(a). So how do we represent a change in quantity demanded? When quantity demanded changes, the curve doesn't

Differentiating Instruction

English Language Learners

To help ELL students, use the following resources, which are provided as part of the *Economics: New Ways of Thinking* program:

- a Spanish glossary in the *Student Text*
- Spanish versions of the Chapter Summaries on an audio CD

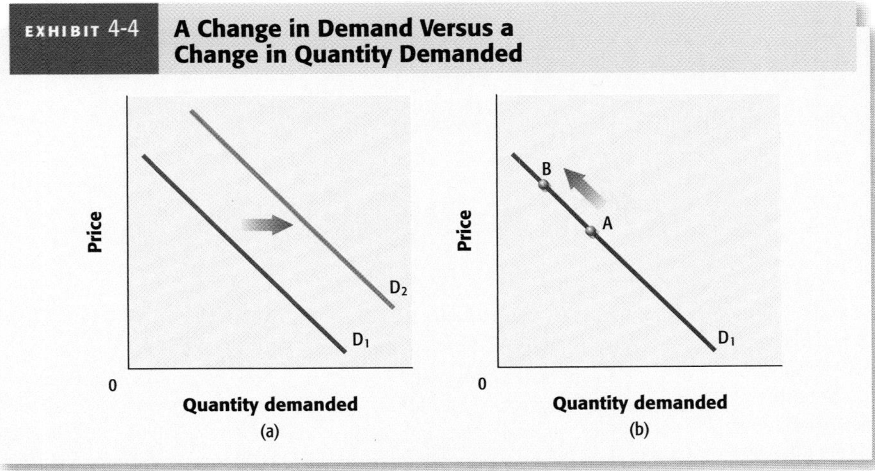

▲ (a) A change in demand refers to a shift in the demand curve. A change in demand can be brought about by a change in a number of factors (income, preferences, prices of related goods, number of buyers, future price). (b) A change in quantity demanded refers to a movement along a given demand curve, which is brought about only by a change in the price of the good.

move right or left. Instead, the only movement is to a different point *along* a given demand curve, which stays in the same place on the graph. See Exhibit 4-4(b).

EXAMPLE: Ian notices that the price of bananas has fallen; as a result, he goes from buying three bananas a week to buying five bananas a week. An economist would say that Ian's *quantity demanded* of bananas has increased (from three to five) as a result of the price of bananas falling. ♦

EXAMPLE: The price of a book was $10 in July and Jeff bought three. The price was $10 in August and Jeff bought four. Economists would say that Jeff's *demand* for books increased between July and August. ♦

SECTION 2 ASSESSMENT

Defining Terms

1. Define:
   a. normal good
   b. inferior good
   c. substitute
   d. neutral good
   e. complement

Reviewing Facts and Concepts

2. Explain what it means if demand increases.
3. Jerry, a comedian, started out doing stand-up comedy and went on to perform on a popular hit television series. As he went from stand-up comedian to TV star, his income increased substantially. During this time, he bought more cars (specifically, Porsches) to add to his collection. For Jerry, what kind of good are Porsches?

Critical Thinking

4. Identify a good that is a substitute for one good and a complement for another. (*Hint*: A Coca-Cola may be a substitute for a Pepsi and a complement for a hamburger.)

Applying Economic Concepts

5. In recent years the price of a computer has fallen. What effect is this price change likely to have on the demand for software? Explain your answer.
6. Graph the following:
   a. an increase in demand
   b. a decrease in demand

Assessment Book

You will find a quiz for this section in the *Assessment Book.*

Reteaching Activity

Direct students to work in pairs to list five examples of goods that are substitutes and five examples of goods that are complements. Ask the pairs to each prepare brief statements describing what will happen to demand if prices are increased on the substitute goods and on the complement goods. Ask a pair to share its statements, and invite the class to fine-tune them if necessary.

Guided Reading

For further reteaching of the key concepts in this section, assign the Outlining Activity and the Just the Facts Handout from the *Guided Reading and Study Guide.*

Defining Terms

1. a. normal good: a good for which demand rises as income rises and falls as income falls; **b. inferior good:** a good for which demand falls as income rises and rises as income falls; **c. substitute:** a similar good; **d. neutral good:** a good for which demand remains unchanged as income rises or falls; **e. complement:** a good that is consumed jointly with another good.

Reviewing Facts and Concepts

2. Answers will vary. Students might say it means that buyers want to buy more of the good at each and every price. They also might mention the factors that cause a shift in demand: income, preferences, prices of related goods, number of buyers, and expectations of future prices.
3. Normal goods.

Critical Thinking

4. Answers will vary.

Applying Economic Concepts

5. Computer hardware and software are complements. With complements, the price of one is inversely related to the demand for the other. Thus, as the price of computers falls, the demand for software is predicted to rise.
6. a. An increase in demand is represented by a rightward shift in a demand curve, such as from D_1 to D_2 in Exhibit 4-3. **b.** A decrease in demand is represented by a leftward shift in a demand curve, such as from D_1 to D_3 in Exhibit 4-3. (Ensure that students label the axes of their diagrams and label all relevant demand curves. They must also show, with arrows, how the demand curve shifts.)

Your Personal Economics

Discussion Starter

Ask students if any of them are considering buying a new computer in the near future. Pose these questions: If a national news agency reported that the price of computers will be higher next year, would you buy one now or wait until next year? How might that news report affect current demand for computers sold in the United States?

Research Activity

Assign each student to conduct an opinion poll on whether the price of houses will continue to skyrocket or decline. Students should survey several adults they know, and should document reasons for each person's opinion. Students may also want to search the Internet for current housing market trends, and use their research to form their own opinions about the issue. Instruct students to compile their data and report back to the class.

Your Personal Economics

Too Good to Be True?

You just learned that buyers' expectations about future prices can affect current demand. If computer buyers think computer prices will be higher next year, they might buy their computers now (at the lower price) instead of next year (at the higher price) Buyers who think computer prices will be lower next year, might hold off buying this year, thinking they will get a lower price next year.

The Tulip Example

Similar thinking has been affecting prices and demand for hundreds of years. In the 1600s in Holland, for example, a tulip craze became so frenzied that some people sold their

businesses and family jewels just to buy a few tulip bulbs. Why would people behave in this way? The answer has to do with what these people thought the future price of tulips would be. They believed that if they bought tulips today at a relatively lower price, they could sell the tulips at a higher price in the future.

Don't Forget Beanie Babies

Now think back to 1998. In that year, many people in the United States were buying Beanie Babies (a small stuffed animal). They believed that Beanie Babies would become

collectors' items, and that the future price of Beanie Babies would be higher than the current price. They thought that if they bought Beanie Babies in 1998, they could turn around and sell those Beanie Babies at a higher price in 1999, or 2000, or in some later year.

Then Came the Internet Bubble

One more example: Internet stocks in the late 1990s. Everyone seemed to be saying that the prices were going to be higher next week or next month and so you ought to buy the stocks as soon as possible. Even though many experts said the stocks were overpriced, people kept buying, thinking that the prices would continue to climb. Many people borrowed money to buy the stocks.

And What About Real Estate Prices?

Well, Beanie Babies, tulips, and many Internet stocks all crashed in price. Beanie Babies that once sold for $100 were selling for $5; tulips that sold for hundreds of thousands of dollars ended up selling for (the equivalent of) a few pennies; and Internet stock prices in some cases went from $400 a share to a few cents a share.

Do you think real estate prices might be similar to these examples? During the period from 2001 to 2005 in many places around the country, all you heard was how home prices were destined—yes, destined—to just keep on rising. It was as if some law—let's call it the law of antigravity—kept pulling prices up, much like the real law of gravity pulls things down. In southern California, especially coastal southern California, it was not uncommon to hear people say, "There is no way

▼ Stock traders such as these participated in the buying surge of Internet stocks in the late 1990s.

Cooperative Learning

Divide students into groups of three or four. Have each group develop two lists. One list will contain items that have increased and then decreased in price. The other list will contain items that are currently increasing in price. Each group should discuss possible reasons why prices decreased on the first list. They should then speculate as to whether items that are currently increasing in price might decrease in price for similar reasons. Have groups report summaries of their discussions to the class.

◀ **Can economists predict *when* real estate prices will rise or fall?**

that houses near the coast are going to go down in price. After all, there's only so much coast to go around." At the time, many people were buying houses not to live in, but to speculate on. In other words, they bought a house in 2003 because they were "certain" they could sell the house in 2004 for a higher price.

Many of these people did just that. Of course, many of the people who bought Beanie Babies, tulips, and Internet stocks did the same thing: they bought low and sold high. Not everybody was so fortunate. In all three crazes—Beanie Babies, tulips, and Internet stocks—some people bought at high prices and ended up selling at low prices.

Will it be the same with houses? It very well could be. It's happened before, and no economic law says it won't happen again.

One Last Point

Consider George. George watches as the price of houses skyrockets. He also notices that house prices are rising much more rapidly than house rents. Based on the discrepancy between the rate of change in house rents and the rate of change in house prices, he is quite sure that sometime in the future house prices will decline (perhaps very quickly).

What George doesn't know is *when* house prices will start to decline. Will the price decline begin next week, next month, next year, or five years from now? It is much harder to predict the timing of an event than it is to predict the event. (The doctor can tell the pregnant woman that she is going to have a baby, but be unsure of the day and time. The weather forecaster is fairly sure that it will rain in the next 24 hours, but he's not sure if the rain will start at 7:08 a.m. or at 9:32 a.m.)

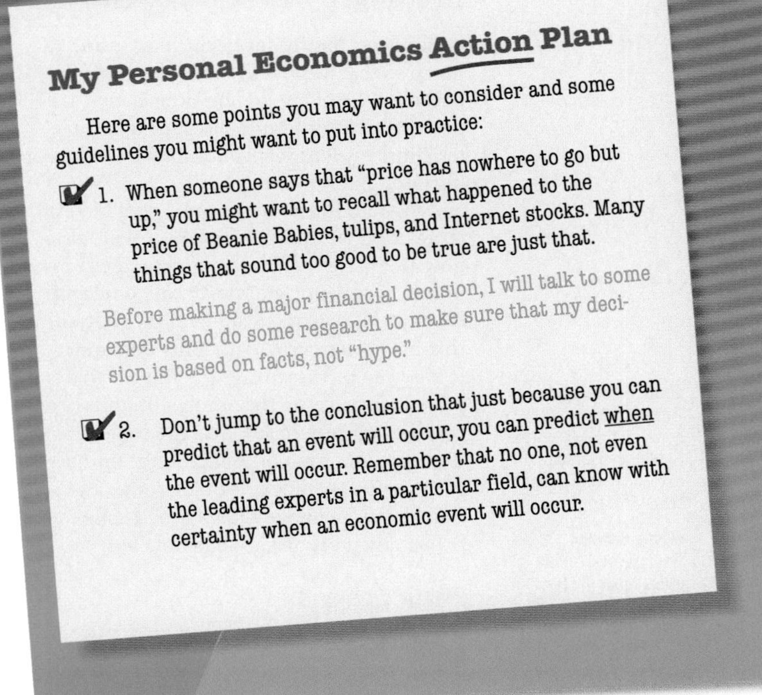

My Personal Economics Action Plan

Here are some points you may want to consider and some guidelines you might want to put into practice:

1. When someone says that "price has nowhere to go but up," you might want to recall what happened to the price of Beanie Babies, tulips, and Internet stocks. Many things that sound too good to be true are just that.

   Before making a major financial decision, I will talk to some experts and do some research to make sure that my decision is based on facts, not "hype."

2. Don't jump to the conclusion that just because you can predict that an event will occur, you can predict when the event will occur. Remember that no one, not even the leading experts in a particular field, can know with certainty when an economic event will occur.

Teaching with Visuals

Economists can research the housing market to determine how big the demand for real estate is, when supply is likely to equal or exceed demand, and what other factors might affect prices, and make predictions based on their findings. However, even leading economists cannot be certain that their predictions are correct.

Discussion Starter

To help students understand that it is harder to predict the timing of an event than it is to predict the event, suggest that they consider the prices of automobiles. Ask students: Do you think automobile sticker prices will go up or down in the future? On what is your opinion based? On a scale of 1 to 10, with 1 standing for "Very Unsure" and 10 standing for "Very Sure," how certain are you of your answer? List students' ratings and calculate the class average.

Then ask students: When do you think prices will change? On what do you base this opinion? How sure are you of this answer? Again list their ratings and calculate the class average.

Compare the average ratings of certainty for each opinion. Your class as a whole should be more sure of its response to the first question; if it is not, point out that the students' responses are an anomaly, and try to find out why they didn't follow the usual pattern.

My Personal Economics Action Plan Instruct students to identify the next major financial decision they might make. Tell them to describe in writing what research they need to do to gather facts, and what experts could give them information and advice concerning the decision. Encourage them to carry out the research and make at least a tentative decision. Invite students to report their plans and decisions back to the class, if they feel comfortable doing so.

SECTION 3

Teacher Support

Focus and Motivate

Section Objectives

After completing this section, students will be able to
- describe elasticity of demand;
- compute elasticity of demand;
- distinguish between elastic, inelastic, and unit-elastic demand;
- list the factors that can change the elasticity of demand; and
- describe the relationship between an increase in price for a good, and higher total revenue.

Economics Around the Clock

Kickoff Activity

Have students reread the 11:35 P.M. scenario in Economics Around the Clock (page 89) and then write their answers to the question that accompanies it.

Invite students to share their answers with the class. Look for responses indicating that the hotel is attempting to increase its value to Evan, so that he might be willing to pay a higher price for a room.

Activating Prior Knowledge

Instruct students to write two or three sentences explaining the differences in meaning between the terms *elastic* and *inelastic,* and guessing at the meanings of the terms *elastic demand, inelastic demand,* and *unit-elastic demand.*

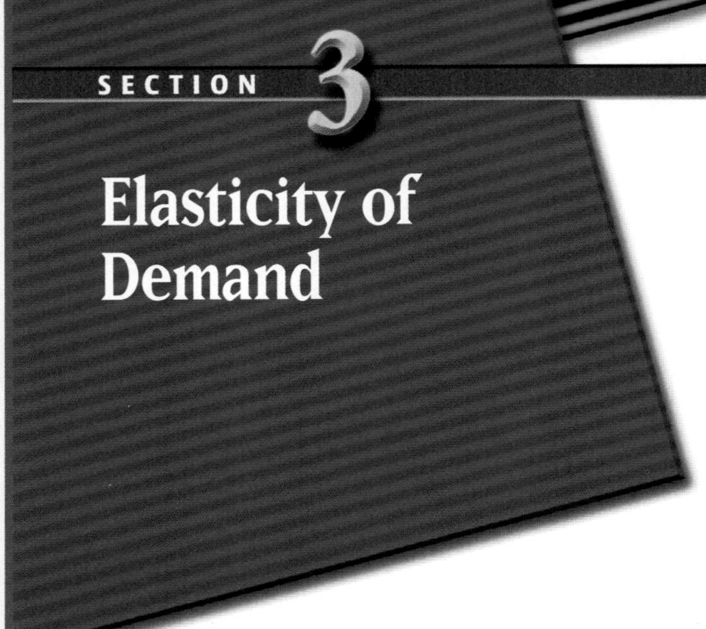

SECTION 3

Elasticity of Demand

Focus Questions
- What is elasticity of demand?
- How do we compute elasticity of demand?
- What does it mean to say that the demand for a good is elastic? Inelastic? Unit elastic?
- What factors can change the elasticity of demand?
- Does an increase in price for a good necessarily bring about a higher total revenue?

Key Terms
elasticity of demand
elastic demand
inelastic demand
unit-elastic demand

What Is Elasticity of Demand?

Suppose Jimmy loves chewing gum, so much so that he buys as many as four or five packs a week. One day he notices that the price of his favorite gum has gone up a quarter. Jimmy will probably now buy less chewing gum. But *how much* less?

This question about Jimmy's gum buying is the kind of question that you will learn how to answer as you study our next economic concept, **elasticity of demand**. Elasticity of demand deals with the relationship between price and quantity demanded. It is a way of measuring the impact that a price change has on the number of units of a good people buy. In some cases a small price change causes a major change in the number of units of a good people buy. In other cases, a small price change causes little change in how many units of a good people buy.

elasticity of demand
The relationship between the percentage change in quantity demanded and the percentage change in price.

elastic demand
The type of demand that exists when the percentage change in quantity demanded is greater than the percentage change in price.

Elastic Demand

Economists have created a way to measure these relationships between price and quantity demanded. They compare the percentage change in quantity demanded of a good to the percentage change in the price of that good. In mathematical terms, here is what elasticity of demand looks like:

$$\text{Elasticity of demand} = \frac{\text{Percentage change in quantity demanded}}{\text{Percentage change in price}}$$

In the equation, the numerator is *percentage change in quantity demanded*, and the denominator is *percentage change in price.* **Elastic demand** exists when the quantity demanded (the numerator) changes by a greater percentage than price (the denominator). For example, suppose the quantity demanded of lightbulbs falls by 15 percent as the price of lightbulbs increases by 10 percent. An economist would say that because the numerator (15%) is greater than the denominator (10%), the demand for lightbulbs is *elastic.* Another way that an economist might say it is that elasticity of demand is greater than 1, because if you divide 15 percent by 10 percent, you get 1.5, which is greater than 1.

Internet Research

Instruct students to use the Internet to find products for which they think there is high demand, low demand, elastic demand, and inelastic demand—one product for each category. Tell them to write brief descriptions of each product, reasons why each product has this type of demand, and what factors might change the demand for each product. Have students create pictures, charts, and graphs showing the results of their research.

Inelastic Demand

Inelastic demand exists when the quantity demanded changes by a smaller percentage than price—that is, when the numerator changes by less than the denominator. Suppose the quantity demanded of salt falls by 5 percent as the price of salt rises by 10 percent. In this case the numerator (5%) is less than the denominator (10%), so the demand for salt is inelastic. An economist could say that elasticity of demand is less than 1 (if you divide 5% by 10% you get 0.5, which is less than 1).

Unit-Elastic Demand

Finally, **unit-elastic demand** exists when the quantity demanded changes by the same percentage as price—that is, when the numerator changes by the same percentage as the denominator. For example, suppose the quantity demanded of picture frames decreases by 10 percent as the price of picture frames rises by 10 percent. The numerator (10%) is equal to the denominator (10%), so the demand for picture frames is unit elastic. According to an economist, elasticity of demand would be equal to 1 (10% divided by 10% equals 1).

When elasticity of demand is greater than 1, we say that demand is elastic. When it is less than 1, we say that demand is inelastic. And finally, when it is equal to 1, we say that demand is unit-elastic. See Exhibit 4-5.

EXHIBIT 4-5 Elasticity of Demand

If demand is . . .	That means . . .
Elastic	Quantity demanded changes by a larger percentage than price. For example, if price rises by 10 percent, quantity demanded falls by, say, 15 percent.
Inelastic	Quantity demanded changes by a smaller percentage than price. For example, if price rises by 10 percent, quantity demanded falls by, say, 5 percent.
Unit-elastic	Quantity demanded changes by the same percentage as price. For example, if price rises by 10 percent, quantity demanded falls by 10 percent.

Elastic or Inelastic?

So, you're probably wondering what products are elastic and which ones are inelastic? One economics study identified oysters, restaurant meals, and automobiles as goods with elastic demand. For these goods, price changes have a strong impact on how much customers will buy. In the same study, coffee, gasoline (for your car), physicians' services, and legal services were identified as goods with inelastic demand. For these products a change in price had less impact on how much customers will buy.

EXAMPLE: A university raises its tuition by 10 percent. As a result, the number of students applying to the university falls by 2 percent. In this situation, we would say that the demand for education at this particular university is inelastic. Why? Because the percentage change in quantity demanded (2%) is less than the percentage change in price (10%). ♦

What Determines Elasticity of Demand?

The demand for some goods (coffee, gasoline at the local gas station, physicians' services) is inelastic, while the demand for other goods (oysters, restaurant meals, and cars) is elastic. Why is the demand for some goods inelastic, while the demand for other goods is elastic? Four factors affect the elasticity of demand: (1) the number of substitutes available, (2) whether something is a luxury or a necessity, (3) the percentage of income spent on the good, and (4) time.

Number of Substitutes

Let's look at two goods: heart medicine and soft drinks. Heart medicine has relatively few substitutes; many people must have it to stay well. Even if the price of heart medicine went up by 50, 100, or 150 percent, the quantity that people demanded probably would not fall by much. Is the demand for heart medicine more likely to be elastic or inelastic? The answer is inelastic. Do you see the reasoning here? The fewer substitutes for a good, the less likely the quantity demanded will change much if the price rises.

inelastic demand
The type of demand that exists when the percentage change in quantity demanded is less than the percentage change in price.

unit-elastic demand
The type of demand that exists when the percentage change in quantity demanded is the same as the percentage change in price.

Teach

Clarifying Terms

After students read the definitions of the terms *elasticity of demand*, *elastic demand*, *inelastic demand*, and *unit-elastic demand* on pages 102–103, tell them to restate the definitions in their own words. Students may think the terms refer just to the pliability of demand. If that is the case, emphasize that the terms refer to relationships between quantity demanded and price.

Reinforcement Activity

Tell students to list five goods on which they spend a small percentage of their money. Then tell them to list five goods on which they spend a large percentage of their income. Afterward ask them what the percentage of income they spend on each of these goods has to do with the elasticity of their demand for that good. For example, students may say that since they spend a very small amount of money on pencils, their demand for pencils is relatively inelastic.

Cross-Curricular Activity

In the material in this section on the elasticity of demand, math plays a dominant role. You might want to review some of the equations with students. If students have trouble with the math involved, especially with the percentages, walk them through the equations using a demand graph that you have drawn on the board. Show, through markings on the graph, the changes that create the percentage changes in quantity demanded and price. Create percentages that are easy to see right away (10%, 50%, etc.). Then have students tell you whether each ratio is elastic, inelastic, or unit-elastic.

ANSWERS TO ECONOMIC THINKING

As China's demand for oil rises, the world demand for oil will also rise. China's rising demand for oil will increase the price you pay for gasoline at the pump.

Reinforcement Activity

Instruct students to clip or copy, from magazines and newspapers, pictures of products that they believe are luxuries. Then have them do the same thing for necessities. Create a bulletin board display with the items provided by students.

Demand for Oil

In recent years, China's demand for oil has been rising. Two reasons: First, about 2.5 million cars are added to China's roads every year. Second, the industrial demand for oil has been rising because China's economy has been rapidly growing.

ECONOMIC THINKING **As China's demand for oil rises, what will happen to the world demand for oil? Although you won't study the topic of *price* until a later chapter, what do you think China's rising demand for oil will do to the price for gasoline you pay at the pump?**

In contrast, a particular soft drink (say Sprite) has many substitutes (Fresca, Mountain Dew, etc.). Therefore, if the price of Sprite rises, we would expect the quanity demanded to fall greatly, because people have many other soft drinks they can choose. Is the demand for a particular soft drink more likely to be elastic or inelastic? The answer is elastic, because the more substitutes there are for a good, the more likely people will buy a lot fewer of the item if the price rises.

Luxuries Versus Necessities

Luxury goods (luxuries) are goods that people feel they do not need to survive. For example, a $70,000 car would be a luxury good for most people. Necessary goods (necessities), in contrast, are goods that people feel they need to survive. Heart medicine may be a necessity for some people. Food is a necessity for everyone.

Generally speaking, if the price of a necessity, such as food, increases, people cannot cut back much on the quantity demanded. (They need a certain amount of food to live.) However, if the price of a luxury good increases, people are more able to cut back on the quantity demanded. Between the two types of goods, luxuries and necessities, the demand for luxuries tends to be elastic; the demand for necessities is more likely to be inelastic.

Percentage of Income Spent on the Good

Claire has a monthly income of $2,000. Of this amount, she spends $10 on magazines and $400 on dinners at restaurants. In percentage terms, she spends one-half of 1 percent of her monthly income on magazines and 20 percent of her monthly income on dinners at restaurants. Suppose the price of magazines and the price of dinners at restaurants both double. What will Claire be more likely to cut back on, the number of magazines she buys or the number of dinners at restaurants?

She will probably reduce the number of dinners at restaurants, don't you think? Claire will feel this price change more strongly because it affects a larger percentage of her income. She may shrug off a doubling in the price of magazines, on which she spends only one-half of 1 percent of her income, but she is less likely to shrug off a doubling in the price of dinners at restaurants, on which she spends 20 percent.

In short, buyers are more responsive to price changes for goods on which they spend a larger percentage of their income. In these cases, the demand is likely to be elastic. Whereas, the demand for goods on which consumers spend a small percentage of their income is more likely to be inelastic.

Time

As time passes, buyers have greater opportunities to change quantity demanded in response to a price change. If the price of electricity went up today and you knew about it, you probably would not change your consumption of electricity much today. By three months from today, though, you would probably have changed it more. As time passes, you have more chances to change your consumption by finding substitutes (natural gas), changing your lifestyle (buying more blankets and turning down the thermostat at night), and similar actions. The less time you have to respond to a price change in a good, the more likely it is that your demand for that good is going to be inelastic.

Background Information: Elasticity and Total Revenue

The relationship between elasticity and total revenue is a basic formulator of price in a free enterprise economy. The law of demand—which specifies that price and quantity demanded move in opposite directions—implicitly assumes that when price changes, *nothing else changes.* In Latin, the term used to denote that nothing else changes is *ceteris paribus* (pronounced "set eris pair abis"). As long as every other part of the equation stays the same *(ceteris paribus)*, by knowing the nature of this relationship, a seller can learn the best price at which to sell the goods or services. So when the law of demand states that as the price of an item falls, people buy more of that item, it is implicitly assuming that nothing else in the world changes.

An Important Relationship Between Elasticity and Total Revenue

Demand is elastic for one good and inelastic for another good. Does it matter? As you just read, it can matter to you as an individual, and it definitely matters to the sellers of goods. In particular, it matters to a seller's total revenue (money sellers receive for selling their goods). To see how elasticity of demand relates to a business's total revenue, let's consider four cases in detail. The cases look at both elastic and inelastic goods and what happens to each when the price rises, and when the price falls.

- **Case 1: Elastic Demand and a Price Increase**
  Javier currently sells 100 basketballs a week at a price of $20 each. His total revenue (price × quanity) per week is $2,000. Suppose Javier raises the price of his basketballs to $22 each, a 10 percent increase in price. As a result, the quantity demanded falls from 100 to 75, a 25 percent reduction. The demand is elastic because the change in quantity demanded (25%) is greater than the change in price (10%). What happened to Javier's total revenue at the new price and quantity demanded? It is $1,650: the new price ($22) multiplied by the number of basketballs sold (75).
  Notice that if demand is elastic, a price increase will lead to a decline in total revenue. Even though he raised the price, Javier's total revenue went down, from $2,000 to $1,650. An important lesson here is that an increase in price does not always bring about an increase in total revenue.

  Elastic demand + Price increase = Total revenue decrease

- **Case 2: Elastic Demand and a Price Decrease**
  In case 2, as in case 1, demand is elastic. This time, however, Javier lowers the price of his basketballs from $20 to $18, a 10 percent reduction in price. We know that if price falls, quantity demanded will rise. Also, if demand is elastic, the percentage change in quantity demanded is greater than the percentage change in price. Suppose quantity demanded rises from 100 to 130, a 30 percent increase. Total revenue at the new, lower price ($18) and higher quantity demanded (130) is $2,340. Thus, if demand is elastic and price is decreased, total revenue will increase.

  Elastic demand + Price decrease = Total revenue increase

- **Case 3: Inelastic Demand and a Price Increase**
  Now let's assume that the demand for basketballs is inelastic, rather than elastic, as it was in cases 1 and 2. Suppose Javier raises the price of his basketballs to $22 each, a 10 percent increase in price. If demand is inelastic, the percentage change in quantity demanded must fall by less than the percentage rise in price. Suppose the quantity demanded falls from 100 to 95, a 5 percent reduction.
  Javier's total revenue at the new price and quantity demanded is $2,090, which

The Bureau of Labor Statistics (BLS) is an agency within the U.S. Department of Labor. The agency collects data on prices in the economy. To see whether consumer prices are rising, falling, or remaining constant, go to the BLS Web site at www.emcp.net/prices. Once there, click on "Inflation & Consumer Spending." Next, scroll down the page until you see "Consumer Price Index (CPI)." The CPI is a measure of the prices of the goods and services purchased by consumers. Have prices risen, fallen, or remained constant in the last month reported? If prices have risen or fallen, by what percentage have they risen or fallen?

Instruct students to each find an advertisement for a sales event in the newspaper and to write a short summary of the advertisement. Then divide the class into groups of three or four and direct each group to decide how the concept of *ceteris paribus* is reflected in the sales events examined by the group members.

Answers will vary depending on the consumer price index information that students find.

Discussion Starter

Have students reread the case studies concerning the relationship between elasticity and total revenue, on pages 105–107. Call on student volunteers to explain each case study in turn. You might invite volunteers to act out the case studies and graph them on the board.

After reading and discussing "An Important Relationship Between Elasticity and Total Revenue," you may want to remind students of the 10:41 A.M. scenario in Economics Around the Clock (page 89) and to discuss their answers to its question.

Students should note that according to the law of demand, the higher the price charged for a good, the fewer units of that good purchased. Higher taxes on cigarettes will raise the price paid for cigarettes, so teens will buy fewer cigarettes. Whether this reduces the amount of money teens spend on cigarettes depends on whether their demand for cigarettes is elastic or inelastic. If inelastic, then a higher price means greater total revenue (or more spent on cigarettes); if elastic, then a higher price means lower total revenue (or less spent on cigarettes).

Teaching with Visuals

After students study Exhibit 4-6 on page 107, instruct them to create their own visuals to explain the relationship between elasticity of demand and total revenue. Suggest that they think of things that are elastic or stretchy, and incorporate them into the illustration. Urge them to be creative—they might come up with cartoon characters or three-dimensional models or a Flash presentation, for example.

Economics in the Real World

After students read this feature, ask them to describe personal experiences in which they have attended a rock concert. Ask whether they agree that rock stars need to know about elasticity of demand, and to explain their responses.

Teaching with Visuals

Ask if students know of any direct connection between economics and Mick Jagger, lead singer for the Rolling Stones. Savvy students might know that he attended the London School of Economics.

ANSWERS TO THINK ABOUT IT **1.** Answers will vary. Understanding elasticity of demand would be important if you wanted to increase total revenue in your business.
2. Answers will vary. Wants are unlimited and resources are limited. People must choose which wants to satisfy.

Application Activity

After reading and discussing Section 3, you may want to assign the Section Activity and the Demand Practice Activity in the *Applying the Principles Workbook.*

Assess

Quick Quiz

The following true-or-false quiz will help you assess student understanding of the material covered in this section.

1. Demand is always inelastic. (False)
2. Unit-elastic demand exists when the quantity demanded is less than the percentage change in price. (False)
3. Time affects the elasticity of demand. (True)
4. The demand for necessities is likely to be inelastic. (True)
5. It doesn't matter if demand is elastic, inelastic, or unit-elastic. (False)

Economics in the Real World

Who's Rockin' with "Elasticity of Demand"?

Rock stars need to know more than how to write and play music. They also need to know about *elasticity of demand*. In fact, a large part of their earnings will depend on whether they know about elasticity of demand.

Suppose you are a rock star. You write songs, record them, and spend 150 days each year on the road performing. Let's say that tonight you will be performing in Chicago. The auditorium there seats 30,000 people. Do you earn more income if all 30,000 seats are sold or if only 20,000 seats are sold?

This question seems a little silly. It seems obvious that you would be better off if you sold more tickets than fewer tickets. Certainly 30,000 would be better than 20,000, wouldn't it?

> "You can't always get what you want
> But if you try sometimes
> You just might find
> You'll get what you need"
> —The Rolling Stones

The obvious answer here is not necessarily correct. The answer really depends on an understanding of elasticity of demand. Let's say that to sell all 30,000 seats, the price per ticket has to be $30. At this ticket price, total revenue, which is the number of tickets sold times the price per ticket, is $900,000.

If the demand for your Chicago performance is inelastic, a higher ticket price will actually raise total revenue. (Remember: Inelastic demand + Price increase = Increase in total revenue.) Suppose you raise the ticket price to $50. At this higher price you will not sell as many tickets as you sold when the price was $30 per ticket. Let's say you sell only 20,000 tickets. You have not "sold out" the auditorium, but it doesn't matter. At a price of $50 per ticket and 20,000 seats sold, total revenue is $1 million—or $100,000 more than it was when you sold out the auditorium.*

Is a sold-out auditorium, then, better than an auditorium that is not sold out? Usually you would think so, but an understanding of elasticity of demand informs us that it may be better to sell fewer tickets at a higher price than to sell more tickets at a lower price. Who would have thought it?

THINK ABOUT IT 1. You may not become a rock star, but you may run your own business someday. Explain why it will be important for you to understand elasticity of demand.

2. What basic economic concept that you learned in Chapter 1 is expressed by the Rolling Stones' lyrics on this page?

*This description assumes that only one ticket price, $30 or $50, can be charged. If more than one ticket price can be charged, then some seats may be sold for $30, some for $40, some for $50, and so on.

is the new price ($22) multiplied by the number of basketballs sold (95). Notice that if demand is inelastic, a price increase will lead to an increase in total revenue. Javier's total revenue went from $2,000 to $2,090 when he increased the price of basketballs from $20 to $22.

Inelastic demand + Price increase = Total revenue increase

Differentiating Instruction

Enrichment and Extension

Present this puzzle: A music group is going to play at an auditorium Friday night. The owner of the auditorium must sell each ticket for the same price. Is the owner necessarily better off if the entire auditorium is filled? What does this situation have to do with elasticity? *(Answer:* The owner is not necessarily better off if she fills the auditorium. She will probably have to sell tickets for a lower price, and the total revenue may then be lower. Suppose the auditorium holds 10,000 people and the owner can sell 10,000 tickets at $10 each, for a total revenue of $100,000. Also suppose that if she increases ticket prices to $20 each, she can sell 7,500 tickets, for a total revenue of $150,000.)

- **Case 4: Inelastic Demand and a Price Decrease**
  Demand is again inelastic, but Javier now lowers the price of his basketballs from \$20 to \$18, a 10 percent reduction in price. We know that if demand is inelastic, the percentage change in quantity demanded is less than the percentage change in price. Suppose quantity demanded rises from 100 to 105, a 5 percent increase. Total revenue at the new, lower price (\$18) and higher quantity demanded (105) is \$1,890. Thus, if demand is inelastic and price decreases, total revenue will decrease.

Inelastic demand + Price decrease = Total revenue decrease

See Exhibit 4-6 for a summary of the four types of relationships between elasticity and revenue.

A Student Asks

QUESTION: *Most people seem to think that if a seller raises the price, the seller's total revenue will automatically rise. But it isn't always true, is it?*

ANSWER: *No, it isn't always true. If demand is inelastic (case 3), then a higher price will lead to a higher total revenue, but if demand is elastic (case 1), a higher price will lead to a lower total revenue.*

EXHIBIT 4-6 Relationship of Elasticity of Demand to Total Revenue

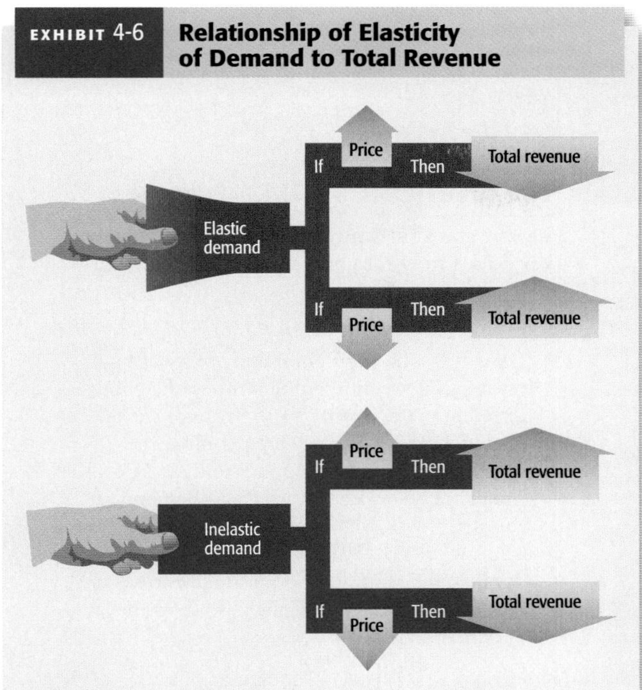

▲ If demand is elastic, price and total revenue move in opposite directions: as price goes up, total revenue goes down, and as price goes down, total revenue goes up. If demand is inelastic, price and total revenue move in the same direction: as price goes up, total revenue goes up, and as price goes down, total revenue goes down.

SECTION 3 ASSESSMENT

Defining Terms

1. Define:
   a. elasticity of demand
   b. unit-elastic demand
   c. inelastic demand
   d. elastic demand

Reviewing Facts and Concepts

2. Does an increase in price necessarily bring about a higher total revenue?
3. The price of a good rises from \$4 to\$4.50, and as a result, total revenue falls from \$400 to \$350. Is the demand for the good elastic, inelastic, or unit-elastic?
4. Good A has 10 substitutes, and good B has 20 substitutes. The demand is more likely to be elastic for which good? Explain your answer.

Critical Thinking

5. How is the law of demand (a) similar to and (b) different from elasticity of demand?

Applying Economic Concepts

6. A hotel chain advertises its hotels as "The Best Hotels You Can Find Anywhere." Does this ad have anything to do with elasticity of demand? If so, what?

Assessment Book

You will find a quiz for this section in the *Assessment Book.*

Reteaching Activity

Direct pairs of students to create their own versions of Exhibit 4-5. The pairs may use the same descriptions on their charts, but they should create examples of specific goods or services, illustrating elastic, inelastic, and unit-elastic demand.

Guided Reading

For further reteaching of the key concepts in this section, assign the Outlining Activity and the Just the Facts Handout from the *Guided Reading and Study Guide.*

SECTION 3 ASSESSMENT ANSWERS

Defining Terms

1. a. elasticity of demand: the relationship between the percentage change in quantity demanded and the percentage change in price; **b. unit-elastic demand:** the type of demand that exists when quantity demanded changes by the same percentage as price; **c. inelastic demand:** the type of demand that exists when quantity demanded changes by a smaller percentage than price; **d. elastic demand:** the type of demand that exists when quantity demanded changes by a larger percentage than price.

Reviewing Facts and Concepts

2. No. The effect on total revenue depends on whether the demand is elastic, inelastic, or unit-elastic.
3. Elastic.
4. The demand for good B is more likely to be elastic. The more substitutes a good has, the higher the likelihood that the quantity demanded of the good will fall off greatly as price rises. And the higher the likelihood that the quantity demanded will fall off greatly, the higher the likelihood that the percentage change in quantity demanded will be greater than the percentage change in price (which is the definition of *elastic demand*).

Critical Thinking

5. (a) The law of demand and the elasticity of demand deal with the same two variables—price and quantity demanded. (b) The law of demand specifies the *direction* that quantity demanded changes as price changes; for example, as price goes up, quantity demanded goes down. The elasticity of demand deals with the *amount* that quantity demanded changes as price changes; for example, if demand is elastic and the price rises by 10%, quantity demanded might fall by 20%.

Applying Economic Concepts

6. When a firm advertises its hotels as "the best," it is trying to get across the message that there are few substitutes for its hotels. After all, there can be only one "best."

CHAPTER 4 Assessment Answers

Economics Vocabulary

1. market; **2.** inferior; **3.** quantity demanded; **4.** law of demand; **5.** law of diminishing marginal utility; **6.** inelastic; **7.** law of demand; **8.** normal; **9.** substitutes; **10.** unit-elastic.

Understanding the Main Ideas

1. The demand for margarine rises.
2. a. The demand curve for apples shifts to the right. **b.** The demand curve for apples shifts to the right. **c.** The demand curve for apples shifts to the right.
3. Students should disagree. If demand is elastic, an increase in price will lower total revenue.
4. a. elastic; **b.** elastic; **c.** unit-elastic.
5. a. Total revenue falls. **b.** Total revenue falls. **c.** Total revenue rises. **d.** Total revenue rises.

Doing the Math

1. 0.583 (*calculation:* $0.07 \div 0.12 = 0.583$).
2. $1,045 (*calculation:* $9.50 × 110 = $1,045).

Working with Graphs and Charts

1. an increase in demand, or a rightward shift in the demand curve.
2. a decrease in demand, or a leftward shift in the demand curve.
3. a movement along a demand curve, or a decrease in quantity demanded.
4. (a) elastic; (b) unit-elastic; (c) inelastic.

Solving Economic Problems

1. It is better to buy stock in a company that produces a normal good. If income is expected to rise, then the demand for a normal good will rise. It is better to buy stock in a company that you expect will have more sales than in one that you expect will have fewer or the same sales (which would be the case with an inferior good or a neutral good, respectively).

Chapter Summary

Be sure you know and remember the following key points from the chapter sections.

Section 1

- Demand is the willingness and ability of buyers to purchase different quantities of a good at different prices during a specific time period.
- A market is any place where people come together to buy and sell goods and services. There are two sides to a market—demand and supply.
- The law of demand says that price and quantity demanded move in opposite directions.
- A demand curve graphically represents the law of demand.

Section 2

- An increase in demand for a good causes the demand curve to shift to the right.
- A decrease in demand causes a leftward shift in the demand curve.
- A change in demand may be caused by changes in income, people's preferences, price of related goods, number of buyers, and future price expectations.
- A change in price is what causes *quantity demanded* to change.

Section 3

- Elasticity of demand deals with the relationship between price and quantity demanded.
- Demand is elastic when quantity demanded changes by a greater percentage than price.
- Demand is inelastic when quantity demanded changes by a smaller percentage than price.
- Elasticity of demand is affected by available substitutes, whether the good is a luxury or necessity, percentage of income spent on the good, and time.

Economics Vocabulary

To reinforce your knowledge of the key terms in this chapter, fill in the following blanks on a separate piece of paper with the appropriate word or phrase.

1. A(n) _______ is any place where people come together to buy and sell goods or services.
2. If, as income rises, demand for a good falls, then that good is a(n) _______ good.
3. According to the law of demand, as the price of a good rises, the _______ of the good falls.
4. According to the _______, price and quantity demanded are inversely related.
5. According to the _______, as a person consumes additional units of a good, eventually the utility gained from each additional unit of the good decreases.
6. Demand is _______ if the percentage change in quantity demanded is less than the percentage change in price.
7. A downward-sloping demand curve is the graphic representation of the _______.
8. For a(n) _______ good, the demand increases as income rises and falls as income falls.
9. If, as the price of good X rises, the demand for Y increases, then X and Y are _______.
10. When demand is _______, the percentage change in quantity demanded is the same as the percentage change in price.

Understanding the Main Ideas

Write answers to the following questions to review the main ideas in this chapter.

1. Margarine and butter are substitutes. What happens to the demand for margarine as the price of butter rises?
2. Explain what happens to the demand curve for apples as a consequence of each of the following.
   a. More people begin to prefer apples to oranges.
   b. The price of peaches rises (peaches are a substitute for apples).
   c. People's income rises (apples are a normal good).

3. "Sellers always prefer higher to lower prices." Do you agree or disagree? Explain your answer.
4. In each of the following, identify whether the demand is elastic, inelastic, or unit-elastic.
   a. The price of apples rises 10 percent as the quantity demanded of apples falls 20 percent.
   b. The price of cars falls 5 percent as the quantity demanded of cars rises 10 percent.
   c. The price of computers falls 10 percent as the quantity demanded of computers rises 10 percent.
5. State whether total revenue rises or falls in each of the following situations.
   a. Demand is elastic and price increases.
   b. Demand is inelastic and price decreases.
   c. Demand is elastic and price decreases.
   d. Demand is inelastic and price increases.

Doing the Math

Do the calculations necessary to solve the following problems.

1. If the percentage change in price is 12 percent and the percentage change in quantity demanded is 7 percent, what is the elasticity of demand equal to?
2. The price falls from $10 to $9.50, and the quantity demanded rises from 100 units to 110 units. What does total revenue equal at the lower price?

Working with Graphs and Charts

Use Exhibit 4-7 to answer questions 1 through 3. (P = Price and Q_d = Quantity demanded)

EXHIBIT 4-7

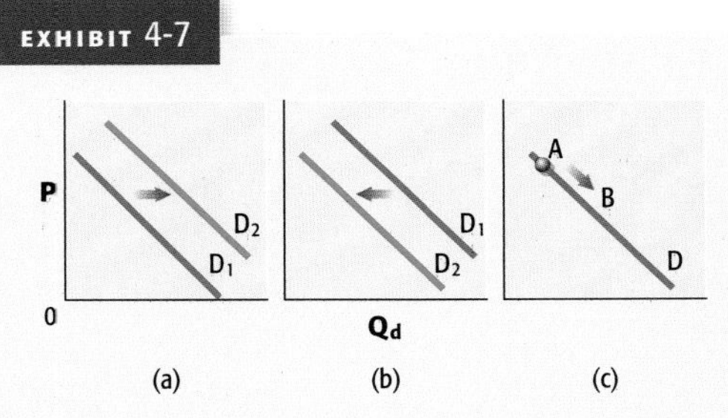

1. What does Exhibit 4-7(a) represent?
2. What does Exhibit 4-7(b) represent?
3. What does Exhibit 4-7(c) represent?

EXHIBIT 4-8

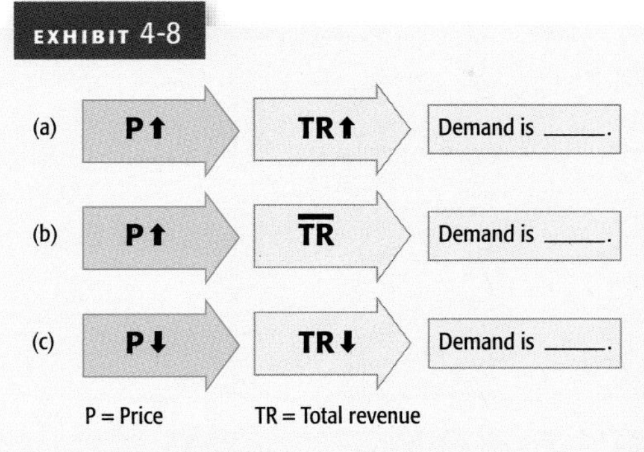

4. In Exhibit 4-8, a downward-pointing arrow (↓) means a decrease, an upward-pointing arrow (↑) means an increase, and a bar (—) over a variable means the variable remains constant (unchanged). Fill in the blanks for parts (a) through (c).

Solving Economic Problems

Use your thinking skills and the information you learned in this chapter to find a solution to the following problem.

1. **Application.** Income in the economy is expected to grow over the next few years. You are thinking about buying stock in a company. Is it better to buy stock in a company that produces a normal, inferior, or neutral good? Explain your answer.

ONLINE emcp.com Practice Tests and Study Guide

Go to www.emcp.net/economics and choose *Economics: New Ways of Thinking*, Chapter 4, if you need more help in preparing for the chapter test.

Chapter 4 Demand 109

Chapter 5 Planning Guide

SECTION ORGANIZER

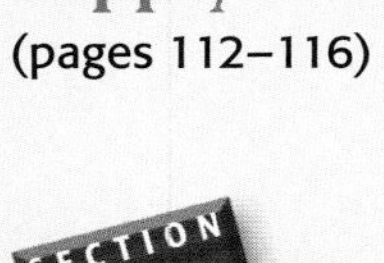

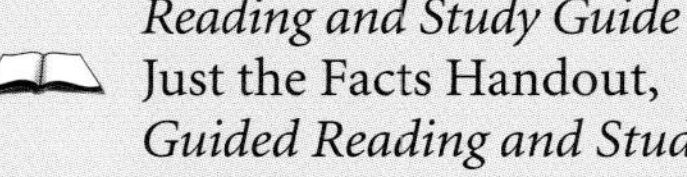

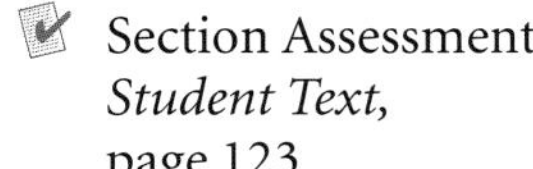

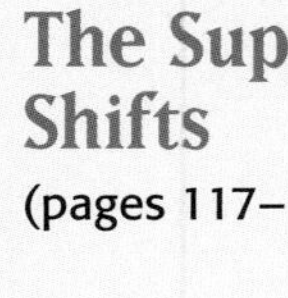

Section	Learning Objectives	Reproducible Worksheets and Handouts	Assessment
SECTION 1 **Understanding Supply** (pages 112–116)	► Explain the law of supply. ► Describe supply curves. ► Describe the difference between a supply schedule and a supply curve.	Section 1 Activity, *Applying the Principles Workbook* Outlining Activity, *Guided Reading and Study Guide* Just the Facts Handout, *Guided Reading and Study Guide*	Section Assessment, *Student Text,* page 116 Quick Quiz, *Annotated Teacher's Edition,* page 115 Section Quiz, *Assessment Book*
SECTION 2 **The Supply Curve Shifts** (pages 117–123)	► Explain the meaning of a supply curve's shifting to the right. ► Explain the meaning of a supply curve's shifting to the left. ► Identify factors that can change supply. ► Identify factors that can change quantity supplied.	Section 2 Activity, *Applying the Principles Workbook* Supply Practice Activity, *Applying the Principles Workbook* Outlining Activity, *Guided Reading and Study Guide* Just the Facts Handout, *Guided Reading and Study Guide*	Section Assessment, *Student Text,* page 123 Quick Quiz, *Annotated Teacher's Edition,* pages 122–123 Section Quiz, *Assessment Book*

CHAPTER AND PROGRAM RESOURCES

Reproducible Chapter Resources and Assessment Materials

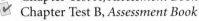

 Graphic Organizer Activity, *Guided Reading and Study Guide*
 Vocabulary Activity, *Guided Reading and Study Guide*
 Working with Graphs and Charts, *Guided Reading and Study Guide*
Practice Test, *Guided Reading and Study Guide*
 Critical Thinking Activity, *Finding Economics*
 Chapter Test A, *Assessment Book*
Chapter Test B, *Assessment Book*

Technology Resources

 *Test Generator CD*
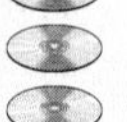 *Spanish Audio Summaries CD*
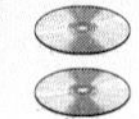 *Marketplace® Audio Lessons CD*
Economic Principles Lectures, Videocassette or DVD

Lesson Planning and Teaching Resources

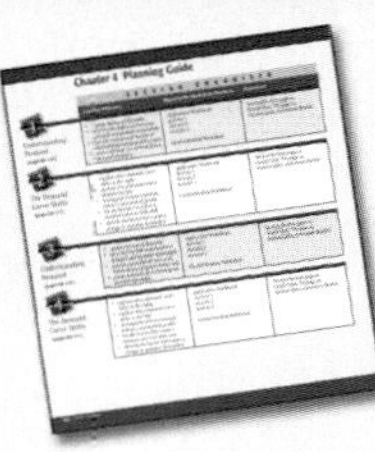

The *Economics: New Ways of Thinking* Teacher Resources include detailed lesson plans for each section in this chapter; the lesson plans are available in print form *(Lesson Plans)* and electronic form. The Teacher Resources also include *Daily Lectures: Overheads and Notes,* which provides prepared overheads and discussion notes covering the key concepts in each section of this chapter.

EMC Publishing Economics Online

Go to Economics Online, at www.emcp.com, for a variety of Internet resources to help you keep your course current and relevant. At Economics Online you will find these items:

- Economics in the News Lessons
- Study Guide Questions
- Practice Tests
- Lesson Plans

Internet Resources

Economics: New Ways of Thinking encourages students to use the Internet to find out more about economics. With the wealth of current, valid information available on Web sites, using the Internet as a research tool is likely to increase your students' interest in and understanding of economics principles and topics. In addition, doing Internet research can help your students form the habit of accessing and using economics information, as well as help them develop investigative skills they will use throughout their educational and professional careers.

To aid your students in achieving these ends, each chapter of *Economics: New Ways of Thinking* includes the addresses of several Web sites at which students will find engaging, relevant information. When students type in the addresses provided, they will immediately arrive at the intended sites. The addresses have been modified so that EMC Publishing can monitor and maintain the proper links—for example, the government site http://stats.bls.gov/ has been changed to www.emcp.net/prices. In the event that the address or content of a site changes or is discontinued, EMC's Internet editors will create a link that redirects students to an address with similar information.

Activities in the *Annotated Teacher's Edition* often suggest that students search the Internet for information. For some activities, you might want to find reputable sites beforehand, and steer students to those sites. For other activities, you might want students to do their own searching, and then check out the sites they have found and discuss why they might be reliable or unreliable.

CHAPTER 5 Overview

Markets have a buying side and a selling side. The previous chapter discussed demand, which is the buying side of the market. This chapter discusses supply, the selling side. The following statements provide brief descriptions of the major concepts covered in each section of this chapter.

Understanding Supply

Section 1 introduces the economic concept of supply. Students will learn the difference between supply and quantity supplied and the differences between a supply schedule and a supply curve.

The Supply Curve Shifts

Section 2 explores the factors that cause a supply curve to shift. These factors include resource prices, technology, taxes, subsidies, quotas, number of sellers, future price, and, in some cases, weather.

CHAPTER 5 Supply

Why It Matters

Just as a coin has two sides, so does a market. A coin has heads and tails; a market has a buying side and a selling side. The previous chapter discussed demand, which is the buying side of the market. This chapter discusses supply, the selling side.

In your life, you will be both buyer and seller. You will buy many goods, and you will also sell some goods. You will certainly end up selling a resource—your labor. In Chapter 4 we learned about you as a buyer. In this chapter, we will have the chance to learn about you as a seller.

These personally autographed guitars are being examined prior to an auction. Before reading this chapter, can you guess how the supply of these guitars will affect the price that people will pay for them in the auction?

Teaching Suggestions from the Author

Students learned about demand in the last chapter, and in this chapter they will learn about supply. I've found that one of the best ways to help students understand supply, the law of supply, and the factors that shift a supply curve is to ask them to put themselves in the shoes of a supplier of some good. Perhaps they produce and sell computers, or they produce and sell furniture. Once they adopt the mindset of a supplier, they have an easier time understanding what will cause them to undertake certain actions.

It s important that students start to explain things in economic terms. They have been studying economics for at least several weeks now, and it is time for them to begin to use the language of economics. If asked

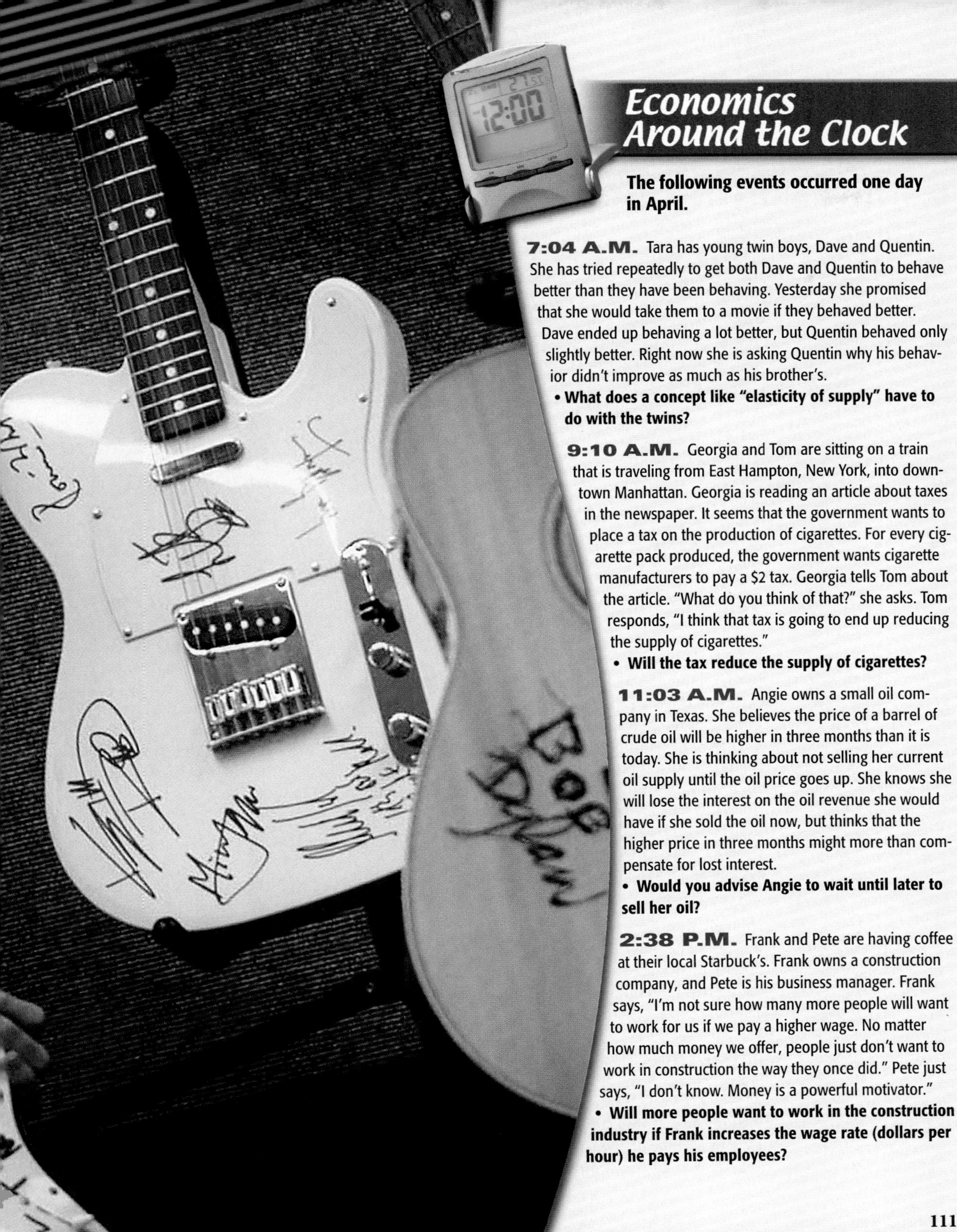

Economics Around the Clock

The following events occurred one day in April.

7:04 A.M. Tara has young twin boys, Dave and Quentin. She has tried repeatedly to get both Dave and Quentin to behave better than they have been behaving. Yesterday she promised that she would take them to a movie if they behaved better. Dave ended up behaving a lot better, but Quentin behaved only slightly better. Right now she is asking Quentin why his behavior didn't improve as much as his brother's.

- **What does a concept like "elasticity of supply" have to do with the twins?**

9:10 A.M. Georgia and Tom are sitting on a train that is traveling from East Hampton, New York, into downtown Manhattan. Georgia is reading an article about taxes in the newspaper. It seems that the government wants to place a tax on the production of cigarettes. For every cigarette pack produced, the government wants cigarette manufacturers to pay a $2 tax. Georgia tells Tom about the article. "What do you think of that?" she asks. Tom responds, "I think that tax is going to end up reducing the supply of cigarettes."

- **Will the tax reduce the supply of cigarettes?**

11:03 A.M. Angie owns a small oil company in Texas. She believes the price of a barrel of crude oil will be higher in three months than it is today. She is thinking about not selling her current oil supply until the oil price goes up. She knows she will lose the interest on the oil revenue she would have if she sold the oil now, but thinks that the higher price in three months might more than compensate for lost interest.

- **Would you advise Angie to wait until later to sell her oil?**

2:38 P.M. Frank and Pete are having coffee at their local Starbuck's. Frank owns a construction company, and Pete is his business manager. Frank says, "I'm not sure how many more people will want to work for us if we pay a higher wage. No matter how much money we offer, people just don't want to work in construction the way they once did." Pete just says, "I don't know. Money is a powerful motivator."

- **Will more people want to work in the construction industry if Frank increases the wage rate (dollars per hour) he pays his employees?**

111

what the law of supply states, a student may answer, "It says that people sell more goods as price goes up." This is, of course, not a wrong answer, but it is phrased slightly differently than an economist would phrase it. An economist would say, "The law of supply holds that as price rises, quantity supplied rises, and as price falls, quantity supplied falls." It is important that students begin to use the phrase "quantity supplied" and to understand the difference between it and "supply."

Introducing the Chapter

The previous chapter discussed one-half of the economic foundation, demand. This chapter will cover the other half, supply. It is impossible to study economics without understanding both of these building blocks of the foundation. While demand deals with the buying side of the market (which students may be more involved in), supply deals with the selling side of the market. Students may initially be unfamiliar with the supply side of the foundation, but once they have learned both sides, the study of economics becomes much easier.

Teaching with Visuals

Students are probably familiar with the word *supply* and may use it to refer to their belongings, for example, a supply of pens and paper. However, in the study of economics, supply takes on a whole new meaning. Economists define supply as the willingness and ability to produce and sell goods. Invite students to predict how the supply of these autographed guitars will affect the prices that people will pay for them in the auction. Many students will correctly predict that a limited supply of autographed guitars will increase the prices of the guitars.

SECTION 1 Teacher Support

Focus and Motivate

Section Objectives

After completing this section, students will be able to
- explain the law of supply;
- describe supply curves; and
- describe the difference between a supply schedule and a supply curve.

Kickoff Activity

Ask students to write the answer to the following question: If the price of a good that a supplier sells goes up, do you think the supplier would want to sell more or fewer units of the good? Explain your answer.

Activating Prior Knowledge

Though the reason why sellers always want to produce and sell more when the price goes up might seem obvious, some students may not understand it. Now that students are familiar with graphs for demand, they may find it easier to comprehend this supply problem if they see a graph illustrating it.

Teach

Discussion Starter

Ask students about factors that might affect a seller's ability and willingness to supply a good or service. These might include resource availability and cost, technology, taxes, quotas, and future price.

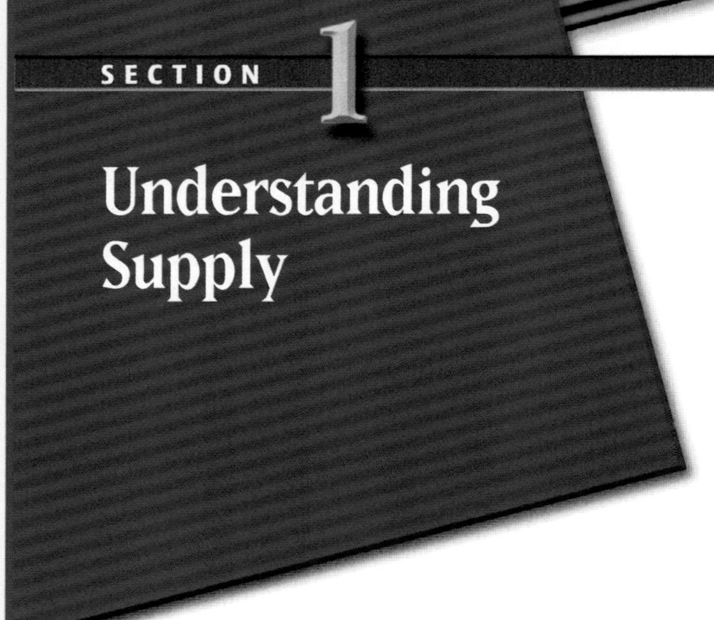

SECTION 1 Understanding Supply

Focus Questions
- What is supply?
- Are all supply curves upward sloping?
- What is the difference between a supply schedule and a supply curve?

Key Terms
supply
law of supply
direct relationship
quantity supplied
supply schedule
supply curve

supply
The willingness and ability of sellers to produce and offer to sell different quantities of a good at different prices during a specific time period.

law of supply
A law stating that as the price of a good increases, the quantity supplied of the good increases, and as the price of a good decreases, the quantity supplied of the good decreases.

direct relationship
A relationship between two factors in which the factors move in the same direction. For example, as one factor rises, the other rises, too.

What Is Supply?

Like the word *demand*, the word **supply** has a specific meaning in economics. It refers to the willingness and ability of sellers to produce and offer to sell different quantities of a good at different prices during a specific time period. The supply of a good or service requires both a supplier's *willingness* and *ability* to produce and sell. Willingness to produce and sell means that the person wants or desires to produce and sell the good. Ability to produce and sell means that the person is capable of producing and selling the good.

EXAMPLE: Jackie is willing to build and sell wooden chairs, but unfortunately she doesn't know *how* to build a chair. In other words, she has the willingness but not the ability. Outcome: Jackie will not supply chairs. ♦

What Does the Law of Supply Say?

Suppose you are a supplier, or producer, of TV sets, and the price of a set rises from $300 to $400. Would you want to supply more or fewer TV sets at the higher price? Most people would say more. If you did, you instinctively understand the **law of supply**, which says that as the price of a good increases, the quantity supplied of the good increases, and as the price of a good decreases, the quantity supplied of the good decreases. In other words, price and quantity supplied move in the same direction. This **direct relationship** can be shown in symbols:

Law of Supply
If P ↑ then Q_s ↑
If P ↓ then Q_s ↓
(where P = price and Q_s = quantity supplied)

When economists use the word *supply*, they mean something different from what they mean when they use the words *quantity supplied*. Again, supply refers to the willingness and ability of sellers to produce and offer to sell different quantities of a good at different prices. For example, a supply of new houses in the housing market means that firms are currently willing and able to produce and offer to sell new houses.

Cooperative Learning

Ask students to form groups of three and brainstorm lists of manufacturing and supply companies in the local area. Have a member of each group contact the public relations department of one of the companies to set up an interview with one of its manufacturing department executives. The class as a whole should prepare questions that relate to how supply is determined. Have the group meet with the executive and, if possible, videotape or audiotape the interview. Have the group write a paragraph or two summarizing the executive's answers and present its findings to the class. Then have the class discuss the differences among their interviews.

Economics in the Real World

Are You Nicer to Nice People?

Business firms supply cars, clothes, food, computers, and much more. The quantity of each good or service they supply depends on price. According to the law of supply, the higher the price, the greater the quantity supplied. In other words, the higher the price of notebook paper, the greater the quantity supplied of notebook paper.

Do you think the law of supply might apply to personal, as well as business, situations? Do you think people might behave differently toward others depending on the reactions to their emotions and behavior? Let's look at some examples of one "product" that people can supply to a greater or lesser degree: niceness.

Wouldn't you say that people can supply different amounts of niceness? Think about your own behavior: You can be very nice to a person, moderately nice, a little nice, or not nice at all. What determines how much niceness you supply to people? (In other words, why are you nicer to some people than to others?)

One factor that may determine how nice you are to someone is how much someone "pays" you to be nice. It may be a stretch, but think of yourself as selling niceness,

in much the same way you might think of yourself selling shoes, T-shirts, corn, or computers. The quantity of each item you supply depends on how much the buyer pays you.

If people want to buy niceness from you, what kind of payment will they offer? A person could come up to you and say, "I will pay you $100 if you will be nice to me," but usually things don't work that way. People buy, and therefore pay for, niceness not with the currency of dollars and cents but with the currency of niceness. In other words, the nicer they are to you, the more they are paying you to be nice to them.

Suppose a person can pay three prices of niceness: the very-nice price (high price), the moderately nice price, and the little-nice price (low price). Now consider two persons, Caprioli and Turen. Caprioli pays you the very-nice price, and Turen pays you the little-nice price. Will you be nicer to Caprioli, who pays you the higher price, or to Turen, who pays you the lower price?

If you answer that you will be nicer to Caprioli, you are admitting that you will supply a greater quantity of niceness to the person who pays you more to be nice. You have found the law of supply in your behavior. Again, you are nicer to those persons who pay you more (in the currency of niceness) to be nice.

THINK ABOUT IT Do you think that when it comes to the quantity supplied of niceness, most people behave in a manner consistent with the law of supply?

Quantity supplied refers to the number of units of a good produced and offered for sale at a specific price. Let's say that a seller will produce and offer to sell five hamburgers when the price is $2 each. Five is the quantity supplied at this price. As you work your way through this chapter, you will see why it is important to know the difference between supply and quantity supplied.

The Law of Supply in Numbers and Pictures

We can represent the law of supply in numbers, just as we did with the law of demand. The law of supply states that as price rises, quantity supplied rises. Exhibit 5-1(a) shows such a relationship. As the price goes up from $1 to $2 to $3 to $4, the quantity supplied goes up from 10 to 20 to 30 to

quantity supplied
The number of units of a good produced and offered for sale at a specific price.

Differentiating Instruction

Visual Learners

There are many different visual representations of supply curves in the supplemental materials for *Economics: New Ways of Thinking.* You might use the *Applying the Principles Workbook* or the *Daily Lectures: Overheads and Notes.* You could also have students practice creating and reading a supply curve using the *Working with Graphs and Charts CD.*

Economics in the Real World

Have students read this feature and make a list of people to whom they are very nice, moderately nice, a little nice, or not nice at all. Ask students why they are nicer to some people than to others. Encourage students to think about whether they are ever paid for being nice in currency other than niceness. For example, students might say that their parents are more likely to award privileges when the students are nice. Point out that students who are nice in order to get more privileges are still obeying the law of supply.

ANSWERS TO THINK ABOUT IT Answers will vary. Invite volunteers to share their experiences with the class.

Reinforcement Activity

Ask students to think about how they treat their friends. Are they nicer to friends who are nicer to them? Tell them to be completely honest. What are some specific acts of niceness that they have recently witnessed?

Cause and Effect

Discuss with students the cause and effect relationship presented in the Economics in the Real World on this page. Use the following questions to generate discussion. If people always respond to "niceness" by being nice, why would anyone not be nice? What are the costs and benefits of being nice to other people?

Clarifying Terms

Ask students to explain the difference between *quantity supplied* and *supply.* Students should recognize that quantity supplied is the number of goods or services actually supplied, and supply is the willingness and ability of sellers to produce and offer goods or services.

Economics in the Real World

After students read this feature, ask them if they were aware that 30-second spots were so lucrative and whether they agree that the chance to earn big profits increases the number of sellers of a good or service.

ANSWERS TO THINK ABOUT IT Answers will vary. Examples are low-fat or low-carbohydrate foods, video-gaming systems, and cellular phones.

Economics Around the Clock

After reading and discussing the law of supply, refer students to the 2:38 P.M. scenario in Economics Around the Clock (page 111) and discuss their answers to the question that accompanies it.

If necessary, remind students that the law of supply states that as the price of a good rises, quantity supplied rises. If the law of supply applies to workers, then as the wage rate offered to workers rises, more workers will offer to work. For example, if the wage rate is $10 an hour, 1,000 individuals might be willing to work, but if the wage rate rises to, say, $20 an hour, then 1,500 individuals might be willing to work.

Prediction Activity

Present students with the following two scenarios. In the first scenario, high school students are not paid to get A's. In the second, they are paid $50 for each A. In which scenario will there be more A's? How does your answer relate to the law of supply?

The answer is that there will be more A's in the second scenario. As the price the student receives for supplying an A rises from $0 to $50, so does the quantity of A's supplied.

Economics in the Real World

Why All the Reality TV Shows?

In 1992, MTV launched a program called *The Real World*. Seven young people from across the country came together in an apartment in New York City. In 2000, CBS launched a show called *Survivor*. The show placed people on an island and then watched as they tried to "outwit, outplay, and outlast" each other for a prize of $1 million.

Both *The Real World* and *Survivor* were reality TV shows. After *Survivor*, it wasn't long before television became deluged with reality shows. In other words, the *supply* of reality shows increased. We will learn in this chapter that one of the factors that can increase supply is the number of sellers. In other words, the greater the number of sellers of a good, the larger the supply of that good. The number of sellers does not increase for no reason; something acts as a catalyst, pushing upward the number of sellers. That thing is profit, which is closely tied to success. The immense popularity of CBS's *Survivor*—as evidenced in its high television ratings—meant that CBS could sell commercial time on the show for huge sums of money, in the process earning high profits.

> ***"Of all seven shows that could be labeled phenomenal hits in the last four years, all but one . . . have been reality shows."***
> —Bill Arter, *New York Times*, May 19, 2003

Soon not only was CBS airing more reality shows, but NBC and ABC quickly came out with reality shows of their own. After all, everyone wanted to earn big profits. Over time, other reality shows hit the air waves: *For Love of Money, Fear Factor, Meet My Folks, The Restaurant, Average Joe, Paradise Hotel, The Amazing Race, Big Brother, The Apprentice, The Bachelor, The Bachelorette, Tommy Lee Goes to College,* and many more. In 2004, four years after the first *Survivor*, some reality shows were earning big profits for their networks. For example, a 30-second spot on *Survivor* was selling for $327,000 and earning CBS an annual profit of $73 million. A

30-second spot on *American Idol*, considered a reality show, was being sold for $414,700 and was earning its company, Fox, $260 million in profit (for the year).

When people wonder where all the reality TV shows are coming from, they are really asking, "What caused the increase in the supply of reality shows?" The answer is that supply increases as the number of sellers (of a good or service) increases. So, what increases the number of sellers of a good or service? The answer is the chance to earn big profits. In short, money.

THINK ABOUT IT One lesson to be learned from the history of reality shows appearing on television is that success is copied. *Survivor* was successful and so it was copied. What other successful products can you think of that have been copied?

supply schedule
A numerical chart illustrating the law of supply.

supply curve
A graph that shows the amount of a good sellers are willing and able to sell at various prices.

40. A numerical chart like this one that illustrates the law of supply is called a **supply schedule.**

We can also show the law of supply in picture form by plotting the data in the supply schedule, as in Exhibit 5-1(b). Point A is the first combination of price and quantity supplied from the supply schedule, with a price of $1 and a quantity supplied of 10. Point B represents a price of $2 and a quantity supplied of 20; Point C, a price of $3 and a quantity supplied of 30; and Point D, a price of $4 and a quantity supplied of 40. Connecting points A through D creates a

Internet Research

Assign students to find online news articles or press releases about new technological products. They can use online news sources or corporate Web sites describing new products. Ask them to explain how each advancement in technology will affect the supply curve for related products or services. How will this product facilitate the production of other items, or how will it help people provide better services?

supply curve, a line that slopes upward (from left to right) and shows the amount of a good sellers are willing and able to sell at various prices. The upward-sloping supply curve in Exhibit 5-1(b) is the graphic representation of the law of supply.

A Vertical Supply Curve

The law of supply, which holds that as price rises, quantity supplied rises, does not hold true for all goods; nor does it hold true over all time periods. First, it does not hold for goods that cannot be produced any longer, such as Stradivarius violins. These violins were made by Antonio Stradivari more than 250 years ago. It is impossible for an additional Stradivarius violin to be produced today, because Stradivari died in 1737. No matter how high the price goes, the quantity supplied cannot increase to more than the total number of Stradivarius violins that currently exist. Thus, the supply curve of Stradivarius violins is not upward sloping but vertical, straight up and down, as shown in Exhibit 5-2(a).

In another example, a theater in St. Louis is sold out for tonight's play. Increasing ticket prices from $40 to $50 would not create additional seats tonight, because time does not allow enlarging the theater to add more seats. For tonight's performance, the supply curve of theater seats is vertical, as illustrated in Exhibit 5-2(b).

EXHIBIT 5-1 Supply Schedule and Supply Curve

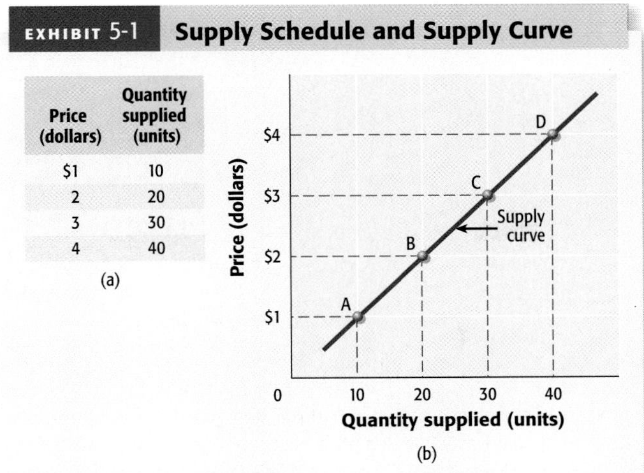

▲ (a) A supply schedule for a good. Notice that as price increases, quantity supplied increases. (b) Plotting the four combinations of price and quantity supplied from part (a), and connecting the points, yields a supply curve.

A Firm's Supply Curve and a Market Supply Curve

Most of the goods supplied in the United States are supplied by business firms. For example, computers are supplied by Dell, Hewlett-Packard, and so on. A firm's supply curve is different from a market supply curve. A firm's supply curve is what it sounds like: it is the supply curve for a particular firm. A market supply curve is the sum of all firms' supply curves.

EXHIBIT 5-2 Supply Curves When No More Can Ever Be Produced or There Is No Time to Produce More

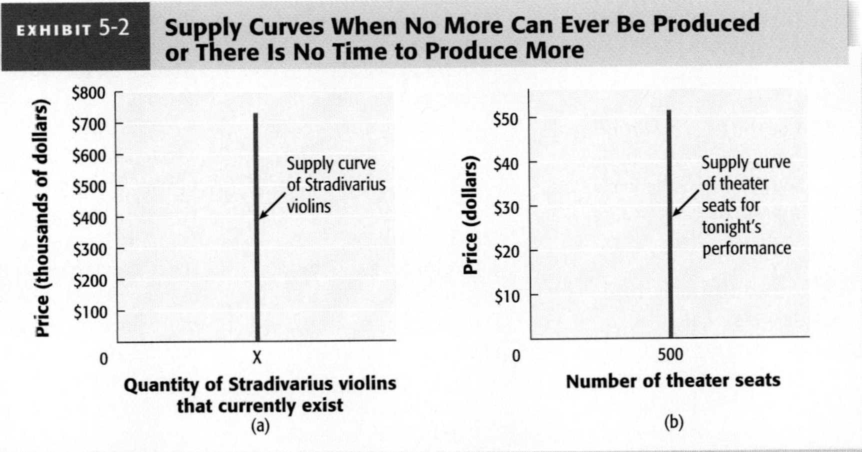

◀ When additional units cannot be produced or there is no time to produce more, the supply curve is vertical.

Background Information: Vertical Supply Curves

Students may be familiar with products that would have a vertical supply curve. Antiques, tickets to sold-out concerts, and so on, would have vertical supply curves. While copies could be made of some items, copies would not affect the prices of the original. Ask students the following questions: Do you or your family own items that might have a vertical supply curve? How do you feel about these items? Why might collecting goods that have a fixed supply (like old baseball cards) be so popular?

Teaching with Visuals

Direct students to Exhibit 5-1. Beginning with point A, ask students to tell you the price and quantity that corresponds with each point. These specifics provide concrete examples of the law of supply: price and quantity supplied move up and down together.

Reinforcement Activity

Ask students if they have ever saved money for a special purchase, only to watch its price increase while they were saving for it. How did this make them feel? What factors might have accounted for the price increase?

Teaching with Visuals

Ask students why the supply curves in Exhibit 5-2 are vertical. They should understand that the supply of these items cannot increase. Students should be aware of the vertical supply curve from going to sold-out concerts or sporting events at which people sell tickets at a higher price than they paid initially. Because of the fixed supply, they can sell the tickets at the higher price.

Application Activity

After reading and discussing Section 1, you may want to assign the Section Activity in the *Applying the Principles Workbook.*

Assess

Quick Quiz

The following true-or-false quiz will help you assess student understanding of the material covered in this section.

1. The law of supply states that as the price goes up, the quantity supplied decreases. (False)
2. Quantity supplied is the number of units of a good produced and offered for sale at a specific price. (True)
3. A supply schedule is a numeric chart that illustrates the law of supply. (True)
4. A supply curve is a graphic representation of the law of supply. (True)
5. A vertical supply curve shows that supply is limited. (True)

Assessment Book

You will find a quiz for this section in the *Assessment Book.*

Reteaching Activity

Use the Section Assessment to gauge which students may need reteaching on this section. Tell those students to imagine they are suppliers of gumballs. Work with them to create a supply schedule indicating the quantity of gumballs they would be willing to supply at various price points.

Guided Reading

For further reteaching of the key concepts in this section, assign the Outlining Activity and the Just the Facts Handout from the *Guided Reading and Study Guide.*

Defining Terms

1. a. supply: the willingness and ability to produce and sell a good; **b. law of supply:** as the price of a good increases, the quantity supplied of the good increases, and as the price of a good decreases, the quantity supplied of the good decreases; **c. direct relationship:** price and quantity supplied move in the same direction; **d. quantity supplied:** the number of units produced and offered for sale at a specific price; **e. supply curve:** a graph showing the amount of a good sellers are willing and able to sell at various prices; **f. supply schedule:** a numerical chart that illustrates the law of supply.
2. Answers will vary.

Reviewing Facts and Concepts

3. a. The law of supply states that price and quantity supplied move in the same direction. Specifically, as price rises, quantity supplied rises, and as price falls, quantity supplied falls. **b.** Price and quantity supplied move in the same direction; as price increases, quantity supplied increases, and as price decreases quantity supplied decreases.
4. No, only upward-sloping supply curves represent the law of supply. For example, the supply curve in Exhibit 5-1 represents the law of supply. Vertical supply curves such as those in Exhibit 5-2 do not represent the law of supply.
5. Answers will vary. An upward-sloping supply curve will exist for any good that can be produced over time. A vertical supply curve will exist for a good that can no longer be produced or for almost any good if time is too short to produce more of the good.

Critical Thinking

6. The price rise is the cause, and the response in quantity supplied is the effect.

Applying Economic Concepts

7. Here the law of supply is applied to the price of labor at McDonald's. If it rises from $6 to $9 per hour, the law of supply predicts that more people will want to work at McDonald's.

EXHIBIT 5-3 From Firms' Supply Curves to Market Supply Curve

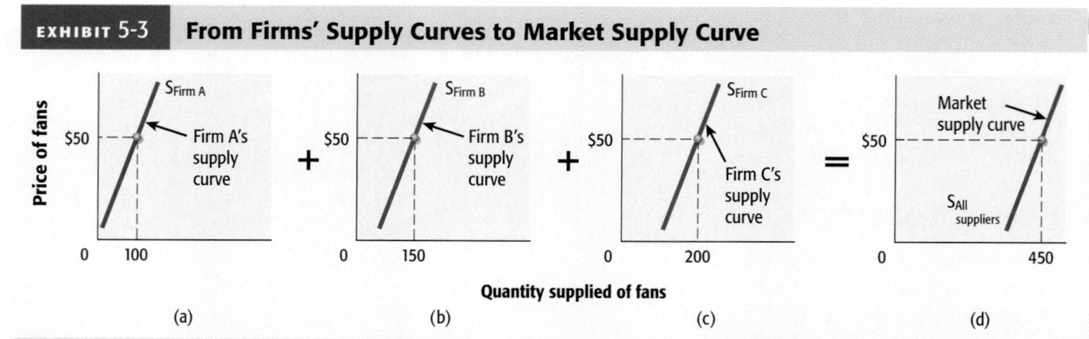

▲ In parts (a) through (c) we show the supply curve for firms A, B, and C, respectively. The market supply curve, shown in part (d), is simply the sum of the firms' supply curves. Stated differently, we know that at a price of $50 per fan, firm A's quantity supplied of fans is 100, firm B's is 150, and firm C's is 200. It follows that all three firms together will offer 450 fans at a price of $50 per fan. This point is identified on the market supply curve in part (d).

EXAMPLE: Suppose that only three suppliers of fans exist in the whole world: firm A, firm B, and firm C. At a price of $50 a fan, quantity supplied is 100 for firm A, 150 for firm B, and 200 for firm C. As a result, the *market supply curve* would have a point representing a price of $50 per fan and a market quantity supplied of 450 fans (100 + 150 + 200).

To see this concept graphically, look at Exhibit 5-3 above. In parts (a) through (c) you see the supply curves for firms A, B, and C, respectively. (To keep things simple, we identify only one point on the supply curve for each firm.) Now look at part (d). Here you can see the *market* supply curve, which is the combination of all the individual market supply curves. ♦

ASSESSMENT

Defining Terms

1. Define:
   - **a.** supply
   - **b.** law of supply
   - **c.** direct relationship
   - **d.** quantity supplied
   - **e.** supply curve
   - **f.** supply schedule
2. Use the term *quantity supplied* correctly in a sentence. Use the word *supply* correctly in a sentence.

Reviewing Facts and Concepts

3. **a.** State the law of supply.
   b. Explain the direct relationship between the price of a good and the quantity supplied.
4. Do all supply curves graphically represent the law of supply? Explain your answer.
5. Identify a good that has an upward-sloping supply curve. Identify a good that has a vertical supply curve.

Critical Thinking

6. Three months ago the price of a good was $4, and the quantity supplied was 200 units. Today the price is $6, and the quantity supplied is 400 units. Did the quantity supplied rise because the price increased, or did the price rise because the quantity supplied increased?

Applying Economic Concepts

7. Suppose three McDonald's restaurants operate in your town, and each pays its employees $6 per hour. If McDonald's started paying $9 per hour to its employees, would more, fewer, or the same number of people want to work for McDonald's, according to the law of supply?

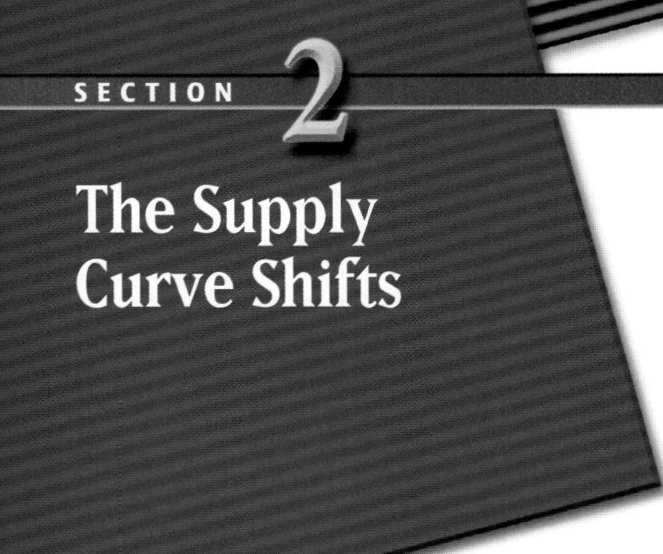

The Supply Curve Shifts

Focus Questions
- What does it mean when a supply curve shifts to the right?
- What does it mean when a supply curve shifts to the left?
- What factors can change supply?
- What factor can change quantity supplied?

Key Terms
technology
advancement in technology
per-unit cost
subsidy
quota
elasticity of supply
elastic supply
inelastic supply

When Supply Changes, the Curve Shifts

Supply can go up, and it can go down. For example, the supply of computers can rise or fall. Every time the supply of a good changes, the supply curve for that good "shifts." By *shift* we mean that it moves; it moves either to the right or to the left.

Change in supply → Shift in supply curve

For example, if the supply of computers increases, the computer supply curve shifts to the right. If the supply of computers decreases, the supply curve shifts to the left. We can understand shifts in supply curves better with the help of Exhibit 5-4.

Look at the curve labeled S_1 in Exhibit 5-4. Suppose this supply curve represents the original (and current) supply of computers. Notice that the quantity supplied at a price of $1,000 is 4,000 computers. Now suppose the supply of computers increases. For whatever reason, people want more computers. This increase in supply is shown by

EXHIBIT 5-4 Shifts in a Supply Curve

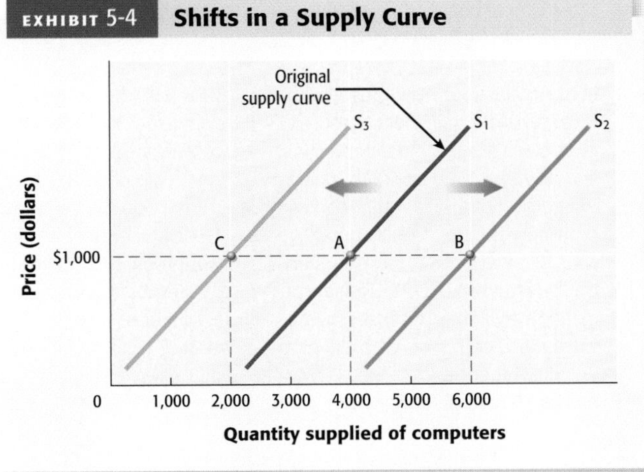

▲ Moving from S_1 (the original supply curve) to S_2 represents a rightward shift in the supply curve. Supply has increased. Moving from S_1 to S_3 represents a leftward shift in the supply curve. Supply has decreased.

the demand curve S_1 shifting to the right and becoming S_2.

What does it mean for a supply curve to shift rightward? The answer is easy if you

Internet Research

Direct students to the Old Farmer's Almanac Web site to look at the long-range weather forecast for their region. If this forecast is accurate, what might they expect to see happen to the supply of agricultural products from their region? How might prices be affected?

SECTION 2

Teacher Support

Focus and Motivate

Section Objectives

After completing this section, students will be able to
- explain the meaning of a supply curve's shifting to the right;
- explain the meaning of a supply curve's shifting to the left;
- identify factors that can change supply; and
- identify factors that can change quantity supplied.

Kickoff Activity

Direct students to reread the 11:03 A.M. scenario in Economics Around the Clock (page 111) and write their answers to its question.

Call on volunteers to share their answers with the class. Students should see that Angie needs to wait until later to sell her oil in order to maximize her oil revenue.

Activating Prior Knowledge

To review some of the concepts presented in the previous chapter, ask students to discuss the conditions that must be present for demand to exist: willingness to purchase and ability to purchase. Students will notice that the same conditions are necessary for supply.

Teach

Teaching with Visuals

Exhibit 5-4 shows what happens to the quantity supplied when the supply curve shifts to the right. Have students brainstorm ideas concerning why the quantity of computers supplied would increase.

Economics in the Real World

Have students read this feature, and then ask them to create a list of other new products similar to TiVo, podcasts, and blogs. What new technology enabled the development of each product? What unfulfilled demand did entrepreneurs see that prompted them to develop each product?

ANSWERS TO THINK ABOUT IT Answers will vary. Invite students to share with the class a new product they would supply.

Background Information

A change in resource prices can change the supply of a good and thus shift the supply curve of the good. Suppose good X is produced in the United States, but one of the resources that is used to produce the good, resource Y, is produced in Bolivia. It follows, then, that what happens in Bolivia can affect markets in the United States. Here's how: The price of the resource (in Bolivia) rises. This causes the supply of good X (in the United States) to fall as producers of X are not willing or able to produce as many of X. Consequently, the price of good X in the United States rises. In other words, if you are a buyer of good X, you now pay a higher price for the good. What has happened in Bolivia affects you, here in the United States.

Economics in the Real World

Where Do TiVo, Podcasts, and Blogs Come From?

It is important to distinguish between *increasing the supply* of a good that has existed for some time (increasing the supply of corn, paper, or shoes) and *creating* the supply of a good that has never existed before. Many goods that we have today—digital video recorders (first introduced by TiVo), podcasts, and blogs, for example—weren't available to us in the past. Where did these goods and the ideas for them come from?

Two answers come to mind: new technology and entrepreneurship. To illustrate how these two factors sometimes work together, consider a blog. A blog, or weblog, is a personal Web site with a dated *log* (diary-like) format that contains commentary and links to other Web sites. Only about 30 blogs existed at the beginning of 1999. Today, you can find millions. The first blogs were hand-coded by Web developers who taught themselves HTML (a markup language designed to create Web pages). Then, programmers created new software programs (a technological development), and entrepreneurs responded to the unfulfilled demand for posting items on the Web, leading to the vast supply of blogs today. Now anyone can go to *Blogger* at www.blogger.com/start and create a blog within minutes.

No digital video recorder (sometimes called a personal video recorder) could exist before the software had been developed to provide programming information and encode data streams. The DVR is a new product brought to us through an advancement in technology, and by the entrepreneurs who saw that the television public wanted more control over their personal television viewing.

Podcasting, which delivers recorded audio programs through the Internet to iPods or other portable music players, would not exist without the software that makes it easy to beam a podcast from a home computer to someone who has signed up to receive it. It would also not exist without the entrepreneurs who saw an unfulfilled demand on the part of consumers for more choices and greater control over their entertainment.

New technology and entrepreneurship—the combination that today gives us many of our new products—are the catalysts behind the *supply* of new products.

THINK ABOUT IT Do you think the technology exists today to develop new products that aren't being developed because entrepreneurs think no one would buy them? What might these new products (that could be developed but aren't being developed) do? Will they brush your teeth for you? Will they make your bed for you? If you were an entrepreneur, what new products would you supply?

again look at Exhibit 5-4 and focus on the horizontal axis and the numbers on it, along the bottom of the graph. What is the quantity supplied on curve S_2 at the price of $1,000? The answer is 6,000 computers. In other words, an increase in supply (or a shift rightward in the supply curve) is the same thing as saying, "Sellers want to sell more of a good at each and every price." In our example, sellers want to sell more computers at $1,000.

How would we graphically represent a decrease in supply? In Exhibit 5-4, again let's suppose that S_1 is our original (and current) supply curve. A decrease in supply is represented as a shift leftward in the supply curve from S_1 to S_3. This decrease in supply means that sellers want to sell less of the good at

Background Information: Taxes, Tariffs, and America's Great Depression

The text discusses both taxes and subsidies as factors that affect supply. A tariff is a tax on foreign-produced (imported) goods.

In June 1930, the Smoot-Hawley Tariff Act became law. It included higher tariffs on many imported goods. Some people thought that the higher tariffs on imported goods would lead Americans to buy fewer imports and more goods produced in the United States. Many people worried that other countries would retaliate with their own high tariffs (which they did), and that global trade would diminish, thus hurting the U.S. economy.

each and every price. Specifically, if we look at the price $1,000, we see that sellers who once wanted to sell 4,000 computers now want to sell 2,000 computers.

Supply increases ⟶ Supply curve shifts rightward
Supply decreases ⟶ Supply curve shifts leftward

What Factors Cause Supply Curves to Shift?

Supply curves do not shift to the right or left without cause. They shift because of changes in several factors. These factors include a change in resource prices, technology, taxes, subsidies, quotas, number of sellers, future price, and weather.

Resource Prices

Chapter 1 identified four resources, or factors of production: land, labor, capital, and entrepreneurship. For now, concentrate on land, labor, and capital. These resources are used to produce goods and services.

When resource prices fall, sellers are willing and able to produce and offer to sell more of the good (the supply curve shifts to the right). The reason is that it is cheaper to produce the good. When resource prices rise, in contrast, sellers are willing and able to produce and offer to sell less of the good (the supply curve shifts to the left); it is more expensive to produce the good.

EXAMPLE: Suppose the cost of labor rises for employees working for a car manufacturer, while everything else remains the same. Wage rates rise from, say, $20 an hour to $22 an hour. As a result, the car manufacturer will produce and offer to sell fewer cars; the supply curve shifts leftward. ◆

Technology

Technology is the skills and knowledge used in production. For example, the technology of farming today is much different from 200 years ago. Today, unlike 200 years ago, tractors, pesticides, and special fertilizers are used in farming.

An **advancement in technology** is the ability to produce more output with a fixed amount of resources. Again, consider farming. With the use of fertilizers and pesticides, farmers today can produce much more output on an acre of land than they could many years ago. This advancement in technology, in turn, lowers the **per-unit cost**, or average cost, of production for farmers. Farmers respond to lower per-unit costs by being willing and able to produce and offer to sell more output. In other words, the supply curve shifts to the right.

"What is wrong with our world is that love is in short supply."
—Anonymous

Taxes

Some taxes increase the per-unit costs. Suppose a shoe manufacturer must pay a $2 tax for each pair of shoes it produces. This "extra cost" of doing business causes the manufacturer to supply less output. (It is similar to the price of a resource rising and thus making it more expensive and less profitable for the producer to manufacture the good. As a result, the producer produces less output.) The supply curve shifts to the left. If the tax is eliminated, the supply curve will shift rightward to its original position.

technology
The body of skills and knowledge concerning the use of resources in production.

advancement in technology
The ability to produce more output with a fixed amount of resources.

per-unit cost
The average cost of a good. For example, if $400,000 is spent to produce 100 cars, the average, or per-unit, cost is $4,000.

BY THE NUMBERS

In 1921, a seller sold something to a buyer for $100. In 2005, a seller sold something to a buyer for $100. Were the two sales, in 1921 and 2005, equivalent? Not at all, because a dollar was worth more in 1921 than in 2005. In fact, a $100 purchase in 1921 was the equivalent of a $1,079.89 purchase in 2005. In other words, buying something for $100 in 1921 was the same as buying something for $1,079.89 in 2005. To find out what any dollar purchase in the past is equivalent to today, go to the Bureau of Labor Statistics inflation calculator at www.emcp.net/inflation. Here we list the 2005 dollar equivalent of several purchases made in 1961. For example, a person who paid $15 for dinner when going out to eat in 1961 would pay $96.22 for an equivalent dinner in 2005.

Good/service	1961 price	2005 equivalent
Dinner	$ 15	$ 96.22
Book	4	25.66
Haircut	3	19.24
Car	3,000	19,244.15
Furniture	500	3,207.36
Hammer	2	12.83
Attorney services	200	1,282.94

Clarifying Terms

Remind students that economists speak using specialized terms. For example, economists say *the supply curve shifts to the right*, but many people might not understand what that means. Ask students to translate that phrase into a phrase that everyone would understand. Students might say that sellers offer more of a good or service at each and every price.

Reinforcement Activity

Ask students to make a list of other goods or services comparing prices in the year they were born with today's dollar equivalent. Have them share their findings with the class.

Economics Around the Clock

Have students reread the 9:10 A.M. scenario in Economics Around the Clock (page 111) and then write their answers to its question.

The answer is yes. The type of tax identified here will reduce the supply of cigarettes. A tax on production makes it more costly to produce goods. As a result, firms are less willing to produce the good, and so the supply curve (for the good) shifts leftward.

The stock market plummeted after the Smoot-Hawley Tariff Act was signed into law, marking the beginning of the Great Depression. Many economists believe that the act was one of the catalysts of the Great Depression, and made it last longer than it would have otherwise.

Thinking Like an Economist

Economists think in terms of incentives and disincentives. More important, they believe that individuals respond to changes in incentives in predictable ways. Recall the discussion of taxes and subsidies with respect to supply. A tax on the production of a good is a disincentive to produce that good. Consequently, economists believe that fewer units of that good will be produced. In contrast, a subsidy on the production of a good is an incentive to produce that good. Consequently, economists believe that more units of that good will be produced as a result. Ask students to think of incentives and disincentives they have received for such acts as earning good grades or breaking their curfews.

Reinforcement Activity

Assign students to use newspapers or magazines to find changes in any of the factors mentioned—resource prices, technology, taxes, subsidies, quotas, number of sellers, or weather—that have affected the supply of a particular good. Direct students to give oral reports on their findings.

After students read the feature, ask them how having this information would have helped Angie in the 11:03 A.M. scenario in Economics Around the Clock (page 111) as she debated whether to sell her oil supply now or wait three months. Would this have made a difference in their advice to Angie to sell now or wait? Invite students to share their answers with the class.

Subsidies

Subsidies have the opposite effect of taxes. A subsidy is a financial payment made by government for certain actions. Suppose the government subsidizes the production of corn by paying corn farmers $2 for every bushel of corn they produce. Farmers will then want to produce more corn at every price, which means the supply curve of corn shifts rightward. Removal of the subsidy causes the supply curve to shift to the left, back to its position prior to the subsidy.

Quotas

Quotas are restrictions on the number of units of a foreign-produced good (import) that can enter a country. For example, suppose Japanese producers are currently sending, and want to continue to send, 100,000 cars to the United States each year. Now suppose the U.S. government imposes a quota on Japanese cars at 80,000 a year. This quota means that no more than 80,000 Japanese cars can be imported into the United States.

subsidy
A financial payment made by government for certain actions.

quota
A legal limit on the number of units of a foreign-produced good (import) that can enter a country.

Economics on the WEB

Suppose you are an oil producer and you want to know the price of oil today and the expected (future) price of oil. Where would you look to find the current and future price of oil? To find the current price, you might go to www.emcp.net/oil. Here you will see the current (or sometimes called *spot*) price for oil, such as Nymex Crude. On the day we checked, the price was $51.25 a barrel. If you want to check the future price of oil, go to www.emcp.net/oil_futures or simply click on "Commodity Futures" in the left margin of your first screen (the screen that shows the current price of crude oil). On the day we checked, the (expected) future price of crude oil was $51.35. Notice that the difference between the current price ($51.25) and the future price ($51.35) is only 10 cents, which means that oil producers don't have much incentive (if any at all) to shift oil from current supply to future supply.

A quota decreases supply, so the supply curve shifts to the left. The elimination of a quota causes the supply curve to shift rightward to its original position.

Number of Sellers

If more sellers begin producing a particular good, perhaps because of high profits, supply increases and the supply curve shifts to the right. If some sellers stop producing a particular good, perhaps because of losses, the supply curve shifts to the left.

Future Price

Sellers who expect the price of a good to be higher in the future may hold back the good now and supply the good to the market in the future. Sellers who expect the price of a good to be lower in the future may want to supply the good now instead of later.

EXAMPLE: Ricky is thinking of selling his house. He just heard that the price of houses is expected to rise three months from today. Instead of offering to sell his house today, he waits until three months later. Why did he wait? Ricky believed the future price of a house would be higher than the current price of a house. Notice that we are talking about a nonperishable good here (houses). In other words, waiting a few months, or even a year, to sell a house doesn't lead to a change in the quality of a house.

A different type of a good is a perishable good, such as eggs. If the egg seller believes that the future price will be higher than the current price of eggs, he may want to hold his eggs off the market today and sell them later. He can't really do that, though, because eggs spoil if kept too long. ♦

Weather (in Some Cases)

Weather can affect the supply of a good. Bad weather reduces the supply of many agricultural goods, such as corn, wheat, and barley. Unusually good weather can increase the supply. Weather can also impact the supply of non-agricultural products, as happens when hurricanes damage fishing boats, shipping docks, and coastal oil refineries.

Cross-Curricular Activity

Ask students to research how natural disasters—like earthquakes, hurricanes, and floods—can affect the supply curve. You might invite a geography teacher to discuss the devastation caused by natural disasters to help students understand the power of nature over the supply of goods and services. Discuss all the different effects of weather, including reallocation of resources, increased taxes, the likelihood of subsidies, and the number of sellers.

What Factor Causes a Change in Quantity Supplied?

We identified the factors (resource prices, technology, etc.) that can cause *supply* to change. As we stated earlier, a change in supply is represented as a shift in the supply curve. The curve moves either right or left. See Exhibit 5-5(a).

But what factor(s) can cause a change in *quantity supplied*? Only one: price. For example, the only thing that can cause sellers to change their quantity supplied of computers is a change in the price of computers. A change in quantity supplied is shown as a movement along a given supply curve. See Exhibit 5-5(b).

Many people are, at first, confused about what leads to a change in quantity supplied and what leads to a change in supply. To many, it seems as if changes in quantity supplied and supply are the same thing.

To make sure you understand the difference, let's look back at a couple of examples in this chapter. Turn back to Exhibit 5-1 on page 115 and look at point A. There you see a price of $1 and a quantity supplied of 10. Now ask yourself what must happen before you can move from quantity supplied of 10 to 20, or from point A to B. Stated differently, what has to change before a move from A to B will happen? The answer is that the price (on the vertical axis) must increase from $1 to $2. In other words, the only factor that will change the quantity supplied of a good is a change in price: the factor that is on the vertical axis.

THE GLOBAL IMPACT: Supply Goes Up, or Down?

On March 21, 2005, Dell Computers opened its third Call Center in India. (A Call Center is a place where people who have purchased Dell computers call if they have technical problems with their computers.) At the time, Dell employed 7,500 people in India and planned to hire about 1,500 more. Dell hires Indians to service U.S. customer calls because it is cheaper to hire Indians than Americans.

ECONOMIC THINKING If Dell keeps its costs of building and servicing computers down, how might this affect the supply of Dell computers for sale?

EXHIBIT 5-5 A Change in Supply Versus a Change in Quantity Supplied

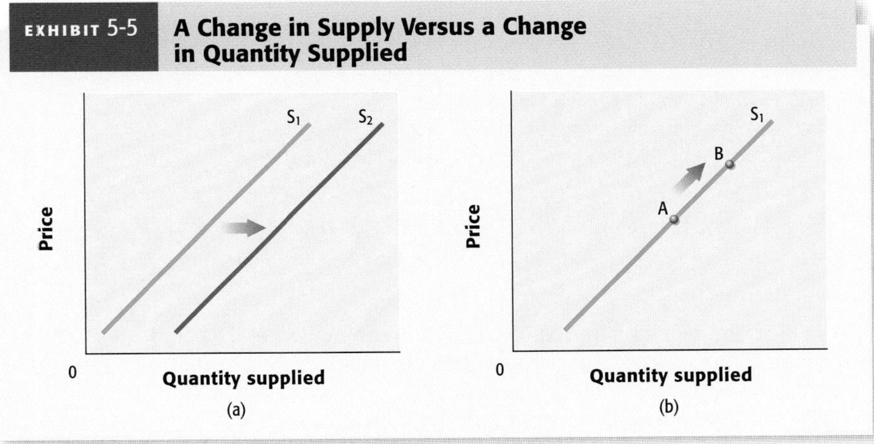

▲ (a) A change in supply refers to a shift in the supply curve. A change in supply can be brought about by a number of factors. (b) A change in quantity supplied refers to a movement along a given supply curve. A change in quantity supplied is brought about *only* by a change in a good's price.

Put students in pairs to read the feature and answer the Economic Thinking question. Ask each pair to make a list of other jobs they've heard about that have been outsourced by American companies to other countries. Then discuss with the class some advantages and disadvantages of outsourcing—both economic and noneconomic.

ANSWERS TO ECONOMIC THINKING Less expensive resources will cause the supply curve to shift to the right—increasing supply—because Dell will have more money to invest in building more computers.

Reinforcement Activity

The United States has a long tradition of creating and then reducing or eliminating tariffs. From the pre-Revolutionary acts of the British Parliament to the trade embargoes of the 20th century, the history of the United States has been affected by economic trade restrictions. Assign students to research particular trade restrictions to determine whether each had a positive or a negative effect on the economy, and why.

Teaching with Visuals

Direct students to compare the information in Exhibit 5-5 with the information in Exhibit 4-4 (page 99). Have them work in pairs to write a short paragraph explaining the difference between a change in supply and a change in demand. Their paragraphs should mention that supply and demand work in opposite directions: an increase in price brings about a decrease in demand and an increase in supply, and vice versa.

Cooperative Learning

Put students in groups of four or five. Have each group choose a good or service that it wants to produce. Each group should then develop a list of specific factors that would shift the supply curve of its good or service to the left, decreasing supply. Then have each group brainstorm ways to overcome the various factors that shifted the supply curve.

Section 2 The Supply Curve Shifts 121

Direct students to read this feature and think about what kind of career they might like to work in for 63 years. What difference would 20 extra years in the workforce make?

ANSWERS TO THINK ABOUT IT Answers will vary. Have them share their opinions with the class. Students should see that the greater the population, the greater demand there is for goods and services. That in turn creates more jobs.

Economics Around the Clock

After reading and discussing "Elasticity of Supply" (pages 122–123), direct students to the 7:04 A.M. scenario in Economics Around the Clock (page 111) and invite them to discuss which boy's supply of good behavior is more likely to be elastic.

The answer is that Dave's quantity of good behavior is more likely to be elastic than Quentin's. Both Dave and Quentin behave better, but Dave behaves a lot better and Quentin behaves only a little better. In other words, Dave's "quantity supplied of good behavior" increases by more than Quentin's. Dave's supply of good behavior is more likely to be elastic (change in quantity supplied is greater than the change in price).

Application Activity

After reading and discussing Section 2, you may want to assign the Section Activity and the Supply Practice Activity in the *Applying the Principles Workbook.*

Assess

Quick Quiz

The following true-or-false quiz will help you assess student understanding of the material covered in this section.

1. Supply has decreased when the curve shifts to the left. (True)

Will You Live to Be 100?

Usually, when we talk about supply, we mean the supply of goods and services. But can an advancement in technology increase the supply of people? One way to increase the supply of people in the world is to increase the length of life. For example, if people start living an average of 100 years instead of 70 years, it means more people in the world.

Michael Rose, a biologist who studies the aging process, found a way to increase the average life span of a fruit fly. The average fruit fly lives for about 70 days, but Rose's fruit flies live for 140 days. If Rose and other like-minded scientists can do for human beings what they have done for fruit flies, then people in the future may live longer lives. According to some scientists working in the area of aging, ages of 100 or 150 years are not unreasonable.

Now suppose that scientists did figure out how to slow the aging process in humans, and people began to live longer. Also suppose that as a result of slowing the aging process, an average 80-year-old in the future felt the same way an average 50-year-old feels today. What economic effects would this change have?

First, longer-living people would probably work for more years than we do today. People today often start full-time work when they are 22 years old and retire at about 65, a work life of 43 years. In the future, they may start work at 22 and retire at 85, a work life of 63 years.

People are resources, and resources are used to produce goods and services. More people working would mean more goods and services. In other words, the current research on aging, if successful, would lead to a greater supply of goods and services in the world.

THINK ABOUT IT Some people believe that the world has only a finite number of jobs, and so with more people—and the same number of jobs—many more people will be unemployed in the future if people live to be 100. The problem with this way of thinking, though, is that in 2005, the population of the United States was greater than it was in 1982, but the unemployment rate in 1982 was higher than the unemployment rate in 2005. Do you think these numbers are evidence that there "are not a finite number of jobs in the world"?

Now let's move over to Exhibit 5-4 on page 117. Take a look at S_1. Ask yourself what has to happen before S_1 shifts to its right and becomes S_2. Does price (on the vertical axis) have to change? No, as you can see in the exhibit, we never change price from $1,000. So, then, you know that a change in a good's actual price isn't what will shift a supply curve. What then does shift a supply curve? The answer is a change in resource prices, technology, taxes, and so on.

elasticity of supply The relationship between the percentage change in quantity supplied and the percentage change in price.

Elasticity of Supply

Chapter 4 discussed elasticity of demand, which deals with the relationship between price and quantity demanded. **Elasticity of supply** is the relationship between the per-

Differentiating Instruction

English Language Learners

To help ELL students, use the following resources, which are provided as part of the *Economics: New Ways of Thinking* program:

- a Spanish glossary in the *Student Text*
- Spanish versions of the Chapter Summaries on an audio CD

centage change in quantity supplied and the percentage change in price. We can look at it as an equation:

$$\text{Elasticity of supply} = \frac{\text{Percentage change in quantity supplied}}{\text{Percentage change in price}}$$

Notice that the equation has a numerator (percentage change in quantity supplied) and a denominator (percentage change in price). **Elastic supply** exists when the quantity supplied changes by a greater percentage than price—that is, when the numerator changes by more than the denominator. For example, suppose the price of lightbulbs increases by 10 percent, and the quantity supplied of lightbulbs increases by 20 percent. The numerator (20%) changes by more than the denominator (10%), so the supply of lightbulbs is elastic.

Inelastic supply exists when the quantity supplied changes by a smaller percentage than price—that is, when the numerator changes by less than the denominator. Finally, *unit-elastic supply* exists when the quantity supplied changes by the same percentage as price—that is, when the numerator changes by the same percentage as the denominator.

EXHIBIT 5-6 Elasticity of Supply

If supply is . . .	That means . . .
Elastic	Quantity supplied changes by a larger percentage than price. For example, if price rises by 10 percent, quantity supplied rises by, say, 15 percent.
Inelastic	Quantity supplied changes by a smaller percentage than price. For example, if price rises by 10 percent, quantity supplied rises by, say, 5 percent.
Unit-elastic	Quantity supplied changes by the same percentage as price. For example, if price rises by 10 percent, quantity supplied rises by 10 percent.

Exhibit 5-6 reviews the definitions of elastic, inelastic, and unit-elastic supply.

EXAMPLE: Firm A currently produces 400 skateboards a day at $50 a skateboard. The price of skateboards increases to $55 a skateboard and the firm then starts producing 420 skateboards a day. Because the quantity supplied of skateboards goes up (5%) by a smaller percentage than the price of skateboards rises (10%), the supply of skateboards is *inelastic*. ♦

elastic supply
The kind of supply that exists when the percentage change in quantity supplied is greater than the percentage change in price.

inelastic supply
The kind of supply that exists when the percentage change in quantity supplied is less than the percentage change in price.

Defining Terms

1. Define:
   a. elastic supply
   b. inelastic supply
   c. per-unit cost
   d. subsidy
   e. quota
   f. technology

Reviewing Facts and Concepts

2. Identify what happens to a given supply curve as a result of each of the following:
   a. Resource prices fall.
   b. Technology advances.
   c. A quota is repealed.
   d. A tax on the production of a good is repealed.
3. If supply increases, does the supply curve shift to the right or to the left?
4. Identify whether a given supply curve will shift to the right or to the left as a result of each of the following:
   a. Resource prices rise.
   b. A quota is placed on a good.
5. Give a numerical example that illustrates elastic supply.

Critical Thinking

6. The previous section explained how a supply curve can be vertical. If a supply curve is vertical, does it follow that supply is (a) elastic, (b) inelastic, (c) unit-elastic, or (d) none of the above? Explain your answer.

Graphing Economics

7. Graph the following:
   a. an increase in supply
   b. a decrease in supply
   c. an increase in the supply of good X that is greater than the increase in the supply of good Y

2. Resource prices affect the supply curve. (True)
3. Advancement in technology will cause the supply curve to shift to the right. (True).
4. Subsidies have the same effect on the supply curve as taxes. (False)
5. Quotas are restrictions on the number of units of a foreign good that can enter the country. (True)

Assessment Book

You will find a quiz for this section in the *Assessment Book.*

Reteaching Activity

Use the Section Assessment to gauge which students need reteaching. Have those students work with partners to create a chart like Exhibit 4-4 for elasticity of supply. Review the charts with each pair of students.

Guided Reading

For further reteaching of the key concepts in this section, assign the Outlining Activity and the Just the Facts Handout from the *Guided Reading and Study Guide.*

Defining Terms

1. a. elastic supply: exists when quantity supplied changes by a larger percentage than price; **b. inelastic supply:** exists when quantity supplied changes by a smaller percentage than price; **c. per-unit cost:** the average cost of a good; **d. subsidy:** a financial payment made by government for certain actions; **e. quota:** a legal limit on the number of units of a foreign-produced good (import) that can enter a country; **f. technology:** the body of skills and knowledge concerning the use of resources in production.

Reviewing Facts and Concepts

2. a. shifts to the right; **b.** shifts to the right; **c.** shifts to the right; **d.** shifts to the right.
3. to the right.
4. a. to the left; **b.** to the left.
5. Answers will vary. The percentage change in quantity supplied must be greater than the percentage change in price.

Critical Thinking

6. It is (b) inelastic because quantity supplied changes by a smaller percentage than price. If the supply curve is vertical, quantity supplied doesn't change no matter how the price changes. Therefore, the percentage change in quantity supplied (0%) is less than the percentage change in price.

Graphing Economics

7. a. The shift from S_1 to S_2 in Exhibit 5-4 represents an increase in supply. **b.** The shift from S_1 to S_3 in Exhibit 5-4 represents a decrease in supply. **c.** The rightward shift in the supply curve for good X should be greater than the rightward shift in the supply curve for good Y.

Section 2 The Supply Curve Shifts 123

Your Personal Economics

Discussion Starter

Ask students the following questions: What does it mean to "invest in yourself"? What are ways you are presently investing in yourself? How could you increase the amount you are investing in yourself?

Research Activity

After students have read "How You Spend Your Time," have them record the number of hours spent on each activity every day for a week. Ask students if there is any time they could reallocate toward something that might provide them with a higher return.

Your Personal Economics

Investing in Yourself

When most people think of investing, they think of investing in such things as stocks, bonds, and real estate. Rarely do we think of investing in ourselves. Investing in yourself, however, is one of the most important things you can do.

Everyone wants a high return from their investments. What could you invest in today—as a high school student—that could provide you with a high return tomorrow? Before we tell you what it is, let's look at how the average 15- to 17-year-old spends his or her time each week.

How You Spend Your Time

According to a University of Michigan study, the average 15- to 17-year-old (in 2002–2003) each week spent 32 hours in school, 4 hours and 47 minutes socializing or visiting with friends, 3 hours playing sports, 1 hour and 17 minutes reading, 2 hours and 45 minutes on the computer, 7 hours eating, 5 hours and 43 minutes doing household work, and 14 hours and 36 minutes watching television.

Let's focus on the 14 hours and 36 minutes a week watching television. Could we reallocate some of the TV time toward something that might provide us with a higher return (than watching television provides us)?

For example, as a high school student, you might be thinking of attending college. Getting into a good college could be the stepping stone to a good-paying job in the future. According to recent data, college graduates earn substantially more over their lifetimes than those with only a high school diploma (see Exhibit 5-7).

▶ It's clear that if you invest more time, effort, and money in your education, your level of income will grow substantially.

EXHIBIT 5-7 Average Annual Earnings by Level of Education

Level of Education	Earnings
Not a high school graduate	$18,826
High school graduate only	$27,280
Some college, no degree	$29,725
Associate's degree	$34,177
Bachelor's degree	$51,194
Master's degree	$60,445
Ph.D. degree	$89,724

Source: Statistical Abstract of the United States, 2004–2005.

You Are Preparing for College, Aren't You?

So, how do you get into a good college? First, you need to have good high school grades. Second, you need to have a reasonably high score on one of the two standardized tests that college-bound high school juniors and seniors take: the SAT and ACT.

Many high school students take these standardized tests without studying for them. They simply get a good night's sleep the night before the test, and then take it.

Think of an alternative way to proceed. Suppose, beginning either at the end of your sophomore year or at the beginning of your junior year of high school, you were to watch 2 hours less of television a week and studied for the SAT or ACT instead.

Now ask yourself how many hours most juniors in high school spend studying for the SAT or ACT. Many say "no more than 5 hours." Yet, the SAT and ACT are important factors considered by college admission offices. (If you have already taken the SAT and ACT, apply the following suggestions to college courses and tests you'll take in the future. If you are a senior and haven't taken them, it's not too late to plan and prepare to take them.)

Are 100 Hours of Studying Too Many?

What if instead of spending only 5 hours studying for the SAT or ACT, a student spent 100 hours studying.

Cooperative Learning

After students have studied Exhibit 5-7, divide them into groups of three or four. Tell each group to develop lists of careers they are interested in pursuing. Then ask them to predict the level of education they will need for that career and the average annual earnings of people in that career. After 15 minutes of brainstorming, invite students to report their list of careers and earnings to the class. Discuss the relationship between annual earnings and education level.

These 100 hours are easily found if the average 15- to 17-year-old would simply cut back his or her TV viewing. If you are the average 15- to 17-year-old, and watch 14 hours and 36 minutes of television a week, consider cutting that down to 12 hours and 36 minutes. With the "freed up" 2 hours, you can now study for the SAT or ACT. In 50 weeks, you would have studied 100 hours. Studying diligently for 2 hours a week for 50 weeks for the SAT or ACT is likely to boost your overall score.

Will you "earn a high return" at the end of the 100 hours? We cannot guarantee how high the return will be (how much you will boost your score over not studying), but certainly it could be substantial. A substantial improvement in your score could pave the way to a good college in your future and everything else that may follow.

The Best Use of Your Time

So how should you proceed if you are now convinced that 2 hours of investing in yourself might bring a higher return than watching an additional 2 hours of television? With respect to either the SAT or ACT, you can go to the appropriate Web sites to see what the tests look like. Go to www.emcp.net/SAT for the SAT. For the ACT, go to www.emcp.net/ACT.

We also strongly urge you to purchase one or two of the test preparation books (on the SAT and ACT) that you can find at almost any bookstore. Most of these test prep books not only provide you with sample tests, but with plenty of study material.

The thing to do once you have purchased these books is to study slowly and carefully. Don't just take the sample tests and put the books away.

You will also find sections in these books on grammar, vocabulary words, critical reading, writing an essay, and more. Read each section carefully, and then read it again. Do all the exercises. Then do them again. Take the sample tests. Then make sure you know what you got wrong on each sample test. Then take more sample tests.

If you simply cut out 2 hours of television a week, and devote that time to studying for the SAT or ACT, you will be surprised how much you learn and how much you can boost your test score.

My Personal Economics Action Plan

Here are some points you may want to consider and some guidelines you might want to put into practice:

1. The average 15- to 17-year-old spends 14 hours and 36 minutes each week watching television. If you do too, then you might want to consider cutting down your TV viewing by 2 hours a week.

   I will reduce my television watching time by ___ hours/___ minutes per day.

2. Spending 100 hours studying for the SAT or ACT can substantially increase your test score. A reasonably high SAT or ACT will increase the probability that you will be admitted to a good college. If you were to spend 2 hours a week for 50 weeks studying for the SAT or ACT, it would mean that you would be studying 100 hours for the test. This is only one-third of the time you put in to an average high school course (if we count in-class time plus homework time.)

   I will devote ___ hours per week studying for ___.

3. We can invest in things (stocks, bonds, gold, real estate), and we can invest in ourselves. Investing in your academic self during your high school years can end up paying a high return in the future. Buy YOU!

   Beginning ______, I will ______ as an investment in myself.

Discussion Starter

To help students realize the power of investing in themselves, have them compare things they can purchase at their current educational level with things they could purchase at a different educational level. Make sure they realize that reallocating a small amount of time now might provide a higher return in the future.

My Personal Economics Action Plan Have each student survey adults they know to determine how their average annual earnings relate to their education level. Students may want to ask follow-up questions, including what adults did to invest academically in themselves when they were 17 or 18 years old. Allow students to report back to the class.

Chapter 5 Supply 125

CHAPTER 5 Assessment Answers

Economics Vocabulary

1. supply schedule; **2.** supply curve; **3.** quantity supplied; **4.** elastic; **5.** inelastic; **6.** Quantity supplied.

Understanding the Main Ideas

1. Supply refers to the willingness and ability of sellers to produce and offer to sell a good or service. Quantity supplied refers to the number of units of a good produced for sale at a specific price.
2. (a) As the price of a good increases, the quantity supplied of the good increases; as the price of a good decreases, the quantity supplied of the good decreases. (b) If P ↑ then Q_S ↑; if P ↓ then Q_S ↓. (c) See Exhibit 5-1(b).
3. No, Luisa is not a supplier of plastic cups. To be a supplier, it is necessary to be both willing and able to produce and offer to sell. Luisa is willing but not able.
4. No. When the supply of a good cannot be increased or there is not enough time to increase it, the supply curve is vertical.
5. Answers will vary. However, the price of the good and the quantity supplied should always go up and down together.
6. a. vertical; **b.** vertical; **c.** upward sloping; **d.** upward sloping; **e.** vertical.
7. When a supply curve shifts to the right, it means that sellers are willing and able to sell more of a good at all prices. When a supply curve shifts to the left, it means sellers are willing and able to sell fewer units of a good at all prices.
8. Any change in price in this range—say, from $10 to $11—will result in a smaller percentage change in quantity supplied.
9. a. The supply of television sets shifts to the right. **b.** The supply of television sets shifts to the right. **c.** The supply of television sets shifts to the left.
10. The chapter discussed seven factors that can change supply: resource prices, advancements in technology, taxes on production, subsidies, quotas, the number of sellers, and weather (in some cases). There is only one factor that can change quantity supplied: price. In other words, the only factor that can change the quantity supplied of apples is the price of apples.
11. a. elastic; **b.** unit-elastic; **c.** elastic.
12. Price is the factor that causes movement along a supply curve.

Doing the Math

1. $100,000. Average cost, or per-unit cost, is the total cost of producing something divided by the number of units produced.
2. Both stores are charging $500 for stereos. This should be reflected in the graph.

CHAPTER 5 ASSESSMENT

Chapter Summary

Be sure you know and remember the following key points from the chapter sections.

Section 1

- The supply of a good or service requires both a supplier's *willingness* and *ability* to produce and sell.
- The law of supply says that price and quantity supplied move in the same direction—as price increases, so does quantity supplied, and vice versa—called a direct relationship.
- Quantity supplied refers to the number of units of a good produced and offered for sale at a specific price.
- The supply curve is an upward-sloping line (from left to right) that shows the amount of a good sellers are willing and able to sell at various prices.
- A market supply curve represents the sum of all individual firms' supply curves for a particular good.

Section 2

- Resource prices, advances in technology, subsidies, quotas, the number of sellers, future price expectations, and weather are all factors that can cause a shift in the supply curve.
- The factor that causes a change in the *quantity supplied* is price.
- The elasticity of supply measures the relationship between the percentage change in price and the percentage change in quantity supplied.
- Supply is elastic when quantity supplied changes by a greater percentage than price.
- Supply is inelastic when quantity supplied changes by a smaller percentage than price.
- Unit-elastic supply exists when quantity supplied changes by the same percentage as price.

Economics Vocabulary

To reinforce your knowledge of the key terms in this chapter, fill in the following blanks on a separate piece of paper with the appropriate word or phrase.

1. A(n) _______ is the numerical representation of the law of supply.
2. A(n) _______ is the graphic representation of the law of supply.
3. According to the law of supply, as price increases, _______ rises.
4. Supply is _______ if the percentage change in quantity supplied is greater than the percentage change in price.
5. Supply is _______ if the percentage change in quantity supplied is less than the percentage change in price.
6. _______ refers to the number of units of a good produced and offered for sale at a specific price.

Understanding the Main Ideas

Write answers to the following questions to review the main ideas in this chapter.

1. Explain the term *supply* as it applies to economics. What is the difference between supply and quantity supplied?
2. Express the law of supply in (a) words, (b) symbols, and (c) graphic form.
3. Luisa is willing but not able to produce and offer to sell plastic cups. Is Luisa a supplier of plastic cups? Explain your answer.
4. Are all supply curves upward sloping? Why or why not?
5. Write out a supply schedule for four different combinations of price and quantity supplied.
6. Identify whether the supply curve for each of the following would be vertical or upward sloping.
   - **a.** desks in your classroom at this moment
   - **b.** seats at a football stadium at this moment
   - **c.** television sets over time
   - **d.** Hewlett-Packard computers over time
   - **e.** Picasso paintings (*Hint*: Picasso is dead.)
7. What does it mean when a supply curve shifts to the right? To the left?

126 Chapter 5 Supply

8. Between the price of $10 and $14, supply is inelastic. What does this statement mean?
9. Explain what happens to the supply curve of television sets as a consequence of each of the following.
   a. Resource prices fall.
   b. A technological advancement occurs in the television industry.
   c. A tax is placed on the production of television sets.
10. Identify the factors that can change supply. Identify the factor that can change quantity supplied.
11. In each of the following cases, identify whether the supply of the good is elastic, inelastic, or unit-elastic.
   a. The price of books increases 10 percent, and the quantity supplied of books increases 14 percent.
   b. The price of bread increases 2 percent, and the quantity supplied of bread increases 2 percent.
   c. The price of telephones decreases 6 percent, and the quantity supplied of telephones decreases 8 percent.
12. What factor causes movement along a supply curve?

Doing the Math

Do the calculations necessary to solve the following problems.

1. A house-building company spends $40 million to produce 400 houses. What is the average cost, or per-unit cost, of a house?
2. Firm A sold 400 stereos for a total of $200,000, and firm B sold 550 stereos for a total of $275,000. Which firm is charging more per unit? Graph the supply curve.
3. If the percentage change in price is 5 percent and the percentage change in quantity supplied is 10 percent, calculate the elasticity of supply.
4. Currently the price of a good is $10, and the quantity supplied is 300 units. For every $1 increase in price, quantity supplied rises by 5 units. What is the quantity supplied at a price of $22?

Working with Graphs and Charts

Use Exhibit 5-8 to answer the following questions. P = price, and Q_s = quantity supplied.

1. What does Exhibit 5-8(a) represent?
2. Which part of Exhibit 5-8 represents a change in supply due to technological advancement?

EXHIBIT 5-8

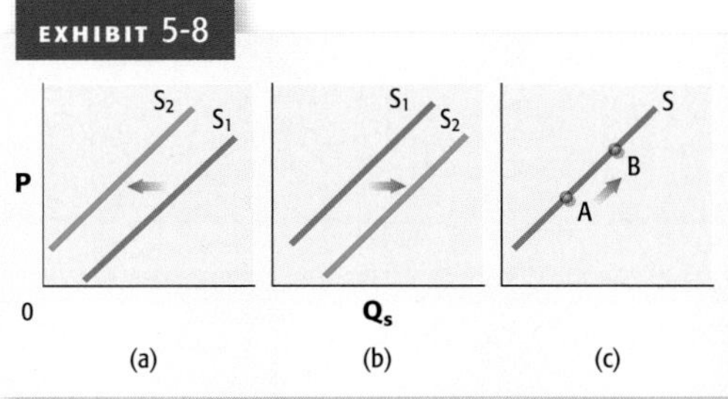

3. What does Exhibit 5-8(c) represent?
4. Which part of Exhibit 5-8 represents a change in supply due to an increase in resource prices?

Solving Economic Problems

Use your thinking skills and the information you learned in this chapter to find solutions to the following problems.

1. **Application.** The law of supply pertains to many goods. For example, if the price of shoes rises, in time the quantity supplied of shoes will rise, too. Devise an experiment to test whether studying for an economics test is subject to the law of supply.
2. **Cause and Effect.** Explain the process by which a tax, applied to the production of a good, changes the supply of the good.

Practice Tests and Study Guide

Go to www.emcp.net/economics and choose *Economics: New Ways of Thinking,* Chapter 5, if you need more help in preparing for the chapter test.

3. 2 (*calculation:* 10% ÷ 5% = 2).
4. 360 units (*calculation:* Increased quantity supplied = current quantity supplied + [5 units × (increased price − current price)] = 300 + [5 units × (22 − 10)] = 300 + [5 units × (12)] = 360).

Working with Graphs and Charts

1. Exhibit 5-8(a) represents a decrease in supply, or a leftward shift in the supply curve.
2. Exhibit 5-8(b) could represent a change in supply due to technological advancement.
3. Exhibit 5-8(c) represents movement along a supply curve, or an increase in quantity supplied.
4. Exhibit 5-8(a) could represent a change in supply due to an increase in resource prices.

Solving Economic Problems

1. Answers will vary. (*Sample answer:* A student keeps a journal of the number of hours she or he studies for an economics test. Let's say the student currently studies an average of 4 hours for every economics test. Next, the teacher increases the reward for a certain performance on the test. Instead of getting only an A for a perfect test, the reward is changed to an A+, something else the student values. If the law of supply holds for studying for an economics test, we should notice that the student will study more than 4 hours for the next test.)
2. If taxes are applied to the production of a good, the good becomes more expensive to produce. As a result, producers will reap lower profits on the good and thus want to produce fewer units of it. At every given price, quantity supplied will decrease. If quantity supplied decreases at every given price, supply will fall.

Chapter 5 Supply 127

Chapter 6 Planning Guide

SECTION ORGANIZER

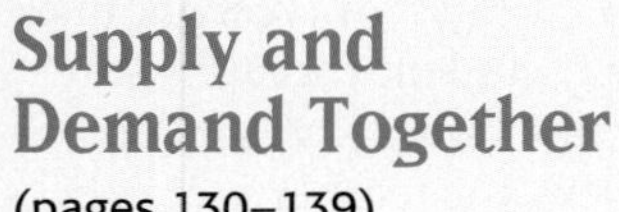

Supply and Demand Together
(pages 130–139)

Supply and Demand in Everyday Life
(pages 140–147)

Section	Learning Objectives	Reproducible Worksheets and Handouts	Assessment
Section 1: Supply and Demand Together (pages 130–139)	▸ Explain how supply and demand together determine price. ▸ Describe what happens to price when the market has a surplus. ▸ Describe what happens to price when the market has a shortage.	Section 1 Activities, *Applying the Principles Workbook* Outlining Activity, *Guided Reading and Study Guide* Just the Facts Handout, *Guided Reading and Study Guide*	Section Assessment, *Student Text,* page 139 Quick Quiz, *Annotated Teacher's Edition,* page 138 Section Quiz, *Assessment Book*
Section 2: Supply and Demand in Everyday Life (pages 140–147)	▸ Provide examples of how supply and demand affect everyday life. ▸ Describe how shortage, surplus, and equilibrium affect special events. ▸ Understand why prices for goods differ from city to city. ▸ Explain the relationship between traffic congestion and supply and demand. ▸ Identify necessary conditions for high income.	Section 2 Activity, *Applying the Principles Workbook* Outlining Activity, *Guided Reading and Study Guide* Just the Facts Handout, *Guided Reading and Study Guide*	Section Assessment, *Student Text,* page 147 Quick Quiz, *Annotated Teacher's Edition,* page 147 Section Quiz, *Assessment Book*

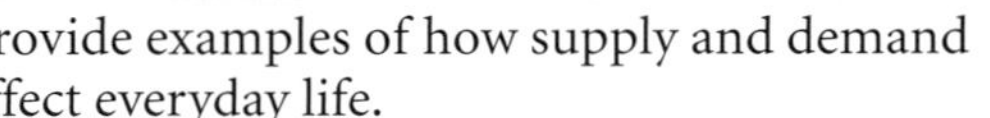

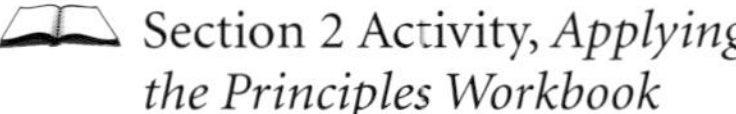

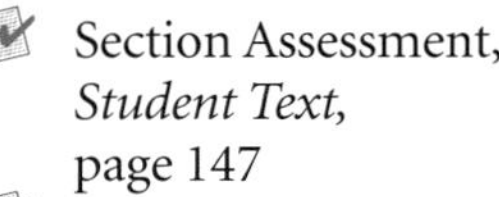

CHAPTER AND PROGRAM RESOURCES

Reproducible Chapter Resources and Assessment Materials

 Graphic Organizer Activity, *Guided Reading and Study Guide*

 Vocabulary Activity, *Guided Reading and Study Guide*

 Working with Graphs and Charts, *Guided Reading and Study Guide*

Practice Test, *Guided Reading and Study Guide*

 Critical Thinking Activity, *Finding Economics*

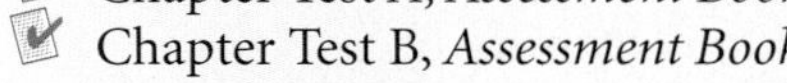

Chapter Test A, *Assessment Book*

Chapter Test B, *Assessment Book*

Technology Resources

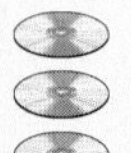

Test Generator CD

Spanish Audio Summaries CD

Marketplace® Audio Lessons CD

Economic Principles Lectures, Videocassette or DVD

Lesson Planning and Teaching Resources

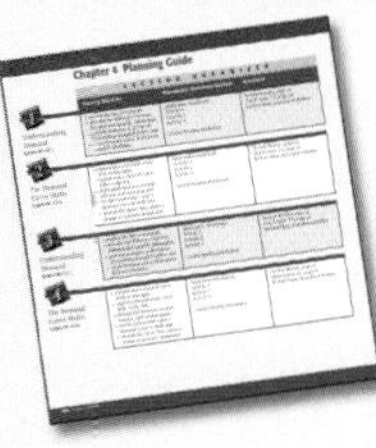

The *Economics: New Ways of Thinking* Teacher Resources include detailed lesson plans for each section in this chapter; the lesson plans are available in print form *(Lesson Plans)* and electronic form. The Teacher Resources also include *Daily Lectures: Overheads and Notes,* which provides prepared overheads and discussion notes covering the key concepts in each section of this chapter.

EMC Publishing Economics Online

Go to Economics Online, at www.emcp.com, for a variety of Internet resources to help you keep your course current and relevant. At Economics Online you will find these items:

- Economics in the News Lessons
- Study Guide Questions
- Practice Tests
- Lesson Plans

Internet Resources

Economics: New Ways of Thinking encourages students to use the Internet to find out more about economics. With the wealth of current, valid information available on Web sites, using the Internet as a research tool is likely to increase your students' interest in and understanding of economics principles and topics. In addition, doing Internet research can help your students form the habit of accessing and using economics information, as well as help them develop investigative skills they will use throughout their educational and professional careers.

To aid your students in achieving these ends, each chapter of *Economics: New Ways of Thinking* includes the addresses of several Web sites at which students will find engaging, relevant information. When students type in the addresses provided, they will immediately arrive at the intended sites. The addresses have been modified so that EMC Publishing can monitor and maintain the proper links—for example, the government site http://stats.bls.gov/ has been changed to www.emcp.net/prices. In the event that the address or content of a site changes or is discontinued, EMC's Internet editors will create a link that redirects students to an address with similar information.

Activities in the *Annotated Teacher's Edition* often suggest that students search the Internet for information. For some activities, you might want to find reputable sites beforehand, and steer students to those sites. For other activities, you might want students to do their own searching, and then check out the sites they have found and discuss why they might be reliable or unreliable.

CHAPTER 6

Overview

This chapter discusses demand and supply together, looks at markets and how they function, and explains how markets determine prices. The following statements provide brief descriptions of the major concepts covered in each section of this chapter.

Supply and Demand Together

Section 1 explains how supply and demand work together to determine market price. Students will learn how an equilibrium price is established, what happens to price when there is a surplus or shortage in the market, and how price controls affect supply and demand.

Supply and Demand in Everyday Life

Section 2 examines real-world scenarios to demonstrate the market forces of supply and demand and price. Students will attain a deeper understanding of supply and demand by examining how they work in arenas with which students are familiar.

CHAPTER 6

Price: Supply and Demand Together

Why It Matters

Markets and prices are a little like the air you breathe—they are everywhere. Anytime you buy or sell something, you will buy or sell that something at a price, in a market.

Supply and demand go together to determine price. What determines the price of the car you buy? Answer: supply and demand. What determines the price that you sell your labor services for? Answer: supply and demand. What determines the price of the house you buy? Answer: supply and demand.

We will learn about supply and demand together in this chapter by looking at several examples from everyday life. We will also learn about price, which is the outcome of demand and supply working at the same time.

This dealer is an expert in fine-crafted art from all over the world. An important part of his job is to arrive at the right price for each object.

Teaching Suggestions from the Author

In my mind, this is the most important chapter in the book. All the fundamentals of supply and demand are here, and the model of how free, competitive markets work is presented. I present the theoretical material in this chapter by asking questions such as the following: What happens in a market if price is above the equilibrium level? What happens in a market if price is below equilibrium level? What happens if there is a shortage in a market? What happens if there is a surplus in the market? What is so special about equilibrium price and quantity?

Then after students understand the theory of supply and demand, and of how markets equilibrate, it is time to have some fun with supply and demand by examin-

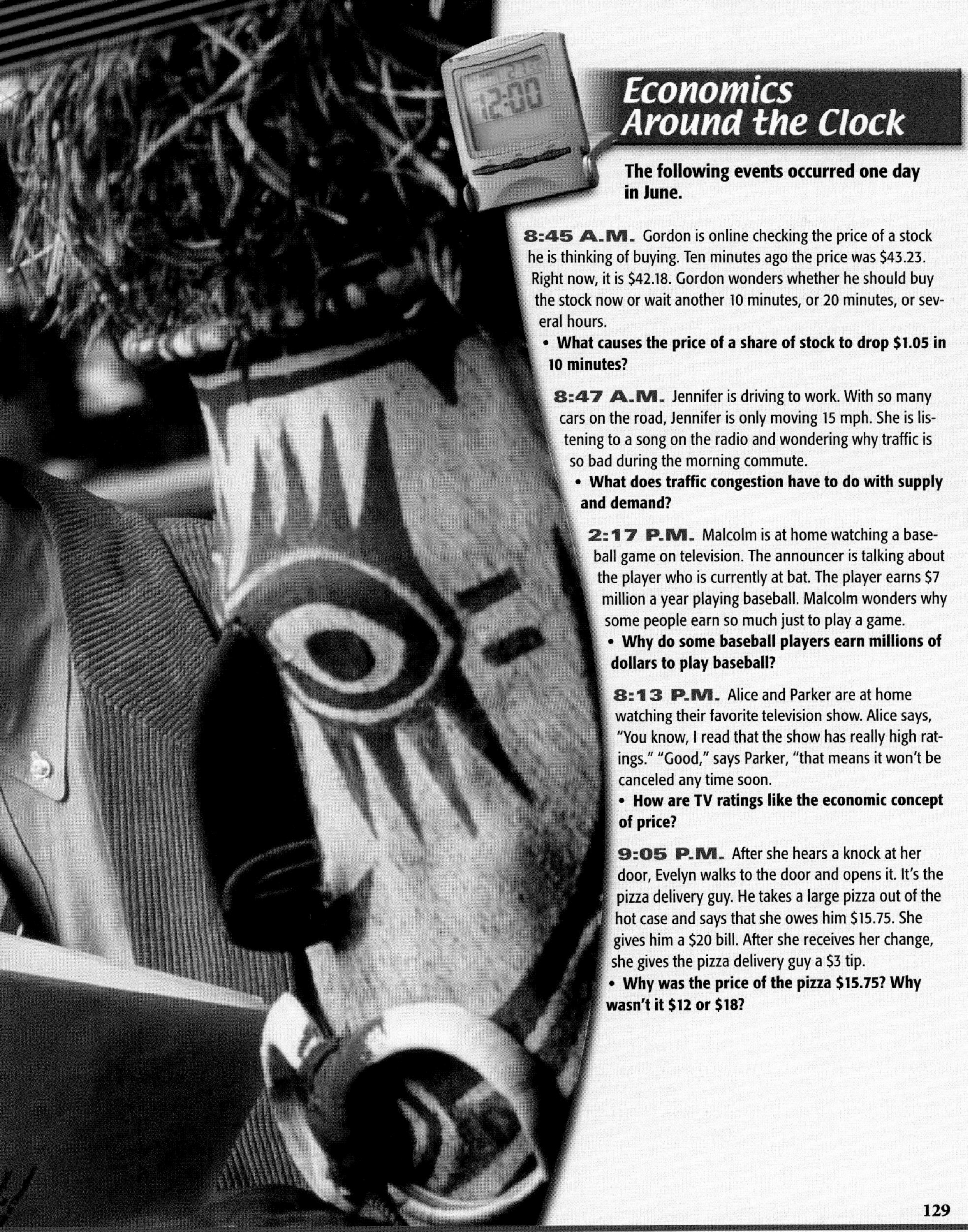

Economics Around the Clock

The following events occurred one day in June.

8:45 A.M. Gordon is online checking the price of a stock he is thinking of buying. Ten minutes ago the price was $43.23. Right now, it is $42.18. Gordon wonders whether he should buy the stock now or wait another 10 minutes, or 20 minutes, or several hours.

- **What causes the price of a share of stock to drop $1.05 in 10 minutes?**

8:47 A.M. Jennifer is driving to work. With so many cars on the road, Jennifer is only moving 15 mph. She is listening to a song on the radio and wondering why traffic is so bad during the morning commute.

- **What does traffic congestion have to do with supply and demand?**

2:17 P.M. Malcolm is at home watching a baseball game on television. The announcer is talking about the player who is currently at bat. The player earns $7 million a year playing baseball. Malcolm wonders why some people earn so much just to play a game.

- **Why do some baseball players earn millions of dollars to play baseball?**

8:13 P.M. Alice and Parker are at home watching their favorite television show. Alice says, "You know, I read that the show has really high ratings." "Good," says Parker, "that means it won't be canceled any time soon.

- **How are TV ratings like the economic concept of price?**

9:05 P.M. After she hears a knock at her door, Evelyn walks to the door and opens it. It's the pizza delivery guy. He takes a large pizza out of the hot case and says that she owes him $15.75. She gives him a $20 bill. After she receives her change, she gives the pizza delivery guy a $3 tip.

- **Why was the price of the pizza $15.75? Why wasn't it $12 or $18?**

ing supply and demand applications. Students will see theory in action and use it to understand their everyday world. After you teach the applications in the chapter, invite students to think up their own supply and demand applications. A few days spent on this exercise are likely to pay high dividends.

Introducing the Chapter

In previous chapters, students learned about two of the building blocks of economics, supply and demand. In this chapter, they will learn what supply and demand create—price. Write the word "price" on the board. Ask students to discuss how important prices are to both buyers and sellers. After the class discussion, explain to students that this chapter will explore how supply and demand work together in our free enterprise economy to determine the prices we pay for goods and services.

Teaching with Visuals

Price is a concept with which students are familiar. Have them look at the photo on this spread and explain how price is important for the art dealer in the photo. Students will probably say that the dealer must be knowledgeable about the value of art from all over the world in order to arrive at the right price for each object.

SECTION 1

Teacher Support

Focus and Motivate

Section Objectives

After completing this section, students will be able to

- explain how supply and demand together determine price;
- describe what happens to price when the market has a surplus; and
- describe what happens to price when the market has a shortage.

Economics Around the Clock

Kickoff Activity

Have students read the 8:45 A.M. scenario in Economics Around the Clock (page 129) and write their answers to the accompanying question.

Invite students to share their answers with the class. Students may predict that changes in the price of a share of stock are determined by changes in the supply and demand of that stock.

Activating Prior Knowledge

To review concepts presented in the previous chapter, give students time to address the following question by creating a visual: What is the relationship between the price of a good and the quantity supplied? Students should draw a supply curve.

SECTION 1

Supply and Demand Together

Focus Questions

- How do supply and demand together determine price?
- What happens to price when the market has a surplus?
- What happens to price when the market has a shortage?

Key Terms

surplus
shortage
equilibrium
equilibrium quantity
equilibrium price
inventory
price ceiling
price floor

Moving to Equilibrium

Imagine a pair of scissors. Which blade does the cutting, the top blade or the bottom? It's impossible to say, isn't it? In much the same way, it is impossible to say whether demand or supply is responsible for the prices we pay for goods and services. The fact is, supply and demand work together to determine price.

To understand exactly how supply and demand work together, imagine that you are at an auction where 40,000 bushels of corn are being sold. All of the potential buyers of corn are sitting in front of computers. At any given price, the buyers simply key in the number of bushels they want to buy. The auction begins with the auctioneer calling out a price of $6. (Follow along in Exhibit 6-1 on the next page as you read about what is happening at the auction.)

surplus
The condition in which the quantity supplied of a good is greater than the quantity demanded. Surpluses occur only at prices *above* equilibrium price.

- At $6 a bushel, the potential buyers think for a second, and then they all enter into their computers the number of bushels they want to buy at that price. The total that the buyers enter is 20,000 bushels, which is the quantity demanded of corn at $6 per bushel (see Exhibit 6-1). The quantity supplied, though, is 40,000. In economics, when quantity supplied is greater than quantity demanded, a **surplus** exists. At a price of $6 per bushel, the surplus equals 20,000 bushels (the difference between the quantity supplied and the quantity demanded). So, what do you think will happen next? The auctioneer, realizing that 20,000 bushels of corn will go unsold at $6, decides to lower the price per bushel to $5.
- At $5 a bushel, the buyers again key in the number of bushels they will buy, and the total increases to 30,000 bushels. This amount still leaves a surplus of corn—specifically, 10,000 bushels. So, what will the auctioneer do? Again, he lowers the price, this time to $2.
- At only $2 a bushel, the buyers want to buy a lot more corn, and the total quantity demanded jumps to 60,000 bushels. At first it sounds like a good thing, but do you see why it is a problem? (Look again at Exhibit 6-1.) Quantity

Internet Research

Guide students in finding online real estate listings for their city or region and comparing the prices for two- or three-bedroom apartments or homes in different neighborhoods. Bring city maps to class so students can see where the listings are actually located. What factors make the prices different? Why does supply and demand differ among neighborhoods? Encourage students to think not only about the overall desirability of living in certain neighborhoods but also about such factors as available land, housing density, and zoning restrictions that may affect housing supply.

demanded is now greater than quantity supplied, a condition that economists call a **shortage**. The auctioneer, realizing that he can't sell 60,000 bushels of corn when he only has 40,000, decides to raise the price to $3.

- As we would expect, when the price goes up, from $2 to $3 a bushel, the buyers want less corn. The quantity demanded falls to 50,000 bushels, but still there is a shortage. So the auctioneer again raises the price, this time to $4.
- At $4 a bushel, the buyers key in a total of 40,000 bushels, exactly the same amount as the auctioneer has to sell. Quantity demanded equals quantity supplied. The auction stops. At this point, but not until this point, economists would say that the corn market is in equilibrium. A market is said to be in **equilibrium** when the quantity demanded of a good equals the quantity supplied. In this example, 40,000 bushels is referred to as the **equilibrium quantity** (the quantity of a good bought and sold in a market that is in equilibrium). The price of $4 is referred to as the **equilibrium price** (the price at which a good is bought and sold in a market that is in equilibrium).

Relationship of quantity supplied (Q_s) to quantity demanded (Q_d)	Market condition
$Q_s > Q_d$	Surplus
$Q_d > Q_s$	Shortage
$Q_d = Q_s$	Equilibrium

When the price was $6 a bushel and there was a surplus of corn, the auctioneer lowered the price. When the price was $2, resulting in a shortage, he raised the price. The behavior of the auctioneer can be summarized this way: If a surplus exists, lower the price; if a shortage exists, raise the price. In this way, the auctioneer moved the corn market into equilibrium.

Not all markets have auctioneers. (When was the last time you saw an auctioneer in the grocery store?) Still, many markets act *as if* an auctioneer is calling out higher and lower prices until equilibrium price is reached. In many real-world markets, prices fall when a surplus occurs and rise when a shortage happens.

EXHIBIT 6-1 Supply and Demand at Work at an Auction

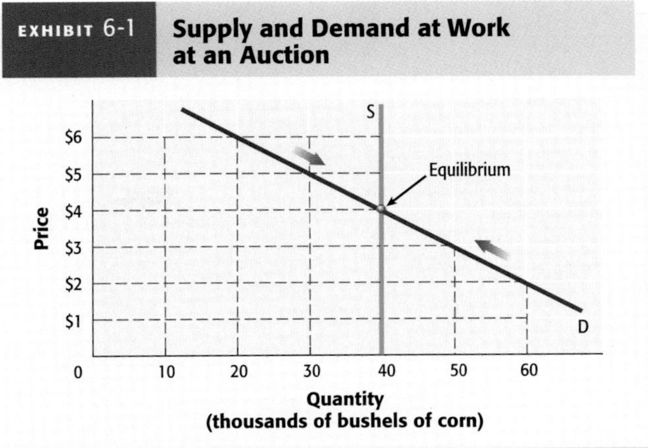

▲ Only at a price of $4 is the quantity demanded equal to the quantity supplied, with neither a surplus nor a shortage.

Why Does Price Fall When a Surplus Occurs?

With a surplus, suppliers will not be able to sell all they had hoped to sell, so their **inventories** (stock of goods on hand) grow beyond the normal level. Storing extra goods can be costly and inefficient; thus sellers want to reduce their inventories. Some will lower prices to do so; some will cut back on producing output; others will do a little of both. As shown in Exhibit 6-2, price and output tend to fall until equilibrium is achieved.

Why Does Price Rise When There Is a Shortage?

With a shortage, buyers will not be able to buy all they had hoped to buy. Some buyers will offer to pay a higher price to get sellers to sell to them rather than other buyers. The higher prices will motivate suppliers to start producing more output. Thus, in a shortage, the tendency is for price and output to rise until equilibrium is achieved (see Exhibit 6-2 on the next page).

shortage
The condition in which the quantity demanded of a good is greater than the quantity supplied. Shortages occur only at prices below equilibrium price.

equilibrium
In a market the point at which the quantity of a good that buyers are willing and able to buy is equal to the quantity that sellers are willing and able to produce and offer for sale (quantity demanded equals quantity supplied).

equilibrium quantity
The quantity of a good that is bought and sold in a market that is in equilibrium.

equilibrium price
The price at which a good is bought and sold in a market that is in equilibrium.

inventory
The stock of goods that a business or store has on hand.

Teach

Discussion Starter

Some students may have participated in auctions, either for livestock or for other items. Have them share their experiences with the class. Ask students how they knew when the equilibrium price was reached for the item up for bid. Students should say that the equilibrium price was reached when the quantity demanded equaled the quantity supplied.

Thinking Like an Economist

Economists think of *equilibrium* the way people think of a magnet. A magnet draws things to it. Markets are drawn toward equilibrium. If there is a shortage in a competitive market, it won't last long. The shortage will turn into equilibrium. Similarly, a surplus in a competitive market won't last long, because the surplus will turn into equilibrium. Invite students to brainstorm situations in which the market is drawn back to equilibrium after prices are set either too high or too low.

Economics Around the Clock

After reading and discussing "Moving to Equilibrium" (pages 130–132), you may want to refer students to the 8:13 P.M. scenario in Economics Around the Clock (page 129) and discuss their answers to the question it poses. Help them understand that when the demand to watch a television show rises, the ratings rise, just as when the demand for a good (apples, oranges, watches) rises, the price rises.

Differentiating Instruction

Kinesthetic and Visual Learners

You may want to pass out wooden rulers to the class so each student can see what equilibrium really is. Tell students that, for this activity, everything on the ruler from zero to six represents the quantity supplied for a good and everything from 6 to 12 represents the quantity demanded. Have them balance the rulers by placing their index finger under the ruler at approximately the six-inch mark. Show students that the ruler can be balanced perfectly on the equilibrium point. Because the quantity demanded equals the quantity supplied, equilibrium is achieved.

Teaching with Visuals

Draw a supply and demand diagram on the board as in Exhibit 6-2. Label the vertical axis "Price" and the horizontal axis "Quantity." Put in an equilibrium price that corresponds to the intersection of supply and demand. Invite students to come to the board and shift the supply or demand curve in one direction or the other. Ask students to explain what happened to supply or demand and to identify the new equilibrium quantity and price.

Reinforcement Activity

Tell students to ask one or two storeowners whether they lower the price when they have a surplus of a good and whether they raise the price when they have a shortage of a good. Allow students to report their findings to the class.

Prediction Activity

Suppose a company's stock sells for $110 a share. The company produces a product that it sells in many countries. One day the company receives some bad economic news: Congress has passed legislation prohibiting it from selling its product in five countries to which it currently sells. Ask students to predict what will happen to the share price of this company's stock.

Students should predict that the share price will decline because the demand for the stock will decrease, and as demand decreases, price falls.

▶ If a surplus occurs, price and quantity of output fall. If a shortage happens, price and quantity of output rise. A price of $10 means neither a surplus nor a shortage, so neither price nor quantity of output changes.

EXHIBIT 6-2 Moving to Equilibrium

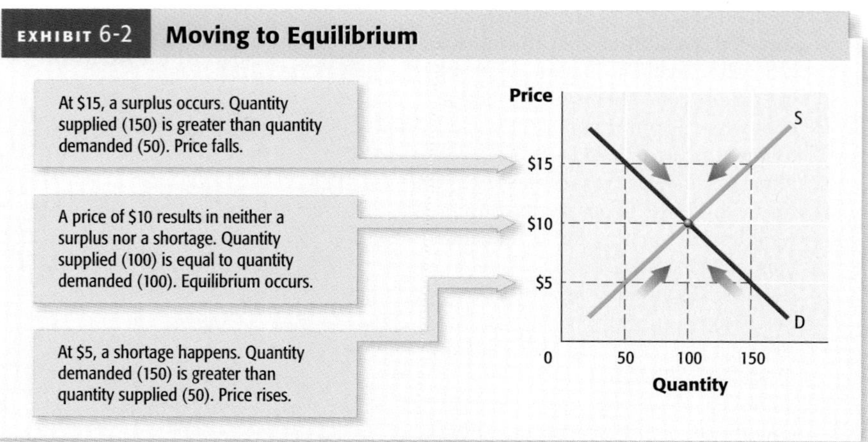

At $15, a surplus occurs. Quantity supplied (150) is greater than quantity demanded (50). Price falls.
A price of $10 results in neither a surplus nor a shortage. Quantity supplied (100) is equal to quantity demanded (100). Equilibrium occurs.
At $5, a shortage happens. Quantity demanded (150) is greater than quantity supplied (50). Price rises.
Price
$15
$10
$5
0
50
100
150
Quantity
S
D

EXAMPLE: We know what a shortage and a surplus look like on a graph, but what do they look like in the real world? Suppose it's Friday night and your school's football team is playing at home. Your school stadium seats 2,000 people but only 500 people are in the stands (350 from your school and 150 from your opponents' school), resulting in a surplus of seats. In other words, the people who wanted to be at the game was a smaller number than seats available in the stands. On the other hand, suppose at another game 2,500 people want to be at the game but the stadium still has only 2,000 seats. Here we see a shortage of seats. Maybe some people will have to stand, or some people will not be admitted to the game. ◆

EXAMPLE: Back when the Soviet Union existed (pre-1989), you could walk around Moscow and find very few people in some shops, but long lines of people inside and outside of other shops. At the time, Soviet officials set the prices of the goods and services sold in the country. Often, the prices they set were not equilibrium prices—prices at which quantity demanded equaled quantity supplied. Where the Soviet officials set the price of a good higher than equilibrium price (say, 100 rubles is the equilibrium price and officials set the price at 250 rubles), there was a surplus of that good. This surplus was evidenced by less of the good being purchased than was available for sale, and therefore, stores with few customers. Where the Soviet officials set the price of a good lower than equilibrium price (say, 100 rubles is the equilibrium price and officials set the price at 30 rubles), there was a shortage of that good. You could "see" a shortage in the form of a long line of people waiting to buy a good that was likely to be "sold out" before they reached the front of the line. ◆

What Causes Equilibrium Prices to Change?

You now know that equilibrium price is determined by both supply and demand. Can you guess what could cause an equilibrium price to change? You probably guessed right—for the equilibrium price to change, either supply or demand would have to change.

Before looking at changes to equilibrium prices, let's review your ability to read graphs showing supply and demand curves. Practice reading these graphs will help you use graphs to determine shortages, surpluses, and ultimately, equilibrium prices.

Look at Exhibit 6-2. Start at a price of $15. To find the quantity demanded, follow the dotted horizontal line over to the demand curve (D). Then follow the dotted vertical line downward to the horizontal (or quantity) axis (50). In this way, you find that the *quantity demanded* at $15 is 50.

Background Information: Equilibrium Prices

In the mid-to-late-1980s, real estate prices in Tokyo were sky high. The demand for land in Tokyo and the supply of land in Tokyo were intersecting at a high equilibrium price. Then, in the early-to-mid-1990s, real estate prices fell dramatically. What happened? Obviously, the supply of land hadn't changed since this was constant. The demand for land had fallen, lowering the equilibrium price of land. Direct students to research house prices around their neighborhoods. Have house values gone up, gone down, or stayed the same over the last 25 years?

How Much Would You Pay for an Ocean View?

Once upon a time, a man bought a house. The house was built on a high cliff overlooking the Atlantic Ocean. The man would get up every morning and drink his coffee as he gazed out over the ocean.

One day a friend visited the man. The friend asked the man how much he thinks he paid for the ocean view he enjoyed daily. The man said, "I didn't pay anything for the view. I bought the house. The view was just there."

The friend asked the man if any houses in the neighborhood were similar to his house but without an ocean view. The man said a house right down the street was exactly like his house but without an ocean view. "Was the price of the house down the street the same as the price of your house?" the friend asked. "No," said the man, "it was $200,000 cheaper."

"Then that is what you paid for the ocean view," the friend said. "If the only difference between your house and the house down the street is the ocean view, then the price difference between the houses is the price of the view." Of course, another way of putting this relationship is to say that the demand for the man's house was greater than the demand for the house down the street because the man's house came with an ocean view and the house down the street didn't. Higher demand for the house with the view means higher price paid for the house with the view.

The man knew that his friend was right. All this time he thought that he simply paid more for his house. Instead, he paid the same dollar price for his house as the person down the street paid for the identical house, and then he "purchased" the ocean view for $200,000.

Now ask yourself if there is anything for you that is similar to what the house was for the man. Do you buy and pay for things that you are unaware of? If you ever paid more for designer jeans than for the identical (and it must truly be "identical") nondesigner jeans, then the price difference is what you paid for the name on the back of the jeans. If you ever paid more for Bayer aspirin than for generic aspirin, then the price difference is what you paid for the name "Bayer." We are not urging you to stop buying designer jeans or Bayer aspirin. Similarly, we are not saying that it is somehow wrong to buy a house with an ocean view. We are simply pointing out what it is you are paying for.

THINK ABOUT IT People who reside in good climate locales often talk about the good climate being "free." Someone might say, "Aren't we lucky to live here? And to think, we don't have to pay a penny for all this good weather." Is it true that they don't pay for the "good weather"?

To find the *quantity supplied* at $15, again start at the price of $15 on the vertical axis, and follow the dotted horizontal line over to the supply curve (S). Then follow the dotted vertical line downward to the horizontal axis. The number here is 150, so the quantity supplied at $15 is 150.

So, at $15, does a surplus or a shortage occur? Because the quantity supplied (150) is greater than the quantity demanded (50), the result is a surplus.

Now let's look at some graphs to see what happens when either supply or demand changes.

Economics in the Real World

Have students read this feature and brainstorm other situations in which they pay for something without knowing that they are doing so.

ANSWERS TO THINK ABOUT IT The answer is no. Houses in good climates are similar to houses with ocean views in that the price of the house in a good climate probably will be higher than the price of that same house in another climate.

Background Information

Perhaps no other scholar introduced the economics profession to as many widely used microeconomic tools as the British economist Alfred Marshall (1842–1924). Two of the most important tools are supply and demand. Marshall compared supply and demand to the two blades of a pair of scissors. Just as it is impossible to say which blade does the actual cutting, it is impossible to say whether demand or supply is responsible for the market price. Some economists before Marshall thought that only the cost of production (reflected in supply) determined price; others thought that only demand determined price. Marshall, however, said that both supply and demand determine price. It is widely acknowledged today that Marshall had it right.

Differentiating Instruction

Kinesthetic and Visual Learners

Allow kinesthetic learners to manipulate the supply and demand curves to find the equilibrium price. Use either a sticky board with materials for curves or direct students to create their own three-dimensional graphs with supply and demand curves. Ask them to show what happens as supply and demand are increased or decreased. Students who create the most imaginative displays should have their work exhibited in the classroom.

Section 1 Supply and Demand Together 133

Discussion Starter

Invite students to imagine that they want to sell an item on an online auction site. Ask them whether they can set any price they like for this item. From the discussion of supply and demand, students should understand that although a seller can set any price, he or she cannot determine the quantity demanded at that price. Ask students what would happen if they set the price too high. Students should recognize that the item will not sell—in other words, the quantity of even one item will not be demanded.

Reinforcement Activity

From time to time, celebrity property is auctioned off at one of the major auction houses. Suggest that students create a list of five things they would be willing to bid on in a celebrity auction and the prices they would be willing to pay for those items. Ask whether they would pay more if someone bid against them; then point out that another bidder increases the demand for the item, increasing the price.

Teaching with Visuals

Learning how the supply and demand curves shift as the two factors change is very important. Students can probably name 10 different situations when the price of something suddenly increased, or times when they wanted to buy something, but the store had run out of its supply. Tell students to prepare their own supply and demand curves based on a real-world situation.

Demand Changes Cause Changes to Equilibrium Price

Exhibit 6-3(a) below shows the demand for and supply of television sets. The original demand curve is D_1, the supply curve is S_1, equilibrium is at point 1, and the equilibrium price is \$300. Now suppose the demand for television sets increases. (Recall from Chapter 4 the factors that can shift the demand curve for a good: income, preferences, prices of related goods, number of buyers, and future price.) The demand curve shifts to the right, from D_1 to D_2. D_2 is now the relevant demand curve. At \$300 per television, the quantity demanded (using the new demand curve, D_2) is 300,000, and the quantity supplied (using the one and only supply curve, S_1) is 200,000.

Because the quantity demanded is greater than quantity supplied, a shortage exists in the television market. Price then begins to rise. As it does, the television market moves to point 2, where it is in equilibrium again. The new equilibrium price is \$400. We conclude that an increase in the demand for a good will increase price, all other things remaining the same.

Now suppose the demand for television sets decreases as in Exhibit 6-3(b). The demand curve shifts to the left, from D_1 to D_2. At \$300, the quantity demanded (using the new demand curve, D_2) is 100,000, and the quantity supplied (again using S_1) is 200,000. Because quantity supplied is greater than quantity demanded, a surplus exists. Price begins to fall. As it does, the television

▶ A change in equilibrium price can be brought about by (a) an increase in demand, (b) a decrease in demand, (c) an increase in supply, or (d) a decrease in supply.

EXHIBIT 6-3 Changes in the Equilibrium Price of Television Sets

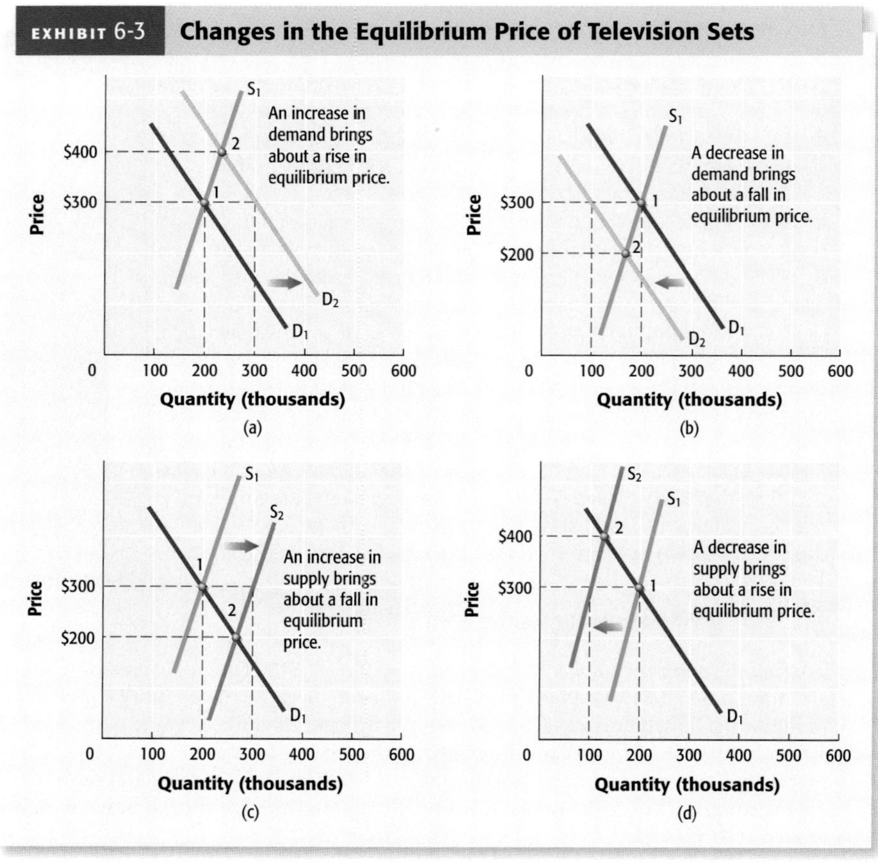

Background Information: Auctions

There are two kinds of auctions: a supply and demand auction, and a reverse auction. In the supply and demand auction process, the seller sets the minimum price and then sells the item at a price higher than the minimum bid. At a reverse auction, especially online auctions, the buyer states the price that he or she is willing to pay for the item, and the seller then decides if he or she wishes to sell at the stated price.

134 Chapter 6 Price: Supply and Demand Together

Do You Speak Economics?

??????????????????

Various language translators are available on the Web. For example, with a Spanish-English translator, you simply key in a statement in English, then click "Free Translation," and the statement is translated into Spanish. "Are you having a good morning?" becomes "¿Tiene usted un buenos días?"

Suppose an English-to-Economics translator were available. How would various statements (that you might hear every day) be translated? Here are a few examples. Do you think it might be in your personal interest to learn to speak Economics?

English
She is very popular in school.
Economics
The ***demand*** to be around her is high relative to the ***demand*** to be around others.

English
We have to do more in Mr. Johnson's class to get an A than we have to do in Mr. Meyer's class to get an A.
Economics
The ***price*** to get an A in Mr. Johnson's class is higher than the ***price*** to get an A in Mr. Meyer's class.

English
I can't get into that class, because it has no open spots.
Economics
The ***quantity demanded*** of seats in that class is greater than the ***quantity supplied***, resulting in a ***shortage*** of seats in that class.

English
They did away with fast food at the school.
Economics
The ***supply*** of fast food at the school dropped to zero.

English
Jake can only come to the party if he brings some food; of course, Stephanie doesn't have to bring anything.
Economics
The ***price*** is higher for Jake to attend the party than for Stephanie.

English
Do you want to dance?
Economics
I have a ***demand*** to be around you. Do you have a ***demand*** to be around me?

English
She broke up with me.
Economics
Her ***demand*** for me fell to zero.

THINK ABOUT IT One purpose of these examples is to show you how much of what you hear in a day has some economic content. Economics appears in more places than you might think. Can you identify some everyday phrase or statement that can easily be translated into "econospeak"?

market moves to point 2, where it is in equilibrium again. The new equilibrium price is $200. A decrease in the demand for a good will decrease price, all other things remaining the same.

EXAMPLE: If you go to the Boston Red Sox Web site you will be able to buy tickets (that some ticket holders want to sell) for various games played at Fenway Park. On the day we checked, the price of a seat in Section 36, Row 19 was $105 if you wanted to see the game between the Boston Red Sox and the Atlanta Braves. If you wanted to see a game between the Boston Red Sox and the New York Yankees the price of a seat in the same section and row was $205. The number of seats in Fenway Park is the same for all games. In other words, the supply curve of seats at Fenway Park is vertical at a little more than 36,000 seats. The demand for games at Fenway differs from game to game,

After reading this feature, students should list benefits of learning to speak Economics. Ask how learning the language of economics might help them make informed decisions on significant financial issues in the future.

ANSWERS TO THINK ABOUT IT Answers will vary. Invite volunteers to share their "econospeak" with the class.

Background Information

There are many different currencies in the world: Mexican pesos, French Francs, Russian rubles, British pounds, Japanese yen, and so on. If you want foreign currency, you have to buy it much the same way you have to buy a computer. The value of a foreign currency is based on the supply or demand for that currency, just like any other good. Whenever the demand for or the supply of a currency changes, its price changes, too. Foreign currencies are very similar to any other good: the equilibrium price will be reached by the market as long as nothing else interferes.

Reinforcement Activity

Assign students to each write a sentence in which they explain the likely effect of long lines of buyers on the equilibrium price of a product.

Cooperative Learning

Divide the class into groups of four or five. Each group member should scan newspapers and newsmagazines for an article or a feature illustrating supply and demand working together. As a group, students should choose the best article and complete the following tasks:

1. Write a summary of the article.
2. Evaluate how this condition affects the local economy.
3. Create a graph illustrating the supply and demand issue in the selected article.

Groups should present their findings to the class.

Direct students to visit the Web site mentioned and follow the directions in this feature. Ask students to draw the supply curve for one of the items they find. Students should draw a vertical supply curve because the supply of any item created before 1900 is fixed. Invite students to explain how bidders affect the demand curve.

Discussion Starter

Students may understand the reasons for changes in equilibrium prices and not even know it. Ask students the following questions about sales that they have seen in the last few days or weeks: What might have happened to supply and demand to cause the sale? How does this change the way you feel about sale prices, if at all?

Cause and Effect

Ask students to bring in advertisements for sales of goods. Most advertisements list both the sale price and the original price. Direct students to graph the supply and demand curves of a sale good and to write a short description of what has happened to supply and demand for that good.

Reinforcement Activity

Street markets and farmers markets are becoming more common in the United States. Ask students to recall a time when they negotiated a lower price from a seller at a market, or to imagine a time when they might have done so. Have them write a sentence about how this negotiation contributed to the forces of supply and demand.

Supply and demand are at work in auctions that take place on the World Wide Web. www.emcp.net/ebay is the address of a popular auction site, eBay. By using the drop-down menu on the left side of your screen, you can browse for various items. Click on "Art," followed by "Antique, Pre-1900." Notice what specific items are being auctioned. Be sure to notice the highest bid for each item, the number of bids, and when the auction ends.

though. For example, the demand for a game with the Yankees is usually greater than the demand for a game with the Braves (in other words, the demand curve for a Yankees game lies to the right of the demand curve for a Braves game). As a result, the ticket price for a Red Sox–Yankees game is usually higher than the ticket price for a Red Sox–Braves game. ♦

EXAMPLE: A hotel in Miami Beach charges $150 a night for a room in June but $250 a night in January. Why the difference? A room is a room is a room, isn't it? Well, yes, a room is a room, but the demand for the room is different at different times of the year. Winter is the "high season" in Miami Beach, because people all over the United States want to escape the cold weather where they live and vacation for a few days in warm Miami Beach. Higher demand translates into higher price. ♦

Supply Changes Cause Changes to Equilibrium Price

Now let's return to Exhibit 6-3. Suppose the supply of television sets increases. (Recall the discussion in Chapter 5 of the factors that can shift the supply curve for a good, including resource prices, technology, taxes, and so on.) The supply curve in Exhibit 6-3(c) shifts to the right, from S_1 to S_2. At $300, the quantity supplied (using the new supply curve, S_2) is 300,000, and the quantity demanded (using D_1) is 200,000. Quantity supplied is greater than quantity demanded, so a surplus exists in the television market. Price begins to fall, and the television market moves to point 2, where it is in equilibrium again. The new equilibrium price is $200. Thus, an increase in the supply of a good will decrease the price, all other things remaining the same.

Now suppose the supply of television sets decreases, as in Exhibit 6-3(d). The supply curve shifts leftward, from S_1 to S_2. At $300, the quantity supplied (using S_2) is 100,000, and the quantity demanded (using D_1) is 200,000. Because quantity demanded is greater than quantity supplied, a shortage exists in the television market. Price begins to rise, and the television market moves to point 2, where it is again in equilibrium at the new equilibrium price of $400. We conclude that a decrease in the supply of a good will increase the price, all other things remaining the same.

EXAMPLE: The supply of oranges in Florida and California is greater in year 2 than in year 1. As a result, the supply curve of oranges in year 2 lies to the right of the supply curve of oranges in year 1. If the demand curve for oranges in both years is the same, then the price of oranges will be lower in year 2 than in year 1. ♦

Changes in Supply and in Demand at the Same Time

Until now, we have looked at cases in which either demand changed and supply remained constant, or supply changed and demand remained constant. In the real world, of course, both demand and supply can change at the same time. Let's look at one case and see how equilibrium price changes as a result.

Look at Exhibit 6-4. Suppose that D_1 and S_1 represent the initial situation in the market, and the resulting equilibrium price is $300. Then both demand and supply increase. Demand increases from D_1 to D_2, and supply increases from S_1 to S_2. Notice that the increase in demand is greater than the increase in supply. In other words, the

Background Information: Supply, Demand, and the California Gold Rush

The California gold rush provides an excellent example of how a dramatic change in supply or demand can lead to equally dramatic price changes. Before the discovery of gold at Sutter's mill, a metal pan sold for 20 cents, which is the equivalent of $3.60 today. After gold was discovered, the demand for metal pans (which were used to "pan" for the gold) increased sharply. The price followed, rising to $15 (equivalent to $270 today). Real estate that cost $16 (the equivalent of $288 today) before gold was discovered jumped to more than $40,000 (more than $750,000 today). Near the mines, a loaf of bread cost 75 cents ($13.50 today). Eggs sold for about $2 each ($36 today), and boots were $100 a pair ($1,800 today).

demand curve shifts further right (from D_1 to D_2) than the supply curve shifts right (from S_1 to S_2). As we can see in the exhibit, equilibrium price rises from $300 to $400. So, if both demand and supply increase and demand increases more than supply, the equilibrium price increases.

The change in equilibrium price will be determined by which changes more, supply or demand. If demand increases more than supply, the equilibrium price goes up. If supply increases more than demand, the equilibrium price will go down.

EXHIBIT 6-4 Changes in Both Supply and Demand

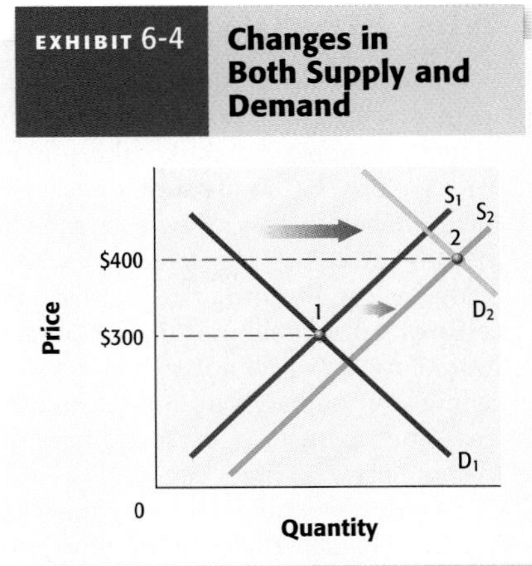

◀ Sometimes supply and demand change at the same time. Here, although both demand and supply increase, demand increases more than supply. As a result, equilibrium price increases.

Does It Matter if Price Is at Its Equilibrium Level?

Think of two different worlds. World 1 has ten markets, each of which is in equilibrium. If all markets are in equilibrium, it means no shortages or surpluses of any good or service. In this world, buyers or sellers have no complaints. Everyone is happy.

World 2 also has ten markets, but in five of the ten markets price is below equilibrium price, and in five markets price is above equilibrium price. In other words, half the markets are in surplus, and half are in shortage. In this world, both buyers and sellers are complaining.

Which world would you rather live in? Can you see why economists think it is important to study and understand price and equilibrium?

Price Is a Signal

You are probably beginning to see that price has certain important jobs that it fulfills in the marketplace. One such job is to provide information, which it does in a kind of "market conversation." For example, suppose for two goods—clocks and books—preferences one day shift against clocks and in favor of books. We know that a change in preferences affects the demand for both clocks and books. The demand for clocks will fall and the demand for books will rise.

What happens to price in each case? As a result of the decreased demand for clocks, the price of clocks falls. Because of the lower price for clocks, the quantity supplied of clocks falls. In other words, clock sellers will respond to the lower price for clocks by offering to sell fewer clocks. (The quantity supplied of clocks is lower at a lower price than at a higher price.)

As a result of the increased demand for books, the price of books rises. Because of the higher price for books, book sellers will offer to sell more books. In other words, book sellers will respond to the higher price of books by offering to sell more books. (The quantity supplied of books is higher at a higher price than at a lower price.)

> *"Teach a parrot to say 'supply and demand,' and you've got an economist."*
> — Economics Joke

Notice how buyers are communicating with sellers. Buyers aren't saying "produce fewer clocks and produce more books," but the result is the same. Instead, buyers are simply lowering the demand for clocks and raising the demand for books. As a result, price goes down for clocks and up for books. Sellers see these price changes and respond to them. They decrease the quantity supplied of clocks and increase the quantity supplied of books. Price, then, acts as a signal that is passed along by buyers to sellers. As price goes down, buyers are saying to sellers "produce less of this good." As price goes up, buyers are saying to sellers "produce more of this good."

In this example, price is a signal that directs the allocation of resources away from clocks and toward books.

Travelers trekking westward often found water in short supply. It was common for them to pay $1 for a glass of water ($18 today). In some cases, the price for a glass of water rose to $100 ($1,800 today).

Reinforcement Activity

Direct students to write a sentence in which they explain how supply and demand relate to equilibrium. Students might write that equilibrium exists in a market when the quantity of a good that buyers are willing and able to buy is equal to the quantity of the good that sellers are willing and able to produce and offer for sale. That is, quantity demanded equals quantity supplied.

Discussion Starter

Invite students to imagine the two worlds discussed on page 137 and discuss the following questions: What would the world that is at complete equilibrium price be like? What kind of place would the other world, with no markets at equilibrium, be? Which world would you rather live in? Why?

Thinking Like an Economist

Economists know that competitive markets, if left unhampered, eventually reach equilibrium. They also know that not all competitive markets reach equilibrium at the same speed. For example, the stock market may go from shortage to equilibrium in a matter of seconds or minutes, whereas the housing market may take months to make a similar move.

Section 1 Supply and Demand Together 137

A Student Asks

You may want to use this A Student Asks to make sure students understand the difference between price ceilings and price floors. Then direct them to the Debating the Issues feature on pages 152–153 for arguments for and against price controls in a specific situation. Afterward lead students to brainstorm other situations in which price controls might be used, and choose one situation for a class discussion on possible positive and negative effects.

Application Activity

After reading and discussing Section 1, you may want to assign the Section Activities in the *Applying the Principles Workbook*.

Assess

Quick Quiz

The following true-and-false quiz will help you assess student understanding of the material covered in this section.

1. When quantity supplied is greater than quantity demanded, a surplus exists. (True)
2. A shortage occurs when quantity demanded is greater than quantity supplied. (True)
3. The price at which a good is bought and sold in a market that is in equilibrium is called the equilibrium price. (True)
4. The stock of goods on hand is called the inventory. (True)
5. If price is too high, there is a surplus; if price is too low, there is a shortage. (True)

price ceiling
A legislated price—set lower than the equilibrium price—above which buyers and sellers cannot legally buy and sell a good.

price floor
A legislated price—set above the equilibrium price—below which buyers and sellers cannot legally buy and sell a good.

What Are Price Controls?

Sometimes government prevents markets from reaching an equilibrium price. For example, suppose that the equilibrium price for a good is $10. It is possible for government officials to pass a law setting the price lower—say, $8. A legislated price that is below the equilibrium price is called a **price ceiling**. A price ceiling is like a ceiling in a room. Just as you cannot go higher than the ceiling in a room, buyers and sellers cannot legally buy and sell a good for a price higher than the price ceiling.

Government could, and sometimes does, legislate a higher (than equilibrium) price—say, $12. A legislated price that is above the equilibrium price is called a **price floor**. A price floor is like a floor in a room. Just as you cannot go lower than the floor in a room, buyers and sellers cannot legally buy and sell a good for a price lower than the price floor.

Let's look at both a price ceiling and price floor graphically. In Exhibit 6-5(a) we show a price ceiling. In the exhibit, $10 is the equilibrium price of the good. You will also notice that the equilibrium quantity is 80. The price ceiling of $8 is below the equilibrium price. What is an effect of the price ceiling? One effect is that a price ceiling creates a shortage in the market. Notice that at $8, quantity demanded (100) is greater than quantity supplied (60), which is the definition of a shortage. Because suppliers only want to supply 60 units at $8, only 60 units are bought and sold. (Sure, buyers may want to buy 100 units at $8, but because suppliers only want to sell 60 units, they decide how much is bought and sold. You can't make suppliers sell more of the good than they want to.)

Now look at Exhibit 6-5(b). Here you see a price floor of $12. What is an effect of the price floor? One effect is that a price floor creates a surplus in the market. Notice that at $12, quantity supplied (98) is greater than quantity demanded (65), which is the definition of a surplus. With the price floor, fewer units are bought and sold. Because buyers only want to buy 65 units at $12, only 65 units are bought and sold.

A Student Asks

QUESTION: *Why does government sometimes impose price controls (price ceilings and price floors)?*

ANSWER: *Sometimes government imposes a price ceiling on a good because it wants to make the good cheaper for*

EXHIBIT 6-5 Price Controls

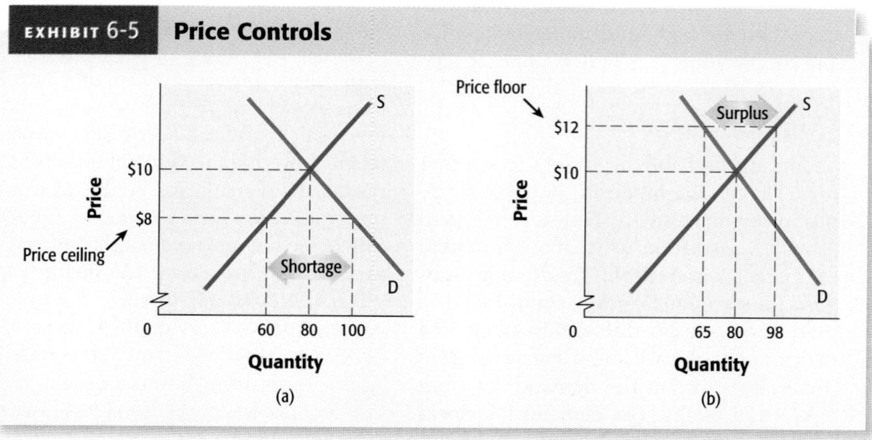

▲ The two types of price controls are price ceilings and price floors. (a) A price ceiling creates a shortage and reduces the quantity of the good bought and sold from what would be the case in equilibrium. (b) A price floor creates a surplus and reduces the quantity of the good bought and sold from what would be the case in equilibrium.

Differentiating Instruction

English Language Learners

To help ELL students, use the following resources, which are provided as part of the *Economics: New Ways of Thinking* program:

- a Spanish glossary in the *Student Text*
- Spanish versions of the Chapter Summaries on an audio CD

consumers to buy. For example, suppose the price of a particular medicine is $200 for a month's supply. Government could impose a price ceiling on this medicine of, say, $100, with the hope that more people will be able to afford the medicine now. Of course, the unintended effect of this lower-than-equilibrium price is that a shortage will result. In other words, some of the people who need the medicine might not be able to buy the medicine at $100 because it is not available.

Sometimes government imposes a price floor because it wants to assist a certain group of producers. For example, farmers sometimes argue that they need to receive a higher dollar price for what they sell. Suppose that the equilibruim price for a bushel of corn is $3. Farmers argue that they can't make a decent living at $3 a bushel. In response, government imposes a price floor of $4 on corn. Government says that no one can buy or sell corn for less than $4 a bushel. The intended effect of the price floor is to help farmers. The unintended effect, though, is to hurt the buyers of corn (they have to pay a higher price). Also, the price floor leads to a surplus of corn.

Price Controls and the Amount of Exchange

Price controls (price ceilings and price floors) bring about less exchange (less trade) than would exist without them. In Figure 6-5(a) the equilibrium quantity traded was 80, but the price ceiling reduced this level to 60. In Figure 6-5(b) the equilibrium quantity traded was 80, but the price floor reduced it to 65.

With this relationship in mind, let's go back to something that you learned about voluntary exchange (or trade) in Chapter 2 and Chapter 3. In those chapters, you learned that exchange is something that makes people better off. If John exchanges his $15 for Yvonne's book, John is, through his actions, saying that he is better off with the book than the $15. At the same time Yvonne is saying that she is better off with the $15 than she is with the book. In other words, exchange is something that makes both parties (the buyer and the seller) better off. If price controls decrease the amount of exchange that occurs, we must conclude that price controls limit the opportunities people have to make themselves better off.

Assessment Book

You will find a quiz for this section in the *Assessment Book.*

Reteaching Activity

Use the Section Assessment to gauge which students may need reteaching on this section. Guide those students in examining Exhibit 6-2. First, ask students to define the words *surplus, shortage,* and *equilibrium.* Then invite students to explain at what prices there is a surplus and at what prices there is a shortage, and why.

Guided Reading

For further reteaching of the key concepts in this section, assign the Outlining Activity and the Just the Facts Handout in the *Guided Reading and Study Guide.*

ASSESSMENT

Defining Terms

1. Define:
   a. shortage
   b. surplus
   c. equilibrium (in a market)
   d. equilibrium quantity
   e. equilibrium price
   f. inventory
   g. price ceiling
   h. price floor

Reviewing Facts and Concepts

2. If demand increases and supply is constant, what happens to equilibrium price?
3. If supply decreases and demand is constant, what happens to equilibrium price?
4. If supply increases and demand is constant, what happens to equilibrium price?
5. If the shortage is 40 units and the quantity supplied is 533 units, then what does quantity demanded equal?
6. If supply decreases by more than demand decreases, what happens to equilibrium price?

Critical Thinking

7. A producer makes 100 units of good X at $40 each. Under no circumstances will he sell the good for less than $40. Do you agree or disagree? Explain your answer.

Graphing Economics

8. Graph the following:
   a. Demand increases in a market.
   b. Supply decreases in a market.
   c. Demand decreases in a market.
   d. Demand increases by more than supply increases in a market.

Defining Terms

1. a. shortage: exists when the quantity demanded of a good is greater than the quantity supplied; **b. surplus:** exists when the quantity supplied of a good is greater than the quantity demanded; **c. equilibrium (in a market):** exists in a market when the quantity supplied of a good equals the quantity demanded of the good; **d. equilibrium quantity:** the quantity of a good that is bought and sold in a market that is in equilibrium; **e. equilibrium price:** the price at which a good is bought and sold in a market that is in equilibrium; **f. inventory:** the stock of goods that a business or store has on hand; **g. price ceiling:** a legislated price that is below the equilibrium price; **h. price floor:** a legislated price that is above the equilibrium price.

Reviewing Facts and Concepts

2. Equilibrium price rises.
3. Equilibrium price rises.
4. Equilibrium price falls.
5. Quantity demanded equals 573 units, or the quantity supplied plus the shortage.
6. Equilibrium price rises.

Critical Thinking

7. Students should disagree. Imagine that on Monday, the equilibrium price of good X is $50. The producer decides to produce 100 units of good X, which takes him from Monday through Thursday. During this time, demand for good X falls, so the new equilibrium price is $35. On Friday, the producer must decide whether to sell the good at $35 per unit even though it cost him $40 per unit to produce the good or not to sell the good at all. He can lose $40 or $5 (*calculation:* $40 – $35 = $5) per unit.

Graphing Economics

8. a. See Exhibit 6-3(a). **b.** See Exhibit 6-3(d). **c.** See Exhibit 6-3(b). **d.** See Exhibit 6-4.

SECTION 2

Teacher Support

Focus and Motivate

Section Objectives

After completing this section, students will be able to

- provide examples of how supply and demand affect everyday life;
- describe how shortage, surplus, and equilibrium affect special events;
- understand why prices for goods differ from city to city;
- explain the relationship between traffic congestion and supply and demand; and
- identify necessary conditions for high income.

Kickoff Activity

Read the following situation to students and have them answer the questions in a paragraph: Suppose tickets to a popular show go on sale at 8 A.M. Monday morning for $50 each. When the booth opens, there is a long line of people waiting to buy tickets. Some people at the far end of the line end up not being able to buy tickets at all. Was the $50 price for a ticket too high, too low, or just right? Explain your answer.

Activating Prior Knowledge

Invite students to share their responses to the Kickoff Activity. Explain to them that running out of tickets is an indicator of a shortage. A shortage occurs only at a price below equilibrium price.

Teach

Discussion Starter

Urge students to think about purchases they made recently. Ask them to explain how supply and demand affected those purchases and whether they would make the same purchases now, knowing what they do about how price is set.

SECTION 2

Supply and Demand in Everyday Life

Focus Questions

- Why do people wait in long lines to buy tickets for some rock concerts?
- Why does a house cost more in San Francisco than in Louisville, but a candy bar costs the same in both cities?
- Why does it cost more to go to the movies on Friday night than on Tuesday morning?
- What does traffic congestion have to do with supply and demand?
- What does trying out for a high school sports team have to do with supply and demand?
- What is the necessary condition to earn a high income?

Why the Long Lines for Concert Tickets?

Suppose tickets for a rock concert go on sale at 8 a.m. on Saturday. A long line of people forms even before the ticket booth opens. The average person has to wait an hour to buy a ticket. Some people don't get to buy tickets at all because the concert sells out before they get to the ticket booth.

Why do so many people wait in line to buy tickets to the rock concert, yet you don't see a long line of people waiting to buy food at the grocery store or TVs at the electronics store? Also, why are some of the people waiting to buy tickets to the rock concert turned away, but no one who wants to buy bread is turned away at the grocery store, and no one who wants to buy a TV set is turned away at the electronics store? The market for the rock concert tickets (at least in this instance) must differ somehow, but how?

In economic terms, when some people go away without being able to buy what they came to buy, it means that quantity demanded exceeds quantity supplied, resulting in a shortage in the market.

You learned earlier that a market shortage causes price to rise. Eventually, it will rise to its equilibrium level. The problem in the rock concert example, though, is that the tickets were bought and sold before the seller realized a shortage of tickets would occur. In hindsight, the seller knows that the price charged for the tickets was too low, and this pricing caused a shortage. If the seller had charged the equilibrium price, he would have encountered no shortage, no long lines, and no one turned away without a ticket.

As shown in Exhibit 6-6, the seller charged $40 a ticket. At this price, quantity demanded (12,500) was greater than quantity supplied (10,000). If the price had been $60 a ticket, quantity supplied (10,000) would have equaled quantity demanded (10,000), and no shortage would have happened.

Why didn't the seller charge the higher equilibrium price, instead of a price that was too low? The seller might have charged the equilibrium price had she known it. Think back to the auctioneer example. Note that the auctioneer did not call out the equilibrium price at the start of the auction. He called out $6, which was too high a price,

Internet Research

Direct students to go to the Web site for Project Vote Smart, look for information on current legislation, and pick as many as three bills that, if passed, might affect the price of some good. Students should briefly summarize the intent of each bill and explain how and why it could affect prices. Then allow students to discuss whether they would pass the bills.

which created a surplus. Later, he called out $2, which was too low a price, causing a shortage. It was only through trial and error that the auctioneer finally hit upon the equilibrium price. Because people come to the grocery store and electronics store to buy goods every day, those stores have countless opportunities to learn by trial and error and adjust their prices to reach equilibrium. The seller of the rock concert tickets did not have the same opportunity.

A Student Asks

QUESTION: *At a concert I attended last month, scalpers were selling tickets for at least $50 more than the original price of the ticket. Tickets that were initially sold for $60 were being sold by scalpers for $110. Aren't the scalpers, in a way, like the auctioneer?*

ANSWER: *Yes. Look again at Exhibit 6-6. We can see that the equilibrium ticket price (for this particular concert) is $60, but the initial ticket seller sells tickets for only $40. What will happen in this case is that someone is likely to buy a ticket (or two, or three, or four) for $40 and then resell the ticket for $60, for a profit of $20 per ticket. Now ask yourself whether this buying and reselling of tickets would happen if all tickets were sold for $60 in the first place. The answer is no. Lesson learned: Scalpers (people who buy and resell tickets at higher prices) will only exist if the good in question was not originally sold at its equilibrium price.*

Look around you. You don't see scalpers when it comes to milk, computers, rugs, shirts, turkey sandwiches, or cups of coffee. No person stands outside a coffee shop and offers to sell you a cup of coffee for $2 more than you can pay for a cup of coffee inside the shop. The reason you don't see any scalpers in these cases is because the prices of the goods are at equilibrium.

Still, you will see a scalper for a rock concert, or some sporting events, or even some plays. Why? Because in these cases, the price initially charged for these events was below the equilibrium price; that is, the price was below the price at which quantity demanded equals quantity supplied.

EXHIBIT 6-6 Rock Concert Ticket Price

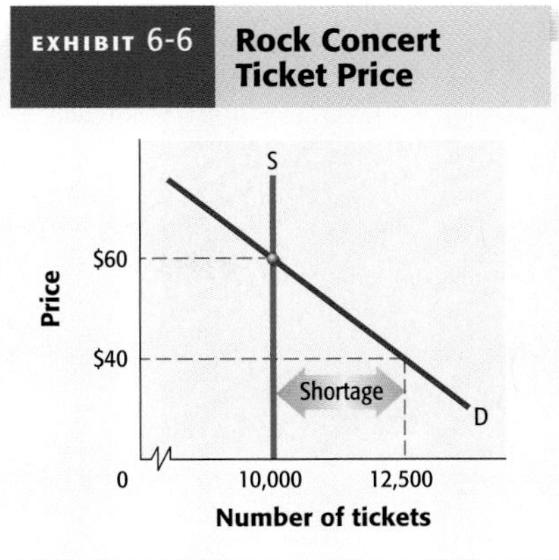

The seller of rock concert tickets sells 10,000 tickets at a price of $40 each. At this price, a shortage occurs; the seller charged too low a price. A price of $60 per ticket would have achieved equilibrium in the market.

The Difference in Prices for Candy Bars, Bread, and Houses

In general, no matter where you go in the United States, the price of a candy bar (pick your favorite brand) is approximately the same. A candy bar in Toledo, Ohio, is approximately the same price as a candy bar in Miami, Florida. This consistency is true for the most part for many other goods, such as a loaf of bread, for example.

But is it true for all goods? What about real estate prices—in particular, the price of a house in San Francisco, California, and the price of a similar house in a similar neighborhood in Louisville, Kentucky? The house in San Francisco will sell for approximately three to four times the price of the house in Louisville. Why, when it comes to candy bars and bread, does a good sell for approximately the same price no matter where it is purchased in the United States, whereas a house purchased in San Francisco is so much more expensive than a similar house in Louisville? Supply and demand give us the answer.

Teaching with Visuals

Remind students that the vertical supply curve means that the supply of tickets is fixed. Supply cannot be shifted left or right.

A Student Asks

You may want to use this A Student Asks to review how supply and demand establish price equilibrium and how the market changes when price changes.

Discussion Starter

Many of the situations in this section will be very familiar to students. Have them share their experiences as each case study is discussed. Ask students how economic thinking is changing the way they think about these common situations.

Reinforcement Activity

Ask students to explain the following scenario in terms of supply and demand: A popular recording artist is on tour. Tickets to see her perform in a large sports arena in St. Louis, MO, cost $40. In Providence, RI, she is performing in a small club, and tickets cost $75. What accounts for the difference in ticket prices?

Background Information: Equilibrium Price

Economists talk about the *law of one price,* meaning that a particular good will sell for the same price no matter where it is sold (exclusive of transportation costs). To illustrate: If prices for cars are higher in Topeka than in Chicago, carmakers will send more cars to Topeka, which will flood the market in Topeka and drive the price down there. Once the prices settle, they should be the same in both cities. The law of one price does not hold true for goods that cannot be moved. For example: The price of a piece of land in Malibu is higher than that of a comparable piece of land in Dallas, because it would be impossible to move the Malibu land (with its view, climate, and so on) to Dallas.

Teaching with Visuals

The price of housing is dependent not only on the size and condition of the house but also upon the amount of land and location. Products that do not differ in price from location to location are cars, clothing, and household goods. Unlike real estate, these items can be moved from location to location.

Discussion Starter

Ask students where they would live if housing costs were the same all over the world. What are some of the factors that would increase the demand for houses in various areas of the world?

A Student Asks

You may want to use this A Student Asks to make sure students understand the role of taxes on price. Remind them of the role taxes play in causing supply curves to shift to the left.

Background Information

The price of oil is affected by international trade and economic activity. Members of the Organization of Petroleum Exporting Countries (OPEC) and non-OPEC oil producing countries were concerned in 1999 when the price of oil fell to around $13 a barrel. They decided that each of their countries would cut back on the supply of oil in hopes prices would rise. Soon the price of oil was in the range of $15 to $17 a barrel. Motorists in the United States soon noticed a rise in the price of gasoline at the pump, from around $1.05 a gallon to about $1.30 a gallon. For this tactic to be successful, the members of OPEC must live up to their cut-back agreements. When they do, the oil supply falls, and prices rise.

▲ Although similar in style and size, houses in different geographic locations often sell at prices differing in the hundreds of thousands of dollars. **What similar products do *not* differ in price from location to location? Why?**

Let's imagine for a second that the price of a candy bar is *not* the same in Toledo as in Miami. At a particular point in time the price for candy bars is $2 in Toledo and $1 in Miami, because the demand for candy bars is higher in Toledo. Knowing what you know now about supply and demand, what do you think will happen?

Given the price difference, the suppliers of candy bars will prefer to sell more of their product in Toledo than in Miami, so the supply of candy bars will increase in Toledo and decrease in Miami. Then what will happen? The price of a candy bars will decrease (say, from $2 to $1.50) in Toledo and increase (say, from $1 to $1.50) in Miami. Only when the prices of candy bars are the same in Toledo and Miami will suppliers no longer have an incentive to rearrange the supply of candy bars in the two cities. The same type of activity would affect the price of bread in the two cities. When suppliers can shift supply from one location to another, price will tend to be uniform for products.

Now consider houses in different cities. Housing prices are much higher in San Francisco than in Louisville because the difference between demand and supply (more demand, less supply) in San Francisco is greater than it is in Louisville. If houses were candy bars or bread, suppliers would shift their supply from Louisville to San Francisco. However, houses are built on land, and the price of the land is part of the price of a house. Naturally, suppliers cannot pick up an acre of land in Louisville and move it to San Francisco.

So, what have we learned? When the supply of a good cannot be moved in response to a difference in price between cities, prices for this good are likely to remain different in these cities.

A Student Asks

QUESTION: *I was in both Oklahoma and California this past summer and the price of gas was higher in California than in Oklahoma. Gas is something that can be moved from place to place (by trucks). So why wasn't the price of gasoline the same in the two locations?*

ANSWER: *Good question. The major reason for the difference you noticed is that taxes on gasoline are different in different states. Many states (and counties too) place an excise tax on gasoline. An excise tax is a tax on the manufacture or sale of a particular good. For example, in Florida gasoline is subject not only to a state excise tax but a county excise tax in many cases as well. State and county excise taxes differ across the country. It so happens that excise taxes on gasoline are less in Oklahoma than in California. This difference in excise taxes often explains why you might pay more for a gallon of gasoline in one state than you pay in another.*

Cross-Curricular Activity

Team with a home economics or business teacher to discuss supply and demand in the supermarket produce section. The home economics or business teacher can have students track fluctuations in the price of produce related to season and crop success, and you reinforce the concepts of supply and demand as well as equilibrium price. You might encourage the home economics teacher to give students practical tips for making good consumer economic decisions concerning produce. To make the team-teaching experience more fun for students, you might also bring in samples of fresh fruit for them to enjoy.

Supply and Demand at the Movies

Have you noticed that the prices for movie tickets can vary? If you want to see a movie on Friday night, you may have to pay $8, but for the same movie at 11:00 a.m. on Tuesday, you may have to pay only $3.50. The difference depends on supply and demand. Certainly the supply of seats in the theater is the same Friday night as Tuesday morning. The demand, however, is different. The demand to see a movie on Friday night is higher than on Tuesday morning, and the higher demand makes for a higher price.

BY THE NUMBERS

What was the ticket price for a movie in 1948? In 1962? In 1974? Here are the "average" ticket prices for the period 1948–2004.

Year	Price	Year	Price	Year	Price
1948	$ .36	1981	$2.78	1994	$4.08
1954	.49	1982	2.94	1995	4.35
1958	.68	1983	3.15	1996	4.42
1963	.86	1984	3.36	1997	4.59
1967	1.22	1985	3.55	1998	4.69
1971	1.65	1986	3.71	1999	5.06
1974	1.89	1987	3.91	2000	5.39
1975	2.03	1988	4.11	2001	5.65
1976	2.13	1989	3.99	2002	5.80
1977	2.23	1990	4.22	2003	6.03
1978	2.34	1991	4.21	2004	6.21
1979	2.47	1992	4.15		
1980	2.69	1993	4.14		

Source: Motion Picture Association of America.

Supply and Demand on a Freeway

Supply and demand are easy to see at a rock concert, a movie theater, or the grocery store. But supply and demand also appear in places we wouldn't initially think to look, such as on a freeway. Suppose a certain supply of freeway space consists of a certain number of lanes and miles. Also, the demand for freeway space is equal to the demand people have to drive on freeways.

The demand to drive on a freeway is not always the same, of course. The demand is higher at 8 a.m. on Monday, when people are driving to work, than at 11 p.m. You can see this demand represented in Exhibit 6-7(a). The supply curve, S_1, represents the

EXHIBIT 6-7 Supply and Demand on a Freeway

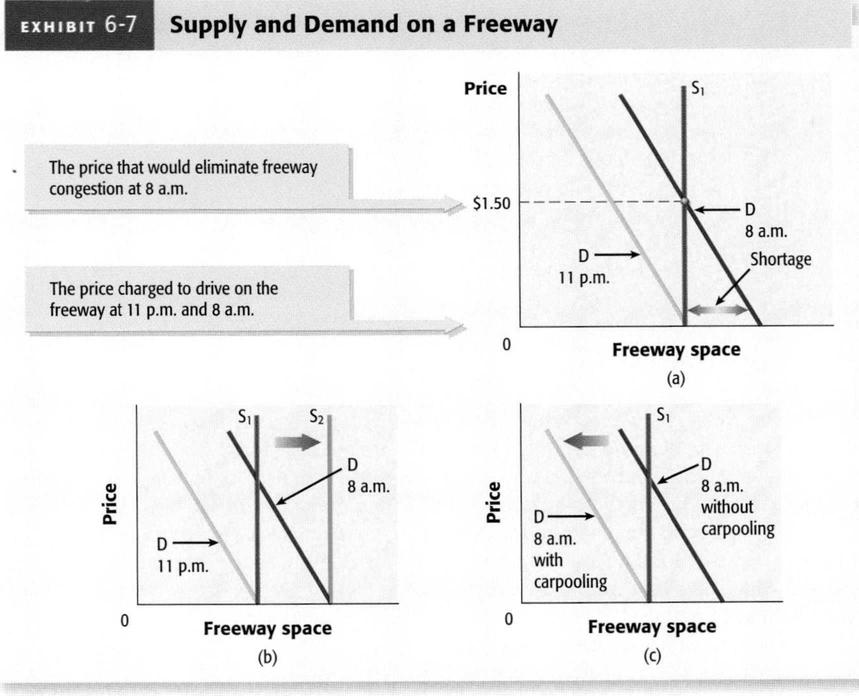

◀ Freeway congestion can be solved by (a) charging a toll, (b) increasing supply, or (c) reducing demand.

Teaching with Visuals

Answers to the questions about movie ticket prices in By the Numbers are as follows: 1948—$0.36, 1962—about $0.82, 1974—$1.89. The average ticket price for the period 1948–2004 is $3.39.

Discussion Starter

Ask students the following questions: How many of you have stood in line at a movie theater waiting to buy tickets? Why didn't you leave and return at a time when there was less demand? In other words, what intangibles made viewing the movie at that particular time more attractive than at other less busy times?

Economics Around the Clock

After students have read some case studies in Section 2, you may want to refer them to the 8:45 A.M. scenario in Economics Around the Clock (page 129) and discuss their answers to the question posed there.

The price of a share of stock is determined by the demand for and the supply of the stock. Obviously, one or the other changed to make the price drop in 10 minutes. For example, the supply of the stock for sale could have increased, thus causing the price to fall.

Internet Research

Direct students to go to the Web site for Ticketmaster and find three events they would like to attend. They should choose a mix of musical, sporting, and other events. Have them record the prices for these events, and ask them to discuss the reasons why they think the prices for these three events differ (if they do) and the reasons why tickets are selling for these prices. What factors might occur to change the pricing of these tickets in the future?

Economics in the Real World

Have students read this feature, and then ask them to consider how supply and demand affects them at the grocery store. Do they hear their parents comment on the price of groceries, or are certain items bought only at certain times?

ANSWERS TO THINK ABOUT IT Answers will vary. The invention of supply and demand would have been comparable in importance to inventions such as the wheel and fire.

Discussion Starter

Ask students the following questions: Have you ever driven on a toll road? If so, why did you choose the toll road over roads you could have driven on for free? Point out that the purpose of tolls is to lessen traffic and save travel time, as well as to raise revenue for transportation improvements.

Who Feeds Cleveland?

Rarely does anyone ask who feeds Cleveland, or who feeds the people in any other city in the world for that matter. Most of us take it for granted that we somehow get fed. We go to the grocery store, we select certain items off the shelves, we pay for those items, and then we go home and eat the food. What more do we need to think about?

To understand just how much is involved, suppose you had the job of feeding Cleveland: You need to tell farmers how much corn, wheat, and soybeans to grow. You need to decide what the right price is for Cheerios and ketchup and milk. (How do you figure out these prices?) You need to send so many boxes of orange juice to various grocery stores. (We wonder whether you might send too much orange juice to one grocery store and not enough to another.)

To get the right amount of food to your local grocery store, literally hundreds of decisions have to be made along the way. Yet, no giant computer decides how much corn and wheat will be grown and how much orange juice will be sent to the grocery store at the corner of 13th Street and Main. No government bureaucracy in Washington, D.C., decides such things. As far as we know, we cannot point to a single person in the world and say, "She feeds Cleveland."

Well, if no one feeds Cleveland, then how does Cleveland get fed? The answer is "supply and demand" feeds Cleveland. That's right, supply and demand, or what we have come to know as "the market." If the demand for Cheerios rises, the price rises, which prompts the manufacturer of Cheerios to produce more Cheerios. If the demand for corn rises, the price rises, which prompts corn farmers to plant and harvest more corn. If the demand for fat-free ice cream falls, then fat-free ice cream stays on the grocery shelves longer, and soon the price drops, which signals to ice cream manufacturers that they shouldn't produce as much fat-free ice cream.

A famous economist once said that if "supply and demand" or "the market" didn't naturally exist, it would have to be invented—and then it would be hailed as the greatest invention the world had ever seen. Of course, the market was not invented, it just is.

Who feeds Cleveland, New York, Chicago, New Orleans, London, Buenos Aires, and Paris?

And who feeds you?

THINK ABOUT IT If the market had been invented, how would it compare to inventions such as the wheel and fire?

supply of freeway space (say, four lanes for 150 miles). The demand curve D (11 p.m.) represents the demand for freeway space at 11 p.m. Monday, and the demand curve D (8 a.m.) represents the demand for freeway space at 8 a.m. Monday. You will notice that the demand at 8 a.m. is greater than the demand at 11 p.m.

What do most people have to pay to drive on the freeway? For most freeways across the country, the price is zero; most freeways do not have tolls.[1] In Exhibit 6-7(a), you will notice that zero price is the equilibrium price at 11 p.m. on Monday. The demand curve for freeway space and the supply curve of freeway space intersect at zero price at

[1] People do pay taxes to build freeways, but this fact is not relevant here. People are not paying a price to drive on freeways, at least not nontoll freeways.

Differentiating Instruction

Kinesthetic and Visual Learners

Students will probably be unaccustomed to thinking of freeway space as a good. Help students visualize this concept by creating a freeway and using toy cars. Use a large plank, perhaps 3 feet by 5 feet, and draw two freeways on it, one marked as a toll road, the other as free. Put as many of the toy cars on the "free" freeway as possible. Leave the toll road empty. How many of the drivers would be willing to spend money to drive without bumper-to-bumper traffic? How much would they be willing to spend? Start at 25 cents per 10 miles and raise the price to see how the demand for traffic-free driving decreases as the price for the toll road increases.

11 p.m. on Monday. In other words, at this time neither a shortage nor a surplus of freeway space exists. People are using the freeway. Traffic is moving freely without congestion.

Now look at the situation at 8 a.m. At zero price—no toll—the quantity demanded of freeway space is greater than the quantity supplied, resulting in a shortage of freeway space. In everyday language, the freeway is congested. If you have ever been in a major traffic jam, you can probably understand that a congested freeway means a shortage of freeway space.

What is the solution to freeway congestion? Two common solutions are building more freeways and having people carpool. One solution deals with the supply side of the freeway market, and the other with the demand side. When people say that we ought to build more freeways, they want to push the supply curve (of freeway space) to the right, shown in Exhibit 6-7(b). If the supply of freeway space shifts from S_1 to S_2, freeway space is able to meet the quantity demanded at zero price at 8 a.m. The problem of freeway congestion is solved.

If more people carpool, then for all practical purposes the demand for freeway space falls as in Exhibit 6-7(c). In other words, if people carpool to such an extent that the demand for driving on the freeway drops by as much as shown in the exhibit, then freeway space is able to meet the quantity demanded at zero price at 8 a.m. The shortage of freeway space again is eliminated.

▲ What factors determine how hard this player has to work and how skilled he has to be to win a position on the team?

Offshoring

In 2003, the McKinsey Global Institute calculated that offshoring (U.S. companies hiring workers in other countries) came with both costs and benefits but that overall the benefits were greater than costs. One benefit, especially noted, was lower costs for U.S. companies.

ECONOMIC THINKING How might lower costs for U.S. companies affect both the supply of goods in the United States and the prices customers pay for those goods?

Of course, as is probably evident now, a third way can be used to get rid of freeway congestion. It has nothing to do with building more freeways or carpooling. Freeway congestion can be eliminated by charging tolls. The tolls bring the freeway market into equilibrium. In other words, as shown in Exhibit 6-7(a), a toll of \$1.50 would eliminate freeway congestion at 8 a.m.

Supply and Demand on the Gridiron

Suppose you want to try out for a high school sport, such as football, volleyball, or golf. How competitive do you have to be to get on the team? It depends on how many open positions are available on the team you want to try out for, as well as how many people are going to try out for those positions. How competitive you must be is a matter of the supply of positions and the demand for positions.

Suppose you want to try out for tight end on the high school football team. The team's coach has decided that he will have three tight ends on the team. In economic terms,

ANSWERS TO ECONOMIC THINKING

Answers will vary. Students should be able to verbalize the concept that lower costs for U.S. companies would result in an increase of supply and a fall in equilibrium price.

Prediction Activity

Present students with the following scenario: Suppose every freeway or highway in your state is turned into a toll road. Furthermore, suppose the toll is mistakenly set at \$2 above equilibrium. What will happen as a result?

The answer is that relatively few people will drive on the freeways and highways. Instead, they will drive on free surface streets. There will be a surplus of space on freeways, but there may be a shortage of space (congestion) on surface streets.

Reinforcement Activity

Students probably will not have thought of economics when they were trying out for sports teams or drama performances. Ask students to name other life experiences that they could explain in terms of supply and demand. Have them share their experiences with the class.

Teaching with Visuals

Answers will vary. Factors such as the number of open positions on the team (supply) and the number of people who are going to try out for those positions (demand) will determine how hard the players have to work and how skilled they have to be to gain a position.

Background Information: Supply, Demand, and the Job Market

Many students will have experienced competitive situations either in sports, drama, or another extracurricular activity for which a limited number of positions are available. Tell students that the same situation occurs when they apply for a job. A manager will review applications and résumés from several people who have applied for the same position and then choose the best qualified. The more applicants, the more likely it is that a very qualified, capable person will be hired. Assign students to research the number of applicants for jobs either at your school or in the community, and ask them how their findings affect their plans for finding work.

Problem Solving

Some of the best teams in high school athletics are found in private schools. While the number of students in most private schools is much smaller than the average number in public high schools, the level of athletics is often superior in private schools. Guide students in an economic discussion of this situation. Ask, What economic factors might account for this?

Students might suggest that private schools make athletic prowess part of the "price" students pay to get into private schools for which demand exceeds supply, or that private schools invest in top-quality sports programs in an effort to increase demand among prospective students who value athletics.

Economics Around the Clock

After reading and discussing "Necessary Conditions for a High Income: High Demand, Low Supply" (pages 146–147) you may want to refer students to the 2:17 P.M. scenario in Economics Around the Clock (page 129) and discuss their answers to its question.

Students should understand that high salaries for baseball players are a matter of simple supply and demand. The demand for major league baseball players is high, and supply is low because few people have the skills required. High demand and low supply are the recipe for a high salary.

Teaching with Visuals

The answer to the photo question on page 147 is that supply and demand determine equilibrium price. In the work world, equilibrium price is equal to salary.

Application Activity

After reading and discussing Section 2, you may want to assign the Section Activity in the *Applying the Principles Workbook.*

we can say that the quantity supplied of tight end positions is three. Suppose that 30 people want to try out for the position of tight end. The quantity demanded of tight end positions is then 30. Because quantity demanded is greater than quantity supplied, a shortage of tight end positions results.

When a shortage of anything occurs in a competitive market, the price of that thing rises. The team's coach, of course, is not going to accept money from the students who want to try out for the team. What he will do is raise the "price" of being a tight end in a different way. People will have to "pay" to be a tight end with hard work and skill. The players who pay more—demonstrate more skill and work harder—will be the ones to make the team as tight ends.

Would these players have to be as good to get on the team if only five people wanted to be a tight end? Not at all. In that case, the shortage of tight end positions would be smaller, and the "price" of being a tight end would not rise as much to bring supply and demand into equilibrium.

Supply and Demand on the College Campus

As you probably know, you do not need the same grade point average (GPA) or standardized test score (SAT or ACT) to get into all colleges. One college may require a GPA of 3.0 and an SAT score of 1550, while another requires a GPA of 3.8 and an SAT score of 2100.[2] Why the difference? Again, the answer is supply and demand. The higher the demand to get into a particular college, the higher its entrance requirements.

Take two colleges, college A and college B. Each college will admit 2,000 students to its entering freshman class next year. Each college charges $5,000 a semester in tuition. The quantity supplied of open spots and the tuition are the same at each college, but suppose the demand to go to college A is three times the demand to go to college B. At college B, 4,000 students apply for 2,000 spots, but 12,000 students apply for 2,000 spots at college A.

[2] The new SAT scores used here first went into effect in March of 2005.

The shortage at college A is greater than the shortage at college B, so the "price" to get into college A will rise by more than it will rise at college B. The "price" of getting into college is usually measured in terms of high school academic performance (in other words, GPA and SAT or ACT scores.) The greater the demand to get into a college compared to supply, the higher the GPA and standardized test scores required to get into that college, or the higher the "price" a student must pay in terms of grades.

EXAMPLE: Suppose a university charges tuition of $12,000 a year and requires a 3.0 GPA and an SAT score of 1900 or higher for admission. Currently, 7,000 students apply for admission each year and 2,000 are admitted. Time passes and the number of applicants rises to 10,000. We know that a rise in the number of applicants is just another way of saying that demand to attend the university increased.

Our study of supply and demand teaches us that if demand rises, tuition will rise too. In other words, tuition might rise to $16,000 a year. Suppose the university chooses not to raise tuition; it maintains tuition at $12,000 a year. Will the standards of admission rise instead? The answer is yes—the university might start requiring a 3.3 GPA and an SAT score of 2000 or higher. ♦

Necessary Conditions for a High Income: High Demand, Low Supply

As consumers, we are used to paying prices. We pay a price to buy a computer, a soda, or a shirt. We sometimes receive prices, too. As a seller of a good, you receive the price that the buyer pays.

Many people do not sell goods; instead, they sell their labor services. The person who works at a fast-food restaurant after school or an attorney at a law firm is selling labor services. The "price" employees receive for what they sell is usually called a wage. A wage, over time, can be referred to as a salary or income. A person who earns a wage of $10 an hour receives a monthly income of $1,600 if he or she works 160 hours a month.

Background Information: Radio Host Incomes

The necessary conditions for high income—high demand, low supply—apply to the career of radio host. The salary range for radio hosts is wide. Disc jockeys in small markets generally earn very little, whereas radio hosts in large markets might earn millions of dollars.

Many more people want to work in radio than there are positions available. Those who do get jobs usually have a college degree in speech, communications, journalism, business, or public relations, or a degree from a broadcasting school. They also have a good, clear, likable voice, creativity, and the ability to ad-lib on the air. Many begin as assistants or interns at small stations, gaining experience they will need as host.

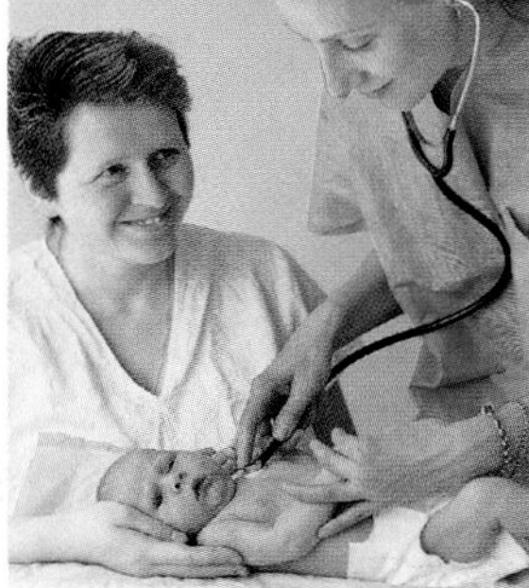

◀ Whether your future occupation is auto mechanic, teacher, doctor, or anything else, your income will be determined by supply and demand. **Can you explain how supply and demand impact wages?**

A wage is determined by supply and demand, just as the price of oranges, apples, or TV sets is. It follows, then, that for someone to receive a high wage, demand must be high and supply low. The higher the demand relative to supply, the higher the wage will be.

To earn a high wage, then, is to perform a job in great demand that not many other people can do. If few know how to do it, supply will be low. Low supply combined with high demand means you will receive a (relatively) high wage.

Consider the wage of a restaurant server versus a computer scientist. The demand is great for both servers and computer scientists. However, a large supply of servers and a not-so-large supply of computer scientists mean that computer scientists earn more than servers.

EXAMPLE: In 2005, Randy Johnson was a pitcher for the New York Yankees. His salary that year was $15,419,815. Why was his salary so high? The answer: high demand, low supply. The demand to watch a good pitcher play in a baseball game is high. The number of people in the world who can pitch a baseball the way Randy Johnson pitches is small. High demand and low supply is the winning combination for a high salary. ♦

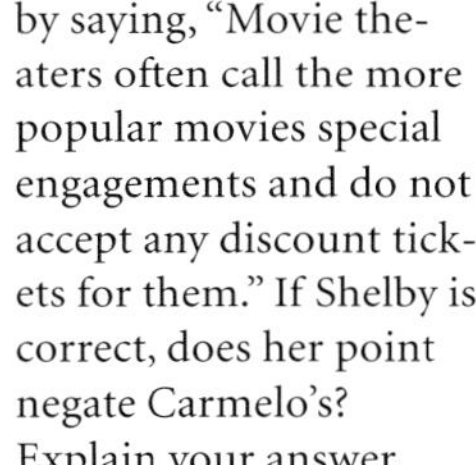

Section 2 Assessment

Reviewing Facts and Concepts

1. A freeway sometimes experiences traffic congestion (bumper-to-bumper traffic) and sometimes very little traffic. Explain why.
2. Housing prices are higher in city X than in city Y. Using the concepts of supply and demand, explain why.
3. Identify whether a shortage, a surplus, or equilibrium exists in the following settings:
   - **a.** Fewer students apply for the first-year class at college X than spaces available.
   - **b.** People who wanted to attend a baseball game were told that tickets had sold out the day before.
   - **c.** Houses for sale used to stay on the market for two months before they were sold. Now they are staying on the market for up to six months, and they still aren't selling.

Critical Thinking

4. Carmelo says, "A movie theater charges the same price for a popular movie as it does for an unpopular movie. Obviously, the movie theater doesn't charge more when demand for the movie is higher than when it is lower." Shelby counters by saying, "Movie theaters often call the more popular movies special engagements and do not accept any discount tickets for them." If Shelby is correct, does her point negate Carmelo's? Explain your answer.

Applying Economic Concepts

5. This section stated that people will earn high incomes if they can supply labor services that not many other people can supply, and for which demand is great. If you choose to go to college, how will this information affect your supply position?

Assess

Quick Quiz

The following true-and-false quiz will help you assess student understanding of the material covered in this section.

1. If there is a shortage in the market, price will fall to equilibrium price. (False)
2. Real estate prices vary because of fixed demand. (False)
3. Tolls alleviate traffic congestion by reducing demand. (True)
4. Movie tickets cost different prices at different times because the supply changes. (False)
5. The demand to drive on freeways is not always the same. (True)

Assessment Book

You will find a quiz for this section in the *Assessment Book.*

Reteaching Activity

Use the Section Assessment to gauge which students may need reteaching on this section. Write the words *shortage* and *price* on the board. Explain that a shortage exists when quantity demanded exceeds quantity supplied. Ask students to explain how price helps eliminate shortages.

Guided Reading

For further reteaching of the key concepts in this section, assign the Outlining Activity and the Just the Facts Handout in the *Guided Reading and Study Guide.*

Section 2 Assessment Answers

Reviewing Facts and Concepts

1. The supply of freeway space is always the same (same number of miles), as is the price to drive on a freeway ($0). The demand is not always the same, though. Traffic congestion is evidence that there is a shortage of freeway space. If there is very little traffic, we might say there is a surplus of freeway space.
2. The reason for the price difference may be that demand for housing is higher in city X than in city Y, that supply is smaller in city X than in city Y, or both.
3. a. surplus; **b.** shortage; **c.** surplus.

Critical Thinking

4. Yes. By not accepting any discount tickets for special engagements (movies that are very popular and therefore have a higher demand than other movies), the theater ensures that the average price of seeing a special-engagement movie is higher than that of other movies.

Applying Economic Concepts

5. A person who goes to college acquires certain skills, information, and knowledge that other people do not have. In effect, going to college decreases the number of people who can do what you do. As a result, one's income will be higher, all other things being the same.

Your Personal Economics

Discussion Starter

Ask students if any of them regularly search the World Wide Web for information on goods and services. Invite those who do to explain the most successful ways of finding the information they need. Encourage students who do not have much Internet experience to think of a purchase they would like to make and to search the Web for information about it, using the tips provided by their classmates.

Research Activity

After students have read the "Buying a Car" scenario in the text, have them decide what kind of car they would like to purchase. Ask them to look on the Internet for information on the car. Next have them research safe cars for teenage drivers and compare that information with their findings on the car they would like to purchase. Now that they have collected this information, ask students what decision they would make concerning the purchase of a car.

Your Personal Economics

The WWW Gets You More for Less

Information is something people will pay to have. We see it a hundred times a day. A person who wants to sell her house will pay a real estate agent to inform her of where the buyers are who want to buy her house. A person who wants to buy bonds and stocks might pay a financial analyst to inform him of the best stocks and bonds to buy. Just as people buy goods and services every day, they also buy information every day.

The World Wide Web

The introduction of the World Wide Web has made it cheaper and easier to acquire certain information. You just need to know where to look.

Buying a Car Let's suppose that Jimmy wants to buy a Honda Accord. The list price of the car is $23,100. But Jimmy wants to know the invoice price; he wants to know what the dealer paid for the car. He can go to www.emcp.net/autobytel and find that the invoice price is $20,788. Knowing the invoice price gives Jimmy information that he didn't have before. It is information that is useful to him when he is negotiating the price he will pay for the car.

Suppose Jimmy just wants to know what cars are especially safe for teenagers. He can go to www.emcp.net/consumerreports and click on "cars for teen drivers." He will then find a list of recommended cars that have advanced safety features and good crash-test results.

Comparing Prices Suppose Katherine wants to buy a television set. Instead of going from store to store to price sets, she can go to www.emcp.net/consumerworld. There she can click on the "Price Checker" for TV sets and in two seconds, she can see a list of 12 or more stores (in her area) that are willing to sell her the TV she is looking at, each listing its price for the TV set.

Suppose Ivan wants to find where he can get gas for as little as possible. He can go to www.emcp.net/firstgov and click on "Find Cheapest Gas Prices." On his next screen he will see a map of the United States. He clicks on his state, New York, and then on his city, Buffalo. Up pops a list of gasoline stations with gas prices per gallon listed.

Background Checks Suppose Melissa is thinking about having a medical operation. She wants to know something about the surgeon who is planning to do the operation. What's his education? Is he a good surgeon? Is he board certified? Have there been any disciplinary actions taken against him? All she needs to do is go to www.emcp.net/healthgrades and click on "Physician Quality Reports." There she can purchase (for about $8) a full report on her surgeon.

College Information Suppose it is Oliver's first year at college and he wants to know what students at his

▶ If you want to get the best deal possible, you have to do some research.

Cooperative Learning

Read "College Information" with students and divide the class into groups of three or four. Tell students to decide what information they want to know about specific colleges. Then have them access the Web to get that information. After 15 minutes of searching, have the groups report their findings to the class.

◀ With so much valuable information available on the Web, there are no excuses for making poor buying decisions.

college think about some of the professors whose courses he wants to take. He can go to www.emcp.net/ratemyprofessors and find out. Once at the site, all he has to do is choose the state, the college, and then the professor. Here's what we found written about one professor: "All we did was watch videos. What a hack." And here's what we found written about another: "Best class I've ever had. Her lectures are clear and she is always there to help you."

Caveat Emptor

When it comes to buying goods and services, it is sometimes good to remember the saying "caveat emptor," which means "let the buyer beware." It means that you, as a buyer, have the responsibility of watching out for yourself. Sellers will not always tell you everything they think you want to know. A car salesperson isn't likely to tell you how poorly the car you're looking at did in the national crash tests. The surgeon isn't likely to tell you that he has two disciplinary actions pending. The gas station isn't likely to advertise that it has some of the highest gas prices in the county.

Many companies will advertise that you can get a "free" credit report from them. An ad might read: "Want to know what your credit report says. Come to our Web site and you'll get a free credit report in minutes."

Fact is, many of the companies that advertise "free" credit reports don't deliver free credit reports. Often once at their sites they will try to get you to sign up for subscription-based services sold by credit bureaus. As of this writing, only one congressionally mandated site, AnnualCreditReport.com, provides a free credit report. Oddly enough, though, if you do a search of "free credit report" on the search engine Google, AnnualCreditReport.com doesn't even make the first page of Google results.

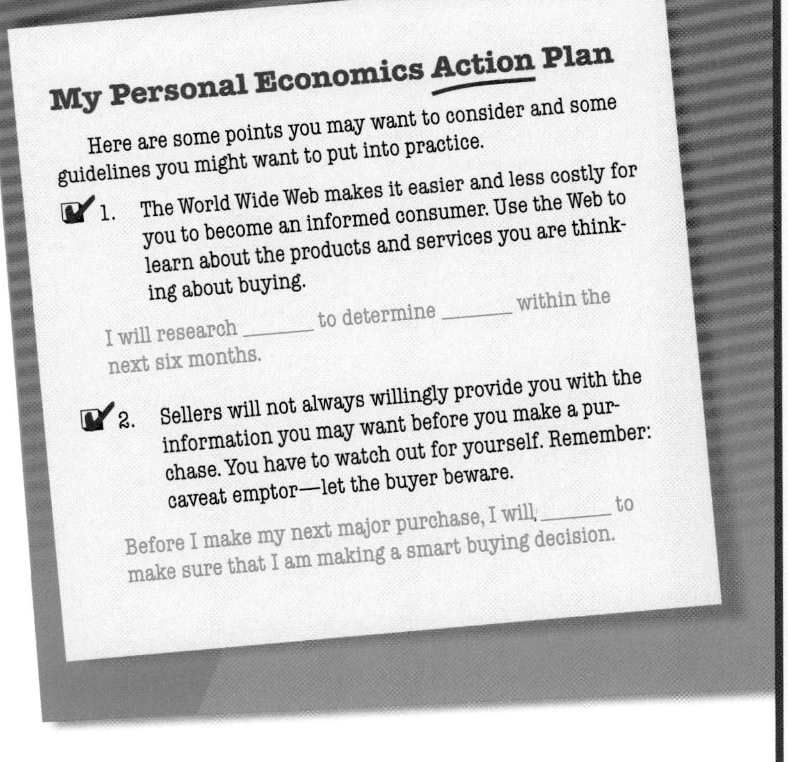

My Personal Economics Action Plan

Here are some points you may want to consider and some guidelines you might want to put into practice.

1. The World Wide Web makes it easier and less costly for you to become an informed consumer. Use the Web to learn about the products and services you are thinking about buying.

   I will research ______ to determine ______ within the next six months.

2. Sellers will not always willingly provide you with the information you may want before you make a purchase. You have to watch out for yourself. Remember: caveat emptor—let the buyer beware.

   Before I make my next major purchase, I will ______ to make sure that I am making a smart buying decision.

Research Activity

To help students realize the power of being an informed consumer, ask them to name an item they want to save money on. Then have them research that item on the Web. Ask whether the information they found has influenced how they will purchase the item.

My Personal Economics Action Plan Assign students to survey their peers about their use of the Web to research purchases. Students should ask peers which purchases they typically research online and which they don't. Students may find their peers are more likely to get information from the Web on some specific items but not on others. Invite students to report back to the class. Compile the class's results into a chart and discuss the overall findings.

Chapter 6 Price: Supply and Demand Together 149

CHAPTER 6 Assessment Answers

Economics Vocabulary

1. surplus; **2.** shortage; **3.** equilibrium; **4.** equilibrium price; **5.** equilibrium quantity; **6.** inventory; **7.** price floor; **8.** price ceiling.

Understanding the Main Ideas

1. If there is a surplus, buyers do not demand the entire quantity produced. To sell the quantity produced, sellers must lower the price until the equilibrium price is reached.
2. A surplus exists at \$5 and \$6. The equilibrium price is \$4, and the equilibrium quantity is 40,000 bushels.
3. Disagree. Markets are sometimes in surplus or shortage. Markets move to equilibrium over time.
4. Answers will vary. Students might say that prices are likely to rise as a result of a shortage.
5. Pens can be moved from city 1, where prices are low, to city 2, where prices are high. This move results in a fall in the supply of pens in city 1 and increase in the supply of pens in city 2. Prices will adjust: the price of pens will rise in city 1 and fall in city 2. In short, the prices of pens in the two cities converge. Houses and the land they occupy cannot be moved, so the supply doesn't shift from one city to another, and the prices don't converge.
6. Marshall's point was that just as it takes two blades (not one alone) of a pair of scissors to cut something, it takes both supply and demand (not one alone) to determine price.
7. a. equilibrium price and quantity rise; **b.** equilibrium price and quantity fall; **c.** equilibrium price falls and equilibrium quantity rises; **d.** equilibrium price rises and equilibrium quantity falls.
8. Check the shelves. If you put item X on the shelves at noon and it is sold out by later that day (nothing is left on the shelves), there is a shortage of X. If you put item Y on the shelves at noon and three days later only two units of Y have been purchased (a lot of Y remains on the shelves), there is some evidence to believe there is a surplus of Y.
9. If demand rises by the same amount as supply rises, then price remains constant. This point is illustrated in Exhibit 6-4.
10. High salaries are a result of high demand and low supply. The basketball players supply a certain level of basketball performance that very few people in the world can supply. Combine this low supply with a high demand for watching basketball, and we now understand why NBA players are paid high salaries.

Doing the Math

1. \$7. At this price, quantity demanded equals quantity supplied, which equals 115 units.

6 CHAPTER 6 ASSESSMENT

Chapter Summary

Be sure you know and remember the following key points from the chapter sections.

Section 1

- Supply and demand work together to determine price.
- A surplus exists when quantity supplied is greater than quantity demanded.
- A shortage exists when quantity demanded is greater than quantity supplied.
- A market reaches equilibrium when the quantity of a good that buyers are willing and able to buy is equal to the quantity of the good that sellers are willing and able to produce and offer for sale, and is shown as the intersection point of the supply and demand curves.
- The cost of storing inventories is part of the reason prices decrease when a surplus occurs.
- A shift in the demand curve will cause prices to increase or decrease.
- A shift in the supply curve will also cause a change in price.
- Governments sometimes legislate price controls: a price ceiling sets a level that a price for a good cannot go above legally, and a price floor is the lowest price at which a good can be sold legally.

Section 2

- A shortage in a market causes price to increase.
- A surplus in a market causes price to decrease.
- The laws of supply and demand affect many areas of our lives: the price of goods and services, the likelihood of getting into a certain university or on a certain sports team, how much traffic is on the roads, and how much money we earn in our jobs.
- All other factors being the same, prices and quantity will always move toward the equilibrium point.

Economics Vocabulary

To reinforce your knowledge of the key terms in this chapter, fill in the following blanks on a separate piece of paper with the appropriate word or phrase.

1. A(n) ______ exists when quantity supplied is greater than quantity demanded.
2. A(n) ______ exists when quantity demanded is greater than quantity supplied.
3. A market is in ______ when quantity demanded equals quantity supplied.
4. The price that exists in a market when quantity demanded equals quantity supplied is called the ______.
5. The quantity that exists in a market when quantity demanded equals quantity supplied is called the ______.
6. In a market, if quantity supplied is currently greater than quantity demanded, a firm's ______ is/are above normal levels.
7. A ______ is a legislated price below which legal trades cannot be made.
8. A ______ is a legislated price above which legal trades cannot be made.

Understanding the Main Ideas

Write answers to the following questions to review the main ideas in this chapter.

1. Explain why price falls when a surplus occurs.
2. Look at the prices listed in Exhibit 6-1. At what prices does a surplus occur? What are the equilibrium price and the equilibrium quantity?
3. "All markets are necessarily in equilibrium at all points in time." Agree or disagree? Explain.
4. What might we see when a market is experiencing a shortage? (Comment: It is not enough to say that quantity demanded is greater than quantity supplied because this answer is simply a definition of shortage. You must identify a tangible event of a shortage.)
5. Pens sell for about the same price in every city in the country, but houses do not. Why?
6. Alfred Marshall, the British economist, compared supply and demand to the two blades of a pair of scissors. Explain his thinking.

150 Chapter 6 Price: Supply and Demand Together

7. Identify what will happen to equilibrium price and equilibrium quantity in each of the following cases:
   a. Demand rises and supply is constant.
   b. Demand falls by more than supply rises.
   c. Supply rises by more than demand rises.
   d. Supply falls and demand is constant.
8. Suppose you are a manager of a grocery store. How would you know which goods were in shortage? In surplus?
9. Both the demand for and the supply of a good rise. Under what condition will the price of the good remain constant?
10. Some National Basketball Association (NBA) players receive annual incomes of several million dollars. Explain their high salaries in terms of supply and demand.

Doing the Math

Do the calculations necessary to solve the following problem.

1. Price is $10, quantity demanded is 100 units, and quantity supplied is 130 units. For each dollar decline in price, quantity demanded rises by 5 units, and quantity supplied falls by 5 units. What is the equilibrium price?

Working with Graphs and Tables

1. Identify the exhibit in the chapter that illustrates the following:
   a. an increase in demand, supply constant
   b. a decrease in supply, demand constant
2. Graphically represent the following:
   a. a decrease in demand, supply constant
   b. an increase in supply, demand constant
   c. a decrease in demand equal to a decrease in supply
3. Explain what is happening in each part, (a)–(d), of Exhibit 6-8.

Solving Economic Problems

Use your thinking skills and the information you learned in this chapter to find solutions to the following problems.

EXHIBIT 6-8

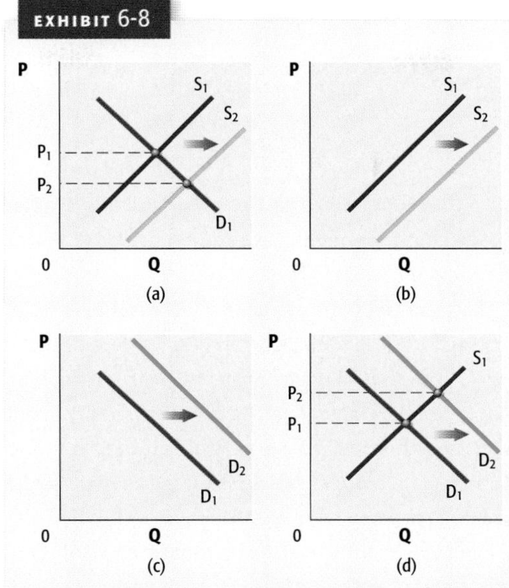

1. **Analysis.** Suppose that in 2005 the average price of a meal at a restaurant was $20, and 50,000 restaurant meals were bought and sold. In 2006 the average price was $22, and 60,000 meals were bought and sold. Which of the following events can explain a higher price and more meals purchased and sold? Explain.
   a. The supply of restaurant meals increased.
   b. The demand for restaurant meals decreased.
   c. The demand for restaurant meals increased.
2. **Cause and Effect.** Suppose the equilibrium price of bread is $2 a loaf. The federal government mandates that no bread can be sold for more than $1 a loaf. How will the market for bread be different from when bread could be purchased and sold for $2? Explain.

ONLINE emcp.com **Practice Tests and Study Guide**

Go to www.emcp.net/economics and choose *Economics: New Ways of Thinking,* Chapter 6, if you need more help in preparing for the chapter test.

Working with Graphs and Tables

1. a. Exhibit 6-3(a); **b.** Exhibit 6-3(d).
2 a. See Exhibit 6-3(b). **b.** See Exhibit 6-3(c). **c.** See Exhibit 6-7(b).
3. (a) An increase in supply lowers the equilibrium price from P_1 to P_2. (b) Supply increases. (c) Demand increases. (d) Demand increases, and equilibrium price rises from P_1 to P_2.

Solving Economic Problems

1. If either event a or event b occurred, the price of a restaurant meal and the number of meals purchased and sold would have fallen. Only with event c would the price rise and more meals be purchased and sold.
2. At $2 a loaf, the quantity demanded of bread equals the quantity supplied. But at $1 a loaf, the quantity demanded is greater than the quantity supplied. (You may want to have students graphically show this.) In short, at $1 there will be a shortage of bread, but at $2 there will be neither a shortage nor a surplus. The lesson here is that below-equilibrium prices (such as $1 for bread in our example) generate shortages. It may not have been the federal government's intention to create a shortage by mandating a $1 price for bread; from its perspective, the shortage may be an unintended effect.

Debating the Issues

Discussion Starters

1. Ask students to summarize the arguments for and against price ceilings. Students should recognize that price ceilings can help provide equal access to goods for those with less money, including, in this case, disaster victims. On the other side of the argument, though, price ceilings can create shortages and long lines. Give students a moment to think of a good they use frequently. Which trade-off would they be willing to make to continue buying that particular good, and why?
2. Ask students to imagine a particular natural disaster that they might experience, and to list several economic concerns they might face in that event.
3. Ask students if they think their opinions on price controls would change if they lost their way of life to a natural disaster. If so, how would their opinions change, and why?
4. What steps might a nation need to take to rebuild its economy after a natural disaster changes demand for a particular good? You might offer a specific example—such as the shortage of natural gas following the flooding of refineries during Hurricane Katrina—and lead the class in a discussion about ways the government could help manage demand for that good.

Debating the Issues

Should There Be Price Controls on Some Goods at Certain Times?

In the summer of 2005, gasoline prices were rising. It was common for people around the country to pay $3 or more per gallon for gasoline.

Then, in the early morning of August 29, 2005, Hurricane Katrina hit the United States and devastated much of the area of the Gulf Coast from New Orleans, Louisiana, to Mobile, Alabama. As a result of Hurricane Katrina, there were breaches in the levee system on the New Orleans side of Lake Pontchartrain, which led to massive flooding and an evacuation of New Orleans.

Just weeks later, Hurricane Rita hit the Gulf Coast area near Galveston, Texas. Hurricane Rita was not as devastating as Katrina, but many of the oil refineries along the coast were put out of commission by the hurricane, further reducing the supply of fuels such as gasoline.

People demanded that something be done. It became common to hear people arguing for price ceilings on gas, on certain food items, and on water. In response, some people argued against price ceilings. Here is what a few people had to say as they discussed the day's news events at their local coffee shop one morning.

Gilberto Vasquez, marketing manager of a fast-food chain

Gasoline prices have risen nearly 70 cents in just the last week. This is getting ridiculous. It used to be that I paid about $25 to fill up and now I'm paying almost $10 more. For many people, this spike in gas prices is adding $100 to $200 a month to the amount of money they have to spend. That is a lot of money. What am I supposed to do? After all I have to do a lot of driving in my job. What do I do, buy less food for my family? My daughter needs braces badly. Does she go without braces? I think the federal government should impose a price ceiling for gas. Maybe the ceiling should be set at 20 cents or 30 cents more than the price used to be, so the oil companies can make some money. But there is no need to let the oil companies gouge us by tacking on 70 cents or $1 more in just one week's time. Did you see the article in the paper this week about one of the oil company's record profits? Don't get me wrong. I don't usually favor government controls. But sometimes I think they are necessary. Why should some people have so much when they are just taking from others?

Winifred Smith, Economics teacher at Jefferson High School

I'm not sure I agree with Gilberto's assumption. He seems to assume that the oil companies can raise the price of gas to anything they want. But if they could do that, why weren't they charging more when the price of gas at the pump was under $2 a gallon? They didn't, I expect, because they couldn't. Supply and demand determine gasoline prices—not the big oil companies. Supply and demand are impersonal forces, they don't have an office anywhere in some building. But people always seem to want to blame someone for their predicament. It is just so easy to blame the oil companies.

Well, suppose, the federal government does slam a price ceiling on gas when it is

Cooperative Learning

Divide the class into groups of three or four. Have the groups brainstorm natural disasters that could strike where they live, and the effects such disasters might have on certain goods. What goods would be in high demand because of the disaster? What trade-offs would the group be willing to make to ensure that people could obtain the goods they wanted and needed? Have the groups share their work with the class.

rising rapidly. If that price ceiling is below the equilibrium price, then simple economics tells us that we are going to have some problems. At a price below equilibrium price, shortages will arise. And with shortages, long lines. I can remember back to the late 1970s when the federal government did place a price ceiling on gas at the pump. Sometimes I had to wait for an hour in line to get gas. I don't want to go back to that.

Patrick Chu, graduate student in physics

Maybe sometimes a long line is better than a high price. Take what happened after Hurricane Katrina or after any natural disaster. All of a sudden, the price of water rises. What the day before cost $2 to buy, now costs $5 or more to buy.

After Katrina hit, many people had to leave their homes. Some went to Houston, Baton Rouge, Atlanta, and other cities. In many of the cities near where cities were devastated, hotel and motel rooms went for higher daily rates. Some of these motel and hotel owners must have said to themselves, "Well, here come all the people leaving New Orleans, so our motel rooms are going to be in high demand, so now is the time to raise the daily rate." It seems to me that these people who raise prices dramatically after a natural disaster are profiting on human misery. They see someone in trouble, they see someone who has no choice but to pay the prices they charge, and they sock it to them.

Maybe there should be a law that after natural disaster, no one can raise the price of anything for at least a month. I think I would be in favor of such a law. We shouldn't allow some people to benefit because other people are in a miserable situation.

Doug Canterfield, salesman

Patrick talks as if price is only there to take money away from some and give to others. Price is a rationing device; that is what all economists teach you. If the demand for water or motel rooms or gasoline is high, and there is only so much supply, then something is going to have to ration these goods. What should the motel owner do? Ration by brute force: if you are stronger than someone else, you get the motel room? By appearance: the prettier you are the more likely you will get a room?

Patrick seems to forget that price has a job to do and if we don't let it do its job—which is rationing—something else is going to have to do the job. Patrick didn't suggest what should become the rationing device for water, or gas, or motel rooms. He simply points a finger at sellers and scolds them.

Anabelle Roberts, high school student

I think some good points have been made on both sides of the issue. I guess I would argue that if people can help one another during a natural disaster, they should. If that means holding prices down, they ought to. After all, presumably the motel owners made money on the day before Hurricane Katrina hit by charging a certain daily rate. Why can't they make money after the hurricane if they charge the same rate?

What Do You Think?

1. Who do you most nearly agree with? Why?
2. What are the strong points of the debate here? The weak points?

Activities for What Do You Think?

1. Conduct a class survey of students' answers to the first question. Chart their opinions to find out the position of the class on price controls on some goods at certain times.
2. Direct students to make lists of the strong points and weak points of the debate. Invite them to share their lists with the class and debate which side of the issue has the most merit.

Closure

Direct students to write a paragraph describing how their opinions on price controls were affected by reading and discussing this Debating the Issues. Have students share their paragraphs with the class. Ask students what particular pieces of information influenced their thinking.

Cooperative Learning

Divide the class into groups of three or four. Assign each group a different natural disaster—for example, a hurricane, a blizzard, a volcanic eruption, a superflood, an extreme drought, and a massive fire. Have each group identify a part of the United States likely to be hit by its assigned disaster. Instruct each group to assume the role of a team of federal officials, and establish guidelines for placing price controls on particular goods at certain times. Have the groups share their guidelines with the class. Discuss similarities and differences in the plans. You might want to outline a general plan that the government could use in deciding price controls with all natural disasters.

UNIT III Preview

Listed below are the chapters included in this unit.

CHAPTER 7
Business Operations

CHAPTER 8
Competition and Markets

CHAPTER 9
Labor, Employment, and Wages

Foundations for the Unit

Unit III concentrates on microeconomics. As pointed out in Chapter 1, it has been said that the tools of microeconomics are microscopes and the tools of macroeconomics are telescopes. In this unit, students will look through microscopes to examine microeconomics—to see a side of the world of business that they may never have seen before. They will begin to see that business decisions are shaped by economic forces that are identifiable, and in many cases predictable.

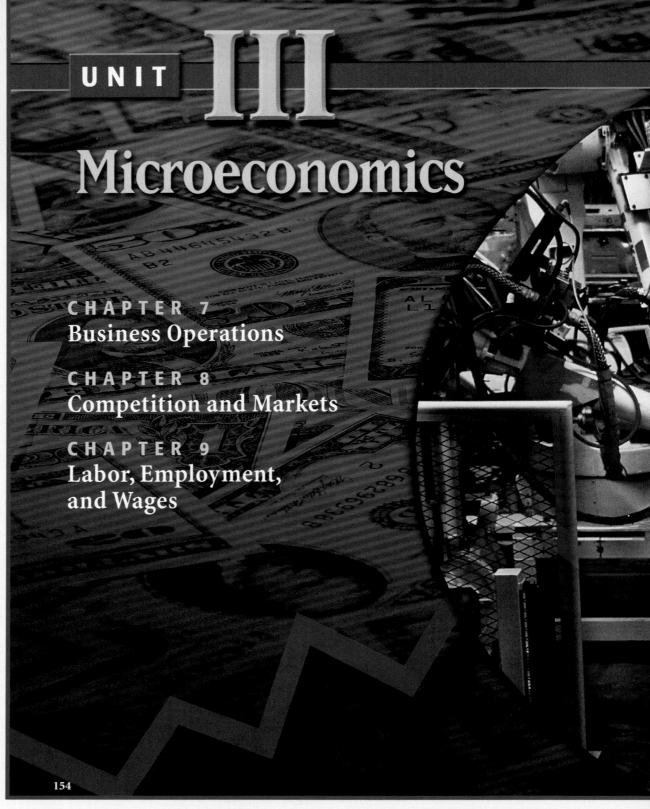

UNIT III Microeconomics

CHAPTER 7
Business Operations

CHAPTER 8
Competition and Markets

CHAPTER 9
Labor, Employment, and Wages

154

Resources for the Unit

Books

Allen, Frederick. *Secret Formula: How Brilliant Marketing and Relentless Sales Made Coca-Cola the Best Known Product in the World*. New York: Harper Business, 1995.

Geiss, Charles R. *Monopolies in America: Empire Builders and Their Enemies from Jay Gould to Bill Gates*. London, England: Oxford University Press, 2000.

Ortega, Robert. *In Sam We Trust: The Untold Story of Sam Walton and Wal-Mart, the World's Most Powerful Retailer*. New York: Times Books, 1999.

Yates, Michael D. *Why Unions Matter*. New York: Monthly Review Press, 1998.

Articles

Ackerman, Elise. "Picking Up the Pace," *U.S. News and World Report,* February 22, 1999.

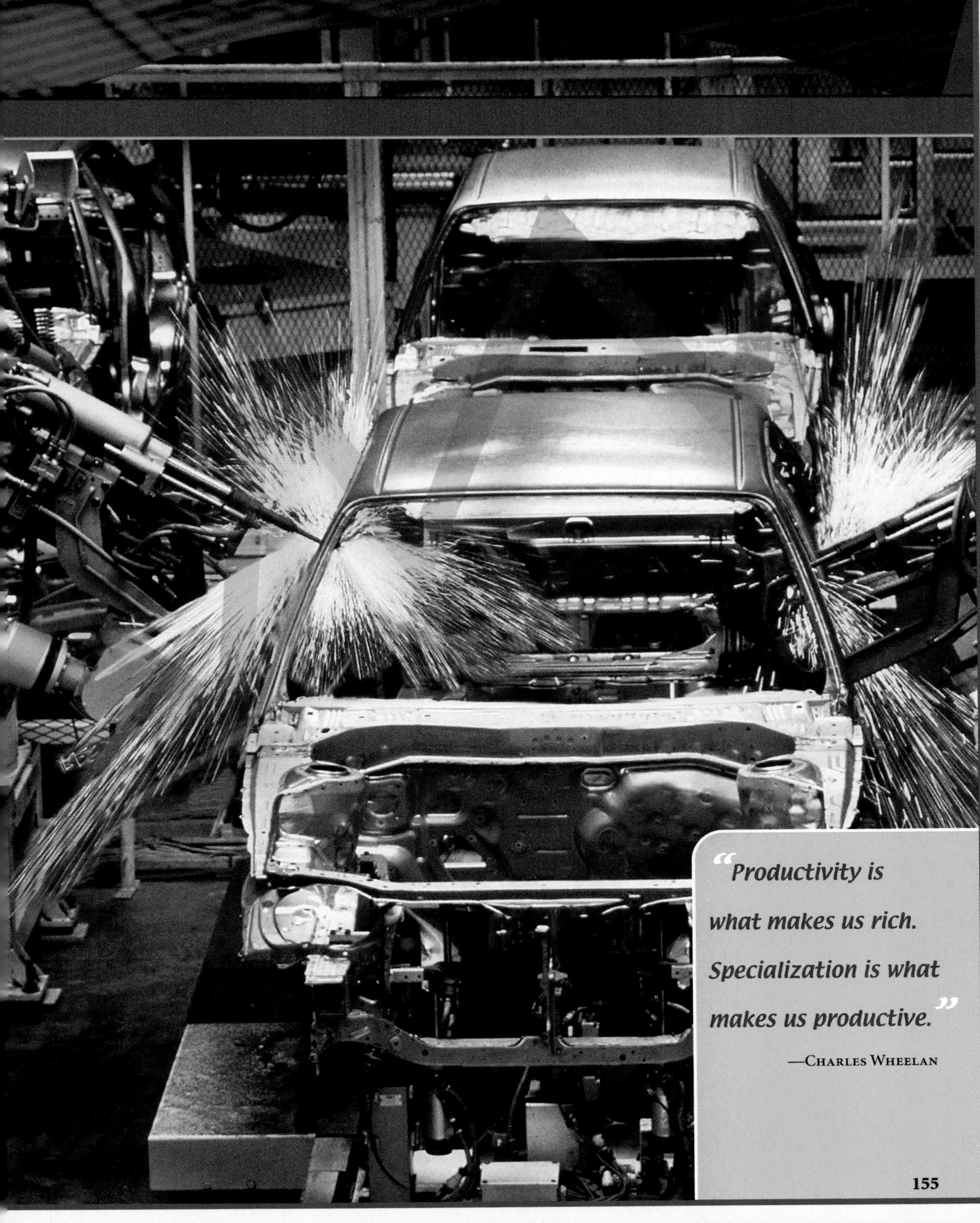

"Productivity is what makes us rich. Specialization is what makes us productive."
—Charles Wheelan
155

Introducing the Unit

You might want to introduce Unit III by writing the word *microeconomics* on the board. Ask students to recall how this word was defined in Chapter 1. Ensure students understand that microeconomics is the branch of economics that deals with human behavior and choices as they relate to relatively small units—the individual, the business firm, the single market. Stress that students should find the material in Unit III useful and informative because each of them, as an individual, represents one of the "relatively small units" that are studied in microeconomics.

Performance Task

Assign students to work in small groups to learn about successful businesses. Each group should choose a business to focus on. For each chapter in this unit, students should gather pertinent information about that business. For Chapter 7, students could explain why the business is structured the way it is. Other topics include strategies that the firm used to maximize profits, an analysis of the firm's competition, and how the firm manages its employees. Each group should write a summary of what its members have learned, including a graph that shows the firm's profits for the last few years. Each group should also predict how its firm's competitive environment might change in the future and what the firm might do to respond to this challenge.

Allen, Jodie T. "These Are the Good Old Days," *U.S. News and World Report,* January 31, 2000.

Slatalla, Michelle. "Online Shopper: Boxed In: Exploring a Big Box Store Online," *New York Times,* January 27, 2000.

Multimedia

Branded: The Power of Brand Names. Three-part series. VHS. British Broadcasting Corporation.

Branding: The Marketing Advantage. Seven-part series. VHS. Films for the Humanities and Sciences.

Market Failure: Externalities and *Market Failure: Monopoly.* In *Introductory Economics.* VHS. Films for the Humanities and Sciences.

Producing. VHS and printed teacher's guide. Films for the Humanities and Sciences.

Chapter 7 Planning Guide

SECTION ORGANIZER

Section	Learning Objectives	Reproducible Worksheets and Handouts	Assessment
 **About Business Firms** (pages 158–171)	▸ Explain why business firms exist. ▸ Describe a sole proprietorship. ▸ Explain how partnerships and corporations are similar and different.	Section 1 Activity, *Applying the Principles Workbook* Outlining Activity, *Guided Reading and Study Guide* Just the Facts Handout, *Guided Reading and Study Guide*	Section Assessment, *Student Text,* page 171 Quick Quiz, *Annotated Teacher's Edition,* page 170 Section Quiz, *Assessment Book*
 **Costs** (pages 172–175)	▸ Describe fixed and variable costs. ▸ Explain what total costs equal. ▸ Explain how to compute fixed cost, variable cost, average total cost, and marginal cost.	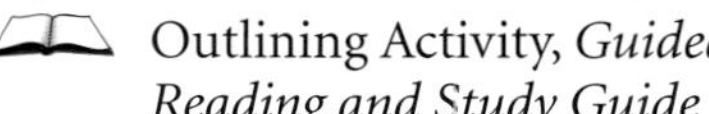 Outlining Activity, *Guided Reading and Study Guide* Just the Facts Handout, *Guided Reading and Study Guide*	Section Assessment, *Student Text,* page 175 Quick Quiz, *Annotated Teacher's Edition,* page 174 Section Quiz, *Assessment Book*
 **Revenue and Its Applications** (pages 176–183)	▸ Explain what total revenue and marginal revenue are. ▸ Explain why a business firm compares marginal revenue with marginal cost when deciding how many units of a good to produce.	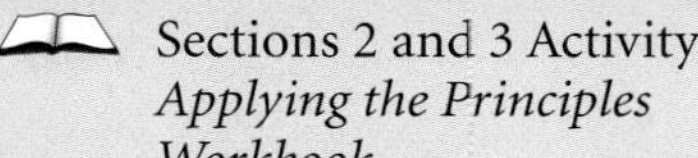 Sections 2 and 3 Activity, *Applying the Principles Workbook* Outlining Activity, *Guided Reading and Study Guide* Just the Facts Handout, *Guided Reading and Study Guide*	Section Assessment, *Student Text,* page 183 Quick Quiz, *Annotated Teacher's Edition,* page 182 Section Quiz, *Assessment Book*

CHAPTER AND PROGRAM RESOURCES

Reproducible Chapter Resources and Assessment Materials

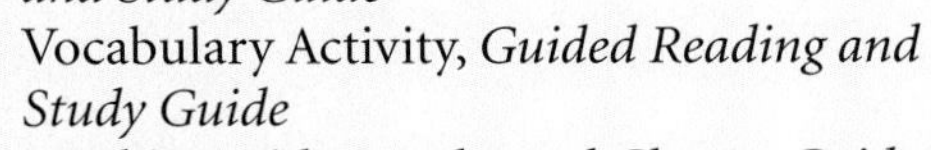

- Graphic Organizer Activity, *Guided Reading and Study Guide*
- Vocabulary Activity, *Guided Reading and Study Guide*
- Working with Graphs and Charts, *Guided Reading and Study Guide*
- Practice Test, *Guided Reading and Study Guide*
- Critical Thinking Activity, *Finding Economics*
- Chapter Test A, *Assessment Book*
- Chapter Test B, *Assessment Book*

Technology Resources

- *Test Generator CD*
- *Spanish Audio Summaries CD*
- *Marketplace® Audio Lessons CD*
- *Economic Principles Lectures, Videocassette or DVD*

Lesson Planning and Teaching Resources

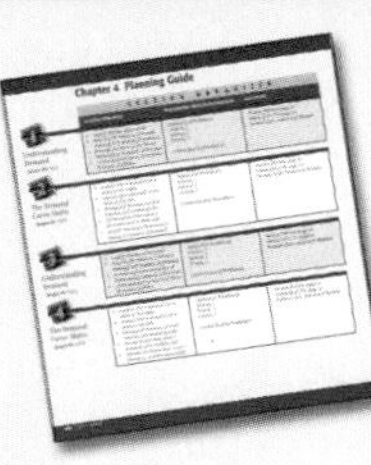

The *Economics: New Ways of Thinking* Teacher Resources include detailed lesson plans for each section in this chapter; the lesson plans are available in print form *(Lesson Plans)* and electronic form. The Teacher Resources also include *Daily Lectures: Overheads and Notes,* which provides prepared overheads and discussion notes covering the key concepts in each section of this chapter.

EMC Publishing Economics Online

Go to Economics Online, at www.emcp.com, for a variety of Internet resources to help you keep your course current and relevant. At Economics Online you will find these items:

- Economics in the News Lessons
- Study Guide Questions
- Practice Tests
- Lesson Plans

Internet Resources

Economics: New Ways of Thinking encourages students to use the Internet to find out more about economics. With the wealth of current, valid information available on Web sites, using the Internet as a research tool is likely to increase your students' interest in and understanding of economics principles and topics. In addition, doing Internet research can help your students form the habit of accessing and using economics information, as well as help them develop investigative skills they will use throughout their educational and professional careers.

To aid your students in achieving these ends, each chapter of *Economics: New Ways of Thinking* includes the addresses of several Web sites at which students will find engaging, relevant information. When students type in the addresses provided, they will immediately arrive at the intended sites. The addresses have been modified so that EMC Publishing can monitor and maintain the proper links—for example, the government site http://stats.bls.gov/ has been changed to www.emcp.net/prices. In the event that the address or content of a site changes or is discontinued, EMC's Internet editors will create a link that redirects students to an address with similar information.

Activities in the *Annotated Teacher's Edition* often suggest that students search the Internet for information. For some activities, you might want to find reputable sites beforehand, and steer students to those sites. For other activities, you might want students to do their own searching, and then check out the sites they have found and discuss why they might be reliable or unreliable.

CHAPTER 7 Overview

This chapter discusses business firms. It explains why business firms exist and describes the different types of business firms. It also discusses how business firms decide what number of units of a good to produce and the number of employees to hire.

SECTION 1 About Business Firms

Section 1 explains why business firms exist and describes the different kinds of business firms that exist.

SECTION 2 Costs

Section 2 covers the difference between fixed and variable costs. It also explores how fixed costs, variable costs, average total costs, and marginal costs are computed.

SECTION 3 Revenue and Its Applications

Section 3 examines total and marginal revenue. It also covers how cost and revenue together determine quantity produced by a firm.

CHAPTER 7 Business Operations

Why It Matters

To understand the life you are living, it is important to understand the institutions that play a big role in our society. One of those institutions is business. Almost every day of your life you come into contact with some kind of business—when you stop for lunch at a fast-food restaurant, buy new shoes at the local mall, or purchase your favorite group's new CD at the electronics store. If you have a part-time job, you are probably working for some kind of local business. This chapter begins to examine business—the institution we all deal with so often.

The owner of this fruit and vegetable market in Bombay, India, appears pleased with his efforts to maximize profits, the goal of all business owners.

Teaching Suggestions from the Author

Some students will go on to major in business administration in college. For these students in particular, this chapter is critical because the basics of business decisions are presented here. The student who understands these basics will have a keener understanding of why businesses do what they do.

I usually begin this chapter by asking students what they think the business world is like. I ask questions such as, Why are some businesses big and others small? Why are there few businesses in some industries and many in other industries? How do businesses decide how many units of a good to produce? For

Economics Around the Clock

The following events occurred one day in November.

8:45 A.M. Jackie started her own business a year ago. Last year she earned $50,032 in profit. This year she hopes to do better. At this moment she is sitting in her office trying to decide whether to hire two more employees. On the one hand, she thinks her business will soon be expanding and she will need two more employees. But on the other hand, she is not sure she can afford to pay the wages of two additional employees.

- **What should Jackie consider when deciding whether to hire additional employees?**

11:09 A.M Carl and Vernon are retired. They meet each Wednesday morning at a local restaurant to have breakfast and talk. Carl says, "I'm not sure what is happening to this country. It looks to me like American firms are just shipping jobs overseas." Vernon nods in agreement and then says, "I guess it is a lot cheaper to hire people in other countries than it is to hire people here. You know, when you can hire someone in another country for $2 an hour, why in the world would you pay $14 an hour here?" Carl says, "I guess it's just good economics to go where your labor cost is low." "I guess," says Vernon.

- **Do U.S. companies always hire workers in countries where the wages are low?**

12:44 P.M. Bob is eating his lunch at a small restaurant near his workplace. He gets a full hour for lunch each day. He looks at his watch, then he calls the server over to order a small dessert. (Bob is trying to lose weight, but now is not the time.) The server comes over and asks, "So are you going to have some dessert today?" Bob says, "I'll have a slice of chocolate cake with vanilla ice cream." "Not in a rush to get back to work?" the server asks. "No," says Bob, "I don't have to punch in."

- **Would Bob be less likely to order dessert if he did have to "punch in" (using a time clock)?**

1:07 P.M. Uri has a hot dog stand in Manhattan. Each day he sells between 300 and 400 hot dogs for $3 each. He just sold a hot dog to one of his regular customers, Sam. As Sam was paying for his hot dog and drink, he says, "You know, Uri, I bet you'd sell a lot more hot dogs if you charged $2.50." Uri just looks at Sam and says, "It's not about selling more hot dogs."

- **If it's not about selling more hot dogs, then what is it about?**

157

Introducing the Chapter

Ask students to list three firms or stores with which they have done business in the last month. Call on students to share their lists of businesses.

Explain that, as students know, there are different types of businesses. In a free enterprise economy, however, there are only three basic forms of business ownership: sole proprietorships, partnerships, and corporations.

In this chapter, students will learn about these three basic forms of business ownership and look at the advantages and disadvantages of each one.

Teaching with Visuals

Business owners face many choices. Where should a business be located, what goods and services are most profitable, and how should the business be organized? Today, of course, businesses face an additional question. Should they be online, traditional, or a combination of both? If these questions are answered well and the business prospers, everyone will be smiling, as shown in this photo.

example, how does a car company know to produce, say, 10,000 cars instead of 20,000?

When students try to answer these questions, they begin to realize that there is more to business than meets the eye. Owning and operating a business does not only consist of coming up with a good product. It is also knowing how to do 101 things, including what resources to buy, how many employees to hire, what price to charge, how many units of a good to produce, and so on.

I often tell students that there is a science of business, just as there is a science of physics, chemistry, or biology. This chapter begins to unlock the secrets of the science of business.

Focus and Motivate

Section Objectives

After completing this section, students will be able to

- explain why business firms exist;
- describe a sole proprietorship; and
- explain how partnerships and corporations are similar and different.

Kickoff Activity

Instruct students to pretend they work at a convenience store, along with three other employees. For employees to get paid, each task on a set list must be completed. If the tasks aren't done, no one gets paid. One day one employee decides not to do any more work. How does this action affect the other employees?

Activating Prior Knowledge

Discuss students' responses to the Kickoff Activity, and explain that in this section, students will learn how business firms are set up to minimize the kind of shirking of responsibilities shown by the lazy employee.

Teach

Discussion Starter

Ask students the following questions: Do you know anyone who owns a business? What business is he or she in? How many employees does she or he have? Is the business a sole proprietorship or a partnership? Invite several local business owners to talk to your class about their businesses and why they formed them as they did.

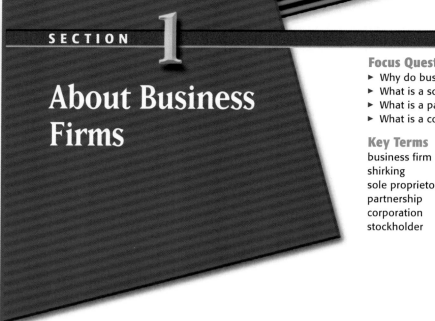

Focus Questions

- Why do business firms exist?
- What is a sole proprietorship?
- What is a partnership?
- What is a corporation?

Key Terms

business firm
shirking
sole proprietorship
partnership
corporation
stockholder
asset
limited liability
board of directors
franchise
franchiser
franchisee

Why Do Business Firms Exist?

Business firms are organizations that use resources to produce goods and services that are sold to consumers, other businesses, or the government. Businesses typically are formed when someone has an idea about how he or she can earn profits by producing and selling a good or service. While many new businesses begin with just one person, most businesses exist because people working together can produce more than the sum of what individuals working alone can produce.

Suppose 10 individuals each fish for a living. Each day each person catches 100 fish. The daily sum of fish caught by these 10 individuals is therefore 1,000 fish. One day one individual says to the others, "Instead of fishing alone, why don't we form a team and fish together? We can specialize in doing different things. One person will make the nets, another person will navigate the boat, some people will cast the nets, and so on. I think that if we work together—if we form a team, so to speak—we will be able to catch 2,000 fish a day."

business firm
An organization that uses resources to produce goods and services that are sold to consumers, other firms, or the government.

Let's suppose this person is correct. Ten people working together can catch more fish (2,000) than the sum of these 10 people working alone (1,000 fish). This would be reason enough for the people to form a team. Another name for this team is a *business firm.* A business firm of people working together can be more effective than a group of people all working individually.

Why Are Bosses Necessary?

Business firms need bosses and employees: people who give the orders and people who carry out the orders. Why are businesses structured this way? Why doesn't everyone have an equal say in what happens in the firm? To answer this question, let's return to our team of fishers.

Suppose that our 10 fishers agree to form a firm and fish together each day. They also agree to split their catch evenly among the 10 of them. If they catch 2,000 fish a day, for example, each person will get 200 fish to sell. Each fish sells for $1, so each person's income will be $200 a day, double the amount they were earning individually.

158 Chapter 7 Business Operations

Cooperative Learning

To own part of a corporation, all one has to do is buy stock in that particular corporation. Some corporations make money, and their stock prices and value go up. At other times, stock prices fall. Bring in a copy of the newspaper financial pages that contain the corporations listed on the NASDAQ and the New York Stock Exchange. Divide students into groups of three or four. Allow each group to choose a corporation. On a weekly basis, invite students to check the stock prices for their corporations. Ask them, if they had purchased real stock, would they have made money, or would they have lost some of their original investment? You might assign students a chart showing the fluctuations in the prices of their two stocks.

Shirking

Things go smoothly for a while. Each day the 10 fishers work together catching fish, and each day they catch 2,000 fish. Then one day one of the 10 individuals, Jake, feels lazy. He comes to work late, takes long breaks, and generally doesn't work as hard as he should. We say he is **shirking**, or putting forth less than the agreed-to effort. Because of Jake's shirking, the fish catch falls to 1,800. Divided 10 ways, each person receives 180 fish, or an income of $180, that day.

Notice that one person, Jake, shirked, but all 10 people had to pay for his shirking. Everyone's income fell by $20 because Jake shirked. When he shirked, Jake received the full benefits of shirking (longer breaks, less work), but he paid only one-tenth of the costs of shirking. Nine-tenths of the shirking costs were paid by the remaining nine persons in the fishing firm, none of whom shirked.

How do you think you would have responded if you were one of the other nine fishers and Jake continued to shirk? Do you think you might have begun shirking? When a person receives the full benefits of his shirking but pays only a fraction of the costs, shirking is likely to increase. No doubt there will be more people shirking than only Jake, and this shirking will further reduce the fish catch. In other words, instead of 1,800 fish a day, the catch will fall to 1,600 as more people shirk, then to 1,400 as even more people shirk, and so on. The increased fish catch (2,000 instead of 1,000), however, was the reason the 10 individuals came together to form a team in the first place. Without added fish, the reason for the firm to exist is gone.

Monitors

How can the 10 members stop the shirking and continue to enjoy the benefits of the added fish catch? One way is to choose one among them to be the monitor—the person in the firm who coordinates team production and seeks to reduce shirking (the boss, in other words). To be effective, this boss must have the ability to fire and hire people. (Can you see the reason for having a boss now?) If Jake is shirking, the boss must be able to fire him and replace him with someone who will not shirk. The threat of dismissal is what reduces shirking in a firm.

How can the monitor, or boss, be kept from shirking? One possibility is to give the monitor an incentive not to shirk by making him or her a *residual claimant* of the firm. A residual claimant receives the excess of revenues over costs (profits) as income. If the monitor shirks, then profits are likely to be lower (or even negative); therefore, the monitor will receive less income.

▲ Few businesses can operate successfully without a boss or bosses. **Can you explain why?**

A Student Asks

QUESTION: *You say, "Once a firm is formed, people in the firm will shirk." You say it as though you know it will happen. How can you be so sure?*

ANSWER: *We can't say that "everybody" will shirk if he or she gets a chance, but it is likely that most people will shirk under the right circumstances. Why is that? Because people value leisure, and what you are doing when you shirk is essentially consuming some leisure. Also, once some people shirk, others naturally begin to feel that they should shirk too, or they end up doing more than their share and getting paid for less of their share. Ask yourself whether you are more likely to shirk in some settings than others. What you will find is that you are more likely to shirk when the costs of shirking (to you) are low and that you are less likely to shirk when the costs of shirking (to you) are high.*

shirking
The behavior of a worker who is putting forth less than the agreed-to effort.

Teaching with Visuals

Having a boss helps prevent employees from shirking.

Prediction Activity

Ask students to consider the following: Suppose that there are two car dealerships, A and B. In A, the members of the sales staff are paid a fixed monthly amount of $2,000 plus a $200 bonus for each car they sell. In B, the salespeople are paid a fixed monthly amount of $2,500, but they do not receive a bonus for each car they sell. In which setting will a member of the sales staff be more likely to shirk?

(*Answer:* A salesperson at dealership B is more likely to shirk. The cost of shirking is higher in A than in B, because if a salesperson shirks at A, he or she may not sell a car and therefore may not get a bonus. Not getting a bonus is the cost of shirking at dealership A. There is no equivalent cost of shirking at dealership B because there is no bonus to forfeit.)

Cause and Effect

Instruct students to think of a business firm as a sports team or a musical band. All members of the firm must be performing at their best in order to produce the best possible good or service. Assign students to create scenarios in which a particular member of a business firm is shirking his or her responsibility. Students should document how well the firm does at its peak and what effect shirking has on the firm's performance.

Differentiating Instruction

Visual Learners

Write the following three headings on the board: "Advantages," "Disadvantages," and "Examples." Then call on students to describe an advantage of a sole proprietorship. As each advantage is described, write that advantage on the board. After you have discussed the advantages, list and discuss disadvantages. Then students can work in pairs to list specific examples of sole proprietorships in your community and to create a visual of each business's primary product or service.

Reinforcement Activity

Ask the sole proprietor of a business in your community to give a short talk to students. To prepare students for the presentation, tell them about the business and the person coming to visit. Assign students to develop a list of two or three questions they would like the business owner to answer. After the proprietor has spoken, ask students to write a one-page paper describing what they learned.

Background Information

Many people think that of the three types of business firms—sole proprietorship, partnership, and corporation—corporations are the most numerous. This is perhaps because they hear and read more about major corporations than about the other two. Point out that sole proprietorships are far more common than corporations, but corporations account for a much larger percentage of total business revenues.

Economics Around the Clock

After reading and discussing "Why Are Bosses Necessary?" (pages 158–160), direct students to the 12:44 P.M. scenario in Economics Around the Clock (page 157).

Answers will vary. Students may say that if Bob's work time isn't monitored by a time clock, it is easier for him to shirk without being caught. If he were caught shirking, he might lose his job.

Teaching with Visuals

Advantages of a sole proprietorship include: easy to form and dissolve; all decision-making power resides with the sole proprietor; profit is taxed only once. Disadvantages include: unlimited liability; limited ability to raise funds for expansion; the business usually ends with the retirement or death of the owner.

For example, in the classroom environment, some students say they end up doing less work and taking things a little easier in class when a substitute teacher is in the class. Why is this? Often the students think that the substitute teacher is here today and gone tomorrow, so they can pretty much do what they want today and get away with it. In anticipation of this behavior, the regular teacher will ask the substitute teacher to give a (graded) quiz to the students. This quiz is supposed to get the students to take the substitute teacher more seriously.

sole proprietorship A business that is owned by one individual who makes all business decisions, receives all the profits or incurs all the losses of the firm, and is legally responsible for the debts of the firm.

Three Types of Firms

Business firms commonly fall into one of three legal categories: sole proprietorships, partnerships, and corporations. Let's look at the similarities and differences of these three types of ownership.

Sole Proprietorships

A **sole proprietorship** is a business that is owned by one individual, who makes all the business decisions, receives all the profits or takes all the losses of the firm, and is legally responsible for the debts of the firm. Many family farms are sole proprietorships, as are many other businesses such as barbershops, restaurants, and carpet-cleaning services. About 18.3 million proprietorships operate in the United States.

Advantages of Sole Proprietorships Certain advantages come with organizing a business as a sole proprietorship.

1. Sole proprietorships are easy to form and to dissolve. To start a sole proprietorship, you need only meet certain broadly defined governmental regulations. Some firms must meet health and zoning regulations; for example, if you are starting a restaurant, you must be sure that the restaurant is clean (a health regulation) and that it is located in an area where restaurants are permitted (a zoning regulation). Also, you need to register the name of the business with local governmental officials. To dissolve a sole proprietorship, you need only to stop doing business.
2. All decision-making power resides with the sole proprietor. If you are the owner of a sole proprietorship, you alone can make all the business decisions. Having no stockholders or partners means that you decide whether to expand your business, buy more supplies, advertise on the radio, and so on. Decisions can be made quickly and easily, since only one person counts—the sole proprietor.
3. The profit of the firm is taxed only once. Among the different types of taxes in the United States are sales taxes, property taxes, corporate income taxes, and personal income taxes. If you are the owner of a sole proprietorship, the profit you earn is counted as your income, and only personal income taxes (taxes paid on your income) apply. Proprietorships do not pay corporate income taxes (taxes paid on a corporation's profits). As you will see, neither do partnerships. Only corporations pay corporate income taxes.

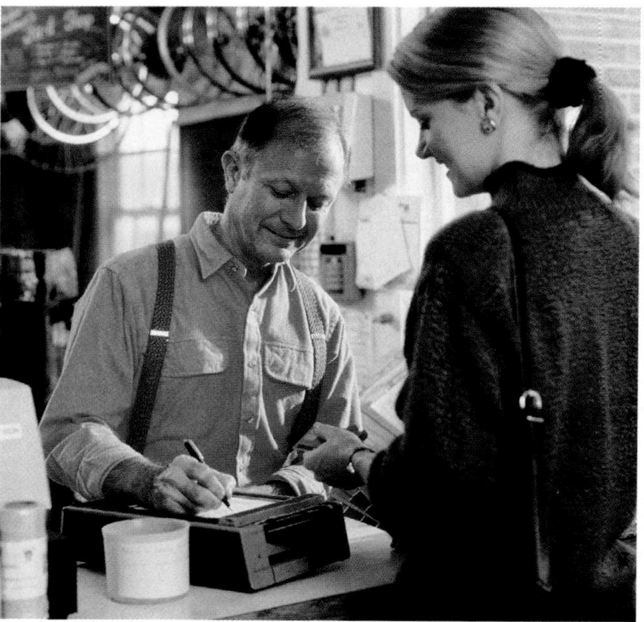

▼ Many small retail businesses, like this bicycle shop, are sole proprietorships. **What are the advantages and disadvantages of a sole proprietorship, as compared to other types of business ownership?**

Cross-Curricular Activity

Invite a business teacher to speak to your class about partnerships. You might wish to discuss the economic advantages and disadvantages of partnerships, and ask students to list partnerships in your community before the visiting teacher comes. The business teacher should discuss the basics of partnerships and partnership law, such as liability and fiduciary relationships. You might ask the business teacher to bring samples of partnership agreements to show your class.

Economics in the Real World

Should NASCAR Be Required for an MBA?

It is the fastest growing sport in America. It is the second most watched sport on television, trailing only pro football. What sport is it? It's NASCAR—National Association of Stock Car Auto Racing.*

What explains the popularity and rapid growth of NASCAR? Some have suggested that it's the danger and drama associated with cars reaching speeds of 190 miles per hour, and life-and-death, win-or-lose decisions being made in milliseconds.

Or maybe—just maybe—it is the economics of competition and cooperation that is visibly noticeable on the racetracks. The same qualities that a driver needs to win stock car races are the qualities one needs to win in the business world. Let's see if we can identify these similar qualities.

At the longer stock car tracks, such as Daytona and Talladega, the way to out-compete your opponents is to out-cooperate them. Specifically, the way to win is to enter into a "draft partnership" with other drivers.

In the 1960s, drivers learned that if one stock car closely followed another, both cars increased their speed. Two cars traveling together in what is called a *draft line* go faster than a single car traveling alone. Drafting explains why you will sometimes see as many as 10 cars, one right behind the other, racing around the track for long periods of time.

When drivers are "drafting," they are cooperating with each other. At a certain point in the race one car in a draft line will form a partnership with another car to pass the front car. The formation of this partnership will often allow a car to pass what was the front car. What we see in these instances is one partnership breaking up and others being formed.

And near the end of the race it is inevitable that cooperation will give way to competition. The second car in a draft line will try to pass the car in front. This is a very technical maneuver, but it is made harder by the first car trying to prevent his former partner from passing.

Lesson learned from stock car racing: Stock car racing is not just a matter of powerful engines, agile handling, expert driving, and fast pit stops. It is a second-by-second knowledge of knowing when to cooperate and when to compete.

The same lesson presents itself in the business world. In the early days of the computer business, Microsoft and Cisco formed partnerships with potential competitors such as Intel, Compaq, and Dell, and did better than Apple, which did not form partnerships. Were Microsoft, Cisco, and others simply forming a "draft line" ?

Moving up the corporate ladder also has characteristics of a "draft line." Often an executive climbs the corporate ladder with selected staff. Often one corporate "draft line" replaces another.

Cooperation and competition are two important processes in economics. People cooperate when they trade with each other, and they compete when they pursue the same customer's dollars. Perhaps this does explain the rise in popularity of NASCAR. People realize that watching and studying stock car races might teach them lessons that lead to success in the business world.

THINK ABOUT IT Are there any "draft lines" in your life? Has it ever been necessary for you to form new partnerships to achieve your goals? Which do you think is most important in achieving success—cooperation or competition?

* This feature draws on two papers: "Fortune 500, Meet Daytona 500," by Charles Duhigg in *Slate*, February 17, 2003, and "Social Science at 190 MPH on NASCAR's Biggest SuperSpeedways," a 2000 Rand Corporation paper by David Ronfeldt.

Economics in the Real World

Ask students to think about other arenas that involve both cooperation and competition.

ANSWERS TO THINK ABOUT IT Answers will vary. Students should be able to back up their opinions with examples.

Discussion Starter

After studying the advantages and disadvantages of being a sole proprietor, have students discuss whether or not they think they would like to be sole proprietors. Ask what goods or services they would provide.

Reinforcement Activity

Tell students to imagine they are sole proprietors of their own businesses. Instruct each student to write a letter to another person, encouraging that person to begin his or her own business. Students should explain the goods and services offered by their own firms, and describe how they run their businesses (accounting, marketing, and so on). They should also explain how they manage their personnel.

Cooperative Learning

Divide students into groups of four or five. Tell them to view themselves as partners in a partnership. Each group should decide what type of partnership it is, such as law, medical, or accounting. Then the group should write five to seven questions its partnership would need to answer—for example: How are we going to generate business? How are we going to decide what our salaries are? How are we going to decide what materials we need to buy? Allow each group to present its questions to the class and explain why it considers these questions important in a partnership.

Activating Prior Knowledge

Discuss with students the concept of liability. Compare the definition given in the text with definitions written by students. Explain that liability is a legal term that has to do with the responsibility to pay debts. Point out that in this chapter they will read about liability as it refers to the owners of differently organized businesses.

Critical Thinking

If one partner in a partnership incurs business debts, all other partners are responsible for those debts. Problems in partnerships may not always occur, but partners need to be prepared for them. Ask students what type of person would make a good partner.

Reinforcement Activity

Direct students to clip articles from the newspaper that relate to failed sole proprietorships, partnerships, or corporations. Assign a short essay in which students summarize what went wrong, and offer their own suggestions for how to fix these problems.

Teaching with Visuals

Advantages of partnerships: benefits of specialization can be realized; only personal income taxes apply to it. Disadvantages: partners in some types of partnerships face unlimited liability; decision making in a partnership can be complicated and frustrating.

Disadvantages of Sole Proprietorships Sole proprietorships have disadvantages, too:

1. The sole proprietor faces unlimited liability. *Liability* is a legal term that has to do with the responsibility to pay debts. Saying that sole proprietors have *unlimited liability* means that their personal assets may be used to pay off the debts of the firm. For example, suppose Arzlani opens her own cookie shop in the shopping mall. A year passes, and she is taking a loss on the business. She is also in debt to her suppliers—the person from whom she buys flour, the person from whom she rents the shop, and so on. Because Arzlani has unlimited liability, her personal assets—such as her car and her house—may have to be sold to pay off her business debts.
2. Sole proprietors have limited ability to raise funds for business expansion. Sole proprietors do not find borrowing funds easy, because lenders are not eager to lend funds to business firms whose success depends on one person. The sole proprietor's sources of money are often limited to personal funds and the funds of close friends and family members.
3. Sole proprietorships usually end with the retirement or death of the proprietor; they have a limited life. When the owner of a sole proprietorship dies, the business "dies" as well. From the point of view of the business community and the firm's employees, this factor is a disadvantage. Employees usually like to work for firms that offer some permanency and the possibility of moving upward.

partnership
A business owned by two or more co-owners, called partners, who share profits and are legally responsible for debts.

Partnerships

A **partnership** is a business that is owned by two or more co-owners, called partners, who share any profits the business earns and are legally responsible for any debts incurred by the firm. You may think of a partnership as a proprietorship with more than one owner. Partnerships include such businesses as some medical offices, law offices, and advertising agencies. Approximately 2.3 million partnerships operate in the United States.

Advantages of Partnerships The advantages of partnerships include the following:

1. In a partnership, the benefits of specialization can be realized. If, for example, one partner in an advertising agency is better at public relations and another is better at artwork, each can work at the tasks for which he or she is best suited. The ad agency then has a better chance of succeeding than if only one person ran it.
2. The profit of the partnership is the income of the partners, and only personal income taxes apply to it. The owners of a partnership, like the owner of a sole proprietorship, pay only personal income taxes. Corporate income taxes do not apply.

Disadvantages of Partnerships Partnerships also have some disadvantages, which include the following:

1. There are two types of partners, general partners and limited partners. *General partners* are partners who are responsible for the management of the firm. They face unlimited liability, just as sole

▼ Chris Feaver and Larry Little were the founding partners of Excite, an Internet company. **Although they have since sold their company, what advantages would Chris and Larry have enjoyed operating their company as a partnership? What would have been the disadvantages?**

Internet Research

Send students to the Internet to learn which large corporations maintain offices or are headquartered in their community. Ask: Do you know people who work for these companies? How significant are these companies in the local economy? How many companies are headquartered in this region? How many corporations just have branches here? Which companies are involved in economic activities that are unique to the region (such as mining)? Which are involved in global activities?

proprietors do. However, unlimited liability is even more of a disadvantage in a partnership than it is in a sole proprietorship. In a sole proprietorship, the proprietor incurs his or her own debts and is solely responsible for them. In a partnership, one general partner might incur the debts, but all general partners are responsible for them. For example, suppose partner Matson incurs a debt by buying an expensive piece of medical equipment without the permission of partners Bradbury and Chan. This is too bad for partners Bradbury and Chan. They are still legally responsible for the debts incurred by Matson.

Although a general partner has unlimited liability, a limited partner does not. The liability of a *limited partner* is restricted to the amount he or she has invested in the firm. Limited partners usually do not participate in the management of the firm or enter into contracts on behalf of the firm.

2. Decision making in a partnership can be complicated and frustrating. Suppose that Smithies, a partner in a law firm, wants to move the partnership in one direction, to specialize in corporate law. Yankelovich wants to move it in another direction, to specialize in family law. Who makes the decision in this tug-of-war? Possibly no one will make the decision, and things will stay as they are, which may not be a good thing for the growth of the partnership.

Corporations

A **corporation** is a legal entity that (1) can conduct business in its own name in the same way that an individual does and (2) is owned by its **stockholders**. Stockholders are people who buy shares of *stock* in a corporation. A share of stock represents a claim on the **assets** of the corporation. (Assets are anything of value to which the firm has legal claim.) A share of stock gives the purchaser a share of the ownership of the corporation. About 5.1 million corporations operate in the United States and account for about 83 percent of all business receipts.

▲ Larry Page (left) and Sergey Brin (right) co-founded Google, Inc., in September of 1998, in Menlo Park, California. **What reasons might they have had for forming a corporation?**

What does it mean when we say that a corporation is a legal entity that can conduct business in its own name? For purposes of the law, a corporation is a living, breathing entity (like an individual), even though in reality a corporation is not a living thing. Let's say that a thousand people want to form a corporation and call it XYZ Corporation. The law treats XYZ Corporation as if it were a person. We can see what this treatment means through an example. Suppose XYZ Corporation has a debt of $3 million and it has only $1 million with which to pay the debt. Legally, the remainder of the debt ($2 million) cannot be obtained from the owners (stockholders) of the corporation. It is the corporation that owes the money, not the owners of the corporation. The owners of the corporation have limited liability.

Advantages of Corporations The advantages of corporations include the following:

1. The owners of the corporation (the stockholders) are not personally liable for the debts of the corporation; they have limited liability. To say that the stockholders have **limited liability** means that they cannot be sued for the corporation's failure to pay its debts. They are not personally responsible for these debts. For example, if Turner is a stockholder in corporation X, and corporation X cannot pay off its creditors, Turner does not have to sell her personal assets (her house, car, and so on) to pay the debts of the corporation. She can

corporation
A legal entity that can conduct business in its own name in the same way that an individual does.

stockholder
A person who owns shares of stock in a corporation.

asset
Anything of value to which the firm has a legal claim.

limited liability
A condition in which an owner of a business firm can lose only the amount he or she has invested (in the firm).

Teaching with Visuals

By forming a corporation, Google's founders could avoid personal liability, the corporation could continue even if they left it, and they could more easily raise funds by using the corporate structure.

Reinforcement Activity

Assign each student to pick one major corporation, such as General Motors, Microsoft, or Xerox, and then find out the number of stockholders in that particular corporation, as well as its current stock price. Students can do their research in the library, on the Internet, or by calling the corporation for the information. They might wish to use *Fortune* magazine and check its *Fortune* 500 listing. Have students share their findings in small groups.

Discussion Starter

Growing numbers of individuals own stocks. Ask students if they know people who own stock in a corporation, or if they themselves own stock. Ask: Why do people invest in the stock market? What are the advantages and disadvantages of owning stock?

Background Information: Double Taxation

We point out in this section that corporations are subject to double taxation, whereas sole proprietorships and partnerships are not. When looking only at the taxation issue, it appears that both sole proprietorships and partnerships are better off than corporations. We have also noted in this chapter that, whereas the owners of sole proprietorships and partnerships have unlimited liability, the owners of corporations have limited liability. Some people have suggested that the owners of corporations have paid for the advantage of limited liability through double taxation.

Section 1 About Business Firms 163

Each year *Fortune* magazine ranks the top 500 corporations in the United States according to revenue. In recent years, the largest revenue-earning corporation in the United States has been General Motors. Tell students to find the most recent list of the *Fortune* 500 by searching the Internet for "list of Fortune 500."

Discussion Starter

Corporations are often involved in local community activities. Direct students to find the names of the top five corporations in their state according to sales revenue. Ask: Are these corporations involved in their communities? In what ways? What motivates corporations to assist communities? What are the benefits and disadvantages to the corporation? Refer students to Milton Friedman's and Ralph Nader's views (page 169) for more information on this topic.

Teaching with Visuals

The change in after-tax profits from the first quarter of 2002 to the first quarter of 2005 was 4.5 cents per $1 of sales.

lose only her investment and nothing more. For example, if she bought fifty shares of stock in the corporation at a price of $10 each, her investment is $500. She may never see this $500 again, but she will lose no more.

2. Corporations continue to exist even if one or more owners sell their shares or die. The corporation itself is a legal entity. Its existence does not depend on the existence of its owners.
3. Corporations are usually able to raise large sums of money by selling stock. Because of limited liability, people are more willing to invest in a corporation than in other business forms. The price of a share of stock may be small, so many more people can afford an investment. Furthermore, they can invest as much or as little as they want; for example, a person may buy either 10 or 1,000 shares of stock in a corporation. In addition, because corporations can sell bonds and issue stock, they have ways of raising money that do not exist for proprietorships or partnerships. (We look at bonds and stocks in more detail later in the chapter.)

Disadvantages of Corporations The disadvantages of corporations include the following:

1. Corporations are subject to double taxation. Suppose XYZ Corporation earns $3 million profit this year. This profit is subject to the corporate income tax. If the corporate income tax rate is 25 percent, then $750,000 is paid in taxes, and $2.25 million remains for *dividends* and other uses. Dividends are shares of the corporation's profits distributed to stockholders.

   Suppose that half of the $2.25 million profit after taxes is distributed to stockholders as dividends. This distribution is considered income for the stockholders and is taxed at personal income tax rates. In short, the $3 million profit was subject to both the corporate income tax and the personal income tax—two taxes, or double taxation. Contrast this situation with the profit earned by a proprietorship, which is subject to only one tax, the personal income tax. Exhibit 7-1 shows after-tax profits per dollar of sales for corporations (that manufacture goods).

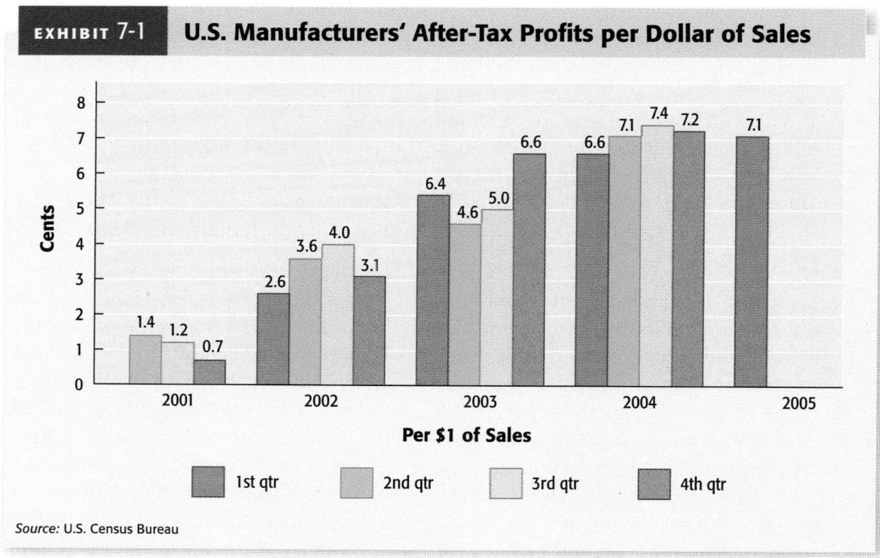

▲ **What was the change in manufacturers' after-tax profits from the first quarter of 2002 to the first quarter of 2005?**

Background Information: Corporations

Corporations originated from joint-stock companies. Medieval guilds and monasteries were the earliest forms of corporations. Business corporations were formed in England in the 16th century to further the country's mercantilist policies. In the late 19th century, industrialization required large sums of capital that could be most easily acquired through the formation of corporations, and the number of new corporations quickly grew. As large corporations emerged, so did monopolies, including Standard Oil and United States Steel. This led, in turn, to antitrust laws, which are meant to control monopoly power and to preserve and promote competition. See the discussions of antitrust laws in Chapter 8 (pages 199–203) for more information.

EXHIBIT 7-2 **Advantages and Disadvantages of Different Types of Business Firms**

Type of business firm	Examples	Advantages	Disadvantages
Sole proprietorship	• Local barbershop • Many restaurants • Family farm • Carpet-cleaning service	• Easy to form and to dissolve. • All decision-making power resides with the sole proprietor. • Profit is taxed only once.	• Proprietor faces unlimited liability. • Limited ability to raise funds for business expansion. • Usually ends with retirement or death of proprietor.
Partnership	• Some medical offices • Some law offices • Some advertising agencies	• Benefits of specialization can be realized. • Profit is taxed only once.	• Partners face unlimited liability (one partner can incur a debt and all partners are legally responsible for payment of the debt). • Decision making can be complex and frustrating.
Corporation	• Hewlett-Packard • Intel • Walt Disney	• Owners (stockholders) have limited liability. • Corporation continues if owners sell their shares of stock or die. • Usually able to raise large sums of money.	• Double taxation. • Corporations are complicated to set up.

▲ A summary of the advantages and disadvantages of the three types of business firms.

2. Corporations are complicated to set up. Corporations are more difficult to organize than sole proprietorships and partnerships, as we discuss next.

Exhibit 7-2 summarizes the advantages and disadvantages of corporations and compares them with the advantages and disadvantages of proprietorships and partnerships.

The Corporate Structure As a group, the stockholders are the most important persons in a corporation. They are its owners, and they elect the members of the board of directors. Voting for the board of directors is usually an annual event, with each stockholder having the right to cast as many votes as he or she has shares of stock. For example, a person with one share of stock has one vote, whereas a person with 10,000 shares of stock has 10,000 votes.

The **board of directors** is an important decision-making body in a corporation that determines corporate policies and goals. It decides what products the corporation will produce and sell, what percentage of the profits of the firm will go to stockholders (as stock dividends), and what percentage will go for modernization and expansion. Also, the board of directors chooses the corporation's top officers, including the president, one or more vice presidents, the secretary, and the treasurer. These officers carry out the day-to-day operations of the corporation. To do so, they often appoint other vice presidents, as well as department heads, who supervise all other employees in their departments. Exhibit 7-3 on the next page shows this structure.

Financing Corporate Activity All firms, whether proprietorships, partnerships, or corporations, can raise money by borrowing from banks and other lending institutions. Only corporations, however, have two other avenues. They can sell bonds (sometimes

board of directors
An important decision-making body in a corporation. It decides corporate policies and goals, among other things.

Reinforcement Activity

Suggest to students that, one evening as they are watching television, they study advertising. On the left side of a piece of paper, they should note the product advertised in each commercial they saw during the course of an hour. On the right side of the paper, they should note the sole proprietorship, partnership, or corporation that produces the product. For example, they might see a commercial for Ford cars. On the left side of the paper, they would write "Ford cars" and on the right side, they would write "Ford Motor Corporation." Students may need to conduct research to find out the name of the business firm that produces the product in the commercial. Allow volunteers to share their findings in class.

Analyzing

Ask students if they think the corporate voting structure is a fair system. Remind them to analyze the problems and benefits of this system. Ask students if they can propose a better system, and if so, how it would work.

Cooperative Learning

Divide the class into groups and assign each group to track the stock of a publicly traded corporation for three weeks. Each group should select a different corporation. Students should list the stock's opening price and keep a daily account of any changes in stock prices. Instruct each group to find out what goods or services the company sells, and write a letter asking for the annual corporate report. Groups should also scan the newspapers to determine if the corporation is in the news. If so, students need to summarize the news stories. Each group will prepare and present an oral report of its findings.

Teaching with Visuals

(Stockholders are placed at the top because they own the company and vote on which directions it will take.) Remind students that the organization chart shown in Exhibit 7-3 is hierarchical. Many new companies, especially those involved in e-commerce, have organizational structures that are quite different than the one shown here. Ask students to describe or create organizational structures of non hierarchical companies. Ask: How might the products or flow of work differ in a non hierarchical company? What factors might cause a business to organize in a non hierarchical structure?

Discussion Starter

Inquire as to whether students know the difference between stocks and bonds. Point out that bonds and stocks are two very different instruments. When an individual buys a bond, he is lending money. When an individual buys stock, she becomes a partial owner of a corporation.

EXHIBIT 7-3 Structure of a Typical Corporation

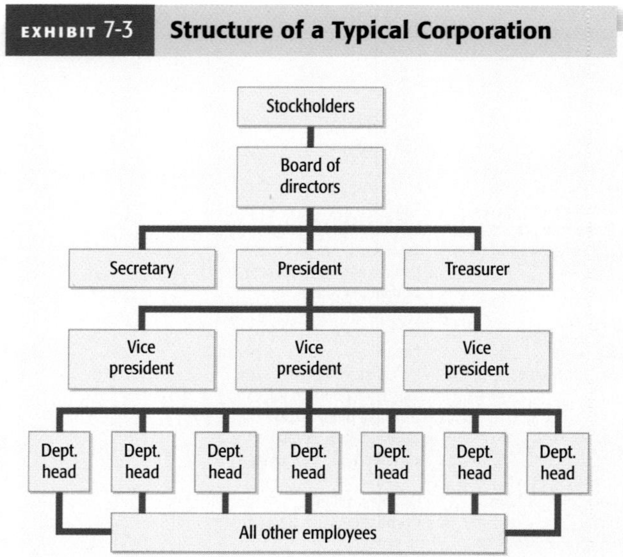

▲ Stockholders occupy the top position in a corporation. They elect the board of directors, which in turn chooses the corporation's top officers (the president and others). **Why do you think the stockholders are placed at the top of the corporate structure?**

referred to as *issuing debt*), and they can issue (or sell) additional shares of stock.

Think of a *bond* as a statement of debt issued by a corporation—an IOU, or piece of paper on which is written a promise to pay. For example, when AT&T issues a bond, it is promising to pay a certain amount of money at a certain time. Here is the process at work:

1. Quentin buys a bond issued by AT&T in the year 2006 for $10,000. The $10,000 is now in the possession of AT&T (the corporation might use the money to help buy new equipment), and the bond (a piece of paper) is in the possession of Quentin.
2. The bond that Quentin has in his hands has a few things written on it. For one thing, it has a dollar figure written on it, called the *face value* (or *par value*) of the bond. We'll say it is $10,000. The percentage written on the bond is called the *coupon rate* of the bond. The coupon rate is the percentage of the face value of a bond that is paid out regularly to the bondholders. For Quentin's bond, we'll say the coupon rate is 8 percent. Finally, a maturity date written on the bond is the date the bond matures, or is paid off by AT&T. We'll say this date is 2016.
3. The bond is a legal promise that AT&T makes to Quentin. The promise has two parts. First, AT&T promises to pay the face value of the bond at the maturity date. Second, it promises to pay the coupon rate, times the face value of the bond, each year until the maturity date. The coupon rate is 8 percent, and the face value of the bond is $10,000; 8 percent of $10,000 is $800, so Quentin receives $800 in the year 2006 and in each year through 2016. (This $800 is called the annual coupon payment.) In 2016, Quentin receives not only $800 but also the face value of the bond, $10,000, because 2016 is the maturity date of the bond.

Instead of selling bonds, AT&T could issue stock to raise money. Remember that a share of stock is a claim on the assets of the corporation that gives the purchaser a share of the ownership of the corporation. Whereas the buyer of a corporate bond is lending funds to the corporation, the buyer of a share of stock is acquiring an ownership right in the corporation. So, if you buy a bond from a corporation, you are a lender, not an owner. If you buy shares of stock in a corporation, you are an owner, not a lender.

The key difference between bondholders and stockholders is that the corporation is under no legal obligation to pay stockholders. Bond purchasers have lent money to the corporation, so the corporation must repay these loans, along with extra payments (such as the $800 Quentin received each year), to the bond purchasers for the use of their money. Stockholders do not lend funds to the corporation; instead, they buy a part of it. If the corporation does well, the value of its stock will rise, and they will be able to sell it at a price higher than the price they paid for it. However, if the corporation does not do well, the value of their stock will fall, and they will most likely have to sell it for less than the purchase price.

Differentiating Instruction

English Language Learners

Guide students in examining Exhibit 7-3, Structure of a Typical Corporation. Allow student volunteers to suggest what each person listed might do or be responsible for. For example, the department head for research and development researches existing products and new technologies in order to develop new products for the company. Reviewing this chart with the class should be beneficial for ELL students, as well as for auditory learners.

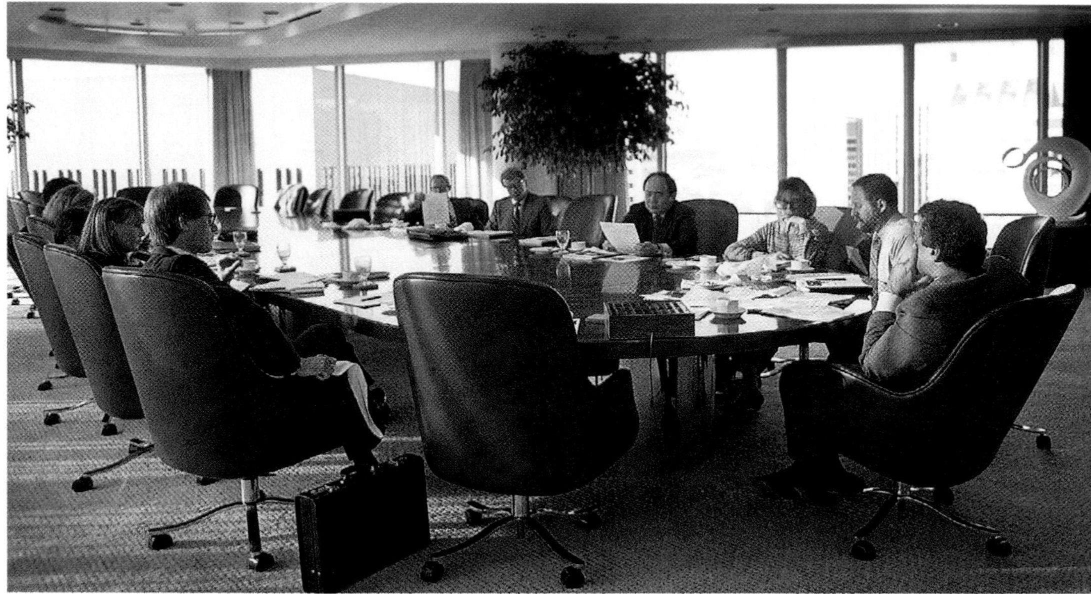

▲ The board of directors are elected to their positions by a vote of the stockholders. **What do you think are the major responsibilities of the board of directors?**

A Student Asks

QUESTION: *I'd like to go back to the example of Quentin buying the bond. He buys the bond in 2006 and the bond matures in 2016—10 years later. Suppose Quentin wants to get the money out of the bond before the 10 years have passed. Can he do this?*

ANSWER: *Yes, he can sell the bond (to anyone willing to buy it) at any time after he purchased it. He does not have to wait for the full 10 years before cashing in the bond. Nothing guarantees, though, that Quentin will sell his bond for the price he paid for it or for more. He might have to sell the bond for less than the purchase price. Why? Because new bonds might have a higher coupon rate than the coupon rate on the (old) bond that Quentin purchased. So he will have to sell his bond for less to compete with the new bonds that are offering a higher coupon rate.*

The Franchise

The franchise is a form of business organization that has become more common in the last 25 years. A **franchise** is a contract by which a firm (usually a corporation) lets a person or group use its name and sell its goods or services. In return, the person or group must make certain payments and meet certain requirements. For example, McDonald's Corporation offers franchises. Individuals can buy the right to use McDonald's name and to sell its products, as long as they meet certain requirements. The corporation, or parent company, is called the **franchiser**; it is the entity that offers the franchise. The person or group that buys the franchise is called the **franchisee**. A few well-known franchises are McDonald's, Burger King, Wendy's, Pizza Hut, Domino's Pizza, and Taco Bell.

franchise
A contract by which a firm (usually a corporation) lets a person or group use its name and sell its goods in exchange for certain payments and requirements.

franchiser
The entity that offers a franchise.

franchisee
The person or group that buys a franchise.

How It Works

The franchise agreement works this way: (1) The franchisee pays an initial fee. (In

Teaching with Visuals

Boards of directors determine corporate policies and goals, such as what percentage of the firm's profits will go to stockholders and what percentage will go for modernization and expansion.

Discussion Starter

Ask students if they would expect bonds that are highly rated to offer a lower coupon rate than bonds that are rated low. Recall that the corporation that issues a bond promises to pay the coupon rate times the face value of the bond each year until the maturity date.

Analyzing

Remind students to read the information concerning the difference between stocks and bonds carefully and critically. Then ask them to make a list of the advantages and disadvantages of buying and owning both stocks and bonds.

Background Information: Corporate Workplaces

Some recently published books and online sources list what some authors believe to be the best corporations for which to work. Ask students what they would find most important in a corporate employer. Some people say corporations have a responsibility to produce a high-quality product, sell it at a reasonable price, help the community, and protect the environment. Others may want high pay and substantial benefits, such as childcare and gym memberships. Tell students to prioritize their lists and then try to find corporations that closely match their lists. You might have students share results of their research in pairs or small groups.

Teaching with Visuals

Answers will vary. Students might say that franchisees benefit from national advertising campaigns, a proven-successful business model, and assistance in training personnel.

Cause and Effect

Guide students in a discussion of the success of some national franchises. Certainly marketing campaigns account for a certain degree of success of these franchises. Ask students to name other causes for this success. (Location, convenience, name recognition, standard quality of food). Help students to see that multiple causation better explains the effect (success) than does a single cause.

Reinforcement Activity

Tell students to work in pairs to list the advantages and disadvantages of managing a chain store, such as The Gap, Barnes and Noble bookstore, or Ann Taylor, versus owning a franchise. When students have finished, compile a class list. Direct students who would prefer to manage a retail store to move to one side of the room, and send students who would prefer to own their own franchise to the other side of the room. Allow a few minutes for discussion within groups, and then one representative from each side should explain the group's reasoning to the class.

▲ The Jack in the Box franchise led the way in developing and expanding drive-thru dining. **If you were going to open a restaurant, why might you consider becoming part of a franchise operation such as Jack in the Box?**

2005 the initial fee for a McDonald's franchise was $45,000.) (2) The franchisee often pays a royalty, or percentage of the profits, to the franchiser for a number of years. At McDonald's in 2005, the royalty rate was 12.5 percent. (3) The franchisee usually agrees to meet certain quality standards decided on by the franchiser. (For example, all McDonald's franchises cook Big Macs for the same length of time.) In return, the franchisee receives from the franchiser the right to use the parent company name, the right to sell a certain product, financial assistance, assistance in training employees and personnel, and national advertising.

Advantages and Disadvantages

Franchises offer several advantages to franchisees. For many franchisees, national advertising is especially important. Consider how many hours of national TV advertising McDonald's buys annually. This advertising benefits its franchisees from Maine to California. Furthermore, with a well-established company such as McDonald's or Burger King, the franchisee buys a business that has been proved successful. Consider the risk of starting your own restaurant compared with the risk of opening a McDonald's or a Burger King. The U.S. Department of Commerce reports that the failure rate is about 12 times higher for independently owned businesses than for franchises.

Of course, franchise business arrangements are not always smooth sailing. Sometimes the franchiser fails to provide the financial and training support the franchisee expects, and occasionally the franchisee does not provide the quality of service and product that the franchiser expects.

A Student Asks

QUESTION: *Is the $45,000 fee the only money one needs to open up a McDonald's?*

ANSWER: *No. A person also needs money to buy goods from the suppliers, to pay a certain amount for the building, and so on. A person needs at least $170,000 (that is not borrowed) to open up a McDonald's. In total a person needs anywhere from $506,000 to $1.6 million to open a McDonald's.*

Background Information: The Small Business Administration

In 1997 President Clinton appointed Aida Alvarez to serve as administrator of the U.S. Small Business Administration. She was the first Hispanic woman to serve in any president's cabinet. The SBA has begun to tap into the extraordinary potential of the increasingly diverse U.S. business community, expand the competitiveness of small businesses, and help ensure that small businesses play a larger role in the global marketplace. Since 1992, the SBA has backed more than $70 billion in small business loans. It has also tripled the number of loans to minorities and women, granting $15 billion to minority-owned businesses and $10 billion in loans to women.

What Is the Ethical and Social Responsibility of Business?

Do businesses have an ethical and social responsibility, and if so, what is it? Here are some different views.

The Nader View

Ralph Nader, the consumer advocate, thinks that businesses do have ethical and social responsibilities. For example, Nader believes that businesses have the responsibility to provide their customers with full information about the products they sell. Ethical companies, says Nader, will often also encourage their customers to "shop around" to make sure they are getting exactly what they want.

According to Nader, businesses should also treat their employees well. For example, businesses should take employee grievances seriously and offer their employees a safe place to work. In addition, when possible, businesses should consider "quality of life" issues (such as employee flex-time, and so on). Nader is also in favor of businesses donating funds to meet social needs in the community.

The Friedman View

According to Milton Friedman, the winner of the 1976 Nobel Prize in economics, "There is one and only one social responsibility of business—to use its resources and engage in activities designed to increase its profits so long as it stays within the rules of the game, which is to say, engages in open and free competition, without deception or fraud." According to Friedman, if a company tried to use government to stifle its competition, that company would not be engaging in open and free competition and therefore would be acting unethically. If a company lied to the buying public about its product, saying the product could provide certain benefits that it actually could not provide, it would be acting unethically.

"Drive thy business or it will drive thee."
—Benjamin Franklin

After a business meets these ethical standards, says Friedman, its job is simple: it should earn as much profit as possible by selling the public something it wants to buy. A business should forget about giving money to the Red Cross, the homeless, or the children's wing of a hospital. All of these organizations are outside its social responsibility.

◀ Avon Products is one of only 19 companies to make *Business Ethics* magazine's list of 100 Best Corporate Citizens in all six years the award has been given. Avon is known for its three-day fund-raising walks for cancer.

Discussion Starter

Question whether students agree with Milton Friedman's statement on page 169 about the ethical and social responsibility of businesses. Ask: Should businesses have the responsibility to make the free enterprise system fair and honest? What kinds of penalties should be enforced for businesses that don't follow the rules? Who should decide the ethics and social responsibilities of businesses? The government? The consumer?

Clarifying Terms

Check student understanding of the following term by asking them to use it in a sentence: *ethics*. *Ethics* is defined as "the principles of conduct governing an individual or a group."

Teaching with Visuals

Ask students to suggest reasons why Avon would like customers to believe that it is a good corporate citizen.

Answers will vary. Students may say that customers might prefer to buy from an ethical company, which leads to higher profits.

Internet Research

Instruct students to pretend that they are going to open a restaurant franchise. They should use the Internet to find out about opening a franchise of a particular restaurant chain such as McDonald's. Students will need to find out: What would they need to have or do to qualify as a franchisee? What benefits would they gain from buying this franchise? How much will they have to pay to acquire the franchise? What would be the pros and cons of owning a franchise of this restaurant chain?

Section 1 About Business Firms 169

Discussion Starter

After students have read the material in the text about asymmetric information, ask them to provide other examples of asymmetric information. Find out whether students believe that the employer described in the text has an ethical responsibility to disclose accurate and complete information to potential employees.

Application Activity

After reading and discussing Section 1, you may want to assign the Section Activity in the *Applying the Principles Workbook*.

Assess

Quick Quiz

The following true-or-false quiz will help you assess student understanding of the material covered in this section.

1. Business firms exist whenever people working together can produce more than the sum of what an individual working alone can produce. (True)
2. The person in the firm who shirks his or her duty is called the monitor. (False)
3. Under a sole proprietorship, all decision-making power resides with the board of directors. (False)
4. In a partnership, the benefits of specialization can be realized.(True)
5. Corporations are subject to triple taxation. (False)

Asymmetric Information

Asymmetric information exists when one party has information that another party to a transaction does not have. For example, let's suppose you are planning to buy a used car from Jack. If Jack has some information about the car that he doesn't pass on to you (the potential buyer), then asymmetric information occurs. The information Jack has but doesn't pass on to you could affect your decision to buy the car. For example, suppose the car has been in an accident, and you don't want to buy a car that has been damaged. Without Jack giving you this piece of information, you might end up buying a car you don't really want to buy.

Asymmetric information can exist in employer-employee situations too. For example, suppose you are being interviewed for a job by a company. The person interviewing you for a job doesn't tell you that a few employees have gotten sick working at the company because of certain pollutants in the air. Here then is an issue of asymmetric information—the employer has some information about the job that he or she isn't passing along to you. Suppose also you wouldn't take this job if you had this information, but without it, you do. The general consensus nowadays is that businesses do have the ethical responsibility to tell their customers and employees everything relevant to either buying a product or taking a job, respectively.

▼ Competition for customers often drives similar firms toward each other. The process by which this happens is described on this page and the next.

Where Will Firms Locate?

Economists often want to know what factors firms consider when deciding where to locate. For example, suppose you wanted to go into the farming business—where would you locate? Obviously you might want to locate where farmland is plentiful and the climate is conducive to growing what you want to grow (wheat, corn, etc.). Or suppose you wanted to open up a car dealership. Where would you locate?

At First, Far Apart

To better understand how firms make location decisions, let's look at a hypothetical situation, as shown in Exhibit 7-4(a). In the exhibit, the letters A through Z represent customers and their locations (say, along a road). You will notice that customers A–Z are evenly distributed along this road. The numbers 1 and 2 represent competing firms, which sell the same goods. They are currently located at extreme ends of the road. If a customer wants to buy a good that either firm 1 or 2 sells, the customer will go to the firm located

EXHIBIT 7-4 The Location of Firms

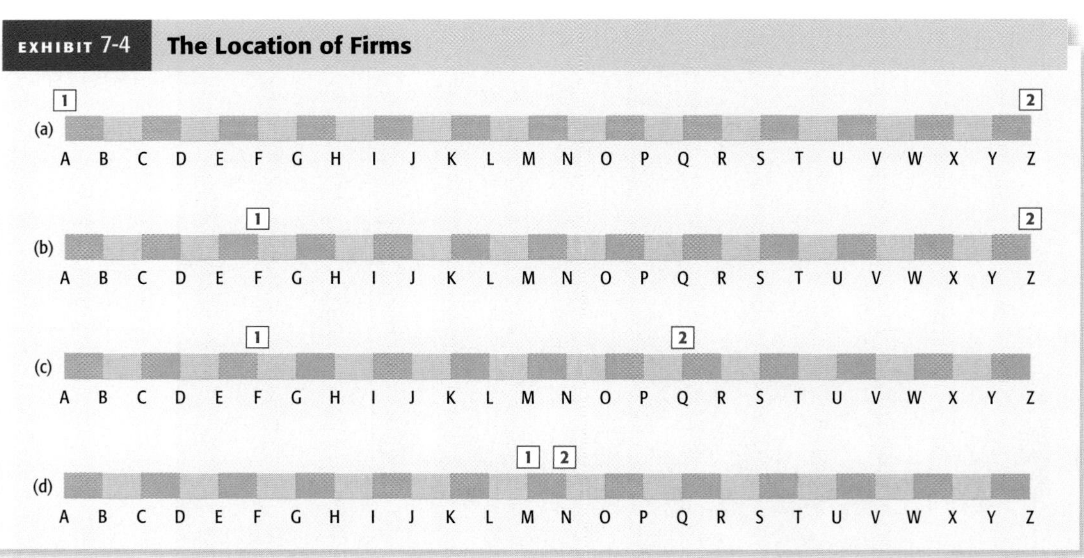

Differentiating Instruction

English Language Learners

To help ELL students, use the following resources, which are provided as part of the *Economics: New Ways of Thinking* program:

- a Spanish glossary in the *Student Text*
- Spanish versions of the Chapter Summaries on an audio CD

closer to him or her. This means that customers A–M will buy from firm 1 and customers N–Z will buy from firm 2. If you count the number of customers that each firm sells to, you will find the number is 13.

One Firm Moves, Then the Other

Now suppose that one day firm 1 moves to a different location, as shown in part (b). Ask yourself how this move serves firm 1's best interest. The answer is that firm 1 takes away customers from firm 2. Now customers A–O are closer to firm 1 than firm 2, so these customers buy from firm 1. Customers Q–Z buy from firm 2 (P isn't counted; he's the same distance from 1 and 2.). In short, firm 1's move put the firm closer to 15 customers instead of 13 customers, leaving 10 customers for firm 2.

Do you think firm 2 will try to counter firm 1's move? It is likely; after all, the firms are competing for customers. Firm 2 moves to a new location, as shown in part (c). Now customers L–Z go to firm 2, leaving customers A–K to go to firm 1. Firm 1 now has only 11 customers and firm 2 has 15.

A Pattern Develops

If you look at what has been happening in parts (a) through (c) of the exhibit, you will notice a pattern. The two firms located on the opposite ends of the road initially, but then the competition for customers moved them closer toward each other. The competition for customers continues. In the end, it is likely that the two firms will be located next to each other, as shown in part (d). At this point, firm 1 will have customers A–M (13 customers) and firm 2 will have customers N–Z (13 customers)—exactly the number of customers each firm started out with in part (a).

What is our conclusion? Simply that similar firms have an incentive to locate near each other. What drives them to this position? The competition for customers.

In the Real World?

Does our theory hold up in the real world? Often, you will notice gas stations located near each other (perhaps, four at an intersection). In many towns, car dealerships are located in the same vicinity, often next to each other. Also, in many towns you will find a certain area of town where many restaurants locate, right next to each other. If you look at major financial firms, you will notice that many of them are headquartered in New York City. In fact, not only are they in the same city, but in the same neighborhood of the same city (near the lower end of Manhattan).

SECTION 1 ASSESSMENT

Defining Terms

1. Define:
   a. sole proprietorship
   b. stock
   c. asset
   d. corporation
   e. partnership
   f. face value
   g. bond

Reviewing Facts and Concepts

2. Under what condition will individuals form a firm?
3. The owners of which types of business organizations face unlimited liability?
4. Which type of business organization accounts for the largest share of total business revenue?
5. Why would a company make a boss (monitor) a residual claimant of the firm?

Critical Thinking

6. Do you think the initial fee for all franchises (McDonald's, Burger King, Play It Again Sports, and so on) is the same? Why or why not?
7. Do you agree or disagree with Milton Friedman's position on the ethical and social responsibility of business? Explain your answer.

Applying Economic Concepts

8. If the face value of a bond is $10,000 and the coupon rate is 5 percent, what is the annual payment to the bondholder?

Assessment Book

You will find a quiz for this section in the *Assessment Book*.

Reteaching Activity

Divide students into groups of three for a debate. Each member of the group should choose a different type of business organization and argue that his or hers is the optimal arrangement.

Guided Reading

For further reteaching of the key concepts in this section, assign the Outlining Activity and the Just the Facts Handout from the *Guided Reading and Study Guide.*

SECTION 1 ASSESSMENT ANSWERS

Defining Terms

Point out that terms b, f, and g are not defined in this chapter; ask students to define only terms a, c, d, and e.

1. a. sole proprietorship: a business that is owned by one individual; **c. asset:** anything of value to which a firm has legal claim; **d. corporation:** a legal entity that can conduct business in its own name in the same way that an individual does; **e. partnership:** a business that is owned by two or more people who share profits and are legally responsible for the company's debts.

Reviewing Facts and Concepts

2. Individuals will form a firm if the sum of what they can produce working together is greater than what they can produce working alone.

3. The owners of sole proprietorships and general partners face unlimited liability.

4. Corporations account for the largest share of total business revenue.

5. The boss would receive more money if the company is more profitable; thus the boss is less likely to shirk.

Critical Thinking

6. No. The initial fee would be determined by supply and demand. The demand for some franchises would be higher than for other franchises, so the initial fee for those franchises would be higher.

7. Answers will vary.

Applying Economic Concepts

8. $500 (*calculation:* $\$10,000 \times 0.05 = \$500$).

SECTION 2 Teacher Support

Focus and Motivate

Section Objectives

After completing this section, students will be able to

- describe fixed and variable costs;
- explain what total costs equal; and
- explain how to compute fixed cost, variable cost, average total cost, and marginal cost.

Kickoff Activity

Since students know what *costs* are and what *fixed* and *variable* mean, let them guess the meaning of these vocabulary terms: *fixed costs* and *variable costs.*

Activating Prior Knowledge

Allow volunteers to share their definitions of fixed and variable costs with the rest of the class. Ask them to think of examples of fixed and variable costs for various businesses.

Teach

Reinforcement Activity

As a classroom activity, ask students to identify the annual costs that their school incurs. They may cite such things as teachers' salaries, electricity, heat for the buildings, paper, chalk, food, and so on. Once students have compiled a list of about 10–15 items, ask students to go back to the list and identify which of the items are variable costs and which are fixed costs.

SECTION 2 Costs

Focus Questions

- What are fixed costs?
- What are variable costs?
- What do total costs equal?
- How do we compute fixed cost, variable cost, average total cost, and marginal cost?

Key Terms

fixed cost
variable cost
total cost
average total cost
marginal cost

Fixed and Variable Costs

All businesses have costs, but not all costs are the same. For example, suppose Maria Torres owns a business that produces a certain kind of toy. In her business, Torres needs a plant, or factory, in which the toy can be produced. She also needs insurance, employees, machines, certain materials for producing the toy (such as plastic and rubber), paper, pens, computers, electricity, and much more. Consider one of the many things Torres needs—a plant. Currently, she rents a plant from Terry Adams. The rental contract specifies that Torres agrees to pay Adams $2,000 rent each month for 12 months.

What if Torres does not want to rent the plant after she has paid only three months' rent? Must she pay rent for the remaining nine months? Given the contract that Torres and Adams entered into, the answer is yes. In other words, no matter whether Torres produces 1 toy, 1,000 toys, 10,000 toys, or even zero toys in the plant each month, she still has the legal obligation to pay rent of $2,000 a month for 12 months.

Costs, or expenses, that are the same no matter how many units of a good are produced are called **fixed costs.** The $2,000 rent is a fixed cost for Torres for a period of 12 months.

EXAMPLE: Bobby pays a business tax of $1,000 a year no matter how many paper boxes he produces and sells. The business tax is a fixed cost. Taryn pays $1,500 in insurance for her small store each year, no matter how much she sells. The $1,500 insurance payment is a fixed cost. ◆

Now suppose Torres employs 10 workers and pays each $50 a day. Her labor cost per day is $500. One day, she gets a special order for many hundreds of toys. To meet the order, she hires five additional workers at $50 per day. As a result, her weekly labor costs increase by $250, to a total of $750. Notice that the increase in labor cost goes along with an increase in the number of toys being produced. Costs, or expenses, that vary, or change, with the number of units of a good produced are called **variable costs.**

If we add fixed costs to variable costs, we have **total costs:**

fixed cost
A cost, or expense, that is the same no matter how many units of a good are produced.

variable cost
A cost, or expense, that changes with the number of units of a good produced.

total cost
The sum of fixed costs plus variable costs.

Internet Research

Instruct students to imagine they are setting up their own businesses in their town. These are the questions they will answer: What type of businesses will you open? What will your fixed costs be? What will your variable costs be? They should find Web pages for local businesses and agencies that would provide the things they would need to open a business, such as office space, office supplies, and telephone service, and answer the following: What will your startup costs be, and approximately how much will your fixed and variable costs be for the first few months? What factors will influence your variable costs?

Total costs = Fixed costs + Variable costs

Suppose we want to compute total costs for a month. If fixed costs are $2,000 for the month and variable costs are $750, then total costs are $2,750 for the month.

EXAMPLE: Jimmy pays $2,000 rent a month on the factory and $1,800 a month for each of the 20 employees he hired. His fixed costs are $2,000 a month, and his variable costs are $36,000 a month. It follows, then, that his total costs are $38,000 a month. ♦

Average Total Cost

Suppose a teacher gives a test to five students. The grades are as follows: 80, 90, 100, 60, and 75. The total number of points—the sum of the individual grades—is 405. To find the average grade, we divide the total, 405, by the number of students, 5. The average grade on the test is 81.

Similarly, to compute the **average total cost** (ATC), or per-unit cost, simply divide total cost (TC) by the quantity of output (Q):

$$\text{Average total cost (ATC)} = \frac{TC}{Q}$$

For example, if total cost is $6,000 and 1,000 units of a good are produced, then average total cost is $6 per unit ($6,000/1,000 = $6).

Marginal Cost: An Important Cost Concept

Marginal cost is an important cost concept in economics. As you will see later, it is one the two factors a business must know about when deciding how much of a good it is best to produce. For now, though, to illustrate what marginal cost is, suppose Torres currently produces 1,000 units of a toy, and total cost is $6,000. She then decides to produce an additional unit of the toy; in other words, she produces one more toy. As a result, total cost rises from $6,000 to $6,008. What is the change in total cost that results from this change in output?

▲ Do you think these workers at a pineapple cannery most likely represent fixed or variable costs?

Well, if total cost was $6,000 and then it rose to $6,008, the change in total cost (from $6,000 to $6,008) must be $8. In other words, total cost has changed by (increased by) $8. This change in total cost that results from producing an additional unit of output is called **marginal cost**. (Every time you read the word *marginal* in economics you should think "additional.") In other words, *marginal cost is the additional cost of producing an additional unit of a good.* In our example, the marginal cost is $8. When you think about marginal cost, focus on the word *change.* Marginal cost describes a change in one thing (total cost) caused by a change in something else (quantity of output).

In economics, the triangle symbol (Δ) means "change in." Thus, when we write

$$\text{Marginal cost (MC)} = \frac{\Delta TC}{\Delta Q}$$

we mean "marginal cost equals the change in total cost divided by the change in quantity of output." We can place the numbers from our example in this equation. ΔTC, the change in total cost, is $8 ($6,008 − $6,000 = $8). ΔQ, the change in quantity produced, is 1 (1,001 − 1,000 = 1):

$$\text{Marginal cost (MC)} = \frac{\$8}{1} = \$8$$

The marginal cost is $8. Exhibit 7-5 reviews the five cost concepts discussed in this section.

average total cost The total cost divided by the quantity of output.

marginal cost The cost of producing an additional unit of a good; the change in total cost that results from producing an additional unit of output.

Teaching with Visuals

The workers most likely represent variable costs, because they may be paid differently for flexible schedules, or because a company may not know how many workers it needs until the work begins.

Discussion Starter

Lead students in brainstorming on the following questions: What are the advantages and disadvantages of a business that has only fixed costs? only variable costs? Could either one of these business scenarios really exist?

Critical Thinking

After students have defined fixed cost, variable cost, and total cost, tell them to continue working to find average total cost for the example given on this page (*calculation:* 6,008 ÷ 1,000 = 6.01). Ask students why a business firm would be interested in finding its average total cost. (Students should be aware that after a business finds its average total cost, it knows what things cost on a per-unit basis.)

Differentiating Instruction

Visual Learners

To illustrate fixed and variable costs, average total costs, and marginal costs, hold a pair of shoes in front of your class. Tell students that the fixed cost to produce 1,000 pairs of shoes was $30,000 for rent and machines. The variable cost was $10,000 for payroll and equipment maintenance. Ask students to find the total cost and the average total cost for a pair of shoes. (*Answers:* Total cost = fixed cost + variable cost = $40,000. Average total cost = $40,000 ÷ quantity = $40.) Tell students that if they wanted to produce one more pair of shoes, the total cost would increase by $50. Ask, What is the marginal cost of this one pair? (*Answer:* $50.)

Economics in the Real World

To see if students understand the concept of marginal cost (as used in this feature), ask for volunteers to explain whether the food or Larry's weight gain represents marginal cost. (Larry's weight gain represents marginal cost; the food represents a change in the quantity of output.)

ANSWERS TO THINK ABOUT IT **1.** Answers will vary. Students might say that Larry could write down all the little items he eats in a week, plus the number of calories in each item. This would help him understand how little things can quickly add up. He could then decide to whittle down the amount of food he eats over time.
2. Answers will vary.

Teaching with Visuals

To reinforce the concepts shown in Exhibit 7-5 (page 175), ask students to work in pairs to write two problems for each of the five types of costs. Have pairs exchange papers and then solve the 10 math problems. (*Example:* If a firm's rent is $1,000 per month, utilities cost $150, and insurance is $75, what are the fixed monthly costs for the firm?)

Assess

Quick Quiz

The following true-or-false quiz will help you assess student understanding of the material covered in this section.

1. All businesses have costs, and all costs are the same. (False)
2. Expenses that are the same, no matter how many units of a good are produced, are called fixed costs. (True)
3. Expenses that change with the number of units produced are called total costs. (False)
4. Average total cost is total cost divided by variable costs. (False)
5. Marginal cost is the additional cost of producing an additional unit of a good. (True)

Economics in the Real World

Why Is It So Easy to Put On Weight?

Some people want to lose weight for health reasons, but they often find this hard to do. Why? Part of the answer has to do with the marginal cost of eating that additional hamburger, or slice of pie, or ice cream cone.

Suppose Larry weighs 200 pounds, and he wants to get down to a weight of 185 pounds for health reasons. When eating, Larry makes incremental (one in a series of many) decisions as opposed to all-or-nothing decisions. An all-or-nothing decision would be deciding whether to eat or not. This decision isn't the one Larry has to make. He knows he is going to eat.

The decision he must make is how much to eat, which is an incremental decision. Does he eat two strips of bacon or just one? Does he have a big piece of cake or a small piece of cake? Does he have three sodas a day or only two?

Suppose the decision in front of Larry is whether to have half tuna sandwich or a whole tuna sandwich. Larry knows that he will eat at least half a tuna sandwich, so the real decision is whether to eat the extra half sandwich. When the increments are small (such as a half sandwich), eating it isn't likely to add much weight. So, for Larry, the marginal cost (in extra weight) of eating the additional half sandwich is likely to be small. Maybe he will be two ounces heavier than he would have been had he not eaten the additional half sandwich.

What happens now is that because all of Larry's decisions about eating are really small incremental decisions (a little larger slice of pie, one more potato chip, one more cookie), it is likely that the marginal cost of each extra unit of food is going to be small. And so Larry will think to himself, *What is a slightly larger slice of pie going to do? Very little.*

Of course, a slightly larger slice of pie will do very little if things stop there. In fact, Larry has a series of incremental decisions to make—one more sip of soda, one more bit of mashed potatoes, one more cookie, and so on. It is only when we add together all the individually tiny incremental decisions that Larry makes do we learn that he has probably eaten more than he wanted to.

Larry's type of thinking is similar to what happens when people litter. They ask themselves, *What will one tiny piece of paper really matter? What will a toothpick thrown on the ground matter?* Well, if only one tiny piece of paper, or one tiny toothpick, was thrown on the ground, it wouldn't matter much. If, however, the same thing happens time after time, the litter is going to build up and then we'll have a lot of trash thrown on the ground.

In summary, a series of tiny incremental decisions decided in a certain way, whether they have to do with eating or littering, can end up producing an aggregate outcome no one really intends. That's why Larry sometimes asks why it is just so hard for him to lose weight when, he says to himself, he wants to lose weight so badly.

THINK ABOUT IT 1. What are some dieting rules that Larry could make for himself that would greatly increase the costs of breaking the rules?

2. Do you ever litter? If so, what have been the costs to you in the situations where you have littered? Could those costs have been increased? If so, how?

EXAMPLE: Harry produced 10 chairs and the total cost is $1,000. Harry goes on to produce one more chair (the 11th chair) and his total cost rises to $1,088. The marginal cost of chairs is $88—the additional cost of producing the additional (which in this case was the 11th) chair. ◆

EXAMPLE: Flight 23 is almost ready to depart for Miami. Currently 98 out of the 100 seats are occupied. Jones walks up to the ticket agent and asks to get on the plane. The ticket agent says that the ticket price is $400. Jones says, "That is an outrageous price to pay to get on a plane that is headed to Miami whether I get on it or not. In fact, the additional cost (marginal cost) for me to travel on the plane is probably near zero. The airline doesn't have to pay anymore for gas, it doesn't have to pay the pilot anymore, it doesn't have to pay the flight attendants anymore, and so on. The only thing it has to do is give me a 'free coke' if I ask for it, and to tell you the truth I don't mind paying for the coke myself. Here's $1.50." Is Jones right? Is the marginal cost of his traveling on the airplane close to zero for the airlines? Yes, he's right. Still, the ticket agent isn't going to be too happy about the $1.50.

EXHIBIT 7-5 Five Cost Concepts

Type of cost	Description	Example
Fixed cost (FC)	Cost, or expense, that does not change as output changes	A firm's monthly rent is a fixed cost.
Variable cost (VC)	Cost, or expense, that changes as output changes	The amount a firm spends on employees' wages is usually a variable cost.
Total cost (TC)	Fixed costs plus variable costs (FC + VC)	If fixed costs equal $2,000, and variable costs equal $4,000, then total cost equals $6,000.
Average total cost (ATC)	Total cost divided by quantity of output $\left(\frac{TC}{Q}\right)$	If total cost equals $6,000, and quantity equals 1,000 units, then average total cost equals $6.
Marginal cost (MC)	Change in total cost divided by change in quantity of output $\left(\frac{\Delta TC}{\Delta Q}\right)$	If total cost equals $6,000 when quantity equals 1,000 units, and total cost equals $6,008 when quantity equals 1,001 units, then marginal cost equals $8.

What is the lesson to learn from this example? The price you pay to travel on an airplane is not necessarily equal to the marginal cost of traveling on the airplane. ◆

SECTION 2 ASSESSMENT

Defining Terms

1. Define:
   a. fixed costs
   b. variable costs
   c. marginal cost

Reviewing Facts and Concepts

2. Give an example of a fixed cost and a variable cost.
3. A firm produces 125 units of a good. Its variable costs are $400, and its total costs are $700. Answer the following questions:
   a. What do the firm's fixed costs equal?
   b. What is the average total cost equal to?
   c. If variable costs were $385 when 124 units were produced, then what was the total cost equal to at 124 units?

Critical Thinking

4. This section discussed both average total cost and marginal cost. What is the key difference between the two cost concepts?

Applying Economic Concepts

5. An airline has 100 seats to sell on a plane traveling from New York to Los Angeles. It sells its tickets for $450 each. At this price, 97 tickets are sold. Just as the plane is about to take off, a person without a ticket says he is willing to pay $150, but not one penny more, to buy a ticket on the plane. The additional cost of the additional passenger (to the airline)—that is, the marginal cost to the airline—is $100. Is it in the best interest of the airline to sell the person a ticket for $150? Explain your answer.

Assessment Book

You will find a quiz for this section in the *Assessment Book.*

Reteaching Activity

Use the Section Assessment to gauge which students may need reteaching on this section. Have those students reexamine Exhibit 7-5. Make sure that each student understands all of the equations and symbols used in the exhibit before you move on to Section 3.

Guided Reading

For further reteaching of the key concepts in this section, assign the Outlining Activity and the Just the Facts Handout from the *Guided Reading and Study Guide.*

SECTION 2 ASSESSMENT ANSWERS

Defining Terms

1. a. fixed costs: the costs (or expenses) that are the same no matter how many units of a good are produced; **b. variable costs:** the costs that change with the number of units produced; **c. marginal cost:** the additional cost of producing an additional unit of a good. Alternatively, it is the change in total cost that results from producing an additional unit of a good.

Reviewing Facts and Concepts

2. Answers will vary. (*Sample answer:* Rent is a fixed cost; wages are a variable cost. There are other examples in the text.)
3. a. $300 (*calculation:* $700 – $400 = $300); **b.** $5.60 (*calculation:* Average total cost = $700 ÷ 125 = $5.60); **c.** $685 (*calculation:* Total cost at 124 units = $300 + $385 = $685).

Critical Thinking

4. With marginal cost, we are considering a change in total cost, given a change in quantity of output. Emphasis is on "change in." With average total cost, we are not concerned with change. Total average cost is the average cost of producing one unit of a good.

Applying Economic Concepts

5. Yes. The airline receives more in additional benefits ($150) than it incurs in additional costs ($100), so it is better off selling the ticket for $150. In other words, if the airline sells the seat, it will make $50.

SECTION 3

Teacher Support

Focus and Motivate

Section Objectives

After completing this section, students will be able to

- explain what total revenue and marginal revenue are; and
- explain why a business firm compares marginal revenue with marginal cost when deciding how many units of a good to produce.

Kickoff Activity

Ask students to write the definition of *revenue.* If they have forgotten, tell them to refer to the glossary. Then, ask them to define *marginal revenue.*

Activating Prior Knowledge

Allow volunteers to share their definitions of *marginal revenue* with the rest of the class. Based on what they learned in the previous section, students should have clear, sound definitions. Tell students that in this section they will apply the word *marginal* to both costs and revenues.

Teach

Discussion Starter

Just as there are two sides to a market, a buying side and a selling side, there are two sides to a business firm: a cost side and a revenue side. The cost side was covered in the previous section of this chapter. Tell students that the revenue side of the relationship will be developed in this section.

SECTION 3

Revenue and Its Applications

Focus Questions

- What is total revenue?
- What is marginal revenue?
- Why does a business firm compare marginal revenue with marginal cost when deciding how many units of a good to produce?

Key Terms

marginal revenue
law of diminishing marginal returns

Total Revenue and Marginal Revenue

In Chapter 3, total revenue was defined as the price of a good times the quantity sold. For example, if the price of a book is $15 and 100 are sold, then total revenue is $1,500. Consider the following: (1) Harris sells toys for a price of $10 each. (2) Harris currently sells 1,000 toys. (3) This means that Harris's total revenue is $10,000. If Harris sells one more toy for $10, what is the change in total revenue that results from the change in output sold?

To answer this question, we first calculate what the total revenue is when Harris sells 1,001 instead of 1,000 toys; it is $10,010. We conclude that the total revenue changes from $10,000 to $10,010 when an additional toy is sold. In other words, a change in total revenue equals $10.

marginal revenue
The revenue from selling an additional unit of a good; the change in total revenue that results from selling an additional unit of output.

The change in total revenue (TR) that results from selling an additional unit of output is **marginal revenue** (MR). In other words, marginal revenue is the additional revenue from selling an additional unit of a good. In the example, $10 is the marginal revenue. We can write it this way:

$$\text{Marginal revenue (MR)} = \frac{\Delta TR}{\Delta Q}$$

Marginal revenue equals the change in total revenue divided by the change in the quantity of output sold.

Firms Have to Answer Questions

If you start up a business, you're going to have to answer certain questions. For example, suppose you start a business producing and selling T-shirts. Someone comes up to you and asks: How many T-shirts are you going to produce each month? What is your answer going to be? Will you say 100, 1,000, or 10,000? How will you go about deciding how many T-shirts you're going to produce? Are you going to put different numbers in a hat and simply draw one out? Whatever number you draw, will that be how many T-shirts you produce? Of course not! So, what are you going to do? How are you

Cooperative Learning

Divide the class into groups of three or four students. Instruct groups to identify situations in which they have said that something is not "worth the effort." Ask what they were talking about. When they say something is not worth the effort, they are saying that the marginal revenue acquired is not worth the additional energy expended. Without even thinking about it, students have been finding marginal revenue for years. Tell groups to pair off and present situations to one another. The goal is to determine if what is gained (the change in total revenue) is worth the cost (the change in quantity).

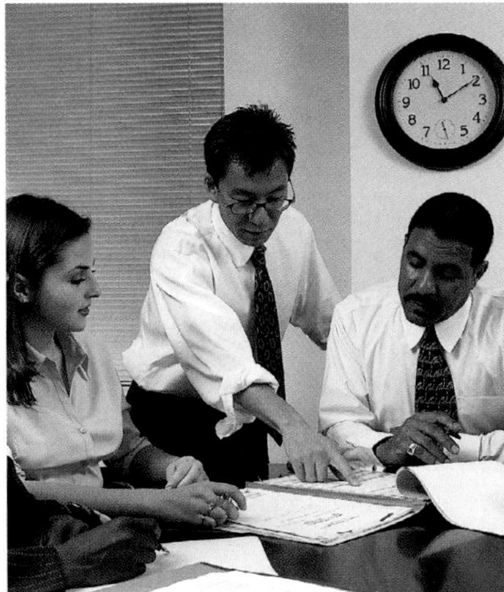

▲ What questions do you think these business executives might be trying to answer?

going to decide how many T-shirts to produce? This is one question that every business firm has to answer:

How much should we produce?

Suppose you decide to produce 1,000 T-shirts a month. Now someone comes up to you and asks: What price will you charge for each T-shirt? What are you going to say? Are you going to say $10, or $10.50, or $15? How will you decide how much to charge for each T-shirt? Here then is a second question every firm has to answer:

What price should we charge?

In this section we will talk more about these two questions.

How Much Will a Firm Produce?

Suppose again that you produce T-shirts. You have to decide how many to produce. What two pieces of information do you need before you can decide how many T-shirts to produce? If you think about it, the answer is fairly simple. You need to know the marginal cost and the marginal revenue for your T-shirts. For example, suppose you are presented with the following data (which is representative of many real-world businesses):

T-shirts	MR	MC
1st	$10	$4
2nd	$10	$6
3rd	$10	$8
4th	$10	$9.99
5th	$10	$11

Having looked at the data, someone asks you: What is the right number of T-shirts for you to produce? What would your answer be? The correct answer is four T-shirts. In other words, you should keep producing T-shirts as long as marginal revenue (additional revenue of producing the additional T-shirt) is greater than the marginal cost (additional cost of producing the additional T-shirt). As long as what comes in through the "revenue door" is greater than what leaves through the "cost door," you ought to keep producing T-shirts. Look at it this way:

$$MR > MC \rightarrow \text{Produce}$$
$$MC > MR \rightarrow \text{Do not produce}$$

Now if you want to produce as long as MR > MC, and you don't want to produce if MC > MR, then ask yourself when you should stop producing. For example, you've already produced, say, 10,000 hats. Should you go ahead and produce one more? The answer is yes as long as marginal revenue is greater than marginal cost—even if the difference between marginal cost and marginal revenue is one penny (as was the case for the fourth T-shirt in the example).

Now suppose the difference is even less than one penny. Suppose it is half a penny. Should you still produce the good? Again the answer is yes. What about one-fourth of a penny? Yes, produce it. You can perhaps see where we are leading. Economists essentially say that it is beneficial to produce as long as marginal revenue is greater than

Teaching with Visuals

Answers will vary, but students might say that they are trying to decide how much of their product to produce and what to charge.

Problem Solving

Point out to students that manufacturers need to answer numerous questions about quantity to produce, price, quality, advertising, and so on. One important question a firm must answer is how many units of a good it should produce. Should it produce as many as it can without looking at what the market will bear? Firms need to be aware of marginal cost and marginal revenue in order to make this decision.

Give students the following information: Cost of a good is $10, price is $20, and base quantity is 1,000. Instruct them to determine the marginal cost and marginal revenue if 1,100 units were produced with a total cost of $12,500. Also ask, Would it be profitable to produce this quantity of the good? (*Answers:* Marginal cost would be $25 per unit and marginal revenue would be $20 per unit. Yes, it would still be profitable to produce this quantity of the good, although the per-unit cost would rise from $10 to $11.36 and the profit margin would decrease from $10,000 to $9,500.)

Differentiating Instruction

Visual Learners

The main thrust of this section is the decision-making process of businesses in terms of their profitability. Students who need more help in mathematics may struggle with this section. Take some extra time showing several examples of the formulas on the board, using pictures of actual products instead of just abstract numbers. Break down each part of the equation so students can see where the numbers are coming from and what they represent. As you finish one example, ask a student to volunteer to come up to the board and work through the finished equation for the class.

Teaching with Visuals

Car manufacturers know that they need to continue increasing production until marginal revenue is no longer greater than marginal cost. They should maximize profits by finding the production level that gives them the most marginal revenue.

Discussion Starter

Ask students if they think that companies want to be as large as possible. Some students may say yes, thinking that with greater size come greater revenues and greater profits. Point out that the objective of the firm is not to become as large as possible, but to maximize profit. Sometimes growth can actually diminish a company's profit.

▲ All companies want to maximize profits and generate the kinds of results you see in the newspaper reports. **How do automobile manufacturers know how many cars to produce and what does that have to do with maximizing profits?**

marginal cost, even if the difference between the two is extremely small. For all practical purposes, then, economists are saying that a business firm should continue to produce additional units of its good until the marginal revenue (MR) is equal to the marginal cost (MC).

In the T-shirt example, we didn't find any unit of T-shirt at which MR = MC, but we did find one where there was only a penny difference. We stopped producing after we had produced the fourth T-shirt because it was as close to MR = MC as we could get.

A Student Asks

QUESTION: *I have known some people who owned businesses and, to tell you the truth, I don't think any one of them even knew what marginal revenue and marginal cost are. You can't expect me to believe that these business owners were producing the quantity of output for which MR = MC if they didn't even know what MR and MC are. Please comment.*

ANSWER: *You don't always have to understand how to do something in order to do it. For example, not many people understand how their legs move to make them walk, or how their lungs behave to make them breathe, but still they walk and breathe. Our guess is that a bird doesn't really understand aerodynamics (which is the study of forces and the resulting motion of objects through the air), but still birds can fly. A business owner may not know what marginal revenue and marginal cost are, but here is what a business owner does know: whether more money is "coming in" than is "going out." And, of course, this is what marginal revenue and marginal cost really are. The additional money coming in is marginal revenue and the additional money going out is marginal cost. As long as a business owner can count, he or she will naturally end up producing the level of output at which MR = MC. Having said all this, let us add that sometimes taking a course in economics or in business formalizes all these "business practices" more effectively. For example, a person who has studied economics would be less likely to make a mistake when determining what quantity of a good to produce than a person who has not studied economics.*

What Every Firm Wants: To Maximize Profit

In Chapter 3 we stated that profit is the difference between total revenue and total cost. For example, if total revenue is $400,000 and total cost is $320,000, then profit is $80,000. The firm wants profit to be as large as possible. An economist states it this way: The business firm wants to maximize profit.

Background Information: Thomas Malthus

Thomas Malthus, a British economist who lived from 1766 to 1834, developed the law of diminishing returns. Malthus argued that land is a fixed resource and when a variable resource (such as labor) is applied to it, at some point the return from the additional quantity of the variable resource will decrease. Malthus was very careful to say that his theory was applicable only under the given technology of his day. Recent economists have tried to disprove the theory but in so doing have applied current technology, something that Malthus could never have foreseen.

178 Chapter 7 Business Operations

Of course if the firm wants to maximize profit, this is just another way of saying that it wants the biggest difference possible between its total revenue and its total cost. For example, given a choice of a total revenue of $1 million or $2 million, a business firm would prefer a total revenue of $2 million (all other things being equal). Or given a choice of a total cost of $250,000 or $500,000, a business firm would prefer a total cost of $250,000 (all other things being equal).

So, maximizing profit is consistent with a firm getting the largest possible difference between its total revenue and its total cost.

Now here is something to think about: Is getting the largest possible difference between total revenue and total cost the same thing as producing the quantity of output at which MR = MC? The answer is that "getting the largest possible difference between total revenue and total cost" is the same thing as producing the quantity of output at which MR = MC. To prove it, again suppose that a business firm's total revenue is $400,000, total cost is $320,000, and profit is $80,000. Now suppose it produces and sells an additional unit of a good. The additional revenue from selling this unit of the good (the marginal revenue) is $40, and the additional cost of producing this unit of the good (the marginal cost) is $10. Total revenue will rise to $400,040 ($400,000 + $40 = $400,040), and total cost will rise to $320,010 ($320,000 + $10 = $320,010). What will happen to profit? It will increase to $80,030 ($400,040 − $320,010 = $80,030). Thus, whenever the firm produces and sells an additional unit of a good and marginal revenue is greater than marginal cost, it is adding more to its total revenue than to its total cost, and therefore it is maximizing profit.

How to Compute Profit and Loss

When a firm computes its profit or loss, it determines total cost and total revenue and then finds the difference:

1. To compute total cost (TC), add fixed cost (FC) to variable cost (VC).

$$TC = FC + VC$$

BY THE NUMBERS

We buy things from stores every day. Some of the businesses that own those stores earn more (per square foot of space and per store) than do others. Here is a list of well-known businesses and the revenue that each earns per store and per square foot of space. Most of the dollar amounts are for 2003.

Company	Revenue per square foot	Revenue per store
Abercrombie and Fitch	$379	$ 2,766,639
Nordstrom	319	37,112,273
Foot Locker	316	1,249,896
Wal-Mart	422	55,924,898
Target	278	32,942,045
Sports Chalet	241	8,816,037
Barnes & Noble	243	5,865,314
Borders	237	6,000,000
Sharper Image	627	2,509,051
Radio Shack	342	829,841
Walgreens	709	7,748,507
Home Depot	370	40,144,000
Krispy Kreme	859	3,952,000
McDonald's	543	1,628,000
Domino's Pizza	527	605,879
Starbucks Coffee	521	781,669

Source: BizStats.com.

2. To compute total revenue (TR), multiply the price of the good (P) times the quantity of units (Q) of the good sold.

$$P \times Q = TR$$

3. To compute profit (or loss), subtract total cost (TC) from total revenue (TR).

$$\text{Profit (or loss)} = TR - TC$$

EXAMPLE: Suppose variable cost is $100 and fixed cost is $400. It follows that total cost is $500. Now suppose that 100 units of a good are sold at $7 each; total revenue is then $700. If we subtract total cost ($500) from total revenue ($700), we are left with a profit of $200. ♦

Teaching with Visuals

Ask students to consider why a business might want to track their revenue per square foot. (*Answer:* Some renters charge by amount of space, so if a company could cut down on space utilized, it might be able to decrease its fixed cost of rent.)

Reinforcement Activity

To show students exactly how profit and loss are determined, create several examples. Supply the class with the fixed cost, variable cost, price, and the quantity produced for an imaginary good. Have students work in pairs to find the total cost, total revenue, and profit or loss. You may even create a game with teams and students racing to find the answers.

Economics Around the Clock

After reading and discussing how much firms should produce, you may want to refer students to the 1:07 P.M. scenario in Economics Around the Clock (page 157), and discuss their answers to its question.

Help students understand that if it were just about selling more hot dogs, or more cars, or more of anything, then sellers would lower their prices dramatically. More hot dogs will be sold at $2 than at $3 a dog; more cars will be sold at $4,000 a car than at $40,000 a car. It is not about selling more, but about profit. Selling more does not come with more profit if the additional revenue earned on the additional unit of the good (the marginal revenue) is less than the additional cost incurred on the additional unit of the good (the marginal cost).

Discussion Starter

Review with students the benefits of hiring additional workers. Ask: What are some of the other benefits to the entire economy when more workers are employed? Are there disadvantages? Also guide students in a discussion of what happens to workers when demand for goods produced by their company declines.

After students have read the feature, ask them to describe personal experiences of friends or relatives who have lost jobs due to global competition. Ask: How did the former employees react? Have they found new jobs? changed careers?

ANSWERS TO ECONOMIC THINKING Answers will vary. Students might suggest that consumers will benefit from lower prices.

Background Information

Businesses want to hire qualified employees who are well suited for the jobs at hand. They hire human resources specialists who recruit and interview employees and advise on hiring decisions. Human resources specialists also provide training and deal with compensation, benefits, and so on.

In the late 1990s, human resources specialists held about 544,000 jobs and were employed in every industry in the United States. For jobs in human resources, employers usually look for college graduates who have majored in business administration, communication, and public administration, among other fields. Many colleges have programs that lead to a degree in personnel, human resources, or labor relations.

How Many Workers Should the Firm Hire?

Wal-Mart has more than 1 million employees. In fact, it has somewhere closer to 1.2 million employees. How does Wal-Mart know how many employees to hire? Did the president of the company simply say one day, "1,199,278 employees sounds like the right number of employees to me, so let's go with it"? We doubt it.

The fact is, every business has to decide how many employees it will hire (just as we learned that every business has to decide how much it will produce). Let's begin the story of how a firm decides how many employees to hire by first discussing the **law of diminishing marginal returns.**

> *"In the business world the rearview mirror is always clearer than the windshield."*
> —Warren Buffet

The name of this "economic law" sounds worse than it is. (If you understood the law of diminishing marginal utility back in Chapter 4, you shouldn't have too much trouble understanding the law of diminishing marginal returns.) It states that if we add additional units of a resource (such as labor) to another resource (such as capital) that is in fixed supply, eventually the additional output produced (as a result of hiring an additional worker) will decrease.

law of diminishing marginal returns
A law that states that if additional units of one resource are added to another resource in fixed supply, eventually the additional output will decrease.

THE GLOBAL IMPACT: Who Benefits?

Increased globalization will place some U.S. companies in a more competitive market setting. A study for the Institute for International Economics found that, between 1979 and 1999, some American workers lost jobs because they worked for U.S. companies that produced goods that couldn't compete in price with foreign-produced imported goods. Many of these workers found other jobs, but 55 percent of those who found new jobs did so at lower pay, and 25 percent took pay cuts of 30 percent or more.

ECONOMIC THINKING Is increased globalization more likely to benefit a larger percentage of U.S. consumers or a larger percentage of U.S. workers?

The best way to illustrate the law is with numbers. Take a look at Exhibit 7-6. Reading across the first row, we see that with zero workers, no output occurs. Now when one worker is added, the quantity of output (shown in the second column) is 5 units. The third column shows the additional output produced as a result of hiring an additional worker. If output is zero with no workers and 5 units with one worker, we conclude that hiring an additional (the first) worker increased output by 5 units.

When a second worker is added, the quantity of output (shown in column 2) increases to 11 units. How much did output increase as a result of an additional (the second) worker? The answer is 6 units, as shown in column 3. If a third worker is added, output rises to 18 units, and the additional output produced as a result of the hiring of an additional (the third) worker is 7 units, as shown in column 3.

Before we go on, notice what has been happening in column 3: the numbers have been increasing, from 0 to 5, then 6, then 7. Notice that when a fourth worker is added, output increases to 23 units; the additional output produced is 5 units, which is *less* than the output produced as a result of adding the third worker.

What we are observing here is the law of diminishing marginal returns, which states that eventually the additional output produced (as a result of hiring an additional worker) will decrease. We added another worker (the fourth worker) here, and the additional output (shown in column 3) decreased from 7 to 5 units. In short, diminishing marginal returns set in with the addition of the fourth worker.

Now what does the law of diminishing marginal returns have to do with hiring employees? The answer is everything, once we turn the factors into dollars. To understand this concept, ask yourself whether you would hire the fourth worker if you owned a business.

To really be able to answer this question, you would first have to ask yourself two questions:

Background Information: U.S. Firms and Mexico

Many foreign countries have lower wages than the United States. This is one benefit to U.S. firms of going to a foreign country and hiring foreign labor, but there are costs, too.

Have students consider the following scenario. Suppose that if a U.S. firm stays in the United States and hires U.S. workers, it will have to pay $10 an hour. If it goes to Mexico and hires Mexican labor, it will have to pay $5 an hour. Wages are two times higher in the United States than in Mexico, so why wouldn't the U.S. firm head for Mexico? The answer is that labor productivity may not be as high in Mexico as in the United States. In the United States, the average worker, working with various capital equipment, can produce 30

180 Chapter 7 Business Operations

1. What do I sell each unit of output for?
2. What do I have to pay to hire the fourth worker?

Suppose you sell each unit of output for $30 and you will have to pay the fourth worker a wage of $70. Would you hire the fourth worker? One way to figure out the answer is to calculate how much "comes in" the door with the fourth worker compared to how much "goes out" the door with the fourth worker. The worker produces 5 more units of output, and you can sell each unit for $30, so the worker really "comes in" the door with $150. You have to pay the fourth worker $70, so the worker "goes out" the door with this amount. Would you be willing to pay someone $70 to get $150 in return? Sure you would, so you should hire the fourth worker.

What is the general rule now for hiring employees? As long as the additional output produced by the additional worker multiplied by the price of the good is greater than the wage you have to pay the worker, then hire the worker. If the additional output produced by the additional worker multiplied by the price of the good is less than the wage you have to pay the worker, then don't hire the worker.

EXHIBIT 7-6 The Law of Diminishing Marginal Returns

(1) Workers	(2) Quantity of output produced each day	(3) Additional output produced (each day) as a result of hiring an additional worker	
0	0 units	0 units	
1	5	5 (5 − 0 = 5)	
2	11	6 (11 − 5 = 6)	Diminishing returns set in
3	18	7 (18 − 11 = 7)	with the addition of the
4	23	5 (23 − 18 = 5) ←	fourth worker.
5	26	3 (26 − 23 = 3)	

▲ As more workers are added (column 1), the quantity of output produced each day rises (column 2). It isn't until the fourth worker that diminishing marginal returns are said to set in.

EXAMPLE: If Bob hires Marianne, output will rise by 7 units a day. Bob can sell each unit of output for $50. To hire Marianne, Bob will have to pay her $200 a day. Should Bob hire Marianne? Sure he should. Output increases by 7 units a day and Bob sells each unit for $50, so Marianne brings $350 a day to Bob. Bob has to pay Marianne only $200 a day. Who wouldn't spend $200 to get $350? ♦

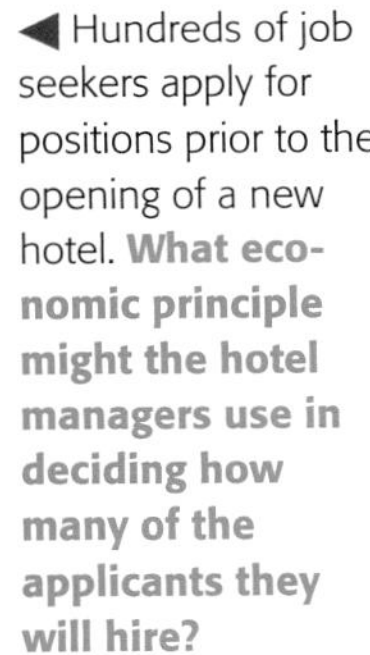

◀ Hundreds of job seekers apply for positions prior to the opening of a new hotel. **What economic principle might the hotel managers use in deciding how many of the applicants they will hire?**

Economics Around the Clock

After reading and discussing "How Many Workers Should the Firm Hire?" (pages 180–181), direct students to reread the 8:45 A.M. scenario in Economics Around the Clock (page 157) and consider its question.

Help students see that Jackie should consider how much output will rise by adding more resources. If the money she makes from the additional output produced by the new worker is more than what she will pay the new worker, Jackie should hire her or him.

Economics Around the Clock

After reading and discussing "How Many Workers Should the Firm Hire?" direct students to reread the 11:09 A.M. scenario in Economics Around the Clock (page 157) and consider its question.

Labor costs in another country may be lower, but sometimes the workers' output is lower, as well. Companies should set up where the most output per dollar can be found.

Teaching with Visuals

The hotel managers could use the law of diminishing marginal returns.

units of good X every hour. In Mexico, the average worker can produce 10 units of good X every hour.

The firm needs to compute its output per dollar of labor cost, which it does by dividing labor productivity by the hourly wage (*calculation:* Output per dollar of labor cost = number of units labor produces per hour ÷ wage rate).

In the United States, the company pays a worker $10 an hour and receives 30 units of good X in return. It produces 3 units per $1 of labor cost. In Mexico, the firm pays a worker $5 an hour and receives 10 units of good X in return, so it produces 2 units per $1 of labor cost. The firm produces more output per dollar in the United States than in Mexico.

Economics in the Real World

Ask students if they had considered homework in these terms before they read this feature.

ANSWERS TO THINK ABOUT IT Yes, the student will study longer. If the student realizes that there are greater benefits to studying economics than he or she thought, the marginal benefit curve in the exhibit shifts upward and to the right. Now it intersects the marginal cost curve to the right of the old intersection point. This new intersection with the horizontal axis corresponds to more hours spent studying.

Reinforcement Activity

Using Exhibit 7-7 as a guide, assign students to create similar marginal benefits curves for their own time to study for the upcoming Chapter 7 test. They should also identify the opportunity costs of studying for the test.

Application Activity

After reading and discussing Sections 2 and 3, you may want to assign the activity for those sections in the *Applying the Principles Workbook.*

Assess

Quick Quiz

The following true-or-false quiz will help you assess student understanding of the material covered in this section.

1. Marginal revenue is the additional revenue from selling an additional unit of a good. (True)
2. Marginal revenue equals the change in total cost divided by the change in total revenue. (False)
3. A firm will produce a good only if a profit will be made. (True)
4. The difference between total cost and total revenue is profit or loss. (True)
5. When one more worker leads to an increase in total revenue, this is an example of the law of diminishing returns. (False)

How Much Time Should You Study?

A business firm can produce anywhere from one to millions of units of a good. What is the right amount? As the chapter explains, it is the amount of the good at which marginal revenue equals marginal cost.

To determine the right amount of something, an economist would say we need to consider marginal costs and marginal benefits. For example, studying, sleeping, eating, working, and vacationing all involve costs and benefits.

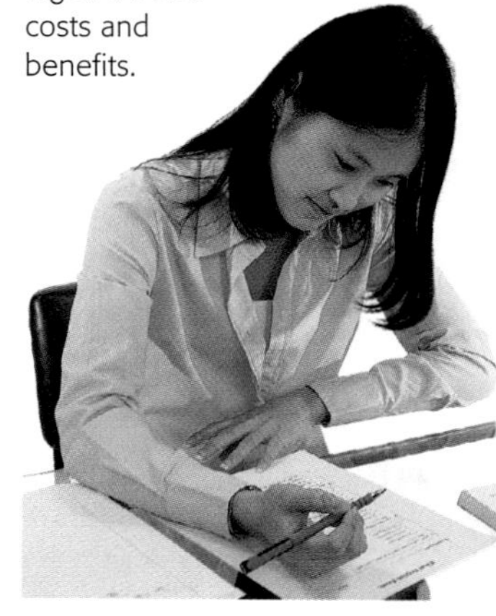

How much of any activity is too little, how much is too much, and how much is the right amount? The answer is simple, says the economist: the right amount of anything is the amount at which the marginal benefits equal the marginal costs.

Suppose the marginal (additional) benefits of studying start out high and decrease with time, as illustrated in Exhibit 7-7 with a downward-sloping marginal benefit curve (for studying). This curve says that you benefit more from the first minute of studying than the second minute, more from the second minute than the third, and so on.

Assume that the marginal costs of studying are constant over time. In other words, you are giving up as much by studying the first minute as the second minute, and so on. In the exhibit, the marginal cost curve (of studying) is horizontal to illustrate this point.

A quick look at Exhibit 7-7 says that the right amount of time to study is two hours. If you study less than two hours (say, one hour), you will forfeit all the net benefits (marginal benefits greater than marginal costs) you could have reaped by studying an additional hour. If you study more than two hours, you are entering into the region where marginal costs (of studying) are greater than marginal benefits. The rule is this: do something as long as marginal benefits are greater than marginal costs, and stop when they are equal.

THINK ABOUT IT Suppose Exhibit 7-7 represents your marginal benefits and marginal costs of studying. In other words, the right amount of time for you to study is two hours. Then one day, your economics teacher talks about the benefits of learning economics. Afterward, you realize that there are more benefits to learning economics than you had thought. Will this change the amount of time you study economics? Explain your answer in terms of Exhibit 7-7.

EXHIBIT 7-7 The Marginal Benefits and Marginal Costs of Studying

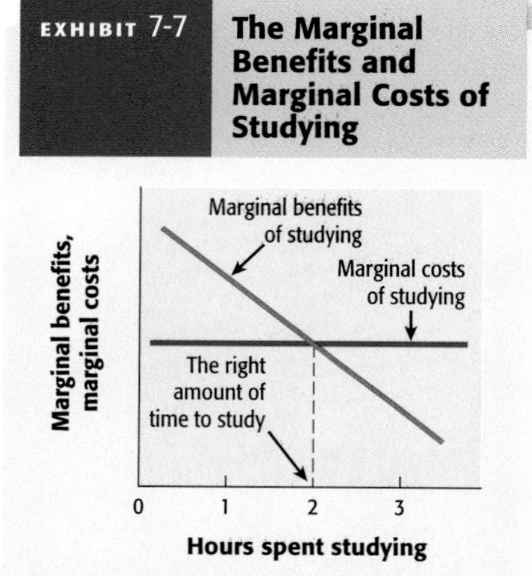

▲ What is the right amount of time to study? Study as long as the marginal benefits of studying are greater than the marginal costs, and quit when the marginal benefits equal the marginal costs. In the diagram, this time comes at two hours of studying.

Cooperative Learning

Students sometimes have a difficult time understanding the law of diminishing returns. Here's an example that may help them understand it. Suppose that a student is at home at night reading a textbook. His objective is to learn certain information to prepare a major term paper. In the first hour he learns 10 pieces of information. In the second hour he learns 15 pieces of information. In the third hour he learns 12 pieces of information, but in the fourth hour he learns only 8 pieces, and in the fifth hour he learns just 6 pieces of new information. Have students work in groups to create a diagram illustrating this example, and brainstorm other examples that could demonstrate the law of diminishing marginal returns.

Reread the previous example from Marianne's point of view. Do you think that Bob is cheating Marianne by paying her only $200 a day? After all, she brings in $350 a day to Bob. Shouldn't Marianne get more than $200 a day if she makes Bob $350 better off a day?

You need to keep in mind that things are a little more complicated than we have made them out to be. Marianne could very well be working with other employees and with certain machines. Not all of what Marianne "produces" for Bob is the result of Marianne's work, and her work alone. She brings "$350 a day to Bob," that is true. But it is really her working with other employees and with certain machinery or tools that ends up producing $350 a day more for Bob.

To illustrate, let's suppose someone goes to work on a farm. We might say that 100 more bushels of wheat were harvested on a given day. Is it that new worker who harvests those 100 additional bushels or is it the new worker using a tractor (which is a capital good) that harvests those 100 additional bushels of wheat? The answer is that it is the new worker using the tractor. The same type of story can be told for Marianne. People don't usually work in isolation from other people or without certain capital goods.

Each year *Fortune* magazine ranks the top 500 corporations in the United States according to revenue. In recent years, a few of the largest revenue-earning corporations in the United States include Wal-Mart, Exxon, General Motors, and Ford Motor Company. If you want to find the most recent list of the Fortune 500, go to www.emcp.net/fortune. If you would like to learn what some of America's highest-paid business executives earn, go to www.emcp.net/forbes and do a site search for "Top Paid CEOs."

ASSESSMENT

Defining Terms

1. Define:
   a. marginal revenue
   b. law of diminishing marginal returns

Reviewing Facts and Concepts

2. The additional output obtained by adding an additional worker is 50 units. Each unit can be sold for $2. Is it worth hiring the additional worker if she is paid $150 a day? Explain your answer.
3. Price is $20 per unit no matter how many units a firm sells. What is the marginal revenue for the 50th unit? Explain your answer.

Critical Thinking

4. This section explained how a firm computes profit. Specifically, it computes total cost and total revenue and then finds the difference. Suppose a firm wants to compute its profit per unit. In other words, instead of computing how much profit it earns in total, it wants to know how much profit it earns per unit. How could the firm go about computing profit per unit? (*Hint:* The answer deals with average total cost.)

Graphing Economics

5. Suppose the marginal benefits of playing tennis are constant for each minute of the first 20 minutes and then steadily decline for each additional minute. The marginal costs of playing tennis are constant. Furthermore, marginal costs are equal to marginal benefits at the 45th minute. Diagrammatically represent the marginal benefits and marginal costs of playing tennis.

Assessment Book

You will find a quiz for this section in the *Assessment Book.*

Reteaching Activity

Use the Section Assessment to gauge which students may need reteaching on this section. Guide those students in rereading the definitions of *marginal revenue* and the *law of diminishing returns.* Make sure that students understand these terms. You might want to pay particular attention to the definition of the *law of diminishing returns* to stress that this law applies when one resource is fixed in supply.

Guided Reading

For further reteaching of the key concepts in this section, assign the Outlining Activity and the Just the Facts Handout from the *Guided Reading and Study Guide.*

Defining Terms

1. a. marginal revenue: the additional revenue from selling an additional unit of a good, or the change in total revenue that results from selling an additional unit of a good; **b. law of diminishing marginal returns:** law stating that as we add additional units of a resource (such as labor) to another resource that is fixed in supply (such as capital), eventually the additional output produced will decrease.

Reviewing Facts and Concepts

2. No. The added benefits of hiring the additional worker are $100; the added costs are $150. Because added costs are greater than added benefits, it is not worth hiring another worker.

3. $20. Total revenue for 49 units is $980, or price ($20) × 49 units. Total revenue for 50 units = $1,000, or price ($20) × 50 units. Because marginal revenue is the change in total revenue that results from selling an additional unit of output, it is $20.

Critical Thinking

4. Average total cost is sometimes called *per-unit cost.* The firm simply subtracts the average total cost from the price it charges for each good to compute profit (or loss) per unit. For example, if price is $10 and the average total cost is $9, then per-unit profit is $1.

Graphing Economics

5. Student graphs should show a steady horizontal line to the 20-minute mark; then the line should decline evenly to the 45-minute mark. See Exhibit 7-7 (page 182) for an example.

CHAPTER 7 Assessment Answers

Economics Vocabulary

1. unlimited, limited; **2.** board of directors; **3.** fixed cost; **4.** marginal cost; **5.** law of diminishing marginal returns; **6.** per-unit cost; **7.** franchiser; **8.** coupon rate; **9.** asset; **10.** personal income.

Understanding the Main Ideas

1. The owners of a partnership have unlimited liability, whereas owners of a corporation have limited liability. Also, the profit of the partnership is the income of the partners, and only the personal income tax is applied to it. The profits of a corporation are taxed twice.
2. Profits of the corporation are taxed as profits (corporate income tax) and as income (dividends to stockholders). The two taxes are the corporate income tax and the personal income tax.
3. \$800 (*calculation:* \$10,000 × 0.08 = \$800).
4. If the sum of what individuals can produce working together (as a team in a firm) is greater than the sum of what they can produce working alone, then a firm will be formed.
5. Mayang is more likely to shirk in setting 2. In setting 1, Mayang obtains all the benefits of her shirking and pays all the costs. In setting 2, she obtains all the benefits of her shirking and pays only one-fifth of the costs. Individuals are predicted to shirk more in settings where they pay a lower fraction of the costs of shirking. In other words, the lower the cost of shirking, the more people will shirk.
6. The bondholder is a lender to the firm. The stockholder is an owner of the firm. Underneath them are the board of directors, president, vice presidents, department heads, and employees. Exhibit 7-3 (page 166) shows this structure.
7. A fixed cost is constant over output, and a variable cost is not. In other words, as output rises, fixed cost remains the same. This is not the case with variable cost, which rises as output rises.
8. Marginal revenue is additional revenue, and marginal cost is additional cost. As long as additional revenue is greater than additional cost, it is worth producing and selling a good. More is coming into the firm than is going out.
9. Yes. As long as the firm's marginal revenue is greater than its marginal cost, it is adding more to its revenue than it is adding to its costs. Therefore, the difference between the two, which is profit, is growing larger.
10. A firm first computes its total cost by summing its fixed and variable costs. It then computes its total revenue by multiplying the price of the good it sells times the number of units it sells. Then it subtracts total cost from total revenue to find profit or loss.

Chapter Summary

Be sure you know and remember the following key points from the chapter sections.

Section 1

- A business is an organization that uses resources to produce goods and services to sell to customers.
- A business needs a boss to efficiently coordinate and direct the activities of others in the organization.
- A sole proprietorship is a business owned by one person who makes the decisions, receives the profits earned, and is liable for the debts of the business.
- A partnership is a business owned by two or more partners who share in the profits and are responsible for any liabilities of the business.
- A corporation is a legal entity formed to conduct business and is owned by individuals who buy shares of the organization.

Section 2

- Fixed costs are expenses that are the same no matter how many units of a good are produced.
- Variable costs are expenses that vary according to the number of units produced.
- Total costs = Fixed costs + Variable costs
- Marginal cost is the additional cost of producing an additional unit of a good.

Section 3

- Firms must answer two essential questions: How much should we produce? and What price should we charge?
- Marginal revenue is the change in total revenue that results from selling an additional unit of output.
- A firm's goal is to maximize profit, which means producing a quantity of output at which marginal revenue equals marginal cost.

Economics Vocabulary

To reinforce your knowledge of the key terms in this chapter, fill in the following blanks on a separate piece of paper with the appropriate word or phrase.

1. In a sole proprietorship and partnership, owners have ______ liability, whereas in a corporation, owners have ______ liability.
2. The stockholders of the firm choose the ______.
3. Total cost equals ______ plus variable cost.
4. The additional cost of producing an additional unit of a good is called ______.
5. The ______ states that if additional units of a resource are added to a resource that is fixed in supply, eventually the additional output produced will decrease.
6. Another term for average total cost is ______.
7. The entity that offers a franchise is called the ______.
8. Ten percent of the face value of a bond is paid out regularly, so 10 percent is the ______ of the bond.
9. A(n) ______ for a firm is anything to which the firm has a legal claim.
10. The tax that a person pays on his or her income is called the ______ tax.

Understanding the Main Ideas

Write answers to the following questions to review the main ideas in this chapter.

1. List and explain two major differences between a corporation and a partnership.
2. To what taxes are we referring when we say that corporations are taxed twice?
3. Suppose a bond has a \$10,000 face value and a coupon rate of 8 percent. What is the dollar amount of each annual coupon payment?
4. Specify the condition under which a firm will be formed.
5. In setting 1, Mayang works for herself. She gets to keep or sell everything she produces. In setting 2, Mayang works with five individuals. Here, she gets to keep one-fifth of everything she produces and of everything that everyone

else produces. In which setting is Mayang more likely to shirk? Explain your answer.

6. What is the relationship between a bondholder and the firm that issued the bond? What is the relationship between a stockholder and the firm that issued the stock?
7. In general, what is the difference between fixed and variable costs?
8. Explain why a firm continues to produce those units of a good for which marginal revenue is greater than marginal cost.
9. A firm will produce and sell units of a good if marginal revenue is greater than marginal cost. Does this strategy have anything to do with the firm's objective to maximize profit? Explain.
10. How does a firm compute its profit or loss?

Doing the Math

Do the calculations necessary to solve the following problems.

1. Calculate the marginal cost for the additional unit in each of the following cases. (TC = total cost, and Q = quantity of output.)
   a. Q = 100, TC = $4,322; Q = 101, TC = $4,376
   b. Q = 210, TC = $5,687; Q = 211, TC = $5,699
   c. Q = 547, TC = $10,009; Q = 548, TC = $10,123
2. Calculate the average total cost in each of the following cases. (TC = total cost, and Q = quantity of output.)
   a. Q = 120, TC = $3,400
   b. Q = 200, TC = $4,560
   c. Q = 150, TC = $1,500
3. The marginal benefit of playing chess (in money terms) is $10 for the first game of chess, $8 for the second, $6 for the third, $4 for the fourth, $2 for the fifth, and $0 for the sixth. The marginal cost of playing chess (in money terms) is always $5. What is the right number of games of chess to play? Explain your answer.
4. Look at Exhibit 7-6. Suppose it costs a firm $45 a day to hire the fifth worker. What does the price of the good the firm produces have to be before it is worth hiring the fifth worker?

Working with Graphs

In Exhibit 7-8, Q = quantity of the good, MC = marginal cost, and MR = marginal revenue. Which part or parts (a–c) illustrate the following?

EXHIBIT 7-8

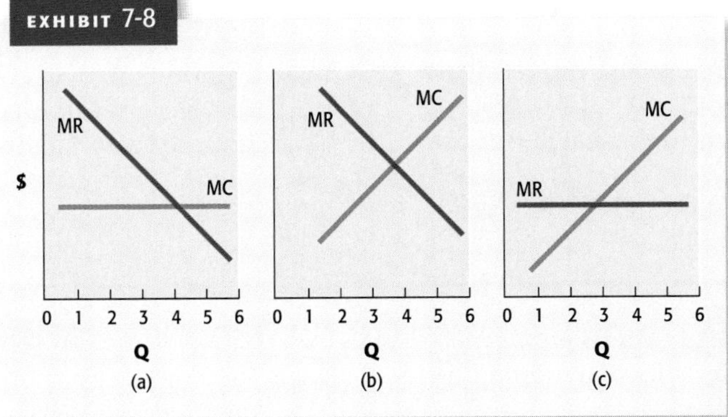

1. Jim pays more to produce the second unit of the good than the first, more for the third than the second, and so on.
2. The additional "benefits" of producing the fourth unit of the good are the same as the additional benefits of producing the fifth.
3. Marginal revenue is constant over a specific quantity of the good produced.
4. Marginal revenue declines as the firm sells additional units of the good.

Solving Economic Problems

1. **Application.** When Dairy Queen first began, it did not require franchisees to handle all Dairy Queen products. In contrast, McDonald's requires its franchisees to handle all of its products. If you were a franchiser, what kind of agreement would you want, and why?

Practice Tests and Study Guide

Go to www.emcp.net/economics and choose *Economics: New Ways of Thinking,* Chapter 7, if you need more help in preparing for the chapter test.

Doing the Math

1. a. $54 (*calculation:* $14, 376 – $4,322 = $54); **b.** $12 (*calculation:* $5,699 – $4,322 = $12); **c.** 114 (*calculation:* 10,123 – 10,009 = 114). **2. a.** $28.33 (*calculation:* $3,400 ÷ 120 = $28.33); **b.** $22.80 (*calculation:* $4,560 ÷ 200 = $22.80); **c.** $10 (*calculation:* $1,500 ÷ 150 = $10). **3.** Three games. For the first three games, marginal benefits are greater than marginal costs. With the fourth game, marginal costs are greater than marginal benefits, so you would not want to play this game. **4.** $15.01. The firm will hire the fifth worker only if it expects greater benefits than costs. Its costs are $45. The fifth worker increases output by 3 units; if the firm can sell each unit for $15, the firm will break even on hiring the fifth worker and therefore be indifferent about hiring the worker or not hiring the worker. One penny more ($15.01 per unit), and the firm will find it in its best interest to hire the fifth worker.

Working with Graphs

1. parts (b) and (c); **2.** part (c); **3.** part (c); **4.** parts (a) and (b).

Solving Economic Problems

1. Answers will vary. Many students will realize the advantages of consistency in all franchises (like McDonald's) so customers know what they are getting if they stop at the franchise. If they didn't know, they might be less likely to stop. This is an argument for each franchise to be just like every other franchise.

Chapter 8 Planning Guide

SECTION ORGANIZER

Section	Learning Objectives	Reproducible Worksheets and Handouts	Assessment
 **A Perfectly Competitive Market** (pages 188–193)	▸ Name the characteristics of a perfectly competitive market. ▸ Provide examples of perfectly competitive markets. ▸ Explain what it means to say that a firm has no control over price. ▸ Describe the role that profit plays in a perfectly competitive market.	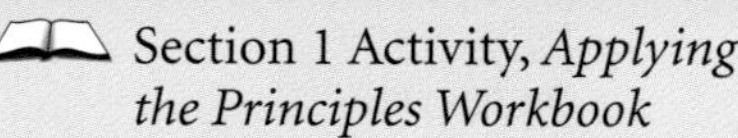 Section 1 Activity, *Applying the Principles Workbook* Outlining Activity, *Guided Reading and Study Guide* Just the Facts Handout, *Guided Reading and Study Guide*	Section Assessment, *Student Text,* page 193 Quick Quiz, *Annotated Teacher's Edition,* page 192 Section Quiz, *Assessment Book*
  **A Monopolistic Market** (pages 194–203)	▸ Describe the characteristics of a monopolistic market. ▸ List some examples of barriers to entry. ▸ Explain whether monopolists ever face competition. ▸ Explain the purpose of antitrust laws. ▸ List some major antitrust laws.	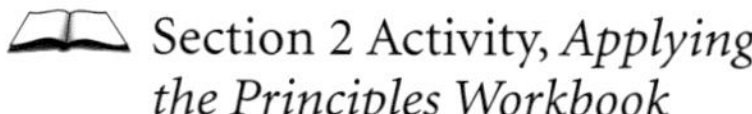 Section 2 Activity, *Applying the Principles Workbook* Outlining Activity, *Guided Reading and Study Guide* Just the Facts Handout, *Guided Reading and Study Guide*	Section Assessment, *Student Text,* page 203 Quick Quiz, *Annotated Teacher's Edition,* page 202 Section Quiz, *Assessment Book*
 **A Monopolistic Competitive Market** (pages 206–210)	▸ Describe the characteristics of monopolistic competition. ▸ List some examples of monopolistic competition. ▸ Explain why monopolistic competitors are price searchers. ▸ Describe how monopolistic competitors answer questions about how much to produce and what price to charge. ▸ Explain the ways the products of monopolistic competitors differ.	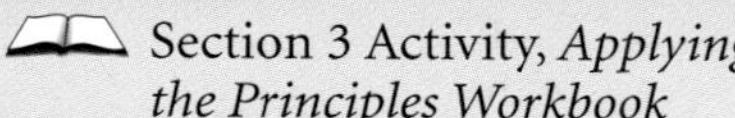 Section 3 Activity, *Applying the Principles Workbook* Outlining Activity, *Guided Reading and Study Guide* Just the Facts Handout, *Guided Reading and Study Guide*	Section Assessment, *Student Text,* page 210 Quick Quiz, *Annotated Teacher's Edition,* page 210 Section Quiz, *Assessment Book*
 **An Oligopolistic Market** (pages 211–219)	▸ Describe the characteristics of an oligopolistic market. ▸ List some examples of an oligopolistic market. ▸ Explain whether sellers in an oligopolistic market are price takers or price searchers. ▸ Explain what cartel agreements are.	 Section 4 Activity, *Applying the Principles Workbook* Outlining Activity, *Guided Reading and Study Guide* Just the Facts Handout, *Guided Reading and Study Guide*	Section Assessment, *Student Text,* page 219 Quick Quiz, *Annotated Teacher's Edition,* page 218 Section Quiz, *Assessment Book*

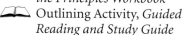

CHAPTER AND PROGRAM RESOURCES

Reproducible Chapter Resources and Assessment Materials

 Graphic Organizer Activity, *Guided Reading and Study Guide*

 Vocabulary Activity, *Guided Reading and Study Guide*

 Working with Graphs and Charts, *Guided Reading and Study Guide*

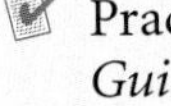 Practice Test, *Guided Reading and Study Guide*

 Critical Thinking Activity, *Finding Economics*

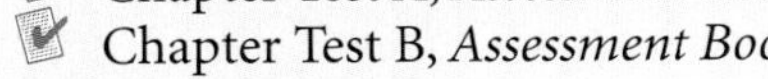 Chapter Test A, *Assessment Book*

Chapter Test B, *Assessment Book*

Technology Resources

 *Test Generator CD*

 *Spanish Audio Summaries CD*

Marketplace® Audio Lessons CD

Economic Principles Lectures, Videocassette or DVD

Lesson Planning and Teaching Resources

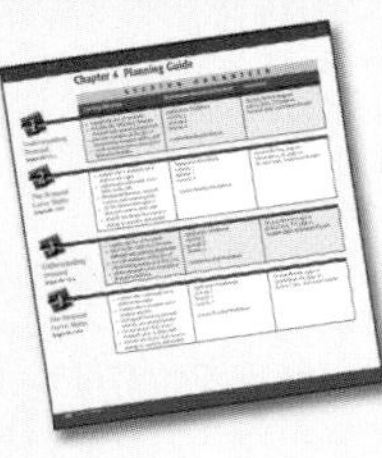

The *Economics: New Ways of Thinking* Teacher Resources include detailed lesson plans for each section in this chapter; the lesson plans are available in print form *(Lesson Plans)* and electronic form. The Teacher Resources also include *Daily Lectures: Overheads and Notes,* which provides prepared overheads and discussion notes covering the key concepts in each section of this chapter.

EMC Publishing Economics Online

Go to Economics Online, at www.emcp.com, for a variety of Internet resources to help you keep your course current and relevant. At Economics Online you will find these items:

- Economics in the News Lessons
- Study Guide Questions
- Practice Tests
- Lesson Plans

Internet Resources

Economics: New Ways of Thinking encourages students to use the Internet to find out more about economics. With the wealth of current, valid information available on Web sites, using the Internet as a research tool is likely to increase your students' interest in and understanding of economics principles and topics. In addition, doing Internet research can help your students form the habit of accessing and using economics information, as well as help them develop investigative skills they will use throughout their educational and professional careers.

To aid your students in achieving these ends, each chapter of *Economics: New Ways of Thinking* includes the addresses of several Web sites at which students will find engaging, relevant information. When students type in the addresses provided, they will immediately arrive at the intended sites. The addresses have been modified so that EMC Publishing can monitor and maintain the proper links—for example, the government site http://stats.bls.gov/ has been changed to www.emcp.net/prices. In the event that the address or content of a site changes or is discontinued, EMC's Internet editors will create a link that redirects students to an address with similar information.

Activities in the *Annotated Teacher's Edition* often suggest that students search the Internet for information. For some activities, you might want to find reputable sites beforehand, and steer students to those sites. For other activities, you might want students to do their own searching, and then check out the sites they have found and discuss why they might be reliable or unreliable.

CHAPTER 8 Overview

This chapter describes each of the four market structures: perfect competition, monopoly, monopolistic competition, and oligopoly. The following statements provide brief descriptions of the major concepts covered in each section of this chapter.

A Perfectly Competitive Market

Section 1 introduces the characteristics of a perfectly competitive market.

A Monopolistic Market

Section 2 examines monopoly, which is the opposite of perfect competition. Students will learn the characteristics of a monopoly and how monopolies come into being, as well as the difference between a government monopoly and a market monopoly.

A Monopolistic Competitive Market

Section 3 explores monopolistic competition—a middle ground between the markets of monopoly and perfect competition. Students will also learn the three conditions that characterize monopolistic competition.

An Oligopolistic Market

Section 4 covers oligopoly. Students will learn the characteristics of the oligopoly and will explore the relationship between oligopoly and cartel.

CHAPTER 8 Competition and Markets

Why It Matters

Sometimes you can negotiate the price you pay for a good. You are about to buy a car, for example. The sticker price is $25,000. You offer the car dealer $23,000. He comes back with $24,500. You say $24,200 and the dealer accepts your offer.

Sometimes you can't negotiate the price you pay. You want to buy a shirt at a store in the mall. The price is $30. You don't say to the clothing salesperson, "I'll pay $25 for the shirt." Instead, you pay $30.

The lesson here is that not all goods are sold in the identical type of market. In some markets, you negotiate price; in others, you don't. Some markets are competitive; others are not. Knowledge of the material in this chapter will help you better understand why markets function in different ways.

This farmer operates in a market that economists call *perfectly competitive*, which means that he is a price taker. You will learn about four different kinds of markets in this chapter.

Teaching Suggestions from the Author

Students often find this an odd chapter. They come to this chapter thinking business is business is business. But that's not true. Every business finds itself in a particular market, and markets are not all alike. For example, there is more competition in some markets than in other markets. There are more sellers in some markets than in other markets. There are more barriers to entering some markets than other markets.

In this chapter we want students to understand that the market in which a firm finds itself will determine how that firm will act. In other words, markets matter to the firm's behavior.

In this chapter you might want to ask students to identify the market structures of well-known firms. In

Economics Around the Clock

The following events occurred one day in July.

9:22 A.M. Barry walks around the car lot looking at new cars. A car salesperson approaches him and asks if he can be of any help. "I'm just looking around," Barry says. "Did you have any specific model in mind?" the car salesperson asks. "Not really," Barry says. The car salesperson walks and talks with Barry as he looks at the different cars on the lot. At one point, the car salesperson nonchalantly asks Barry what he does for a living.

- **Why did the car salesperson ask Barry what he does for a living?**

10:04 A.M. Melissa loves to read. She is currently in her local bookstore looking at the newest fiction. Melissa reads the first few pages of a book by one of her favorite authors. She then closes the book and checks the price—$29.99. She wonders whether she should buy it. On the one hand, she really wants the book. On the other hand, it's expensive and she knows that she could wait until the book comes out in paperback. It would be much more affordable then.

- **Why do book publishers publish the exact same book in hardcover and in paperback, but come out with the hardcover edition months before the paperback edition?**

7:34 P.M. Ethan is at Petco Park in San Diego watching the San Diego Padres play the Milwaukee Brewers. He is thinking about going to the concession stand and buying a hamburger, some peanuts, and a soft drink. The price of the hamburger is $6.50, a bag of peanuts is $5.00, and a soft drink is $3.75. The total price for the three items is $15.25. "That is a lot of money," Ethan thinks to himself. "I don't know why food is so expensive at a baseball game."

- **Why is food so expensive at a baseball park?**

9:59 P.M. George is getting ready to take his medicine. He heard a news report on television earlier this evening saying that the company that produces his medicine actually sells the medicine for much less in foreign countries than it does in the United States. He pays $95 for a month's supply, but understands that if he lived in India he could buy the same medicine for the equivalent of $30.

- **Why does George, in the United States, pay more for the same medicine that a person in India buys for much less?**

Introducing the Chapter

Remind students that the previous chapter discussed the three types of business firms. Several of the activities asked students to identify examples of businesses that typified each one of the business types. Explain to students that they might keep those same businesses in mind as they examine competition and markets in Chapter 8.

Also remind students that economics often applies very specific meanings to commonly used words. In this chapter, students will learn about the specific meaning that economics applies to the word *competition*.

Teaching with Visuals

Students will learn about a variety of markets in this chapter. Have them look at the photo on this spread and think about the differences between wheat and, say, automobiles. What does it mean to say these products belong to different markets?

what kind of market structure does Microsoft find itself? In what kind of market structure does General Motors find itself? Afterward, you may want to ask students how a firm that finds itself in a monopolistic market might behave if it found itself in an oligopolistic market, or in a perfectly competitive market.

Finally, it is always important to talk about competition when discussing market structures. You might want to ask students if the nature of competition differs between a perfectly competitive market and a monopolistic competitive market, or between a monopolistic market and a monopolistic competitive market.

 187

SECTION 1

Teacher Support

Focus and Motivate

Section Objectives

After completing this section, students will be able to

- name the characteristics of a perfectly competitive market;
- provide examples of perfectly competitive markets;
- explain what it means to say that a firm has no control over price; and
- describe the role that profit plays in a perfectly competitive market.

Economics Around the Clock

Kickoff Activity

Direct students to the 9:22 A.M. scenario in Economics Around the Clock (page 187), and invite them to write their answers to the accompanying question.

Allow students to share their answers with the class. They may guess that the salesperson is trying to determine how much Barry has to spend on a car.

Activating Prior Knowledge

Invite students to list the three types of business firms they studied in Chapter 7. Tell them that each of these firms operates in a market structure.

Teach

A Student Asks

You might want to use this A Student Asks to make sure that students understand that economists can distinguish between markets, and that students will learn to distinguish one market from another, as well.

SECTION 1

A Perfectly Competitive Market

Focus Questions

- What are the characteristics of a perfectly competitive market?
- What are some examples of perfectly competitive markets?
- What does it mean to say that a firm has no control over price?
- What role does profit play in a perfectly competitive market?

Key Terms

market structure
perfectly competitive market
price taker

Four Types of Markets

The more than 25 million businesses in the United States include car companies, bookstores, clothing stores, grocery stores, hair salons, restaurants, and more. Not every one of the 25 million businesses operates in the same kind of market.

Economists talk about the different types of market structures. **Market structures** are defined by their characteristics, such as the number of sellers in the market, the product that sellers produce and sell, and how easy or difficult it is for new firms to enter the market. You will learn about four types of markets—perfectly competitive, monopolistic, monopolistic competitive, and oligopolistic—in this chapter.

market structure
The setting in which a seller finds itself. Market structures are defined by their characteristics, such as the number of sellers in the market, the product that sellers produce and sell, and how easy or difficult it is for new firms to enter the market.

For now, think of each of the four kinds of markets the way you might think of four different rooms in a house. Each room is similar to and different from every other room. All rooms have floors and ceilings, but not all rooms are painted the same color, or are the same size.

It's the same with markets. They have some things in common (they all have buyers and sellers), and a few things that differ. Let's begin by discussing our first market, the perfectly competitive market.

A Student Asks

QUESTION: *For me, as a buyer, almost all markets seem the same. For example, I can't tell much difference between the market for books and the market for skateboards. In both markets, if I want to buy something, I pay the price that is charged. What are economists looking at to distinguish one market from another?*

ANSWER: *What you implied about markets—they all seem the same—can be said about other things too. Someone might say that he can't tell much difference between two shirts. But, on a closer look, one shirt might be cotton and the other flannel, or one might be a short-sleeve shirt and the other a long-sleeve shirt. It is the same with markets: the closer you look at them, the more differences you can find. Economists look*

Differentiating Instruction

English Language Learners

This chapter might contain a number of terms that are difficult for students with limited English proficiency. Assign these students to work in pairs to make a list of the key terms. Students should define the terms both in English and in their native languages, if appropriate. Then, on their own, they should write new sentences that show that they understand both the meaning of the word and how to use the word correctly in English. You might also ask them to provide clear, concrete examples of the terms on their lists. When you have finished the chapter, quiz these students on the words on their lists.

at a variety of things to distinguish between markets, such as how many sellers there are in a market (many, a few, only one), how many buyers in a market, and whether sellers sell the same good or a slightly differentiated good. You will see more of the differences as you progress through this chapter.

▲ Many different kinds of stores sell many different products in a typical modern mall. **Do you think any of the markets represented by these stores and products are perfectly competitive markets? If so, what four characteristics must be present?**

Characteristics of a Perfectly Competitive Market

Economists categorize markets according to their characteristics. Here are four characteristics of a **perfectly competitive market**.

1. The market has many buyers and many sellers.
2. All firms sell identical goods.
3. Buyers and sellers have relevant information about prices, product quality, sources of supply, and so on.
4. Firms have easy entry into and exit out of the market.

EXAMPLE: Jones is a wheat farmer, or a producer and seller of wheat. Does Jones sell his wheat in a perfectly competitive market? In other words, is the wheat market a "perfectly competitive market"? To answer this question we have to determine whether the wheat market has the four characteristics that any perfectly competitive market has. First, does it have many buyers and many sellers of wheat? The answer is yes; so the first characteristic holds for the wheat market. Second, do all wheat sellers sell the same wheat? For a given type of wheat, the answer is yes. It would be impossible, for example, to tell Jones's wheat from any other farmer's wheat. So, the second characteristic of a perfectly competitive market holds. Third, do buyers and sellers of wheat possess information on the quality of wheat, prices of wheat, and so on. The answer is yes. For example, wheat farmers often get up in the morning and check the daily wheat report. They know what price wheat is selling for on that given day. So, the third characteristic of a perfectly competitive market holds. Fourth, is entry into and out of the wheat market easy? In other words, is it easy for Jones to leave the farming business if he wants to, and would it be easy for others (if they wanted to) to get into the farming business. The answer is yes. Nothing prevents Jones from deciding to no longer be a farmer and nothing prevents you or anyone else from being a wheat farmer. If an accountant at an accounting firm wants to quit his job tomorrow, buy some land in Iowa, and start wheat farming, she is free to do just that. You might say it is expensive to get into farming, so doesn't that make it hard to get into farming? It may be expensive, but what economists mean when they say that there is "easy entry and exit" is that no entity prevents the entry into or exit from a market. For example, government doesn't prevent individuals from going into farming if they want. So, the fourth characteristic of a perfectly competitive market is met. We can conclude then the wheat market is a perfectly competitive market. ♦

perfectly competitive market
A market structure characterized by (1) many buyers and many sellers, (2) all firms selling identical goods, (3) all relevant information about buying and selling activities available to buyers and sellers, and (4) easy entry into and easy exit out of the market.

Teaching with Visuals

Student answers will vary. If they answer yes, then they should list the four characteristics of a perfectly competitive market.

Discussion Starter

Guide students in a discussion of the word *competition*. Ask them to define the word in as many ways as they can, and list the definitions on the board. Then explain that in this chapter they will be looking at competition from an economist's point of view.

Discussion Starter

Guide students in a discussion of the characteristics of perfect competition. Have students identify examples of markets that might be perfectly competitive. Examine each example in light of the four characteristics to determine if the example qualifies as a perfectly competitive market.

Background Information: Perfect Competition

Sometimes people believe that sellers can sell their goods at any price they desire. A discussion of perfect competition will reveal that this is not the case. For example, a firm that finds itself in a perfectly competitive market can sell its goods only at the market price. Point out to students that the market price has been determined by the impersonal forces of supply and demand. Thousands of sellers and thousands of buyers come together and determine the equilibrium or market price through quantity demanded and quantity supplied. No single seller or buyer sets price. The entire market does.

Discussion Starter

Write the following statement on the board: "In the perfectly competitive market, there is only one price." Ask students if they agree or disagree with this statement. Students should understand that while the possibility of multiple prices exists, there is only one price that will maximize profit and bring demand.

Reinforcement Activity

The markets for agricultural goods (such as wheat and corn) are considered perfectly competitive markets. Direct students to prepare a short essay on one of these markets. The essay should describe what a farmer must do to produce the product, the price of the product, who buys this product, and any variable conditions that might affect quantity and/or price. If your students live in an agricultural area, this could be a particularly interesting project.

Clarifying Terms

Perfectly competitive firms are price takers—sellers who can sell their output at the equilibrium price but can sell none of the output at a higher price. They must take the price that the market offers; if they try to sell at a higher price, they will be unable to sell any of their products.

Teaching with Visuals

The markets for corn and wheat are perfectly competitive because they meet the four characteristics. Because sellers of these commodities must sell at the equilibrium or market price, they are price takers.

Sellers in a Perfectly Competitive Market Are Price Takers

Because of the four characteristics of a perfectly competitive market, sellers in this market end up being **price takers**. It is similar to saying that a person who exercises daily, eats healthfully, and always gets enough sleep will end up being healthier than if the person didn't do these things. Certain things follow from certain characteristics. When it comes to the perfectly competitive market, its characteristics determine that a seller in this market will be a price taker. A price taker is a seller that can only sell his or her goods at the equilibrium price (think back to Chapter 6 where we explained how the equilibrium price came to exist). In other words, suppose Jones, the farmer, is a price taker. What does this mean for him? It means that he gets up in the morning, turns on the radio or television, and finds out what today's equilibrium price for wheat is. If it is, say, $5 a bushel, Jones will have to sell his wheat at this price and no other price.

price taker
A seller that can sell all its output at the equilibrium price but can sell none of its output at any other price.

Now consider another price taker, this time in a market other than the wheat market. Consider Brown, who owns 1,000 shares of Disney stock. One day Brown decides to sell her stock (just like Jones might have decided to sell his wheat). Brown goes online and checks the current (equilibrium) price of Disney stock. If it is $27.80, then this is the price Brown must "take" if she wants to sell her stock. She won't be able to sell her stock for even one penny more.

▼ Sellers of commodities such as corn and wheat are price takers. **Can you explain why?**

A Student Asks

QUESTION: *Aren't all sellers price takers? Don't all sellers have to sell their goods at the equilibrium price determined by supply and demand?*

ANSWER: *No. Think of the difference between the seller of stock or wheat and the seller of, say, books. The stock seller can only sell her stock at one price—the equilibrium price. Charge one penny higher, and she can't sell any stock. The wheat seller can only sell his wheat at one price—the equilibrium price. Charge one penny higher, and he can't sell any wheat. But the seller of books can sell books at various prices, although the bookseller can't sell as many books at a higher price as at a lower price.*

Can Price Takers Sell for Less than the Equilibrium Price?

So we learned that if Jones, the farmer, and Brown, the stock seller, want to sell what they own (wheat and stock) they will have to sell at the equilibrium price in their respective markets, and not at one penny more. What happens if they want to sell for one penny less? If the equilibrium price of Disney stock is $27.80, can't Brown sell her stock at $27.50 (for 30 cents less)? Yes, she can. No buyer is going to turn down a lower price. The point is that Brown has no reason to offer to sell her stock at a price lower than the equilibrium price. After all, she can sell all her stock at the equilibrium price of $27.80. So, two points are true for every price taker:

1. He or she cannot sell for a price higher than equilibrium price.
2. He or she will not sell for a price lower than equilibrium price.

190 Chapter 8 Competition and Markets

Cooperative Learning

Divide students into groups of four or five and assign each group to develop a product that could exist in a perfectly competitive market. Once each group has developed and named its product, have it name an initial price and identify the factors that determine that price. Once groups have determined an equilibrium price, ask each group to explain what would happen to its place in the market if it raised its price, and if it lowered the price.

EXAMPLE: Patty owns 10 ounces of gold that she wants to sell. She checks the daily (equilibrium) price for gold on a particular day; it is $418. She will have to sell her gold for $418 an ounce. If, by chance, she charges a higher price—say, $420—she won't sell even an ounce of gold at that price. Patty is a price taker. ♦

Must a Perfectly Competitive Market Possess All Four Characteristics?

Recall that a perfectly competitive market has four characteristics. Is a real-world market still a perfectly competitive market if it doesn't perfectly match these four characteristics? For example, suppose a market has characteristics 1, 2, and 4 (you may want to look back to refresh your memory on the four characteristics of a perfectly competitive market), but only slightly satisfies characteristic 3. Does it follow that because this market doesn't satisfy all four characteristics 100 percent that it isn't a perfectly competitive market? The answer is no.

Think about this old saying: If it looks like a duck and quacks like a duck, it is probably a duck. The same thing holds for markets too. If a seller is a price taker—that is, if he or she can only sell at the equilibrium price—then for all practical purposes this seller is operating in a perfectly competitive market. Rephrasing the duck saying, we get: If a seller is a price taker, then it is operating in a perfectly competitive market.

What Does a Perfectly Competitive Firm Do?

As we said in the previous chapter, every firm has to answer certain questions. Two questions we identified are:

1. How much of our product do we produce?
2. What price do we charge for our product?

How does a perfectly competitive firm answer the first question of how much to produce? It answers it the way any firm would answer it. It produces the quantity of output at which marginal revenue (MR) equals marginal cost (MC).

How does the perfectly competitive firm answer the second question of what price to charge? Because it is a price taker, it has no choice in the matter: It sells its product for the equilibrium price determined in the market. If the equilibrium price is $10, then that is the price it charges, not $10.01 or $9.99.

So, to summarize answers to the two questions: (1) perfectly competitive firms produce the quantity of output at which marginal revenue equals marginal cost; (2) they charge the equilibrium price for their product.

EXAMPLE: Market A is a perfectly competitive market. Currently, the equilibrium price is $10. The total revenue and marginal revenue data for one seller in this market look like the following:

Units of output	Total revenue	Marginal revenue
1	$10	$10
2	20	10
3	30	10

This firm's total cost and marginal cost data look like the following:

Units of output	Total cost	Marginal cost
1	$ 6	$ 6
2	14	8
3	24	10

▲ **If this manufacturer operates in a perfectly competitive market, how does it decide what price to charge for its products?**

Teaching with Visuals

The manufacturer has no choice in the matter; it checks the equilibrium price and must accept it.

Reinforcement Activity

Ask students if they would like to sell in a perfectly competitive market. What do they think the advantages would be for the price takers? What would be the disadvantages? If the market price does not change and everyone's product is the same, is the market a good market in which to be? Then ask students if they would like to be a buyer in a perfectly competitive market. What would be the advantages and disadvantages?

Critical Thinking

The firms in a perfectly competitive market must answer the two questions of how much of a good to produce and how much to charge for that good. No matter what the company decides, the market has already set the equilibrium price. Ask students to imagine ways that a business can deviate from perfect competition in order to make more profit, and what might happen if it takes those steps. Students should realize that as soon as a business differentiates its product, that seller is no longer competing in a perfectly competitive market, because it no longer fits the third characteristic of a perfectly competitive market.

Cooperative Learning

The stock market or the commodities markets are great examples of perfectly competitive markets. Divide the class into groups of three or four. Have the groups track a particular stock or commodity for a period of a week. Does the price change during the week? What quantity of stock or commodity is sold during the week? If possible, have a stockbroker or commodities trader come to your class to discuss how these markets work. Have the groups prepare questions the day before the visit so that both the class and your guest speaker are prepared.

Teaching with Visuals

Competitors are likely to enter the market.

Application Activity

After reading and discussing Section 1, you may want to assign the Section Activity in the *Applying the Principles Workbook.*

Assess

Quick Quiz

The following true-or-false quiz will help you assess student understanding of the material covered in this section.

1. In perfect competition, there are few buyers and many sellers. (False)
2. In perfect competition, all firms sell identical goods. (True)
3. All firms are price takers in a perfectly competitive market. (True)
4. Only three of the four characteristics must be met for a market to be considered a perfectly competitive market. (False)
5. If price falls in perfect competition, firms will enter the market. (False)

Now ask what quantity of output this firm will produce. You know that it wants to produce the quantity of output at which marginal revenue equals marginal cost: MR = MC occurs at a quantity of 3 units. Now ask what price it will charge for each of the 3 units it sells. Because the firm is a price taker, it takes the equilibrium price of $10. So, it produces 3 units and charges a price of $10 for each unit.

How much profit does this firm earn? We know that profit is the difference between total revenue and total cost. When the firm produces 3 units of output its total revenue is $30 and its total cost is $24, so it follows that this firm's profit is $6. ◆

A Student Asks

QUESTION: *How did you get the dollar amounts in the marginal revenue (MR) column and in the marginal cost (MC) column?*

ANSWER: *Remember from Chapter 7 that marginal revenue is the additional revenue from producing an additional unit of a good. Notice that when the firm sells 1 unit of the good its total revenue is $10 and when it sells 2 units of a good its total revenue is $20. What is the additional revenue generated due to selling the additional unit (the second unit)? Obviously the answer is $10. The same holds going from selling 2 units to 3 units. The total revenue for the firm when it sells 2 units is $20 and it is $30 when it sells 3 units; therefore the additional revenue due to selling the additional unit (the third unit) is $10. Here is the MR equation from Chapter 7:*

Marginal revenue (MR) $= \Delta TR/\Delta Q$

As to the dollar amounts in the marginal cost (MC) column, we just made up these dollar amounts. Often, in the real world, marginal cost rises as a firm produces additional units of a good, so we had the marginal cost dollar amounts rise in our example.

Profit Is a Signal in a Perfectly Competitive Market

Suppose 200 sellers operate in market X, a perfectly competitive market. Each of the sellers produces good X and sells it for its current equilibrium price, $10. Furthermore, all 200 firms earn profits. Will things stay as they are currently? Not likely.

According to the fourth characteristic of a perfectly competitive market, easy entry is an aspect of a perfectly competitive market. In other words, firms that are currently not in market X can easily get into that market. Nothing is holding them out. As long as sellers are earning profits in that market, the answer is yes.

As new firms enter market X, the number of firms in the market increases, say from 200 to 250. With more firms, the supply of good X increases. (Remember from Chapter 5 that as the number of sellers increases, the supply of the good increases too—the supply curve shifts rightward.) When the supply of a good rises, equilibrium price falls. Furthermore, as price falls, so does profit. Profit, remember, is total revenue (price times number of units sold) minus total cost. In this case, as price falls, so do total revenue and profit.

How long will new firms keep entering market X? Until they see no reason to do

▲ What is likely to happen if this fast-food restaurant's profits begin to climb?

Differentiating Instruction

English Language Learners

To help ELL students, use the following resources, which are provided as part of the *Economics: New Ways of Thinking* program:

- a Spanish glossary in the *Student Text*
- Spanish versions of the Chapter Summaries on an audio CD

192 Chapter 8 Competition and Markets

so—that is, until the competition eliminates the profit. When profit falls to zero and total revenue exactly equals total cost, firms will no longer have a monetary incentive to enter market X.

In a perfectly competitive market, then, profit acts as a signal to firms that are currently not in the market. It says, "Come over here and get me." As new firms gravitate toward the profit, they increase the supply of the good that is earning profit and thus lower its price. As they lower its price, the profit dissipates. The process ends when firms no longer see an incentive to enter the market to obtain profit:

Profit exists → New firms enter the market → Supply rises → Price falls → Price falls until firms no longer see an incentive to enter the market

A Student Asks

QUESTION: *Can you give us some examples of profit (in a market) that signals other firms to enter into the the market, ultimately reducing the price that consumers pay?*

ANSWER: *Think about the prices you sometimes pay for new goods (goods that have just been introduced). When the VCR was introduced, its price was more than $1,000. The profit in the VCR market acted as a signal to new firms to enter that market. As they did, the supply of VCRs went up and the price of VCRs fell. You can buy one today for about $60. The same thing happened in the market for calculators (the early ones with numerous functions sold for about $400), the market for personal computers, the market for DVD players, and many more markets.*

Profits May Be Taxed Away

Suppose we go back to the point in time when the 200 firms in market X were all earning profits. Now suppose a member of Congress says, "The firms in market X are earning huge profits. They do not deserve them; they just happened to be in the right place at the right time. The government needs some additional money for some new programs, so we ought to tax these profits. I propose a special tax on these profits of 100 percent."

Congress goes along with this member, enacts a special tax on the profits of the firms in market X, and taxes away these profits. With the profits taxed away, the reason for firms not currently in market X to enter it is gone. If no new firms enter market X, the supply of good X will not rise, and the price of good X will not then fall. This situation leaves consumers paying a higher price than they would have paid if the profits of the 200 firms had not been taxed away.

The intended effect was to tax away the profits of the 200 firms and to generate new revenue for the government. The unintended effect was that consumers ended up paying a higher price for good X than they would have paid without the tax.

SECTION 1 ASSESSMENT

Defining Terms

1. Define:
   a. price taker
   b. market structure
   c. perfectly competitive market

Reviewing Facts and Concepts

2. What is easy entry into a market and easy exit out of the market?
3. What quantity of output does a perfectly competitive firm produce? What price does it charge for its product?

Critical Thinking

4. Some of the 200 firms in market X, a perfectly competitive market, are incurring losses. How will these losses influence (a) exit out of the market, (b) the supply of the good produced in the market, and (c) the price of the good? Explain your answers.

Applying Economic Concepts

5. How can a seller determine whether it is a price taker?

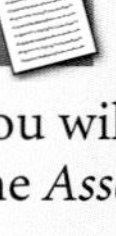

Assessment Book

You will find a quiz for this section in the *Assessment Book.*

Reteaching Activity

Use the Section Assessment to gauge which students may need reteaching on this section. Ask those students whether sellers in perfect competition have control over price, and work with them to write explanations of their answers.

Guided Reading

For further reteaching of the key concepts in this section, assign the Outlining Activity and the Just the Facts Handout from the *Guided Reading and Study Guide.*

SECTION 1 ASSESSMENT ANSWERS

Defining Terms

1. a. price taker: a seller that cannot sell any of its product at a price above equilibrium price and won't sell any of its product at a price below equilibrium price, and therefore sells all its product at the equilibrium price; **b. market structure:** the particular environment or setting a firm finds itself in, the characteristics of which influence the firm's pricing and output decisions; **c. perfectly competitive market:** a market that consists of the following four characteristics: (1) the market has many buyers and many sellers; (2) all firms sell identical goods; (3) buyers and sellers have relevant information about prices, product quality, sources of supply, and so on; and (4) firms have easy entry into and exit out of the market.

Reviewing Facts and Concepts

2. Easy entry and easy exit mean that there is nothing stopping firms from getting into a market or leaving it.
3. It produces the quantity of output at which marginal revenue equals marginal cost. It charges the equilibrium price as determined in the market by supply and demand.

Critical Thinking

4. The firms that incur losses will (a) exit the market, because exit is easy in a perfectly competitive market. This will lead to (b) a reduction in the supply of the good produced in the market, which in turn will lead to (c) a higher price for the good.

Applying Economic Concepts

5. It could offer to sell its product for a price above equilibrium price. If it can sell some of its product for a price above equilibrium price, it is not a price taker. If it cannot sell anything above equilibrium price, it is a price taker.

SECTION 2 Teacher Support

Focus and Motivate

Section Objectives

After completing this section, students will be able to

- describe the characteristics of a monopolistic market;
- list some examples of barriers to entry;
- explain whether monopolists ever face competition;
- explain the purpose of antitrust laws; and
- list some of the major antitrust laws.

Kickoff Activity

Have students brainstorm associations with the word *monopoly*. Most students will think of the famous board game Monopoly.

Activating Prior Knowledge

Invite students to share their ideas generated during the Kickoff Activity. Most will mention the board game, and many will already have a simplistic understanding of what a monopoly is in economic terms. Explain to students that in this section they will learn what an economist associates with the word *monopoly*.

Teach

Discussion Starter

Direct students to read aloud the characteristics of a monopoly listed on this page. Ask them to think of markets that might qualify as monopolies. Examples include utilities such as gas, electricity, and cable in regions where only one company is permitted to provide these goods.

SECTION 2 A Monopolistic Market

Focus Questions

- What are the characteristics of a monopolistic market?
- What are examples of barriers to entry?
- Do monopolists ever face competition?
- What purpose do antitrust laws serve?
- What have been some of the major antitrust laws?

Key Terms

monopolistic market
barrier to entry
price searcher
public franchise
natural monopoly
antitrust law

Characteristics of a Monopoly

The three characteristics of a **monopolistic market** include the following:

1. The market consists of one seller.
2. The single seller sells a product that has no close substitutes.
3. The **barriers to entry** are high, which means that entry into the market is extremely difficult.

monopolistic market A market structure characterized by (1) a single seller, (2) the sale of a product that has no close substitutes, and (3) extremely high barriers to entry.

barrier to entry Anything that prohibits a firm from entering a market.

price searcher A seller that can sell some of its output at various prices.

How Monopolists Differ from Perfect Competitors

Perfectly competitive firms are price takers. A monopoly firm (or monopolist) is a **price searcher**. In contrast with a price taker, a price searcher can sell some of its product at various prices (for example, at $12, $11, $10, $9, and so on) Whereas a price taker has to "take" one price—the equilibrium price—and sell its product at that price, the price searcher has a list of prices from which to choose. The price searcher "searches" for the best price, the price that generates the greatest profit or, in some cases, the price that minimizes losses.

Which of the many possible prices is the best price? To answer this question, back up and consider the questions that the monopoly firm, like any firm, has to answer: (1) How much do we produce? (2) How much do we charge? The monopoly firm, like any firm, will produce that quantity of output at which marginal revenue equals marginal cost.

Now suppose that for a monopoly firm this quantity turns out to be 20,000 units. What is the best price to charge for each unit? The best price turns out to be the highest price at which all 20,000 units can be sold. If only 15,000 units of the 20,000 units are sold at a price of $14, then $14 is not the best price. But if at $13, all 20,000 units can be sold, then $13 is the best price. Again, the monopoly firm seeks to charge the best price possible, which is the highest price at which it can sell its entire output.

Here is the problem for the monopolist: It does not know what its best price is. So, it has to search for it through a process of trial and error. It may charge one price this week, only to change it next week. Over time, a

Background Information: The Monopoly Game

The game that we know and play today as Monopoly has a very cloudy past. While some people say it was invented in the 1930s, others can show a direct line back to a game invented by a young woman in 1903. What is not in doubt is the fact that Monopoly has sold over 200 million copies worldwide. The blocks on the original board are representations of streets in Atlantic City, New Jersey, but versions have been developed for many cities all over the world—and even for the Star Wars universe!

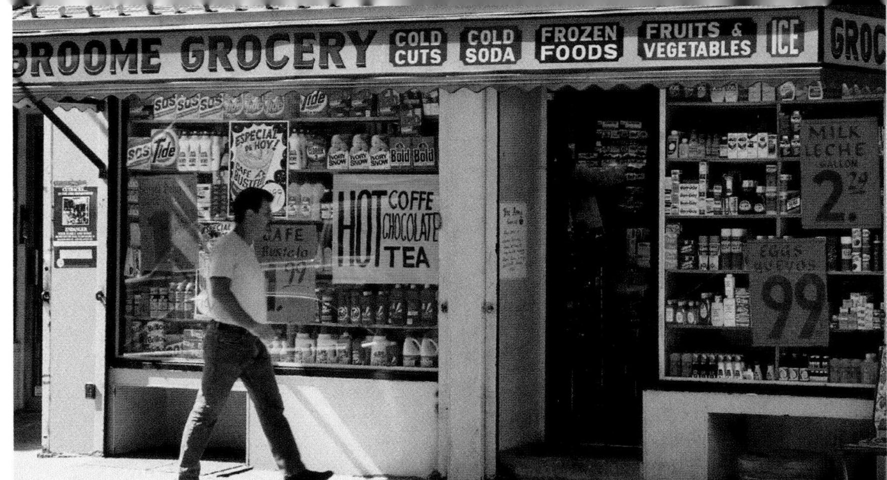

◀ How might the owner of this small, neighborhood store have a monopoly?

monopoly firm finds the highest price at which it can sell its entire output.

EXAMPLE: Suppose you are taking a long drive along a route that has only one gas station. The sign reads: Last Chance for Gas for 100 Miles. Gasoline is a product with very few substitutes. You can't put water in your gas tank and hope that the car will run. The gas station is a local monopolist; in other words, it's not that it is the only gas station in the world, but it is the only gas station in a certain small part of the world. The gas station owner decided that the best quantity of gas for her to sell is 400 gallons. Now, of course, she wants to find the highest price per gallon at which she can sell all 400 gallons. She may have to "search" for this price. Is $2.76 too low? Is $3.18 too high? It is likely that through trial and error she will eventually figure out what the highest price is at which she can sell all 400 gallons of gas. ♦

A Student Asks

QUESTION: *You mentioned that the gas station is a local monopolist. I am interested in the word "local" here. Do you mean to imply that a seller might be a monopolist in one area but not in another?*

ANSWER: *Yes. Think of a small grocery store instead of a gas station. The small grocery store might be the only grocery store in 10 square miles, but not the only grocery store in 20 square miles. Or think of a bookstore on a university campus. Many university campuses have only one bookstore that sells the textbooks that students buy. Some would consider the bookstore in this setting a monopolist. Of course, with the introduction of the Internet, this bookstore isn't as much a monopolist today as it might have been in years gone by. Today, students can buy many of their textbooks online, either directly from the publisher or from an online bookstore.*

How Selling Corn or Stock Differs from Selling Cable Television Service

Perhaps nothing brings home the difference between a perfectly competitive seller (a price taker) and a monopoly seller (a price searcher) than placing yourself in the role of each. First, suppose you are a corn farmer in Iowa. You just harvested 100,000 bushels of corn, and you want to sell them as quickly as possible. It's easy to determine at what price you sell your corn: you just check the newspaper or listen to the crop report on the radio or TV news to see what price corn is selling at. That's the price you take for your corn.

Now say you own a cable television company. In many towns only one cable company

Teaching with Visuals

The store might have a local monopoly if it is the only such store in the area.

Cause and Effect

In its position as a price searcher, the monopoly firm will fluctuate the price of its good or service to find the equilibrium price for the quantity supplied. Ask students to describe how supply and demand affect the selling price of a monopolistic good or service.

Discussion Starter

Ask students which market they would rather sell their products in, a perfectly competitive market or a monopolistic market? What are the advantages and disadvantages to each type of market?

Cross-Curricular Activity

The U.S. economic system is based on the principles of free enterprise. At times in our history, certain businesses have grown into monopolies. Invite a history teacher to your class to discuss the development of monopolies in the United States, especially focusing on the late 19th-century "barons of business," John D. Rockefeller, J. P. Morgan, and Andrew Carnegie. If possible, have the history teacher also discuss the laws and regulations that have limited the growth of monopolies in our country.

Reinforcement Activity

The example of the medical monopolist is a good one for students to think about. If a company discovers a new cure for a previously incurable disease, could it charge as much as $1 million for each dose? Assign students to research the discovery of new cures in order to determine whether the discovering company or individual set a price that would dramatically increase company profits. Ask students why a company might not set such a high price.

Discussion Starter

Prompt students to identify situations in which the equilibrium price for a good produced by a monopolist is less than its average cost. Ask them why a monopoly seller might continue to produce in a market in which it was not making a profit. Students might mention start-up monopolistic companies with new products for which demand is small but growing. These companies might tolerate losses in a particular market in order to drive competitors out of business.

Teaching with Visuals

Use Exhibit 8-1 to make sure students understand that monopolistic markets do have limits on the prices that can be charged for their products.

is allowed to serve a certain geographic area; therefore, you are a monopolist. (Although with satellite TV, the local cable company is probably less of a monopolist than it once was.) The cable wire has been laid across town, and you are ready for business. What do you charge for your cable service? The answer is not so easy this time. No "cable television report" provides the market with information the way a crop report does. Thus, even though it is rather easy for firms to determine their selling prices in perfectly competitive markets, price determination is not so easy in monopolistic markets.

Is the Sky the Limit for the Monopolist?

Suppose a pharmaceutical company recently invented a new medicine that cures arthritis. With respect to this medicine, the pharmaceutical company is a monopolist; it is the only seller of a medicine that has no close substitutes. Can the pharmaceutical company charge any price it wants for the medicine? For example, can it charge $5,000 for one bottle (24 pills) of medicine? If your answer is yes, ask yourself whether the company can charge $10,000 for one bottle. If your answer is still yes, ask yourself whether the company can charge $20,000 for one bottle.

The purpose of these questions is to get you to realize that monopolists do face a limit as to how high a price they can charge. The sky is not the limit. At some high prices in our example, no one, not even someone who suffers greatly from arthritis pain, is willing to buy the medicine.

The monopolist is limited by the "height" of the demand curve it faces. What do we mean by the "height" of the demand curve? Suppose the demand curve in Exhibit 8-1 is the demand curve for the medicine that cures arthritis and that the pharmaceutical company has decided to produce 500,000 bottles of medicine. As you can see, the highest price (per bottle) that can be charged for each bottle of 500,000 bottles is determined by the height of the demand curve, $100 per bottle. The sky is not the limit; the height of the demand curve (at the quantity of output the firm wants to sell) is the limit.

A Monopoly Seller Is Not Guaranteed Profits

Most people think that if a firm is a monopoly seller, it is guaranteed to earn profits. This assumption is not true, however; no monopoly seller is guaranteed profits. A firm earns profits only if the price it sells its good for is above its average total cost. For example, if a firm sells its good for $10 and average total cost (per-unit cost) is $6, then it earns $4 profit per unit. If it sells 1,000 units, its profit is $4,000.

The monopolist sells its product for the highest price possible, but nothing guarantees that this price is greater than the monopoly seller's average total cost. If it is not, the monopoly seller does not earn any profits. If average total cost for the monopoly seller is actually higher than the highest possible price for which it sells its product, the monopoly seller earns a loss (not a profit). If this situation continues, the monopoly seller will go out of business.

EXAMPLE: Tony has gone into business; he sells a good that no one else sells.

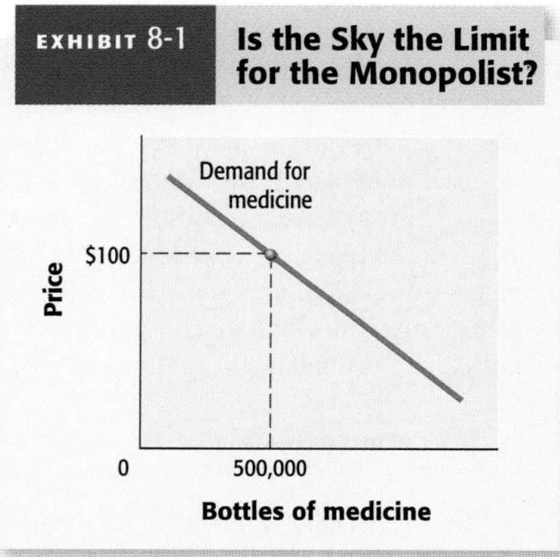

▲ Once a monopoly firm decides on its quantity of output, it is limited to the highest price it can charge (per unit) for the product. Specifically, it is limited by the height of the demand curve. In this case the monopoly firm decides to produce 500,000 bottles of medicine. The highest price it can charge (per unit) and sell this output is $100 per bottle.

Cooperative Learning

Direct students to work in pairs to identify three monopolies. Students should refer to the three characteristics of a monopoly listed on page 194. Examples include local public utility companies. In many areas there is only one water company, one gas company, and one electric company. Encourage students to look beyond the public utility market and try to find other examples of monopolies in the economy.

196 Chapter 8 Competition and Markets

Because he is the only one who sells this particular good, his friend refers to him as a monopolist. Is Tony guaranteed profit because he is the only seller of a particular good? Not necessarily. It turns out that no one demands the good that Tony sells. In other words, a seller could possibly be a monopolist and not sell anything. The objective many sellers set for themselves is to be a monopolist with respect to a good for which demand is high. ♦

◀ A cable TV company may have a monopoly in a certain geographic area. **Are there any barriers to entry here?**

Barriers to Entry

Suppose firm X is a monopolist. It is currently charging a relatively high price for its product and earning large profits. Why don't other businesses enter the market and produce the same product as firm X? As noted earlier, one of the three characteristics of a monopolistic market is high barriers to entry. They include legal barriers, a monopolist's extremely low average total costs, and a monopolist's exclusive ownership of a scarce resource.

Legal Barriers

Legal barriers to entry in a monopoly market include public franchises, patents, and copyrights. A **public franchise** is a right granted to a firm by government that permits the firm to provide a particular good or service and excludes all others from doing so. Potential competition is thus eliminated by law.

For example, as stated earlier, in many towns only one cable company is allowed to service a particular geographic area. This company has been given the exclusive right to produce and sell cable television. If an organization other than the designated company were to start producing and selling cable television, it would be breaking the law.

Another example of a legal barrier is the restriction the U.S. government has placed on private mail carriers. Only the U.S. Postal Service can deliver first-class mail. Also, some towns make it illegal for more than one company to collect trash.

In the United States, a patent is granted to the inventor of a product or process for 20 years. For example, a pharmaceutical company may have a patent on a medicine. During this time, the patent holder is shielded from competitors; no one else can legally produce and sell the patented product or process.

Copyrights give authors or originators of literary or artistic productions the right to publish, print, or sell their intellectual productions for a period of time. With books, either the author or the company that publishes the book holds the copyright. For example, the publishing company holds the copyright to this textbook—it owns the right to reproduce and sell copies of this book. Anyone else who copies the book or large sections of it to sell or simply to avoid buying a copy is breaking the law.

Extremely Low Average Total Costs (Low Per-Unit Costs)

Chapter 7 described average total cost as total cost divided by quantity of output, also called per-unit cost. For example, if total cost is $1,000 and quantity of output is 1,000 units, then average total cost is $1 per unit.

In some industries, firms have an average total cost that is extremely low—so low that no other firm can compete with this firm. To see why, let's consider the relationship of average total cost and price. A business will earn a per-unit profit when it sells its product for a price that is higher than its average total cost. For example, if price is

public franchise
A right granted to a firm by government that permits the firm to provide a particular good or service and excludes all others from doing so.

Teaching with Visuals

Yes, the cable TV company has probably been granted a legal monopoly for that area.

Critical Thinking

Assign students to research monopolies that have existed in the United States, including those discussed by the history teacher in the Cross-Curricular Activity at the bottom of page 195. Urge students to consider, as part of their research, whether each business created a barrier to prevent competitors from entering the market or whether the barrier was created by an outside force.

Reinforcement Activity

Direct students to list the three characteristics of a monopoly and give one example of a monopolistic market.

Internet Research

Have students search the Internet for an example of a patent or a copyright that has helped to provide an individual or a company with a monopoly. Tell students to write a one-page paper about that person or company. Ask students to examine how copyright or patent law provides a legal barrier to entry by the monopolist. Also ask students to explain what the time limitation is to the copyright or patent. Have students predict what will happen to the market for the product after its copyright or patent expires.

Economics in the Real World

After students read this feature, ask them why some college administrations grant monopolies to college bookstores. Students might suggest that the campus has space for only one bookstore or that the college is getting some benefit from the bookstore in order to enforce barriers to entering the market.

ANSWERS TO THINK ABOUT IT Answers will vary, but students could spend some time searching the Internet to help them answer this question. Ask students to share the results of their research with the class.

Background Information

Is the Internet the enemy of geographic monopolies? Imagine that you live in a small town in Italy, Japan, or the United States, and that this town has only one bookstore. The bookstore can be said to be a geographic monopoly—that is, it is the only seller of books within a certain geographical area. Enter the Internet. Now there is a substitute for the one bookstore in town (assuming you have an Internet connection), and the local store no longer has a monopoly.

Economics in the Real World

Will the Internet Bring an End to Monopolies?

Many college campuses have only one bookstore. Professors tell the campus bookstore manager the books they want their students to buy, and the bookstore orders the books. During the first weeks of classes, students usually go to the bookstore and buy the books they need. They often complain about the high price of textbooks; it is not uncommon for textbooks to sell for $100 or more.

Many college students feel that to a large degree, the campus bookstore acts as a monopolist. It is a single seller of a good (required textbooks) that has no substitutes (the student has to buy the book the professor is using in class, not a book that is similar). Usually the university administration will not allow more than one bookstore on campus (so barriers to entry are high). In a way, we might consider the campus bookstore a local or geographic monopoly: it is the single seller of a good with no good substitutes and high barriers to entry in a certain location—the university campus.

Enter the Internet, which has, to a large degree, destroyed many local or geographic monopolies. College students no longer have to buy their textbooks from their campus bookstore. They can buy them from an online bookstore such as Amazon.com, which often discounts the books it sells. In other words, the Internet essentially eliminates the barrier to entering any campus's textbook market.

Similarly, some people think that the Internet eliminates local monopolies in cars, although the case is less strong here. Suppose you live in a town with only one Ford dealership. It is true that the dealership may be the sole seller of Fords within a certain area (say, a radius of 40 miles), but substitutes for a Ford (for example, a Honda) are available. Nevertheless, it is possible for a single Ford dealership to have a certain degree of monopoly power. If you want a Ford, you are inclined to go to that Ford dealership.

Again, the Internet changes that situation. First, at various online sites you can obtain the invoice price of any car you are thinking about buying. Second, you can contact Ford dealers in nearby areas via the Internet and ask them if they are willing to sell you a Ford for, say, $1,500 over invoice price. Now, instead of negotiating with the only Ford dealership in town, you can negotiate with several dealerships over the Internet.

THINK ABOUT IT The Internet is used to weaken local (or geographic) monopolies in textbooks and cars. Can you identify any other kinds of local monopolies threatened by the Internet?

$10 and average total cost is $4, then per-unit profit is $6.

Some companies may have such a low average total cost that they are able to lower their prices to a very low level and still earn profits. Consequently, competitors may be forced out of business. Suppose 17 companies are currently competing to sell a good. One of the companies, however, has a much lower average total cost than the others. Say company A's average total cost is $5, whereas the other companies' average total cost is $8. Company A can sell its good for $6 and earn a $1 profit on each unit sold. Other companies cannot compete with it. In the end, company A, because of its low average total cost, is the only seller of the good; such a firm is called a **natural monopoly**.

natural monopoly A firm with such a low average total cost (per-unit cost) that only it can survive in the market.

Internet Research

Request that students find out how they would go about registering a patent and a copyright. They can visit the Web sites of the U.S. Patent and Trademark Office and the U.S. Copyright Office. Ask them to list the steps they would need to take to apply for each one and then explain the reasons why patents and copyrights exist and their effects on competition.

EXAMPLE: Three companies, A, B, and C, all sell a particular good. The per-unit costs of company A are $4 while the per-unit costs for B and C are $7. Currently, all three companies sell their good for a price of $10. In time, company A lowers its price to $6, but companies B and C cannot follow suit. For them to lower price to $6 would mean they would incur a $1 per-unit loss on each item they produce and sell. Because of its lower price, customers start buying from company A instead of from B and C. In time, companies B and C go out of business. ♦

Exclusive Ownership of a Scarce Resource

It takes oranges to produce orange juice. Suppose one firm owned all the oranges; it would be considered a monopoly firm. The classic example of a monopolist that controls a resource is the Aluminum Company of America (Alcoa). For a long time, this company controlled almost all sources of bauxite (the main source of aluminum) in the United States, making Alcoa the sole producer of aluminum in the country from the late nineteenth century until the 1940s.

Government Monopoly and Market Monopoly

Sometimes high barriers to entry exist because competition is legally prohibited, and sometimes they exist for other reasons. Where high barriers take the form of public franchises, patents, or copyrights, competition is legally prohibited. In contrast, where high barriers take the form of one firm's low average total cost or exclusive ownership of a resource, competition is not legally prohibited. In these cases, no law keeps rival firms from entering the market and competing, even though they may choose not to do so.

Some economists use the term *government monopoly* to refer to monopolies that are legally protected from competition. They use the term *market monopoly* to refer to monopolies that are not legally protected from competition.

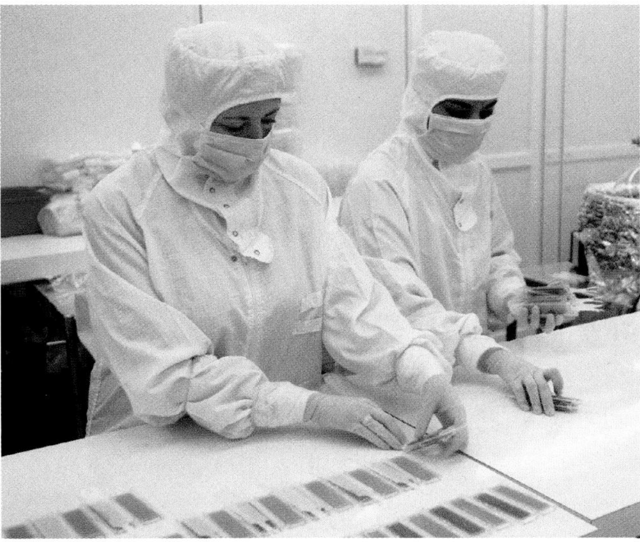

▲ Research companies often obtain patents on their products, which prevent other companies from entering the market for a specified time period. **Do you think such barriers to entry are necessary? Explain.**

Antitrust and Monopoly

One of the stated objectives of government is to encourage competition so that monopolists do not have substantial control over the prices they charge. Let's look briefly at some of the issues involved in maintaining competition.

Antitrust Laws

The government tries to meet its objectives through its **antitrust laws**, laws meant to control monopoly power and to preserve and promote competition. Following are descriptions of some of the major antitrust laws. Exhibit 8-2 provides a quick look at a time line for the implementation of these laws.

The Sherman Antitrust Act The Sherman Antitrust Act (or, simply, the Sherman Act) was passed in 1890, a time when there were numerous mergers between companies. A merger occurs when one company buys more than half the stock in another company, putting two companies under one top management. At the time of the Sherman Act, the organization that two companies formed by combining to act as a monopolist was called a *trust*, which in turn gave us the word *antitrust*.

antitrust law
Legislation passed for the stated purpose of controlling monopoly power and preserving and promoting competition.

Teaching with Visuals

Answers will vary, but students might say that the barriers to entry are necessary to allow companies to recover their research costs.

Reinforcement Activity

Ask students to write a one-page essay answering the following question: What do you consider the benefits and costs of a patent law that gives the inventor of a product or process a monopoly position for 20 years? Why would this be important to inventors? Students should see that patents provide incentives for inventors by virtually guaranteeing that they will be able to sell their inventions at higher prices than they would be able to charge in a perfectly competitive market.

Economics Around the Clock

After reading and discussing the first part of Section 2, direct students to reread the 7:34 P.M. scenario in Economics Around the Clock (page 187) and write an answer to the question that accompanies it.

Students should see that the concession firm operating in the baseball stadium has a monopoly on the sale of concessions. This means that it is a price searcher and can charge the highest price at which people are willing and able to purchase a sufficient amount of each type of food.

Cross-Curricular Activity

Team with a history teacher from your school to discuss both the economics and the technology involved in a historical example of government monopoly and market monopoly.

The history teacher might discuss the evolution of the steam engine from the first one built by Thomas Newcomen to those that powered steamboats such as Robert Fulton's steamboat and later steam locomotion.

You might encourage students to look at the economic impact of each of these innovations and at the resources that were used in producing these products.

Teaching with Visuals

Invite students to research the historical factors that contributed to the monopolies each of these antitrust acts was developed to break up. Then allow students to speculate about monopolies that might emerge owing to recent technological, legal, or other changes, as well as the laws that might be necessary to regulate them.

Reinforcement Activity

Allow students to look through newspapers and magazines to see if they can find any mention of antitrust activities. Two of the best newspapers and magazines to have students look through are the *Wall Street Journal* and *Fortune* magazine. Invite students to report their findings to the class.

Reinforcement Activity

Students can show they understand the four points of the Clayton Act by creating role-playing activities in which one of the points is acted out. For example, one student could act out a tying contract by telling a store owner that she will get a much better deal on pencils if she buys the paper, erasers, and pens as well.

EXHIBIT 8-2 Antitrust Acts

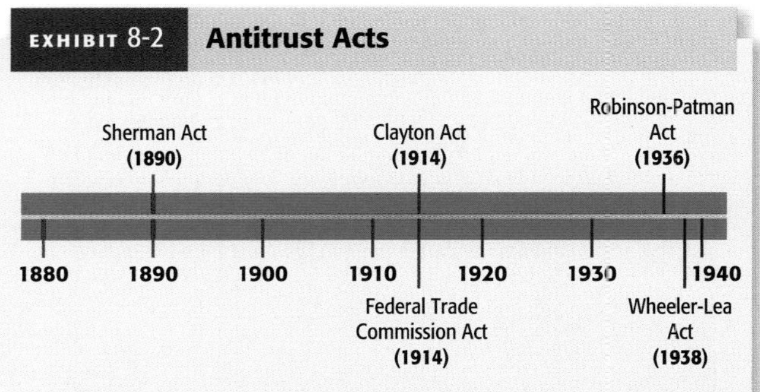

▲ Major antitrust acts in U.S. history include the Sherman Act, the Clayton Act, the Federal Trade Commission Act, the Robinson-Patman Act, and the Wheeler-Lea Act.

The Sherman Act contains two major provisions:

1. "Every contract, combination in the form of trust or otherwise, or conspiracy, in restraint of trade or commerce . . . is hereby declared to be illegal."
2. "Every person who shall monopolize, or attempt to monopolize, or combine or conspire with any other person or persons to monopolize any part of the trade or commerce . . . shall be deemed guilty of a misdemeanor."

Together, these two provisions state that either attempting to become a monopolist or trying to restrain trade is illegal.

The Clayton Act The Clayton Act of 1914 made certain business practices illegal when their effects "may be to substantially lessen competition or tend to create a monopoly." Here are two practices that were prohibited by the act:

1. *Price discrimination.* Price discrimination occurs when a seller charges different buyers different prices for the same product and when the price differences are not related to cost differences. For example, if a company charges you $10 for a product and charges your friend $6 for the same product, and there is no cost difference for the company in providing the two of you with this product, then the company is practicing price discrimination. (You will learn more about price discrimination near the end of the chapter.)
2. *Tying contracts.* A tying contract is an arrangement whereby the sale of one product depends on the purchase of some other product or products. For example, suppose the owner of a company that sells personal computers and computer supplies agrees to sell computers to a store only if the store owner agrees to buy paper, desk furniture, and some other products, too. This agreement is a tying contract, and it is illegal under the Clayton Act.

The Federal Trade Commission Act The Federal Trade Commission Act, passed in 1914, declared that "unfair methods of competition in commerce" were illegal. In particular, the act was designed to prohibit aggressive price-cutting acts, sometimes referred to as cutthroat pricing.

EXAMPLE: Suppose you own a business that produces and sells tires. A competitor begins to drastically lower the prices of the tires it sells. From your viewpoint, your competitor may be engaged in cutthroat pricing. From the viewpoint of the consumer, your competitor is simply offering a good deal. The FTC officials, who enforce the Federal Trade Commission Act, will have to decide. If they believe your competitor is cutting its prices so low that you will have to go out of business and that it intends to raise its prices later, when you're gone, they may decide that your competitor is violating the act. ♦

Some economists have noted that the Federal Trade Commission Act, like other antitrust acts, contains vague terms. For instance, the act does not precisely define what "unfair methods of competition" consist of. Suppose a hotel chain puts up a big, beautiful hotel across the street from an old, tiny, run-down motel, and the old motel ends up going out of business. Was the hotel chain employing "unfair methods of competition" or not?

The Robinson-Patman Act The Robinson-Patman Act was passed in 1936 in an attempt to decrease the failure rate of small businesses by protecting them from the competition of large and growing chain stores. At that time in our economic history, large chain stores had just arrived on the scene.

Internet Research

Direct students to search the Web using the keywords *monopolies, mergers,* and *antitrust,* to learn more about antitrust law. Ask students to identify a merger that is being discussed in the news, and to answer these questions about it: What are the names of the companies involved? Why are they merging? Who will control the new company formed by the merger?

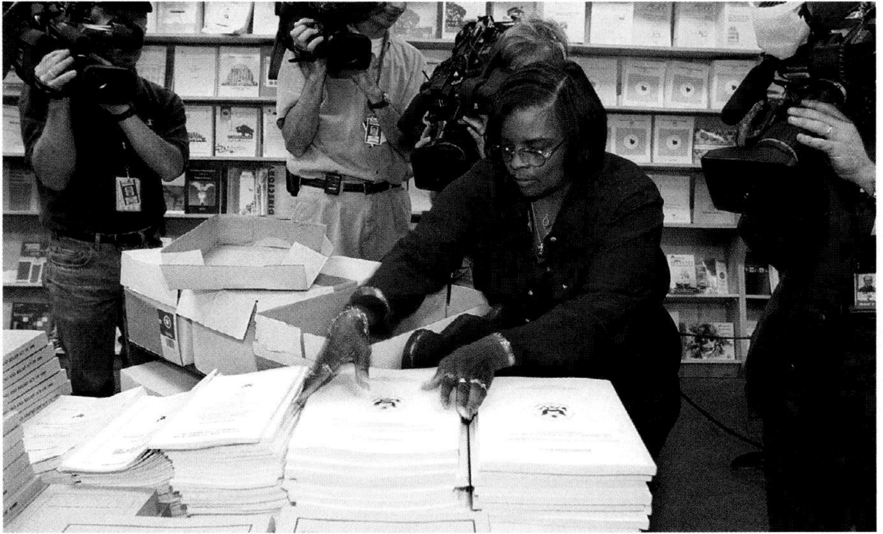

◀ Copies of Judge Thomas Penfield Jackson's ruling against Microsoft in November of 1999 were in high demand. The case was one of the major antitrust cases of the twentieth century. **What would a company have to do to be guilty of antitrust violations?**

They were buying goods in large amounts and were sometimes being offered price discounts from their suppliers. The chain stores began to pass on the price discounts to their customers. The small businesses were not being offered the price discounts and thus found it increasingly difficult to compete with the chain stores. The Robinson-Patman Act prohibited suppliers from offering special discounts to large chains unless they also offered the discounts to everyone else.

Many economists believe that rather than preserving and strengthening competition, the Robinson-Patman Act limited it. The act, they say, seemed more concerned about a particular group of competitors (small businesses) than about the process of competition.

The Wheeler-Lea Act The Wheeler-Lea Act, passed in 1938, empowered the Federal Trade Commission (FTC), a government agency, to deal with false and deceptive acts or practices by businesses. Major actions by the FTC in this area have involved advertising that the agency has deemed false and deceptive.

The Issue of Natural Monopoly

Instead of applying antitrust laws to natural monopoly, often what government does is impose some kind of regulation on the natural monopolist. For example, instead of allowing the natural monopoly to charge any price it wants, government often sets the price that the natural monopoly can charge. Alternatively, sometimes government specifies a certain rate of profit the natural monopoly can earn.

There are often unintended effects of government regulation of natural monopolists. For example, suppose government states that the natural monopolist can only charge a price of $2 above costs. If the natural monopolist knows that it can always charge a price of $2 higher than costs, it will have little, if any, incentive to keep its costs down. In the end, consumers may end up paying high prices because the natural monopolist knows that no matter what its costs are, it can always charge a price $2 higher (than costs). Similarly, if a natural monopoly is guaranteed a certain rate of profit, it will have little incentive to hold down its costs.

Are Antitrust Laws Always Applied Properly?

People are inclined, perhaps, to believe that when the government enforces the antitrust laws, it does so properly. Government may be seen as riding into the market on a white horse, preventing monopolies from running roughshod over consumers. In reality, the record of government in this area is mixed. Sometimes government,

Teaching with Visuals

A company would have to either enter into an agreement or conspiracy to restrain trade, or monopolize, attempt to monopolize, or conspire to monopolize any part of trade.

Discussion Starter

Antitrust laws are designed to create a free enterprise system that is open and competitive. Since the laws are applied by the government and the government is made up of people, it is very possible that the laws could be used to a political end. Invite students to discuss possible solutions to this problem. Challenge them to think of ways of ensuring that the laws are applied as intended.

Background Information: Price Discrimination

Price discrimination occurs when a seller charges different buyers different prices for the same product when the price differences are not related to cost differences. The Clayton Act deems price discrimination illegal when it substantially lessens competition. Students may find it interesting and fun to find examples of price discrimination. Ask students to come up with examples of when they think price discrimination should be allowed. For example, some people might say that if a medical doctor wants to charge a poor person for a medical visit, the doctor should be allowed to do so—even if this is an act of price discrimination. You may want to ask students what they think about this.

After students have read this feature, ask them to think about why the barriers to entry are so high and why this situation hasn't changed.

ANSWERS TO THINK ABOUT IT Students should agree. The high price of a taxi medallion keeps many people out of the taxi business. In turn, this keeps the supply of taxis lower. A lower supply results in higher taxi fares.

Reinforcement Activity

Have students research the cost of beginning and maintaining a taxi service in their own communities. Would the owner need a taxi medallion?

Discussion Starter

Ask students why it would matter if several universities charged the same tuition, paid the same salaries, and gave identical financial aid packages. What problems could arise? Students should see that, among other things, without competition among universities, prospective university students would face higher prices.

Application Activity

After reading and discussing Section 2, you may want to assign the Section Activity in the *Applying the Principles Workbook.*

Assess

Quick Quiz

The following true-or-false quiz will help you assess student understanding of the material covered in this section.

1. There is only one seller in a monopoly. (True)
2. Monopoly firms are price takers. (False)
3. A monopoly seller is not guaranteed profits. (True)
4. The Sherman Antitrust Act contains two major provisions. (True)
5. The Clayton Act of 1914 made price discrimination illegal. (True)

Why So Much for Such a Short Ride?

??????????????????

It is easy for new firms to enter some markets and difficult for them to enter others. Difficulty in entering a market is usually caused by the existence of some barrier to entry. Of course, not all barriers to entry are the same. One kind is created through legal means. For example, when the government specified that no firm can compete with the U.S. Postal Service in the delivery of first-class mail, it effectively created a legal barrier to entering the business of delivering first-class mail.

Suppose you go to New York City. You visit Rockefeller Center and Madison Square Garden; you take a tour of the Empire State Building and the Statue of Liberty; you go to a Broadway play at night. In your travels around New York City, you notice taxicabs picking up and delivering people. You wonder what you or anyone else would need to do to enter the taxicab market in New York City.

Let's list the things that sound reasonable. You would need a car and a driver's license. Perhaps the city of New York would want to make sure that you did not have a criminal record, so you might need to pass a personal background check.

In reality, the Taxi and Limousine Commission in New York City requires that you also have a taxi license, called a taxi medallion. It is similar to a business license: you need it to lawfully operate a taxicab business in New York City. In 2003 the price of a taxi medallion was $220,214.

The high price of a taxi medallion acts as a barrier to entering the taxicab market in New York City. Who gains and who loses as a result of this barrier to entry? The beneficiaries are clearly the current owners of taxicab businesses. Because of such a high barrier to entering the taxicab business, the supply of taxis on the streets of New York City is less than it otherwise would be. If supply is lower than it would be, then prices are higher. In other words, the price of a taxi ride in New York City is likely to be less if a taxi medallion cost, say, $300 than if it cost $220,000. At the latter price, fewer people will be entering the taxicab business and expanding the supply of taxis for hire. The losers are (1) people who would like to enter the taxicab business but cannot and (2) the taxi riders who pay higher prices because of the somewhat restricted entry into the taxicab business.

THINK ABOUT IT As a result of the high price of a taxi medallion, taxi fares are higher than they would be if taxi medallion prices were lower. Do you agree or disagree?

through its enforcement of the antitrust laws, promotes and protects competition, and sometimes it does not.

EXAMPLE: In 1967, the Salt Lake City–based Utah Pie Company charged that three of its competitors in Los Angeles were practicing price discrimination, which is deemed illegal by the Clayton Act. Specifically, the three competitors were charged with selling pies in Salt Lake City for lower prices than they were selling them near their plants of operation. The U.S. Supreme Court ruled in favor of Utah Pie.

What were the facts? Were the three competitors from Los Angeles running Utah Pie out of business? Were they hurting consumers by charging low prices? Some economists have noted that Utah Pie actually charged lower prices for its pies than did its competitors and that it continued to increase its sales volume and earn a profit during the time its competitors were supposedly exhibiting anticompetitive behavior. These economists suggest that Utah Pie was simply trying to use the antitrust laws to hinder its competition. ♦

Now consider a case in which most economists believe that the antitrust laws were applied properly. For many years, the upper-level administrators of some of the top universities—Brown, Columbia, Cornell, Dartmouth, Harvard, MIT, Princeton, University of Pennsylvania, and Yale—met to discuss such things as tuition, faculty salaries, and financial aid. There seemed to be evidence that these meetings occurred because the universities were trying to align tuition, faculty raises, and financial need. For example, one of the universities wanted to raise faculty salaries by more than the others but was persuaded not to do so. Also at these meetings, the administrators would compare lists of applicants to find the names of students who had applied to more than one of their schools (for example, someone might have applied to Harvard, Yale, and MIT). The administrators would then adjust their financial aid packages for that student so that no university was offering more than another.

▲ Richard Branson, CEO of Virgin Atlantic Airlines, testifies against an airline industry merger before a Senate subcommittee on antitrust in 2001.

The U.S. Justice Department charged the universities with a conspiracy to fix prices. Eight of the universities settled the case by agreeing to cease *colluding* (making secret agreements that effectively reduce competition) on tuition, salaries, and financial aid. MIT pursued the case to the U.S. Supreme Court. In 1992, the Supreme Court ruled against MIT, saying that it had violated antitrust laws.

SECTION 2 ASSESSMENT

Defining Terms

1. Define:
   a. barrier to entry
   b. natural monopoly
   c. price searcher
   d. antitrust law

Reviewing Facts and Concepts

2. When it comes to determining the quantity of goods to produce, how is a monopolist like a perfect competitor?
3. A monopolist is a price searcher. For what price is the monopolist searching?
4. A company advertises its product in a deceptive manner. Which antitrust act would apply to this action?

Critical Thinking

5. Firm A is a perfectly competitive firm, and firm B is a monopoly firm. Both firms are currently earning profits. Which firm is less likely to be earning profits in the future? Explain your answer.

Applying Economic Concepts

6. The demand for the good that firm A sells does not rise or fall during the month. Firm A raises its price at the beginning of the month and lowers its price at the end of the month. What might explain firm A's pricing behavior?

Assessment Book

You will find a quiz for this section in the *Assessment Book.*

Reteaching Activity

Use the Section Assessment to gauge which students may need reteaching on this section. Guide those students in reading the three conditions that characterize monopoly. Then ask students to provide examples of barriers to entry that might allow monopolies to thrive.

Guided Reading

For further reteaching of the key concepts in this section, assign the Outlining Activity and the Just the Facts Handout from the *Guided Reading and Study Guide.*

SECTION 2 ASSESSMENT ANSWERS

Defining Terms

1. a. barrier to entry: prohibits a firm from entering a market; **b. natural monopoly:** a firm that has such a low average total cost (per-unit cost) that it alone can survive in a market; **c. price searcher:** a seller that can sell some of its product at various prices; **d. antitrust law:** legislation passed to control monopoly power and preserve and promote competition.

Reviewing Facts and Concepts

2. Both a monopolist and a perfect competitor produce the quantity of output at which marginal revenue equals marginal cost.

3. The monopolist is searching for the best price to charge for the product it produces and sells. The best price turns out to be the highest per-unit price at which it can sell its entire output.

4. The Wheeler-Lea Act prohibits false advertising.

Critical Thinking

5. Firm A, the perfectly competitive firm, is less likely to be earning profits in the future. In perfect competition, there is easy entry into the market, whereas in monopoly, there are high barriers to entering the market. This difference matters. Firms will enter the perfectly competitive market, and, eventually, firm A's profits will decrease. Firms will be unable (or unlikely) to enter the monopoly market and compete away firm B's profits.

Applying Economic Concepts

6. Firm A may be a price searcher; the changes in the price of the good it sells may reflect its search for the best price.

Your Personal Economics

Discussion Starter

Ask students if any of them have ever seen something on the Internet or received a letter or an e-mail that seemed suspicious. What kind of offer was it? What seemed suspicious about it?

Research Activity

Have each student survey several adults they know to determine whether any have seen the type of scam discussed in the feature or some other type of scam. Students should find out the nature of the scam and whether any of the people they surveyed were victimized. Have students compile their data and report back to the class.

Your Personal Economics

Don't Fall for an Old Scam

One day you receive a letter in the mail. The letter is from an investment advisor who says that he can predict what will be good investments in the near future.

The Setup

At this point, like most people would be, you are skeptical. Having anticipated your skepticism, the investment advisor goes on to say in his letter that he is going to make a prediction about next week's price of gold. He predicts that it will rise. It costs you nothing to wait to see if the price of gold rises, so you do.

Next week, the price of gold rises. Soon after, you get another letter from the investment advisor. He reminds you that he wrote you last week and predicted a rise in the price of gold. He reminds you that things happened as he said they would. Just to prove to you, once again, that he can predict increases and decreases in the price of gold, he tells you that next week the price of gold will fall. Sure enough, the price of gold does fall the next week.

Again, you get a letter from the advisor. Again he reminds you that he correctly predicted the change in the price of gold in two consecutive weeks. He makes a third prediction. He predicts that next week the price of gold will rise again. Sure enough, he is right a third time.

The Hook

The final letter you get from the advisor reminds you that he predicted the change in gold in three consecutive weeks. He asks whether you are convinced that he can predict what will and will not be good investments. He also asks you for $1,000, after which he promises to send you a weekly update of his investment advice. He says that if you only follow his "crystal-ball advice" you can turn a little money into a lot.

Don't Be Fooled

Now if you are thinking that you should go along and send in the $1,000, think again. What the investment advisor has just done is make a promise to you that he cannot possibly keep. He can't really predict the good investments time after time.

But he's done it, you say. You saw him do it with your own two eyes. He didn't just say he could predict the change in the price of gold, he did it.

◀ Be skeptical of any get-rich offers you receive in the mail. If it sounds too good to be true, it probably is.

Cooperative Learning

Divide students into groups of three or four. Have each group look through magazines and newspapers to find three advertisements for questionable business ventures. Each group should discuss the characteristics of the offers. Have the groups compare and contrast the advertisements. How are they different? How are they similar?

▲ Even reputable newspapers and magazines contain ads for questionable business ventures. Investigate the company before giving them your money if you have any doubts.

How It Works

Here is how he did it. Before you got your first letter from the investment advisor, he wrote 10,000 letters. Half of the letters predicted an increase in the price of gold next week, and half predicted a decrease. The investment advisor kept a record of the people to whom he sent each letter. When the price of gold went up the next week, he then wrote the people who got the "price-is-going-up" letter again. He did not write to the "price-going-down" people.

In the second round of letters he predicted a rise in price to half the people and a decline in price to the other half. When the price of gold went down, he then wrote the people who got the "price-is-going-down" letter again, but did not write again to the "price-going-up" people.

He repeated this process one more time. To half of the people receiving the third round of letters he predicted another fall in the price of gold. To the other half he predicted a rise in the price of gold. When the price of gold rose, he then wrote the people who got the "price-is-going-up" letter—one of whom was you—and told you how he had predicted things correctly three times in a row. Then came the request for money—he urged you to pay him $1,000 for his investment advice.

So, you see, the investment advisor never really predicted anything. He just wrote a lot of letters, predicting a higher price of gold in half of the letters and predicting a lower price of gold in the other half. To the people who received the "correct prediction," he wrote again. He wasn't predicting the future, he was covering all bases. He was running a scam.

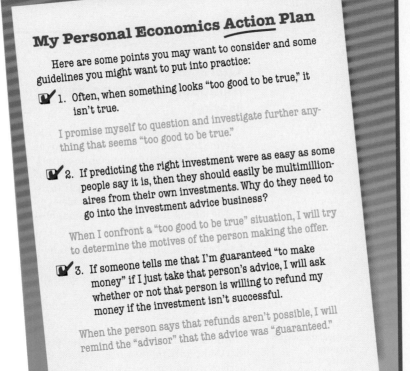

My Personal Economics Action Plan

Here are some points you may want to consider and some guidelines you might want to put into practice:

1. Often, when something looks "too good to be true," it isn't true.

   I promise myself to question and investigate further anything that seems "too good to be true."

2. If predicting the right investment were as easy as some people say it is, then they should easily be multimillionaires from their own investments. Why do they need to go into the investment advice business?

   When I confront a "too good to be true" situation, I will try to determine the motives of the person making the offer.

3. If someone tells me that I'm guaranteed "to make money" if I just take that person's advice, I will ask whether or not that person is willing to refund my money if the investment isn't successful.

   When the person says that refunds aren't possible, I will remind the "advisor" that the advice was "guaranteed."

Discussion Starter

Ask students the following questions about how they think the "scam industry" has changed because of the Internet and e-mail: Is it easier or more difficult for scammers to reach a large group of potential victims? How might the cost of operating scams have been affected by technology? Would it be easier or more difficult to stop the proliferation of questionable ventures sent by e-mail than by letter?

My Personal Economics Action Plan Discuss with students some of the common characteristics of scam offers. Invite students to brainstorm ways to identify and respond to questionable business ventures.

Chapter 8 Competition and Markets 205

SECTION 3

Teacher Support

Focus and Motivate

Section Objectives

After completing this section, students will be able to

- describe the characteristics of monopolistic competition;
- list some examples of monopolistic competition;
- explain why monopolistic competitors are price searchers;
- describe how monopolistic competitors answer questions about how much to produce and what price to charge; and
- explain the ways the products of monopolistic competitors differ.

Kickoff Activity

Define the term *oxymoron* as "a combination of contradictory words." Ask students to make a list of five to 10 oxymoronic expressions, such as "make haste slowly" and "a cruel kindness."

Activating Prior Knowledge

The previous section tells students that there is little or no competition in a monopoly. The title of this section, however, is not an oxymoron. Point out to students that *monopolistic competition* has a very specific definition in economics.

Teach

Discussion Starter

Assign students to read the characteristics of monopolistic competition. Then have them try to identify existing markets that have all these characteristics.

SECTION 3

A Monopolistic Competitive Market

Focus Questions

- What are the characteristics of monopolistic competition?
- What are some examples of monopolistic competition?
- Are monopolistic competitors price takers or price searchers?
- How do monopolistic competitors answer questions about how much to produce and what price to charge?
- What are some ways in which the products of monopolistic competitors differ?

Key Term

monopolistic competitive market

Characteristics of a Monopolistic Competitive Market

Between perfect competition at one extreme and monopoly at the other, there are two types of markets: monopolistic competitive and oligopolistic. In this section you will learn about monopolistic competition. In the next section we will examine oligopolies.

The three characteristics of a **monopolistic competitive market** are as follows:

1. The market includes many buyers and many sellers.
2. Firms produce and sell slightly differentiated products.
3. Firms have easy entry into and exit out of the market.

monopolistic competitive market
A market structure characterized by (1) many buyers and many sellers, (2) the production and sale of slightly differentiated products, and (3) easy entry into and easy exit from the market.

Notice that two of the characteristics (the first and third) are the same as found in a perfectly competitive market (a perfectly competitive market has many buyers and sellers and easy entry and exit). One characteristic (the second characteristic) is not found in either a perfectly competitive or monopolistic market.

Monopolistic Competitive Firms Are Price Searchers

Firms in a monopolistic competitive market are price searchers. Why do we consider them price searchers? Because they sell a slightly differentiated product.

Suppose firm A is a monopolistic competitive firm or seller. It is currently producing and selling good A at $40 per unit. At this price, it sells 1,000 units a week. If it raises its price to $45, it is likely to still sell some of its product (say, 700 units), because what it sells is not identical to any other product in the market. In other words, consumers will not be able to shift wholly from buying good A to buying an identical good; good A is slightly different from all other goods.

EXAMPLE: In many cities and towns, you will find a good number of Italian and Mexican restaurants. One restaurant that serves Italian-style food may be similar to, but not identical with, another restaurant that serves Italian-style food. These restaurants operate in a monopolistic competitive market. ♦

Cooperative Learning

Divide the class into groups of three or four. Have each group research a business that functions in a monopolistic competitive market and describe how the market possesses the three characteristics of monopolistic competitive markets. Once all the groups have presented their research, lead a class discussion that focuses on the similarities and differences among the businesses.

What Do Monopolistic Competitive Firms Do?

Like perfectly competitive firms and monopoly firms, monopolistic competitive firms have to answer two questions: (1) How much do we produce? and (2) What price do we charge? They answer the first question the same way every firm answers it: they produce the quantity of output at which marginal revenue equals marginal cost. They answer the second question the same way monopoly sellers answer it: by searching for the highest price per unit at which they can sell their entire output. If they produce 10,000 units of their good, they search for the highest per-unit price at which they can sell all 10,000 units.

▲ Do you think the owner of this restaurant is a price taker or a price searcher?

A Student Asks

QUESTION: *What use is it to me to know that one seller (say, a wheat farmer) operates in a perfectly competitive market and another seller (a restaurant) operates in a monopolistic competitive market?*

ANSWER: *What this information helps you understand is why the prices you pay are what they are. Suppose a number of sellers are selling a particular good for the same price. (Every seller is charging $100.) When some people see all the same prices, they sometimes jump to the conclusion that the sellers agreed among themselves to sell the good for the same price. In other words, people think they colluded on price. Of course, another explanation that you learned from our discussion of a perfectly competitive market is that all sellers sometimes sell the good for the same price because they have no other choice. In other words, no collusion is involved at all. It's just that the sellers are operating in a perfectly competitive market.*

Suppose you wonder why some medicines are priced as high as they are. Some of the high price has to do with the patents that pharmaceutical companies hold—patents that hold other sellers out of the market (for a period of time). Or suppose you learn that in your town only one cable company has the right to provide cable TV services. Would you have known how this type of monopoly would affect your monthly cable bill? Now you know that limiting entry to a market (for good reasons or bad reasons) always results in higher prices than would have existed had entry not been limited.

We do not expect that as the years pass, you will go around in your daily life pointing out which companies are perfectly competitive companies, and which companies are monopolists, and so on. That is not the reason for learning this material. The reason is to understand "how things work" in a part of the world that you might not have understood before.

How Are Monopolistic Competitors' Products Different?

When we say that one product is slightly *different* from another product, to what are we referring? When we say that McDonald's hamburgers are slightly different from Burger King's hamburgers, for example, the

Teaching with Visuals

The owner is a price searcher. Ask students to use the three characteristics of monopolistic competitive markets to explain how they know that restaurants in their communities compete in a monopolistic competitive market.

Clarifying Terms

The root *differ* means "not the same" so the term *differentiated* means "distinctive or different in nature." Remind students that they already know the words *different* and *differ,* which contain the same root.

Analyzing

Now that students have looked at three different types of markets, have them identify which market would be most advantageous if they went into business. From the class discussion, you will be able to determine whether students understand the differences among these three types of markets.

Background Information: Monopolistic Competitive Firms

Students are surrounded by monopolistic competitive firms every day of their lives. From gasoline to fast food, many markets exist in monopolistic competition. Ask students to answer the following questions about one product they have purchased in the last two weeks from a monopolistic competitive market: What other varieties of that same product exist? How do the other varieties compare in price? How can products that are only slightly different from each other have such a range of prices? Why did you choose to buy the particular product you did?

Reinforcement Activity

Brainstorm with students various ways that monopolistic competitors differentiate their products from one another, recording students' ideas on the board. Ask: What are the most common ways of differentiating products? Which are the most unique? Lead students to see how packaging, advertising, location, and other factors can make essentially similar products seem very different. Remind students that as long as customers perceive the products to be different, monopolistic competitors can still charge different prices for their goods.

Background Information

Students should be aware that all firms must answer the same two questions no matter in which type of market they compete: How much do we produce? and What price do we charge? The major difference between the three types of markets is how they answer those two questions. In a monopolistic competitive market, they answer the second question the same way that monopoly sellers do: by price searching.

Teaching with Visuals

Answers will vary. Students might suggest that cell phones differ in brand name, appearance, accompanying calling plans, and optional features.

word *different* refers to taste and appearance. McDonald's hamburgers look and taste slightly different (to most people) from Burger King's hamburgers. Products can differ in other ways, too. For example, consider a particular brand of gasoline sold at a gas station at Third Avenue and Main Street and at a gas station at Ninth Avenue and Main Street. Is the gasoline at the two stations identical? Certainly the physical properties are the same, but the gasoline is sold at different locations, and the locational differences may affect the choices of the buyers of the gasoline. For example, suppose the gas station at Third and Main is in a dangerous neighborhood, and the gas station at Ninth and Main is in a safe neighborhood. Consumers may perceive gas sold in a safe neighborhood as slightly different from gas sold in a dangerous neighborhood. In other words, the location at which a product is sold may be enough to differentiate one physically identical product from another.

Monopolistic competitors' products, then, can be different in any way that is perceived as different by consumers. If location makes a difference to consumers, then two physically identical products sold at different locations are slightly different products. If different credit terms, sales service, or delivery options make two physically identical products different in the minds of consumers, then they are slightly different products. In short, when it comes to buying products, the physical properties of a product may not be all that matters to consumers. How the product is packaged, where it is purchased, from whom it is purchased, and whether it is delivered may all matter (make a difference) to consumers.

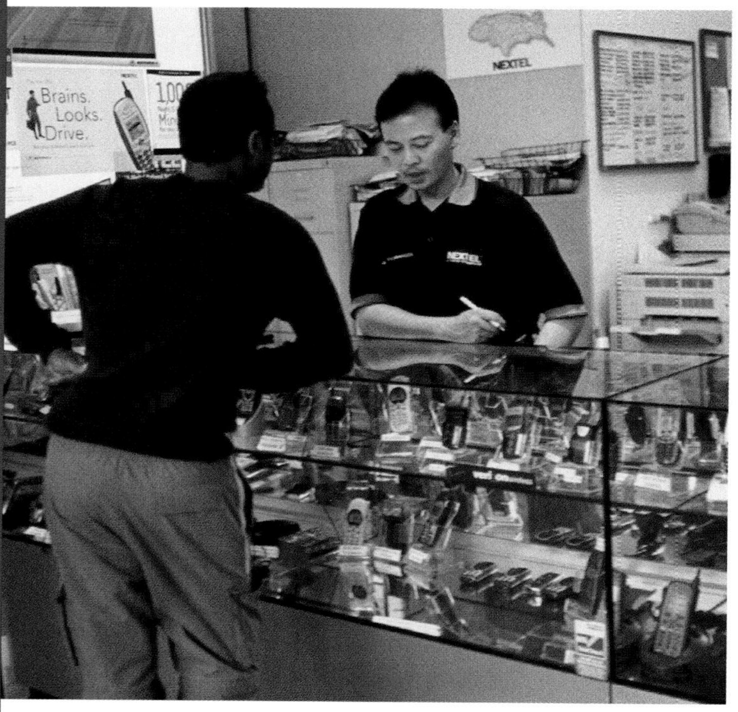

▼ Customers have many different features to choose from when buying a new cell phone. **In what ways might the phones differ, in addition to the features of the phone itself?**

Many Monopolistic Competitors Would Rather Be Monopolists

Suppose you own a business that is considered a monopolistic competitive firm. Your business is one of many sellers, you sell a product slightly differentiated from the products of your competitors, and entry into and exit from the industry is easy. Would you rather your business was a monopolist firm instead? Wouldn't it be better for you to be the only seller of a product than to be one of many sellers?

Most business owners would say it is indeed better to be a monopolist firm than a monopolistic competitive firm, because they believe that as a monopolist they would face less competition. How do monopolistic competitors go about trying to become monopolists?

Some monopolistic competitors use advertising. If a monopolistic competitor can, through advertising, persuade the buying public that its product is more than slightly differentiated from those of its competitors, it stands a better chance of becoming a monopolist. For example, many firms produce men's and women's jeans, and many people think the jeans produced by these firms look very much alike. How, then, does any one of the firms differentiate its product from the pack? Some companies add designer labels to their jeans to suggest that they are uniquely desirable.

Internet Research

Ask students to search the Internet for online stores that are involved in monopolistic competition with one another. For example, they might look for online music or bookstores. Have them explain the evidence suggesting monopolistic competition. Then ask them to explain how each store differentiates itself from its competition and what one of the stores could do if it wanted to become a monopoly in that market.

A Student Asks

QUESTION: *Are you suggesting that it is wrong or uneconomical to buy designer jeans?*

ANSWER: *Not at all. People may get "utility" or "satisfaction" from wearing designer jeans. It is not the job of the economist to tell consumers how they should get their satisfaction. Sometimes people buy, say, designer clothes because they feel it sets them apart from others, or because their friends are wearing designer clothes, or because they feel better about themselves if they are wearing a particular item with a monogram. We are not saying that any of these preferences are wrong. We are simply pointing out that sellers will sometimes try to differentiate their products (from their competitors' products) by adding a particular label, or coming up with a particular "motto" ("Just Do It"), and other such things. It is up to the consumer to decide whether the designer label, the motto, or anything else is worth the (sometimes) higher price. It might be a bland world indeed if all shirts were green, all jeans were the same cut, and all MP3 players were the same color.*

Go to www.emcp.net/bloomberg.com/ and find today's price of gold. Are the sellers of gold price takers or price searchers? Explain your answer. Next, go to Amazon.com in the United States (www.emcp.net/amazon.com) and in the United Kingdom (www.emcp.net/amazon_uk). Find the price of the most recent Harry Potter book in both pounds and dollars. Next, go to www.emcp.net/currency and find today's dollar price for a pound. Next, multiply it by the pound price of the Harry Potter book. Is the price of the Harry Potter book in the United States and the United Kingdom the same? On the day we looked, the dollar price of *Harry Potter and the Half-Blood Prince* was $17.99, and the pound price was £9.99. The dollar price of a pound was $1.8233. Multiplying $1.8223 by 9.99, we get $18.20. In other words, Harry Potter was selling for $17.99 in the United States and for $18.20 in the United Kingdom.

What Matters Is How Much Competition a Seller Faces

One of the major differences between sellers in different types of markets is how much competition a seller in each market faces. How much competition a seller faces—much, some, very little, none—principally depends on two factors: how close to unique a seller's product is, and how easy it is for new sellers to enter the market.

In a perfectly competitive market, a seller does not produce and sell a unique product at all: it produces and sells a product *identical* to that of other sellers. This means the seller is in a competitive position. If it raises the price of its product by only one penny over equilibrium price, consumers can turn to other sellers to purchase the identical product. A seller in a perfectly competitive market faces stiff competition from other sellers currently in the market, as well as potentially stiff competition from new sellers who may join the market. After all, a perfectly competitive market has easy entry into the market.

Things are somewhat different for the monopolistic competitive seller. This seller does not face as much competition from current sellers, because it produces and sells a product that is slightly different from that of other sellers. A rise in the price of its good will not cause all its customers to leave it and head for its competitors. Still, the monopolistic competitor has the same problem as the perfect competitor when it comes to potential

◀ **Why might a jean manufacturer create a designer label for its jeans?**

A Student Asks

Explore the value that students place on various company logos and mottos, by asking students how much more they would be willing to pay to get a brand-name product.

Teaching with Visuals

Some companies add designer logos to suggest that their jeans are uniquely desirable—in other words, to differentiate them in the market.

Have students read this feature on page 210 and discuss why taxes might be higher in Sweden and Belgium than in other nations. Help students make the connection between higher taxes and more government services.

ANSWERS TO ECONOMIC THINKING Answers will vary. Students might suggest that nations with high taxes will be forced to lower their tax rates to keep companies and workers in their country. On the other hand, countries that use higher tax revenues to provide better services to citizens might attract more citizens that way.

Teaching with Visuals

In response to the photo on page 210, students should say that the painkiller market is monopolistic competitive. Types of painkillers are slightly differentiated and sell for different prices.

Application Activity

After reading and discussing Section 3, you may want to assign the Section Activity in the *Applying the Principles Workbook.*

Cooperative Learning

Divide the class into groups of three or four and have each group pick a type of good. Remind students to look not only at physical products like hats and bicycles, but also at services like movie theaters and automobile mechanics. Then have each group formulate a list of ways that monopolistic competitors differentiate their versions of this good or service. If students notice that companies—for example, movie theaters—sell the exact same good for different prices, ask them how that can be. Have each group present its findings to the class.

Assess

Quick Quiz

The following true-or-false quiz will help you assess student understanding of the material covered in this section.

1. There are many buyers and sellers in monopolistic competition. (True)
2. Monopolistic competitive firms are price searchers. (True)
3. Location can be a differentiating factor in two products. (True)
4. Most monopolistic competitors would rather be monopolies. (True)
5. A monopoly seller faces less competition than a monopolistic competitor. (True)

Assessment Book

You will find a quiz for this section in the *Assessment Book.*

Reteaching Activity

Use the Section Assessment to gauge which students may need reteaching on this section. Have those students create a chart that shows the conditions for each type of market. In both markets, there are many sellers and buyers, and entry into and exit from the market are easy. The difference is that in monopolistic competition, firms produce slightly different products, and in perfect competition, the products are identical.

Guided Reading

For further reteaching of the key concepts in this section, assign the Outlining Activity and the Just the Facts Handout from the *Guided Reading and Study Guide.*

Lower Taxes?

In 2001, a worker in Belgium paid 55 cents in taxes out of every $1 earned. In the same year, a worker in Ireland paid 25 cents in taxes out of every $1 earned. Going back a few years, in the late 1990s, several major Swedish companies said they were likely to leave Sweden because taxes were high. Mainly they were talking about taxes on personal income (earned by workers and owners of the companies). In Sweden, in 2001, a worker paid 48 cents in taxes for every $1 earned. Keep in mind that a job activity that requires only a computer screen, a telephone, and a modem can be located anywhere in the world. Today, with lower telecommunication costs, companies and workers find it easier to locate anywhere in the world. They have an increased ability to "vote with their feet," which means if they don't like it one place, they can move somewhere else.

ECONOMIC THINKING Will this increased ability to vote with one's feet, which is a characteristic of globalization, cause taxes in many high-tax countries to drop? Might the high-tax country lower its taxes in order to keep companies and workers in the country?

competitors because of easy entry into a monopolistic competitive market, just as in a perfectly competitive market. New sellers can be just around the corner waiting to take away some of a current monopolistic competitor's business.

▲ How would you categorize the pain killer market—perfectly competitive, monopoly, or monopolistic competitive? Explain.

How much competition does a monopoly seller face? It faces less competition than either a perfect competitor or a monopolistic competitor. It sells a product that has no close substitutes. Consumers buying from monopoly sellers have fewer options available to them than they do when they buy from perfect competitors or monopolistic competitors. For example, if a monopolistic competitor raises price too high, provides poor service, or lowers quality, many consumers will choose to walk away and buy from the seller's competition. It's not that easy to walk away from a monopoly seller, because no sellers sell a close substitute for the monopoly seller's products. In short, the monopoly seller does not have to be afraid of competition, because it really doesn't have much. Furthermore, competition is not likely to increase because of barriers to entering the monopoly market.

Section 3 Assessment

Reviewing Facts and Concepts

1. What three conditions characterize a monopolistic competitive market?
2. How might monopolistic competitors' products be slightly different?
3. A monopolistic competitive market shares some things with a perfectly competitive market and some things with a monopolistic market. Explain.

Critical Thinking

4. In what way or ways are a monopolist, a monopolistic competitor, and a perfect competitor alike?

Applying Economic Concepts

5. Identify an action of a real-world monopolistic competitor that is trying to turn itself into a monopolist.

Section 3 Assessment Answers

Reviewing Facts and Concepts

1. Monopolistic competitive markets are characterized by many buyers and many sellers, slightly differentiated products, and easy entry into and exit from the market.
2. They can be different in any way that is perceived as different by consumers. Factors may include location, service, or perceived quality.
3. In both monopolistic competition and perfect competition there are many buyers and many sellers, along with easy entry into and exit from the market. In both monopolistic competition and monopoly, firms are price searchers.

Critical Thinking

4. There are many ways in which they are alike: Both try to maximize profit, try to minimize cost, want to sell their output for the highest price possible, and produce the quantity of output at which marginal revenue is equal to marginal cost. You may want to give students full credit if they identify any two ways in which the various sellers are alike.

Applying Economic Concepts

5. Answers will vary. Answers should relate to an attempt to get a product to be perceived by buyers as unique.

210 Chapter 8 Competition and Markets

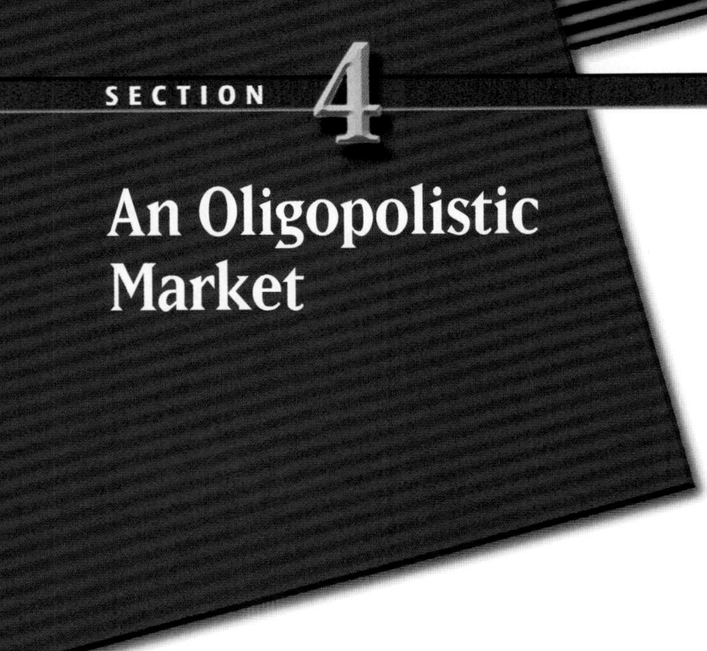

SECTION 4

An Oligopolistic Market

Focus Questions

- What are the characteristics of an oligopolistic market?
- What are some examples of an oligopolistic market?
- Are sellers in an oligopolistic market price takers or price searchers?
- What are cartel agreements?

Key Terms

oligopolistic market
cartel agreement
price discrimination

Characteristics of an Oligopolistic Market

The following three conditions characterize an **oligopolistic market**:

1. It has few sellers.
2. Firms produce and sell either identical or slightly differentiated products.
3. The barriers to entry are significant, which means that entry into the market is difficult.

Exhibit 8-3 lists the conditions that characterize each of the four markets discussed in this chapter.

Oligopolistic Firms Are Price Searchers

Like monopolistic and monopolistic competitive firms, oligopolistic firms are price searchers. In other words, they have some control over the price they charge. They can raise the price of their good and still sell some of the good they produce (which is not the case for a price taker).

How Much Competition Do Oligopolists Face?

The last section developed a way to think about sellers in various markets. We think about, or categorize, sellers according to *how much* competition they face. In turn, how much competition a seller faces depends on how close to unique a seller's product is and how easy it is for new sellers to enter the market and compete with it. With this information as background, let's discuss oligopoly.

How close to unique is an oligopolist's product? According to the conditions that characterize oligopoly, an oligopolist's product is not unique. Some oligopolists produce an identical good (e.g., steel), and others produce a slightly differentiated product (e.g., cars). We would expect, then, that an oligopolistic seller faces fairly intense competition from current sellers. For example, Ford Motor Company faces stiff competition from General Motors. In the world market for cars, Ford faces extremely stiff competition from Japanese

oligopolistic market
A market structure characterized by (1) few sellers, (2) the production and sale of either identical or slightly differentiated products, and (3) significant barriers to entry.

Cooperative Learning

Divide the class into three groups and assign each one of the three following industries to research: breakfast cereal, farm machinery, and soaps and detergents. Each group should research how well that industry meets the three conditions that characterize oligopoly. They should also list the names of the firms that dominate the particular industry and some of the products produced with their specific prices. Encourage the groups to prepare oral reports with visual aids.

SECTION 4

Teacher Support

Focus and Motivate

Section Objectives

After completing this section, students will be able to

- describe the characteristics of an oligopolistic market;
- list some examples of an oligopolistic market;
- explain whether sellers in an oligopolistic market are price takers or price searchers; and
- explain what cartel agreements are.

Kickoff Activity

Write the following statement on the board for students to answer: "Write the names of five U.S. car manufacturers."

Activating Prior Knowledge

List the names of U.S. car manufacturers on the board as students volunteer them. Point out to students that there are relatively few manufacturers producing the vast number of cars in the United States. Explain to students that these manufacturers are oligopolists, and that in this section they will learn more about oligopoly markets.

Teach

Discussion Starter

For each characteristic of oligopoly listed here, ask students if that particular characteristic is more closely associated with perfect competition or monopoly. You may want to refer students to Exhibit 8-3 to see a direct correlation among the four types of markets.

Teaching with Visuals

In class, invite students to name between 10 and 20 large and small items found in most households, including automobiles, televisions, washing machines, and toothbrushes. Ask students to decide in which market structure these items are sold.

Reinforcement Activity

One of the most famous oligopolies in the U.S. economy is the soft drink market. Two companies, the Coca-Cola Company and PepsiCo, control approximately 75% of the soft drink market through a pure oligopoly. They control the majority of brand names that you see in restaurants and supermarkets. To show that oligopolies can sell identical to slightly differentiated products, stage the famous blind cola taste test. Ask students how different the products actually are and how these companies truly differentiate their products.

EXHIBIT 8-3 Conditions That Characterize Various Markets

Market	Number of sellers	Type of product	Barriers to entry	Control over price	Examples of products and services sold in this type of market
Perfectly competitive	Many	Identical	No barriers	No control	Wheat, corn, stocks
Monopolistic	One	Unique	Extremely high barriers	Considerable amount of control	Water, electricity, delivery of first-class mail
Monopolistic competitive	Many	Slightly differentiated	No barriers	Yes, but not as much as in monopoly	Clothing, meals at restaurants
Oligopolistic	Few	Identical or slightly differentiated	Significantly high barriers	Yes, but not as much as in monopoly	Cars, cereal

car companies such as Toyota, Nissan, Honda, and Mitsubishi.

Where the oligopolistic seller does not face too much competition is from potential sellers. It is difficult to enter an oligopolistic market, so current oligopolistic sellers are shielded from new sellers to some degree.

A Student Asks

QUESTION: *I always thought that the more sellers in a given market (for example, the more sellers of, say, computers), the more competition in that market. Now it sounds like there can be quite a bit of competition in a market even with only two or three sellers. Is this statement correct?*

ANSWER: *Yes. Competition can exist in a market with three sellers and with 300 sellers. For example, think back to the days of only three television networks: ABC, NBC, and CBS. The three networks stiffly competed with each other. Today more competition in the television market exists largely because of cable. Still, the television market experienced competition before cable.*

Identifying Oligopolistic Industries

Economists determine whether a market is oligopolistic by looking at the percentage of sales accounted for by the top four firms in the industry. If only a few firms account for a large percentage of sales, then the market is considered oligopolistic. For example, suppose an industry consists of 10 firms, and the total revenue of the industry is $100 million. The four firms with the highest sales generate $80 million in revenue. In other words, the top four firms account for 80 percent of total revenues in the industry (because $80 million is 80 percent of $100 million), and the industry is dominated by the top four firms. It is an example of an oligopolistic market.

Now consider a real-world example. The U.S. automobile industry is largely made up of General Motors, Ford Motor Company, and Chrysler (or DaimlerChrysler) Corporation. Together, these three firms account for about 90 percent of American-made cars sold in the United States. Other examples of oligopolistic markets include industries that produce cigarettes, tires and inner tubes, breakfast cereals, farm machinery, and soap and detergents.

Differentiating Instruction

Kinesthetic and Visual Learners

Invite students to create their own versions of the table in Exhibit 8-3. Encourage students to use visuals to trigger their memories of each market's characteristics. For example, students might create a three-dimensional table with actual products as samples. Decorate your room with these representations of the exhibit.

212 Chapter 8 Competition and Markets

Oligopoly and Interdependence: Looking over Your Shoulder

Oligopoly differs from other market structures in terms of the number of sellers. Both perfectly competitve and monopolistic competitive markets include many sellers, and a monopolistic market has only one seller. Only an oligopolistic market consists of a *few* sellers.

Will a seller act differently if it is one of only a few sellers than if it is one of many? Some evidence indicates that when a seller is one of only a few sellers, it is more likely to base its behavior on what other sellers do than if it is one of many sellers. Consider the airline market, which is considered to be oligopolistic. If one airline lowers its ticket prices, other airlines are likely to do the same.

▲ The cereal market is an oligopolistic market. **Can you name the firms that dominate this market?**

Cartels

It is easier for the few sellers in an oligopolistic market to get together and discuss common issues than for the many sellers in either a perfectly competitive or a monopolistic competitive market to do the same. Why would sellers that compete with each other want to get together in the first place? One of the various reasons may be that they want to try to eliminate or reduce the competition they present to one another.

Each year, the three major car companies compete with one another on such things as price, quality, style, and service. Over the years they realized that the competition between them actually helps the car consumer and hurts them. In the boardroom of one of the car companies, the chief executive officer (CEO) says, "Every time our competitors lower prices, we have to do the same thing; every time they come up with a new sport utility vehicle or a better or safer sedan, we have to do the same thing. All this competition is great for the consumer, but it's not so good for our profits."

Suppose the CEO calls a meeting with the CEOs at the other two major car companies. They get together for a nice lunch somewhere and talk over their problems. At the end of the lunch they all agree that the competition among them is helpful to consumers but not so helpful to them, so they should try to reduce some of this competition. Specifically, they decide to keep prices where they currently are (no more discounts) and to stop coming up with new car models for the next two years.

The three CEOs have entered into a **cartel agreement**, an agreement that specifies that they will act in a coordinated way to reduce the competition among them and (they hope) raise their profits. In the United States, cartel agreements are illegal. But suppose that they were not illegal, so nothing prevented the CEOs from making the cartel agreement. What then? Many people would say that the CEOs would be successful at reducing their competition and increasing their profits. In other words, the cartel agreement would harm consumers and help the three car companies.

This answer assumes that the three car companies would actually hold to the cartel agreement. However, firms that enter into cartel agreements often break them. To see why, put yourself in the place of one of the

cartel agreement
An agreement that specifies how the firms that entered into the agreement will act in a coordinated way to reduce the competition among them.

Teaching with Visuals

Students will probably name General Mills and Kellogg.

Background Information

Note that the four market structures discussed in this chapter have names that may counter the expectations of laypeople. For example, consider perfect competition and oligopoly. The layperson understands competition in an oligopolistic market better than in a perfectly competitive market. Everybody knows that car companies compete with each other, but rarely do we think of a farmer (a seller in a perfectly competitive market) competing with another farmer.

Discussion Starter

Encourage students to identify as many oligopolistic markets as they can. What do these markets have in common? Do they have all of the characteristics of true oligopolies?

Internet Research

Tell students to visit www.emcp.net/autobytel.com and search by make of car. Students should choose one or two makes and compare the cars made by different companies. How similar or different are the cars in each category? What characteristics of oligopoly do students notice when comparing these car models? Have them find one car that appears significantly different from the others and determine what the manufacturer did to differentiate this car from others manufactured by companies in the oligopoly.

Teaching with Visuals

Answers will vary, but students might say that cartels would reduce competition and harm consumers.

Discussion Starter

Invite students to imagine that they are major producers of personal and handheld computers. Ask them what the advantages and disadvantages would be to forming a computer cartel.

▲ The Organization of Petroleum Exporting Countries (OPEC) is a cartel. Here OPEC president, Indonesian oil minister Purnomo Yusgiantoro, opens an OPEC meeting at its headquarters in Vienna. **Why do you think cartels are illegal in the United States?**

three automobile company CEOs. You return to your office after lunch with the other CEOs. You start to think about the cartel agreement you just entered into and say to yourself, "I know I promised not to lower prices and not to develop any new model cars, but suppose I forget what I promised. Suppose I develop new car models and release them to the market next year. If my competitors hold to the cartel agreement, they will not release new models next year, and I will be the only car company with new models. My company should be able to take business away from our competitors. Instead of not competing with my competitors, why don't I just try to run them out of business?"

> ***"People of the same trade seldom meet together, even for merriment and diversion, but the conversation ends in a conspiracy against the public, or in some contrivance to raise prices."***
>
> —Adam Smith

Each of the CEOs feels a strong monetary incentive to break the promise made with the other CEOs. Each is likely to break the agreement in the hope of getting rid of his or her competition, once and for all. If all three break the agreement out of self-interest, the agreement is gone. The three car companies are back where they started, competing with each other.

Even if cartel agreements were not illegal, they probably would not be much of a problem for consumers. Certainly sellers in the same market might try to make cartel agreements and would want them to hold, but it is not likely that they would hold. After all, once the agreement was made, each seller that entered into it would feel a sharp monetary incentive to break it and make itself much better off at the expense of its competitors. It's nearly impossible for companies to turn their backs on the chance to get rid of their competition.

Is It Buyers Against Sellers or Sellers Against Sellers?

The noneconomist may think that the best interests of consumers or buyers are pitted against the best interests of producers or sellers. They may believe that buyers want to buy high-quality products at low prices. Sellers want to produce cheap products and sell them for high prices. Whatever is good for buyers is bad for sellers, and whatever is good for sellers is bad for buyers. In short, buyers and sellers are on different sides of the fence; it's sellers against buyers.

Putting things this way makes it sound as if buyers and sellers are natural enemies and always at war. However, this view does not accurately represent the forces at work. The real war may not be between buyers and sellers but among sellers. Sellers may indeed be on one side of the fence and buyers on the other side, but not all the sellers on the same side of the fence are happy with one another. Some want to get rid of other sellers so that there will be fewer sellers on the selling side of the fence. General Motors wants to get rid of Toyota so there will be fewer car companies. Dell wants to get rid of Hewlett-Packard so there will be fewer computer manufacturers. NBC wants to get rid of CBS; and NBC, CBS, and ABC wish that cable television had never come to exist.

Sellers may (initially) have interests opposed to those of consumers, but it does not mean sellers will get what they want at the expense of consumers. Often, what keeps sellers in line is other sellers—either other sellers currently in the market or sellers who

Differentiating Instruction

Enrichment and Extension

OPEC (the Organization of the Petroleum Exporting Companies) is one of the most powerful cartels in the world. It controls a large percentage of the world's oil supply and has done so since the 1960s. Assign some of your more advanced students to research the OPEC countries and see what effects OPEC has had on the world's oil market. Allow students to share their results with the class.

may one day enter the market. In other words, it is the threat of actual or potential competition from other sellers that ends up aligning the interests of sellers with buyers. It is competition between sellers that keeps downward pressure on prices (sellers want to underprice their competitors) and on costs (if sellers can lower their costs, then they have a better chance of outcompeting their competitors).

A Student Asks

QUESTION: *What about underhanded, manipulative sellers who try to scam buyers?*

ANSWER: *Probably all buyers have come across sellers that haven't told them everything they would like to know about a product, or tried to get them to buy something they might not have wanted, or tried to cheat them in some way. Nothing we have said is meant to imply that unscrupulous sellers do not exist. What we are suggesting, though, is that what essentially keeps sellers in line, and trying to serve the buying public, is not a seller's "big heart," but the competition it faces from other sellers. In other words, fewer sellers and less competition would mean a lot more "underhanded, manipulative sellers" in the world.*

Price Discrimination

Price discrimination exists when a seller charges different prices to different buyers, and the price differences do not reflect cost differences. Suppose a movie theater charges children $4 to see a movie and charges adults $8 to see a movie. If the movie theater experiences absolutely no cost difference when it comes to children and adults, this situation would be an example of price discrimination.

Now suppose a company runs two small grocery stores: one on the east side of town and one on the west side of town. In the grocery store on the east side of town it charges $3 for a loaf of bread, but on the west side of town it charges $2.50 for the same loaf of bread. Is this situation an example of price discrimination? Well, it could be, but not necessarily. In this town, the crime rate is higher on the east side than on the west side, which means the insurance rates for the company are higher on the east side of town. As a result, it may be more costly to sell bread on the east side of town than on the west side of town, and this higher cost is reflected in the higher price of bread on the east side of town. The difference in price here is not an example of price discrimination.

When we have price discrimination, though, we need to ask two important questions: (1) Why would a seller want to price discriminate? (2) Under what conditions can a seller price discriminate?

price discrimination
Practice by which a seller charges different prices (to different buyers) for the product it sells when the price differences do not reflect cost differences.

Why Discriminate?

A seller would want to price discriminate if it increased total revenue. Look at the following three points on a market demand curve.

Point	Price	Quantity demanded
A	$10	1
B	8	2
C	6	3

As you can see, price and quantity demanded move in the opposite direction according to the law of demand, which says that more is purchased at lower prices than at higher prices.

▼ **Would CNN's coverage of news events, such as Barack Obama's speech at the Democratic National Convention in 2004, improve or decline if Fox News and MSNBC went off the air?**

Discussion Starter

Competition between sellers can be quite obvious. In recent years, the two major soft drink companies have developed advertising campaigns directed against one another. Invite students to name other markets where the sellers have used advertising to downgrade their competition.

A Student Asks

Ask students to think of examples of ways that competition keeps sellers "in line."

Teaching with Visuals

Answers will vary. Students might say that the quality of CNN's coverage of news events might decline with less competition.

Cooperative Learning

Divide students into groups of three or four. Ask each group to find an example of price discrimination in your community. Ask the groups to answer two questions: Why does the seller discriminate, and What conditions make it possible for the seller to do so? Explain to students that these two questions are essential to understanding why price discrimination occurs.

Economics *in the* Real World

After students have read this feature, ask them to suggest reasons why some people believe that coupon clipping is not worth their time. How might such people otherwise spend their time?

ANSWERS TO THINK ABOUT IT Answers will vary, but students might suggest that people in their late sixties might be more likely to use coupons because many are on a fixed income and because they typically have more free time than do people in their thirties.

Clarifying Terms

Check students' understanding of the following term by asking them to use it in a sentence: *discrimination* (to show prejudice against someone or something). Challenge students to use the term in a way that is not necessarily negative.

Economics Around the Clock

After reading the introductory paragraphs to the section "Price Discrimination" (page 215), direct students to reread the 10:04 A.M. scenario in Economics Around the Clock (page 187) and to write an answer to its question.

Students may point out that when a publisher produces a more expensive hardcover edition first, it hopes to attract both buyers who are willing to pay more for it and buyers who would rather pay less for a paperback but don't want to wait. By later offering the paperback edition to satisfy those who are willing to wait for it, the publisher covers a broad market and maximizes revenue.

Economics *in the* Real World

Do You Sometimes Choose to Pay Higher Prices?

As you know, one of the conditions of price discrimination is that the seller be able to distinguish among customers who would be willing to pay different prices.

Ask yourself whether people who value their time highly are more willing to pay a higher price for a product than people who do not. Some sellers think so. They argue that people who place a high value on their time want to economize on the shopping time connected with the purchase of the product. If sellers want to price discriminate between these two types of customers—charging more to customers who value time more and charging less to customers who value their time less—they must determine the category into which each of their customers falls.

How would you go about making this determination if you were a seller? What many sellers do is place cents-off coupons in newspapers and magazines. They think that people who value their time relatively low will spend it clipping and sorting coupons. People who place a relatively high value on their time will not.

In effect, the process works in a similar way at your local grocery store.

- The posted price for all products is the same for all customers.
- Both Linda and Josh put the cereal in their shopping carts.
- When Linda goes through the checkout, the clerk asks her if she has any coupons. Linda says no, so Linda pays the posted price.
- When Josh goes through the checkout, he says he has a coupon for the cereal, and so he ends up paying a lower price than Linda paid.

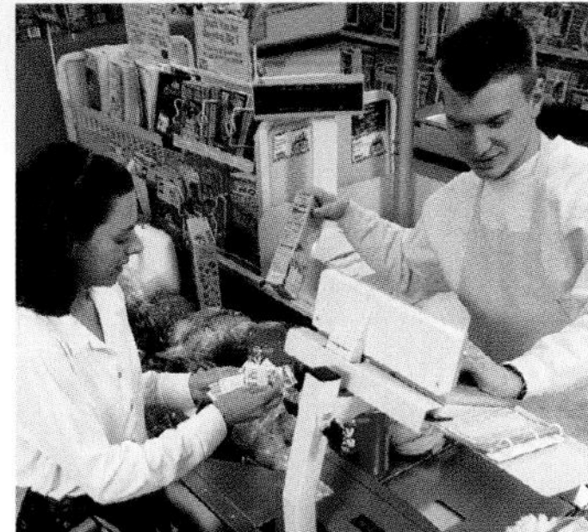

THINK ABOUT IT Do you think that people in their thirties are more or less likely to use coupons than people in their late sixties? Explain your answer.

Now suppose the seller can only charge one price and wants to sell 3 units of the good. What price will the seller charge? The answer is $6, because only at $6 will 3 units of the good be purchased. (If the seller charges $8, only 2 units will be purchased.) The total revenue for this seller is $18, which is the price of the good ($6) times the quantity bought (3).

Now suppose this seller can price discriminate, or charge one price to one buyer and a different price to another buyer. The seller will charge one buyer $10 (because from our table we know that at least one buyer is willing and able to pay $10 for the good—after all, we can see that the quantity demanded is 1 at a price of $10), and then charge another buyer $8 (because we know that that the price of the good has to be $8 before another person will buy the good). The seller charges a third person $6 (because we know that the price of the good has to be $6 before a third person will buy the good). What is the seller's total revenue now? It is the sum of $10 and $8 and $6, or $24.

In other words, if the seller does not (or cannot) price discriminate, and charges the same price to all customers, total revenue is $18. But if the seller can and does price discriminate, charging different prices to different customers, total revenue increases by $6 to a total of $24.

Background Information: Price Discrimination and the Clayton Antitrust Act

The Clayton Antitrust Act of 1914 made certain business practices, including price discrimination, illegal. The law prohibits "any person engaged in commerce…to discriminate in price between different purchasers of commodities of like grade and quality…where the effect of such discrimination may be substantially to lessen competition or tend to create a monopoly in any line of commerce."

The Clayton Act was passed to supplement the Sherman Antitrust Act. Many legal cases were brought under the Clayton Act to curb price discrimination and other conduct considered unlawful under its provisions.

It would seem, then, that every seller in the world would want to price discriminate. In fact, every seller does want to price discriminate—but not every seller can. Certain conditions must be present.

Factors Allowing Price Discrimination

First, different customers must be willing and able to pay different prices for a good. In other words, one person is willing and able to pay $10 for the good, but another person is only willing and able to pay $8 for the good.

Second, the seller requires a way to tell who is willing to pay $10 and who is only willing to pay $8. (By the way, buyers don't willingly give up this information.)

Third, it has to be impossible, or extremely costly, for the good that is purchased by one customer to be resold to another. For example, suppose the person who bought the good at $6 (in the example earlier) could buy 3 units of the good at this price. Then this buyer could turn around and sell one unit of the good to another buyer for, say, $10, and one unit of the good to still another buyer for $8. Instead of the seller capturing the "$6 added revenue" from price discrimination, it goes instead to one buyer.

Where Does Price Discrimination Occur?

Think of the places where you might see price discrimination. Often restaurants will sell a dinner to an older person for less than it will sell the same dinner to a younger person. In other words, the older person gets the "senior discount." Here is an example where the good the older person buys is not usually resold. We have never seen an older person in a restaurant buy the salmon and vegetables for $15 and then try to sell it for $20 to the person at the next table.

As we mentioned earlier, we sometimes see price discrimination at a movie theater. Young kids are often charged less than adults. Again, little if any reselling is going on here. A kid doesn't typically buy 100 tickets for $4 each and then stand outside the movie theater selling them for, say, $7 each.

▲ **Can you think of ways in which this major retailer, which sells men's and women's fashions at its Web site and in stores across the country, might practice price discrimination?**

You will also sometimes see price discrimination at a pharmacy. An older person may perhaps pay a lower price for a medicine than a younger person. Here again reselling of the medicine is unlikely. Older people (and younger people too) only buy medicine they seem to need. Did you ever see an older person standing outside of the pharmacy offering a 40-year-old his or her high blood pressure medicine for a lower price than the 40-year-old has to pay?

Why Not Higher Prices for Everyone?

Here's something to consider, though: why does the seller charge a lower price to some customers than to others. For example, if the older person would pay $20 for the salmon and vegetables, why charge $15? If the young kid would pay $8 to get into the movie, why charge $4? The answer is because the seller believes that older persons (on average) won't pay $20 for the salmon and vegetables and that young kids (on average) won't pay $8 to get into the movie.

> ***"If you wish to prosper, let your customer prosper."***
> —Frederic Bastiat

It's not that the seller is trying to "do a favor" for the older person or the young

Teaching with Visuals

Answers will vary, but students might say that because the store has locations across the nation it can more easily discriminate according to median income.

Economics Around the Clock

You may want to remind students of the 9:59 P.M. scenario in Economics Around the Clock (page 187), and discuss their answers to the question that accompanies it.

Help students see that pharmaceutical companies will try to price discriminate. If the highest price people in relatively poor countries are willing and able to pay for medicine is lower than the highest price people in rich countries are willing and able to pay for medicine, then a pharmaceutical company may end up charging individuals in the rich country a higher price for the same medicine.

Cases could be brought by individuals who alleged that they had suffered from anticompetitive activities or by the federal government.

After passing the Clayton Act, Congress created the Federal Trade Commission to enforce antitrust law. The FTC can temporarily halt suspected anticompetitive activities pending investigation and potential legal action by the Justice Department.

After students have read this feature, ask them to provide reasons why a seller should or should not be allowed to discriminate by zip code.

ANSWERS TO THINK ABOUT IT Answers will vary.

A Student Asks

Make sure students understand that sellers engage in price discrimination to maximize revenue, not to make up for revenue lost by selling to some groups at lower prices.

Teaching with Visuals

Answers to the question accompanying the photograph on page 219 will vary. Students might say that because medical providers treat some people at lower prices, they need to make up lost revenue by setting higher prices for other people. An economist would disagree, explaining that medical providers charge the highest prices they can to each group they serve.

Application Activity

After reading and discussing Section 4, you may want to assign the Section Activity in the *Applying the Principles Workbook.*

Assess

Quick Quiz

The following true-or-false quiz will help you assess student understanding of the material covered in this section.

1. Entry into and exit from an oligopolistic market is easy. (False)
2. Oligopolistic firms can control the prices they charge. (True)
3. Cartel agreements are designed to maximize competition. (False)
4. Competition between sellers helps keep sellers' interests aligned with buyers' interests. (True)
5. The primary purpose of price discrimination is to maximize revenue. (True)

Could Your ZIP Code Cost You?

In 2000, Amazon.com, the large online seller of books and more, was charging different prices for its new DVDs. Some customers were charged a higher price than other customers. In other words, it looked as if Amazon.com was price discriminating. Amazon.com said that it was not; it said that it was engaged in a random "price test," to find out what customers were willing and able to pay for DVDs.

If you frequent an online seller regularly, as many people do who buy books from Amazon.com, it is possible for the online seller to acquire certain information about your buying habits. For example, it is not difficult for an online seller to know the dollar amount of your purchases and the frequency of your purchases. For example, almost any online bookseller you deal with will know your buying history with it.

Also, because online sellers must send you (through the mail) the products you buy, they naturally know your ZIP code. Once an online seller knows your ZIP code, it is fairly easy to find the median family income earned in that ZIP code. At the Bureau of the Census Web site (www.emcp.net/census), you can key in the ZIP code and it will provide income information. For example, by keying in the ZIP code "90029," we learned that the median family income is $87,416. By keying in the ZIP code "24108" we learned that the median family income is $66,678. An online seller could easily link your name to your ZIP code so that the next time you visit its site, you see the prices for that particular ZIP code. (Might people who live in Beverly Hills, California, be willing and able to pay higher prices for books and DVDs than people who live in a small, rural town in the Midwest?)

As far as we know, no seller does what we have suggested here. However, it doesn't mean that it might not become a topic of discussion in the months and years ahead.

THINK ABOUT IT What is your opinion of price discriminating according to ZIP code?

kid. It's that the seller has some reason to believe that the older person will not buy the dinner unless it is priced at, say, $15. How does the seller know? It might be because at $20 a dinner, very few older persons show up to buy the meal, but at $15 a dinner, many do. The situation is similar with the movie theater and the young kids. It might be that if the price is $8 for adults and for kids, few young kids would show up at the movies. Parents might leave their kids at home, or with a babysitter, if they have to pay $8 for their young kids, but will bring their kids along to the movie if the price is $4 for the kids.

A Student Asks

QUESTION: *Does one buyer end up paying a higher price because some other buyer pays a lower price? For example, does some 30-year-old end up paying more for a dinner because some people get a "senior discount"?*

ANSWER: *No, but most people seem to think it works this way. The seller wants to charge both the 30-year-old and the older person the highest price each is willing and able to pay. If possible, the seller would charge the older person $20 for the dinner*

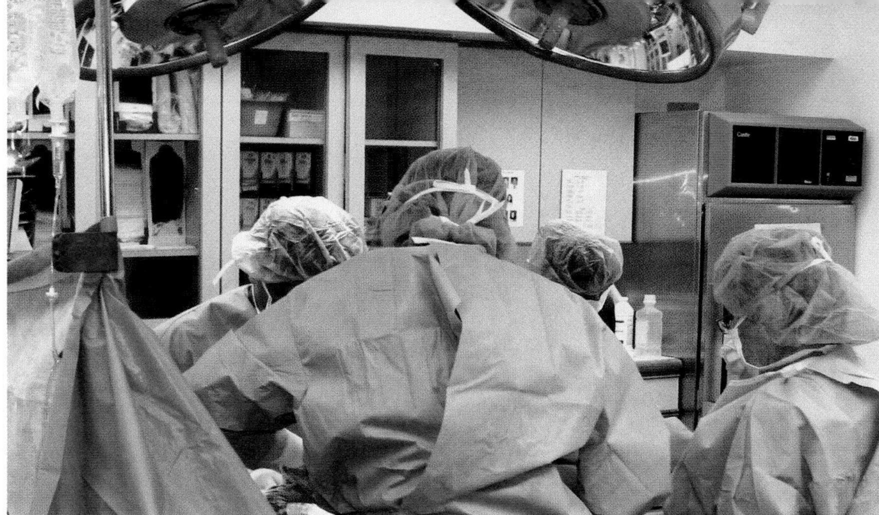

◀ Do you think some people pay more for a medical procedure because others pay less? How might an economist answer this question?

instead of $15. If the seller did charge $20 to the older person, that seller wouldn't then be content enough to charge the 30-year-old only $18 for the dinner. The seller would still charge the 30-year-old $20 for the dinner. Again, the objective is to charge everyone the highest price he or she is willing and able to pay, no matter what someone else pays.

Price Discrimination and the Law

The general perception is that price discrimination is illegal in the United States. It is illegal under certain conditions. For example, it is illegal if a seller price discriminates, and, as a result, injures competition (which usually means reducing the amount or intensity of competition in the market). It is also usually illegal if one of the discriminating sales crosses state lines (for example, when a seller sells a good for less in one state than in another state and the difference in price is not warranted by a difference in costs). Price discrimination is not usually deemed illegal by government authorities if no injury occurs to competition or if the seller can show that charging a lower price to some customers is necessary to adequately compete in the market.

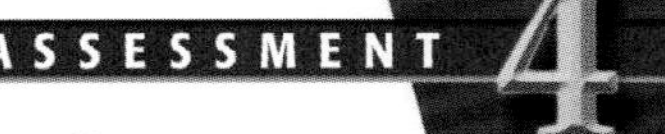

SECTION 4 ASSESSMENT

Defining Terms

1. Define:
   a. oligopolistic market
   b. cartel agreement
   c. price discrimination

Reviewing Facts and Concepts

2. Why might a firm that voluntarily entered into a cartel agreement decide to cheat on (or breach) the agreement?
3. Why are oligopolistic firms price searchers?
4. What conditions are necessary before a seller can practice price discrimination?

Critical Thinking

5. If perfectly competitive firms are price takers, and monopolistic, monopolistic competitive, and oligopolistic firms are price searchers, then it follows that three times as many firms in the real world are price searchers than are price takers. Do you agree or disagree? Explain your answer.

Applying Economic Concepts

6. Someone tells you that the firms in a particular industry are all selling their products for the same prices. Does it follow that the firms have entered into a cartel agreement?

Assessment Book

You will find a quiz for this section in the *Assessment Book.*

Reteaching Activity

Use the Section Assessment to gauge which students may need reteaching on this section. Invite those students to create an imaginary company and explain why its market is oligopolistic. Then invite students to explain how and why their company might use price discrimination and whether doing so would be legal in its case.

Guided Reading

For further reteaching of the key concepts in this section, assign the Outlining Activity and the Just the Facts Handout from the *Guided Reading and Study Guide.*

SECTION 4 ASSESSMENT ANSWERS

Defining Terms

1. a. oligopolistic market: a market structure in which there are few sellers, sellers produce and sell either identical or slightly differentiated products, and there are significant barriers to entry; **b. cartel agreement:** an agreement that specifies that firms will act in a coordinated way to reduce the competition among them so that their profits will rise; **c. price discrimination:** discrimination occurring when a seller charges different buyers different prices for the same product when the price differences are not related to cost differences.

Reviewing Facts and Concepts

2. The firm would find itself in a different position before and after the agreement. Before, it would want the agreement to reduce its competition with other firms. After, it might realize that it could benefit at the expense of the others by violating the agreement.

3. Oligopolistic firms are price searchers because they may sell some of their output at various prices.

4. Different customers must be willing and able to pay different prices for a good; the seller must be able to tell how much different customers are willing to pay; and it has to be impossible, or extremely costly, for the good purchased by one customer to be resold to another.

Critical Thinking

5. Students should disagree. The question does not specify the percentage breakdown among the four types of firms. The statement would be true only if firms were distributed equally among the four market types, which would not necessarily be the case.

Applying Economic Concepts

6. No. Firms may sell their products for the same prices although they have not entered a cartel agreement. For example, perfectly competitive firms must sell their products for the same equilibrium price.

CHAPTER 8 Assessment Answers

Economics Vocabulary

1. price taker; **2.** monopoly; **3.** price searcher; **4.** government monopoly; **5.** natural monopoly; **6.** monopolistic competition; **7.** oligopoly; **8.** cartel; **9.** public franchise.

Understanding the Main Ideas

1. In perfect competition, there are many sellers of identical products. Furthermore, buyers have all relevant information that relates to price. It follows that if firm A tries to sell its product for one penny more, buyers will know this, and they will simply buy from one of the many other sellers.
2. A monopoly seller is a price searcher because it can sell some of its product at various prices. This means that it can raise its price and still sell some of its product.
3. Students should agree. The perfectly competitive firm sells its product for the equilibrium price, which is the highest price for which it can sell its product. A monopoly firm tries to sell the quantity of output it has produced for the highest price possible.
4. Per-unit profit is the difference between price and average total cost (or per-unit cost). For example, if price is $10 and per-unit cost is $4, then profit per unit is $6. Now suppose there are 10 firms, A through J. Firm A has an average total cost of $2, and every other firm has an average total cost of $6. It follows that firm A can lower its price to, say, $5, earn a profit per unit of $3, and eliminate its competition (which cannot lower the price to $5 and still earn a profit). Thus, once firm A has eliminated its competition, its low average total costs act as an impediment or barrier for other firms entering the market.
5. It is difficult for other firms to enter the monopoly market and compete away the profits of the monopoly seller because of extremely high barriers to entry.

CHAPTER 8 ASSESSMENT

Chapter Summary

Be sure you know and remember the following key points from the chapter sections.

Section 1

- The four types of market structure are perfectly competitive, monopolistic, monopolistic competitive, and oligopolistic markets.
- A perfectly competitive market has many buyers and sellers who have relevant information about prices, quality, and other factors; its firms sell identical goods; and market entry and exit are easy.

Section 2

- A monopolistic market consists of one seller of a good that has no good substitute in a market with high barriers to entry.
- A monopoly firm searches for the price at which it can maximize its profits.
- Some barriers to entry into a monopolistic market are legal barriers.

Section 3

- A monopolistic competitive market includes many buyers and sellers; firms produce and sell slightly differentiated products; and market exit and entry are easy.
- Monopolistic competitive firms are price searchers because of the slight differentiation in their products.
- Like other firms, monopolistic competitive firms must answer the questions of how much to produce and what price to charge.

Section 4

- An oligopolistic market has few sellers, firms sell either identical or slightly differentiated goods, and market entry and exit are difficult.
- Oligopolistic firms have some control over the price they charge.
- The barriers to market entry limit the amount of potential competition for oligopolistic firms.

Economics Vocabulary

To reinforce your knowledge of the key terms in this chapter, fill in the following blanks on a separate piece of paper with the appropriate word or phrase.

1. A(n) ______ is a seller that can sell all its output at the equilibrium price but none at 1 penny higher.
2. The conditions that characterize ______ include one seller, no close substitutes for the good the seller sells, and high barriers to entry.
3. A(n) ______ can sell some of its output at various prices, although it sells less output at higher prices.
4. A(n) ______ is a monopoly that is legally protected from competition.
5. A company that ends up being the only seller of a good because of its low average total cost is called a(n) ______.
6. The conditions that characterize ______ include many buyers and sellers, firms that sell slightly differentiated products, and easy entry into and exit from the market.
7. The conditions that characterize ______ include few sellers, firms that produce and sell either identical or slightly differentiated products, and significant barriers to entry.
8. An agreement among firms that specifies that they will act in a coordinated way to reduce the competition between them is called a(n) ______ agreement.
9. A(n) ______ is a right granted to the firm by the government that permits the firm to provide a particular good or service and excludes all others from doing so.

Understanding the Main Ideas

Write answers to the following questions to review the main ideas in this chapter.

1. Firm A is a perfectly competitive firm. Why can't it sell its product for 1 penny higher than the equilibrium price?
2. Why is a monopoly seller a price searcher?
3. In at least one sense, a perfectly competitive firm is like a monopoly firm. Each firm sells its

6. A tying contract is an arrangement whereby the sale of one product depends on the purchase of some other product or products. Tying contracts are prohibited by the Clayton Act.
7. They can be different in terms of features, location, proximity, accompanying services, and so on.
8. The two determinants are how close to unique a seller's product is and how easy it is for new sellers to enter the market and compete with it.
9. There are few sellers in oligopoly and many sellers in monopolistic competition. It is easier for a few sellers to get together and reach agreement than for many sellers to get together and reach agreement. For example, it is easier to get three car companies together than hundreds of clothing companies.
10. A firm would cheat on or break a cartel agreement to make itself better off. The opportunity to

product for the highest price possible. Do you agree or disagree? Explain your answer.

4. How can low average total costs (per-unit costs) act as a barrier to entry?
5. What keeps any profits the monopoly seller is earning from being competed away?
6. What is a tying contract, and which antitrust act deems it illegal?
7. Firms in a monopolistic competitive market produce slightly different products. In what ways might these products differ?
8. What are the two principal determinants of how much competition a seller in a market faces?
9. Why might a cartel agreement be more likely in an oligopolistic market than in a monopolistic competitive market?
10. Explain why a firm that entered into a cartel agreement would cheat on or break that agreement.
11. Can every seller price discriminate? Explain.

Doing the Math

Do the calculations necessary to solve the following problems.

1. A monopoly seller produces and sells 1,000 units of a good at a price of $49.99 per unit. Its total cost is $30,000. How much profit does it earn?
2. A firm can sell 1 unit of good X at $40, and it can sell one additional unit for every $1 reduction in price. Its marginal cost is constant at $34. How many units of the good should the firm produce?

Working with Graphs and Tables

1. Exhibit 8-4(a) partly describes what happens in a competitive market when firms earn high profits. Fill in the missing boxes A through C.
2. Exhibit 8-4(b) partly describes what happens in a competitive market when firms in a market earn losses. Based on your knowledge of what happens when firms earn high profits, fill in the missing boxes D and E.

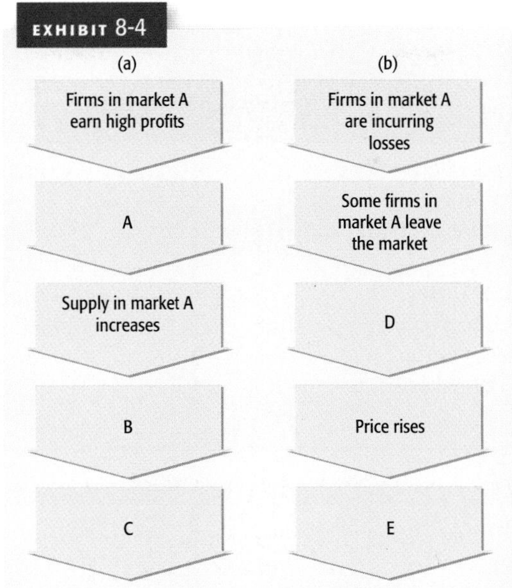

Solving Economic Problems

Find solutions to the following problems.

1. **Application.** Lam goes to a car dealership to look at cars. The salesperson shows him the cars he wants to see and drive. The salesperson asks Lam what he does for a living. What is the economic reason for asking this question?
2. **Analysis.** Firm A has been producing and selling good A in market A for 10 years. Recently, other firms moved into market A and started to produce good A. Firm A asked the government to restrict the number of firms that can enter the market. Why would firm A want to restrict entry into the market?

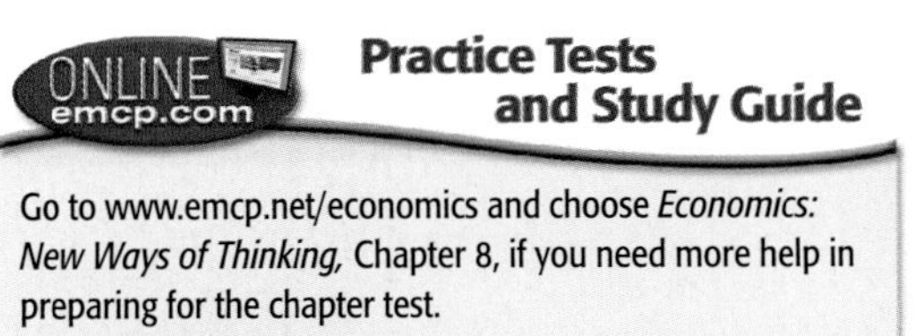

eliminate the competition is too hard for most firms to turn away from.

11. Not every seller can discriminate. Three conditions must be present: different customers must be willing and able to pay different prices for a good; the seller must be able to tell how much different customers are willing to pay; and it has to be impossible, or extremely costly, for the good that is purchased by one customer to be resold to another.

Doing the Math

1. $19,990. Total revenue resulting from the sale of 1,000 goods at $49.99 each would be $49,990. Profit = total revenue – total cost, or $19.990.

2. 4 units. To find out how many units a firm should produce, we need to find that quantity of output at which marginal revenue is equal to marginal cost. In the problem, marginal cost is given at $34, which leaves the student to find marginal revenue. At 1 unit and a price of $40, total revenue is $40. At 2 units and a price of $39, total revenue is $78, and marginal revenue is $38 ($78 – $40 = $38). At 3 units and a price of $38, total revenue is $114, and marginal revenue is $36 ($114 – $78 = $36). At 4 units and a price of $37, total revenue is $148, and marginal revenue is $34. Because at 4 units marginal revenue equals marginal cost, 4 units is what the firm should produce.

Working with Graphs and Tables

1. A. New firms enter the market. B. Price falls. C. Profit declines.
2. D. Supply falls. E. Losses decline, or losses turn into profits.

Solving Economic Problems

1. The economic reason for asking the question is to gauge the price Lam can pay for the car. Look at it this way: Car dealerships want to sell their cars for the highest price possible, but they do not know what this price is. Is the highest price possible for the car $30,000 or $31,000? The salesperson may want to get a feel for how high a price a person can pay. Finding out what the person does for a living, and thus how much the person probably makes, may help in this regard. Of course, ability to pay and willingness to pay are two different things. It does not necessarily follow that because a person can pay a higher price, he or she will do so.
2. Easy entry into the market means firm A faces greater competition and lower profits. Firm A may want to restrict entry into market A so that if it does earn profits, it can continue to earn profits instead of having them competed away by new firms entering the market and producing the same good it produces.

Chapter 8 Competition and Markets 221

Chapter 9 Planning Guide

SECTION ORGANIZER

SECTION 1 — What Determines Wages? (pages 224–235)

SECTION 2 — Labor and Government Regulation (pages 238–247)

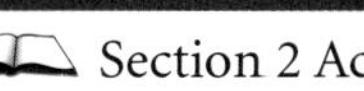

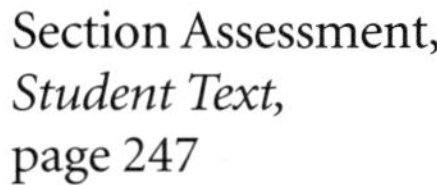

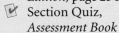

Section	Learning Objectives	Reproducible Worksheets and Handouts	Assessment
What Determines Wages? (pages 224–235)	► Explain what the demand curve for labor looks like. ► Explain what the supply curve for labor looks like. ► Explain why wage rates differ. ► Describe nonmoney benefits and how they factor into comparisons between jobs. ► Identify factors that determine how much a person earns.	Section 1 Activity, *Applying the Principles Workbook* Outlining Activity, *Guided Reading and Study Guide* Just the Facts Handout, *Guided Reading and Study Guide*	Section Assessment, *Student Text,* page 235 Quick Quiz, *Annotated Teacher's Edition,* page 234 Section Quiz, *Assessment Book*
Labor and Government Regulation (pages 238–247)	► Describe how labor unions affect labor demand and supply. ► Explain what union and closed shops are. ► Identify states that have right-to-work laws. ► Provide examples of the unintended effects of regulation.	Section 2 Activity, *Applying the Principles Workbook* Outlining Activity, *Guided Reading and Study Guide* Just the Facts Handout, *Guided Reading and Study Guide*	Section Assessment, *Student Text,* page 247 Quick Quiz, *Annotated Teacher's Edition,* pages 246–247 Section Quiz, *Assessment Book*

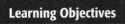

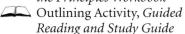

CHAPTER AND PROGRAM RESOURCES

Reproducible Chapter Resources and Assessment Materials

 Graphic Organizer Activity, *Guided Reading and Study Guide*

 Vocabulary Activity, *Guided Reading and Study Guide*

 Working with Graphs and Charts, *Guided Reading and Study Guide*

Practice Test, *Guided Reading and Study Guide*

 Critical Thinking Activity, *Finding Economics*

 Chapter Test A, *Assessment Book*

Chapter Test B, *Assessment Book*

Technology Resources

 *Test Generator CD*

Spanish Audio Summaries CD

 *Marketplace® Audio Lessons CD*

Economic Principles Lectures, Videocassette or DVD

Lesson Planning and Teaching Resources

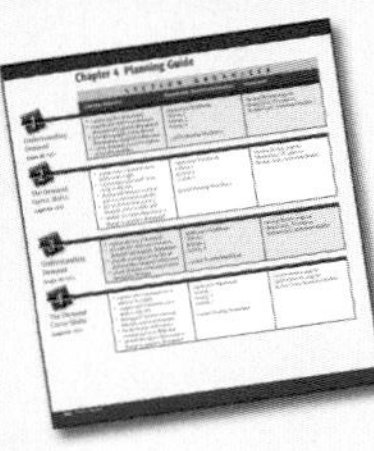

The *Economics: New Ways of Thinking* Teacher Resources include detailed lesson plans for each section in this chapter; the lesson plans are available in print form *(Lesson Plans)* and electronic form. The Teacher Resources also include *Daily Lectures: Overheads and Notes,* which provides prepared overheads and discussion notes covering the key concepts in each section of this chapter.

EMC Publishing Economics Online

Go to Economics Online, at www.emcp.com, for a variety of Internet resources to help you keep your course current and relevant. At Economics Online you will find these items:

- Economics in the News Lessons
- Study Guide Questions
- Practice Tests
- Lesson Plans

Internet Resources

Economics: New Ways of Thinking encourages students to use the Internet to find out more about economics. With the wealth of current, valid information available on Web sites, using the Internet as a research tool is likely to increase your students' interest in and understanding of economics principles and topics. In addition, doing Internet research can help your students form the habit of accessing and using economics information, as well as help them develop investigative skills they will use throughout their educational and professional careers.

To aid your students in achieving these ends, each chapter of *Economics: New Ways of Thinking* includes the addresses of several Web sites at which students will find engaging, relevant information. When students type in the addresses provided, they will immediately arrive at the intended sites. The addresses have been modified so that EMC Publishing can monitor and maintain the proper links—for example, the government site http://stats.bls.gov/ has been changed to www.emcp.net/prices. In the event that the address or content of a site changes or is discontinued, EMC's Internet editors will create a link that redirects students to an address with similar information.

Activities in the *Annotated Teacher's Edition* often suggest that students search the Internet for information. For some activities, you might want to find reputable sites beforehand, and steer students to those sites. For other activities, you might want students to do their own searching, and then check out the sites they have found and discuss why they might be reliable or unreliable.

CHAPTER 9 Overview

There are many markets in the economy. This chapter discusses the labor market, the market in which wages are determined. It discusses the demand for and supply of labor, and how wages are determined. It also discusses the history of the labor union movement in the United States.

What Determines Wages?

Section 1 deals with labor, which, like any other resource, exists within a market. Students will learn how the forces of supply and demand affect the labor market. These forces determine an equilibrium price (or wage) for labor. Students will also learn what money and nonmoney benefits are and how they affect wages.

Labor and Government Regulation

Section 2 explores the organization of workers into labor unions, which changed the market for labor. Students will learn the history of labor unions and how they affect the labor market.

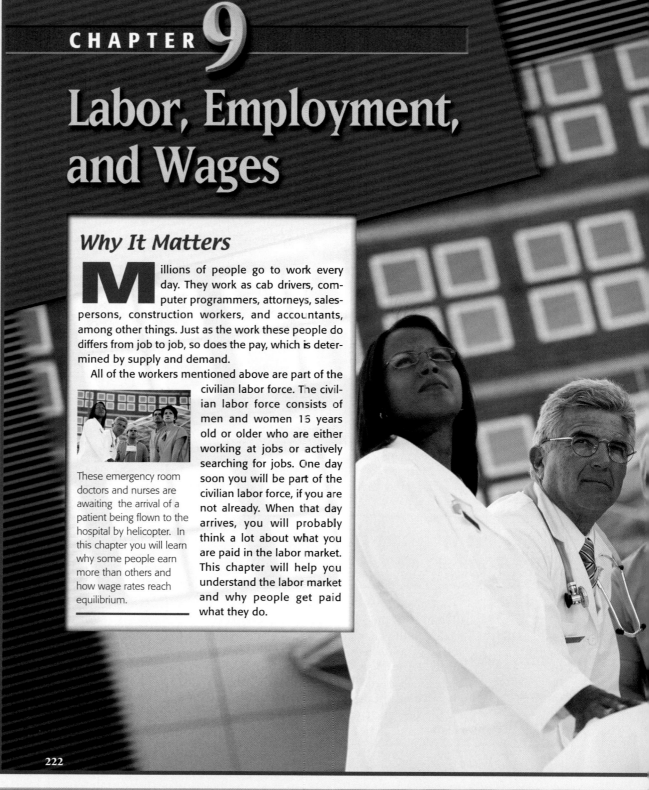

CHAPTER 9 Labor, Employment, and Wages

Why It Matters

Millions of people go to work every day. They work as cab drivers, computer programmers, attorneys, salespersons, construction workers, and accountants, among other things. Just as the work these people do differs from job to job, so does the pay, which is determined by supply and demand.

All of the workers mentioned above are part of the civilian labor force. The civilian labor force consists of men and women 16 years old or older who are either working at jobs or actively searching for jobs. One day soon you will be part of the civilian labor force, if you are not already. When that day arrives, you will probably think a lot about what you are paid in the labor market. This chapter will help you understand the labor market and why people get paid what they do.

These emergency room doctors and nurses are awaiting the arrival of a patient being flown to the hospital by helicopter. In this chapter you will learn why some people earn more than others and how wage rates reach equilibrium.

222

Teaching Suggestions from the Author

One way to get students interested in the material in this chapter is to start with this question: How many of you are interested in the amount of money you will earn on a job? Tell students that in this chapter they'll learn about factors that determine wage rates.

Alternatively, you can start by asking students to give reasons why baseball stars, basketball stars, and movie stars earn as much as they do. This can often stimulate a classroom discussion. Some students will say that baseball stars are not worth what they are paid. Other students may argue that baseball stars are worth what they are paid. Ask all of these students to explain why.

You may also want to ask students how much discretion employers have over the salaries that they pay their

Economics Around the Clock

The following events occurred one day in September.

7:14 A.M. Blake is up and watching television. He hears a story about professional basketball players and the high salaries they earn. Blake, an avid basketball fan, wonders why some people end up making so much money.

- **Is Blake part of the reason that professional basketball players earn high incomes?**

8:44 A.M. Emily and her best friend, Karen, are having a cup of coffee at work. They talk about a TV documentary they saw last night about new immigrants to the United States. Emily says, "I thought the documentary made some good points—points I was unaware of." "I know," said Karen. "I didn't know that new immigrants could end up causing our wages to go down." "But I don't think that is what the documentary said," says Emily. "I thought it said that new immigrants could, but need not lower peoples' wages, and not necessarily everyone's wages—just some people's wages."

- **What effect does immigration have on wages?**

10:56 A.M. Jill works as an accountant in Atlanta. Her annual salary is $82,000. She just got off the phone with an accounting firm in Milwaukee. The vice president of the accounting firm in Milwaukee offered her a salary of $100,000 if she would come and work for the firm. The Milwaukee firm has a reputation for disgruntled employees. Jill is thinking of turning down the offer.

- **Would Jill be wrong to turn down the job in Milwaukee?**

5:03 P.M. Stephen is 16 years old and works at a grocery store every day after school. He bags groceries and stocks food. He earns the minimum wage. Right now he is cleaning up in the back room of the store. A coworker of his just came into the back room. Stephen looks over and asks his coworker how much he is getting paid. The coworker says, "Same as you, the minimum wage." "I wish I made a little more at this job," Stephen says. "So do I," says the coworker.

- **Would Stephen have a job at the grocery store if the minimum wage were raised to $3 higher than it currently is?**

Introducing the Chapter

Write the word "labor" on the board. Ask students to name the first three words that come to their minds when they think of labor. Note that many times students' responses will reflect negative connotations.

To give students a balanced perspective on labor, you might point out that President Ulysses S. Grant said, "Labor disgraces no man; unfortunately you can occasionally find men who disgrace labor."

Ask students what they think Grant meant by this statement. Explain that this chapter looks at the labor force, examining both those who are employed and those who are unemployed.

Teaching with Visuals

Workers in specialized fields such as the medical industry are in high demand. Owing to low supply, these workers are able to command high salaries. Ask your students to name other occupations where the demand for skilled workers is greater than the supply. Ask students how this affects wage rates. Using their knowledge of supply and demand, students should conclude that as demand for labor increases, wage rates increase, and vice versa.

employees. For example, can an employer pay an employee less than the market-determined wage, or are employers forced to pay the market-determined wage?

Finally, it is always good to ask students to think about what they need to do early in life to earn a good salary as an adult. Examine the correlation between education and wages, as well as between work experience and wages. What factors are the most important in determining wages? Have students explain why.

SECTION 1 Teacher Support

Focus and Motivate

Section Objectives

After completing this section, students will be able to

- explain what the demand curve for labor looks like;
- explain what the supply curve for labor looks like;
- explain why wage rates differ;
- describe nonmoney benefits and how they factor into comparisons between jobs; and
- identify factors that determine how much a person earns.

Economics Around the Clock

Kickoff Activity

Instruct students to respond in writing to the 5:03 P.M. scenario in Economics Around the Clock (page 223).

Invite students to share their answers with the class. Students should come up with the concept that employers would hire more people at a lower wage rate than at a higher wage rate.

Activating Prior Knowledge

To review supply and demand concepts presented in previous chapters, ask students to create a visual aid explaining the relationship between wage and supply and demand. Divide students into small groups to present their visual aids.

SECTION 1 What Determines Wages?

Focus Questions

- What does the demand curve for labor look like?
- What does the supply curve for labor look like?
- Why do wage rates differ?
- What are nonmoney benefits and how do they factor into comparisons between jobs?
- What factors will determine how much you will earn?

Key Terms

wage rate
derived demand
minimum wage law

Supply and Demand in the Labor Market

In Chapters 4 and 5 you learned about demand and supply. In particular, you learned how both supply and demand affect prices for goods or products—such things as apples, cars, and houses. Supply and demand can also be used to analyze how we determine the price of a resource, or factor of production, such as labor.

People who demand labor are usually referred to as employers, and people who supply labor are employees. Looking at employers and employees in this way, we can create a demand curve and a supply curve showing the price of labor. The price of labor is called the **wage rate**.

wage rate
The price of labor.

The demand curve for labor is downward sloping (left to right), as shown in Exhibit 9-1. A downward-sloping demand curve indicates that employers will be willing and able to hire more people at lower wage rates than at higher wage rates. For example, employers are willing and able to hire more workers if the wage rate is $7 per hour than if the wage rate is $10 per hour.

EXAMPLE: Jack owns a small hotel. Currently, he employs four persons to clean rooms. He pays each person $80 a day. If he could pay each worker only $60 a day, he would hire five instead of four persons to clean rooms. ♦

The supply curve for labor, in contrast, is upward sloping (left to right), as shown in Exhibit 9-2. More people will be willing and able to work at higher wage rates than at lower wage rates. In the exhibit, more people are willing and able to work if the wage rate is $10 per hour than if the wage rate is $7 an hour. For example, Pam is not willing to work as a salesperson in a clothing store if the store pays $7 an hour. However, she is willing to work as a salesperson in a clothing store if the store pays $10 an hour.

How the Equilibrium Wage Rate Is Established

Recall from Chapter 6 that the equilibrium price is the price at which the quantity demanded of a good equals the quantity supplied. Suppose $14 is the equilibrium

Background Information: Supply, Demand, and Teen Labor

Students may be interested to know how supply and demand affect teen labor. Despite steady and strong job growth for civilian employment in recent years, teens have been unable to capture a substantive share of the new employment opportunities. Employment rates seem to vary across gender and racial and ethnic groups, with millions of teens being unutilized or underutilized in summer and year-round employment. Recent studies indicate a clear need for job opportunities for teens on a year-round basis. Some experts agree Congress could propose programs such as increased job placement efforts and a targeted job stimulus bill to expand teen employment opportunities.

EXHIBIT 9-1 The Demand for Labor

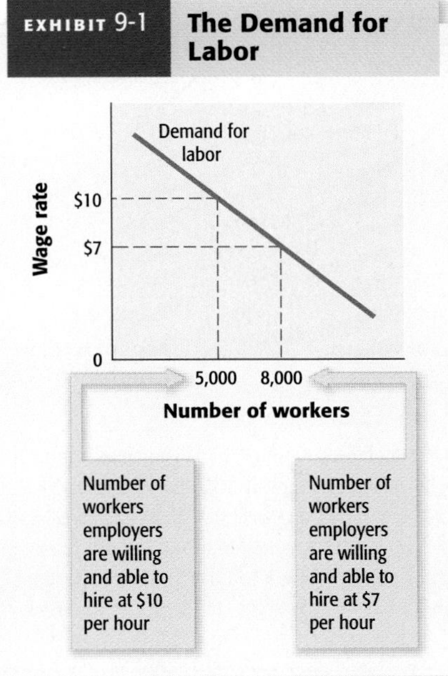

▲ A downward-sloping demand curve indicates that employers hire more people at lower wage rates.

EXHIBIT 9-2 The Supply of Labor

Supply of labor

Wage rate

$10

$7

0

4,000 7,000

Number of workers

Number of workers willing and able to work at $7 per hour

Number of workers willing and able to work at $10 per hour

▲ An upward-sloping supply curve indicates that more people are willing and able to work at higher wage rates.

price of compact discs; at this price, the number of compact discs that sellers are willing and able to sell equals the number of compact discs that buyers are willing and able to buy.

Similarly, in the labor market, the equilibrium wage rate is the wage at which the quantity demanded of labor equals the quantity supplied of labor. Stated differently, it is the wage rate at which the number of people employers are willing and able to hire is the same as the number of people who are willing and able to be hired. In Exhibit 9-3(a) on the next page, when the wage rate is $9, the number of people who are willing and able to work (quantity supplied equals 7,000) is greater than the number of people employers are willing and able to hire (quantity demanded equals 3,000). It follows that $9 is not the equilibrium wage rate; at $9, the market has a surplus of labor.

In Chapter 6, you learned that when a surplus of a good occurs, the price of the good falls. Things are similar in a competitive labor market. When the market has a surplus of labor, the wage rate falls:

Quantity supplied of labor > Quantity demanded of labor = Surplus of labor

Surplus of labor → Wage rate falls

Now consider Exhibit 9-3(b). The wage rate is $7, and the number of people employers are willing and able to hire (6,000) is greater than the number of people who are willing and able to work (4,000). Thus, $7 is not the equilibrium wage rate. At $7, the market experiences a shortage of labor, so the wage rate rises:

Quantity demanded of labor > Quantity supplied of labor = Shortage of labor

Shortage of labor → Wage rate rises

Teach

Discussion Starter

Some students have undoubtedly considered what kinds of jobs they would like to have when they get older. Ask students what jobs they would like to have when they are 29 years old, along with their reasons for wanting that job, and what they think a person with that job earns today.

Teaching with Visuals

To ensure that students understand Exhibits 9-1 and 9-2, instruct them to re-create them on their own paper. Then instruct them to plot various points. For example, how many workers would be willing and able to work for $15 per hour? How many would be willing and able to work for $5 per hour?

Discussion Starter

Point out to students that the salaries, incomes, or wages of different people vary. For example, medical doctors earn more than bank tellers do. Also, some professional baseball players earn far more than most doctors do. Ask students to discuss why these differences exist. Guide students in a discussion about why wages differ for different lines of employment.

Analyzing

Divide students into pairs to list factors that make some professions more valuable than others, and that account for differences in wages. Obviously, education and skill sets are factors. As an example of salary variations, ask students why a skilled saddle maker or weaver can sometimes earn as much as a lawyer or doctor.

Internet Research

If demand for a good increases, it usually follows that the demand for the labor that produces that good increases, and the wage rate for workers who produce that good increases. Ask students to suppose the demand for computers increases, increasing the demand for people who produce computers. The wage rate for these positions will rise. Direct students to the Internet to find articles on products for which the demand is increasing and for which demand for labor is increasing. Allow students to share their findings in small groups.

Section 1 What Determines Wages? 225

Teaching with Visuals

If students have difficulty understanding the three charts shown in Exhibit 9-3, review how equilibrium prices are established. Remind students that labor is a good, or commodity, with variable rates. Equilibrium price for labor is established just as equilibrium price is established for other goods.

Reinforcement Activity

Instruct students to copy and share with the class articles from newspapers or magazines that relate to people earning different incomes. For example, one student may find an article from a newspaper stating that a business executive earns $100,000 per year, or that a professional baseball player earns $5 million per year. Ask students to offer economic explanations for the salaries. You might make a bulletin-board display of the articles.

Some people believe that a celebrity who earns a very high annual income is not worth that much money. An economist would say, however, that this person's income is often a reflection of supply and demand forces. Ask students to consider whether they agree or disagree as they present their articles to the class. Also ask students whether they believe it is fair or unfair to allow supply and demand to operate in the labor market.

EXHIBIT 9-3 Finding the Equilibrium Wage Rate

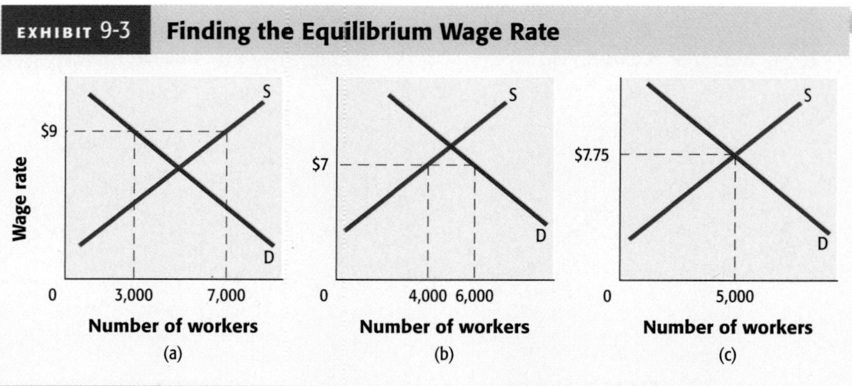

▲ (a) At $9 per hour, the number of people willing and able to work (7,000) is greater than the number employers are willing and able to hire (3,000). We conclude that $9 is not the equilibrium wage rate. (b) At $7 per hour, the number of people employers are willing and able to hire (6,000) is greater than the number willing and able to work (4,000). We conclude that $7 is not the equilibrium wage rate. (c) At $7.75 per hour, the number of people willing and able to work (5,000) is the same as the number employers are willing and able to hire (5,000). We conclude that $7.75 is the equilibrium wage rate.

In Exhibit 9-3(c), the wage rate is $7.75, and the number of people employers are willing and able to hire (5,000) equals the number of people who are willing and able to work (5,000). We conclude that $7.75 is the equilibrium wage rate. At this level the wage rate neither rises nor falls because the market has no shortage or surplus of labor.

Why Do Some People Earn More than Others?

If you convert a daily salary or a monthly salary into hours, you can find out how much a person earns on an hourly basis. This figure is that person's wage rate. For example, suppose someone earns $4,000 per month and works 160 hours a month. Her wage rate is $25 an hour.

> ***"Pleasure in the job puts perfection in the work."***
> — ARISTOTLE

Now some people earn a higher wage rate than others. For example, some people earn $100 an hour while other people earn $8 an hour. Why the big difference? Supply and demand help us to understand why some people earn higher wages than others. First, suppose that the demand for every type of labor is the same—the demand for accountants is the same as the demand for construction workers, and so on. Now suppose we learn that the equilibrium wage rate for accountants is higher than that for construction workers. If demand for the two types of labor is the same, how can we explain the difference in wage rates? Obviously, the supply of accountants and the supply of construction workers must not be the same. If accountants earn more than construction workers, it must be because the supply of accountants is less than the supply of construction workers. We conclude that *wage rates can differ because the supply of different types of labor is not the same.*

Suppose instead that the supply of different types of labor is the same—for example, suppose the supply of bank tellers is the same as the supply of grocery store cashiers. If grocery store cashiers earn more than bank tellers, then what could possibly explain the difference? Obviously, the demand for bank tellers and grocery store cashiers must not be the same. We conclude that *wage rates can differ because the demand for different types of labor is not the same.*

As an aside, you may be interested in knowing the average hourly earnings of

Differentiating Instruction

Kinesthetic and Visual Learners

If students have difficulty understanding the information presented in Exhibit 9-3, assign students to make their own 3-D graphs with materials they can manipulate upward and downward on a graph. Then ask students to explain what wages and number of workers would be at various points along the curves.

workers in different industries. In 2003, in construction it was $18.95; manufacturing, $15.74; financial activities, $17.13; leisure and hospitality, $8.76; and business and professional services, $17.20.

A Student Asks

QUESTIONS: *Many physicians earn less than many major league baseball players, but shouldn't they earn more? After all, major league baseball players are just playing a game. At least some physicians are saving lives.*

ANSWER: *Your question takes us beyond the confines of economics. It's sort of like asking a physicist if we would be better off if dynamite didn't blow up. Some things just are. It is a fact that the average major league baseball player earns more than the average physician, and it is not so much the economist's job to pass judgment on this point, as it is to explain why. Addressing the "why part" has to do with supply and demand. If a lot more people could do what major league baseball players do (a lot more supply of major league baseball players), you can be sure they would earn less than they currently do. Or, if, for example, people stopped watching baseball games (the demand for baseball games falls off), baseball salaries would decline. As things are now, though, the demand for baseball players is high and the supply of them is low, and so they earn more than most people earn.*

Are Money Benefits the Only Thing That Matters?

Suppose Smith is offered two jobs, A and B. In job A, he will earn an annual income of $100,000 and in job B, $40,000. Which job will he choose? Most people would say that he will choose job A because it pays a higher income. Smith won't necessarily choose job A, however, because a higher income (more money per year) is not the only thing that matters to people. Also important are what people are doing in their jobs, who their coworkers are, where they have to work, how many hours a week they have to work, how much vacation time they receive, and more. In short, if everything between the two jobs, A and B, is the same except that job A pays $100,000 and job B pays $40,000, then certainly Smith will choose job A over job B. However, usually not everything is the same between two jobs.

Let's suppose that Smith chooses job B (the lower-paying job) over job A. He tells us that he chose the lower-paying job because he likes the job so much more. In job B he is doing something that he has always wanted to do, he works with nice people, he gets one month of vacation each year, and he is enormously stimulated by what he does. In contrast, in job A he would have been doing something both boring and tedious to him, he would have worked with people he did not really like (especially his boss), and he would have had only two weeks of vacation each year. On top of all this, he would have had to work 10 hours more each week in job A than he has to work in job B, and he would have had much less job security. Thus, job A pays more than job B, but job A does not have the nonmoney benefits that job B has.

All jobs come with both money benefits and nonmoney benefits. Look at it this way:

Benefits in a job =
Money benefits (income) + Nonmoney benefits

▼ Being able to afford a trip to a seaside resort is of no value if your job prevents you from getting away. **What are some nonmoney benefits of a job?**

A Student Asks

You may want to use this A Student Asks to make sure that students understand how supply and demand determine the salaries of major league baseball players.

Discussion Starter

Guide students in a discussion of nonmoney benefits. Create a class list of nonmoney benefits other than those listed in the text.

Critical Thinking

Ask students to imagine that they have just been offered three jobs. The first one is in their hometown and would pay $30,000 a year. The second job pays $50,000, but is more than two thousand miles from their home. The third job would only pay about $25,000, but it is in the most beautiful location in the nation. Ask: Which one would you choose? Is there any other information you would need before making a decision? How much does the location of the position (a nonmoney benefit) have to do with your acceptance of the position?

Teaching with Visuals

Answers will vary. Students should be able to create a list of several nonmoney benefits of a job.

Differentiating Instruction

English Language Learners

To help ELL students better understand this information, tell them to read through this chapter and list the words with which they are unfamiliar. In this chapter, there are many terms and phrases that may be difficult for students to comprehend. Create a list of these terms and then work through them with students. Have students make flash cards of words on the list and work in pairs to quiz each other on these concepts before they move on to the next chapter.

Economics in the Real World

After students have read this feature, ask them if they have had a personal experience in which their productivity was closely linked to monetary benefits. Ask if they think it is fair for some people to receive a higher wage for less productivity.

ANSWERS TO THINK ABOUT IT Answers will vary.

Discussion Starter

Ask students what they think would be the single most important nonmoney benefit for themselves. Ask how much money they would be willing to give up to attain this benefit.

After students have read and discussed "Are Money Benefits the Only Thing That Matters?" (pages 227–229), instruct them to discuss their answers to the 10:56 A.M. scenario in Economics Around the Clock (page 223).

You might point out that when deciding whether to accept a job, Jill considers both the money benefits and the nonmoney benefits of the job, not just one or the other. Students can think of it this way: Jill is not "wrong" to turn down a job that pays more because the nonmoney benefits she receives in her current job could more than compensate her for any money income she would lose by turning down another job.

Economics in the Real World

Do You Want the 1st or the 43rd Pick in the NFL Draft?

??????????????????

Each year the National Football League (NFL) conducts a draft in which the 32 teams take turns picking the best college players. Most people assume that the players picked earlier are the better football players. For this reason, where a player is picked in the draft largely determines that player's starting salary: the earlier chosen, the higher the salary.

After studying the NFL draft, two economists argue that how valuable a player is to a team depends on how productive the player is, and how much he is paid. For example, player 1 might perform better than player 2, but be paid *twice* as much as player 2. But unless player 1 is twice as valuable on the field as player 2, then either he is being "overpaid" or player 2 is being "underpaid."

The economists collected data from the last 17 drafts and tried to figure out which draft picks were the "best" for the amount of money they were paid. The economists tried to identify not the best overall player, but the "best per dollar" player.

What did they discover? The best per dollar player is not usually the first pick in the first round. Instead, the best pick per dollar is usually the 43rd person picked, which is the 11th pick in the second round. In 2004, this pick went to the Dallas Cowboys, who took running back Julius Jones. Jones ran for 819 yards and scored seven touchdowns in eight games. Cost to Dallas for Jones's six-year contract: a very reasonable $4.37 million (the first pick that year, Eli Manning, received a six-year, $54 million contract).

The strategy outlined by the economists—go with lower-priced players in the second round rather than higher-priced players in the first round—is said to have been the strategy employed by General Manager Bobby Beathard of the Washington Redskins in the 1980s. He often traded away his first-round picks for lower-priced picks in later rounds. The team Beathard built using this strategy won three Super Bowls. In more recent years, the New England Patriots won three Super Bowl titles in four years led by quarterback Tom Brady, who wasn't drafted until the sixth round.

So, if the economists are right, why are many teams paying too much for some of the early picks in the draft? Some have speculated that it is difficult to correctly estimate an athlete's worth over time, as compared to other types of employees. For example, could you estimate a typist's productivity over time? A typist who types 60 words this year is likely to type 60 words next year and 60 words the year after. His or her work environment and skills might improve modestly, but will probably be fairly constant from one year to the next.

The productivity of football players, on the other hand, seems to be very different. A football player usually plays with different team members and for different coaches from one year to the next, both of which impact the player's performance. It is also the case that injuries and age can have a major impact on a player's performance, much more significantly than in other occupations.

Since the two economists published their research, a number of NFL teams have contacted them for advice. It will be interesting to see which teams, if any, continue to overpay top picks. And by the way, how has your favorite team done in recent drafts?

We might expect that in some fields productivity is more closely linked to pay than in other fields. For example, we would expect it to be closely linked in a field where it is easy to measure productivity and less closely linked in a field where it is hard to measure productivity. In what fields do you think it might be hard to measure productivity?

Cooperative Learning

Divide the class into small groups and assign each group to select and research three occupations. For each occupation, students should find out the skills required, working conditions, employment opportunities, training and advancement, and earnings. Explain to the groups that for more information, they can refer to Bureau of Labor Statistics on the U.S. Department of Labor's Web site.

228 Chapter 9 Labor, Employment, and Wages

Certainly job A comes with higher money benefits (higher income) than job B, but (as far as Smith is concerned) it also comes with lower nonmoney benefits than job B. Because Smith chose job B (the $40,000 job) over job A (the $100,000 job), the nonmoney benefits in job B must have been higher than the nonmoney benefits in job A.

How much higher must they have been, in a dollar amount? The answer is at least $60,000 higher. To understand why, consider what Smith has "paid" by choosing job B over job A. He has paid $60,000 a year, because he has given up the opportunity to earn $60,000 more a year in job A. Therefore, the nonmoney benefits of job B must have been worth at least $60,000 to Smith. This means that job B "pays" more, as long as we understand that a person in a job is paid in terms of both money and nonmoney benefits.

EXAMPLE: Kevin graduates from college in a year. His father has always wanted him to go to medical school. One of the reasons his father wants him to go to medical school is because doctors earn a relatively high salary. An orthopedic surgeon, for example, can earn $600,000 a year. Kevin doesn't really want to go to medical school. It's not that he thinks he would find being a doctor uninteresting, it's just that he doesn't want to work as hard as one needs to work to become a physician. He would have to go to four years of medical school, then serve an internship and residency, then, perhaps, end up working 60 to 80 hours a week for years. According to Kevin, "There is more to life than just money."

Here, then, is an example of a person who considers more than just the money benefits in a job; Kevin considers the nonmoney benefits too. Even though being a medical doctor comes with high money benefits, it doesn't come with enough "nonmoney benefits" for Kevin. Obviously, Kevin is willing to trade off some money benefits he would receive as a doctor for greater nonmoney benefits in some other job. ♦

Each year, *Parade* magazine interviews people in a variety of jobs. It is mainly concerned with what people in various occupations earn. If you go to www.emcp.net/parade, you can see the wage rates for various occupations.

A Student Asks

QUESTION: *I thought economics was about money—specifically, the more money the better. Am I wrong here?*

ANSWER: *It is one thing to say "the more money the better" and quite another to say "the more money the better, all other things being equal." The economist will make the second statement but not the first. In other words, what the economist means here is that if two jobs, A and B, are exactly alike except for the fact that job A pays more than B, then job A is a better job than job B.*

The Demand for a Good and Wage Rates

Eva works in a radio factory. Suppose the demand for radios decreases as shown on the next page in Exhibit 9-4(a). What do you think will happen to Eva? If the demand for radios decreases, radio manufacturers do not need to hire as many workers, so the demand for workers decreases, as shown in Exhibit 9-4(b). As the demand for these workers decreases and the supply stays constant, the wage rate decreases.

Because the demand for labor is dependent upon the demand for the good or service labor produces, the demand for labor is often referred to as a **derived demand**. A derived demand is a demand that is the result of some other demand.

derived demand A demand that is the result of some other demand.

Background Information

Some people believe that labor productivity is lower in one country or one part of the country than in another. The perception could be that people do not work as hard in some areas as they do in others. Actually, labor productivity has more to do with incentives, education, and whether or not factories are highly industrialized and well equipped than with the innate productivity of people who live and work in a particular region.

Ask students if they have ever seen *Parade* magazine's interviews about occupations and earnings. Ask how this Web site and its information can help them.

A Student Asks

You may want to use this A Student Asks to make sure students understand the significance of the phrase "all things being equal."

Reinforcement Activity

One of the factors that determine how much money you will earn is the location of your job. Students may not be aware of the large salary differences that sometimes exist, based solely on geographic location. For example, a tax manager for a bank in the Midwest would make, on average, $57,200. On the West Coast, the same position would pay, on average, $62,300. Assign students to research two or three jobs and find the differences in salaries in various areas of the nation. Some of this information is available on the Internet.

Cooperative Learning

Divide the class into groups of three or four. Ask groups to select a particular industry or factory, and research the average wages of the workers in that industry or factory over the past five years. Groups should prepare demand curves based on the salaries and output of the chosen industry or factory. If salaries have varied, students can write an explanation of the changes. Groups should be prepared to share their visuals (demand charts) with the class and give an oral report of their findings. After students have finished, lead them in analyzing which industries have had the most variance and the least variance, and ask them to make predictions about the factors that might account for this.

Teaching with Visuals

Discuss with students both charts in Exhibit 9-4 to ensure that everyone in the class comprehends them. Have students recreate both (a) and (b) on their own paper and add quantity and dollar amounts. Then ask students to plot particular points along the curves.

Prediction Activity

Instruct students to consider this scenario: Jim is offered two jobs, A and B. Job A pays $50,000 a year, and job B pays $60,000 a year. The nonmoney benefits in the two jobs are the same. Cindra is offered two jobs, C and D. Job C pays $50,000 a year, and job D pays $60,000 a year, but the nonmoney benefits in the two jobs are not the same. Is it as easy to predict which job Cindra will choose as it is to predict which job Jim will choose? Why or why not?

(*Answer:* It is easier to predict which job Jim will choose. We predict he will choose job B, because it has the same nonmoney benefits as job A, but offers more money. It is impossible to predict accurately which job Cindra will pick. Job C pays less than job D, but it is possible that the nonmoney benefits in job C are much greater for her than the money benefits in job D. If this were the case, then most likely Cindra would choose job C. We do not know, however, the value (in dollars) of the nonmoney benefits in each job.)

Reinforcement Activity

Productivity is measured both for individuals and for nations. Assign students to compare a particular nation's productivity figures with those of the United States. Ask: Which is higher? Why? Encourage students to prepare oral reports with visuals to share with the class.

Teaching with Visuals

Answers will vary. Students should include factors such as demand for labor services, supply of labor offered, productivity, education level, and skill development.

EXHIBIT 9-4 The Demand for Radios, the Demand for the Workers Who Produce the Radios, and Their Wage Rates

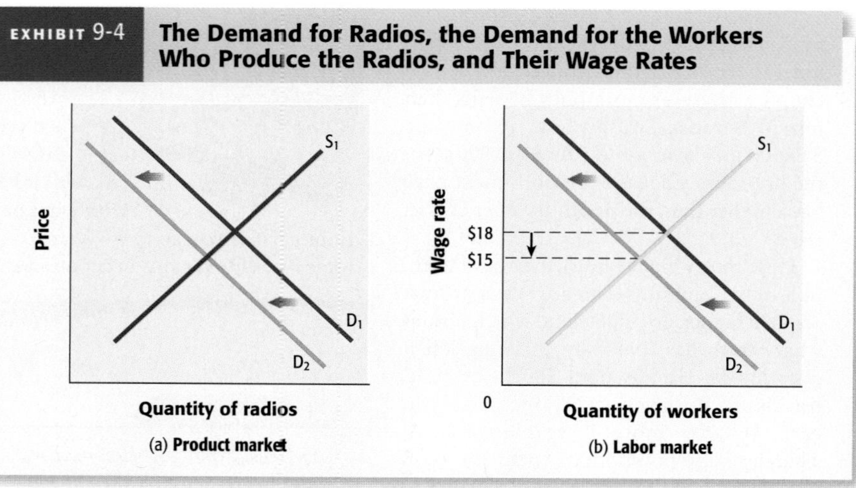

▶ The demand for radios affects the demand for the workers who produce the radios and their wages. In this example, when the demand for radios falls, the demand for workers also falls, causing wage rates to fall from $18 to $15 per hour.

EXAMPLE: Carl plays ice hockey. If the demand to watch ice hockey games falls (perhaps people switch from watching ice hockey to watching more basketball), then the demand for hockey players will fall too. As a result, Carl's wage rate will fall. ◆

What Will You Earn?

If you are reading this book as part of a high school course, you are somewhere between the ages of 14 and 18. Let's jump ahead 15 years, when you will be between 29 and 33 years old. At that time, you will be working at some job and earning some wage rate or salary. You could be earning anywhere between, say, $20,000 and $500,000 a year. What will determine the amount you will earn?

▶ **How much do you think you would earn as an automobile mechanic? What are some of the factors that would determine your wage rate?**

Your wage rate (and salary) depends on a number of things, one of which is the demand for your labor services. The demand for you may be high, low, or medium. The higher the demand for you, the higher your wage rate will be. Obviously, you want the demand for you to be as high as possible.

Two factors will make the demand for your labor services high: (1) the demand for the good you produce, and (2) your productivity. The greater the demand for the product you produce, the greater is the demand for your labor services. If you produce attorney services and attorney services are in high demand, then you are in high demand, too. If you produce telephones and telephones are in low demand, then you will be in low demand, too.

The second factor that relates to the demand for you as an employee is your productivity. The more productive you are at what you do, the greater the demand for you. Suppose that two people can produce accounting services. One, however, can produce twice as many accounting services per hour as the other. It follows, then, that the faster accountant will be in greater demand by accounting firms.

A number of factors can influence your productivity. One factor is your innate abil-

Background Information: Gender and Wages

Gender is another significant factor that accounts for wage differences in the United States. For example, in 2003, women who worked full-time earned only 80 cents for every dollar earned by men. In 1980, the difference was even greater; women earned only 60% as much as men. Gender differences exist in other countries as well. For example, in South Korea women earn 60% as much as men; in France, 80%; in the Philippines, 91%; and in Australia, 102%. Ask students to list factors explaining why women often make less than men, and why they tend to make more than men in Australia.

Are Entertainers Worth Millions?

A television news anchor announces a particular sports star's new salary: $10 million a year. The anchor goes on to say that a particular TV star will now earn $1 million per episode, and a movie star will get $20 million for his next movie.

When looking at these large salaries, it is natural to ask whether the people who receive them are worth the money they are paid. Is anyone worth $1 million per episode or $10 million to play one season of baseball?

Would an economist say these high salaries are justified? Let's explore the question by laying out a possible set of facts.

Suppose you are the president of NBC, and a star of one of your hit shows is asking for $1 million per episode. Whether you pay it depends on whether the star is worth $1 million per episode. But how do you determine whether she is worth $1 million?

First, you ask yourself what would happen to the ratings of the show if the star were no longer on it. Suppose you think the ratings would drop. If they dropped, you could not charge as much for a 30-second commercial. Currently, a 30-second spot on a top-rated television show sells for about $450,000. For 10 30-second commercials, the revenue is $4.5 million.

Suppose that without the star on the television show you think that ratings would drop so that you could charge only $200,000 for a 30-second commercial. With 10 commercials, this price would reduce revenue to $2 million. In short, with the star the network earns revenue of $4.5 million an episode, and without the star it would earn revenue of $2 million per episode, a difference of $2.5 million. If the star left, revenue would drop by $2.5 million.

Is it worth paying $1 million to the star to prevent losing $2.5 million in revenue? The answer is yes. As long as the additional revenue that the star generates (in this case, an additional $2.5 million) is greater than the star's salary (in this case, $1 million), then the star is worth what she is paid.

THINK ABOUT IT Sometimes a large difference separates what a star earns from what others who work with the star earn. For example, in 2005, Shaquille O'Neal, who played with the Miami Heat (NBA basketball team) earned $30,466,072. Another player, Dorrell Wright, earned $1,032,200. What explains such a large difference between what a star earns and what those who work with the star earn?

ity; you may simply have been born with a great ability to organize people, play baseball, sing a song, or write a story. A second factor is how much effort you put into developing your skills. You may have worked hard developing and perfecting your ability to produce a service, whether it is attorney services, teaching services, or medical services. Third, your productivity is affected by the quality and length of your education. The higher the quality of your education and the more education you have, the more productive you will be (all other things being equal). In fact, statistics show that as one's educational level rises, so does one's income. In summary, the demand for you (as an employee) will rise with the demand for the product or service you produce and your productivity.

Of course, your wage (or salary) in the future depends not only upon how high or low the demand for you is in the future but

Prompt students to think of their favorite athlete or TV star and to guess what the star earns annually. Ask if students think the high salaries of such people are justified.

ANSWERS TO THINK ABOUT IT Answers will vary. Students should understand that a highly paid star presumably brings in much higher revenue for the team than other players on the team.

Economics Around the Clock

After reading and discussing "Are Entertainers Worth Millions?" ask students to discuss their answers to the 7:14 A.M. scenario in Economics Around the Clock (page 223).

Basketball players in the NBA earn high salaries because the demand for them is high and the supply of them is low. Part of the reason the demand is high is because so many people enjoy watching professional basketball—one of whom is Blake. If basketball had fewer fans like Blake, basketball players wouldn't earn as much as they do.

Discussion Starter

The salaries for professional sports and Hollywood stars are so high that many people cannot fathom the amounts of money that they earn. When you think that a professional basketball star could make $15 million in one season, the number seems inconceivable. However, when broken down over an 82-game season, that would be approximately $182,926.83 a game, or $3,810.90 a minute, or $63.50 a second. Make sure students can see, even through these enormous numbers, that the market of supply and demand can still support these salaries.

Internet Research

Assign students to go online to find the 10 to 20 highest-paid executives in the United States. Assign students to select one of these businesspeople and conduct online research about the company for which the executive works, and, if possible, find a biographical sketch of the person. In small groups, allow students to share the results of their research and explain why they believe the executives earn such high salaries.

Teaching with Visuals

Answers will vary. Students should see that Hudson's high wages are a result of high demand combined with low supply.

Can the demand for football in other countries affect the salary of a football player in the United States? It certainly can. To illustrate, consider the Super Bowl, which is broadcast around the world. There seems to be a demand by people in other countries for watching American football. If that demand were to fall, foreign TV ratings of the Super Bowl would fall, reducing the amount firms would pay to advertise during the Super Bowl. This would reduce the earnings of the football teams, and teams would not be willing to pay the same salaries to football players. Teams would pay players less.

Reinforcement Activity

Instruct students to write a sentence in which they define the role of the equilibrium wage rate in the supply and demand for labor.

▶ Actress Kate Hudson attends a screening of *Elizabethtown* in Toronto in September 2005. **What qualities do you think contribute to Kate's earning more than most people her age?**

also upon the number of people who can do what you do. In short, it also depends on supply. For example, the demand for you may be high, but if the supply is high too, you are not likely to earn a high wage. High wages are the result of high demand combined with low supply.

> ***"I'm living so far beyond my income that we may almost be said to be living apart."***
> — E. E. CUMMINGS

Why is supply high in some labor markets and low in others? The supply of labor offered in a particular labor market is the result of a number of factors, one of which is the ability to perform a particular service. For example, more people can work as restaurant servers than as brain surgeons. Similarly, more people can drive trucks than can argue and win difficult law cases before the U.S. Supreme Court. These statements do not put a value judgment on work as a restaurant server or truck driver. They simply report the fact that some tasks can be completed by more people than others. All other things being equal, the fewer people who can do what you do, the higher your wage (or salary) will be.

EXAMPLE: Orthopedic surgeons earn a lot of money each year because they possess the three factors necessary to generate a high income. First, they are part of a (medical) team that produces health services, a service that is in high demand. Second, orthopedic surgeons are productive. Third, not many people can do what they do (supply is low). In short, as was stated earlier, the combination of high demand for the good or service produced, high productivity, and a situation where not many people can do what one does, results in a high salary. ♦

minimum wage law A federal law that specifies the lowest hourly wage rate that can be paid to workers.

Government and the Minimum Wage

The **minimum wage law** sets a wage floor—that is, a level below which hourly wage rates are not allowed to fall. The law, passed during the Great Depression of the

BY THE NUMBERS

Every two years the U.S. Department of Labor publishes an interesting book titled the *Occupational Outlook Handbook*. You can see the most current edition of the book at www.emcp.net/jobs. If you are planning your work future, this book will be especially important to you. It identifies the median salary, job growth, and educational requirements of almost every job you can think of. Want to know how much a mathematician earns? Go to the handbook. Want to know what the educational requirements are for a teacher? Go to the handbook. Here are the 10 occupations that the Bureau of Labor Statistics predicts will be the fastest growing during the period 2002–2012.

Occupation	Growth rate (%) during the period 2002–2012
Medical assistants	59
Network systems and data communications analysts	57
Physician assistants	49
Social and human service assistants	49
Home health aides	48
Medical records and health information technicians	47
Physical therapist aides	46
Computer software engineers, applications	46
Computer software engineers, systems software	45
Physical therapist assistants	45

Cooperative Learning

Divide students into small groups and assign each group a job category in which people tend to earn high salaries (entertainment, music, athletics, television, journalism). Each group should identify five to 10 well-known people in that field and research the annual salaries of each. Each group should create a visual documenting the salaries. Ask groups to prepare and present oral reports to show their visuals and provide explanations for salary differences among the people they have researched.

◀ This worker is paid the minimum wage at a sporting goods store near his home. **How do you think he would be affected if the government raised the minimum wage by $2 an hour?**

1930s, initially established a minimum wage of 25 cents an hour. In 2005, the federal minimum wage was $5.15 an hour. Some states, such as California, Washington, and Massachusetts, set their minimum wage rate higher than the federal rate. (An employee who is tipped, such as a restaurant server, is only required to be paid $2.13 an hour in wages if that amount plus the tips received equals at least the federal minimum wage. Also, a minimum wage of $4.25 per hour applies to young workers under the age of 20 during their first 90 consecutive calendar days of employment.)

The U.S. Congress determines the minimum wage. Earlier, however, you read that supply and demand determine wage rates. So what really does determine wage rates—the government or supply and demand? The fact is that supply and demand usually, but not always, determine wages.

Suppose that in a particular labor market the equilibrium wage rate is $4.10 an hour. In other words, the demand curve and the supply curve of labor intersect at a wage rate of $4.10. Congress then argues that a wage rate of $4.10 an hour is too low, and it orders employers to pay employees at least $5.15 an hour. This rate is now the minimum wage. It becomes unlawful to pay an employee less than this hourly wage.

Many people would agree with Congress that a wage of $4.10 an hour is simply too low. Economists, however, are not so interested in whether Congress is justified in setting a minimum wage as they are in knowing the *effects* of setting the minimum wage rate above the equilibrium wage rate. They know what the intended effects are, but they also wonder about the unintended effects. For example, will employers hire as many workers at the minimum wage rate of $5.15 as they would at the equilibrium wage rate of $4.10? Remember, the demand curve for labor is downward sloping (from left to right). As the wage rate falls, employers will hire more workers; and as the wage rate rises, they will hire fewer workers. Thus, a minimum wage rate set by Congress above the equilibrium wage rate will result in employers being willing and able to hire fewer workers.

A Student Asks

QUESTION: *Without a minimum wage law, wouldn't employers pay next to nothing for unskilled labor?*

ANSWER: *Suppose 100 people are working and earning the minimum wage of $5.15 an hour. First ask whether these people are worth $5.15 an hour. The answer has to be yes, because no employer would pay someone $5.15 an hour unless the employee was worth $5.15 an hour to the employer.*

Now let's ask ourselves whether the people who are not worth $5.15 an hour to an employer are working when the minimum wage is in existence. The answer is no. For example, Jack, 16 years old, may be worth $4.90 an hour, but not worth $5.15, so if the employer has to pay Jack $5.15 an hour he will not hire

Teaching with Visuals

Student answers will vary. Students should understand that if the minimum wage were raised, employers might hire fewer workers.

Economics Around the Clock

After reading and discussing "Government and the Minimum Wage" (pages 232–233), instruct students to discuss their answers to the 8:44 A.M. scenario in Economics Around the Clock (page 223). The effect immigration has on wages depends on whether immigration increases the supply of labor by more than, less than, or equal to how much it increases the demand for labor.

Cause and Effect

Many students may think that the minimum wage only increases earnings and has no effect on employment rates. Have students evaluate this scenario and determine the effect on wages and employment rates: A company has enough money to pay $28 an hour in wages. It has five employees, all of whom make $5.60 an hour working full time. What would happen if the government raised the minimum wage to $7 an hour? to $8 an hour? How would such an increase affect the company and its workers?

A Student Asks

You may want to use this A Student Asks to make sure students understand the intended and unintended effects of the minimum wage law.

Cooperative Learning

Some students may have already worked at full-time positions in the summer and perhaps hold down jobs during the school year. Divide the class into groups, making sure that there is at least one student who has worked in each group. Assign groups to create lists of costs and benefits of working, including the lost time from school studies and the chance to make their own money. Stress that you are not necessarily endorsing working during school, but at some point in time all of them will have a job, and will have to give up something else to have it.

Ask students to provide some examples of U.S. companies hiring foreign labor. Ask, What is the role of productivity in hiring foreign labor?

ANSWERS TO ECONOMIC THINKING Students should conclude that the difference between foreign wages and U.S. wages would fall.

Prediction Activity

Instruct students to think about the following question: The prices of goods and services are rising, but money wages do not seem to be rising at the same pace. What will happen to real wages in the near future? (*Answer:* Because it costs more in money wages to purchase goods and services, real wages will fall.)

Teaching with Visuals

The answer to the question accompanying the photo on page 235 is that increasing prices at the pump will cause this person's real wages to fall.

Application Activity

After reading and discussing Section 1, you may want to assign the Section Activity in the *Applying the Principles Workbook.*

Assess

Quick Quiz

The following true-or-false quiz will help you assess student understanding of the material covered in this section.

1. The price of labor is called the derived demand. (False)
2. The equilibrium wage rate is established where the quantity demanded of labor equals the quantity supplied of labor. (True)
3. Location could be a nonmoney benefit. (True)
4. If the demand for a good increases, the wage for the producers of that good decreases. (False)
5. The minimum wage law sets a wage floor. (True)

Wages Around the World

Today the average worker in the United States earns more per hour than the average worker in India, China, Mexico, and many other countries. This comparison does not mean that U.S. companies will hire only foreign labor, because sometimes the foreign labor is not as productive as the U.S. labor. However, when the high U.S. worker productivity does not compensate for the high wage cost of U.S. labor, U.S. companies will hire foreign labor instead of U.S. labor. As a result of U.S. companies hiring foreign labor, the demand for the foreign labor rises.

ECONOMIC THINKING What do we expect to happen to the gap between U.S. wages and foreign wages? Suppose some U.S. companies start hiring workers in India because they are as productive as U.S. workers but earn lower wages. Will the difference between the U.S. wage and the Indian wage rise, fall, or stay constant?

him in the first place. Now ask what happens if the minimum wage is scrapped. Do the 100 people who were earning $5.15 find themselves earning only $2 an hour? Not at all. If they were hired when the wage rate was mandated at $5.15, then they truly must be worth $5.15 an hour, and if someone offers them $2 an hour, they will simply move to work for someone who pays them their market wage of $5.15 an hour.

Scrapping the minimum wage law will not lower the wage rate for workers currently earning the minimum wage; instead, it will bring people into the labor force who weren't previously worth the minimum wage. It brings Jack into the market, because now an employer is willing to hire Jack if he can pay him $4.90 an hour. Most likely, in time Jack will acquire new skills that will make him worth more (to an employer), and he will earn a higher wage.

Two Types of Wages: Money and Real

Suppose Patel earns $9 an hour in 2004 and $12 an hour in 2005. Is she better off in 2004 or in 2005? The obvious answer seems to be that she is better off in 2005, when she earns the higher wage rate. This answer, however, assumes that the prices of the goods and services she buys in 2004 and 2005 are the same, but they may not be. Prices may be higher in 2005 than 2004. Whether Patel is better off in 2005 than 2004 depends on how much her wages increased compared to the increase in prices.

We can measure a person's wage rate in terms of money (for example, $9 or $11 per hour) or in terms of what the wages will buy. Measuring a person's wage rate in terms of money gives us the person's *money wage* (sometimes the *money wage* is called the *nominal wage*). Measuring a person's wage rate in terms of what it buys gives us the person's *real wage.* Can a person's money wage rise while the person's real wage falls? Let's look at an example.

EXAMPLE: Suppose the only good that Patel buys is chocolate bars. In 2004, chocolate bars sell for $1 a bar. With a wage rate of $9 an hour, Patel can buy 9 chocolate bars an hour. In 2005, chocolate bars are $2 a bar; with $12 an hour, Patel can buy 6 chocolate bars an hour. Patel went from earning $9 to $12 an hour, but her real wage fell from 9 chocolate bars an hour to 6 chocolate bars an hour. Everyone talks in terms of money wages ("I earn $10 an hour"), but our real wage is far more important because it measures what we can do with the money wage we receive.

We are paid in money wages, so how do we compute our real wages so that we can see how much better off or worse off we are in terms of buying power from one period to the next? We computed Patel's real wage in 2004 versus 2005 by simply dividing the money wage in each year by the price of a chocolate bar in each year. In the real world, of course, people do not simply buy chocolate bars; they buy a variety of goods. The government measures the "average price" of these goods, usually called a price index.

Differentiating Instruction

English Language Learners

To help ELL students, use the following resources, which are provided as part of the *Economics: New Ways of Thinking* program:

- a Spanish glossary in the *Student Text*
- Spanish versions of the Chapter Summaries on an audio CD

One particularly well-known price index is the *Consumer Price Index*, or *CPI*. Perhaps you heard a television newscaster say, "The government reported today that the CPI rose by 4 percent over the year." In other words, prices, on average, are 4 percent higher this year than last year.

The government computes the CPI on an annual basis. Therefore, we can compute our real wage by simply dividing our money wage in a given year by the CPI in the same year:

$$\text{Real wage} = \frac{\text{Money wage}}{\text{CPI}}$$

For example, suppose in 2002 a person earned a wage rate of $20 an hour, and the CPI was 177. The person's real wage was 0.113. In percentage terms, it is 11.3 percent—but 11.3 percent of what? In the chocolate bar example, it would be 11.3 percent of one chocolate bar. But we aren't talking about chocolate bars here; we are talking about many goods. Think of the 0.113, then, as 11.3 percent of one unit of a composite good. This composite good is a little food, a little housing, and a little entertainment all rolled up into one. With $20 an hour, then, a person can purchase 11.3 percent of one unit of the composite good.

▲ **How does increasing prices at the pump affect this person's real wage?**

Now suppose the person's wage rate rises to $30 in 2005. Furthermore, let's suppose that the CPI in 2005 turns out to be 190. What, then, is the person's real wage? If we divide $30 by 190, we get 0.1578, or 15.78 percent of one unit of a composite good.

Is the person's real wage higher in 2002 or in 2005? The answer is 2005. In 2002, the real wage rate is 11.3 percent of one unit of a composite good, and in 2005 it is 15.78 percent of one unit of a composite good. ♦

Section 1 Assessment

Defining Terms

1. Define:
   a. wage rate
   b. derived demand
   c. minimum wage law
2. Give an example of a money wage and a real wage.

Reviewing Facts and Concepts

3. In a competitive labor market, suppose the quantity demanded of labor is greater than the quantity supplied. What will happen to the wage rate? Explain.
4. John is paid $7 an hour, and Kimsan is paid $23 an hour. In general, why does Kimsan earn more than John?
5. Mauricio accepts a job that pays $35,000 a year instead of a job that pays $80,000 a year. What do the nonmoney benefits in the $35,000 job equal (at minimum)? Explain your answer.

Critical Thinking

6. If major league baseball becomes less popular, what will happen to players' salaries? Explain your answer.

Applying Economic Concept

7. Over the past three years, Rachel's money wage increased by 10 percent, and prices increased by 13 percent. Has Rachel's real wage increased, decreased, or remained stable? Explain your answer.

Assessment Book

You will find a quiz for this section in the *Assessment Book.*

Reteaching Activity

Use the Section Assessment to gauge which students may need reteaching on this section. Have those students work in pairs to complete the following sentences (the correct answers are provided for your reference):

1. The wage rate is the price of labor.
2. When there is a surplus of labor, the wage rate falls.
3. Wage rates may differ because demand conditions for different types of labor are not the same or because the supply conditions for different types of labor are not the same.

Guided Reading

For further reteaching of the key concepts in this section, assign the Outlining Activity and the Just the Facts Handout from the *Guided Reading and Study Guide.*

Section 1 Assessment Answers

Defining Terms

1. a. wage rate: the price of labor; **b. derived demand:** demand that is the result of some other demand; **c. minimum wage law:** federal law that specifies the lowest hourly wage rate that can be paid to workers.
2. A person's money wage is the amount the person is paid in dollars; "$4 an hour" is a money wage. Real wage is a measurement of what money wage can buy in terms of goods and services; "3 units of good X" is a real wage.

Reviewing Facts and Concepts

3. The wage rate will rise. The price of labor rises when a shortage in the labor market occurs.
4. Demand and supply conditions in John's labor market are different from Kimsan's. Wage rates are a reflection of supply and demand. If rates differ among competitive labor markets, it is because the supply and demand conditions differ.
5. Nonmoney benefits at the $35,000 job equal $45,000 in money benefits. Nonmoney benefits include, but are not limited to, location, vacation time, and management.

Critical Thinking

6. If major league baseball loses popularity, salaries fall. The demand for major league baseball players is derived from the demand for baseball. If baseball becomes less popular, the demand for baseball falls. If the demand for baseball falls, the demand for baseball players falls. If the demand for baseball players falls, their salaries will fall.

Applying Economic Concepts

7. Rachel's real wage has decreased. A person's real wage can be viewed as a ratio, with money wages as the numerator and a price index as the denominator. If the numerator rises by less than the denominator, then the ratio becomes smaller, or the real wage falls.

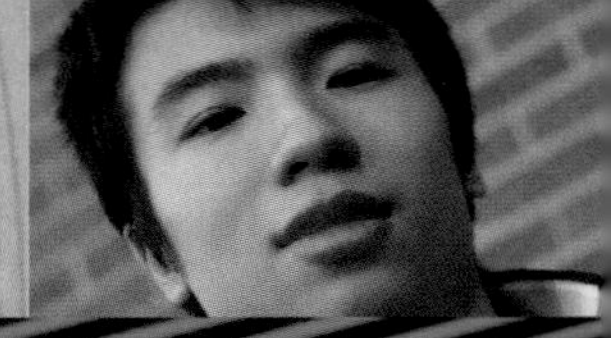

Your Personal Economics

Discussion Starter

Inquire as to whether students have ever thought about multiplying themselves. Ask: How could you do that? What role could education play in multiplying yourselves? For students who have not thought of education in this way, suggest that they reconsider the value of education.

Research Activity

After students have studied the table in the text, direct them to the Internet to research the same information for the years between 2003 and current year. They should investigate these questions: Did the unemployment rate pattern stay the same each year? Did the median weekly earnings pattern stay the same each year? Ask students how this information could be useful to them at this time in their lives.

Your Personal Economics

Education—It's Like Multiplying Yourself

Here is what possibly could be one of the most important tables you will ever see. It is from the U.S. Bureau of Labor Statistics.

More Money, More Security

This table shows you the unemployment rate and the median weekly earnings in 2003 for individuals with various levels of education. For example, the average person with some high school but no diploma earned $396 a week in 2003 and had an unemployment rate of 8.8 percent. Now notice what happens as one's educational level rises. First, his or her weekly earnings rise. Second, the unemployment rate falls. In other words, *more education brings a higher income and a*

▼ Diplomas can double your earnings.

Education attained	Unemployment rate in 2003	Median weekly earnings in 2003
Doctoral degree	2.1%	$1,349
Master's degree	2.9	1,064
Bachelor's degree	3.3	900
Associate degree	4.0	672
Some college, no degree	5.2	622
High school graduate	5.5	554
Some high school, no diploma	8.8	396

Cooperative Learning

Divide students into groups of three or four. Tell each group to draw the same comparisons as the text, using median weekly earnings of the current year. The group should calculate lifetime earnings for an 18-year-old working for 48 years, for someone with a bachelor's degree working for 43 years, and for someone with a master's degree working for 41 years. After 15 minutes, let all groups report their calculations to the class.

smaller probability of being unemployed.

In fact, as you get more education, it is like multiplying yourself. To see how, let's suppose you compare your earnings under two scenarios. In the first you have some high school (but no diploma). In the second case, you earn a master's degree.

An Important Comparison

Let's assume that you have some high school (only), and you start working when you are 18 and stop working when you are 65. You will earn an average of $396 a week for 48 years. This yields a total of $988,416 in lifetime earnings (before taxes).

Now let's assume you have a master's degree. Getting this degree means that you will work for fewer years because you must go to college to earn a bachelor's degree (that's 4 or 5 years) and then on to graduate school to earn a master's degree (let's say 2 years). So, in total, you will work 6 to 7 years less. You will earn, then, an average of $1,064 a week for, say, 41 years. The total ends up being $2,268,448 in lifetime earnings (before taxes).

Now we know that your lifetime earnings with a master's degree ($2,268,448) are more than double your lifetime earnings with only some high school ($988,416). What do these comparisons mean then? Simply that a master's degree gives you the ability to create another one of yourself. In other words, when you go into the labor market with only some high school, it is like one of you going to work. But when you go into the labor market with a master's degree, it is like two of you going to work. It's you and your double.

My Personal Economics Action Plan

Here are some points you may want to consider and some guidelines you might want to put into practice:

1. The more education you have, the higher your lifetime earnings likely will be.

   I will graduate from high school with the highest possible grade point average.

2. The more education you have, the less likely you will be unemployed.

   After graduating from high school, I will enroll in ______ to get a degree in ______.

3. Going from a high school diploma to a master's degree is equivalent to creating a double of yourself.

   After graduating from ______, I will assess my options for graduate school and make a decision to obtain a graduate degree in ______ by the time I am ______ years old.

4. Some people say they don't like school and would rather go to work as soon as possible. Look at it this way. Whether you are in school or working at a job, you have something to do eight hours a day. It's not a choice between going to school and doing nothing; the choice is between learning eight hours a day or working eight hours a day. Sometimes learning looks a lot better when you see at it as a substitute for work (instead of as a substitute for leisure).

   I will substitute learning for working ______ hours a day for ______ years so that I can earn twice as much money in my lifetime.

Discussion Starter

To help students realize the power of using education to multiply themselves, ask them to list necessities that can be purchased with wages, such as a house, a car, and food. Invite them to put a dollar amount on each necessity. Then instruct students to calculate how much money is left from weekly earnings after subtracting money for necessities. Ask them to do this for each of the three educational levels. Then have students compare the money left from the weekly earnings in each educational level situation. Ask students if this information changed their minds about education. Ask what they can do now to earn a good salary as an adult.

My Personal Economics Action Plan Instruct students each to survey adults they know to determine if the adults experience the same pattern of more education bringing a higher income. Students may want to ask follow-up questions to determine what kinds of situations break the pattern. Allow students to report their findings in small groups.

SECTION 2 Teacher Support

Focus and Motivate

Section Objectives

After completing this section, students will be able to

- describe how labor unions affect labor demand and supply;
- explain what union and closed shops are;
- identify states that have right-to-work laws; and
- provide examples of the unintended effects of regulation.

Kickoff Activity

Invite students to respond in writing to the following question: What is a labor union? Allow volunteers to share their answers with the rest of the class. Knowing how well your students understand labor unions and their activities will be helpful as you decide how best to present this material.

Activating Prior Knowledge

To an economist, the minimum wage law is neither a good law nor a bad law. It is a law that has consequences; specifically, because of it, fewer persons will end up working than would work without it. Ask students' opinions on whether the law is worth keeping.

Teach

Discussion Starter

Ask students if they know of anyone who is a member of a labor union. One student may say her father belongs to a labor union. Another may say his next-door neighbor belongs to a labor union. Invite students to share what they know about labor unions. Ask if labor unions help working men and women, and if so, in what ways they help workers.

SECTION 2 Labor and Government Regulation

Focus Questions

- How do labor unions affect labor demand and supply?
- What is a union shop? Closed shop?
- How many states have right-to-work laws?
- What are some of the unintended effects of regulation?

Key Terms

labor union
closed shop
Taft-Hartley Act
union shop
strike
right-to-work law

Some Practices of Labor Unions

One objective of a **labor union** may be to obtain higher pay for its members. The union then must direct its activities to increasing the demand for its labor, decreasing the supply of its labor, or both.

labor union
An organization that seeks to increase the wages and improve the working conditions of its members.

closed shop
An organization that hires only union members.

Taft-Hartley Act
An act, passed in 1947 by the U.S. Congress, which made the closed shop illegal and gave states the right to pass right-to-work laws. These right-to-work laws prohibit employers from establishing union membership as a condition of employment.

union shop
An organization that requires employees to join the union within a certain period after being hired.

The Demand for Union Labor

As stated earlier, if the demand for a good decreases, then the demand for the labor that produces the good decreases, too. For example, if the demand for cars decreases, then the demand decreases for the workers who produce cars. If the demand for cars increases, of course, the demand increases for the workers who produce cars.

With that relationship in mind, suppose you are a union worker in the U.S. automobile industry, centered in Detroit, Michigan. Would you want the demand for American-made cars to increase, stay constant, or decrease? Obviously, you would want the demand for American-made cars to increase, because you know that if it increases, the demand for your labor increases, too. As the demand for your labor increases, your wage rate increases, all other things remaining the same.

For this reason your labor union might try to increase the demand for the product it produces. It might launch an advertising campaign urging people to purchase only union-produced goods. For example, television commercials in the past have urged people to "look for the union label"—in other words, buy union-made goods. Also, when U.S. union workers are in competition with workers in other countries (for example, U.S. car workers are in competition with Japanese car workers), an advertising campaign might urge people to buy goods "made in the U.S.A."—another union slogan in the recent past.

The Supply of Union Labor

Just as a labor union tries to increase the demand for its labor, it also tries to decrease labor supply. Suppose you work as a truck driver. Would you prefer to be one of a thousand truck drivers in the United States or one of ten thousand truck drivers? Your answer probably is one of a thousand,

Internet Research

Direct students to visit the Web sites for several major labor unions, such as the Teamsters and United Auto Workers. Assign them to find out what services the unions provide for their members, and what activities and actions unions are involved in. Students should write a page explaining the effects that these services and activities might have on wages for both union and nonunion workers in these industries.

because you know that the lower the supply of truck drivers, the higher your wage rate, all other things remaining the same.

Some people criticize labor unions for trying to control the supply of labor at times. In the past, some unions supported **closed shops**, organizations that hire only union members. To work for these companies, people would first have to join the labor union. The labor union, in turn, might hold down the number of workers who could join (and thus work in the particular industry) in order to keep the supply of workers in that industry low and keep wage rates high. The union could perhaps do this by limiting membership or requiring long training periods. Today, the closed shop is illegal. It was prohibited by the **Taft-Hartley Act**, passed by the U.S. Congress in 1947.

The **union shop**, however, is legal in many states. A union shop does not require individuals to be union members in order to be hired, but it does require employees to join the union within a certain period of time after being hired. Labor unions favor union shops, because if everyone working in a particular trade or industry has to become a member of the union within a certain period of time, the labor union gains greater control over the supply of labor. For example, consider the **strike**, a work stoppage called by union members to put pressure on an employer. It is easier for the union to call a strike if everyone in a particular trade or industry is a member of the union.

Today, 22 states have passed **right-to-work laws**, which make it illegal to require union membership for purposes of employment. In short, in states with right-to-work laws, the union shop is illegal. Exhibit 9-5 shows the states with right-to-work laws. Also, today approximately 12.5 percent of all workers are members of unions.

▲ **Why do you think these union workers oppose free trade?**

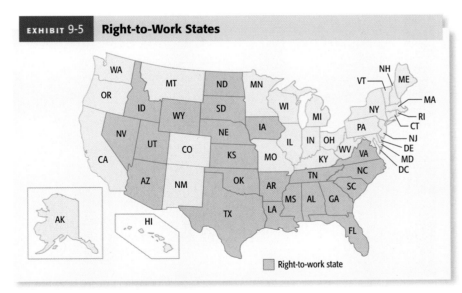

EXHIBIT 9-5 Right-to-Work States

WA, OR, CA, ID, NV, MT, WY, UT, AZ, CO, NM, ND, SD, NE, KS, OK, TX, MN, IA, MO, AR, LA, WI, IL, MI, IN, OH, KY, TN, MS, AL, GA, FL, SC, NC, VA, WV, PA, NY, VT, NH, ME, MA, RI, CT, NJ, DE, MD, DC, AK, HI

Right-to-work state

◀ Union shops are illegal in the 22 states with right-to-work laws.

strike
A work stoppage called by union members to put pressure on an employer.

right-to-work law
A state law that prohibits the practice of requiring employees to join a union in order to work.

Teaching with Visuals

Answers will vary. Students should see that unions try to increase the demand for labor and decrease labor supply. Free trade would jeopardize that effort.

Discussion Starter

Strikes and work slowdowns have become common tools for organized labor. What other tools might labor unions employ to improve working conditions for their members?

Reinforcement Activity

The Taft-Hartley Act is discussed briefly on page 239. Ask students to research this act. Instruct them to either turn in their work or share their findings with the rest of the class. Remind students to include what happened in that period of U.S. history that caused the government to pass this act. Stress the importance of placing legislative acts in a correct historical perspective.

Background Information: Strikes

Strikes have generally been peaceful, but there are exceptions. You might want to review the history of the strike at the McCormick Harvester Works in Chicago on May 3, 1886, when one worker was killed and several were injured. A public meeting was called at Chicago's Haymarket Square the next day to protest the killing of the worker. That rally ended in violence. When police marched into the square to break up the meeting, someone in the crowd threw a dynamite bomb. Seven people were killed by the bomb, and four more people were killed in the ensuing exchange of gunfire between the police and armed men in the crowd. At least 60 people were injured.

Unions' Effects on Union and Nonunion Wages

On average, do union workers receive higher pay than comparable nonunion workers? (By saying *comparable nonunion workers*, we are comparing union and nonunion workers who do essentially the same work.) One important economics study concluded that over the period from 1920 to 1979, the average wage of union members was 10 to 15 percent higher than that of comparable nonunion labor. That is, for every $100 earned by nonunion labor, comparable union labor earned between $110 and $115. In 2004, the U.S. Bureau of Labor Statistics reported that mean weekly earnings for union workers were about 27 percent higher than for nonunion workers.

An economic reason supports these results. Suppose the labor force has 100 persons; 25 are members of a union, and 75 are not. We assume that each of the 100 persons can work in either the union or the nonunion part of the economy. Furthermore, we assume that each of the 100 persons currently earns a wage rate of $15.

Suppose now that the labor union (of which 25 persons are members) calls a strike and ends up bargaining its way to a wage rate of $20. At $20 per hour, the businesses that currently employ union labor workers do not wish to employ as many persons as they wished to employ at a wage rate of $15, so a few of the union workers get fired. Let's say that five workers get fired.

The five union workers who were fired seek jobs in the nonunion part of the economy. As a result, the supply of persons in the nonunion part rises (from 75 to 80). An increase in the supply of labor puts downward pressure on wage rates in the nonunion part of the economy. The wage rate moves down from $15 to $13. Can you see from this example how unions are likely to affect wages of both union and nonunion workers?

Two Views of Labor Unions

There are two major views of labor unions' effects on production and efficiency. The traditional view holds that labor unions are an obstacle to establishing reasonable work standards and thus make companies that employ union labor less competitive. For example, suppose some members of a plumbers' union work for a manufacturing company. The union may insist that in this company only a plumber (and no one else) can change the washer on a leaky faucet. Union critics argue that such rigid staffing requirements are unreasonable and that they

▶ Members of this union are picketing nonunion workers at the Port of Long Beach in California. **How might this type of activity benefit the union workers?**

Cause and Effect

Labor unions are sometimes blamed for things they do not cause. For example, some people will argue that because labor unions bargain for higher wages and businesses end up paying the higher wages and charging higher prices, labor unions cause inflation. However, this is not true. Inflation is caused by other factors.

Background Information

In August 1997, union workers employed by United Parcel Service went on strike, primarily to protest UPS's increased use of part-time workers. The strike, which lasted 16 days, was the largest in more than a decade. It was also highly successful, in part because of its effect on businesses that depended on UPS for deliveries.

Teaching with Visuals

You may want to make sure that students understand the meaning of the term *picketing*. Answers will vary. Students should note that the purpose of this type of activity is to attract negative press and to pressure companies into using union labor.

Background Information: César Chávez, Migrant Farm Worker and Labor Leader

César Estrada Chávez (1927–1993) was born into a California migrant family who traveled to pick fruits and vegetables during the harvest. After completing the eighth grade, César quit school and worked full-time in the fields. He protested the low pay and poor working conditions of the migrant workers, forming a labor organization, the National Farm Workers Association (NFWA), which later became the United Farm Workers (UFW).

In 1965, Chávez and the NFWA led a strike of California grape pickers to demand higher wages. He encouraged Americans to boycott table grapes as a show of support. In 1970, with 17 million people supporting the grape boycott, the growers signed an

240 Chapter 9 Labor, Employment, and Wages

Will You Sleep Less if You Earn More?

Do you remember from Chapter 1 that the opportunity cost of something is the most valued opportunity or alternative you have to give up (or forfeit) to do something? For example, if you were not reading this chapter right now, you might be talking to a friend on the telephone; thus, "talking to a friend on the telephone" is the opportunity cost to you of reading this chapter.

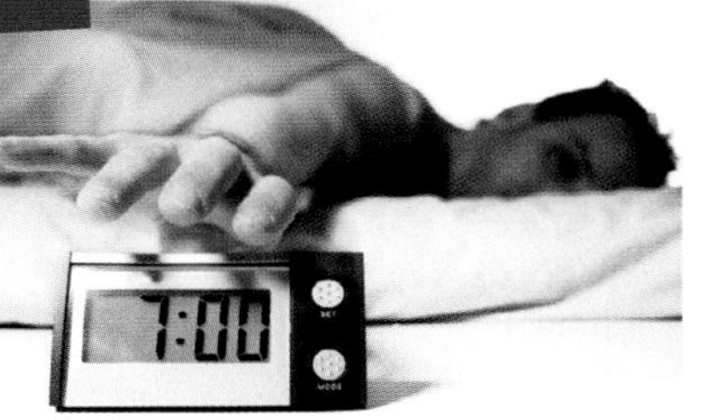

Now let's see if we can tie together opportunity cost, education, and wage rates with the number of hours a person sleeps. We know that as educational achievement rises, a person's wage rate rises. It is possible to view a person's wage rate as the opportunity cost of not working. In other words, a person who earns $20 an hour when she is working is forfeiting this amount when she chooses not to work. It follows, then, that people who earn relatively high wages have higher opportunity costs of not working than do people who earn relatively low wages. For example, the person with the doctorate (who earns $32.27 an hour) forfeits more than the person with only the high school diploma (who earns $10.71 an hour) when that person does not work.

One of the things we do when we do not work is sleep. It follows that the opportunity cost of sleeping is higher for the person with more education and higher wages than for the person with less education and lower wages. An economist would predict that the higher the opportunity cost of sleeping, the less one will sleep. If the economist is correct, we should see that individuals who are more educated and earn higher incomes will sleep less than those who are less educated and earn lower incomes.

More education → Higher wages → Higher opportunity cost of not working → Higher opportunity cost of sleeping →Sleep less

Two economists, J. Biddle and D. Hammermesh, did present evidence that on average, sleep is related to education and wage rates. They found that more-educated people earn more and sleep less than less-educated people who earn less. They sleep 14 minutes less for each year of additional schooling. In short, more education may be good for your wallet, but it's not so good for your sleep.

THINK ABOUT IT Blackwell has a high school diploma, earns $10 an hour, and sleeps 8 hours a night. Nitobe has a doctorate, earns $100 an hour, and sleeps 8 hours and 30 minutes a night. Both Blackwell and Nitobe are the same age. If our evidence is correct, does it mean that the Biddle and Hammermesh evidence must be incorrect?

make these companies less competitive in a world economy. When a company loses its competitive edge, it may go out of business.

A newer view says that the labor union is a valuable collective voice for its members. Evidence in some industries indicates that union firms have a higher rate of productivity than nonunion firms. Economists explain this difference by saying that the labor union acts as a collective voice mechanism for its members. Without a labor union, some argue, workers who were disgruntled with their jobs, who felt taken advantage of by their employers, or who felt unsafe in their work would leave their jobs and seek work elsewhere. This "job exiting" comes at a cost. It raises training costs for the firm and results in lengthy job searches during which those searching for jobs are not producing goods. Such costs can be

agreement with Chávez's union; the strike had lasted five years. Today Chávez is given credit for bringing to the attention of the U.S. public the poor working conditions of migrant workers, and for initiating the process that led to improved working conditions.

Economics in the Real World

Ask students to estimate the number of hours of sleep they get during a school week. Ask if they get less sleep during the week because they are studying.

ANSWERS TO THINK ABOUT IT Answers will vary. Students must understand that the study looks at averages, and that any average statistic may have varying evidence.

Analyzing

We have presented two views of labor unions: the traditional view and the new view. Assign a one-page essay defending one of the two views and pointing out the weaknesses of the other view. Alternatively, you can ask students to find examples (in books, magazines, newspapers, or the Internet) of either of the two views. Invite students to report their findings to the class.

Discussion Starter

Instruct students to discuss their views on labor unions after reading this section. Some students may have family members who have been involved in unions, but make sure students can support their opinions on whether labor unions are a positive or a negative force in the U.S. economy.

Reinforcement Activity

This part of the text highlights an interesting period in U.S. history. Instruct students to research different organizations or laws discussed on these pages. For example, students may research the American Federation of Labor, the Wagner Act, or the Congress of Industrial Organizations. Point out to students that the history of labor unions is mixed—at times it seems that labor unions are mistreated and at other times that labor unions take harsh measures against industries and individual businesses.

Analyzing

For the most part, only labor has been unionized, but there are notable exceptions. More than one million teachers belong to the American Federation of Teachers, a union. Some engineers belong to the International Association of Mechanics and Aerospace Workers, and some doctors and dentists belong to the Union of American Physicians and Dentists. Guide students in a discussion about why highly educated professionals might choose to join a union.

Teaching with Visuals

Discuss with students the impact images such as this may have had on people's opinions of unions.

reduced, it is argued, when a labor union provides a collective voice for its members. Instead of individual employees discussing sensitive employment matters with their employers, the labor union does it for them. Overall, the labor union makes the employees feel more confident, less intimidated, and more secure in their work. Such positive feelings usually mean happier, more productive employees.

A Brief History of the Labor Movement

National unionism began to emerge in the United States after the Civil War. Because labor unions greatly affect the U.S. economy, you should be aware of some of the key events in the development of these unions.

The Knights of Labor

In 1869, a union called the Knights of Labor was organized. Seventeen years later, in 1886, its membership totaled approximately 800,000. The Knights of Labor welcomed anyone who worked for a living—farmers, skilled workers, and unskilled workers—with a few exceptions, such as liquor dealers. The group called for higher wages and an eight-hour working day.

On May 4, 1886, approximately 100,000 members of the Knights of Labor demonstrated in front of the McCormick Harvester Works in Haymarket Square in Chicago. Someone tossed a bomb into the crowd, causing a riot in which several people were killed. Public sentiment soon turned against the Knights of Labor, although no wrongdoing on its part was proved. The union began to lose membership, and in 1917 it collapsed.

The American Federation of Labor

The American Federation of Labor (AFL) was formed in 1886 under the leadership of Samuel Gompers, who ran the organization until his death in 1924. Gompers believed that the AFL should consist mainly of skilled workers. Membership was approximately 2 million in 1904, rising to 5 million in 1920 and then falling to 3 million in 1930. Its activities were almost solely directed to lobbying for better pay and improved working conditions for its members.

▶ Dozens of people were killed at the Haymarket Riot in Chicago in 1886. Many Americans came to associate unions with violence and radical ideas as a result of events such as this, although no wrongdoing by the union was ever proved.

Cross-Curricular Activity

Invite a government teacher from your school to discuss labor unions. While you could discuss the economic effects of labor unions, the government instructor could address labor unions' impact on the political world and the free-speech issues that relate to strikes and picket lines, as well as labor unions as an interest group. Both you and the government teacher should encourage students to share their perceptions of unions and union membership.

Early Court Decisions

In the early days of the labor union movement, the courts treated unions as illegal conspiracies. Union leaders were regularly prosecuted and sued for damages. For example, in an important case decided by the Supreme Court of Massachusetts in 1842, the court ruled that unions were not illegal, but that certain union practices were. Later, the Sherman Antitrust Act, which was passed by Congress in 1890, began to be applied to labor unions, although many persons said that Congress had only intended it to be applied to businesses. The Sherman Act declared that "every person who shall . . . combine or conspire with any other person or persons, to monopolize any part of the trade or commerce . . . shall be guilty of a misdemeanor."

During the early 1900s, *injunctions* were used against labor unions to prevent strikes and some other activities. (Injunctions are court orders that were originally designed to prevent damage to property when it was thought that other court processes would be too slow.) Because of the use of injunctions by employers during this period, labor unions found it difficult to strike.

The Norris-LaGuardia and Wagner Acts

The legal climate in which labor unions operated changed dramatically in 1932 with the passage of the Norris-LaGuardia Act by the U.S. Congress. The main purpose of the act was to restrain the use of injunctions. It declared that workers should be "free from the interference, restraint, or coercion of employers" in choosing their union representatives.

In 1935 Congress passed the Wagner Act, which required employers to bargain in good faith with workers; the act also made it illegal for employers to interfere with their employees' rights to organize or join a union. In addition, the act set up the National Labor Relations Board (NLRB) to investigate unfair labor practices. Union membership grew by leaps and bounds as a result of the Norris-LaGuardia and the Wagner acts.

◀ John L. Lewis formed the Congress of Industrial Organizations (CIO). **What difference of opinion led Lewis and others to split with the AFL and form the CIO?**

The Congress of Industrial Organizations

Because of the better legal climate for labor unions after passage of the Norris-LaGuardia and Wagner acts, a push was made to unionize major industries such as steel and automobiles. This trend caused some discontent within the AFL. The union was largely made up of craft unions—unions of individuals who practice the same craft or trade (for example, plumbers' union, electricians' union, carpenters' union). Some people within the AFL wanted to unionize people only into craft unions. Others wanted industrial unions—unions that include everyone in a particular industry, whether or not they all practice the same craft. For example, people doing many different jobs in the automobile industry would belong to the same union. In 1938, John L. Lewis of the United Mine Workers broke with the AFL and formed the Congress of Industrial Organizations (CIO). The CIO successfully unionized the steel, rubber, textile, meatpacking, and automobile industries along industrial union lines.

For a time, both the AFL and the CIO increased their memberships. After World War II, however, membership in the CIO began to decline. Some thought that the bickering between the two unions was the cause. In 1955, the AFL, a craft union, and the CIO, an industrial union, merged under the leadership of George Meany into the AFL-CIO.

Teaching with Visuals

Some AFL members wanted industrial unions, while others believed unions should remain for a particular craft or trade. John L. Lewis and others formed the CIO, which unionized along industrial lines. The AFL unionized people mainly into craft unions.

Discussion Starter

Ask students if they would rather live in a country without labor unions or in a country with labor unions, and to state their reasons for their positions. Students may point to the fact that unions can make working conditions more secure and democratic than they may otherwise be. Other students may point out that labor unions can cause inefficiencies and that they sometimes employ tactics with which an individual may not agree in order to achieve their ends.

Reinforcement Activity

Ask students the following questions: What is a union shop? What does it have to do with a right-to-work state?

Background Information: PATCO

Students may not realize that air traffic controllers were, at one time, unionized. In 1981, nearly 12,000 members of the Professional Air Traffic Controllers Organization (PATCO) walked off their jobs. President Reagan had little sympathy for labor unions and warned the striking workers to return to their jobs or face dismissal. The workers were dismissed and initially replaced by military personnel. The resulting change in personnel resulted in major delays in air travel, which caused the public to lose sympathy for the striking members of PATCO. Discuss with students the importance of public support for strikes and striking workers, if a strike is to be successful.

Reinforcement Activity

Instruct students to research one of these two regulatory agencies: OSHA (Occupational Safety and Health Administration) or the CPSC (Consumer Products Safety Commission). They should research when these agencies were formed, what duties are carried out by these agencies, and so on. Each student should pair up with someone who studied the other agency and share her or his findings.

Discussion Starter

How much government regulation is enough? How much is too much? Direct students who believe that the government has too many regulations to stand on one side of the classroom. Students who believe that the government has just enough or too few regulations should stand on the other side of the classroom. Allow students on both sides to take turns sharing their opinions about government regulations. If a student's argument persuades another student to change his or her opinion, the student with the changed opinion may change sides of the room. It will be interesting to note how many students change their opinions about government regulation, and whether most students favor a lot of regulation or whether most would favor less regulation.

The Taft-Hartley Act

The congressional sentiment that made the Wagner Act possible in 1935 began to shift after World War II. A few particularly damaging strikes in 1946 set the stage for the Taft-Hartley Act in 1947. This act gave states the right to pass right-to-work laws, which prohibit unions from requiring employers to make union membership a condition of employment.

The Landrum-Griffin Act

Congress passed the Landrum-Griffin Act in 1959 with the intent of policing the internal affairs of labor unions. The act calls for regular union elections and secret ballots, and it requires union leaders to report on their unions' finances. It also prohibits former convicts and communists from holding union office. The Landrum-Griffin Act was passed because the U.S. public became concerned during the late 1950s that some labor union leaders had misappropriated funds and were involved in corruption.

The Growth in Public Employee Unions

A public employee union is a union whose members work for the local, state, or federal government. By far the most important development in the labor movement in the 1960s and 1970s was the sharp growth in public employee union membership. The main issue raised by public employee unions is the right to strike. These unions feel they should be able to exercise this right, but their opponents argue that public sector strikes—by police officers or firefighters, for example—could have a crippling effect on society.

Government Regulation

In the United States, government often regulates business and labor practices. We already discused in the previous chapter how government might regulate a natural monopoly firm. In Chapter 3, we discussed how government often regulates business when it comes to issues such as air quality.

Government also regulates labor markets, with regard to issues such as hiring practices and safety regulations. For example, the Occupational Safety and Health Administration (OSHA) is a regulatory government agency that is concerned with protecting workers against occupational injuries and illnesses. The Consumer Product Safety Commission (CPSC) specifies minimum standards for potentially unsafe products. A business firm cannot simply make any type of toy to sell, but only toys that are not likely to harm the children who use them. The Environmental Protection Agency (EPA) regulates the amount of pollution business firms can emit into the air or rivers.

Not everyone agrees as to the value of government regulation. Some people argue that most regulation is too costly to taxpayers. The proponents of regulation counter that even though the costs are high, the benefits are higher. They say, for example, that highway fatalities would be 40 percent higher in the absence of automobile safety features mandated through regulation. They also say that mandated childproof lids resulted in 90 percent fewer child deaths caused by accidental swallowing of poisonous substances. Proponents of regulation also say that restrictions on the use of asbestos save between 630 and 2,553 persons from dying of cancer each year.

EXAMPLE: In 1987 Beech-Nut Nutrition Corporation, a baby food manufacturer, pleaded guilty to 215 felony counts. (A felony is a major crime.) The company had sold millions of containers of sugar water and flavoring that it had labeled "100 percent apple juice." ◆

EXAMPLE: Cordis Corporation produced and sold thousands of pacemakers that it knew were defective. Many of the pacemakers failed, and the company ended up pleading guilty to 25 criminal violations. ◆

Government regulation, whether it has to do with prices and profits, consumer information, or working standards, continues to be a major topic of debate. The next section explains why.

Cooperative Learning

You might want to organize a union day in your classroom to show students how unions work. Divide the class into three groups, and have each group select a name for its union, along with two or three leaders. Instruct each union to draw up a mission statement and list its particular goals for improving conditions in the school or classroom. Unions should set a membership fee and present it along with arguments for joining the organization. Then have the unions compete for members. Students can change unions, joining the one that appeals to them most. Discuss with students which union each one joined and why. Ask how the benefits promised by that union compared with the fee charged for membership.

When Is $50,000 Not $50,000?

A person can live in many different places in the United States. Depending on where you live, you may end up paying more or less for certain goods and services. For example, the median house price in Boston is much higher than the median house price in Lexington, Kentucky. Health care costs are higher in New York City than in Birmingham, Alabama.

What all this means is that a dollar in one place may get you more or less than it gets you in another place. Suppose you live and work in Seattle, Washington, where you earn an annual income of $50,000. You are thinking of moving to Bridgeport, Connecticut. You wonder whether $50,000 in Bridgeport will do as much for you as it does in Seattle. The answer is that it will do more for you. In fact, an annual salary of $39,646 in Bridgeport, Connecticut, will get you everything that an annual salary of $50,000 will get you in Seattle.

Now let's say that instead of moving from Seattle to Bridgeport, you are thinking of moving to Thousand Oaks, California. Will $50,000 in Thousand Oaks buy you what it does in Seattle? The answer is no. You will need $57,074 in Thousand Oaks, California, to do what $50,000 did in Seattle, mostly because housing costs are higher in Thousand Oaks than in Seattle.

Numerous cost-of-living calculators are available on the Web to help you figure out what you will need to earn in various cities to have the standard of living you have in your current city. You can find these calculators by going to any search engine and keying in "cost-of-living calculator." One can be found at www.emcp.net/costofliving.

Interesting, you say, but how does all this information relate to reading this book in high school as a part of an economics course? Well, one day you're going to be working at some job earning a salary. You may get a higher-paying job offer in another city. Is getting a raise of $10,000 going to be worth your moving? You will want to see what the cost of living is like in the city you are thinking of moving to. You may have to call up your prospective employer in the new city and tell him or her that even with the $10,000 raise, your standard of living is going down because of the higher housing and health costs in the new city. For example, it would take an additional $27,000 over a $50,000 salary earned in Seattle to maintain one's standard of living in San Francisco.

▲ How do you think the cost of living in Kansas City (left) might compare with the cost of living in New York City (right)? Where can you find specific comparisons?

THINK ABOUT IT If it takes $2 in city A to do what $1.40 does in city B, then in which city do you think nurses will earn a higher annual income?

Economics in the Real World

Ask students to name a salary they would like to earn in the future. Then have them name two cities in which they would like to live. Ask: In which city would your salary buy more?

ANSWERS TO THINK ABOUT IT Students should see that nurses will probably earn a higher annual income in city A.

Discussion Starter

Ask how many students live in an apartment or house that their family rents from someone else. Ask if they are aware of how much notice they would have to give if they wanted or needed to move out. Assign students to research how much apartments and houses cost to rent around your school or city. Ask, How would the level of rent be affected by a change in rental regulations that lessened the length of notice a landlord could demand?

Reinforcement Activity

Public utility commissions are government groups that regulate public utility companies. Pose the following questions to students: It has been argued that if a public utility commission sets a certain limit on the profit rate a public utility may earn, the public utility will have little incentive to hold down its costs. Do you agree or disagree? Explain your answer.

Discussion Starter

Rules and regulations are not foreign topics to students. Ask: What rules and regulations can you think of? (*Sample answers:* things like dress codes, curfews, and rules of the road.) What kinds of activities are these rules and regulations supposed to regulate?

Cooperative Learning

Divide students into small groups and assign each group a different union to research. Students should find mission statements, history, number of members, dues or fees, and the process by which one joins the union. Students should also find out if the union has ever gone on strike or used work stoppages to try to better conditions for its members. Have students prepare visuals to explain and support their research and invite them to present their findings to the class.

Teaching with Visuals

Answers will vary. Students should see that there are costs and benefits of government regulation, which affects goods and services.

Costs and benefits of government regulation have a global impact. The owners of firms will pick up and leave a country if that country's regulations become too stiff. There is an old saying, "People vote with their feet." What this means is that if people don't like something in one place, and believe that things are better in some other place, they will simply leave one place and move to the other. If regulations become too stiff in Canada, Canadian firms will move to other countries (such as the United States). If regulations become too stiff in the United States, no doubt some U.S. firms will move to other countries.

Teaching with Visuals

Answers will vary. Students should be able to identify environmental regulations; for example, requirements that businesses purchase antipollution devices and that car manufacturers improve their products' fuel economy.

Application Activity

After reading and discussing Section 2, you may want to assign the Section Activity in the *Applying the Principles Workbook.*

Assess

Quick Quiz

The following true-or-false quiz will help you assess student understanding of the material covered in this section.

1. A union can raise the demand for a product through advertising. (True)
2. Labor unions try to increase the labor supply. (False)
3. On average, union workers receive higher pay than comparable nonunion workers do. (True)

▶ Toyota's Prius hybrid sedans roll off the production line at the Tsutsumi plant in Toyota City, in western Japan. **Have government regulations in the United States impacted the sales of Toyota's Prius?**

The Costs and Benefits of Government Regulation

Suppose a business firm is polluting the air with smoke from its factories. The government passes an environmental regulation requiring that this business firm purchase antipollution devices that cut down on the smoke emitted into the air. What are the benefits of this kind of regulation? First is cleaner air, which may lead to fewer medical problems in the future. For example, in some U.S. cities, the pollution from cars and factories causes people to cough, feel tired, and experience eye discomfort. Some of these people have continuing medical problems from constantly breathing dirty air. Government regulation that ends up reducing the amount of pollution in the air surely helps these people, reducing lost work time and health care costs.

▼ **What have governments done to solve problems such as poor air quality?**

Regulation may also benefit the environment and thus the people who enjoy a clean environment. For example, some air pollution can harm birds and destroy certain types of plants and trees. Cleaner air may ensure more birds singing and prettier trees to view.

Regulation, however, does not come with benefits only. It comes with costs, too. For example, a business firm that incurs the cost of required antipollution devices experiences a rise in its overall costs of production. As a result, the business firm may produce fewer units of its product, which raises its product price and results in some workers losing their jobs.

If you are a worker who loses your job, you may view the government's insistence that business install pollution devices differently than if you are a person suffering from weak lungs. If you have weak lungs, less pollution may be the difference between your feeling

246 Chapter 9 Labor, Employment, and Wages

Internet Research

Direct students to the Web sites for federal regulatory agencies such as the Environmental Protection Agency and the Food and Drug Administration. Students should learn about the kinds of regulations created by the agency they have chosen. Then they should choose three regulations and write an oral report outlining the costs and benefits of each. Allow students to share their findings with the class.

well or sick. If you are a worker for the business firm, less pollution may end up costing you your job. Ideally, you may prefer to have a little less pollution in your neighborhood, but not at the cost of losing your job.

Where do economists stand on these issues? Are they for or against government regulation of the type described? They are neither for nor against such regulation; the job of the economist is continually to point out both the benefits and the costs of regulation. To the person who sees only the costs, the economist asks, "But what about the benefits?" And to the person who sees only the benefits, the economist asks, "But what about the costs?" The economist then goes on to outline the benefits and costs as accurately as possible.

Unintended Effects of Regulation

In addition to outlining the benefits and costs of regulation, the economist tries to point out the sometimes unintended consequences of regulation. The government, which often regulates the manufacturers of automobiles by imposing fuel economy standards on cars, may state that new cars must get an average of 40 miles per gallon instead of, say, 30 miles per gallon. Many people say that this regulation is good. They reason that if car companies were made to produce cars that got better mileage, people would not need to buy and burn as much gasoline. With less gasoline burned, less pollution would be produced.

It is not guaranteed to work out this way, though. If car companies produced cars that were more fuel efficient, people would have to buy less gasoline to take them from one place to another. The cost per mile of traveling would fall, so people might begin to travel more. Leisure driving on Saturday and Sunday might become more common, people might begin to drive farther on vacations, and so on. If people began to travel more, the gasoline saving that resulted from the higher fuel economy standards might be offset or even outweighed. More gasoline consumption due to more travel would mean more gas burned and more pollutants ending up in the air. In other words, a regulation requiring car companies to produce cars that get better fuel mileage might have an unintended effect.

SECTION 2 ASSESSMENT

Defining Terms

1. Define:
   a. Taft-Hartley Act
   b. right-to-work law
   c. union shop
2. What is the difference between a union shop and a closed shop?

Reviewing Facts and Concepts

3. Labor union A wants to increase the demand for its member workers. Identify two things the union can do to try to achieve this outcome.
4. Is the union shop illegal in right-to-work states?
5. What did the Norris-LaGuardia Act accomplish?
6. How does the economist view government regulation?

Critical Thinking

7. Do you think it was right for the courts, in the early days of labor unions, to issue injunctions that prevented strikes and other union activities? Why or why not?
8. "If the government imposes higher fuel economy standards, the amount of pollution produced by automobiles will undoubtedly become less." Do you agree or disagree? Explain your answer.

Applying Economic Concepts

9. The members of labor union X produce cars in the United States for sale in the United States only. The U.S. Congress is contemplating imposing a quota, restricting the number of foreign-produced cars that can be sold in the country. Are the members of labor union X likely to support or not support this action? Explain your answer.

SECTION 2 ASSESSMENT ANSWERS

Defining Terms

1. a. Taft-Hartley Act: prohibited closed shops, and gave states the right to pass right-to-work laws; **b. right-to-work law:** made it illegal to require union membership for purposes of employment; **c. union shop:** an organization that does not require individuals to be union members in order to be hired, but requires membership within a certain period of time after being hired.

2. Closed shops are organizations that hire only union members. Union shops don't require membership to be hired, but employees must join within a certain period of time after being hired.

Reviewing Facts and Concepts

3. The labor union can gain greater control over the supply of labor, and increase the demand for the product it produces.

4. The Knights of Labor was organized in 1886. (False)

5. The Wagner Act required employers to bargain in good faith with workers. (True)

Assessment Book

You will find a quiz for this section in the *Assessment Book.*

Reteaching Activity

Use the Section Assessment to gauge which students may need reteaching on this section. Ask those students to explain the difference between a closed shop and a union shop. Go over the answers with students. After you are sure that students understand the distinction, remind them that the closed shop was outlawed by the Taft-Hartley Act.

Guided Reading

For further reteaching of the key concepts in this section, assign the Outlining Activity and the Just the Facts Handout from the *Guided Reading and Study Guide.*

4. Yes, in states with right-to-work laws, union shops are illegal.

5. The Norris-LaGuardia Act restrained the use of injunctions, giving workers the freedom to choose their union representatives.

6. Economists are not for or against government regulation, but point out the costs and benefits of regulation.

Critical Thinking

7. Answers will vary.

8. Answers will vary. Students should see that there may be unintended effects of higher fuel economy standards.

Applying Economic Concepts

9. Labor union X is likely to support the quota on foreign-produced cars because when supply decreases for foreign cars, demand for union X cars should increase.

CHAPTER 9 Assessment Answers

Economics Vocabulary

1. minimum wage law; **2.** closed shop; **3.** strike; **4.** wage rate; **5.** union shop; **6.** Taft-Hartley Act.

Understanding the Main Ideas

1. If there is a surplus in the labor market, the wage rate will fall. If there is a shortage, the wage rate will rise.
2. Disagree. The supply of John's labor services could be lower than the supply of Wilson's services.
3. Agree. The reason is that the demand curve for labor is downward sloping. Fewer people will be hired at higher wages than at lower wages.
4. Most studies conclude that unions raise the wages for union labor and decrease the wages for comparable nonunion labor. Unions reduce the supply of workers in the union sector and indirectly increase the supply of workers in the nonunion sector.
5. Demand is changed by the productivity of labor and the change in the demand for the good or service that labor produces.
6. Yes. If price decreases, then real wage can increase even if money wage decreases. For example: If a person's money wage rate is $10 an hour and the price of the only good the person buys, X, is $1, then the person's real wage is 10 units of X. If the person's money wage rate falls to $8 an hour and the price of X falls to $0.50, then the person's real wage increases to 16 units of X.
7. The traditional view identifies labor unions as an obstacle to establishing reasonable work standards; it generally sees labor unions in negative terms. The new view sees labor unions in a positive light. Unions play the role of collective-voice mechanism for their members, representing workers in negotiations with management. This representation makes workers feel more comfortable in their jobs, more productive, and less likely to quit their jobs.

CHAPTER 9 ASSESSMENT

Chapter Summary

Be sure you know and remember the following key points from the chapter sections.

Section 1

- People who demand labor are employers.
- People who supply labor are employees.
- The price of labor is called the wage rate.
- The equilibrium wage rate occurs at the point where the quantity of labor supplied equals the quantity of labor demanded.
- Wage rates differ because the supply and the demand for different types of labor are not the same.
- A job's benefits come in both money and nonmoney forms.
- Labor is a derived demand—the result of the demand for a good.
- The minimum wage rate is a government-set wage floor.
- Money wages are the actual dollars received for doing a job.
- Real wages are the value of the dollars in terms of what they buy.
- The Consumer Price Index (CPI) is the average price, or index, of a group of goods.

Section 2

- A labor union seeks to increase the wages and improve the working conditions of its members.
- A closed shop is an organization that hires only union members; the Taft-Hartley Act makes closed shops illegal.
- A union shop requires union membership within a certain period after taking a job.
- Right-to-work laws, in place in many states, make it illegal to require union membership for a specific job.
- Unions began to emerge in the United States after the Civil War and experienced many ups and downs in labor's history.

Economics Vocabulary

To reinforce your knowledge of the key terms in this chapter, fill in the following blanks on a separate piece of paper with the appropriate word or phrase.

1. The _______ sets a level below which wage rates are not allowed to fall.
2. A(n) _______ is an organization that hires only union members.
3. A _______ is a tactic used by unions to put pressure on employers by having workers refuse to work.
4. The price of labor is called the _______.
5. A(n) _______ is an organization that requires employees to join the union within a certain period of time after being hired.
6. The _______, which was passed in 1947, gave the states the right to pass right-to-work laws.

Understanding the Main Ideas

Write answers to the following questions to review the main ideas in this chapter.

1. In a competitive labor market, what happens to the wage rate when a surplus of labor occurs? A shortage of labor?
2. John earns a higher wage rate than Wilson. It necessarily follows that the demand for John's labor services is greater than the demand for Wilson's labor services. Do you agree or disagree? Explain your answer.
3. If the minimum wage rate is higher than the equilibrium wage rate, fewer people will be hired because the cost of labor is too high. Do you agree or disagree? Explain your answer.
4. What are unions' effects on union wages? On nonunion wages? Explain your answers.
5. Identify two factors that can change the demand for labor.
6. Can a person's money wage decrease at the same time his or her real wage increases? Explain.
7. Outline the traditional view and the new view of labor unions.
8. Outline the details of the Wagner Act.
9. What is a public employee union?

248 Chapter 9 Labor, Employment, and Wages

8. The Wagner Act required employers to bargain in good faith with workers and made it illegal for employers to interfere with their employees' rights to organize or join a union. Also, it set up the National Labor Relations Board to investigate unfair labor practices.
9. It is a union whose members work for the local, state, or federal government.
10. Wages will remain the same.
11. Disagree. Economists are neither for nor against regulation of business and labor. Their job is to point out the costs and benefits of regulation.

Doing the Math

1. $28,000 (*calculation:* $60,000 – $32,000 = $28,000).

10. If the demand for labor increases by the same amount as the supply of labor increases, will wages rise, fall, or remain the same?
11. "Economists are against regulation of business and labor." Do you agree or disagree with this statement? Explain your answer.

Doing the Math

Do the calculations necessary to solve the following problems.

1. Alicia turned down a job that pays \$60,000 a year for a job that pays \$32,000 a year. The nonmoney benefits in the lower-paying job equal at least what dollar amount?
2. In year 1, Bob earns \$1,000 a month when the CPI is 130. In year 2, Bob earns \$1,500 a month when the CPI is 135. In which year is Bob's real income higher? What percentage higher?

Working with Graphs and Tables

Graphically represent the following.

1. The equilibrium wage rate is currently \$10 an hour. The demand for labor increases by more than the supply of labor increases. The new equilibrium wage rate is \$12. Be sure to label your axes.
2. The demand for labor falls by more than the supply of labor rises.
3. The demand for labor rises by the same amount as the supply of labor rises.
4. In Exhibit 9-6, the original demand and supply curves are labeled D_1 and S_1, and the new demand and supply curves are labeled D_2 and S_2. In parts (a) through (d), identify what will happen to the equilibrium wage as a result of the change in demand, supply, or both.

EXHIBIT 9-6

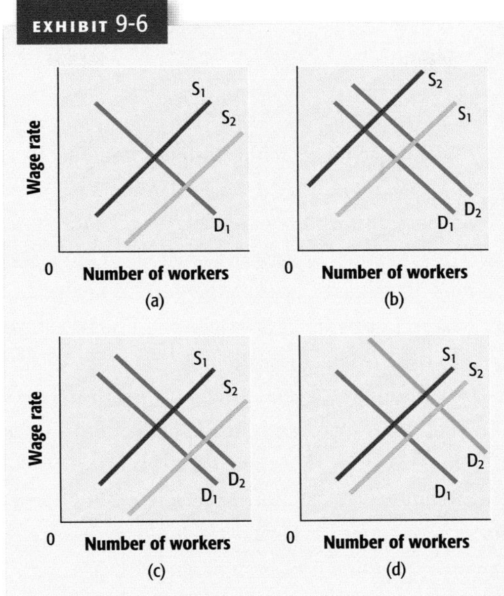

Solving Economic Problems

Use your thinking skills and the information you learned in this chapter to find solutions to the following problems.

1. **Application.** Suppose you are an economist hired by a labor union that is currently negotiating wages with management. Current union members are paid \$18 an hour. The objective of the labor union executives is to make sure that over the next year, their members' wages do not fall in real terms. The CPI in the current year is 179, and the expected CPI next year is 190. What money wage would maintain the real wage of the union members?
2. **Analysis.** Three jobs, A, B, and C, all pay the same salary, \$70,000 a year. What additional information do you need to decide which of the three jobs is the best job for you?

Practice Tests and Study Guide

Go to www.emcp.net/economics and choose *Economics: New Ways of Thinking,* Chapter 9, if you need more help in preparing for the chapter test.

2. Real income per month in year 1 is \$1,000 ÷ 130, or 7.69. Real income per month in year 2 is \$1,500 ÷ 135, or 11.11. Thus, real income per month in year 2 is 44.47% higher.

Working with Graphs and Tables

1.

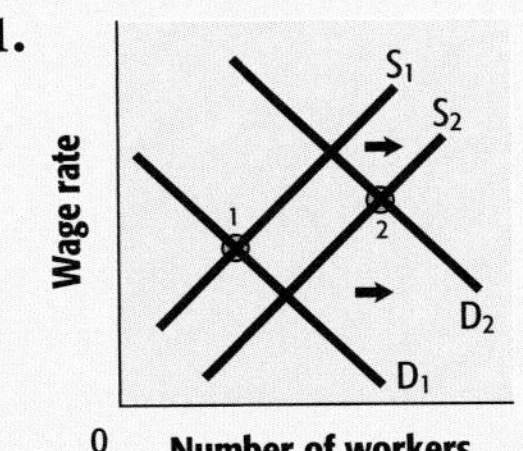

2.

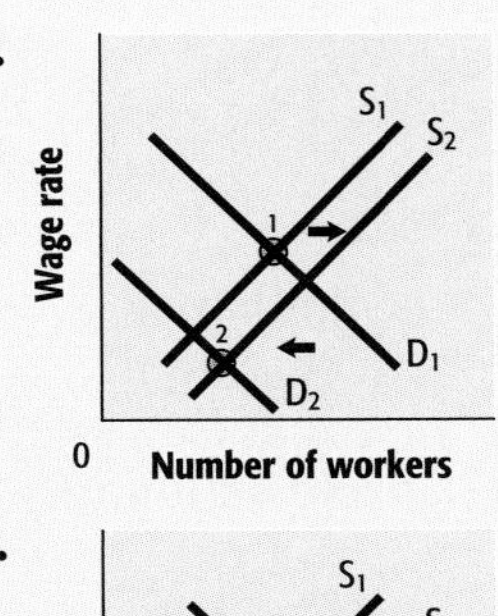

3.

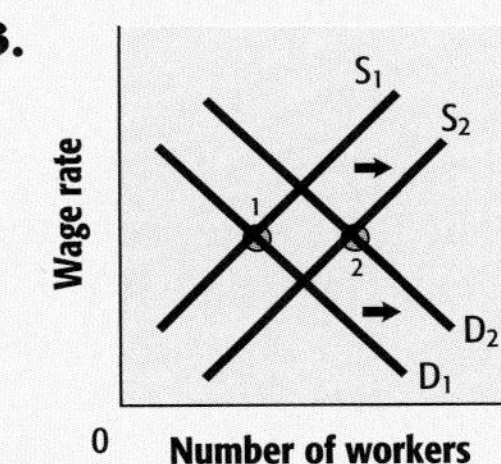

4. (a) The wage rate will fall; (b) The wage rate will rise; (c) The wage rate will fall; (d) The wage rate will rise.

Solving Economic Problems

1. The current real wage is \$18 ÷ 179, or 0.10. If the denominator (CPI) next year will be 190, then the money wage must be \$19 to keep the real wage (0.10) constant.

2. You need to know the dollar value of the nonmoney benefits in each job. The best job for you is the job with the highest overall benefits, as measured by you.

Debating the Issues

Discussion Starters

1. Ask how many students have worked for minimum wage. Allow volunteers to share their personal experiences working at a job that paid minimum wage.

2. Ask students how productivity relates to minimum wage. Instruct them to consider the following scenario. Student A is motivated to attract the attention of his or her employer by being a "self-starter" with high productivity. Student B does the minimum to meet the job description, knowing that he or she will collect the minimum wage. If you were an employer, which student would you want to work for you? Which student's work ethic would encourage you to pay more than minimum wage?

3. Ask students the following questions: Does a person's value to an employer depend on minimum wage? What other things would make a person valuable to an employer? Does a person's "worth" increase just because minimum wage increases? How could a person be worth more to an employer, deserving an increase in pay?

4. What are some trade-offs of having a minimum wage in effect?

Debating the Issues

Should There Be a Minimum Wage?

Like many high school students, you may have a job and work after school. If so, there is a good chance that you earn the minimum wage, which is set by the U.S. Congress. It is against the law for employers to pay workers less than the minimum wage. If the minimum wage is $5.15 an hour, then it is unlawful for an employer to pay an employee less than this amount.

Do you think that a minimum wage is good for workers and good for the economy, too? Some people argue in favor of it; other people argue against it. Some people argue that the minimum wage should be raised; other people argue that it should not be. Let's listen in on a conversation between Mike and Mrs. Peters. Mrs. Peters owns a small bakery in town. Mike, 17 years old, works at the hardware store three doors down from the bakery. Mike currently earns the minimum wage.

Mrs. Peters: How are you doing today, Mike? What can I get for you?

Mike: I'll have a chocolate éclair and a milk. And, by the way, I'm doing pretty well today. On my way to work I heard that Congress is thinking of raising the minimum wage. That will mean more money for me.

Mrs. Peters: I think the minimum wage is something that sounds better than it is.

Mike: What do you mean? What could possibly be wrong with the minimum wage?

Mrs. Peters: Well, for one thing, it goes against the whole idea of free enterprise. Under free enterprise, employers and employees should be able to make their own deals. They shouldn't have government telling them how much to pay.

Mike: But if there weren't a minimum wage, employers would pay their employees next to nothing. Perhaps instead of my earning $6 an hour, I'd earn $2 an hour.

Mrs. Peters: Okay, let's say that you are earning $6 an hour. Along comes the government and tells your employer that he has to pay you $7.50 an hour. Jim may decide to fire you. It may be worth it for Jim to pay you $6 an hour, but not $7.50 an hour. Has the minimum wage helped you? I don't think so. I think it has priced you out of a job.

Mike: But it's possible that I'll keep my job as the wage goes from $6 to $7.50. Fact is, I may be worth $7.50 an hour, but Jim is paying me only $6 an hour so he can earn higher profits. What the minimum wage does is simply force Jim to pay me what I'm worth.

Mrs. Peters: If you were really worth $7.50 an hour, you would be earning $7.50 an hour right now. The boss who thinks you are worth $7.50 an hour would simply offer you that amount to come work for him instead of working for Jim. That's how he would compete you away from Jim.

But let's go with what you say. Let's suppose that Congress tells your employer he has to pay you $7.50 an hour. And let's suppose you keep your job. That doesn't mean some people won't lose their jobs. Everyone knows that employers hire more people at lower wages than at higher wages. As wages go up, they are going to hire fewer people. In other words, some of the people working at the lower wages will be fired.

Differentiating Instruction

Enrichment and Extension

1. Instruct students to prepare and conduct a survey of the adults they know on the subject of whether there should be a minimum wage. After students collect their data, have them create a visual that displays the results of the survey. You might create a class bulletin board for these visuals.

2. Assign students to write a rap song or poem that expresses their opinions of minimum wages. Allow class time for volunteers to present their songs. After the presentations, let the class vote on the best song or poem, and allow its writer to teach it to the class.

Mike: I don't think anyone has to lose his job as the wage goes up. Employers will simply end up with lower profits.

Mrs. Peters: That might work if you're talking about Microsoft or General Motors, but what about Joe's Pizza or the corner deli? Some companies are just squeaking by, so that any mandated cost increase will hurt them. They will try to cut their costs by firing some people.

The other thing is that not all businesses are faced with the same set of circumstances. Circumstances may differ from one region of the country to another. The economy may be booming in the Southwest and businesses can easily pay higher wages. But the economy may be sluggish in the Midwest and businesses can't pay higher wages. A set minimum wage that every business has to pay, no matter what its circumstances, doesn't take this into account.

Mike: I don't know, I hear what you are saying, but I still think that without the minimum wage, too many employers would squeeze their employees.

Mrs. Peters: Mike, there are whole industries in this country where the minimum wage is not relevant. No one who works for an accounting firm is paid the minimum wage, no one who works as a computer scientist is paid the minimum wage, no one who works as an attorney is paid the minimum wage. All these people earn much more than the minimum wage. Do they earn more because government has ordered the companies to pay them more than the minimum wage? Not at all. The government hasn't said a thing. The companies simply pay them more because they can't hire these people without paying more. It is a matter of supply and demand, Mike. Companies have to pay the wages that are determined in the market by the forces of supply and demand.

Mike: Oh, come on. You know there is a big difference between what an attorney earns and what I earn. The minimum wage law isn't there to protect attorneys, accountants, and computer scientists. It is there to protect the little guy. The guy without much skill or experience.

Mrs. Peters: But, that's just the point. The minimum wage doesn't protect this person. It often just prices him out of a job. You can't make employers pay more for a person than that person is worth to them. If a person is worth only $5 an hour to an employer, and the government says you have to pay this person $7 an hour, you know what is going to happen? That person is going to go without a job.

What Do You Think?

1. Who do you think makes the stronger argument, Mike or Mrs. Peters? Defend your answer.
2. What are Mike's strong points? Weak points? What are Mrs. Peters's strong and weak points?
3. Do you think the minimum wage should be raised, left where it currently is, or eliminated altogether? Explain your answer.

Activities for What Do You Think?

1. Label three different points in the room with the following signs: "Minimum Wage Should Be Raised," "Minimum Wage Should Be Left Alone," and "Minimum Wage Should Be Eliminated." Then have students move to the label with which they most agree. Allow students five minutes to list reasons why they voted for that label. Let each group present its reasons to the class, and then vote again to see if opinions change.
2. Divide students into groups of three or four to write scripts to act out. Skits should show real-life examples of the minimum wage either working or failing. Allow time for students to present their skits to the class.

Closure

Assign students to write short essays describing their current opinions on minimum wage. They should describe any previous opinions, along with what changed their minds. Allow students to share these essays with partners.

Preview

Listed below are the chapters included in this unit.

CHAPTER 10
Money, Banking, and the Federal Reserve System

CHAPTER 11
Measuring Economic Performance

CHAPTER 12
Economic Changes and Cycles

CHAPTER 13
Fiscal and Monetary Policy

CHAPTER 14
Taxing and Spending

Foundations for the Unit

In Unit IV we shift our focus from microeconomics to macroeconomics. We put away the microscopes we used to examine the discrete components of economics and take out telescopes with which to see the aggregate picture of economics. Throughout this unit, you may find that it is useful for students to watch nightly newscasts and to read the front page of daily newspapers. Many macroeconomic topics will be highlighted in headlines and discussed in news stories.

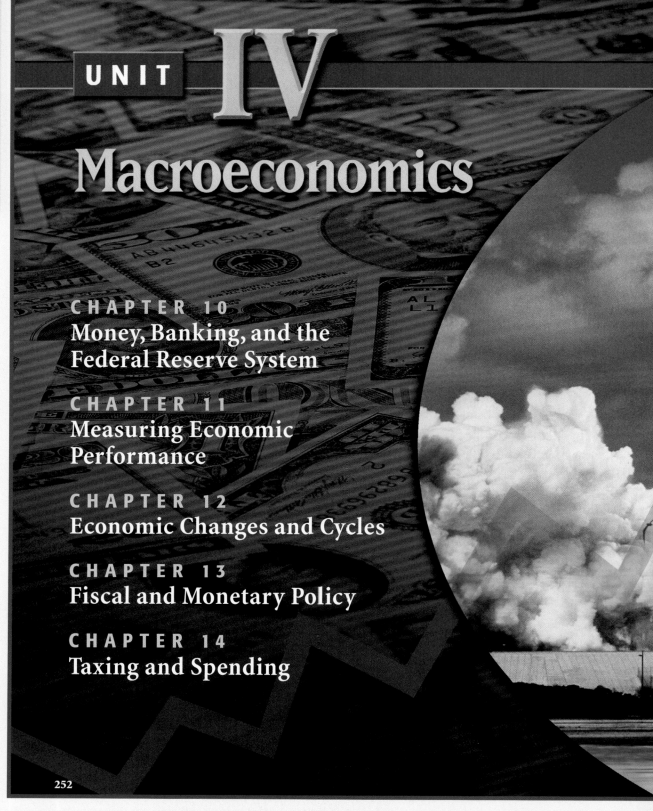

UNIT IV Macroeconomics

CHAPTER 10
Money, Banking, and the Federal Reserve System

CHAPTER 11
Measuring Economic Performance

CHAPTER 12
Economic Changes and Cycles

CHAPTER 13
Fiscal and Monetary Policy

CHAPTER 14
Taxing and Spending

252

Resources for the Unit

Books

Beard, Charles A. *An Economic Interpretation of the Constitution of the United States.* New York: Free Press, 1986.

DuBoff, Richard B. *Accumulation and Power: An Economic History of the United States.* Armonk, NY: M. E. Sharpe, 1989.

Galbraith, John Kenneth. *The Affluent Society*. New York: Houghton Mifflin, 1998.

Morris, Charles R. *Money, Greed and Risk: Why Financial Crises and Crashes Happen*. New York: Times Books, 1999.

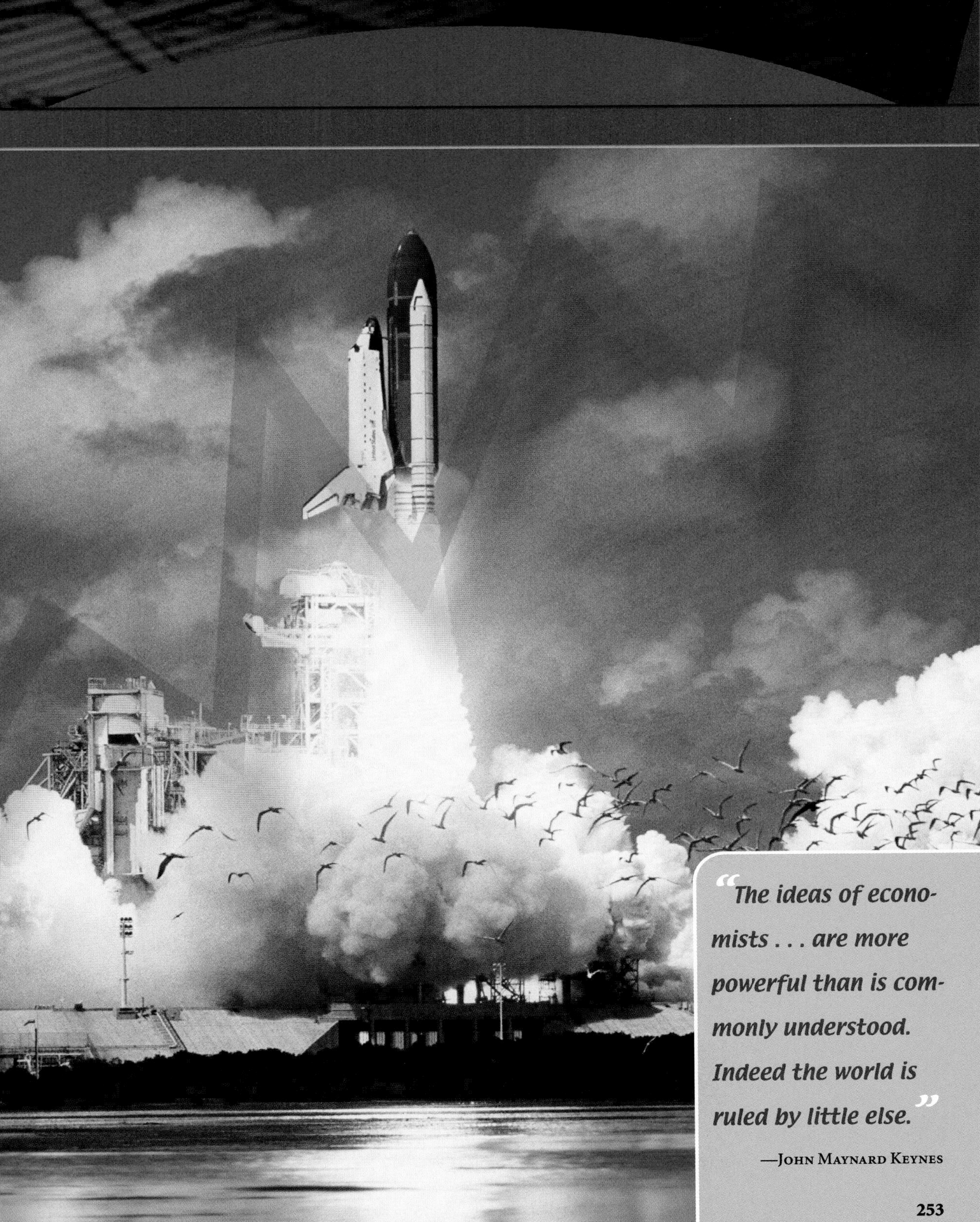

"The ideas of economists . . . are more powerful than is commonly understood. Indeed the world is ruled by little else."

—John Maynard Keynes

253

Introducing the Unit

You might want to introduce Unit 4 by calling for students to demonstrate by a show of hands whether they have already taken a government course. Point out that students who have already taken government will probably be familiar with many of the concepts discussed in this unit. Explain that this is because macroeconomics deals with the state of a nation's economic health. That economic health is usually a topic of great concern for both those who are serving in public office and those who hope to be elected to public office.

Performance Task

Assign students to work in small groups to create their own portraits of the nation's economic health. For each chapter in this unit, students should collect and analyze pertinent national economic statistics. For Chapter 10, students could collect figures relating to the current money supply. Groups should present these figures graphically; write a summary of what is presented in their graphs, including calculations showing the percentage changes, and so on; and write an analysis stating what the figures mean in terms of the United States' economic health. Other topics might include the current discount rate, the current gross domestic product and consumer price index, the current inflation rate and unemployment rate, and the current national debt.

Articles

Gergen, David. "No Time for Complacency," *U.S. News and World Report,* March 29, 1999.

Grant, James. "Future Shock at the Fed," *New York Times,* October 26, 2005.

Greenman, Catherine. "Filing Your Taxes Online: It's Faster, More Accurate and Welcomed by I.R.S." *New York Times,* January 27, 2000.

Healey, Matthew. "This Pile of Scrap Once Cast a Fortune in Notes," *New York Times,* December 19, 2005.

Multimedia

Economics U$A: The Banking System. VHS. The Annenberg/CPB Projects.

Chapter 10 Planning Guide

SECTION ORGANIZER

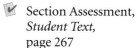

Section	Learning Objectives	Reproducible Worksheets and Handouts	Assessment
 **The Origins of Money** (pages 256–262)	▸ Describe what a barter economy is. ▸ Explain how money emerged from a barter economy. ▸ Describe what money is. ▸ Explain what gives money its value. ▸ Describe the functions of money.	Section 1 Activity, *Applying the Principles Workbook* Outlining Activity, *Guided Reading and Study Guide* Just the Facts Handout, *Guided Reading and Study Guide*	Section Assessment, *Student Text,* page 262 Quick Quiz, *Annotated Teacher's Edition,* page 261 Section Quiz, *Assessment Book*
 **The Money Supply** (pages 263–267)	▸ Explain what the money supply consists of. ▸ Explain what a Federal Reserve note is. ▸ Describe what "money" is and what it is not. ▸ Explain what causes interest rates to change.	 Section 2 Activity, *Applying the Principles Workbook* 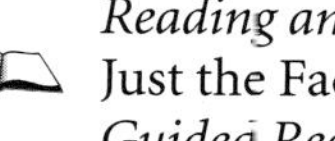 Outlining Activity, *Guided Reading and Study Guide* Just the Facts Handout, *Guided Reading and Study Guide*	Section Assessment, *Student Text,* page 267 Quick Quiz, *Annotated Teacher's Edition,* page 266 Section Quiz, *Assessment Book*
 **The Federal Reserve System** (pages 270–273)	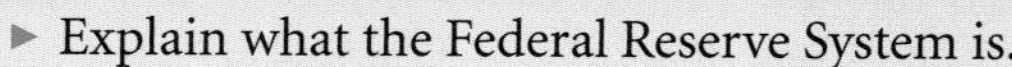 ▸ Explain what the Federal Reserve System is. ▸ State how many persons sit on the Board of Governors of the Federal Reserve System. ▸ Describe the major responsibilities of the Federal Reserve System. ▸ Describe how the check-clearing process works.	 Section 3 Activity, *Applying the Principles Workbook* 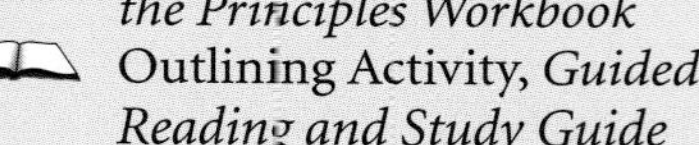 Outlining Activity, *Guided Reading and Study Guide* Just the Facts Handout, *Guided Reading and Study Guide*	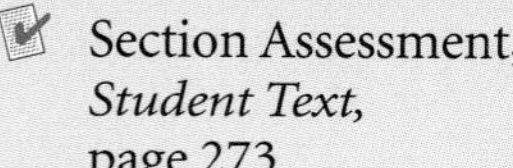 Section Assessment, *Student Text,* page 273 Quick Quiz, *Annotated Teacher's Edition,* page 272 Section Quiz, *Assessment Book*
 **The Money Creation Process** (pages 274–279)	▸ Explain what total reserves equal. ▸ Explain what required and excess reserves are. ▸ Describe how banks use checking accounts to increase the money supply. ▸ Describe what banks do with excess reserves. ▸ Calculate the maximum change in the money supply resulting from bank loans.	 Section 4 Activity, *Applying the Principles Workbook*  Outlining Activity, *Guided Reading and Study Guide*  Just the Facts Handout, *Guided Reading and Study Guide*	Section Assessment, *Student Text,* page 279 Quick Quiz, *Annotated Teacher's Edition,* page 278–279 Section Quiz, *Assessment Book*
  **Fed Tools for Changing the Money Supply** (pages 280–283)	▸ Describe how a change in the reserve requirement changes the money supply. ▸ Explain how an open market operation changes the money supply. ▸ Explain how a change in the discount rate changes the money supply.	 Section 5 Activity, *Applying the Principles Workbook*  Outlining Activity, *Guided Reading and Study Guide* Just the Facts Handout, *Guided Reading and Study Guide*	Section Assessment, *Student Text,* page 283 Quick Quiz, *Annotated Teacher's Edition,* page 282 Section Quiz, *Assessment Book*

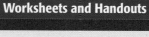

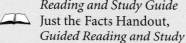

CHAPTER AND PROGRAM RESOURCES

Reproducible Chapter Resources and Assessment Materials

Graphic Organizer Activity, *Guided Reading and Study Guide*

Vocabulary Activity, *Guided Reading and Study Guide*

Working with Graphs and Charts, *Guided Reading and Study Guide*

Practice Test, *Guided Reading and Study Guide*

Critical Thinking Activity, *Finding Economics*

Chapter Test A, *Assessment Book*

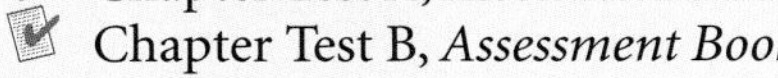
Chapter Test B, *Assessment Book*

Technology Resources

Test Generator CD

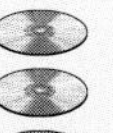
Spanish Audio Summaries CD

Marketplace® Audio Lessons CD

Economic Principles Lectures, Videocassette or DVD

Lesson Planning and Teaching Resources

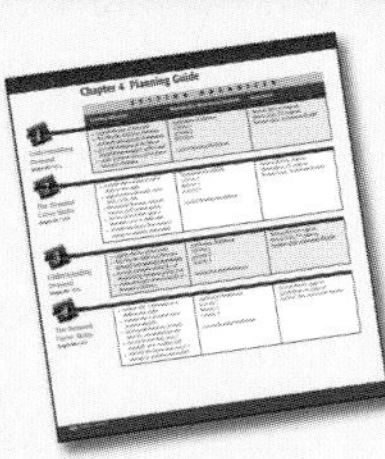

The *Economics: New Ways of Thinking* Teacher Resources include detailed lesson plans for each section in this chapter; the lesson plans are available in print form *(Lesson Plans)* and electronic form. The Teacher Resources also include *Daily Lectures: Overheads and Notes,* which provides prepared overheads and discussion notes covering the key concepts in each section of this chapter.

EMC Publishing Economics Online

Go to Economics Online, at www.emcp.com, for a variety of Internet resources to help you keep your course current and relevant. At Economics Online you will find these items:

- Economics in the News Lessons
- Study Guide Questions
- Practice Tests
- Lesson Plans

Internet Resources

Economics: New Ways of Thinking encourages students to use the Internet to find out more about economics. With the wealth of current, valid information available on Web sites, using the Internet as a research tool is likely to increase your students' interest in and understanding of economics principles and topics. In addition, doing Internet research can help your students form the habit of accessing and using economics information, as well as help them develop investigative skills they will use throughout their educational and professional careers.

To aid your students in achieving these ends, each chapter of *Economics: New Ways of Thinking* includes the addresses of several Web sites at which students will find engaging, relevant information. When students type in the addresses provided, they will immediately arrive at the intended sites. The addresses have been modified so that EMC Publishing can monitor and maintain the proper links—for example, the government site http://stats.bls.gov/ has been changed to www.emcp.net/prices. In the event that the address or content of a site changes or is discontinued, EMC's Internet editors will create a link that redirects students to an address with similar information.

Activities in the *Annotated Teacher's Edition* often suggest that students search the Internet for information. For some activities, you might want to find reputable sites beforehand, and steer students to those sites. For other activities, you might want students to do their own searching, and then check out the sites they have found and discuss why they might be reliable or unreliable.

CHAPTER 10 Overview

This chapter defines money. It discusses the history of money as well as the purposes that money serves today. Additionally, this chapter explains banking, the Federal Reserve System, and how the changing money supply affects our lives. The following statements provide brief descriptions of the major concepts covered in each section of this chapter.

The Origins of Money

Section 1 teaches students about the origins of a money economy and explains the various functions of money. Students might not be aware that there was a time when money did not exist.

The Money Supply

Section 2 explores the components of money supply and the difference between money and near-money. Students learn to determine whether savings accounts, credit cards, and debit cards are money.

The Federal Reserve System

Section 3 discusses the major responsibilities of the Federal Reserve System and explains the system's role in the U.S. economy.

The Money Creation Process

Section 4 explores the ways modern banks work. Students learn the differences between total reserves, required reserves, and excess reserves.

CHAPTER 10 Money, Banking and the Federal Reserve System

Why It Matters

Suppose that tomorrow morning you woke up, and all the money in the world was gone. It disappeared. How would the world be different? Would it be a better or a worse place to live? Would people be more greedy, less greedy, or about the same? Would people work harder, or work less?

When someone mentions the word *money*, you might think of a $20 bill. Money is cold, hard cash to most of us, but money involves much more than that $20 bill. In this chapter you will begin to find out about the story of money. You will learn how money came into existence and the purposes it serves today. You will also learn about banking and the Federal Reserve System, which work together to change the amount of money in circulation at any given time. As you complete the chapter, you will begin to see how the changing money supply can affect your life in the years to come.

Many people, when they think about banks, think of safe, secure places to keep their money and other valuables. But banks do much more than store money. They also participate in the process of creating money and regulating our money supply—activities that have a major impact on our economy.

254

Teaching Suggestions from the Author

Most students are naturally interested in a chapter that is concerned with money. I usually tell students that in this chapter we are going to put money under a microscope and examine it. We are going to try to explain why money came into existence, what gives money value, and so on.

One of the first things that I do to get students' attention and to show them that there's more to money than they know, is to take out a dollar bill and ask, "What is this called?" They will often say, "It is called a dollar bill." Then I point out the actual words at the top of the bill. The words read "Federal Reserve

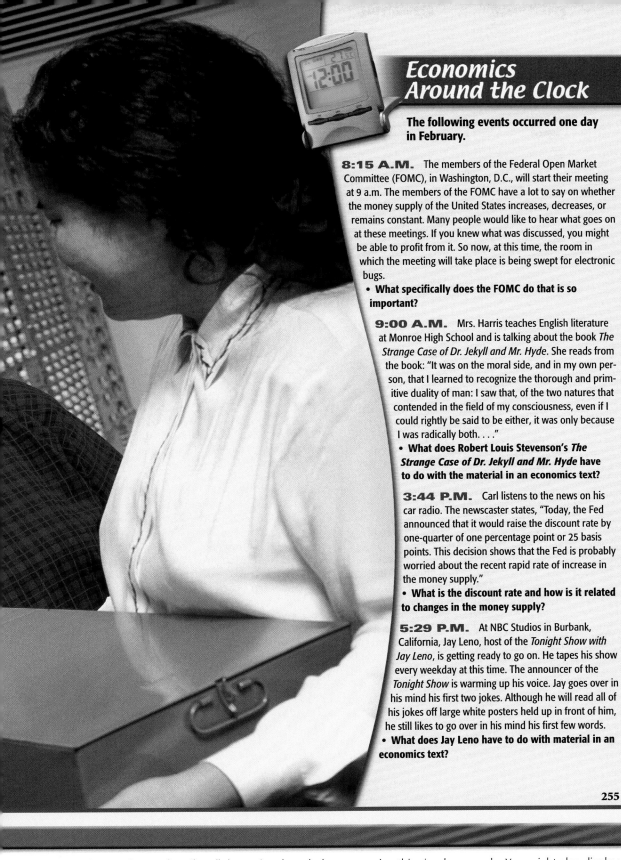

Economics Around the Clock

The following events occurred one day in February.

8:15 A.M. The members of the Federal Open Market Committee (FOMC), in Washington, D.C., will start their meeting at 9 a.m. The members of the FOMC have a lot to say on whether the money supply of the United States increases, decreases, or remains constant. Many people would like to hear what goes on at these meetings. If you knew what was discussed, you might be able to profit from it. So now, at this time, the room in which the meeting will take place is being swept for electronic bugs.

- **What specifically does the FOMC do that is so important?**

9:00 A.M. Mrs. Harris teaches English literature at Monroe High School and is talking about the book *The Strange Case of Dr. Jekyll and Mr. Hyde*. She reads from the book: "It was on the moral side, and in my own person, that I learned to recognize the thorough and primitive duality of man: I saw that, of the two natures that contended in the field of my consciousness, even if I could rightly be said to be either, it was only because I was radically both. . . ."

- **What does Robert Louis Stevenson's *The Strange Case of Dr. Jekyll and Mr. Hyde* have to do with the material in an economics text?**

3:44 P.M. Carl listens to the news on his car radio. The newscaster states, "Today, the Fed announced that it would raise the discount rate by one-quarter of one percentage point or 25 basis points. This decision shows that the Fed is probably worried about the recent rapid rate of increase in the money supply."

- **What is the discount rate and how is it related to changes in the money supply?**

5:29 P.M. At NBC Studios in Burbank, California, Jay Leno, host of the *Tonight Show with Jay Leno*, is getting ready to go on. He tapes his show every weekday at this time. The announcer of the *Tonight Show* is warming up his voice. Jay goes over in his mind his first two jokes. Although he will read all of his jokes off large white posters held up in front of him, he still likes to go over in his mind his first few words.

- **What does Jay Leno have to do with material in an economics text?**

Fed Tools for Changing the Money Supply

Section 5 combines what was taught in Sections 3 and 4. Here students learn about the Fed's tools for changing the monetary supply and enacting monetary policy.

Introducing the Chapter

Draw a large dollar symbol on the board, and underneath the symbol write the word "money." Next to the symbol, write this question: "How many of you expected money to be the basic subject of this course?" Many students will respond in the affirmative. Point out that money was not even mentioned in the definition of economics given in Chapter 1. (That definition states that economics is the science that studies the choices that people make when trying to satisfy their wants in a world of scarcity.)

You might want to explain to students that just as the definition of economics may have turned out to be different from their expectations, so might their study of money in this chapter hold some surprises.

Teaching with Visuals

Students are probably familiar with many of the services offered by banks. The rental of safety deposit boxes is only one such service. Ask students to suggest other services offered by banks.

Note." Sometimes I describe all the national symbols on the dollar bill. Most students have never before considered these words and symbols. This example shows them that they do not know as much about money as there is to know. I often find that they become much more interested in the material in this chapter after seeing this simple example. You might also display a credit card and lead students in a discussion of whether it is money and what its actual value is.

SECTION 1

Teacher Support

Focus and Motivate

Section Objectives

After completing this section, students will be able to

- describe what a barter economy is;
- explain how money emerged from a barter economy;
- describe what money is;
- explain what gives money its value; and
- describe the functions of money.

Kickoff Activity

Before class, write the following instruction on the board: "Describe what you think life would be like in a world where money did not exist." (Essentially, you are asking students to describe what life would be like in a barter economy.) When class begins, tell students to write out their answers.

Activating Prior Knowledge

Ask for student volunteers to share their responses to the Kickoff Activity. Explain that in a barter economy, or in a world with no money, it would take longer to make daily transactions than it does today in our money economy.

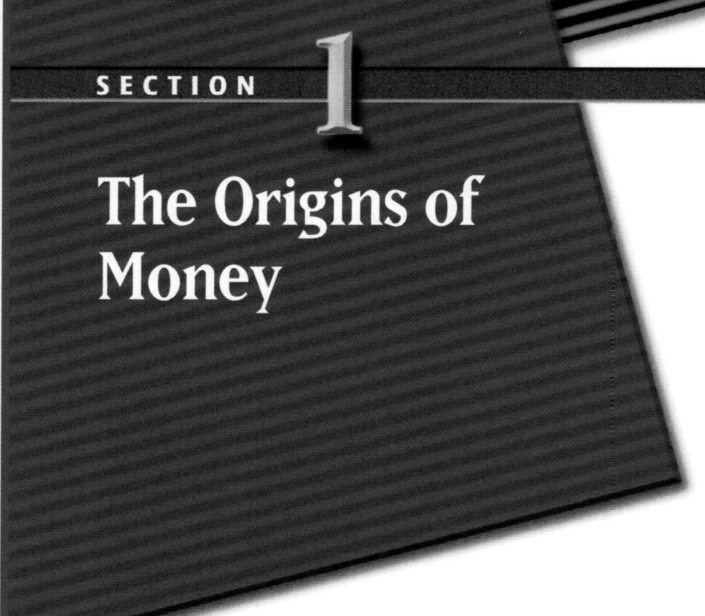

SECTION 1

The Origins of Money

Focus Questions

- What is a barter economy?
- How did money emerge out of a barter economy?
- What is money?
- What gives money its value?
- What are the functions of money?

Key Terms

barter economy
transaction costs
money
medium of exchange
unit of account
store of value
fractional reserve banking

What's It Like Living in a Barter Economy?

A **barter economy** is an economy with no money. The only way you can get what you want in a barter economy is to trade something you have for it. Suppose you have apples and want oranges. You trade two apples for three oranges.

Life in a barter economy can be difficult. It can take a lot of time and effort to get what you want. Suppose you produce utensils such as forks, spoons, and knives. No one can live on utensils alone, so you set out to trade your utensils for bread, meat, and other necessities. You come across a person who bakes bread and ask if he is willing to trade some bread for some utensils. He says, "Thank you very much, but no. I have all the utensils I need." You ask him what he would like instead of utensils. He says he would like to have some fruit, and that if you had fruit he would be happy to trade bread for fruit.

You go on your way and find another person with bread. You ask her if she wants to trade bread for utensils. Like the first person, she says no, but she would be happy to trade bread for meat if you had any. You do not, so you move on to find another person who, you hope, will be willing to trade bread for utensils.

What is the problem here? You encounter people who have what you want but (unfortunately for you) don't want what you have. (You find the person who has the bread that you want, but this person doesn't want the utensils that you have.) What makes living in a barter economy difficult is that many of the people you want to trade with don't want to trade with you.

In this type of situation, trade is time consuming. It could take all day, if not longer, to find a person who wants to trade bread for utensils. Economists state the problem this way: the **transaction costs** of making exchanges are high in a barter economy. Think of the transaction costs as the time and effort you have to spend before you can make an exchange. If the transaction costs could somehow be lower, trading would be easier.

barter economy
An economy in which trades are made in goods and services instead of in money.

transaction costs
The costs associated with the time and effort needed to search out, negotiate, and consummate an exchange.

Cooperative Learning

Ask students to bring something to class that they no longer need, use, or want. You might want to put a value limit (say, $10) on each item they bring. (Used CDs might be good tools for this exercise.) Once you have discussed the text information on bartering, tell students you are going to allow 15 minutes for them to barter with classmates to secure an item they want that someone else has brought to sell. When time has ended, ask students to share their experience. Have them tell how many trades it took before they actually got the item they wanted.

EXAMPLE: Taylor wants to buy a house and a gallon of milk. He has to do more to buy a house than he has to do to buy a gallon of milk. To buy a house, he has to find the house, inspect the house, bargain on the price of the house, take out a loan to buy the house, and much more. To buy a gallon of milk, he simply walks into a grocery store, pays at the counter, and walks out. The transaction costs of buying a house are greater than the transaction costs of buying a gallon of milk. ♦

How and Why Did Money Come to Exist?

How can an individual living in a barter economy reduce the transaction costs of making exchanges? In a barter economy with, say, 100 goods, some goods are more readily accepted in exchange than others. For example, good A might be accepted (on average) every tenth time it is offered in exchange, while good B might be accepted every seventh time. If you are going out today to trade in a barter economy, which good, A or B, would you prefer to have in your possession? The answer is B, because it is more likely to be accepted in a trade than A. In other words, to reduce the transaction costs of making exchanges, it is better to offer B than A.

Before you can offer B, though, you have to have it. So suppose someone offers to trade good B for your utensils. You don't really want to consume good B (in the same way that you want to consume bread), but you realize that good B will be useful in making exchanges. You accept the trade because later you will use good B to lower the transaction costs of getting what you want.

Once some people begin accepting a good because it reduces the transaction costs of exchange, others will follow. After you accepted good B, it had greater acceptability than it used to have. Because you accepted it, even though it wasn't the good you really wanted, perhaps it will be accepted every sixth time now instead of every seventh time. This greater acceptability makes good B more useful to other people than it was previously. Then, when Pheng accepts good B, it is even more likely that someone else will accept good B. Can you see what is happening? That you accepted good B made it more likely that Pheng would accept it. That Pheng accepted it made it more likely that someone else would accept it. Eventually, everyone will accept good B in exchange. When this time arrives—when good B is widely accepted in exchange—good B is called money. **Money** is any good that is widely accepted in exchange and in the repayment of debts. Historically, goods that evolved into money included gold, silver, copper, rocks, cattle, and shells, to name only a few.

EXAMPLE: You are on an island with 10 other people without money. You start to make trades with the others on the island—some shells for some mango, two small bluish fish for one large reddish fish, some rocks for some seaweed. One day you learn that of all things on the island, a coconut is more widely accepted in exchange than anything else. In other words, if you have a coconut to trade, six out of every 10 people will trade with you, but for other items (shells, fish, rocks) only four, or fewer, out of every 10 people will trade with you. You realize that those coconuts can make it a whole lot easier to trade: "I had better always accept a coconut (in a trade) when someone offers one to me because I can then turn around and use the coconut to get what I

▲ These Native Americans are trading furs with explorer Henry Hudson. **What were some disadvantages of living in a barter economy?**

money
A good that is widely accepted for purposes of exchange and in the repayment of debt.

Teach

Teaching with Visuals

Some disadvantages of living in a barter economy were that bartering took a lot of time and effort, and transaction costs were high.

Discussion Starter

Ask students to provide a definition of a barter economy. You might want to read aloud the section "What's It Like Living in a Barter Economy?" (pages 256–257). Explain that a barter economy is a system in which people trade goods for goods, goods for services, and services for services. Ask students what might be some of the problems of living in a barter economy. Try to help them understand that making everyday exchanges in a barter economy would be very time-consuming.

Cause and Effect

Although some people believe that government created money, we see that money emerged out of a need for a simpler, more expedient method of exchange. The barter economy was slow and at times tedious. The need for a more effective method of exchange caused paper and coin money to evolve. Instruct students to research the history of money to discover when the shift from bartering to a simpler method of exchange occurred, and what other changes this shift caused.

Reinforcement Activity

Barter economies do not have to be countrywide. Whenever students trade a good or service for a good or service from another person, that is bartering. Ask students to think about the last time they bartered with someone. Have them describe the situation and decide whether the exchange was equal in value—that is, a fair exchange—for both parties.

Cross-Curricular Activity

You might want to invite a world or U.S. history teacher to your class to discuss bartering as it took place in another time period. For instance, you could ask the visiting teacher to discuss bartering or commodity money used by the early colonists. Information such as what was considered a valuable commodity to be used for trade would be interesting, or the teacher could discuss items that were scarce and in high demand during that period. You may want to assign a project in which individual students or groups of students research that historical period and expand on the information they gained from the lecture.

Teaching with Visuals

A few items that people have used for money are silver, copper, rocks, cattle, and shells.

Critical Thinking

Pose this scenario to students: Suppose you woke up tomorrow morning and no money existed. How would your life be different? What good or goods do you think would evolve as money? Students might suggest that their CDs and other such items would take on greater value in a barter economy.

Critical Thinking

Ask students what gives money its value. Some may say that gold backing gives money its value. However, the U.S. dollar is no longer backed by gold. What gives money its value is the fact that other people will accept it for purposes of exchange. Money is valuable to John because Susan will accept it for purposes of exchange. Point out that an intangible—something that exists even if we cannot see it or touch it—gives money its value.

Background Information

Over the years, many different items have been used as mediums of exchange and as stores of value. This was especially true in the preindustrial world. One example was the obsidian (a type of volcanic glass) that was used for making stone tools. Obsidian was found in only a few areas, so people had to trade for it. Sometimes a piece of obsidian would be traded hundreds of miles away from its source before it reached its final destination. Instruct students to divide into groups of three or four and research some other form of "money" that was used in an earlier historic period. Ask the groups to present their findings in class.

▲ This woodcut shows men panning for gold in California in the 1850s. **What materials, other than gold, have people used for money?**

want from others." So you start accepting coconuts in trade, even though you don't like coconuts, and because you do, the acceptability of coconuts is now even greater than before. Then someone else sees that the acceptability of coconuts is on the rise, and so she begins accepting coconuts in all trades. On it goes until almost everyone realizes that it is in their best interests to accept coconuts. Coconuts are now money. ♦

What Gives Money Value?

Forget coconuts. Let's turn to a $10 bill. Is a $10 bill money? The $10 bill is widely accepted for purposes of exchange, of course, and therefore it is money.

What gives money (say, the $10 bill) its value? Like good B and the coconuts in the earlier examples of a barter economy, our money (today) has value because of its general acceptability. Money has value to you because you know that you can use it to get what you want. You can use it to get what you want, however, only because other people will accept it in exchange for what they have.

EXAMPLE: Imagine a time in the future. Ryan begins to walk to a local shopping center. On the way, he stops by the convenience store to buy a doughnut and milk. He tries to pay for the food with two $1 bills. The owner of the store says that he no longer accepts dollar bills in exchange for what he has to sell. This story repeats itself all day with different store owners; no one is willing to accept dollar bills for what he or she has to sell. Suddenly, dollar bills have little or no value to Ryan. If he cannot use them to get what he wants, they are simply paper and ink, with no value at all. ♦

EXAMPLE: Between 1861 and 1865, during the Civil War, in the South Confederate notes (Confederate money) had value because Confederate money was accepted by people in the South for purposes of exchange. Today in the South, Confederate money has little value (except for historical collections), because it is not widely accepted for purposes of exchange. You cannot pay for your gasoline at a service station in Alabama with Confederate notes. ♦

Are You Better Off Living in a Money Economy?

The transaction costs of exchange are lower in a money economy than in a barter economy. In a barter economy, not everyone you want to trade with wants to trade with you. In a money economy, however, everyone you want to buy something from wants what you have—money. In short, a willing trading partner lowers the transaction costs of making exchanges.

Lower transaction costs translate into less time needed for you to trade in a money economy than in a barter economy. Using money, then, frees up some time for you. With that extra time, you can produce more of whatever it is you produce (accounting services, furniture, computers, or novels), consume more leisure, or both. In a money economy, then, people produce more goods and services and consume more leisure than they would in a barter economy. The residents of money economies are richer in goods, services, and leisure than the residents of barter economies.

The residents of money economies are more specialized, too. If you lived in a barter economy, it would be difficult and time consuming to make everyday transactions. You probably would produce many things yourself rather than deal with the hardship of

Internet Research

Direct students to search for Web sites that allow users to trade goods and services in a virtual barter economy, and to find answers to questions like these: What types of goods and services are being traded? Does making this type of site available seem like a good idea? What could be the advantages and disadvantages of trading versus using money to buy something over the Internet? Have students discuss their responses or write them down. Then challenge pairs of students to design their own barter Web sites, identifying particular products and services for inclusion and explaining their choices.

Economics in the Real World

Would You Hear Hip-Hop in a Barter Economy?

Suppose one of today's hip-hop artists lived in a barter economy. Would he still be a hip-hop artist?

Before we answer this question, let's look at what an average day, living in a money economy, looks like for a hip-hop artist. He has to work on writing songs, rehearsing songs, planning for a tour, working on a video. So much of his day is wrapped up in his highly specialized work of being a hip-hop artist.

Would he be engaged in the same activities if he lived in a barter economy? Probably not. A typical day might go like this. He wakes up, eats breakfast, and then sees if he can trade a little of his hip-hop for some goods. He meets a woman with bread and asks if she is willing to trade some bread for a little hip-hop. The person tells the hip-hop artist that she is not interested in making a trade. She says she doesn't care much for hip-hop.

Onward the hip-hop artist goes, trying to find someone who will trade goods for hip-hop. He might run into a few people, but we can be sure that by the end of the day the hip-hop artist finds it fairly hard to make simple exchanges: a song for some steak, a song for some fruit, a song for a shirt.

What is likely to happen to the hip-hop artist? He will quickly recognize how difficult making trades is and decide to make a lot of what he needs to survive himself. He might start making his own bread and his own clothes instead of trying to trade hip-hop for each. In short, in a barter economy, because trade is so difficult and time consuming, people are likely to try to produce for themselves the things they need. In the end, the hip-hop artist is so busy making bread, clothes, and so on that he really doesn't have much time to work on his hip-hop. As a result, hip-hop is likely to go by the wayside. Soon, he is no longer a hip-hop artist, but just another person producing many of the things he needs.

The lesson learned? Few people would specialize in a barter economy to the degree they do in a money economy. After all, what is the probability that everyone whose goods you want will want the one thing that you produce?

In a money economy, in contrast, everyone is willing to trade what they have for money. The risk in specializing is less than in a barter economy, so people produce one thing (hip-hop songs, attorney services, corn, and so on), sell it for money, and then use the money to make their preferred purchases.

Jay-Z on stage. **Would Jay-Z be a hip-hop artist in a barter economy?**

THINK ABOUT IT Do you think specialization is more likely in a large city (such as New York City) or a small city (some city with a population under 7,000 persons for example)? Explain your answer. Also, do you think the fact that you can buy goods online makes it more likely or less likely that you will specialize? Explain your answer.

producing only one good and then trying to exchange it for so many other goods. In other words, the higher the transaction costs of trading, the less likely you would want to trade, and the more likely you would produce the goods that you would otherwise have to trade for.

In a money economy, however, it is neither difficult nor time consuming to make everyday transactions. The transaction costs

Economics in the Real World

After students have read this feature, ask them what other goods or services that we enjoy today might not be available in a barter economy.

ANSWERS TO THINK ABOUT IT Answers will vary. Students might say that specialization is more likely in a large city where the variety of people may be interested in a variety of goods and services. The ease of buying and selling goods online also encourages specialization by making those goods available to a wider population with wider interests.

Economics Around the Clock

You may want to refer students to the 9:00 A.M. and 5:29 P.M. scenarios in Economics Around the Clock (page 255), and discuss their answers to the accompanying questions.

Lead students to understand that Robert Lewis Stevenson would probably never have written *The Strange Case of Dr. Jekyll and Mr. Hyde* had he not lived in a money economy, and that likewise, Jay Leno would not be a comedian if he did not live in a money economy. If Stevenson and Leno had lived in a barter economy, they would have been too busy making trades and trying to be self-sufficient to specialize in writing a book or creating comedy. Specialization often is the result of living in a money economy.

Background Information: Barter Economies

The Internet is causing a resurgence of the barter economy. Corporations are now using several Web sites designed to allow trade of products as diverse as office furniture and hotel rooms, for a small trading fee charged by the Web host. Some 250,000 U.S. companies already barter independently or through barter exchanges. Until 1982, business-to-business bartering was an underground economy that encouraged tax evasion. In 1982, President Reagan signed the Tax Equity and Fiscal Responsibility Act, which opened the door to corporate bartering. Some experts suggest that it could be possible for big corporations to stop using cash altogether!

Teaching with Visuals

This transaction would be much more difficult without money because the parties to it would each have to have something that the other wanted.

Discussion Starter

The text details the three functions of money. To help students gain a better understanding of this concept (which is that money is more than just a means by which they can purchase a new CD), ask them to think of a time when they exercised each of the three functions in the past two weeks. (*Possible answer:* medium of exchange: purchased a CD; unit of account: priced a certain dress or stereo; store of value: chose to save for a particular purchase in the future.) Invite students to share their experiences with the class.

Reinforcement Activity

Every day, students use money in each of the three ways discussed in the text. They pay for their lunches, compare prices, and maybe put money in a savings account. Tell students to create a chart with three heads: "Medium of Exchange," "Unit of Account," and "Store of Value." Then assign them to keep track of the ways they used money for three days and to log those ways in their charts. At the end of the three days, discuss their results.

▲ Money lowers the transaction costs of making exchanges. **How much more difficult would this transaction be without money?**

of exchange are low compared to what they are in a barter economy. You have the luxury of specializing in the production of one thing (fixing faucets, writing computer programs, teaching students), selling that one thing for money, and then using the money to buy whatever good or service you want to buy.

In only very few places in the world today is barter still practiced. In those places, you will find that the people have a low standard of material living, and they are not nearly as specialized as they are in money economies.

What Are the Three Functions of Money?

Money has three major functions: a medium of exchange, a unit of account, and a store of value.

medium of exchange Anything that is generally acceptable in exchange for goods and services.

unit of account A common measurement used to express values.

store of value Something with the ability to hold value over time.

Money as a Medium of Exchange

A **medium of exchange** is anything that is generally acceptable in exchange for goods and services. As we have seen, then, the most basic function of money is as a medium of exchange. Money is part of (present in) almost every exchange made.

Money as a Unit of Account

A **unit of account** is a common measurement used to express values. Money functions as a unit of account, which means that all goods can be expressed in terms of money. For example, we express the value of a house in terms of dollars (say, $280,000), the value of a car in terms of dollars (say, $20,000), and the value of a computer in terms of dollars (say, $2,000).

Money as a Store of Value

A good is a **store of value** if it maintains its value over time. Money serves as a store of value. For example, you can sell your labor services today, collect money in payment, and wait for a future date to spend the money on goods and services. You do not have to rush to buy goods and services with the money today; it will store value to be used at a future date.

To say that money is a store of value does not mean that it is necessarily a constant store of value. Let's say that the only good in the world is apples, and the price of an apple is $1. Julio earns $100 on January 1, 2006. If he spends the $100 on January 1, 2006, he can buy 100 apples. Suppose he decides to hold the money for one year, until January 1, 2007. Suppose also that the price of apples doubles during this time to $2. On January 1, 2007, Julio can buy only 50 apples. What happened? The money lost some of its value between 2006 and 2007. If prices rise, the value of money declines.

When economists say that money serves as a store of value, they do not mean to imply that money is a *constant* store of value, or that it always serves as a store of value equally well. Money is better at storing value at some times than at other times. (Money is "bad" at storing value when prices are rapidly rising.)

For a summarized comparison of the three major functions of money, see Exhibit 10-1.

A Student Asks

QUESTION: *Can money lose its value very fast over a short period of time?*

ANSWER: *Money will lose its value fairly quickly (and therefore not be a good store of value) any time prices rise quickly over*

Differentiating Instruction

Visual and English Language Learners

Students are learning about the three major functions of money. Ask them to create a poster using pictures to exhibit all the functions of money. Each item on the exhibit should be labeled by function along with a short description of it. This activity will be particularly useful for visual learners and those who have difficulty comprehending English.

a short period of time. A classic example is Germany in 1923 when prices were rising so quickly, and money was losing its value so fast, that workers in Germany were being paid (with money) three times a day. They might be paid in the morning, use the money right away to buy goods, then be paid in the afternoon, use that money right away to buy goods, and so on. In other words, if they waited too long to use the money they were paid, prices would have risen by so much that the amount of money they had wouldn't buy much. So they ended up spending their money almost as quickly as they received it.

Who Were the Early Bankers?

Our money today is easy to carry and transport, but it was not always that way. For example, when money was principally gold coins, carrying it was neither easy nor safe. Gold is heavy, and transporting thousands of gold coins is an activity that could easily draw the attention of thieves. Thus, individuals wanted to store their gold in a safe place. The person most individuals turned to was the goldsmith, someone already equipped with safe storage facilities. Goldsmiths were the first bankers. They took in other people's gold and stored it for them.

To acknowledge that they held deposited gold, goldsmiths issued receipts called *warehouse receipts* to their customers. For example, Adam might have a receipt from the goldsmith Turner stating that he deposited 400 gold pieces with Turner. Before long, people began to circulate the warehouse receipts in place of the gold itself (gold was not only inconvenient for customers to carry, but also inconvenient for merchants to accept). For instance, if Adam wanted to buy something for 400 gold pieces, he might give a warehouse receipt to the seller instead of going to the goldsmith, obtaining the gold, and then delivering it to the seller. Using the receipts was easier than dealing with the gold itself for both parties. In short, the warehouse receipts circulated as money—that is, they became widely acceptable for purposes of exchange.

Goldsmiths began to notice that on an average day, few people came to redeem their receipts for gold. Most individuals were simply trading the receipts for goods. At this stage, warehouse receipts were fully backed by gold. The receipts simply represented, or stood in place of, the actual gold in storage.

EXHIBIT 10-1 The Major Functions of Money

Function	Definition	Example
Medium of exchange	Anything that is generally acceptable in exchange for goods and services	John uses money to buy haircuts, books, food, CDs, and computers. Money is the medium of exchange.
Unit of account	Common measurement in which values are expressed	The price of a candy bar is \$1, and the price of a book is \$14. The exchange value of both goods is measured by dollars (unit of account). Notice that exchange values can be compared easily when money is used. In this example, the book has 14 times the exchange value of the candy bar.
Store of value	An item that maintains value over time	Phil has a job and gets paid \$100. He could use \$100 to buy a ski jacket that he wants, but he decides not to. Instead, he saves the \$100 and buys the ski jacket six months later. For Phil, money has acted as a store of value over the six-month period.

◀ This table summarizes the major functions of money.

Teaching with Visuals

Encourage students to re-create Exhibit 10-1 using their own words and examples. Then display their examples on a bulletin board in the classroom.

Teaching with Visuals

The answer to the question accompanying the illustration on page 262 is that goldsmiths were among the first bankers because they kept gold for others, in the process passing out receipts that began to circulate. Eventually, goldsmiths began to lend out gold to earn interest.

Application Activity

After reading and discussing Section 1, you may want to assign the Section Activity in the *Applying the Principles Workbook.*

Assess

Quick Quiz

The following true-or-false quiz will help you assess student understanding of the material covered in this section.

1. A barter economy is difficult because not everyone wants to trade for what you have to offer. (True)
2. The money economy appeared because of individual self-interest. (True)
3. Money has value because you can use it to get the things you want. (True)
4. The most basic function of money is as a medium of exchange. (True)
5. Banks create money by holding on reserve all the money deposited with them and lending none. (False)

Internet Research

Instruct students to locate the Web site for a bank in their community and to find out about different types of accounts they could open there. Encourage them to make brochures for other teenagers that explain their banking options. The purpose of the brochures is to help students understand the ways that having a bank account can help them save and earn money.

Assessment Book

You will find a quiz for this section in the *Assessment Book.*

Reteaching Activity

Use the Section Assessment to gauge which students may need reteaching on this section. Lead those students in a brainstorming session on the term *bartering*. Ask what type of bartering they are involved in today, if any.

Guided Reading

For further reteaching of the key concepts in this section, assign the Outlining Activity and the Just the Facts Handout in the *Guided Reading and Study Guide.*

▲ A goldsmith's shop of the sixteenth century. **Why were goldsmiths among the first to become bankers?**

Some goldsmiths, however, began to think, "Suppose I lend out some of the gold that people have deposited with me If I lend it to others, I can charge interest for the loan. And since receipts are circulating in place of the gold, I will probably never be faced with redeeming everyone's receipts for gold at once." Some goldsmiths did lend out some of the gold deposited with them and collected the interest on the loans. The consequence of this lending activity was an increase in the supply of money, measured in terms of gold and paper receipts. Remember, both gold and paper warehouse receipts were widely accepted for purposes of exchange.

fractional reserve banking
A banking arrangement in which banks hold only a fraction of their deposits and lend out the remainder.

A numerical example can show how the goldsmiths' activities increased the supply of money. Suppose the world's entire money supply is made up of 100 gold coins. Now suppose the owners of the gold deposit their coins with the goldsmith. To keep things simple, suppose the goldsmith gives out 1 paper receipt for each gold coin deposited. In other words, if Flores deposits 3 coins with a goldsmith, she receives 3 warehouse receipts, each representing a coin.

The warehouse receipts begin to circulate instead of the gold itself, so the money supply consists of 100 paper receipts, whereas before it consisted of 100 gold coins. Still, the number is 100. So far, so good.

Now the goldsmith decides to lend out some of the gold and earn interest on the loans. Suppose Robert wants to take out a loan for 15 gold coins. The goldsmith grants the loan. Instead of handing over 15 gold coins, though, the goldsmith gives Robert 15 paper receipts.

What happens to the money supply? Before the goldsmith went into the lending business, the money supply consisted of 100 paper receipts. Now, though, the money supply has increased to 115 paper receipts. The increase in the money supply (as measured by the number of paper receipts) is a result of the lending activity of the goldsmith.

The process described here was the beginning of **fractional reserve banking**. We live under a fractional reserve banking system today. Under a fractional reserve banking system, such as the one that currently operates in the United States, banks (like the goldsmiths of years past) create money by holding on reserve only a fraction of the money deposited with them and lending the remainder.

ASSESSMENT

Defining Terms

1. Define:
   a. barter economy
   b. transaction costs
   c. money
   d. medium of exchange
   e. unit of account
   f. store of value
   g. fractional reserve banking

Reviewing Facts and Concepts

2. What gives money its value?
3. Money serves as a unit of account. Give an example to illustrate what this means.
4. What does it mean to say that the United States has a fractional reserve banking system?

Critical Thinking

5. Is specialization in a money economy more or less likely to happen than in a barter economy?

Defining Terms

1. a. barter economy: an economy in which trades are made in goods and services instead of in money; **b. transaction costs:** the costs associated with the time and effort needed to search out, negotiate, and consummate an exchange; **c. money:** a good that is widely accepted for purposes of exchange and in the repayment of debt; **d. medium of exchange:** anything that is generally acceptable in exchange for goods and services; **e. unit of account:** a common measurement in which values are expressed; **f. store of value:** something that holds value over time; **g. fractional reserve banking:** a banking arrangement in which banks hold only a fraction of their deposits and lend out the remainder.

Reviewing Facts and Concepts

2. General acceptability gives money its value.

3. Answers will vary. Students should express the value of something in terms of money.

4. Having a fractional reserve banking system means that banks create money by holding on reserve only a fraction of the money deposited with them and lending the remainder.

Critical Thinking

5. Specialization is more likely to happen in a money economy because people do not need to spend as much time producing goods for their own use.

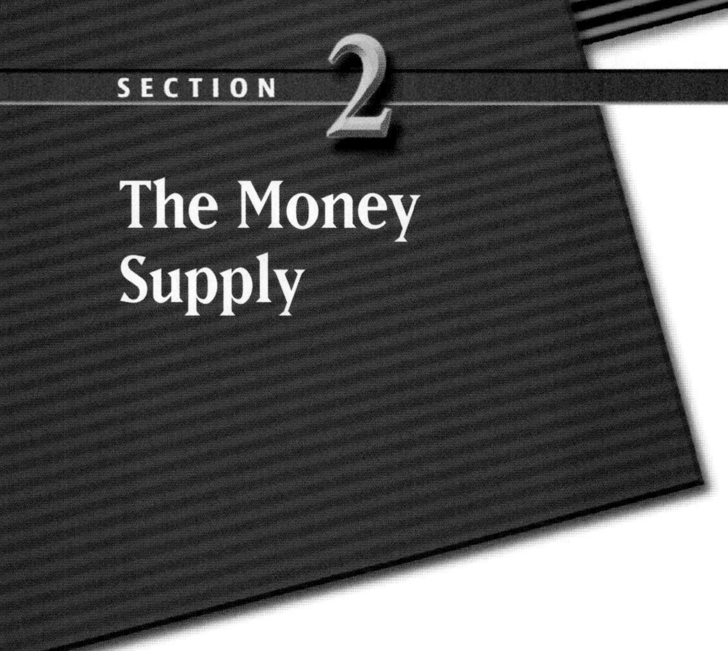

The Money Supply

Focus Questions

- What does the money supply consist of?
- What is a Federal Reserve note?
- What is and what is not "money"?
- What causes interest rates to change?

Key Terms

money supply
currency
Federal Reserve note
demand deposit
savings account
near-money
loanable funds market

What Are the Components of the Money Supply?

The most basic **money supply**—sometimes referred to as M1 (M-one)—consists of three components we will soon identify. Other "money supplies" besides M1 include a broader measure of the money supply called M2 (M-two). For purposes of simplicity, when we discuss the money supply in this text, we are referring to M1. The M1 in the United States is composed of (1) currency, (2) checking accounts, and (3) traveler's checks.

1. *Currency.* **Currency** includes both coins (such as quarters and dimes) minted by the U.S. Treasury and paper money. The paper money in circulation consists of **Federal Reserve notes.** If you look at a dollar bill, you will see at the top the words "Federal Reserve Note." The Federal Reserve System, which is the central bank of the United States (discussed in a later section), issues Federal Reserve notes.
2. *Checking accounts.* Checking accounts are accounts in which funds are deposited and can be withdrawn simply by writing a check. Sometimes checking accounts are referred to as **demand deposits**, because the funds can be converted to currency on demand and given to the person to whom the check is made payable. For example, suppose Malcolm has a checking account at a local bank with a balance of $400. He can withdraw up to $400 currency from his account, or he can transfer any dollar amount up to $400 to someone else by simply writing a check to that person.
3. *Traveler's checks.* A traveler's check is a check issued by a bank in any of several denominations ($10, $20, $50, and so on) and sold to a traveler (or to anyone who wishes to buy it), who signs it at the time it is issued by the bank and then again in the presence of the person cashing it.

In August 2005, $710 billion in currency was in circulation, along with $619 billion in

money supply
The total supply of money in circulation, composed of currency, checking accounts, and traveler's checks.

currency
Coins issued by the U.S. Treasury and paper money (called Federal Reserve notes) issued by the Federal Reserve System.

Federal Reserve note
Paper money issued by the Federal Reserve System.

demand deposit
An account from which deposited funds can be withdrawn in currency or transferred by a check to a third party at the initiative of the owner.

Focus and Motivate

Section Objectives

After completing this section, students will be able to

- explain what the money supply consists of;
- explain what a Federal Reserve note is;
- describe what "money" is and what it is not; and
- explain what causes interest rates to change.

Kickoff Activity

Prompt students to name all the ways that they pay for goods and services and collect payments from others. Without comment or discussion, list the responses on the board as students call them out.

Activating Prior Knowledge

Refer to the list you compiled during the Kickoff Activity. Ask students which of the items listed would be considered money. Put an *M* next to each of those items. Then go back through the list and discuss why their responses are correct or incorrect.

Some students may say that credit cards are money. Acknowledge that like money, credit cards are widely accepted for purposes of exchange. But also explain that there is a difference between credit cards and money. Only money can ultimately be used to pay off debts. A credit card is an instrument that allows a person to take out a loan from the bank that issued the card. A credit card is not money.

Teach

Discussion Starter

Many students think of money as only currency (paper bills and coins). Ask students, What is the money supply? Read aloud the definition of *money supply* from page 263 of the text. Stress that the money supply is more than just currency or cash. It is currency, checking accounts, and traveler's checks combined. All three are money. Some students may have questions or ask about credit cards. Tell them they will be learning more about credit and debit cards in this section.

Discussion Starter

Ask students if they have a savings account. Did they set it up themselves or did their parents set it up for them? Do they know how much money is in the account? How often do they check the balance on the account? What is the current interest rate? If some students have trouble answering these questions, encourage them to find out more about saving money.

EXHIBIT 10-2 Components of the Money Supply

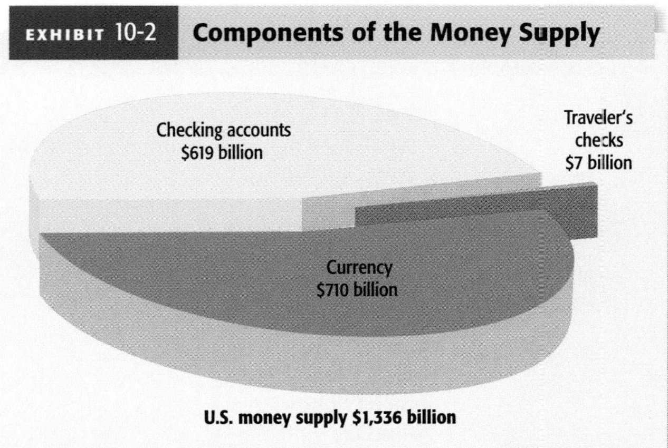

▲ The money supply consists of currency, checking accounts (balances), and traveler's checks. The amounts shown represent the money supply in August 2005.

checking accounts, and $7 billion in traveler's checks. Altogether, the money supply equaled $1,336 billion (see Exhibit 10-2).

You might be wondering why debit cards aren't mentioned; after all, you can buy products with a debit card in the same way that you can with currency. Do you see why the debit cards aren't included in our list? They are already represented in checking accounts. When you use a debit card, money is removed from your checking account in the same way that it is when you write a check.

Another card that some people might in the future think of as currency are smart cards. A *smart card* resembles a credit card in shape and size, but it is not just a simple piece of plastic the way a credit card is. Inside it is an embedded 8-bit microprocessor. A smart card can be used for many things, and it can hold significant amounts of data. For purposes here, though, we need to point out that a monetary value can be placed on a smart card (much like a monetary value can be placed on a card at a video arcade), and then the card can be used to make on-the-spot purchases, much like currency is used for the same thing.

savings account
An interest-earning account.

near-money
Assets, such as nonchecking savings accounts, that can be easily and quickly turned into money.

A Student Asks

QUESTION: *I am used to thinking that only the cash and change I have in my wallet is money. Are we saying cash is only one component of money?*

ANSWER: *Yes, that is exactly what we are saying. Remember that money is anything that is widely accepted in exchange and in the repayment of debt. The cash and change in your wallet (the currency in your wallet) is widely accepted in exchange and in the repayment of debt, so it is money. The check you might write out for $100 is also accepted in exchange and in the repayment of debt, so it is money. Traveler's checks are also widely accepted in exchange and in the repayment of debt, so they are money too. In summary, money consists of currency plus checking accounts plus traveler's checks.*

Is a Savings Account Money?

A **savings account** is an interest-earning account. For example, if you have $400 in your savings account and the annual interest rate you are paid is 6 percent, in a year your savings account will increase to $424. With some savings accounts, you can write checks; others you cannot. Savings accounts on which you can write checks fall into the category of checking accounts, which were discussed earlier. A passbook savings account is an example of a nonchecking savings account. When you deposit your money into a passbook savings account, you are given a small booklet in which deposits, withdrawals, and interest are recorded.

A nonchecking savings account is not considered money because it is not widely accepted for purposes of exchange. No person can go into a store, show the salesperson the balance in a passbook savings account, and buy a $40 sweater. However, nonchecking savings accounts are considered **near-money**. Near-money is anything that can be relatively easily and quickly turned into money. A person cannot buy a sweater by telling the salesperson that she has so much "money" in her passbook savings account, but she can go to the bank and request that her nonchecking savings be returned to her in currency ("I'll take it in twenties").

Internet Research

Direct students to the Federal Deposit Insurance Corporation (FDIC) Web site to find out when the agency was established, why it exists, and what it does. Ask students to imagine that the FDIC suddenly ceased to exist—what might be the consequences? Tell them to write essays examining these possibilities.

BY THE NUMBERS

The money supply has been increasing in the United States over time. The following table shows the money supply figures for the years 1989–2005. (The figure for 2005 was reported in August 2005.) All numbers are in billions of dollars. Is the money supply in a following year always higher than the money supply in a prior year? If you want to find the most recent money supply figures, you can go to www.emcp.net/federalreserve and click on Table 1.

Year	Money supply (billions of dollars)
1989	$ 793
1990	825
1991	897
1992	1,025
1993	1,129
1994	1,150
1995	1,126
1996	1,079
1997	1,072
1998	1,094
1999	1,122
2000	1,087
2001	1,179
2002	1,216
2003	1,299
2004	1,367
2005	1,336

Are Credit Cards Money?

You're out on a Friday night with your friends eating pizza. Someone asks, "Anyone here got any money?" You say, "I have a credit card." Your friends say, "Good enough."

Is a credit card money? After all, it is often referred to as "plastic money," and most retailers accept credit cards as payment for purchases. On closer examination, we can see that a credit card is not money.

Consider Tina, who decides to buy a pair of shoes. She hands the shoe clerk her Visa card and signs for the purchase. Essentially, what the Visa card allows Tina to do is take out a loan from the bank that issued the card. The shoe clerk knows that this bank has, in effect, promised to pay the store for the shoes. At a later date, the bank will send Tina a credit card bill. At that time, Tina will be required to reimburse the bank for the shoe charges, plus interest (if her payment is made after a certain date). Tina is required to discharge her debt to the bank with money, such as currency or a check written on her checking account.

Can you see that a credit card is not money? Money has to be both widely used for exchange and be used in the repayment of debt. A credit card is not used to repay debt but rather to incur it. It is an instrument that makes it easier for the holder to

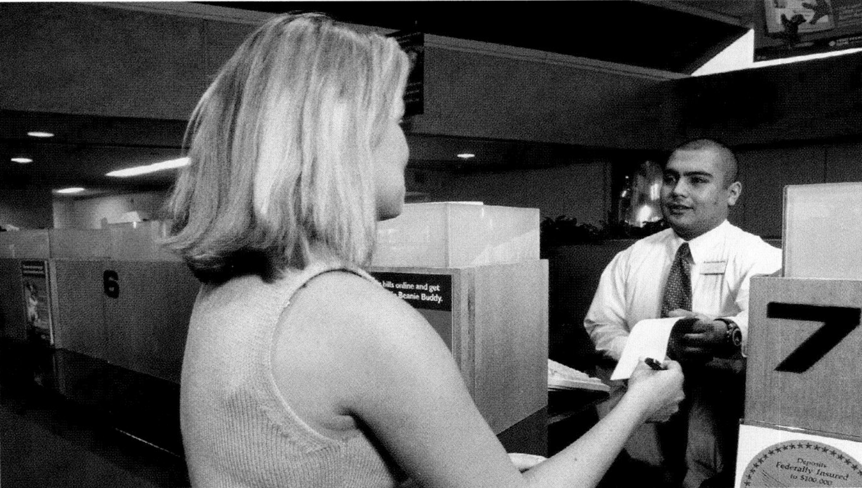

◀ Today, if you have near-money, you can quickly and easily turn it into money, either at the bank or through your online banking service. **What is near-money?**

Reinforcement Activity

Encourage students to gather from various banks information concerning minimum balances, interest rates, incentives, and benefits of opening and maintaining a savings account. Invite them to bring in brochures from the banks or printouts from the banks' Web sites. Then instruct everyone to look through all the materials and each choose the bank that offers the best savings account for him or her. Direct students to write a paragraph naming the account they would like to put their money in and explaining why they chose it.

Teaching with Visuals

Near-money is anything that can easily and quickly be turned into money.

Cooperative Learning

Numerous sources report money supply figures. Two print sources are the *Economic Report of the President* and the *Survey of Current Business*. Newspaper sources include the *New York Times* and the *Wall Street Journal*. A number of Web sites also provide money supply information. Divide the class into groups of three or four students. Have each group find recent money supply figures, and discuss its findings in a one-page report. Insist that students substantiate their findings by listing the sources they used.

Economics in the Real World

After students have read this feature, ask them why, do they think, cigarettes rather than some other item became "money" in prison camps.

ANSWERS TO THINK ABOUT IT The prisoners accepted the cigarette as money because it was universally recognized as having value. They set the exchange rate for other goods to the cigarette.

Teaching with Visuals

The answer to the question for the photograph on page 267 is that a credit card cannot be used to pay a debt; a credit card incurs debt.

Application Activity

After reading and discussing Section 2, you may want to assign the Section Activity in the *Applying the Principles Workbook.*

Assess

Quick Quiz

The following true-or-false quiz will help you assess student understanding of the material covered in this section.

1. One component of the money supply is traveler's checks. (True)
2. Of the three major components of the money supply, the currency component was the largest in August 2005. (True)
3. A nonchecking savings account is considered money. (False)
4. A credit card is money. (False)
5. Use of a credit card places a person in debt that needs to be paid off with money. (True)

Assessment Book

You will find a quiz for this section in the *Assessment Book.*

What Is Money in a Prisoner of War Camp?

During World War II, an American, R. A. Radford, was captured and imprisoned in a prisoner of war (POW) camp. During his stay, he noted that the Red Cross would periodically distribute to the prisoners packages that contained goods such as cigarettes, toiletries, chocolate, cheese, margarine, and tinned beef. Not all the prisoners had the same preferences: some liked chocolate but did not like cigarettes, whereas others liked cigarettes but did not like cheese. Soon, the prisoners began to barter-trade with each other. One prisoner, who had cigarettes and wanted more chocolate, would try to find another prisoner who wanted less chocolate and more cigarettes.

▲ Cigarettes were money in prisoner of war camps.

As this chapter explained, barter is a more time-consuming and difficult way to trade than trading with money. Soon the prisoners no longer bartered goods; they used money instead. The money was not U.S. dollars, French francs, German marks, or British pounds. In fact, it was not any national money at all; cigarettes emerged as the money in the POW camp. They were widely accepted for purposes of exchange. Soon chocolate bars, cheese, and other goods were quoted in "cigarette prices": 10 cigarettes for a chocolate bar, 20 cigarettes for cheese, and so on.

THINK ABOUT IT Why did the cigarette rather than the chocolate or cheese become money?

obtain a loan. The use of a credit card places a person in debt, which he or she then has to repay with money.

Don't think of the card as money because it isn't money. Think of it as what it is—a piece of plastic that allows you to take out a loan from the bank that issued the card.

In other words, when you hand the credit card to the cashier to pay for the pizza, or shoes, or new CD, it is you and the bank standing up there in front of the cashier—not just you alone. The bank is saying to you, "Here, we are going to lend you some 'money' to pay for the item. Oh, and by the way, we want you to pay us back later, with interest."

To get a better understanding of credit cards, turn to page 268 and read about "The Psychology of Credit Cards" in the "Your Personal Economics" feature.

Borrowing, Lending, and Interest Rates

As you know, when a person uses a credit card, he or she is actually borrowing funds from a bank. In other words, the person is a borrower and the bank is a lender. Often, when loans are made, an interest rate must be paid for the loan.

Now if we look at interest rates (for loans) over time, we see that sometimes interest rates are higher than at other times. For example, in the 1970s, interest rates were relatively high. In 2004, interest rates were relatively low.

Why are interest rates high at some times and low at other times? The answer has to do with supply and demand, which you learned about in Chapters 4 through 6. Interest rates are determined in the **loanable funds**

loanable funds market The market for loans. There is a demand for loans (stemming from borrowers) and a supply of loans (stemming from lenders). It is in the loanable funds market where the interest rate is determined.

Differentiating Instruction

Kinesthetic Learners and Enrichment and Extension

For one week, create an imaginary bank with accounts for your class. Each student should have a savings account and a checking account (with checkbook and debit card). Instruct students to make imaginary purchases with their imaginary checkbooks and debit cards, and to keep track of their balances. Set a minimum balance on their savings accounts, and then allow students to transfer money from their savings accounts into their checking accounts. At the end of the week have students prepare a statement like the monthly statements that banks send to customers, and turn in their checkbooks, passbooks, and statements for evaluation.

◀ Credit cards are not money—they cannot be used to repay debt. **What is the relationship between credit cards and debt?**

market in much the same way that apple prices are determined in the apple market, computer prices are determined in the computer market, and house prices are determined in the housing market.

The loanable funds market includes a demand for loans and a supply of loans. The demanders of loans are called borrowers; the suppliers of loans are called lenders. Through the interaction of the demand for and supply of loans, the interest rate is determined.

What happens if the demand for loans rises? Obviously, if the demand for loans rises and the supply remains constant, the price of a loan, which is the interest rate, rises. What happens if the demand for loans falls? The interest rate falls. What happens if the supply of loans rises? The interest rate falls. What happens if the supply of loans falls? The interest rate rises.

Sometimes people make a distinction between short-term interest rates and long-term interest rates. The terms *short* and *long* refer to the time period of the loan. For example, if you were to take out a six-month loan, it would likely be referred to as a short-term loan, in contrast to, say, a 30-year loan, which would be referred to as a long-term loan. The interest rate you paid (as a borrower) for the six-month loan would be referred to as a short-term interest rate; the interest rate you paid for the 30-year loan would be referred to as a long-term interest rate.

> *"There is only one way to have your cake and eat it too: Lend it out at interest."*
>
> — Anonymous

Section 2 Assessment

Defining Terms

1. Define:
   - **a.** money supply
   - **b.** currency
   - **c.** Federal Reserve note
   - **d.** demand deposit
   - **e.** savings account
   - **f.** near-money

Reviewing Facts and Concepts

2. What is the official name for a "dollar bill"? (*Hint:* Look at a dollar bill and see what is written at the top.)
3. What is the difference between near-money and money?

Critical Thinking

4. Credit cards are widely accepted for purposes of exchange, yet they are not money. Why not?

Applying Economic Concepts

5. Take a look at a Federal Reserve note. On it, you will read the following words: "This note is legal tender for all debts, public and private." What part of the definition of money does this message refer to?

Reteaching Activity

Use the Section Assessment to gauge which students may need reteaching on this section. With a group of those students, write the words "currency," "checking accounts," and "traveler's checks" on the board. Call on volunteers to explain the meanings of these terms. Draw a large circle around all three of these terms and label this circle "The Money Supply." Explain to students again that the money supply equals the total amount of currency, checking accounts, and traveler's checks.

Guided Reading

For further reteaching of the key concepts in this section, assign the Outlining Activity and the Just the Facts Handout in the *Guided Reading and Study Guide.*

Section 2 Assessment Answers

Defining Terms

1. a. money supply: the total supply of money in circulation, composed of currency, checking accounts, and traveler's checks; **b. currency:** coins issued by the U.S. Treasury and paper money issued by the Federal Reserve System; **c. Federal Reserve note:** paper money issued by the Federal Reserve System; **d. demand deposit:** an account from which deposited funds can be withdrawn in currency or transferred by a check to a third party at the initiative of the owner; **e. savings account:** an interest-earning account; **f. near-money:** an asset, such as a nonchecking savings account, that can easily and quickly be turned into money.

Reviewing Facts and Concepts

2. A dollar bill is officially called a Federal Reserve note.

3. Money is anything that is widely accepted for purposes of exchange. Near-money is not widely accepted for exchange purposes, but it can easily and quickly be turned into money.

Critical Thinking

4. To be money, a good has to be widely used for purposes of exchange and must be used in the repayment of debt. Credit cards are not used to repay debt; they are used to obtain loans. When you receive a loan, you have incurred a debt. You cannot pay off one debt with another debt. For example, if you owe $500 on a Visa card, you cannot say to the bank that issued the card, "Let me pay off the $500 I owe you by charging it to my MasterCard card." Instead, you have to repay the debt with money.

Applying Economic Concepts

5. Money is any good that is widely used for purposes of exchange and in the repayment of debt. The inscription on the Federal Reserve note refers to the latter part of the definition (the repayment of debt).

Your Personal Economics

Discussion Starter

Ask students if they know anyone who has owed a considerable amount of money because he or she was careless with a credit card. Caution them not to name names, and ask how those people found themselves in that situation.

Research Activity

Assign students to each research how many credit cards the average American has and to answer questions like these: Has this number increased or decreased during the last 10 years? Has individual credit card debt increased or decreased during this period? What effects have these changes had on the economy? on society as a whole? on individual people? Compare students' findings in a class discussion.

Teaching with Visuals

Answers will vary. Students may say that their decision will depend on whether they paid for the original ticket with cash or a credit card, and on whether they will purchase a replacement with cash or a credit card.

Your Personal Economics

The Psychology of Credit Cards

If you work to earn $50, do you use the money in the same way that you would use a $50 gift? Many economic studies show that people often are more serious with money they earn than with money they win or receive as a gift. In reality, a dollar is a dollar is a dollar, no matter from where it came. But in everyday life, we see a dollar earned as somehow different from a dollar won.

$100 "Out the Window"

Suppose you plan to go to a concert, and the ticket costs $100. You buy the ticket on Monday to attend the concert on Friday. When Friday night comes, you realize you lost the ticket. Assuming that tickets are still available, do you buy another? Answer the question before reading further.

Now let's change the circumstances. Suppose instead of buying the ticket on Monday, you plan to buy it on Friday, right before the concert. At the ticket window on Friday night, you realize that on your way to the concert you lost $100 out of your wallet. You brought plenty of money so you still have enough to buy the ticket. Do you buy it?

▼ **If you lost your ticket to this concert, would you buy another?**

The Economist Says...

According to economists, the two settings present you with the same choice. In both settings, you have to spend another $100 to see the concert. Because the two settings present you with the same choice, economists argue that you will behave the same in the two settings. If you decide not to buy another ticket in the first setting, then you shouldn't in the second. If you do decide to buy another ticket in the first setting, then you should in the second.

But in Real Life...

People don't seem to behave the way that economists predict, however. Many people, when asked the two questions in this example, say that they will not buy a second ticket if they lost the first ticket, but they will buy a ticket if they lost $100. Why? These people argue that spending an additional $100 on an additional ticket is like spending $200 to see the concert, which is too much to pay. However, they don't see themselves spending $200 to see the concert when they lose $100 on the way to the concert and pay $100 for a ticket. To these people, the situations are completely different.

Economists say that the people who answer the two questions differently—although both settings offer the same basic choice—are *compartmentalizing*. They are treating two $100 amounts differently, as if they come from two different compartments. The concert ticket example shows that people do compartmentalize when it comes to money. They don't always treat a dollar in the same way.

Cash Versus Credit Cards

With this example in mind, let's compare using cash to using a credit card. Say a person has $500 in cash and a credit card in her wallet. She wants to purchase something that costs $480. She could use the cash to make the purchase, or she could put the purchase on her credit card (and pay off the credit card later). In this situation, many people will say that it is somehow easier to use the credit card than to pay cash. When they pay cash, they say, they have a harder time making the decision to purchase the item. Somehow it seems more real to them; somehow the purchase seems more expensive.

You and Your Lending Partner

It may be easier to use a credit card than to pay cash, but it certainly is not cheaper. In fact, it can be more expensive. If you don't pay credit card balances off monthly, you will end up paying interest on the loan the bank provided you via your credit card purchase.

Cooperative Learning

Divide students into groups of three or four. Direct the groups to each compare credit cards offered by three different companies. Ask students to note the cards' interest rates, late fees, annual fees, and fees for cash advances. Tell students to be sure that they read the fine print of the credit card agreements. Which card offers the best deal? What in the fine print surprised the group? Allow the groups to summarize their findings for the class.

▲ You must either pay for something when you buy it or pay later. If you pay later, you often pay more.

In a sense, when you buy something with a credit card, two people, not one, stand in front of the cashier making the purchase. First is you, handing over your credit card. Plus, "standing" next to you, is "your partner" representing the bank. This imaginary partner is there with you, issuing you a loan to make the purchase with the credit card. Later, your " partner" from the bank will come back to you and ask to be repaid for the loan, with interest. In other words, a $100 item will cost you $100 if you pay in cash, but it could cost you $110 if you pay with a credit card ($100 for the purchase and $10 interest paid for the $100 loan).

An Expensive Lesson

Making a credit card purchase might be easier (for you) than a cash purchase of the same denomination, but often it is a costlier purchase. Not realizing this can lead to serious financial trouble, as far too many people have learned the hard way.

Consider Kevin (a real person whose name has been changed). He went off to college with a credit card. The first two months at college he used the credit card for all his purchases—many purchases. Kevin purchased new clothes, took his friends out to eat regularly, and bought an expensive television for his dorm room.

When Kevin received the credit card bill, he was shocked at just how much he had spent. (It seemed so easy to spend when he was out with his friends having a good time.) He said he felt as if someone else had spent the money. In his words, "It felt like I was getting things for free." Now Kevin certainly was smart enough to know that he wasn't getting anything for free, but he wasn't stating what he knew, he was telling us how he felt. Looking back, he realized his compartmentalizing caused him to buy a lot more than he would have if he paid in cash. In the end he had to work many more hours (than he had wanted to) to pay off his credit card bill.

My Personal Economics Action Plan

Here are some points you may want to consider and some guidelines you might want to put into practice.

1. Someone once said that if you know where the holes are, you are less likely to step in them. Does this observation apply to credit cards? If you know that credit cards can be abused, then you are less likely to get into financial trouble with credit cards.

   I will not use a credit card instead of a check or cash until I am ______ years old and have proven to myself that I am financially responsible.

2. Keep in mind that people do sometimes compartmentalize. For them, a dollar is not always a dollar. The truth of the matter is, people are deceiving themselves: A dollar is a dollar is a dollar.

   In the future, I will spend only ______ percent of money gifts I receive, and I will save ______ percent.

3. If you use a credit card to buy something that costs $100, you may end up paying more than $100 for the item. Generally speaking, using a credit card to buy something makes that something costlier than using cash.

   I will not use a credit card unless I know for sure that I will be able to pay my bill in full when it comes.

Discussion Starter

After students have read "You and Your Lending Partner," ask: Have you ever thought about credit cards in this way? What do you think about the idea of having a "partner" present at every purchase? Do any of you find this idea a bit disconcerting? Why or why not?

My Personal Economics Action Plan Encourage students to identify scenarios in which it might not be a good idea to use a credit card. Also suggest that they name circumstances under which using a credit card might be acceptable. Arrange for students to report their thoughts to the class.

SECTION 3

Teacher Support

Focus and Motivate

Section Objectives

After completing this section, students will be able to

- explain what the Federal Reserve System is;
- state how many persons sit on the Board of Governors of the Federal Reserve System;
- describe the major responsibilities of the Federal Reserve System; and
- describe how the check-clearing process works.

Kickoff Activity

Write the following question on the board: "The central bank of the United States, called the Federal Reserve System, serves as the lender of last resort. What do you think is the meaning of this statement?" Give students five minutes to think about the question.

Activating Prior Knowledge

Invite students to share their responses to the Kickoff Activity. Ensure students understand that the Federal Reserve System is an important part of government. As a *lender of last resort,* its function is to lend money to banks that are suffering cash management problems. Ask why other banks might not loan money to banks with cash management problems.

Teach

Discussion Starter

Ask whether students have heard "the Fed" being discussed in the news and what they think the Fed does.

SECTION 3

The Federal Reserve System

Focus Questions

- What is the Federal Reserve System (the Fed)?
- How many persons sit on the Board of Governors of the Federal Reserve System?
- What are the major responsibilities of the Federal Reserve System?
- How does the check-clearing process work?

Key Terms

Federal Reserve System (the Fed)
Board of Governors of the Federal Reserve System
Federal Open Market Committee (FOMC)
reserve account

What Is the Federal Reserve System?

In 1913, Congress passed the Federal Reserve Act. This act set up the **Federal Reserve System**, which began operation in 1914. (The popular name for the Federal Reserve System is "**the Fed**.") The Fed is a *central bank,* which means it is the chief monetary authority in the country. A central bank has the job of determining the money supply and supervising banks, among other things. Today, the principal components of the Federal Reserve System are (1) the Board of Governors, and (2) the 12 Federal Reserve district banks.

Federal Reserve System (the Fed) The central bank of the United States.

Board of Governors of the Federal Reserve System The governing body of the Federal Reserve System.

Board of Governors

The **Board of Governors of the Federal Reserve System** controls and coordinates the Fed's activities. The board is made up of seven members, each appointed to a 14-year term by the president of the United States with Senate approval. The president also designates one member as chairperson of the board for a 4-year term. The Board of Governors is located at 20th Street and Constitution Avenue in Washington, D.C.

A Student Asks

QUESTION: *Do other countries have a Federal Reserve System?*

ANSWER: *As stated earlier, the Federal Reserve System is a central bank, and other countries do have central banks. Whereas we, in the United States, call our central bank the Federal Reserve System, in most other countries the central bank is either called "the central bank" or "the bank" of that particular country. For example, the Bank of Japan, the Bank of Ghana, the Central Bank of Iceland, and so on.*

The 12 Federal Reserve District Banks

The United States is broken up into 12 Federal Reserve districts. Exhibit 10-3 shows the boundaries of these districts. Each district has a Federal Reserve district bank. (Think of the Federal Reserve district banks as "branch

Cooperative Learning

Students often learn and retain information best through firsthand exposure to a concept. If you live near a Federal Reserve district bank, contact the bank and schedule a tour for your class. Before the trip, have students work in groups of three or four to develop specific questions they would like to ask. In the class period following the visit, tell the groups to write short reports on what they learned, and to describe specifically to anything they discovered about a Federal Reserve bank or the Federal Reserve System that was not discussed in the text.

EXHIBIT 10-3 **Federal Reserve Districts and Federal Reserve Bank Locations**

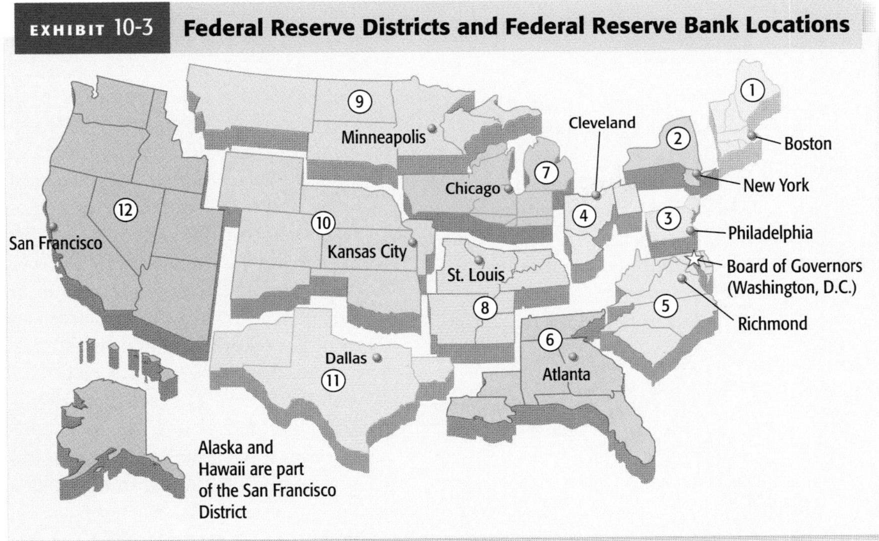

offices" of the Federal Reserve System.) Each of the 12 Federal Reserve district banks has a president. Which Fed district do you live in?

An Important Committee: The FOMC

The major policy-making group within the Fed is the **Federal Open Market Committee (FOMC)**. A later part of this chapter will consider what the FOMC does, but for now you need only note that the FOMC is made up of 12 members. Seven of the 12 members are the members of the Board of Governors. The remaining five members come from the ranks of the presidents of the Federal Reserve district banks.

What Does the Fed Do?

The following is a brief description of six major responsibilities of the Fed.

1. *Control the money supply.* A full explanation of how the Fed controls the money supply comes later in the chapter.
2. *Supply the economy with paper money (Federal Reserve notes).* As stated in an earlier section, the pieces of paper money we use are Federal Reserve notes. Federal Reserve notes are printed at the Bureau of Engraving and Printing in Washington, D.C. The notes are issued to the 12 Federal Reserve district banks,

Federal Open Market Committee (FOMC)
The 12-member policy-making group within the Fed. This committee has the authority to conduct open market operations.

◀ The Federal Reserve Board controls the nation's money supply, but the Fed does not actually print money. **What government agency is responsible for printing our paper money?**

Teaching with Visuals

Exhibit 10-3 shows the Federal Reserve districts and the cities in which the Fed banks are located. Ask: Which district is your school in? Where is the closest Federal Reserve bank?

Discussion Starter

Tell students that there is one bank that is more important than all other banks in the United States. This is the central bank of the United States, the Federal Reserve System. Ask students what they think a central bank would do that a regular commercial bank would or could not do. In other words, what makes a central bank special? Point out that one major feature is that it has the ability to control the money supply.

Teaching with Visuals

The Bureau of Engraving and Printing is responsible for printing paper money in the United States.

Internet Research

You may want to suggest that students visit additional Web sites to enhance their study of this chapter. Have students go to the Board of Governors of the Federal Reserve System's Web site to find out more about the structure and functions of the Fed. Encourage them to make posters or diagrams that clearly illustrate the Fed's different roles. The visuals should be geared toward a general audience that doesn't know anything about the Fed and its functions. You might arrange for pairs or groups of students to give brief presentations about the Fed to classes of younger students.

After students have read this feature, ask them to think about why China might be interested in opening up its banking sector.

ANSWERS TO ECONOMIC THINKING Answers will vary. Students might suggest that efforts to increase international trade motivate nations to open up their banking sectors.

Teaching with Visuals

Instruct students to re-create Exhibit 10-4 (page 273) for specific banks in their Federal Reserve district. Or suggest that they look at a check that has cleared and use the signatures and stamps on the check to trace the check's path through the clearing process.

Application Activity

After reading and discussing Section 3, you may want to assign the Section Activity in the *Applying the Principles Workbook.*

Assess

Quick Quiz

The following true-or-false quiz will help you assess student understanding of the material covered in this section.

1. The Federal Reserve Act was passed in Congress in 1913. (True)
2. The president of the Board of Governors is elected by the people. (False)
3. There are 15 Federal Reserve districts in the United States. (False)
4. The major policy-making group in the Fed is the FOMC. (True)
5. The Fed has six major responsibilities. (True)

Economics on the WEB

You can read the bios of the members of the Board of Governors at www.emcp.net/Board. The Fed operates an educational Web site at www.emcp.net/federalreserveeducation. Go there and click "American Currency Exhibit" to see some of the various currencies used in the United States at various times. You may want to click "In Plain English: Making Sense of the Federal Reserve."

reserve account
A bank's checking account with its Federal Reserve district bank.

which keep the money on hand to meet the demands of the banks and the public. For example, suppose it is the holiday season, and people are going to their banks and withdrawing greater than usual numbers of $1, $5, and $20 notes. Banks need to replenish their supplies of these notes, and they turn to their Federal Reserve district banks to do so.

THE GLOBAL IMPACT

Banks Becoming Partners

As the globalization trend continues, countries will open up their banking sectors to the outside world. For example, on April 21, 2005, the Hangzhou City Commercial Bank, a local bank in Zhejiang Province, east China, and the Commonwealth Bank of Australia signed an agreement on strategic cooperation. The Australian bank purchased a 19.9 percent interest in the Chinese bank for 625 million yuan ($75 million). One of the reasons an Australian bank might want to be partners with a Chinese bank is because lending activities might be more advantageous (at some points in time) in China than in Australia.

ECONOMIC THINKING **What might stimulate more of these types of bank partnerships in the future?**

The Federal Reserve district banks meet this cash need by supplying more paper money. (Remember, the 12 Federal Reserve district banks do not print the paper money; they only supply it.)

3. *Hold bank reserves.* Each commercial bank that is a member of the Federal Reserve System is required to keep a **reserve account** (think of it as a checking account) with its Federal Reserve district bank. For example, a bank located in Durham, North Carolina, would be located in the fifth Federal Reserve district, which means it deals with the Federal Reserve Bank of Richmond (Virginia). The local bank in Durham must have a reserve account, or checking account, with this reserve bank. Soon we will see what role a bank's reserve account with the Fed plays in increasing and decreasing the money supply.

4. *Provide check-clearing services.* When someone in Miami (Florida) writes a check to a person in Savannah (Georgia), what happens to the check? The process by which funds change hands when checks are written is called the check-clearing process. The Fed plays a major role in this process. Here is how it works (see Exhibit 10-4):

   a. Suppose Harry writes a $1,000 check on his Miami bank and sends it by mail it to Ursula in Savannah. To record this transaction, Harry reduces the balance in his checking account by $1,000. In other words, if his balance was $2,500 before he wrote the check, it is $1,500 after he wrote the check.
   b. Ursula receives the check in the mail. She takes the check to her local bank, endorses it (signs it on the back), and deposits it into her checking account. The balance in her account rises by $1,000.
   c. Ursula's Savannah bank sends the check to its Federal Reserve district bank, which is located in Atlanta. The Federal Reserve Bank of Atlanta increases the reserve account of the

Differentiating Instruction

English Language Learners

To help ELL students, use the following resources, which are provided as part of the *Economics: New Ways of Thinking* program:

- a Spanish glossary in the *Student Text*
- Spanish versions of the Chapter Summaries on an audio CD

Savannah bank (Ursula's bank) by $1,000 and decreases the reserve account of the Miami bank (Harry's bank) by $1,000.

   d. The Federal Reserve Bank of Atlanta sends the check to Harry's bank in Miami, which then reduces the balance in Harry's checking account by $1,000. Harry's bank in Miami either keeps the check on record or sends it along to Harry with his monthly bank statement.

5. *Supervise member banks.* Without warning, the Fed can examine the books of member commercial banks to see what kind of loans they made, whether they followed bank regulations, how accurate their records are, and so on. If the Fed finds that a bank has not followed established banking standards, it can pressure the bank to do so.
6. *Serve as the lender of last resort.* A traditional function of a central bank is to serve as the "lender of last resort" for banks suffering cash management problems. For example, let's say that bank A lost millions of dollars and finds it difficult to borrow from other banks. At this point, the Fed may step in and act as lender of last resort to bank A. In other words, the Fed may lend bank A the funds it wants to borrow when no one else will.

EXHIBIT 10-4 The Check-Clearing Process

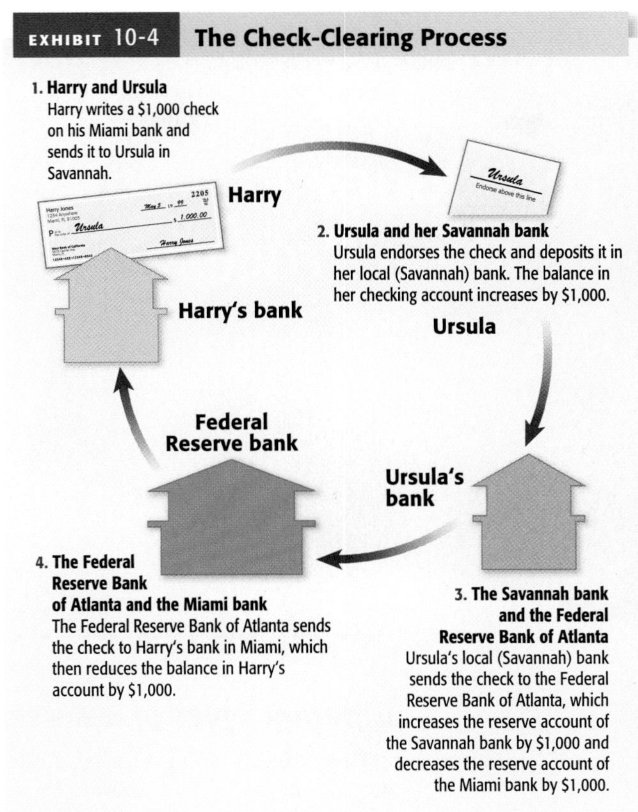
1. Harry and Ursula
Harry writes a $1,000 check on his Miami bank and sends it to Ursula in Savannah.
Harry
2. Ursula and her Savannah bank
Ursula endorses the check and deposits it in her local (Savannah) bank. The balance in her checking account increases by $1,000.
Harry's bank
Ursula
Federal Reserve bank
Ursula's bank
4. The Federal Reserve Bank of Atlanta and the Miami bank
The Federal Reserve Bank of Atlanta sends the check to Harry's bank in Miami, which then reduces the balance in Harry's account by $1,000.
3. The Savannah bank and the Federal Reserve Bank of Atlanta
Ursula's local (Savannah) bank sends the check to the Federal Reserve Bank of Atlanta, which increases the reserve account of the Savannah bank by $1,000 and decreases the reserve account of the Miami bank by $1,000.

▲ An example showing how the check-clearing process works.

SECTION 3 ASSESSMENT

Defining Terms

1. Define:
   a. Federal Open Market Committee (FOMC)
   b. Federal Reserve System (the Fed)
   c. Board of Governors of the Federal Reserve System
   d. reserve account

Review Facts and Concepts

2. In what year did the Fed begin operating?
3. Explain how a check is cleared.
4. What does it mean when we say the Fed is the lender of last resort?

Critical Thinking

5. Economists speak about printing, issuing, and supplying paper money. Are these different functions? Where is each function performed?

Applying Economic Concepts

6. Do you think banks need the Fed to act as "lender of last resort" more often during good economic times or bad economic times? Explain your answer.

Assessment Book

You will find a quiz for this section in the *Assessment Book.*

Reteaching Activity

Use the Section Assessment to gauge which students may need reteaching on this section. Ask those students to list the six major responsibilities of the Federal Reserve System. (*Answer:* Control the money supply, supply the economy with paper money, hold bank reserves, provide check-clearing services, supervise member banks, and serve as the lender of last resort.)

Guided Reading

For further reteaching of the key concepts in this section, assign the Outlining Activity and the Just the Facts Handout in the *Guided Reading and Study Guide.*

SECTION 3 ASSESSMENT ANSWERS

Defining Terms

1. a. Federal Open Market Committee (FOMC): the 12-member policy-making group within the Fed that has the authority to conduct open market operations; **b. Federal Reserve System (the Fed):** the central bank of the United States; **c. Board of Governors of the Federal Reserve System:** the governing body of the Federal Reserve System; **d. reserve account:** a checking account that a commercial bank has with its Federal Reserve district bank.

Reviewing Facts and Concepts

2. The Fed began operating in 1914.

3. See Exhibit 10-4 on this page for the explanation.

4. Being the lender of last resort means that the Fed has the responsibility of lending banks money when no one else will.

Critical Thinking

5. Yes, printing, issuing, and supplying paper money are different functions. In the United States, paper money is actually printed (produced) by the Bureau of Engraving and Printing in Washington, D.C. It is then issued by the Bureau of Engraving and Printing to various Federal Reserve district banks. For example, the Bureau of Engraving and Printing may issue (send) $200 million of paper money to the Federal Reserve District Bank of San Francisco. The district bank then supplies the paper money to commercial banks, which supply it to the public.

Applying Economic Concepts

6. Most likely banks will need the Fed as a "lender of last resort" during bad economic times. If people and businesses cannot repay their loans, banks lose money and need assistance from the Fed.

SECTION 4

Teacher Support

Focus and Motivate

Section Objectives

After completing this section, students will be able to

- explain what total reserves equal;
- explain what required and excess reserves are;
- describe how banks use checking accounts to increase the money supply;
- describe what banks do with excess reserves; and
- calculate the maximum change in the money supply resulting from bank loans.

Kickoff Activity

Write the following question on the board before students come to class, and tell them to answer it in writing: "What's the first thing you think of when you hear the phrase 'creating money'?"

Activating Prior Knowledge

Allow time for students to share their responses to the Kickoff Activity. Students may say that the first thing that comes to their minds is printing money. Some may think of counterfeiting money. Make the point that banks do not have the ability, or the right, to print money. In short, we are trying to distinguish between printing money and creating money. One can create money without printing currency, by creating checking accounts or demand deposits. Remind students once again that money is more than currency.

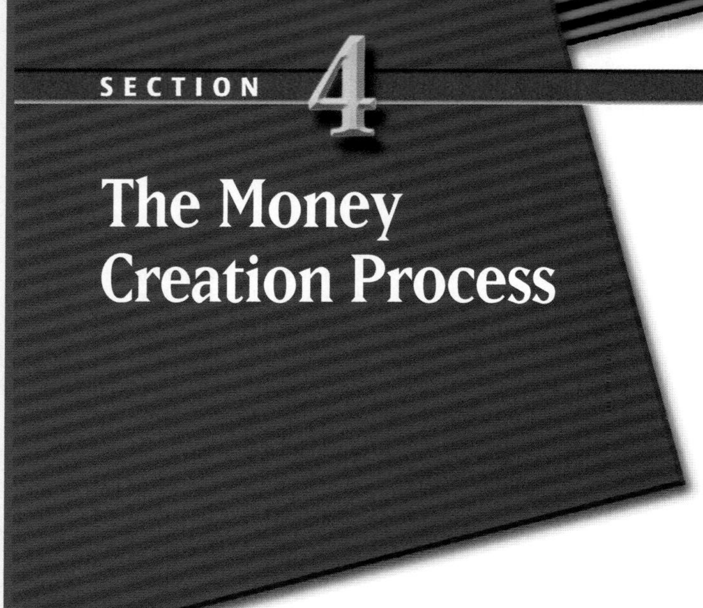

SECTION 4

The Money Creation Process

Focus Questions

- What do total reserves equal?
- What are required reserves? Excess reserves?
- How do banks use checking accounts to increase the money supply?
- What do banks do with excess reserves?
- Knowing the reserve requirement, how can you calculate the maximum change in the money supply resulting from bank loans?

Key Terms

total reserves
required reserves
reserve requirement
excess reserves

Different Types of Reserves

Here you are going to learn how the money supply in the United States is increased (more money) and decreased (less money). Before you can understand the difference, it is important to know the different types of a bank's reserves. The following points and definitions are crucial to an understanding of how the money supply rises and falls.

1. The previous section mentioned that each member bank has a reserve account, which is simply a checking account that a commercial bank has with its Federal Reserve district bank. If we take the dollar amount of a bank's reserve account and add it to the cash the bank has in its vault (called, simply enough, vault cash), we have the bank's **total reserves**.

total reserves
The sum of a bank's deposits in its reserve account at the Fed and its vault cash.

required reserves
The minimum amount of reserves a bank must hold against its deposits as mandated by the Fed.

reserve requirement
The regulation that requires a bank to keep a certain percentage of its deposits in its reserve account with the Fed or in its vault as vault cash.

Total reserves = Deposits in the reserve account at the Fed + Vault cash

EXAMPLE: The president of bank A, a small commercial bank, notes that the bank has $15 million in its (bank) vault. (In other words, if the bank were robbed right now, the most the thieves would get is $15 million.) The bank president also notes that the bank has $10 million in its reserve account at the Fed. If we add the vault cash of $15 million (the money in the vault) to the $10 million deposit in the reserve account, we get a total of $25 million. This dollar sum—$25 million—is the bank's total reserves. ♦

2. A bank's total reserves can be divided into two types: required reserves and excess reserves. **Required reserves** are the amount of reserves a bank must hold against its checking account deposits, as ordered by the Fed. For example, suppose bank A holds checking account deposits (checkbook money) for its customers totaling $100 million. The Fed requires, through its **reserve requirement**, that bank A hold a percentage of this total amount in the form of reserves—that is, either as deposits in its reserve account at the Fed or as vault cash

Internet Research

Counterfeiting has a long history in the United States. Early on, banks often issued their own money, and it was difficult for people to know which bills were real and which were fake. By the time of the Civil War, experts estimate that one-third of all currency in the United States was counterfeit. In 1863, the government adopted a national currency in an attempt to solve the problem, but it soon had to establish the Secret Service as the number of forgeries continued to grow. Modern counterfeiters use computers, scanners, and digital imaging software to create realistic fakes. For more information, direct students to the counterfeiting information at the U.S. Secret Service's Web site.

(because both of these are reserves). If the reserve requirement is 10 percent, bank A is required to hold 10 percent of $100 million, or $10 million, in the form of reserves. This $10 million is called required reserves.

Required reserves =
Reserve requirement × Checking account deposits

3. **Excess reserves** are the difference between total reserves and required reserves. For example, if total reserves equal $25 million and required reserves equal $10 million, then excess reserves would be $15 million. See Exhibit 10-5 for a review of these points.
4. Banks can make loans with their excess reserves. For example, if bank A has excess reserves of $15 million, it can make loans of $15 million.

(You may not realize it, but you just read a very short but very important section of this chapter. In this section you were introduced to four new terms—total reserves, required reserves, reserve requirement, and excess reserves. If you are not absolutely sure what each term refers to, you should go back and read this section again. These four terms will be used often in the discussion that follows. You don't want to be in the thick of the discussion asking yourself, "What are required reserves again?")

How Banks Increase the Money Supply

Earlier we said that the money supply is the sum of three components: currency (coins and paper money), checking account deposits, and traveler's checks. For example, $710 billion in currency, $619 billion in checking account deposits, and $7 billion in traveler's checks mean that the money supply is $1,336 billion. You will recall that checking account deposits are sometimes referred to as demand deposits because a checking account contains funds that can be withdrawn not only by a check but also on demand.

Banks (such as your local bank down the street) are not allowed to print currency. Your bank cannot legally print a $10 bill. (No matter how hard you look, you are not going to find a money-printing machine in the bank.) However, banks can create checking account deposits (checkbook money), and if they do, they increase the money supply. The following discussion explains the process.

Creating Checking Account Deposits

To see how banks use checking account deposits to increase the money supply, let's imagine a fictional character named Fred. (His name rhymes with Fed for a reason you will learn later.) Fred is somewhat of a magician: he can snap his fingers and create a $1,000 bill out of thin air. On Monday

excess reserves Any reserves held beyond the required amount.

EXHIBIT 10-5 Reserves: Total, Required, and Excess

Kind of reserves	What it equals	Numerical example
Total reserves	Total reserves = Deposits in the reserve account at the Fed + Vault cash	Deposits in the reserve account = $10 million Vault cash = $15 million **Total reserves = $25 million**
Required reserves	Required reserves = Reserve requirement × Checking account deposits	Reserve requirement = 10% Checking account deposits = $100 million **Required reserves = $10 million**
Excess reserves	Excess reserves = Total reserves − Required reserves	Total reserves = $25 million Required reserves = $10 million **Excess reserves = $15 million**

◀ A summary of the different types of reserves.

Teach

Discussion Starter

After students read the section "Different Types of Reserves" and the definition for *excess reserves,* ask: Why, do you think, is it important for banks to know the amount of excess reserves they have available? How could a bank increase its excess reserves? Why would banks choose to increase their excess reserves?

Reinforcement Activity

To help students grasp the concept of how money is created, ask them to research the subject. Encourage them to visit a local bank or to conduct Internet research to gather data. You may ask students to write a one-page report or to share their findings orally in class.

Teaching with Visuals

Suggest that students re-create Exhibit 10-5 on their own paper to keep as a reference while studying this chapter. Remind students that the excess reserves are the amount of money the bank can loan out. Bankers need to monitor their excess reserves very carefully.

Differentiating Instruction

Kinesthetic Learners

Bring a set of Monopoly money to class to teach students the difference between total reserves, required reserves, and excess reserves. Urge students to imagine that the tray of money is a bank. Give several students each two random bills and tell the students to deposit these amounts in the bank. Then instruct them to find the total reserves of the bank, the required reserves for that new account, and the excess reserves from that initial deposit. Call on each student to go through this process so that all can become more familiar with these terms. You might wish to divide the class into groups for this activity, appointing one student in each group to serve as the banker.

Cause and Effect

There is an obvious cause-and-effect relationship between total reserves and excess reserves. Have students create their own examples that illustrate the relationship between changes in total reserves and excess reserves.

Teaching with Visuals

It may seem hard to understand that a deposit of $1,000 results in the creation of $10,000. Guide the class in a discussion in which each student explains one part of Exhibit 10-6. As the table is being explained, lead students to restate it in their own words and to re-create the table on the board.

morning at 9:00, outside bank A, Fred snaps his fingers and creates a $1,000 bill. He immediately walks into the bank, opens up a checking account, and tells the banker that he wants the $1,000 deposited into his checking account. The banker gladly complies. Entry (a) in Exhibit 10-6 shows this deposit.

Now what does the bank physically do with the $1,000 bill? It places it into its vault, which means the money found its way into vault cash, which is part of total reserves. (Total reserves = Deposits in the reserve account at the Fed + Vault cash.) Thus, if vault cash goes up by $1,000, total reserves increase by the same amount. (If you need to check back to the earlier equations to see this total, do it now.)

To keep things simple, let's assume that bank A had no checking account deposits before Fred walked into the bank. Now it has $1,000. Also, let's say that the Fed set the reserve requirement at 10 percent. What are bank A's required reserves? Required reserves equal the reserve requirement multiplied by checking account deposits. Bank A's $1,000 × 10 percent = $100, which is the amount bank A has to keep in reserve form—either in its reserve account at the Fed or as vault cash. Look at entry (b) in Exhibit 10-6.

Currently, however, bank A has more than $100 in its vault; it has the $1,000 that Fred handed over to it. What, then, do its excess reserves equal? Because excess reserves equal total reserves minus required reserves, it follows that the bank's excess reserves equal $900, the difference between $1,000 (total reserves) and $100 (required reserves), as in entry (c) in Exhibit 10-6.

What Does the Bank Do with Excess Reserves?

What does bank A do with its $900 in excess reserves? It creates new loans with the money. For example, suppose Alexi walks into bank A and asks for a $900 loan. The loan officer at the bank asks Alexi what she wants the money for. She tells the loan officer she wants a loan to buy a television set, and the loan officer grants her the loan.

▶ Follow this diagram and the explanation in the text to see how banks increase the money supply.

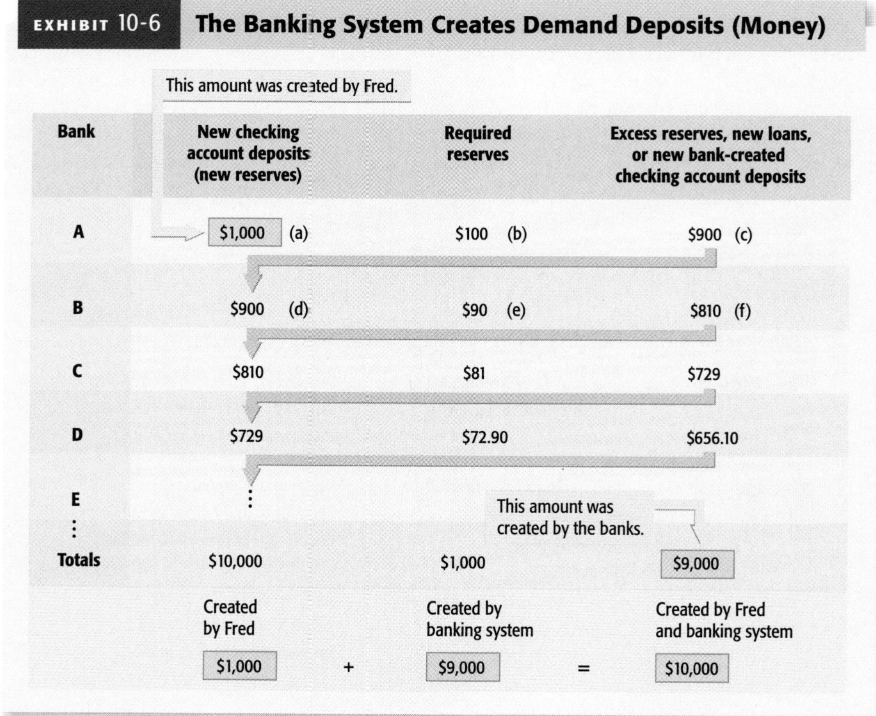

EXHIBIT 10-6 The Banking System Creates Demand Deposits (Money)
This amount was created by Fred.
Bank
New checking account deposits (new reserves)
Required reserves
Excess reserves, new loans, or new bank-created checking account deposits
A $1,000 (a) $100 (b) $900 (c)
B $900 (d) $90 (e) $810 (f)
C $810 $81 $729
D $729 $72.90 $656.10
E
This amount was created by the banks.
Totals $10,000 $1,000 $9,000
Created by Fred
Created by banking system
Created by Fred and banking system
$1,000 + $9,000 = $10,000

Cross-Curricular Activity

Invite a U.S. history teacher to your class to talk about the details of the Depression of 1893, the fight for metals, and the election of 1896. These historical events relate directly to how the money supply should or should not be handled. There are many interesting angles to this story that students can relate to the information in this chapter. If you wish, assign students to prepare a short oral presentation on one person or one event of the time, accepted by you, and ask students to present their reports when the history teacher is present. The teacher can then give helpful hints on the history, and you can evaluate students' performances.

Some people may think that at this point the loan officer of the bank simply walks over to the bank's vault, takes out $900 in currency, and hands it to Alexi. It does not happen this way. Instead, the loan officer opens up a checking account for Alexi at bank A and informs her that the balance in the account is $900. See entry (c) in Exhibit 10-6. In other words, banks give out loans in the form of checking account deposits. (This point is important to remember as we continue.)

What has bank A done by opening up a checking account (with a $900 balance) for Alexi? It has, in fact, increased the money supply by $900. Remember that the money supply consists of (1) currency, (2) checking account deposits, and (3) traveler's checks. When bank A opens up a checking account (with a balance of $900) for Alexi, the dollar amount of currency has not changed, nor has the dollar amount of traveler's checks. The only thing that has changed is the dollar amount of checking account deposits, or checkbook money. It is $900 higher, so the money supply is $900 higher, too.

At this point you might ask, "But isn't the $900 Alexi receives from the bank part of the money that Fred deposited in the bank?" To say that Fred does not have the $1,000 anymore, but Alexi has $900 of it, is not exactly correct. Fred does not have the $1,000 in currency anymore, but he does still have $1,000. In other words, he doesn't have the $1,000 on him, in his wallet. It is now in the bank vault. He does have a checking account with a balance of $1,000. Alexi now has $900 in her checking account as well, an additional $900, created by the bank, that did not exist before.

A Student Asks

QUESTION: *Does the bank have to create a loan with its excess reserves?*

ANSWER: *No, it does not have to create a loan with its excess reserves, but lending money is what banks do. That is how banks generate income. A bank is a business like any other business, trying to make a profit. Banks extend loans to customers to earn income in much the same way that a farmer grows and sells corn to earn an income. If a bank were to hold on to its excess reserves, it would be ignoring an opportunity to earn income.*

▲ Bank employees must decide what to do with the bank's excess reserves. The bank's success depends on these people being able to make good loans with the excess reserves.

What Happens After a Loan Is Granted?

So far, Alexi is given a loan in the form of a $900 balance in a new checking account. She now goes to a retail store and buys a $900 television set. She pays for the set by writing out a check for $900 drawn on bank A. She hands the check to the owner of the store, Roberto.

At the end of the business day, Roberto takes the check to bank B. For simplicity's sake, we assume that checking account deposits in bank B equal zero. Roberto, however, changes this situation by depositing the $900 into his checking account. See entry (d) in Exhibit 10-6.

At this point, the check-clearing process (described earlier) kicks in. Bank B sends the check to its Federal Reserve bank, which increases the balance in bank B's reserve account by $900. At the same time, the Federal Reserve bank decreases the funds in bank A's reserve account by $900. Once the Federal Reserve bank increases the balance in bank B's reserve account, total reserves for

Reinforcement Activity

To reinforce student understanding of how banks create money, ask students to read the explanation in the text, then go to one other source (they may choose to visit someone in a local bank or research the Internet) to ask that person or source for further information or details. Ask students to describe the process, in their own words, in a one-page written report or in an oral presentation.

Background Information: Lending Practices

The fine line between increasing the money supply and engaging in dangerous lending practices might have been crossed in the Great Depression. By 1934, more than 6,000 banks had stopped conducting business. The shutdowns created a national crisis as depositors tried to recoup their losses and people stood in large groups outside of closed banks trying to get the money they had deposited in savings and checking accounts. To control the run on banks, President Franklin D. Roosevelt declared a bank holiday on March 6, 1933. Have students research this period of banking history. Guide the class in a discussion of the role of reserve requirements and federal regulations in the banking industry.

Economics in the Real World

After students have read this feature, ask them for reasons why companies outside of the English-speaking world might be interested in hiring people who can speak English.

Teaching with Visuals

Answers will vary. Students might mention that they are more likely to communicate with someone who speaks the same language that they speak, because doing so requires less time and effort.

ANSWERS TO THINK ABOUT IT Answers will vary. Students might say that more and more people are using English.

Discussion Starter

One difficult thing for students to understand is that banks can create money simply by creating checking accounts or demand deposits for customers. Perhaps this is hard to understand because students often think of money only as currency. Remind students that checks are money. The money supply consists of currency, plus checking accounts, plus traveler's checks.

Application Activity

After reading and discussing Section 4, you may want to assign the Section Activity in the *Applying the Principles Workbook.*

Assess

Quick Quiz

The following true-or-false quiz will help you assess student understanding of the material covered in this section.

1. Total reserves can be divided into required reserves and excess reserves. (True)
2. Banks are allowed to print currency. (False)
3. When banks create demand deposits, there is more money in the economy. (True)

Economics in the Real World

How Is the English Language Like Money?

Money emerged (or evolved) out of a barter economy. In a barter economy many goods were traded. One good, among all goods, was more widely accepted for purposes of exchange. People started holding this good to reduce their transaction costs. Soon, everyone was accepting this good for purposes of exchange and thus it became money.

Have you ever thought that the same process might be at work when it comes to various languages? Many languages are spoken in the world today. A few languages are widely spoken, such as Spanish and English. Increasingly, though, one language is becoming the language that you hear spoken all over the world, and that language is English.

You can see English on posters in India, Japan, China, and many other countries. You can hear English in pop songs sung in Tokyo, Hong Kong, Mexico City, and Moscow. English is the language of 98 percent of German research physicists. It is the official language of the European Central Bank, even though the bank is in Frankfurt, Germany. English is found in official documents in Phnom Penh, Cambodia. Alcatel, a French telecommunications company, uses English as its internal language.

In a barter economy, we know that the more people who accept a particular good in exchange, the more other people will accept that good in exchange. Might the same be the case of a language? Might it be the case that the more people (as a percentage of the world's population) who speak English, the more people will want to learn and speak English? Just as money lowers the transaction costs of making exchanges, English might lower the transaction costs of communicating.

▲ **How might the fact that these young ladies in Agra, India, speak English lower transaction costs for you?**

THINK ABOUT IT Is the world evolving toward one universal language and is that language English? Explain your answer.

bank B rise by $900. (Total reserves = Deposits in the reserve account at the Fed + Vault cash.) Again, see entry (d) in Exhibit 10-6.

What happens to the checking account deposits at bank B? They rise to $900, too. Bank B is required to keep a percentage of the checking deposits in reserve form. If the reserve requirement is 10 percent, then $90 has to be maintained as required reserves as in entry (e) in Exhibit 10-6. The remainder, or excess reserves ($810), can be used by bank B to extend new loans or create new checking account deposits (which are money), as in entry (f) in Exhibit 10-6. The story continues in the same way with other banks (banks C, D, E, and so on).

A Student Asks

QUESTION: *In the story so far, bank A creates a loan, then bank B creates a loan, then bank C creates a loan and so on. Does this process ever stop?*

ANSWER: *Yes, it stops when the dollar amounts that a bank can lend out become tiny. For example, notice that*

Cooperative Learning

Divide the class into two equal groups. The first person in group 1 should ask the first person in group 2 a question that relates to the information in Section 4. For example, she might ask, What are total reserves? or What are excess reserves? Students should give examples to illustrate their answers. If the first person in group 2 gets the correct answer, his side gets one point. If not, his side neither loses nor gains a point. The process continues with the first person in group 2 asking the first person in group 1 a question, and so on. At the end of the allotted time, the side with the most points wins.

bank A created a loan of $900, but bank B created a loan of only $810, and bank C created a still smaller loan of $729. In other words, the loans become smaller and smaller. At some point, the dollar amount becomes so small that it doesn't make sense to create a loan.

How Much Money Was Created?

So far, bank A created $900 in new loans or checking account deposits, and bank B created $810 in new loans or checking account deposits. If we continue by bringing in banks C, D, E, and so on, we will find that all banks together—that is, the entire banking system—create $9,000 in new loans or checking account deposits (money) as a result of Fred's deposit. This dollar amount is boxed in Exhibit 10-6. This $9,000 is new money—money that did not exist before Fred snapped his fingers, created $1,000 out of thin air, and then deposited it into a checking account in bank A.

The facts can be summarized as follows:

1. Fred created $1,000 in new paper currency (money) out of thin air.
2. After Fred deposited the $1,000 in bank A, the banking system as a whole created $9,000 in additional checking account deposits (money).

Thus, Fred and the banking system together created $10,000 in new money. Fred created $1,000 in currency, and the banking system created $9,000 in checking account deposits. Together, they increased the money supply by $10,000.

You can use the following simple formula to find the (maximum) change in the money supply ($10,000) brought about in the example:

Change in money supply = 1/Reserve requirement × Change in reserves of first bank

In the example, the reserve requirement was set at 10 percent (0.10). The reserves of bank A, the first bank to receive the injection of funds, changed by $1,000. Put the data into the formula:

Change in the money supply =
1/0.10 × $1,000 = $10,000

The idea here is that $1,000 created by Fred ends up increasing the money supply by a specific multiple (in this example, the multiple is 10).

SECTION 4 ASSESSMENT

Defining Terms

1. Define:
   a. total reserves
   b. required reserves
   c. reserve requirement
   d. excess reserves

Reviewing Facts and Concepts

2. Fred creates $2,000 in currency with the snap of his fingers and deposits it in bank A. The reserve requirement is 10 percent. By how much does the money supply increase?
3. Bank A has checking account deposits of $20 million, the reserve requirement is 10 percent, vault cash equals $2 million, and deposits in the reserve account at the Fed equal $1 million. What do required reserves equal? What do excess reserves equal?

Critical Thinking

4. The numerical examples in this section always had banks creating loans (new checking account deposits) equal to the amount of excess reserves they held. For example, if bank A had $900 in excess reserves, it would create new loans equal to $900, not something less. In reality, banks may not lend out every dollar of their excess reserves, but they usually come close. Why would a bank want to lend out nearly all (if not all) of its excess reserves?

Applying Economic Concepts

5. Is a $100 check money? Explain.

4. Money supply consists of currency, checking accounts, and traveler's checks. (True)
5. A bank creates new loans with excess reserves. (True)

Assessment Book

You will find a quiz for this section in the *Assessment Book.*

Reteaching Activity

Use the Section Assessment to gauge which students may need reteaching on this section. Write these terms on the board: "total reserves," "required reserves," and "excess reserves." Assign students to work with partners to define each term. Then reread the material on the money creation process to these students, having them supply their definitions each time one of these words is used.

Guided Reading

For further reteaching of the key concepts in this section, assign the Outlining Activity and the Just the Facts Handout from the *Guided Reading and Study Guide.*

SECTION 4 ASSESSMENT ANSWERS

Defining Terms

1. a. total reserves: a bank's deposits in its reserve account at the Fed and its vault cash; **b. required reserves:** the minimum amount of reserves a bank must hold against its deposits as mandated by the Fed; **c. reserve requirement:** the regulation that requires a bank to keep a certain percentage of each dollar deposited in the bank in its reserve account at the Fed or in its vault as vault cash; **d. excess reserves:** any reserves held beyond the required amount.

Reviewing Facts and Concepts

2. $20,000 *(calculation:* Change in the money supply = 1 ÷ 0.10 × $2,000 = $20,000).
3. $1 million *(calculations:* Required reserves = reserve requirement × checking account deposits = 0.10 × $20 million = $2 million; Excess reserves = total reserves – required reserves = ($1 million + $2 million) – $2 million = $1 million).

Critical Thinking

4. When a bank lends a dollar, it can charge interest. Banks are trying to generate interest earnings by creating loans with excess reserves.

Applying Economic Concepts

5. Yes. Money is anything that is widely accepted for purposes of exchange and in the repayment of debt. Checks are widely accepted for purposes of exchange (you can use a check to buy a television set, a computer, or groceries) and in the repayment of debt; therefore, checks are money.

SECTION 5 Teacher Support

Focus and Motivate

Section Objectives

After completing this section, students will be able to

- describe how a change in the reserve requirement changes the money supply;
- explain how an open market operation changes the money supply; and
- explain how a change in the discount rate changes the money supply.

Economics Around the Clock

Kickoff Activity

Direct students to reread the 3:44 P.M. scenario in Economics Around the Clock (page 255) and then write their answers to its question.

Invite students to share their answers with the class. If they struggle with the meaning of the term *discount rate,* point them to the definition on page 282, which says it is the interest rate that the Fed charges a bank for a loan. From the scenario, students might guess that increasing this rate decreases the money supply, and vice versa.

Activating Prior Knowledge

At the beginning of class, ask students to write an answer to the following question: What do you think the term *monetary policy* means? Allow time for students to share their answers. Explain that in this section students will be learning that *monetary policy* refers to the deliberate control of the money supply by the Fed.

SECTION 5 Fed Tools for Changing the Money Supply

Focus Questions

- How does a change in the reserve requirement change the money supply?
- How does an open market operation change the money supply?
- How does a change in the discount rate change the money supply?

Key Terms

open market operations
federal funds rate
discount rate

Changing the Reserve Requirement

Think of the Fed as having three "buttons" to push. Every time it pushes one of the three buttons, it either raises or lowers the money supply. The first button is the reserve requirement button. To understand how a change in it can change the money supply, let's consider three cases. In each case, the money supply is initially zero, and $1,000 is created out of thin air. The difference in the three cases is the reserve requirement, which is 5 percent in the first case, 10 percent in the second, and 20 percent in the third. Let's calculate the change in the money supply in each of the three cases. For these calculations we will use the formula you learned in the last section:

Change in money supply = 1/Reserve requirement × Change in reserves of first bank

Case 1: (Reserve requirement = 5%);
Change in money supply = 1/0.05 × $1,000 = $20,000

Case 2: (Reserve requirement = 10%);
Change in money supply = 1/0.10 × $1,000 = $10,000

Case 3: (Reserve requirement = 20%);
Change in money supply = 1/0.20 × $1,000 = $5,000

Note that the money supply is the largest ($20,000) when the reserve requirement is 5 percent. The money supply is the smallest ($5,000) when the reserve requirement is 20 percent. You can see that the smaller the reserve requirement, the bigger the change in the money supply. So, ask yourself what happens to the money supply if the reserve requirement is lowered? Obviously, the money supply must rise. What happens to the money supply if the reserve requirement is raised? Obviously, the money supply must fall.

Thus, the Fed can increase or decrease the money supply by changing the reserve requirement. If the Fed decreases the reserve requirement, the money supply increases; if it increases the reserve requirement, the money supply decreases.

Lower reserve requirement → Money supply rises

Raise reserve requirement → Money supply falls

Cooperative Learning

Divide students into an even number of groups of four or five. Ask half of the groups to find a reason for the Fed to increase the money supply, and ask the other half to find a reason for the Fed to decrease the money supply. Have each group develop a role-play that demonstrates its reasoning and decision. Discuss the possible economic conditions of these actions. Challenge students to determine the current economic conditions, and ask them if they think the Fed should increase, decrease, or maintain the money supply. Students should justify their answers with logic and reasoning.

A Student Asks

QUESTION: *Why would the Fed want to increase or decrease the money supply? Why not simply leave the money supply alone?*

ANSWER: *You are asking a question about monetary policy, a topic we will discuss more fully in a later chapter. For now, though, let us just say that the Fed may increase or decrease the money supply to deal with some economic problem. For example, if businesses are not doing well, and the unemployment rate is rising, the Fed might want to increase the money supply to stimulate consumer spending.*

Open Market Operations

The second button the Fed can "push" to change the money supply is the open market operations button. Remember that earlier we mentioned an important committee in the Federal Reserve System, the Federal Open Market Committee (FOMC). This committee of 12 members conducts **open market operations**. Open market operations are simply the buying and selling of government securities by the Fed. Before we discuss open market operations in detail, we need to provide some background information that relates to government securities and the U.S. Treasury.

The U.S. Treasury is an agency of the U.S. government. The Treasury's job is to collect the taxes and borrow the money needed to run the government. Suppose the U.S. Congress decides to spend $1,800 billion on various federal government programs. The U.S. Treasury has to pay the bills. It notices that it collected only $1,700 billion in taxes, which is $100 billion less than Congress wants to spend. It is the Treasury's job to borrow the $100 billion from the public. To borrow this money, the Treasury issues or sells government (or Treasury) securities to members of the public. A government security is no more than a piece of paper promising to pay a certain dollar amount of money in the future; think of it as an IOU statement.

The Fed (which is different from the Treasury) may buy government securities from any member of the public or sell them. When the Fed buys a government security, it is said to be conducting an *open market purchase.* When it sells a government security, it is said to be conducting an *open market sale.* These operations affect the money supply.

open market operations Buying and selling of government securities by the Fed.

Open Market Purchases

Let's say that you currently own a government security, which the Fed offers to purchase from you for $10,000. You agree to sell your security to the Fed. You hand it over, and in return you receive a check made out to you for $10,000.

It is important to realize where the Fed gets this $10,000. It gets the money "out of thin air." Remember Fred, who had the ability to snap his fingers and create a $1,000 bill out of thin air? Obviously, no such person has this power. The Fed, however, does have this power—it can create money "out of thin air."

How does the Fed create money out of thin air? Think about the answer in this way: You have a checking account, and the Fed has a checking account. Each account has a certain balance (amount in the account). The Fed can take a pencil and increase the balance in its account at will—legally. You, on the other hand, cannot, nor can anyone

▼ These clerks at the Chicago Board of Trade are buying and selling U.S. Treasury bonds. **Why does the U.S. Treasury issue bonds?**

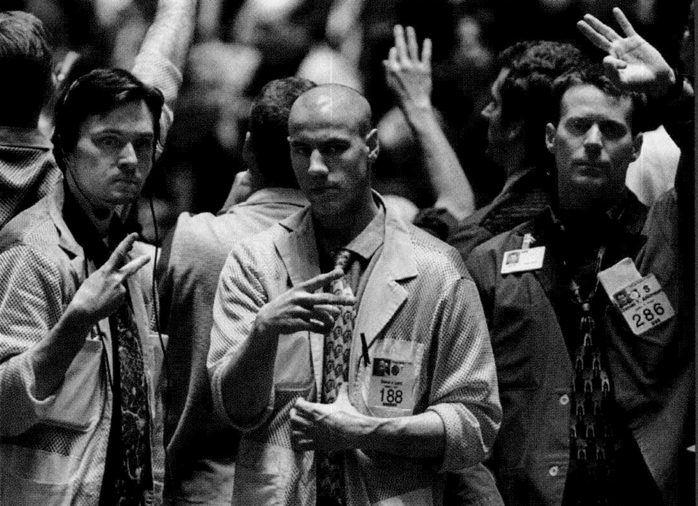

Teach

Discussion Starter

Ask students if they know how the Fed controls the money supply. Ensure that they know that the Fed can do this in one of three ways: by changing the reserve requirement, by conducting open market operations, or by changing the discount rate. All three ways are discussed in this section. Open market operations is the tool most commonly used by the Fed to change the money supply. Changing the discount rate and changing the reserve requirement are used less often. Remind students that the FOMC (Federal Open Market Committee) is the committee that conducts open market operations.

Discussion Starter

Discuss with students the concepts of state and federal budget excesses and deficits. Pose questions like these: What are government excesses and deficits? What happens to government-sponsored programs when there is a deficit? What happens when there is an excess?

Economics Around the Clock

Direct students to reread the 8:15 A.M. scenario in Economics Around the Clock (page 255) and then write their answers to its question.

Allow students to share their answers with the class. Ensure that they know that the FOMC buys and sells government securities. Ask why, do they think, secrecy is so important for the committee's meeting.

Teaching with Visuals

The U.S. Treasury issues bonds to raise the revenue that the federal government needs.

Teaching with Visuals

Answers will vary. Students might say that banks can borrow from the Fed at the discount rate.

Analyzing

Tell students to check the newspaper or Internet to find the most recent federal funds rate and discount rate. Post their findings on the board and compare the two rates. Lead students in a discussion of what any difference between the rates means. (*Answer:* If the discount rate is greater than the federal funds rate, the Fed is telling banks that it does not want them to borrow from it, and therefore it does not want to increase the money supply. If the discount rate is less than the federal funds rate, the Fed is telling commercial banks that it wants them to borrow from it, and thus it wants to increase the money supply.)

Application Activity

After reading and discussing Section 5, you may want to assign the Section Activity in the *Applying the Principles Workbook.*

Assess

Quick Quiz

The following true-or-false quiz will help you assess student understanding of the material covered in this section.

1. The FOMC conducts open market operations, buying and selling government securities. (True)
2. When the Fed buys and sells government securities, it does not affect the money supply. (False)
3. The Fed and the Treasury are actually the same governmental department. (False)
4. An open market sale reduces the money supply. (True)
5. If bank A borrows money from the Fed, the interest rate is called the federal funds rate. (False)

▶ The Federal Reserve Bank of Chicago. **What are some of the functions this bank performs for the commercial banks in its district?**

else. If you decide to pencil in a new balance and then write a check for an amount you don't have in your checking account, your check bounces and you pay the bank a penalty charge. Fed checks do not bounce. The Fed can, and does, create money at will "out of thin air."

Let's return to the example of an open market purchase. Once you have the $10,000 check from the Fed, you take it to your local bank and deposit it in your checking account. The total dollar amount of checking account deposits in the economy is now $10,000 more than before the Fed purchased your government security. Because no other component of the money supply (not currency or traveler's checks) is less, the overall money supply has increased.

Open market purchase → Money supply rises

Open Market Sales

Suppose the Fed has a government security that it offers to sell you for $10,000. You agree to buy the security. You write out a check to the Fed for $10,000 and give it to the Fed. The Fed, in return, turns the government security over to you. Next, the check is cleared, and a sum of $10,000 is removed from your account in your bank and transferred to the Fed. Once this sum is in the Fed's possession, it is removed from the economy altogether. It is as if it disappears from the face of the earth. As you might have guessed, the Fed also has the power to make money disappear into thin air.

federal funds rate
The interest rate one bank charges another for a loan.

discount rate
The interest rate the Fed charges a bank for a loan.

The total dollar amount of checking account deposits is less than before the Fed sold you a government security. An open market sale reduces the money supply.

Open market sale → Money supply falls

Changing the Discount Rate

The third button the Fed can push to change the money supply is the discount rate button. Suppose bank A wants to borrow $1 million. It could borrow this dollar amount from another bank (say, bank B), or it could borrow the money from the Fed. If bank A borrows the money from bank B, bank B will charge an interest rate for the $1 million loan. The interest rate charged by bank B is called the **federal funds rate**. If bank A borrows the $1 million from the Fed, the Fed will charge an interest rate, called either the *primary credit rate* or the **discount rate**.

Whether bank A borrows from bank B or from the Fed depends on the relationship between the federal funds rate and the discount rate. If the federal funds rate is lower than the discount rate, bank A will borrow

Internet Research

Direct students to search an online news source for articles about the Fed's actions regarding the interest rates (the discount rate) over the past 6–12 months. Assign them to write a one-page report addressing these questions: Has the Federal Reserve changed interest rates during this period? If so, why? If not, why not? Has there been any discussion of interest rates or the discount rate in the news lately? What change, if any, might the Fed make in the near future? What might be the consequences of the Fed's making that change today?

from bank B instead of from the Fed. (Why pay a higher interest rate if you don't have to?) If, however, the discount rate is lower than the federal funds rate, bank A will probably borrow from the Fed.

Whether bank A borrows from bank B or from the Fed has important consequences. If bank A borrows from bank B, no new money enters the economy. Bank B simply has $1 million less, and bank A has $1 million more; the total hasn't changed.

If, however, bank A borrows from the Fed, the Fed creates new money in the process of granting the loan. Here is how it works: the bank asks for a loan, and the Fed grants it by depositing the funds (created out of thin air) into the reserve account of the bank. For example, suppose the bank has $4 million in its reserve account when it asks the Fed for a $1 million loan. The Fed simply changes the reserve account balance to $5 million.

If the Fed lowers its discount rate so that it's lower than the federal funds rate, and if banks then borrow from the Fed, the money supply will increase.

Lower the discount rate → Money supply rises

If the Fed raises its discount rate so that it is higher than the federal funds rate, banks will begin to borrow from each other rather than from the Fed. At some point, though, the banks must repay the funds they borrowed from the Fed in the past (say, funds they borrowed many months ago), when the discount rate was lower. When the banks repay these loans, money is removed from the economy, and the money supply drops. We conclude that if the Fed raises its discount rate relative to the federal funds rate, the money supply will eventually fall.

Raise the discount rate → Money supply falls

See Exhibit 10-7 for a review.

EXHIBIT 10-7 Fed Monetary Tools and Their Effects on the Money Supply

Fed monetary tool	Money supply
Open market operation	
Buys government securities	Increases
Sells government securities	Decreases
Reserve requirement	
Raises reserve requirement	Decreases
Lowers reserve requirement	Increases
Discount rate	
Raises discount rate (relative to the federal funds rate)	Decreases
Lowers discount rate (relative to the federal funds rate)	Increases

▲ This table summarizes the ways in which the Fed can change the money supply.

SECTION 5 ASSESSMENT

Defining Terms

1. Define:
   a. discount rate
   b. federal funds rate
   c. open market operation

Reviewing Facts and Concepts

2. The Fed wants to increase the money supply.
   a. What can it do to the reserve requirement?
   b. What type of open market operation can it conduct?
   c. What can it do to the discount rate?

3. The Fed conducts an open market sale. Does the money for which it sells the government securities stay in the economy? Explain your answer.

Critical Thinking

4. When the Fed conducts an open market purchase, it buys government securities. As a result, the money supply rises. Could the Fed raise the money supply by buying something other than government securities? For example, suppose the Fed were to buy apples instead of government securities. Would apple purchases (by the Fed) raise the money supply? Explain your answer.

Applying Economic Concepts

5. If the Fed wants the money supply to rise by a ridiculously high percentage—say, 1 million percent—could it accomplish this objective? Explain your answer.

Assessment Book

You will find a quiz for this section in the *Assessment Book.*

Reteaching Activity

Use the Section Assessment to gauge which students may need reteaching on this section. Ask students to look at Exhibit 10-7. As students look at each of the ways the Fed can increase or decrease the money supply, invite them to explain some of these processes in greater detail.

Guided Reading

For further reteaching of the key concepts in this section, assign the Outlining Activity and the Just the Facts Handout in the *Guided Reading and Study Guide.*

SECTION 5 ASSESSMENT ANSWERS

Defining Terms

1. a. discount rate: the interest rate the Fed charges a bank for a loan; **b. federal funds rate:** the interest rate one bank charges another bank for a loan; **c. open market operation:** the buying and selling of government securities by the Fed.

Reviewing Facts and Concepts

2. a. lower the reserve requirement; **b.** an open market purchase; **c.** lower the discount rate relative to the federal funds rate.

3. No. When the Fed sells a government security, it collects the funds from the purchaser and removes those funds from the economy. It is as if the funds do not exist. They are in no one's checking account, they do not belong to any bank, and no one has ownership over them. For all practical purposes, they have disappeared.

Critical Thinking

4. Apple purchases by the Fed would increase the money supply. It is not so important *what* the Fed buys as it is *how* the Fed buys what it buys. The Fed buys whatever it buys with money created out of thin air. In other words, it simply changes the balance in its own account to reflect whatever dollar amount it wants.

Applying Economic Concepts

5. Yes. Nothing was said in the chapter to indicate that there is a limit to how much money the Fed can create. It is unlikely, but the Fed could increase the money supply by 1 million percent if it wanted to. How does the Fed raise the money supply? By lowering the reserve requirement, lowering the discount rate, or conducting an open market purchase.

CHAPTER 10 Assessment Answers

Economics Vocabulary

1. barter economy; **2.** medium of exchange; **3.** fractional reserve banking; **4.** money supply; **5.** open market operation; **6.** Board of Governors; **7.** excess reserves; **8.** Required reserves; **9.** federal funds rate; **10.** discount rate.

Understanding the Main Ideas

1. Money here is principally functioning as a medium of exchange.
2. In a barter economy, goods were traded for goods, services were traded for services, and so on. Individuals tried to make their daily trading easier. Therefore, they began to accept the good that was more acceptable than other goods. As some people did this, others began to do this as well, until the good was widely accepted for purposes of exchange. At this point, it was considered money.
3. The funds in the checking account belong to the owner and can be obtained on demand.
4. Currency consists of paper money and coins.
5. The check-clearing process is shown in Exhibit 10-4, page 273.
6. Boston, New York City, Philadelphia, Cleveland, Richmond, Atlanta, Chicago, St. Louis, Minneapolis, Kansas City, Dallas, and San Francisco.
7. a. Total reserves = deposits in the reserve account at the Fed + vault cash; **b.** Required reserves = reserve requirement × checking account deposits; **c.** Excess reserves = total reserves – required reserves.
8. (a), (c), and (e).
9. To understand what this means, consider the following scenario: Bank A has a reserve account with the Fed. The balance in the account is $10 million. Next, the Fed buys government securities worth $2 million from bank A. Bank A turns over the securities to the Fed, and the Fed must now pay the bank. How does the Fed pay the bank? It simply goes to the reserve account of the bank and changes the balance to $12 million ($2 million more than previously existed). Where did the Fed get the $2 million it deposited into the bank's reserve account? Out of thin air.
10. The Fed buys government securities and pays for them by creating money out of thin air. (See the answer to question 9 for an explanation of what "creating money out of thin air" means.) This act increases the reserves of banks. The banks then have excess reserves that they loan out. As they create new loans, they create new checking account deposits, and checking account deposits are money.
11. As the reserve requirement is lowered, the money supply increases; as the reserve requirement is increased, the money supply decreases.
12. The Fed is signaling that it does not want to increase the money supply.

Chapter Summary

Be sure you know and remember the following key points from the chapter sections.

Section 1

- Transaction costs—the time and effort required in an exchange—are high in a barter economy.
- Money is any good that is widely accepted in exchange and in repayment of debts.
- The value of money comes from its general acceptability in exchange.
- Money has three major functions: a medium of exchange, a unit of account, and a store of value.
- Early bankers were goldsmiths who gave the customers a warehouse receipt for the gold they stored with the goldsmith.

Section 2

- The most basic money supply in the United States is called M1 (M-one).
- M1 consists of currency, checking accounts, and traveler's checks.
- Currency is coins and paper money, or Federal Reserve notes.
- Checking accounts are also known as demand deposits, money deposited that can be withdrawn by writing a check.
- A traveler's check is issued by a bank in specific denominations and sold to travelers for their use.
- A savings account is considered near-money.
- Credit cards are not money because they cannot be used as repayment of debt.

Section 3

- As a central bank, the Federal Reserve System is the chief monetary authority in the country.
- The Federal Reserve's main activities include the following: control the money supply, supply the economy with paper money, hold bank reserves, provide check-clearing services, supervise member banks, and act as lender of last resort.

Economics Vocabulary

To reinforce your knowledge of the key terms in this chapter, fill in the following blanks on a separate piece of paper with the appropriate word or phrase.

1. A(n) ______ is an economy in which trades are made in terms of goods and services instead of money.
2. Anything that is generally accepted in exchange for goods and services is a(n) ______.
3. A banking arrangement in which banks hold only a fraction of their deposits and lend out the remainder is referred to as ______.
4. The ______ is composed of currency, checking accounts, and traveler's checks.
5. When the Fed buys or sells government securities, it is conducting a(n) ______.
6. The governing body of the Federal Reserve System is the ______.
7. Total reserves minus required reserves equals ______.
8. ______ are the minimum amount of reserves a bank must hold against its checking account deposits, as mandated by the Fed.
9. The interest rate that one bank charges another bank for a loan is called the ______.
10. The interest rate that the Fed charges a bank for a loan is called the ______.

Understanding the Main Ideas

Write answers to the following questions to review the main ideas in this chapter.

1. A person goes into a store and buys a pair of shoes with money. Is money here principally functioning as a medium of exchange, a store of value, or a unit of account?
2. Explain how money emerged out of a barter economy.
3. Why is a checking account sometimes called a demand deposit?
4. What is currency?
5. Explain how a check clears. Illustrate this process using two banks in the Federal Reserve district in which you live.

6. List the locations of the 12 Federal Reserve district banks.
7. State what each of the following equals:
   a. total reserves
   b. required reserves
   c. excess reserves
8. Determine which of the following Fed actions will increase the money supply: (a) lowering the reserve requirement, (b) raising the reserve requirement, (c) conducting an open market purchase, (d) conducting an open market sale, (e) lowering the discount rate relative to the federal funds rate, (f) raising the discount rate relative to the federal funds rate.
9. What do we mean when we say that the Fed can create money "out of thin air"?
10. Explain how an open market purchase increases the money supply.
11. What is the relationship between changes in the reserve requirement and changes in the money supply?
12. Suppose the Fed sets the discount rate much higher than the existing federal funds rate. With this action, what signal is the Fed sending to banks?

Doing the Math

Do the calculations necessary to solve the following problems.

1. A tiny economy has the following money in circulation: 25 dimes, 10 nickels, 100 one-dollar bills, 200 five-dollar bills, and 40 twenty-dollar bills. In addition, traveler's checks equal $500, balances in checking accounts equal $1,900, and balances in savings accounts equal $2,200. What is the money supply? Explain your answer.
2. A bank has $100 million in its reserve account at the Fed and $10 million in vault cash. The reserve requirement is 10 percent. What do total reserves equal?
3. The Fed conducts an open market purchase and increases the reserves of bank A by $2 million. The reserve requirement is 20 percent. By how much does the money supply increase?

Working with Graphs and Tables

1. In Exhibit 10-8, fill in the blanks (a), (b), and (c).

EXHIBIT 10-8

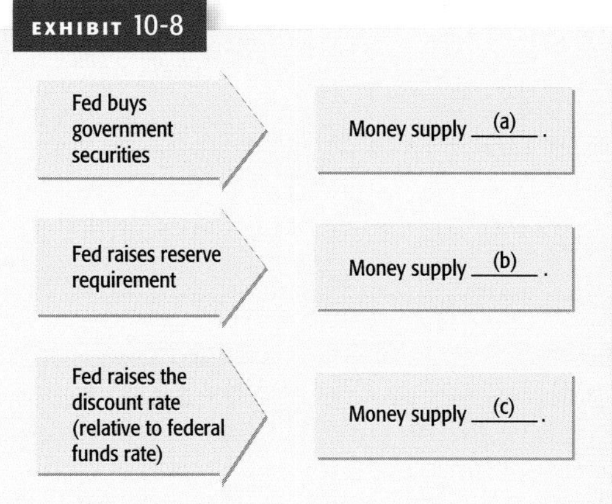

Solving Economic Problems

Use your thinking skills and the information you learned in this chapter to find solutions to the following problems.

1. **Cause and Effect.** In year 1, reserves equal $100 billion, and the money supply equals $1,000 billion. In year 2, reserves equal $120 billion, and the money supply equals $1,200 billion. Did the greater money supply in year 2 cause the higher dollar amount of reserves, or did the higher dollar amount of reserves cause the greater money supply? Explain.
2. **Writing.** Write a one-page paper about something you enjoy that would not exist in a barter economy. Explain why it would not exist.

Practice Tests and Study Guide

Go to www.emcp.net/economics and choose *Economics: New Ways of Thinking,* Chapter 10, if you need more help in preparing for the chapter test.

Working with Graphs and Tables

1. (a) rises or increases; (b) falls or decreases; (c) falls or decreases.

Solving Economic Problems

1. The higher reserves caused the greater money supply. Here is how it works: The Fed does something to increase reserves in the banking system (say it undertakes an open market purchase).With more reserves, banks end up with greater excess reserves. With greater excess reserves, they can offer more loans. More loans mean more checking account deposits, and more checking account deposits mean more money.
2. Students will write a one-page paper about something they enjoy that would not exist in a barter economy. The paper should explain why the item would not exist.

Doing the Math

1. The money supply, as defined in the text, is equal to currency plus checking accounts plus traveler's checks. In this problem, currency equals $1,903, checking account balances equals $1,900, and traveler's checks equals $500. It follows that the money supply equals the sum of these dollar amounts, or $4,303.
2. $110 million *(calculation:* Total reserves = deposits in the reserve account at the Fed + vault cash = $100 million + $10 million = $110 million).
3. $10 million *(calculation:* Change in money supply = (1 ÷ reserve requirement) × change in reserves of first bank = (1 ÷ 0.20) × $2 million = 5 × $2 million = $10 million).

Chapter 11 Planning Guide

SECTION ORGANIZER

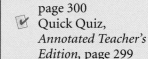

Section	Learning Objectives 	Reproducible Worksheets and Handouts	Assessment
 **National Income Accounting** (pages 288–292)	▸ Define GDP. ▸ Explain why only final goods and services are computed in GDP. ▸ List what is omitted from GDP. ▸ Explain the difference between GDP and GNP.	 Section 1 Activity, *Applying the Principles Workbook*  Outlining Activity, *Guided Reading and Study Guide* Just the Facts Handout, *Guided Reading and Study Guide* 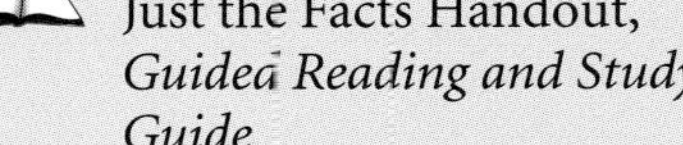	Section Assessment, *Student Text,* page 292 Quick Quiz, *Annotated Teacher's Edition,* page 291 Section Quiz, *Assessment Book*
 **Measuring GDP** (pages 293–296)	▸ List the four sectors of the economy. ▸ Describe consumption, investment, government purchases, export spending, and import spending. ▸ Explain how GDP is measured. ▸ Describe per capita GDP. 	 Section 2 Activity, *Applying the Principles Workbook*  Outlining Activity, *Guided Reading and Study Guide*  Just the Facts Handout, *Guided Reading and Study Guide*	Section Assessment, *Student Text,* page 296 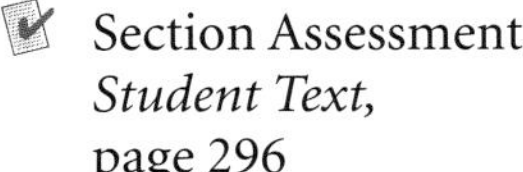 Quick Quiz, *Annotated Teacher's Edition,* page 295 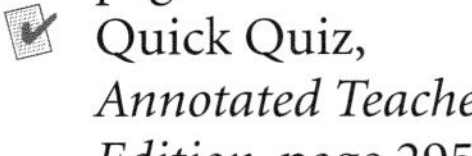 Section Quiz, *Assessment Book*
 **Real GDP** (pages 297–300)	▸ Name the two variables involved in calculating GDP. ▸ Explain whether we would automatically know why GDP is higher in some years than others. ▸ Describe the difference between GDP and real GDP. ▸ Explain how economists go about computing real GDP.	 Section 3 Activity, *Applying the Principles Workbook*   Outlining Activity, *Guided Reading and Study Guide* Just the Facts Handout, *Guided Reading and Study Guide*	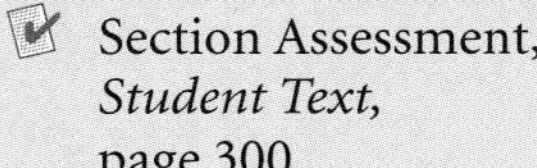 Section Assessment, *Student Text,* page 300 Quick Quiz, *Annotated Teacher's Edition,* page 299 Section Quiz, *Assessment Book*
 **Measuring Price Changes and the Unemployment Rate** 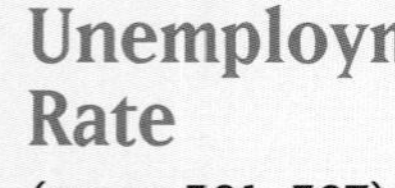 (pages 301–307)	▸ Explain what the consumer price index is and how it is calculated. ▸ Distinguish between an aggregate demand curve and an aggregate supply curve. ▸ Explain how the employment rate and unemployment rate are calculated.	 Section 4 Activity, *Applying the Principles Workbook*  Outlining Activity, *Guided Reading and Study Guide* Just the Facts Handout, *Guided Reading and Study Guide*	Section Assessment, *Student Text,* page 307 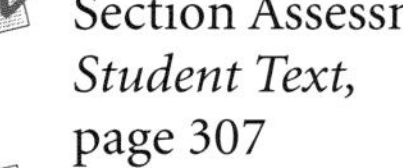 Quick Quiz, *Annotated Teacher's Edition,* page 306 Section Quiz, *Assessment Book*

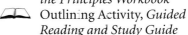

CHAPTER AND PROGRAM RESOURCES

Reproducible Chapter Resources and Assessment Materials

 Graphic Organizer Activity, *Guided Reading and Study Guide*
 Vocabulary Activity, *Guided Reading and Study Guide*
 Working with Graphs and Charts, *Guided Reading and Study Guide*
 Practice Test, *Guided Reading and Study Guide*
 Critical Thinking Activity, *Finding Economics*
Chapter Test A, *Assessment Book*
 Chapter Test B, *Assessment Book*

Technology Resources

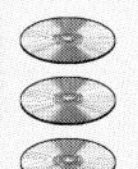

- *Test Generator CD*
- *Spanish Audio Summaries CD*
- *Marketplace® Audio Lessons CD*
- *Economic Principles Lectures, Videocassette or DVD*

Lesson Planning and Teaching Resources

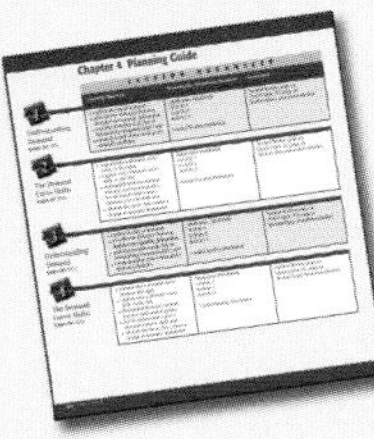

The *Economics: New Ways of Thinking* Teacher Resources include detailed lesson plans for each section in this chapter; the lesson plans are available in print form *(Lesson Plans)* and electronic form. The Teacher Resources also include *Daily Lectures: Overheads and Notes,* which provides prepared overheads and discussion notes covering the key concepts in each section of this chapter.

EMC Publishing Economics Online

Go to Economics Online, at www.emcp.com, for a variety of Internet resources to help you keep your course current and relevant. At Economics Online you will find these items:

- Economics in the News Lessons
- Study Guide Questions
- Practice Tests
- Lesson Plans

Internet Resources

Economics: New Ways of Thinking encourages students to use the Internet to find out more about economics. With the wealth of current, valid information available on Web sites, using the Internet as a research tool is likely to increase your students' interest in and understanding of economics principles and topics. In addition, doing Internet research can help your students form the habit of accessing and using economics information, as well as help them develop investigative skills they will use throughout their educational and professional careers.

To aid your students in achieving these ends, each chapter of *Economics: New Ways of Thinking* includes the addresses of several Web sites at which students will find engaging, relevant information. When students type in the addresses provided, they will immediately arrive at the intended sites. The addresses have been modified so that EMC Publishing can monitor and maintain the proper links—for example, the government site http://stats.bls.gov/ has been changed to www.emcp.net/prices. In the event that the address or content of a site changes or is discontinued, EMC's Internet editors will create a link that redirects students to an address with similar information.

Activities in the *Annotated Teacher's Edition* often suggest that students search the Internet for information. For some activities, you might want to find reputable sites beforehand, and steer students to those sites. For other activities, you might want students to do their own searching, and then check out the sites they have found and discuss why they might be reliable or unreliable.

CHAPTER 11 Overview

This chapter discusses several of the measurements that economists consider when determining the health of the economy. One measurement is total output, or the total market value of all goods and services in the United States. Another measurement is overall prices in the economy. The following statements provide brief descriptions of the major concepts covered in each section of this chapter.

National Income Accounting

Section 1 explains what the gross domestic product is and how it reflects the federal economy.

Measuring GDP

Section 2 explores the four sectors of the economy and how per-capita GDP is determined.

Real GDP

Section 3 deals with calculating real GDP. This calculation is necessary for tracking the growth of GDP precisely from one year to the next.

Measuring Price Changes and the Unemployment Rate

Section 4 introduces students to the consumer price index, which shows how prices change over time.

CHAPTER 11 Measuring Economic Performance

Why It Matters

If you go to the doctor for a checkup, she will take your vital signs—your temperature, your blood pressure, and your pulse rate. When it comes to the economy, economists do much the same. This chapter discusses many of the measurements that economists make to determine the health of the economy.

First, economists want to measure the total output of the economy. They want to measure the total market value of all the goods and services produced annually in the United States. Think of it in this way: each year, people in the United States produce goods and services—cars, houses, computers, attorney services, and so on. Economists want to know the total dollar value of all these goods and services.

This relatively small transaction is but one of millions that economists account for each year to measure the economy's activity.

Another vital sign that economists want to monitor is prices. Are prices in the economy rising? If so, how fast are they rising? Are they rising by 1 percent, 3 percent, or 5 percent? Are prices falling? If so, how fast are they falling?

As you read this chapter, think of the economy as a patient in a doctor's office. Instead of the doctor checking out the economy, an economist will take the economy's "pulse," "height and weight," and other vital signs. In later chapters you will learn more about the remedies economists prescribe for an unhealthy economy.

Teaching Suggestions from the Author

I've found that one of the best ways to get students interested in the material in this chapter is to first get them to see why it is so important to measure a few particular items.

Every student has something he or she feels is important to measure. It may be her performance on a biology test or his performance on the baseball field. It may be the temperature outside or the number of days until semester break. I ask students why it is important for them to measure and quantify certain things. Often, they say it is so that they can plan their lives better, add some certainty to their lives, or simply to know what is going on.

The same things apply when economists measure GDP, real GDP, and prices. It has to do with being able

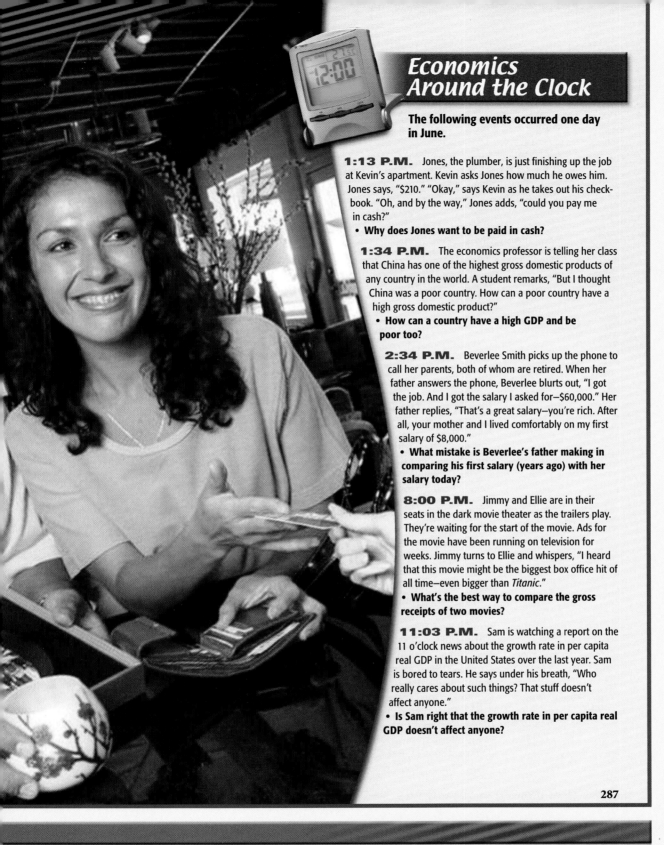

Economics Around the Clock

The following events occurred one day in June.

1:13 P.M. Jones, the plumber, is just finishing up the job at Kevin's apartment. Kevin asks Jones how much he owes him. Jones says, "$210." "Okay," says Kevin as he takes out his checkbook. "Oh, and by the way," Jones adds, "could you pay me in cash?"

- **Why does Jones want to be paid in cash?**

1:34 P.M. The economics professor is telling her class that China has one of the highest gross domestic products of any country in the world. A student remarks, "But I thought China was a poor country. How can a poor country have a high gross domestic product?"

- **How can a country have a high GDP and be poor too?**

2:34 P.M. Beverlee Smith picks up the phone to call her parents, both of whom are retired. When her father answers the phone, Beverlee blurts out, "I got the job. And I got the salary I asked for—$60,000." Her father replies, "That's a great salary—you're rich. After all, your mother and I lived comfortably on my first salary of $8,000."

- **What mistake is Beverlee's father making in comparing his first salary (years ago) with her salary today?**

8:00 P.M. Jimmy and Ellie are in their seats in the dark movie theater as the trailers play. They're waiting for the start of the movie. Ads for the movie have been running on television for weeks. Jimmy turns to Ellie and whispers, "I heard that this movie might be the biggest box office hit of all time—even bigger than *Titanic*."

- **What's the best way to compare the gross receipts of two movies?**

11:03 P.M. Sam is watching a report on the 11 o'clock news about the growth rate in per capita real GDP in the United States over the last year. Sam is bored to tears. He says under his breath, "Who really cares about such things? That stuff doesn't affect anyone."

- **Is Sam right that the growth rate in per capita real GDP doesn't affect anyone?**

to plan better and to know what is going on. Ask students to keep this in mind as they read the chapter. You might also want to discuss with them how certain things are measured. Baseball scores are very different from counting days until the holidays, and different ways of measuring or keeping track of the measurements are needed.

Introducing the Chapter

Before you begin to teach this chapter, you might want to hold up a ruler for the class to see. Ask students to tell you what this tool is used for. Then ask them to name other devices that we use for measurement purposes. Explain that in this chapter they will be looking at some of the tools that economists use to measure the economy. Tell them that just as we have many tools to help us measure things like distance, economists have a variety of tools to measure an economy.

Teaching with Visuals

The terms *gross domestic product*, *consumer price index*, and *real gross domestic product* might seem like a foreign language to students. However, they will learn that every time they go shopping, they contribute to the GDP.

SECTION 1 Teacher Support

Focus and Motivate

Section Objectives

After completing this section, students will be able to

- define GDP;
- explain why only final goods and services are computed in GDP;
- list what is omitted from GDP; and
- explain the difference between GDP and GNP.

Kickoff Activity

Write the following on the board for students to answer while attendance is being taken: "Suppose the government wants to measure all the production that occurs in the U.S. economy. How do you think the government would do this?"

Activating Prior Knowledge

Allow volunteers to share their responses to the Kickoff Activity. Students may have a difficult time answering this question. To simplify it, ask students to think of their classroom as a mini-economy. Each student produces something in the mini-economy and buys goods from other students. Ask them how they would measure the total output produced in their mini-economy. For example, suppose that in their mini-economy they produce 25 bicycles, three cars, and four bushels of wheat. The way to measure the total production of that economy is to take each one of those quantities of goods and multiply it by its particular price, and then add all dollar amounts to get a total.

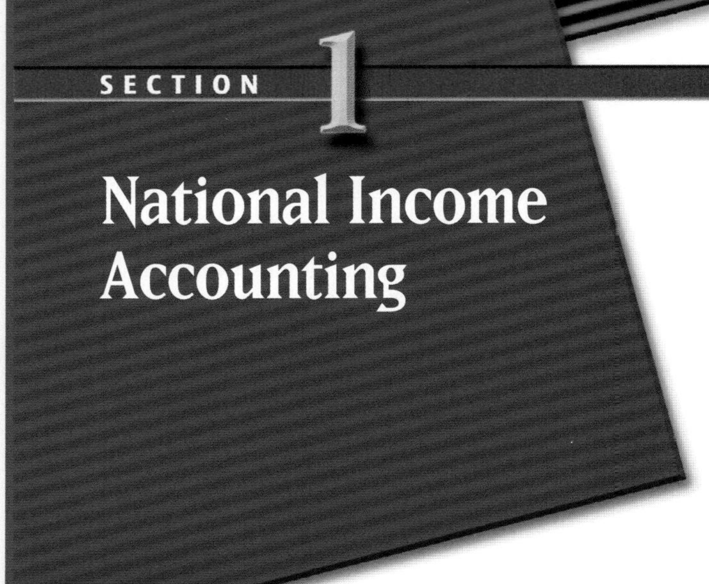

SECTION 1 National Income Accounting

Focus Questions

- What is GDP?
- Why are only final goods and services computed in GDP?
- What is omitted from GDP?
- What is the difference between GDP and GNP?

Key Terms

gross domestic product (GDP)
double counting

What Is Gross Domestic Product?

A family has an income. For example, the annual income of the Smith family might be $90,000. A country has an income too, but we don't call it an income. Instead, we call it *gross domestic product.* **Gross domestic product (GDP)** is the total market value of all final goods and services produced annually in a country. (Note: Sometimes GDP is referred to as *nominal* GDP. This is sometimes done to distinguish it from *real* GDP, which we will discuss later.)

gross domestic product (GDP)
The total market value of all final goods and services produced annually in a country.

Suppose in a tiny economy only three goods are produced in these quantities: 10 computers, 10 cars, and 10 watches. We'll say that the price of a computer is $2,000, the price of a car is $20,000, and the price of a watch is $100. If we wanted to find the GDP of this small economy—that is, if we wanted to find the total market value of the goods produced during the year—we would multiply the price of each good times the quantity of the good produced and then add the dollar amounts. (See Exhibit 11-1.)

1. *Find the market value for each good produced.* Multiply the price of each good times the quantity of the good produced. For example, if 10 computers are produced and the price of each is $2,000, then the market value of computers is $20,000.
2. *Sum the market values.*

Here are the calculations:

Market value of computers =
$2,000 × 10 computers = $20,000

Market value of cars =
$20,000 × 10 cars = $200,000

Market value of watches =
$100 × 10 watches = $1,000

Gross domestic product =
$20,000 + $200,000 + $1,000 = $221,000

This total, $221,000, is the gross domestic product, or GDP, of the tiny economy.

EXAMPLE: A tiny economy has two goods, A and B. It produces 100 units of A and 200 units of B this year. The price of A is

Differentiating Instruction

Visual Learners

For students who have difficulty understanding the terms *gross domestic product, final goods,* and *intermediate goods,* assign them to make a three-part pictorial or collage. One section should be labeled "GDP," and students should draw or affix 10–20 pictures of items included in the GDP. They should then pictorially distinguish between final and intermediate goods, showing in their visual illustrations the relationships between the intermediate and the final good.

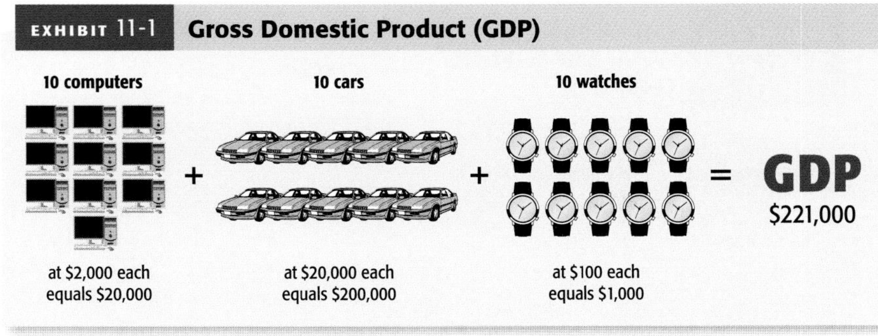

◀ In our tiny example economy, the only goods produced are computers, cars, and watches. To calculate the GDP, we multiply the quantity of each good by its price, then sum the dollar amounts.

$4 and the price of B is $6. It follows that its GDP is $1,600. We got this dollar figure by finding the market value of A ($4 × 100 units = $400), the market value of B ($6 × 200 units = $1,200), and then adding the two values. ♦

Why Count Only Final Goods?

The definition of GDP specifies "final goods and services"; GDP is the total market value of all *final* goods and services produced annually in a country. Economists often distinguish between a *final good* and an *intermediate good.*

A final good is a good sold to its final user. When you buy a hamburger at a fast-food restaurant, for example, the hamburger is a final good. You are the final user; no one uses (eats) the hamburger other than you.

An intermediate good, in contrast, has not reached its final user. For example, consider the bun that the restaurant buys and on which the hamburger is placed. The bun is an intermediate good at this stage, because it is not yet in the hands of the final user (the person who buys the hamburger). It is in the hands of the people who run the restaurant, who use the bun, along with other goods (lettuce, mustard, hamburger meat), to produce a hamburger for sale.

When computing GDP, economists count only final goods and services. If they counted both final and intermediate goods and services, they would be **double counting**, or counting a good more than once.

Suppose that a book is a final good and that paper and ink are intermediate goods used to produce the book. In a way, we can say that the book is paper and ink (book = paper + ink). If we were to calculate the GDP by adding together the value of the book, the paper, and the ink (book + paper + ink), we would, in effect, be counting the paper and ink twice. Because the book is paper and ink, once we count the book, we have automatically counted the paper and the ink. It is not necessary to count them again.

EXAMPLE: A car is made up of many intermediate goods: tires, engine, steering wheel, radio, and so on. When computing GDP, we count only the market value of the car, not the market value of the car plus the market value of the tires, engine, and other intermediate goods. ♦

A Student Asks

QUESTION: *I assume that each country in the world computes its GDP. Why is GDP so important?*

ANSWER: *Countries are interested in computing their GDP for much the same reason that individuals are interested in knowing their income. Just as knowledge of your income from one year to the next lets you know "how you're doing," GDP does much the same for countries. Exhibit 11-2 on the next page shows the GDP for certain countries and for the world in 2004.*

double counting
Counting a good more than once in computing GDP.

Teach

Teaching with Visuals

Invite students to look over the items included and omitted from the GDP in Exhibit 11-1. Ask students how many of the items in the exhibit apply to them. Prompt them to explain how those items are connected to the gross domestic product.

Reinforcement Activity

Direct students to look through newspapers and news magazines to see if they can find a dollar figure for the current gross domestic product. GDP is often reported in newspapers, especially business newspapers such as the *Wall Street Journal.*

Discussion Starter

Ask students if they can see why figuring a true GDP can be overwhelming. Ask: How many products, including their prices, can you name? How many of these products do you think will be sold in a year? Make a list on the board, and calculate a few more involved artificial GDPs with students.

Internet Research

Assign students to find recent GDP statistics on the Web. Ask students to look at the components included in the GDP figures. Ask: What are the most significant components of our country's output? What is the difference between durable and nondurable goods? What are the differences between goods and services? What is meant by *investment?*

Reinforcement Activity

Write the name of each student on a separate piece of paper and put all the names into a hat. Pull out the first name and ask that student why one of the factors is omitted from the GDP. For example, ask: Why are illegal goods and services omitted from the GDP? Why are the sales of used goods omitted from the GDP? If the student answers the question correctly, his or her name stays out of the hat. If the answer is incorrect, the name goes back in the hat. Choose another name, and continue until all the factors have been identified.

Economics Around the Clock

Lead students in a discussion of their answers to the 1:13 P.M. scenario in Economics Around the Clock (page 287).

Help them see that if Kevin pays Jones in cash, there will be no record of this transaction, which means it will not be counted in the GDP. Jones might want to do this because it means he won't have to pay taxes on this income.

▶ **Why do countries think it is important to keep track of their GDP?**

EXHIBIT 11-2 GDP in 2004, the World and Selected Countries

Country or World	GDP (in trillions of dollars)
World	$55.50
United States	11.75
China	7.26
Japan	3.75
India	3.32
Germany	2.36
United Kingdom	1.78
France	1.74
Italy	1.61
Brazil	1.49
Russia	1.41
Canada	1.02
Mexico	1.01

Source: CIA World Factbook, 2005.

Does GDP Omit Anything?

Some exchanges that take place in an economy are omitted from the GDP measurement. The following are not included when calculating GDP.

Illegal Goods and Services

For something to be included in the calculation of GDP, that something has to be capable of being counted. Illegal trades are not capable of being counted, for obvious reasons. For example, when someone makes an illegal purchase, no record is made of the transaction. The criminals involved in the transaction do everything in their power to prevent anyone from knowing about the transaction.

EXAMPLE: As you know, it is illegal in the United States to buy and sell drugs such as cocaine, heroin, and methamphetamine. Suppose a person pays $400 to buy some of an illegal drug. This $400 is not counted in GDP. If, however, the person spends $40 to buy a book, this $40 is counted in GDP. It is not illegal to buy a book. ♦

A Student Asks

QUESTION: *Obviously, illegal transactions occur in the United States every day (such as dollars exchanged for illegal drugs), and other transactions that occur are "under the table" (such as a person being paid for his services in cash instead of with a check). Do economists know what percentage of all transactions these types of transactions account for?*

ANSWER: *Both illegal transactions and legal transactions that government authorities do not know about (such as cash transactions that do not include a receipt) make up what is called the underground economy. Some economists estimate that the underground economy in the United States is about 13 percent of the regular economy. In other words, for every $100 transaction in the regular economy, there is a $13 transaction in the underground economy. Keep in mind, though, that it is somewhat difficult to get a really good estimate of the underground economy because, by definition, it is largely invisible to economists. It is difficult to count what people are trying to prevent you from counting.*

Transactions of Legal Goods and Services with No Record

Suppose a gardener goes to someone's house and offers to mow the lawn and prune the shrubbery for $35 a week. The person agrees. The gardener then asks that he be paid in cash instead of by check and that no written record of the transaction be made. In other words, no sales receipt is provided. Again the person agrees. The payment for these gardening services does not find its way into GDP. A cash payment and no sales receipt mean that no evidence shows that a transaction was ever made.

Some Nonmarket Goods and Services

Some goods and services are traded, but not in an official market setting. Let's say that Eileen Montoya cooks, cleans, and takes

Background Information: Nonmarket Goods and Services

Currently, nonmarket goods and services are not counted in the GDP. For example, if a man or woman stays at home and cooks and cleans, the value of these services is not computed into the GDP. Some people have said that by not counting these services in the GDP, we devalue the activities that are performed by these people. For example, society does not perceive a homemaker's work in the home as being as valuable as a person's work in the marketplace. Ask students if they would be in favor of counting nonmarket goods and services in the GDP, assuming that it were possible to do so. Ask them to give reasons for their positions.

care of all financial matters in the Montoya household. She is not paid for doing these activities; she does not receive a weekly salary from the family. Because she is not paid, the value of the work she performs is not counted in GDP.

EXAMPLE: Jayne has three young boys, ages 2 to 6. She cuts their hair every few weeks. The "market value" of these haircuts is not counted in GDP. However, if Jayne took her boys to a barber, and he cut their hair, what the barber charged for haircuts would be counted in GDP. ♦

Sales of Used Goods

Suppose you buy a used car tomorrow. Will this purchase be recorded in this year's GDP statistics? No, a used car does not enter into the current year's statistics because the car was counted when it was originally produced.

EXAMPLE: Mario just sold his 2002 Toyota to Jackson for $7,000. This $7,000 is not counted in GDP. ♦

Stock Transactions and Other Financial Transactions

Suppose Elizabeth buys 500 shares of stock from Keesha for a price of $100 a share. The total price is $50,000. The transaction is not included in GDP, because GDP is a record of goods and services produced annually in an economy. A person who buys stock is not buying a product but rather an ownership right in the firm that originally issued the stock. For example, when a person buys Coca-Cola stock, he is becoming an owner of the Coca-Cola Corporation.

Government Transfer Payments

In everyday life, one person makes a payment to another usually in exchange for a good or service. For example, Enrique may pay Harriet $40 to buy her old CD player.

When the government makes a payment to someone, it often does not get a good or service in exchange. When this happens, the payment is said to be a government transfer payment. For example, the Social Security check that 67-year-old Frank Simmons receives is a government transfer payment. Simmons, who is retired, is not currently supplying a good or service to the government in exchange for the Social Security check. Because GDP accounts for only current goods and services produced, and a transfer payment has nothing to do with current goods and services produced, transfer payments are properly omitted from GDP statistics. See Exhibit 11-3 for a review of items omitted from GDP.

Quite a bit of economic data can be found on the Web. Go to the Economic Statistics Briefing Room at www.emcp.net/employment and click on "Employment" if you want to find the current civilian labor force, number of persons unemployed, and unemployment rate. Click on "Prices" if you want to find the one-month change in the CPI. If you want to find the most current GDP figures, go to the Bureau of Economic Analysis at www.emcp.net/GDPfigures and click on "Frequently Requested NIPA Tables" and then "Gross Domestic Product."

EXHIBIT 11-3 What the GDP Omits

Item	Example
Illegal goods and services	A person buys an illegal substance.
Legal goods and services with no record of the transaction	A gardener works for cash, and no sales receipt exists.
Some nonmarket goods and services	A family member cooks, cleans, and mows the lawn.
Sales of used goods	You buy a used car.
Stock transactions and other financial transactions	You buy 100 shares of stock in a company.
Government transfer payments	Frank Simmons receives a Social Security check.

Direct students to look up GDP figures. Ask: What was the GDP for the third quarter of 2005? What was the change for "Structures" from the first quarter of 2005 to the third quarter?

Teaching with Visuals

Exhibit 11-3 lists examples of items that are not included in the GDP. Have students re-create this table for themselves, listing the same items but different examples.

Application Activity

After reading and discussing Section 1, you may want to assign the Section Activity in the *Applying the Principles Workbook.*

Assess

Quick Quiz

The following true-or-false quiz will help you assess student understanding of the material covered in this section.

1. GDP is the total market value of all final goods and services produced monthly in an economy. (False)
2. A final good is a good sold to its final user. (True)
3. When a restaurant pays for steak, this is a final good. (False)
4. Sales of used goods are omitted from the GDP calculations. (True)
5. GDP only measures economic activity within the boundaries of the country it is measuring. (True)

Cooperative Learning

Divide the class into groups of four or five. Tell each group that it will be looking at the concept of final goods and services and double counting. Instruct each group to choose a final good that it can bring to class or find around the room. You might encourage students to bring in appropriate goods that are not of excessive value. As a group, members should examine the good and try to name what other goods went into producing it. For example, if the good that is brought to class is a radio, some of the goods used to produce it might be plastic and wires. Each group should make a list of these goods used in producing its final good. Have each group choose a speaker to report its findings to the class.

Section 1 National Income Accounting 291

Assessment Book

You will find a quiz for this section in the *Assessment Book.*

Reteaching Activity

Use the Section Assessment to gauge which students may need reteaching on this section. For those students, write the following on the board: "The gross domestic product is the total market value of final goods and services produced annually in an economy. The gross domestic product is often simply called the GDP." Ask students to explain each statement. Go over their answers to be sure they understand the meaning of GDP.

Guided Reading

For further reteaching of the key concepts in this section, assign the Outlining Activity and the Just the Facts Handout from the *Guided Reading and Study Guide.*

EXHIBIT 11-4 Gross National Product Does Not Equal Gross Domestic Product

GNP

Total market value of final goods and services produced by U.S. citizens (wherever they reside–the United States, France, Mexico, etc.)

≠

GDP

Total market value of final goods and services produced within the borders of the United States (by both citizens and noncitizens)

▲ The producer's *citizenship* matters in computing GNP. The producer's place of *residence* matters in computing GDP.

The Difference Between GDP and GNP

Economists, government officials, and members of the public talk about GDP when they want to discuss the overall performance of the economy. They might say, "GDP has been on the rise" or "GDP has been declining a bit." It was not always GDP that these individuals talked about, though. They used to talk about GNP, the gross national product. (In some international publications, you will read about gross national income, or GNI, instead of gross national product, GNP.)

What is the difference between GDP and GNP? GNP measures the total market value of final goods and services produced by U.S. citizens, no matter where in the world they reside. GDP, in contrast, is the total market value of final goods and services produced within the borders of the United States, no matter who produces them.

Suppose a U.S. citizen owns a business in Japan. The value of the output she is producing in Japan is counted in GNP because she is a U.S. citizen, but it is not counted in GDP because it was not produced within the borders of the United States. Now suppose a Canadian citizen is producing goods in the United States. The value of his output is not counted in GNP because he is not a U.S. citizen, but it is counted in GDP because it was produced within the borders of the United States. (See Exhibit 11-4.)

EXAMPLE: José is a Mexican citizen working in the United States. The dollar value of what he produces is counted in the U.S. GDP. Sabrina is a U.S. citizen living and working in Brazil. The dollar value of what she produces (in Brazil) is counted in U.S. GNP. ♦

SECTION 1 ASSESSMENT

Defining Terms

1. Define:
   a. gross domestic product (GDP)
   b. double counting

Reviewing Facts and Concepts

2. In a simple economy, three goods are produced during the year, in these quantities: 10 pens, 20 shirts, and 30 radios. The price of pens is $4 each, the price of shirts is $30 each, and the price of radios is $35 each. What is GDP for the economy?
3. Why are only final goods and services computed in GDP?
4. Which of the following are included in the calculation of this year's GDP?
   a. Twelve-year-old Bobby mowing his family's lawn
   b. Terry Yanemoto buying a used car
   c. Barbara Wilson buying 100 shares of Chrysler Corporation stock
   d. Stephen Sidwhali's receipt of a Social Security check
   e. An illegal sale at the corner of Elm and Jefferson

Critical Thinking

5. What is the difference (for purposes of measuring GDP) between buying a new computer and buying 100 shares of stock?

Applying Economic Concepts

6. The government does not now include the housework that a person does for his or her family as part of GDP. Suppose the government were to include housework. How might it go about placing a dollar value on housework?

SECTION 1 ASSESSMENT ANSWERS

Defining Terms

1. a. gross domestic product (GDP): the total market value of all final goods and services produced annually in a country; **b. double counting:** counting a good more than once. When the GDP is calculated, only final goods are counted, thus eliminating double counting.

Reviewing Facts and Concepts

2. $1,690 (*calculation:* 10 pens × $4 = $40; 20 shirts × $30 = $600; 30 radios × 35 = $1,050; $40 +$600 + $1,050 = $1,690).

3. If we counted intermediate goods as well as final goods and services, we would be counting some goods twice, that is, double counting.

4. None of the items listed is included in calculating the GDP.

Critical Thinking

5. The computer purchase is a part of the GDP, but the stock purchase is not. A person who buys stock is not buying a good that was produced. Instead, he is buying an ownership right in a company that produces certain goods and services.

Applying Economic Concepts

6. The government could find out how much a person would have to pay someone to do his or her housework. How much would Jones, for example, have to pay to have someone wash his clothes, tidy up the house, cook his meals, and so on? Then this dollar amount would be added to the GDP.

SECTION 2

Measuring GDP

Focus Questions

- What are the four sectors of the economy?
- What are consumption, investment, government purchases, export spending, and import spending?
- How is GDP measured?
- What is per capita GDP?

Key Terms

consumption
investment
government purchases
export spending
import spending

How Is GDP Measured?

The GDP of the United States today is more than $12 trillion. How did economists come up with this figure? What exactly did they do to get this dollar amount?

First, economists break the economy into four sectors: the household sector, the business sector, the government sector, and the foreign sector. Next, they state a simple fact: the people in each of these sectors buy goods and services—that is, they make expenditures.

Economists give names to the expenditures made by each of the four sectors. The expenditures made by the household sector (or by consumers) are called **consumption**. The expenditures made by the business sector are called **investment**, and expenditures made by the government sector are called **government purchases**. (Government purchases include purchases made by all three levels of government—local, state, and federal.) Finally, the expenditures made by the residents of other countries on goods produced in the United States are called **export spending**. Exhibit 11-5 on page 294 gives examples of goods purchased by households, businesses, government, and foreigners.

Consider all the goods and services produced in the U.S. economy in a year: houses, tractors, watches, restaurant meals, cars, computers, plasma television sets, DVDs, iPods, cell phones, and much, much more. Suppose someone from the household sector buys a DVD. This purchase falls into the category of *consumption*. When someone from the business sector buys a large machine to install in a factory, the purchase is considered an *investment*. If the U.S. government purchases a tank from a company that produces tanks, the purchase is considered a *government purchase*. If a person living in Sweden buys a U.S.-produced sweater, this purchase is considered spending on U.S. exports and therefore is registered as *export spending*.

All goods produced in the economy must be bought by someone in one of the four sectors of the economy. If economists simply sum the expenditures made by each sector—that is, if they sum consumption, investment, government purchases, and export spending—they will be close to computing the GDP.

consumption Expenditures made by the household sector.

investment Expenditures made by the business sector.

government purchases Expenditures made by the government sector. Government purchases do not include government transfer payments.

export spending The amount spent by the residents of other countries for goods produced in the United States.

Differentiating Instruction

Visual Learners

Divide students into four groups. Each group will create a poster for one sector of the economy. Students can bring in photographs or small items that represent their assigned sector and glue them to the posters. Once the posters are completed, you may choose to display them in the classroom. Students should identify each of the items on the posters and explain why it fits within that particular sector of the economy. Ask: Are there any items that appear in more than one of the sectors? If so, how is this possible? Is it possible for a good to appear in all four of the sectors of the economy? Why or why not?

SECTION 2

Teacher Support

Focus and Motivate

Section Objectives

After completing this section, students will be able to

- list the four sectors of the economy;
- describe consumption, investment, government purchases, export spending, and import spending;
- explain how GDP is measured; and
- describe per capita GDP.

Kickoff Activity

Write the following question on the board for students to answer: "Do you think people who live in a country with a large GDP are better off than people who live in a country with a small GDP? Explain your answer."

Activating Prior Knowledge

Allow volunteers to share their responses to the Kickoff Activity. Their answers should touch on the idea that neither is necessarily better, because GDP does not take into account nonmaterial goods and services. Nor does it take into account how the GDP is distributed among the population.

Teach

Discussion Starter

Invite students to discuss the products they have purchased in the last month. Are these items reflective of consumption or import spending?

Teaching with Visuals

Instruct students to look at Exhibit 11-5. Ask them which expenditure of the GDP is the most important to the determination of the GDP. The answer is consumption.

Reinforcement Activity

Obtain a copy of the *Economic Report of the President,* either from your school library or from the Internet. Ask students to locate in that document current dollar figures for the components of the GDP: consumption, investment, government expenditures, and imports and exports.

What goes on in the United States affects the GDP in, say, Mexico, and what goes on in Mexico affects the GDP in, say, the United States. This is obvious once we note that the GDP for any country is equal to C + I + G + EX – IM. When Mexicans buy more goods from the United States, exports in the United States (EX) rise and the U.S. GDP rises. When Americans buy more goods from Mexico, exports in Mexico rise and Mexico's GDP rises. In short, by affecting the exports of a country, importing countries affect the exporting country's GDP.

A Student Asks

You may want to use this A Student Asks to make sure that students understand the difference between the two meanings of the word *investment.*

EXHIBIT 11-5 The Expenditures Made by the Four Sectors of the Economy

Sector of the economy	Name of expenditures	Definition	Examples
Household	Consumption	Expenditures made by the household sector on goods for personal use	TV sets, telephones, clothes, lamps, cars
Business	Investment	Expenditures made by the business sector on goods used in producing other goods; also includes business inventories	Tools, machines, factories
Government	Government purchases	Expenditures made by federal, state, and local governments	Paper, pens, tanks, planes
Foreign	Exports	Expenditures made by foreigners for American-made goods	Cars, wheat, computers
	Imports	Expenditures made by Americans for foreign-made goods	Cars, radios, computers

They are only close, however; they still need to adjust for U.S. purchases of foreign-produced goods. For example, if Cynthia in Detroit purchases a Japanese-made television set for $500, this $500 TV purchase would not be included in GDP because GDP is a measure of goods and services produced annually in a country. Specifically, the U.S. GDP is a measure of goods and services produced annually in the territorial area we know as the United States. Cynthia's TV was not produced in the United States, so it is not part of U.S. GDP. Spending by Americans for foreign-produced goods is called **import spending**.

To compute U.S. GDP, then, we need to sum consumption (C), investment (I), government purchases (G), and export spending (EX), and then subtract import spending (IM). We can now write GDP in symbol form:

$$GDP = C + I + G + EX - IM$$

For example, in the first quarter of 2005, consumption in the United States was $8.534 trillion,[1] investment was $2.085 trillion, government purchases were $2.260 trillion, export spending was $1.210 trillion, and import spending was $1.938 trillion. Thus we can calculate GDP to be $12.151 trillion (see Exhibit 11-6).

A Student Asks

QUESTION: *Earlier you stated that investment is defined as the expenditures made by the business sector. For example, if a business buys a new machine, the purchase of the machine is considered an investment. I think in the everyday world people use the word "investment" a little differently than the word is being used here. Am I right?*

ANSWER: *Yes, you are right. For example, in the everyday world, someone might say, "I made a good investment last week. I bought stock in the stock market." The economist, however, is not using the word "investment" in this way. Again, what an economist means when he or she uses the word "investment" is the expenditures made by a business—for example, a business buying a factory, or more robotics, and so on.*

import spending The amount spent by Americans for foreign-produced goods.

[1] These quarter figures for consumption, investment, and so on have been annualized. This means that for all practical purposes you can consider these quarter figures to be fairly representative of the relevant annual figures. Think of it this way. Suppose that in the first three months of the year (the first quarter of the year) you spend $400 on consumption goods. If you buy the same amount in the next three quarters, your annual expenditure on consumption goods will be $1,200. So, when we say that the quarter figures have been annualized, we are saying that instead of using the $400 figure, we are using the $1,200 figure.

Cooperative Learning

Divide students into groups of two or three and let each group choose a U.S. state other than their own. Tell students that people often have misconceptions about the industries that are most important in a state. For example, many people assume that there are only two major industries in Texas (oil and cattle), but in fact its major products and services also include natural gas, cotton and other farm items, steel, banking, insurance, and tourism. Instruct students to find out the largest and most important industries for their chosen state and the GDP of that state. Then provide students with the same information for their own state. Ask students: How do the industries and GDP of our own state compare with those of the states you have researched?

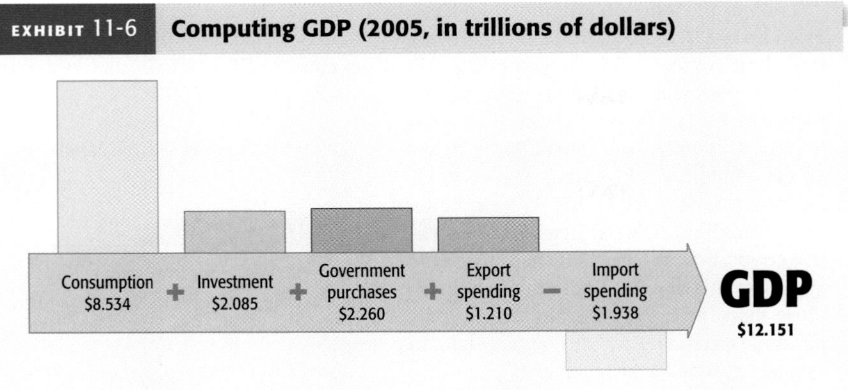

EXHIBIT 11-6 **Computing GDP (2005, in trillions of dollars)**

◀ To calculate GDP we add several expenditures, then subtract one. **What is the expenditure that we subtract rather than add?**

Is Every Good That Is Produced Also Sold?

Our definition of GDP is the total market value of all final goods and services *produced* annually in an economy. However, we measured the GDP by finding out how much the four sectors of the economy *spend* on goods and services. Suppose something is produced but not purchased. Is it included in GDP or not? For example, a car company produces 10,000 new cars this year, but the household sector chooses to buy only 8,900 of the 10,000 cars. That means that some cars (1,100) were produced but not sold. Do these cars get counted in GDP?

The answer is yes, because the government statisticians who measure GDP assume that everything that is produced is purchased by someone. For purposes of calculating GDP, the government statisticians assume that the car company "purchased" the 1,100 cars that the car company did not sell.

EXAMPLE: Nigel owns his own sock factory. Last year he produced 100,000 pairs of socks. He sold 80,000 pairs to people. That left 20,000 pairs of socks produced but unsold (as far as Nigel is concerned). Government statisticians view these 20,000 pairs of socks as having been produced by Nigel and as having been "purchased" by Nigel. How many pairs of socks are counted in GDP: 80,000 or 100,000? Answer: 100,000. ◆

A Student Asks

QUESTION: *How do government statisticians know about the 20,000 pairs of socks in inventory? After all, they would have to know about them in order to count them in GDP.*

ANSWER: *When Nigel produced the 100,000 pairs of socks he had to pay workers to produce them. These workers earned incomes that were reported to the government for tax purposes. Roughly, by comparing expenditures with incomes the government statisticians can get an idea of what was produced but not sold. Suppose you paid $1,000 to workers but only sold goods totaling $40. This difference indicates the production of some goods that didn't end up getting sold.*

GDP Versus Quality of Life

In 2004, the U.S. GDP was more than six times larger than the GDP of France. Does it follow that because Americans live in a country with a higher GDP than the French, Americans are better off than the French? If your answer is yes, then you have made the mistake of equating a higher GDP with being better off or having greater well-being. Greater production of goods and services is only one of the many factors that contribute to being better off or possessing greater well-being.

Teaching with Visuals

We subtract import spending. To help students understand the calculations of GDP, bring in objects to represent each factor in the equation. You might use bread for consumption, a stapler for investment, a ream of paper for the government (all those forms), a toy car for export spending, and anything from a foreign country for import spending. Guide students in a discussion of how these items are reflected in the GDP.

Economics Around the Clock

After students have read Section 2, ask them to discuss their answers to the 1:34 P.M. scenario in Economics Around the Clock (page 287).

Answers may vary. Students might suggest that just because a country has a high GDP, it might not have a high per capita GDP. China has a very large population, so its per capita GDP might be smaller than that of another country.

Application Activity

After reading and discussing Section 2, you may want to assign the Section Activity in the *Applying the Principles Workbook.*

Assess

Quick Quiz

The following true-or-false quiz will help you assess student understanding of the material covered in this section.

1. Economists break the economy into three sectors: household, government, and business. (False)
2. If a person living in Sweden purchases a U.S.-produced television, that is regarded as U.S. import spending. (False)
3. According to GDP figures, every good that is produced by the economy is sold. (True)
4. A higher GDP necessarily means a happier life. (False)
5. Americans are better off than the French on the basis of both countries' GDPs. (False)

Cooperative Learning

Divide students into groups to develop lists of the industries they feel are important in their local community. Have a volunteer list the industries on the board. Then, as a class, try to rank the industries in the community in terms of number of employees. To follow up on this activity, you might ask students to contact the local Chamber of Commerce or Board of Trade to check the accuracy of the list. Ask students to research these questions: Were any industries left off this list? Are there any industries on the list that really do not belong? Perhaps you could arrange to have a representative from one of the industries visit your class and discuss the role and importance of that industry in the community.

Assessment Book

You will find a quiz for this section in the *Assessment Book.*

Reteaching Activity

Use the Section Assessment to gauge which students may need reteaching on this section. Guide those students in using the formula on page 294 to compute the GDP. Write the math equation on the board as you discuss it, so students can better make the connection. Give students various sample problems and have them calculate the GDPs with numbers you supply.

Guided Reading

For further reteaching of the key concepts in this section, assign the Outlining Activity and the Just the Facts Handout from the *Guided Reading and Study Guide.*

Look at the issue on an individual basis. Franklin has $1 million in the bank, owns a large home, drives a luxury car, and works 70 hours per week. He has little time to enjoy nature or his family. In contrast, Harris has $100 in the bank, owns a small home, drives an old car, and works 30 hours a week. He has much time to enjoy life. Who is better off—Franklin or Harris? In terms of expensive goods, Franklin certainly has more than Harris; in this one respect, Franklin benefits more than Harris. In terms of leisure time, though, Harris is better off than Franklin. In overall terms—taking everything into account—we cannot say who is better off.

Similarly, we simply cannot say whether Americans are better off than the French on the basis of their GDPs. All we can say for sure is that Americans live in a country in which greater production exists. Being better off takes into account much more than simply how much output is produced.

In assessing a country's GDP, its population also must be considered. Suppose country X has double the GDP of country Y, but its population is three times as large. This would mean that on a per-person basis (the same as a *per capita* basis) each person has fewer goods and services (on average) in country X than in country Y. In short, a bigger country GDP does not necessarily mean a bigger per capita GDP.

Per capita GDP = GDP/Population

A Student Asks

QUESTION: *What are some countries of the world that have a high per capita GDP?*

ANSWER: *In 2004, Luxembourg had the highest per capita GDP at $58,900. The United States was second at $40,100. Norway was fourth at $40,000, Switzerland was tenth at $33,800, and Canada was fifteenth at $31,500. The country with the lowest per capita GDP was East Timor at $400. To find the current rank ordering of countries according to per capita GDP, go to the CIA World Factbook at www.emcp.net/GDPrank. (If you want to check a different year, simply change the year in the Web address.)*

Section 2 Assessment

Defining Terms

1. Define:
   a. consumption
   b. investment
   c. government purchases
   d. export spending
   e. import spending

Reviewing Facts and Concepts

2. Why is import spending subtracted from the sum of consumption, investment, government purchases, and export spending in computing GDP?
3. Suppose consumption is $2,000 billion, investment is $700 billion, government purchases are $1,200 billion, export spending is $100 billion, and import spending is $150 billion. What does GDP equal?
4. A computer company produces 25,000 computers this year and sells 22,000 to its customers. According to government statisticians, however, all 25,000 computers have been purchased. How do the statisticians reach this conclusion?

Critical Thinking

5. Suppose country X has a GDP that is three times larger than that of country Y. Are the people in country X better off than the people in country Y? Explain your answer.

Applying Economic Concepts

6. A family has six people, five of whom produce goods and services that are sold directly to consumers. One person in the family is too young to work. How would you go about measuring the family's "GDP"?

Section 2 Assessment Answers

Defining Terms

1. a. consumption: expenditures made by the household sector; **b. investment:** expenditures made by the business sector; **c. government purchases:** expenditures made by the government sector; **d. export spending:** the amount spent by the residents of foreign countries on goods produced in the United States; **e. import spending:** the amount spent by residents of the United States on goods produced in foreign countries.

Reviewing Facts and Concepts

2. Imports are not produced in the United States, and to find the GDP, we must subtract what Americans spend on foreign-produced goods.
3. $3,850 billion (*calculation:* C + I + G + EX – IM = $2,000 billion + $700 billion + $1,200 billion + $100 billion – $150 billion = $3,850 billion).
4. Government statisticians say that if any goods are produced by a company but are not sold, the remaining goods are considered to be purchased by the company itself.

Critical Thinking

5. Not necessarily. *Better off* is a subjective term. Even if everyone in country X had three times as many goods and services as everyone in country Y, the people in country X are not necessarily better off than the people in country Y. Maybe the people in country X have to work long and hard hours for what they get, and they have very little leisure time. Furthermore, if the population of country X is four times that of country Y, then the per capita GDP is lower in country X than country Y.

Applying Economic Concepts

6. GDP is the total market value of all final goods and services produced annually in an economy. If the economy were a "family economy," we would compute the market value of what each family member produces and then sum each value to get the family's GDP.

SECTION 3

Real GDP

Focus Questions

- What two variables are involved in calculating GDP?
- If GDP is higher in one year than another, do we automatically know why it is higher?
- What is the difference between GDP and real GDP?
- How do economists go about computing real GDP?

Key Terms

base year
real GDP

The Two Variables of GDP: P and Q

When we computed GDP in a simple, one-good economy, we multiplied two variables to find GDP: price (P) and quantity (Q). If either of the two variables rises and the other remains constant, GDP will rise.

To see how this relationship works, look at the following chart:

Price	Quantity	GDP
$10	2	$20
$15	2	$30
$10	3	$30

With a price of $10 and a quantity of 2, GDP is $20. When the price rises to $15 but the quantity is held constant at 2, GDP rises to $30. Finally, if the price is constant at $10 and the quantity increases to 3, GDP again is $30. Clearly, an increase in either price or quantity will raise GDP.

Suppose someone then told you that GDP was $20 one year and $30 the next year. You would have no way of knowing whether GDP increased because price increased, because quantity of output increased, or because both price and quantity increased. On the other hand, if price was held constant and GDP increased, would you know what caused the rise in GDP? If price is held constant, then any rise in GDP must be due to a rise in quantity, of course.

How can we keep price constant? Economists do it by computing GDP for each year—2003, 2004, 2005, and so on—using the prices that existed in one particular year in the past, called the **base year**, chosen as a point of reference for comparison. Economists who compute GDP this way are said to be computing real GDP (GDP measured in base-year, or constant, prices). GDP is equal to price in the current year times quantity in the current year, but **real GDP** is equal to price in the base year times quantity in the current year.

Let's again assume that we have a simple, one-good economy that produces only watches. In Exhibit 11-7, on page 298, column 1 lists several years, column 2 gives the price of watches in these years, and column 3 gives the quantity of watches

base year
In general, a benchmark year–a year chosen as a point of reference for comparison. When real GDP is computed, the outputs of different years are priced at base-year levels.

real GDP
Gross domestic product (GDP) that has been adjusted for price changes; GDP measured in base-year, or constant, prices.

Background Information: Real GDP

If students question the importance of the information about real GDP, tell them the following: When choosing the base year, economists choose a year in which sharp changes in major economic factors do not appear. For example, if in one year prices are skyrocketing, and in another year prices are stable, economists are much more likely to pick the second as the base year—the year against which other years are measured.

SECTION 3

Teacher Support

Focus and Motivate

Section Objectives

After completing this section, students will be able to

- name the two variables involved in calculating GDP;
- explain whether we would automatically know why GDP is higher in some years than others;
- describe the difference between GDP and real GDP; and
- explain how economists go about computing real GDP.

Kickoff Activity

Ask students to respond in writing to the following question while attendance is being taken: What two things can increase GDP?

Activating Prior Knowledge

Invite students to discuss their responses to the Kickoff Activity. Students' answers should reflect that if prices go up, GDP will increase, and/or if output goes up, GDP will increase.

Teach

Discussion Starter

Ask students for a reason why most economists use real GDP instead of GDP when talking about the economy. They should recognize that most economists do so because an increase in prices and/or output will increase GDP, whereas only an increase in output will increase real GDP.

Cause and Effect

To show the relationship between price and quantity, write the following problem on the board: "The given price for 1,000 units of a good produced last year was $5. This year, the price is $5.50 and the quantity produced is 750." Ask students which year had the higher GDP. (*Answer:* Last year's GDP of $5,000 was higher than this year's GDP of $4,125.) Ask students which was the higher real GDP. (*Answer:* The real GDP of last year, $5,000, was higher than that of this year, $3,750.) What would happen to the comparison if the quantity produced in the second year was 1,200? (*Answer:* Both GDP and real GDP would increase.)

Instruct students to reread and discuss their answers to the accompanying question to the 11:03 P.M. scenario in Economics Around the Clock (page 287).

Help students understand that Sam is not right. A small increase in the per capita real GDP growth rate can make a huge difference in the standard of living enjoyed by people.

Reinforcement Activity

Ask students to demonstrate their understanding of this section by writing a sentence or two explaining how real GDP differs from GDP. Their answers should reflect that while GDP is the total market value of all final goods and services produced annually in the economy, real GDP makes adjustments for changes in price and output.

EXHIBIT 11-7 Computing GDP and Real GDP in a Simple, One-Good Economy

(1) Year	(2) Price of watches	(3) Quantity of watches produced	(4) GDP	(5) Real GDP
1987	$20	—	Price in current year × Quantity in current year	Price in 1987 × Quantity in current year
2003	$50	1,900	$50 × 1,900 = $95,000	$20 × 1,900 = $38,000
2004	$60	2,000	$60 × 2,000 = $120,000	$20 × 2,000 = $40,000
2005	$70	1,855	$70 × 1,855 = $129,850	$20 × 1,855 = $37,100

▲ Column 4 computes the GDP for a simple, one-good economy. The price in the current year is multiplied by the quantity produced in the current year. Column 5 computes real GDP by multiplying the price in 1987 (the base year for purposes here) by the quantity produced in the current year. Economists prefer working with real GDP to working with GDP because they know that if real GDP in one year is higher than real GDP in another year, output is greater in the year with the higher real GDP.

produced in these years. Column 4 shows GDP for each year. (GDP equals the current-year price times the current-year quantity of watches.)

Between 1990 and 2003, prices increased about 43 percent. This increase doesn't mean that the price of every single good or service went up 43 percent during this period. The prices of some goods went up more than the prices of other goods, and the prices of some goods actually fell. Here is the percentage increase or decrease in the prices of a few selected items during this time period. In particular, notice what happened to college tuition.

Food and beverages	↑ 36%
New cars	↑ 10
Prescription drugs	↑ 80
Hospital services	↑ 121
Men's clothes	↓ 1.6
Women's clothes	↓ 7.4
Airline fares	↑ 56
Cable TV	↑ 95
College tuition	↑ 130

Real GDP is shown in column 5. To calculate it, we multiply the price of watches in our chosen base year of 1987 by the current-year quantity. For example, to get real GDP in 2003, we take the quantity of watches produced in 2003 and multiply it by the price of watches in 1987.

A quick look at real GDP figures tells us that because real GDP in 2004 ($40,000) is higher than that in 2003 ($38,000), the quantity of watches produced in 2004 must have been greater than the quantity of watches produced in 2003. A look at the quantities in column 3 confirms this assumption. Also, because the real GDP figure for 2005 ($37,100) is lower than that for 2004 ($40,000), the quantity of watches produced in 2005 must have been lower than the quantity of watches produced in 2005. Again, column 3 confirms this lower production.

Finally, in computing real GDP for 2003, 2004, and 2005 we multiplied the quantity of watches produced in each year times the price of watches in 1987, the base year. Thus, another way to define real GDP is *GDP in base-year prices* or, if 1987 is the base year, for example, *GDP in 1987* prices.

Background Information: Healthy Laborers

One way of producing more goods and services, and therefore increasing real GDP, is to increase the number of people working. Obviously, people cannot work if they are dead. In the past, many people died young, often of things that are readily and easily cured today.

Consider the case of Nathan Rothschild, who in 1836 was said to be the richest man in the world. At the time, he was suffering from an inflammation that a German physician had diagnosed as a boil. When Rothschild got steadily worse, a surgeon opened and cleaned the wound, but it was too late. The "boil" was an abscess, and the poison from it had gotten into Rothschild's body. On July 28, 1836, Rothschild died of an infection that today is routinely cured by antibiotics.

Is There Real GDP Growth in Your Future?

Suppose you heard on the radio that per capita real GDP grew by 2.3 percent last year in the United States. Does this percentage matter to you? Life goes on pretty much the same way, right? You didn't get a pay raise at your part-time job, nobody bought you a new car, you still have to go to school every day and do homework. So what does it matter?

Well, real GDP growth in one year may not matter much, but how much it grows over time should matter to you. How much per capita real GDP grows during your lifetime will greatly influence the kind of life you live.

You may be a bit skeptical about this, so let's take a quick look at the history of real GDP. Little per capita real GDP growth occurred from the year A.D. 1 to about 1500. A person living in, say, 1300 didn't have a much different standard of living from a person living in the year 70. It was fairly common during the years of little to no growth in per capita real GDP for a son or daughter to have the same standard of living as his or her great-great-great-great grandmother or grandfather. Today, it's different. For example, your standard of living is much higher than the standard of living of the people who lived in the United States during the Revolutionary War, Civil War, World War I, and World War II. And we are not just talking about the fact that you enjoy some goods today that people in the Revolutionary War did not (such as cell phones, computers, and so on).

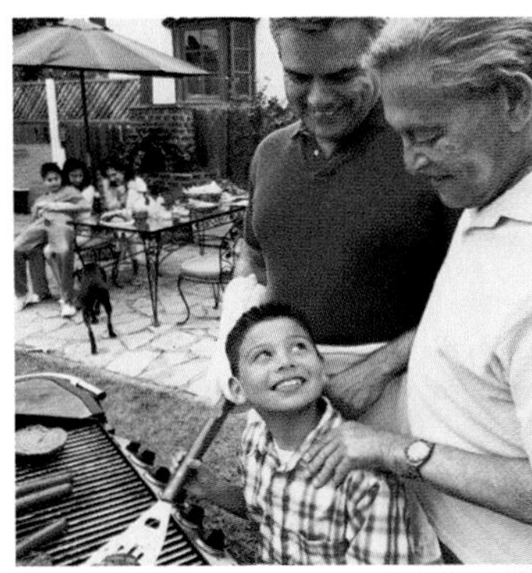

Growth in Material Wealth Across Centuries, 1000–2000

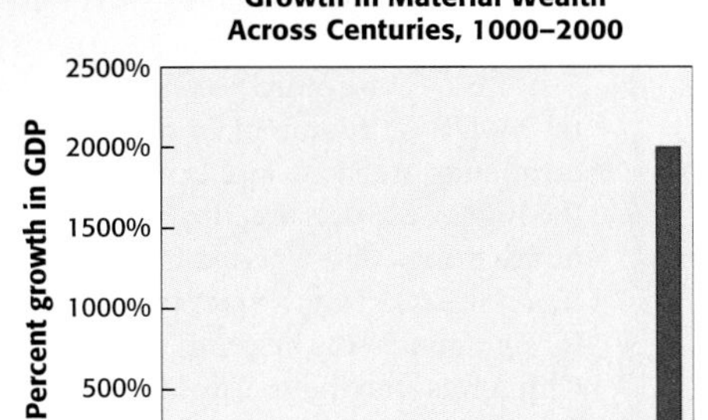

Source: Figure courtesy of Brad de Long, University of California–Berkeley.

Now let's suppose that we look at the case for someone who is born today. If the annual growth rate of per capita real GDP is 1.1 percent, this person will be 65 years old before his or her standard of living (as measured by per capita real GDP) would have doubled. But if the annual growth rate of per capita real GDP is just 1 percent higher, at 2.1 percent, this person will only be 34 years old when his or her standard of living has doubled. If the person lives to 68 years old, this person will have seen his or her standard of living double twice.

Think of what this "doubling" means for you. You are, say, 17 years old. If you live to the age of 77, your standard of living will have doubled twice if the annual per capita real GDP growth rate is 2.1 percent, but it will have only doubled once if it is 1.1 percent. In other words, just a little more growth in per capita real GDP can make a huge difference in the life you live. As an aside, the per capita real GDP growth rate in the United States was 2 percent in 2003 and 3.3 percent in 2004. What will future growth rates be like? We don't know, but we can say if the future is more like 2004 than 2003, we will double our standard of living 15 years earlier (by 2025 instead of 2040). The difference is going to matter to your standard of living when you retire.

THINK ABOUT IT A well-known economist once said that if he had to pick a country for his children to be born in, it would be a country with a high annual growth rate in per capita real GDP. What do you think about his statement?

Rothschild's fate was not uncommon in the early 1800s. People also commonly died of gastrointestinal infections, which were often transmitted from human waste to hands to food to digestive tracts. The main reasons for this transmission were woolen underwear (which caused people to itch) and a lack of mass-produced soap.

Two chief products of the Industrial Revolution were cheap, washable cotton (which does not scratch) and mass-produced soap. These products dramatically reduced the transmission rates of gastrointestinal infections. After their introduction, people ended up living and working longer, which meant that more goods and services could be produced.

Ask students to study the chart in this feature. Allow volunteers to suggest reasons why material wealth grew so rapidly during the 20th century.

ANSWERS TO THINK ABOUT IT Answers will vary. Students might say that the economist knows that the standard of living in the country with a high annual growth rate in per capita real GDP will mean that his children will experience a higher standard of living.

ANSWERS TO ECONOMIC THINKING

The answer to this feature on page 300 is that if foreign countries bought less from the United States, the U.S. GDP would go down.

Application Activity

After reading and discussing Section 3, you may want to assign the Section Activity in the *Applying the Principles Workbook.*

Assess

Quick Quiz

The following true-or-false quiz will help you assess student understanding of the material covered in this section.

1. To find real GDP, you must know a good's current price. (False)
2. Real GDP is more accurate than GDP because it holds price constant. (True)
3. If real GDP is higher in one year than another, it means the price for the good increased. (False)
4. Real GDP shows the change in quantity. (True)
5. The base year is the year that price is taken from to calculate real GDP. (True)

Assessment Book

You will find a quiz for this section in the *Assessment Book.*

Reteaching Activity

Use the Section Assessment to gauge which students may need reteaching on this section. The difference between real GDP and GDP can be difficult for some students to understand. Review Exhibit 11-7 with those students, and give them some new sample numbers for columns (2) and (3) to provide more practice finding GDP and real GDP. Two variables are used to compute GDP—price and quantity. Real GDP takes into account price changes in order to paint a more accurate portrait of any change in the quantity of final goods and services produced in an economy in one year. In other words, with real GDP, economists can see if the number of final goods and services has grown or shrunk.

Guided Reading

For further reteaching of the key concepts in this section, assign the Outlining Activity and the Just the Facts Handout from the *Guided Reading and Study Guide.*

Exports and GDP

In 2005, the countries of South Korea, Taiwan and Japan each found that about 20 percent of their exports were going to China. How much a country exports affects a country's GDP. We know that a country's GDP is the sum of consumption, investment, government purchases, and exports minus imports. Thus, the higher exports are, the higher a country's GDP. One of the things that worried South Korea, Taiwan, and Japan in 2005 was the fact that China's importation of foreign goods was beginning to slow. In other words, China was starting to buy less from South Korea, Taiwan, and Japan.

ECONOMIC THINKING If this were to continue, we could expect the GDP of these countries to decline, all other things being equal. If foreign countries started buying less from the United States, how would the U.S. GDP be affected?

EXAMPLE: A country produces one good, X, which it sells for $4 in 1990, $8 in 1999, and $10 in 2005. It produces 40 units of X in 1990, 45 units in 1999, and 40 units in 2005. If 1990 is designated as the base year, what is the real GDP in each of the three years we designated: 1990, 1999, and 2005?

To find out, we simply multiply the quantity of X the country produces in each year by the price it sells X for in the base year. For example, the real GDP in 1990 is $4 times 40 units, which equals $160. The real GDP in 1999 is $4 times 45 units, which equals $180. The real GDP in 2005 is equal to $4 times 40 units, which is $160. Notice that the real GDP is the same in both 1990 and 2005. ◆

You may be wondering how economists decide what year will be the base year when calculating real GDP. Unfortunately there is no easy answer to this question. The base year has to be a year in the past, but not too far in the past. For example, no economist would choose 1865 as a base year because that is too long ago. The economic world then was much different from today. Economists generally want the base year to be a year in the near past in which no major economic events were occurring. They try not to pick a year in which there were large increases in prices or high unemployment. Aside from those factors, however, choosing the base year is somewhat arbitrary. Several years in the immediate past might fit the bill, but one gets chosen over the others.

ASSESSMENT

Defining Terms

1. Define:
   a. base year
   b. real GDP

Reviewing Facts and Concepts

2. Gross domestic product is $6,000 billion in one year and $6,500 billion the next year. Is output necessarily higher in the second year than in the first? Explain your answer.
3. Why do economists compute real GDP?
4. When real GDP increases, which variable, P or Q, is increasing?

Critical Thinking

5. Can GDP go up at the same time that real GDP goes down? Explain your answer.

Applying Economic Concepts

6. An economist wants to know whether the "average person" in country X has more goods and services to consume than the "average person" in country Y. Do you recommend that the economist look at per capita GDP or per capita real GDP? Explain your answer.

ASSESSMENT ANSWERS

Defining Terms

1. a. base year: a benchmark year, a year chosen as a point of reference for comparison; **b. real GDP:** GDP that has been adjusted for price changes; GDP measured in base-year, or constant, prices.

Reviewing Facts and Concepts

2. No, output is not necessarily higher in the second year than in the first. Prices could be higher.

3. Economists compute real GDP because they want to see what is happening to production over time. The GDP does not provide that information.

4. When real GDP increases, the variable Q is increasing. The variable P is held constant.

Critical Thinking

5. Yes, GDP can go up at the same time that real GDP goes down. GDP is price × quantity, and real GDP is simply quantity (holding prices constant). If quantity goes down, the real GDP falls. The GDP does not necessarily fall, though, because prices can go up by more than quantities go down.

Applying Economic Concepts

6. It is better to look at per capita real GDP, because real GDP measures output, whereas GDP measures output and prices. In short, just because GDP and per capita GDP can rise does not ensure that there is any more output for anyone to consume. When real GDP rises, in contrast, there must be more output.

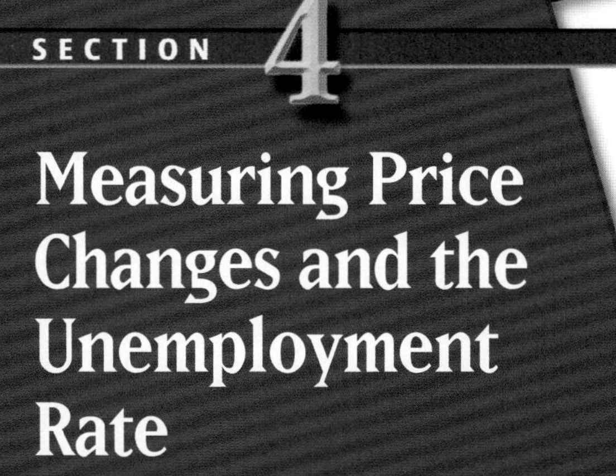

SECTION 4 Measuring Price Changes and the Unemployment Rate

Focus Questions

- What is the consumer price index?
- How is the consumer price index calculated?
- What is the aggregate demand curve?
- What is the aggregate supply curve?
- How do we calculate the unemployment rate?
- How is the employment rate calculated?

Key Terms

price index
consumer price index (CPI)
aggregate demand curve
aggregate supply curve
unemployment rate
employment rate

Calculating the Change in a Single Price

Suppose that in 2004 a Honda Accord was priced at \$20,000, and in 2005 a Honda Accord was \$21,500. By what percentage did the price of a Honda Accord increase? Here is the formula we use to determine the percentage change in price:

$$\text{Percentage change in price} = \frac{\text{Price in later year} - \text{Price in earlier year}}{\text{Price in earlier year}} \times 100$$

If we fill in the numbers, we get the following:

$$\text{Percentage change in price} = \frac{\$21{,}500 - \$20{,}000}{\$20{,}000} \times 100 = 7.5\%$$

The Consumer Price Index

In the previous example, we found the percentage increase in a single price from one year to the next. Economists are much more interested, though, in what happens to prices in general than in what happens to a single price. Before they can calculate the change in prices from one year to the next, they need to compute a **price index**, the average price level. The most widely cited price index is the **consumer price index (CPI)**. You might have heard a newscaster say, "Today it was reported in Washington that the consumer price index has risen 3.2 percent on an annual basis." Let's look at how the CPI is computed and what it means.

EXAMPLE: If you are reading this book, you were probably born around 1989. Let's take the CPI in 1989, which was 121.1. Now let's find the latest CPI data we can find (at the time of this writing). The CPI for April 2005 was 194.6. (If you want to find a more recent CPI, we will give you a Web address shortly.) Now let's calculate how much prices (as measured by the CPI) went up between 1989 and April 2005. The calculation is $[(194.6 - 121.1)/121.1] \times 100$, which is 60.69 percent. This means what cost \$1 when you were born would now cost (on average) about \$1.61. ♦

price index
A measure of the price level, or the average level of prices.

consumer price index (CPI)
The most widely cited price index.

Cooperative Learning

Divide the class into groups of three or four students. Instruct the groups to research the consumer price index. Ask them to consider how changes in the consumer price index affect their lives and their parents' lives. For example, they might explore how buying power is affected by a rise in the consumer price index. Allow groups to present their findings in class.

SECTION 4 Teacher Support

Focus and Motivate

Section Objectives

After completing this section, students will be able to

- explain what the consumer price index is and how it is calculated;
- distinguish between an aggregate demand curve and an aggregate supply curve; and
- explain how the employment rate and unemployment rate are calculated.

Kickoff Activity

Ask students the following question at the beginning of class: You may hear on the news that prices are 5% higher this year than last year. How do you think government goes about measuring the change in prices from one year to the next?

Activating Prior Knowledge

Invite students to share their responses to the Kickoff Activity. They will learn on page 302 that government workers use a representative group of goods called the *market basket*. They compare the prices of this basket from year to year.

Teach

Reinforcement Activity

To give students more practice with determining price changes, bring a weekend advertisement into class that shows original prices and sale prices. Have students find the percentage change in price for each item.

Reinforcement Activity

Assign students to look through newspapers for reports of a change in prices of all goods in an economy or any mention of the consumer price index (CPI). Instruct them to share their findings in small groups.

Teaching with Visuals

To provide students more practice with calculating the consumer price index and to help ensure that they understand this concept, create your own market basket of items and discuss it with the class. Make sure you have clear base-year prices and current year prices. Then tell students to do the same with five to 10 products whose base-year prices they know or can find. Invite students to share their information, what they included in their market baskets, and what they used as base-year prices. As a class, compare students' individual CPIs. Are they all in the same range?

A Student Asks

QUESTION: *If what cost $1 when I was born now costs $1.61, does that mean I am worse off today than someone in 1989? It would seem so—after all I have to pay $1.61 for the same thing that someone in 1989 paid $1 for.*

ANSWER: *Prices are higher today than they were in 1989, but incomes are higher too. Whether you are worse off than the person living in 1989 depends on how much incomes rose compared to how much prices rose.*

Suppose a person earned $100 in 1989 and the average price was $1 per unit. That person could buy 100 units of a good. Now suppose a person earns $161 today and the average price of goods is $1.61. Well, then, the person can still buy 100 units of a good. In other words, a person whose income rises by the same rate as prices is no better and no worse off.

Again suppose a person earned $100 in 1989 and the average price of goods was $1. The person could buy 100 units of a good. Now suppose a person earns $150 today and the average price of goods is $1.61. Now the person can buy only 93 units of a good. A person who is able to buy less today than in 1989 is worse off. This situation happens when one's income rises by less than prices rise.

The CPI is calculated by the U.S. Bureau of Labor Statistics. The bureau uses a sampling of thousands of households and determines what these consumers paid for a representative group of goods called the *market basket.* This amount is compared with what a typical "consumer unit" paid for the same market basket in 1982–1984. (A consumer unit is a household of related or unrelated individuals who pool their money. In the last survey, the average consumer unit was made up of 2.6 people.)

Calculating the CPI involves this process:

1. Calculate the total dollar expenditure on the market basket in the base year and the total dollar expenditure on the market basket in the current year.
2. Divide the total current-year expenditure by the total base-year expenditure, and multiply by 100.

Exhibit 11-8 provides an example. To simplify things, we'll say that the market

▶ If you have some basic information, you can use these steps to calculate the CPI.

EXHIBIT 11-8 Calculating the Consumer Price Index

	(1) Goods in the market basket	(2) Price in base year	(3) Base-year expenditure (1) × (2)	(4) Price in current year	(5) Current-year expenditure (1) × (4)
Step 1: Calculate the total dollar expenditure on the market basket in the base year and the current year. These amounts are calculated in column 3 ($150) and column 5 ($180), respectively.	10 CDs	$13	10 × $13 = $130	$15	10 × $15 = $150
	5 T-shirts	$4	5 × $4 = $20	$6	5 × $6 = $30
			$150 **Total dollar expenditure on the market basket in the base year**		$180 **Total dollar expenditure on the market basket in the current year**

Step 2: Divide the total dollar expenditure on the market basket in the current year by the total dollar expenditure on the market basket in the base year, and then multiply by 100.

$$CPI_{\text{current year}} = \frac{\text{Total dollar expenditure on the market basket in current year}}{\text{Total dollar expenditure on the market basket in base year}} \times 100$$

$$= \frac{\$180}{\$150} \times 100$$

$$= 120$$

Cooperative Learning

Divide the class into groups of three or four students. Direct the groups to the Web site of the U.S. Bureau of Labor Statistics, and then, under the "CPI" section, tell them to select "Tables Created by the BLS." Ask: Has the consumer price index ever fallen from year to year? What year saw the greatest drop? Ask groups to choose a year that the CPI fell and to research why it might have fallen that year. Allow them to present their findings to the class.

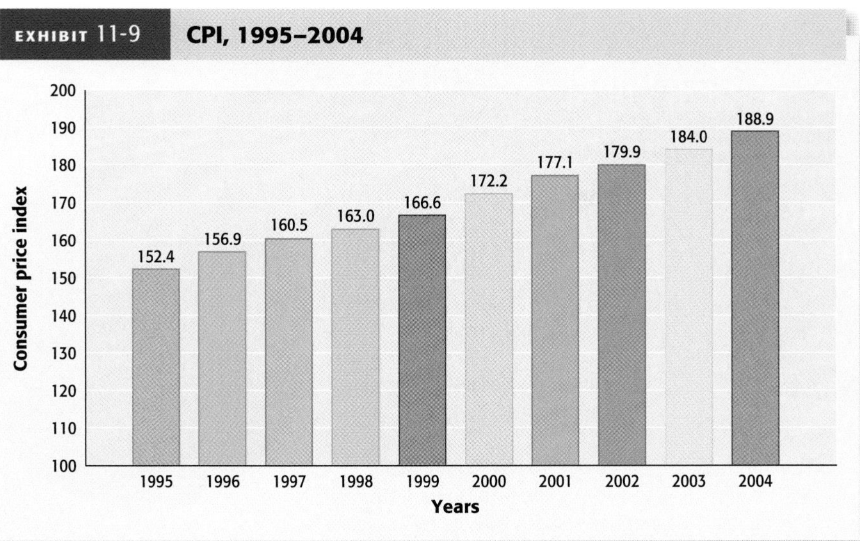

◀ Taken individually the CPI numbers mean very little. **What can you learn by comparing the numbers?**

basket is made up of only two goods instead of the hundreds of items that it actually contains. Our market basket will contain 10 CDs and five T-shirts.

The total dollar expenditure on the market basket in the base year is found by multiplying the quantity of each good in the market basket (column 1) times the price of that good in the base year (column 2). A look at column 3 shows us that $130 was spent on CDs and $20 was spent on T-shirts, for a total dollar expenditure of $150.

Next, the total dollar expenditure on the market basket in the current year is found by multiplying the quantity of each good in the market basket (column 1) times the price of that good in the current year (column 4). A look at column 5 shows us that $150 was spent on CDs and $30 was spent on T-shirts, for a total dollar expenditure of $180.

Now, we divide the total current-year expenditure, $180, by the total base-year expenditure, $150, and then multiply by 100:

$$\$180/\$150 \times 100 = 120$$

The CPI for the current year is 120.

Notice that the CPI is just a number. What does this number tell us? By itself, the CPI number tells us little. It is only when we compare one CPI number with another that we learn something. (See Exhibit 11-9.) For example, in the United States in 2003, the CPI was 184.0. One year later, in 2004, the CPI was 188.9. The two CPI numbers can be used to figure out the percentage by which prices increased between 2003 and 2004 in the same way we determined the percentage increase for a single price:

$$\text{Percentage change in CPI} = \frac{CPI_{\text{later year}} - CPI_{\text{earlier year}}}{CPI_{\text{earlier year}}} \times 100$$

If we fill in the numbers, we get the following:

$$\text{Percentage change in CPI} = \frac{188.9 - 184.0}{184.0} \times 100 = 2.66\%$$

Determining the Quantity of Goods and Services and the Price Level

Chapter 4 explained that the two sides to every market are a demand side and a supply side. We represent the demand in a market with a downward-sloping demand curve

Teaching with Visuals

Ask students to refer to Exhibit 11-9 and find the percentage increase in the CPI for each year shown. Ask: In what year is the highest percentage increase found? What is the highest percentage increase? The highest percentage increase is found in 2000, and it is 3.36% (*calculation:* $[(CPI_{\text{later year}} - CPI_{\text{earlier year}}) \div CPI_{\text{earlier year}}] \times 100$ = percentage increase in CPI; $[(172.2 - 166.6) \div 166.6] \times 100 = 3.36\%$).

Reinforcement Activity

Ask students why it is important to find out if prices are changing from one month to the next or from one year to the next. Students might say that workers need to know that prices are going up so that they can more readily bargain for higher wages. If they didn't know that prices were rising, they wouldn't as readily ask for higher wages. In short, knowing what is happening to prices tells us what is happening to our standard of living. Suppose prices go up and our wages are constant; then we know that our standard of living is declining.

Internet Research

Direct students to the Web site of the U.S. Bureau of Labor Statistics. They should find the "CPI" section, then select "Tables Created by the BLS." Have students graph the average percentage changes for a 20-year period. Ask them to analyze their graphs and explain what economic factors might contribute to the CPI's high and low points during this period.

Economics in the Real World

This feature may be a good beginning point for comparing prices of various products over time. One fun way to do this is to assign students to look at old newspapers or catalogs for prices and then have them use the CPI formula to find how much the product would cost today. This can be even more interesting when the product still exists, manufactured by the same firm.

ANSWERS TO THINK ABOUT IT If a house cost \$45,000 in 1970, the price of the house in 2005 dollars would be approximately \$231,666.66 (*calculation:* \$45,000 × (194.6 ÷ 37.8)).

Economics Around the Clock

Discuss students' answers to the 2:34 P.M. scenario in Economics Around the Clock (page 287).

Help them realize that Beverlee's father's mistake is that he is comparing his salary, earned many years ago when prices were lower, with Beverlee's salary, earned today when prices are much higher. It is not the correct comparison to make. It would be better to convert both his salary and Beverlee's salary into today's dollars and then compare them. We have practiced this in two Economics in the Real World features in this chapter: the one on movies and the one on President Kennedy's salary.

Economics in the Real World

Did President Kennedy Earn More than Today's President?

Today, the president of the United States earns an annual salary of \$400,000. In 1962, when John F. Kennedy was president, he earned \$100,000. Would you say that the president today is paid four times more than President Kennedy was paid?

At first glance, it may seem that today's president is paid more than Kennedy. We need to keep in mind, however, that when Kennedy was president the prices of goods and services were much lower than today. In 1962, \$100,000 would buy much more than \$100,000 will buy today. The question is, would it buy four times as much in 1962 as it will buy today?

To get some idea of what a \$100,000 salary in 1962 would equal in today's dollars, economists use the following formula:

$$\text{Salary in today's dollars} = \text{Salary in earlier year} \times (CPI_{today}/CPI_{1962})$$

Suppose that by "today" we mean 2005. We want to find out what Kennedy's 1962 salary is equal to in 2005 dollars. The CPI in April 2005 was 194.6, and the CPI in 1962 was about 30. Filling in the formula, we see that Kennedy's salary in 1962 is equivalent to earning \$648,667 in 2005.

$$\text{Salary in today's dollars} = \$100,000 \times (194.6/30) = \$648,667$$

President Kennedy, in 1962, earned more than the president today earns, in terms of purchasing power. Kennedy earned the equivalent of \$648,667 in today's (2005) dollars, and the president today earns \$400,000. In other words, Kennedy was paid the equivalent of \$248,667 more than the president today is paid.

THINK ABOUT IT Suppose a house cost \$45,000 in 1970, and the CPI in 1970 was 37.8. What is the price of the house in 2005 dollars (CPI in 2005 = 194.6)?

(left to right) and the supply in a market with an upward-sloping supply curve (left to right). As you may recall, equilibrium price and quantity in a market (the point at which the demand curve and the supply curve intersect) are determined by the forces of supply and demand.

What holds for a market holds for an economy, too; any economy has a demand side and a supply side, as illustrated in Exhibit 11-10. The demand side is represented by the **aggregate demand curve**, which shows the quantity of goods and services that buyers are willing and able to buy at different price levels. (Sometimes the quantity of goods and services is simply referred to as output or as real GDP.) The supply side is represented by the **aggregate supply curve**, which shows the quantity of goods and services, or output, that producers are willing and able to supply at different price levels. The equilibrium price level and equilibrium quantity of goods and services are determined by the forces of aggregate demand and aggregate supply.

The forces of aggregate demand and supply determine the equilibrium price level and equilibrium quantity of goods and services (equilibrium output) in an economy. The equilibrium price level (P_E in Exhibit 11-10) and the equilibrium quantity of goods and services, or output (Q_E in Exhibit

aggregate demand curve
A curve that shows the quantity of goods and services that buyers are willing and able to buy at different price levels.

aggregate supply curve
A curve that shows the quantity of goods and services that producers are willing and able to supply at different price levels.

Internet Research

Instruct students to browse online news sources to find examples of current events that could change the aggregate supply or aggregate demand curves. Ask them to list their findings, along with an explanation of the effect that each of the events might have on either of these two curves. Ask them to use specific information about supply and demand that they have learned from their textbook.

EXHIBIT 11-10 Aggregate Demand and Aggregate Supply

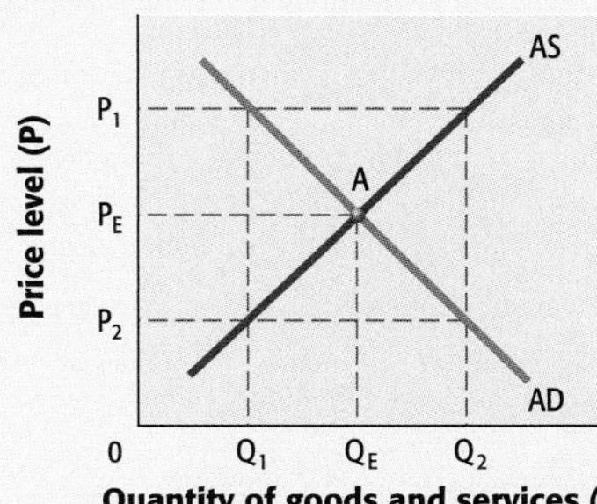

	When price level is	Buyers are willing and able to buy	Sellers are willing and able to sell	Remarks
Look at AD only	P_1	Q_1	—	Buyers are willing and able to buy more at lower price levels than at higher price levels.
	P_2	Q_2	—	
Look at AS only	P_1	—	Q_2	Sellers are willing and able to produce and sell more at higher price levels than at lower price levels.
	P_2	—	Q_1	
Look at AD and AS together	P_1	Q_1	Q_2	Buyers are willing and able to buy less than sellers are willing and able to produce and sell.
	P_2	Q_2	Q_1	Buyers are willing and able to buy more than sellers are willing and able to produce and sell.
	P_E	Q_E	Q_E	At equilibrium, buyers are willing and able to buy the same amount as sellers are willing and able to produce and sell.

◀ Equilibrium in an economy comes about through the economic forces of aggregate demand (AD) and aggregate supply (AS). The economy is in equilibrium at point A in the exhibit.

11-10), come to exist over time. For example, at P_1 the quantity demanded of goods and services (Q_1) is less than the quantity supplied of goods and services (Q_2), resulting in a surplus of goods and services. As a result, the price level drops. At a lower price level, people buy more goods and services, and producers produce less. The surplus begins to disappear because of these actions on the part of buyers and sellers. (Buyers are helping to eliminate the surplus by buying more, and sellers are helping to eliminate the surplus by producing less.)

At P_2, the quantity demanded of goods and services (Q_2) is greater than the quantity supplied (Q_1), which means a shortage of goods and services. Thus, the price level rises, people buy fewer goods and services, and producers produce more. The shortage begins to disappear because of the actions of buyers and sellers. (Buyers are helping to eliminate the shortage by buying less, and sellers are helping to eliminate the shortage by producing more.) Only at P_E is the quantity of goods and services supplied equal to the quantity of goods and services demanded; both are Q_E.

Aggregate supply and demand are influenced by a number of factors and act as an influence on some other factors. One of the factors that aggregate supply and demand impact is unemployment, which we discuss next.

Teaching with Visuals

In this chapter we have studied three major topics: GDP, real GDP, and the consumer price index. All three of these can be seen in Exhibit 11-10. In the exhibit, the price level is on the vertical axis; the quantity of goods and services, or real GDP, is on the horizontal axis; and GDP is simply the product of what is on the vertical axis (P) and the horizontal axis (Q).

Discussion Starter

Ask students to define an aggregate demand curve and an aggregate supply curve. Encourage them to put the definitions in their own words and to give examples. The aggregate demand / aggregate supply framework is used often in economics. Tell students that understanding this concept is very important, and that they will use it in a future chapter.

Background Information: Movie Sales

Once students have worked on the CPI formula for calculating current dollars, they should be able to apply it to anything, including blockbuster movies of the past. Some Disney movies, including *Snow White and the Seven Dwarfs, Fantasia, 101 Dalmatians, Bambi, Mary Poppins,* and *Sleeping Beauty* are among the highest grossing movies of all time in current dollars. Ask students why they think these movies have grossed so much money. The answer is that copies of these movies continue to sell in stores while other classic movies do not have current sales.

Economics in the Real World

Ask if students were surprised to learn that *Gone with the Wind* is the top-grossing movie of all time. Which movie did they think would be the top earner?

ANSWERS TO THINK ABOUT IT Answers will vary.

Economics Around the Clock

Invite students to share their answers to the 8:00 P.M. scenario in Economics Around the Clock (page 287). Make sure they understand that to compare the profits of the two movies, we should convert the gross receipts into today's dollars.

Application Activity

After reading and discussing Section 4, you may want to assign the Section Activity in the *Applying the Principles Workbook.*

Assess

Quick Quiz

The following true-or-false quiz will help you assess student understanding of the material covered in this section.

1. The average price level is known as the price appendix. (False)
2. The consumer price index is calculated by the U.S. Treasury. (False)
3. The quantity of goods and services is simply referred to as output. (True)
4. An upward sloping aggregate supply curve indicates that producers are willing and able to produce and offer to sell a greater quantity of goods at higher price levels than at lower price levels. (True)
5. The forces of aggregate demand and supply determine the equilibrium price level and equilibrium quantity of goods and services in an economy. (True)

Economics in the Real World

What Is the All-Time Top-Grossing Movie?

Someone comes up to you and asks what is the top-grossing movie of all time in the United States. Do you know the answer? As of this writing, it is *Titanic*, which grossed $660 million in the United States and $1.8 billion worldwide. Some other movies that make the 10 top-grossing movies in the United States list include *Star Wars* (1977), *Shrek 2*, *E.T.*, and *Spider-Man*.

A slight problem arises when we realize that movies in the top 10 list were released in different years. For example, *Titanic* was released in 1997, *Star Wars* was released 20 years earlier in 1977, and *E.T.* was released in 1982. Now not only were ticket prices different in these different years, but the prices of almost all goods and services were different too. For example, the CPI in 1977 was 58.5, but it was 94.3 in 1982, and 160.5 in 1997.

If we simply compare the gross receipts for movies in different years—without taking into account that prices are different in different years—we are making an inaccurate comparison. It is like comparing apples with oranges. To make an accurate and reasonable comparison, we need to convert the gross receipts for all movies (no matter what year the movie was released) into today's dollars. When we do, *Titanic* falls from the top of the list. In fact, it falls all the way to sixth place. The top-grossing movie of all time in the United States turns out to be *Gone with the Wind*, which was released in 1937. *Star Wars* (1977) comes in second and *The Sound of Music* comes in third.

THINK ABOUT IT The list of the top 100 movies of all time is released periodically, but rarely is any attempt made to convert the gross receipts of each movie into today's dollars. Why do you suppose they aren't compared in terms of today's dollars?

Who Are the Unemployed?

Look at Exhibit 11-11 on the next page, which shows the employment status of the entire United States population. Notice at the far left of the exhibit the total population, which is then divided into two broad groups. One group consists of persons under 16 years of age, in the armed forces, or in a mental or correctional facility. The other group, which consists of all others in the total population, is called the *noninstitutional adult civilian population.*

> ***"The study of economics won't necessarily keep you out of the unemployment line, but at least if you're there, you'll understand why."***
> — ANONYMOUS

Now take the noninstitutional adult civilian population and divide it into two groups: persons *not in the labor force* and persons in the *civilian labor force*. The persons not in the labor force are those who are neither working nor looking for work. Retired persons fall into this category, as do those engaged in homemaking in their own homes and persons who choose not to work.

Finally, persons in the civilian labor force can be divided into two groups: they are either *employed* or *unemployed.*

Civilian labor force =
Unemployed persons + Employed persons

Differentiating Instruction

English Language Learners

To help ELL students, use the following resources, which are provided as part of the *Economics: New Ways of Thinking* program:

- a Spanish glossary in the *Student Text*
- Spanish versions of the Chapter Summaries on an audio CD

EXHIBIT 11-11 **Breakdown of the Total U.S. Population by Employment Status**

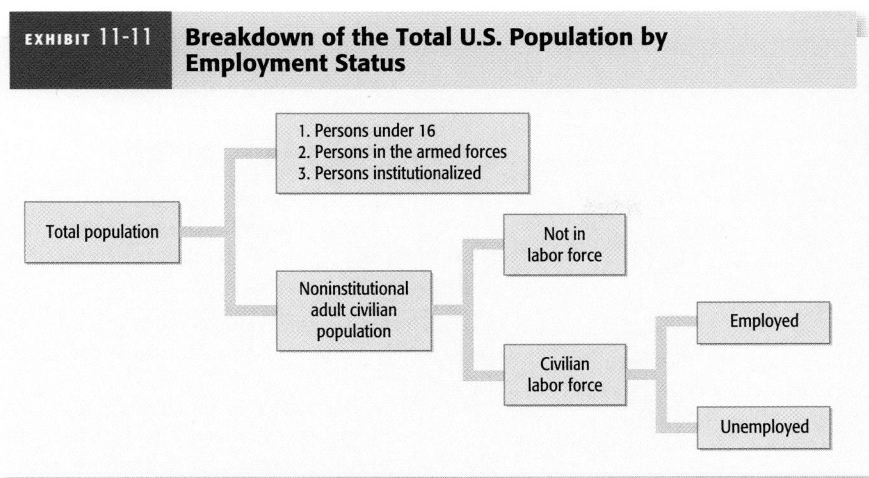

◀ **In which of the boxes shown in the exhibit do you belong? Think of different people you know and try to determine which category they are currently in.**

The Unemployment and Employment Rates

The **unemployment rate** is the percentage of the civilian labor force that is unemployed. It is equal to the number of unemployed persons divided by the civilian labor force.

Unemployment rate =
Unemployed persons/Civilian labor force

For example, if the civilian labor force totals 10 million, and the number of persons unemployed is 1 million, then the unemployment rate is 10 percent. Exhibit R-14 in the Databank at the back of the book shows the unemployment rate in the United States in each year during the period 1980–2005.

The **employment rate** is the percentage of the noninstitutional adult civilian population that is employed. It is equal to the number of persons employed divided by the number of persons in the noninstitutional adult civilian population:

Employment rate = Employed persons/
Noninstitutional adult civilian population

unemployment rate
The percentage of the civilian labor force that is unemployed.

employment rate
The percentage of the noninstitutional adult civilian population that is employed.

Defining Terms

1. Define:
   - **a.** price index
   - **b.** consumer price index
   - **c.** aggregate demand curve
   - **d.** aggregate supply curve
   - **e.** unemployment rate
   - **f.** employment rate

Reviewing Facts and Concepts

2. Suppose the CPI was 143 in year 1 and 132 in year 2. Did prices rise or fall between year 1 and year 2?
3. The noninstitutional adult civilian population is 120 million, the number of unemployed persons is 5 million, and the number of employed persons is 60 million. What is the unemployment rate?

Critical Thinking

4. What can cause the equilibrium price level to rise? What can cause the equilibrium quantity of goods and services (in the economy) to fall? (*Hint:* Look at Exhibit 11-10.)

Applying Economic Concepts

5. Smith earned $40,000 in 2003 and $50,000 in 2004. The CPI was 184.0 in 2003 and 188.9 in 2004. Using the data presented, how can Smith figure out whether his earnings went up by more than, less than, or equal to the change in prices?

Assessment Book

You will find a quiz for this section in the *Assessment Book.*

Reteaching Activity

Use the Section Assessment to gauge which students may need reteaching on this section. With those students, review the paragraph on page 303 that begins with "Notice that the CPI is just a number." Make sure that students understand the usefulness of the CPI when used to track prices over time.

Guided Reading

For further reteaching of the key concepts in this section, assign the Outlining Activity and the Just the Facts Handout from the *Guided Reading and Study Guide.*

Defining Terms

1. a. price index: a measure of the price level, or the average level of prices; **b. consumer price index:** the most widely cited price index; **c. aggregate demand curve:** shows the quantity of goods and services that buyers are willing and able to buy at different price levels; **d. aggregate supply curve:** shows the quantity of goods and services that producers are willing and able to supply at different price levels; **e. unemployment rate:** the percentage of the civilian labor force that is unemployed; **f. employment rate:** percentage of the noninstitutional adult civilian population that is employed.

Reviewing Facts and Concepts

2. Prices fell.

3. The unemployment rate is 4% (*calculation:* UR = 5 million ÷ 120 million = 0.04).

Critical Thinking

4. The equilibrium price level will rise if (a) the aggregate demand curve shifts to the right or (b) the aggregate supply curve shifts to the left. The equilibrium quantity of goods and services will fall if (a) the aggregate demand curve shifts to the left or (b) the aggregate supply curve shifts to the left.

Applying Economic Concepts

5. Smith needs to do two things. First, he needs to figure out the percentage increase in his earnings from one year to the next (*calculation:* ($50,000 – $40,000) ÷ $40,000 × 100% = 25%). Next, he must figure out the percentage increase in prices from one year to the next (*calculation:* 188.9 – 184 ÷ 184 × 100% = 2.66%). From there, he needs to compare the percentage increase in his earnings with the percentage increase in prices. He can then see that his earnings went up by a greater percentage than prices increased.

CHAPTER 11 Assessment Answers

Economics Vocabulary

1. GDP; **2.** GNP; **3.** double counting; **4.** consumption; **5.** investment; **6.** base year; **7.** aggregate demand curve; **8.** Aggregate demand, aggregate supply; **9.** Real GDP; **10.** government purchases; **11.** export spending; **12.** employment rate.

Understanding the Main Ideas

1. Government transfer payments are unrelated to the production of goods and services.
2. The GDP measures output produced within the borders of a country; the GNP measures the output produced by the citizens of a country, no matter where they reside. The GDP is relevant to geography; the GNP is relevant to citizenship.
3. There is no record of illegal transactions.
4. Stock transactions simply bring about a change in the ownership of assets; there is no production.
5. A final good is in the hands of a consumer or end user of the good. An intermediate good is not.
6. Real GDP figures have been adjusted for price changes. When an economist sees that the real GDP is higher in year 2 than in year 1, she knows why: quantity of output is higher in year 2. But when an economist sees that the GDP is higher in year 2 than in year 1, she does not know why. It could be because quantity of output is higher, because prices are higher, or because both are higher. An economist has greater certainty with real GDP than with GDP.
7. Exhibit 11-6 shows that consumption is the largest spending component of GDP.
8. Because GDP = C + I + G + EX – IM, if import spending (IM) rises and nothing else changes, then GDP falls.
9. The unemployment rate is the percentage of the civilian labor force that is not employed. Unemployment rate = unemployed persons ÷ civilian labor force. The employment rate is the percentage of the noninstitutional adult civilian population that is employed. Employment rate = employed persons ÷ noninstitutional adult civilian population.
10. No, it is not possible, because Unemployment rate = unemployed persons ÷ civilian labor force.

Doing the Math

1. $6 trillion (*calculation:* $3.2 trillion + $1.2 trillion + $1.9 trillion + $1.5 trillion – $1.8 trillion = $6 trillion).
2. 162.5 (*calculation:* for the base year, x = 10 × $1 = $10; y = 15 × $2 = $30; and x + y = $10 + $30 = $40; for the current year, x = 10 × $2 = $20;

CHAPTER 11 ASSESSMENT

Chapter Summary

Be sure you know and remember the following key points from the chapter sections.

Section 1

- Gross domestic product (GDP) is the total market value of all final goods and services produced annually in a country.
- Some exchanges, such as illegal transactions and those with no record, are omitted from the GDP measurement.

Section 2

- Economists break the economy into four sectors: household, business, government, and foreign.
- To compute U.S. GDP we need to sum consumption (C), investment (I), government purchases (G), and export spending (EX), and then subtract import spending (IM).
- Greater production of goods and services (higher GDP) is a factor that contributes to people being better off.

Section 3

- Real GDP is equal to price in the base year times quantity in the current year.
- Economists use a base year to analyze changes in production and prices.

Section 4

- To calculate the change in prices from one year to the next, economists compute a price index.
- The consumer price index (CPI) is calculated by sampling households to determine what consumers paid for a group of goods called the market basket.
- The forces of an economy's aggregate demand and supply determine the equilibrium price level and equilibrium quantity of goods and services.
- The unemployment rate equals the unemployed persons divided by the civilian labor force.

Economics Vocabulary

To reinforce your knowledge of the key terms in this chapter, fill in the following blanks on a separate piece of paper with the appropriate word or phrase.

1. The total market value of all final goods and services produced annually in an economy is called ______.
2. The total market value of all final goods and services produced annually by the citizens of a country, no matter where in the world they reside, is called ______.
3. Counting a good more than once in computing GDP is called ______.
4. The household sector makes expenditures called ______.
5. The business sector makes expenditures called ______.
6. Real GDP is measured in ______ prices.
7. The ______ shows the quantity of goods and services that buyers are willing and able to buy at different price levels.
8. ______ and ______ go together to determine the equilibrium price level and the equilibrium quantity of goods and services in an economy.
9. ______ is GDP that has been adjusted for price changes.
10. ______ refers to expenditures made by the government sector.
11. Expenditures made by the people in foreign countries who are buying U.S.-produced goods are called ______.
12. The ______ is the percentage of the noninstitutional adult civilian population that is employed.

Understanding the Main Ideas

Write answers to the following questions to review the main ideas in this chapter.

1. Why does the GDP omit government transfer payments?
2. What is the difference between GDP and GNP?
3. Why does GDP omit illegal transactions?
4. Why does GDP omit stock transactions?

5. What is the difference between an intermediate good and a final good?
6. Why does an economist prefer to work with real GDP figures over GDP figures?
7. Which spending component of GDP is the largest?
8. What happens to GDP if import spending rises and no other spending component of GDP changes?
9. What is the unemployment rate? The employment rate?
10. Is it possible for the unemployment rate to rise as the number of unemployed persons falls? Explain.

Doing the Math

Do the calculations necessary to solve the following problems.

1. Using the following data, compute the GDP: consumption = $3. 2 trillion; government purchases = $1.2 trillion; export spending = $1.9 trillion; import spending = $1.8 trillion; and investment = $1.5 trillion.
2. A tiny economy produces 10 units of good X and 15 units of good Y. Base-year prices for these goods are $1 and $2, respectively. Current-year prices for these goods are $2 and $3. What is the CPI?
3. Using the data in question 2, what does real GDP equal?
4. In Exhibit 11-8, change the prices in column 2 to $14 for CDs and $6 for T-shirts. Change the prices in column 4 to $17 for CDs and $8 for T-shirts. Now calculate the CPI.
5. The CPI is 143 in year 1 and 132 in year 2. By what percentage have prices fallen?
6. Total population = 145 million; noninstitutional adult civilian population = 135 million; persons not in the labor force = 10 million; unemployed persons = 7 million. Using these data, compute the following:
   a. The unemployment rate
   b. The employment rate
   c. The civilian labor force

Working with Graphs and Tables

Look at Exhibit 11-12. Fill in each blank, (a) through (f), with the correct dollar amount.

EXHIBIT 11-12

Goods in market basket	Price in base year	Base-year expenditure	Price in current year	Current-year expenditure
10 X	$4	(b)	(c)	$50
12 Y	(a)	$120	$12	(d)

Total dollar expenditure on market basket in current year = (e)

Total dollar expenditure on market basket in base year = (f)

Solving Economic Problems

1. **Cause and Effect.** Does a higher GDP cause higher prices, or do higher prices cause a higher GDP? Explain your answer.
2. **Writing.** Find a recent copy of the Economic Report of the President in your library or on the Web at www.emcp.net/economicreport. Click on "Downloadable Reports/Tables." Next, click the most recent year under "Downloadable Entire Reports." The report contains chapters on different economic topics. Choose one of the chapters to read; then write a two-page paper that briefly explains the content of the chapter.
3. **Economics in the Media.** Find a story or article in your local newspaper that addresses one of the following: GDP, real GDP, CPI, unemployment rate, consumption spending, investment spending, or government spending. Explain what was said in the story or article.

Practice Tests and Study Guide

Go to www.emcp.net/economics and choose *Economics: New Ways of Thinking,* Chapter 11, if you need more help in preparing for the chapter test.

Working with Graphs and Tables

(a) $10 (*calculation:* $120 ÷ 12 = $10); (b) $40 (*calculation:* 10 × $4 = $40); (c) $5 (*calculation:* $50 ÷ 10 = $5); (d) $144 (*calculation:* 12 × $12 = $144); (e) $194 (*calculation:* $50 + $144 = $194); (f) $160 (*calculation:* $40 + $120 = $160).

Solving Economic Problems

1. Price is a component of GDP; GDP is not a component of price. It follows, then, that higher prices cause a higher GDP.
2. Answers will vary.
3. Answers will vary.

y = 15 × $3 = $45; and $20 + $45 = $65. $65 ÷ 40 × 100 = 162.5).
3. $40 (*calculation:* Real GDP for good X = $1 × 10 units = $10; Real GDP for good Y = $2 × 15 units = $30; Total real GDP for both X and Y = $10; + $30 = $40).
4. 123.53 (*calculation:* Total dollar expenditure (TDE) for base year = ($10 × $14) + ($5 × $6) = $140 + $30 = $170; TDE for current year = ($10 × $17) + ($5 × $8) = $170 + $40 = $210; (Total current year expenditure ÷ total base year expenditure) × 100 = ($210 ÷ $170) × 100 = 123.53).
5. Prices have fallen by 7.69% (*calculation:* ($132 – $143) ÷ $132 × 100 = 7.69).
6. a. 5%; **b.** 87%; **c.** $125 million.

Chapter 12 Planning Guide

SECTION ORGANIZER

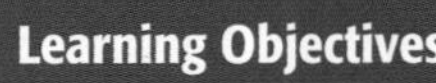

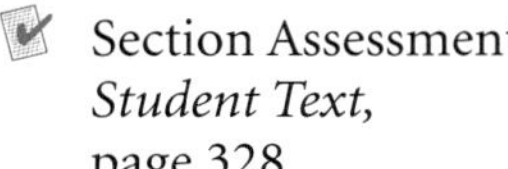
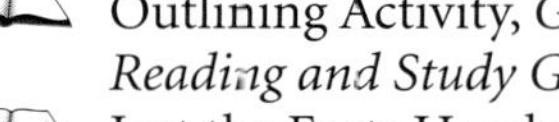

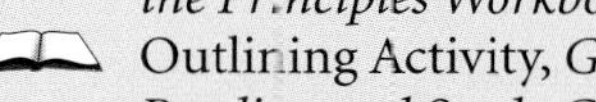

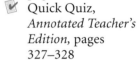

Section	Learning Objectives	Reproducible Worksheets and Handouts	Assessment
SECTION 1 **Inflation and Deflation** (pages 312–322)	▸ Describe inflation. ▸ Explain how inflation is measured. ▸ Identify causes of inflation. ▸ Describe deflation. ▸ Identify causes of deflation.	Section 1 Activity, *Applying the Principles Workbook* Outlining Activity, *Guided Reading and Study Guide* Just the Facts Handout, *Guided Reading and Study Guide*	Section Assessment, *Student Text,* page 322 Quick Quiz, *Annotated Teacher's Edition,* pages 321–322 Section Quiz, *Assessment Book*
SECTION 2 **Business Cycles** (pages 323–328)	▸ Describe a business cycle. ▸ Explain how economists forecast business cycles. ▸ Identify some economic indicators. ▸ Identify some causes of business cycles. ▸ Explain how politics cause upward and downward movements in the economy.	Section 2 Activity, *Applying the Principles Workbook* Outlining Activity, *Guided Reading and Study Guide* Just the Facts Handout, *Guided Reading and Study Guide*	Section Assessment, *Student Text,* page 328 Quick Quiz, *Annotated Teacher's Edition,* pages 327–328 Section Quiz, *Assessment Book*
SECTION 3 **Economic Growth** (pages 329–335)	▸ Describe the difference between absolute real economic growth and per capita real economic growth. ▸ Explain the purpose of the Rule of 72. ▸ Explain whether small differences in economic growth matter. ▸ Identify causes of economic growth. ▸ Explain arguments against economic growth.	Section 3 Activity, *Applying the Principles Workbook* Outlining Activity, *Guided Reading and Study Guide* Just the Facts Handout, *Guided Reading and Study Guide*	Section Assessment, *Student Text,* page 335 Quick Quiz, *Annotated Teacher's Edition,* pages 334–335 Section Quiz, *Assessment Book*

CHAPTER AND PROGRAM RESOURCES

Reproducible Chapter Resources and Assessment Materials

 Graphic Organizer Activity, *Guided Reading and Study Guide*

 Vocabulary Activity, *Guided Reading and Study Guide*

 Working with Graphs and Charts, *Guided Reading and Study Guide*

 Practice Test, *Guided Reading and Study Guide*

 Critical Thinking Activity, *Finding Economics*

Chapter Test A, *Assessment Book*

Chapter Test B, *Assessment Book*

Technology Resources

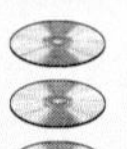 *Test Generator CD*

Spanish Audio Summaries CD

Marketplace® Audio Lessons CD

Economic Principles Lectures, Videocassette or DVD

Lesson Planning and Teaching Resources

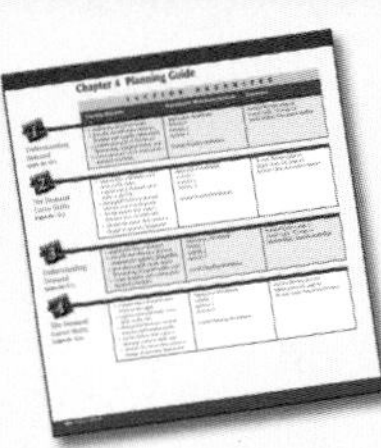

The *Economics: New Ways of Thinking* Teacher Resources include detailed lesson plans for each section in this chapter; the lesson plans are available in print form *(Lesson Plans)* and electronic form. The Teacher Resources also include *Daily Lectures: Overheads and Notes,* which provides prepared overheads and discussion notes covering the key concepts in each section of this chapter.

EMC Publishing Economics Online

Go to Economics Online, at www.emcp.com, for a variety of Internet resources to help you keep your course current and relevant. At Economics Online you will find these items:

- Economics in the News Lessons
- Study Guide Questions
- Practice Tests
- Lesson Plans

Internet Resources

Economics: New Ways of Thinking encourages students to use the Internet to find out more about economics. With the wealth of current, valid information available on Web sites, using the Internet as a research tool is likely to increase your students' interest in and understanding of economics principles and topics. In addition, doing Internet research can help your students form the habit of accessing and using economics information, as well as help them develop investigative skills they will use throughout their educational and professional careers.

To aid your students in achieving these ends, each chapter of *Economics: New Ways of Thinking* includes the addresses of several Web sites at which students will find engaging, relevant information. When students type in the addresses provided, they will immediately arrive at the intended sites. The addresses have been modified so that EMC Publishing can monitor and maintain the proper links—for example, the government site http://stats.bls.gov/ has been changed to www.emcp.net/prices. In the event that the address or content of a site changes or is discontinued, EMC's Internet editors will create a link that redirects students to an address with similar information.

Activities in the *Annotated Teacher's Edition* often suggest that students search the Internet for information. For some activities, you might want to find reputable sites beforehand, and steer students to those sites. For other activities, you might want students to do their own searching, and then check out the sites they have found and discuss why they might be reliable or unreliable.

CHAPTER 12 Overview

This chapter identifies some causes and effects of inflation and deflation, and discusses business cycles and economic growth. The ups and downs of business cycles, changes in real gross domestic product (GDP), and changing standards of living create the economic environment in which we spend much of our lives.

Inflation and Deflation

Section 1 discusses the concepts of inflation and deflation. Students will learn what causes inflation and deflation, how they are measured, and what their effects are.

Business Cycles

Section 2 examines the business cycle, which is one of the predicting tools of economists. Students will learn the phases of the business cycle and how economists use various indicators to forecast business cycles.

Economic Growth

Section 3 explores economic growth. Students will learn the difference between absolute real economic growth and per-capita economic growth. They will also discover how the production possibilities frontier shows what absolute real economic growth looks like.

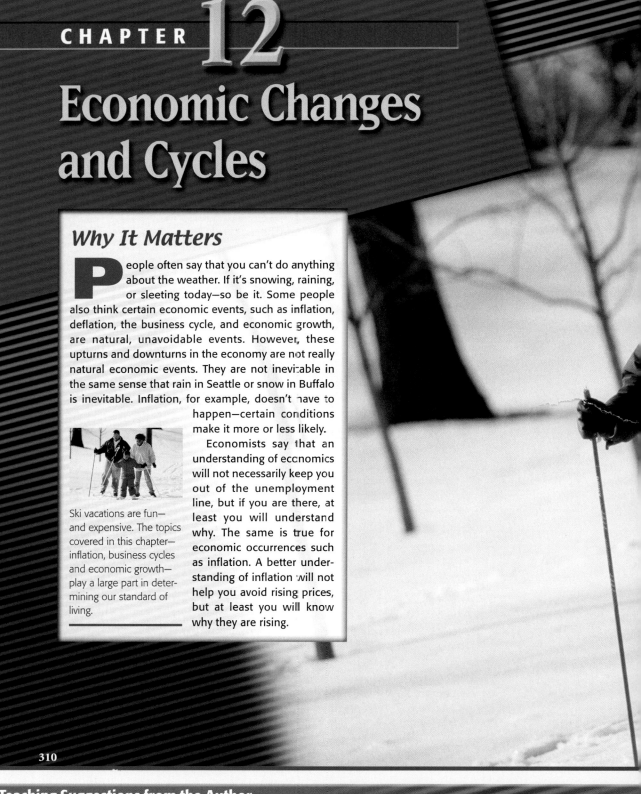

CHAPTER 12 Economic Changes and Cycles

Why It Matters

People often say that you can't do anything about the weather. If it's snowing, raining, or sleeting today—so be it. Some people also think certain economic events, such as inflation, deflation, the business cycle, and economic growth, are natural, unavoidable events. However, these upturns and downturns in the economy are not really natural economic events. They are not inevitable in the same sense that rain in Seattle or snow in Buffalo is inevitable. Inflation, for example, doesn't have to happen—certain conditions make it more or less likely.

Economists say that an understanding of economics will not necessarily keep you out of the unemployment line, but if you are there, at least you will understand why. The same is true for economic occurrences such as inflation. A better understanding of inflation will not help you avoid rising prices, but at least you will know why they are rising.

Ski vacations are fun—and expensive. The topics covered in this chapter—inflation, business cycles and economic growth—play a large part in determining our standard of living.

Teaching Suggestions from the Author

This chapter presents the main topics of concern for macroeconomists—inflation, deflation, business cycles, and economic growth.

I like to begin a discussion of inflation and deflation by asking students to define each and to identify causal factors for each. It is then a good idea to talk about the personal costs of each. How are people harmed by inflation? Are people harmed by deflation? Does the state of the economy matter to one's standard of living? Does it matter to one's happiness?

Increasingly, business cycles and economic growth have come to be the most important topics of study in macroeconomics. Economists know that the standard of living of a people depends largely on the economy's

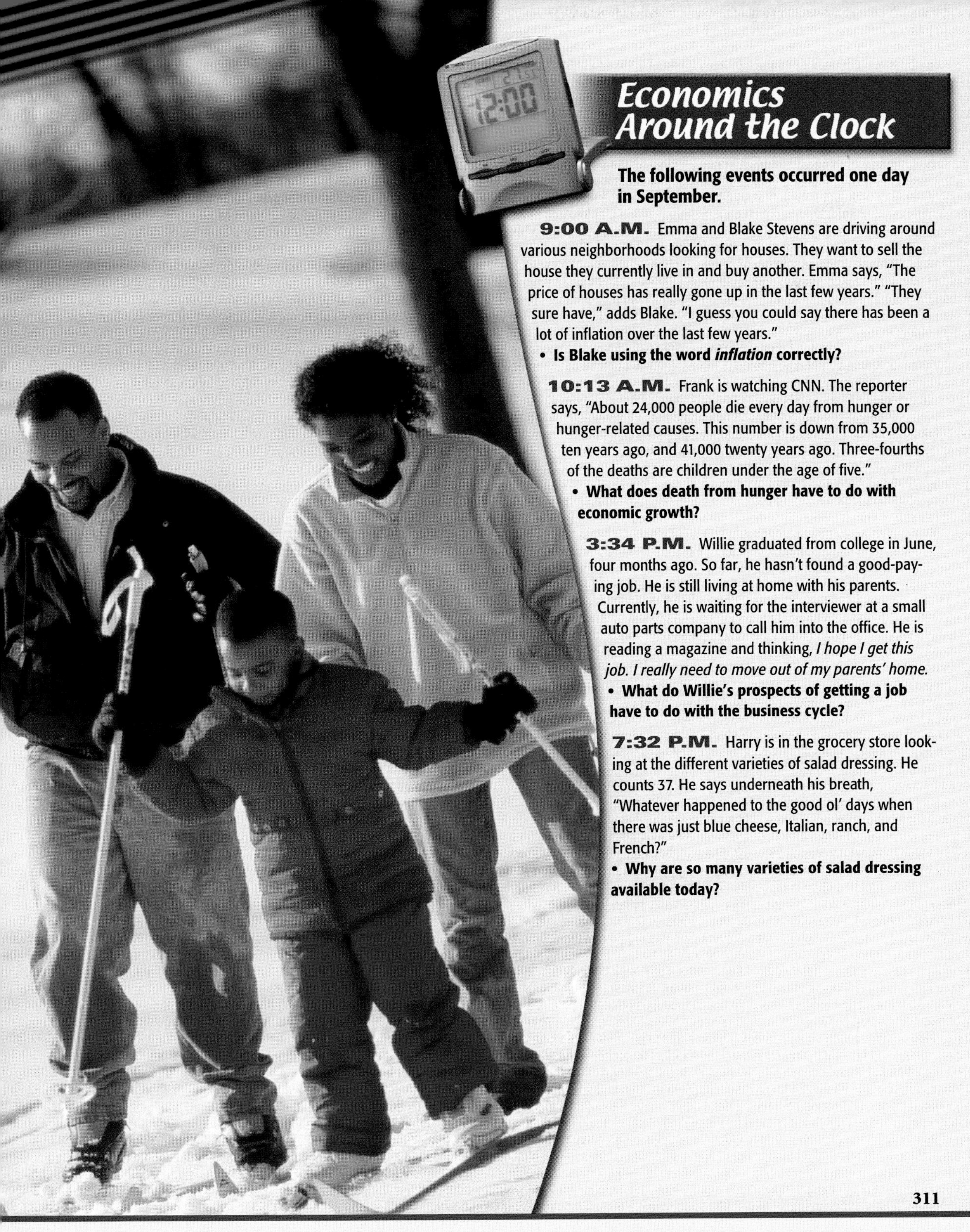

Economics Around the Clock

The following events occurred one day in September.

9:00 A.M. Emma and Blake Stevens are driving around various neighborhoods looking for houses. They want to sell the house they currently live in and buy another. Emma says, "The price of houses has really gone up in the last few years." "They sure have," adds Blake. "I guess you could say there has been a lot of inflation over the last few years."

- **Is Blake using the word *inflation* correctly?**

10:13 A.M. Frank is watching CNN. The reporter says, "About 24,000 people die every day from hunger or hunger-related causes. This number is down from 35,000 ten years ago, and 41,000 twenty years ago. Three-fourths of the deaths are children under the age of five."

- **What does death from hunger have to do with economic growth?**

3:34 P.M. Willie graduated from college in June, four months ago. So far, he hasn't found a good-paying job. He is still living at home with his parents. Currently, he is waiting for the interviewer at a small auto parts company to call him into the office. He is reading a magazine and thinking, *I hope I get this job. I really need to move out of my parents' home.*

- **What do Willie's prospects of getting a job have to do with the business cycle?**

7:32 P.M. Harry is in the grocery store looking at the different varieties of salad dressing. He counts 37. He says underneath his breath, "Whatever happened to the good ol' days when there was just blue cheese, Italian, ranch, and French?"

- **Why are so many varieties of salad dressing available today?**

growth rate. Adam Smith, the famous 18th-century economist, wanted to know why some nations are rich and some nations are poor. This has been a key macroeconomic question for over two centuries. Ask students what they think determines the wealth and poverty of nations.

Introducing the Chapter

To introduce Chapter 12, you might want students to focus on just how important inflation, deflation, business cycles, and economic growth are as political issues. Ask students what they think are some of the larger issues facing this country today. Students may include such issues as crime, violence, racism, drugs, poverty, homelessness, AIDS, and so on. Have a volunteer list students' responses on the board.

After you have compiled a reasonably lengthy list, have students read Why It Matters on page 310. Point out that inflation, deflation, business cycles, and economic growth seem to be difficult to understand at first but knowing how the economy changes over time may give students peace of mind when the fluctuation affects them. Some economists, like Ray Fair of Yale University, think that the economy is directly linked to the person Americans elect as president. You might encourage students to see that many of the social issues are also linked to inflation and unemployment. For example, you might point out that some people argue for a direct link between the crime rate and the unemployment rate.

Teaching with Visuals

Many families like to take regular vacations. Ask students if they think there is a direct relationship between a family's standard of living and the kinds of vacations that the family takes. In what ways would the family's standard of living affect how the family members spend their leisure time?

SECTION 1

Teacher Support

Focus and Motivate

Section Objectives

After completing this section, students will be able to
- describe inflation;
- explain how inflation is measured;
- identify causes of inflation;
- describe deflation; and
- identify causes of deflation.

Economics Around the Clock

Kickoff Activity

Direct students to read the 9:00 A.M. scenario in Economics Around the Clock (page 311) and write their answers to the question. Invite them to share their answers with the class.

Students should see that Blake is not using the word *inflation* correctly. Inflation refers to an increase in the general level of prices, not to an increase in the price of one good. Blake and Emma are talking about the prices of houses. Increased housing prices do not necessarily indicate that the average price of all goods and services combined has risen.

Activating Prior Knowledge

Students often instinctively understand inflation and the effects of inflation. They may know of times when the income in their household does not change, but the cost of goods and services increases. Ask students to identify situations where they were aware of inflation and its effects on them personally.

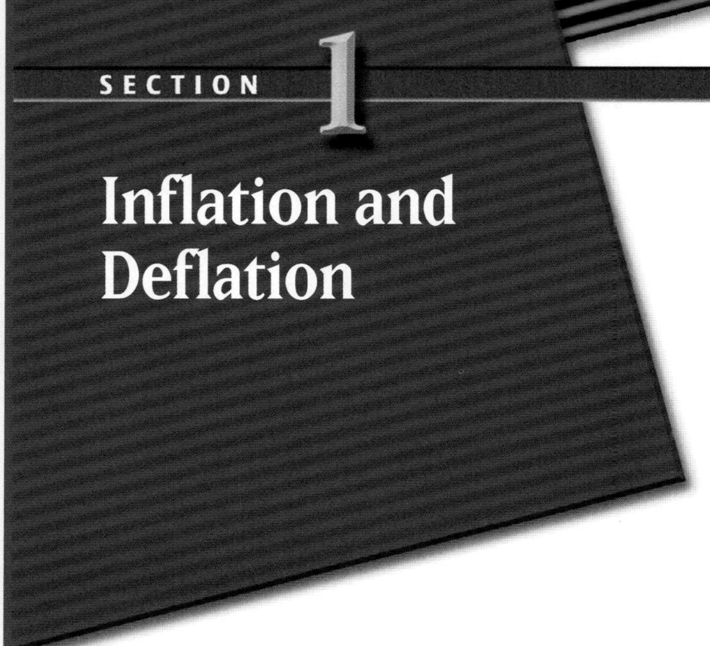

SECTION 1

Inflation and Deflation

Focus Questions
- What is inflation?
- How is inflation measured?
- What causes inflation?
- What is deflation?
- What causes deflation?

Key Terms
inflation
demand-side inflation
supply-side inflation
velocity
simple quantity theory of money
hedge
deflation

What Is Inflation?

Each good produced and sold in the economy has a price. An average of all these prices is called the *price level.*

When someone says that the price level increased, it means that the prices of goods produced and sold in the economy are higher *on average* than they were previously. This does not necessarily mean that every single price in the economy is higher—only that on average, prices are higher. **Inflation** is defined as an increase in the price level.

inflation
An increase in the price level, or average level of prices.

EXAMPLE: Suppose that an economy has three goods (A, B, C), and the prices of the goods are currently $1, $2, and $3, respectively. The average price of these three goods is $2. Now suppose prices change to $1.50, $2.99, and $2.50, respectively. Notice that two prices increased and one decreased. The new average price is $2.33. Because the new average price is higher than the old average price, we have inflation. Notice that it is possible to have inflation even if some prices fall. ♦

How Do We Measure Inflation?

How do we determine whether an economy experienced inflation? If the price level increased, then inflation occurred; if it did not increase, then no inflation occurred.

Chapter 11 explained that the consumer price index (CPI) is used to measure the price level. Suppose the CPI last year was 180, and the CPI this year is also 180. Did inflation occur between the two years? The answer is no, because the price level (as measured by the CPI) did not increase.

Suppose, though, that the CPI was 180 last year and is 187 this year. The increase in the CPI means that inflation occurred between the two years.

It is usually not enough just to know whether inflation occurred. People often want to know how much inflation occurred—they want to measure the rate of inflation. We can find the inflation rate between two years by using the same formula we used in Chapter 11 to find the percentage change in the CPI:

Differentiating Instruction

English Language Learners

Some students may have difficulty understanding the difference between inflation and an increase in price of various items—in other words, between *price* and *price level.* Make sure that students recognize that there is a difference between an increase in the price of a single good and inflation. When the price of houses or tires or cars goes up, it does not necessarily follow that inflation is occurring. As the prices of cars and tires and houses go up, the prices of other goods could be coming down, so that there would be no net increase in the price level. It is only when the price level, or prices on average, increases that inflation is indicated.

Inflation rate =

$$\frac{\text{CPI later year} - \text{CPI earlier year}}{\text{CPI earlier year}} \times 100$$

Filling in the numbers, we get the following:

Inflation rate =

$$\frac{187 - 180}{180} \times 100 = 3.89\%$$

A positive change (rise) in the CPI means inflation occurred; the inflation rate is 3.89 percent.

Exhibit 12-1 shows the CPI over the period 1913 to 2005. As you can see, the CPI rose only slightly during the period from 1913 to 1968, but then begins to increase substantially after that date. One way to interpret this graph is an indicator of what happens to the value of the dollar over time. When the CPI rises, that simply means that a dollar buys less than it used to buy. So, as the CPI rises (in Exhibit 12-1), the value of the dollar falls.

Exhibit 12-2 on the next page shows the inflation rate in the United States during the period from 1960 to 2005. Notice the inflation rate in the late 1970s and early 1980s compared with today.

Demand-Side Versus Supply-Side Inflation

Chapters 4 and 5 discussed supply and demand in a market setting. When the demand for a good increases and supply remains the same, price increases; and when the supply of a good decreases and demand remains the same, price increases. Chapter 11 introduced the concept of supply and demand in an economy. The demand side of the economy was represented by *aggregate demand*, and the supply side of the economy was represented by *aggregate supply*.

Inflation, which is an increase in the price level, can originate on either the demand side or the supply side of the economy. Consider Exhibit 12-3(a), which depicts an aggregate demand curve (AD_1) and an aggregate supply curve (AS_1). The equilibrium price level is P_1. Suppose aggregate demand increases; the aggregate demand curve shifts rightward, from AD_1 to AD_2.

EXHIBIT 12-1 Consumer Price Index (CPI), 1913–2005

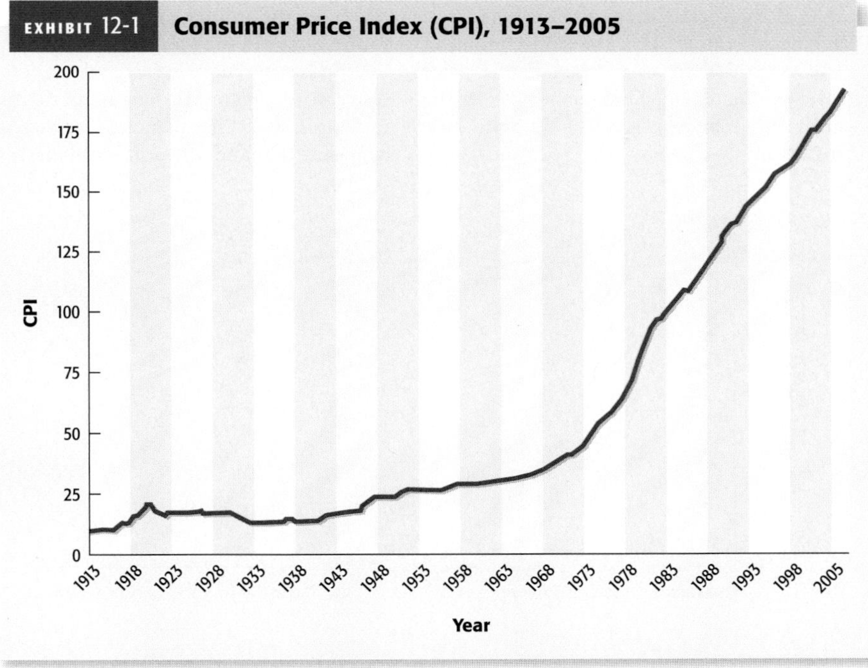

◀ **How would you describe the relationship between the value of the dollar and the CPI?**

Teach

Discussion Starter

Inflation is an increase in the average level of prices. Students may more easily see this phenomenon on the larger scale. Prices have changed a lot since 1950 for products that students still purchase, like soft drinks, shirts, and automobiles. Ask students if they believe that the general price level has risen in the last 50 years or just the price of a few, particular goods and services.

Teaching with Visuals

Students should understand that when the CPI rises, the value of the dollar falls.

Background Information: Inflation and Long Lines

In some countries, prices and wages are set by the government. Markets do not determine prices through the forces of supply and demand; government officials do.

When aggregate demand rises or aggregate supply falls in such countries, price level cannot rise, so inflation results in longer lines of people waiting to buy goods. Instead of prices serving to ration goods, the first-come-first-served (FCFS) rule rations goods, and long lines of people appear. The longer the line is, the higher the inflation rate must be.

Reinforcement Activity

Allow students to look through current newspapers (if the inflation rate is high) or newspapers from earlier years, particularly the late 1970s (if the inflation rate is not high), to find stories on inflation. Assign written reports on their findings or ask students to present findings to the class.

Teaching with Visuals

Exhibit 12-3 shows the two ways the price level can increase—an increase in aggregate demand or a decrease in aggregate supply. Help students understand how these increases in the price level originate.

▶ This graph charts the inflation rate over a 45-year period.

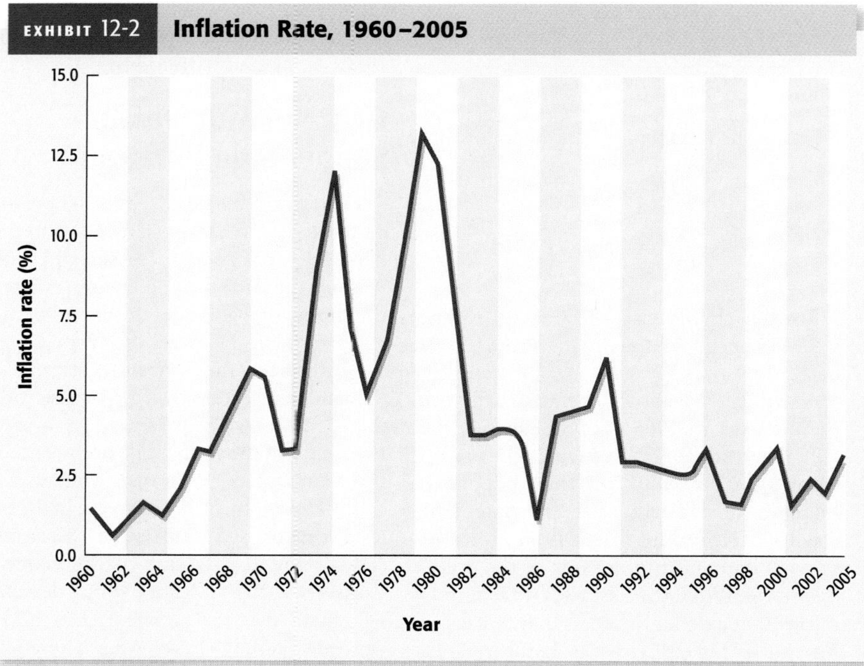

Consequently, the price level increases, from P_1 to P_2. The increase in the price level indicates that inflation occurred. We conclude that if aggregate demand increases and aggregate supply stays the same, inflation will occur. When an increase in the price level originates on the demand side of the economy, economists call it **demand-side inflation**.

demand-side inflation An increase in the price level that originates on the demand side of the economy.

One of the things that can cause demand-side inflation is an increase in the money supply. For example, suppose the Fed increases the money supply. The result is more money in the economy, and so people end up buying more goods and services. In other words, aggregate demand in the economy rises. As a consequence of the increased aggregate demand, the price level increases.

▶ An increase in the price level can be caused by an increase in aggregate demand, or AD, as shown in part (a), or by a decrease in aggregate supply, or AS, as shown in part (b).

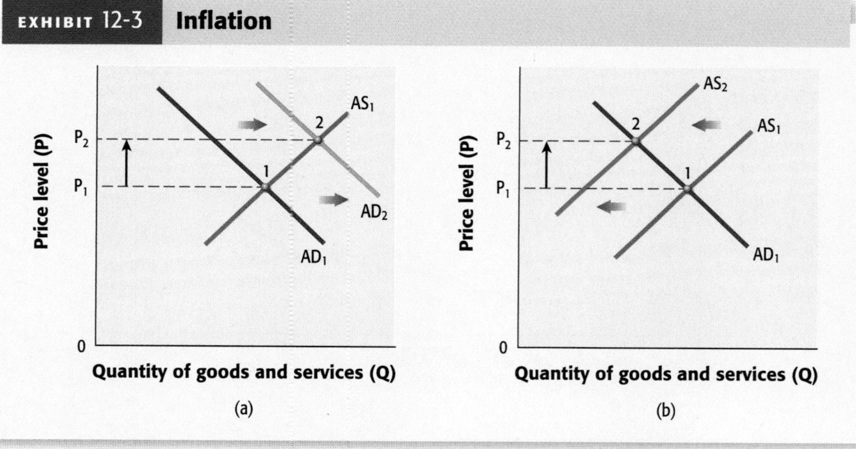

Internet Research

Direct students to use Exhibit 12-2 to examine the inflation rates over the last 20 years. Then have them write paragraphs describing what most likely happened to unemployment rates during these years and why. Finally, direct them to the Web site of the U.S. Department of Labor, Bureau of Labor Statistics, to check their predictions against actual unemployment statistics. Tell them to summarize their findings in a second paragraph.

Exhibit 12-3(b) shows a decrease in aggregate supply, from AS_1 to AS_2. As a result of this decrease, the price level increases, from P_1 to P_2. Again, the increase in price level indicates that inflation occurred. Thus, if aggregate supply decreases and aggregate demand stays the same, inflation will occur. An increase in the price level that originates on the supply side of the economy is called **supply-side inflation**. One of the things that can cause supply-side inflation is a major drought that lowers the output of agricultural goods. As a result the supply of goods in the economy is smaller, and the price level increases.

A Student Asks

QUESTION: *What if both aggregate demand and aggregate supply increase? Will this cause inflation?*

ANSWER: *It depends on how much aggregate demand increases compared to a specific increase in aggregate supply. For example, look at Exhibit 12-4. Initially, the economy is at point 1, and the price level is P_1. Then both aggregate demand and aggregate supply increase, so both the AD and AS curves shift rightward, to AD_2 and AS_2, respectively. Notice, though, that aggregate demand increases more; its curve shifts rightward by more than the aggregate supply curve shifts rightward. In this case, the increase in the price level from P_1 to P_2 indicates inflation.*

EXHIBIT 12-4 Aggregate Demand Increases by More than Aggregate Supply

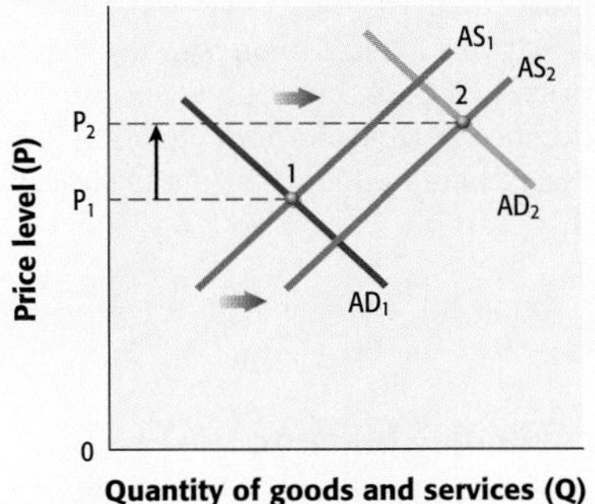

When aggregate demand (AD) increases by more than aggregate supply (AS), the price level (P) increases; we have inflation.

The Simple Quantity Theory of Money

The simple quantity theory of money presents a clear picture of what causes inflation. Before examining this theory, though, we must know something about velocity and the exchange equation.

Velocity

The average number of times a dollar is spent to buy final goods and services is called **velocity**. To illustrate the concept of velocity, consider a tiny economy with only five \$1 bills. In January, the first of the \$1 bills moves from Maria's hands to Nancy's hands to buy a newspaper. Then, in June, it goes from Nancy's hands to Bob's hands to buy a bagel. And in December, it goes from Bob's hands to Tu's hands to buy a used paperback book. Over the course of the year, this \$1 bill has changed hands three times. The other \$1 bills also change hands during the year. The second bill changes hands five times; the third, six times; the fourth, three times; and the fifth, three times. Given this information, we can calculate the number of times the average dollar changes hands in purchases. We do so by finding the sum of the times each dollar changed hands ($3 + 5 + 6 + 3 + 3 = 20$ times) and then dividing by the number of dollars (5). The answer is 4, which is the velocity in this example.

The Exchange Equation

In the exchange equation

$$M \times V = P \times Q$$

M stands for the money supply, V stands for velocity, P stands for the price level or average price, and Q stands for the quantity of output (quantity of goods and services). M times V must equal P times Q. To see why, think of the equation on a personal basis. Suppose you have \$40; this amount is your

supply-side inflation An increase in the price level that originates on the supply side of the economy.

velocity The average number of times a dollar is spent to buy final goods and services in a year.

Teaching with Visuals

Exhibit 12-4 illustrates inflation as it would occur when aggregate demand increases by more than aggregate supply. Ask students to explain why this would cause inflation.

Critical Thinking

Assign students to come up with a visual representation of velocity. Students might perform a role-play like the following one: Three people stand in front of the class. The first person has a dollar in her hand. She gives it to the second person, and then the second person gives it to the third person. Ask the class what the velocity is in this example. (*Answer:* 2.)

Reinforcement Activity

Write the exchange equation on the board. Put values into the various parts of the equation and ask students to find the remaining values. For example, if you were to write $P = 7$, $Q = 10$, and $M = 14$, then students would need to solve to find V, which would equal 5.

Reinforcement Activity

To reinforce inflation concepts, have students work with partners to complete the following sentences. Answers are given for your reference.

1. Demand-side inflation is an <u>increase</u> in the price level that originates on the demand side of the economy.
2. An increase in the <u>price</u> level that originates on the <u>supply</u> side of the economy is called supply-side inflation.

Background Information: The Simple Quantity Theory of Money

The simple quantity theory of money was put forth by classical economists. One of the leading proponents of the simple quantity theory of money was Irving Fisher (1867–1947), a British economist and mathematician. Many of the ideas of these early economists have been updated by modern economists and now serve as the building blocks of modern economic theory. Some economists today still adhere to the simple quantity theory of money.

Section 1 Inflation and Deflation 315

Prediction Activity

Ask students to predict what will happen to the price level as a result of each of the following situations.

1. The money supply decreases.
2. Velocity increases.
3. The quantity of goods and services decreases.

(*Answers:* **1.** Price level decreases. **2.** Price level increases. **3.** Price level increases.)

Reinforcement Activity

Ask students how inflation is like theft. Some people have suggested that inflation robs people of some of the purchasing power of their money. To illustrate, suppose you have $100. With a 10% inflation rate, your $100 will buy less than it would have with zero inflation. The goods that you could have purchased without inflation can no longer be purchased. Ask students whether those goods were "stolen."

Clarifying Terms

Help students understand the phrase *strictly proportional. Strictly* means "exactly" or "precisely," and *proportional* means "having the same or a constant ratio." To ensure students' understanding of the phrase, invite volunteers to use it in a couple of original sentences.

Teaching with Visuals

Since Exhibit 12-5 begins with the exchange equation, review with students the variables used in the equation: [M = money], V = velocity, P = price level or average price, and Q = quantity of output (quantity of goods and services).

money supply (M). You spend the $40 one time, so velocity (V) is 1. You spend the $40 on 5 books, so 5 is the quantity of goods and services you purchase—it is your Q in the exchange equation. Now ask yourself what P must equal, given that M is $40, V is 1, and Q is 5. If you spend $40 on 5 books, the average price per book must be $8. P must be $8, because $8 times 5 books equals $40. Here is the exchange equation using the numbers in this example:

$$M(\$40) \times V(1) = P(\$8) \times Q(5 \text{ books})$$
$$\$40 = \$40$$

Explaining Inflation

simple quantity theory of money
A theory that predicts that changes in the price level will be strictly proportional to changes in the money supply.

The **simple quantity theory of money** is used to explain inflation. The theory begins by making two assumptions: that velocity (V) is constant and that the quantity of output or goods and services (Q) is constant. Let's set V at 2 and Q at 100 units. These numbers will remain constant throughout our discussion.

Suppose the money supply (M) equals $500. If V is 2 and Q is 100 units, then the price level must equal $10:

$$M(\$500) \times V(2) = P(\$10) \times Q(100 \text{ units})$$
$$\$1{,}000 = \$1{,}000$$

Now suppose the money supply increases from $500 to $1,000, a doubling of the money supply. As stated earlier, velocity and output are constant. Velocity (V) is still 2, and output (Q) is still 100 units. The price level (P), however, increases to $20:

$$M(\$1{,}000) \times V(2) = P(\$20) \times Q(100 \text{ units})$$
$$\$2{,}000 = \$2{,}000$$

In other words, if the money supply doubles (from $500 to $1,000), the price level doubles (from $10 to $20; see Exhibit 12-5).

▶ This exhibit outlines the basics of the simple quantity theory of money. Start with M × V = P × Q. Then, if V and Q are held constant, it follows that a change in the money supply (M) will lead to a strictly proportional change in the price level (P).

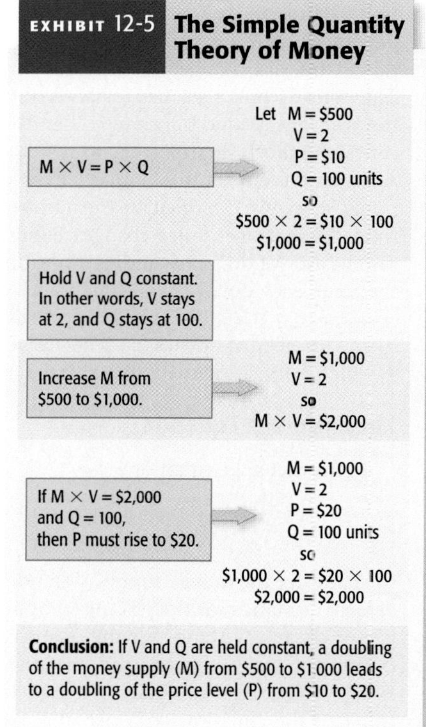

EXHIBIT 12-5 The Simple Quantity Theory of Money
M × V = P × Q
Let M = $500
V = 2
P = $10
Q = 100 units
so
$500 × 2 = $10 × 100
$1,000 = $1,000
Hold V and Q constant. In other words, V stays at 2, and Q stays at 100.
Increase M from $500 to $1,000.
M = $1,000
V = 2
so
M × V = $2,000
If M × V = $2,000 and Q = 100, then P must rise to $20.
M = $1,000
V = 2
P = $20
Q = 100 units
so
$1,000 × 2 = $20 × 100
$2,000 = $2,000
Conclusion: If V and Q are held constant, a doubling of the money supply (M) from $500 to $1,000 leads to a doubling of the price level (P) from $10 to $20.

In Theory The simple quantity theory of money states that changes in the money supply will bring about *strictly proportional changes* in the price level. For example, if the money supply increases by 100 percent, the price level will increase by 100 percent; and if the money supply increases by 20 percent, the price level will increase by 20 percent.

Real-World Application In the real world, the strict proportionality between changes in the money supply and the price level does not usually hold. An increase in the money supply of, say, 10 percent does not usually bring about a 10 percent increase in the price level.

What we do see in the real world is that the greater the increase in the money supply, the greater the increase in the price level. For example, a nation that increased its money supply by 30 percent would usually have a greater increase in its price level (its inflation rate) than a nation that increased its money supply by 20 percent. This finding is consistent with the "spirit" of the simple quantity theory of money. After all, the theory says that changes in the money supply bring about strictly propor-

Cross-Curricular Activity

Team with a math teacher to discuss inflation. You can open the lesson by helping students recall and understand the definitions of important terms, such as *velocity, quantity of output, money supply,* and *price.* The math instructor can then walk students through the equations in this chapter, helping them with the basic math concepts inherent in each of the economic formulas. Give students time to create their own problems with these variables and exchange them with other students in the class.

tional changes in the price level, so it follows that larger changes in the money supply should bring about larger changes in the price level.

EXAMPLE: The money supply in country A rises by 10 percent and the money supply in country B rises by 2 percent. Let's also assume that velocity is constant and the output of goods and services in each country is constant. In which country would we predict the higher inflation rate, A or B? Well, according to the simple quantity theory of money, the greater the increase in the money supply, the greater the inflation rate, so we would predict a higher inflation rate in country A. ♦

A Student Asks

QUESTION: *How long after the money supply rises does the price level rise? Is it the next day?*

ANSWER: *A lag occurs between the time the money supply rises and the price level rises. That lag is usually between 10 months to 18 months. In other words, if the money supply rises in January, prices might not go up until October.*

The Effects of Inflation

We tend to think that inflation affects only the buyer of goods, as when a person pays $60 instead of $50 a week for groceries. In truth, however, people are affected by inflation in many other ways as well.

Inflation and Individuals on Fixed Incomes

Denise has lived on a fixed income for the last 10 years; that is, every year for the past 10 years, her income has been the same. However, each year for the past 10 years, the price level increased and inflation occurred. Thus inflation lowered the purchasing power of Denise's money. She can buy fewer units of goods with a given amount of money than she could previously buy, and her material standard of living is reduced.

Inflation and Savers

On January 1, Lorenzo puts $2,000 into a savings account that pays 6 percent interest. On December 31, he removes $2,120 from the account ($2,000, which is the original amount, and $120 in interest). Suppose that during the year prices did not increase at all—an inflation rate of 0 percent. Saving made Lorenzo better off, because at the end of the year he can purchase $120 more of goods and services than he could at the beginning of the year.

"By a continuing process of inflation, governments can confiscate, secretly and unobserved, an important part of the wealth of their citizens."
—JOHN MAYNARD KEYNES, ECONOMIST

Now suppose instead that during the year, prices increased by 10 percent—an inflation rate of 10 percent. How much money would Lorenzo need at the end of the year to buy exactly what $2,000 could buy at the beginning of the year? If prices had increased by 10 percent, he would need 10 percent more money, or a total of $2,200. Instead of having $2,200, Lorenzo has only $2,120 from his savings account; he must settle for purchasing $80 less of goods and services than he could at the beginning of the year. Because the inflation rate of 10 percent was greater than the interest rate of 6 percent that Lorenzo earned on his savings, he ended up worse off. It is clear that inflation hurts savers.

If inflation persists, however, it is customary for financial institutions to compete for customers by offering an interest rate that

▼ Many senior citizens live on a fixed income. **How would their grocery shopping be affected by the combination of a fixed income and inflation?**

A Student Asks

Make sure students understand that increases in the money supply do not immediately result in higher prices.

Reinforcement Activity

Invite students to consider the following scenario: Someone tells you that she paid $30,000 for a house in 1960. That sounds like very little to pay for a house, but 1960 was a long time ago, when prices were not as high as they are today.

To figure out what you would have to pay today for the same house, visit the U.S. Bureau of Labor Statistics Web site and go to the Consumer Price Index Inflation Calculator. Fill in the calculator with the relevant data and then answer this question: What would you have to pay in the most recent year identified to buy the same house that was bought for $30,000 in 1960?

Critical Thinking

Guide students in a discussion of inflation rates versus savings rates. In the example given in the text, Lorenzo does lose some purchasing power. Ask, What might Lorenzo, or others, do to protect himself against high inflation rates? Students might say that individuals can put their money in an investment account that typically yields an interest rate comparable to or higher than the rate of inflation.

Teaching with Visuals

A fixed income is a problem during periods of inflation because the income does not rise in relation to rates of inflation. This means senior citizens would have less money to spend on groceries.

Differentiating Instruction

English Language Learners

Students who have difficulty reading English and those who have difficulty understanding graphs and mathematical formulas may have difficulty understanding Exhibit 12-5. Pair students to practice solving for one of the four variables by substituting different money supplies, velocities, prices, and quantities.

Section 1 Inflation and Deflation 317

Economics in the Real World

Ask students if they have experienced grade inflation and, if so, whether they were aware that their relative standing in school had not gone up. Discuss similarities and differences between grade inflation and price inflation.

ANSWERS TO THINK ABOUT IT Answers will vary.

Discussion Starter

Ask students to vote on whether they would like to have their grades inflated. Then require students to give reasons for their answers and write the reasons on the board in two columns—pro and con. After you've listed all the reasons, take another vote to see how many would still want to have their grades inflated. Lead students to explain why their vote changed or stayed the same.

Reinforcement Activity

Grade inflation may seem like a good idea to students. However, it can create a false sense of security: "I am getting better grades without studying harder, so why put in the effort?" Students should understand that an inflated grade does not indicate knowledge of the subject matter or an ability to use its concepts out in the world. Ask students to compare the subjects in which they studied hard and truly learned in school, with subjects in which they may have gotten a good grade but learned very little.

Problem Solving

People often talk about inflation as if it is a bad thing. In light of this belief, discuss with students the following question: What is so bad about inflation? Students may answer that it makes it difficult for people to plan their expenditures. For example, someone may plan to buy a house in three years at a price of $150,000, but by then, with inflation, the price of houses may rise to a level they can't afford.

Grade Inflation: When Is a B+ No Better than a C?

Inflation can sometimes be deceptive. Suppose that Lavotka produces and sells motorcycles. The average price for one of his motorcycles is $10,000. Unknown to Lavotka, the Fed increases the money supply. Months pass, and then one day Lavotka notices that the demand for his motorcycles has increased. He raises the price of his motorcycles and earns a higher dollar income.

Lavotka is excited about earning more income, but he soon realizes that the prices of many of the things he buys increased, too. Food, clothing, and housing prices are all higher. Lavotka is earning a higher dollar income, but he is also paying higher prices. In relative terms, his financial position may be the same as it was before he increased the price of his motorcycles; for example, if his income went up by 10 percent, and prices also increased by 10 percent, he would be no better off.

Grade inflation also exists. Suppose that instead of teachers giving out the full range of grades, A through F, they start to give out only grades A through C. As a result, the average grade given out rises, resulting in grade inflation. (Just as price inflation is a higher average price, grade inflation is a higher average grade.)

Grade inflation can be just as deceiving as price inflation. Suppose you get higher grades without studying more. Your average grade goes from a C to a B+. Your relative standing in school has not gone up, however, unless only your grades, and no one else's grades, have risen (or your grades have risen by more than other persons' grades). Because everyone is getting higher grades, you may just be maintaining your relative position. In other words, if you are now earning a B+ instead of a C, other people may be earning an A instead of a B+. In a class of 30 students, with the teacher giving out the full range of grades (A through F), you might have been ranked tenth in the class. Now, in the same class of students, with the teacher giving only grades A through C, you might be earning higher grades but still be ranked tenth in the class.

THINK ABOUT IT What do you think might be the cause of grade inflation? What might be the effects of grade inflation?

has been adjusted upward by the inflation rate. Suppose financial institutions would offer a 4 percent interest rate next year if prices were going to stay the same as this year (meaning no inflation). However, they anticipate a 5 percent inflation rate during the year. Many institutions will begin to compete for customers by offering a 9 percent interest rate, the sum of the interest rate they would offer if prices did not change plus the anticipated inflation rate (4% + 5% = 9%).

Inflation and Past Decisions

Inflation often turns past decisions into mistakes. Consider the building contractor who last year signed a contract to build a shopping mall for $30 million. He agreed to this dollar figure based on his estimates of what it would cost to buy the materials and hire the labor to build the mall. He estimated $28 million in costs. All of a sudden, inflation hits. Prices of labor, concrete, nails, tile, and roofing rise. Now the

Internet Research

A good activity to get students to think globally is to have them research the inflation rates in other countries. If they can get this data, they should then try to find data on the growth rate in the money supply in the same countries and determine whether higher rates in the money supply correspond to higher inflation rates. They should research how the inflation rates of other countries affect the United States.

contractor realizes it will cost him $31 million to build the mall. He looks back on his decision to build the mall for only $30 million as a mistake—a costly mistake for him.

Inflation and Hedging Against Inflation

What do individuals in an inflation-prone economy do that individuals in a stable-price economy do not do? They try to **hedge** against inflation. In hedging, people try to avoid or lessen a loss by taking some counterbalancing action. They try to figure out what investments offer the best protection against inflation. Would gold, real estate, or fine art be the best hedge? People travel to distant cities to hear "experts" talk about inflation. They subscribe to numerous newsletters that claim to predict future inflation rates accurately. All this action obviously requires an expenditure of resources. Resources, we remind ourselves, that are expended in the effort to protect against inflation can no longer be used to build factories or produce houses, shoes, or cars. Thus, one effect of inflation is that it causes individuals to try to hedge against it, thereby diverting resources away from being used to produce goods.

What Is Deflation?

Deflation is the opposite of inflation. **Deflation** is defined as a decrease in the price level, or the average level of prices. We measure deflation the same way we measured inflation, by finding the percentage change in prices or the CPI between years. For example, suppose the CPI in year 1 is 180, and it is 175 in year 2. What is the change in the CPI? Here is the formula again:

$$\text{Deflation rate} = \frac{\text{CPI later year} - \text{CPI earlier year}}{\text{CPI earlier year}} \times 100$$

Filling in the numbers yields the following:

$$\text{Deflation rate} = \frac{175 - 180}{180} \times 100 = -2.8\%$$

A negative (downward) change in the CPI indicates deflation. The deflation rate is 2.8 percent. Notice that when we calculated the deflation rate we had a minus sign in front of the percentage change. However, when you speak of a deflation rate, you don't usually mention the minus. In other words, you would not say, "The deflation rate is minus 2.8 percent." It is understood that deflation refers to a decrease in the price level, so you would simply say, "The deflation rate is 2.8 percent."

Demand-Side Versus Supply-Side Deflation

Just like inflation, deflation can originate on either the demand side or the supply side of the economy. Consider Exhibit 12-6(a) on the next page, which shows an aggregate demand curve (AD_1) and an aggregate supply curve (AS_1). The equilibrium price level is P_1. Suppose the aggregate demand curve decreases and shifts from AD_1 to AD_2. Consequently, the price level decreases from P_1 to P_2. Because the price level decreased, deflation occurred. We conclude that if aggregate demand decreases and aggregate supply stays the same, deflation will occur. One of the things that can cause aggregate demand to fall is a decrease in the money supply, so a decrease in the money supply can cause deflation.

Next, consider an increase in aggregate supply, from AS_1 to AS_2 in Exhibit 12-6(b). As a result, the price level drops from P_1 to P_2. Again, because the price level decreased, deflation occurred. If aggregate supply increases and aggregate demand stays the same, deflation will occur. One of the things that can cause deflation (from the supply side) is an increase in technology that makes it possible to produce more goods and services with the same level of resources.

A Student Asks

QUESTION: *I often read about and hear people on the news talking about inflation, but rarely do I hear a mention of deflation. Why don't they talk about deflation?*

hedge
To try to avoid or lessen a loss by taking some counterbalancing action.

deflation
A decrease in the price level, or average level of prices.

Discussion Starter

After students have read the section "The Effects of Inflation," ask them to list some of the ways inflation directly affects their lives. Allow students to list the effects on the board.

Reinforcement Activity

Have students define *inflation* in their own words and then write a sentence in which they use the term.

Background Information

The following example illustrates how the rate of growth in the money supply in one country can affect another country's economy.

A person in Great Britain can buy good X from a seller in the United States or in France. Currently, the price of good X is the same in both countries. The person in Great Britain is indifferent as to where he buys the good, so he buys the good from the seller in France. Later, the money supply in France rises, and the result is inflation. The price of good X rises in France; the price of good X stays the same in the United States. If exchange rates are slow to change, the person in Great Britain now finds that good X is cheaper if he buys it from a seller in the United States.

Reinforcement Activity

Ask students to make a list of metaphors to describe deflation. An example might be a helium balloon that drops toward the floor as it deflates.

Clarifying Terms

Students need to understand several economic concepts they may have struggled with earlier in this section. Have them describe how CPI, aggregate demand, aggregate supply, and the simple quantity theory of money are related to the concept of deflation.

Background Information: High Rates of Inflation

High rates of inflation have occurred several times in the past century and can, according to many economists, lead to an unstable or even volatile political situation. Assign students to find examples of instability that is a result (in part) of inflation throughout history. Allow students to report their findings to the class.

Discussion Starter

Prompt students to brainstorm events and developments that might cause deflation. Students might mention a stock market crash, a sharp decrease in the money supply by the Fed, and a technological development that dramatically increases aggregate supply.

Reinforcement Activity

Ask students to define the term *deflation* and to show how to find the deflation rate.

Reinforcement Activity

Direct students to Exhibit 12-1 on page 313. Challenge them to use the consumer price index figures to determine which years experienced an inflationary economy and which experienced deflationary economy.

▶ Deflation can be caused by a decrease in aggregate demand as shown in part (a), or by an increase in aggregate supply as shown in part (b).

EXHIBIT 12-6 **Deflation**

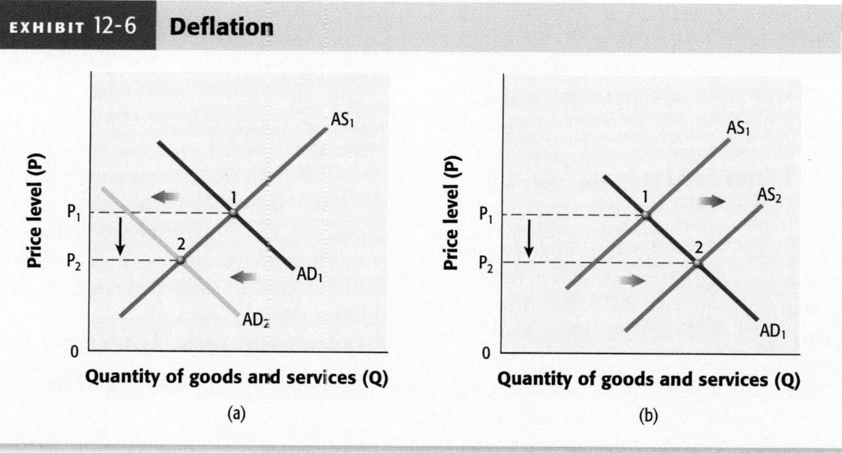

ANSWER: *You haven't heard people talking about deflation for a very simple reason—there hasn't been any deflation for some time. In the recent economic history of the United States, we have not had a period of deflation; instead, we have had an extended period of low inflation. Go back to Exhibit 12-2 and look at the inflation rate for the different years, 1960 through 2005. Notice that in every year during this period, inflation—not deflation—occurred.*

Perhaps we should be asking why inflation—but not deflation—has been the more common condition to appear on the economic scene. Much of the answer to this question has to do with increases in the money supply (M) as compared to increases in output (Q). Often the Fed will increase the money supply at a faster rate than the growth of output rises.

QUESTION: *I noticed that computer prices are lower in recent years. For example, a few years ago a computer cost $2,000. Today you can get the same computer for, say, $700. Would you call this trend "computer deflation"?*

ANSWER: *The price of one good falling does not constitute deflation. Remember, you need a decline in the price level, or in the average price of goods, before you can say deflation occurred.*

Simple Quantity Theory of Money and Deflation

Just as the simple quantity theory of money can be used to explain inflation, it can be used to explain deflation, too. Suppose the money supply (M) equals $500, velocity (V) equals 2, and quantity of goods and services (Q) is 100 units. We know that M × V must equal P × Q, so the price level (P) must equal $10.

M($500) × V(2) = P($10) × Q(100 units)
$1,000 = $1,000

Suppose the money supply drops to $250, and all other things remain the same. What happens to the price level? It must drop to $5:

M($250) × V(2) = P($5) × Q(100 units)

In other words, a fall in the money supply will bring about deflation (assuming that velocity and the quantity of goods and services do not change).

A Major Effect of Deflation

When prices fall, they do not all fall at the same time. This situation often presents a problem. For example, suppose Latoya produces wooden tables. To produce wooden tables, she needs wood, glue, and laborers. In short, in her business Latoya is interested

Cross-Curricular Activity

It can be difficult for students to understand what living in a period of deflation is like. Invite a history teacher to the class to talk about deflationary periods in U.S. history. The teacher might want to focus on the deflation that occurred during the Financial Panic of 1893 or the Great Depression. After the teacher's presentation, ask students to search the Internet or the library for first-hand testimony of what it was like to live during a deflationary period. Ask students to share what they have learned with the class.

Economics in the Real World

Can You Have "Too Much Money"?

??????????????????

Suppose someone has $20,000. We ask that person if he would prefer to have $50,000 instead. His first response is to ask us what he has to do to get the extra money. We say nothing. He quickly smiles and says, "Sure, I'll take the extra money."

No one, it seems, turns down money for doing nothing in return. More money is always better than less money.

Now what is odd is that even though an individual may never have "too much money," the sum of individuals (the society) may have "too much money." To understand how, all that is needed are two things: first, a short history lesson, and second, an understanding of the simple quantity theory of money.

In 1923, prices were rising quite rapidly in Germany. Not by 10 percent or 20 percent a year, but by 41 percent a day. In 1946 in Hungary, prices were tripling each day. Both situations are examples of hyperinflation.

To understand what this type of increase means, consider a modern-day example. Suppose a hamburger cost $2 today, but that the price of the hamburger triples every day. In just nine days a hamburger will cost $13,122. Think of what this increase would do to a person with a savings account of $13,122. It would surely reduce the buying power of that savings account.

Ask yourself what would happen in a society that experienced this kind of hyperinflation. History shows us that such societies tend to be composed of fearful, uncertain individuals who cannot predict what tomorrow will bring. One economist argued that the German hyperinflation destroyed much of the wealth of the middle classes in Germany and made it easier for the Nazis to gain power. If he is correct, rapid

increases in prices are more destructive than anyone could imagine.

What caused the hyperinflation in Germany? It is simple: too much money. The German government was increasing the money supply at an astronomical rate: that's what caused prices to soar. Prices rose by *854 billion percent* in the five-month period from July to November 1923.

You might think that you could never possibly have too much money. But what many of us forget is that when we think that we can never get enough money, we are assuming that the nation's money supply remains constant. In other words, you are assuming that you have $4 million more, and that collectively everyone else has $4 million less.

Think of the difference in effects between (1) your having $4 million more and collectively everyone else having $4 million less; and (2) you and everyone else having $4 million more. In the first case, the nation's money supply stays the same and so do prices. It's just that you have $4 million more to spend for goods whose prices have not changed. In the second case, the nation's money supply increases by $4 million times the population. In the United States, we would multiply $4 million times a population of about 300 million. That means the money supply increases by 12 followed by 14 zeros. You can expect prices to rise so fast and so high that soon you'll be paying hundreds of thousands of dollars for a hamburger.

What is the lesson? For the individual, there may not be such a thing as "too much money." For the sum of individuals—for a society—there is.

THINK ABOUT IT Can you think of other things for which more is better for the individual but more is not necessarily better for the "sum of individuals"?

Economics in the Real World

After students read this feature, ask if they think they could ever have too much money. Invite them to paraphrase the reason why it is possible for a country to have too much money.

ANSWERS TO THINK ABOUT IT Answers will vary.

Cause and Effect

Divide the class into pairs and give the pairs time to invent their own imaginary businesses similar to Latoya's wooden table business in "A Major Effect of Deflation." Then have them imagine what would happen if deflation struck. First, have them suppose that the prices of the goods they need for their operation fell before the price of the good they sell fell. Then have them imagine that the price of the good they sell dropped first. What would happen to their business in each scenario?

Teaching with Visuals

The answer to the question accompanying the photograph on page 322 is that deflation might hurt the construction company if prices of the houses the company is building fall more quickly than prices of the supplies the company needs to build the houses.

Application Activity

After reading and discussing Section 1, you may want to assign the Section Activity in the *Applying the Principles Workbook.*

Assess

Quick Quiz

The following true-or-false quiz will help you assess student understanding of the material covered in this section.

1. Inflation is an increase in the price level. (True)
2. Inflation can originate either on the supply side or on the demand side. (True)

Cooperative Learning

Divide students into three groups to study instances of hyperinflation. Assign one group to 1920s Germany, one to 1940s Hungary, and one to 1980s Brazil. Each group should create a chart or graph to show the rate of inflation and the rate of growth in the money supply. Allow each group to present to the class its visuals as well as an oral report on the causes of the hyperinflation and the methods the government used to deal with it.

3. Deflation can only originate on the supply side of the economy. (False)
4. Inflation generally hurts savers. (True)
5. A negative change in the consumer price index leads to deflation. (True)

Assessment Book

You will find a quiz for this section in the *Assessment Book*.

Reteaching Activity

Use the Section Assessment to gauge which students may need reteaching on this section. With those students, review the concepts of CPI, aggregate supply, and aggregate demand. Then help students create graphs showing how increases and decreases in aggregate supply and aggregate demand affect inflation and deflation.

Guided Reading

For further reteaching of the key concepts in this section, assign the Outlining Activity and the Just the Facts Handout from the *Guided Reading and Study Guide*.

▲ The company developing this section of new homes must invest considerable resources to purchase the land, materials, and labor needed to build the homes. **How might deflation create a financial hardship for the company?**

in four prices: the prices of wooden tables, wood, glue, and laborers. She is interested in the price of wooden tables because it relates to her total revenue. For example, if the price of wooden tables is $100 and she sells 50, her total revenue is $5,000. If the price of wooden tables is lower, at $40, her total revenue is $4,000.

Latoya is interested in the price of wood, glue, and laborers because these prices relate to her total cost. The higher these prices, the higher her overall costs.

Suppose that the money supply in the economy drops, and deflation occurs. Furthermore, not all prices fall at the same time. The price of wooden tables falls first, and the prices of wood, glue, and laborers fall many months later.

What happens to Latoya as a result of the price of wooden tables falling but the prices of wood, glue, and laborers staying constant (for a few months)? Her total revenue falls, but her total costs stay the same. As a result, her profits fall—so much that Latoya ends up getting out of the business of producing wooden tables. She closes up shop, lays off the workers she currently employs, and looks for different work.

In short, when prices do not fall at the same time, deflation can lead to firms going out of business and workers being laid off. Because it is unusual for all prices to fall at the same time, these results are common in deflation.

SECTION 1 ASSESSMENT

Defining Terms

1. Define:
   a. inflation
   b. demand-side inflation
   c. supply-side inflation
   d. velocity
   e. simple quantity theory of money
   f. hedge
   g. deflation

Reviewing Facts and Concepts

2. The CPI is 167 in year 1 and 189 in year 2. What is the inflation rate between the two years?
3. The CPI is 180 in year 1 and 174 in year 2. What is the deflation rate between the two years?
4. "An increase in the money supply is more likely to cause supply-side inflation than demand-side inflation." Do you agree or disagree? Explain your answer.
5. Explain how a change in aggregate demand and aggregate supply can cause deflation.

Critical Thinking

6. A theory that predicts that changes in the money supply bring about strictly proportional changes in the price level also predicts that larger changes in the money supply should bring about larger changes in the price level. Do you agree or disagree? Explain your answer.

Applying Economic Concepts

7. The simple quantity theory of money assumes that velocity and the quantity of goods and services are constant. Suppose we drop the second assumption, and something happens so that the quantity of goods and services in the economy falls. What will happen to the price level?

SECTION 1 ASSESSMENT ANSWERS

Defining Terms

1. a. **inflation:** an increase in the price level, or average level of prices; **b. demand-side inflation:** an increase in the price level that originates on the demand side of the economy; **c. supply-side inflation:** an increase in the price level that originates on the supply side of the economy; **d. velocity:** the average number of times a dollar is spent to buy final goods and services in a year; **e. simple quantity theory of money:** a theory that predicts that changes in the price level will be strictly proportional to changes in the money supply; **f. hedge:** to try to avoid or lessen a loss by taking some counterbalancing action; **g. deflation:** a decrease in the price level, or the average level of prices.

Reviewing Facts and Concepts

2. 13.17%. See the formula on page 313.
3. 3.33%. See the formula on page 319.
4. Students should disagree. An increase in the money supply is more likely to cause demand-side inflation.
5. A decrease in aggregate demand will cause deflation. An increase in aggregate supply will also cause deflation.

Critical Thinking

6. Students should agree. For example, this theory predicts that a 10% increase in the money supply will cause a 10% rise in the price level, and a 20% increase in the money supply will cause a 20% rise in the price level.

Applying Economic Concepts

7. The price level will rise. If M and V are constant and Q falls, P must rise.

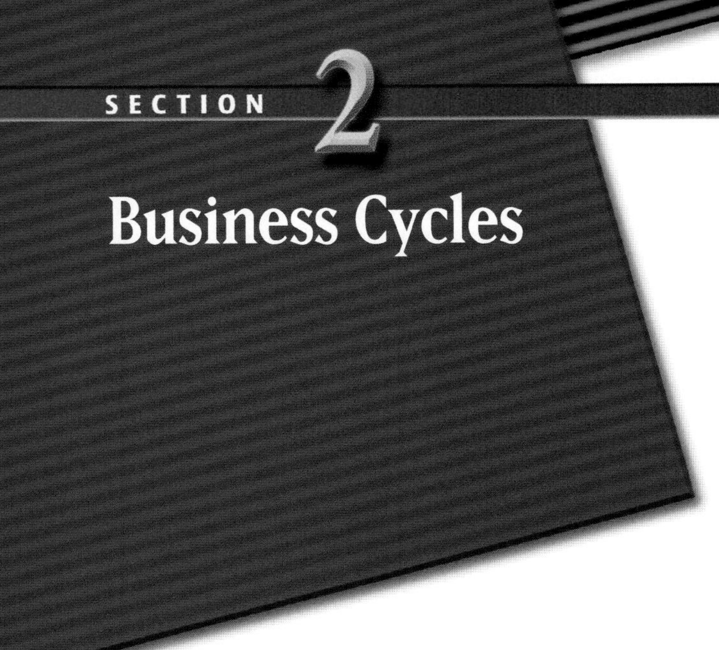

Business Cycles

Focus Questions
- What is a business cycle?
- How do economists forecast business cycles?
- What are some economic indicators?
- What causes business cycles?
- How does politics cause upward and downward movements in the economy?

Key Terms
business cycle
recession

What Is a Business Cycle?

Chapter 11 discussed both GDP and real GDP. As you recall, GDP is the total market value of all final goods and services produced annually in a country. Real GDP is simply GDP adjusted for price changes. To calculate real GDP, we take the quantity of goods and services produced in a country in a current year and multiply by the prices that existed in a base year:

$$\text{Real GDP} = P_{\text{Base Year}} \times Q_{\text{Current Year}}$$

If real GDP is on a roller-coaster—rising and falling and rising and falling—the economy is said to be incurring a **business cycle**. Economists usually talk about four or five phases of the business cycle. Five phases are identified here and in Exhibit 12-7.

1. *Peak.* At the peak of a business cycle, real GDP is at a temporary high (Q_1 in Exhibit 12-7).
2. *Contraction.* If real GDP decreases, the economy is said to be in a contraction. If real GDP declines for two consecutive quarters (with four quarters in a year), the economy is said to be in a **recession**. Usually when the economy contracts (real GDP falls), the unemployment rate rises. A higher unemployment rate not only hurts those who are unemployed, but it hurts the country as a whole. More unemployment means fewer goods and services are being produced, and therefore the overall material standard of living of people declines.

business cycle
Recurrent swings (up and down) in real GDP.

recession
A slowdown in the economy marked by real GDP falling for two consecutive quarters.

EXHIBIT 12-7 The Phases of the Business Cycle

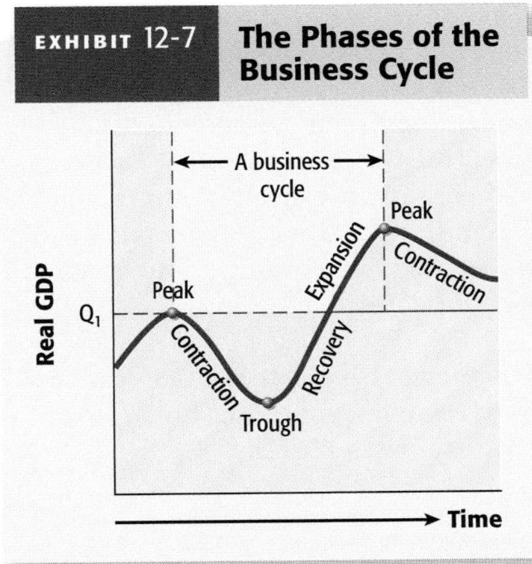

◀ The phases of a business cycle include the peak, contraction, trough, recovery, and expansion. A business cycle is measured from peak to peak.

Cooperative Learning

To help students better understand business cycles of the past, have them research the Great Depression and the New Deal legislation that was intended to increase demand and spur economic activity. After students have completed their research, have them work in pairs to create wall posters showing the business cycle from the peak of the 1920s through the Great Depression to the boom period of WWII. You may want them to indicate on this cycle the names of the major pieces of New Deal legislation that apply.

SECTION 2

Teacher Support

Focus and Motivate

Section Objectives

After completing this section, students will be able to
- describe a business cycle;
- explain how economists forecast business cycles;
- identify some economic indicators;
- identify some causes of business cycles; and
- explain how politics cause upward and downward movements in the economy.

Economics Around the Clock

Kickoff Activity

Direct students to read "What Is a Business Cycle?" on pages 323–324, followed by the 3:34 P.M. scenario in Economics Around the Clock (page 311). Then discuss the answer to the question that follows that scenario.

Students should remember that a business cycle includes five stages. If Willie is looking for a job during the contraction stage of the business cycle, his chances of getting a job are less than if he is looking for a job during the expansion stage of the business cycle.

Activating Prior Knowledge

Many students will have heard the terms *economic recovery, recession,* and *depression.* Ask them to discuss their associations with these terms.

Teach

Teaching with Visuals

Suggest that students depict the business cycle using images that will help them remember the meanings of the phases. You can hang their representations of the business cycles around the room.

Discussion Starter

Tell students that a business cycle is measured from one period of prosperity to another. It begins with a peak period. As the economy contracts, a recession may occur, which may turn into a depression. The lowest point is the trough. Next comes the period of recovery, which then leads to another peak. Ask students where they believe we are in the current business cycle, and why they think so.

Clarifying Terms

Some students may have trouble understanding the terms *peak, contraction, trough, recovery,* and *expansion*. Allow students to substitute their own words for these terms. List these substitutions under each term on a wall chart, and assure students that they will have opportunities to learn the standard terms as they study this section.

Make sure students understand that economic problems in one country can have significant effects on the economies of other nations.

ANSWERS TO ECONOMIC THINKING Those countries would not be able to buy as many goods from the United States. This would negatively affect the U.S. economy.

Reinforcement Activity

The text uses the metaphor of the flu to help students understand the concepts of leading, coincident, and lagging indicators. Ask students what other metaphors would work to describe these concepts.

3. *Trough.* The low point in real GDP, just before it begins to turn up, is called the trough of the business cycle.
4. *Recovery.* The recovery is the period when real GDP is rising; it begins at the trough and ends at the initial peak. For example, the recovery in Exhibit 12-7 extends from the trough to where real GDP is again at Q_1.
5. *Expansion.* The expansion refers to increases in real GDP beyond the recovery. In Exhibit 12-7, it refers to increases in real GDP above Q_1.

An entire business cycle is measured from peak to peak.

Forecasting Business Cycles

Economists try to predict changes in the economy. Comparing the economy to your health might help you see how they go about making their predictions.

Think of yourself when you have the flu. Your illness usually has three stages: (1) when you are coming down with the flu, (2) when you have the flu, and (3) when you are getting over the flu but still do not feel like your old self. Each stage includes a sign or indicator of what is happening.

Flu Signs

In the first stage, when you are coming down with the flu, you feel a little sluggish and tired. We might call this condition a *leading indicator* of the flu, in that it precedes the flu; it lets you know what is coming.

In the stage when you have the flu, you feel achy, and you might have a fever. We could call this condition a *coincident indicator* of the flu, in that it coincides with having the flu.

Finally, during the period when you are getting over the flu, your temperature returns to normal. You are slightly more alert, but you do not have all your energy back. We could call this condition a *lagging indicator* of the flu. Thus, we established a few indicators of your health and sickness.

Economic Indicators

Similarly, economists devised a few indicators of the health and sickness of the economy—*leading, coincident,* and *lagging* indicators. These indicators do what their names suggest: *lead* economic upturns or downturns (in real GDP), *coincide* with economic upturns or downturns, and *lag* behind economic upturns and downturns.

We would expect a leading indicator to rise before an upturn in real GDP and to fall before a downturn in real GDP. A coincident indicator should reach its high point at the same time as a peak of a business cycle and reach its low point with the trough of a business cycle. Finally, we would expect a lagging indicator to reach its high sometime after the peak of a business cycle and to reach its low sometime after the trough.

Leading economic indicators tend to be more often cited in the news than either coincident or lagging indicators, perhaps because people seem particularly interested in predicting or forecasting the future. They want to know what lies ahead—contraction or expansion. What will the economic future hold?

THE GLOBAL IMPACT

One Country Affects the Other

In 2003, *The Economist* reported that "Japan and Germany together make up about 20% of global output. And they are both in a mess." In a world of economic integration, in a global economy, if two major economies are "both in a mess" they can affect other economies. When countries are doing poorly economically, they often do not buy as many goods from other countries. In other words, their imports can fall. However, an import for one country is an export for another country. When some countries stop buying as much, other countries necessarily stop selling as much.

ECONOMIC THINKING **What might happen to the U.S. economy if the economies of China, India, Japan, Germany, and Mexico were to falter?**

Internet Research

Direct students to use the Internet to find out whether the stock market is currently up or down. They can find stock market information from a variety of Internet sources, including Yahoo! Finance. After they look at a few of the composite indices for the past year, ask them to explain what this market trend suggests about the phase of the business cycle the economy is in and may be about to enter. Guide them in discussing whether we are probably in an expansion, a contraction, or a recovery.

NON SEQUITUR
by WILEY
BECAUSE THE RATES ARE BETTER AND THE MARKET ANALYSIS IS JUST AS ACCURATE...
Madam Moestreet's ASTROLOGICAL and ECONOMIC FORECASTS
WILEY 10-6
©1998 Wiley Miller / Dist. by Universal Press Syndicate

A few of the leading indicators include stock prices, the money supply (in inflation-adjusted dollars), consumer expectations, and average weekly hours worked in manufacturing. For example, a stock market that is up generally reflects good economic times ahead, and a stock market that is down generally reflects bad economic conditions to come.

An increase in average weekly hours worked reflects good times ahead. The reasoning is that when good things are happening in the economy—when sales and profits are expected to rise—companies will adjust upward the number of hours their employees work before hiring more people. Similarly, a decline in average weekly hours worked reflects bad times ahead. When this indicator goes down, it usually means that sales and profits are expected to fall, and companies are cutting back on the number of hours their employees work.

A Student Asks

QUESTION: *I have two questions. First, has the United States experienced many business cycles?*

ANSWER: *Between 1854 and 2001, the United States experienced 32 business cycles. The average business cycle—from peak to peak—has been 53 months. If you would like to see the dates of the 32 business cycles in U.S. history, you can go to www.emcp.net/businesscycles.*

QUESTION: *Second question: is an economic contraction the same thing as a recession?*

ANSWER: *A contraction refers to a declining period of real GDP. In Exhibit 12-7 on page 323, it is simply the declining part of the curve. Usually, when the decline is relatively mild (like going down a slide with only a slight incline) we often call the contraction a recession. For example, if real GDP drops by 2 percent, for two consecutive quarters, we would say the economy is in a recession. If the decline in real GDP is sharp (like going down a steep slide), we usually call the contraction a depression.*

What Causes the Business Cycle?

Since the end of World War II, the United States has gone through 10 business cycles. What causes a business cycle? As you might expect, different economists identify different causes of the business cycle.

Money Supply

Some economists believe that changes in the money supply cause economic contractions and expansions. For example, when either the absolute money supply drops (say from $1,200 billion down to $1,150 billion) or the growth rate in the money supply

Background Information

To help students understand a business cycle, share the following scenario with them: Suppose there is an economic contraction in Asia. As a result, incomes in Asia are falling. With lower incomes, Asians buy fewer goods from the United States, and so U.S. exports decline. Since GDP = C + I + G + (EX – IM), a decline in exports (EX) will lower U.S. GDP. In short, because of the economic contraction in Asia, U.S. GDP declines.

A Student Asks

You may want to use this A Student Asks to make sure students understand the difference between a recession and a depression.

Reinforcement Activity

The National Bureau of Economic Research (NBER) is a private, nonprofit, nonpartisan research organization dedicated to promoting a greater understanding of how the economy works. One of the many things that the NBER does is determine the dates of the different phases of the business cycle. For example, it might determine that the peak of a given business cycle was in a certain month and year. Go to the NBER Web site at www.emcp.net/nber.org to find the business cycle that took place during the Great Depression, from 1929 to 1933. According to the NBER, how many months was the Great Depression, from peak to trough? The answer is 43 months; in other words, the contraction phase known as the Great Depression lasted for 43 months.

Background Information: Real GDP

Most economists use *real* GDP instead of GDP when talking about the economy. This is because an increase in prices and/or output will increase GDP, whereas only an increase in output will increase real GDP. The difference between real GDP and GDP can be a difficult concept for some students to grasp. Remind them that two variables are used to compute GDP—price and quantity. It is important to understand that real GDP takes into account price changes in order to paint a more accurate portrait of any change in the quantity of final goods and services produced in an economy in one year.

Section 2 Business Cycles 325

Teaching with Visuals

Answers will vary, but students should see that an increase in government spending on road construction will create jobs for people who will spend money on goods and services, potentially leading to an increase in economic activity.

Discussion Starter

Economists use economic indicators to make educated guesses about how the economy will react to various stimuli. Ask students if they can think of another subject in school in which they must gather data to support an educated guess. Discuss whether economics is a science or an art.

Prediction Activity

Have students consider this scenario and the questions that follow it: The chair of the Board of Governors of the Federal Reserve System goes before Congress and says that the Fed is likely to sharply cut back the growth rate of the money supply in the next few months. What do you predict will happen to real GDP? to the unemployment rate?

Students should predict an economic contraction. This means real GDP will decline and the unemployment rate will rise.

Cause and Effect

Invite students to brainstorm events that might affect the current economic situation (oil embargo, new microprocessor, election year, natural disaster, etc.) and then determine the effect of each event on the business cycle.

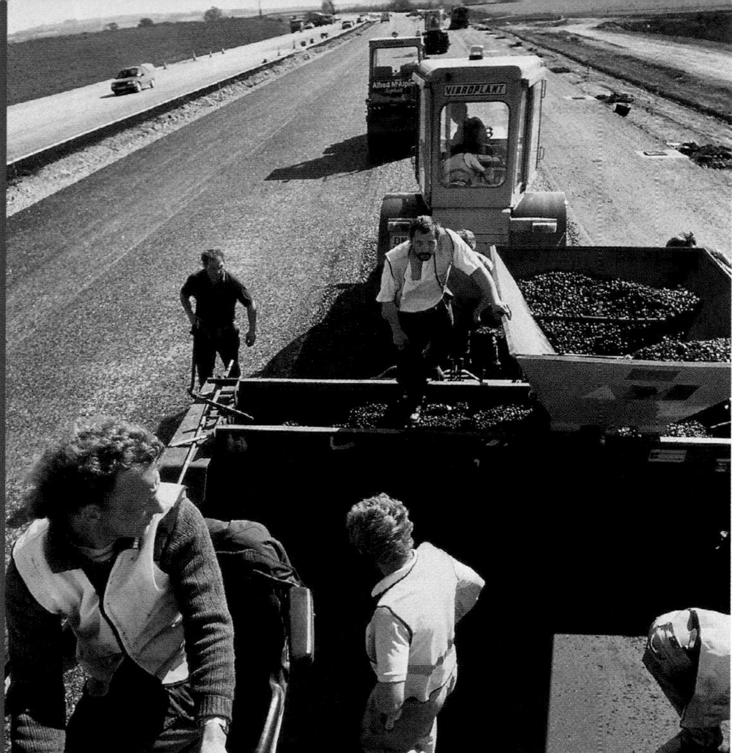

▲ **How might changes in government spending on road construction affect the economy?**

declines (say from 5 percent down to 1 percent), people end up buying fewer goods and services, and the economy falls into a contraction. In contrast, an increase in the money supply means more buying, and leads to an economic expansion.

These economists say the ups and downs of the business cycle are caused by the erratic behavior of the monetary authorities or the Fed. Sometimes the Fed puts the monetary accelerator to the floor, dramatically increasing the money supply and causing expansion. At other times it slams on the monetary brakes, causing the money supply to drop and the economy to dive into a contraction.

EXAMPLE: Suppose the money supply goes up in one six-month period, and then down in the next six-month period, and then up again in the next six-month period. This up and down movement in the money supply is what causes the up and down in economic activity (real GDP) according to some economists. In a way, increasing the money supply acts as a "stimulant" to the economy and reducing the money supply acts as a "depressant" on the economy. ♦

Business Investment, Residential Construction, and Government Spending

Some economists point to changes in business investment (firms cut back on buying factories and machinery), residential construction (contractors stop building as many homes), or government spending (government spending is cut substantially) as the cause of a business cycle. For example, a contraction might result from a cutback in business investment or government spending that lowers aggregate demand in the economy. With lower aggregate demand, firms do not sell as many goods and services, so they end up firing workers. Fired workers do not have the income they once had, so overall income in the economy falls. With a lower income, people do not buy as many goods. Thus the initial cut in spending results in even further declines in spending, and the economy falls deeper into recession. Things are reversed when either the business sector or government starts to spend more.

EXAMPLE: Suppose the federal government is spending $1.5 trillion a year and then it cuts back to $1.1 trillion. According to some economists, this cutback in government spending can reduce the overall demand for goods and services in the economy, and lead to a decline in economic activity. Similarly, they argue that a rise in government spending could lead to a pickup in economic activity. ♦

Politics

Some economists believe that at least some business cycles have been caused by politicians trying to get reelected to office. Suppose it is a year or so before the members of Congress will be running for reelection. They know that their chances of reelection are greater if the economy is in good shape on election day. To this end, they pass more spending bills in Congress, hoping to increase aggregate demand in the economy. With greater aggregate demand, they reason, firms will sell more goods and services and hire more workers. People will

326 Chapter 12 Economic Changes and Cycles

Background Information: Economist Irving Fisher and the Depression

How hard is it to predict downturns in the economy? For Irving Fisher (1867–1947) it was rather hard, which says a lot about how hard it is for others.

Fisher, who taught at Yale University, was one of the most respected economists of his day. But even he did not predict the Great Depression. Just two days before the major stock market crash, the "first shot" of the Great Depression, Fisher said that the stock market would continue to rise and that no problems lay ahead for the economy. Taking his own advice, Fisher lost a lot of money in the stock market.

Was Fisher a bad economist? Not at all; in fact, he is regarded as one of the best economists who has ever

Did the Great Depression Change the Country?

The most severe contraction that the U.S. economy has endured began in 1929 and ended in 1933 (the worst years of the Great Depression). In fact, that contraction was so deep and long that many people believe it changed the way people viewed free enterprise.

Before the Great Depression, most people believed that the economy was self-correcting or self-regulating. The economy could "heal itself" if it got "sick." Just like the human body can cure itself of certain ailments (such as a cold or the flu), so could the economy cure itself if it found itself in a contraction or a business slump. For example, in a business slump, wages and interest rates fall, and firms start hiring more workers and start investing more. In time, a bad situation turns into a good one. Obviously, if the economy is self-correcting, government has little, if any, role to play. Government need not intervene and try to fix the economy because the economy will soon fix itself.

The Great Depression changed this view. For many people, it was proof that a free enterprise economy was not only unstable but also unable to heal itself. Government intervention in the economy came to be viewed as necessary to prevent it from collapsing.

This view opened the door to the government's intervening in and managing the economy. Many government programs ("New Deal" programs) that began during the administration of President Franklin Delano Roosevelt probably would not have had wide public support before the Great Depression. Coming when they did, however, Roosevelt's government programs were seen by many as ultimately saving people from the ravages of a free enterprise economy that wasn't working.

Some economists argued against this view. Milton Friedman, for example, argued that the Great Depression was not so much the fault of a free enterprise economy as it was the fault of the Federal Reserve System. He argued that it was the Fed's cutting back the money supply by about one-third during the years of the Great Depression, and not the free market economy, that made the contraction so severe. Friedman's view is accepted by many economists today, but it was not widely understood in the 1930s through the 1960s.

THINK ABOUT IT Anton says that people change their view of how the world works only after experiencing a crisis that their view cannot explain. Frances says that people change their view of how the world works only through education. Which person are you more likely to agree with, and why?

have jobs and income. When times are good, voters are more likely to reward the people in office who (they believe) made this possible.

Of course, things may get out of hand after the election. The greater aggregate demand can cause inflation (as we saw in earlier in the chapter). Congress may then reverse its strategy by trying to cut spending to lower aggregate demand and cool off the economy. If Congress cuts spending too much, though, the economy could slide into a contraction.

lived. Even the best economists have trouble making consistently accurate economic predictions.

If all economists could make consistently accurate predictions about the stock market, what would you expect to see in the world? (*Answer:* You would expect to see a lot of wealthy economists!)

Before they read this feature, invite students to share what they know about the Great Depression and how it affected people's lives. Ask them what they think it would be like to live without having enough money for household expenses. Then ask what they think it would be like for employers not to be able to hire workers because there is no money in circulation. Urge students to imagine how their present lifestyle would change if there were another depression.

ANSWERS TO THINK ABOUT IT Answers will vary.

Reinforcement Activity

Invite one or two students to give an oral report on how the economic policy of the United States both contributed to and alleviated the Great Depression. Then assign all students to graph the business cycle in the United States from 1925 to 1945. Discuss with students the impact of the Depression and World War II on the business cycle.

Teaching with Visuals

The answer to the photo question on page 328 is that Hurricane Katrina affected the economy by restricting needed imports, interrupting industrial production, and knocking out city services that maintain healthy living conditions.

Application Activity

After reading and discussing Section 2, you may want to assign the Section Activity in the *Applying the Principles Workbook.*

Assess

Quick Quiz

The following true-or-false quiz will help you assess student understanding of the material covered in this section.

1. The length of a typical business cycle is 10 years. (False)

2. Three types of economic indicators are leading, lasting, and coincident. (False)

3. Money supply and politics are causes of business cycles. (True)
4. Stock prices are leading indicators. (True)
5. Real GDP goes up during the contraction phase of the business cycle. (False)

Assessment Book

You will find a quiz for this section in the *Assessment Book.*

Reteaching Activity

Use the Section Assessment to gauge which students may need reteaching on this section. Direct those students to examine Exhibit 12-7. On their own paper, have them list the five phases of the business cycle shown in the exhibit and, next to each, an event in history that will remind them of that phase.

Guided Reading

For further reteaching of the key concepts in this section, assign the Outlining Activity and the Just the Facts Handout from the *Guided Reading and Study Guide.*

▶ In 2005 Hurricane Katrina caused over 1,000 deaths and billions of dollars in damages, including the flooding and evacuation of the important port city of New Orleans. **What impact can such an event have on the economy?**

EXAMPLE: Every two years, the members of the House of Representatives and one-third of U.S. senators are up for reelection. Suppose the economy is contracting currently: real GDP is declining, more people are becoming unemployed, and so on. The members of Congress are afraid that if election day comes during poor economic times, they will not be reelected to office. So, prior to election day, they decide to pass various spending bills, including more money for national defense, more money for Medicare, more money for education, and more money for highway development. As a result, some economists argue that economic activity will pick up, but they also remind us that the motivation for the pickup in economic activity was the reelection prospects of members of Congress. ♦

Innovation

Some economists believe that major innovations are the seeds of business cycles. For example, a company develops a major new technology or product, and its sales skyrocket. To stay competitive, other companies must try to copy what the innovator has done or come up with a better innovation themselves. For a time, these copycat firms invest heavily to maintain their market positions relative to the innovator. In time, though, investment spending tends to slow, and the economy turns down.

Supply Shocks

Some economists argue that the contraction phase of the business cycle is brought about by major supply-side changes in the economy that reduce the capacity of the economy to produce. For example, a war can destroy factories and people and lower the productive capacity of an economy. Consider a major cutback in oil production brought on by conflict in the Middle East. With less oil, which is an important resource in the production process, the productive capability of the economy declines. Firms end up producing less, so they fire some of their workers. Real GDP goes down, and the unemployment rate goes up.

SECTION 2 ASSESSMENT

Defining Terms

1. Define:
   a. business cycle
   b. recession

Reviewing Facts and Concepts

2. What are the five phases of a business cycle?
3. If the initial peak of a business cycle was January 1, year 1, the trough was July 1, year 2, and the final peak was July 1, year 4, how long was the contraction (in months)?
4. What is a coincident indicator?

Critical Thinking

5. One leading indicator is average weekly hours worked. If this indicator rises, what does it indicate about the future performance of the economy? Explain your answer.

Applying Economic Concepts

6. One explanation of the business cycle is that changes in business investment, residential construction, or government spending cause the business cycle. If this explanation is correct, how could you use this information to determine whether it is a good time or bad time to buy stocks in the stock market?

SECTION 2 ASSESSMENT ANSWERS

Defining Terms

1. a. business cycle: recurrent swings (up and down) in real GDP; **b. recession:** a slowdown in the economy marked by real GDP falling for two consecutive quarters.

Reviewing Facts and Concepts

2. The five phases are peak, contraction, trough, recovery, and expansion.
3. The contraction lasted 18 months.
4. A coincident indicator is an indicator that reaches its high when the economy is at the peak of a business cycle and reaches its low when the economy is at the trough of a business cycle.

Critical Thinking

5. It indicates that the future economic performance is likely to be good. That is, the economy will be in recovery or expansion. If firms expect greater sales and profits in the future, they ask their present workforce to work longer hours. This is what the indicator measures.

Applying Economic Concepts

6. If spending is down, then the economy is headed downward. If spending is far enough down, perhaps a contraction is in the future. A contraction would be bad for businesses and the stocks that they issue. Now is probably not the time to buy stocks. Instead, now might be the right time to sell stocks. Conversely, if spending is up, the economy may be about to improve, in which case buying stocks would make sense.

SECTION 3

Economic Growth

Focus Questions

- What is the difference between absolute and real economic growth?
- What is the purpose of the Rule of 72?
- Do small differences in economic growth rates matter?
- What causes economic growth?
- Why might someone argue against economic growth?

Key Terms

absolute real economic growth
per capita real economic growth
human capital

What Is Economic Growth?

So far in this chapter we talked about inflation (increase in the price level), deflation (decrease in the price level), and the business cycle (real GDP on a roller-coaster ride: going up and down).

The last topic we need to discuss is economic growth. Specifically, we can talk about absolute real economic growth and per capita real economic growth. **Absolute real economic growth** is an increase in real GDP from one period to the next. For example, if real GDP was $10.2 trillion in year 1 and $11.1 trillion in year 2, the economy experienced absolute real economic growth. See Exhibit 12-8 on the next page for real GDP over the period 1980–2005. **Per capita real economic growth** is an increase from one period to the next in per capita real GDP, which is real GDP divided by population:

$$\text{Per capita real GDP} = \frac{\text{Real GDP}}{\text{Population}}$$

For example, if in year 1 per capita real GDP is $23,000 and it is $25,000 in year 2, then the economy experienced per capita real economic growth.

Per Capita Real GDP Growth and the Rule of 72

In Chapter 11, the Economics in the Real World feature on page 299 explained the effects of real GDP growth. In that example, we looked at what happens when the annual growth rate of per capita real GDP is 1.1 percent. A person born today will be 65 years old before his or her standard of living (as measured by per capita real GDP) will double. But if the annual growth rate of per capita real GDP is just 1 percent higher, at 2.1 percent, this person will be only 34 years old when his or her standard of living doubles. If the person lives to 68 years old, this person will see his or her standard of living double twice.

How do we know that a person will be 65 years old before his or her standard of living would double (assuming per capita real GDP grows at a rate of 1.1 percent)? We use the Rule of 72, which says that the way to find out the time required for any variable to double is simply to divide its percentage

absolute real economic growth
An increase in real GDP from one period to the next.

per capita real economic growth
An increase from one period to the next in per capita real GDP, which is real GDP divided by population.

SECTION 3

Teacher Support

Focus and Motivate

Section Objectives

After completing this section, students will be able to

- describe the difference between absolute real economic growth and per capita real economic growth;
- explain the purpose of the Rule of 72;
- explain whether small differences in economic growth matter;
- identify causes of economic growth; and
- explain arguments against economic growth.

Economics Around the Clock

Kickoff Activity

Have students reread the 7:32 P.M. scenario in Economics Around the Clock (page 311) and guess the answer to the question given. Help them see that a wide product selection often indicates economic growth.

Activating Prior Knowledge

Review the phases of the business cycle. Then ask students how the business cycle might be affected by inflation and deflation. Note that if inflation is caused by an increase in the money supply, allowing people to buy more, economic growth may result. Deflation might have the opposite effect.

Internet Research

Direct students to the U.S. Department of Commerce Bureau of Economic Analysis Web site to view the chart showing the GDP for the past few years. Ask students to print this chart or re-create it on their own paper. Students should label the different phases of the business cycle and identify the phase the country appeared to be in during the last financial quarter shown on the chart. Ask students to share their charts with the class.

Teach

Teaching with Visuals

Student explanations may vary. Increases in real GDP are more important to economists because they present a more accurate picture of actual increases in products and services.

Discussion Starter

Ask students if absolute real or per capita real growth is a better indicator of a country's standard of living. They will probably say that per capita economic growth is a better indicator because it keeps pace with the growth of the population. If population grows at a higher rate than does absolute real economic growth, the country will experience negative per capita economic growth.

Clarifying Terms

If students have difficulty understanding the meaning of *absolute real economic growth, per capita real economic growth,* and *production possibilities frontier*, you might discuss each term as a class. Then ask students to write definitions for the terms in their own words.

Discussion Starter

Ask students if a country that experiences more economic growth than another country is better off, and if so, how. Students will probably say economic growth benefits a country by providing residents of the country with more goods and services, access to more jobs, and so on.

Background Information

The Kirov Works in St. Petersburg, Russia, once produced military equipment, and now produces farm machinery. This change may have had a positive impact on economic growth in Russia. With advanced machinery, farm productivity increases. With increased productivity, the country can better serve the needs of its own people and export excess crops.

Teaching with Visuals

Students will probably say the farmer lives in a country with low economic growth.

▶ **Which would most economists say is more important—increases in GDP or increases in real GDP? Explain.**

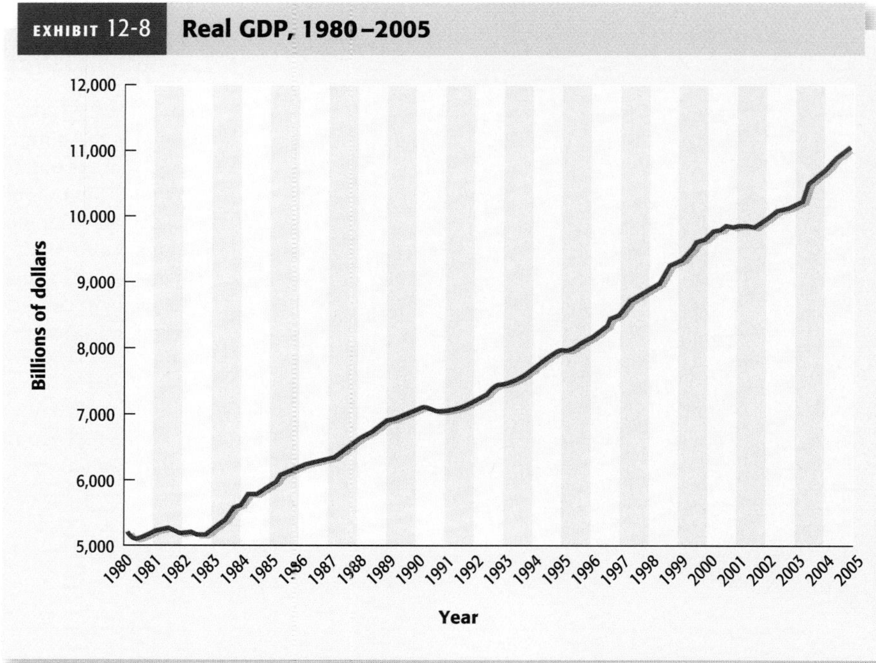

growth rate (expressed as a whole number, not a decimal) into 72.

Rule of 72 = 72/Growth rate =
Number of years for a variable to double

If you earn an annual interest rate of 5 percent on a savings account, how many years will it take for the money you deposit into the account to double? The answer is 14.4 years because 72 divided by 5 is 14.4. Or suppose your weight increases by 2 percent per year. How many years will it be before your weight doubles? The answer is 36 years because 72 divided by 2 is 36.

▶ **Based on what you have learned about real GDP and one's standard of living, do you think this farmer lives in a country with relatively high or low economic growth?**

Background Information: The Rule of 72

The Rule of 72 is a valuable tool for students to understand and to apply. It can be used to project population growth, investment performance, and so on. Just divide 72 by the known growth rate and you can determine the amount of time it will take the variable to double. Students do need to realize, however, that they must use annual growth rates or compounded interest rates in this formula. They also must realize that the Rule of 72 assumes that the growth rate will remain constant. Allow students to experiment with this formula using economic growth rates of various countries.

Economic Growth and a Production Possibilities Frontier

In Chapter 1, we defined the *production possibilities frontier (PPF)*. You might remember that the PPF shows us all possible combinations of two goods that an economy can produce in a certain period of time. (If you have forgotten how we derived the PPF, you might want to go back to Chapter 1 and review the material. We are assuming in our discussion here that you remember the details of a PPF.)

Using a PPF, in Exhibit 12-9, we can show what absolute real economic growth looks like. Economic growth can occur from a position either below or on the PPF.

Economic Growth from a Position Below the PPF

An economy can be located on or below its PPF. For example, an economy could be located at either point A or point B in Exhibit 12-9(a). Suppose an economy is located at point A, a point below the PPF. Obviously at this point some resources in the economy remain unused, because only when the economy is on the PPF are all resources fully used. At point A the economy is producing 100 units of X and 100 units of Y, but it can produce more with the resources it has; it can produce 150 units of X and 200 units of Y by using all its resources and producing at point B.

A movement from point A to point B is evidence of economic growth. More of both goods are produced at point B than at point A. This means that real GDP is higher at point B than point A.

Economic Growth from a Position on the PPF

Now suppose the economy is located at point B in Exhibit 12-9(b), on PPF_1, producing 150 units of X and 200 units of Y. How does an economy that is currently on its production possibilities frontier experience economic growth? Obviously, the only way is to shift its PPF to the right, say, from PPF_1 to PPF_2. In other words, if an economy is already on its PPF, the only way it can experience economic growth is if its PPF shifts rightward. Then, as we see in Exhibit 12-9(b), the economy can move from point B to point C (where more goods are produced and the real GDP is higher).

What Causes Economic Growth?

What factors cause economic growth of the type shown in Exhibit 12-9(b), that is, economic growth brought on by a rightward shift in the PPF? A few factors that can affect

EXHIBIT 12-9 Economic Growth from a Position Below and On a PPF

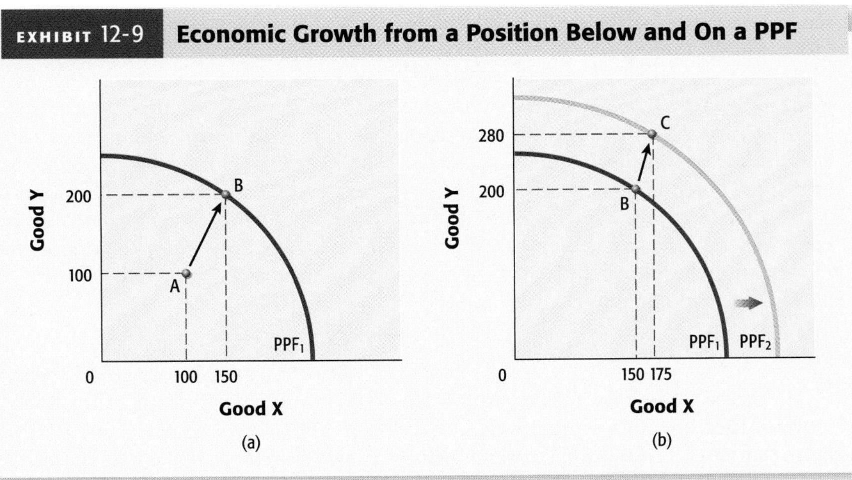

◀ Economic growth can occur from a position below the PPF as shown in part (a) or from a position on the PPF as shown in part (b).

Economics Around the Clock

After reading and discussing the first part of this section, you may want to refer students to the 10:13 A.M. scenario in Economics Around the Clock (page 311) and discuss their answers to the question that accompanies it.

Help students realize that economic growth, especially if we are talking about per capita real economic growth, is generally associated with less hunger. Hunger and hunger-related diseases are often found in countries that have not experienced much per capita real economic growth.

Critical Thinking

Economic growth may produce consequences that students have not considered. Some economists say that a country that experiences great economic growth not only has more goods and services to consume, but also provides more effectively for those who cannot provide for themselves. A rich country has a greater ability to provide for the poor and homeless than a poor country does, if it has the will to do so. Ask students whether they agree with this view, and encourage them to think of other consequences of economic growth.

Reinforcement Activity

Production possibility frontiers show the opportunity costs of producing one product over another. Direct students to reread the Chapter 1 section on opportunity cost, pages 7–10.

Background Information: Global Economic Growth

Students might find it interesting to compare economic growth in other countries with growth in the United States during the same period. Have students consult the *Economic Report of the President* in the school or city library, or on the Internet, to find this information. Alternatively, they may want to look at the *Statistical Abstract of the U.S.* for this information. Ask students to prepare written reports or create graphs that clearly show similarities and differences in the growth of various countries.

Section 3 Economic Growth 331

Teaching with Visuals

Capital investment causes economic growth by combining workers with more capital goods to increase labor productivity. The workers with the construction machinery in the photograph are more productive than the farmer who works without machinery.

Background Information

Remind students that although using capital goods, such as machines, does increase productivity, such goods are expensive. Poor nations are in a catch-22 situation. They usually have inexpensive (but often untrained) labor, but scarce capital to purchase the machines needed to become more productive and thus profitable when competing against productive, capital-intensive labor.

▶ Capital investment can lead to increases in productivity and growth. **Explain how capital has made workers in this photograph more productive than the farmer shown on page 330.**

growth are natural resources, labor, capital, human capital, technological advances, and incentives.

Natural Resources

With more natural resources, a country can produce more goods and services. For this reason, people often think that countries with a plentiful supply of natural resources experience economic growth, whereas countries that are short of natural resources do not. In reality, however, some countries with an abundant supply of natural resources have experienced rapid economic growth in the past (such as the United States), and some have experienced no growth or only slow growth. Also, some countries that are short of natural resources, such as Singapore, have grown quickly in the past.

Natural resources are neither sufficient nor necessary for economic growth. However, it is still more likely for a country rich in natural resources to experience growth, all other things being equal. In other words, if two countries, A and B, are the same in nearly all aspects except that A has more natural resources than B, then A is likely to grow more than B.

Labor

With more labor, it is possible to produce more output. In other words, we can get more output with 100 people working than with 70 working. More labor, by itself, however, is not what matters most to the economic growth. More important is the productivity of the labor. Government statisticians measure labor productivity by dividing the total output produced by the number of hours it takes to produce the output:

$$\text{Labor productivity} = \frac{\text{Total output produced}}{\text{Total hours it takes to produce total output}}$$

For example, if \$6 trillion of output is produced in 200 billion labor hours, then labor productivity is \$30 per hour.

An increase in labor productivity causes economic growth. The real question, then, is how an economy can achieve an increase in labor productivity. One way is through increased education and training. Another way is through capital investment. Combining workers with more capital goods tends to increase the labor productivity of the workers. For example, a farmer with a tractor is more productive than a farmer without one, and an accountant with a computer is more productive than an accountant without one.

Capital

As just mentioned, capital investment can lead to increases in labor productivity and therefore to increases in output or real GDP. However, more capital goods do not just fall

332 Chapter 12 Economic Changes and Cycles

Internet Research

Assign students a particular country. Have them find the country's investment as percentage of GDP for the current year, and if possible, for the 1990–2000 decade. Students might begin their investigation using the Internet search engine of their choice. As part of this assignment, you might wish to invite volunteers to describe the steps they took to find this data.

Can Economic Growth Eliminate Politics?

Liberal and conservative politicians sometimes want different things for their constituents and for society as a whole. Sometimes it seems as if these politicians are at opposite ends of a rope, each pulling the rope in a different direction and engaging in a political tug-of-war.

Suppose the U.S. production possibilities frontier is PPF_1 in Exhibit 12-10. The economy is currently at point A, producing and consuming 10 units of good X and 10 units of good Y.

The liberals would prefer to be at point L, producing and consuming 15 Y and only 5 X. The conservatives, however, would prefer to be at point C, producing and consuming 15 X and only 5 Y. In other words, the liberals are pulling in the direction of L, and the conservatives are pulling in the direction of C. Each is trying to influence politicians and citizens to "vote" for a different combination of goods than exists at the status quo point, point A.

If no economic growth occurs and the economy remains on PPF_1, the liberals cannot get what they want without the conservatives becoming unhappy. Similarly, without economic growth, the conservatives cannot get what they want without the liberals becoming unhappy.

EXHIBIT 12-10 Liberals, Conservatives, and Economic Growth

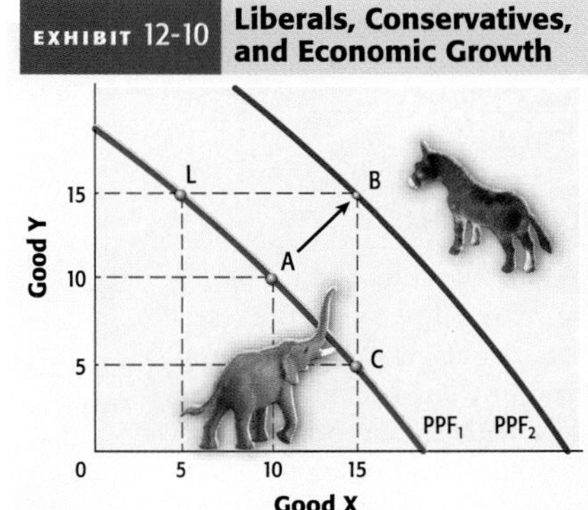

Both liberals and conservatives can get what they want, however, with economic growth. As we know, economic growth shifts the PPF rightward from PPF_1 to PPF_2. Now it is possible for society to move from point A (on PPF_1) to point B (on PPF_2). Notice that at point B, both liberals and conservatives get what they want. Liberals get 15 Y and conservatives get 15 X. In other words, economic growth can end the political tug-of-war between liberals and conservatives for awhile. We say "awhile" because soon after the economy is located at point B, it is likely that liberals will want to move up PPF_2 to get more Y and the conservatives will want to move down PPF_2 to get more X.

Specifically, what goods or services do you think liberals want more of? What goods or services do you think conservatives want more of? Might economic growth eventually make political differences irrelevant?

from the sky. Recall from an earlier chapter that getting more of one thing often means forfeiting something else. To produce more capital goods, which are not directly consumable, present consumption must be sacrificed. Consider Robinson Crusoe, alone on an island and fishing with a spear. He must give up some of his present fish to take time to weave a net (a capital good) with which he hopes to catch more fish.

Human Capital

Production of goods and services requires not only physical or tangible capital (a machine, for example), but also human capital. **Human capital** consists of the knowledge and skill that people obtain from education, on-the-job training, and work experience. It also consists of such things as honesty, creativity, and perseverance—traits that lend

human capital
The knowledge and skill that people use in the production of goods and services; also includes honesty, creativity, and perseverance—traits that lend themselves to finding work.

After students have read this feature, ask them if they know of any tug-of-war between politicians over economic issues. Invite volunteers to describe such situations. Then choose one or two and discuss how economic growth might have satisfied both sides.

ANSWERS TO THINK ABOUT IT Answers will vary. Some students might say that economic growth can make political differences irrelevant only for a while.

Analyzing

Point out that sometimes the Fed increases the money supply even though doing so is likely to cause some inflation. Ask students the following questions: Given what you know about the relationship between capital and economic growth, why would the Fed increase the money supply? How does this help the economy? Students may say that increasing the money supply increases available capital and fuels economic growth.

Discussion Starter

After students read the section "Human Capital" is an outstanding time to remind them of the importance of an educated workforce. The better educated an individual is, the higher her or his productivity will be, and the greater his or her income is likely to be. On the larger scale, an educated workforce leads to higher economic growth.

Cooperative Learning

The text discusses some factors that affect economic growth—natural resources, labor, capital, human capital, technological advances, and incentives. Divide the class into six groups, and assign each group to one of these six factors. Each group should brainstorm examples of the factor it has been assigned and report its ideas to the class.

Section 3 Economic Growth 333

Reinforcement Activity

The world is in danger of running out of some natural resources. Guide students in creating a list of natural resources and determining which are renewable.

Analyzing

In Chapter 2, students learned about some differences between free enterprise and socialism. In this chapter, they are learning that incentives affect economic growth. Ask students how they think the incentives structure differs between free enterprise and socialism, and how this difference might affect the economic growth rate of the two economic systems. You might also ask students whether they think incentives other than money can stimulate economic growth, and to name other incentives if they can think of any.

Background Information

Draw students' attention to the second worry about future economic growth. Discuss the role that the U.S. government plays in providing or controlling resources. For example, the government sets aside vast tracts of land as national forests. Ask students to provide examples of local government control of resources.

Teaching with Visuals

Answers to the question accompanying the picture on page 335 will vary. Students might say increased pollution is one potential cost of economic growth.

Application Activity

After reading and discussing Section 3, you may want to assign the Section Activity in the *Applying the Principles Workbook.*

Assess

Quick Quiz

The following true-or-false quiz will help you assess student understanding of the material covered in this section.

1. Absolute real economic growth is an increase in real GDP from one period to the next. (True)

themselves to finding work. Human capital is part of a person and cannot be separated from him or her the way physical or tangible capital can be. (You can separate a person from a machine but you cannot separate a person from his or her education, skills, and other personal qualities.)

Many economists argue that human capital is related to economic growth. Generally speaking, the more human capital a group of people have, the greater economic growth will be. It is important to point out how important human capital is to economic growth. Some countries, lacking natural resources, have experienced economic growth by relying on a well-trained, educated, hardworking, and conscientious labor force. For example, in the past, the so-called "Asian tigers" (Hong Kong, Singapore, South Korea, and Taiwan) experienced economic growth in this way.

> ***"In a modern economy, human capital is by far the most important form of capital increasing wealth and growth."***
>
> GARY BECKER, ECONOMIST

Technological Advances

Technological advances make it possible to obtain more output from the same amount of resources. Compare the amount of work that can be done by a business that uses computers with the amount accomplished by a business that does not.

Technological advances may be the result of new capital goods or of new ways of producing goods. The use of computers is an example of a technological advance that is the result of a new capital good. New and improved management techniques are an example of a new way of producing goods.

Technological advances usually result from companies and countries investing in research and development (R&D). R&D is a general term that encompasses such things as scientists working in a lab to develop a new product and managers figuring out, through experience, how to motivate employees to work to their potential.

Incentives

Some economists have argued that economic growth first appeared in areas that directed people to effective economic projects. In other words, economic growth developed where people were given the incentive to produce and innovate.

Consider two incentive structures: In one, people are allowed to keep the full monetary rewards of their labor, and in the other, people are allowed to keep only half. Many economists would predict that the first incentive structure would stimulate more economic activity than the second, all other things being the same. Individuals invest more, take more risks, and work harder when the incentive structure allows them to keep more of the monetary rewards of their investment, risk taking, and labor.

BY THE NUMBERS

The table below shows the U.S. absolute economic growth rate (percentage change in real GDP) in the period 1990–2004.

Year	Absolute economic growth rate
1990	1.9%
1991	−0.2
1992	3.3
1993	2.7
1994	4.0
1995	2.5
1996	3.7
1997	4.5
1998	4.2
1999	4.5
2000	3.7
2001	0.8
2002	1.6
2003	2.7
2004	4.2

Two Worries About Future Economic Growth

Two worries commonly crop up in discussions of economic growth. One concerns the costs of growth. Some individuals argue that more economic growth means more pollution, more factories, more crowded cities, more emphasis on material goods and getting ahead, more rushing around, more

Background Information: Journalism and Business Cycles

Newspaper reporters are members of the educated workforce. Many major in journalism, English, history, economics, or political science, and they have good listening and writing skills. They gather information and write stories about local, state, national, and international events and present points of view on various current issues.

Reporters have to research stories quickly to meet deadlines, and go places that they would sometimes rather not go. Their working hours vary, and they may work long into the night. They also get to meet interesting people and act as current-day historians.

Ask students to explain how a newspaper reporter's job is linked to the ups and downs of a business cycle.

psychological problems, more people using drugs, more suicides, and so on. They argue for less growth instead of more.

Others maintain that no evidence indicates economic growth (or faster, as opposed to slower, economic growth) causes any or all of these problems. They argue that growth brings many positive things: more wealth, less poverty, a society that is better able to support art projects and museums, a society more likely to protect the environment, and so forth.

The debate between those who favor more growth and those who favor less is complex. Economists have joined in, as have psychologists, biologists, sociologists, and many others. The debate promises to continue for a long time.

The second worry concerns the relationship between economic growth and the future availability of resources. Some people believe that continued economic and population growth will hasten the time when there will be no more natural resources, clean air, or pure water, and no more land for people to live on comfortably. These people urge social policies that will slow growth and preserve what we have.

Critics of this position often charge that such "doomsday forecasts," as they have come to be called, are based on unrealistic assumptions, oversights, and flimsy evidence. For example, economist Julian Simon pointed out that, contrary to popular opinion, population growth does not hinder economic growth, nor does it increase the incidence of famine. Furthermore, he points out that natural resources are not becoming increasingly more scarce. In fact, Simon had a wager with Paul Ehrlich, author and professor of population studies and biological sciences, about the relative price of natural resources in the period 1980–1990. Ehrlich said that natural resources were becoming increasingly more scarce and therefore would rise in price during this period. Simon, to the contrary, said that natural resources were becoming more plentiful and would actually fall in price. Simon won the bet easily.

▲ What potential costs of economic growth come to mind as you look at this photograph?

SECTION 3 ASSESSMENT

Defining Terms

1. Define:
   a. absolute real economic growth
   b. per capita real economic growth
   c. human capital

Reviewing Facts and Concepts

2. Can real GDP rise as per capita real GDP falls? Explain your answer.
3. You put $1,000 into a savings account that pays an interest rate of 6 percent annually. How many years before your savings doubles?

Critical Thinking

4. Natural resources are neither necessary nor sufficient for economic growth. Explain.
5. Can labor productivity decline as total output is rising? Explain your answer.

Applying Economic Concepts

6. What do you see as the costs of economic growth? What do you see as the benefits?

SECTION 3 ASSESSMENT ANSWERS

Defining Terms

1. a. absolute real economic growth: an increase in the real GDP from one period to the next; **b. per capita real economic growth:** an increase from one period to the next in real GDP divided by population; **c. human capital:** the knowledge and skill that people use in the production of goods and services; also includes honesty, creativity, and perseverance—traits that lend themselves to finding work.

Reviewing Facts and Concepts

2. Yes. If the population rises by a greater percentage than the real GDP, then per capita GDP falls as real GDP rises.
3. The Rule of 72 indicates that it would take 12 years for the money to double.

2. The way to find out the time required for any variable to double is called the Rule of 72. (True)
3. Economic growth shifts the production possibilities frontier to the left. (False)
4. Technological advances are not a factor that can affect growth. (False)
5. One of the worries that surfaces in discussions of economic growth concerns the availability of future resources. (True)

Assessment Book

You will find a quiz for this section in the *Assessment Book.*

Reteaching Activity

Use the Section Assessment to gauge which students may need reteaching on this section. Guide those students in examining Exhibit 12-9 and ask them what could make the PPF shift to the right? (*Answer:* an increase in resources.) What could make the PPF shift to the left? (*Answer:* a decrease in resources.) Have students reread the subsection "What Causes Economic Growth?"

Guided Reading

For further reteaching of the key concepts in this section, assign the Outlining Activity and the Just the Facts Handout from the *Guided Reading and Study Guide.*

Critical Thinking

4. This statement means that a country does not need plentiful natural resources in order to grow and a country that has plentiful natural resources is not guaranteed to grow.
5. Yes. Labor productivity is equal to total output produced divided by the total hours it takes to produce the total output. If total output rises but total hours rises by a greater percentage, then labor productivity will decline.

Appying Economic Concepts

6. Answers will vary.

Your Personal Economics

Discussion Starter

Ask students if they have ever thought of themselves in terms of being human capital and what it means to them personally to do so. In other words, what is the value in thinking of themselves that way?

Research Activity

After students have read the section on specific and generic capital, have them research at least five jobs they might be interested in pursuing in the future. Have them chart the generic and specific human capital they would gain from each job. Then ask students to use their findings to determine which of the jobs they listed would best prepare them to enter a variety of industries. Invite students to report their findings to the class.

Teaching with Visuals

Answers will vary.

Your Personal Economics

Your Goal: Generic, Not Specific, Human Capital

As you learned in reading this chapter, human capital refers to the knowledge and skills that people use to produce goods and services. Economists talk about two types of human capital: specific and generic. What's the difference? An economist once explained it by saying that specific human capital is an employee knowing where the restroom is; generic human capital is knowing how to read signs on doors.

Specific Capital

Anybody who works for a business acquires certain specific human capital; he or she learns certain things that are useful and important in that particular business. Suppose you go to work for a company that produces movies. You may learn how movies are made, how they are distributed, what makes some movies more profitable than others. You will also learn certain things about the people who work in the movie industry. No doubt, you will have much more specific knowledge about the movie industry than many people have.

Now ask yourself how transferable that specific human capital will be. In other words, will it be easy or hard for you to transfer the knowledge and skills—the human capital—you acquired in the movie industry? If it is hard to transfer, then it is likely that the human capital you acquired is specific—that is, it can only be used in that particular industry. If it is easy to transfer, then it is likely that the human capital you acquired is generic and can be used in almost any industry.

Comparing Specific to Generic Capital

As another example, let's look at two jobs: one as a machine operator at a car plant and the other as a computer programmer. It is likely that the machine operator has specific human capital. He can operate a particular machine in an auto plant, but he can't transfer this knowledge and skill to operating a different kind of machine in a non-auto plant. On the other hand, it is likely that the computer programmer has generic human capital. She can transfer her knowledge and skills in computer programming among a number of different industries.

▶ **Compare the two types of human capital—specific and general—that you would acquire as a pizza delivery person.**

Human Capital and Unions

How might these differences between specific and generic human capital affect unionism in the United States? Unionism tends to be strong and visible in manufacturing, where it is likely that workers have specific human capital. Unionism does not tend to be strong or visible in computer programming, where it is likely that workers have generic human capital.

Why is unionism in one place and not in the other? Some economists say unionism appears where workers need strong bargaining muscle (the places where the workers have specific human capital). If you have generic human capital, strong bargaining muscle is less crucial because you can work for so many different companies in so many different industries.

In recent years, the percentage of the labor force that is unionized declined. For example, in 1983, 20.1 percent of the labor force was

Cooperative Learning

After reading "Learning to Solve Problems," divide students into groups of three or four. Assign each group a different section of the required courses listed in your school's graduation plan—for example, mathematics, sciences, history, language arts, fine arts, and physical education. Have each group review the courses in its assigned section, and create a list of human capital assets, both specific and generic, to be gained by taking those courses. After 15 minutes, call the groups to report to the class.

▲ **Why do higher level math courses contribute to your generic human capital?**

Sometimes students take an algebra, trigonometry, or chemistry course in high school and wonder what good that course will ever be to them in the "real world." You might hear statements such as, "I don't know what use algebra is going to be to me when I'm out in the real world working," or "I'll never use what I learned in chemistry ever again. I don't plan to be a chemist." Well, you may not plan to be an algebra teacher or a chemist, but it doesn't mean the "thinking skills" you acquire learning algebra or chemistry are not useful in the "real world." Thinking skills, after all, are what transfer easily among jobs. It is becoming increasingly more important in the U.S. economy to know how to solve many problems than how to solve a single problem. But to solve many problems, one has to have good thinking skills.

unionized. By 2003, that percentage fell to 12.9 percent. Why the decline over the years? Some suggested it is because production in the United States moved from manufacturing to service sector jobs, which means that generic human capital became more important than specific human capital.

Learning to Solve Problems

This trend away from specific human capital and toward generic human capital is likely to continue. Now, perhaps more than ever before, it is important to acquire generic human capital. You need to acquire—while in school—as much generic human capital as possible. You need to acquire the skills and knowledge that more and more employers want—critical thinking skills, an ability at mathematics, an ability to write and reason clearly. You want to acquire the knowledge and skills that are in high demand in a world that is coming to value generic human capital more than specific human capital.

My Personal Economics Action Plan

Here are some points you may want to consider and some guidelines you might want to put in practice:

1. You may never solve a geometry problem after completing your high school geometry course. The type of thinking you learn while studying geometry, however, can be very useful in the world in which you will live and work.

   I will take __________ and __________, which will be challenging courses for me, but will help me learn generic thinking skills.

2. During your work life, the persons who possess generic human capital that can be transferred from industry to industry are likely to earn more and possess greater job security than those who possess only specific human capital.

   I will evaluate each course I take and each job at which I work to determine whether or not I am gaining specific or generic human capital.

Teaching with Visuals

Higher-level math courses develop students' ability to solve many kinds of problems.

Discussion Starter

To help students realize the importance of human capital, ask them to create a personal human capital profile on themselves. Have them include knowledge and skills obtained from education, on-the-job training, if applicable, and any work experience that they have had. Also, have them include personal traits that lend themselves to finding work. Ask students how this activity increased their knowledge about their personal human capital. How could having this human capital profile help them in applying for future jobs?

My Personal Economics Action Plan Have each student survey several adults to determine how human capital is evident in the adults' jobs. They may need to ask follow-up questions to determine if the job has specific capital or generic capital. Allow students to report back to the class.

Differentiating Instruction

English Language Learners

To help ELL students, use the following resources, which are provided as part of the *Economics: New Ways of Thinking* program:

- a Spanish glossary in the *Student Text*
- Spanish versions of the Chapter Summaries on an audio CD

CHAPTER 12 Assessment Answers

Economics Vocabulary

1. demand-side inflation; **2.** supply-side inflation; **3.** velocity; **4.** simple quantity theory of money; **5.** deflation; **6.** peak; **7.** expansion; **8.** trough; **9.** absolute real economic; **10.** per-capita real GDP.

Understanding the Main Ideas

1. Inflation is an increase in the price level. Deflation is a decrease in the price level.
2. Yes. An increase in aggregate demand causes inflation, while a decrease in aggregate demand causes deflation.
3. During inflation, money cannot transfer as many goods from other people to you.
4. Suppose a firm produces good X with resources A, B, and C. If prices fall but the price of good X falls before the prices of A, B, and C fall, then it is likely that the firm's total revenue will fall as its total costs remain constant. This situation will lower profits. As a result of lower profits, the firm may reduce the number of workers it hires or go out of business altogether. Either way, some people are fired from their jobs. In the interim, at least, unemployment rises.
5. The money supply could increase.
6. The assumptions are that velocity and the quantity of goods and services are constant. The theory predicts that changes in the money supply will bring about strictly proportional changes in the price level.
7. The inflation rate will be higher after year 4. The simple quantity theory of money holds that money supply changes bring about strictly proportional changes in the price level.
8. Yes. An increase in aggregate supply causes deflation, while a decrease in aggregate supply causes inflation.
9. With less aggregate demand or total spending in the economy, there is less buying of goods and services. Fewer goods and services bought means there is less need to have people who produce these goods and services working for you.
10. Inflation lowers the standard of living of people on fixed incomes by reducing their purchasing power. They can transfer fewer goods and services from others to themselves. Inflation hurts savers by lowering the purchasing power of the dollars they are saving.
11. The more incentive people have to produce and innovate, the more economic growth there is likely to be.
12. The Fed alternates between increasing and decreasing the money supply. When it increases the money supply, people buy more goods and services, and there is an economic recovery or expansion. By alternately increasing and decreas-

Chapter Summary

Be sure you know and remember the following key points from the chapter sections.

Section 1

- Inflation is an increase in the price level.
- A positive change (rise) in the consumer price index means inflation occurred.
- When an increase in the price level occurs because of increased demand, economists call it demand-side inflation.
- When an increase in the price level occurs because of decreased supply, it is called supply-side inflation.
- In the exchange equation, money supply (M) multiplied by velocity (V) equals price (P) times quantity of output (Q).
- Deflation is a decrease in the price level.

Section 2

- The recurrent swings in an economy's real GDP are known as a business cycle.
- Economists identify five phases of a business cycle: (1) peak, (2) contraction, (3) trough, (4) recovery, and (5) expansion.
- Economists use leading indicators, including stock prices, money supply, consumer expectations, and manufacturing labor hours worked, to forecast the direction the economy is heading.
- Various theories are used to explain the phases of the business cycle, including changes in the money supply, levels of business investment and government spending, politics, innovation, and supply shocks.

Section 3

- Absolute real economic growth is an increase in real GDP from one period to the next, whereas per capita real economic growth is an increase in real GDP divided by population.
- Economic growth is the result of a number of factors, including the supply of natural resources, labor productivity, capital investment, human capital/experience, technological advances, and incentives to produce.

Economics Vocabulary

To reinforce your knowledge of the key terms in this chapter, fill in the following blanks on a separate piece of paper with the appropriate word or phrase.

1. Aggregate demand rises, and the price level rises. This scenario is an example of ______
2. Aggregate supply falls, and the price level rises. This is an example of ______.
3. The average number of times a dollar is spent to buy final goods and services in a year is called ______.
4. The ______ predicts that changes in the price level will be strictly proportional to changes in the money supply.
5. ______ is a decrease in the price level or average level of prices.
6. Real GDP is at a temporary high if it is at the ______ of a business cycle.
7. The ______ of a business cycle refers to increases in real GDP beyond the recovery.
8. If real GDP is at the low point of the business cycle, it is in the ______.
9. An increase in real GDP from one period to the next is referred to as ______ growth.
10. Real GDP divided by population is called ______.

Understanding the Main Ideas

Write answers to the following questions to review the main ideas in this chapter.

1. What is the difference between inflation and deflation?
2. Can both inflation and deflation be caused by changes in aggregate demand? Explain your answer.
3. How does inflation reduce the value or purchasing power of money?
4. Explain how deflation can lead to an increase in unemployment.
5. What might happen on the demand side of the economy to cause inflation?
6. What are the assumptions of the simple quantity theory of money? What is its prediction?

UNDERSTANDING AND APPLICATION

7. In year 1 the Fed increases the money supply 10 percent, and in year 4 it increases the money supply 20 percent. Following which year is the inflation rate likely to be higher if the simple quantity theory of money predicts well? Explain your answer.
8. Can both inflation and deflation be caused by changes in aggregate supply? Explain your answer.
9. Explain why the unemployment rate might rise if aggregate demand falls.
10. Explain how inflation affects both individuals on fixed incomes and savers.
11. How do incentives affect economic growth?
12. Explain how the Fed can cause a business cycle.
13. What is human capital and how does it relate to economic growth?

Doing the Math

Do the calculations necessary to solve the following problems.

1. The CPI is 145 in year 1 and 154 in year 2. What is the inflation rate between the two years?
2. The money supply is $2,000, velocity is 2, and the quantity of goods and services is 500 units. According to the exchange equation, what is the average price of a good?
3. Real GDP in year 1 is $4,233 billion, and in year 2 it is $4,456 billion. The population is 178 million in year 1 and 182 million in year 2. What is the per capita real GDP in each year? Did per capita real economic growth occur?
4. If positive absolute real economic growth and negative per capita real economic growth occur at the same time, what is the relationship between the change in real GDP and the change in population?

Working with Graphs and Tables

1. Illustrate the following:
   a. demand-side inflation
   b. supply-side inflation
2. In Exhibit 12-11 identify each of the following:
   a. point A
   b. point B
   c. point C to D
   d. point A to D
   e. point B to C

EXHIBIT 12-11

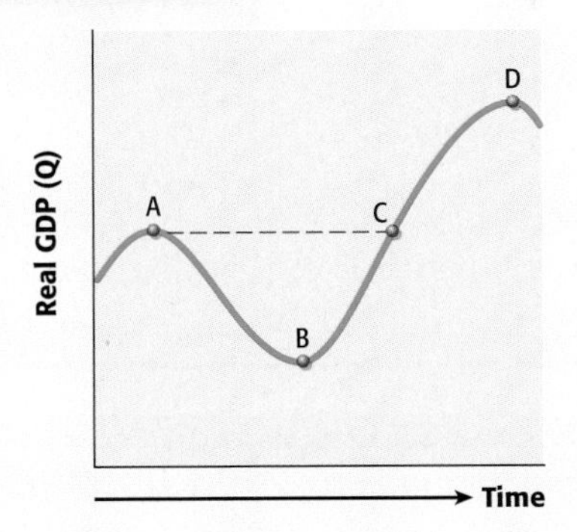

Solving Economic Problems

Use your thinking skills and the information you learned in this chapter to find solutions to the following problems.

1. **Application.** Explain how knowledge of the exchange equation can be used to explain both inflation and deflation.
2. **Analysis.** Can inflation occur in the face of an increase in the quantity of goods and services? Explain your answer.
3. **Cause and Effect.** Do higher interest rates cause higher inflation, or does higher inflation cause higher interest rates? Explain your answer.
4. **Economics in the Media.** Find a newspaper article that discusses economic growth. Identify and discuss the details of the article.

Practice Tests and Study Guide

Go to www.emcp.net/economics and choose *Economics: New Ways of Thinking,* Chapter 12, if you need more help in preparing for the chapter test.

ing the money supply, the Fed influences ups and downs in the economy.
13. Human capital is knowledge and skill that people use in the production of goods and services. It also includes traits such as honesty, creativity, and perseverance that lend themselves to finding work. Economic growth relies on the human capital of a well-trained, educated, hardworking, and conscientious labor force.

Doing the Math

1. *6.2% (calculation:* [(154 – 145) ÷ 145] × 100 = 6.2%).
2. *$8 (calculation:* If $2,000 × 2 = P × 500, then P = $8).
3. In year 1, per-capita real GDP is $23,780.89 (*calculation:* $4,233 billion ÷ $178 million). In year 2 it is $24,484.51 (*calculation:* $4,456 billion ÷ $182 million). The per capita real GDP is greater in year 2 than in year 1, so there has been per capita real economic growth.
4. The percentage increase in population has to be greater than the percentage increase in real GDP.

Working with Graphs and Tables

1. a. See Exhibit 12-3(a). **b.** See Exhibit 12-3(b).
2. a. the peak of a business cycle; **b.** the trough of a business cycle; **c.** the expansion phase of the business cycle; **d.** an entire business cycle (peak to peak); **e.** the recovery phase of a business cycle.

Solving Economic Problems

1. Inflation and deflation deal with changes in the price level. Inflation is an increase in the price level, and deflation is a decrease in the price level. The price level (P) appears in the exchange equation: M × V = P × Q. Using the exchange equation, we can explain both increases and decreases in the price level. For example, an increase in the money supply will raise the price level, while a decrease in the money supply will lower the price level.
2. The question is really asking whether the price level can go up at the same time as the quantity of goods and services rises. Certainly this situation is possible; an increase in aggregate demand that is greater than an increase in aggregate supply will bring this about.
3. Higher inflation causes higher interest rates. The text stated, "If inflation persists, it is customary for financial institutions to compete for customers by offering an interest rate that has been adjusted upward by the inflation rate." If interest rates are being adjusted upward by the inflation rate, then the higher the inflation rate, the higher the interest rate. In other words, higher inflation causes higher interest rates.
4. Answers will vary.

Chapter 13 Planning Guide

SECTION ORGANIZER

Section	Learning Objectives	Reproducible Worksheets and Handouts	Assessment
 **Fiscal Policy** (pages 342–350)	▸ Explain what fiscal policy is. ▸ Describe fiscal policies aimed at reducing unemployment. ▸ Describe fiscal policies aimed at reducing inflation. ▸ Define *crowding out* and *crowding in.* ▸ Explain how taxes can affect the supply side of the economy. 	Section 1 Activity, *Applying the Principles Workbook* Outlining Activity, *Guided Reading and Study Guide* Just the Facts Handout, *Guided Reading and Study Guide*	Section Assessment, *Student Text,* page 350 Quick Quiz, *Annotated Teacher's Edition,* page 349 Section Quiz, *Assessment Book*
 **Monetary Policy** (pages 351–356)	▸ Describe the type of monetary policy used to reduce unemployment. ▸ Describe the type of monetary policy used to reduce inflation. ▸ Explain how monetary policy reduces unemployment and inflation. ▸ Explain the purpose of the exchange equation.	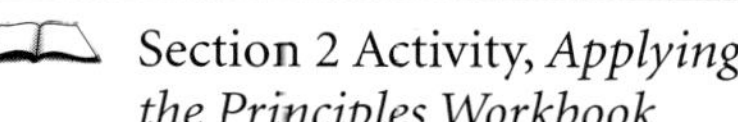 Section 2 Activity, *Applying the Principles Workbook* Outlining Activity, *Guided Reading and Study Guide* Just the Facts Handout, *Guided Reading and Study Guide*	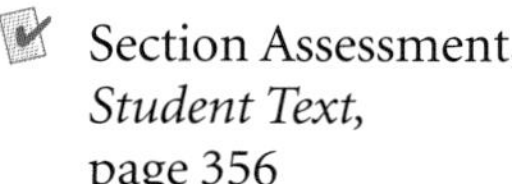 Section Assessment, *Student Text,* page 356 Quick Quiz, *Annotated Teacher's Edition,* page 356 Section Quiz, *Assessment Book*
 **Stagflation: The Two Problems Appear Together** (pages 357–361)	▸ Explain why the output of goods and services rises before prices when the money supply rises. ▸ Explain why the output of goods and services falls before prices when the money supply falls. ▸ Explain what causes stagflation.	Section 3 Activity, *Applying the Principles Workbook* Outlining Activity, *Guided Reading and Study Guide* Just the Facts Handout, *Guided Reading and Study Guide*	Section Assessment, *Student Text,* page 361 Quick Quiz, *Annotated Teacher's Edition,* page 360 Section Quiz, *Assessment Book*

CHAPTER AND PROGRAM RESOURCES

Reproducible Chapter Resources and Assessment Materials

 Graphic Organizer Activity, *Guided Reading and Study Guide*
 Vocabulary Activity, *Guided Reading and Study Guide*
 Working with Graphs and Charts, *Guided Reading and Study Guide*
 Practice Test, *Guided Reading and Study Guide*
 Critical Thinking Activity, *Finding Economics*
 Chapter Test A, *Assessment Book*
Chapter Test B, *Assessment Book*

Technology Resources

Test Generator CD
Spanish Audio Summaries CD
Marketplace® Audio Lessons CD
Economic Principles Lectures, Videocassette or DVD

Lesson Planning and Teaching Resources

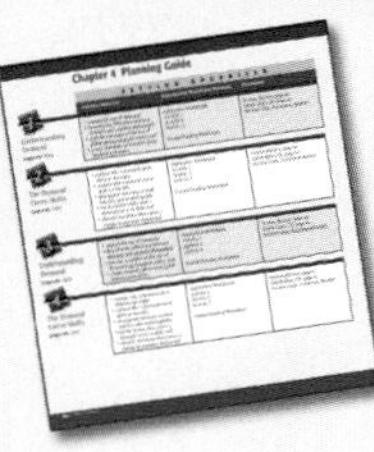

The *Economics: New Ways of Thinking* Teacher Resources include detailed lesson plans for each section in this chapter; the lesson plans are available in print form *(Lesson Plans)* and electronic form. The Teacher Resources also include *Daily Lectures: Overheads and Notes,* which provides prepared overheads and discussion notes covering the key concepts in each section of this chapter.

EMC Publishing Economics Online

Go to Economics Online, at www.emcp.com, for a variety of Internet resources to help you keep your course current and relevant. At Economics Online you will find these items:

- Economics in the News Lessons
- Study Guide Questions
- Practice Tests
- Lesson Plans

Internet Resources

Economics: New Ways of Thinking encourages students to use the Internet to find out more about economics. With the wealth of current, valid information available on Web sites, using the Internet as a research tool is likely to increase your students' interest in and understanding of economics principles and topics. In addition, doing Internet research can help your students form the habit of accessing and using economics information, as well as help them develop investigative skills they will use throughout their educational and professional careers.

To aid your students in achieving these ends, each chapter of *Economics: New Ways of Thinking* includes the addresses of several Web sites at which students will find engaging, relevant information. When students type in the addresses provided, they will immediately arrive at the intended sites. The addresses have been modified so that EMC Publishing can monitor and maintain the proper links—for example, the government site http://stats.bls.gov/ has been changed to www.emcp.net/prices. In the event that the address or content of a site changes or is discontinued, EMC's Internet editors will create a link that redirects students to an address with similar information.

Activities in the *Annotated Teacher's Edition* often suggest that students search the Internet for information. For some activities, you might want to find reputable sites beforehand, and steer students to those sites. For other activities, you might want students to do their own searching, and then check out the sites they have found and discuss why they might be reliable or unreliable.

CHAPTER 13 Overview

This chapter introduces the ways that government can intervene in the economy. Two principal means are through fiscal policy and monetary policy. Fiscal policy deals with changes in taxes and government spending. Monetary policy deals with changes in the money supply. The following statements provide brief descriptions of the major concepts covered in each section of this chapter.

Fiscal Policy

Section 1 defines and describes fiscal policy. It also explains both expansionary and contractionary fiscal policy.

Monetary Policy

Section 2 explores monetary policy. It discusses the different types of monetary policy as well as how monetary policy is used.

Stagflation: The Two Problems Appear Together

Section 3 deals with the definition and causes of stagflation.

CHAPTER 13 Fiscal and Monetary Policy

Why It Matters

In the past, people in the United States thought that government had no right to try to manage the economy. Government was simply there to provide goods (such as national defense) that the economy could not produce itself. Today, many people believe that if something is wrong with the economy, the government should get to work on it. Government should manage the economy. Specifically, if inflation occurs, government should get rid of it; if the level of unemployment is too high, government should lower it; if economic growth is weak, government should give the economy a boost.

Government uses monetary and fiscal policy to try to manage the economy at times. Do monetary and fiscal policy always work as hoped? Not always. This chapter helps you understand the technical details and effects of monetary and fiscal policy.

In October of 2005 President Bush nominated economist Ben Bernanke to replace Alan Greenspan as Federal Reserve chairman. In this chapter you will learn about the important decisions that the Federal Reserve chairman must make about the expansion and contraction of the nation's money supply.

Teaching Suggestions from the Author

In this chapter, we present students with an introduction to fiscal and monetary policy. One key point we make is that fiscal policy is effective depending upon the conditions that exist. For example, fiscal policy will be effective at changing total spending in the economy if there is no crowding out or crowding in. One of the best things that you can do before teaching this chapter is to get students to think in terms of conditions. In other words, X will occur if Y happens first, or Z will occur if A happens first.

Ask students to give you examples of if-then statements. For example, if it rains, then we cannot have the picnic. If you do not study for a test, then you will not do well. If you do not drive carefully, then you might

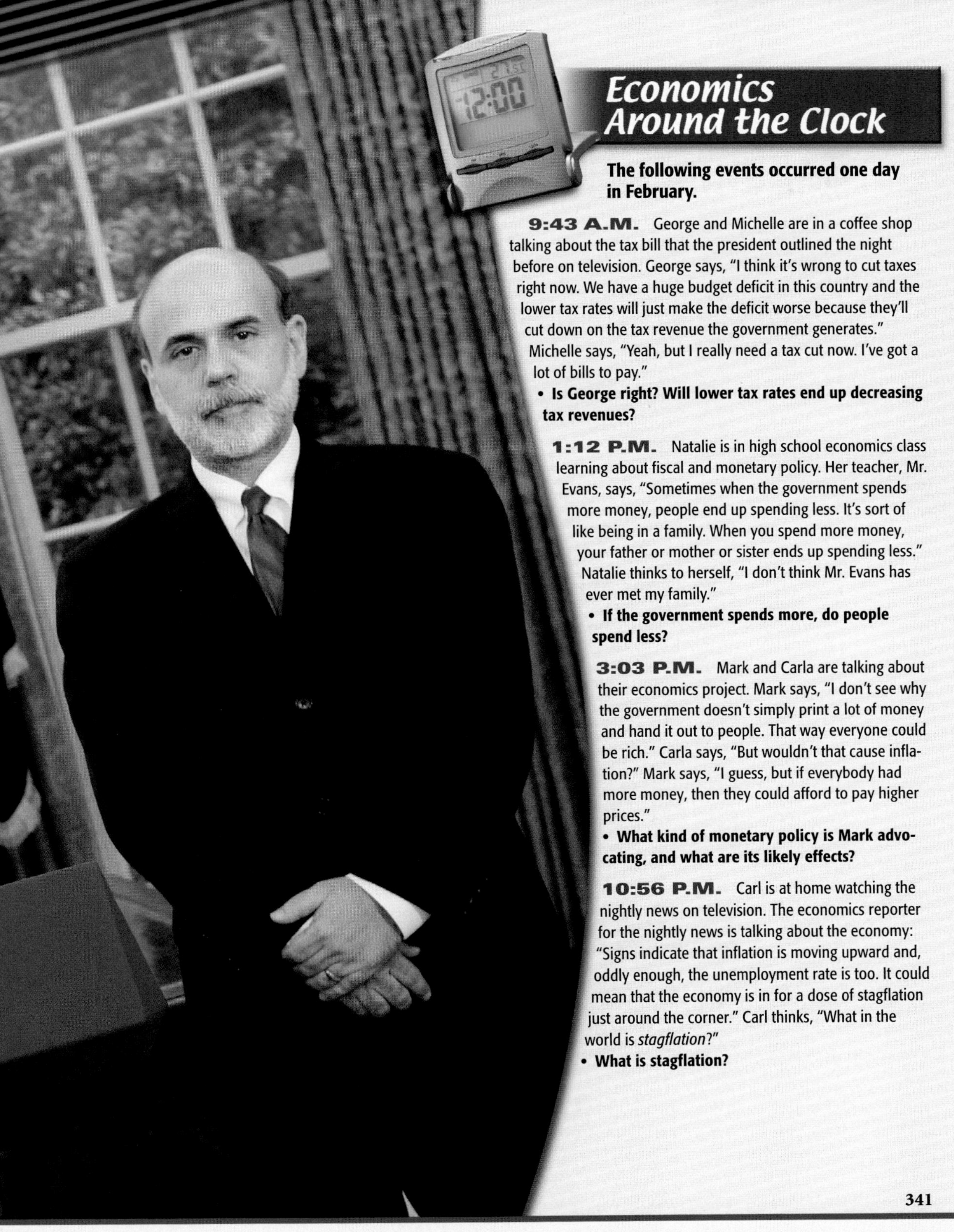

Economics Around the Clock

The following events occurred one day in February.

9:43 A.M. George and Michelle are in a coffee shop talking about the tax bill that the president outlined the night before on television. George says, "I think it's wrong to cut taxes right now. We have a huge budget deficit in this country and the lower tax rates will just make the deficit worse because they'll cut down on the tax revenue the government generates." Michelle says, "Yeah, but I really need a tax cut now. I've got a lot of bills to pay."

- **Is George right? Will lower tax rates end up decreasing tax revenues?**

1:12 P.M. Natalie is in high school economics class learning about fiscal and monetary policy. Her teacher, Mr. Evans, says, "Sometimes when the government spends more money, people end up spending less. It's sort of like being in a family. When you spend more money, your father or mother or sister ends up spending less." Natalie thinks to herself, "I don't think Mr. Evans has ever met my family."

- **If the government spends more, do people spend less?**

3:03 P.M. Mark and Carla are talking about their economics project. Mark says, "I don't see why the government doesn't simply print a lot of money and hand it out to people. That way everyone could be rich." Carla says, "But wouldn't that cause inflation?" Mark says, "I guess, but if everybody had more money, then they could afford to pay higher prices."

- **What kind of monetary policy is Mark advocating, and what are its likely effects?**

10:56 P.M. Carl is at home watching the nightly news on television. The economics reporter for the nightly news is talking about the economy: "Signs indicate that inflation is moving upward and, oddly enough, the unemployment rate is too. It could mean that the economy is in for a dose of stagflation just around the corner." Carl thinks, "What in the world is *stagflation*?"

- **What is stagflation?**

Introducing the Chapter

To introduce this chapter, you might write the words *fiscal policy* and *monetary policy* on the board. Explain to students that these terms represent two types of government policy designed to meet economic goals. Ask students what types of goals they think the government might be trying to meet.

Answers will vary. They might include reducing inflation, reducing unemployment, or promoting absolute real economic growth. Tell students to skim the Key Terms on page 342. Ask them to predict what they will learn in this chapter.

Teaching with Visuals

Direct students' attention to the picture of President Bush and Ben Bernanke on this spread, and read the caption on page 340. Ask students what qualities Bush would have considered in picking a new Federal Reserve chairman and why each quality is important to the position.

have an accident. You could brainstorm a list of situations with students and write the list on the board. Introducing this type of if-then thinking in advance will make it easier for all students to understand the material in this chapter.

SECTION 1

Teacher Support

Focus and Motivate

Section Objectives

After completing the section, students will be able to

- explain what fiscal policy is;
- describe fiscal policies aimed at reducing unemployment;
- describe fiscal policies aimed at reducing inflation;
- define *crowding out* and *crowding in*; and
- explain how taxes can affect the supply side of the economy.

Kickoff Activity

Ask students the following questions: Why would the government want to increase spending in the economy? What do you think the government can do to increase spending in the economy?

Activating Prior Knowledge

Allow students to discuss their answers to the questions in the Kickoff Activity. Answers will vary. Students might mention increasing government spending and cutting taxes.

Teach

Teaching with Visuals

After students examine Exhibit 13-1, ask for volunteers to explain the difference between expansionary and contractionary fiscal policies.

SECTION 1

Fiscal Policy

Focus Questions

- What is fiscal policy?
- What type of fiscal policy does government use to try to reduce unemployment?
- What type of fiscal policy does government use to try to reduce inflation?
- What are crowding out and crowding in?
- How can taxes affect the supply side of the economy?

Key Terms

fiscal policy
expansionary fiscal policy
contractionary fiscal policy
crowding out
crowding in
after-tax income
Laffer curve

Two Types of Fiscal Policy

Fiscal policy deals with government spending and taxes. If government increases spending, reduces taxes, or both, government is said to be implementing **expansionary fiscal policy**. The objective of this type of policy is to increase total spending in the economy to reduce the unemployment rate. For example, suppose government is currently spending $1,800 billion a year and it increases its spending to $1,900 billion a year. This act is called expansionary fiscal policy.

fiscal policy
Changes government makes in spending or taxation to achieve particular economic goals.

expansionary fiscal policy
An increase in government spending or a reduction in taxes.

contractionary fiscal policy
A decrease in government spending or an increase in taxes.

EXHIBIT 13-1 Two Types of Fiscal Policy

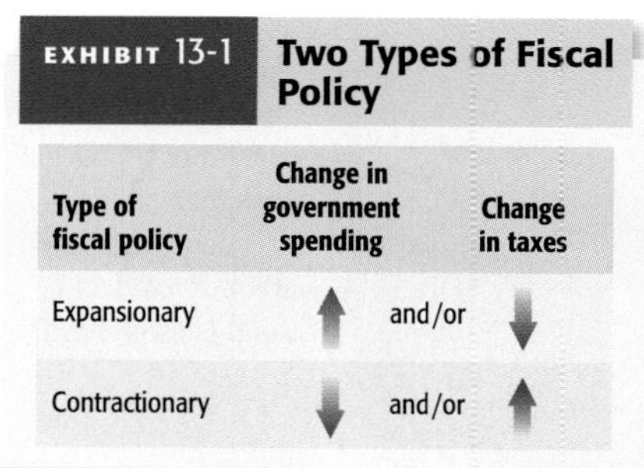

Type of fiscal policy	Change in government spending		Change in taxes
Expansionary	↑	and/or	↓
Contractionary	↓	and/or	↑

If government decreases spending, raises taxes, or both, government is said to be implementing **contractionary fiscal policy**. The objective is to reduce total spending in the economy in order to reduce inflation. For example, suppose government is currently spending $1,800 billion a year and it reduces its spending to $1,700 billion a year. This act is called contractionary fiscal policy. (The two types of fiscal policy discussed here are summarized in Exhibit 13-1.)

Expansionary Fiscal Policy and the Problem of Unemployment

Suppose the unemployment rate in the economy is 8 percent and government sets a goal of getting the unemployment rate down to 5 percent. Does it have any economic tools to help it get the unemployment rate down? Some economists say that the answer is yes. Government can use the tool of expansionary fiscal policy. Here is how these economists explain it.

342 Chapter 13 Fiscal and Monetary Policy

Differentiating Instruction

Visual Learners

To ensure that students understand the concepts of both expansionary and contractionary fiscal policy, assign them to create two political cartoons that clearly illustrate both concepts. For example, students could create a political cartoon about unemployment and the solution of expansionary fiscal policy. They could create another cartoon showing prices or interest rates skyrocketing with the government trying to use contractionary fiscal policy to contain the problem.

- A high unemployment rate is the result of people not spending enough money in the economy. In other words, if people spend more money, firms will sell more goods, and they will have to hire more people to produce the goods (in the process lowering the unemployment rate).
- To reduce the unemployment rate, Congress should implement expansionary fiscal policy—that is, it should increase government spending, lower taxes, or both. If it chooses to increase government spending instead of lowering taxes, government can choose to spend more on health care, education, national defense, and many other needed programs.
- An increase in government spending means more spending in the economy. For example, suppose that at current prices the government is spending $1,800 billion, business is spending $1,200 billion (buying factories, machines, and materials), and consumers are spending $6,000 billion (buying television sets, clothes, computers, and other goods). Total spending at current prices is $9,000 billion. If government decides to increase its spending by $200 billion, to $2,000 billion, then total spending increases to $9,200 billion.
- As a result of the increase in total spending, firms sell more goods.
- When firms start to sell more goods, they have to hire more workers to produce the additional goods. The unemployment rate goes down as a result of more people working.

A Student Asks

QUESTION: *Let me see if I have this right. The reason the unemployment rate is high (at 8 percent) is because there is not enough spending (buying) in the economy. So the government boosts spending and the unemployment rate comes down.*

ANSWER: *Yes, that is essentially it. An analogy comes to mind. Suppose a person is feeling sluggish. The reason he is feeling sluggish is because he isn't getting enough vitamins. So the doctor boosts his vitamin intake and he feels better. Expansionary fiscal policy works the same way. The patient (the economy) is sluggish (it has too high an unemployment rate). The doctor (the government) says the sluggishness will go away if vitamins (increased spending) are added to the diet. As a result the patient (the economy) gets better (its unemployment rate drops).*

▲ The government builds submarines to bolster our national defense. **What other reason might the government have for deciding to build the submarine?**

The Issue of Crowding Out

Some economists do not agree that things will turn out the way they were just presented. They say that when government spends more, total spending in the economy does not necessarily increase. They bring up the issue of **crowding out**, which occurs when increases in government spending lead to reductions in private spending (spending made in the private sector by consumers and businesses).

Suppose that currently in the economy, $60 million is spent on an average day. We'll say that $45 million is spent by the private sector (households and businesses buying such things as television sets, houses, and

crowding out
The situation in which increases in government spending lead to reductions in private spending.

Teaching with Visuals

Answers will vary. Students might say that another reason to increase defense spending is to lower unemployment.

Reinforcement Activity

Allow students to look through newspapers and business magazines to see if they can find any mention of fiscal policy, increases or decreases in taxes, or increases or decreases in government spending. Have them report their findings to the class.

Clarifying Terms

You may want to provide students with the definition of the word *fiscal*—"relating to financial matters, especially taxation, public revenue, or public debt."

Internet Research

Ask students to use the Internet to find out about the most recent actions of the Federal Reserve with regard to interest rates. When was the last time the Fed raised or lowered interest rates? Ask students to explain how this action might affect inflation and unemployment. Of what type of fiscal policy would this be an example? They should be sure to discuss the concepts of crowding in and crowding out.

Teaching with Visuals

Answers will vary. Students might say that the parents would take advantage of the better public education by reducing spending on private education. If enough people respond this way, the reduction in private spending will offset the increase in public spending.

Cause and Effect

Assign students to research the current fiscal policy of the U.S. government. They can determine this either by looking at recent fiscal policy decisions or by studying economic positions expressed in party platforms. Ask students the following questions: What would be the effect on the economy if Congress changed legislation to spend more? To spend less and cut government programs? Which of these would be expansionary fiscal policy, and which would be contractionary?

Discussion Starter

Students may be intrigued by the concept of crowding out. Guide them in a discussion of how and why this can occur. Have students examine other segments of the economy (besides education) where crowding out might occur. For example, you might discuss health care or public safety spending.

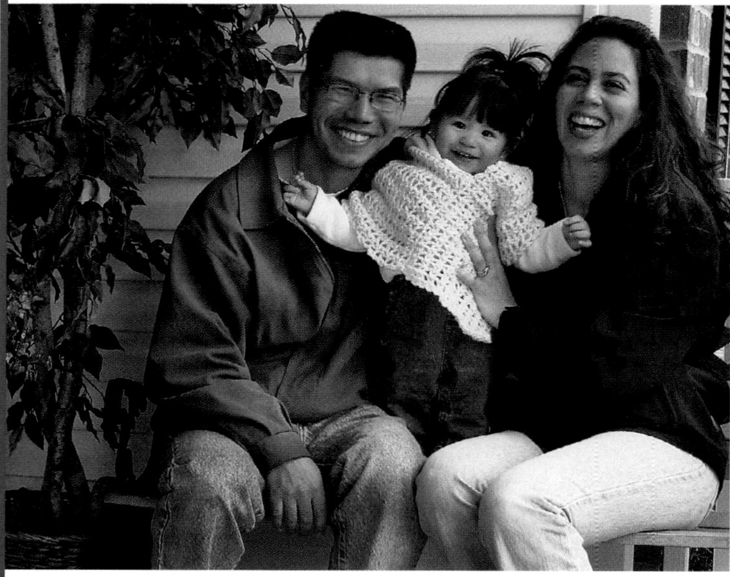

▲ **Suppose that to boost the economy the federal government decides to increase its spending on preschool education by $2 billion. How might this young family and others like it spoil the government's strategy? What do economists call this sort of activity?**

factories), and $15 million is spent by government (buying such things as defense and education). Suppose now that government decides to increase its spending on education, raising its average daily spending to $17 million. What is the consequence? Does total spending rise to $62 million ($17 million in public spending plus $45 million in private spending)?

Not necessarily, say some economists. Because government spends more on education, people may decide to spend less on education. Specifically, because government spends more on public schools and public school teachers, people may decide they can spend less on private schools and private school teachers. As a result, private spending will drop from $45 million to $43 million. Total spending therefore will remain at $60 million ($17 million in government spending plus $43 million in private spending).

In this example, where an increase of $2 million in government spending causes a $2 million decline in private spending, we have *complete crowding out*; each dollar increase in government expenditures is matched by a dollar decrease in private spending. With complete crowding out, an increase in government expenditures does not lead to an increase in total spending in the economy. Thus, it does not affect unemployment.

As another example, if the government spends an extra $2 million, and consumers and businesses spend less—but not $2 million less—*incomplete crowding out* is the result. When a decrease in private spending only partially offsets the increase in government spending, increased government spending does raise the total spending in the economy.

EXAMPLE: The unemployment rate is high at 9 percent. The government wants to bring it down to 5 percent. The government therefore enacts expansionary fiscal policy by raising its daily spending by $10 million a day. As a result, the private sector lowers its spending by $10 million a day. Did total spending in the economy go up? No. It's just that more government spending was completely offset by less private sector spending. Because every added dollar of government spending was offset by one less private sector dollar, we have *complete crowding out.* ♦

A Student Asks

QUESTION: *Can you explain crowding out using your vitamin comparison?*

ANSWER: *Yes, but with a modification. Let's say that we can get vitamins in two different ways. The first way is by having your body produce vitamins itself, using the food that you eat. The second way is the way we all know—getting vitamins through a vitamin pill. Now let's say the patient is sluggish because he lacks vitamins. The doctor gives him some vitamin pills. Now, because the doctor gives the patient some vitamin pills, the patient's body "decides" it is going to produce fewer vitamins itself. Crowding out happens in the same way. The government does X, but because the government is doing X now, when it wasn't before, the private sector no longer does X, or it doesn't do as much X as it used to do.*

Differentiating Instruction

Kinesthetic Learners

Reinforce the meanings of the terms in this section by tossing a tennis ball to a student. If the student drops the ball, she or he must define a term, such as *fiscal policy, expansionary fiscal policy, contractionary fiscal policy, crowding out, incomplete crowding out, crowding in, incomplete crowding in, zero crowding in, consumption, after-tax income, tax revenues,* or *Laffer curve.* If the student catches the ball, he or she chooses a classmate who must define the term. You might also ask students to give examples of terms or phrases. (For example, *complete crowding out* occurs when the government spends an additional dollar, and the private sector then reduces its expenditures by a dollar.)

Can Batman Crowd Out the Box Office?

The movie *Batman Begins* was released in June 2005. In its first five days of release, it earned $72.9 million.

Looking at these dollar amounts, some people would say that *Batman Begins* contributed to a higher total dollar amount spent on movies (in 2005). However, an increase in total movie spending is not inevitable after a blockbuster release. Some crowding out in movies may work in one of two ways.

Suppose the movie-going public spends an average of $70 million each weekend on movies when about 10 different movies are playing. Let's also assume that the $70 million is evenly distributed across all 10 movies, so each movie earns $7 million. So what happens when a blockbuster, like *Batman Begins*, is released? Does the total spent go up, or does Batman simply take more than one-tenth of the $70 million? Maybe it earns $20 million (instead of $7) and the nine remaining movies evenly divide up the remaining $50 million. In other words, spending on *Batman* comes at the expense of other movies. Blockbuster spending crowds out nonblockbuster spending in much the same way that government spending can crowd out household spending.

Of course, things don't have to work this way. Because of the blockbuster, total spending on movies on the blockbuster weekend may rise. In other words, the movie-going public may increase the amount it spends on movies in the first few weekends after a blockbuster is released. Spending may rise to, say, $90 million each weekend for three consecutive weekends. Once the "blockbuster effect" wears off, however, spending may fall below the usual $70 million per weekend—say, to $50 million per weekend for a few weekends. The blockbuster spending still crowds out nonblockbuster spending, although not as quickly. This crowding out occurs over a six-week period instead of during a given week.

Alternatively, a blockbuster may not crowd out nonblockbuster movie spending but may crowd out nonmovie spending. Suppose that because of a blockbuster, spending on movies actually does rise over a year. The new weekend average goes from $70 million to $80 million. Because people are spending more on movies, they spend less on other things, such as eating out and attending concerts. In other words, movie spending crowds out nonmovie spending. One sector in the economy (the movie sector) expands as another sector contracts.

THINK ABOUT IT A blockbuster movie is released on a given weekend, and the owner of the coffee shop next door to the theater says, "We're going to get a lot of business this weekend; in fact, I think this new blockbuster will increase our annual revenues." Is the coffee shop owner correct about the blockbuster increasing annual revenues?

Contractionary Fiscal Policy and the Problem of Inflation

Chapter 12 stated that inflation (increases in the price level) can occur when the aggregate demand in the economy grows faster than the aggregate supply in the economy. In other words, inflation is the result of *too much spending* in the economy compared to the quantity of goods and services available for purchase. Some economists describe inflation as "too much money chasing too few goods." Many of these economists argue that the way to get prices down in the economy is to reduce spending, which they say can be done

Ask students what the effect would be if two blockbusters were released the same weekend. Urge students to consider whether movie studios have an incentive to avoid releasing blockbusters at the same time.

ANSWERS TO THINK ABOUT IT Not necessarily. The coffee shop may have better-than-average business on the weekend that the blockbuster movie is first released (say, weekend 25), but, if there is crowding out, less-than-average business on some weekends in the future (say, weekends 32, 34, and 35). Overall, the average weekend business and annual revenues may not change.

Thinking Like an Economist

Tell students that if they were to ask an economist a question, they would probably get a conditional answer. For example, suppose they asked an economist if expansionary fiscal policy will bring about more spending in the economy. The economist might say that it will, given the condition that complete crowding out does not occur. In other words, if complete crowding out occurs, then expansionary fiscal policy will not increase spending in the economy; but if complete crowding out does not occur, then expansionary fiscal policy will increase spending in the economy. Some people, hearing this conditional answer, may think the economist simply cannot give a direct answer, but this is not the case at all. The economist is simply specifying the conditions under which expansionary fiscal policy works and the conditions under which it does not work. Put students in groups and assign each group to find examples of economists' using conditional answers. Allow groups to present their findings to the class.

Background Information: Conditional Answers

Economists provide conditional answers because conditions change—often quickly and frequently. Economists can speak without conditions only if they can be certain that nothing else will change. (Economists use the Latin phrase *ceteris paribus,* or "all else being equal," to describe this state.) As students study fiscal policy, they need to remember that the success of any fiscal policy is conditional. Expansionary and contractionary fiscal policy are used to help keep the economy flowing as well as can be expected. But, economists also keep in mind that *ceteris paribus* does not always exist in the real U.S. economy.

Clarifying Terms

Encourage students to draw pictures that will help them remember the meanings of *contractionary* and *expansionary.*

Prediction Activity

Stop students before they read "The Issue of Crowding In," and have them use what they know about crowding out to predict what crowding in is. If students need a hint, tell them that complete crowding in eliminates the effectiveness of a reduction in government spending.

Economics Around the Clock

Direct students to the 1:12 P.M. scenario in Economics Around the Clock (page 341), and discuss their answers to the question provided there.

Students should note that when the government spends more, it is possible that people will spend less. If they do, economists say that government spending has "crowded out" some private spending.

through contractionary fiscal policy. Here are the points they make:

- Inflation is the result of too much spending in the economy. So, if people spent less money, firms would initially sell fewer goods. The firms would end up with a surplus of goods in their warehouses. To get rid of their goods, they would have to lower prices.
- To get prices down, Congress should implement contractionary fiscal policy by decreasing government spending, raising taxes, or both. Let's suppose that government cuts its spending.
- The decrease in government spending means less overall spending in the economy. To illustrate, suppose that at current prices the government is spending $1,800 billion, business is spending $1,200 billion, and consumers are spending $6,000 billion. Total spending at current prices is $9,000 billion. Government decides to cut its spending by $200 billion. Now total spending decreases to $8,800 billion.
- As a result of the decrease in total spending, firms initially sell fewer goods.
- When they sell fewer goods, firms end up with surplus goods on hand. The inventories in their warehouses and factories rise above a desired level, so to get rid of the unwanted inventory (the surplus goods), firms lower prices.

A Student Asks

QUESTION: *If high unemployment was similar to having "too few vitamins" (to return to the story of a person's health and the doctor), would inflation be similar to having "too many vitamins"?*

ANSWER: *Yes, and so the "cure" for too many vitamins is for the doctor to cut back on the number of vitamin pills she recommends that you take each day. That would be similar to the government reducing its spending (enacting contractionary fiscal policy).*

crowding in
The situation in which decreases in government spending lead to increases in private spending.

The Issue of Crowding In

As with expansionary fiscal policies, some economists do not agree that things will turn out the way they are supposed to with contractionary fiscal policies. They say that if government reduces its spending, total spending in the economy will not necessarily decline. They point out that **crowding in** occurs when decreases in government spending lead to increases in private spending.

Suppose government decreases its spending on public education by $2 million. As a result, people turn to private education, increasing their purchases of it by $2 million. This dollar-for-dollar trade-off is referred to as *complete crowding in*; for every $1 decrease in government spending on education, private spending on education increases $1. Because of complete crowding in, total spending in the economy does not change. Thus, if complete crowding in occurs, a decrease in government spending will not lead to a decrease in total spending in the economy, so it will not bring prices down.

It is possible that *crowding in* is not complete. In other words, it is possible to have *incomplete crowding in* or *zero crowding in.* With zero crowding in, private spending remains constant for every $1 cut in government spending. Incomplete crowding in means that for every $1 cut in government spending, private spending rises by less than $1. For example, for every $1 decrease in government spending on education, private spending on education may rise by, say, 60 cents. With either zero or incomplete crowding in, a decrease in government spending will lead to a decrease in total spending in the economy, so it will bring prices down. (Exhibit 13-2 summarizes the effectiveness of fiscal policy under various conditions.)

A Student Asks

QUESTION: *I've noticed in our discussion of fiscal policy so far, that you say some economists think one way, but then other economists disagree with them. Is there much disagreement among economists?*

Differentiating Instruction

Visual Learners

Creating a pictorial representation often helps visual learners focus on and retain information. Assign students to create two cartoons, one that illustrates the concept of crowding in and one that illustrates the concept of crowding out. Give students an opportunity to explain their cartoons to the class.

ANSWER: *Yes, economists frequently disagree—especially when it comes to macroeconomic issues such as what causes inflation and how fiscal policy works. Economists have different ideas about what will cure the economy's ills, in much the same way that doctors often disagree about a patient's illness and the best remedy. High school and college economic students have always yearned for their teachers to simply tell them how the economy works, in much the same way that a math teacher might teach them how to solve for X in the following equation: 2X + 1 = 5. Things aren't quite as simple or as neat and tidy in economics.*

Are economists simply not smart enough to figure out exactly how the economy works? It is probably not that. The economy, like the human body, is a complicated mechanism. We know a lot more about it today than we used to, but it is still not easy to figure out exactly how it works.

Fiscal Policy and Taxes

The discussion up to this point focused on either an increase or a decrease in government spending. Besides changing its spending, government can also change taxes. Changes in taxes are different from spending changes in that tax changes can affect two sides of the economy, rather than just one. Changes in taxes can affect the spending (demand) side of the economy and the producing (supply) side of the economy.

How Taxes Can Affect the Spending (Demand) Side of the Economy

You may remember from Chapter 11 that economists designate four sectors in the economy: the household sector, the business sector, the government sector, and the foreign sector. For now, let's look at just the household sector (also called consumption) and assume that no crowding out or crowding in occurs.

EXHIBIT 13-2 The Effectiveness of Fiscal Policy

Objective	Policy	Condition existing	Does the policy affect total spending in the economy?	Does the policy meet the objective (as stated in the first column)?
Reduce unemployment	Expansionary fiscal policy (as measured by an increase in government spending)	No crowding out	Yes	Yes
	Same as above	Complete crowding out	No	No
	Same as above	Incomplete crowding out	Yes	Yes

(a)

Objective	Policy	Condition existing	Does the policy affect total spending in the economy?	Does the policy meet the objective (as stated in the first column)?
Reduce inflation	Contractionary fiscal policy (as measured by a decrease in government spending)	No crowding in	Yes	Yes
	Same as above	Complete crowding in	No	No
	Same as above	Incomplete crowding in	Yes	Yes

(b)

◀ (a) The degree of crowding out determines the effectiveness of expansionary fiscal policy.
(b) The degree of crowding in determines the effectiveness of contractionary fiscal policy.

Problem Solving

Invite students to imagine they are government officials with some influence over fiscal policy. Tell students that inflation is high, and ask them how they would solve this problem and what conditions would have to be in place for the solution to work. Then tell students that the unemployment rate has skyrocketed. Ask them what they would suggest to solve this problem and why.

Teaching with Visuals

The information in Exhibit 13-2 will help students clearly grasp the differences between expansionary and contractionary fiscal policies. Review each part of the chart with students to ensure that they understand differences between the two.

Cross-Curricular Activity

Invite a government teacher to your class to discuss fiscal policy. You might wish to introduce the topic by quickly reviewing the aims of fiscal policy as well as the definitions of contractionary fiscal policy and expansionary fiscal policy. The government teacher can then discuss the mechanics of implementing fiscal policy, including the president's budget proposals, significant lobbies, congressional battles, and final adoption. You might ask the government teacher to stress how particular interest groups and party loyalties can influence fiscal policy.

Reinforcement Activity

Tell students to search newspapers and magazines for articles about taxation and its effects on the economy. If you are teaching this class during or near an election period, there should be a lot of information on the proposed taxation policies of the candidates and their implications.

A Student Asks

Lead students in a discussion of the advantages and disadvantages of cutting taxes at different rates according to income level.

Reinforcement Activity

Assign students to research the sales tax rates for every state in the United States. Which states have the highest sales tax rates? Which have the lowest? Try to find the annual sales tax revenue for each state as well. Which states have the highest total and per capita revenue from sales tax? Guide students in a discussion of the benefits citizens garner from their taxes. Then have students decide if they would raise or lower the sales tax in their state. Ask them to identify advantages of either change.

Economics Around the Clock

After students read "Tax Rates and Tax Revenues" (pages 349–350), refer them to the 9:43 A.M. scenario in Economics Around the Clock (page 341) and discuss their answers to the question provided there.

Note that George may be right: lower tax rates can lower tax revenues. However, George is not necessarily right. Sometimes lower tax rates can actually raise tax revenues, if the lower rates motivate people to generate more income. Whether tax revenues rise or fall depends on the percentage reduction in the tax rate compared with the percentage increase in income. For example, if the tax rate drops by 5%, but income rises by 15%, then tax revenues will rise.

Members of the household sector get most of the money they spend on goods and services from their income. However, people do not get to spend all the income they earn; part of it goes to pay taxes. The part left over is called **after-tax income**.

Let's say that the average household spends 90 percent of its after-tax income and saves the rest. (In other words, out of every $1 earned, it spends 90 cents and saves 10 cents.) Now suppose the average household earns $60,000 a year and pays $15,000 in taxes. The household has an after-tax income of $45,000. If the household spends 90 percent of its after-tax income, then $40,500 ($45,000 × 0.90 = $40,500) is spent on goods and services. If the economy includes, say, 50 million households, the entire household sector spends the following on consumption: 50 million × $40,500 = $2,025 billion.

What happens if government lowers taxes? For example, suppose it lowers taxes such that the average household no longer pays $15,000 in taxes but rather pays $10,000 in taxes. After-tax income now rises from $45,000 to $50,000. If the average household continues to spend 90 percent of its income, it now spends $45,000 ($50,000 × 0.90 = $45,000) on goods and services. If we multiply this amount times 50 million households, we get $2,250 billion. In other words, as a result of a decrease in taxes, consumption spending has risen from $2,025 billion to $2,250 billion. If no other sector's spending in the economy falls, then total spending in the economy rises as a result of a tax cut.

The increase in total spending means that firms sell more goods. When firms start to sell more goods, they hire more workers to produce the additional goods. The unemployment rate goes down as a result of more people working.

Would things work in the opposite direction if taxes were raised? Most economists think so. A rise in taxes would lower after-tax income, thus lowering consumption spending. A reduction in consumption spending, in turn, would lower total spending in the economy.

after-tax income
The part of income that's left over after taxes are paid.

EXAMPLE: The unemployment rate is high and the government wants to lower it. The government chooses to use expansionary fiscal policy; that is, it will either raise government spending or lower taxes or do some combination of both. Let's say it decides to cut taxes. As a result of cutting taxes, individuals have more after-tax income. Suppose the average taxpayer ends up with an extra $100 a month in after-tax income. What does she do with this extra $100 after-tax income? She might save part of it, but then she probably spends some of it too. This extra spending means that businesses will end up selling more goods and services. As a result, they will have to hire more workers to produce the additional goods and services. In the end, the unemployment rate drops. ♦

A Student Asks

QUESTION: *When the government cuts taxes, does it cut the taxes on all income groups the same? For example, suppose one person earns $1 million a year and another person earns $50,000 a year. Do both persons have their taxes cut by the same dollar amount or by the same percentage?*

ANSWER: *No, not necessarily. It could be that everyone's taxes go down by, say, 5 percent, or it could be that some people's taxes go down by 4 percent, others by 5 percent, and so on. Depending on how Congress writes the tax law, everyone could receive the same tax cut, or many different groups of people could all receive different amounts of cuts.*

How Taxes Can Affect the Producing (Supply) Side of the Economy

How much would anyone work if income taxes were 100 percent? In other words, if out of every $1 a person earned, he or she had to pay the full $1 in taxes, how many hours a week would the person work? Of course, no one would work if he or she had to pay 100 percent of earnings in taxes. It

Cooperative Learning

Divide students into small groups and assign each group to re-create Exhibit 13-2 on a large piece of construction paper. For each column, students should provide illustrations that they believe explain or represent the textual information they have copied. Have groups justify the illustrations they have used. Post the results in the classroom.

stands to reason, then, that people would work more as the income tax rate came down from 100 percent. For example, people might work more at a 40 percent tax rate than at a 70 percent tax rate.

We can also look at this concept in terms of after-tax income. The higher your after-tax income, the more you are willing to work; the lower your after-tax income, the less you are willing to work. In other words, we would expect a much more industrious, hard-working, long-working labor force when the average income tax rate is, say, 20 percent than when it is 70 percent. It follows, then, that the supply of goods and services in the economy will be greater (the aggregate supply curve shifts rightward) when taxes are lower than when they are higher.

Tax Rates and Tax Revenues

Many people think that a tax rate cut results in lower tax revenues for the government, but it is not necessarily true. Tax cuts can lead to lower or to higher tax revenues.

If Smith is a representative taxpayer who earns $2,000 each month and pays an average tax rate of 40 percent, then he pays $800 in taxes. His after-tax income is $1,200.

Tax revenue = Average tax rate × Income

Now suppose the average tax rate is cut to 35 percent. Does it follow that tax revenues will decline? Not necessarily. As was stated earlier, tax cuts often stimulate more work, and more work leads to more income. Suppose, as a result of the tax cut, Smith works more and earns $2,500 a month, an increase in his income of $500 a month. Now he pays 35 percent of $2,500 in taxes, or $875, and he is left with an after-tax income of $1,625.

Thus, at a tax rate of 40 percent Smith paid $800 in taxes, but at a tax rate of 35 percent he paid $875 in taxes. So, in this example, if Smith is the representative taxpayer, a *tax rate cut* will actually *increase tax revenues*. The government will take in more tax money with a tax cut, not less money, because the rise in income was greater than the tax cut. Income rose from $2,000 to $2,500 a month, which is a 25 percent increase. The tax rate cut was from 40 to 35 percent, which is a 12.5 percent cut. In other words, as long as income rises by more than the taxes are cut, tax revenues will rise.

Consider what could have happened, though. Suppose Smith's income had risen from $2,000 to $2,100 (a 5 percent rise in income) instead of to $2,500. At a tax rate of 35 percent and an income of $2,100, Smith pays $735 in taxes. In other words, he pays less in taxes at a lower tax rate. If he is the representative taxpayer, it follows that lower tax rates generate lower tax revenues, because the rise in income (5 percent) is less than the tax rate cut (12.5 percent).

A group of economists, called *supply-side economists*, believe that cuts in high tax rates can generate higher tax revenues, whereas cuts in low tax rates generate lower tax revenues. To illustrate, Exhibit 13-3(a) starts at a relatively high tax rate of 90 percent (point A). A tax rate cut to 80 percent raises tax revenue from $700 billion to $1,000 billion. Lower tax rates go together with higher tax revenues.

Alternatively, Exhibit 13-3(b) starts at a relatively low tax rate of 20 percent (point A). A tax rate cut to 10 percent lowers tax

▼ Most people assume that the higher the tax rates, the more tax revenue the government collects. **Can you explain why this is not necessarily the case?**

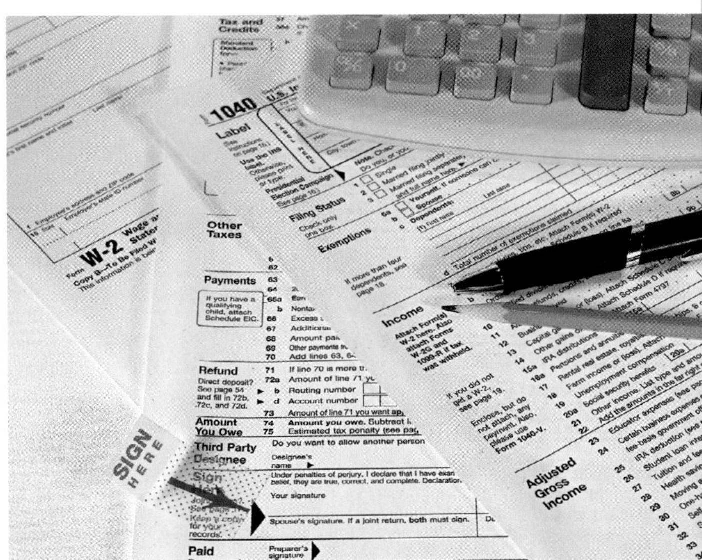

Teaching with Visuals

Tax revenues might fall as a result of a higher tax rate because people might be less motivated to work and thus generate lower income on which to be taxed.

Application Activity

After reading and discussing Section 1, you may want to assign the Section Activity in the *Applying the Principles Workbook.*

Assess

Quick Quiz

The following true-or-false quiz will help you assess student understanding of the material covered in this section.

1. If government spending is increased and taxes are increased, it is expansionary fiscal policy. (False)
2. Expansionary fiscal policy brings up the issue of crowding out. (True)
3. If the inflation rate is high, government may implement contractionary fiscal policy. (True)
4. Incomplete crowding in will make contractionary fiscal policy ineffective. (False)
5. Tax cuts always lead to lower tax revenues. (False)

Assessment Book

You will find a quiz for this section in the *Assessment Book.*

Background Information: Taxes and the Middle Class

Middle-class families in some states pay more taxes than middle-class families in other states. For example, in 2000, middle-class families in Alaska, Idaho, Maine, Minnesota, New York, North Carolina, Oregon, Utah, Virginia, and Wisconsin paid what are considered to be very high taxes. Middle-class families in other states, including Florida, Nevada, New Hampshire, North Dakota, Pennsylvania, Texas, and Wyoming paid very low taxes. Discuss with students reasons that might account for these differences in taxes.

Section 1 Fiscal Policy 349

Reteaching Activity

Use the Section Assessment to gauge which students may need reteaching on this section. Give those students each a balloon and ask the students to inflate the balloons. This is expansionary. Instruct them to let the air out of the balloons, and explain that this is contractionary. Ask students to relate this activity to fiscal policy.

Guided Reading

For further reteaching of the key concepts in this section, assign the Outlining Activity and the Just the Facts Handout from the *Guided Reading and Study Guide*.

EXHIBIT 13-3 A Hypothetical Laffer Curve

▲ The Laffer curve represents the relationship between tax rates and tax revenues that some economists believe exists. Starting at relatively high tax rates, a *tax rate cut* will generate *higher tax revenues*. For example, as shown in (a), the tax rate is cut from 90 percent to 80 percent and tax revenues rise. Starting at relatively low tax rates, a *tax rate cut* will generate *lower tax revenues*. For example, as shown in (b), the tax rate is cut from 20 percent to 10 percent and tax revenues fall. The Laffer curve is named after economist Arthur Laffer.

Laffer curve
The curve, named after economist Arthur Laffer, that shows the relationship between tax rates and tax revenues. According to the Laffer curve, as tax rates rise from zero, tax revenues rise, reach a maximum at some point, and then fall with further increases in tax rates.

revenue from $1,000 billion to $700 billion. This time, lower tax rates are accompanied by lower tax revenues.

The curve in Exhibit 13-3 is called the **Laffer curve**, after economist Arthur Laffer. The Laffer curve simply illustrates the relationship that some economists believe exists between tax rates and tax revenues.

In Exhibit 13-3, you will notice that tax revenue is maximized at a tax rate of 50 percent. No one knows whether it is maximized at 50 percent; specific tax rates were added to the Laffer curve drawn here merely for explanatory purposes. As far as anyone knows, tax revenue may be maximized at some tax rate higher or lower than 50 percent.

SECTION 1 ASSESSMENT

Defining Terms

1. Define:
   a. fiscal policy
   b. expansionary fiscal policy
   c. contractionary fiscal policy
   d. crowding out
   e. crowding in
   f. after-tax income
   g. Laffer curve

Reviewing Facts and Concepts

2. What is contractionary fiscal policy, and why is it likely to be used?
3. Give a numerical example of complete crowding out.
4. Even though changes in government spending principally affect the demand side of the economy, a change in taxes can affect both the demand side and the supply side of the economy. Do you agree or disagree? Explain your answer.

Critical Thinking

5. Is expansionary fiscal policy always effective at increasing total spending in the economy and decreasing unemployment? Explain your answer.

Applying Economic Concepts

6. Someone says, "If the federal government cuts income tax rates, tax revenues will rise." Might this person be wrong? Explain your answer.

SECTION 1 ASSESSMENT ANSWERS

Defining Terms

1. a. fiscal policy: changes government makes in spending or taxation to achieve particular macroeconomic goals; **b. expansionary fiscal policy:** increases in government spending or a reduction in taxes; **c. contractionary fiscal policy:** decreases in government spending or an increase in taxes; **d. crowding out:** refers to increases in government spending that may lead to reductions in private spending; **e. crowding in:** refers to decreases in government spending that may lead to increases in private spending; **f. after-tax income:** income after taxes have been taken out; **g. Laffer curve:** a diagram that shows the relationship between tax rates and tax revenues.

Reviewing Facts and Concepts

2. It is a decrease in government spending and/or an increase in taxes. It is used to reduce total spending and thereby to reduce inflation.

3. Government spends $10 billion more, and the private sector spends $10 billion less.

4. Students should agree. Government spending is one of the four components of total spending in the economy. If there is incomplete or no crowding out, a rise in government spending will raise total spending in the economy. A change in total spending affects the demand side of the economy. A change in taxes can affect the demand side by affecting after-tax income. It affects the supply side by affecting the incentive to work and produce goods.

Critical Thinking

5. No. Its effectiveness depends on whether there is complete crowding out or not. If for every $1 increase in government spending, private spending decreases by $1, then a rise in government spending will not decrease unemployment.

Applying Economic Concepts

6. The person might be wrong. If the tax rate falls on the upward-sloping portion of the Laffer curve, an income tax rate cut will lower tax revenues.

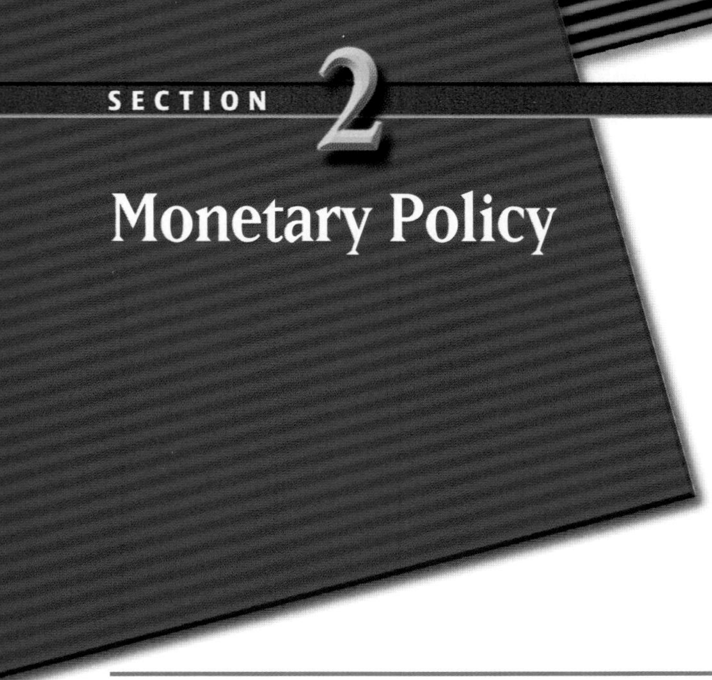

SECTION 2

Monetary Policy

Focus Questions

- What type of monetary policy is used to reduce unemployment?
- What type of monetary policy is used to reduce inflation?
- How does monetary policy reduce unemployment and inflation?
- What is the purpose of the exchange equation?

Key Terms

monetary policy
expansionary monetary policy
contractionary monetary policy

Two Types of Monetary Policy

Monetary policy deals with changes in the money supply. If the Fed increases the money supply, it is implementing **expansionary monetary policy**. Its objective is to increase total spending in the economy to reduce the unemployment rate. If the Fed decreases the money supply, it does so to reduce total spending and thereby reduce inflation. In this case it is implementing **contractionary monetary policy**.

Expansionary Monetary Policy and the Problem of Unemployment

Many economists believe expansionary monetary policy works to lower the unemployment rate in the following manner:

- The Fed increases the money supply.
- A greater money supply is usually associated with greater total spending in the economy. (There is more money to spend.)
- As a result of increased spending in the economy, firms begin to sell more products.
- As firms sell more products, they hire more workers, thus lowering the unemployment rate.

The issue of crowding out does not arise in monetary policy. If the Fed increases the money supply, no one need spend less; there is simply more money to spend.

Because crowding out is not an issue with expansionary monetary policy, many economists argue that an increase in the money supply will increase total spending in the economy, which will indirectly lower the unemployment rate.

EXAMPLE: The Fed meets and decides that the unemployment rate in the economy is too high. The Fed wants to lower the unemployment rate. It decides to enact expansionary monetary policy—in other words, it decides to increase the money supply. In an earlier chapter, you learned the Fed can increase the money supply by (1) lowering the reserve requirement, (2) undertaking an open market sale, or (3) lowering the

monetary policy
Changes the Fed makes in the money supply.

expansionary monetary policy
An increase in the money supply.

contractionary monetary policy
A decrease in the money supply.

Differentiating Instruction

English Language Learners

Some terms and phrases in this chapter may be difficult for students to understand. Encourage students to rephrase, in their own words, difficult words and phrases in this chapter. For example, they might say that *expansionary fiscal policy* is "a plan for expanding the amount of money that people spend in the economy." Then review the concepts behind the terms and phrases. On the board, draw the three-way connection between the original terms, the students' phrases, and the concept the term or phrase represents.

SECTION 2

Teacher Support

Focus and Motivate

Section Objectives

After completing the section, students will be able to

- describe the type of monetary policy used to reduce unemployment;
- describe the type of monetary policy used to reduce inflation;
- explain how monetary policy reduces unemployment and inflation; and
- explain the purpose of the exchange equation.

Kickoff Activity

Have students answer the following at the beginning of class: In an earlier chapter, you learned that the Federal Reserve can increase or decrease the money supply. What do you think the effects on the economy are of changing the money supply?

Activating Prior Knowledge

Allow students to share their responses to the Kickoff Activity. Some of their responses may reflect the following: increasing the money supply will increase the amount of spending in the economy; decreasing the money supply will decrease the amount of spending in the economy.

Teach

Reinforcement Activity

The economist Milton Friedman is closely associated with the topic of monetary policy. Assign students to research the life and work of Milton Friedman and either present their findings to the class or turn in their work.

Economics in the Real World

Ask for volunteers to share instances in which their families moved or experienced a similarly significant life change in response to an economic situation.

ANSWERS TO THINK ABOUT IT **1.** Answers will vary. **2.** Answers will vary.

Economics in the Real World

Can Monetary Policy Determine Eye Color?

Scientists sometimes use the term *butterfly effect* to express the idea that small changes can be catalysts for huge changes (that are far removed in time and space from the initial small change). To illustrate, suppose a butterfly is flying over the equator. It flaps its wings as its flies. The flap of a butterfly's wings is a tiny thing, but it could be just enough (at a particular place and time) to cause a small change in the weather, which could ultimately change the weather conditions around the world. A butterfly flapping its wings over Brazil could be the catalyst that ends up producing a hurricane off the coast of Florida.

Some people use the butterfly effect to explain why it is so hard to predict the future. After all, if something as small as a butterfly flapping its wings can make the difference between a hurricane and no hurricane, then how many other little things in the world can upset one's predictions?

People also use the butterfly effect to explain how a change in one place—far away from a person—can end up affecting that person's life. These people might even say that a change in monetary policy can affect a person's life, maybe even yours.

Take the case of Caroline, who is 17 years old. Caroline has blue eyes. One day someone asks her why she has blue eyes. She says it is because both her mother and father have blue eyes.

Now we ask ourselves how Caroline's mother and father met. It turns out that they met in Denver. Her mother was a college student at the time and her father was working on a construction crew building apartment buildings. When we dig deeper, we learn that the only reason Caroline's father was in Denver is because he couldn't find work in his hometown, Austin, Texas. Why couldn't he find work in Austin? Well, at the time, the economy was depressed and the unemployment rate was high.

Reacting to this state of affairs, the Fed decided to increase the rate of growth in the money supply. The "new money" the Fed created found its way initially to Denver, and so the Denver economy started moving upwards before many other local economies. The man who was to become Caroline's father, who was living in Austin at the time, heard that jobs were plentiful in Denver and so he went there looking for a job.

In other words, if the Fed hadn't increased the money supply, the Denver economy might not have started booming (when it did). And if Denver's economy hadn't begun to boom, Caroline's father may not have gone to Denver, where he met and married Caroline's mother. And if they hadn't met, they would not have had Caroline—who, we remember, has blue eyes because both her mother and father have blue eyes.

Or does Caroline have blue eyes because of the Fed enacting monetary policy?

THINK ABOUT IT 1. Try to find butterfly effects in your life. How many can you come up with?

2. Create a story in which a change in fiscal or monetary policy causes what would seem to be an unrelated event (similar to Caroline's having blue eyes).

Background Information: John Maynard Keynes

John Maynard Keynes (1883–1946) is considered one of the greatest economists of all time. Before Keynes, most economists thought it was impossible for insufficient spending within an economy to cause high unemployment. They said that if people were spending too little, firms would simply lower prices, and people would start buying more goods.

Keynes argued that even if people were not spending much money, firms such as car manufacturers might not lower prices because doing so would necessitate reducing wages. If wages could not be cut, the car manufacturer might not lower prices.

Why wouldn't wage rates decrease? You would think that a representative of the car manufacturer could go discount rate. In time, the money supply rises. People have more money to spend, and so they spend it. As a result, firms sell more goods and services. To produce the additional goods and services, the firms have to hire more people. In the end, the unemployment rate drops. ♦

A Student Asks

QUESTION: *Do the president or members of Congress have anything to do with monetary policy?*

ANSWER: *No, strictly speaking monetary policy is under the jurisdiction of the Fed (which we discussed in Chapter 10). The president and the members of Congress deal with fiscal policy, the Fed with monetary policy.*

Contractionary Monetary Policy and the Problem of Inflation

Many economists believe contractionary monetary policy works to reduce inflation in the following manner:

- The Fed decreases the money supply, perhaps by conducting an open-market sale. (Open-market sales are discussed in Chapter 10.)
- A smaller money supply is usually associated with lower total spending in the economy. (There is less money to spend.)
- As a result of the decrease in spending in the economy, firms begin to sell less.
- As firms sell fewer products, their inventories in the warehouses rise. To get rid of surplus goods, firms reduce prices (or they at least stop raising prices).

Exhibit 13-4 summarizes expansionary and contractionary monetary policies.

Monetary Policy and the Exchange Equation

The exchange equation, introduced in Chapter 12, states that the money supply (M) times velocity (V) is equal to the price level (P) times the quantity of goods and services produced (Q):

$$M \times V = P \times Q$$

Some economists say that the objective of monetary policy, pure and simple, is to maintain a stable price level—in other words, keep P constant in the exchange equation. If this objective is met, then neither inflation (P rising) nor deflation (P falling) occurs.

Suppose maintaining a stable price level is the objective. How should the Fed go about meeting it? To answer this question, we must realize that if $M \times V = P \times Q$, then

$$\%\Delta M + \%\Delta V = \%\Delta P + \%\Delta Q$$

where Δ stands for "change in." In other words, the percentage change in the money supply plus the percentage change in velocity equals the percentage change in the price

The Federal Open Market Committee (FOMC) largely determines monetary policy in the United States. Visit the Web site for the FOMC at www.emcp.net/fomc.
Who are the current members of the FOMC?

▼ Expansionary monetary policy is used to reduce unemployment; contractionary monetary policy is used to reduce inflation.

EXHIBIT 13-4 The Effectiveness of Monetary Policy

Objective	Policy	Does the policy affect total spending in the economy?	Does the policy meet the objective?
Reduce unemployment	Expansionary monetary policy	Yes	Yes
Reduce inflation	Contractionary monetary policy	Yes	Yes

to the workers and say, "I need to lower car prices so that people will buy more cars. That way we can avoid layoffs." Keynes said that workers would initially resist wage cuts, thinking that the car manufacturer was trying to pay them less to earn higher profits.

If wages are not coming down quickly and sellers are not reducing prices, people might be laid off from their jobs because consumers are not spending enough for full employment to exist. Keynes argued that at this point, total spending in the economy had to be increased. Government had to either increase its spending or lower taxes. Critics, however, argue that Keynes's proposal did not take into account crowding out: if government spends more, consumers and businesses will spend less.

A Student Asks

Use this A Student Asks as an opportunity to review the difference between fiscal policy and monetary policy.

Visit the Web site www.emcp.net/fomc for a current list of FOMC members, and use this list to check students' answers.

Economics Around the Clock

Refer students to the 3:03 P.M. scenario in Economics Around the Clock (page 341), and discuss their answers to the question provided there.

Be sure students understand that Mark is advocating expansionary monetary policy. Advocating large increases in the money supply, as Mark is doing, is likely to lead to a high inflation rate. Think of it in terms of the exchange equation: $M \times V = P \times Q$. If the money supply (M) rises sharply, and V and Q are relatively constant, then prices (P) will rise sharply.

Economics in the Real World

Ask students whether they think this is a plausible interpretation of *The Wonderful Wizard of Oz.* Clarify any parts of the interpretation students find confusing.

ANSWERS TO THINK ABOUT IT Answers will vary. Students might say that Baum seemed to be aware of the role that the money supply part of the equation plays in the economy, even if he wasn't aware of the exact exchange equation.

Discussion Starter

You might want to show clips from the movie *The Wizard of Oz* to illustrate the symbolism in Baum's book. After students have watched the clips, discuss the gold standard once again with the class.

What Is *The Wizard of Oz* Really About?

??????????????????

For most people, *The Wizard of Oz* is the story of a young girl, Dorothy, who travels a yellow brick road to Emerald City, where she encounters a wizard (who really isn't a wizard). But *The Wizard of Oz* is really a story about monetary policy in the United States about 1893.

The country had fallen into an economic depression. The stock market had crashed, banks had failed, many workers had been laid off. Some people blamed the bad times on the gold standard. The gold standard was a monetary arrangement where gold backed paper money, and so a major way to get more paper money was to get more gold.

Now many people at the time said that the economic bad times would disappear if only people had more money to spend. They didn't have any more money to spend because the government had already printed up all the paper money it could, given its gold supply. What to do? Some suggested that the government should use both gold and silver to back paper money, and not only gold. With gold and silver backing the paper money supply, more money could be printed, turning the bad economic times into good economic times.

One of the champions of the so-called silver movement was William Jennings Bryan, who was the Democratic candidate for the U.S. presidency in 1896. A big supporter of Bryan was L. Frank Baum, the author of *The Wonderful Wizard of Oz*, which was the book that was the basis for the 1939 movie *The Wizard of Oz*.

In the book and movie, Dorothy represents William Jennings Bryan.

Both Dorothy and Bryan were young (Bryan was 36 years old when he ran for the presidency). The cyclone in the book and movie transports Dorothy to Oz in much the same way that the delegates at the Democratic convention lifted Bryan into the world of presidential politics. (Oz is the abbreviation for ounces, as in an ounce of gold or an ounce of silver, the common measurement for these two metals.)

As Dorothy begins her travels to the Emerald City (which represents Washington, D.C.) with her dog Toto (who represents the Democratic Party) to meet the Wizard of Oz, she travels down a yellow brick road. The yellow brick road represents the gold standard. On her way, she meets a scarecrow (who represents the farmers of the day), a tin man (who represents the manufacturing workers of the day), and a cowardly lion (who represents the Populist Party of the time). The Populist Party was often represented in cartoons of the day as a lion. It was said to be cowardly because it didn't have the courage to wage an independent campaign for the presidency in 1896.

The message was clear, according to Baum. Jennings, along with the farmers, manufacturers, the Populist Party, and the Democratic Party, would travel along the road of the gold standard to Washington, D.C., and make things right.

Once Dorothy reaches the Emerald City, however, she and the others are denied their wishes, just as Bryan is denied the presidency. (He loses the election.)

All is not over though. Dorothy still must battle with the Wicked Witch of the West, who wears a golden cap (the gold standard). When the witch sees Dorothy's silver shoes (they were ruby shoes in the movie but silver shoes in the book), she desperately wants them for their magical quality. Unfortunately for the witch, Dorothy kills the Wicked Witch of the West, and then clicks her silver slippers together. The silver slippers take her back home, where all is right with the world.

THINK ABOUT IT Do you think Baum had any knowledge of the exchange equation? Explain your answer.

Internet Research

Tell students to use the Internet to find out more about differing economic theories concerning monetary policies. They should search for sites discussing Keynes, Friedman, and other prominent economists. Have them write papers comparing and contrasting at least two of these theories. They should be sure to discuss the differing views on the relationship of fiscal policy to inflation and unemployment.

level plus the percentage change in the quantity of goods and services. For example, if the money supply grows by, say, 3 percent, and velocity rises by 1 percent, then it means a 4 percent change on the left-hand side of the exchange equation. Ask yourself how much the right-hand side must rise now (because the right-hand side will always equal the left-hand side). The answer is 4 percent.

The exchange equation can be rearranged in a way that shows how the percentage change in the money supply is calculated. Subtracting %ΔV from both sides gives us:

$$\%\Delta M = \%\Delta P + \%\Delta Q - \%\Delta V$$

With this equation in mind, suppose that the average annual changes in velocity and quantity of goods and services are as follows:

1. %ΔV = 1%
2. %ΔQ = 3%

Now let's assume that the objective is to hold the price level stable:

3. Objective: %ΔP = 0%

Given 1 through 3, how much should the Fed increase the money supply so that the price level does not change? The answer is 2 percent:

$$\begin{array}{cccc} \%\Delta M = & \%\Delta P + & \%\Delta Q - & \%\Delta V \\ \downarrow & \downarrow & \downarrow & \downarrow \\ 2\% = & 0\% + & 3\% - & 1\% \end{array}$$

Some economists propose that monetary policy should be implemented this way—that is, put on automatic pilot. The Fed should simply compute the average annual change in velocity and in the quantity of goods and services, set the percentage change in prices equal to 0 percent, and calculate the money supply change accordingly. The Fed should not fiddle with the money supply from month to month or year to year. It should not increase it sometimes and decrease it other times.

Will such a policy always yield stable prices? Probably not, because in some years V and Q will change by more or less than the average annual rate. For example, if the average annual change in velocity is 1 percent, some years it might change by, say, 2 percent or 0.5 percent. Economists who support this type of monetary policy, however, say that the changes in V and Q will be close enough to their average annual changes that we will

▼ Meeting of the members of the Federal Reserve Board in Washington, D.C. **How might this meeting affect the price you pay for the goods you buy?**

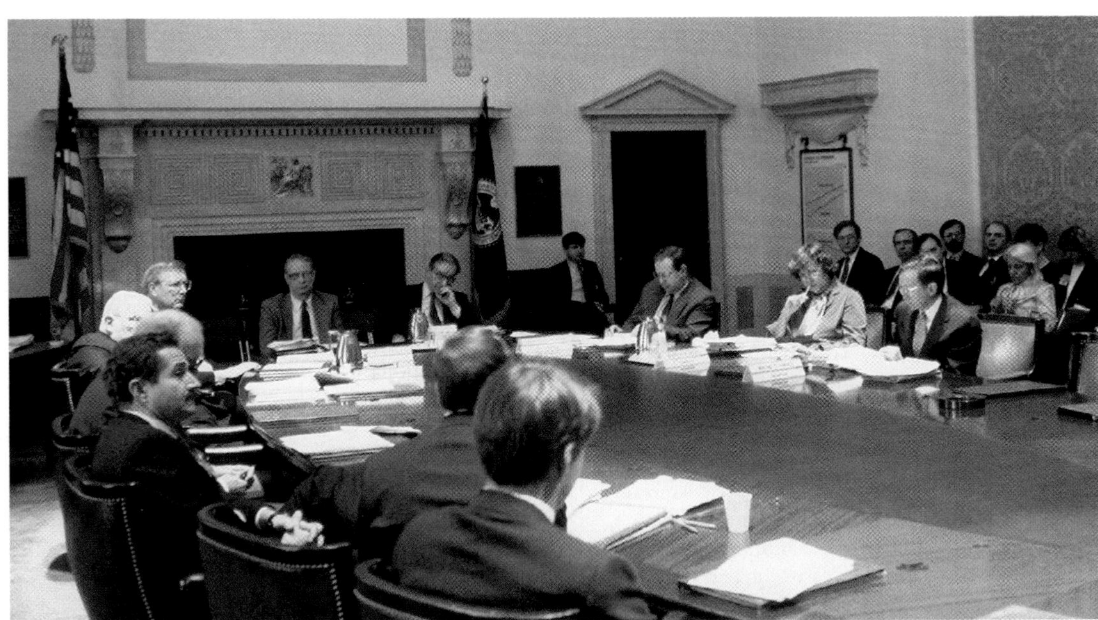

Reinforcement Activity

If students have trouble with the section "Monetary Policy and the Exchange Equation" (pages 353–356), have them review the section in Chapter 12 on the simple quantity theory of money (pages 315–316). Create several problems using various values for the percentage changes in money supply, velocity, price level, and quantity of goods and services produced. Call on students to work through the problems on the board.

Teaching with Visuals

If the Fed decreases the money supply, prices should drop to help firms sell their rising inventories.

Application Activity

After reading and discussing Section 2, you may want to assign the Section Activity in the *Applying the Principles Workbook.*

Cooperative Learning

Divide the class into two groups. Have one group gather information that supports the idea that the monetary policy should be put on "automatic pilot" as described in the text. Assign the other group to research counterarguments to this idea. Have each side present their findings to the class. Then lead a class discussion about whether the Fed should continue its practice of adjusting the money supply from time to time.

Assess

Quick Quiz

The following true-or-false quiz will help you assess student understanding of the material covered in this section.

1. Expansionary monetary policy does nothing to reduce unemployment. (False)
2. Contractionary monetary policy does nothing to reduce inflation. (False)
3. Some economists believe that monetary policy should be placed on automatic pilot. (True)
4. As a result of contractionary monetary policy, firms sell fewer goods. (True)
5. Decreasing the money supply counts as expansionary monetary policy. (False)

Assessment Book

You will find a quiz for this section in the *Assessment Book*.

Reteaching Activity

Use the Section Assessment to gauge which students may need reteaching on this section. Work with those students to create flowcharts showing what happens to the economy during times of expansionary monetary policy and during times of contractionary monetary policy.

Guided Reading

For further reteaching of the key concepts in this section, assign the Outlining Activity and the Just the Facts Handout from the *Guided Reading and Study Guide*.

come close to keeping prices stable if we simply put money supply changes (monetary policy) on automatic pilot.

A Student Asks

QUESTION: *It seems to me that you are saying that the president, the members of Congress, and the Fed can use economic policy (fiscal or monetary) to get rid of almost any economic sickness—high unemployment or high inflation. It is as if the government always has the right economic medicine to cure the economy of what ails it. But if it does, then why does the economy stay sick sometimes?*

ANSWER: *Well, think about these factors: First, not all economists agree that government does have the right medicine. For example, go back to our discussion of fiscal policy. Some economists thought the medicine of "expansionary fiscal policy" would not cure the economy of high unemployment because of crowding out.*

Second, sometimes economic policies are enacted too early or too late. Just like a medicine that will not cure a patient whose disease has gone too far, sometimes something similar happens in economics.

Third, sometimes economic policies are not as precise as we need them to be. For example, suppose the unemployment rate is high and the Fed wants to lower it. We know that it will enact expansionary monetary policy—it will raise the money supply. But suppose it raises the money supply too much. It could raise the money supply by more than is necessary and end up solving the high unemployment problem but causing a new problem to take its place—the problem of high inflation. It would be similar to giving a human patient too much of a medicine, and in the process of curing one disease it produces a different health problem at the same time. Think of it this way: the right amount of an antibiotic can make you well, but too much of an antibiotic can make you sick. Even the best doctors are not always sure which antibiotic or how much of it is just the right amount for a particular patient.

Section 2 Assessment

Defining Terms

1. Define:
   a. expansionary monetary policy
   b. contractionary monetary policy

Reviewing Facts and Concepts

2. Explain how expansionary monetary policy can lower the unemployment rate.
3. The objective is to keep prices stable. Suppose the average annual change in velocity is 1 percent, and the average annual change in the quantity of goods and services is 4 percent. By what percentage should the Fed increase the money supply?

Critical Thinking

4. What evidence would be inconsistent with the theory that predicts lower inflation through contractionary monetary policy?
5. What evidence would support the theory that lower inflation will result from contractionary monetary policy?

Applying Economic Concepts

6. Suppose the Fed sets as its single objective the stabilization of the price level. To this end, it decides to automatically increase the money supply by 2 percent each year based on an average annual change in velocity of 1 percent and an average annual change in the quantity of goods and services of 3 percent. If current-year velocity is above its average annual rate, what will happen?

Section 2 Assessment Answers

Defining Terms

1. a. expansionary monetary policy: an increase in the money supply; **b. contractionary monetary policy:** a decrease in the money supply.

Reviewing Facts and Concepts

2. The Fed increases the money supply. When it does this, the increase leads to greater total spending in the economy. Because of increased spending, firms sell more products. As firms sell more products, they hire more workers, and thus the unemployment rate drops.
3. The formula on page 355 indicates that to keep prices stable, the Fed should increase the money supply by 3%.

Critical Thinking

4. If the money supply were decreased and lower prices did not follow, it would be evidence that is inconsistent with the stated theory.
5. A decrease in the price level would support the stated theory.

Applying Economic Concepts

6. If current-year velocity is above the average annual rate of 2%, then the price level will rise—in other words, inflation will occur.

SECTION 3

Stagflation: The Two Problems Appear Together

Focus Questions

- When the money supply rises, why does the output of goods and services rise before prices?
- When the money supply falls, why does the output of goods and services fall before prices?
- What causes stagflation?

Key Terms

stagflation
stop-and-go, on-and-off monetary policy

Rising Unemployment and Inflation (at the Same Time)

For many years, economists believed that the economy would experience either high inflation or high unemployment, but not both at the same time. Moreover, they believed that inflation and unemployment moved in opposite directions. As the inflation rate increased, the unemployment rate decreased; and as the inflation rate decreased, the unemployment rate increased. Economists thought that inflation and unemployment were on opposite ends of a seesaw.

Real-world data appeared to support this view. For example, during most of the 1960s, inflation and unemployment moved in opposite directions. But in the 1970s, the inflation-unemployment trade-off disappeared for a few years. Instead of moving in opposite directions, inflation and unemployment began to move in the same direction—specifically, they both began to increase. The economy began to experience high inflation and high unemployment at the same time, or **stagflation**.

A Student Asks

QUESTION: *I have heard about the economic problems of inflation and high unemployment, but I haven't heard much about stagflation. Is stagflation a rare economic problem?*

ANSWER: *Compared to both the problem of inflation and the problem of high unemployment, stagflation is a rare economic problem. For example, we haven't experienced stagflation in the United States since the mid to late 1970s. Of course, the fact that it hasn't occurred for over 25 years doesn't mean stagflation might not be a problem in the future.*

How Money Changes Affect the Economy

Some economists believe that stagflation is the result of a **stop-and-go, on-and-off monetary policy**. Before we examine their position, though, it is important that we look at the sequence of effects that monetary policy has on the economy.

stagflation
The occurrence of inflation and high unemployment at the same time.

stop-and-go, on-and-off monetary policy
An erratic monetary policy.

Cross-Curricular Activity

Invite an American history teacher to class to discuss the political, social, and economic culture of the 1970s. Make sure she or he discusses the conflict in Southeast Asia, the Watergate Scandal, the oil crisis, and other issues that may have contributed to the feelings of disillusionment that many people in the United States experienced at that time. After the history teacher has discussed the historical context, you can connect the context to the economic realities by using charts that show the inflation rate and the unemployment rate over the same period. Discuss with students the relationship between governmental actions, political crises, and the economy.

Focus and Motivate

Section Objectives

After completing the section, students will be able to

- explain why the output of goods and services rises before prices when the money supply rises;
- explain why the output of goods and services falls before prices when the money supply falls; and
- explain what causes stagflation.

Kickoff Activity

Ask students the following question at the beginning of class: What do you think stagflation is?

Activating Prior Knowledge

Invite students to share their ideas about the term *stagflation*. Be sure they know that stagflation is the simultaneous occurrence of high inflation and unemployment.

Teach

Critical Thinking

Some people say that incumbent politicians at the national level are not likely to be reelected if stagflation exists. Ask students whether they think the state of the economy influences how people vote, and if so, how. Students should understand that people dislike both inflation and unemployment, but when the two occur together, people have so much to dislike that they often take their anger out on incumbent politicians.

Economics in the Real World

Ask students volunteers to offer additional reasons why it would be worthwhile to understand the basics of economics.

ANSWERS TO THINK ABOUT IT Answers will vary. Most students will probably say that it is easier for politicians to say economically incorrect things to an ignorant public than to a public that could catch them making mistakes.

Discussion Starter

Students often begin their study of economics without understanding how economic policy affects them. Ask students to reflect on whether their views of the relevance of economics have changed during the semester.

Tell students that what happens in Washington, D.C., in terms of monetary or fiscal policy does indeed affect them. Economists believe that fiscal policy and monetary policy can affect the total spending in the economy. This, in turn, affects how many goods and services are bought. Students will eventually be producers of goods and services or will work for firms that produce goods and services, so these policies affect them.

Economics in the Real World

Why Does the Public Know So Little About Economic Policy?

Did you realize that you may be on your way to becoming an economic policy advisor? For example, here are some economic questions you know the answers to.

- What is expansionary monetary policy? (An increase in the money supply.)
- How does the Fed change the money supply? (By changing the reserve requirement, conducting open market operations, or by changing the discount rate.)
- Will a cut in tax rates always lower tax revenues? (No, not always.)

Why do you know the answers to these questions, but most people do not? The obvious answer is that you are currently taking an economics course and you have some incentive to learn economics—if you don't learn it your economics grade is going to be low.

Suppose economics were not a course you had to take in high school. Would you have gone to a bookstore, purchased a book on economics, and started to read it? If you are like most people, your answer is "no." The reason you, and others, would not have learned about economics is because it would not have seemed worth it to you. The costs of learning economics would have been greater than the benefits.

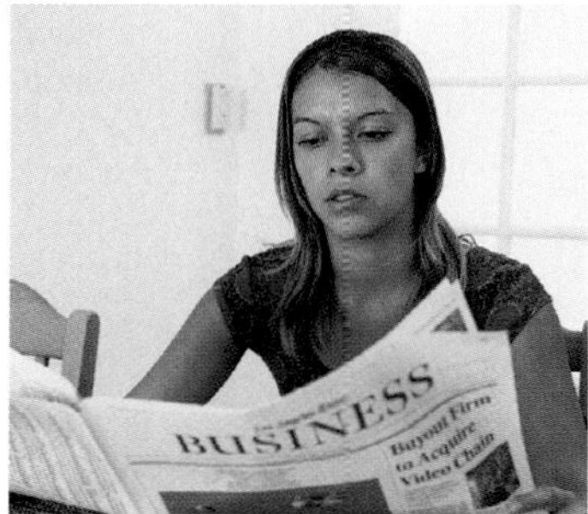

The author of this text does not know much about geology. He could, if he wanted to, learn about geology. The reason he doesn't is because (for him) the costs of learning geology are higher than the benefits.

When people choose not to learn something (that they have an ability to learn), economists say they are exhibiting *rational ignorance*. Rational ignorance is different from ignorance. For example, suppose that someone named Smith tries to learn astrophysics, but can't. In this case we could say that Smith is ignorant when it comes to astrophysics. A person is *rationally ignorant,* however, if he can learn something but chooses not to. Everyone—and we do mean everyone—is rationally ignorant when it comes to some things.

When it comes to economics, many people are rationally ignorant. But why?

Well, let's consider *expansionary fiscal policy* as an example. Many people will not be able to tell you what it is. That's because they decided that even if they know about it, they can't change it. It's sort of like the weather. Why take a big interest in it if you can't change it? It is what it is.

Of course, just because you can't change something (the weather or fiscal policy in the United States, for example), it doesn't mean that it doesn't affect you. The rain, snow, and sunshine affect your day, and fiscal policy can affect your life.

Sometimes *knowing* that something can affect your life will make all the difference. A person checks the weather report because she wants to know if she should take an umbrella to work tomorrow. You might want to check the money supply figures to know whether an "inflation storm" is beginning to build. (Maybe I should buy the car now before inflation hits.) You might want to keep an eye on Congress and the president to get a feel about whether taxes are going up or down. (I might want to take on less overtime work this year when income taxes are high and take on more overtime work next year when taxes are low.)

THINK ABOUT IT If the public is largely rationally ignorant when it comes to economic policy, is it easier or harder for national politicians to say economically incorrect things?

Internet Research

The severe economic problems and the recession that most Asian nations experienced in the late 1990s had global implications. Assign students to select a particular country in Asia and, using the Internet, learn how the recession has impacted that country and, in turn, how the economic problems in that country have affected the United States.

▲ An increase in the money supply will likely cause an increase in spending, which in turn causes an increase in production and employment. **In this situation what usually happens to prices, and when does it happen?**

Most economists agree that changes in the money supply affect both prices and the output of goods and services, but that output is affected before prices. For example, when the Fed increases the money supply, total spending in the economy increases. As a result, firms sell more goods. Consequently, they begin to hire more laborers and produce more output. It is only later that prices rise.

Why does output rise before prices? Because when firms begin to sell more, they do not know at first whether this increase is temporary or permanent. Thinking it may be temporary ("It was a good sales week, but next week may not be so good"), firms do not yet want to change prices. If they raise prices and later learn that the higher sales were only a quirk, they may become less competitive.

Consider Yoko, who owns a pizza restaurant. In an average week, she sells 400 pizzas at an average price of $6. This week, she sells 550 pizzas. Yoko does not know why she did so well this week. People may be getting tired of hamburgers, or people may be getting tired of eating at home, or the Fed may have raised the money supply and increased total spending.

Yoko could immediately raise the price of her pizzas from $9 to $11, but suppose her higher-than-average sales do not last. If this week's higher sales are only temporary and she raises her price to $11 (while her competitors keep their prices the same), Yoko may hurt her business. She is therefore likely to be cautious and wait to see what happens. If sales continue at 550 a week, maybe after a few weeks she will raise her price. But if sales drop back to 400 a week, she will keep the price as it is. We can conclude that given an increase in the money supply, output is likely to go up before prices do.

Similarly, when the money supply decreases, output is affected before price. Suppose that instead of selling her average of 400 pizzas this week, Yoko sells only 250 pizzas. She does not know why sales are lower than average; she just knows they are. She reduces her output of pizzas and perhaps

Teaching with Visuals

Prices usually increase after firms conclude that the increase in their output will be permanent.

Reinforcement Activity

Invite students to imagine that they are small-business owners in the market of their choice. Then have them imagine that demand suddenly increases or decreases. Ask them what they will do as a result and why they might wait before changing prices.

Economics Around the Clock

Direct students to read the 10:56 P.M. scenario in Economics Around the Clock (page 341), and tell them to write down how they would explain stagflation to Carl.

Answers will vary. Essentially, students should explain that stagflation occurs when inflation and high unemployment happen simultaneously.

Internet Research

Assign students to use the Internet to locate inflation and unemployment statistics, and ask them to determine whether the United States has experienced stagflation since the 1970s. If stagflation has occurred in recent years, what are some of the reasons this economic situation arose? If not, what might have changed since the 1970s to help improve the U.S. economy?

Section 3 Stagflation: The Two Problems Appear Together 359

Ask students how many of them were aware of China's role in keeping prices low before reading this feature. Encourage students to think about what else China's significant role in keeping inflation low means about that nation's power in the global economy.

ANSWERS TO ECONOMIC THINKING Answers will vary. Students might say that China's presence has made the Fed's job easier by helping to keep inflation low.

Teaching with Visuals

Answers to the photo question on page 361 will vary. The unemployed workers might say that they were laid off to increase company profits. Economists might say that they were laid off because aggregate demand decreased.

Application Activity

After reading and discussing Section 3, you may want to assign the Section Activity in the *Applying the Principles Workbook.*

Assess

Quick Quiz

The following true-or-false quiz will help you assess student understanding of the material covered in this section.

1. Economists have always understood the concept and possibility of stagflation. (False)
2. Some economists believe that stagflation is a result of a stop-and-go monetary policy. (True)
3. Stagflation is a combination of inflation and low unemployment. (False)
4. Some economists believe that a marked decrease in aggregate supply can also cause stagflation. (True)
5. When there is a decrease in the money supply, output is affected before price. (True)

China and U.S. Prices

Monetary policy is sometimes used to reduce a country's inflation rate. For example, if the inflation rate is high in a country, that country's central bank may enact contractionary monetary policy. But, as *The Economist* reported in 2005, "Central bankers in countries such as the United States and Canada like to take all the credit for the defeat of inflation, but China has given them a big helping hand in recent years. China's ability to produce more cheaply has pushed down the prices of many goods worldwide. . . . For instance, the average prices of shoes and clothing in America have fallen by 10% over the past ten years—a drop of 35% in real [inflation-adjusted] terms."

ECONOMIC THINKING **Has the economic presence of China in the global economy in recent years made the Fed's job of maintaining price stability easier, harder, or not affected it at all?**

cuts back on overtime for her employees. She does not immediately reduce the price, though, because she cannot be sure whether the lower-than-average sales will continue. She does not want to lower the price until she is sure that the demand for her good has fallen. We conclude that given a decrease in the money supply, output is likely to go down before prices do.

EXAMPLE: Elizabeth owns a hair salon. Last week she did better than she has ever done. It seemed as if business was booming. She is not quite sure what caused the booming business. She takes a wait-and-see attitude. She hires more hair cutters, but she doesn't raise prices—at least not yet. Now suppose time passes, and Elizabeth has the worst business week of her life. People canceled their appointments right and left and weren't rescheduling. Elizabeth is not quite sure what happened. Again, she adopts a wait-and-see attitude. She cuts back the hours of a few hair cutters, but she doesn't lower prices yet. ♦

What Causes Stagflation?

Some economists believe stagflation is caused by a *stop-and-go, on-and-off monetary policy* (an erratic monetary policy) that was defined earlier. They describe what happens as follows:

- The Fed increases the money supply. It pushes the monetary accelerator to the floor, which first raises output and then raises prices.
- Time passes. The increased money supply raises the price level—that is, it causes inflation.
- At the same time people are dealing with the high inflation, the Fed reduces the money supply. It presses on the monetary brakes. As a result, output is affected first, and it falls. Because of less output, fewer people are required to work in the factories. Unemployment rises.

Notice that in the economy, inflation is coupled with a cutback in output and an increase in unemployment. The previous monetary policy (money supply up) caused the high inflation, and the current monetary policy (money supply down) caused the high unemployment. The economy is experiencing the effects of both monetary policies, or stagflation.

Not all economists agree with this description of the cause of stagflation or believe it is the only cause. Some economists maintain that a marked decrease in aggregate supply (perhaps due to a fall in the market supply of a major resource, such as oil) can also cause stagflation.

EXAMPLE: Think of things happening along a time line. It is January and the Fed increases the money supply. Let's say that prices are starting to head upward by April. Then in May, the Fed decreases the money supply. Soon after, in July, output is headed down and so the unemployment rate rises. (Less output means fewer people needed to produce the output.) Is anything else happening in July? Yes, remember prices started heading up back in April, and they are continuing to rise in July. So what does July look like? July is a month of rising unemployment (caused by the

Background Information: Keynesian Economics and Stagflation

In the Keynesian view of the economy, stagflation could not occur. There could be a choice between high inflation and high unemployment, but the two would never happen together. The simultaneous high inflation and high unemployment experienced by the United States in the late 1970s and early 1980s partly discredited the Keynesian view.

money supply decrease in May) and rising prices (caused by the money supply increase in January). ◆

A Student Asks

QUESTION: *It seems to me that monetary policy is important. If the money supply is too high, we seem to get inflation. If it is too low, we might end up with high unemployment. If it goes from up to down too quickly (stop and go, on and off) we get stagflation. Do I have this right? Is the money supply a big factor in what happens in the economy?*

ANSWER: *Most economists would say that it is. Think of it in extreme terms for a few minutes. Suppose the money supply were cut in half overnight. Wouldn't that cut spending in the economy dramatically and result in high unemployment? Suppose the money supply were raised by 50 percent overnight. Wouldn't that lead to a high rate of inflation? Now, in reality, the Fed does not raise or lower the money supply by these large percentages, but that doesn't mean the smaller changes in the money supply that the Fed makes do not have consequences.*

Most people are used to thinking that what the president does, or what the members of Congress do, is all that matters to the state of the economy. But what the Fed does is extremely important to the state of the economy. Some people call the chair of the Fed the second most powerful person in the country, after the president, because that person has a big part in directing the monetary policy of the country.

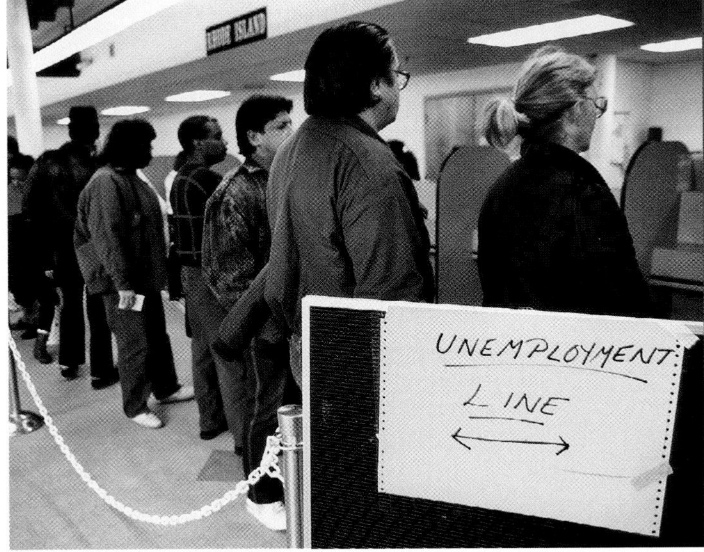

▲ These people are in line to apply for unemployment benefits. **What are some reasons these people might give if asked why they had lost their jobs? What reasons might an economist give?**

Section 3 Assessment

Defining Terms

1. Define:
   a. stagflation
   b. stop-and-go, on-and-off monetary policy

Reviewing Facts and Concepts

2. In the past how did economists view the relationship between unemployment and inflation? When did economic events begin to change this view?
3. Does a decrease in the money supply cause a change in output, prices, or both?
4. When the money supply increases, output rises before prices. Why?
5. Explain in detail how some economists believe the Fed causes stagflation. What is an alternative view of what causes stagflation?

Critical Thinking

6. Because firms adjust output before prices, what information do they lack?

Applying Economic Concepts

7. What effect, if any, do you think stagflation plays in the reelection prospects of the president of the United States?

Assessment Book

You will find a quiz for this section in the *Assessment Book.*

Reteaching Activity

Use the Section Assessment to gauge which students may need reteaching on this section. Make sure that those students understand that stagflation occurs when prices rise, causing inflation, and then aggregate demand falls, causing output to fall before price.

Guided Reading

For further reteaching of the key concepts in this section, assign the Outlining Activity and the Just the Facts Handout from the *Guided Reading and Study Guide.*

Section 3 Assessment Answers

Defining Terms

1. a. stagflation: the occurrence of inflation and high unemployment at the same time; **b. stop-and-go, on-and-off monetary policy:** an erratic monetary policy in which the money supply is increased, then decreased, and so on.

Reviewing Facts and Concepts

2. Economists believed that they moved in opposite directions. The concurrent appearance of inflation and high unemployment in the 1970s changed this view.

3. A decrease in the money supply leads to lower output, which will eventually lead to lower prices.

4. When firms begin to sell more, they do not know whether this increase is temporary or permanent. Because it may be temporary, they do not want to change prices, so they adjust output, not prices.

5. Some economists believe that stop-and-go, on-and-off monetary policy causes stagflation. The money supply increases, so firms sell and produce more. When higher sales appear to be permanent, firms raise prices, causing inflation. Then the Fed reduces the money supply. Firms sell less and cut back on production. They fire some workers; unemployment rises. Higher prices are occurring at the same time as higher unemployment. Some economists argue that a marked decrease in aggregate supply can also cause stagflation.

Critical Thinking

6. Firms do not know whether a rise or fall in sales is temporary or permanent. Only time will provide the company with this information.

Applying Economic Concepts

7. Answers will vary. Generally, bad economic times are thought to hurt an incumbent president's chances of reelection.

CHAPTER 13 Assessment Answers

Economics Vocabulary

1. complete crowding out; **2.** contractionary monetary; **3.** expansionary monetary; **4.** complete crowding in; **5.** Stagflation; **6.** Fiscal policy; **7.** Laffer curve; **8.** after-tax income; **9.** expansionary fiscal; **10.** contractionary fiscal.

Understanding the Main Ideas

1. The objective of contractionary fiscal policy is to reduce total spending. If there is complete crowding in, a reduction in government spending will simply be offset by an increase in private spending, making contractionary fiscal policy ineffective.

2. Most economists believe the cause of stagflation is stop-and-go, on-and-off monetary policy. The inflation part of stagflation is caused by increases in the money supply. The unemployment part of stagflation is caused by decreases in the money supply.

3. The money supply increases. As a result, total spending increases, firms sell more goods, they hire more workers, and the unemployment rate decreases.

4. The money supply decreases, which reduces total spending in the economy. Firms sell fewer goods. Inventories rise. Firms decide to lower prices to rid themselves of their surplus goods, and inflation decreases.

5. A reduction in income tax rates leaves more after-tax income for people, so they end up spending more. This is how an income tax rate cut affects the demand side of the economy. A tax cut also motivates people to work more and produce more goods, affecting the supply side of the economy.

6. She does not know if the demand for her hotel has gone up or if this week is simply an above-average week. If she raises the rent too fast, she may become less competitive.

7. Government increases its spending. As a result, there is more spending in the economy. As a result of more spending in the economy, firms sell more goods, they hire more workers, and the unemployment rate goes down.

8. Expansionary monetary policy would probably make the inflation part of stagflation worse.

9. No, not necessarily. A cut in tax rates can increase or decrease tax revenues depending on whether the percentage increase in income (as a result of the tax cut) is greater than the percentage reduction in the tax rate. If it is, then tax revenues rise; if it is not, then tax revenues fall.

10. The inflation part of stagflation is caused by increases in the money supply. The unemployment part of stagflation is caused by decreases in the money supply.

13 CHAPTER 13 ASSESSMENT

Chapter Summary

Be sure you know and remember the following key points from the chapter sections.

Section 1

- Government increases in spending and reduction in taxes are considered expansionary fiscal policy, whereas decreases in spending and increases in taxes are contractionary fiscal policy.
- Expansionary fiscal policy is believed to reduce the unemployment rate.
- Crowding out suggests that increased government spending reduces private spending.
- A contractionary fiscal policy is believed to reduce inflation.
- Crowding in occurs when decreases in government spending lead to increases in private spending.
- Supply-side economists believe that cuts in high tax rates can generate higher tax revenues, whereas cuts in low tax rates generate lower tax revenues, as demonstrated by the Laffer curve.

Section 2

- Monetary policy deals with changes in the money supply.
- Expansionary monetary policy can help reduce unemployment and does not involve crowding out because the money supply is increased.
- Contractionary monetary policy works to reduce inflation by reducing the money supply, which leads to a decrease in spending and a decrease in prices.

Section 3

- High inflation and high unemployment at the same time is known as stagflation.
- Most economists agree that changes in the money supply affect both prices and the output of goods and services, and that output is affected before prices.
- Stop-and-go, on-and-off monetary policy is an erratic policy in which the Fed alternately increases and decreases the money supply.

Economics Vocabulary

To reinforce your knowledge of the key terms in this chapter, fill in the following blanks on a separate piece of paper with the appropriate word or phrase.

1. The scenario in which government spending increases by $1 and, as a result, private spending decreases by $1 is called ______.
2. If the Fed decreases the money supply, it is implementing a(n) ______ policy.
3. If the Fed increases the money supply, it is implementing a(n) ______ policy.
4. The scenario in which government spending decreases by $1 and, as a result, private spending increases by $1 is called ______.
5. ______ is the simultaneous occurrence of inflation and high unemployment.
6. ______ refers to changes government makes in spending, taxation, or both to achieve particular macroeconomic goals.
7. The ______ expresses the relationship that some economists believe holds between tax rates and tax revenues.
8. Income minus taxes is ______.
9. If the government increases its spending or lowers taxes, it is implementing a(n) ______ policy.
10. If the government decreases its spending or raises taxes, it is implementing a(n) ______ policy.

Understanding the Main Ideas

Write answers to the following questions to review the main ideas in this chapter.

1. Explain how complete crowding in affects contractionary fiscal policy.
2. In general, what is the cause of stagflation?
3. Explain the process by which expansionary monetary policy reduces the unemployment rate.
4. Explain the process by which contractionary monetary policy reduces inflation.
5. How can changes in income tax rates affect both the supply side and the demand side of the economy?

UNDERSTANDING AND APPLICATION

6. Rosa Jenkins, who owns a hotel, rented out a higher-than-average number of rooms this week. Why is she likely to wait awhile before she raises the room rent?
7. Describe the process by which expansionary fiscal policy reduces unemployment (assuming no crowding out or incomplete crowding out).
8. Explain why expansionary monetary policy is probably not a solution to stagflation.
9. Do lower tax rates mean lower tax revenues? Explain your answer.
10. What causes the inflation part of stagflation? What causes the unemployment part of stagflation?

Doing the Math

Do the calculations necessary to solve the following problems.

1. Suppose the average tax rate is 20 percent, and tax revenues are $800 billion. What does (taxable) income equal?
2. Suppose the average tax rate is 25 percent, and tax revenues equal $600 billion. If the average tax rate falls to 20 percent, how much will (taxable) income have to increase in order to keep tax revenues unchanged?

Working with Graphs and Tables

1. If the objective is to maintain price stability, by what percentage should the money supply change in cases A through D in Exhibit 13-5?
2. Using Exhibit 13-6, answer the following questions.
   a. What happens to tax revenues as the tax rate is lowered from E to D?
   b. What happens to tax revenues as the tax rate is increased from A to B?
   c. What is the tax rate at which tax revenues are maximized?
   d. What happens to tax revenues as the tax rate is increased from D to E?

EXHIBIT 13-5

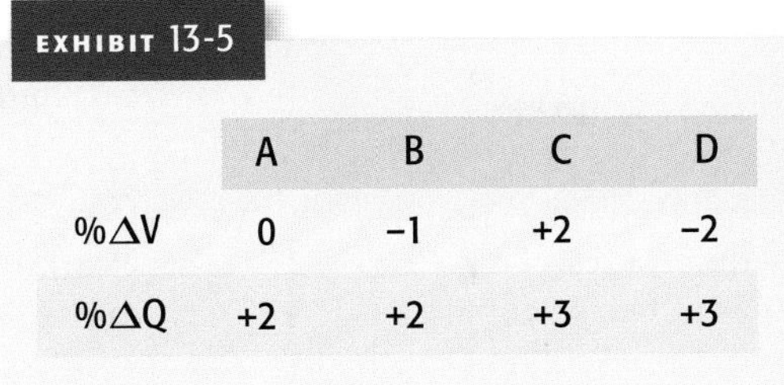

	A	B	C	D
%ΔV	0	−1	+2	−2
%ΔQ	+2	+2	+3	+3

EXHIBIT 13-6

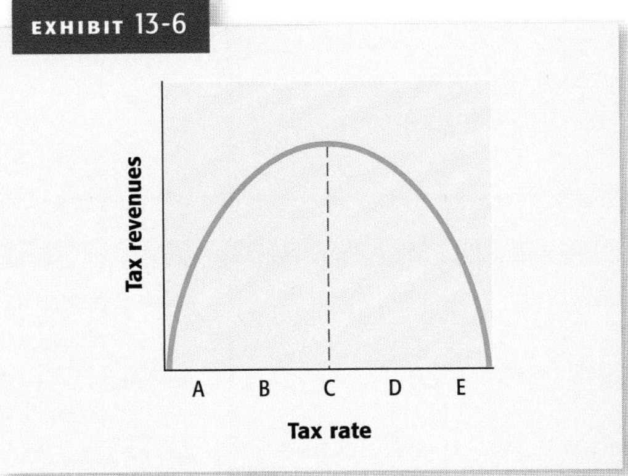

Solving Economic Problems

Use your thinking skills and the information you learned in this chapter to find solutions to the following problems.

1. **Application.** It is sometimes said that making consistently accurate predictions in economics is difficult. Based on your reading of this chapter, give an example that illustrates this point.
2. **Writing.** Based on your reading of the chapter, write a one-page paper that addresses this question: *Why do economists differ in their views on the effects of fiscal policy actions?*

ONLINE emcp.com **Practice Tests and Study Guide**

Go to www.emcp.net/economics and choose *Economics: New Ways of Thinking,* Chapter 13, if you need more help in preparing for the chapter test.

Solving Economic Problems

1. Answers will vary. It is difficult to predict what will happen to tax revenues if tax rates are lowered. The answer depends on whether the increase in taxable income (as people are motivated to work more) is greater than, less than, or equal to the cut in taxes. If we knew which of the three possibilities would materialize, an accurate prediction would be forthcoming. Because we do not, we cannot be sure that our "best guess" of which condition will hold will be the "right guess" and therefore give us an accurate prediction.
2. Answers will vary. Here are some points students might make: (1) Economists don't know whether there will be complete crowding out, incomplete crowding out, or no crowding out. Which condition exists can determine whether expansionary fiscal policy is effective at changing total spending or not. (2) Economists do not know whether there will be complete crowding in, incomplete crowding in, or no crowding in. Which condition exists can determine whether contractionary fiscal policy is effective at changing total spending or not. (3) Economists do not know whether a cut in tax rates will generate a proportionately larger or smaller rise in taxable income and therefore a rise or fall in tax revenues. The general answer here is that any time economists have several possible conditions to choose from, different economists will choose different options. Consequently, economists will have different views on what is likely to happen to the economy in the future.

Doing the Math

1. $4,000 billion (*calculation:* $800 billion = 0.20 × X; therefore, X = $4,000 billion).
2. $600 billion. If a 25% tax rate generates $600 billion in tax revenues, taxable income must equal $2,400 billion. An income of $3,000 billion is required before a 20% tax rate will generate $600 billion in tax revenues. The difference between $3,000 billion and $2,400 billion is $600 billion.

Working with Graphs and Tables

1. A. 2%; **B.** 3%; **C.** 1%; **D.** 5%.
2. a. tax revenues increase; **b.** tax revenues increase; **c.** tax revenues are maximized at tax rate C; **d.** tax revenues fall.

Chapter 13 Fiscal and Monetary Policy 363

Chapter 14 Planning Guide

SECTION ORGANIZER

Section	Learning Objectives	Reproducible Worksheets and Handouts	Assessment
 **Taxes** (pages 366–373)	▸ List the three major federal taxes. ▸ Describe the three types of taxes people pay in addition to the three major federal taxes. ▸ Explain the purpose of the alternative minimum tax. ▸ Explain how proportional, progressive, and regressive income taxation differ. ▸ Engage in an informed discussion about fair taxation.	Section 1 Activity, *Applying the Principles Workbook* Outlining Activity, *Guided Reading and Study Guide* Just the Facts Handout, *Guided Reading and Study Guide*	Section Assessment, *Student Text,* page 373 Quick Quiz, *Annotated Teacher's Edition,* page 372 Section Quiz, *Assessment Book*
 **The Budget: Deficits and Debt** (pages 376–385)	▸ Describe how the federal government spends its tax revenues. ▸ Define *balanced budget, budget deficit,* and *budget surplus.* ▸ Explain the relationship between deficits and the national debt. ▸ Describe some of the issues connected with budget surpluses.	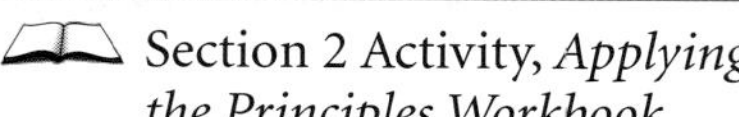 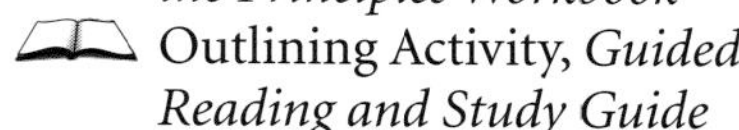 Section 2 Activity, *Applying the Principles Workbook* Outlining Activity, *Guided Reading and Study Guide* Just the Facts Handout, *Guided Reading and Study Guide*	Section Assessment, *Student Text,* page 385 Quick Quiz, *Annotated Teacher's Edition,* pages 384–385 Section Quiz, *Assessment Book*

CHAPTER AND PROGRAM RESOURCES

Reproducible Chapter Resources and Assessment Materials

 Graphic Organizer Activity, *Guided Reading and Study Guide*

 Vocabulary Activity, *Guided Reading and Study Guide*

 Working with Graphs and Charts, *Guided Reading and Study Guide*

 Practice Test, *Guided Reading and Study Guide*

 Critical Thinking Activity, *Finding Economics*

 Chapter Test A, *Assessment Book*

Chapter Test B, *Assessment Book*

Technology Resources

 *Test Generator CD*

 *Spanish Audio Summaries CD*

Marketplace® Audio Lessons CD

Economic Principles Lectures, Videocassette or DVD

Lesson Planning and Teaching Resources

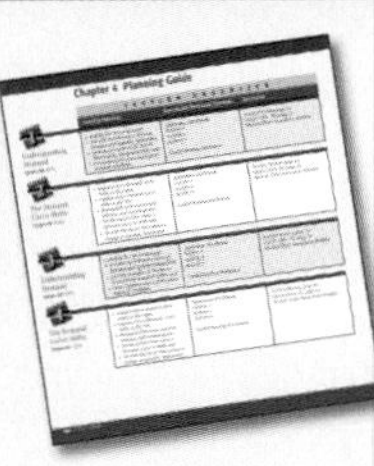

The *Economics: New Ways of Thinking* Teacher Resources include detailed lesson plans for each section in this chapter; the lesson plans are available in print form *(Lesson Plans)* and electronic form. The Teacher Resources also include *Daily Lectures: Overheads and Notes,* which provides prepared overheads and discussion notes covering the key concepts in each section of this chapter.

EMC Publishing Economics Online

Go to Economics Online, at www.emcp.com, for a variety of Internet resources to help you keep your course current and relevant. At Economics Online you will find these items:

- Economics in the News Lessons
- Study Guide Questions
- Practice Tests
- Lesson Plans

Internet Resources

Economics: New Ways of Thinking encourages students to use the Internet to find out more about economics. With the wealth of current, valid information available on Web sites, using the Internet as a research tool is likely to increase your students' interest in and understanding of economics principles and topics. In addition, doing Internet research can help your students form the habit of accessing and using economics information, as well as help them develop investigative skills they will use throughout their educational and professional careers.

To aid your students in achieving these ends, each chapter of *Economics: New Ways of Thinking* includes the addresses of several Web sites at which students will find engaging, relevant information. When students type in the addresses provided, they will immediately arrive at the intended sites. The addresses have been modified so that EMC Publishing can monitor and maintain the proper links—for example, the government site http://stats.bls.gov/ has been changed to www.emcp.net/prices. In the event that the address or content of a site changes or is discontinued, EMC's Internet editors will create a link that redirects students to an address with similar information.

Activities in the *Annotated Teacher's Edition* often suggest that students search the Internet for information. For some activities, you might want to find reputable sites beforehand, and steer students to those sites. For other activities, you might want students to do their own searching, and then check out the sites they have found and discuss why they might be reliable or unreliable.

CHAPTER 14 Overview

This chapter introduces the federal government's taxing and spending activities. It describes what taxes the government applies and how the government spends tax revenues. It also examines the national debt, as well as the effects of both a budget surplus and a budget deficit. The following statements provide brief descriptions of the major concepts covered in each section of this chapter.

Taxes

Section 1 describes the types of taxes that exist. It also explains the difference among proportional, progressive, and regressive income taxation.

The Budget: Deficits and Debt

Section 2 answers the following questions: What is a balanced budget? What is a budget deficit? What is a budget surplus? What is the relationship between deficits and the national debt? What are some issues connected with budget surpluses?

CHAPTER 14 Taxing and Spending

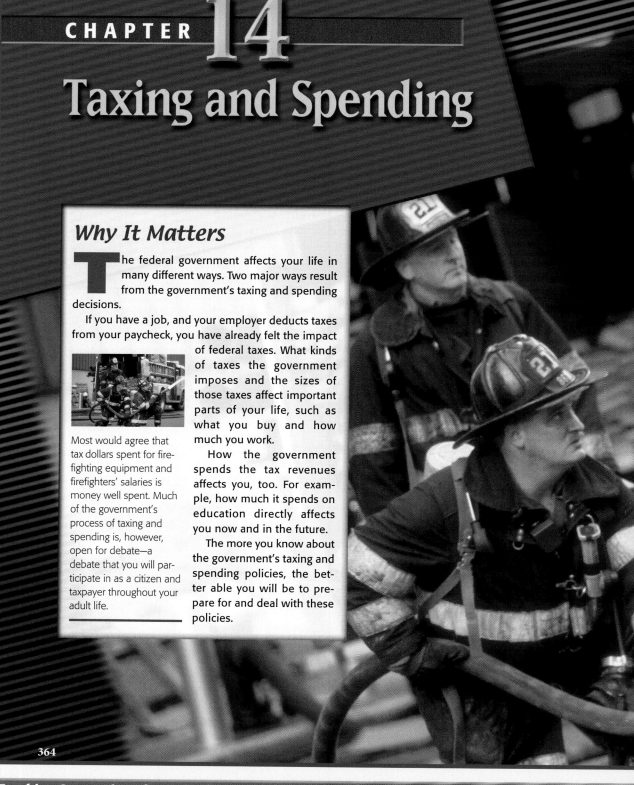

Why It Matters

The federal government affects your life in many different ways. Two major ways result from the government's taxing and spending decisions.

If you have a job, and your employer deducts taxes from your paycheck, you have already felt the impact of federal taxes. What kinds of taxes the government imposes and the sizes of those taxes affect important parts of your life, such as what you buy and how much you work.

How the government spends the tax revenues affects you, too. For example, how much it spends on education directly affects you now and in the future.

The more you know about the government's taxing and spending policies, the better able you will be to prepare for and deal with these policies.

Most would agree that tax dollars spent for fire-fighting equipment and firefighters' salaries is money well spent. Much of the government's process of taxing and spending is, however, open for debate—a debate that you will participate in as a citizen and taxpayer throughout your adult life.

Teaching Suggestions from the Author

Many students see this as a very practical chapter. It discusses taxes and government spending. Students seem to have a natural interest in knowing about these two subjects. They want to know what taxes are paid, how much revenue selective taxes raise, how the federal government spends money, and so on.

Students also seem interested in the national debt and, perhaps to a lesser degree, Social Security. These are two other topics discussed in this chapter.

It is a good idea to start things off by talking generally with students about taxes. Do they think the average taxpayer pays too much in taxes? How much do

Economics Around the Clock

The following events occurred one day in October.

5:30 P.M. As the Stevens family eats dinner, Mary Stevens tells the family about something she read today in *Time* magazine. Mary says, "I read today that the rich in America are getting richer and the poorer are getting poorer." "I don't think that's true," Frank Stevens, Mary's husband, says. Jimmy, the littlest Stevens in the family asks, "What's for dessert?"

- **Are the rich getting richer and the poor getting poorer?**

5:32 P.M. Vernon and Maria Cole are eating dinner. Maria says, "I think we spend too much money in this country on national defense. We ought to spend less on national defense and more on education, health care, and environmental concerns." Vernon says, "How much do we spend on national defense?" "I don't know," Maria says, "but I'm sure it's a lot."

- **How much does the federal government spend on national defense?**

6:04 P.M. Clark and Eddie, two friends at college, are eating dinner together in the dining hall. "I found it interesting," says Eddie, "that Russia has a flat tax." "What's so interesting about that?" Clark asks. "Well," says Eddie, "Russia used to be part of the Soviet Union, a communist country, and a flat tax is usually associated with countries where low taxes are all the rage. I don't know, it just seems to me that a flat tax and a formerly communist country don't go together."

- **What is a flat tax, and what countries in the world have a flat tax?**

7:16 P.M. The Martinez family is eating dinner. Elise Martinez says, "I heard today that the federal government pays hardly anything for education. I think that is wrong. If the federal government doesn't pay for education, who does?" Ken Martinez, Elise's husband, says, "I agree with you. I bet the federal government spends more on road construction than education. And educating our kids is perhaps the most important job we have."

- **Does the federal government spend little on education?**

Introducing the Chapter

To introduce Chapter 14, you might write the words "taxation without representation" on the board. Ask, Where have you heard that phrase before? (*Answer:* Students should be familiar with this famous phrase from their study of U.S. history.) Stress that taxes are almost always seen as a burden. The types of unfair taxes that the British imposed on the American colonies were sufficient to act as a catalyst for the War for Independence. Ask, Can you think of any other famous quotes regarding taxes? Answers will vary. They might include Benjamin Franklin's frequently quoted statement, "In this world nothing is certain but death and taxes." Explain that taxes, along with deficits and debt, are a main topic of this chapter. You might ask students to skim the lists of Key Terms for the chapter and then ask for student volunteers to share what types of things they expect to learn from this chapter.

Teaching with Visuals

Direct students' attention to the image on these pages. Ask students what other government services they think are necessary.

they think the average taxpayer pays? Do they think Social Security will be there for them when they retire? Why or why not?

Sometimes it is a good idea to start off this chapter with a more philosophical discussion. Ask students what they think government should do. Should government provide roads and national defense only, or should it provide education, too? Should it provide health care, scholarships for college, and food for people with low incomes? Some students will think government should provide many services; other students will disagree. Try to get students to engage in a debate on the government's proper role before they read this chapter.

SECTION 1

Teacher Support

Focus and Motivate

Section Objectives

After completing this section, students will be able to

- list the three major federal taxes;
- describe the three types of taxes people pay in addition to the three major federal taxes;
- explain the purpose of the alternative minimum tax;
- explain how proportional, progressive, and regressive income taxation differ; and
- engage in an informed discussion about fair taxation.

Kickoff Activity

Ask students to explain what they know about taxes and to list as many different types of taxes as they can.

Activating Prior Knowledge

Invite students to share their responses to the Kickoff Activity. You may want to create a list of taxes on the board, from the information contributed by students. For every tax that students list, ask them if they know how that tax is assessed, and write the correct response on the board next to the tax. For example, personal income tax is applied to income, and sales tax is applied to the purchase of goods and services.

SECTION 1

Taxes

Focus Questions

- What are the three major federal taxes?
- What are three types of taxes people pay in addition to the three major federal taxes?
- What is the purpose of the alternative miniumum tax?
- How do proportional, progressive, and regressive income taxation differ?
- What is a fair tax?

Key Terms

proportional income tax
progressive income tax
regressive income tax

Three Major Federal Taxes

The government has three levels: federal, state, and local. At the federal level are three major taxes: the personal income tax, the corporate income tax, and the Social Security tax. In 2005, the federal government took in tax revenues of $2,057 billion. Of this total, about 92.3 percent was from personal income, corporate income, and Social Security taxes. Exhibit 14-1 shows the estimates of the Congressional Budget Office for the tax revenue that each of the three taxes will generate from 2006 to 2011.

▼ Here are the federal tax projections made by the Congressional Budget Office for the years 2006–2011.

EXHIBIT 14-1 Federal Tax Projections, 2006–2011 ($ billions)

Taxes	2006	2007	2008	2009	2010	2011
Personal income	$ 986	$1,082	$ 1,172	$1,265	$1,362	$ 1,561
Corporate income	226	226	237	246	249	254
Social Security	833	833	918	962	962	1,054
Other	167	167	181	188	188	193
Total	$2,212	$2,308	$2,508	$2,661	$2,761	$3,062

Personal Income Tax

The personal income tax is the tax a person pays on his or her income. A federal personal income tax is applied by the federal government, and many (but not all) states have a personal income tax. At the federal government level, the personal income tax raised $899 billion in 2005, which accounted for approximately 44 percent of total federal tax revenue that year. In other words, for every $1 the federal government received in taxes in 2005, 44 cents of that dollar came from the personal income tax.

Corporate Income Tax

The tax corporations pay on their profits is the corporate income tax. The federal government applies a corporate income tax, as do many states. At the federal government level, the corporate income tax raised $216 billion in 2005. This amount was about 10.3 percent of the total federal tax revenue in 2005.

Cooperative Learning

Divide the class into groups. Each group is to research the taxing and budgeting process for one country other than the United States. Group members should decide which country to research, then find the following information for their country: What types of taxes does the government impose? How is the budget prepared? Does this country currently have a budget deficit or surplus? How do the taxing and budgeting in this country compare to those in our own country? Each group should prepare its findings to be given as a brief oral report and should use visual aids to enhance the report.

Social Security Tax

The Social Security tax is a federal government tax placed on income generated from employment. Half of the tax is placed on the employer, and half is placed on the employee. In 2005, at the federal government level, the Social Security tax raised approximately $790 billion, or about 38 percent of the total federal tax revenue. (See Exhibit 14-2.)

A Student Asks

QUESTION: *Don't tax revenues steadily climb for the U.S. government? In other words, aren't tax revenues always higher for a later year than an earlier year?*

ANSWER: *Over a long period of time, tax revenues rise, but tax revenues in a later year are not always higher than in an earlier year. For example, in 2000, federal tax revenues were $2,025 billion, but in 2001 they fell to $1,991.2 billion. One year later, in 2002, they fell again to $1,853.2 billion. In other words, federal tax revenues fluctuate.*

EXHIBIT 14-2 Where the Money Comes From

Personal income tax	Corporate income tax	Social Security tax	Other taxes

Source: U.S. Bureau of the Census.

▲ For each dollar the federal government raises from taxes, 44 percent comes from the personal income tax, 10.3 percent comes from the corporate income tax, 38 percent comes from the Social Security tax, and 7.7 percent comes from other federal taxes. (These percentages are for 2005.)

Three Other Taxes

The taxes just described are not the only taxes people pay. In most states, people must also pay a state income tax. In addition, other major taxes are sales taxes, excise taxes, and property taxes.

Sales Tax

Sales taxes are applied to the purchase of a broad range of goods—cars, computers, clothes, books, and so on—when they are purchased. State governments typically raise tax revenue through sales taxes. The federal government does not collect a (national) sales tax.

Sales taxes differ among states. For example, in Florida the sales tax rate is 6 percent, but in Georgia it is 4 percent. In most states, food purchases (at a grocery store) are not subject to the sales tax, although some states tax food sales at a rate that is lower than the regular sales tax. In most states, no sales tax is charged for prescription drugs.

Excise Tax

Excise taxes are taxes placed on the purchase of certain goods, such as tobacco products and gasoline. Every time people buy gasoline at a gas station, they pay an excise tax. The federal government applies excise taxes, as do many states.

EXAMPLE: Edward goes to the gas station and fills up his car with gas. He looks at the price per gallon: $2.75. He might not realize it, but an excise tax is included in that $2.75 per gallon. Both federal and state excise taxes apply on gasoline. While the federal tax is uniform across the country, the state excise taxes vary from state to state. To pick one state, Connecticut, the sum of federal and state excise taxes on a gallon of gasoline is about 50 cents. In other words, out of every gallon of gas purchased in the state of Connecticut, 50 cents goes for excise taxes. ♦

"The hardest thing in the world to understand is the income tax."
—ALBERT EINSTEIN

Property Tax

Property tax is a tax on the value of property (such as a home). It is a major revenue source for state and local governments.

EXAMPLE: Yvonne buys a house. In the state in which she lives, the property tax rate is 1.25 percent of the market price of the house. She paid $300,000 for her house, so her property taxes each year amount to $3,750, or $312.50 a month. ♦

Teach

Teaching with Visuals

Exhibit 14-1 (page 366) shows the federal tax projections for the years 2006–2011. Ask students which tax brings in the most revenue for government. (*Answer:* personal income tax.) Ask: Did you notice that the dollar amounts for all the taxes increase each year? To what do you attribute the increase? Do you think taxes will be raised each year, or could there be other reasons? Students may suggest that the increases occur because there will be more taxpayers contributing to the revenue.

Teaching with Visuals

To help students better understand the breakdown of government revenue from taxes, you might want to create, on the board or on an overhead transparency, a pie chart that shows the information in Exhibit 14-2. If possible, color the segments of the pie chart differently, so that students can easily see the different percentages of taxes paid.

Discussion Starter

Ask students if they can list some of the things that are done with tax money. Possible answers include paying for schools, highways, national defense, and interest on the national debt. Suggest that although many people don't like to pay taxes, most do like the things that taxes buy. For instance, Julio may not want to pay taxes, but he likes the fact that tax money is used to provide national defense; Jane doesn't like to pay taxes, but she likes the fact that taxes provide some people with health care. Help students to see that the economist tries to look at both sides of the coin, both costs and benefits.

Reinforcement Activity

Ask students to review the list of six taxes discussed on pages 366–367. Instruct them to identify which taxes they have paid, either by working at jobs or by purchasing goods and services.

Differentiating Instruction

English Language Learners

One method for assisting English language learners is to read the chapter's Key Terms and their definitions aloud before assigning the chapter. Reading these words aloud will help students to "hear" them as they read the text. You might also use the Spanish glossary from the back of the *Student Text,* and the Spanish versions of the Chapter Summaries on an audio CD, which are provided as part of the *Economics: New Ways of Thinking* program. Another way of helping English language learners is to go over all Section Assessment and Chapter Assessment answers orally.

Economics in the Real World

Ask students if it had occurred to them before reading this feature that the employers' Social Security tax burden is actually carried by employees, to some extent. Ask if students think that the way Social Security is funded should be modified in any way, and discuss any ideas for change that they offer.

ANSWERS TO THINK ABOUT IT Agree. This feature showed that the tax was placed fully on the buyers of labor, which affected the demand for labor. But if we affect the demand for labor, we also affect the wage rate, because the wage rate is determined by both the demand for and the supply of labor. The wage rate is earned by the suppliers of labor, so indirectly the suppliers of labor have been affected by something that initially affected the demand side of the market.

Economics in the Real World

Are You Paying Someone Else's Taxes?

Since the inception of Social Security, the Social Security tax has been split between the employer and the employee. For example, in 2005, the Social Security tax rate was 12.4 percent. Half of this tax, or 6.2 percent, was placed on the employer, and the other half was placed on the employee. In other words, the employee was expected to pay $6.20 per $100 of gross earnings (up to a limit), as was the employer.

It is commonly believed that if a tax is placed on someone, then that someone actually pays the tax. However, the placement of a tax is different from the payment of a tax. Just because the government places a tax on Anderson, it does not necessarily follow that Anderson pays the tax. The same is true for the Social Security tax. Just because the government places half the tax on the employer does not necessarily mean that the employer pays the tax.

To better understand this concept, suppose the Social Security tax is $2 a day and that $1 of the tax is placed on the employer and $1 placed on the employee. An earlier chapter explained that wage rates are determined by supply and demand. For example, the demand for labor and the supply of labor go together to determine the wage rate. Suppose that the equilibrium wage rate before the tax is placed on the employer is $10 an hour.

What will the tax that is placed on the employer do to the employer's demand for labor? A tax will lower the employer's demand for labor. Employers will not want to hire as many employees as they might otherwise, if they have to pay a $1 tax per employee per day.

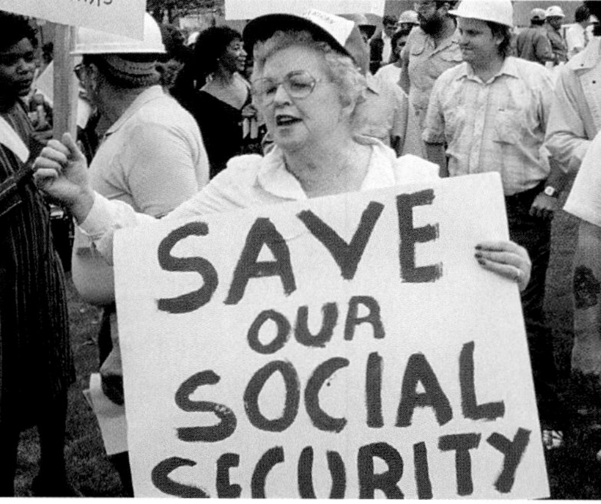

In other words, as a result of the Social Security tax being fully placed on the employer, the demand for labor falls. Now if the demand for labor falls, and the supply of labor is constant, we know (through our supply-and-demand analysis) that the wage rate will fall, say, from $10 an hour to $9.35 an hour.

So, in our example, have employees paid for any of the Social Security tax that was placed on the employer? Yes, they have paid in terms of lower wages. In other words, without the tax, employees' wages would be higher ($10 an hour) than they are with the tax ($9.35 an hour). Some of the Social Security tax (in our example, 65 cents of the $1 tax) is paid for by the employees in the form of lower wages, even though the tax was placed on the employer.

The first moral of the story is this: many people think that the employer pays half the Social Security tax and the employee pays the other half when, in fact, the employee ends up paying more than half the Social Security tax. The employee pays the employee half of the tax, and then pays some of the employer's part of the tax in the form of (earning) lower wages.

Second moral of the story: the legislature can place a tax on anyone it chooses, but it is not the legislature that determines who pays the tax. The laws of economics (in this case, the laws of demand and supply) determine who pays the tax.

THINK ABOUT IT Every market has two sides: a demand side (buying side) and a supply side (selling side). If a tax is placed on one side of the market, it can affect the other side. Do you agree or disagree? Explain your answer.

Internet Research

You may want students to use the Internet to find information and additional resources to enhance their study of this chapter. Direct students to search the Internet for sites that provide assistance in filing federal income tax returns or that provide tax advice. Ask them to list the types of services that these sites offer and to explain what tax-related concerns people appear to have. Instruct students to locate an IRS Form 1040 online and to assess whether they think it would be easy or difficult to do their own taxes. If they have ever filed their own taxes, ask what was easy or difficult about doing so.

The Alternative Minimum Tax

The alternative minimum tax (AMT) is a tax that some people have to pay on top of their regular income tax. The original idea behind the tax was to prevent persons with high incomes from paying little or no taxes because of their claiming certain tax benefits. Congress enacted the AMT in 1969 following testimony by the secretary of the Treasury that 155 people with adjusted gross income above $200,000 had paid zero federal income tax on their 1967 tax returns.

How It Works

The name—alternative minimum tax—comes from the way the tax is designed to work. In short, for a given income, a minimum tax is computed; then, if you are paying at least that amount of taxes, you don't pay the alternative minimum tax, but if you are not paying at least that amount, you do.

Suppose the minimum amount of taxes usually paid by a person earning $75,000 a year is $15,000. This $15,000 becomes the benchmark against which others are measured. If Smith, who earns $75,000, is not paying at least $15,000 in taxes, then he is subject to the alternative minimum tax. If Jones, who earns $75,000, is paying at least $15,000 in taxes, then he is not subject to the alternative minimum tax.

Why It Is Affecting More People

When the alternative minimum tax was first put into place in 1969, fewer than 1 percent of all taxpayers were affected by it. Today, more than 3 percent pay AMT. If the alternative minimum tax retains its current structure, 20 percent of taxpayers, or 30 million Americans, will be subject to it by 2010. By 2015, the AMT will affect 50 million people.

What happened? Why have so many more people fallen under the umbrella of the alternative minimum tax in recent years? Two factors are responsible.

Inflation The first is inflation. Because of inflation, individuals find that their dollar incomes increase. Think of it this way: A person sells apples at 20 cents each. Inflation raises the prices of most goods, including apples, which rise to a price of 30 cents each. Before inflation, the apple seller received an "income" of 20 cents an apple; now she receives an "income" of 30 cents an apple.

The regular income tax is adjusted for inflation; the government doesn't simply look at your higher dollar income and conclude that you are better off because of it. Government realizes that although you have a higher dollar income, prices are higher too, and your higher dollar income might not buy you any more at the higher prices than your lower dollar income bought you at lower prices.

Even though the regular income tax is adjusted for inflation, the AMT is not. When inflation raises a person's dollar income, it moves him upward toward the income level at which the alternative minimum tax kicks in.

Tax Cuts The second factor causing more people to be subject to the AMT is the income tax cuts in 2001 and 2003. We realize this statement sounds odd, but keep in mind that the federal income tax cuts in 2001 and 2003 were made in the regular income tax, not in the AMT. Because taxpayers must pay the greater of either their AMT or regular income tax liability, the decline in regular income tax liability without any change in the AMT pushed many taxpayers into the AMT. In other words, what the regular income tax cuts gave with one hand were (for many people) taken away by the AMT with the other hand.

A Student Asks

QUESTION: *Is everybody subject to the AMT, or only people above a certain income?*

ANSWER: *Only persons above a certain income. In 2006, that income is $67,890 for a person filing jointly with two children.*

Reinforcement Activity

Tell students that only 19,000 people paid the AMT in 1970, but more than 30 million are projected to pay it in 2010. Assign students to prepare one-page persuasive essays about the AMT and what they believe its future should be. They should answer this question: Do you think that the AMT will be adjusted for inflation, abolished, or changed in some other way? Students should back up their ideas with evidence from the text or from outside research.

A Student Asks

You might want to use this A Student Asks to make sure that students understand that more taxpayers will be facing this tax in coming years.

Cross-Curricular Activity

Throughout this text we have discussed the role of government numerous times. There is a divergence of opinion regarding to what degree the government should be involved in the economy. You may want to invite a government teacher to your class to provide more insight into the subject. Then, divide your class into two teams and ask one team to be in favor of more government control and the other team to be opposed. Give students time to research their side of the issue and prepare to support it in a debate. Encourage students to use primary source documents and visual aids in arguments. Each team should select two speakers who will debate the team's perspective.

Teaching with Visuals

Answers to the question with Exhibit 14-3 will vary.

Teaching with Visuals

A flat tax is the same as a proportional tax. Answers to the question accompanying Exhibit 14-4 will vary. Students might say that tax revenues would fall because the tax rate would be lower for higher-earning individuals.

Economics Around the Clock

Invite students to discuss their answers to the 6:04 P.M. scenario in Economics Around the Clock (page 365).

Students may respond that a flat tax is another name for a proportional income tax. A flat, or proportional tax, is one in which all taxpayers pay the same tax rate no matter what their income. For example, both the person who earns $1 million a year and the person who earns $50,000 a year pay the same tax rate of, say, 18%.

Reinforcement Activity

Students may not be aware that the United States has a progressive tax bracket structure. They may not know the percentage breakdown for the tax rates and that the amount someone pays is based on their yearly taxable income figure. Ask students to do research to determine: the percentage tax bracket rates; the income range for the tax brackets; and the tax bracket containing the smallest portion and the one with the largest portion of the American population. Students can acquire this information from the Internal Revenue Service and the U.S. Bureau of the Census. The results of their fact-finding activity will be a good base for class discussion.

proportional income tax An income tax that everyone pays at the same rate, whatever the income level.

progressive income tax An income tax whose rate increases as income level rises. Progressive income tax structures are usually capped at some rate.

regressive income tax An income tax whose rate decreases as income level rises.

Proportional, Progressive, and Regressive Income Taxes

Income taxes can be proportional, progressive, or regressive. See Exhibit 14-3.

Proportional Income Taxation

With a **proportional income tax**, everyone pays taxes at the same rate, whatever the income level. For example, if Kuan's taxable income is $100,000, she will pay taxes at the same rate as Arehart, who has a taxable income of $10,000. Suppose this rate is 10 percent. Kuan then pays $10,000 in income taxes, and Arehart pays $1,000. Notice that Kuan, who earns ten times as much as Arehart, pays ten times as much in taxes ($10,000 as opposed to $1,000). However, Kuan pays at exactly the same rate—10 percent—as Arehart. Sometimes a proportional income tax is called a *flat tax*, because everyone pays the same flat tax rate. Interestingly enough, many (but not all) countries that today have a flat tax system were once communist countries. In Exhibit 14-4 you will find a list of some countries with flat taxes.

A common, but mistaken, belief is that a flat tax is necessarily a low tax. It does not have to work this way. For example, some people today think that Lithuania's flat tax of 33 percent is too high. (See Exhibit 14-4.)

EXHIBIT 14-3 Three Income Tax Structures

Proportional	Progressive	Regressive
Same tax rate for every taxpayer. Tax rate remains constant as taxable income rises.	Tax rate rises as taxable income rises.	Tax rate falls as taxable income rises.

▲ Do you think that one of these types of income tax makes more sense or is more fair than the others? If so, explain.

EXHIBIT 14-4 Countries with a Flat Tax

Country	Rate	Year introduced
Estonia	26%	1994
Lithuania	33	1994
Latvia	25	1995
Russia	13	2001
Serbia	14	2003
Ukraine	13	2004
Slovakia	19	2004
Georgia	12	2005
Romania	16	2005

▲ A flat tax is the same type of tax as which of the three taxes described in Exhibit 14-3? If the U.S. government switched from its current tax structure to a flat tax, do you think it would see tax revenues rise, fall, or stay the same? Explain.

Progressive Income Taxation

A **progressive income tax** is a tax that people pay at a higher rate as their income levels rise. Suppose that Davidson pays taxes at the rate of 10 percent on a taxable income of $10,000. When his income doubles to $20,000, he pays at a rate of 12 percent. A progressive income tax is usually capped at some tax rate; it rises to some rate and then stops. For instance, perhaps no one will pay at a rate higher than 35 percent, no matter how high his or her income.

The United States has a progressive income tax structure. For example, in 2005, the tax rates were 10, 15, 25, 28, 33, and 35 percent. If you would like to find out whether the tax rate structure is the same today, go to www.emcp.net/taxrate and key in "tax rates" in the Search box. A list of documents will then come up. Pick the document that specifies the tax rates for the current year, such as tax rates for 2006.

Regressive Income Taxation

With a **regressive income tax**, people pay taxes at a lower rate as their income levels rise. For example, Lowenstein's tax rate is 10 percent when her income is $10,000 and 8 percent when her income rises to $20,000.

Cooperative Learning

Exhibit 14-3 defines proportional, progressive, and regressive tax structures. Divide the class into three groups and assign one of the tax structures to each group. Each group should research its particular tax structure to find information about where and how this tax structure has been used and how effective it has been. Cap off the activity by encouraging the three groups to debate the merits of the different tax structures.

370 Chapter 14 Taxing and Spending

Economics in the Real World

Do Tax Rates Affect Athletic Performance?

On Sunday, May 29, 2005, Danica Patrick became the first woman to lead the Indianapolis 500 and the highest-finishing (fourth) woman in the race's history. Leading as late as Lap 193 in the 200-lap race, Patrick's winnings that day were $378,855. As of June 2005, her racing winnings totaled $613,755.

Now let's turn to Maria Sharapova, tennis star, who on June 13, 2005, was ranked second in the World Tennis Association rankings. Her tennis prize money as of that day (in 2005) was $1,012,721. (Her income was much higher for 2005 if we take into account endorsements.)

By the standards of most people, both Danica Patrick and Maria Sharapova were having a good year in 2005. Both were earning quite a bit of money. However, money earned and money kept are two different things. One can earn a million dollars, but because of taxes, one doesn't keep a million dollars.

If we calculate Danica Patrick's taxes on her total winnings of $613,755 (as of a certain date), and Sharapova's taxes on $1,012,721, what would they be?

Because we do not know the financial particulars of either of these women athletes, we have to make some rough estimates. For example, we do not know the actual dollar deductions or exemptions for either person, so we will assume that each takes the $5,000 standard deduction and the $3,200 personal exemption only, for a total of $8,200 for each person.

If we subtract this dollar amount from Patrick's winnings (as of June 2005), it leaves her with a taxable income of $605,555. Now if we consult the 2005 IRS tax table, we learn that for anyone who earns more than $326,450 a year, she must pay in federal income taxes "$94,727.50 plus 35 percent of everything over the amount of $326,450." Danica Patrick owes taxes equal to $94,727.50 + 0.35(605,555 – $326,450). Her tax liability amounts to $192,414.25. If we subtract this amount from her gross earnings of $613,755, Danica Patrick is left with $421,340.75.

What about Sharapova? If we subtract our $8,200 in deductions and exemptions from her gross tennis earnings (as of a certain date), we are left with a taxable income of $1,004,521. Her tax liability is $94,727.50 + 0.35(1,004,521 – $326,450), or $332,052.35. If we subtract her tax liability from her gross income of $1,012,721, her after-tax income is $680,668.65. Keep in mind, also, that we did not calculate the state income tax that both Patrick and Sharapova might have to pay. Our after-tax dollar amounts are higher than they would be after state income taxes were paid.

Both Danica Patrick and Maria Sharapova, you will notice, had to pay in taxes 35 percent of everything they earned over $326,450. For every dollar they earn over this amount, 35 cents has to be paid in taxes to the federal government. Suppose that Sharapova is playing tennis and the winning prize is $1 million. As she is playing tennis, she ought to think of a prize somewhat smaller. How much smaller? Thirty-five percent smaller—the prize for her, after she pays her taxes on the $1 million prize, would be $650,000.

THINK ABOUT IT Suppose Danica Patrick and Maria Sharapova had to pay 70 cents out of every dollar earned over $326,450. Do you think it would affect Patrick's desire to race cars or Sharapova's desire to play tennis? Explain your answer.

Economics in the Real World

Ask students to pick a professional athlete of their choice and compute the athlete's approximate federal tax liability in the last year.

ANSWERS TO THINK ABOUT IT Answers will vary. Students may believe that a tax rate of 70% might act as a disincentive for these athletes to compete once they had earned $326,450.

Internet Research

Tell students that they will carry out research on regressive taxes. Instruct them to choose a state and find out that state's sales tax rate. Next, ask them to research whether these rates have increased, decreased, or stayed the same over the last 10 years. Students should find reasons why the rates have or have not changed during this period. Allow students to present their findings to the class.

Teaching with Visuals

Exhibit 14-5 shows the increase in the number of days a taxpayer has to work to pay his or her taxes. Ask students to look carefully at the exhibit. In what period of time was the increase the biggest? (*Answer:* From 1995 to 2000 the increase was nine days.) What period saw the greatest decrease? (*Answer:* From 2000 to 2004 the decrease was 18 days.)

Teaching with Visuals

Exhibit 14-6 (page 373) shows which income groups pay the most taxes in the United States. The answers to the questions posed with this exhibit are as follows: The percentage of the total tax bill was higher than the percentage of total income for five groups, or all groups except the bottom 50%. The percentage difference was greatest for the top 10%.

It might help students understand the figures if you change some of the percentages to fractions. For example, the top 1% pays nearly ⅓ of the taxes, and the top 5% pays over ½ of the taxes. You might also create a pie chart with this information to help students get a visual understanding of the information.

Application Activity

After reading and discussing Section 1, you may want to assign the Section Activity in the *Applying the Principles Workbook.*

Assess

Quick Quiz

The following true-or-false quiz will help you assess student understanding of the material covered in this section.

1. There are five major taxes at the federal government level. (False)
2. The federal government and some states apply an excise tax on some items. (True)
3. The alternative minimum tax is a tax that everyone pays on top of their regular income tax. (False)
4. With a proportional income tax, everyone pays at the same rate. (True)

A Student Asks

QUESTION: *I know the federal income tax in the United States is progressive, but aren't some taxes in the United States regressive? Do some taxes "hit" poor people harder than rich people?*

ANSWER: *A state sales tax is an example of a tax that is regressive. To understand this concept, suppose a state sales tax is 6 percent. In other words, for every $1 purchase, a person will pay 6 cents in state sales tax. Now suppose that two individuals, A and B, each buy a $1,000 computer. Both will end up paying a state sales tax of $60. Because A has a larger income than B has, A will pay a smaller percentage of A's income in sales taxes than B will. For example, if A's income is $5,000 a month and B's income is $3,000 a month, then $60 is 1.2 percent of $5,000, but it is 2.0 percent of $3,000.*

▼ This exhibit shows the number of days an average taxpayer has to work to pay his or her taxes in selected years. In 1980 it was 112 days. In 2005 it was 107 days.

How Long Do You Have to Work to Pay All Your Taxes?

Individuals, then, pay an assortment of taxes to the federal, state, and local government. How many days each year does the average person have to work to pay all his or her taxes? It was calculated that if a person began work on January 1, 2005, he or she would have to work until April 17, 2005, before earning enough to pay all taxes owed. Exhibit 14-5 shows how long the average taxpayer had to work to pay taxes in selected years. We should mention that the number of days a person has to work to pay his or her entire tax bill differs between states, because taxes are higher in some states than in other states. If you want to find out how many days a person in your state has to work to pay all his or her taxes, you can go to www.emcp.net/taxes and click on your state. For example, in Nebraska a person works from January 1, 2005, to April 13, 2005, to pay all of his or her taxes for the year. In New York, a person works until April 29.

EXAMPLE: The average worker works about 35 hours a week, 49 weeks a year, or about 1,715 hours a year spent working. How many of those hours are spent working in order to earn enough money to pay one's total tax bill (for the year)? The answer is about 490 hours, or slightly more than 28 percent of all working hours. Or you can look at it this way: If you start work at 9 a.m. each day, take an hour for lunch, and leave work at 5 p.m., you work from 9 a.m. to a few minutes before 11 a.m. each day in order to pay your taxes. After 11 a.m., what you earn stays with you. ♦

EXHIBIT 14-5 How Many Days Do You Have to Work to Pay Your Taxes?

Year	Number of days spent working to pay all federal, state, and local taxes	Time period
1980	112	January 1–April 21
1985	108	January 1–April 18
1995	115	January 1–April 25
2000	124	January 1–May 3
2004	106	January 1–April 15
2005	107	January 1–April 17

A Student Asks

QUESTION: *If the average person in the United States had to work from January 1, 2005, until April 17, 2005, to pay his or her taxes, that is 107 days. How long does the average person have to work to pay for other things, such as housing, food, and clothes?*

ANSWER: *The average person works 65 days a year to pay for housing and housing operation. You might be interested in knowing how long the average person works to purchase other things. For example, medical care, 52 days a year; food, 31 days a year; clothing and accessories, 13 days a year; recreation, 22 days. So, you can see that taxes take a major part of most people's income.*

Cross-Curricular Activity

Invite an American history teacher from your school to the class to discuss how the tax burden has fallen across society during the nation's history. Make sure she or he touches on the history of the income tax—why it was considered necessary and how people reacted to it. After the history teacher has discussed the historical facts, you can connect these facts to economic realities by using charts to show how tax rates have changed throughout U.S. history.

Who Pays What Percentage of Federal Income Taxes?

Do the wealthy in the United States pay their fair share of taxes? Polls taken in the United States indicate that most people think that the wealthy do not pay their fair share.

Several issues are important in the discussion of taxes and the share paid by different income groups. First, it is important to define what we mean by "wealthy Americans." Are wealthy Americans those persons who are in the top 1 percent of income earners, or top 5 percent, or top 10 percent?

Second, it is important to define what we mean by a "fair share" of taxes. For example, is it unfair if wealthy Americans pay only 5 percent of all federal income taxes, but fair if they pay 20 percent?

Third, it is important to get some idea of what wealthy Americans pay in taxes compared to what they earn in income.

Let's compare tax data for people in different income groups (see Exhibit 14-6). How does each income group's share of income compare to its share of taxes? Do you notice a pattern with regard to the average tax rates for the different groups? After studying the data, do you have an opinion about whether or not the wealthy pay a fair share of the total income tax?

EXHIBIT 14-6 Federal Individual Income Tax Categories

Income group	Income split point	Group's share of total U.S. income	Group's share of federal income taxes	Average tax rate
Top 1%	above $285,424	16.12%	33.71%	27.25%
Top 5%	above $126,525	30.55%	53.80%	22.95%
Top 10%	above $ 92,663	41.77%	65.73%	20.51%
Top 25%	above $ 56,401	64.37%	83.90%	16.99%
Top 50%	above $ 28,654	85.77%	96.50%	14.66%
Bottom 50%	below $ 28,654	14.23%	3.50%	3.21%

Source: Internal Revenue Service (2003).

▲ This exhibit compares the amount of total U.S. income earned to the amount of taxes paid for by selected income groups. The "Income split point" (second column) is simply a term for the amount of income a person had to earn to be in a particular group. For example, a person had to earn *at least* $285,424 to be in the top 1% of earners. Note from the last column, reading from the bottom up, that the more money a person earns, the higher average tax rate the person pays. **For how many groups was the percentage of the total tax bill higher than the percentage of total income? For which group was this percentage difference the greatest?**

SECTION 1 ASSESSMENT

Defining Terms

1. Define
   a. proportional income tax
   b. progressive income tax
   c. regressive income tax

Reviewing Facts and Concepts

2. What three federal taxes together account for approximately 92.3 percent of federal government tax revenues?
3. Which federal tax raises the greatest tax revenue?
4. What percentage of the year did the average taxpayer have to work in 2000 to pay all his or her taxes?

Critical Thinking

5. "It is possible for a high-income earner to pay more in taxes than a low-income earner under a regressive income tax." Do you agree or disagree? Explain your answer.

Applying Economic Concepts

6. Is a sales tax regressive, proportional, or progressive? Explain your answer.

Assessment Book

You will find a quiz for this section in the *Assessment Book.*

Reteaching Activity

Use the Section Assessment to gauge which students may need reteaching on this section. Ask those students to list and describe the three major federal taxes.

Guided Reading

For further reteaching of the key concepts in this section, assign the Outlining Activity and the Just the Facts Handout from the *Guided Reading and Study Guide.*

SECTION 1 ASSESSMENT ANSWERS

Defining Terms

1. a. proportional income tax: a tax structure in which a person pays the same tax rate no matter what his or her income is; **b. progressive income tax:** a tax structure in which a person pays a higher tax rate as his or her income rises; **c. regressive income tax:** a tax structure in which a person pays a lower tax rate as his or her income rises.

Reviewing Facts and Concepts

2. Personal income tax, corporate income tax, and Social Security tax account for 92.3% of federal tax revenue.

3. According to Exhibit 14-2, the personal income tax raises the greatest revenue.

4. The average taxpayer had to work 124 days to pay all his or her taxes in 2000. This is 34% of 365 days (1 year).

Critical Thinking

5. Agree. Under a regressive income tax, a person's tax rate goes down as income rises, but it is still possible for a high-income earner to pay more in taxes than a low-income earner. For example, suppose the tax rate for a person who earns $10,000 is 10%, and the tax rate for a person who earns $100,000 is 5%. The person with the lower income pays $1,000 in taxes, and the person with the higher income pays $5,000 in taxes.

Applying Economic Concepts

6. A sales tax is regressive. To illustrate, suppose there are two people, Smith and Jones. Smith earns $10,000 a year, and Jones earns $100,000 a year. Both Smith and Jones buy good X for $40. The sales tax on the good is $5. The $5 sales tax is a larger percentage of Smith's income than Jones's income, which means that the sales tax is regressive.

Your Personal Economics

Discussion Starter

Ask volunteers to describe their experiences in preparing and filing a federal income tax return. (You might want to make clear to students that they do not have to volunteer this information.) Ask students: Did you prepare the return yourself, or did you ask for the assistance of a tax preparer, accountant, or other adult? Did you use tax software? How did the difficulty of completing the form compare with the difficulty of taking an economics test?

Research Activity

Instruct each student to conduct an opinion poll on whether federal income tax forms are too complex. Students should survey several adults they know to determine opinions, and reasons for each person's opinion. Students may want to search the Internet to see what other people's opinions are on this issue. Ask students to compile their data and then report back to the class.

Your Personal Economics

Filing an Income Tax Return

If you haven't already, you will soon have to file an annual federal income tax return. Is it hard to do? In most cases, it is not hard at all. You have taken numerous tests in high school that are much harder than filing your tax return.

How should you proceed? New software programs are available for you to use, or you can complete your tax returns yourself. Even if you use the software, make sure you understand the process behind filing your return.

An Overview

Let's look at the big picture of what you will be doing. First, you will identify all the income you earned in a given year. Let's say this amount is $50,000. Second, you subtract certain dollar items from this $50,000. These items come with different names: exemptions, deductions, adjustments. Third, you end up with a certain dollar amount of taxable income. Let's say this amount is $40,000. Fourth, you simply consult an IRS tax table to see how much you will pay in taxes based on this taxable income.

These simple steps are really all there is to it. It is a matter of a little addition and subtraction and consulting one (fairly simple) tax table.

The Step-by-Step Process

Now let's outline the steps in a little more detail.

1. Gather together all your tax documents. They include things such as your W2 statement (a statement you receive from your employer stating how much you earned during the year).
2. Most likely, the first several years you will be able to use Form 1040EZ, which is the simplest form. For example, you can use this form if you earned less than $100,000 during the year, do not plan to claim any dependents (anyone who is dependent upon you for some support), and have interest income of $1,500 or less. If you are unsure of which form to file, go to www.emcp.net/taxforms.
3. Go to www.emcp.net/printtaxforms and print off one or two copies of the correct form.
4. Start filling out the form. Take things slowly, line by line.
5. You need to determine your filing status. You must file as one of the following: a single person, head of household, qualifying widow, married filing jointly, or married filing separately.
6. You next claim an exemption for yourself and for any dependents you may have. You cannot claim a personal exemption for yourself if anyone, such as your parents, has claimed you as a dependent.
7. You must state the amount of income you earned in the last year. Your W2 form comes in handy here. It identifies the dollar amount of income you earned working at your job.
8. You may also list certain adjustments to your income. These adjustments include expenses that you incurred over the year (moving expenses, tuition and

Cooperative Learning

Divide students into groups of four or five. Assign each group a different portion of a 1040 Form. Instruct groups to look for places in the form that might be difficult for taxpayers to understand. Ask groups what kind of information the IRS is looking for in that portion of the form. Allow each group to make a presentation to the class, explaining the portion of the 1040 it was assigned.

fees deduction, health savings account deductions, and more) that will lower your taxable income and thus reduce the amount of taxes you must pay.

9. You may take the standard deduction (which is something else that will lower your taxable income). The amount of standard deduction you take depends upon your filing status.
10. If you do not take the standard deduction, you may take certain "itemized deductions" instead. Like exemptions, adjustments, and the standard deduction, itemized deductions lower your taxable income and thus lower the amount of taxes you must pay.
11. At this point, you add up all your exemptions, deductions, and adjustments and subtract them from your total income. What is left is your taxable income.
12. To figure out how much you have to pay in taxes, you consult a tax table. These tables can be found at www.emcp.net/taxtables or in the tax booklet that you received from the IRS.

The accompanying table is for a single person filing in 2005. Using the table, you can figure your tax liability. For example, let's suppose your taxable income was $40,000. Using the table, we see that $40,000 falls between $29,700 and $71,950. Therefore your tax liability is $4,090 plus 25 percent of the amount over $29,700. If we subtract $29,700 from your taxable income of $40,000, the amount is $10,300. Twenty-five percent of $10,300 is $2,575. So $4,090 + $2,575 = $6,665, the amount you owe in taxes.

13. It is also likely that you paid taxes throughout the year. You have probably noticed that a certain amount of money is deducted from your paychecks to pay federal income taxes. Let's say the total amount of taxes deducted from your paychecks over the year was $6,000. Given that you already paid $6,000 of the $6,665 you owe in taxes, you now need to write out a check to the IRS for $665.
14. If by chance, the total amount of taxes deducted from your paychecks over the year was $7,000, then you paid more in taxes than you owe. You will be entitled to a tax refund of $335.
15. Finally, you can file your tax return over the phone, online, or via regular mail.

If taxable income is over–	But not over–	The tax is:
$0	$7,300	10% of the amount over $0
$7,300	$29,700	$730 plus 15% of the amount over 7,300
$29,700	$71,950	$4,090 plus 25% of the amount over 29,700
$71,950	$150,150	$14,652.50 plus 28% of the amount over 71,950
$150,150	$326,450	$36,548.50 plus 33% of the amount over 150,150
$326,450	no limit	$94,727.50 plus 35% of the amount over 326,450

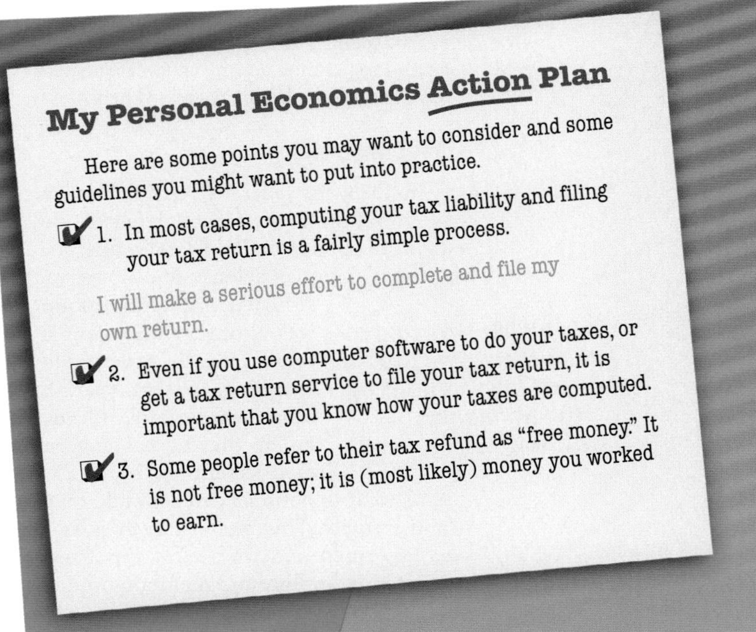

My Personal Economics Action Plan

Here are some points you may want to consider and some guidelines you might want to put into practice.

1. In most cases, computing your tax liability and filing your tax return is a fairly simple process.

I will make a serious effort to complete and file my own return.

2. Even if you use computer software to do your taxes, or get a tax return service to file your tax return, it is important that you know how your taxes are computed.
3. Some people refer to their tax refund as "free money." It is not free money; it is (most likely) money you worked to earn.

Discussion Starter

Remind students that when they work as an employee, taxes will be taken out of their paychecks over the course of the year. If they are self-employed, taxes will not be taken out. However, self-employed individuals do have to make quarterly payments to the federal government (assuming they earn more than a certain amount). Ask students why they think the government requires taxpayers to pay so far in advance of April 15, the day tax returns must be postmarked. Ask: Can you think of any downsides to paying in advance? Are there any benefits to taxpayers or to the federal government?

My Personal Economics Action Plan Lead students in brainstorming ways that they might be able to prepare for paying federal income taxes. Ask students to consider the pros and cons of using tax software versus retaining the services of a tax professional. Ask students to suggest ways they might save money on their federal income taxes.

SECTION 2 Teacher Support

Focus and Motivate

Section Objectives

After completing this section, students will be able to

- describe how the federal government spends its tax revenues;
- define *balanced budget, budget deficit,* and *budget surplus;*
- explain the relationship between deficits and the national debt; and
- describe some of the issues connected with budget surpluses.

Economics Around the Clock

Kickoff Activity

Direct students to read the 5:32 P.M. scenario in Economics Around the Clock (page 365).

Tell students that about a fifth of the federal budget is devoted to defense and homeland security. Ask students to suggest reasons why that might be so and to evaluate whether or not it is appropriate.

Activating Prior Knowledge

Take time to have student volunteers share their responses to the Kickoff Activity. Tell them they will be learning more about how the federal government allocates funds as they study this section.

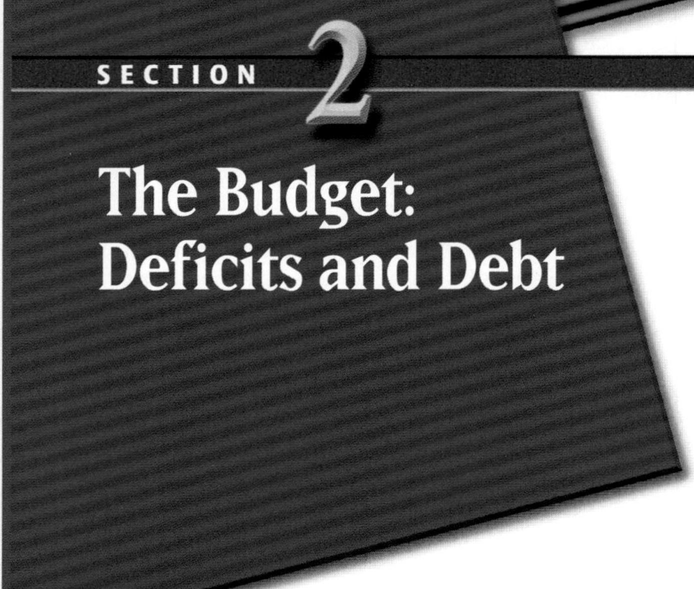

SECTION 2 The Budget: Deficits and Debt

Focus Questions

- How does the federal government spend its tax revenues?
- What is a balanced budget? A budget deficit? A budget surplus?
- What is the relationship between deficits and the national debt?
- What are some issues connected with budget surpluses?

Key Terms

national debt
budget deficit
budget surplus

How Does the Federal Government Spend Money?

In 2005, the federal government spent approximately $2,451 billion. How was this money spent? The federal government breaks down its spending according to categories, a few of which are briefly discussed here.

National Defense

In 2005, the federal government spent $497 billion on national defense (and about $31 billion on homeland security). If we sum national defense and homeland security, this total amount was about 21.5 percent of total federal government spending in that year. In other words, out of every dollar the federal government spent in 2005, 21.5 cents went to national defense and homeland security. This money largely goes to pay the men and women in the armed services and to buy and maintain military weapons.

> *"It's a billion here and a billion there; the first thing you know it adds up to real money."*
> —Senator Everett Dirksen

Income Security, Retirement, and Disability

Income security refers to government programs such as housing assistance, food and nutrition assistance for the poor, unemployment compensation (for those persons who have lost their jobs), food stamps, child nutrition programs, federal employee disability payments, and so on. The federal government spent $197 billion on income security in 2005. On other retirement and disability programs it spent $147 billion. The sum total here is $344 billion or 14 percent of total federal government spending.

Social Security

The federal government in 2005 spent $516 billion on Social Security payments, which largely go to retired persons. These payments were a little more than 21 percent of total federal government spending.

Medicare

In 2005, the federal government spent $297 billion on Medicare, which is hospital

Background Information: Social Security and Retirement

Students might question the importance of Social Security taxes, believing that they're too young to be worrying about retirement. Tell them that during the past several years, however, there has been some concern about whether Social Security will "run out" of funds or offer decreased benefits in the future. Most people agree that Social Security will still exist in the future, but the program may be changed.

Students need to realize that Social Security should be used as part but not all of their financial planning for retirement. They need to begin planning for their retirement with funds in addition to Social Security.

376 Chapter 14 Taxing and Spending

◀ It is likely that many of these senior citizens participate in the federal government's Medicare program. In 2005 the federal government spent $297 billion on Medicare.

and medical insurance for Social Security beneficiaries. This amount was 12.1 percent of total federal government spending.

Net Interest on the National Debt

When the government spends more money than it receives in tax revenues, it is said to run a budget deficit. For example, if the government spends $2,000 billion and its tax revenue is $1,800 billion, the budget deficit is $200 billion. The government has to borrow the $200 billion, in much the same way that people have to borrow money if their expenditures are greater than their income. The federal government borrowed much money over the years; on October 24, 2005, its total debt—referred to as the **national debt**—was $8,009 billion or $8.009 trillion. If you want to know what the national debt is today, go to www.emcp.net/nationaldebt. This Web site will show you the national debt to the penny.

The federal government has to pay interest on this debt, in much the same way that people make interest payments on their general credit card bills (such as Visa or MasterCard). In 2005, the interest payment the government had to make on the national debt was approximately $177 billion, or 7.2 percent of total federal government spending.

If we combine national defense spending, spending on homeland security, income security spending, spending on retirement and disability, Social Security spending, Medicare spending, and spending on the national debt, we see that we have accounted for 75.8 percent of all federal government spending. Just looking at national defense (plus homeland security) and Social Security (plus Medicare) accounts for over half of all federal spending, at a total of 54.6 percent.

Exhibit 14-7 shows projected federal government spending for the period from 2006 to 2011.

national debt
The sum total of what the federal government owes its creditors.

EXHIBIT 14-7 Projected Federal Government Spending

Year	Projected spending (billions of dollars)
2006	$2,511
2007	2,625
2008	2,754
2009	2,881
2010	3,008
2011	3,157

Source: Internal Revenue Service (2005).

Teach

Discussion Starter

In this section students learn how much money is spent in different major categories of federal government spending. Ask students if they would allocate tax dollars in a different way, and if so, why. Make it clear that there is no incorrect point of view and that differences in opinion are welcome.

Reinforcement Activity

Allow students to work in groups of four or five to learn about last year's national debt. Pose questions like these for them to explore: What was the total dollar amount of the national debt? How did it rank historically with the national debts of previous years? Why is the debt so large? Allow the groups to present their findings to the class.

Teaching with Visuals

As students look at Exhibit 14-7, ask them where the money for the increased government spending will come from. (*Answer:* The money will come from tax revenue.) Do students think this means that taxes will go up? Why or why not?

Help students understand that even without raising taxes, the government receives more tax revenue in years when the U.S. economy is strong.

Background Information: Medicare

Medicare, which is the nation's largest health insurance program, is administered by the Health Care Financing Administration. Medicare covers millions of Americans. In addition to insuring Social Security beneficiaries aged 65 and older, Medicare also provides for some disabled people under age 65 and for people with permanent kidney failure treated with dialysis or a transplant. To be eligible for Medicare, a person or his or her spouse must have worked for at least 10 years in Medicare-covered employment and be a citizen or permanent resident of the United States.

A Student Asks

You might want to use this A Student Asks as an opportunity for students to examine their state's spending on education. Direct students to www.emcp.net/schools, and then ask them the following questions: How does our state compare with other states? Do you think that we are spending an appropriate amount on education in this state? Why or why not?

Economics Around the Clock

After students read A Student Asks on this page, refer them to the 7:16 P.M. scenario in Economics Around the Clock (page 365) and discuss their answers to the question provided there.

In 2002, the federal government allocated about 2.2% of its total spending to elementary and secondary education, which is a relatively small percentage. However, most educational spending is the responsibility of state governments and comes out of state budgets.

A Student Asks

QUESTION: *Does the federal government spend much on education? What percentage of total federal spending goes for education?*

ANSWER: *In 2002, the federal government spent approximately $54.6 billion on elementary and secondary education, which was about 2.2 percent of total federal spending. Keep in mind, though, that most spending on elementary and secondary public education occurs at the state level. In other words, state governments are the major spenders on education. Spending on education usually takes the biggest slice of a state government's budget. In 2002, per-student spending in a public school was $7,524. In other words, it takes about that much to educate you if you are in a public school. If you would like some detailed data on schools in your state, you can go to www.emcp.net/schools. Once there, simply click on the state you are interested in. You will find information on total number of schools in your state, total number of students, total number of teachers, pupil/teacher ratio, total dollar amount spent on education, and much more.*

The Costs and Benefits of Government Spending Programs

According to economists, a government spending program is not worth pursuing unless the benefits of that program outweigh the costs. In other words, if the program generates $100 billion in benefits and costs $40 billion, then we have $60 billion in net benefits, and the program is worth pursuing.

In reality, though, things don't always turn out this way. Sometimes spending programs that have greater costs than benefits get passed in Congress. Why? Let's look at the following example.

Person	Benefits	Costs	Vote
A	$130	$100	Yes
B	120	100	Yes
C	102	100	Yes
D	50	100	No
E	10	100	No

Five people, A–E, are represented in the table above. Suppose these people are considering buying a statue for their town square, the total cost of which is $500. They have agreed that if they decide to buy the statue, they will split the cost equally, each member paying $100. Now, they take a vote on whether or not to buy the statue. How will each person vote? Each person has to compare his or her personal benefits from the statue to the personal costs. In this case, their costs are all the same—$100. But to determine the benefits, each person must place a dollar value on what he or she thinks the benefits are worth. This dollar amount is essentially what the person is willing to pay for the statue. If the person's benefits are greater than the costs, the person will vote yes for the statue; if the person's benefits are less than the costs, the person will vote no.

As you can see in the table, persons A, B, and C vote yes for the statue because for each of them the benefits are greater than the costs. Persons D and E vote no because for them benefits are less than costs—they don't believe they will receive $100 worth of benefits from the statue.

More yes votes (3) than no votes (2) means the community of five persons buys the statue. Notice one thing, however: the total benefits to the community of five persons is less than the total cost to the community of five persons. Even though the total benefits ($412) are less than the total costs ($500), the community buys the statue.

On a personal level, you would never buy anything if the total benefits to you were less than the total costs. However, the government buys things every day where the total benefits are less than the costs, because government decides whether something will be bought based on voting. And voting, as we showed, can lead to things being bought even though the total benefits of something are less than the total costs.

Cooperative Learning

Divide the class into groups and ask each group to discuss how things might be different if there were no national debt. Ask groups to decide how they would spend an extra $8,009 billion if they were the government. Would they spend it on education or on programs to help poor people? Would they return it to the taxpayers to spend as they saw fit? Each group should itemize how it would redistribute the money and draw up a chart showing its spending plan. Then a representative from each group should present the group's ideas to the class.

Economics in the Real World

Would We All Be Better Off Without Show-Offs?

Thorstein Veblen (1857–1929), an economist, believed that people sometimes buy goods for the wrong reasons. He coined the term *conspicuous consumption*—that is, purchasing designed to show off or to display one's status.

Consider the fact that today you can buy several different makes of watches, two of which are a Timex and a Rolex. A Timex costs under $100, and a Rolex costs many thousands of dollars. Both brands of watches keep good time, but the Rolex does something else: it "says" that you have the money to buy something expensive. In other words, a Rolex is a status symbol.

In 2005, Tom Cruise and Katie Holmes, both movie actors, got engaged (to be married). Tom Cruise gave Katie Holmes a 4-carat diamond engagement ring. Cost: $200,000.

Does our culture today promote status? Some economists believe that it does. The race for status, these economists contend, is a relative race and is wasteful.

Some economists argue that the race for status comes with certain opportunity costs, one of which is lost leisure. If we try to leapfrog each other, we work harder and longer to achieve a status position we could all achieve at lower cost.

Another opportunity cost of the race for status may be that society has to do without certain goods that it wants. For example, suppose society wants the government to spend more money on medical research, education, and infrastructure. Currently, three individuals—A, B, and C—are locked into a race for status with the other two. A is richer than B, and B is richer than C, so A can buy more status goods (big houses, fancy cars, etc.) than B, who can buy more status goods than C.

Suppose the government proposes that it increase taxes on each of the individuals by 10 percent. A, B, and C argue against the higher tax rate because it reduces their ability to buy status goods. They fail to realize, however, that even though higher tax rates may make it less likely that each individual can buy as many status goods, their relative positions in the race for status will not change. After the higher taxes are paid, A will still have a higher after-tax income than B, who will have a higher after-tax income than C. Higher taxes will not stop the race for status, nor will higher taxes prevent anyone from showing off. The higher taxes simply reduce the amount of money that the individuals can spend in their race to show off.

Are any benefits derived from the higher taxes? According to some economists, the additional tax revenue can finance more medical research, education, and infrastructure. In other words, some benefits may come from using higher taxes to slow down the race for status.

One criticism of this reasoning is that the additional tax funds may not be used in the way people want them to be used. The funds may go for "public conspicuous consumption," such as expensive federal buildings, and other similar things. The critics also point out that higher taxes dampen people's incentives to produce, which may lead to less economic growth and wealth in the future. Finally, the critics point out that if the race for status is hobbled by higher taxes, the race will not slow down; it will simply take a different form. Instead of competing for status in terms of goods, people will compete for status in terms of power over others. In the end, the critics argue, it may be better to have people compete for status by buying goods than by trying to control others.

THINK ABOUT IT Do people in your high school try to achieve status by purchasing certain goods? If so, what goods?

Economics in the Real World

Before discussing this Economics in the Real World feature, you might ask students what the phrase "keeping up with the Joneses" means. If students have not heard this phrase, encourage them to ask parents or other adults the following questions about it: What does it mean? Is it intended as a compliment? Then discuss with students how the phrase relates to the topic of this feature.

ANSWERS TO THINK ABOUT IT Answers will vary. Students might mention certain types of clothing or shoes, electronic equipment such as MP3 players or video games, and even cars.

Internet Research

Request that students locate Web sites discussing the federal budget and online news articles discussing politicians' views on how federal funds should be spent. Instruct them to read the articles for answers to these questions: What ideas are proposed? What are the general political leanings of the different groups supporting each proposal? Ask students to keep track of proposals supported mostly by Democrats, those supported mostly by Republicans, and those supported mostly by other political parties. Hold a class debate in which students argue the pros and cons of one proposal for change.

Some countries have high taxes and other countries have low taxes. For example, in the late 1990s, taxes in Singapore, Switzerland, Ireland, Chile, Ecuador, and the United States were relatively low compared with taxes in Finland, Denmark, Portugal, Greece, and Syria. Generally, economists find that countries with relatively low taxes experience more rapid economic growth than countries with relatively high taxes. On the other hand, countries with relatively high taxes often provide their residents with more government services.

At the Congressional Budget Office (www.emcp.net/budget) you will find a host of budgetary data (data on tax revenues, government spending, etc.). Go to the site. Once there, click on "Current Budget Projections." Next, scroll down the page and find the following: (1) Projected individual income tax revenue in 2010; (2) Individual income taxes as a percentage of GDP in 2005; (3) Projected spending on Medicare in 2008.

The Budget Process

Just as individuals may have budgets in which they specify how they will spend their incomes—such as $300 a month for food and $100 a month for clothes—the federal government has a budget, too. In the federal budget, the federal government specifies how it will spend the money it has. It may decide to spend $250 billion on national defense, $100 billion on health care, and so on.

It Begins with the President

Preparing a budget and passing it into law is a long process. It begins with the president of the United States, who, with others in the executive branch of government, prepares the budget. The president's budget recommends to Congress how much should be spent for such things as national defense and income security programs. The president must submit the budget to Congress on or before the first Monday in February of each year.

Disagreements and Compromises

Once the president's budget is in the hands of Congress, it is scrutinized by the members of the many congressional committees and subcommittees. The Congressional Budget Office advises the members of the committees and subcommittees on technical details of the president's budget.

Members of Congress may disagree with the president about how money should be spent. For example, the president may want to spend more money for health care than do many members of Congress.

Disagreements may also arise over how much tax revenue is likely to be raised over the next few months. Perhaps the president estimated that the federal government will take in $2,100 billion in tax revenues, but Congress estimated tax revenues to be $1,900 billion. Both the executive and legislative branches must estimate tax revenues, because no one knows for sure how the economy will perform. For example, if the economy is sluggish and many millions of people are out of work, less income is earned, and thus income taxes will be down. Many details of the president's budget may be changed to reflect compromises between the president and Congress.

Public Opinion Counts

Where are the American people in the budget process? Do they have a role to play? Once the president submits a budget to Congress, the people get a chance to hear about it. Usually numerous newspaper stories and newscasts cover the president's proposals. The American people can write to or call their congresspersons and express their preferences on the president's budget. Also during this time, special-interest groups may lobby members of Congress and express their preferences on the president's budget.

The Budget Becomes Law

Congress is obligated to pass a budget by the beginning of the fiscal, not the calendar, year. (A calendar year begins on January 1 and runs through December 31; a fiscal year can begin on the first day of another month and run for the next 12 months. The fiscal year under which the federal government operates begins on October 1 and runs through September 30.) Once Congress passes the budget, the details of spending outlined in the budget become law for that fiscal year. Then, the whole process begins again in only a few months.

Background Information: The President

Students have already learned that the president is responsible for preparing the nation's annual budget. But do they know that the president is also looked upon as being the nation's economic leader? The public, Congress, and the business and labor communities increasingly look to the president to lower unemployment, fight inflation, keep taxes down, and promote economic growth. The Employment Act of 1946 created the Council of Economic Advisors to give the president economic advice. Ask students how they think the current president is doing as the nation's economic leader and whether the president seems to be getting good advice from the Council of Economic Advisors.

Splitting the Check: Do You Order Lobster or a Hamburger?

Suppose you and five friends go out to dinner. In setting A, you and your friends agree to pay for your own meals. If you have lobster for dinner, you pay for lobster. If you have a hamburger for dinner, you pay for the hamburger. The same holds for your friends.

In setting B, you and your friends agree to split the bill evenly. If the total bill comes to $150, then you will split this bill six ways ($25 each).

Now in which of the two settings, A or B, do you think (1) you will order more expensive food and (2) the total bill will be higher?

In other words, do you think you will order a more expensive meal when you have to pay for what you order, or when you pay one-sixth of what everyone orders?

Do you think the total bill will be greater when everyone pays for what he or she ordered, or when everyone pays an equal share?

One might think that a person would buy exactly the same meal in both settings, and so the total bill in both settings will be the same. However, some evidence indicates that people seem to buy more expensive things (food, clothes, etc.) when they view themselves as paying a fraction of the cost.

Think of it this way. If you are considering the lobster, and you know that you will have to pay for it, you consider the full price of the lobster—say, $35. If, however, you agree to split the bill, then the price (to you) of purchasing lobster is not $35, but one-sixth of $35, which is $5.83. Few people will choose the lobster at a price of $35, but many will at $5.83.

What holds for you holds for everyone at the dinner table. Because splitting the bill causes the items on the menu to appear cheaper (for each individual), each individual is more likely to buy expensive meals. But if everyone buys meals they wouldn't likely buy if they had to pay the full price, the dinner total is likely to be high indeed.

The dinner under two different settings goes a long way to explaining why government spending can zoom upward quickly. As you saw in Exhibit 14-7 on page 377, projected federal government spending in 2006 is $2,511 billion. But the people who lobby government for benefits aren't paying for all the benefits that they may receive. For example, let's say that the farmers ask Congress for subsidies. If Congress and the president agree to the subsidies, the taxpayers will have to foot the bill. Now the farmers are taxpayers, so they will have to pay for some of the benefits they receive. But they only pay for a fraction of the benefits they receive in a country with more than

100 million taxpayers. For the farmers this is like going to dinner with 100 million people at the table, all having agreed to split the check.

Now if 100 million people are going to split the check, anything you order is going to be cheap indeed. What's the lobster cost now? Dessert? I'll have 15.

In politics, almost everyone has an incentive to order big off the government menu. Yet, if everyone has an incentive to order big, and does order big, the total spending bill is going to be huge.

THINK ABOUT IT Why do you think people sometimes agree to split the check evenly rather than deciding that each individual will pay his or her exact share? Does splitting the check lead to a higher total?

Economics in the Real World

Ask students to think of other areas of government spending that benefit a particular group at the expense of the broad base of taxpayers. Encourage them to consider positive aspects of these situations, as well as negative aspects. For example, few of us have ever heard of Jumping Frenchmen of Maine, a rare disorder that causes an extreme reaction to unexpected noises or sights. Without government funds, it is unlikely that the very small percentage of the population suffering this condition would find the resources to search for a treatment or cure.

ANSWERS TO THINK ABOUT IT Answers will vary. Students might say that diners who are in a hurry will tend to agree to split the check evenly rather than take the time after the meal to identify each person's charges on the bill. Some might think that if people agree before the meal to split the bill, the total might be higher because people will feel more comfortable ordering expensive items knowing that the total will be divided evenly among everyone. Others might think the opposite—that people will want to be sure no one is overburdened by the cost of the meal, and will therefore order a less expensive meal in an effort to keep the total down.

Cooperative Learning

In many countries, the governments in power have had to take severe steps to curb runaway inflation, help decrease unemployment, and stabilize the economy. Divide the class into groups of three to four students. Have each group pick one of the following countries where this has occurred: Argentina, Ecuador, Zimbabwe, or Germany following World War I. Ask them to prepare brief oral reports outlining the government's actions to stabilize the country's economy and what the political, social, and economic results were.

Economics Around the Clock

You may want to refer students to the 5:30 P.M. scenario in Economics Around the Clock (page 365) and discuss their answers to the question that follows it.

Note that if we define the rich as the top 1% of income earners, and we look at certain select years, the top 1% of income earners are earning more of the total income pie today than they have in some years in the past. For example, in 1980, the top 1% earned 8.46% of the income pie, but in 2002, that percentage had risen to 16.2%. If you compare the situation in 2000 with the situation in 2002, however, the rich are not getting richer. In 2000, the top 1% earned 20.81% of total income, but in 2002, they earned only 16.2% of the total.

▲ President Bush confers with members of his cabinet regarding the budget. The president is obligated to submit his budget recommendations to Congress on or before the first Monday in February each year.

What Is a Fair Share?

Most people say that it is only right for everyone to pay his or her fair share of taxes. The problem is, how do we decide what a fair share is? And who decides? Historically, two principles of taxation touch on this issue: the benefits-received principle and the ability-to-pay principle.

Benefits-Received Principle

The benefits-received principle holds that a person should pay in taxes an amount equal to the benefits he or she receives from government expenditures. For example, if you drive often on government-provided roads and highways, you ought to pay for the upkeep of the roads. This goal is usually met through the excise tax on gasoline. People who drive a lot buy a lot of gas, so they pay more in gas taxes than people who drive very little. Because gas tax revenues are used for the upkeep of the roads, the major users of the roads end up paying the bulk of road upkeep costs.

Ability-to-Pay Principle

With some government-provided goods, it is easy to figure out roughly how much someone benefits. For instance, in the roads-and-highways example, we can assume that the more a person drives on the road or highway, the more benefit he or she obtains from it.

With other government-provided goods, however, it is not as easy to relate benefits received to taxes paid. For example, we could say that almost all Americans benefit from national defense, but we would have a hard time figuring out how much one person benefits compared to another person. Does Jackson, down the street, benefit more than, less than, or the same as Paul, who lives up the street? The benefits-received principle is hard to implement in such cases.

Often, the ability-to-pay principle is used instead. This principle says that people should pay taxes according to their abilities to pay. Because a rich person is more able to pay taxes than a poor person, a rich person should pay more taxes than a poor person. For example, a millionaire might pay $330,000 a year in income taxes, whereas a person who earns $50,000 a year might pay $8,000.

BY THE NUMBERS

The federal income tax came into existence in 1913. In that year, the top tax rate that anyone paid was 7 percent. As you learned in this chapter, the top (stated) tax rate today is 35 percent. The top tax rate has been different in different years. The following list shows the top tax rate for a few selected years.

Year	Top Tax Rate
1913	7.0%
1916	15.0
1919	73.0
1922	58.0
1929	24.0
1938	79.0
1944	94.0
1952	92.0
1962	91.0
1967	70.0
1986	50.0
1999	39.6
2005	35.0

Cross-Curricular Activity

Invite students to brainstorm questions about the history, political implications of, and controversy around taxation according to the "benefits-received" and the "ability-to-pay" principles. Then invite a history teacher and a government teacher to join you in a panel discussion in which you answer students' questions. Give the other teachers copies of the questions in advance so that they can research answers to them.

382 Chapter 14 Taxing and Spending

▲ One would expect that the people living in the houses on the left are more able to pay taxes than the people who live in the housing shown on the right. **Do you think the people living in the more expensive housing should have to pay a higher percentage of their income in taxes? If so, why?**

Budgets: Balanced and in Deficit

Adam Smith, the eighteenth century economist, said, "What is prudence in the conduct of every private family, can scarce be folly in that of a great kingdom." In other words, if it is right and reasonable for a family to do something, it is probably also right and reasonable for a great nation to do the same. If it is right for a family to save and avoid debt, then it is right for a nation to do the same.

For many years this notion carried over to the discussions of U.S. federal budget policy. Most people believed that the federal budget should be balanced—that is, government expenditures should be equal to tax revenues. **Budget deficits**, which occur when government expenditures exceed tax revenues, were acceptable, but only during wartime. (As an aside, a **budget surplus** exists if tax revenues exceed government expenditures.)

The Great Depression

Conditions began to change around the time of the Great Depression (1929–1933), a period of great economic distress in this country. During this time, unemployment skyrocketed, the production of goods and services plummeted, prices fell, banks closed, and companies went bankrupt. Until this time, many people in the United States thought that free enterprise was a stable, smooth mechanism. The economic downturn of the Great Depression gave these people cause for doubt, however, and slowly many previously accepted ideas of budget policy began to be discarded. One notion in particular that fell by the wayside was the idea that the federal budget should be balanced. People began to accept budget deficits as a way of reducing unemployment.

Reducing Unemployment

What do budget deficits have to do with reducing unemployment? Suppose the federal budget is balanced. Government spending is $2,000 billion, and tax revenues are $2,000 billion. However, unemployment is high, say, about 10 percent. The president, along with Congress, wants to reduce the unemployment rate by implementing expansionary fiscal policy (increase government spending or decrease taxes). Together, they decide to increase government spending to $2,200 billion. Tax revenues, we'll assume, remain constant at $2,000 billion. In this instance, expansionary fiscal policy leads to a budget deficit.

Many people came to see budget deficits as necessary, given the high unemployment that plagued the economy. According to them, the choice was simple: (1) either keep the federal budget balanced and suffer high unemployment (and the reduced output of goods and services that results), or (2) accept the budget deficit and reduce the unemployment rate. For many people, it was "better to balance the economy than to balance the budget." Exhibit 14-8 shows projected budget deficits from 2006 to 2011.

budget deficit
The situation in which federal government expenditures are greater than federal government tax revenues.

budget surplus
The situation in which federal government expenditures are less than federal government tax revenues.

Teaching with Visuals

Answers will vary.

Differentiating Instruction

English Language Learners

Students may have some difficulty understanding the terminology used in this discussion, yet they can easily understand the concept of debt. Ask students what would happen if you were to charge them $5 for every imaginable minor rule violation (chewing gum, not having a pencil out when class began, talking, etc.). It would not be long before their debt to you became unpayable. When the federal debt becomes unpayable, the government, unlike most consumers and businesses, can delay payments until future years.

Critical Thinking

After students have read "Higher Future Taxes" (pages 384–385), ask whether they think it is fair or unfair that they may be paying for debt that their parents' and grandparents' generations incurred. Encourage them to consider the benefits they receive from the spending that contributed to the national debt.

Students might benefit from doing more research on this topic and sharing their findings with the class. See the Internet Research activity below.

After students have read this feature on page 385, ask whether they think that the difference in taxes from nation to nation will increase or decrease. (*Sample answer:* The difference will decrease. If globalization continues, differences between tax levels might decrease because it will be easier for firms to move to nations with lower taxes.)

ANSWERS TO ECONOMIC THINKING Answers will vary. Students might say that many of these nations will have to lower taxes.

Teaching with Visuals

Discuss with students the photo and accompanying question on page 385. Answers to the question will vary.

Application Activity

After reading and discussing Section 2, you may want to assign the Section Activity in the *Applying the Principles Workbook.*

Assess

Quick Quiz

The following true-or-false quiz will help you assess student understanding of the material covered in this section.

1. If the federal government spends more than it receives in tax revenues, it has to borrow the difference and incur a debt. (True)

2. To determine *per capita national debt,* we divide the national debt by the U.S. population. (True)

EXHIBIT 14-8 Projected Federal Budget Deficits, 2006–2011

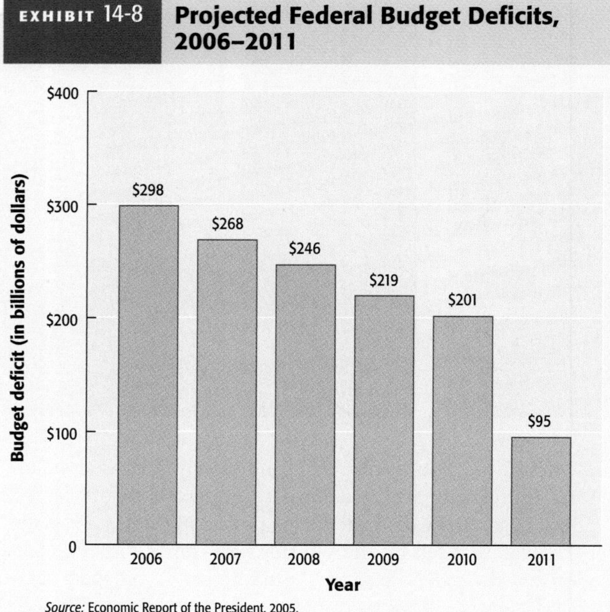

▲ These projections can change from year to year as economic conditions change and as Congress passes new tax laws.

A Student Asks

QUESTION: *Do all economists think that enacting expansionary fiscal policy (even if it causes a budget deficit) is the way to reduce the unemployment rate?*

ANSWER: *No. Remember what we said in the last chapter. Some economists believe that if the government spends more (enacts expansionary fiscal policy by raising its spending), members of the private sector (you, for example) will spend less. In the case of complete crowding out (a term from the last chapter), $1 more spent by the government will lead to $1 less spent by the private sector. This means no additional spending occurs in the economy to push the unemployment rate down.*

National Debt

The only way an individual can spend more than he or she earns is to borrow the difference and incur a debt. (We are ruling out monetary gifts to this person.) For example, if Harry earns $30,000 a year and spends $32,000, he would have had to borrow $2,000. This $2,000 is Harry's debt.

What is true for Harry is true for the federal government. If it spends more than it receives in tax revenues, it has to borrow the difference and incur a debt. Of course, another way to say this is that every time the federal government runs a deficit, it has to borrow money and incur a debt. In short, deficits lead to debt. The debt of the federal government is called the *national debt.*

As we stated earlier, the national debt as of October 24, 2005, was $8.009 trillion. If we divide the national debt by the U.S. population, we get *per capita national debt,* which is approximately $25,950. The per capita national debt is sometimes referred to as each "citizen's share" of the national debt.

A Student Asks

QUESTION: *Will I have to pay off some of the national debt one day?*

ANSWER: *Whenever you pay federal taxes, you are helping to pay off the national debt. Remember, one of the spending categories of the federal government is "net interest on the national debt." In 2005, this amounted to $177 billion. Whoever paid federal taxes that year helped pay off some of the national debt.*

Higher Future Taxes

When the government spends more than it collects in tax revenues, it has to borrow the difference. Deficits lead to debt. But what does debt lead to? Some economists argue that it leads to higher taxes in the future.

When the government borrows the money to pay for the excess of its spending over tax revenues, it has to borrow that money from people. Those people will have to be repaid one day; the debt has to be paid off. (If you borrowed money from a bank, you would have to repay the money one day, with interest.) What happens when the government's debt has to be paid off? Taxes must be used, so taxes have to be higher than they would have been had the debt not been incurred in the

384 Chapter 14 Taxing and Spending

Internet Research

Have students locate Web sites and news articles related to the budget deficit and the balanced budget debate. Direct students to write an overview of the issues concerning the deficit and to explain viewpoints on the issue of whether there should be a constitutional amendment to balance the budget. Encourage students to become aware of differences between the positions of different political parties on this issue.

first place. Some economists say that as far as future taxpayers are concerned, current budget deficits are a form of "taxation without representation."

EXAMPLE: Suppose that in a particular year a government needs $2.0 trillion to buy all the different things that year, and to pay interest on its national debt. The government calculates that it would need only $1.9 trillion in taxes were in not for the interest on the debt. Taxpayers would be able to keep $0.1 trillion for themselves if the government had not gone into debt.

Is it ethical for one generation to buy things that another generation ends up partly paying for? Some people say no, but others say it depends on whether what the first generation buys benefits the next generation. For example, suppose the present generation decides to buy an interstate freeway system for $10 billion. The present generation decides to pay $2 billion itself through taxes and to borrow $8 billion. The present generation knows that the future generation will have to pay off the $8 billion (plus interest), but it reasons that the future generation will use the freeway system, so it should pay for some of it. If the current generation purchased $10 billion of something from which only it could benefit, the situation would be different. ♦

THE GLOBAL IMPACT

Tax Advantages

Globalization sometimes makes it easier for a company to lower its taxes. Firms might design a good in one country, manufacture it in another, and sell it in a third. This approach gives these firms some flexibility in lowering their tax bills by shifting operations from country to country. For example, foreign subsidiaries of U.S. companies often report higher profits in low-tax countries and lower profits in high-tax countries.

ECONOMIC THINKING **How do you expect the high-tax countries to respond to growing difficulties in collecting taxes in a global economy?**

▶ If the government spends more than it takes in, it incurs a debt that must be paid off eventually. **Do you think it's fair to pass on to the next generation the responsibility for paying off this debt?**

SECTION 2 ASSESSMENT

Defining Terms

1. Define:
   a. national debt
   b. budget deficit
   c. budget surplus

Reviewing Facts and Concepts

2. How does the federal government spend its tax revenues?
3. How are current budget deficits linked to higher taxes in the future?
4. What was the public debt equal to on June 22, 2005?

Critical Thinking

5. What do people mean when they say that it is better to balance the economy than to balance the budget?

Applying Economic Concepts

6. Suppose the Fed were to create enough money to pay off the entire public debt. What would happen to prices? Explain your answer.

3. Higher interest rates are one effect of balanced budgets. (False)
4. When overall spending exceeds tax revenues, the government has a budget surplus. (False)
5. All economists agree that it is better to have a budget deficit and reduce unemployment than to maintain a balanced budget. (False)

Assessment Book

You will find a quiz for this section in the *Assessment Book*.

Reteaching Activity

Use the Section Assessment to gauge which students may need reteaching on this section. Instruct those students to draft a $2,000 billion budget showing how they would allocate government spending for the next year. Then ask them to explain what would happen if they needed more than $2,000 billion or less than $2,000 billion to meet all expenses.

Guided Reading

For further reteaching of the key concepts in this section, assign the Outlining Activity and the Just the Facts Handout from the *Guided Reading and Study Guide.*

SECTION 2 ASSESSMENT ANSWERS

Defining Terms

1. a. national debt: the total debt owed by the federal government; **b. budget deficit:** the situation in which a federal government's spending is greater than its tax revenues; **c. budget surplus:** the situation in which a federal government's spending is less than its tax revenues.

Reviewing Facts and Concepts

2. A few of the key spending categories are national defense; income security, retirement, and disability; Social Security; Medicare; and net interest on the national debt.
3. Budget deficits increase the national debt, which needs to be paid off in future years. Taxes will have to be higher in future years in order to pay off the national debt.
4. $7.785 trillion. (To find this answer, students can follow the links from www.emcp.net/nationaldebt, which is mentioned on page 377 of the *Student Text.*)

Critical Thinking

5. They mean that when unemployment is high, it is better to run a budget deficit, stimulate spending in the economy, and (one hopes) bring the unemployment rate down rather than to maintain a balanced budget at the expense of continued high unemployment.

Applying Economic Concepts

6. If the Fed created enough money to pay off the public debt, the increased money supply would lead to a rise in demand in the economy. As a consequence of the increased demand, prices would rise.

Section 2 The Budget: Deficits and Debt 385

CHAPTER 14 Assessment Answers

Economics Vocabulary

1. budget deficit; **2.** flat; **3.** regressive; **4.** ability-to-pay principle; **5.** benefits-received principle; **6.** benefits-received; **7.** corporate income; **8.** budget deficit; **9.** progressive.

Understanding the Main Ideas

1. The three major types of federal taxes are personal income tax, corporate income tax, and Social Security tax.
2. State governments typically collect sales taxes.
3. Inflation and tax cuts are responsible for the widening reach of the alternative minimum tax.
4. A budget deficit can be reduced or eliminated if government spending falls, tax revenues rise, or both occur.
5. If the current generation spends $100 billion in one year and taxes itself just $75 billion, it runs a budget deficit of $25 billion. This $25 billion has to be borrowed and paid back at a later date. The future generation ends up paying back the $25 billion plus interest.
6. Smith meant that if it is right and good to do X in a family, then it is likely to be right and good to do X in the nation.
7. The Congressional Budget Office advises the members of the congressional committees and subcommittees on technical details of the president's proposed budget.
8. A calendar year runs from January 1 to December 31; a fiscal year may run from the first of any month through the end of the month preceding it.
9. Personal income tax, corporate income tax, and Social Security tax raise more than 90% of federal tax revenues.
10. It is impossible to tell. To tell, we would have to know the tax rate and the taxable income for each person.
11. The benefits-received principle holds that a person should pay in taxes an amount equal to the benefits he or she receives from government expenditures.

14 CHAPTER 14 ASSESSMENT

Chapter Summary

Be sure you know and remember the following key points from the chapter sections.

Section 1

- The three main forms of federal taxes are personal income tax, corporate income tax, and Social Security tax.
- Personal income tax is the tax a person pays on his or her income.
- The tax corporations pay on their profits is the corporate income tax.
- The Social Security tax is a tax placed on income generated from employment.
- With a proportional income tax, everyone pays taxes at the same rate, whatever the income level.
- With a progressive income tax, the form of income tax used in the United States, people pay at a higher rate as their income levels rise.
- With a regressive income tax, people pay taxes at a lower rate as their income levels rise.

Section 2

- The federal government breaks down its spending according to categories. The major categories include national defense; income security, retirement, and disability; Social Security and Medicare; and interest on the national debt.
- According to economists, a government spending program is not worth pursuing unless the benefits of that program outweigh the costs; but the system of voting to decide on spending means costs of approved projects are sometimes greater than the benefits.
- The government prepares a budget that indicates how it will spend its tax revenues.
- Budget deficits occur when government expenditures exceed tax revenues; budget surpluses occur when revenues are greater than expenditures.
- When the government borrows money to pay for excess spending, it has to borrow that money from people who will have to be repaid.

Economics Vocabulary

To reinforce your knowledge of the key terms in this chapter, fill in the following blanks on a separate piece of paper with the appropriate word or phrase.

1. A(n) ______ exists when government spending is greater than tax revenues.
2. A proportional tax is sometimes called a(n) ______ tax.
3. A tax rate that falls as income rises is a(n) ______ tax.
4. The ______ is the idea that each person should pay taxes according to his or her ability to pay.
5. The ______ is the idea that each person should pay taxes according to the benefits that he or she receives from government expenditures.
6. A gas tax is consistent with the principle of ______ taxation.
7. The ______ tax is applied to corporate profits.
8. A(n) ______ exists if federal government spending is greater than federal government tax revenues.
9. A tax rate that rises as income rises is a(n) ______ tax.

Understanding the Main Ideas

Write answers to the following questions to review the main ideas in this chapter.

1. What are the three major types of federal taxes?
2. Which level of government—federal, state, or local—typically collects sales taxes?
3. Name two factors that have caused more and more people to pay the alternative minimum tax.
4. In what ways can a budget deficit be reduced or eliminated?
5. Explain how a budget deficit can cause a future generation to pay for what a current generation buys.
6. What did Adam Smith mean when he said, "What is prudence in the conduct of every private family, can scarce be folly in that of a great kingdom"?
7. What role does the Congressional Budget Office (CBO) play in the budget process?

12. With a flat tax, everyone pays taxes at the same rate.

Doing the Math

1. The personal income tax will account for $1,265 of the total tax revenues of $2,661, or 47.5%.
2. To pay off 1980 taxes, the representative taxpayer worked 112 of 365 days, or 31% of the year.
3. Spending is expected to increase from $2,754 billion to $2,881 billion, or by $127 billion. The increase of $127 billion is 4.61% of $2,754 billion, so the correct answer is 4.61%.

Solving Economic Problems

1. Reducing the property tax makes it more beneficial to own property. The demand for property

8. What is the difference between a calendar year and a fiscal year?
9. What three federal taxes raise more than 90 percent of all federal tax revenues?
10. Smith paid $40,000 in federal income taxes, and Abuel paid $20,000. Is the income tax progressive, proportional, or regressive, or is it impossible to tell? Explain your answer.
11. Explain the benefits-received principle of taxation.
12. What is a flat tax?

Doing the Math

Do the calculations necessary to solve the following problems.

1. According to Exhibit 14-1, what percentage of total taxes is the personal income tax projected to account for in 2009?
2. According to Exhibit 14-5, approximately what percentage of a year did the representative taxpayer work to pay his or her taxes in 1980?
3. According to Exhibit 14-7, what percentage increase in government spending is expected between 2008 and 2009?

Solving Economic Problems

Use your thinking skills and the information you learned in this chapter to find solutions to the following problems.

1. **Application.** Suppose a local government were to lower the property tax from 1.25 percent of the assessed value of property to, say, 0.75 percent. How might this affect the price of property? Explain your answer.
2. **Cause and Effect.** Do you think a proportional tax or a progressive tax is more likely to lead to unequal after-tax pay? Explain your answer.
3. **Writing.** Write a one-page paper outlining your arguments either for or against the benefits-received principle of taxation.
4. **Economics in the Media.** Find an article in the local newspaper that addresses the current state of the federal budget, personal income taxes, sales taxes, or the national debt. Identify the major ideas of the article.

Working with Graphs and Tables

1. Look at Exhibit 14-9(a) below. Each bar represents a certain type of federal income tax in 2005. Identify the kind of tax that goes with each bar.
2. Look at Exhibit 14-9(b). Each bar (A, B, and C) represents a certain federal spending program in 2005. Identify the program that goes with each bar.

EXHIBIT 14-9

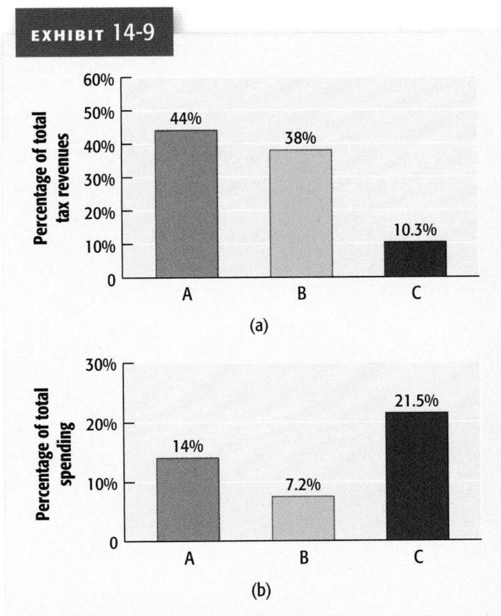

Practice Tests and Study Guide

Go to www.emcp.net/economics and choose *Economics: New Ways of Thinking,* Chapter 14, if you need more help in preparing for the chapter test.

would increase, and therefore the price of property would rise. It may not rise by the amount of the tax reduction, though. In other words, if the property tax reduces taxes by, say, $5,000 on a given piece of property, it does not follow that the price of the property will rise by $5,000.

2. A progressive tax is more likely to lead to unequal after-tax pay because the tax rates increase as income rises.

3. Answers will vary.

4. Answers will vary.

Working with Graphs and Tables

1. Bar A is the personal income tax; bar B is the Social Security tax; bar C is the corporate income tax.

2. Bar A is income security, retirement, and disability; bar B is net interest on the national debt; and bar C is national defense.

Chapter 14 Taxing and Spending 387

Debating the Issues

Discussion Starters

1. Ask students if they know of anyone who benefits from government-provided services. If so, ask what services those people receive. (Caution students not to name names or otherwise identify the people they are talking about.) Allow these students to share with the class what they know and understand about these services.

2. Invite students to consider and respond to the following scenarios:

Student A's grandmother lives alone and receives a modest Social Security pension. The pension barely covers her living expenses. What would happen to student A's grandmother if she did not have the Social Security pension from the government?

Student B is the oldest child in a family of two parents and four younger siblings. The combined household income is below the poverty level, and the family must depend on food stamps to feed their family each month. What would happen to student B's family if they had no food stamps?

Student C's uncle had a serious accident and is unable to hold a full-time job. He receives a disability check from the government each month, but it isn't enough to cover household expenses. What would happen to his family if he did not receive the disability check from the government?

If you were a government official, what would you say to people who wanted to cut social services that benefit the underprivileged and elderly? How would you decide which social services to limit in order to stay within the budget?

3. Ask students the following questions: How much help should the government provide to its citizens? Could providing national defense be considered help for a nation's citizens? Should the government have an emergency fund for citizens who suffer from natural disasters?

Debating the Issues

What Is Government's Role When It Comes to the Economy?

People often disagree as to what the federal government's role should be regarding the economy. For example, some people argue that the federal government should try to stabilize the economy. These people say that if the economy is in a recession, the government should implement expansionary monetary and fiscal policy to stimulate the economy. This may mean increasing the money supply and cutting taxes to stimulate spending. Others argue that if the government hadn't implemented the wrong monetary and fiscal policies in the past, there would be no recession to combat. The question becomes: does government mainly make the patient (the economy) sick, or does it mainly make the patient (the economy) well when it is sick?

Sometimes people disagree about what goods and services the federal government should provide to the citizens. Is it government's role to deliver the mail and care for the sick and elderly, or is it better if government limited itself to building the roads and providing for the national defense? How much or how little should government do? Let's listen in to what some people have to say.

Hamid Khatami, computer consultant

It seems to me that the Great Depression settled the issue of government's role in the economy. I believe that if government hadn't come to the rescue, and provided people with jobs, and stimulated spending in the economy, that the Great Depression would have gone on much longer than it did.

Before the Great Depression, many people used to think that a free enterprise economy could take care of itself. It wouldn't produce too much inflation and it wouldn't bring on an economic contraction. Well, then, how do you explain the Great Depression? The unemployment rate rose to 25 percent during that time. The government had to do something.

Francine Watermaker, registered nurse

I'm not sure that Hamid has the explanation of the Great Depression correct. I don't think it was free enterprise that failed. I think it was government doing the wrong things. It was the government overspending in the 1920s and planting the seeds of the economic contraction. It was the government placing high tariffs on imported goods and making the contraction worse than it would have been. It was the Fed cutting the money supply too much. If anything, the Great Depression was a failure of government, not free enterprise. The way I see it, government makes more problems for the economy than it solves. Sure, the government can do some things right, but government today is into more things than it can do. I am in favor of the government limiting itself to doing what individuals or businesses can't do. For example, I don't believe that either individuals or businesses can supply the country with the national defense that it needs. National defense then should be left to government. Use the tax money to provide for the national defense, not to subsidize the farmers. And in my opinion, it doesn't make sense for the government to be involved in programs such as Medicare and Social Security.

Differentiating Instruction

Enrichment and Extension

Hold a mock political election in which students as candidates campaign on positions regarding governmental involvement in the economy. Begin by deciding what type of political office the class will fill—national president? city mayor? Then assign students to write campaign speeches and deliver them to the class. After all speeches have been given, allow the class to vote for the candidate who had the most convincing speech. Consider rewarding the winner with a seat of honor in front of the class and with the power to grant a small favor to the class, such as allowing five minutes of free talk.

Yong Kim, retired attorney

Here's what I would like to know. If government is so bad—as Francine seems to imply—why has this country been as militarily and economically strong for so long? We have the largest economy in the world and we have the strongest and most capable military in the world. And we've done both of these things at the same time that the federal government has been getting bigger. If government bigness is so bad, how does someone explain that our economy is as strong and as big as it is?

Nancy Owens, college student

I think Yong is making a mistake here. Just because you see two things at the same time, or nearly the same time, it doesn't mean that one is the cause and the other is the effect. There are more dogs in the United States today than there were in 1950. Does it follow that a rising dog population is what causes the economy to be strong? Not at all. There are a lot of things that happen at around the same time that have nothing to do with each other.

But I have a better point to make with respect to Yong's comment. Isn't it possible that we would have an even stronger economy, and a mightier military, if the government hadn't grown so large? With a smaller, less intrusive government, perhaps our economy would be even larger than it is today. And perhaps our military would be even stronger.

Blanca Sanchez, physician

I think what we are talking about here is that neither free enterprise nor government is perfect at doing everything. Sometimes the free enterprise economy does need government to help it out. For instance, when the economy is slumping, or we need something that free enterprise won't produce, such as protection against terrorists, government needs to step in.

But certainly this doesn't mean that government has been perfect. Government can make mistakes. I think government can implement the wrong monetary policy—perhaps causing high inflation. I believe that government may implement a particular fiscal policy that doesn't work because of, say, complete crowding out. My guess is that sometimes government does more to make things worse than to make things better.

Maybe what we are learning over time is what government should and should not do, and what free enterprise should and should not do. In other words, maybe the last 50 years have been a learning period for us.

What Do You Think?

1. What is your opinion as to the proper role for government, especially when it comes to economic issues?
2. What goods and services do you think government should provide (using taxpayer money)? Is there anything that government currently does that you don't think it should do? Explain your answer.

Activities for What Do You Think?

1. Divide students into two groups to debate the following proposition: the government needs more control over the economy.

Allow students time to organize their points in the debate, and to decide who will present each side. Give each side five to seven minutes to present its case. Allow enough time for debriefing and closure at the end of the class period.

2. Have students create posters of services they think the government should provide. (These can be services currently provided or services not currently provided.) Display the posters at the front of the class. Also ask students to create separate posters on services the government provides that they think it shouldn't. Display these at the back of the class. Compare the two groups of posters. Are some services listed in both groups? If so, you might hold a class vote to decide where those services should remain.

Closure

Instruct students to write a page describing how their opinions on this issue were affected by reading and discussing Debating the Issues. They should include what information from the text or discussion influenced their thinking.

Differentiating Instruction

Enrichment and Extension

Divide students into groups of three or four. Tell each group to decide on a position for or against more government involvement in the economy. Then ask each group to compose a cheer for its position, and allow the groups to present their cheers to the class.

Listed below are the chapters included in this unit.

CHAPTER 15

International Trade and Economic Development

CHAPTER 16

Stocks and Bonds

Foundations for the Unit

With Unit V, we enlarge our focus in order to study the world through economics. Increasingly, because of technological breakthroughs in science, communication, and other areas, the world seems to be a smaller place. Today, economic events in one part of the world can almost instantaneously affect economic events in another part of the world. All of us, economists, politicians, businesspeople, teachers, and more, are quickly discovering that the Disney song is accurate—"It's a small world, after all." This unit will help students begin to understand the realities of our new global economy.

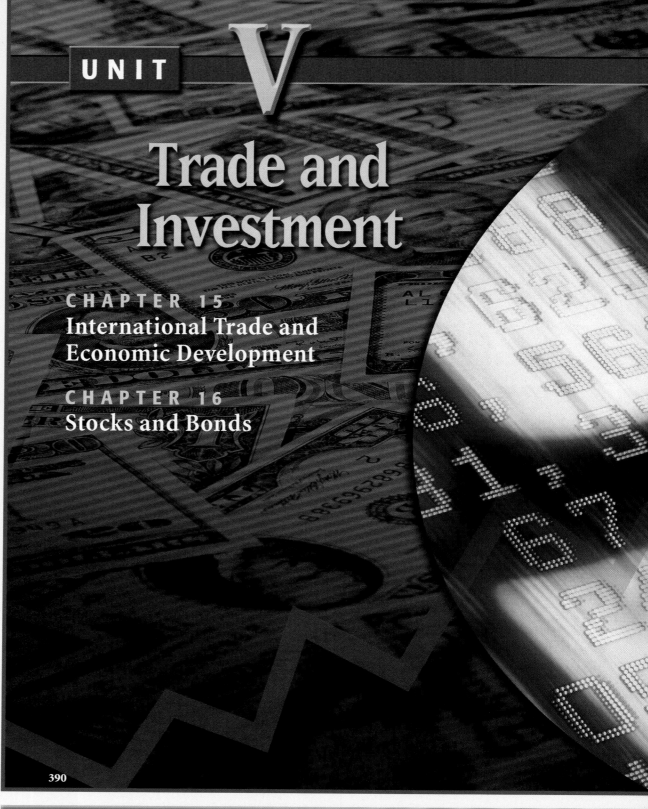

UNIT V

Trade and Investment

CHAPTER 15
International Trade and Economic Development

CHAPTER 16
Stocks and Bonds

390

Resources for the Unit

Books

Ashworth, William. *A Short History of the International Economy Since 1850.* London, England: Longman Publishing, 1987.

Heilbroner, Robert L. *The Making of an Economic Society.* Englewood Cliff, NJ: Prentice-Hall, Inc., 1962.

Mantle, Jonathan. *Car Wars: 50 Years of Greed, Treachery and Skullduggery in the Global Market.* New York: Arcade Publishers, 1996.

Articles

Cohen, Warren. "Up, Up, and Away," *U.S. News and World Report,* November 2, 1998.

Editorial Desk. "The Ragged March to Markets," *New York Times,* November 11, 1999.

Rohter, Larry. "Outlook 2000: International: After a Hard Year, Latin America Looks for Better Times," *New York Times,* December 20, 1999.

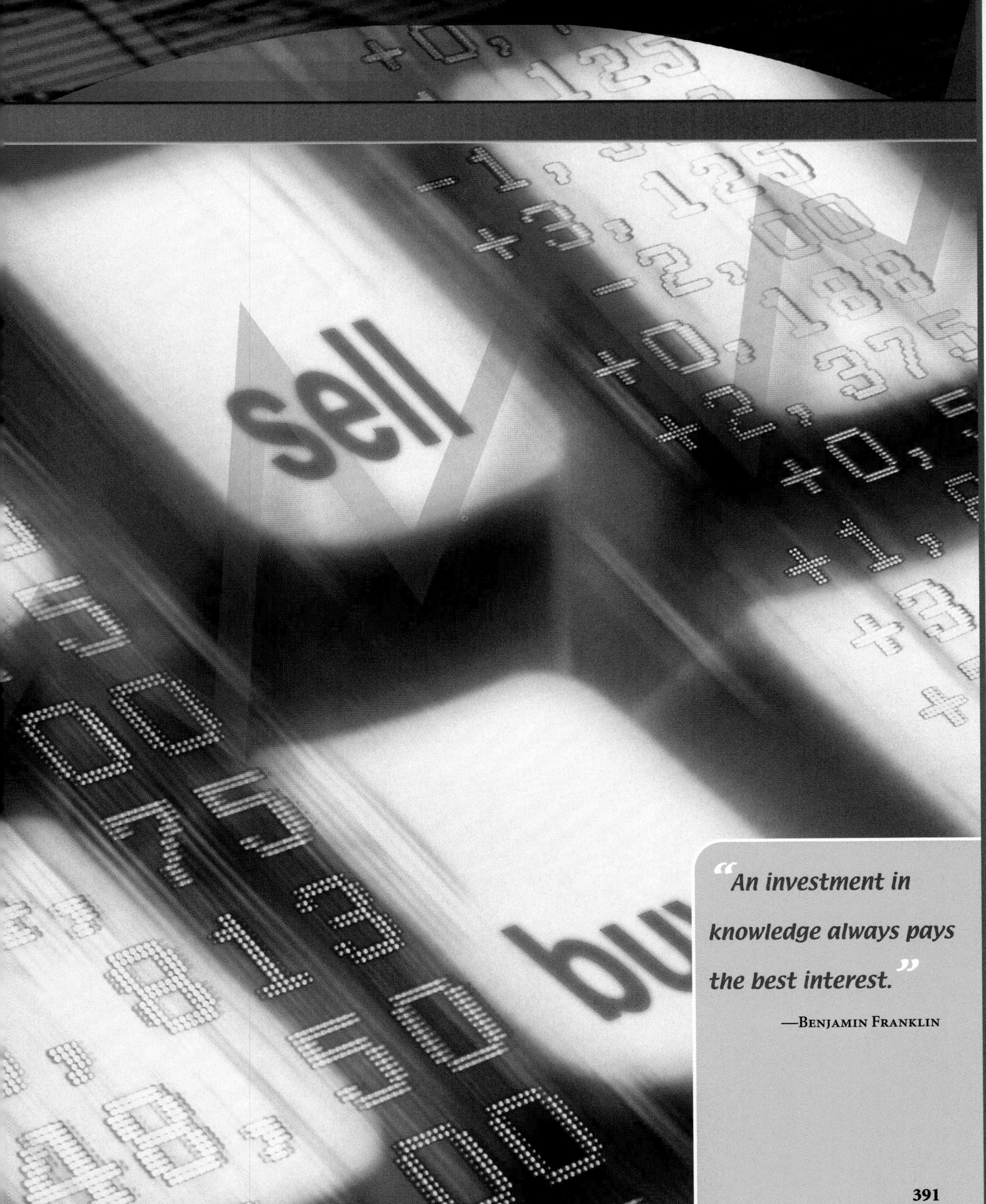

"An investment in knowledge always pays the best interest."

—Benjamin Franklin

Introducing the Unit

To introduce Unit V, you might read aloud the following: "Many economists define globalization as a process by which individuals and businesses in any part of the world are much more affected by events elsewhere in the world than they used to be." Ask your students where they might have heard this before. Students might recall that this definition of globalization was presented in Chapter 2. Stress to students that the material in this unit should help them to get a better economic view of our world. Point out that the more we know about the other players in the global economy, the better equipped we will be to succeed in the global economy.

Performance Task

The performance task for Unit V can best be performed cooperatively. Working in groups, students should identify a country of the world they wish to study. For this country, they should develop an economic atlas, including such data as pertinent economic statistics (data might include real GDP for the country and for other selected neighboring countries, currency, and other statistics relating to economic health and standard of living); a brief summary of the country's economic history; a brief description of the country's governmental and economic systems; and maps showing important natural resources, crops, and industries for the country. Each group should present an oral report of its findings to the class. Encourage students to discuss the cultures of their chosen countries in their reports. Additionally, students might want to prepare and share with the class selected foods native to the countries they have studied.

Multimedia

Interest Rates and Exchange Rates. In *Introductory Economics.* VHS. Films for the Humanities and Sciences.

Is America Number One? Understand the Economics of Success. VHS. Films for the Humanities and Sciences.

Stabilization Policy for a Small Open Economy. In *Introductory Economics.* VHS. Films for the Humanities and Sciences.

Thinking Globally: Effective Lessons for Teaching about the Interdependent World Economy. CD-ROM. National Council on Economic Education.

Chapter 15 Planning Guide

SECTION ORGANIZER

Section	Learning Objectives	Reproducible Worksheets and Handouts	Assessment
International Trade (pages 394–406)	► Describe what goods are major U.S. exports and imports. ► Explain what comparative advantage is.	Section 1 Activity, *Applying the Principles Workbook* Outlining Activity, *Guided Reading and Study Guide* Just the Facts Handout, *Guided Reading and Study Guide*	Section Assessment, *Student Text,* page 406 Quick Quiz, *Annotated Teacher's Edition,* page 405 Section Quiz, *Assessment Book*
Trade Restrictions (pages 407–414)	► Define *tariff* and *quota.* ► Explain how tariffs and quotas affect prices. ► Explain why the government imposes tariffs and quotas if they are harmful to U.S. consumers. ► Describe the effect that tariffs had on the Great Depression. ► Describe the arguments for and against trade restrictions.	Section 2 Activity, *Applying the Principles Workbook* Outlining Activity, *Guided Reading and Study Guide* Just the Facts Handout, *Guided Reading and Study Guide*	Section Assessment, *Student Text,* page 414 Quick Quiz, *Annotated Teacher's Edition,* page 413 Section Quiz, *Assessment Book*
The Exchange Rate (pages 415–419)	► Define *exchange rate.* ► Explain what it means to say that a currency appreciates in value. ► Explain what it means to say that a currency depreciates in value.	Section 3 Activity, *Applying the Principles Workbook* Outlining Activity, *Guided Reading and Study Guide* Just the Facts Handout, *Guided Reading and Study Guide*	Section Assessment, *Student Text,* page 419 Quick Quiz, *Annotated Teacher's Edition,* page 418 Section Quiz, *Assessment Book*
Economic Development (pages 422–425)	► Explain what a less-developed country is. ► Understand why some countries are rich while others are poor. ► Describe why savings accounts are important to economic development. ► List a few factors that aid economic development.	Section 4 Activity, *Applying the Principles Workbook* Outlining Activity, *Guided Reading and Study Guide* Just the Facts Handout, *Guided Reading and Study Guide*	Section Assessment, *Student Text,* page 425 Quick Quiz, *Annotated Teacher's Edition,* page 424 Section Quiz, *Assessment Book*

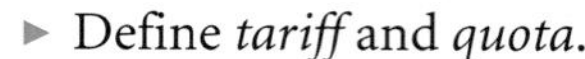

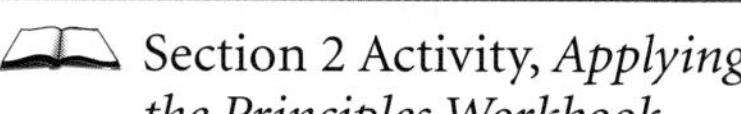

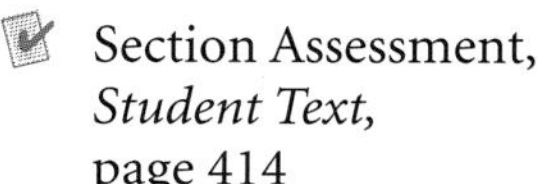

CHAPTER AND PROGRAM RESOURCES

Reproducible Chapter Resources and Assessment Materials

 Graphic Organizer Activity, *Guided Reading and Study Guide*

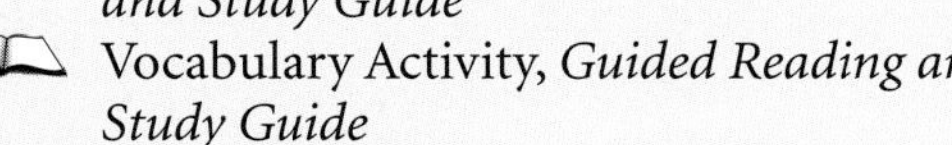 Vocabulary Activity, *Guided Reading and Study Guide*

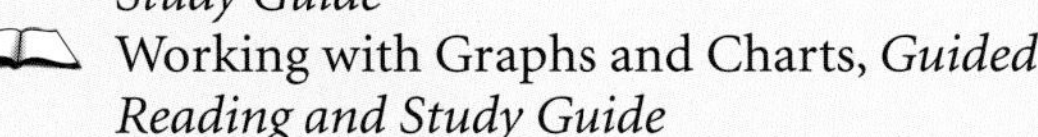 Working with Graphs and Charts, *Guided Reading and Study Guide*

 Practice Test, *Guided Reading and Study Guide*

Critical Thinking Activity, *Finding Economics*

Chapter Test A, *Assessment Book*

Chapter Test B, *Assessment Book*

Technology Resources

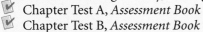

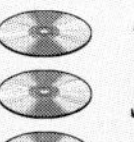 *Test Generator CD*

Spanish Audio Summaries CD

Marketplace® Audio Lessons CD

Economic Principles Lectures, Videocassette or DVD

Lesson Planning and Teaching Resources

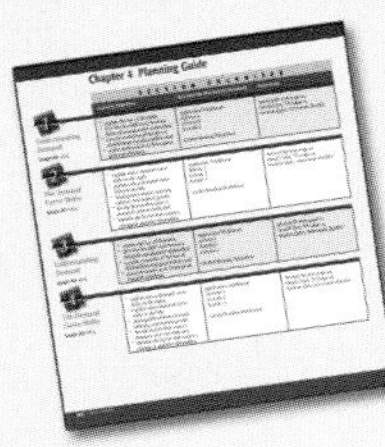

The *Economics: New Ways of Thinking* Teacher Resources include detailed lesson plans for each section in this chapter; the lesson plans are available in print form *(Lesson Plans)* and electronic form. The Teacher Resources also include *Daily Lectures: Overheads and Notes,* which provides prepared overheads and discussion notes covering the key concepts in each section of this chapter.

EMC Publishing Economics Online

Go to Economics Online, at www.emcp.com, for a variety of Internet resources to help you keep your course current and relevant. At Economics Online you will find these items:

- Economics in the News Lessons
- Study Guide Questions
- Practice Tests
- Lesson Plans

Internet Resources

Economics: New Ways of Thinking encourages students to use the Internet to find out more about economics. With the wealth of current, valid information available on Web sites, using the Internet as a research tool is likely to increase your students' interest in and understanding of economics principles and topics. In addition, doing Internet research can help your students form the habit of accessing and using economics information, as well as help them develop investigative skills they will use throughout their educational and professional careers.

To aid your students in achieving these ends, each chapter of *Economics: New Ways of Thinking* includes the addresses of several Web sites at which students will find engaging, relevant information. When students type in the addresses provided, they will immediately arrive at the intended sites. The addresses have been modified so that EMC Publishing can monitor and maintain the proper links—for example, the government site http://stats.bls.gov/ has been changed to www.emcp.net/prices. In the event that the address or content of a site changes or is discontinued, EMC's Internet editors will create a link that redirects students to an address with similar information.

Activities in the *Annotated Teacher's Edition* often suggest that students search the Internet for information. For some activities, you might want to find reputable sites beforehand, and steer students to those sites. For other activities, you might want students to do their own searching, and then check out the sites they have found and discuss why they might be reliable or unreliable.

CHAPTER 15 Overview

This chapter discusses international trade and introduces the information necessary to answer such questions as these: Why do people in different countries trade with each other? Is it bad economic news if a country buys more from other countries than it sells to other countries? What causes the value of the U.S. dollar to rise and fall on foreign exchange markets? The following statements provide brief descriptions of the major concepts covered in each section of this chapter.

International Trade

Section 1 explores what imports and exports are. This section also explains comparative advantage.

Trade Restrictions

Section 2 explains the concepts of tariff and quota, as well as how tariffs and quotas affect price.

The Exchange Rate

Section 3 discusses the exchange rate and what it means when a currency appreciates or depreciates in value.

Economic Development

Section 4 explores economic growth and the ways in which less-developed countries become developed.

CHAPTER 15 International Trade and Economic Development

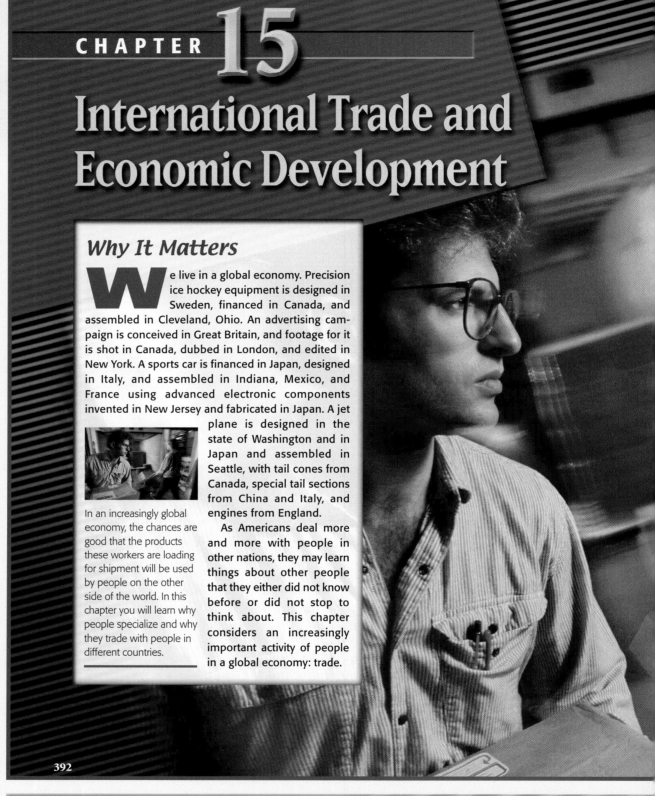

Why It Matters

We live in a global economy. Precision ice hockey equipment is designed in Sweden, financed in Canada, and assembled in Cleveland, Ohio. An advertising campaign is conceived in Great Britain, and footage for it is shot in Canada, dubbed in London, and edited in New York. A sports car is financed in Japan, designed in Italy, and assembled in Indiana, Mexico, and France using advanced electronic components invented in New Jersey and fabricated in Japan. A jet plane is designed in the state of Washington and in Japan and assembled in Seattle, with tail cones from Canada, special tail sections from China and Italy, and engines from England.

In an increasingly global economy, the chances are good that the products these workers are loading for shipment will be used by people on the other side of the world. In this chapter you will learn why people specialize and why they trade with people in different countries.

As Americans deal more and more with people in other nations, they may learn things about other people that they either did not know before or did not stop to think about. This chapter considers an increasingly important activity of people in a global economy: trade.

Teaching Suggestions from the Author

One thing that helps pique student interest in international trade is learning about different countries and different people. When students realize that other countries are fascinating places, and that other people can be interesting, exciting, and different, they develop an appreciation for what international trade is all about. One thing you might want to do is assign students to choose a country in which they think they might be interested, and ask them to do a little research on it, to find out what its products are and what its people are like. Usually, once students learn about a country and its people, they are much more receptive to the idea of trading with the people of that country. What they learn

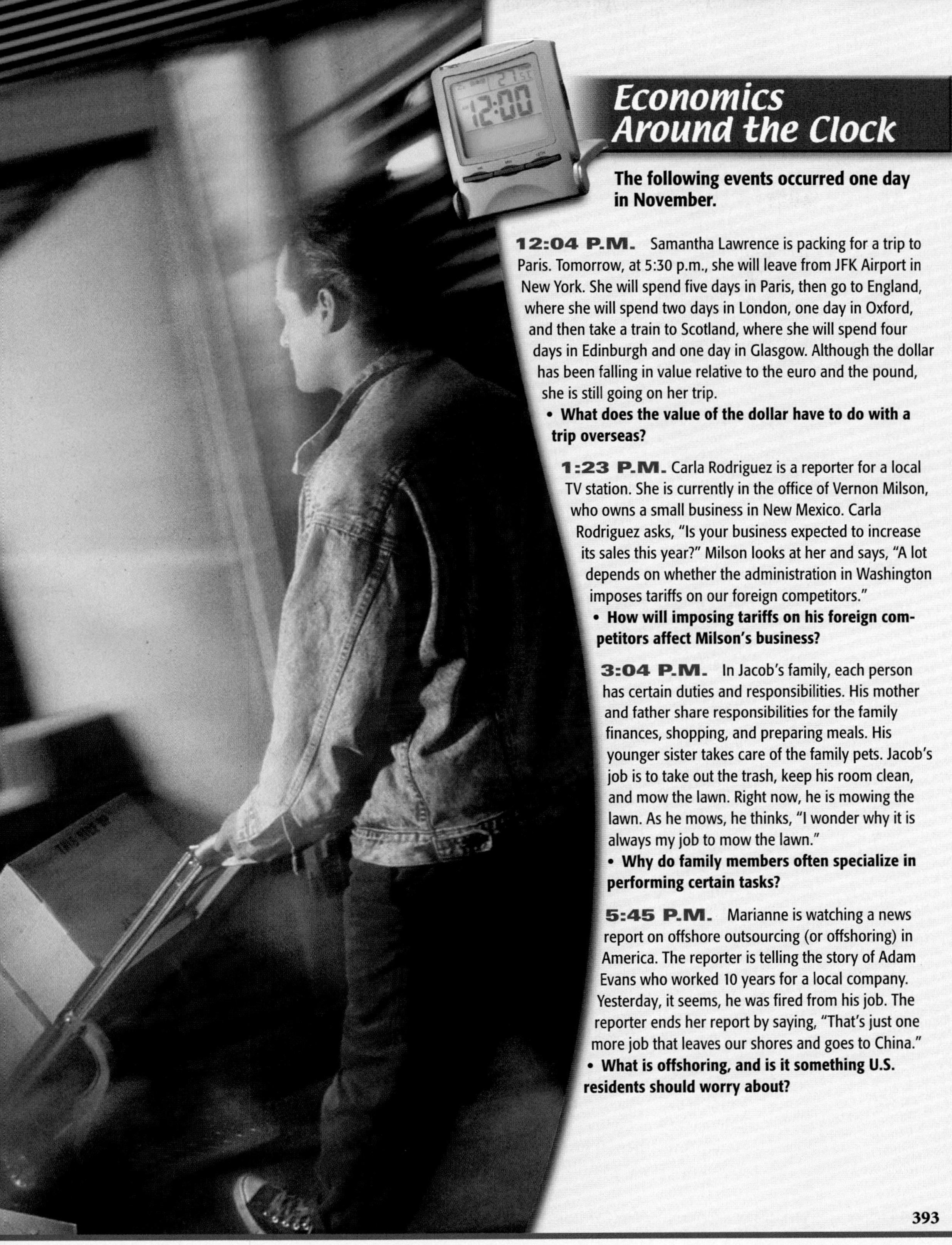

Economics Around the Clock

The following events occurred one day in November.

12:04 P.M. Samantha Lawrence is packing for a trip to Paris. Tomorrow, at 5:30 p.m., she will leave from JFK Airport in New York. She will spend five days in Paris, then go to England, where she will spend two days in London, one day in Oxford, and then take a train to Scotland, where she will spend four days in Edinburgh and one day in Glasgow. Although the dollar has been falling in value relative to the euro and the pound, she is still going on her trip.

- **What does the value of the dollar have to do with a trip overseas?**

1:23 P.M. Carla Rodriguez is a reporter for a local TV station. She is currently in the office of Vernon Milson, who owns a small business in New Mexico. Carla Rodriguez asks, "Is your business expected to increase its sales this year?" Milson looks at her and says, "A lot depends on whether the administration in Washington imposes tariffs on our foreign competitors."

- **How will imposing tariffs on his foreign competitors affect Milson's business?**

3:04 P.M. In Jacob's family, each person has certain duties and responsibilities. His mother and father share responsibilities for the family finances, shopping, and preparing meals. His younger sister takes care of the family pets. Jacob's job is to take out the trash, keep his room clean, and mow the lawn. Right now, he is mowing the lawn. As he mows, he thinks, "I wonder why it is always my job to mow the lawn."

- **Why do family members often specialize in performing certain tasks?**

5:45 P.M. Marianne is watching a news report on offshore outsourcing (or offshoring) in America. The reporter is telling the story of Adam Evans who worked 10 years for a local company. Yesterday, it seems, he was fired from his job. The reporter ends her report by saying, "That's just one more job that leaves our shores and goes to China."

- **What is offshoring, and is it something U.S. residents should worry about?**

Introducing the Chapter

A good way to begin a study of Chapter 15 is to ask students to list the many foreign-made products that they or their families own. Allow only two minutes for this exercise. Call on volunteers to read their lists to the class. After students have begun to see the tremendous number of foreign products that are available in our country, ask them another question: Which products that are produced in the United States do you think are exported? Allow students to share their responses. Emphasize that international trade is one of the most important aspects of the global economy. Explain that in this chapter students will study international trade.

Teaching with Visuals

Because of international trade, many items are sent around the world. Huge container ships are filled with cars, appliances, electronic parts, clothing, and food. The goods eventually find their way to us, coast to coast.

about one country can then be generalized to other countries around the world.

You might ask students to prepare maps of their selected countries, showing major cities, geographical features, and natural resources.

SECTION 1 Teacher Support

Focus and Motivate

Section Objectives

After completing this section, students will be able to

- describe what goods are major U.S. exports and imports; and
- explain what comparative advantage is.

Kickoff Activity

Write the following question on the board for students to answer: "Why, do you think, do countries produce only some goods and not all goods that they need or want? For example, the United States produces cars but not bananas. Why doesn't it produce both cars and bananas?"

Activating Prior Knowledge

Invite students to share their responses to the Kickoff Activity. Some students will say the reason that the United States does not produce bananas is because it doesn't have the proper climate. Remind students that bananas can be produced in the United States under hothouse conditions. The point is, though, that this would be too expensive to do. Try to communicate to students the idea that countries produce and export those goods that they can produce more cheaply than other countries. Countries import goods that they can buy more cheaply than they can produce themselves.

SECTION 1 International Trade

Focus Questions

- What goods are major U.S. exports?
- What goods are major U.S. imports?
- What is comparative advantage?

Key Terms

exports
imports
balance of trade
absolute advantage
specialize
comparative advantage
outsourcing

Why Do People in Different Countries Trade with Each Other?

We have international trade for the same reason we have domestic trade (trade within a country). Individuals trade to make themselves better off. Frank and Nate, who live in Fargo, North Dakota, trade because both value something the other has more than they value something of their own. For example, perhaps Frank trades $10 for Nate's book. On an international scale, Elaine in the United States trades with Cho in China because Cho has something that Elaine wants and Elaine has something that Cho wants.

Obviously, different countries have different terrains, climates, and resources. It follows that some countries will be able to produce some goods that other countries cannot produce or can produce only at extremely high cost. For example, Hong Kong has no oil, and Saudi Arabia has a large supply of oil. Bananas do not grow easily in the United States, but they flourish in Honduras. Americans could grow bananas if they used hothouses, but it is cheaper for them to buy bananas from Honduras than to produce bananas themselves.

Sometimes we forget how many goods we use each day are purchased from people living in other countries. Our alarm clock might be produced in Belgium, our shoes in China, our watch in Switzerland. Take a look sometime at all the goods you use each day. How many are produced in foreign countries?

exports
Goods produced in the domestic country and sold to residents of a foreign country.

What Are Exports and Imports?

Exports are goods that are produced in the domestic country and sold to residents of a foreign country. For example, if residents of the United States (the domestic country) produce and sell computers to people in France, Germany, and Mexico, then computers are a U.S. export. In April 2005, the value of U.S. exports was $106.4 billion, which means that U.S. residents produced and sold $106.4 billion worth of U.S. goods and services to people in other countries—in just one month. Major U.S. exports include automobiles, computers, aircraft, corn, wheat, soy-

Differentiating Instruction

Visual Learners

Assign students to make a collage that can be used as a bulletin board display. You could assign each student to make an individual poster, or you could ask students to bring in copies of photos of both consumer items and raw materials, and create a large cooperative collage. Collages should be divided into two sections, imports and exports. On the import side, students can affix pictures of goods imported by the United States. On the export side, students can display goods exported by the United States.

beans, scientific instruments, coal, machinery, and plastic materials.

Imports are goods produced in foreign countries and purchased by residents of the domestic country. For example, if residents of the United States (the domestic country) buy coffee from Colombia, then coffee is a U.S. import. In April 2005, the value of U.S. imports was $163.4 billion; U.S. residents, again, in just one month, bought $163.4 billion worth of goods and services from people in other countries. Major U.S. imports include petroleum, clothing, iron, steel, office machines, footwear, fish, coffee, and diamonds.

Exhibit 15-1 shows the value of exports and the value of imports for the period from 1980 to 2005. Exhibit 15-2 on the next page shows the number of imported cars in each year during the same period.

imports
Goods produced in foreign countries and purchased by residents of the domestic country.

EXHIBIT 15-1 Value of U.S. Exports and Imports, 1980–2005

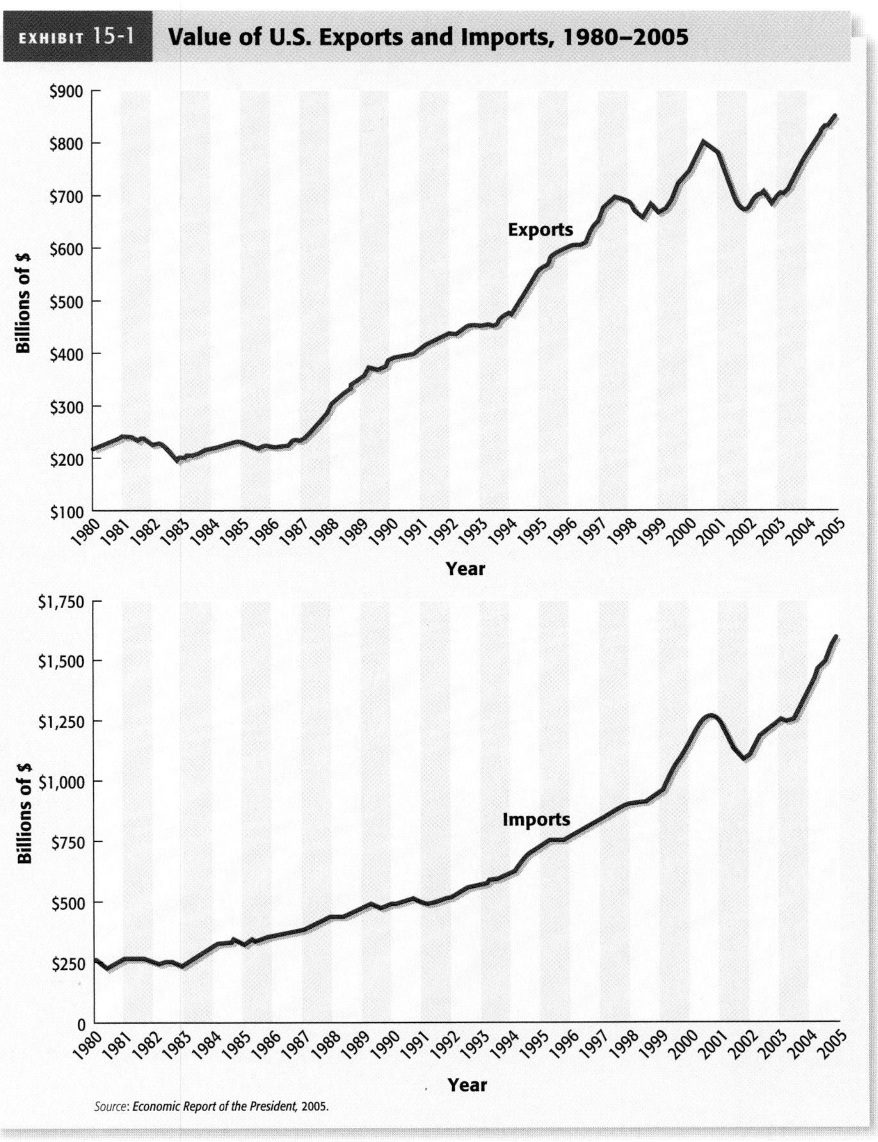

Source: *Economic Report of the President*, 2005.

◀ **Which had the biggest percentage increase from 1980 to 2005—exports or imports? Based on your earlier study of GDP, did this difference contribute to an increase or decrease in the GDP?**

Teach

Discussion Starter

Ask students why they think people in one country trade with people in another country. In short, what is the motivation behind international trade? The answer is that people in one country trade with people in another country for the same reason people in one country trade with people in the same country: to make themselves better off.

Teaching with Visuals

Imports had the bigger percentage increase from 1980 to 2005. Import spending is subtracted from the GDP, so the increased spending on imports contributed to a decrease in the GDP.

Internet Research

Instruct students to look at the Web site for the United States Export-Import Bank. Ask them to find out what the function of the Export-Import Bank is. Divide students into groups to prepare brief presentations highlighting two small business ideas that they believe should qualify for the support of the U.S. Export-Import Bank.

Teaching with Visuals

Answers will vary. Students might suggest that domestic car manufacturers produced cars that appealed more to consumers.

Analyzing

In the 1990s the United States ran trade deficits. In other words, the United States imported more goods than it exported. Ask students how a trade deficit affects the economy. How does a trade surplus affect the economy?

▶ Why do you think the number of cars imported to the U.S. declined during the period from the late 1980s to mid-1990s?

EXHIBIT 15-2 Number of Imported Cars, 1980–2005

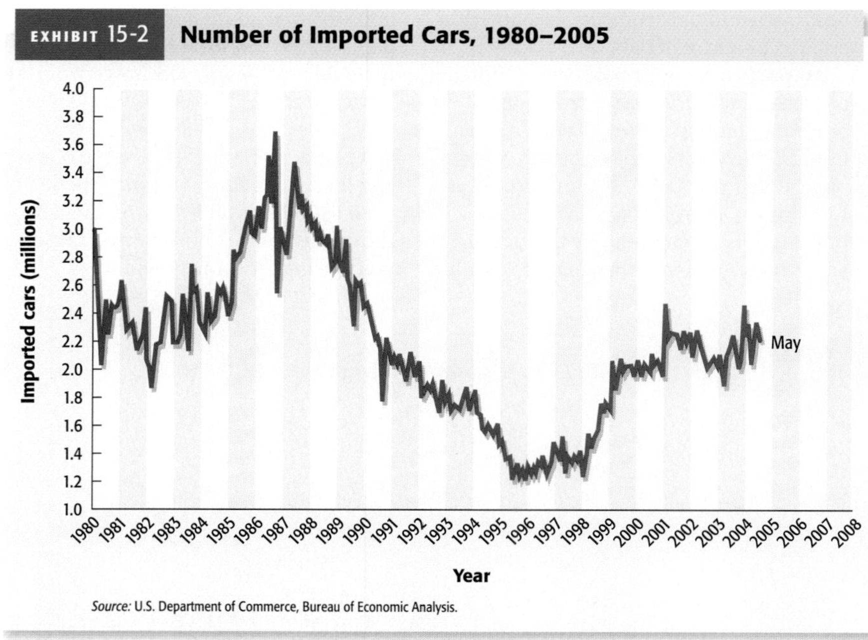

Source: U.S. Department of Commerce, Bureau of Economic Analysis.

A Student Asks

QUESTION: *I noticed that the value of exports in April 2005 was less than the value of imports. In other words, Americans bought more from people in other countries than the people in other countries bought from Americans. Does it happen this way in most months?*

ANSWER: *Yes, in the recent history of the United States, during most months, Americans buy more from people in other countries than people in other countries buy from Americans.*

balance of trade
The difference between the value of a country's exports and the value of its imports.

▼ The United States is a major importer of bananas.

Balance of Trade

A country's **balance of trade** is the difference between the value of its exports and the value of its imports.

Balance of trade =
Value of exports − Value of imports

For example, if the value of a country's exports is, say, $300 billion (for the year) and the value of its imports is $200 billion, then the country has a positive balance of trade ($100 billion) or is said to have a *trade surplus.* If the value of a country's exports is $100 billion and the value of its imports is $210 billion, then the country has a negative balance of trade (–$110 billion) or is said to have a *trade deficit.*

A Student Asks

QUESTION: *What is the recent trade history of the United States? Has it mostly had a trade surplus or trade deficit?*

ANSWER: *From 1946 through 1970, the United States had a trade surplus.*

Background Information: Specialization

Government officials of a country do not sit down with piles of cost data and determine what their country should specialize in producing, and then decide to trade. Countries do not plot production possibilities frontiers on graph paper or formally calculate opportunity cost. Instead, it is the desire of individuals to make a dollar, a franc, a pound, or a yen that determines the pattern of international trade; it is the desire for profit that determines what a country specializes in and trades.

Beginning in 1971 (and with the exception of 1973 and 1975) it has had a trade deficit. If you would like to check the status of U.S. exports and imports for the latest month and year, you can go to the U.S. Census Bureau (Foreign Trade Statistics) at www.emcp.net/exports_imports. As an aside, you may be interested in knowing which countries the United States trades with often and in a large way. These countries include Canada, Germany, Mexico, Japan, United Kingdom, and China. If you would like to find the trade balance between the United States and any country in particular, you can go to www.emcp.net/tradebalance and simply click on the relevant country. For example, in April 2005, the United States sold $3.4 billion worth of goods to China and bought $18.1 billion worth of goods from China. In other words, for that month, the United States had a trade deficit of -$14.7 billion with China.

▲ This worker is testing new computers at a Dell manufacturing plant in Texas. The U.S exports large numbers of computers every year.

Absolute and Comparative Advantage

Suppose that using the same quantity of resources as Japan, the United States can produce either of the following two combinations of food and clothing:

- Combination A: 150 units of food and 0 units of clothing
- Combination B: 100 units of food and 25 units of clothing

Suppose that Japan, using the same quantity of resources as the United States, can produce either of the following two combinations of food and clothing:

- Combination C: 30 units of food and 120 units of clothing
- Combination D: 0 units of food and 180 units of clothing

When a country can produce more of a good than another country using the same quantity of resources, it is said to have an **absolute advantage** in the production of that good. In our example, the United States has an absolute advantage in producing food, because the maximum amount of food it can produce (150 units) is greater than the maximum amount of food Japan can produce (30 units). Japan, in contrast, has an absolute advantage in producing clothing, because the maximum amount of clothing it can produce (180 units) is greater than the maximum amount of clothing the United States can produce (25 units).

Suppose that in year 1, Japan and the United States do not trade with each other. Instead, each nation decides to produce some quantity of each good and consume it. The United States produces and consumes combination B (100 units of food and 25 units of clothing), and Japan produces and consumes combination C (30 units of food and 120 units of clothing).

In year 2, things change. Each country decides to **specialize** in the production of one good and then trade some of it for the other good. Which good—clothing or food—should the United States specialize in producing? Which good should Japan specialize in producing?

In general, a country should specialize in the production of the good in which it has a **comparative advantage**—the good it can produce at a lower opportunity cost.

Determining Opportunity Cost

Recall from Chapter 1 that the opportunity cost of producing a good is what is given up to produce that good. For example, if Julio gives up the opportunity to

absolute advantage
The situation in which a country can produce more of a good than another country can produce with the same quantity of resources.

specialize
To do only one thing. For example, when a country specializes in the production of a good, it produces only that good.

comparative advantage
The situation in which a country can produce a good at lower opportunity cost than another country.

Economics Around the Clock

Invite students to discuss their answers to the 3:04 P.M. scenario in Economics Around the Clock (page 393).

Students may answer that family members often end up specializing in that thing in which they have a comparative advantage. In the end, if individuals specialize in their comparative advantage, the work often gets done in less time.

Reinforcement Activity

Direct students to look through newspapers and magazines to find stories that relate to the international economy and international trade. Ask them to write one-page papers on the stories of their choice. Allow students to read their papers aloud in small groups, and encourage other students in the groups to ask questions and make comments.

Cooperative Learning

Divide the class into small groups. Each group should choose two imports and research where these products originated. Groups should then seek to find price data, so they can compare the price of the imported product with its American-made counterpart. Students should try to answer the following questions about the import they research: How much does it cost? How does this cost compare to an American-made counterpart, if any exists? Invite groups to share their findings with the class in the form of oral reports. Encourage students to include a map of the country of origin of each of their imported products, as well as any other visual aids they can prepare to support their presentation.

Reinforcement Activity

Remind students that they first learned about the concept of opportunity cost in Chapter 1 of this text. Here we see this concept again. Stress to students how important the concept of opportunity cost is in economics. Ask students to list all of the different ways that opportunity cost has impacted their study of economics thus far.

Critical Thinking

Exhibit 15-2 on page 396 shows that the United States imports many automobiles. U.S. companies also, of course, produce many automobiles each year. Ask students: Does the United States have a comparative advantage in producing cars? Does Japan or Germany? Answers will vary. Some factors students should consider include costs of producing and importing cars, and of materials and workers needed.

BY THE NUMBERS

The United States buys more from the entire world than the world buys from it. In other words, the United States has a trade deficit. But it doesn't follow that the United States buys more from every country in the world than every country in the world buys from it. For example, in 2003, Australia bought more from the United States than the United States bought from Australia. In the same year, though, the United States bought more from China than China bought from the United States. Here is a list of the top five countries that the United States bought more from in 2003. The trade deficit (in dollars) that the United States had with that particular country is provided.

China:	−$123.9 billion
Japan:	−$65.9 billion
Canada:	−$54.3 billion
Mexico:	−$40.6 billion
Germany:	−$39.1 billion

produce three towels if he produces a blanket, then the opportunity cost of the blanket is three towels.

What is the opportunity cost of producing food for the United States? What is the cost for Japan? We know that the United States can produce either combination A (150 units of food and 0 units of clothing) or combination B (100 units of food and 25 units of clothing). Suppose it is producing combination B. What are the benefits and costs of deciding to produce combination A instead? By producing combination A, the country will make itself better off by 50 additional units of food, but it will have to give up 25 units of clothing to do so. In other words, for every 1 extra unit of food, it will have to give up ½ unit of clothing. In economic terms, for the United States, the opportunity cost of 1 unit of food is ½ unit of clothing.

The process is similar for Japan. We know that Japan can produce either combination C (30 units of food and 120 units of clothing) or combination D (0 units of food and 180 units of clothing). Suppose it is producing combination D. What are the benefits and costs of deciding to produce combination C instead? By producing combination C, Japan will make itself better off by 30 additional units of food, but it will have to give up 60 units of clothing to do so. In other words, for every 1 extra unit of food, it will have to give up 2 units of clothing. In economic terms, for Japan, the opportunity cost of 1 unit of food is 2 units of clothing. Thus the opportunity cost of producing 1 unit of food (F) is ½ unit of clothing (C) for the United States and 2 units of clothing for Japan:

Opportunity cost of 1 unit of food
United States: 1F = ½C
Japan: 1F = 2C

We conclude that the United States can produce food more cheaply than Japan. In other words, the United States has a comparative advantage in food production. Food, then, is what the United States should specialize in producing. If we followed this procedure for clothing production, we would find that Japan could produce clothing more cheaply than the United States. The opportunity cost of producing 1 unit of clothing is 2 units of food for the United States and ½ unit of food for Japan.

Opportunity cost of 1 unit of clothing
United States: 1C = 2F
Japan: 1C = ½F

Therefore, Japan has a comparative advantage in clothing production. Clothing, then, is what Japan should specialize in producing.

EXAMPLE: Country A can produce either (1) 40X and 20Y or (2) 80X and 0Y. Country B can produce either (1) 20X and 20Y or (2) 40X and 0Y. What is the opportunity cost of producing 1X for both countries, A and B? To find it for country A, we realize that when it goes from producing 40X to 80X, it ends up not producing 20Y. So, country A gets 40 more X at the cost of 20 fewer Y. In other words, for every 2 more X it gets, it gives up 1Y. Or, to state it differently, for every 1 more X it gets, it gives up ½Y. In short, the opportunity cost of 1X is ½Y.

Now let's look at things for country B. When it goes from producing 20X to 40X it gives up producing 20Y. In other words, to

Background Information: The *CIA World Factbook*

The *CIA World Factbook* is a useful, easily accessible resource for information about imports and exports, and the current dollar amount the United States gains from these exports. According to the *CIA World Factbook,* in 2003 the United States exported billions of dollars worth of agricultural products. These exports included wheat, grains, corn, fruit, cotton, beef, pork, poultry, dairy products, and fish. To find current figures, check the *World Factbook* online.

398 Chapter 15 International Trade and Economic Development

To Mow, or Clean, or Both?

Fourteen-year-old Steve and twelve-year-old Danny are brothers. Their father just told them that each week they must complete two tasks: clean their rooms and mow the lawn. The following table shows how many minutes it takes each brother to do each task:

	Time to clean both rooms	Time to mow lawn
Steve	100 minutes	60 minutes
Danny	100 minutes	120 minutes

Although both Steve and Danny take the same time to clean both rooms, Danny is slower mowing the lawn than Steve. For one, he takes a lot more breaks when mowing the lawn than Steve does.

Steve and Danny wonder how they should go about doing what their father told them they need to do. They realize they could each do half of each task, or they could simply split the tasks and each do one. Which is the better way to proceed?

Suppose each of the brothers does half of each task. Steve spends 50 minutes on his half of cleaning the rooms, and Danny spends 50 minutes, which is a total of 100 minutes to clean the rooms. Then Steve spends 30 minutes mowing his half of the lawn, and Danny spends 60 minutes mowing, a total of 90 minutes of mowing. To complete both tasks it takes 100 minutes plus 90 minutes, or 190 minutes.

Now suppose that Steve only mows the lawn (he specializes), and Danny only cleans the rooms (he specializes). It takes Steve 60 minutes to mow the lawn, and it takes Danny 100 minutes to clean the rooms, which is a total of 160 minutes.

The choice is between 190 minutes or 160 minutes. To save time, the brothers should do what each

has a *comparative advantage* in doing, specialize in one task, and get their duties completed 30 minutes faster, leaving them much more time to do what they want.

THINK ABOUT IT In many families, people have certain things that they do and no one else does. For example, a husband may cook and the wife may wash the dishes; a husband may mow the lawn and the wife may wash the clothes. Do you think the jobs that each family member does are the result of comparative advantage or something else? Explain your answer.

produce 20 more X, it must forfeit 20Y, or for every 1 more X it has to give up 1Y. In short, the opportunity cost of 1X is 1Y.

Who is the low-cost producer of X, country A or B? It is country A, because it gives up less (½Y) to produce 1 more X. ◆

Benefits of Specialization and Trade

Suppose we look at two countries, Japan and the United States. Currently, we assume that each country can produce some food and some clothing. Here are the combinations of the two goods that each country can produce.

United States	Japan
A: 150 food, 0 clothing	C: 30 food, 120 clothing
B: 100 food, 25 clothing	D: 0 food, 180 clothing

Now let's consider two cases for both the United States and Japan. In the first case, Exhibit 15-3(a) on the next page, neither Japan nor the United States specializes in

Economics in the Real World

Ask students if, before reading this feature, they had ever thought of dividing chores in this way. Ask, Do any of you think you might try to figure out the comparative advantages of various tasks with a sibling?

ANSWERS TO THINK ABOUT IT Answers will vary. Comparative advantage may play a role in deciding who does which chore, but in the past, household tasks have often been divided along gender lines. Women have been expected to cook or clean, and men have been expected to mow lawns or fix things. These days, other factors may play bigger parts.

Reinforcement Activity

Ask students to respond in writing to the following question: How do opportunity costs relate to the concept of comparative advantage? The answer is that comparative advantage is the situation in which one country can produce a good at a lower opportunity cost than another country.

Background Information: Imports and Exports

Although the United States exports goods around the globe, and imports come from many countries, the United States does have several significant trading partners. As of 2004, 23% of our exports go to Canada, 14% to Mexico, 7% to Japan, and 4.4% to the United Kingdom. The balance of our exports is widely dispersed. The United States receives 17% of its imports from Canada, 14% from China, 10% from Mexico, and 9% from Japan. Exports total approximately $800 billion every year, while imports total approximately $1.5 trillion per year.

Teaching with Visuals

Assign students the task of re-creating the information in Exhibit 15-3, substituting Mexico or a European country for Japan. Students should show the goods most often involved in trade between that country and the United States. Students should also show comparative advantages in their visuals.

▶ Countries can have more of each good if they specialize in the production of the good for which they have a comparative advantage. They can then trade some of that good for other goods.

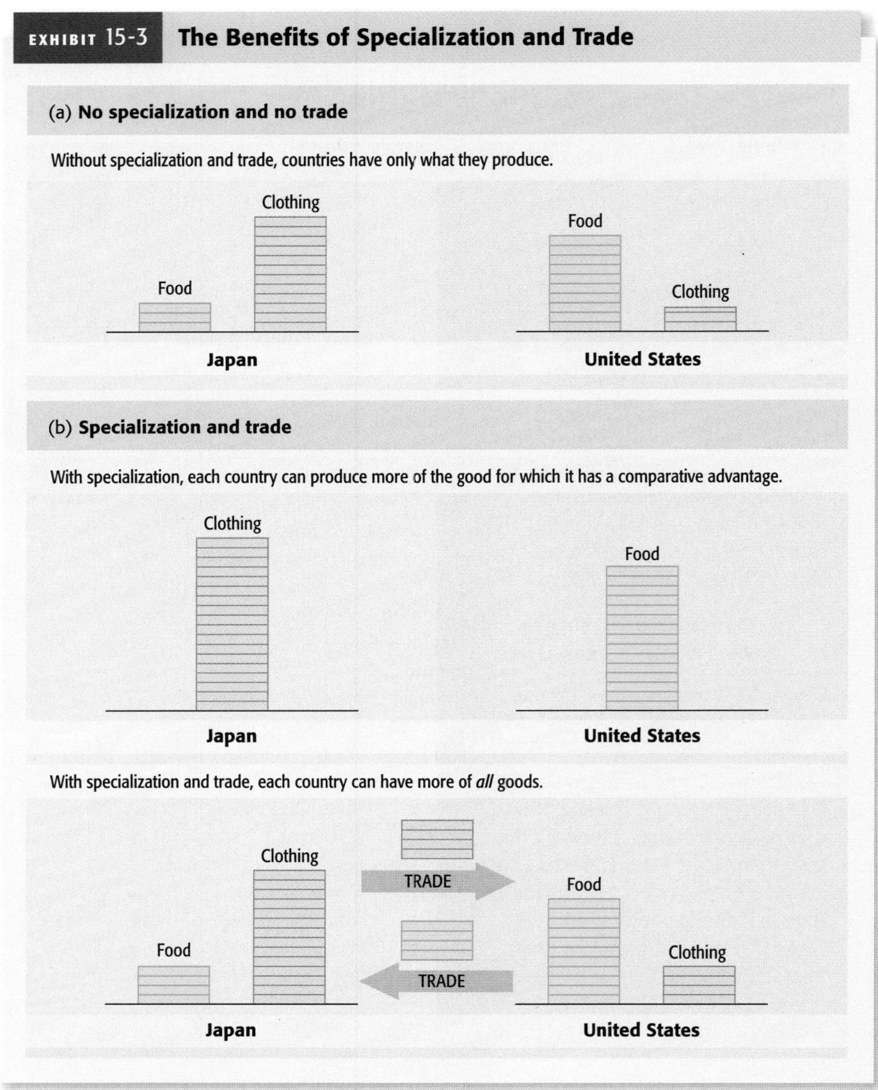

EXHIBIT 15-3 The Benefits of Specialization and Trade
(a) No specialization and no trade
Without specialization and trade, countries have only what they produce.
Food
Clothing
Japan
Food
Clothing
United States
(b) Specialization and trade
With specialization, each country can produce more of the good for which it has a comparative advantage.
Clothing
Japan
Food
United States
With specialization and trade, each country can have more of all goods.
Food
Clothing
TRADE
TRADE
Japan
Food
Clothing
United States

the production of either good (thus, both produce some amount of each good), and the two countries do not trade. In this case, the United States produces combination B (100 units of food and 25 units of clothing), and Japan produces combination C (30 units of food and 120 units of clothing).

No specialization and no trade
United States: 100F + 25C
Japan: 30F + 120C

In the second case, in Exhibit 15-3(b), each country specializes in the production of the good in which it has a comparative advantage, and then it trades some of that good for the other good. The United States produces combination A (150 units of food and 0 units of clothing), and Japan produces combination D (0 units of food and 180 units of clothing).

Then the countries decide that the United States will trade 40 units of food to Japan in return for 40 units of clothing.

Cooperative Learning

Divide the class into groups of three or four students. Tell each group to research a different trading partner of the United States. Groups should research the following questions: In what types of goods does the nation specialize? Does it carry on a significant trade in these items with the United States? Ask students to find the most current data of what types of goods are traded between that nation and the United States. Allow groups to present their findings to the class.

Countries trade
40F for 40C

After trade, the United States ends up with 110 units of food and 40 units of clothing. Japan, in turn, ends up with 40 units of food and 140 units of clothing.

Specialization and trade
United States: 110F + 40C
Japan: 40F + 140C

In which case are Japan and the United States better off? The answer is the second case in which they specialize and then trade. In the first case (no specialization and no trade), the United States ended up with 100 units of food and 25 units of clothing, whereas in the second case, it ended up with 110 units of food and 40 units of clothing. In other words, through specialization and trade, the United States ended up with more of both food and clothing.

Benefits to United States of specialization and trade
10 more units of F
15 more units of C

The same is true for Japan. In the first case, it had 30 units of food and 120 units of clothing, whereas it ended up with 40 units of food and 140 units of clothing in the second case, through specialization and trade.

Benefits to Japan of specialization and trade
10 more units of F
20 more units of C

Thus, if countries specialize in the production of the goods in which they have a comparative advantage and then trade some of these goods for other goods, they can make themselves better off.

A Student Asks

QUESTION: *Suppose one country in the world is better at producing all goods. In other words, it can produce more of all goods with a given amount of resources. Would this country still be better off trading with other countries?*

ANSWER: *Yes. Instead of thinking of this example on a country basis, let's think of it on an individual basis. Suppose a person is a brain surgeon. She is a very good brain surgeon, but then she is good at almost everything she does. For example, not only is she a good brain surgeon, but she's also good at changing the oil in her car, washing her clothes, cleaning her house, mowing the lawn, fixing the faucet in the bathroom, and so on. Does it follow that because she is, say, better than most plumbers when it comes to fixing bathroom faucets, that she should fix her own bathroom faucet instead of calling a plumber? Not at all. Most likely she can benefit from calling a plumber and devoting her time to brain surgery instead of fixing the faucet. Our point is a simple one. Even if you find a person who is better at doing everything than everyone else, still this person is made better off by doing the one thing he or she is the best at doing, and purchasing the services of other people to do other things.*

The same thing is true for a country. Even if one country could produce everything better than other countries, still it would benefit this country to do what it does best, and then trade with other countries.

A Student Asks

QUESTION: *I have another question about trade. Isn't it the case that if we (in the United States) don't produce as many different goods as we can, we will simply be shipping jobs out of the country? For example, although it might be costly to produce bananas in the United States, some Americans would be working in the banana industry in the United States if we produced bananas. Now no one works in the banana industry in the United States, but people in Honduras are working in the banana industry. Isn't it better for Americans to keep the jobs at home?*

Prediction Activity

Present the following scenario to the class: Carlos and Kim are married. Carlos can wash the dishes in 20 minutes and cut the lawn in 30 minutes. Kim can wash the dishes in 40 minutes and cut the lawn in 40 minutes. If Carlos and Kim decide to specialize in doing certain tasks, ask students who they predict will cut the lawn, and who they think will wash the dishes.

Carlos has a comparative advantage in washing the dishes. We predict that Carlos will therefore wash the dishes and Kim will cut the lawn. If they specialize this way, Carlos will spend 20 minutes washing the dishes and Kim will spend 40 minutes cutting the lawn, for a total of 60 minutes. This is less than the 70 minutes it would take if Kim washed the dishes and Carlos cut the lawn. It is also less time than if Carlos and Kim decided to split tasks. In this case, Carlos would spend 10 minutes washing the dishes and complete half the dishes, and Kim would spend 20 minutes completing the other half. Carlos would then spend 15 minutes cutting half the lawn, and Kim would spend 20 minutes cutting the other half. The total time it would take to do the dishes and cut the lawn would be 65 minutes. To recap, specializing in the task in which you have a comparative advantage minimizes the time it takes to complete tasks.

A Student Asks

You might want to use the first A Student Asks on this page to make sure that students understand the analogy between the brain surgeon and a nation that is good at producing all goods.

Internet Research

The International Trade Administration of the U.S. Department of Commerce compiles trade statistics. Have students go to its Web site and click on "Trade Statistics," then "National Trade Data," and finally "Global Patterns of U.S. Merchandise Trade." This allows students to see the trade balance and imports and exports displayed on a map. Ask students what the U.S. balance of trade was for the latest year published.

Economics Around the Clock

Invite students to discuss their answers to the 5:45 P.M. scenario in Economics Around the Clock (page 393).

The answer to the first question is that offshoring occurs when a domestic company hires persons in another country to do certain work activities. Should U.S. residents worry about offshoring? Answers will vary. Students may say that offshoring comes with benefits and costs. It definitely involves some costs for American workers, but it also provides benefits for American consumers.

outsourcing
The term used to describe work done for a company by another company or by people other than the original company's employees.

ANSWER: *First, you shouldn't assume that if Americans are not working in the banana industry that they are not working at all. Americans not working in the banana industry might be working in some other industry. Second, it is not so much a matter of "keeping the jobs at home," as it is making sure Americans are doing the jobs they are best at doing. It may be relatively costly for Americans to work at producing bananas, but relatively cheap—in opportunity cost terms—for Americans to work at producing computer software, cars, or movies.*

Even without international trade, the composition of jobs in the United States changes. For example, in 1929, 22 percent of the workforce was made up of farmers. That percentage was down to 16.2 percent in 1945, and today it is about 2.4 percent.

No doubt someone in the 1940s, complaining about the declining employment of farmers in the United States, said something like, "We can't have people leaving the ranks of the farmers; it will be the end of America." But it wasn't the end of America. Agricultural production in the United States boomed at the same time as the number of farmers decreased (in both absolute and relative terms) in America. Many of the people who would have been farmers turned out instead to be teachers, doctors, accountants, engineers, plumbers, construction workers, taxi drivers, and so on.

Our point is a simple one: even without any international trade, the composition of the labor force will change over time. At one time in the United States, no one was working in the computer software industry because there were no computers. Today, thousands are employed in this industry. At one time in the United States, no one was employed in the auto industry because there were no cars. Today thousands are employed in this industry.

Outsourcing and Offshoring

A controversial issue has come to America: outsourcing and offshoring. Before examining this issue, let's make sure you know the difference between these two terms.

Understanding the Difference

Suppose a company called "Adams Software" is located in Greensboro, North Carolina. Let's say the company has 100 employees. One day the president of the company decides to hire some people in, say, Seattle, Washington, to do some work for the company. Because the president is hiring some workers who are not formal employees of the company in Greensboro, he is said to be *outsourcing* jobs. In short, **outsourcing** is the term used to describe work done for a company by either another company or by people other than the original company's employees.

Recall from Chapter 2 that when a company outsources certain work to individuals in another country, it is said to be engaged in *offshore outsourcing* or *offshoring*. For example, if Dell, Inc., in Texas, hires people in India to answer customers' calls, then Dell is offshoring.

Sometimes people use the word *outsourcing* when the correct word to use is *offshoring*. For example, it is not uncommon to hear a person say, "Yes, many U.S. companies are outsourcing jobs to India and China." Once again, if we are talking about individuals being hired in another country (a country other than the United States), the correct word is *offshoring*.

Jobs Are Lost

It is not uncommon for Americans to be concerned about offshoring. Think of an extreme case. A person in Montana goes to college to learn software engineering. After having studied four or five years in college, she gets her degree and is ready to work. Then, just as she goes into the job market, she finds out that many of the companies she is seeking employment with are hiring software engineers in, say, India. Why? Because software engineers in India earn

Differentiating Instruction

Enrichment and Extension

Encourage students to read *The World Is Flat: A Brief History of the Twenty-first Century,* by Thomas L. Friedman (New York: Farrar, Straus and Giroux, 2005). Challenge them to take notes on issues related to the topics of this chapter as they read. Also instruct each of them to write three or four questions about those issues that would be good for use in a book group discussion. For example, they might ask, What does Friedman mean when he says the world is flat? When students have completed their reading and their questions, gather participants in a circle for a discussion of the book. You might host this discussion outside of class, in a relaxed environment with refreshments.

◀ Indian employees at a call center in Bangalore, India, provide service support to international customers. **Why would a company in Germany, Russia, or the United States, for example, hire Indian workers, rather than workers in their own country, to handle these calls?**

lower salaries than software engineers in the United States.

It is easy to see why our software engineer from Montana might be disheartened by what has happened. Here she went to college, thinking that a job would be awaiting her when she graduated, but many of the jobs were "shipped" overseas.

Will these kinds of things happen in a free global economy? Yes they will. In fact, they have happened. Is this a personal tragedy for some people, such as our software engineer from Montana? No doubt it is. What happens to the software engineer is not the full story, though. There is more to tell.

Some Benefits

First, offshoring is not something that only happens in the United States. Yes, U.S. companies can and do hire individuals who live in other countries. It's also the case, however, that foreign companies hire individuals who work in the United States. In short, offshoring is a two-way street.

Second, offshoring often benefits consumers. How so? U.S. companies outsource certain work activities only if it is less costly for them to hire foreign labor than U.S. labor (assuming the quality of the labor in the two countries is the same). In other words, the motivation behind offshoring is the attempt to lower costs (and thus raise profits). As we know from an earlier chapter, lower costs shift the supply curve (of the good) to the right. Do you remember what happens if the supply curve shifts to the right? The price of the good will fall. In other words, consumers will end up paying lower prices.

Opportunity Costs Play a Role

Offshoring is nothing more than those persons producing things that they can produce at a lower cost than other people. It is simply *comparative advantage* at work.

Looking at it this way sheds some light on the case of the Montana software engineer. When we last discussed her situation, the job she was seeking had been offshored to India. The reason: Indian software engineers earn less than American software engineers.

But couldn't the software engineer from Montana have offered to work for the same wage that the Indian software engineer agreed to work for? Let's say this wage was $600 a week. The answer, of course, is yes. So why didn't she offer to do this? Why didn't she simply say that if the Indian software engineer is willing to work for $600 a week, then so is she?

The reason is because she must have had a better alternative open to her than working for $600 a week. If she didn't, then she would have offered to work for the same wage as the Indian software engineer. In other words, here is her priority list:

Teaching with Visuals

Workers in India are probably willing to work for lower wages.

Reinforcement Activity

Tell students that although many workers in India are willing to work for lower wages than workers in the United States, there may be other reasons that U.S. companies prefer to offshore jobs there. Ask students what some of those reasons might be. Answers will vary. Students might suggest the presence of an educated workforce and low political barriers.

Cooperative Learning

Remind students that offshoring does not occur only in the United States. Divide the class into groups of four or five students. Instruct each group to choose a company that offshores jobs to the United States. Each group should research the following questions: What product or service does the company offer? When and why did it begin offshoring jobs to the United States? Has the offshoring produced any sort of political backlash in the company's home nation? Invite groups to present their findings to the class.

Teaching with Visuals

The offshoring of these jobs means that some U.S. engineers might not land jobs that pay as highly as they had hoped. Other engineering jobs that still pay better than the jobs in India are probably still available.

A Student Asks

You might want to use this A Student Asks to remind students that U.S. companies do not automatically send jobs overseas if wage levels are slightly lower in other nations. Companies have to consider other factors, such as political barriers, language barriers, or costs of relocating some personnel.

Reinforcement Activity

Tell students to work in groups of three or four to find newspaper or magazine articles about offshoring. Ask, What kind of jobs are being lost, and where are the jobs going? Urge students to think about how the offshoring of these jobs might affect consumer prices. Allow groups to present their findings to the class.

▲ These software engineers in Bangalore, India, work for an Indian software company that has about 300 clients around the world, including U.S. companies Bank of America and Citigroup. **Because Bank of America and Citigroup have chosen to offshore these jobs, it doesn't necessarily follow that U.S. software engineers have no jobs at all. Explain.**

Top choice:
Work as a software engineer for $1,000 a week

Second choice:
Work at job X for $700 a week

Third choice:
Work as a software engineer for $600 a week (which is the same wage an Indian software engineer is receiving)

She initially goes after her top choice and learns that it is no longer open to her. She doesn't go for her third choice, though, because she has a second choice that is better.

In other words, our software engineer from Montana doesn't choose to work at the same wage as the Indian software engineer because her opportunity costs are greater than his. We are not suggesting that offshoring does not hurt her. Her hurt comes in the form of earning $700 a week instead of $1,000 a week. It's just that now we understand her options are not between (1) working for $1,000 a week and (2) not working. Her options are between (1) working for $1,000 a week and (2) working for $700 a week. In other words, her options are not as black-and-white or as extreme as we perhaps initially thought.

One final point to consider is that even though offshoring lowers our Montana software engineer's income by $300 a week, it lowers the U.S. company's costs by $400 a week (per software engineer hired in India instead of the United States). In other words, costs of the company fall by more than income falls. And, as we said earlier, if the company operates in a competitive environment—where prices tend to fall to a level just sufficient enough to cover costs—then we can expect a decline in prices to follow.

A Student Asks

QUESTION: *I think part of this story is unrealistic. You say that if the software engineer from Montana wanted to work for $600, she could have told the U.S. company offshoring jobs to India. Then she would have worked at $600 an week. But I have never heard of a person going into a company and offering to work for the same wage as a person in India, or China, or any other country. Isn't this unrealistic?*

ANSWER: *In a way, you are right. Very few, if any, people will send the following e-mail to the president of a company that is offshoring jobs.*

Dear President:

I know you have been offshoring jobs to India because you can hire labor in India at a lower wage than you can hire labor here in the United States. I also know that the wage isn't the only thing that matters to you—productivity matters too. So it must be the case that Indian labor is as productive as U.S. labor—but just costs less. I can see why you are doing what you are doing. If I were in your shoes, and had to answer to the stockholders, I would probably do the same thing.

So here's the deal: I will work for the same wage you are paying the software engineers in India. Here is my phone number and e-mail address.

I hope to hear from you soon.

Signed,
Software engineer from Montana

But even though e-mails like this one are rarely sent, if the message in the letter is the same message on the minds of enough American software engineers, you can be sure the president of the company is going to hear it. He or she might not

Differentiating Instruction

English Language Learners

To help ELL students, use the following resources, which are provided as part of the *Economics: New Ways of Thinking* program:

- a Spanish glossary in the *Student Text*
- Spanish versions of the Chapter Summaries on an audio CD

hear it in an e-mail, or on the phone, but he or she will hear it in board meetings. U.S. companies have a monetary incentive to learn what wages they have to pay. If many American software engineers will work for the same wage as Indian engineers, then U.S. companies will be aware of this fact. Then they will hire Americans because often the cost of setting up an operation overseas is expensive and problematic (especially problematic if foreign government issues must be worked out).

The Costs of Offshoring Are Easier to See than the Benefits

Our economic discussion of offshoring mentions some benefits and costs to offshoring. One huge cost came to the software engineer who ended up earning $700 a week instead of $1,000 a week. Some benefits came in the form of lower prices for consumers. In addition, we learned that offshoring is a two-way street.

The biggest practical problem with offshoring is that the costs are much easier to see than the benefits. For this reason, many people come away thinking that offshoring is nothing but costs.

Think of yourself watching the TV news one night. A news reporter tells you the story of our software engineer from Montana who went to college and then couldn't get a job as a software engineer earning $1,000 a week because so many U.S. companies decided to hire Indian software engineers instead. The news report makes the picture easy to see. The software engineer from Montana on your screen is a real person—just like you. If you are an empathic sort of person, you can feel some of the pain and heartbreak that she must be going through.

What you don't see at that moment on television, or perhaps read about in the newspaper the next day, is that just as U.S. companies offshore jobs to India, some foreign companies offshore jobs to the United States. In other words, you don't see the American who is working for a foreign company. His or her story is rarely told on the TV news.

You also don't see the lower prices that often result from offshoring. As far as you know, prices just keep going up and up and up. So where are the lower prices that offshoring is creating for American buyers? The problem here is that two things are

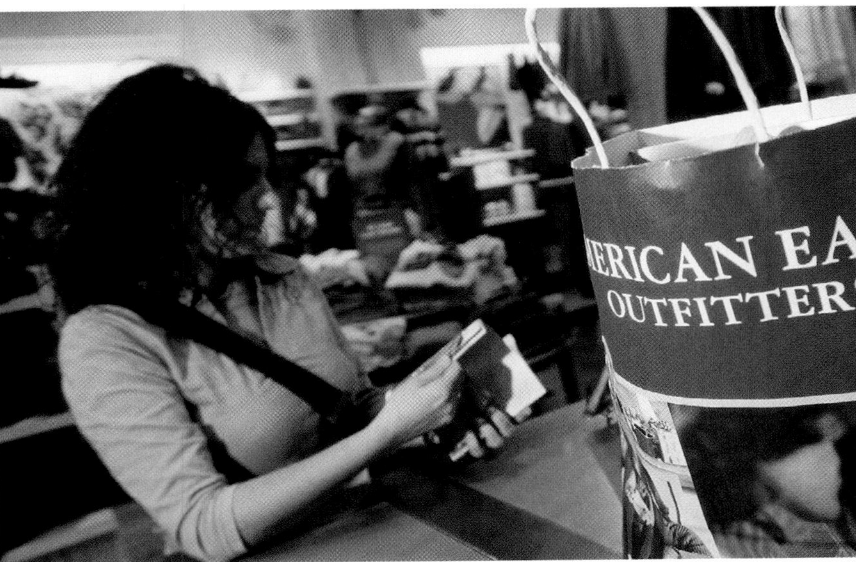

◀ As she shops, why might this American consumer fail to realize that she will be benefiting from the process of offshoring if she decides to make the purchase?

Cooperative Learning

Divide the class into two groups, and tell them that they will need to prepare for a debate about offshoring. At issue: Is offshoring good for the United States? Give the groups several days to research the pros and cons of their sides. Then act as a moderator for the debate. Make sure that most of the students have input. When the debate has concluded, ask students whether their opinions about offshoring changed while they prepared for or participated in the debate.

Teaching with Visuals

The consumer might not be aware that the item she is about to buy is made more affordable by offshoring. Offshoring helps to keep the cost of goods low by keeping labor costs low.

Application Activity

After reading and discussing Section 1, you may want to assign the Section Activity in the *Applying the Principles Workbook.*

Assess

Quick Quiz

The following true-or-false quiz will help you assess student understanding of the material covered in this section.

1. Exports are goods that are produced in foreign countries and sold to residents of the domestic country. (False)
2. Balance of trade is the difference between the value of a country's exports and its imports. (True)
3. An absolute advantage means that one country can produce more of a good using the same quantity of resources than another country. (True)
4. Opportunity costs are very important in determining comparative advantage. (True)
5. Countries with comparative advantages in goods should not specialize in any one product. (False)

Assessment Book

You will find a quiz for this section in the *Assessment Book.*

Reteaching Activity

Use the Section Assessment to gauge which students may need reteaching on this section. For those students, write the phrase "balance of trade" on the board. Draw a traditional scale. Tell students that the right side of the scale represents exports and the left side represents imports. Invite students to come to the board to draw weights on the scale to represent both favorable and unfavorable trade balances.

Guided Reading

For further reteaching of the key concepts in this section, assign the Outlining Activity and the Just the Facts Handout from the *Guided Reading and Study Guide.*

happening at the same time, which make it difficult to see what is happening to prices because of offshoring. The first thing that is happening is that the Fed, which we discussed in an earlier chapter, is busy raising the money supply (most months). The increased money supply is putting upward pressure on prices. At the same time, offshoring is putting downward pressure on prices. The problem, however, is that net prices keep rising because the money supply effect pushing prices upward is stronger than the offshoring effect pushing prices downward. It is as if the money supply raises the price of a good $3 at the same time that offshoring lowers the price $1. What will be the end result? It's going to rise by $2. (Think of a person throwing buckets of water on a fire. The fire still flames, but not by as much as it would if no water had been thrown on the water.)

If all we can really see are the costs of offshoring, then it is likely that many Americans will rally against it. They might vote for politicians who speak out against it, they might march in the street against U.S. companies that practice it. Would their behavior be different if they saw the whole picture instead of only the cost side of the picture?

A Student Asks

QUESTION: *I think that if your job were on the line, you would be more anti-offshoring than you seem to be. Isn't it easy for someone to talk about the benefits (to others) of offshoring if he or she is not the one losing a job?*

ANSWER: *You bring up an interesting point. I think I might be less likely to bring up the benefits of offshoring if I were the person losing a job. It doesn't mean the benefits of offshoring are not there, however. Remember, no economist is telling you that offshoring is all benefits or all costs; the economist is simply telling you that the situation involves both costs and benefits. An economist then usually goes on to say that the costs are often more visible than the benefits, such that the benefits are often ignored in our daily conversations while the costs are not. At the end of the day, you have every right to be either "for" or "against" offshoring. We are simply outlining the benefits and costs of offshoring so that you can make an informed choice.*

SECTION 1 ASSESSMENT

Defining Terms

1. Define:
   - **a.** exports
   - **b.** imports
   - **c.** balance of trade
   - **d.** absolute advantage
   - **e.** comparative advantage
   - **f.** specialize

Reviewing Facts and Concepts

2. Suppose the United States can produce either 90 apples and 20 oranges or 80 apples and 30 oranges. What is the opportunity cost of producing 1 apple?
3. Suppose Japan can produce either 100 cars and 30 television sets or 80 cars and 60 television sets. What is the opportunity cost of producing 1 television set?
4. What does it mean to say that country A has a comparative advantage in the production of computers?

Critical Thinking

5. Jones is an attorney, and Smith is a gardener. Jones, however, is better at gardening than Smith is at gardening. Essentially, he can do what needs to be done in the garden in 30 minutes, whereas it takes Smith one hour. Does it follow that Jones should do his own gardening instead of hiring Smith to do it? Explain your answer.

Applying Economic Concepts

6. How would you go about computing the opportunity cost (in dollars) of studying for a test?

Defining Terms

1. a. exports: goods that are produced in the domestic country and sold to residents of a foreign country; **b. imports:** goods produced in foreign countries and purchased by residents of the domestic country; **c. balance of trade:** the difference between the value of a country's exports and imports, can be either positive or negative; **d. absolute advantage:** the situation in which a country can produce more of a good than another country with the same quantity of resources; **e. comparative advantage:** the situation in which a country can produce a good at lower opportunity cost than another country; **f. specialize:** to do only one thing.

Reviewing Facts and Concepts

2. 1 orange (*calculation:* The opportunity cost of producing 10 more apples is not producing 10 oranges; $10 \div 10 = 1$).
3. $\frac{2}{3}$ car (*calculation:* $100 - 80 = 20$ cars; $60 - 30 = 30$ television sets; $20 \div 30 = \frac{2}{3}$ car).
4. It means that country A is the low-cost producer of computers, or that country A can produce computers most cheaply.

Critical Thinking

5. No. Just because Jones is better at gardening than Smith, it does not follow that he should do his own gardening instead of hiring Smith. Jones may have a higher opportunity cost of gardening than Smith. He may have to give up one-half hour of work as an attorney (at $150 a half hour) if he does his own gardening. If it takes Smith one hour to garden and he charges $30 an hour, then Jones would be better off working as an attorney for one-half hour, earning $150, paying Smith $30, and keeping $120.

Applying Economic Concepts

6. Estimate how many hours of study it takes to achieve a certain grade on the test. For example, suppose it takes John two hours of study to get a B on a test, and it takes Karie one hour of study to get a B on the same test. Find out what each could earn in an hour. Suppose John and Karie could each earn $5 an hour. The opportunity cost (in dollars) of studying to get a B is $10 (2 hours × $5 an hour) for John and $5 (1 hour × $5 an hour) for Karie.

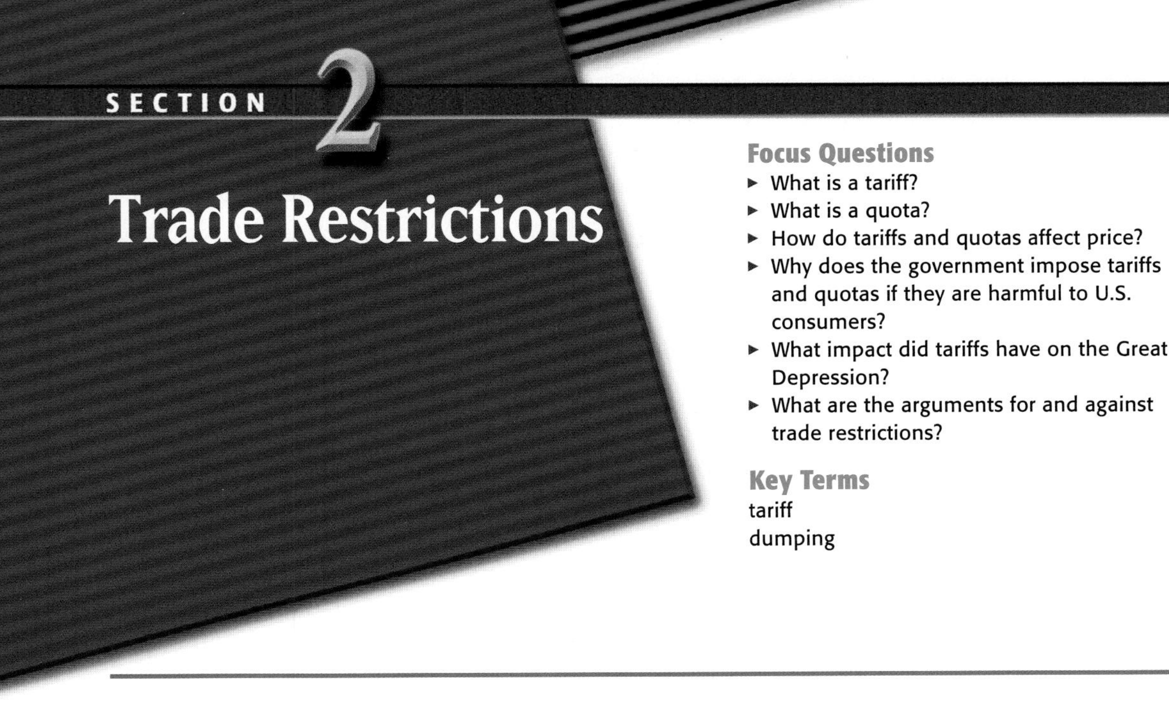

SECTION 2

Trade Restrictions

Focus Questions

- What is a tariff?
- What is a quota?
- How do tariffs and quotas affect price?
- Why does the government impose tariffs and quotas if they are harmful to U.S. consumers?
- What impact did tariffs have on the Great Depression?
- What are the arguments for and against trade restrictions?

Key Terms

tariff
dumping

Trade Restrictions: Tariffs and Quotas

Tariffs and quotas are the two major types of trade restrictions. A **tariff** is a tax on imports. For example, currently some Americans buy cars made in Japan, which are considered imports. Let's say each car sells for $22,000. Now suppose the U.S. government places a $1,000 tariff on each car, raising the price of a Japanese car from $22,000 to $23,000. As a result, Americans will buy fewer Japanese cars. (Remember the law of demand: As price rises, quantity demanded falls.)

A *quota* is a legal limit on the amount of a good that may be imported. Suppose Japan is sending 300,000 cars into the United States each year. The U.S. government decides to set a quota, or legal limit, on Japanese cars at 200,000 cars per year. In short, the U.S. government says it is legal for Japan to send 200,000 cars each year to the United States, but not one car more.

The effect of the quota is to raise the price of Japanese cars. With a smaller supply of Japanese cars and with demand for Japanese cars constant, the price of Japanese cars will rise. (Recall that when the supply of a good falls and the demand for the good remains the same, the price of the good rises.) In effect, then, both tariffs and quotas raise the price of the imported good to the U.S. consumer.

The U.S. Government and Producer Interests

If tariffs and quotas result in higher prices for U.S. consumers, why does the government impose them? Government is sometimes more responsive to producer interests than consumer interests. In other words, government may be more responsive to U.S. car manufacturers than to U.S. car consumers. To see why, suppose 100 U.S. producers produce good X and 20 million U.S. consumers consume good X. The producers want to protect themselves from foreign competition, so they lobby for, and receive, tariffs on foreign goods that compete with what they sell. As a result, consumers end up paying higher prices. We'll say that consumers end up paying $40 million more, and producers end up receiving $40 million

tariff
A tax on imports.

Differentiating Instruction

English Language Learners

It is possible that English language learners will have trouble with the concepts presented in this chapter. To help those students understand this information, you might call on student volunteers to read the chapter aloud. Each time the volunteer comes across vocabulary that may be unfamiliar to ELL students, stop the volunteer and ask the class to help you define the word. At the end of each section, you might also call on class members to help summarize that part of the text. By explaining new vocabulary and providing summaries, you will aid those students for whom English is a second language.

SECTION 2

Teacher Support

Focus and Motivate

Section Objectives

After completing this section, students will be able to

- define *tariff* and *quota;*
- explain how tariffs and quotas affect prices;
- explain why the government imposes tariffs and quotas if they are harmful to U.S. consumers;
- describe the effect that tariffs had on the Great Depression; and
- describe the arguments for and against trade restrictions.

Kickoff Activity

Present students with the following question: Someone in society has to ask for the tariffs and quotas that we see placed on some foreign goods. In the United States, who are these people and why do they ask for tariffs and quotas?

Activating Prior Knowledge

Allow volunteers to share their responses to the Kickoff Activity. Answers will vary. Some students will probably say that U.S. producers of goods may ask for tariffs and quotas on their foreign competitors' goods. Some students may say that, at times, labor unions will ask for tariffs and quotas on foreign goods in order to secure their members' jobs.

Teach

Teaching with Visuals

The government might be responding to pressure from the steel industry. Answers will vary as to whether students would vote for tariffs.

Critical Thinking

Ask students if producers and consumers share an interest in having tariffs and quotas applied to important goods. The answer is no. Whereas producers may want tariffs and quotas, consumers will not. As we show in this section, domestic producers are helped by tariffs and quotas, but consumers end up paying higher prices.

▲ Why might the U.S. government place tariffs on imported steel? If you were a member of Congress, would you vote for or against such tariffs?

more, for good X than they would have if the tariffs had not been imposed. If we equally divide the additional $40 million received among the 100 producers, we find that each producer receives $400,000 more as a result of tariffs. If we equally divide the additional $40 million paid among the 20 million consumers, we find that each customer pays $2 more as a result of tariffs. A producer is likely to think, "I should lobby for tariffs, because if I am effective, I will receive $400,000 more." A consumer is likely to think, "Why should I lobby against tariffs? If I am effective, I will save myself only $2. It is not worth my lobbying to save $2." In short, the benefits of tariffs are concentrated on *relatively few producers,* and the costs of tariffs are spread over *relatively many consumers.* This situation makes each producer's gain relatively large compared with each consumer's loss. Producers will probably lobby government to obtain the relatively large gains from tariffs, but consumers will not lobby government to avoid paying the small additional amount added by tariffs.

Politicians, who generally respond to the most vocal interests, hear from those people who want the tariffs but not from those people who are against them. Politicians may thus mistakenly assume that consumers' silence means that they accept the tariff policy, when in fact they may not. They may simply not find it worthwhile to do anything to fight the policy.

A Student Asks

QUESTION: *Can you give me an example of producer interests getting the tariffs they seek?*

ANSWER: *In 2002, the federal government placed tariffs on imported steel. The steel tariffs were in response to what the domestic (U.S.) steel industry was asking for at the time. As a result of the tariffs, consumers ended up paying more for such goods as cars. A* USA Today *article stated the following about the tariffs: "The tariffs will undoubtedly be passed on to consumers, but the [Bush] administration did not estimate by how much. Critics say the action will raise prices to consumers on items ranging from cars, houses, and appliances. One critical study suggested the average family of four would spend up to $283 more a year." In late 2003, the tariffs on steel that were imposed in 2002 were ended.*

A Student Asks

QUESTION: *Don't tariffs sometimes save American jobs, though? Didn't the steel tariffs save some American jobs?*

ANSWER: *Yes, it is possible for tariffs to save some American jobs, but the question for an economist is: At what cost? For example, the Institute for International Economics estimated that the steel tariffs saved 1,700 jobs in the steel industry, but at the cost to consumers (in the form of higher prices) of $800,000 per job. In other words, U.S. consumers ended up paying $800,000 in higher prices for every one job they saved*

Internet Research

In the fall of 1999, the World Trade Organization held its Ministerial Conference in Seattle. Thousands of protesters also went to Seattle to demonstrate against the WTO. Instruct students to use the Internet to find at least two Web sites or articles in favor of the WTO and two opposed to this organization. Ask students to imagine that their parents or friends have asked them to explain what happened in Seattle, and to write papers summarizing what they have learned. They should conclude by explaining whether, had they been in Seattle at that time, they think they would have joined the protestors or the contingent supporting the WTO.

in the steel industry. Or look at it this way. The average job saved in the steel industry was a job that paid $50,000 to $55,000 a year. In short, tariffs ended up causing American consumers to pay $800,000 in higher prices in order to save a $50,000–$55,000 job.

One of the lessons we introduced in the first chapter of this book is that economists want to look at the entire picture, not only part of it. Tariffs can save jobs, which is certainly part of the picture of tariffs. But another part is that tariffs drive up prices for consumers. Tariffs can also make it more expensive for other American producers to produce goods. For example, even though tariffs on steel might have helped the U.S. steel industry, they certainly hurt the U.S. car industry (because car producers buy steel). It is important, when discussing tariffs and quotas, to make sure to identify all of their effects.

Tariffs and the Great Depression

In January 1929, many members of Congress became disturbed over the increase in imports into the United States. Willis Hawley, the chairman of the House Ways and Means Committee, introduced a bill in Congress to deal with this apparent problem. It came to be known as the Smoot-Hawley Tariff Act, which proposed substantially higher tariffs on many imported goods. It was thought with higher tariffs on imported goods, Americans would buy fewer imports and more goods produced in the United States. This outcome, some thought, would be good for the country.

Although the Smoot-Hawley Tariff Act was not signed into law until June 17, 1930, its passage was likely, and many people in the country suspected it would become law long before it did. Some people thought it would be bad for business in the United States. They thought that other countries would retaliate with their own high tariffs (which they did), and that global trade would diminish, thus hurting the U.S. economy. (If other countries imposed high tariffs on U.S. goods, then Americans would not be able to sell as much abroad.)

"Trade barriers are chiefly injurious to the countries imposing them."
— John Stuart Mill

Some economists blame the sharp decline in the stock market in 1929—which some say dates the beginning of the greatest economic decline in the nation's history, the Great Depression—on the foregone conclusion that Congress would pass, and the president would sign, the Smoot-Hawley Tariff Act. Many economists today believe that the act not only served as one of the catalysts of the Great Depression but also made the Great Depression last longer than it would have otherwise.

Arguments for Trade Restrictions

Do tariffs and quotas exist only because government is sometimes more responsive to producer interests than consumer interests? Not at all; they exist for other reasons, too.

The National-Defense Argument

It is often argued that certain industries—such as aircraft, petroleum, chemicals, and weapons—are necessary to the national defense and therefore deserve to be protected from foreign competition. For example, suppose the United States has a comparative

▼ Why might a country that produces oil place a tariff or quota on imported oil?

Reinforcement Activity

When some people talk about free trade, tariffs, and quotas, they make it sound as if it is "us" against "them." Often, this is not the way it is. For example, suppose there is a Toyota dealership in a city. Americans work for that dealership. Ask students to suppose that U.S. auto manufacturers lobby government to have tariffs placed on Japanese imported cars. Ask, Is this really a matter of "us" against "them"? Some students might suggest that it is a case of "us" against "us." For example, aren't the U.S. auto manufacturers hurting the people in the United States who work for the Toyota dealership?

Economics Around the Clock

Invite students to discuss their answers to the 1:23 P.M. scenario in Economics Around the Clock (page 393).

Students may answer that tariffs make foreign goods more expensive to purchase, thus moving American consumers away from foreign-produced goods and toward domestic goods.

Teaching with Visuals

The country might place a tariff or quota on imported oil to keep the cost of oil high, or it might do so because it believes that the production of oil is imperative to its national defense.

Cross-Curricular Activity

Invite a government teacher from your school to speak to your class about the North American Free Trade Agreement that was passed in 1993. The political debates about this agreement were heard for years before the agreement could actually be put into effect. Ask the teacher to discuss what has happened in the years since the signing. Has the agreement paid dividends for all sides, as it was advertised to do? Who is benefiting the most from NAFTA?

Economics in the Real World

Question students about the pros and cons of offshoring grading. Ask, for example: Will your school district save money? How might these savings be used?

ANSWERS TO THINK ABOUT IT Answers will vary. Students might reply that jobs that require personal interaction will not be offshored.

Reinforcement Activity

Instruct students to look through newspapers and magazines for articles about any of the arguments for trade restrictions mentioned in the text. Divide students into small groups or partnerships to share their findings, or ask them to turn in their work for evaluation.

Economics in the Real World

Might Someone in India Grade Your Homework?

A person walks into a hospital to have a magnetic resonance imaging (MRI) test. In an MRI test, the area of the body being studied is positioned inside a strong magnetic field. The MRI detects changes in the normal structure and characteristics of organs or other tissues. These changes may indicate diseases caused by trauma, infection, inflammation, or tumors.

The information from an MRI scan is often saved and stored on a computer. Then it is sent electronically to someone who studies the scan and reports on what he or she sees. The person who examines the MRI scan can be anywhere in the world. Often the person is located in another country.

What happens with MRI scans today might happen with your five-page essays or homework assignments in the future. The teacher in high school spends most of the day teaching and discussing the material—economics, history, mathematics. Homework assignments, essays, tests, and all other assignments are scanned into a computer and then electronically sent to graders in India, Ireland, or even Russia. The only proviso is that the grader has to know the material the student is being tested on and reads and writes English. (By the way, this same process is effectively what happens when you write the essay for the SAT. Your essay is scanned into a computer and sent to a grader who can live anywhere in the United States. Well, if your essay can be sent to anyone in the United States, it can also be sent to anyone in the world.)

It may just be cheaper to grade this way than to have your teacher take out time to grade your work. Of course, if you had a problem with your grader in India or Ireland, your teacher in your high school would be the one to speak with. He or she could change the grade if need be.

The computer and the Internet combine to make some things possible that weren't possible before, such as separating teaching from grading—because the computer and the Internet effectively overcome the hurdle of location. The teacher doesn't have to be the same person as the grader when the grader can get your work in the time it takes to scan and send a document.

In the future, you might just see a greater specialization of tasks than ever experienced before. Instead of a teacher being a teacher and a grader and a recorder of grades, a teacher may just teach. Others will grade, and still others will record grades, and so on.

THINK ABOUT IT What work activities are unlikely to be offshored? Is it more likely that an accountant's work will be offshored or a medical physician's work?

advantage in the production of wheat, and China has a comparative advantage in the production of weapons. Should the United States specialize in the production of wheat and then trade wheat to China in exchange for weapons? Many Americans would answer no; they maintain it is too dangerous to leave weapons production to another country, whether that country is China, France, or Canada.

The national-defense argument may have some validity, but even valid arguments may be overused or abused. Industries that are not necessary to the national defense may still argue for trade restrictions placed on imported goods. For example, in the past, the national-defense argument has been used by some firms in the following industries: pens, pottery, peanuts, candles, thumbtacks, tuna fishing, and pencils. It is difficult

Background Information: European Union

The European Economic Community, which became the European Union, was created in 1957. Today, the EU consists of 25 countries and almost half a billion people. In June 1998, the European Monetary Institute became the European Central Bank. A major economic development of the European Union was the adoption of a single currency, the euro. In 2002, the euro became the currency used by most of these countries.

to believe that these goods are necessary to the national defense.

The Infant-Industry Argument

Alexander Hamilton, the first U.S. secretary of the Treasury, argued that "infant," or new, industries often need to be protected from older, more established foreign competitors until the new industries are mature enough to compete on an equal basis. Today, some persons voice the same argument. The infant-industry argument is clearly an argument for only temporary protection from foreign producers. Critics charge, however, that once an industry is protected from foreign competition, removing the protection is almost impossible. The once-infant industry will continue to argue that it is not yet old enough to go it alone.

The Antidumping Argument

Dumping is selling goods in foreign countries at prices below their costs and below the prices charged in the domestic (home) market. For example, if Germany sells a German-made car in the United States for a price below the cost to produce the car and at a price below what it sells the car for in Germany, then Germany is said to be dumping cars in the United States. Critics of dumping say that dumpers (in our example, Germany) seek only to get into a market, drive out U.S. competitors, and then raise prices. However, some economists point out that such a strategy is not likely to work. Once the dumpers have driven out their competition and raised prices, their competition is likely to return. The dumpers, in turn, will have obtained only a string of losses (by selling below cost) for their efforts. Second, opponents of the antidumping argument point out that U.S. consumers benefit from dumping by paying lower prices.

The Low-Foreign-Wages Argument

Some people argue that U.S. producers can't compete with foreign producers because U.S. producers pay high wages to their workers, and foreign producers pay low wages to their workers. The U.S. producers insist that free trade must be restricted, or they will be ruined.

What the argument overlooks is the reason U.S. wages are high and foreign wages are low: productivity. High wages and high productivity usually go together, as do low wages and low productivity. Suppose a U.S. worker who receives $20 per hour produces 100 units of good X per hour; the cost per unit is 20 cents. A foreign worker who receives $2 per hour produces 5 units of good X per hour. The cost per unit is 40 cents—twice as high as for the U.S. worker. In short, a country's high-wage disadvantage may be offset by its productivity advantage. (See Exhibit 15-4 for the hourly compensation paid to production workers in different countries.)

dumping
The sale of goods abroad at prices below their costs and below the price charged in domestic (home) markets.

▼ Hourly compensation includes wages; premiums; bonuses; vacation, holidays, and other leave; insurance; and benefit plans.

EXHIBIT 15-4 Hourly Compensation for Production Workers, Selected Countries

Country	Hourly compensation for production workers (in dollars)
Australia	$ 20.05
Austria	25.38
Belgium	27.73
Canada	19.28
Denmark	32.18
Finland	27.17
France	21.13
Germany	29.91
Ireland	19.14
Italy	18.35
Japan	20.09
Korea, South	10.28
Mexico	2.48
Netherlands	26.84
New Zealand	11.13
Norway	31.55
Portugal	6.23
Singapore	7.41
Spain	14.96
Sweden	25.18
Switzerland	27.87
Taiwan	5.84
United Kingdom	20.37
United States	21.97

Source: U.S. Bureau of Labor Statistics, 2003.

Teaching with Visuals

Ask students to compare the hourly wages of workers in the United States with those of workers in Mexico, Singapore, and Taiwan. Discuss with students the ways these differences might lead to offshoring.

Reinforcement Activity

Instruct students to find the hourly compensation for production workers in some countries not listed in Exhibit 15-4. One place to look is the *Statistical Abstract of the United States.*

Internet Research

Assign students the task of going online to find the most recent wages (hourly compensation) reported for workers in the countries listed in Exhibit 15-4. Then tell students to create charts showing both the figures given here and the newer figures. Ask: Is there a difference? Has there been real growth in income? Have workers' wages held steady, according to the CPI? Allow students to present their findings in small groups, and then guide the class in a discussion of the results of their research.

Teaching with Visuals

Answers will vary.

Critical Thinking

Some people suggest that we are moving toward more and larger free trade areas in the world. Others say that, in short order, we will be moving in the other direction, toward greater protectionism. Ask students what they think. Allow them to discuss or debate the issue and give reasons for their positions.

Reinforcement Activity

Assign students to research one of the following: the European Union, NAFTA, or GATT. They should investigate the following questions: Who is in this group? What sets this group apart from the rest of the world?

Discussion Starter

Ask students if they would be willing to move to another country if the jobs there paid more money. Ask, Why does it not necessarily follow that a high hourly compensation makes for a better standard of living?

Discussion Starter

Some people have made the argument that the United States has a moral obligation to help citizens of poor countries economically. Other people disagree. Ask students to research and debate this issue.

▲ **Suppose tariffs have been imposed on these goods. In your opinion, what would be a good reason, or reasons, to impose tariffs?**

Look at it this way. If firms always sought out the lowest cost labor in the world (and didn't account for the productivity of the labor), then almost nothing would be produced in countries such as the United States, Belgium, and Australia.

The Tit-for-Tat Argument

Some people argue that if a foreign country uses tariffs or quotas against U.S. goods, the United States ought to apply equal tariffs and quotas against that foreign country, in the hope that the foreign country will lower or eliminate its trade restrictions. According to this tit-for-tat argument, we should do to them as they do to us.

> ***"Protectionism [trade restrictions] will do little to create jobs and if foreigners retaliate, we will surely lose jobs."***
> — Alan Greenspan

Critics of this type of policy argue that a tit-for-tat strategy has the potential to escalate into a full-blown trade war. For example, suppose China places a tariff on American-made radios. The United States retaliates by placing a tariff on Chinese-made radios. China then reacts by placing a tariff on American-made clothes, the United States retaliates by placing a tariff on Chinese-made clothes, and so on. At some point, it might be difficult to figure out who started what.

A Student Asks

QUESTION: *Doesn't the United States need to be concerned with what other countries do? After all, if other countries impose tariffs on U.S.-made goods, doesn't the United States have to retaliate? If other countries dump goods in the United States, doesn't the United States have to retaliate in some way? It's sort of like having someone hit you in the face, and you just say "hit me some more." Don't you have to defend yourself?*

ANSWER: *If you look at it in terms of the United States as an individual and other countries are individuals too, then you get the conclusion you have reached. That comparison may not be the best one to use here. Take tariffs for example. If China imposes tariffs on the United States, you say that the United States should retaliate and impose tariffs on China. Certainly the United States can do that, but it isn't only hurting Chinese producers when it does that. It is also hurting American consumers. Simply put, if the United States retaliates against other countries for the tariffs they have imposed, American consumers get hurt in the crossfire.*

Consider what happens if Japan dumps some goods in the United States (sells at a price below cost). That action might hurt U.S. producers (that compete with Japan), but it helps U.S. consumers because they are the ones who pay the low prices. So dumping is not really like getting a slap in our collective face. It is a slap in the face to our producers, but it is a pat on the back as far as our consumers go. What we are trying to point out is that this whole issue of international trade and trade restrictions is not quite as black-and-white as it might first appear.

EXAMPLE: Suppose Kelly is a domestic producer of good X. Currently, the United States imposes a high tariff on good X if it is produced in any foreign country. Kelly benefits from the tariff because the tariff simply makes any foreign-produced good X less

Cooperative Learning

The text provides some basic information about the European Union. Obviously there is much more written, and to be written, on this union and on its currency, the euro. Divide the class into groups of four or five students. Direct each group to research one facet of the European Union that interests them, such as the history, the struggles, the arguments, or how a nation joins, and assign reports on the findings. You might schedule time in the school library for groups to conduct research.

competitive with the good X that Kelly produces. Now suppose one day that a study shows that American consumers are annually paying an extra $400,000 to increase Kelly's profits from $10 a year to $100,000 a year. This news is broadcast all over the television and radio news, and finally the Congress of the United States decides to consider eliminating the tariffs on good X. Kelly may know that the country, as a whole, benefits more from eliminating the tariff than keeping it, but Kelly certainly doesn't benefit more. Kelly may lobby to keep the tariff, even though more Americans are hurt by it than are helped by it. ♦

▲ These Chinese workers are inspecting shoes that will be exported all over the world. **Why might some countries impose tariffs on the shoes? How might China respond?**

International Economic Integration

One of the hallmarks of a global economy is economic integration, the combining of nations to form either a *common market* or a *free trade area.* In a common market, the member nations trade without restrictions, and all share the same trade barriers with the outside world. For example, suppose countries A, B, C, D, E, and F formed a common market. They would eliminate all trade barriers among themselves (free trade would exist), but they would have common trade barriers with all other nations. Thus, any tariffs placed on country Z's goods would apply in all member countries.

A major common market is the European Union (EU), which consists of 25 countries (as of this writing; two more countries are expected to join in 2007). Currently, the euro is a common currency in 12 of the 25 countries of the EU.

In a free trade area, in contrast to a common market, trade barriers among the member countries are eliminated, and each country is allowed to set its own trade rules with the rest of the world. For example, if both country G and country D are part of a free trade area, country G might place tariffs on country Z's goods (country Z is not a member of the free trade area), while country D does not.

A major free trade area created by the North American Free Trade Agreement (NAFTA) includes Canada, Mexico, and the United States. NAFTA took effect in 1994. In 2005, the U.S. Congress passed the Central American-Dominican Republic Free Trade Agreement (CAFTA-DR). The CAFTA-DR is a free trade agreement between the countries of the United States, Costa Rica, El Salvador, Guatemala, Honduras, Nicaragua, and the Dominican Republic. As of this writing, CAFTA-DR is not in effect. It will be as soon as the legislatures of Costa Rica, the Dominican Republic, and Nicaragua approve it. Once approved and implemented, it will reduce barriers to trade between the signing countries.

International Organizations

Many economists predict that countries are likely to join in common markets and free trade areas in the near future. Increasingly, countries of the world are finding that it is in their best interests to lower trade barriers between themselves and their neighbors.

The World Trade Organization (WTO) provides a forum for its member countries (148 countries in mid-2005) to discuss and negotiate trade issues. It also provides a system for adjudicating trade disputes. For example, suppose the United States claimed that the Canadian government was preventing U.S. producers from openly selling their goods in Canada. The WTO would look at the matter, consult trade experts, and then decide the issue. A country that is found engaging in unfair trade can either desist from this practice or face appropriate retaliation from the injured party.

Teaching with Visuals

Answers will vary. Students may say that countries might want to protect their shoe industry from Chinese competitors. China might respond by passing tariffs of its own.

Reinforcement Activity

During the last half of 1993, there was much debate in the United States over the advantages and disadvantages of NAFTA. Assign students to look at newspapers from this time period and then write two- to three-page papers outlining the debate. Students should address these questions: What did proponents of NAFTA believe? What did opponents of NAFTA argue?

Teaching with Visuals

The answer to the question with the photo on page 414 is that the major economic purpose of the European Union is to provide a common market, in which member nations trade freely among themselves and all enforce the same barriers to trade with nonmember nations.

Application Activity

After reading and discussing Section 2, you may want to assign the Section Activity in the *Applying the Principles Workbook.*

Assess

Quick Quiz

The following true-or-false quiz will help you assess student understanding of the material covered in this section.

1. A quota is a tax on imports. (False)
2. Tariffs and quotas only exist because government is sometimes more responsive to producer interests than consumer interests. (False)
3. Alexander Hamilton argued that "infant" industries needed protection from established foreign competitors. (True)
4. In a common market, all member nations trade without restrictions. (True)
5. Dumping is selling goods in foreign countries at prices below their costs and below prices charged in the domestic market. (True)

Internet Research

Students are probably not too familiar with the workings of the International Monetary Fund or the World Bank. Ask students to search the Internet for an example of how one of these organizations is assisting a particular nation. Assign students one-page papers summarizing their findings, including background information about the particular challenges facing the nation.

Assessment Book

You will find a quiz for this section in the *Assessment Book.*

Reteaching Activity

Use the Section Assessment to gauge which students may need reteaching on this section. For those students, write the words "tariff" and "quota" on the board. Ask which term refers to a legal limit on the amount of a good that may be imported. (*Answer:* quota.) Then ask which term refers to a tax on imports? (*Answer:* tariff.)

Guided Reading

For further reteaching of the key concepts in this section, assign the Outlining Activity and the Just the Facts Handout from the *Guided Reading and Study Guide.*

Section 2 Assessment Answers

Defining Terms

1. a. tariff: a tax on imports; **b. dumping:** the sale of goods abroad at prices below their costs and below the price charged in domestic markets.

Reviewing Facts and Concepts

2. A tariff raises the price of imported goods.

3. The infant-industry argument says that "infant," or new, industries often need to be protected from older, more established foreign competitors until they are mature enough to compete on an equal basis. Critics argue that once an industry is protected from foreign competition, removing the protection is almost impossible.

4. The tit-for-tat argument says that if one country uses tariffs or quotas against U.S. goods, the United States ought to apply equal tariffs or quotas against that foreign country's goods. Critics argue that the tit-for-tat strategy can escalate into a full-blown trade war.

Critical Thinking

5. 500,000. The cost of the policy is $2 per person in group A. At this low cost, it is unlikely that individuals in group A will find it in their best interest to lobby against the policy. If group B is made up of 50 million people, the benefits per person are $2, but if group B is made up of 500,000 persons, the benefits per person are $200. The members of group B are more likely to lobby in favor of $200 benefits, and with lobbying, the policy has a greater probability of being passed.

Applying Economic Concepts

6. Domestic producers have a monetary incentive to try to restrict the importing of goods that compete with the goods they produce. For example, U.S. shoe manufacturers are better off if Americans cannot buy foreign produced shoes, or if shoes produced overseas are very expensive. To this end, domestic producers may claim that a foreign competitor is dumping, when in fact it is not.

▶ A meeting of the European Parliament in Strasbourg, France. This body of the European Union cannot initiate legislation, but it can amend or veto policies. **What is the major economic purpose of the European Union?**

Two other prominent international organizations are the World Bank and the International Monetary Fund (IMF). The World Bank, officially known as the International Bank for Reconstruction and Development (IBRD), is the biggest development bank in the world. Its primary function is to lend money to the world's poor and less-developed countries. The money for lending comes from rich member countries, such as the United States, and from selling bonds and lending the money raised through bond sales. The World Bank usually makes loans for economic development projects that are expected to produce a return sufficient to pay back the loan.

The IMF is an international organization that, among other things, provides economic advice and temporary funds to nations with economic difficulties. It has been referred to as a "doctor called in at the last minute." When a country is in economic difficulty, the IMF might submit a list of economic reforms for it to follow, such as cutting excessive government spending to reduce budget deficits or decreasing the growth rate of the money supply. The IMF often lends funds to a country in economic trouble on the condition that its economic advice is followed.

A country's acceptance of IMF reforms is usually a signal to other international organizations, such as the World Bank, that the country is serious about getting its economic house in order. The World Bank may then provide long-term funding.

Section 2 Assessment

Defining Terms

1. Define:
   a. tariff
   b. dumping

Reviewing Facts and Concepts

2. What effect does a tariff have on the price of imported goods?
3. First state, and then evaluate, the infant-industry argument for trade restrictions.
4. First state, and then evaluate, the tit-for-tat argument for trade restrictions.

Critical Thinking

5. Consider a policy that effectively transfers $100 million from group A to group B. Suppose that group A is made up of 50 million people. Is the policy more likely to be passed and implemented if the number of people that make up group B is 50 million or 500,000? Explain your answer.

Applying Economic Concepts

6. How might domestic producers of a good abuse the antidumping argument for restricted trade?

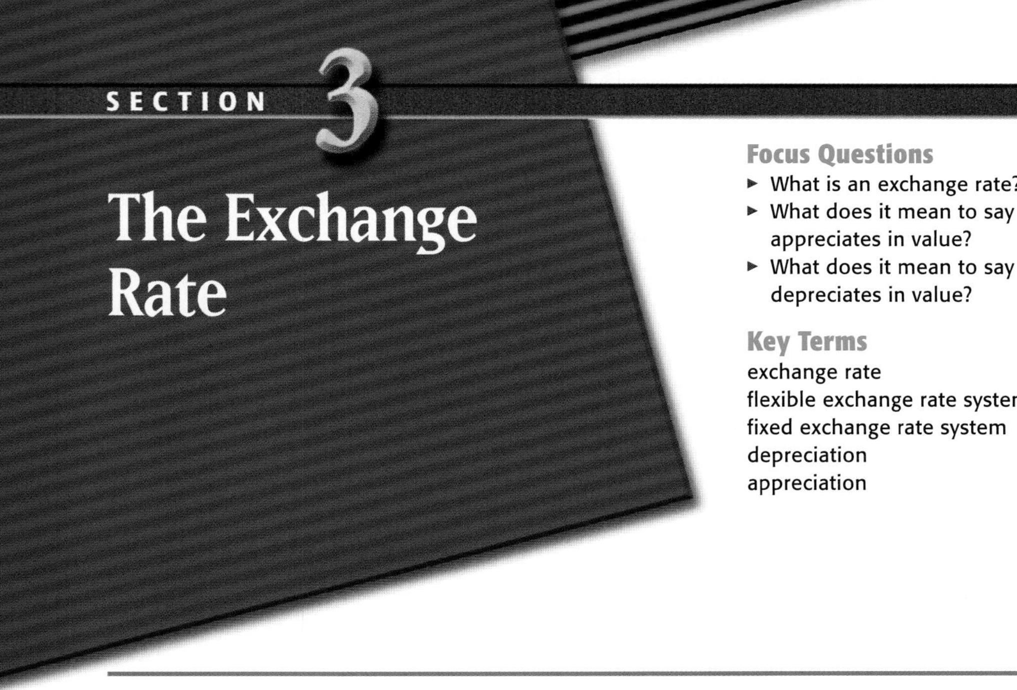

SECTION 3

The Exchange Rate

Focus Questions

- What is an exchange rate?
- What does it mean to say that a currency appreciates in value?
- What does it mean to say that a currency depreciates in value?

Key Terms

exchange rate
flexible exchange rate system
fixed exchange rate system
depreciation
appreciation

What Is an Exchange Rate?

The **exchange rate** is the price of one nation's currency in terms of another nation's currency. Suppose you take a trip to Italy. To buy goods and services, you will need to have the currency used in Italy, the basic unit of which is the euro. (The monetary symbol for the euro, €, simply looks like a C with two lines through the middle.) Therefore, you will need to exchange your dollars for euros.

Suppose you want to exchange $200 for euros. How many euros you will get depends on the exchange rate, which may be determined in two ways: by the forces of supply and demand under a **flexible exchange rate system** or by government under a **fixed exchange rate system**. Suppose the exchange rate is currently $1 for €0.80. For every $1 you have, you will get €0.80 in exchange, so you will receive €80 in exchange for $100. (Exhibit 15-5 on the next page shows the value of the U.S. dollar in terms of eight foreign currencies on October 28, 2005.)

EXAMPLE: Just as people buy goods (like a chair or a TV set), people can buy foreign money too. Americans can buy euros, pesos, yen, and so on. When Americans buy, say, euros, they have to pay some price. The dollar price they have to pay for a euro is called the exchange rate. Suppose an American is in Italy and sees an item for sale. Its price: €100 (100 euros). The American asks himself how much this is in dollars. If the exchange rate is, say, $1 = €0.80, he knows that for every $1 he has he will get €0.80 in exchange. To get 100 euros, then, the American will have to pay $125. ♦

A Student Asks

QUESTION: *How did €100 turn out to be $125? Will you go over the calculation?*

ANSWER: *Keep in mind that any exchange rate can be expressed two ways, not just one. For example, here is one way to express the dollar-euro exchange rate: $1 = €0.80.*

This expresses the exchange rate between dollars and euros in terms of one dollar. Instead, suppose we want to express the exchange rate between dollars and euros in terms of one euro: we

exchange rate
The price of one country's currency in terms of another country's currency.

flexible exchange rate system
The system whereby currency exchange rates are determined by the forces of supply and demand.

fixed exchange rate system
The system whereby currency exchange rates are fixed, or pegged, by countries' governments.

SECTION 3

Teacher Support

Focus and Motivate

Section Objectives

After completing this section, students will be able to

- define *exchange rate*;
- explain what it means to say that a currency appreciates in value; and
- explain what it means to say that a currency depreciates in value.

Kickoff Activity

Ask students the following question: What do you think it means if a person buys currencies?

Activating Prior Knowledge

Allow volunteers to share their responses to the Kickoff Activity. They may answer that there is a foreign exchange market. In this market, currencies of different countries are bought and sold.

Teach

Discussion Starter

Lead students in a discussion about their experiences in traveling to other countries. Ask: How did you handle money during your travels? Did you convert the value of a dollar to the value of the foreign currency with a calculator, or did you do the calculations in your head?

Internet Research

Ask students to imagine that they have just found a wallet in the street. It's full of money, but from several different countries—perhaps it belongs to someone on a world tour. Of course, they're going to turn it in to the police…but in case it isn't claimed, they want to know how much money they'll get to keep. Direct them to a currency-exchange Web site (such as CNN's Currencies page) to find out how many dollars they would have if they exchanged the money today and the wallet contains 1,200 Japanese yen, 500 French francs, 55 British pounds, 200 Australian dollars, and 450 Mexican pesos. Answers will vary depending on current exchange rates.

Section 3 The Exchange Rate 415

Teaching with Visuals

Ask students why it is important to know exchange rates, especially if one is planning a trip to a foreign country.

Economics Around the Clock

Lead students in a discussion of their answers to the question accompanying the 12:04 P.M. scenario in Economics Around the Clock (page 393).

Students may answer that the value of the dollar will determine the cost of anything Samantha purchases overseas. If the value of the dollar is low, it will cost Samantha more in American dollars to purchase the same items.

EXHIBIT 15-5 Exchange Rates

Country/ region	Currency	Currency units per U.S. dollar
China	yuan	8.08
European Union	euro	0.82
Australia	dollar	1.33
Sweden	krona	7.88
India	rupee	45.04
Mexico	peso	10.83
Japan	yen	115.54
Great Britain	pound	0.56

▲ If you travel outside the United States or invest in foreign businesses, you will want to know the exchange rate for your U.S. currency. The values for the dollar are for selected currencies on October 28, 2005. On that day, it took 10.83 Mexican pesos to buy one U.S. dollar. The rate is probably different today because the exchange rates are constantly changing.

simply divide $1 by the number of euros it takes to obtain that one dollar. Here is the arithmetic: $1/0.80 = $1.25. In other words €1 = $1.25. We are saying, then, that (a) $1 = €0.80 and (b) €1 = $1.25 are exactly the same thing.

If your objective is to find out how much of your money you have to pay to buy a foreign good, you need to follow three simple steps:

1. Find the current exchange rate. (Exchange rates are often quoted in the daily newspaper and online.)
2. Figure out how much of your money it takes to buy 1 unit of the foreign money.
3. Multiply the price of the foreign good by your answer to #2.

Let's rework the previous example, showing each step.

1. We identified the current exchange rate as $1 = €0.80.
2. We need to identify how much of our money (U.S. money) it takes to buy 1 unit of the foreign money. In other words, we need to know how many dollars and cents it takes to buy 1 euro. We can figure this out from the exchange rate identified in #1. We currently know that $1 buys €0.80, but we don't know how many dollars and cents it takes to buy 1 euro. To find out, we simply divide $1 by the number of euros it takes to buy $1: $1/0.80 = $1.25. In other words, it takes $1.25 to buy 1 euro.
3. We now multiply the price of the foreign good (€100) times our answer in #2 ($1.25), and we get $125.

Consider another problem. Suppose someone from Italy comes to the United States and wants to buy an American good priced at $200. If the exchange rate is $1 = €0.80, how may euros does the person have to give up to buy a $200 item? Let's calculate things from the perspective of the Italian. In other words, we will put ourselves in the shoes of the Italian.

1. We know the exchange rate is $1 = €0.80.
2. We know how much it takes of our currency ("our currency" this time is the euro because we are the Italian) to buy $1. It takes €0.80.
3. We multiply the price of the American good ($200) times our answer in #2 (€0.80). This gives us €160.

Note: These calculations are not hard, it's just that you are unaccustomed to making them. Going between currencies is a little like translating from one language into another. First you have to listen to the foreign language, understand what is being said, and then find the words in your native language that correspond to the foreign words. Just as it takes some time to learn how to translate a language, it takes some time to learn how to go from one currency to another. Go over the examples a few more times to get the hang of it.

Appreciation and Depreciation

Suppose that on Tuesday the exchange rate between euros and dollars is $1 for €0.80. By Saturday, the exchange rate has changed to $1 for €0.70. On Saturday, then,

Differentiating Instruction

Visual Learners

In an effort to expose students to different currencies and let students see what they look like, ask those in your school who have traveled to foreign countries to bring samples of the currency from those countries to class. Ask: What do you notice about other countries' currencies? What do you find most similar and most different about the foreign currencies? Why, do you think, has the United States been so hesitant to move new coins into its own economy?

Can Big Macs Predict Exchange Rates?

In an earlier chapter, we explained why goods that can be easily transported from one location to another usually sell for the same price in all locations. For example, if a candy bar can be moved from Atlanta to Wichita, then we would expect the candy bar to sell for the same price in both locations. Why? Because if the candy bar is priced higher in Wichita than Atlanta, people will move candy bars from Atlanta (where the price is relatively low) to Wichita to fetch the higher price. In other words, the supply of candy bars will rise in Wichita and fall in Atlanta. These changes in supply in the two locations affect the price of the candy bars in the two locations. In Wichita the price will fall and in Atlanta the price will rise. This price movement will stop when the price of a candy bar is the same in the two locations.

Now consider a good that is sold all over the world, McDonald's Big Mac. Suppose the exchange rate between the dollar and the yen is \$1 = ¥100 and the price of a Big Mac in New York City is \$3 and ¥400 in Tokyo. Given the exchange rate, is a Big Mac selling for the same price in the two cities? The answer is no. In New York, it is \$3, but in Tokyo it is \$4 (the price in Tokyo is ¥400 and \$1 = ¥100). Stated differently, in New York \$1 buys one-third of a Big Mac, but in Tokyo \$1 buys only one-fourth of a Big Mac.

Will Big Macs be shipped from New York to Tokyo to fetch the higher price? No, the exchange rate is likely to adjust in such a way so that the price of a Big Mac is the same in both cities.

Now ask yourself what the exchange rate has to be between the dollar and yen before the Big Mac is the same dollar price in New York and Tokyo. Here are three different exchange rates. Pick the correct one.

(a) \$1 = ¥133.33
(b) \$1 = ¥150.00
(c) \$1 = ¥89.00

The answer is (a), \$1 = ¥133.33. At this exchange rate, a Big Mac in New York is \$3 (as we stated earlier), and a Big Mac in Tokyo that is ¥400 is \$3 (once we have computed its price in dollars). Here are the steps: (1) The exchange rate is \$1 = ¥133.33; (2) 1 yen is equal to \$0.0075; (3) \$0.0075 × 400 yen is \$3.

The *purchasing power parity theory* in economics predicts that the exchange rate between two currencies will adjust so that, in the end, \$1 buys the same amount of a given good in all places around the world. In other words, if the exchange rate is initially \$1 = ¥100 when a Big Mac is \$3 in New York and ¥400 in Tokyo, it will change to become \$1 = ¥133.33. In other words, the dollar will soon appreciate relative to the yen.

The Economist, a well-known economics magazine, publishes what it calls the "Big Mac index" each year. It shows what exchange rates currently are and it shows what a Big Mac costs in different countries (just as we did here). Then it predicts which currencies will appreciate and depreciate based on this information. *The Economist* does not always predict accurately, but it does do so in many cases.

In other words, if you want to predict whether the euro, pound, or peso is going to appreciate or depreciate in the next few months, looking at exchange rates in terms of the price of Big Mac will be a useful source of information.

THINK ABOUT IT Suppose a Big Mac costs \$3 in New York City and 4.25 Swiss francs in Zurich. Also, suppose \$1 = 1.25 francs. Based on our discussion, do you expect the franc to appreciate or depreciate? Explain your answer.

Ask students why they think *The Economist* chose Big Macs as a way to compare currencies.

ANSWERS TO THINK ABOUT IT At \$1 = 1.25 francs and a price of 4.25 Swiss francs for a Big Mac, a Big Mac costs \$3.40 in Zurich—40 cents more than in New York City. The exchange rate will have to change to \$1 = 1.42 francs before a Big Mac costs the same in New York City and Zurich. The dollar will appreciate, and the franc will depreciate.

Reinforcement Activity

Instruct students to find the current numbers for the Big Mac index on *The Economist's* Web site. Create a chart in class to show the purchasing power parity theory to all of your students. Ask: Where is a Big Mac the cheapest in U.S. dollars? Where is it the most expensive? How might you use this index to predict the appreciation or depreciation of the foreign currency listed in Exhibit 15-5 over the next year?

Reinforcement Activity

After discussing "Appreciation and Depreciation" (pages 416–418), instruct students to look through newspapers and magazines to see if they can find any mention of the terms *appreciation* or *depreciation*. Invite them to explain what is being discussed in the articles.

Differentiating Instruction

Enrichment and Extension

The text presents several scenarios related to the appreciation and depreciation of the dollar. Direct students to Exhibit 15-5 (page 416) and propose several problems for them to solve. For example, a book costs \$22 in the United States, in U.S. dollars. How much will a consumer pay in French francs for the same book? How much would someone using Canadian dollars have to pay for the same book? Create several problems for students to solve, including those involving appreciation and depreciation.

Discussion Starter

Guide students in a discussion of appreciation and depreciation, using numerical examples. After solving a few problems students will better understand these two concepts.

ANSWERS TO ECONOMIC THINKING

The answer to the first question in this feature on page 419 is yes, globalization can affect wages in China. Answers to the second question may vary. Students might say that if there is a possibility that jobs could be moved to a country with even lower wages, wages in China might stay constant.

Application Activity

After reading and discussing Section 3, you may want to assign the Section Activity in the *Applying the Principles Workbook.*

Assess

Quick Quiz

The following true-or-false quiz will help you assess student understanding of the material covered in this section.

1. The exchange rate is the price of one nation's currency in terms of another nation's currency. (True)
2. A government can fix the exchange rate for its currency. (True)
3. Appreciation is an increase in the value of one currency relative to others. (True)
4. When domestic currency depreciates, it is cheaper to buy foreign-produced goods. (False)
5. To buy goods in foreign countries, you will usually need to exchange your dollars for pounds. (False)

▶ Many people speculate in currencies, attempting to make a profit by buying and selling certain currencies at opportune times. Most people, however, are interested in exchange rates only when they travel to foreign countries.

a dollar buys fewer euros than it did on Tuesday. When this situation happens, economists say that the dollar has depreciated relative to the euro. **Depreciation** is a decrease in the value of one currency relative to other currencies. A currency has depreciated if it buys less of another currency.

Appreciation is the opposite—an increase in the value of one currency relative to other currencies. A currency has appreciated if it buys more of another currency. For example, if the exchange rate goes from $1 for €0.80 to $1 for €0.90, the dollar buys more euros and therefore has appreciated in value.

depreciation A decrease in the value of one currency relative to other currencies.

appreciation An increase in the value of one currency relative to other currencies.

EXAMPLE: Suppose the exchange rate between the U.S. dollar and the Mexican peso is $1 = 10 pesos on Wednesday. So, if you have $1 you can get 10 pesos in exchange for it. Suppose two days later, on Friday, the exchange rate is $1 = 9 pesos; if you have $1 you can get 9 pesos for it. The dollar got more pesos in exchange for it on Wednesday than on Friday. We would say, then, that the dollar depreciated between Wednesday and Friday. ♦

If the Dollar Depreciates, Foreign Goods Are More Expensive

Suppose you and a friend take a trip to Mexico City this summer. In Mexico City, you come across a jacket that you want to buy. The price tag reads 1,000 pesos; what is the price in dollars? To find out, you need to know the current exchange rate between the dollar and the peso. Suppose it is $1 = 10 pesos; for every dollar you give up, you get 10 pesos in return. In other words, you will pay $100 (which is the same as 1,000 pesos) to buy the jacket. You decide to buy the jacket. Here are the steps to the calculation: (1) the exchange rate is $1 = 10 pesos; (2) if we divide $1 by 10, we learn how much we have to pay for 1 peso, which is 10 cents; (3) we multiply 10 cents times 1,000 pesos, which equals $100.

A week passes, and you and your friend are still in Mexico City. Your friend likes your jacket so much that he decides to buy one, too. You and your friend return to the

Background Information: Financial Stability

Some economists believe that countries most prone to financial crises and instability have three major flaws in their economies. First, they have insufficient cash reserves to defend or support their currency. Secondly, the banks are weak, and finally, they have a recent history of sharp currency inflation. Countries that have high cash reserves coupled with strong banks and only mild currency appreciation have not suffered from financial crises like those that plagued Mexico and Asia in the 1990s.

store and find the exact jacket for sale, still for 1,000 pesos. You tell your friend that he will have to pay \$100 for the jacket. However, you are wrong, because the dollar-peso exchange rate changed since last week. Now it is \$1 = 8 pesos. In other words, the dollar has depreciated relative to the peso, because this week each dollar buys fewer pesos than it did last week.

What will the jacket cost in dollars this week? The answer is \$125. Here are the steps to the calculation: (1) we know the exchange rate is \$1 = 8 pesos; (2) if we divide \$1 by 8, we learn how much we pay to pay for 1 peso, which is 12.5 cents; (3) we multiply 12.5 cents times 1,000 pesos and get \$125. Your friend says that he was willing to buy the jacket for \$100, but that he is not willing to pay \$125 for the jacket. The economic concept illustrated by this example is simply that when one's domestic currency depreciates (as the dollar did in the example), it becomes more expensive to buy foreign-produced goods.

Dollar depreciates → Foreign goods become more expensive

The flip side of this concept is that when one's domestic currency appreciates, it becomes cheaper to buy foreign-produced goods. Suppose the dollar-peso exchange rate changed to \$1 = 12 pesos. Now a jacket with a price tag of 1,000 pesos would cost \$83.33.

Dollar appreciates → Foreign goods become cheaper

THE GLOBAL IMPACT

Reduced Bargaining Power

According to *The Economist*, "The entry of China's vast army of cheap workers into the international system of production and trade has reduced the bargaining power of workers in developed economies [such as the United States]. Although the absolute number of jobs outsourced from developed countries to China remains small, the threat that firms could produce offshore helps to keep a lid on wages." In other words, workers in countries such as the United States are afraid to push for higher wages from their employers because the threat of moving jobs to China hangs over their heads.

ECONOMIC THINKING If globalization can affect wages in the United States, can it affect wages in China too? Would you expect with increased globalization that wages in China will rise, fall, or stay constant?

SECTION 3 ASSESSMENT

Defining Terms

1. Define:
   a. exchange rate
   b. flexible exchange rate system
   c. depreciation
   d. appreciation

Reviewing Facts and Concepts

2. If the exchange rate is \$1 = ¥129 (yen) and the price of a Japanese good is ¥7,740, what is the equivalent dollar price?
3. If the exchange rate is \$1 = £0.6612 (pounds) and the price of a U.S. good is \$764, what is the equivalent pound price?

Critical Thinking

4. Steve, an American in London, wants to buy a British-made sweater. The current price of the sweater is £40. Would Steve be better off if the exchange rate is \$1 = £0.87 or \$1 = £0.77? Explain your answer.

Applying Economic Concepts

5. Are more Americans likely to travel to Mexico when the peso has appreciated relative to the dollar or when the peso has depreciated relative to the dollar? Explain your answer.

Assessment Book

You will find a quiz for this section in the *Assessment Book.*

Reteaching Activity

Use the Section Assessment to gauge which students may need reteaching on this section. In particular, try to ascertain that students understand how to calculate exchange rates. Give struggling students five to 10 problems to solve, and allow them to work in pairs to find the correct solutions.

Guided Reading

For further reteaching of the key concepts in this section, assign the Outlining Activity and the Just the Facts Handout from the *Guided Reading and Study Guide.*

SECTION 3 ASSESSMENT ANSWERS

Defining Terms

1. a. exchange rate: the price of one country's currency in terms of another country's currency; **b. flexible exchange rate system:** a system in which currency exchange rates are determined by the forces of supply and demand; **c. depreciation:** a decrease in the value of one currency relative to other currencies; **d. appreciation:** an increase in the value of one currency relative to other currencies.

Reviewing Facts and Concepts

2. \$60 (*calculation:* 7,740 ÷ 129 = 60).
3. £505.16 (*calculation:* 764 × 0.6612 = 505.16).

Critical Thinking

4. Steve is better off if the exchange rate is \$1 = £0.87. At this exchange rate, he pays \$45.97 for the sweater. If the exchange rate is \$1 = £0.77, he pays \$51.95 for the sweater.

Applying Economic Concepts

5. More Americans are likely to travel to Mexico at a time when the peso has depreciated. If the peso has depreciated relative to the dollar, it follows that the dollar has appreciated relative to the peso. An appreciated dollar means that Americans get more pesos for their dollars than before, which makes Mexican goods less expensive. Point out that when the dollar is strong against a foreign currency, U.S. travelers to that country benefit.

Your Personal Economics

Discussion Starter

Ask students if they know anyone who has had their job offshored. Ask: What kind of work did the person do? Do you know why the job was offshored? Has the person found other employment, and if so, is it in the same field?

Research Activity

After students have read the feature, ask them to pick one of the 10 professions discussed. Ask students to update the figures given in the text, including the number of people working in that profession, their median annual salary, and the predicted number of people in that profession in 10 years. Divide students into small groups to report their data.

Teaching with Visuals

Medical specialists may perform some tasks from a distance; in this case, the X-rays might have been sent through the mail or Internet, to be read by specialists in another location. Lawyers must be present in court to present their cases, but they review legal documents and prepare their cases at other locations.

Your Personal Economics

Jobs: Location Matters . . . Sometimes

When it comes to some jobs, location matters. When it comes to other jobs, location does not matter. Let's look at some examples of both situations. Understanding the difference may help you choose a career with greater job security.

Location Matters

If you are sick, and need a doctor, you prefer to have a doctor close to you. If you live in Salem, Virginia, you will probably want a doctor who works in Salem, Virginia, not in Bangkok, 8,914 miles away.

If you need a plumber, you will probably want a plumber close by, not one on the other side of the world. If you want to go out to eat, you will most likely go to a restaurant near where you live, not one on the other side of the world.

When it comes to some services, you want the provider to be near you. So if you are at point X, you want your provider to be near point X too.

Location Doesn't Matter

When it comes to buying a book, it may not matter to you where the book seller resides, as long as you can get the book fairly quickly. When it comes to someone answering your technical computer questions, it may not matter where the technician lives. As long as the technician speaks your language, listens well, and gives clear and concise instructions, you probably don't care where he or she is located.

Offshoring/Outsourcing

When a provider's (supplier's, worker's) location is important to you, you can be fairly sure that the kind of job the provider performs will not be offshored to another country. When a provider's location is not important to you, the probability of the provider's job being offshored rises.

In 2004, *Forbes* magazine ran a story titled "Ten Professions Not Likely to Be Outsourced." Here is the list:

1. **Chief Executive Officer (of a company)**. In 2002, 553,000 chief executive officers in the United States headed various companies. That number was expected to rise to 645,000 in 2012. Although many CEOs earn million-dollar salaries, the median salary in 2002 was $126,000. Why won't the jobs of CEOs be offshored? Essentially because they are at the head of the company.
2. **Physician and Surgeon.** In 2002, physicians and surgeons numbered 583,000, with an increase to 697,000 expected by 2012. The median pay in 2002 was $138,000. (Within the medical field, salaries vary widely. For example, orthopedic surgeons may earn $200,000–$300,000 more than a psychiatrist.) Why won't such jobs be offshored? It is hard to perform surgery at a distance of greater than a few feet.
3. **Pilot, Co-Pilot, and Flight Engineer.** In 2002, for the 79,000 pilots, co-pilots, and flight engineers the median annual salary was $109,000. Why won't these jobs be offshored? Because you need someone in the cockpit to fly the plane.
4. **Lawyer.** In 2002, 695,000 lawyers earned a median annual salary of $90,000. In 2012, the number of lawyers is predicted to

◀ Does location matter in these occupations?

Cooperative Learning

Divide students into groups of four or five. Ask each group to research two professions that experts think are likely subjects for outsourcing in coming years. Allow groups to present their findings to the class. Once all the groups have completed their presentations, lead a class discussion of common characteristics among the professions that make them likely candidates for outsourcing. Write these characteristics on the board as students identify them.

increase to 813,000. Today, many aspects of the legal profession can be outsourced or offshored (research, transcription, document preparation), but the actual practice of the law, and trying a case in front of a judge, is something that cannot be outsourced or offshored.

5. **Computer and Information Systems Manager.** In 2002, 284,000 individuals were employed in this profession. By 2012, that number is expected to be 387,000. The 2002 median annual salary was $85,000. It is true that software development has been offshored (to some extent), but the people who make strategic decisions and oversee the day-to-day operations are staying put in order to be of assistance to higher-level executives when making key company decisions.
6. **Sales Manager.** Total employment of 343,000 in 2002 was predicted to increase to 448,000 in 2012. The 2002 median annual salary was $75,000. Many companies need a sales staff and an on-site person to manage them. Often, customers in one country like to deal with salespeople in the same country, who have a familiarity with the language, customs, business practices, and so on.
7. **Pharmacist.** The current number of pharmacists employed (230,000 in 2002) is expected to rise to 299,000 by 2012. The 2002 median annual salary was $77,000. Although you can today buy drugs from other countries, it is unlikely that the U.S. government will allow too much drug importation. In addition, in many cases the role of the pharmacist is becoming increasingly consultative—people like to ask him or her about their new medicine and its interactions with other medicines, about suggestions concerning various health issues, and so on.
8. **Chiropractor.** Total employment in 2002 was 49,000; in 2012, it is expected to be 60,000. The 2002 median annual salary was $65,000. It is difficult to get someone in another country to fix your back if you are thousands of miles away.
9. **Physician's Assistant.** In 2002, 63,000 physician's assistants were employed. This number is predicted to rise to 94,000 by 2012. The 2002 median annual salary was $65,000. Because physician's assistants function like quasi-doctors, they need to be near the patient. Performing physical exams is difficult at a distance.
10. **Education Administrator, Elementary and Secondary School.** In 2002, education administrators numbered 217,000; in 2012, the number is predicted to be 262,000. The 2002 median annual salary was $71,000. Although some electronic learning (e-learning) is occurring at the college level, not much is found at the elementary and secondary school level. Especially for the lower grades of education, it seems critically important to have live teachers teaching. These teachers will continue to report to on-site education administrators.

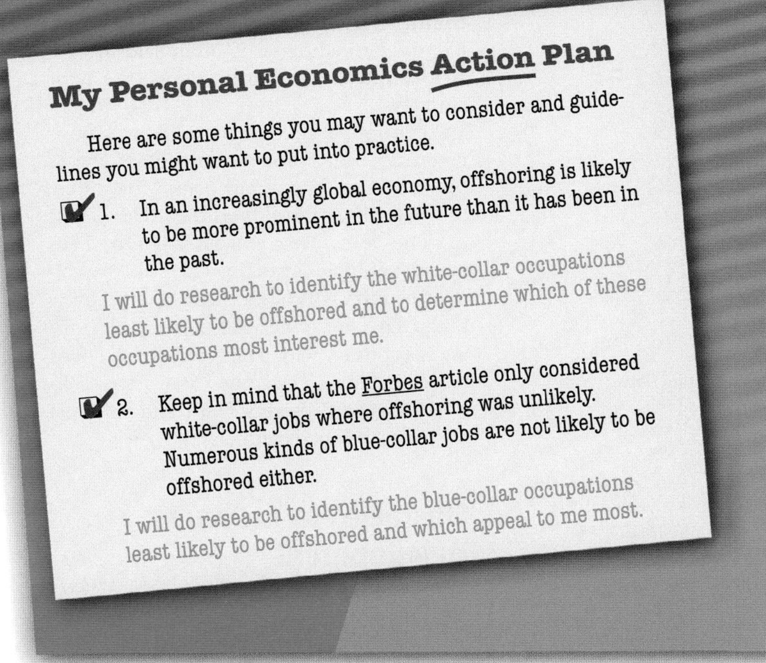

My Personal Economics Action Plan

Here are some things you may want to consider and guidelines you might want to put into practice.

1. In an increasingly global economy, offshoring is likely to be more prominent in the future than it has been in the past.

   I will do research to identify the white-collar occupations least likely to be offshored and to determine which of these occupations most interest me.

2. Keep in mind that the Forbes article only considered white-collar jobs where offshoring was unlikely. Numerous kinds of blue-collar jobs are not likely to be offshored either.

   I will do research to identify the blue-collar occupations least likely to be offshored and which appeal to me most.

Discussion Starter

Direct students' attention again to the list of occupations not likely to be offshored. Ask if students can think of ways that some aspects of these professions could be offshored. For example, a person overseas could examine scanned versions of the often thousands of documents that must be reviewed before a legal case goes to trial, or medical records could be reviewed outside the United States. As an alternative, remind students of the list that the class developed of occupations likely to be offshored. Ask, Are there aspects of these professions that are not likely to be offshored?.

My Personal Economics Action Plan Ask if students are interested in pursuing careers not listed in this feature. If so, ask what steps they could take to lower the chances that jobs in that field be offshored.

SECTION 4 Teacher Support

Focus and Motivate

Section Objectives

After completing this section, students will be able to

- explain what a less-developed country is;
- understand why some countries are rich while others are poor;
- describe why savings accounts are important to economic development; and
- list a few factors that aid economic development.

Kickoff Activity

Write the following question on the board for students to answer: "What do you think life would be like in a poor country?"

Activating Prior Knowledge

Invite students to share their responses to the Kickoff Activity. Tell them that, in economics, a poor country is more often referred to as a less-developed country (LDC) or an underdeveloped country.

Teach

Discussion Starter

Help students brainstorm obstacles to economic development. Assign each student to prepare an individual list to share with the class. Then allow students to share their ideas in a group discussion and write lists on the board. Tell students that in this section they will learn some of the obstacles that less-developed countries face as they move toward becoming developed countries.

SECTION 4 Economic Development

Focus Questions

- What is a less-developed country?
- Why are some countries rich and others poor?
- What is the vicious circle of poverty?
- Why are savings accounts important to economic development?
- What are a few factors that aid economic growth and development?

Key Terms

developed country
less-developed country
population growth rate

How Countries Are Classified

The layperson often talks about "rich" countries and "poor" countries. For example, the United States is often said to be a rich country; Ethiopia is said to be a poor country.

Economists talk about rich and poor countries, too, although they do not always use the terms *rich* versus *poor*. More often, they talk about **developed countries** (DCs) or more-developed countries (MDCs) versus **less-developed countries** (LDCs) A developed country is a country that has a relatively high GDP per capita; a less-developed country is a country with a relatively low GDP or GNP per capita. The United States is a developed country, whereas Haiti and Ethiopia are less-developed countries.

developed country A country with a relatively high per capita GDP.

less-developed country A country with a relatively low per capita GDP.

population growth rate The birthrate minus the death rate.

Obstacles to Economic Development

Why are some countries poor while others are rich? Here are some factors to consider.

Rapid Population Growth The population growth rate is typically higher in less-developed countries than in developed countries. The population growth rate in developed countries has been about 0.5 to 1 percent, compared with about 2 to 3 percent for less-developed countries.

The **population growth rate** is equal to the birthrate minus the death rate.

Population growth rate = Birthrate − Death rate

If in country X the birthrate is 3 percent in a given year and the death rate is 2 percent, the population growth rate is 1 percent.

What caused the relatively high population growth rate in the less-developed countries? First, the birthrate tends to be higher than in developed nations. In countries where financial assistance such as pensions and Social Security do not exist and where the economy revolves around agriculture, children are often seen as essential labor and as security for parents in their old age. In this setting, people tend to have more children.

Second, in the past few decades, the death rate has fallen in the less-developed coun-

Differentiating Instruction

Visual and English Language Learners

To help visual learners and those who have difficulty comprehending English to better understand the information in this section, try the following activity. Bring in pictures of street scenes from all around the world. These are readily available in newspapers, magazines, and sometimes on the Internet. Show each picture to the class and ask if, based on the scene, the picture appears to have been taken in a developed country or an LDC. Request that students explain their choices and their reasoning.

tries, largely because of medical advances. The combination of higher birthrates and declining death rates explains why the population grows more rapidly in less-developed nations than in developed nations.

Is a faster population growth rate always an obstacle to economic development? The fact that many of the countries with the fastest-growing populations are relatively poorer on a per capita basis than those countries with the slowest-growing populations is not proof that rapid population growth causes poverty. Many of the developed countries today witnessed faster population growth rates when they were developing than the less-developed countries do today.

Low Savings Rate A farmer with a tractor (which is a capital good) is likely to be more productive than one without a tractor, all other things being equal. Now consider a farmer who cannot afford to buy a tractor. This farmer may decide to borrow the money from a bank. The bank gets the money it lends from the people who have savings accounts at the bank. Savings, then, are important to economic growth and development. If savings rate is low, banks will not have much money to lend, and capital goods such as tractors (which increase productivity) will not be produced and purchased.

Some economists argue that the less-developed countries have low savings rates because the people living in them are so poor that they cannot save. In short, they earn only enough income to buy the necessities of life—shelter and food—leaving no "extra income" left over to save. This situation is called the *vicious circle of poverty*: less-developed countries are poor because they cannot save and buy capital goods, but they cannot save and buy capital goods because they are poor.

Other economists argue, though, that being poor is not a barrier to economic development. They say that many nations that are rich today, such as the United States, were poor in the past but still managed to become economically developed.

▲ This family lives in Bangladesh, an overpopulated country in which two-thirds of the people work in agriculture. Political instability and corruption have also hindered economic development.

Cultural Differences Some less-developed countries may have cultures that retard economic growth and development. For example, some cultures are reluctant to depart from the status quo (the existing state of affairs). People may think that things should stay the way they always have been; they view change as dangerous and risky. In such countries, it is not uncommon for people's upward economic and social mobility to depend on who their parents were rather than on who they themselves are or what they do. Also, in some cultures the people are fatalistic by Western standards. They believe that a person's good or bad fortune in life depends more on fate or the spirits than on how hard the person works, how much he or she learns, or how hard he or she strives to succeed.

Political Instability and Government Seizure of Private Property Individuals sometimes do not invest in businesses in less-developed countries because they are afraid either that the current government leaders will be thrown out of office or that the government will seize their private property. People are not likely to invest their money in places where the risk of losing it is high.

High Tax Rates Some economists argue that high tax rates affect economic development. Economist Alvin Rabushka studied the tax structures of 54 less-developed countries between 1960 and 1982 and categorized each

Reinforcement Activity

Instruct students to check the *Statistical Abstract of the United States* to find countries with low per capita GDPs, and then list 10–15 countries and the per capita GDP in each. Let volunteers report their findings to the class.

Problem Solving

Remind your students that when a country has an economic obstacle, the country is not necessarily less developed than another country. Instruct students to research five countries, including at least one country that exhibits one of the obstacles presented on these pages. Then ask students to determine whether these countries are developed or less-developed. Ask: Are all of these obstacles apparent in all of these countries? How do the statistics used to measure developed countries versus LDCs compare among these five countries? Which of these countries should truly be considered developed? Allow students to present their findings to the class or in small groups.

Analyzing

Some less-developed countries have cultures that retard economic growth and development. In a way, this might sound like a criticism of these countries. The question arises: Might a country's particular traditions be more important than its economic growth? The answer to this question is subjective. Ask students to discuss the issue. For example, suppose the tradition in one country is to take every other day off to rest and relax. In such a country, economic growth would be lower than in a country in which people work five or six days a week. Ask, Is there anything necessarily wrong with the culture in which people traditionally take every other day off from work? Why or why not?

Internet Research

Direct students to the IDB Population Pyramid site of the U.S. Census Bureau to find the population pyramids for three less-developed (such as Angola, Nepal, and Honduras) and one developed country (such as the United States). They will see that a population pyramid shows a country's age distribution for men and women. Ask them to compare and contrast the three population pyramids and to explain what the pyramids indicate about each country's future economic growth potential. Ask, What might a youthful population today predict about a country's future economic circumstances and needs?

Section 4 Economic Development 423

Teaching with Visuals

A country might not achieve a high rate of economic growth because its people's upward economic and social mobility depends on who their parents were, or because the culture believes that fortune depends on fate.

Discussion Starter

Review with students the ways taxes can benefit or hurt economic conditions. Ask them to explain why low tax rates, like those in Hong Kong, encourage economic growth. Governments that need more capital might need or want to demand higher tax rates, resulting in low per capita income growth.

Reinforcement Activity

Assign students to make a list of where their 10 favorite or most-used items were produced. Many electronic products come from Asia. Shoes and clothing are produced worldwide and then imported into our country. Remind students that a major benefit of free trade is that these products are available to them at affordable costs.

Application Activity

After reading and discussing Section 4, you may want to assign the Section Activity in the *Applying the Principles Workbook.*

Assess

Quick Quiz

The following true-or-false quiz will help you assess student understanding of the material covered in this section.

1. Free trade allows residents of a country to buy inputs from the cheapest supplier. (True)
2. High taxes provide a greater incentive for workers to work in order to pay their taxes. (False)
3. Allowing foreign countries to invest promotes growth and development. (True)
4. The more difficult it is to obtain a business license, the more new businesses will develop. (False)
5. Protecting private property stimulates economic growth. (True)

▶ In some cultures people value the status quo over change. **What are some other cultural reasons for a country not achieving a high rate of economic development and growth?**

country as a high-, low-, or medium-tax-rate nation. Rabushka found that Hong Kong, with the lowest tax rates, had the highest growth rate in per capita income during the period under study. Generally, low-tax countries had an average growth rate in per capita income of 3.7 percent, and high-tax countries had a per capita income growth rate of 0.7 percent.

Factors That Aid Growth and Development

Can a poor country follow a certain recipe in order to become a rich country? Some economists believe so. They argue that poor countries can become rich countries if they do certain things. Here are some factors that economists emphasize.

Free Trade Countries can hinder or promote international trade. For example, they hinder it when they impose tariffs or quotas on imports. They promote it when they eliminate tariffs, quotas, or anything else that prevents the free flow of resources and goods between countries. Free trade promotes the production of goods and services in a country and therefore spurs growth and development in two ways. Free trade allows residents of a country to buy inputs from the cheapest supplier, no matter where in the world it is located. Free trade also opens up a world market to domestic firms.

Low Taxation Generally, a country with relatively low taxes provides a greater incentive to workers to work and more incentive to investors to invest than does a country with relatively high taxes. As discussed earlier in the chapter, low-tax countries had an average growth rate in per capita income that was substantially higher than the average growth rate in per capita income of high-tax countries.

Absence of Restrictions on Foreign Investment
Some countries prevent foreigners from investing in their countries. For example, country X may pass a law stating that no one from any other country can invest there. Such restrictions on foreign investment often hamper economic growth and development. Allowing foreigners to invest in a country, to start or expand businesses, promotes growth and development.

Absence of Controls on Bank Lending Activity
Banks channel funds from those who save to those who want to invest and produce. In some countries, government tells banks to whom they can and cannot lend. For example, banks may not be able to lend to automobile manufacturers but be permitted to lend to steel manufacturers. Such restrictions may arise because the government in the country is trying to promote a particular industry.

Controls of this type often hinder growth and development. Banks have a monetary incentive to search out those individuals, firms, and industries that can repay any loans received. Often, these individuals, firms, and industries are the ones likely to be

Cooperative Learning

Divide students into small groups and assign each group four or five different countries. Each student in the group should research one of the factors that aid economic development and growth for the assigned countries. Groups should address the following questions: If a country does not have all the factors for economic development outlined in the text, is it doomed to economic failure? How many of these factors might a country need to implement to achieve economic success? If a country has already implemented these strategies, has it achieved, or will it achieve, economic success? Have each group prepare a chart showing each country's economic development strategies and the group's predictions for the country's future.

the most successful at producing goods and services and at generating employment.

Absence of Wage and Price Controls The free market determines equilibrium prices and wages. When government "overrides" the market and imposes controls on prices and wages, production usually suffers. Suppose the market wage for workers in a particular industry is $10 an hour, and the market price for the good produced in the industry is $40. At current wages and prices, firms are earning just enough profit to continue in business. Now suppose government says that these firms have to pay a minimum of $12 an hour to their workers and that they cannot charge more than $38 for their goods. It is likely that the firms will go out of business; the goods and services they once produced will no longer exist.

The United States usually exports more agricultural products than it imports, but it usually imports more manufactured goods than it exports. If you want to find the balance of trade for manufactured goods and for agricultural products, you can go to www.emcp.net/balanceoftrade and click on "U.S. Trade in Goods." At this site you can also find the top 50 purchasers of U.S. exports and the top 50 suppliers (to the United States) of imports. In 2004, the top three purchasers of U.S. exports were (in order) Canada, Mexico, and Japan. The top three suppliers of imports (to the United States) were Canada, China, and Mexico.

Simple, Easy Business Licensing Procedures Most countries require a person to have a business license before starting a business. In some countries, obtaining a business license is easy, involving the filling out of a few papers and payment of a nominal fee. In other countries it involves visiting government offices, filling out numerous documents, bribing government officials, and so on. The easier and cheaper it is to obtain a business license, the more new businesses will pop up. Historically, new businesses often promoted economic growth and development.

Protecting Private Property People will not work hard or invest in businesses unless they are reasonably sure that the property they amass from such endeavors is protected from expropriation (seizure by the government). Countries that protect private property often develop faster than those that do not.

SECTION 4 ASSESSMENT

Defining Terms

1. Define
   a. developed country
   b. less-developed country
   c. population growth rate

Reviewing Facts and Concepts

2. Why might people in less-developed countries have more children than people in developed countries?
3. What are some of the benefits of free trade to a less-developed country?

Critical Thinking

4. In country A, the government does not protect private property, taxes are high, and quotas and tariffs are imposed on imported goods. In country B, the government does protect private property, taxes are low, and free trade is practiced. In which country do you expect economic growth and development to be the stronger? Explain your answer.

Applying Economic Concepts

5. In this section we defined a poor or less-developed country as a country with a low per capita GDP. Does it follow that the people in a country with a low per capita GDP are not as happy as the people in a country with a high per capita GDP? Explain your answer.

Assessment Book

You will find a quiz for this section in the *Assessment Book.*

Reteaching Activity

Use the Section Assessment to gauge which students may need reteaching on this section. Instruct those students to work in groups to create a list of the ways that less-developed countries can develop. Students should include specific examples to illustrate the steps these countries could take to further economic growth and development.

Guided Reading

For further reteaching of the key concepts in this section, assign the Outlining Activity and the Just the Facts Handout from the *Guided Reading and Study Guide.*

SECTION 4 ASSESSMENT ANSWERS

Defining Terms

1. a. developed country: a country with a relatively high per capita GDP; **b. less-developed country:** a country with a relatively low per capita GDP; **c. population growth rate:** the birthrate minus the death rate.

Reviewing Facts and Concepts

2. In less-developed countries, the economy is often based on agriculture, and there are no pensions or social security programs to speak of. Children are more likely to be seen as necessary to help work on the farms and to take care of their parents in old age.
3. Free trade allows residents of a country to buy inputs from the cheapest supplier, no matter where in the world it is located; free trade opens a world market to domestic firms.

Critical Thinking

4. Economic growth and development is likely to be stronger in country B. According to most economists, there is ample evidence to support the view that countries grow and develop when private property is protected, when taxes are low, and when free trade is practiced.

Applying Economic Concepts

5. No. Happiness involves more than a high per capita GDP.

CHAPTER 15 Assessment Answers

Economics Vocabulary

1. tariff; **2.** quota; **3.** comparative advantage; **4.** balance of trade; **5.** Dumping; **6.** Absolute advantage; **7.** Appreciation; **8.** exchange rate; **9.** Depreciation; **10.** less-developed country; **11.** population growth rate.

Understanding the Main Ideas

1. If the demand increases for pesos, the price of a peso will rise. For example, instead of 1 peso = \$0.25, 1 peso = \$0.30. When a peso fetches more of another currency, it has appreciated in value.
2. The United States has a comparative advantage in food, Japan in clothing.
3. The low-foreign-wages argument states that U.S. producers cannot compete with companies in other countries that pay lower wages.
4. It means the United States is the low-cost producer of computers, or that the United States produces computers most cheaply.
5. A tariff raises the price of imported goods, so consumers would be expected to buy fewer imported goods. Therefore, consumers would buy fewer imported cars if a tariff were imposed on them.
6. Agree. To illustrate, suppose the exchange rate goes from £1 = \$1.75 to £1 = \$2. The pound has appreciated, because it now fetches more dollars and cents. The flip side of the coin is that the dollar fetches fewer pounds. At the first exchange rate, \$1 exchanges for £0.57 (that is, if £1 = \$1.75, then it follows that \$1 = £0.57), whereas at the second exchange rate, \$1 exchanges for £0.50.
7. Critics of the low-foreign-wages argument say that producers care about more than simply wages; they care about productivity, too. If foreign workers earn low wages and are less productive than U.S. workers who earn high wages, it is possible that a company would prefer to pay high wages to a productive workforce rather than pay low wages to a less productive workforce.

15 CHAPTER 15 ASSESSMENT

Chapter Summary

Be sure you know and remember the following key points from the chapter sections.

Section 1

- Exports are goods that are produced in the domestic country and sold to residents of a foreign country.
- Imports are goods produced in foreign countries and purchased by residents of the domestic country.
- A country's balance of trade is the difference between the value of its exports and imports.
- Countries specialize in production of goods in which they have comparative advantage.

Section 2

- Tariffs and quotas are the two major types of trade restrictions.
- A tariff is a tax on imports; a quota is a limit on the amount of a good that may be imported.

Section 3

- The exchange rate is the price of one nation's currency in terms of another nation's currency.
- Depreciation is a decrease in the value of one currency relative to other currencies.
- Appreciation is an increase in the value of one currency relative to other currencies, meaning it buys more of another currency.

Section 4

- A developed country is one with a relatively high GDP per capita; a less-developed country is one with a relatively low GDP or GNP per capita.
- Obstacles to economic development include rapid population growth, low savings rate, cultural beliefs, political instability and seizure of property, and high tax rates.
- Factors that aid development include free trade, low taxation, few restrictions on foreign investment or control on bank lending, absence of wage and price controls, easy business licensing procedures, and protection of private property.

Economics Vocabulary

To reinforce your knowledge of the key terms in this chapter, fill in the following blanks on a separate piece of paper with the appropriate word or phrase.

1. A(n) ______ is a tax on imports.
2. A legal limit on the amount of a good that may be imported (into a country) is called a(n) ______.
3. Country A has a(n) ______ in the production of a good if it can produce the good at lower opportunity cost than country B.
4. The ______ is the difference between the value of exports and the value of imports.
5. ______ refers to the sale of goods abroad at prices below their costs and below the price charged in the domestic market.
6. ______ refers to the situation in which a country can produce more of a good than another country can produce with the same quantity of resources.
7. ______ refers to an increase in the value of one currency relative to other currencies.
8. If one dollar buys two pesos, it is called the ______ between dollars and pesos.
9. ______ refers to a decrease in the value of one currency relative to other currencies.
10. A ______ is a country with a low per capita GDP.
11. The birthrate minus the death rate equals the ______.

Understanding the Main Ideas

Write answers to the following questions to review the main ideas in this chapter.

1. If exchange rates under a flexible exchange rate system are determined by the forces of supply and demand, will an increase in the demand for pesos cause the peso to appreciate or depreciate? Explain your answer.
2. The United States can produce either combination A (100 units of food and 0 units of clothing) or combination B (80 units of food and 20 units of clothing). Japan can produce combination C (80 units of food and 0 units of clothing)

8. –\$107 billion (*calculation:* Exports – imports = balance of trade). The United States has a negative balance of trade.
9. The national-defense argument states that certain industries should be protected because they are essential to the security of the United States.
10. A culture that would foster economic development would be one that was not afraid to depart from the status quo, took risks, and was not fatalistic. A culture that might hinder economic development would be the opposite. It would not want to move away from the status quo, it would shun risks, and it would be fatalistic. (That is, it would believe that a person's good or bad fortune in life depended more on fate or the spirits than on such things as how hard a person works.)

or combination D (75 units of food and 10 units of clothing). Which country has a comparative advantage in the production of food? Which country has a comparative advantage in the production of clothing?

3. State the low-foreign-wages argument for trade restrictions.
4. What does it mean to say that the United States has a comparative advantage in the production of computers?
5. After a tariff is imposed on imported cars, would you expect consumers to buy more or fewer imported cars, all other things remaining the same? Explain your answer.
6. If the pound appreciates relative to the U.S. dollar, the dollar must depreciate relative to the pound. Do you agree or disagree? Explain your answer.
7. What do critics of the low-foreign-wages argument for trade restrictions say?
8. If the value of U.S. exports is $103 billion and the value of U.S. imports is $210 million, what does the balance of trade equal?
9. State the national-defense argument for trade restrictions.
10. Describe a culture that would foster economic development. Describe a culture that would hinder economic development.
11. Is a fast-growing population necessarily an obstacle to economic development? Explain your answer.

Doing the Math

Do the calculations necessary to solve the following problems.

1. If the price of an Irish sweater is €30 and the dollar-euro exchange rate is $1 = €0.70, what does the sweater cost in dollars?
2. If the price of a U.S. car is $20,000 and the dollar-yen exchange rate is $1 = ¥129, what does the car cost in yen?
3. If the United States can produce either 20 units of clothing and 40 units of food or 60 units of clothing and 0 units of food, what is the opportunity cost of producing 1 unit of food?
4. If Brazil can produce either 100 units of clothing and 0 units of food or 30 units of clothing and 50 units of food, what is the opportunity cost of producing 1 unit of clothing?

Solving Economic Problems

Use your thinking skills and the information you learned in this chapter to find solutions to the following problems.

1. **Application.** Suppose the United States buys 1 million cars from Japan each year. If the dollar depreciates relative to the yen, will Americans buy more or fewer than 1 million cars from Japan? Explain your answer.
2. **Analysis.** Suppose that U.S. imports currently equal U.S. exports. Explain how a fall in the value of the dollar in comparison to other currencies can affect the current U.S. balance of trade.
3. **Cause and Effect.** Over a six-month period you notice that the dollar appreciates in value compared to other currencies and that the U.S. balance of trade goes from zero to −$30 billion. You suspect some relationship exists between the change in the value of the dollar and the U.S. balance of trade. Did the change in the balance of trade cause the change in the value of the dollar, or did the change in the value of the dollar cause the change in the balance of trade? Explain your answer.
4. **Writing.** Suppose the people in Houston buy more goods from the people in Los Angeles than vice versa. This is not "news." Write a one-page paper that answers this question: Why is a city-to-city trade balance not news but a country-to-country trade balance is?

Practice Tests and Study Guide

Go to www.emcp.net/economics and choose *Economics: New Ways of Thinking,* Chapter 15, if you need more help in preparing for the chapter test.

11. No, many of the developed countries today witnessed faster population growth rates when they were developing than the less-developed countries do today. Also, some countries with high-density populations are richer than some countries with low-density populations.

Doing the Math

1. $42.85 (*calculation:* 30 ÷ 0.7 = 42.85).
2. 2.58 million yen (*calculation:* 20,000 × 129 = 2.58 million).
3. 1 unit of clothing (*calculation:* 20 ÷ (60 – 40) = 1).
4. 0.71 unit of food (*calculation:* 50 ÷ (100 – 30) = 0.71).

Solving Economic Problems

1. The United States will buy fewer than 1 million cars. If the dollar depreciates relative to the yen, the price of Japanese cars increases for Americans. As a result of the higher price of Japanese cars, Americans will buy fewer (according to the law of demand).
2. If the dollar depreciates in comparison to other currencies, it follows that other currencies appreciate in value. A depreciated dollar makes foreign-produced goods more expensive for Americans and makes U.S. goods cheaper for foreigners. As a result of more-expensive foreign imported goods, Americans will buy fewer imports. As a result of less-expensive U.S. goods, foreigners will buy more U.S. goods. Conclusion: U.S. exports will rise, and U.S. imports will fall. As a result, the United States will have a positive balance of trade.
3. The change in the value of the dollar caused the change in the balance of trade. To understand this concept, remember that if the dollar appreciates in value, foreign goods become cheaper for Americans, who therefore buy more foreign (imported) goods. In contrast, because the dollar has appreciated, some foreign currencies have depreciated (relative to the dollar). This situation has made it more expensive for foreigners to buy U.S. goods; therefore, they cut back on their purchases of U.S. goods. As a result, the United States exports fewer goods. To put things together, the dollar appreciation stimulates import buying and restrains export selling. We started with a zero balance of trade (where value of exports equals value of imports), so now the value of imports must be greater than the value of exports, and the United States must be running a negative balance of trade.
4. Answers will vary. Students may suggest that different currencies are involved when different countries are involved. Thus no one cares if some Americans buy more from some other Americans, but they do care if Americans buy more from the Japanese, Mexicans, or English.

Chapter 16 Planning Guide

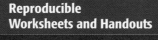

SECTION ORGANIZER

Section	Learning Objectives	Reproducible Worksheets and Handouts	Assessment
 **Stocks** (pages 430–441)	▸ Define stocks. ▸ Describe where and how stocks are bought and sold. ▸ Explain the Dow Jones Industrial Average. ▸ Understand what it means to "buy the market."	Section 1 Activity, *Applying the Principles Workbook* Outlining Activity, *Guided Reading and Study Guide* Just the Facts Handout, *Guided Reading and Study Guide*	Section Assessment, *Student Text,* page 441 Quick Quiz, *Annotated Teacher's Edition,* page 440 Section Quiz, *Assessment Book*
 **Bonds** (pages 442–449)	▸ Define bonds. ▸ Identify the factor that determines the rating of a bond. ▸ Explain the relationship between interest rates and the price of bonds. ▸ Identify various types of bonds. ▸ Explain the relationship between risk and return. ▸ Explain why financial markets are important.	 Section 2 Activity, *Applying the Principles Workbook* 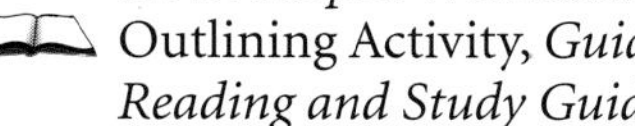 Outlining Activity, *Guided Reading and Study Guide* Just the Facts Handout, *Guided Reading and Study Guide*	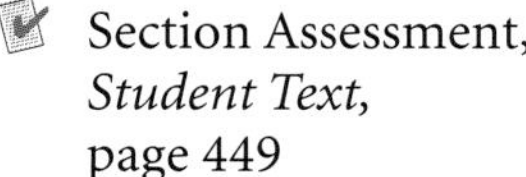 Section Assessment, *Student Text,* page 449 Quick Quiz, *Annotated Teacher's Edition,* page 448 Section Quiz, *Assessment Book*
 **Futures and Options** (pages 450–455)	▸ Explain futures contracts. ▸ Explain why people buy futures contracts. ▸ Explain a currency futures contract. ▸ Explain an options contract. ▸ Describe the difference between a put option and a call option. ▸ Identify the reason an investor would use a put or a call option.	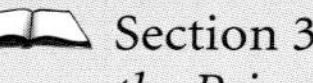 Section 3 Activity, *Applying the Principles Workbook* Outlining Activity, *Guided Reading and Study Guide* Just the Facts Handout, *Guided Reading and Study Guide*	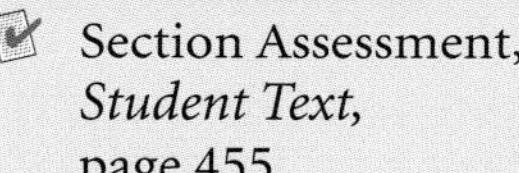 Section Assessment, *Student Text,* page 455 Quick Quiz, *Annotated Teacher's Edition,* pages 454–455 Section Quiz, *Assessment Book*

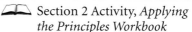

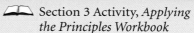

CHAPTER AND PROGRAM RESOURCES

Reproducible Chapter Resources and Assessment Materials

 Graphic Organizer Activity, *Guided Reading and Study Guide*

 Vocabulary Activity, *Guided Reading and Study Guide*

 Working with Graphs and Charts, *Guided Reading and Study Guide*

Practice Test, *Guided Reading and Study Guide*

 Critical Thinking Activity, *Finding Economics*

 Chapter Test A, *Assessment Book*

Chapter Test B, *Assessment Book*

Technology Resources

 *Test Generator CD*

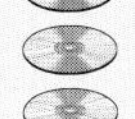 *Spanish Audio Summaries CD*

Marketplace® Audio Lessons CD

Economic Principles Lectures, Videocassette or DVD

Lesson Planning and Teaching Resources

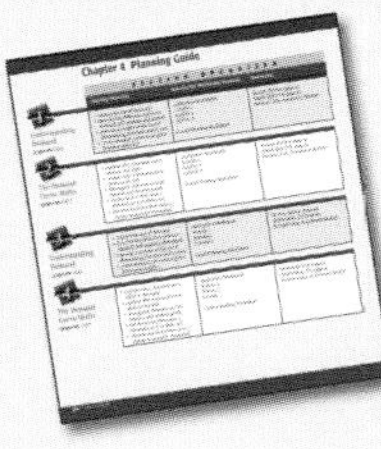

The *Economics: New Ways of Thinking* Teacher Resources include detailed lesson plans for each section in this chapter; the lesson plans are available in print form *(Lesson Plans)* and electronic form. The Teacher Resources also include *Daily Lectures: Overheads and Notes,* which provides prepared overheads and discussion notes covering the key concepts in each section of this chapter.

EMC Publishing Economics Online

Go to Economics Online, at www.emcp.com, for a variety of Internet resources to help you keep your course current and relevant. At Economics Online you will find these items:

- Economics in the News Lessons
- Study Guide Questions
- Practice Tests
- Lesson Plans

Internet Resources

Economics: New Ways of Thinking encourages students to use the Internet to find out more about economics. With the wealth of current, valid information available on Web sites, using the Internet as a research tool is likely to increase your students' interest in and understanding of economics principles and topics. In addition, doing Internet research can help your students form the habit of accessing and using economics information, as well as help them develop investigative skills they will use throughout their educational and professional careers.

To aid your students in achieving these ends, each chapter of *Economics: New Ways of Thinking* includes the addresses of several Web sites at which students will find engaging, relevant information. When students type in the addresses provided, they will immediately arrive at the intended sites. The addresses have been modified so that EMC Publishing can monitor and maintain the proper links—for example, the government site http://stats.bls.gov/ has been changed to www.emcp.net/prices. In the event that the address or content of a site changes or is discontinued, EMC's Internet editors will create a link that redirects students to an address with similar information.

Activities in the *Annotated Teacher's Edition* often suggest that students search the Internet for information. For some activities, you might want to find reputable sites beforehand, and steer students to those sites. For other activities, you might want students to do their own searching, and then check out the sites they have found and discuss why they might be reliable or unreliable.

CHAPTER 16 Overview

Stocks and bonds are an important commodity for both businesses and individuals. This chapter describes the different kinds of stocks and bonds and discusses their role in the economic system.

Stocks

Section 1 of this chapter discusses the stock market—how to buy and sell stock, how to predict changes in stock value, and what it means when changes occur.

Bonds

This section will answer questions about bonds and the bond market. Students will learn how to buy and sell bonds and the relationship between interest rates and bond prices.

Futures and Options

The final section of this chapter details investments known as futures and options. It will discuss the differences between futures and options and the risks and benefits of investing in each.

CHAPTER 16 Stocks and Bonds

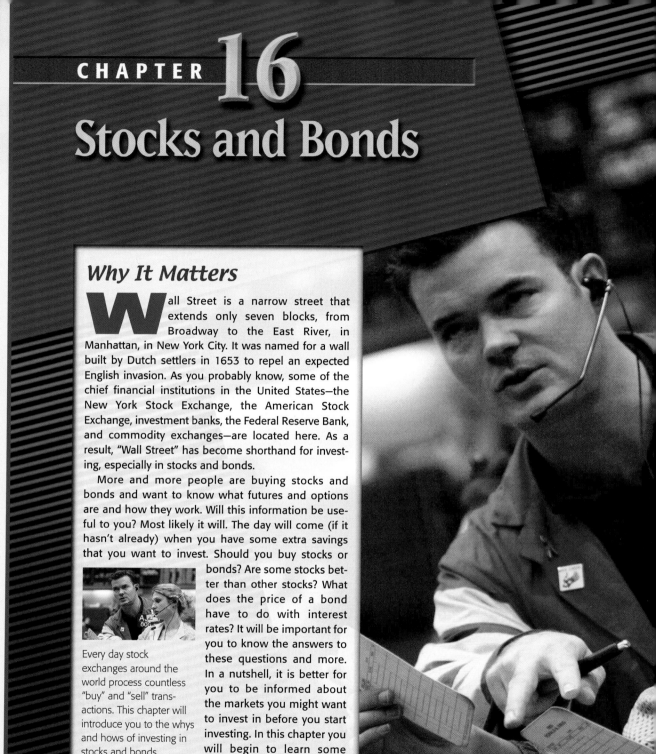

Why It Matters

Wall Street is a narrow street that extends only seven blocks, from Broadway to the East River, in Manhattan, in New York City. It was named for a wall built by Dutch settlers in 1653 to repel an expected English invasion. As you probably know, some of the chief financial institutions in the United States—the New York Stock Exchange, the American Stock Exchange, investment banks, the Federal Reserve Bank, and commodity exchanges—are located here. As a result, "Wall Street" has become shorthand for investing, especially in stocks and bonds.

More and more people are buying stocks and bonds and want to know what futures and options are and how they work. Will this information be useful to you? Most likely it will. The day will come (if it hasn't already) when you have some extra savings that you want to invest. Should you buy stocks or bonds? Are some stocks better than other stocks? What does the price of a bond have to do with interest rates? It will be important for you to know the answers to these questions and more. In a nutshell, it is better for you to be informed about the markets you might want to invest in before you start investing. In this chapter you will begin to learn some investment basics.

Every day stock exchanges around the world process countless "buy" and "sell" transactions. This chapter will introduce you to the whys and hows of investing in stocks and bonds.

Teaching Suggestions from the Author

Students of today are somewhat different from students of 20 or even 10 years ago. Today, students hear much about the stock market, the bond market, futures, and options. Every night on the news the anchor reports whether the Dow (Dow Jones Industrial Average) is up or down. Every night the anchor reports on the NASDAQ (National Association of Securities Dealers Automated Quotations). Students know that investing in the stock market has become a boom industry in the United States. They know that thousands of people today invest online.

Students come to this chapter with a natural curiosity. They want to know what the Dow is and why it goes up and down. They want to know what the NASDAQ is.

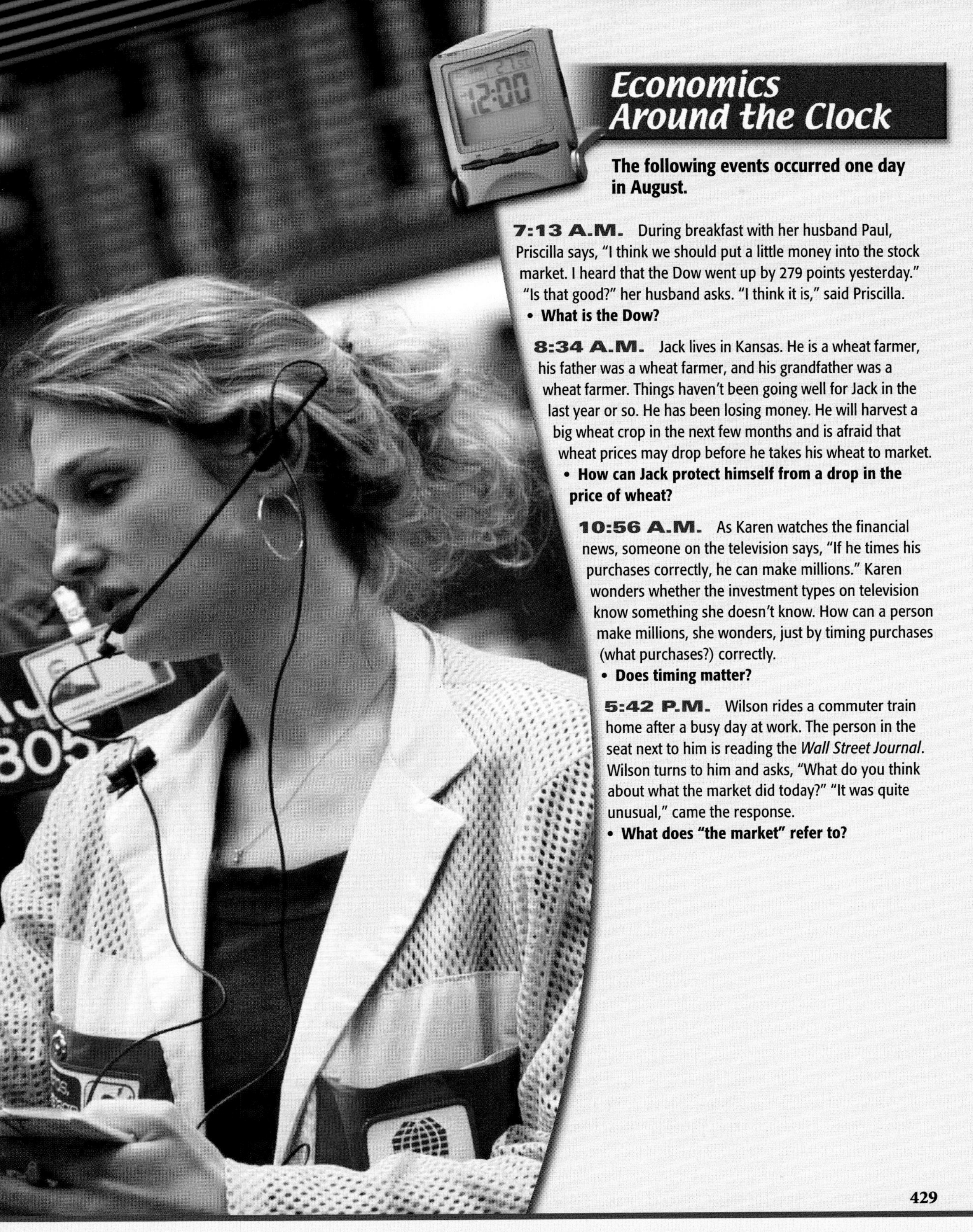

Economics Around the Clock

The following events occurred one day in August.

7:13 A.M. During breakfast with her husband Paul, Priscilla says, "I think we should put a little money into the stock market. I heard that the Dow went up by 279 points yesterday." "Is that good?" her husband asks. "I think it is," said Priscilla.
- **What is the Dow?**

8:34 A.M. Jack lives in Kansas. He is a wheat farmer, his father was a wheat farmer, and his grandfather was a wheat farmer. Things haven't been going well for Jack in the last year or so. He has been losing money. He will harvest a big wheat crop in the next few months and is afraid that wheat prices may drop before he takes his wheat to market.
- **How can Jack protect himself from a drop in the price of wheat?**

10:56 A.M. As Karen watches the financial news, someone on the television says, "If he times his purchases correctly, he can make millions." Karen wonders whether the investment types on television know something she doesn't know. How can a person make millions, she wonders, just by timing purchases (what purchases?) correctly.
- **Does timing matter?**

5:42 P.M. Wilson rides a commuter train home after a busy day at work. The person in the seat next to him is reading the *Wall Street Journal*. Wilson turns to him and asks, "What do you think about what the market did today?" "It was quite unusual," came the response.
- **What does "the market" refer to?**

Introducing the Chapter

Over the lifetime of your students, the Dow Jones Industrial Average, a leading indicator for the New York Stock Exchange, has risen more than 10,000 points. People have become very excited over the rising stock market, and in fact, overexcitement has caused the stock market to have huge fluctuations, much larger than the dip in 1929. This chapter was written to give students a sense of how the stock market works.

Teaching with Visuals

The trading floor of the New York Stock Exchange is a hectic place. People working on the floor carry out the many stock purchases and sales that take place each day.

They want to learn how to buy stocks (even if they don't have the money right now to buy stocks). They want to know the difference between a bond and a stock or between a future contract and an option.

I've often thought that we can do our students a big service if we get them to develop the habit of keeping track of financial matters. We can instill that habit in them if we present the material in this chapter in an interesting and exciting way.

SECTION 1 Teacher Support

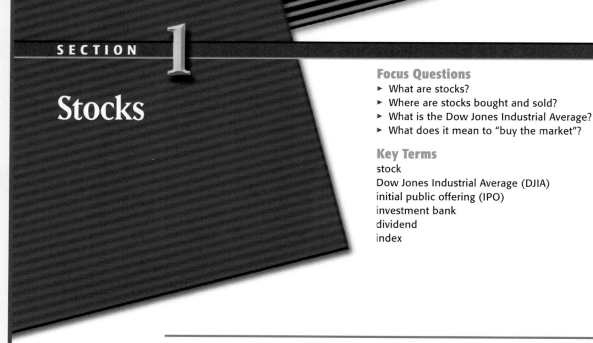

Focus and Motivate

Section Objectives

After completing this section, students will be able to
- define stocks;
- describe where and how stocks are bought and sold;
- explain the Dow Jones Industrial Average; and
- understand what it means to "buy the market."

Economics Around the Clock

Kickoff Activity

Refer students to the 7:13 A.M. scenario in Economics Around the Clock (page 429) and tell them to guess the answer to the question, using their prior knowledge of the stock market.

Activating Prior Knowledge

Discuss students' guesses about what the Dow is. Invite volunteers to share any experiences with the stock market that they have had themselves or through their parents. Tell students that the Dow refers to the Dow Jones Industrial Average (DJIA), a weighted average of 30 widely traded stocks on the New York Stock Exchange. The Dow is viewed as an indicator of day-to-day stock market activity.

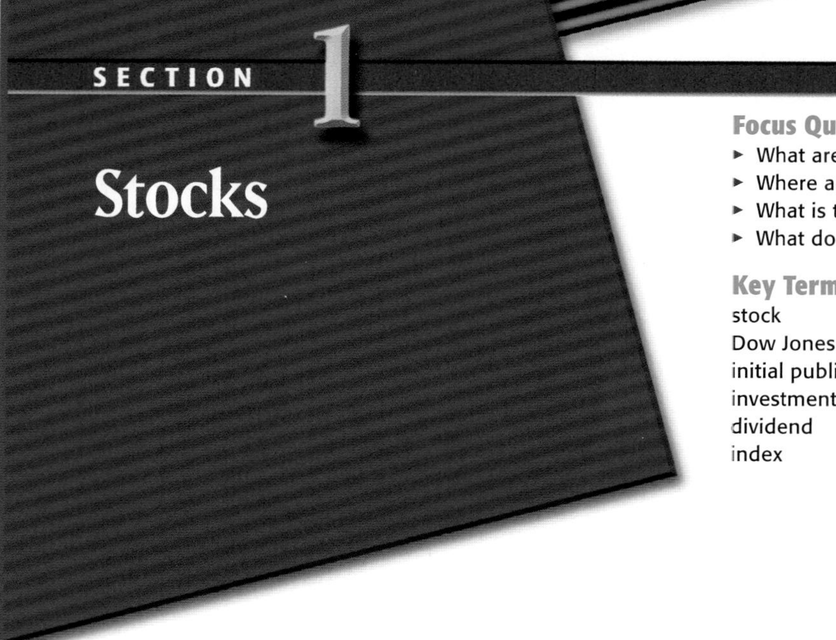

SECTION 1 Stocks

Focus Questions
- What are stocks?
- Where are stocks bought and sold?
- What is the Dow Jones Industrial Average?
- What does it mean to "buy the market"?

Key Terms
stock
Dow Jones Industrial Average (DJIA)
initial public offering (IPO)
investment bank
dividend
index

Financial Markets

Everyone has heard of stocks and bonds. Everyone knows that stocks and bonds can be sold and purchased, but not everyone knows the economic purpose served by stocks and bonds.

Buying and selling stocks and bonds occurs in a financial market. Financial markets serve the purpose of channeling money from some people to other people. Suppose Jones saved $10,000 over two years and that Smith is just starting a new company. Smith needs some money to get the new company up and running. On the other hand, Jones would like to invest the savings and receive a return. Jones and Smith may not know each other; in fact, they may live on opposite ends of the country. What a financial market does, though, is bring these two people together. It allows Jones either to invest in Smith's company or to lend Smith some money. For example, Jones might buy stock in Smith's company or perhaps buy a bond that Smith's company is issuing. In this chapter you will learn more about the ways in which people like Smith and Jones help each other through use of the financial markets.

stock
A claim on the assets of a corporation that gives the purchaser a share of the corporation.

What Are Stocks?

What does it mean when someone tells you that she owns 100 shares of a particular stock? For example, suppose Jane owns 100 shares of Yahoo! stock. It means that she is a part owner in Yahoo!, Inc., which is a global Internet media company that offers a network of World Wide Web programming. A **stock** is a claim on the assets of a corporation that gives the purchaser a share in the corporation.

Jane, in this example, is not an owner in the sense that she can walk into Yahoo! headquarters (in Santa Clara, California) and start issuing orders. She cannot hire or fire anyone, and she cannot decide what the company will or will not do over the next few months or years. Still, she is an owner, and as an owner she can, if she wants, sell her ownership rights in Yahoo!. All she has to do is find a buyer for her 100 shares of stock. Most likely, she could do so in a matter of minutes, if not seconds.

Background Information: New York Stock Exchange

For more than 100 years, the main measuring stick for the New York Stock Exchange has been the Dow Jones Industrial Average. For the first 50 of those years, the Dow grew relatively slowly. In fact, with a starting index of 40.94 points on May 26, 1896, the Dow had only gained 460 points by March 12, 1956. In the next 40 years, the Dow increased from 500 points to almost 6,000 in October of 1996. In December 2005 it was over 10,000.

A Student Asks

QUESTION: *If I buy shares of stock, do I have to hold on to them for any set period of time? Also, where can I buy shares of stock?*

ANSWER: *No, you can buy shares of stock at 10:12 in the morning and sell those shares five minutes later if you want to. As for buying stock, you can buy stock through a stock broker—in person, on the phone, or online. For example, many people today buy stocks from an online broker. They simply go online, open an account with an online broker, deposit funds into that account, and then buy and sell stock.*

▲ The interior and exterior of the New York Stock Exchange. Stocks of close to 3,000 companies, valued at nearly $20 trillion, are traded on the exchange.

Where Is Stock Bought and Sold?

You know where groceries are bought and sold—at the grocery store. You know where clothes are bought and sold—at the clothing store. But where are stocks bought and sold?

Let's go back in time to help answer the question. In 1792, 24 men met under a buttonwood tree on what is now Wall Street in New York City. They essentially bought and sold stock (for themselves and their customers) at this location. Someone might have said, "I want to sell 20 shares in company X. Are you willing to buy these shares at $2 a share?"

From this humble beginning came the New York Stock Exchange (NYSE). Every weekday (excluding holidays) men and women meet at the NYSE in New York City and buy and sell stock.

Suppose you own 100 shares of a stock listed on the NYSE. Do you have to go to the NYSE in New York to sell it? No, you would simply contact a stock broker (either over the phone, in person, or online) and he or she would convey your wishes to sell the stock to a person at the NYSE itself. That person at the NYSE would then execute your order.

In addition to the NYSE where stocks are bought and sold, other stock exchanges and markets also serve as a place to trade stocks and bonds, including the American Stock Exchange (AMEX) and the NASDAQ (pronounced NAZ-dak) stock market. NASDAQ stands for National Association of Securities Dealers Automated Quotations. Buying and selling stock on the NASDAQ does not take place the same way it takes place on the NYSE. Instead of the buying and selling occurring in one central location, NASDAQ is an electronic stock market with trades executed through a sophisticated computer and telecommunications network. The NYSE might in fact change to this kind of market in the near future. Instead of people meeting together in one location to buy and sell stock, they could simply do it electronically.

Increasingly, Americans are not only buying and selling stocks on U.S. stock exchanges and markets, but in foreign stock exchanges and markets too. For example, an American might buy a stock listed on the German Stock Exchange, the Montreal Stock Exchange, or the Swiss Exchange.

The Dow Jones Industrial Average (DJIA)

You may have heard news commentators say, "The Dow fell 302 points on heavy trading." They are talking about the Dow Jones Industrial Average. The **Dow Jones Industrial Average (DJIA)** first appeared on the scene more than 100 years ago, on

Dow Jones Industrial Average (DJIA)
The most popular, widely cited indicator of day-to-day stock market activity. The DJIA is a weighted average of 30 widely traded stocks on the New York Stock Exchange.

Teach

Discussion Starter

Explain to students that stocks are simply claims of ownership in a corporation. Remind them also that due to the telecommunications revolution, stocks can be bought and sold anywhere a stock market exists. Ask students to make a list of companies in which they would like to have partial ownership by buying stock.

A Student Asks

Later in this section, students will learn how to access a stock broker's services.

Background Information

The difference between the NASDAQ Stock Market and the New York Stock Exchange is that the NYSE is housed in an actual building on Wall Street, and NASDAQ is an electronic stock market with trades executed through computer and telecommunications software.

Cooperative Learning

Divide students into groups of three or four. Each group should research one major stock exchange and then create a visual representation of how the stock market works. They can show the process on a chart or poster or they can act out all of the actions in the stock market. Allow students to be as creative as possible but at the same time accurately represent how each market works. Make sure each group shows how its market is different from the other markets.

Teaching with Visuals

Charles Dow created the Dow Jones Industrial Average to convey information about what was happening in the stock market. It serves the same purpose today.

Discussion Starter

Ask students if they think that there is a need for multiple stock exchanges. Encourage them to identify advantages and disadvantages of having multiple exchanges, and then of having a single exchange. Students might mention that if all stocks were sold on a single exchange, the list of offerings would be enormous, and buyers and sellers might be more likely to overlook small offerings from small companies.

Reinforcement Activity

Charles Henry Dow was co-founder of Dow Jones & Company and creator of the Dow Jones Industrial Average. He began his journalism career as a reporter with the *Springfield* (MA) *Daily Republican* and soon became an assistant editor. In 1875 he left Springfield to join the Providence (RI) *Morning Star and Evening Press*. There he met Edward Jones, and in 1882 they formed Dow Jones & Company. In 1896 Dow came up with the idea for the Dow Jones Industrial Average.

Allow students to work in groups to research more information about Charles Dow and Edward Jones. They can present their information to the class in oral presentations.

Prediction Activity

Invite students to consider the following scenario: It has just been announced that personal income in the United States is higher than expected. Do you predict that this announcement will have any effect on the Dow? Explain your answer.

Students should understand that a higher-than-expected increase in personal income often causes the Dow to rise. Stock investors think that higher incomes will cause people to spend more, and more spending is good for business. Therefore, investors think this would be a good time to buy stock, and stock prices rise as demand increases.

EXHIBIT 16-1 The 30 Stocks of the Dow Jones Industrial Average

3M Company	Intel Corporation
Alcoa Incorporated	International Business Machines Corporation
Altria Group, Inc.	J. P. Morgan Chase and Company
American Express	Johnson & Johnson
American International Group, Inc.	McDonald's Corporation
Boeing Company	Merck & Company, Inc.
Caterpillar Incorporated	Microsoft Corporation
Citigroup Incorporated	Pfizer Incorporated
Coca-Cola Company	Procter & Gamble Company
DuPont	SBC Communications Incorporated
Exxon Mobil Corporation	United Technologies Corporation
General Electric Company	Verizon Communications, Inc.
General Motors Corporation	Wal-Mart Stores Incorporated
Hewlett-Packard Company	Walt Disney Company
Home Depot Incorporated	
Honeywell International, Inc.	

▲ **Why did Charles Dow create the Dow Jones Industrial Average? What purpose does it serve today?**

May 26, 1896. It was devised by Charles H. Dow. Dow took 11 stocks, summed their prices on a particular day, and then divided by 11. The "average price" was the DJIA. (Some of the original companies included American Cotton Oil, Chicago Gas, National Lead, and U.S. Rubber.)

When Charles Dow first computed the DJIA, the stock market was not highly regarded in the United States. Prudent investors bought bonds, not stocks. Stocks were thought to be the area in which speculators and conniving Wall Street operators plied their trade. It was thought back then that Wall Streeters managed stock prices to make themselves better off at the expense of others. A lot of gossip surrounded what was and was not happening in the stock market.

Dow devised the DJIA to convey some information about what was actually happening in the stock market. Before the DJIA, people had a hard time figuring out whether the stock market, on average, was rising or falling. Instead, they only knew that a particular stock went up or down by so many cents or dollars. Dow decided to find an average price of a certain number of stocks (11) that he thought would largely mirror what was happening in the stock market as a whole. With this number, people could then have some sense of what the stock market was doing on any given day.

Today, the DJIA consists of 30 stocks, which are widely held by individuals and institutional investors. See Exhibit 16-1. This list can and does change from time to time, as determined by the editors of the *Wall Street Journal*.

You may think that the DJIA is computed by summing the prices of stocks and dividing by 30, but it is not quite that simple today. A special divisor is used to avoid distortions that can occur, such as companies splitting their stock shares. Exhibit 16-2 shows the Dow Jones Industrial Average during the period 1928 through June 2005.

In addition to the DJIA, other prominent stock indices (beside the Dow) are cited in the United States. A few include the NASDAQ Composite, the Standard & Poor's 500, the Russell 2000, and the Wilshire 5000. Other prominent stock indices around the world include the Hang Seng (in Hong Kong), the Bovespa (Brazil), IPC (Mexico), BSE 30 (India), CAC 40 (France), and so on.

Different economic consulting firms attempt to find out what influences the Dow: What causes it to go up? What causes it to go down? According to many economists, the Dow is closely connected to changes in such things as consumer credit, business expectations, exports and imports, personal income, and the money supply. For example, increases in consumer credit are expected to push up the Dow, the thought being that when consumer credit rises, people will buy more goods and services, which is good for the companies that sell goods and services. When consumer credit falls, the reverse happens.

Differentiating Instruction

Kinesthetic Learners

If you show students a videotape of the floor of a stock exchange, they will see people flashing hand signals to each other. Ask students why flashing hand signals would be so important on the stock market floor. (*Answer:* Brokers need to be able to communicate across distances in a loud environment.) Have some of your kinesthetic learners research the hand signals of the trading floor and their meanings. They can come to class and demonstrate the signals for the rest of the students.

EXHIBIT 16-2 **Dow Jones Industrial Average: 1928–June 2005***

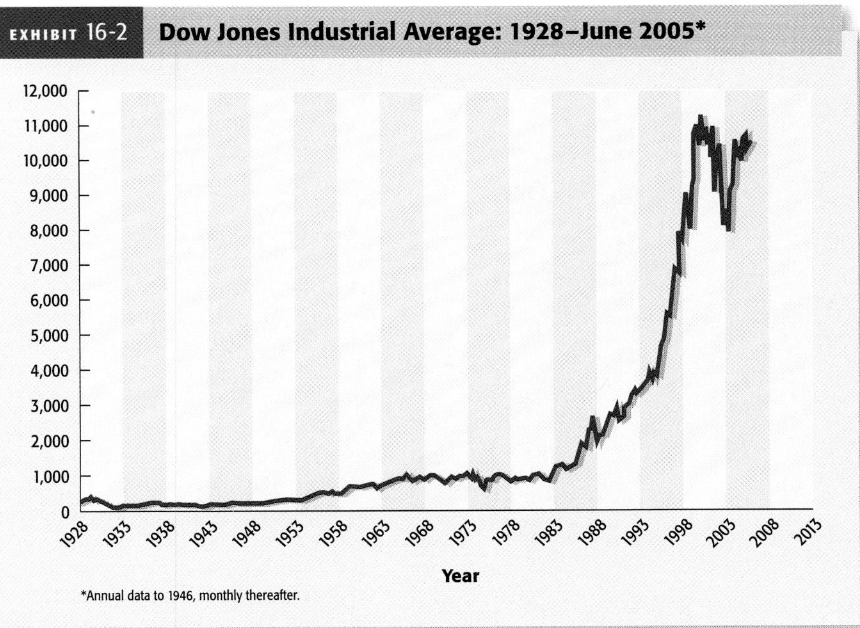

*Annual data to 1946, monthly thereafter.

◀ **When would have been a good time to have purchased shares in the companies making up the DJIA? When would have been a good time to sell? (There's more than one answer to each question.)**

A Student Asks

QUESTION: *I own a few stocks as a result of some gifts I received from my grandparents. None are included in the Dow Jones Industrial Average. Does it affect me when the Dow goes up or down, even if I do not own any of the stocks that make up the DJIA?*

ANSWER: *It doesn't affect you if we are looking at daily changes, but if we are talking about a long decline or a long rise in the DJIA, then it indirectly affects you. Many economists say that what happens in the stock market—or to the DJIA—is a sign of future economic events. In other words, if the DJIA goes down over time, it indicates that the economic future is somewhat depressed; if it goes up over time, it indicates that the economic future looks good. The economic future, good or bad, is something that does affect you. It affects prices you pay, how easy or hard it is to get a job, how large or small a raise in income you get, and so on.*

How the Stock Market Works

Suppose a company wants to raise money so that it can invest in a new product or a new manufacturing technique. It can do one of three things to get the money. First, it can go to a bank and borrow the money. Second, it can borrow the money by issuing a bond (a promise to repay the borrowed money with interest; you will learn more about bonds later in the chapter). Third, it can sell or issue stock in the company, or put another way, it sells part of the company. Stocks are also called *equity* because the buyer of the stock has part ownership of the company.

"Everyone has the brainpower to follow the stock market. If you made it through fifth-grade math, you can do it."
— PETER LYNCH

When a company is initially formed, the owners set up a certain amount of stock, which is worth little. The owners of the company try to find people (usually friends and associates) who would be willing to buy the stock (on the hopes that one day it will be worth something). It would be nearly

A Student Asks

You may want to use this A Student Asks to make sure students understand that daily changes in stock value are normal and that long-term investors are more affected by broad changes over time.

Teaching with Visuals

Have students study Exhibit 16-2 and then answer the questions. Answers will vary. Students should understand that it makes sense to buy stock when values are low and sell stock when values are high.

Reinforcement Activity

The Dow Jones Industrial Average is an average of 30 stocks. Assign students to research how these stocks have been determined over the years and answer the following questions: Are there any stocks that have remained the same through the entire history of the Dow? Which of the current stocks has been a part of the Dow for the longest time? For the shortest time?

Economics Around the Clock

After reading and discussing financial markets, you may want to refer students to the 5:42 P.M. scenario in Economics Around the Clock (page 429) and discuss their answers to the question provided there.

Students should recognize that in the context of financial issues, *the market* usually refers to a stock index, such as the Dow or the Standard & Poor's 500. When the Dow goes down, someone might say, "The market is down today."

Differentiating Instruction

Kinesthetic and Visual Learners

Play a stock market game like the following one: Tell students they have a fixed amount of play money to invest, and set an end date at which the game will be over. Assign students to research companies and buy imaginary stocks with this money. To add more interest to the game, allow students to set up their own imaginary companies and then buy capital, monitor their investments over the course of the game, and sell and trade stock (with you serving as the broker) to increase their holdings. Give students a certain amount of time each day (and perhaps before and after school) to make their trades. On the last day of the game, students sell their stock at that day's values, and the one with the most money wins a prize.

Teaching with Visuals

Answers will vary. Students will probably say the founding partners of Google needed additional money to expand the business and increase profits.

Reinforcement Activity

In the last few years, some companies and their stocks have been so anticipated that their initial public offering prices have skyrocketed past usual numbers. Some companies have raised their IPO several times before their stock was actually sold because the demand for it was perceived as being very high. Assign students to research some recent IPOs and answer the following questions: What is the highest IPO stock price you found? Would you be willing to spend that kind of money for one share of stock that had never been traded before? What information would influence your decision?

Background Information

Ask students whether events in other countries might influence the Dow. Give them this example of one way foreign events influence the index: Suppose we learn that one of the companies currently listed in the Dow will face stiffer competition in Spain next year because of the emergence of a new company there. As a result, the market value of its stock falls and, because it is one of the 30 stocks that compose the Dow, the Dow ends up dropping.

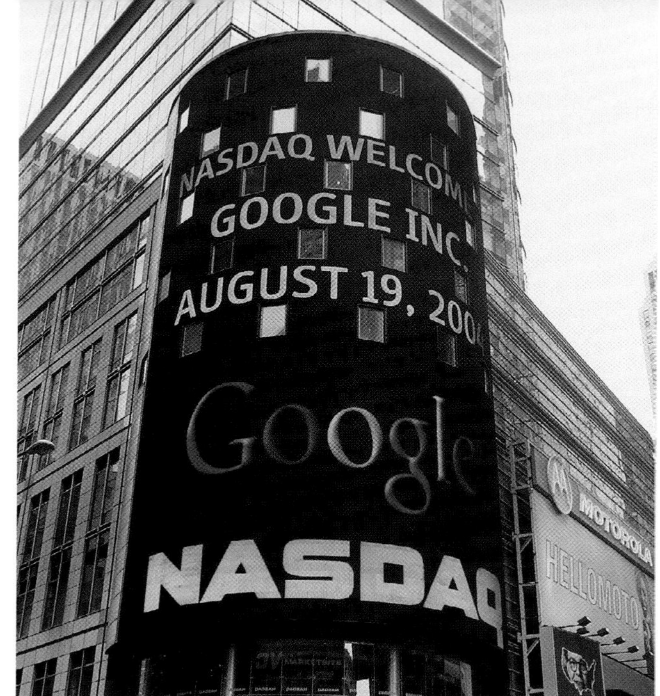

▲ The IPO for Google took place on August 19, 2004. **Why do you think the founding partners of Google decided to sell stock in their company?**

impossible in these early days of the company for anyone who owned stock to sell it. For example, if Alvarez owned 100 shares of some new company that almost no one had heard of, hardly anyone would be willing to pay any money to buy the stock.

As the company grows, and needs more money, it may decide to offer its stock on the open market. In other words, it offers its stock to anyone who wants to buy it. By this time, the company may be better known, making people more willing to buy it. The company makes what is called an **initial public offering (IPO)** of its stock. The process is quite simple. Usually an **investment bank** sells the stock for the company for an initial price, say $10 a share. How do you find out about an IPO? They are announced in the *Wall Street Journal.*

initial public offering (IPO)
A company's first offering of stock to the public

investment bank
Firm that acts as an intermediary between the company that issues the stock and the public that wishes to buy the stock.

When an IPO occurs for a stock, it is usually traded on a stock exchange or in an electronic stock market. Sometimes the stock that initially sold for $10 will rise in price and sometimes it will fall like a rock. It all depends on what people in the stock market think the company that initially issued the stock will do in the future.

If they think the company is destined for big earnings, the stock will likely rise in price. If they think the company is destined for losses, or only marginal earnings, the stock will likely fall in price. In a way, you can think of trading stock in much the same way you think about trading baseball cards, or paintings, or anything else. The price depends on the forces of supply and demand. If demand rises, and supply is constant, then the price of the stock will rise. If demand falls, and supply is constant, then the price of the stock will fall.

Sometimes people buy certain stocks because they hear that other people are buying the stock and because they think that the stock is "hot." In other words, it is popular and everyone wants it. In the 1990s, some of the Internet stocks fit this description. Stocks such as Yahoo!, Amazon.com, and eBay were bought because people thought the Internet was the wave of the future and almost anything connected with the Internet was destined for great profit.

More often, though, people buy a particular stock if they think that the earnings of the company that initially issued the stock are likely to rise. After all, remember that a share of stock represents ownership in a company. The more profitable that company is expected to be, the more likely people are going to want to own that company, and therefore the greater the demand for the stock of that company.

EXAMPLE: Suppose William Welch started a company in 1895. Through the years, the company was passed down to family members. In 2005, the family members running the company want to expand it to two, three, or four times its current size. Where might they get the money for this expansion? One way is by selling shares in the company, that is, by issuing stock in the company. Once they issue shares in the company to the public, the company is no longer solely family owned. Now many of the public own part of it too. ♦

People who work on Wall Street often use their own "language." For "translations" of some of that language, see Exhibit 16-3 on page 436.

Cooperative Learning

Divide students into groups of three or four. Tell them they are now a financial advisory board that wants to help Kirk (the investor) with his investment portfolio. Kirk has $50,000 to invest and no previous experience with the stock market.

Instruct students to prepare different strategies for Kirk, detailing how he could invest his money and how much he could expect in returns. Tell students that the more specific they are with the suggestions on the investments Kirk should make, and the higher the returns, the more likely Kirk will hire them as his financial advisors. Have them prepare and turn in a summary of their advice to Kirk.

434 Chapter 16 Stocks and Bonds

Economics in the Real World

Was the Great Crash the Culprit?

On Thursday, October 24, 1929, the *New York Times* ran a headline that read "Prices of Stocks Crash in Heavy Liquidation." Elsewhere in the *Times* a headline read "Many Accounts Wiped Out." These headlines referred to the stock market crash (sometimes simply called the Great Crash) that began on that October day in 1929 and continued on October 28 and 29.

In some historical accounts and in the minds of many members of the public, the stock market crash in 1929 was what caused the Great Depression that followed. However, this cause-and-effect assumption is not true, and it points out the *post hoc ergo propter hoc* logical fallacy. *Post hoc ergo propter hoc* is Latin for "After this, therefore as a result of this." Stated differently, it means "That which comes before another must be its cause." For example, if X comes before Y, then X is the cause of Y. This statement is not necessarily true.

Think of some simple examples. The teacher gives you a test before it rains, but the teacher's giving you a test does not cause the rain. Similarly, just because the stock market crash came before the many years of the Great Depression does not necessarily mean that the stock market crash caused the Great Depression. In fact, most economists believe that both the stock market crash and the Great Depression (with such things as rising unemployment and falling incomes) were effects of the same causes. In other words, the same factors caused both the stock market crash and the Great Depression.

However, the stock market crash did change the psychological mind-set of the people living in the late 1920s. Gone were the good times of the Roaring Twenties; a dark economic cloud seemed to descend. It is interesting how many people failed to see the dark economic cloud on the horizon. Irving Fisher, perhaps the best-known American economist of the day, said just a week before the crash, "Stock prices have reached what looks like a permanently high plateau. I expect to see the stock market a good deal higher than it is today within a few months." Fisher ended up losing a fortune in the stock market crash.

Other people who did not see the crash coming were Myron Forbes, who was president of Pierce Arrow Motor Company, and E. H. H. Simmons, president of the New York Stock Exchange. Also, Winston Churchill, who until earlier that year had served for five years as the chancellor of the exchequer, an important financial position in Great Britain, was in America just a few weeks before the crash and had written to his wife telling her how well they were doing in the stock market. On October 24, 1929, when word got out that the stock market was crashing, thousands of people gathered on Wall Street to witness events. One of those people, Winston Churchill (who later became prime minister of Great Britain in 1940) watched from the visitors' gallery of the New York Stock Exchange as his fortune disappeared on the trading floor below.

THINK ABOUT IT Predicting stock market movements is often difficult. Why do you think it is difficult?

Economics in the Real World

After students have read this feature, ask them to share what they know about the Great Depression. Ask students to answer questions like these: Suppose you were a wealthy teen living in October 24, 1929; how would your lifestyle have changed had your family lost its fortune in the stock market crash? How might the Great Depression have changed the psychological mind-set of people living in the late 1920s?

ANSWERS TO THINK ABOUT IT Answers will vary. Students will probably say it is impossible for economists to make long-term predictions about the stock market because stock prices are affected by many events, some of them impossible to predict.

Discussion Starter

Ask students if they ever traded anything, like sports memorabilia or food at lunch. If so, were they certain they were getting the better end of the deal? How could they tell? Remind students that when stocks are traded, the value does not always increase.

Reinforcement Activity

To make sure students understand how the price of a stock is determined, have them write one or two sentences explaining the process. If they have trouble, direct them to page 434.

Internet Research

There are many Internet sites that can help in predicting the stock market. Remind students that the best way to predict the future of a stock is to be informed about the current nature of the company and its history in the market. Some companies are seasonal and by looking at a chart of their earnings you may be able to predict when that stock is most profitable. Charting Web sites offer all kinds of free information on the recent history of a stock and its industry.

Discussion Starter

Buying and selling stock online has become one of the most popular pastimes of Americans. It can become very dangerous however. Ask students to think about what problems could occur if an ill-informed person were to trade without getting advice.

Background Information

Knowing a stock's history is very important in predicting what will happen with the stock in the future. Often a broker will look at the stock's previous performance over a certain period of time to get a sense of how the stock price will change in the near future.

Reinforcement Activity

Allow students to demonstrate understanding of the material presented in this section by writing one or two sentences to define stocks.

Discussion Starter

Allow students to watch or listen to financial news, and ask them to keep track of things that they understand because they have read this section—that is, things they wouldn't have understood before reading this section. Ask them to comment on how the stock market is related to the economic health of the United States.

EXHIBIT 16-3 Translating Financial Talk

Term	Meaning
after the bell	Refers to the time after the bell sounds and the stock market is closed until the next trading day.
air pocket stock	A stock that plunges fast and furiously, much like an airplane that hits an air pocket.
Bo Derek	A slang term used to refer to a perfect stock or investment; named after the movie actress who starred in the 1979 movie *10*.
big board	The nickname for the New York Stock Exchange.
bull and bear markets	Terms used to describe the direction the market is moving. A bull market is one in which prices are expected to rise. A bear market is one in which prices are expected to fall. The terms *bull* and *bear* come from the way these animals attack their opponents: the bull puts its horns up in the air and a bear moves its paws down (across its opponent).
casino finance	An investment strategy that is considered extremely risky.
deer market	A flat market where not much is happening and investors are usually timid. It is neither a bull nor bear market.
eat well, sleep well	A phrase describing two different strategies for investing. When it comes to investing, no one gets anything for nothing. If you want a high return, you usually have to assume some risk. If you don't want to take on much risk, then you will likely have a low return. In short, high risk comes with high return, and low risk comes with low return. "Eat well, sleep well" captures this idea: do you want a risky investment that may end up feeding you well, or do you want a safe investment that lets you sleep at night?
falling knife	A stock whose price has fallen significantly in a short time. Someone might say, "Don't try to catch a falling knife" (because you can hurt yourself).
Goldilocks economy	An economy that is not too hot or too cold, but is just right. People often referred to the economy in the mid-to-late 1990s in the U.S. as the Goldilocks economy.
lemon	A disappointing investment.
love money	Money given by family or friends to a person to start a business.
Nervous Nellie	An investor who isn't comfortable with investing, mainly because of the risks.
sandwich generation	A phrase that refers to people usually of middle age who are "sandwiched" between their children and their parents by the demands of care and support for these two groups of people.
Santa Claus rally	A jump in the price of stocks that often occurs during the week between Christmas and New Year's.
short selling	A technique used by investors who are trying to benefit from a falling stock price. For example, suppose Brian believes that stock X will soon fall in price. He borrows the stock from someone who currently owns the stock with the promise to return the stock later. He then sells the (borrowed) stock, hoping to buy back enough shares later at a lower price to return to the original owner.
war babies	A name given to stocks issued by companies that produce military hardware (tanks, airplanes, etc.).

Why Do People Buy Stock?

Millions of people, in countries all over the world, buy stock every day. Why do they do it? They do it based on a couple of reasons. Some people buy stocks for the **dividends**, which are payments made to stockholders based on a company's profits.

dividend
A share of the profits of a corporation distributed to stockholders.

EXAMPLE: Suppose company X issued 1 million shares of stock purchased by different people. Each year the company tabulates its profit and loss, and when it earns a profit, it divides up much of the profit among the owners of the company as dividends. This year's dividend might be $1 for each share of stock a person owns. So, if Florian owns 50,000 shares of stock, she will receive a dividend check for $50,000. ♦

The other reason to buy stock is for the expected gain in its price. Stockholders can make money if they buy shares at a lower price and sell at a higher price.

EXAMPLE: Kristor buys 100 shares of Microsoft stock today. He thinks that the company is going to do well and that a year from now he can sell the stock for as much as $50 more a share than he purchased it. In other words, he hopes to earn $5,000 on his stock purchase. ♦

People also sell stock for many reasons. Smith might sell her 100 shares of IBM because she currently needs the money to help her son pay for college. She also might sell the stock in order to help put together a down payment for a house. Another common reason for selling stock is that the stockholder thinks that the stock is likely to soon go down in price. In other words, it is better today to sell at $25 a share than to sell one week from now at $18 a share.

Differentiating Instruction

Kinesthetic and Visual Learners

Students may not realize that it is possible to buy and sell stock in foreign stock markets. We have discovered in our earlier chapters how interrelated the world is economically and how the fluctuations in one country's economic stability can have far-reaching effects. Tell students to track stocks of companies that produce substitutes for U.S. goods. Students might track Peugeot as an example of the foreign automobile market and compare it to General Motors stock. Visual learners can reflect their work in the form of a chart or graph.

A Student Asks

QUESTION: *Suppose I buy 100 shares of stock at a price of $40 a share. The stock goes down in price to $32. Shouldn't I wait until the share price rises to $40 or higher before I sell it?*

ANSWER: *When it comes to stock, what goes down is not guaranteed to go up. In other words, even if the stock's price has gone down by $8, it might go down more. You want to always look forward to the future (not backward to the past) when deciding whether to sell a stock. If you see reasons for the price to fall even farther, it is better to sell at $32 (and take a $8 per share loss) than to sell at $25 and take a bigger loss. If you believe the price will eventually rise, then you would want to hold on to the stock.*

How to Buy and Sell Stock

Buying and selling stock is relatively easy. You can buy or sell stock through a full-service stock brokerage firm, a discount broker, or an online broker. With all varieties of brokers, you usually open an account by depositing a certain dollar amount into it, most commonly between $1,000 and $2,500. Once you open an account, you can begin to trade (buy and sell stock).

With a full-service broker, you may call up on the phone and ask your broker to recommend some good stock. Your broker, usually called an *account representative*, might say that you should buy X, Y, or Z stock. You may ask why these stocks are good ones to buy. He may say that the research department in the firm has looked closely at these stocks and believes they are headed for good times. The analyst's reasons could be based on the current economic situation in the country, the level of exports, the new technology that is coming to market, and so on.

If you do not require help to buy stocks, you can go either to a discount broker or to an online broker. You can call up a discount broker the same way you called up a full-service broker and tell the broker that you want to buy or sell so many shares of a given stock. The broker will simply execute the trade for you. He or she is not there to offer any advice.

The same process can be undertaken online. You go to your broker's Web site, log in by entering your username and password, and then buy or sell stock. You may submit an order to buy 100 shares of stock X. Your online broker will register your buy request and then note when it has been executed. Your account, easily visible online, will show how much cash you have in it, how many shares of a particular stock you hold, and so on.

Deciding Which Stocks to Buy

You can use various methods to decide which stocks to purchase. The first way is to simply buy shares of stock that you think are going to rise in price. So you might buy 50 shares of Microsoft, 100 shares of General Electric, and 500 shares of Disney.

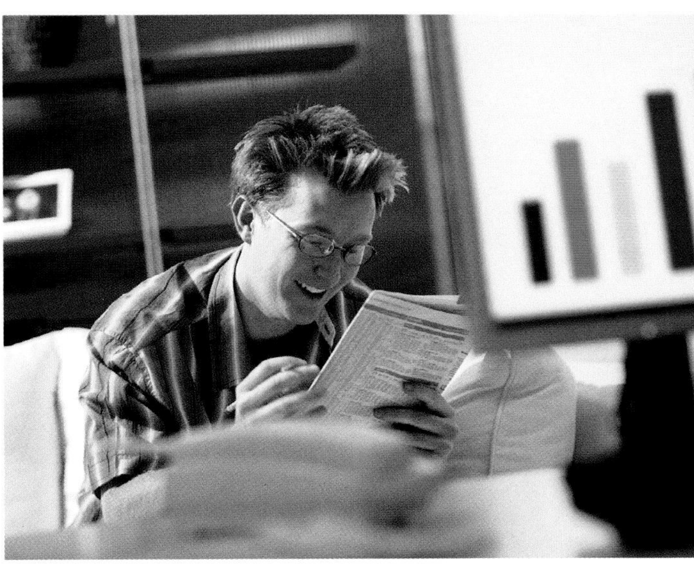

▲ It's fun to check your stocks each day in the paper or on your computer—when they're going up. It's not so much fun if they are going down. Get some expert advice and do some research before you buy.

Background Information

Ask students whether they have ever saved something of value, and if so, how long they saved it, why they did so, and how difficult it was to do so. Point out that it is sometimes very hard to be patient with stocks, but that patience and the use of long-term investment strategies are key to being successful in the market. Explain that if you own stock in a company and the price triples in two weeks for some reason, it may seem like a great time to sell. But it's possible that the price could continue to rise—or it could fall just as quickly. Historically, over the long term, stock prices have gone up. However, investing in the stock market is not a reliable way of making a lot of money in the short term.

Reinforcement Activity

Assign students to watch the markets for four or five countries in addition to markets in the United States and to track whether fluctuations in one market affect the other markets. You might want to check the markets in class every day and perhaps graph them as time progresses.

Internet Research

Direct students to visit the Dow Jones Industrial Average Web site to learn more about the Dow. Have them create reports with text, charts, and other visual aids that explain to beginning investors what the Dow is all about. Their reports should answer the following questions: What does the Dow show? How does the Dow differ from other indices? How much has the Dow fluctuated in the past century? What stocks are currently traded? What stocks were originally traded? What do the types of stocks originally and currently traded reveal about changes to the economy since the Dow was created?

Background Information

Some students might be thinking that they can make millions on the stock market overnight. Remind students that there are literally millions of people invested in the stock market who have the exact same information as they have and have not made millions.

Investing in stocks and bonds is a long-term investment. Some stocks can open at a low price and then shoot up over the next week, but many of these will slip below their initial value in a matter of months.

Reinforcement Activity

There are many mutual funds companies to choose from in the stock market. Assign students to research the leading mutual fund companies and then track their successes or failures over a period of time. Then encourage students to analyze the companies' Web sites as to how accurately they present their track record.

Reinforcement Activity

Many people invest in mutual funds through company retirement accounts or individual retirement accounts (IRAs). Assign students to interview adults they know, to find out how various retirement programs work. Students might talk with parents or other relatives, teachers, family friends, bankers, human resource professionals, or financial advisors. Students could also consult popular financial books such as those by Suze Orman. Allow students to share their results with the class or in small groups.

▲ Rather than trying to select the biggest winners, some investors choose to "buy the market." If the market as a whole does well, these investors do well.

Mutual Funds

Another way is to invest in a stock mutual fund, which is collection of stocks. The fund is managed by a fund manager who works for a mutual fund company. For example, Smith may operate mutual fund Z at mutual fund company Z. If you put, say, $10,000 in mutual fund Z, you are in effect buying the stocks in that fund. Let's say that fund consists of stocks A, B, C, W, and X at the current time. The fund manager may, on any given day, buy more of A and sell some of B, or sell all of C and add stock D to the fund portfolio.

It is up to the fund manager to do what he or she thinks is best to maximize the overall returns from the fund. As a buyer of the fund, you put your money in the fund manager's hands. Mutual fund companies often advertise the records of their fund managers. They might say, "Our fund managers have the best record on Wall Street. Invest with us and get the highest returns you can." You may be prompted to put your money in the hands of the "experts" because you feel they know better than you what stocks to buy and sell and when to do each.

index
A portfolio of stocks, which represents a particular market or a portion of it, used to measure changes in a market or an economy.

Buying the Market

You could use another strategy, though, and buy the stocks that make up a stock index. An **index** is basically a portfolio of stocks that represent a particular market or a portion of it, used to measure changes in a market or an economy. Earlier, we discussed the DJIA. The DJIA is a stock index. It gives us information on the performance of the 30 stocks that make up the Dow. Another index is the Standard & Poor's 500. This index is a broad index of stock market activity because it is made up of 500 of the largest U.S. companies. Another broad-based stock index is the Wilshire 5000, which consists of the stocks of about 6,500 firms.

A particularly easy way to get a composite type of fund is to buy what are called "Spyders." The term *Spyders*, or SPDRs, which stands for "Standard & Poor's Depository Receipts," are securities representing ownership in the SPDR Trust. The SPDR Trust buys the stocks that make up the Standard & Poor's (S&P) 500 index. Spyders are traded under the symbol SPY. When this book was being written, Spyders were selling for about $120 a share. Spyders cost one-tenth of the S&P index (total of the share prices of the stocks in the S&P). For example, if the S&P index is 1,200, then a Spyder will sell for $120.

When you buy Spyders, you are buying the stock of 500 companies. Because you are buying the stock of so many companies, you are said to be "buying the market."

EXAMPLE: Jack decides to "buy the market" instead of buying a few individual stocks. He checks on the current price of Spyders. He sees the current price is $120.16 per share. He decides to buy 100 shares, for a total price of $12,016. His online broker charges him a small commission for this stock purchase. ♦

A Student Asks

QUESTION: *Is it a good idea to buy stock?*

ANSWER: *A lot depends on such factors as your age (are you at the beginning of your work career or near the end), your income, and how much you can afford to invest in the stock market. There is no guarantee that stock that you buy will go up in price. However, generally it is the case that stock prices increase over the long run.*

Differentiating Instruction

Kinesthetic and Visual Learners

Economic concepts such as the bull and bear stock market have often been represented in political cartoons. Cartoons can present difficult subjects in a clear way. Have an art teacher come into your class and assist students in creating an economic cartoon to help them understand some facet of the stock market. After students have finished their cartoons, invite volunteers to explain their work to the rest of the class. Display the cartoons around the room. With permission, you may also create transparencies of some cartoons for use in future classes.

Picking Stocks: Darts or Analysts?

Let's say that you just inherited some money and decide that you would like to buy some stock. What's your investment strategy?

- You could pick and buy certain individual stocks yourself.
- You could buy shares in a mutual fund. You would invest your money in a fund created by the so-called Wall Street experts.
- A third option would be to buy a stock index fund, such as the 30 stocks that make up the DJIA, or the 500 stocks that make up the Standard & Poor's 500.

Most people think stock mutual funds do better than the stock index funds because the experts pick the stocks that make up the funds. These experts make it their business to study stocks day and night. Right?

Enter Burton Malkiel, a professor of financial economics at Princeton University. He has shown that a person who invested $10,000 in 1969 in the Standard & Poor's 500 stock index fund (which is not managed by the experts) would have seen its value increase to $310,000 by mid-1984. But the person who invested $10,000 in 1969 in the average actively managed fund would have seen its value increase to $170,000, or $140,000 less than the stock index fund.

Many rigorous studies confirm Malkiel's results. For now, though, consider a rather informal study done by editors at *Forbes* magazine. They would pin the stock market page of the newspaper to the back of an office door and throw darts at it. Then they would invest "play money" in each of the stocks the dart hit. At the same time, they would invest the same amount of "play money" in the stock picks of some of the best-known stock pickers on Wall Street. At the end of the year, they would check to see which group of stocks (dart-picked or expert-picked) did better. Over the years, few highly trained professionals did as well as the darts.

To understand why throwing darts will often beat the experts, consider the stocks of two companies, IBM and Ford. Suppose that on a given day each stock sells for $100 a share. Then one day IBM announces a major breakthrough in computer technology. On the same day, Ford has to recall one of its best-selling cars. In other words, the IBM news is good and the Ford news is bad.

What will happen to each company's stock? No doubt IBM stock will be bid up in price and Ford stock will be bid down in price. At the end of the day, IBM will sell for more than $100 and Ford will be selling for less than $100. The prices of the two stocks will keep adjusting until it is no better to buy IBM stock than Ford stock. In the end it will be no better to buy Ford at the lower price than IBM at the higher price.

As long as stock prices adjust quickly—and evidence indicates that they do—then no stock will be better than or worse than any other stock. If all stocks are alike once their prices have adjusted to good and bad news, then even a monkey throwing darts can pick stocks as well as Wall Street experts.

You can test this yourself. Pick 10 stocks using the dart method. Invest $100 play money in each stock. Next, go online and search for "top stock picks." Invest $100 play money in the same number of top picks as dart-picked stocks. Compare the results.

THINK ABOUT IT If stock pickers can do no better (and sometimes worse) than throwing darts at the stock market page, then why do you think some people still pay the experts to pick stocks for them?

Economics in the Real World

After students read this feature, allow them to test the dart method using $100 of play money, as suggested in the feature. When students have completed the test, ask them whether they would use the dart method to invest in stocks.

ANSWERS TO THINK ABOUT IT Answers will vary. Students will probably say that experts have valuable knowledge to use when choosing stocks.

Background Information

People who have stocks usually watch NASDAQ reports closely because a rapidly declining market might be an economic indicator of a larger problem.

Internet Research

Tell students to select one or two companies that are listed on the New York Stock Exchange or NASDAQ and track the stock prices for those companies in the newspaper for a week. At the same time, have them track the prices of the same stocks online. Then have them answer the following questions: Which source gives them the most up-to-date information? Which is easier to use? Are the figures reported the same? Which do they think they would use if they were intending to purchase or monitor stock prices? Why?

A Student Asks

You may want to use this A Student Asks to make sure students understand there are no guarantees about the future of stock prices.

Reinforcement Activity

Invite students to bring to class the financial or business section of a newspaper and locate the stock reports. Ask which market seems to have the most stocks listed within it. Direct students to compare the amount and type of information presented for each market.

Discussion Starter

Ask students the following questions after they have read through this section: How would they invest their money in stocks? Would they put their money into individual stocks or would they rather use a mutual fund? Would they invest it themselves or would they have someone manage their money for them?

Application Activity

After reading and discussing Section 1, you may want to assign the Section Activity in the *Applying the Principles Workbook.*

Assess

Quick Quiz

The following true-or-false quiz will help you assess student understanding of the material covered in this section.

1. The NYSE is the largest marketplace for the sale and purchase of stocks in the world. (True)
2. There are still 11 companies in the Dow Jones Industrial Average. (False)
3. One reason to buy stock is for the expected gain in its price. (True)
4. Spyders are stock guides that give information to stockholders. (False)
5. The yield of a stock is the dividend divided by the closing price. (True)

If you want to find the current price of a particular stock, go to Yahoo! Finance at www.emcp.net/stockprices. At the top of the page you will find a search box. Put the symbol in the box and click GO. If you don't know the symbol for the stock, click "Symbol Lookup." Also, the homepage of Yahoo! Finance lets you know how the DJIA is doing.

If you want to find the current price of commodities, metals (gold and silver), and other such things, go to Bloomberg.com at www.emcp.net/marketdata and click on "Market Data." The left side of the page provides selections from which to choose.

Finally, a good investment dictionary and education site on investing can be found at Investopedia.com at www.emcp.net/investing. See the top of the page for various topics.

For example, suppose we look at the S&P Index during the period 1926–2004. The data here show a 70 percent likelihood of earning a positive investment return over a one-year period, but an 86.5 percent chance of a positive investment return if you held the stocks in the index over a five-year period. The probability of a positive return went up to 97.1 percent if you held the stocks for 10 years. In other words, the longer you hold stocks in the stock market, the more likely you will earn a positive return.

How to Read the Stock Market Page

Suppose you purchased some stock and now you want to find out how it is doing. Is it rising or falling in price? Is it paying a dividend? How many shares were traded today?

One of the places you can find the answers to these questions, and more, is the newspaper. Turn to the stock market page in the newspaper. (Keep in mind that many newspapers are online.) You will see something similar to what you see in Exhibit 16-4. The descriptions that follow focus on the last stock (in bold type) as an example.

- **52W high.** This column provides the high price of the stock during the past year or past 52 weeks. For our example stock, you see the number "51.25," which is $51.25.
- **52W low.** This column provides the low price of the stock during the past 52 weeks. For our example stock, you see the number "27.69," which is $27.69.
- **Stock.** In this column you see "Rockwell," which is either an abbreviation of the name of the company or the full name of the company whose stock you are studying. The company here is Rockwell Automation Incorporated.
- **Ticker.** In this column you see "ROK," which is the stock or ticker symbol for Rockwell Automation Incorporated.
- **Div.** In this column, the number, in this case "1.02," indicates that the last annual dividend per share of stock was $1.02. For example, a person who owned 5,000 shares of Rockwell Automation stock would have received $1.02 per share or $5,100 in dividends. (If this space is blank, then the company does not currently pay out dividends.)
- **Yield %.** The yield of a stock is the dividend divided by the closing price.

Yield = Dividend per share/Closing price per share

The closing price of the stock (shown in one of the later columns) is 47.54, or $47.54. If we divide the dividend ($1.02) by the closing price ($47.54), we get a yield of 2.1 percent. A higher yield is better, all other things being the same.

- **P/E.** The PE ratio, or price-earnings ratio, is obtained by taking the latest closing price per share and dividing it by the latest available net earnings per share. In other words,

Differentiating Instruction

English Language Learners

Some of the terms and phrases in this chapter of the text may be difficult for some of your students. Encourage students to rephrase, in their own words, some of the more difficult words and phrases in this chapter. Then, using their new definitions, review the concepts behind the terms and phrases. On the board, draw the three-way connection between the original terms, the students' phrases, and the concept the term or phrase represents.

EXHIBIT 16-4 **Reading the Stock Market Page of a Newspaper**

(1) 52W high	(2) 52W low	(3) Stock	(4) Ticker	(5) Div	(6) Yield %	(7) P/E	(8) Vol 00s	(9) High	(10) Low	(11) Close	(12) Net chg
45.39	19.75	ResMed	RMD			57.5	3831	42.00	39.51	41.50	−1.90
11.63	3.55	Revlon A	REV				162	6.09	5.90	6.09	+0.12
77.25	55.13	RioTinto	RTP	2.30	3.2		168	72.75	71.84	72.74	+0.03
31.31	16.63	RitchieBr	RBA			20.9	15	24.49	24.29	24.49	-0.01
8.44	1.75	RiteAid	RAD				31028	4.50	4.20	4.31	+0.21
38.63	18.81	RobtHall	RHI			26.5	6517	27.15	26.50	26.50	+0.14
51.25	**27.69**	**Rockwell**	**ROK**	**1.02**	**2.1**	**14.5**	**6412**	**47.99**	**47.00**	**47.54**	**+0.24**

◀ The text on the opposite page and this page explains how to read and understand the information about stocks found in the newspaper.

PE = Closing price per share/Net earnings per share

A stock with a PE ratio of 14.5, like the one here, means that the stock is selling for a share price that is 14.5 times its earnings per share. What does this number tell us about the stock? Let's suppose that most stocks have a PE ratio of 14.5. In comparison, let's say stock X has a PE ratio of 50. What would make stock X have a PE ratio so much higher than most stocks? A high PE ratio usually indicates that people believe the stock will experience higher than average growth in earnings. Whether they are right remains to be seen.

- **Vol 00s.** Volume in the hundreds, or 6412 here, translates to 641,200. In other words, 641,200 shares of this stock were traded (bought and sold) on this particular day.
- **High.** This number, 47.99, stands for the high price the stock traded for on this particular day, which translates to $47.99 for this stock.
- **Low.** This number is the low price the stock traded for on this particular day. The number is 47.00 and translates to $47.00.
- **Close.** The number here—47.54, or $47.54—is the share price of the stock when trading stopped this particular day.
- **Net chg.** Net change is the difference between the current closing price and the previous day's closing price. The number here is +0.24, which translates to $0.24, meaning that the price of the stock on this particular day closed 24 cents higher than it did the day before.

"Wall Street is the only place that people ride to in a Rolls Royce to get advice from those who take the subway."
— Warren Buffet

ASSESSMENT

Defining Terms

1. Define:
  a. investment bank
  b. dividend

Review Facts and Concepts

2. What information did Charles Dow convey with the Dow Jones Industrial Average?

3. What does it mean to "buy the market"?

4. Does your probability of earning a positive return by buying (and selling) stocks go up or down the longer you hold the stocks (before selling)?

Critical Thinking

5. Suppose that for 500 stocks, the share price of each stock rises on Monday. Does everyone in the stock market believe that stocks are headed even higher, since no one would buy a stock if he or she thought share prices were headed lower?

Applying Economic Concepts

6. Which of the two stocks has a bigger gap between its closing price and net earnings per share: Stock A with a PE ratio of 17 or Stock B with a PE ratio of 45?

Assessment Book

You will find a quiz for this section in the *Assessment Book.*

Reteaching Activity

Use the Section Assessment to gauge which students may need reteaching on this section. With those students, create a large chart that resembles the stock market page with a column for the stock, symbol, and so on. Guide students as they identify each column in their own words and then describe what the number in the column represents. Make another chart that shows the applicable equations.

Guided Reading

For further reteaching of the key concepts in this section, assign the Outlining Activity and the Just the Facts Handout from the *Guided Reading and Study Guide.*

Defining Terms

1. a. investment bank: a firm that acts as an intermediary between a company that issues a stock and the public that wishes to buy the stock; **b. dividend:** a share of the profits of a corporation distributed to stockholders.

Reviewing Facts and Concepts

2. He conveyed information on how the stock market, on average, was doing. Was it rising? falling? holding constant?

3. It means to invest in a composite fund representing stock of many companies.

4. Your probability goes up because stock prices generally increase over the long run.

Critical Thinking

5. No. The stock market is made up of buyers and sellers. If one person buys 100 shares of stock, there must be someone who sells 100 shares of stock. The people who sold probably think that share prices are going to fall. If they had thought otherwise, they would have waited to sell in order to get a higher return.

Applying Economic Concepts

6. Stock B has a bigger gap. The PE ratio is the closing price of the stock divided by the net earnings per share. Stock B has a closing price 45 times larger than net earnings, while stock A has a closing price 17 times larger than net earnings.

SECTION 2
Teacher Support

Focus and Motivate

Section Objectives

After completing this section, students will be able to

- define bonds;
- identify the factor that determines the rating of a bond;
- explain the relationship between interest rates and the price of bonds;
- identify various types of bonds;
- explain the relationship between risk and return; and
- explain why financial markets are important.

Kickoff Activity

Encourage students to think about these questions at the beginning of class: We have learned in this course that economists have their own definitions for many words. What meanings do you know for the word *bond?* How might the word relate to financial markets?

Activating Prior Knowledge

Discuss students' answers to the questions in the Kickoff Activity. Encourage students to think about how the word *bond* sometimes implies a trust relationship. In an economist's way of thinking, a bond is an IOU, or a promise to pay, typically issued by companies, governments, or government agencies as a way of borrowing money.

Teach

A Student Asks

To help students understand how someone who buys a bond is a lender, invite two volunteers to act out the transaction described in A Student Asks.

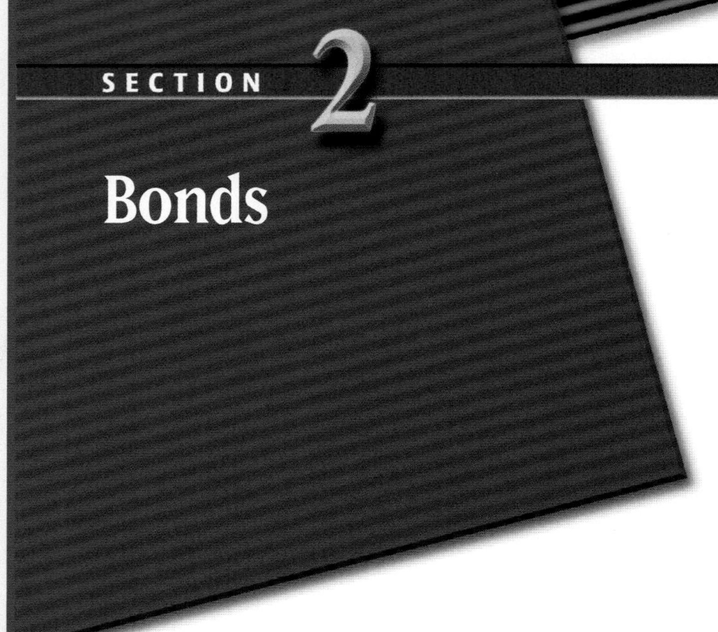

SECTION 2
Bonds

Focus Questions

- What are bonds?
- What factor determines the rating of a bond?
- What is the relationship between interest rates and the price of bonds?
- What are the various types of bonds?
- What is the relationship between risk and return?
- Why are financial markets important?

Key Terms

bond
face value (par value)
coupon rate
yield

What Is a Bond?

Suppose a company in St. Louis wants to build a new factory. How can it get the money to build the factory? You will recall that companies use three principal ways to raise money. First, they can go to a bank and take out a loan. Second, they can issue stock or, in other words, sell ownership rights in the company. Third, they can issue bonds. A **bond** is simply an IOU, or a promise to pay. Typically, bonds are issued by companies, governments, or government agencies. In each case, the purpose of issuing a bond is to borrow money. The issuer of a bond is a borrower. The person who buys the bond is a lender.

bond
An IOU, or a promise to pay, issued by companies, governments, or government agencies for the purpose of borrowing money.

face value (par value)
Dollar amount specified on a bond. The total amount the issuer of the bond will repay to the buyer of the bond.

A Student Asks

QUESTION: *I don't quite understand how a person who buys something (like a bond) can be called a lender. I thought that when you lend money to someone you just turn over money to that person and he or she pays you back later.*

ANSWER: *Suppose a friend asks to borrow $10, and tells you that he will pay you back $11 next month if you lend him the $10 today. You say okay and hand over $10. Now suppose your friend takes out a piece of paper, and writes the following on it: "I owe the person who returns this piece of paper one month from today a total of $11." Then he signs his name and gives the piece of paper to you. For all practical purposes, that piece of paper is a bond (an IOU statement) and you, by purchasing the IOU, have become a lender.*

The Components of a Bond

The three major components of a bond are face (par) value, maturity date, and coupon rate.

The **face value**, or **par value**, of a bond is the total amount the issuer of the bond will repay to the buyer of the bond. For example, suppose Dawson buys a bond from company Z. Let's say that the face value of the bond is $10,000. It follows that company Z

Background Information: Bonds and the Military

During the crisis of the American Revolution, the government of the colonies needed to build funds to support its effort against the British. The government tried to raise money by selling bonds, pieces of paper that people buy at a set price, knowing that they can exchange their bonds for a profit after a certain amount of time. This practice was not as successful as it is now, and the government had to look to other means to finance its military.

promises to pay Dawson $10,000 at some point in the future.

The *maturity date* is the day when the issuer of the bond must pay the buyer of the bond the face value of the bond. For example, suppose Dawson buys a bond with a face value of $10,000 that matures on December 31, 2015. On that date, he receives $10,000 from the issuer of the bond.

The **coupon rate** is the percentage of the face value that the bondholder receives each year until the bond matures. For example, suppose Dawson buys a bond with a face value of $10,000 that matures in 5 years and has a coupon rate of 10 percent. He receives a coupon payment of $1,000 each year for 5 years.

EXAMPLE: Jackie buys a bond with a face value of $100,000 and a coupon rate of 7 percent. The maturity date of the bond is 10 years from today. Each year, for the next 10 years, Jackie receives 7 percent of $100,000 from the issuer of the bond. This amounts to $7,000 a year for each of 10 years. In the tenth year, she also receives $100,000 from the bond issuer. With respect to this bond, the maturity date is 10 years, the coupon rate is 7 percent, and the face value is $100,000. ♦

Bond Ratings

Bonds are rated or evaluated. The more likely the bond issuer will pay the face value of the bond at maturity and will meet all scheduled coupon payments, the higher the bond's rating. Two of the best known ratings are Standard & Poor's, and Moody's. A bond rating of AAA from Standard & Poor's or a rating of Aaa from Moody's is the highest rating possible. A bond with this rating is one of the most secure bonds you can buy; the bond issuer is almost certain to pay the face value of the bond at maturity and meet all scheduled coupon payments.

Bonds rated in the B to D category are lower-quality bonds than those rated in the A category. In fact, if a bond is rated in the C category it may be in default (the issuer of the bond cannot pay off the bond) and if it is rated in the D category, it is definitely in default.

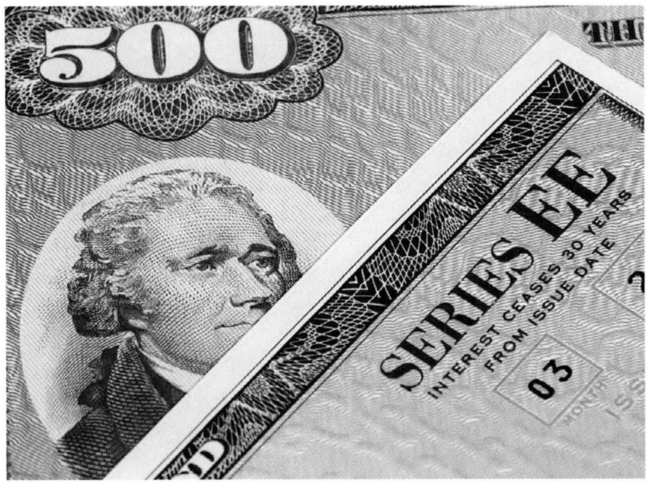

▲ An effective, practical way for young people to begin saving and investing is to buy U.S. savings bonds. Issued by the U.S. government, these bonds can be purchased in smaller, more affordable denominations than most other bonds.

A Student Asks

QUESTION: *Suppose I want to buy a bond issued by some corporation. Would I buy the bond from the corporation itself or from someone else (say, for example, from a person who had purchased a bond from the corporation at an early time)?*

ANSWER: *If the corporation is currently issuing (selling) bonds, you could buy the bond from the corporation. You would purchase them through a broker who is finding buyers for the bonds the corporation wants to sell. If the corporation is not currently issuing bonds, you could buy the bond from someone who purchased and still holds the bond bought from the corporation at an earlier date.*

Primary market *and* secondary market *are the terms that apply here. If you are buying a bond that is newly issued, you are buying it in the primary market; if you are buying a bond from someone who currently owns the bond, you are buying it in the secondary market. By far, most bond and stock purchases occur in the secondary market.*

coupon rate
The percentage of the face value that the bondholder receives each year until the bond matures.

Reinforcement Activity

Students may be aware of bonds as they relate to school bond issues or education bonds voted on in state or local elections. Have some students interview school, local, and state government officials to find out what school or education bonds really are and how they are used. You can have other students talk to local corporate leaders to discuss how bonds are used in the corporate world. Allow students to report their findings to the class and answer the more applicable of the following two questions: Do you think education or school bonds are a good way of raising money? Are corporations successful making money with the sale of corporate bonds?

A Student Asks

You may want to use this A Student Asks to make sure students understand the difference between primary and secondary markets.

Discussion Starter

Ask students the following questions: Which would you rather buy—a B-rated bond with a $10,000 face value and an 8% coupon rate, or an AAA-rated bond with a $10,000 face value and a 4% coupon rate? Why?

Differentiating Instruction

Visual Learners

Have the class register for and participate in the InvestSmart Market Simulation on the Internet. They can first review the stock market basics and view the "real life examples." Then register the class as a group, and have them go through the simulation. This site also includes lesson plans. If you do not have Internet capabilities in your classroom or your school, develop a stock market game using the information found here and the daily newspaper.

Section 2 Bonds 443

Critical Thinking

After students read A Student Asks, which deals with the relationship between coupon rates and interest rates, have them consider the following scenario: Vera buys a $10,000 corporate bond with a 5% coupon rate. The next year, interest rates on savings accounts go up to 7%. What will this mean for the company if it wants to issue more $10,000 bonds? (*Answer:* It will need to offer a coupon rate of at least 7%.) What will it mean for the value of Vera's bond? (*Answer:* She will not be able to sell it for the full $10,000 because people can buy $10,000 bonds from the company at a 7% coupon rate. She will have to sell it for less money than she paid.)

Reinforcement Activity

Have a student come to the board and show how market forces affect the prices of bonds. He or she should be able to create a graph that shows that the price of a bond goes up in response to rising demand relative to supply. Invite another student to the board. As a class, assign a face value and a coupon rate to a bond. Then ask the student to find the yield on that bond over one year.

A Student Asks

You may want to use this A Student Asks to make sure students understand the concept of coupon rates, how they are set, and the role of the bond issuer.

▲ Two of the best known bond ratings are Standard & Poor's and Moody's, both of which have informative Web sites.

Bond Prices and Yields

The price that a person pays for a bond depends on market conditions. The greater the demand for the bond relative to the supply, the higher the price. The price is important because it determines the yield that the bondholder receives on the bond.

Let's suppose that Sonya is currently the owner of a bond with a face value of $1,000 and a coupon rate of 5 percent. She decides to sell this bond to Joshua for $950. Now we know that the coupon payment on this bond will be 5 percent of $1,000 each year, or $50. In other words, Joshua can expect to receive $50 each year. However, the **yield** on the bond is the coupon payment divided by the price paid for the bond.

yield
Equal to the annual coupon payment divided by the price paid for the bond.

Yield = Annual coupon payment/Price paid for the bond

In this example it is $50/$950, or 5.26 percent. For the bond buyer, higher yield is better. (Sometimes, in everyday language, people talk about the yield on the bond as being the same as the interest rate. For example, someone might ask "What is the yield on that bond?" when they are actually referring to the interest rate.)

Now suppose that Joshua paid $1,100 for the bond instead of $950. In this case the yield would be $50/$1,100, or 4.54 percent. In other words, as the price paid for the bond rises, the yield declines.

When are the coupon rate and yield the same? Obviously they are the same when the price paid for the bond equals the face value. For example, consider a bond with a face value of $1,000 and a coupon rate of 5 percent. If the bond is purchased for $1,000, then the yield ($50/$1,000), which is 5 percent, is equal to the coupon rate.

EXAMPLE: Robin buys a bond with the face value of $10,000 for $9,000. The coupon rate on the bond is 4 percent. Because the coupon rate is 4 percent, Robin receives 4 percent of $10,000 (the face value of the bond), or $400, each year through the time when the bond matures. Because Robin bought the bond for a price lower than the face value, the bond's yield will be higher than the coupon rate. To find the yield, we divide the annual coupon payment of $400 by the price of the bond ($9,000), giving us a yield of 4.4 percent. ◆

A Student Asks

QUESTION: *Can a bond issuer set the coupon rate at anything he or she wants? If so, why wouldn't the bond issuer always set the coupon rate at something like 1 percent?*

ANSWER: *The answer has to do with competition. Suppose company A needs to borrow $1 million and decides to issue $10,000 bonds. The only way anyone would be willing to buy one of these bonds (lend the company $10,000) would be if the company promised the buyers a rate of return comparable to the interest rate they could get if they simply put the money in a savings account. In other words, the company has to set the*

Background Information: Financial Journalists

Financial journalists work at newspapers, magazines, television networks, cable television stations, and many other places. Most have attended college and majored in journalism, with perhaps a second major or a minor in business or economics.

As with many jobs, networking can be an important part of getting a job in the field. Many financial journalists first serve as interns at newspapers or television networks while in college. They also work on college newspapers to gain experience and publish work that can be submitted when interviewing for their first post-college jobs. Employers interviewing financial journalists look for an ability to write well, a solid knowledge of

Are Economists Poor Investors?

You might think that economists would do pretty well in the stock market compared to the average person. After all, their job is to understand how markets work and to study key economic indicators.

So how do you explain a May 11, 2005, *Los Angeles Times* article titled "Experts Are at a Loss on Investing"? The article looked at the investments of four economists—all Nobel Prize winners in Economics. Not one of them said that he invests the way he should invest, and none of them seemed to be getting rich through their investments. In other words, often a big difference separates knowing what to do from doing it.

Harry M. Markowitz won the Nobel Prize in Economics in 1990. He won the prize for his work in financial economics; he is known as the father of "modern portfolio theory," the main idea being that people should diversify their investments.

Did Markowitz follow his own advice? Not really. Most of his life he put half of his money in a stock fund and the other half in a conservative, low-interest investment. Markowitz, age 77 at the time, says, "In retrospect, it would have been better to have been more in stocks when I was younger."

George Akerlof, who won the Nobel Prize in Economics in 2001, invested most of his money in money market accounts, which tend to have relatively low interest rate returns (but are safe). Akerlof, when confronted with this fact, said, "I know it's utterly stupid."

Clive Granger, who won the Nobel Prize in Economics in 2003, was asked about his investments. He said, "I would rather spend my time enjoying my income than bothering about investments."

Daniel Kahneman, who won the Nobel Prize in Economics in 2002, said the following about his investments: "I think very little about my retirement savings, because I know that thinking could make me poorer or more miserable or both."

Keep in mind what we said in an earlier chapter: almost every activity comes with both benefits and costs. Benefits can come from investing wisely, but certain costs are involved too. It takes time to find out about various investments, to research them, and to keep informed on how they are doing.

The actions of our four Nobel Prize winners also point out something else. As we said once before, many people think that economics is simply about money and money matters. It is not. It is about utility and happiness and making oneself better off. Each of our four Nobel Prize winners might not have been doing the best thing for his wallet, but certainly each knew it and continued on the same path anyway. In other words, each was willing to sacrifice some money in order to live a preferred lifestyle.

What is the lesson for you? Should you care nothing about your investments and hope that your financial future will take care of itself? Or should you spend time regularly watching, researching, and evaluating various investments that either you have made or plan to make? Neither extreme is too sensible. It is not a matter of either one or the other. It is possible to learn enough about investments to protect yourself from the financial uncertainties of the future, but not spend so much time worrying about the future that you don't enjoy the present.

THINK ABOUT IT Sometimes people choose not to learn about various investments because they think what they need to learn is too difficult to understand. A person might say, "Learning about stocks and bonds, and put options, and other such things is just beyond me." What do you think?

economics and business, initiative, good ideas, and the ability to be part of a team.

With the increasing use of the Internet for investment, many people are investing their money from home. Television financial journalists such as Louis Rukeyser have become mainstays for these at-home investors. Assign students to research some financial journalists and determine their qualifications to report investment and financial news.

Economics in the Real World

After students have read this feature, ask them why, do they think, the economists interviewed have, in their own opinions, invested badly. Invite students to consider how much time they want to devote to investing when they have the money. Ask students to explain what it means to say that economics is about "utility, happiness, and making oneself better off." Then ask whether they agree, and why or why not.

ANSWERS TO THINK ABOUT IT Answers will vary. Invite volunteers to share their answers with the class.

Reinforcement Activity

In order to give students a good idea of how stocks and bonds differ, have them create a chart with stocks on one side and bonds on the other. Then have them answer the following questions for both stocks and bonds:

1. What does the investment represent?
2. How is the price determined?
3. How is profit gained?
4. Is there a chance to lose the principal investment?
5. How do interest rates affect the price?

Cause and Effect

Tell students that they are going to buy bonds from a corporation. They have $10,000 to spend. What should they check next? (*Answer:* The interest rate.) Why is this information important? (*Answer:* The coupon rate should match or exceed the interest rate.) What would happen if they buy the bonds and interest rates go up 2%? (*Answer:* As the interest rate rises, the price of old or existing bonds falls. Interest rates and the price of old or existing bonds move in opposite directions.)

Reinforcement Activity

Ask students why timing is so important in buying and selling bonds. They should say that bond prices are based on interest rates, so to make a profit on the buying and selling of bonds you need to understand the relationship between bond prices and interest rates. As interest rates rise, the prices of old or existing bonds fall.

Economics Around the Clock

After reading and discussing the topics in this section, you may want to refer students to the 10:56 A.M. scenario in Economics Around the Clock (page 429) and discuss their answers to the question provided.

Students should understand that yes, timing can matter a lot. Ideally, when investing in stocks, bonds, real estate, or whatever, one wants to "buy low" and "sell high." In other words, one wants his or her buying and selling activities to be timed just right so that buying corresponds to "low price" and selling corresponds to "high price."

Prediction Activity

One of the most used strategies in bond investing is interest rate anticipation. Investors will try to predict the coming interest rate and tie their investment strategy into their predictions. The interest rate may seem easy to predict; after all, it can only go up, down, or stay the same. Find the prime rate (or the interest rate of the local bank) and find out how often it changes. Encourage students to predict the changes based on what they have learned in the course.

Teaching with Visuals

Answers will vary. Students may say traders would need to know the face value of a bond, the maturity date, current yield, volume, close, the net change, and the tax liability.

coupon rate in such a way that it can attract people to its bonds. If people are earning, say, 5 percent, on their savings account, they will not lend money to the company unless the company pays a coupon rate of at least 5 percent. In short, the coupon rate is set at a competitive level and not at just any level the company wants to set it.

Types of Bonds

As stated earlier, bonds are typically issued by companies, governments, and government agencies. This section briefly describes some of the many types of bonds that these entities issue.

Corporate Bonds A corporate bond is issued by a private corporation. It is typical to find a corporate bond with a $10,000 face value. Corporate bonds may sell for a price above or below face value depending on current supply and demand conditions for the bond. The interest that corporate bonds pay is fully taxable.

Municipal Bonds Municipal bonds are issued by state and local governments. States may issue bonds to help pay for a new highway. Local governments may issue bonds to finance a civic auditorium or a sports stadium. Many people purchase municipal bonds because the interest paid on the bonds is not subject to federal taxes.

Treasury Bills, Notes, and Bonds When the federal government wants to borrow funds, it can issue Treasury bills (T-bills), notes, or bonds. The only difference between bills, notes, and bonds is their time to maturity. Although called by different names, all are bonds. Treasury bills mature in 13, 26, or 52 weeks. Treasury notes mature in 2 to 10 years, and Treasury bonds mature in 10 to 30 years. Treasury bills, notes, and bonds are considered safe investments because it is unlikely that the federal government will default on its bond obligations. After all, the federal government has the power to tax to pay off bondholders.

Inflation-Indexed Treasury Bonds In 1997, the federal government began to issue inflation-indexed bonds. The first indexed bonds issued matured in 10 years and were available at face values as small as $1,000. The difference between an inflation-indexed Treasury bond and a Treasury bond that is not indexed is that an inflation-indexed Treasury bond guarantees the purchaser a certain real rate of return, but a nonindexed Treasury bond does not. For example, suppose you purchase an inflation-indexed, 10-year, $1,000 bond that pays 4 percent coupon rate. If no inflation occurs, the annual interest payment will be $40. On the other hand, if the inflation rate is, say, 3 percent, the government will "mark up" the value of the bond by 3 percent—from $1,000 to $1,030. Then it will pay 4 percent on this higher dollar amount. So instead of paying $40 each year, it pays $41.20. By increasing the monetary value of the security by the rate of inflation, the government guarantees the bondholder a real return of 4 percent.

▲ If one of these traders was buying bonds for you, what information do you think he would need to have about the bonds being considered for purchase?

Cooperative Learning

Divide students into four groups, and assign each of the groups a type of bond listed on page 446. Each group should research what the bond is, how to buy it, and the tax liability associated with it. Then the group should identify five examples of its assigned bond and chart out the symbol, coupon rate, maturity date, current yield, volume, close, and net change. The group can present this information to the rest of the class.

▲ At City Hall in New York City the city government might decide that the city needs a new football stadium and that the best way to finance construction of the stadium would be to sell bonds. **What do we call the type of bonds that the city would sell?**

How to Read the Bond Market Page

If you turn to the bond market page of the newspaper, you can find information about the different types of bonds. If you want to invest in bonds, you will need to know how to read the information that relates to both corporate bonds and Treasury bonds. First let's look at corporate bonds.

Corporate Bonds

Not all publications will present corporate bond information in exactly the same format. The format we show you here is most common.

(1) Bonds	(2) Cur. Yld.	(3) Vol	(4) Close	(5) Net Chg.
PacBell 6 5/8 34	6.7	115	99 1/2	−3/4

In the first column you find three pieces of information. The first is the abbreviation for the company that issued the bond. Here you see "PacBell," which stands for Pacific Bell, the telecommunications company. Next to that you see "6 5/8," which indicates the coupon rate of the bond. Next you see "34," the year the bond matures, which in this case it is 2034.

In the second column you find the current yield. (We showed how to compute the yield on a bond earlier.) This current yield means that if the bond is purchased today (hence the word *current*), it will provide a yield of 6.7 percent.

In the third column you find the volume of sales in dollars for a particular day. The number here is 115, so the dollar volume today is $115,000.

The fourth column indicates the closing price for the bond on this particular day: 99 1/2. Bond prices are quoted in points and fractions; each point is $10. Thus, 99 1/2 is $999.50 ($99.5 \times 10 =$ $999.50).

In the fifth column we see the net change for the day. The "−3/4" means the price on this day was $7.50 lower than it was the day before.

Treasury Bonds

Not all publications present Treasury bond information in exactly the same format. The following format is common.

(1) Rate	(2) Maturity	(3) Bid	(4) Ask	(5) Chg	(6) Yield
7 3/4	Feb. 09	105:12	105:14	−1	5.50

Teaching with Visuals

New York would sell municipal bonds to finance the construction of a stadium.

Background Information

Municipal bonds are popular because the interest paid on them is not subject to federal taxes.

Reinforcement Activity

Direct students to look over the bond report in a major newspaper, like the *Wall Street Journal*. Have them select three bonds and reproduce the chart from the newspaper on a separate piece of paper. Have them identify the type of each bond as well as the coupon rate, the maturity date, the yield, the price of the bond today, and the price of the bond yesterday.

Cross-Curricular Activity

Ask the government teacher from your school to come into your class to talk about the uses of bonds by the federal government. Have the teacher discuss the historical significance of government bonds, including war bonds, and the financial rewards that the government has gathered by selling bonds. Require students to prepare questions beforehand to allow the teacher time to research answers and statistics on government bonds that have been issued. After the teacher has discussed the political implications of bonds, you can talk about the economic implications.

Teaching with Visuals

Answers will vary. Ask students to share their answers and explain.

Reinforcement Activity

Invite the financial journalist for your local newspaper, radio, or television station into your class to discuss the bond market. Students should prepare questions ahead of time to give the visitor the chance to prepare answers for the class.

After students read this feature on page 449, ask them if they ever thought about buying stock in a company located in another part of the world.

ANSWERS TO ECONOMIC THINKING Answers to the first question may vary. Students might say that it would make sense to buy Brazilian or Italian stock instead of a U.S. stock because the foreign stock might yield a higher return. The answer to the second question is no, the rates of return for all stocks from around the world would not be the same.

Application Activity

After reading and discussing Section 2, you may want to assign the Section Activity in the *Applying the Principles Workbook.*

Assess

Quick Quiz

The following true-or-false quiz will help you assess student understanding of the material covered in this section.

1. The face value of a bond is also called the par value. (True)
2. The more likely the bond issuer will default on the face value of the bond, the higher the bond's rating. (False)
3. Coupon rate and yield are the same when the price paid for the bond equals the face value. (True)
4. Bond issuers can set any coupon rate they like. (False)
5. Inflation-indexed treasury bonds guarantee bondholders a real return based on inflation. (True)

▼ Storing your valuables in a lock box is safe and secure but offers no return on your assets. Buying high-risk stocks and bonds, on the other hand offers an opportunity for high returns—and high losses. **What sort of investment strategy do you think is the wisest?**

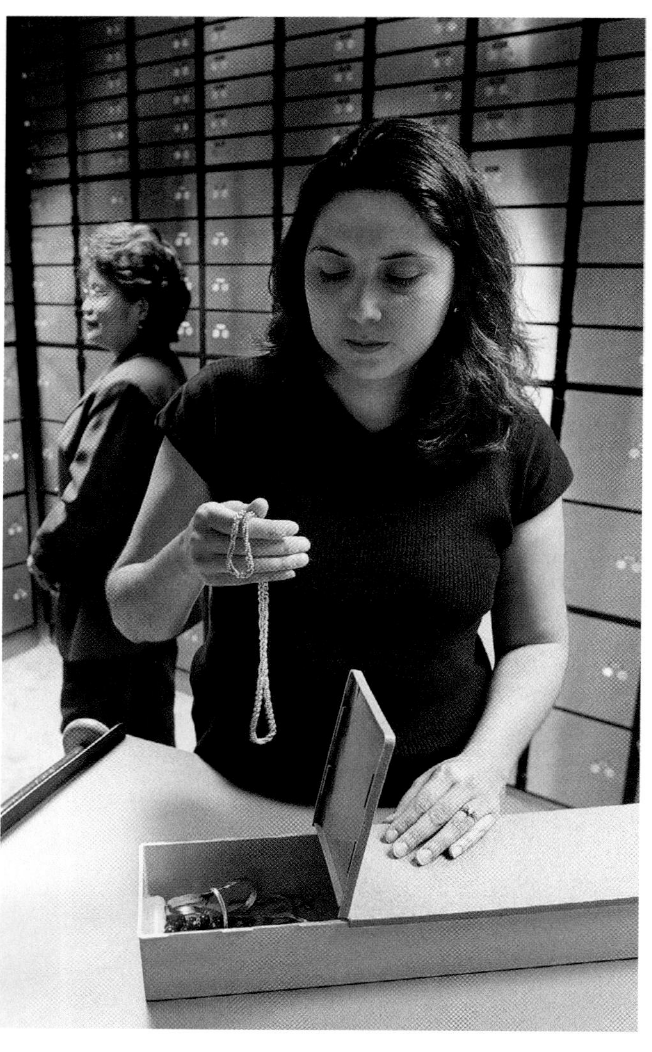

In the first column we find the coupon rate of the bond. This Treasury bond pays $7\frac{3}{4}$ percent of the face value of the bond in annual interest payments.

In the second column we learn when the bond matures. This Treasury bond matures in February 2009.

In the third column we learn how much the buyer is willing to pay for the bond (the price you will receive if you sell it). The number here is 105:12. The number before the colon is multiplied by 10, and the number after the colon stands for 32nds of $10. Therefore, first multiply 105 × $10, which gives you $1,050. Then, since 12/32 is 0.375, multiply 0.375 times $10, giving you $3.75. Add the $3.75 to $1,050 to get $1,053.75.

The fourth column indicates how much the seller is asking for the bond. In other words, it is the price you will pay to the seller if you buy the bond. In this case, it is $1,054.37.

In the fifth column the change in the price of the bond from the previous trading day is quoted in 32nds. It follows then that a –1 means that the price of the bond fell by 1/32nd of $10 or approximately 32 cents from the previous day.

Finally, yield, which is based on the ask price, is the return a person who buys the bond today (at the ask price) and holds it to maturity will realize. For this bond, the yield is 5.50 percent.

Risk and Return

We discussed stocks in the first section of this chapter and bonds in the second. The common denominator between both these sections is that people buy stocks or bonds for the return. Simply stated, they buy stocks and bonds in the hope that they will "make money."

We need to keep in mind that stocks and bonds often come with different risk and return factors. For example, it might be much riskier to buy stock in a new company than it is to buy a Treasury bond issued by the U.S. Treasury. You can be fairly sure that the U.S. Treasury is going to pay off that bond; after all, the U.S. government has the ability to tax people. However, you can't be so sure you'll have a positive return on the stock you buy in the new company. You might buy the stock for $10 one day, and three days later it falls to $1 and stays at that price (or thereabouts) for 10 years.

Back in Chapter 1 we mentioned a well-known principle in economics: There is no such thing as a free lunch. Applied to stocks and bonds (or any investment), it means that you never get something for nothing. In short, higher returns come with higher risks and lower returns come with lower risks. Treasury bonds, for example, will often pay (relatively) low returns because they are so safe (risk-free).

Differentiating Instruction

English Language Learners

To help ELL students, use the following resources, which are provided as part of the *Economics: New Ways of Thinking* program:

- a Spanish glossary in the *Student Text*
- Spanish versions of the Chapter Summaries on an audio CD

What Would Life Be Like Without Financial Markets?

In Section 1, you learned that the purpose of a financial market (such as the stock or bond market) is to channel money from some people to others. Now you have a better idea of how this process happens. People with saved funds might buy stock in a company that wants the money to buy a piece of machinery or a new plant. Similarly, people with saved funds might buy bonds (and therefore lend money) from a company that wants to borrow the money to buy a piece of machinery or a new plant.

To see just how important financial markets are, imagine a world without them. Suppose that in this world you are a person with a great idea for a new product. The only problem is that it is almost impossible for you to save enough money (on your current salary) to develop, produce, and sell the new product. In a world without financial markets, you have nowhere to turn. You can't issue stock in your new company because no stock market provides a place of trade. You can't borrow the funds because no bond market provides a place of exchange. So, your good idea is never acted upon. Society never gets the new product.

In a world of financial markets, though, the people with the good ideas can be matched up with the people who saved funds that they would like to invest. As a result, society ends up with more goods and services than otherwise would be the case.

Stocks Around the World

In February 2005, 11,000 investors from 22 countries met at the World Money Show in Orlando, Florida, to get investment advice from advisers from around the world. In a global economy, as opposed to a national economy, investors set out to find the best return for their money—no matter where that may take them. One easy way to accomplish this goal is to purchase ADRs, which stands for American Depository Receipts. An ADR is certificate issued by a U.S. bank; the ADR represents a specified number of shares (or one share) in a foreign stock that is traded on a U.S. stock exchange. Envision a world where anyone can easily buy stock issued by any company in the world. In other words, it is as easy to buy stock issued by a company in your hometown as it is to buy stock issued by a company in Moscow.

ECONOMIC THINKING Why might it make more sense to sometimes buy a Brazilian or Italian stock instead of a U.S. stock? Would you predict that the rates of return for all stocks (around the world) would be the same?

Defining Terms

1. Define:
   a face value of a bond
   b. coupon rate of a bond
   c. yield

Review Facts and Concepts

2. a. Is an issuer of a bond a lender or borrower?
   b. Is a buyer of a bond a lender or borrower?
3. If the face value of a bond is $10,000 and the annual coupon payment is $600, then what is the coupon rate?
4. If the annual coupon payment is $500 and the price paid for the bond is $9,544, then what is the yield?

Critical Thinking

5. "If you can predict interest rates, then you can earn a fortune buying and selling bonds." Do you agree or disagree? Explain your answer.

Applying Economic Concepts

6. Why might a person purchase an inflation-indexed Treasury bond?

Assessment Book

You will find a quiz for this section in the *Assessment Book.*

Reteaching Activity

Use the Section Assessment to gauge which students may need reteaching on this section. Show those students a single line of a bond market page from the newspaper. Have them identify aloud what each column means and how it is calculated.

Guided Reading

For further reteaching of the key concepts in this section, assign the Outlining Activity and the Just the Facts Handout from the *Guided Reading and Study Guide.*

Defining Terms

1. a. face value of a bond: the amount the issuer of the bond will repay to the buyer of the bond on the maturity date; **b. coupon rate of a bond:** the percentage of the face value that the bondholder receives each year until the bond matures; **c. yield:** equal to the annual coupon payment divided by the price paid for the bond.

Reviewing Facts and Concepts

2. a. borrower; **b.** lender.
3. 6% (*calculation*: $600 ÷ $10,000 = 6%).
4. 5.24% (*calculation*: $500 ÷ $9,544 = 5.24%).

Critical Thinking

5. Students should agree. As interest rates rise, bond prices fall, and as interest rates fall, bond prices rise. The objective is to buy bonds when they are low and sell them when they are high. If a person could predict interest rates, he would buy bonds when he thought interest rates were at their highest (because at this time bonds would be at their lowest), and he would sell bonds when he thought interest rates were at their lowest (because bonds would be at their highest). Buying low and selling high consistently is the way to earn a fortune.

Applying Economic Concepts

6. Inflation-indexed Treasury bonds guarantee the purchaser a certain real rate of return. The government increases the monetary value of the security by the rate of inflation, thereby guaranteeing the bondholder a real rate of return.

SECTION 3

Teacher Support

Focus and Motivate

Section Objectives

After completing this section, students will be able to

- explain futures contracts;
- explain why people buy futures contracts;
- explain a currency futures contract;
- explain an options contract;
- describe the difference between a put option and a call option;
- identify the reason an investor would use a put or a call option.

Kickoff Activity

Invite students to predict the economic meanings of the following terms: *futures* and *options*. Allow students to discuss their answers. Remind students that in an economic way of thinking, many words have definitions that may differ from the definitions with which they are familiar. Have them preview the definitions of these terms on pages 450 and 454 and use each in a sentence that illustrates its economic definition.

Activating Prior Knowledge

To review previous sections, direct students to compare stocks and bonds, noting their similarities and differences.

Teach

Discussion Starter

As you discuss with students exactly what a futures contract is, ask them why someone would want to buy or sell a product at today's prices in the future. What chances are the buyer and the seller taking? What is each hoping for? Ask students whether they would be willing to take these kinds of chances.

SECTION 3

Futures and Options

Focus Questions

- What is a futures contract?
- Why do people buy futures contracts?
- What is a currency futures contract?
- What is an options contract?
- What is a put option?
- What is a call option?
- What is the major reason that an investor would decide to make use of either a put or call option?

Key Terms

futures contract
option

Futures

Myers is a miller. He buys wheat from the wheat farmer, turns the wheat into flour, and then sells the flour to the baker. Obviously he wants to earn a profit for what he does. But how much, if any, profit he earns depends on the price at which he can buy the wheat, and the price at which he can sell the flour.

Now suppose Myers enters into a contract with a baker. Myers promises to deliver to the baker 1,000 pounds of flour in six months. At the current wheat price, $3 a bushel, Myers knows he can earn a profit on his deal with the baker. But he doesn't need the wheat now; he needs it in about 6 months. What will the price of wheat be then? If it is, say, $2 a bushel, then Myers will earn more profit on the deal with the baker. But if it is, say, $4 a bushel, then he will lose money on the deal. Myers's problem is that he doesn't know what a bushel of wheat will sell for in six months.

futures contract
Agreement to buy or sell a specific amount of something (commodity, currency, financial instrument) at a particular price on a stipulated future date.

Myers decides to buy a futures contract in wheat. A **futures contract** is a contract in which the seller agrees to provide a particular good (in this case, wheat) to the buyer on a specified future date at an agreed-upon price. For example, Myers might buy bushels of wheat now, for a price of $3 a bushel, to be delivered to him in six months.

Who would sell Myers the futures contract? A likely possibility would be a speculator, someone who buys and sells commodities to profit from changes in the market. A speculator assumes risk in the hope of making a gain.

Suppose Smith, a speculator, believes that the price of wheat six months from now is going to be lower than it is today. She may look at things this way: "The price of wheat today is $3 a bushel. I think the price of wheat in six months will be close to $2 a bushel. Why not promise the miller that I will deliver him as much wheat as he wants in six months if, in return, he agrees today to pay me $3 a bushel for it? Then, in six months, I will buy the wheat for $2 a bushel, sell it to the miller for $3 a bushel, and earn myself $1 profit per bushel."

Myers, the miller, and Smith, the speculator, enter into a futures contract. Myers buys 200 bushels of wheat for delivery in six months; Smith sells 200 bushels of wheat for delivery in six months.

Internet Research

Direct students to use the Internet to research the job of floor trader. They should write a one- or two-page essay answering the following questions: Would you like this type of job? Do you think you have the type of personality to be an effective trader? Students should also list the things they would and wouldn't like about the job. Then they should list the additional topics they would want to learn about before feeling prepared to become a trader.

What does each person get out of the deal? Myers, the miller, gets peace of mind. He knows that he will be able to buy the wheat at a price that will let him earn a profit on his deal with the baker. Smith takes a chance, which she is willing to take, for the chance of earning a profit.

EXAMPLE: Wilson is a farmer, who grows primarily corn. The current price of corn is $2.34 a bushel. Wilson doesn't have any corn to sell right now, but she will in two months. She hopes that between now and then, the price of corn won't fall, say, to something under $2. She decides to enter into a futures contract in corn. She promises to deliver 5,000 bushels of corn two months from now for $2.34 a bushel. Johnson, a speculator in corn, decides that this deal is a good one for him because he believes that in two months the price of a bushel of corn will rise to $3.14. So Wilson and Johnson enter into a futures contract. Two months pass and the price of corn drops to $2.10. Johnson turns out to be wrong about the price rising. So, Wilson delivers 5,000 bushels of corn to Johnson, for which Johnson pays Wilson $2.34 a bushel (total: $11,700) as agreed. Then Johnson turns around and sells the corn for $2.10 a bushel (receiving $10,500). Johnson loses $1,200 on the deal. ♦

A Student Asks

QUESTION: *In the example, the price of corn went down. It could have gone up, though. In this case, would Wilson, the farmer, have lost money?*

ANSWER: *Let's suppose that the price of corn rose to $4. In this case, Wilson would have delivered 5,000 bushels of corn to Speculator Johnson for $2.34 a bushel, and then Johnson would have turned around and sold the corn for $4 a bushel. In this case, Speculator Johnson earned the difference between $4 and $2.34—or $1.66—for every one of the 5,000 bushels, for a total of $8,300.*

Did Wilson, the farmer, lose this $8,300? In a way she did. She didn't lose it in the sense that it was once in her pocket and now it isn't. She lost it in the sense that it could have been in her pocket (if she hadn't entered into the futures contract with Johnson) and now it isn't.

This situation might be okay with Wilson. Wilson, remember, may not want to be in the speculating business. She might want to only be worried about growing and selling corn and nothing else. Maybe she doesn't want to be involved in speculating on the price of corn. In other words, maybe she is willing to "give up" $8,300 now and then so that she can sleep soundly at night and not worry constantly about possible price declines.

▲ You may remember from Chapter 8 that this wheat farmer is a price taker. He has to sell his wheat at the equilibrium price—not a penny more or less. **How might a farmer reduce the uncertainty in the wheat market?**

Currency Futures

A futures contract can be written for wheat, as we have seen, or for a currency, a stock index, or even bonds. Here is how a currency futures contract works.

Suppose Bill owns a Toyota dealership in Tulsa, Oklahoma. It is currently May and Bill is thinking about a shipment of Toyotas he plans to buy in August. He knows that he must buy the Toyotas from Japan with yen, but he has a problem. At the present time, the dollar price of yen is $0.012. Bill wonders

Teaching with Visuals

Use the Economics Around the Clock activity below for a thorough discussion of the question provided with the photograph.

Economics Around the Clock

After reading and discussing "Futures," you may want to refer students to the 8:34 A.M. scenario in Economics Around the Clock (page 429) and discuss their answers to the question provided there.

Students should say that Jack could enter into a futures contract, promising to deliver so many bushels of wheat in the future for a predetermined set price. This would protect him against a potential drop in the price of wheat.

Problem Solving

Invite students to suppose that they are looking to trade in some type of agricultural future for a product commonly produced in your area. Ask students what they would need to know before they got involved in trading futures for that product. Allow students to work on this problem on their own and then come together as a class to discuss their thoughts.

Answers will vary. Students might mention that they should know the current price of the product, a list of factors that affect the supply of that product (weather, insects, seed supply) and demand for the product (dietary trends), and any other information that might help them predict the supply and demand for the product, and thus the equilibrium price in the future.

Background Information: Futures and Options

If students question the importance of learning about futures and options, tell them that options and futures are two of the riskiest ways to invest money. Professional advisors and brokers want investors to be made aware of several cardinal rules of investing. The rules include these:

1. Never invest more than you are able to lose. No one can completely predict the market, especially not in terms of futures and options.
2. Be aware of costs attached to the trade itself, like commissions.
3. Make sure you know where your money is; don't assume the broker is working in your best interests.

Reinforcement Activity

Because of the highly volatile nature of the futures market, trading without the help of an advisor or broker is not recommended. The general policy of "buying low and selling high" can be even faster in futures because as a speculator, you set your own prices for buying and selling—which means that you make your buy and sell decisions ahead of time and do not usually spend time making them at the time of the purchase or sale. It's very important to have a constant eye on your portfolio and to know what is happening in the market. Assign students to monitor the futures market in the newspaper for three days, or, if possible, have them check the market on the Internet twice a day. Ask, How much do the prices for futures change over a three-day period?

Teaching with Visuals

Answers will vary. Invite students to share their answers with the class.

what the price of yen will be in August when he plans to make his purchase. Suppose the dollar price of yen rises to $0.018. If the price of the yen goes up, then instead of paying $30,000 for a Toyota priced at 2.5 million yen, he would have to pay $45,000.

What can Bill do? He could purchase a futures contract today for the needed quantity of yen in August. Who is willing to sell this contract? Obviously someone who thinks the dollar price of yen will go down between now and August. For example, Julie may think to herself, "I think the dollar price of yen will go down between now and August. Therefore, I will enter into a contract with Bill stating that I will give him 2.5 million yen in August for $30,000, the exchange rate specified in the contract being 1 yen = $0.012. If I am right, and the actual exchange rate at the time is 1 yen = $0.011, then I can purchase the 2.5 million yen for $27,500, and fulfill my contract with Bill by turning the yen over to him for $30,000. I walk away with $2,500 profit."

EXAMPLE: Suppose you check the dollar price of a euro today and find that it is 83 cents. In other words, for every 83 cents, you get 1 euro in return. Let's say that you believe that in three months you will have to pay $1.10 to buy a euro. With this belief in mind, you enter into a futures contract: essentially, you say that you are willing to buy $10 million worth of euros three months from now for 83 cents a euro. Who might be willing to enter into this contract with you? Anyone who thinks the dollar price of a euro will be lower (not higher) in three months. Suppose you and this other person enter a contract. You promise to buy $10 million worth of euros in three months (at 83 cents a euro) and this other person promises to sell you $10 million worth of euros in three months (at 83 cents a euro).

Three months pass and we learn that it takes 97 cents to buy a euro (not 83 cents and not $1.10). What happens now? The person who entered into a contract with you has to buy $10 million worth of euros at an exchange rate of 97 cents = 1 euro. For $10 million, he gets 10,309,278 euros. He then turns these euros over to you and gets 83 cents for every euro, which gives him $8,556,701. Obviously this person has taken a loss; he spent $10 million to get $8,556,701 in return—a loss of $1,443,299.

What about you? You now have 10,309,278 euros for which you paid $8,556,701. How many dollars will you get if you sell all those euros? Well, since you get 97 cents for every euro, you will get approximately $10 million. Are you better off or worse off now? You are better off by $1,443,229. ♦

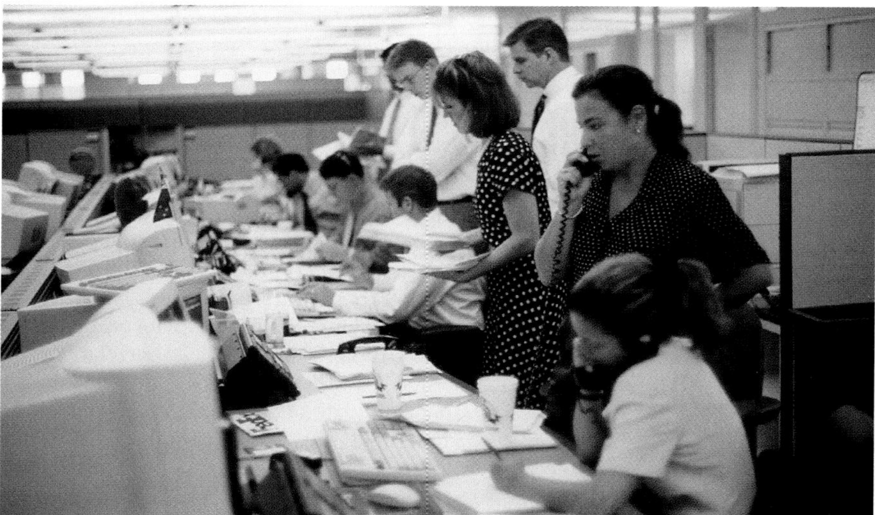

▶ Thousands of people work in the financial industry helping people trade almost anything they want to trade—stocks, bonds, wheat, gold, or money, for example. **Do you think you would enjoy this type of work?**

Background Information: Online Trading

According to leading sources, U.S. families are managing an increasing number of online accounts. Right now, most American investors are passive investors, allowing their financial advisors and 401(k) fund managers to move their investments. Soon, analysts believe, more people will take control of their own investments through online brokerages. The lure of big payoffs has more and more Americans checking their investments every day and moving their money for the big score. However, it is more likely that the people who move their money will lose rather than make money in the long run.

Economics in the Real World

Want to Make $1.3 Quadrillion?

??????????????????

At the close of the twentieth century, the editors of the financial magazine *The Economist* identified the highest returning investments for each year, beginning in 1900 and ending in 1999. For example, the highest-returning investment in 1974 was gold, in 1902 it was U.S. Treasury bills, and in 1979 it was silver.

The editors then asked how much income a person would have earned at the end of 1999 if she had invested $1 in the highest-returning investment in 1900, and then taken the returns from that investment and invested it in the highest-returning investment in 1901, and so on for each year during the century. After taxes and dealer costs, she would have earned $1.3 quadrillion. (Quadrillion comes after trillion. In 2004, Bill Gates, the richest person in the world, had $47 billion, so $1.3 quadrillion is 27,659 times what Bill Gates has.) What is the lesson? With perfect foresight (or with a crystal ball that always correctly tells you what the highest-returning investment of the year will be), one would be rich beyond his or her imagination.

After the editors ran their experiment, they changed it. They went back and asked themselves what one would have earned over the twentieth century if, instead of investing in the highest-returning investment in a given year, she invested in it one year late. In other words, if X is the best investment in 1956, then invest in it in 1957.

Why did the editors choose to proceed this way? Because they believed that many people only invest in a "hot" investment when it is too late. In other words, they invest in it after they have heard about it, but investing in it after they have heard about it is usually too late. Think of an investment as a mountain. Going up the mountain is comparable to increasing returns on the investment; going down the mountain is comparable to decreasing returns. It's only when the investment is near its peak that many people hear about it. Then it's too late, with no place to go but down.

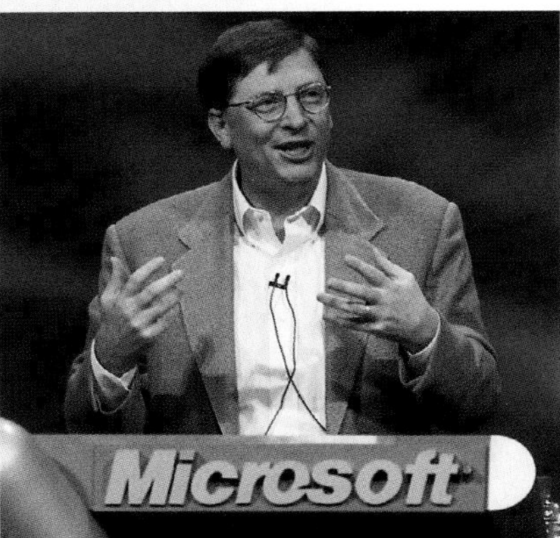

Here's an example. A person with a crystal ball, or with perfect foresight, would have invested in the Polish stock market in 1993, when no one was talking about it, and reaped a 754 percent gain. The typical investor would have invested in it one year later, in 1994, when everyone was talking about it. The problem is that the Polish stock market fell by 55 percent in 1994.

So, what would the person who is always one year late have earned over the twentieth century? After taxes and dealer costs, $290.

What are the economic lessons here? First, the best investments are often the ones that you don't hear about until it is too late. Second, ignoring the first lesson, and thinking that a popular investment is necessarily a good investment, is often the way to low returns.

THINK ABOUT IT Many people seem to think that when it comes to investments, whatever an investment did last year will be what it does this year. If it went up by 30 percent last year, well then it has to go up this year by 30 percent. Consider the words of Warren Buffet, one of the most successful investors of all times. "If past history was all there was to the game, the richest people would be librarians." What do you think: does anything guarantee that the future will look exactly like the immediate past?

Economics in the Real World

Instruct students to read this feature. Then ask students how likely it is that anyone would make $1.3 quadrillion on a $1 investment. Ask students whether they think that any investment—whether small or large—is better than no investment at all.

ANSWERS TO THINK ABOUT IT Answers will vary. Students should see that there are no guarantees in investing, and that the future will not look exactly like the immediate past.

Reinforcement Activity

Speculators are people who buy and sell commodities to profit from changes in the market. They hope that the price of the good will decrease in the future, earning them a profit. They assume risks in the hope of making a gain.

Ask students if, considering the financial risks involved, they think being a speculator is a good job to have. Also ask them what a person would need in order to have this kind of job.

Answers will vary. One thing a person needs to have for a speculating job is a financial reserve to absorb losses. There are no guarantees of profits in the market.

Cross-Curricular Activity

Some newspapers and online brokerages have started to use decimal points rather than fractions on their stock pages. Ask students to bring in the financial section of a newspaper. Have a math teacher come into your class to show students how to convert the fractions into decimals. Once they have learned to do that, suggest that students work on additional pages of the newspaper, converting fractions into decimals or vice versa. Ask students which format they find easier to understand.

Reinforcement Activity

Ask students the following questions: When would a buyer exercise a call option? When would a buyer exercise a put option? (*Answer:* A buyer would exercise a call option if the price of the specified stock increases. A buyer would exercise a put option if the price of the specified stock decreases.)

Cause and Effect

In today's business market, employees commonly receive stock options as bonuses. Ask students to predict what could happen to the stock price if employees exercise their option, or purchase the stock. Students might point out that demand for the stock will rise—and that if demand increases while supply remains the same, the price of the stock will rise.

Reinforcement Activity

Guide students in reviewing the different kinds of investing. Ask if they would like to invest, and what kind of investments they would make. Remind them that when they invest, they should do so wisely and under the supervision of a qualified professional.

Teaching with Visuals

No, clients do not already own the stock in question. Answers will vary. Students should see that the call option gives clients a chance to watch a stock's performance without spending a lot of money.

Application Activity

After reading and discussing Section 3, you may want to assign the Section Activity in the *Applying the Principles Workbook.*

Assess

Quick Quiz

The following true-or-false quiz will help you assess student understanding of the material covered in this section.

1. In a futures contract, the seller would be someone who does not mind assuming the risk of a change in prices. (True)

Options

An **option** is a contract that gives the owner of the option the right, but not the obligation, to buy or sell shares of a stock at a specified price on or before a specified date. The two types of options are calls and puts.

option
Contract that gives the owner the right, but not the obligation, to buy or sell shares of a good at a specified price on or before a specified date.

Call Options

Call options give the owner of the option the right to buy shares of a stock at a specified price within the time limits of the contract. The specified price at which the buyer can buy shares of a stock is called the *strike price.* For example, suppose Brown buys a call option for $20. The call option specifies that she can buy 100 shares of IBM stock at a strike price of $150 within the next month. If the price of IBM stocks falls below $150, Brown doesn't exercise her call option. She simply tears it up and accepts the fact that she has lost $20. If she still wants to buy IBM stock, she can do so through her stockbroker as she normally does and pay the going price, which is lower than $150. If the price rises above $150, she exercises her call option. She buys the stock at $150 a share and then turns around and sells it for the higher market price. She has made a profit.

If Brown buys a call option, then someone must sell it to her. Who would sell her a call option? Any person who thought the option wouldn't be exercised by the buyer. For example, if Jackson believed that the price of IBM was going to fall below $150, then he would gladly sell a call option to Brown for $20, thinking that the option would never be exercised. That's $20 in his pocket.

Put Options

Put options give the owner the right, but not the obligation, to sell (rather than buy, as in a call option) shares of a stock at a strike price during some period of time. For example, suppose Martin buys a put option to sell 100 shares of IBM stock at $130 during the next month. If the share price rises above $130, Martin will not exercise his put option. He will simply tear it up and sell the stock for more than $130. On the other hand, if the price drops below $130, then he will exercise his option to sell the stock for $130 a share. Who buys put options? People who think the price of the stock is going to decline.

Who sells put options? Obviously, the people who think the price of the stock is going to rise. Why not sell a put option for, say, $20, if you believe that the price of the stock is going to rise and the buyer of the put option is not going to exercise the option?

▼ **If these traders are buying call options, do their clients already own the stock in question? Why do you think someone would buy an option on a stock rather than the stock itself?**

A Student Asks

QUESTION: *I've heard some people talk about getting part of their pay or a bonus in the form of stock options. I've heard that some people make a lot of money through stock options. What are these options?*

ANSWER: *A stock option gives an employee the right to buy a specific number of shares of stock at a price specified by the employer. The "price" specified by the employer is often the current market price of the stock when the stock option is issued. The hope for the employee is that the market price will rise over time. For example, if the stock option specifies the price of $10 a share, the employee has the right to buy the stock at $10. Now suppose time passes and the market price of the stock rises to $40. What can the employee do now? He or she can buy the stock for $10 a share and then turn around and sell it for $40 a share.*

Cooperative Learning

Divide students into small groups. Assign half of the groups to write scenarios in which someone might want to enter into a futures contract. Assign the other half of the groups to write scenarios in which someone might want to purchase options. Encourage students to write some scenarios that focus on the speculator and some that focus on the other party. Then have groups trade scenarios and explain what each party hopes for in each transaction.

How You Can Use Call and Put Options

Suppose you think a certain stock is going to rise in price during the next few months. Currently, the stock sells for $250 a share. You don't have enough money to buy many shares of stock, but you would like to benefit from what you expect will be a rise in the price of the stock. What can you do? You can buy a call option. A call option will sell for a fraction of the cost of the stock. So, with limited resources, you decide to buy the call option, which gives you the right to buy, say, 100 shares of the stock at $250 anytime during the next three months.

Wait a minute. If you don't have the money to buy the stock at $250 a share now, why does anyone think you will have the money to buy the stock at $250 in a few months? Well, you don't have to buy the stock. If you are right that the price of the stock will rise, then the call option you are holding will become worth more to people. In other words, if you bought the option when the price of the stock was $250, and the stock rises to $300, then your call option has become more valuable. You can sell it and benefit from the uptick in the price of the stock.

Alternatively, let's say you expect the price of the stock to fall. Then you can buy a put option. In other words, you buy the right to sell the stock for $250 anytime during the next three months. If the price does fall, then your option becomes more valuable. In fact, the further the price falls, the more valuable your put option becomes. People who have the stock and want to sell it for a price higher than it currently brings on the market will be willing to buy your put option from you for some price higher than the price you paid.

EXAMPLE: The current price of a call option for AT&T stock is $10, while the current price of the AT&T stock is $100. Ginny decides to buy a call option for $10. This call option gives her the right to buy AT&T at a price of $100. Five months pass and the price of AT&T shares has risen to $150. If Ginny wants to, she can exercise her call option to buy AT&T stock at $100. In other words, she can spend $100 to buy a share of stock, which she can turn around and immediately sell for $150, making a profit of $50 per share. ◆

BY THE NUMBERS

The left side of the following table shows the top 10 days for the largest point gains in the Dow. For example, the Dow went up by 499.19 points on March 16, 2000. Keep in mind that the largest point gain in a day is not the same as the largest percentage gain in a day. We show the top 10 days for the largest percentage gain on the right side of the table.

Largest Point Gains			Largest Percentage Gains		
Rank	Date	Point Change	Rank	Date	Percentage Change
1	03/16/00	499.19	1	03/15/33	+15.34
2	07/24/02	488.95	2	10/6/31	+14.87
3	07/29/02	447.49	3	10/30/29	+12.34
4	04/05/01	402.63	4	09/21/32	+11.36
5	04/18/01	399.10	5	10/21/87	+10.15
6	09/08/98	380.53	6	08/3/32	+9.52
7	10/15/02	378.28	7	02/11/32	+9.47
8	09/24/01	368.05	8	11/14/29	+9.36
9	10/01/02	346.86	9	12/18/31	+9.35
10	05/16/01	342.95	10	02/13/32	+9.19

SECTION 3 ASSESSMENT

Defining Terms

1. Define:
   a. futures contract
   b. option

Review Facts and Concepts

2. Why might a person buy a futures contract?
3. Why might a person buy a call option?

Critical Thinking

4. "The currency speculator who sells futures contracts assumes the risk that someone else doesn't want to assume." Do you agree or disagree? Explain your answer.

Applying Economic Concepts

5. If you thought the share price of a stock was going to fall, would you buy a call option or a put option?

2. It is not possible to create a currency futures contract. (False)
3. There are two types of options, call options and push options. (False)
4. Call options give the owner the right to buy shares of a stock at a strike price during some period of time. (True)
5. You can make money with options without having to buy the stocks. (True)

Assessment Book

You will find a quiz for this section in the *Assessment Book.*

Reteaching Activity

Use the Section Assessment to gauge which students may need reteaching on this section. Divide students into groups and research the differences between futures and options. Why aren't these investments as steady as bonds or stocks?

Guided Reading

For further reteaching of the key concepts in this section, assign the Outlining Activity and the Just the Facts Handout from the *Guided Reading and Study Guide.*

SECTION 3 ASSESSMENT ANSWERS

Defining Terms

1. a. futures contract: a contract in which the seller agrees to provide a particular good to the buyer on a specified future date at an agreed-upon price; **b. option:** a contract that gives the owner the right, but not the obligation, to buy or sell shares of a stock at a specified price on or before a specified date.

Reviewing Facts and Concepts

2. A person might buy a futures contract in order to lock in a price in advance. In the text, Myers, a miller, buys a futures contract for wheat delivery at a certain price. Myers buys the futures contract because he wants to be assured of the price he will pay for the wheat.

3. A person might buy a call option because she or he thinks a particular stock will rise in price in the future but does not have enough money to buy the stock itself. Buying a call option is a way to benefit from an expected increase in price at a fraction of what it would cost to actually buy the stock.

Critical Thinking

4. Students should agree. The following illustrates the point: Jack sells Japanese television sets. He expects to buy a shipment of TVs in four months. The price he pays for the TVs will depend on the exchange rate between the yen and the dollar. He does not want to take a chance that the exchange rate will turn against him—that the dollar will depreciate and he will have to pay more for yen—so he buys a currency futures contract. The seller of the contract locks in a price per yen for Jack and, by doing this, assumes the risk of exchange rate changes herself.

Applying Economic Concepts

5. Students should say they would buy a put option.

CHAPTER 16 Assessment Answers

Economics Vocabulary

1. the market; **2.** yield; **3.** bond; **4.** yield; **5.** municipal; **6.** Treasury notes; **7.** futures contract.

Understanding the Main Ideas

1. Financial markets serve the purpose of channeling money from some people to other people.
2. You are buying ownership in the company.
3. The New York Stock Exchange (NYSE), the American Stock Exchange (AMEX), and the National Association of Securities Dealers Automated Quotations (NASDAQ) are three places where stocks are bought and sold.
4. Charles Dow created the Dow Jones Industrial Average to convey some information about what was actually happening in the stock market.
5. The Dow Jones Industrial Average can be seen as an "average price" of 30 key stocks. When the DJIA rises by 100 points, it means this average price has risen by $100. In general, when the DJIA rises, it costs more to buy the 30 stocks that make up the DJIA.
6. Dividends and expected gain in the stock's price are two reasons to buy stock.
7. The price of a stock is determined by the forces of supply and demand. If demand rises, and supply is constant, then the price of the stock will rise. If demand falls, and supply is constant, then the price of the stock will fall.
8. If you invest in a mutual fund, you are buying the stock of the companies that make up the fund. For example, if mutual fund A is made up of companies that sell Internet technology and you invest in mutual fund A, then you are buying stock of the companies that make up the fund (and sell Internet technology). If you invest in a stock index fund, you are investing in the companies that make up the stock index. For example, if you buy Spyders, you are buying stock in the five hundred companies that make up the Standard & Poor's 500 index.

CHAPTER 16 ASSESSMENT

Chapter Summary

Be sure you know and remember the following key points from the chapter sections.

Section 1

- Financial markets serve the purpose of channeling money from some people to other people.
- A stock is a claim on the assets of a corporation that gives the purchaser a share (ownership) in the corporation.
- Stocks are bought and sold on exchanges and markets such as the New York Stock Exchange.
- Some people buy stocks for the dividends, which are payments made to stockholders based on a company's profits, or to make money by buying shares at a lower price and selling at a higher price.

Section 2

- A bond is simply an IOU, or a promise to pay, typically issued by companies, governments, or government agencies.
- The three major components of a bond are face or par value, maturity date, and coupon rate.
- The price that a person pays for a bond depends on market conditions: the greater the demand for the bond relative to the supply, the higher the price.
- The yield on the bond is the coupon payment divided by the price paid for the bond.

Section 3

- In a futures contract, a seller agrees to provide a particular good to the buyer on a specified future date at an agreed-upon price.
- An option is a contract giving the owner the right, but not the obligation, to buy (a call option) or sell (a put option) a particular good at a specified price on or before a specified date.

Economics Vocabulary

To reinforce your knowledge of the key terms in this chapter, fill in the following blanks on a separate piece of paper with the appropriate word or phrase.

1. If a person buys Spyders, she is buying a stock index, sometimes referred to as buying ______.
2. The ______ of a stock is the dividend divided by the closing price.
3. A(n) ______ is an IOU, or a promise to pay.
4. The ______ on a bond is equal to the annual coupon payment divided by the face value of the bond.
5. A(n) ______ bond is a bond issued by a state or local government.
6. The federal government issues bonds of different maturities. Bonds with a maturity of 2 to 10 years are called ______.
7. A(n) ______ is a contract in which the seller agrees to provide a particular good to the buyer on a specified future date at an agreed-upon price.

Understanding the Main Ideas

Write answers to the following questions to review the main ideas in this chapter.

1. What is the purpose of financial markets?
2. If you buy a stock are you lending money to the company issuing the stock, or are you buying ownership in the company?
3. Name three places where stocks are bought and sold.
4. Why did Charles Dow create the Dow Jones Industrial Average?
5. What does it mean if the Dow Jones Industrial Average rises by, say, 100 points in a day?
6. What are the two reasons to buy stock?
7. What determines the price of a stock?
8. What does it mean if someone invests in a mutual fund? In a stock index fund?
9. "The stock market may not be the best place to put your money in the short run, but it is a pretty good place to put your money in the long run." What does this statement mean?

456 Chapter 16 Stocks and Bonds

9. The statement refers to the fact that over the short run, the stock market goes up and down. In other words, you could buy stocks with an average price of $100 in year 1, and in year 2 the average price may have fallen to $76. However, while there are both ups and downs in the stock market in the short run (say, from one year to the next, or even over a five- to 10-year period), the trend line for the stock market has been up. In other words, if you were to buy stocks in year 1 and sell them in year 25, you could be fairly sure that if the future is like the past, the stock market will be higher in year 25 than in year 1.
10. It means that the stock is selling for a share price that is 33 times higher than its earnings per share.
11. The three components of a bond are face value, the total amount the issuer of the bond will repay to the buyer of the bond; maturity date, the date

UNDERSTANDING AND APPLICATION

10. The PE ratio of a stock is 33. What does this number mean?
11. List and define the three major components of a bond.
12. Name two of the best known bond ratings services.
13. What determines whether a bond will have a good rating or a poor rating?
14. What is the yield of a bond?
15. Would you buy or sell bonds if you expected the interest rate to rise? Explain your answer.
16. If your city needed to raise money, what kind of bond would it issue?
17. What is a Treasury bill?
18. Suppose you are the type of person who likes to take chances, and you are not afraid of risk. Are you likely to receive higher or lower returns on your investments? Explain.
19. What is a futures contract? Give an example of a situation in which someone might buy such a contract. Why would this person buy the contract?
20. What is a call option? Why might someone buy a call option rather than stock shares?

Doing the Math

Do the calculations necessary to solve the following problems.

1. Assume that you own 1,250 shares of stock X. You just read in the newspaper that the dividend for the stock is $3.88 per share. What did you earn in dividends?
2. The closing price of a stock is $90.25. The stock is paying a dividend of $3.50. What is the yield of the stock?
3. The closing price of the stock is $66.40, and the net earnings per share is $2.50. What is the stock's PE ratio?
4. The face value of a bond is $10,000 and the annual coupon payment is $850. What is the coupon rate?
5. Let's say that a person buys a bond that matures in 10 years and pays a coupon rate of 10 percent. The face value of the bond is $10,000. How much money will the bondholder receive in the tenth year?

Solving Economic Problems

Use your thinking skills and the information you learned in this chapter to find solutions to the following problems.

1. **Application.** In Chapter 10 you learned how the Fed decides to change the money supply. Suppose that the Fed decides to increase the money supply. How do you think this action will affect the stock market?
2. **Analysis.** If bonds and stocks are substitutes, then what should we see happen as bonds offer higher returns?
3. **Cause and Effect.** Suppose that there is no cause-effect relationship between the current condition of the federal budget (deficit, balance, or surplus) and the Dow Jones Industrial Average. If so, what would we expect to see in the real world?
4. **Writing.** Write a one-page paper discussing the factors that you think will influence the stock market over the next several years. Explain how the factors that you have identified will cause people to want to buy more stocks, sell more stocks, or turn entirely to other types of investments.
5. **Economics in the Media.** Check the newspaper and find the Dow Jones Industrial Average (DJIA) for the most recent date.
6. **Economics in the Media.** Check the newspaper and find the current stock price for five of the 30 companies that compose the DJIA.
7. **Economics in the Media.** Find an article in the newspaper or a story on television news that mentions one of the following: stock market, bond market, put option, call option, DJIA, S&P 500, or NASDAQ. Discuss the contents of the article or story.

Practice Tests and Study Guide

Go to www.emcp.net/economics and choose *Economics: New Ways of Thinking,* Chapter 16, if you need more help in preparing for the chapter test.

when the issuer must pay the buyer the face value of the bond; and coupon rate, the percentage of the face value of the bond that the bondholder receives each year until the bond matures.
12. Standard & Poor and Moody are two of the best-known bond ratings services.
13. The rating depends upon how likely it is that the bond will be paid off. The more likely it will be paid off, the better the rating.
14. The yield of a bond is the coupon payment divided by the price paid for the bond.
15. Interest rates and bond prices move in opposite directions. If you expected interest rates to rise, then it follows that you would expect bond prices to fall. If you own bonds, it is best to sell bonds now, before the price falls.
16. If your city needed to raise money, it would issue municipal bonds.
17. A Treasury bill is a bond issued by the federal government. The government issues Treasury bills when it wants to borrow funds. Treasury bills mature in 13, 26, or 52 weeks.
18. You are likely to receive higher returns. Higher returns come with higher risks, and lower returns come with lower risks.
19. A futures contract is a contract in which the seller agrees to provide a particular good to the buyer on a specified future date at an agreed-upon price. Examples will vary.
20. A call option is a contract that gives the owner the right to buy shares of stock at a specified price within the time limits of the contract. Call options usually cost less than stock shares.

Doing the Math

1. $4,850 (*calculation:* 1,250 × $3.88 = $4,850).
2. 3.88% (*calculation:* $3.50 ÷ $90.25 = 3.88%).
3. 26.56 (*calculation:* $60.40 ÷ $2.50 = 26.56).
4. 8.5% (*calculation:* $850 ÷ $10,000 = 8.5%).
5. He or she will receive $10,000 plus a $1,000 coupon payment, for a total of $11,000.

Solving Economic Problems

1. When the Fed increases the money supply, there is obviously more money in the economy. Some of this added money will be spent on houses, clothes, new businesses, and most likely, stock purchases. Increases in the money supply are likely to stimulate buying activity in the stock market, driving stock market prices upward.
2. As bonds offer higher returns, we should see people getting out of stocks (selling stocks) and into bonds (buying bonds).
3. We should see that changes in the Dow are unrelated to changes in the state of the budget. In other words, the Dow will rise or fall whether or not the budget is balanced, is in deficit, or is in surplus.
4. Answers will vary.
5. Answers will vary.
6. Answers will vary.
7. Answers will vary.

Chapter 16 Stocks and Bonds 457

Debating the Issues

Discussion Starters

1. Ask students to define the terms *tariffs* and *quotas* in their own words. Ask them why the United States would impose tariffs and quotas on goods produced in other countries.
2. Ask students if they know of someone who lost his or her job owing to an influx of imported goods. How did the loss of job affect the person and his or her family?
3. One perception is that tariffs and quotas protect American workers, producers, and consumers. Is this true? Ask students how they think American workers, producers, and consumers are protected through tariffs and quotas.
4. Ask students to think of benefits of free trade for American workers, producers and consumers. Does free trade offer benefits for students and their families personally? Have them share that information with the class.

Debating the Issues

Is Free Trade the Best Policy for the United States?

Oklahoma can't impose a tariff or quota on goods produced in Wisconsin, but the United States can and does impose tariffs and quotas on goods produced in other countries. For example, the United States currently imposes tariffs on garments, textiles, sugar, and many other goods produced in other countries. In other words, free trade exists among the states of the United States, but not among countries of the world. Do you think there should be free trade among countries, as there is among states? The issue has both opponents and proponents.

One day in November, two high school debate teams met and debated the issue of free trade. The question before each team was, Is free trade the best policy for the United States? Here is what four of the debaters, two from each team, had to say.

Alycyn Waldrop, Addison High School Debate Team

When I go to the store to buy something new, whether it be a pair of running shoes or a portable telephone, I want to buy the best product for the lowest price. That's my objective, plain and simple. I have a better chance of meeting that objective living in a world of free trade than living in a world where countries impose tariffs and quotas on each other's goods. Free trade maximizes competition, which is what guarantees me the highest quality goods at the lowest possible price.

Suppose there are 40 running shoe companies in the world, 10 in the United States and 30 in other countries. Am I, as a consumer, better off if all 40 companies sell their shoes in the United States, or if only the 10 U.S. companies sell their shoes in the United States? The answer is obvious. I am better off when 40 companies, domestic and foreign alike, compete for my business, than when only 10 domestic companies compete for it. Free trade is the policy that maximizes choice for the consumer. It guarantees high quality goods at reasonable prices.

Mike Saunders, Spring Valley High School Debate Team

If every country in the world practiced free trade, then perhaps free trade would be the best policy for the United States. But that's not the case. That's not the world we live in, and we shouldn't pretend that it is. When other countries impose tariffs and quotas on our goods, that hurts our industries and our workers, and we should retaliate in kind.

Suppose the German government places a tariff on American cars imported into Germany. As a result, the price of American cars rises in Germany and Germans buy more German cars and fewer American cars. Since U.S. car companies sell fewer cars, they will have to lay off some of their workers. The people who are laid off are Americans, not Germans. In other words, some Americans will lose their jobs because the German government decided to impose tariffs on American cars.

Is this fair? Should the U.S. government practice free trade when another country doesn't? Should our government sit back and do nothing as the German government puts Americans out of work?

I for one don't think so. A policy of "give and take" would be more acceptable to me. If Germany practices free trade with

Differentiating Instruction

Enrichment and Extension

Divide students into groups of three or four. Each group will imagine it is a business that produces a particular good. Then each group will decide if its business profits from a free trade policy or would do better with a tariff and quota system. The group will list reasons for its decision. Have students share their decisions with the class.

us, then we should practice free trade with Germany. But if Germany doesn't practice free trade with us, then we shouldn't practice free trade with them. We have to be realistic, and we have to protect ourselves.

Sylvia Minors, Addison High School Debate Team

I disagree. I think that practicing free trade is a little like practicing honesty—you should do it even if others don't. If 10 people tell lies, it doesn't follow that the best thing you can do is tell a lie, too.

If most countries impose tariffs and quotas, it doesn't follow that the United States should do likewise. The United States should practice free trade even if every other country in the world imposes tariffs and quotas on all products being imported. That's because the United States prospers through free trade, even when other countries do not practice it.

Suppose there are five countries in the world. Four of the countries impose tariffs and quotas; one country, the United States, does not. Certainly foreign tariffs and quotas hurt U.S. producers and workers, but the U.S. government can't make things better for our producers and workers by making our consumers worse off. And that is exactly what the U.S. government would be doing if it retaliated by imposing tariffs and quotas on foreign goods. Then, not only would U.S. producers and workers be hurt by foreign tariffs and quotas, but U.S. consumers would also be hurt by U.S. tariffs and quotas on foreign goods. If the choice is between hurting producers and workers or hurting producers, workers, and consumers, it is better to hurt as few people as possible.

Here's what it comes down to: The best policy is for every country in the world to practice free trade. The second best policy is for the United States to practice free trade, even if no other country in the world practices it. The worst policy is for the United States to impose tariffs and quotas on foreign goods simply because other countries impose tariffs and quotas on our goods.

Madison Golecke, Spring Valley High School Debate Team

United States policy shouldn't protect the interests only of consumers; it should protect the interests of consumers, producers, and workers. When other countries impose tariffs and quotas on U.S.-produced goods, those countries hurt our producers and our workers. These countries should bear the economic consequences. There must be a price for such actions, or these countries will continue to make themselves better off at the expense of American producers and workers. The higher the price of imposing tariffs and quotas on U.S.-produced goods, the less likely foreign countries will do so.

The way to ensure free trade is for the United States to give other countries a taste of their own medicine. If they practice free trade with us, then we should practice free trade with them. If they impose tariffs and quotas on our goods, we should do the same to their goods.

What Do You Think?

1. Should the United States practice free trade even if other countries do not? Explain your thinking.
2. Is the world moving toward or away from greater free trade? Give some examples from recent news stories to support your answer.

Activities for What Do You Think?

1. Label two points in the room with "Yes" and "No." Then ask students to "vote with their feet" by moving to one of the two labels in the room to answer this question: Should the United States practice free trade even if other countries do not? Allow the groups five minutes to compile their reasons for voting for that opinion. Then have each group spend one minute presenting its reasons to the class. Conduct another class vote to see if there is any change in the voting.

2. Divide students into groups of three or four to discuss whether the world is moving toward or away from free trade. Require that students cite specific examples to substantiate the group's opinion. Each group can then create a skit to share its opinion with the class.

Closure

Direct students to write a paragraph describing how their opinions on this issue were affected by reading Debating the Issues and discussing it with the class. Ask those students whose opinions changed what information influenced their thinking.

Personal Finance Handbook

In this handbook you will find background information and tips that will help you get the most from your money. You will also find guidelines to help you begin planning for your future, with a focus on the years immediately following your graduation from high school.

The topics covered in the handbook, appearing alphabetically, are:

You will find additional information and tips on practical, day-to-day issues in the *Personal Economics* features that appear throughout this text. Your teacher may have already assigned some of the features. If, at a particular point, you wish to refer back to the information contained in these features, here is a list of the features with corresponding page numbers:

While you will find the information and tips in this handbook useful, keep in mind that you have easy access to the most up-to-date information available through the Internet (that's the topic of the *Personal Economics* feature on page 148). As you know, in a world of scarcity it is crucial that we make the most of our limited resources, and taking time to acquire all the relevant information is necessary if you hope to maximize your own personal resources.

Avoiding Telemarketing Fraud and Swindles

Each day in the United States, thousands of telephone calls are made in attempts to sell something. Some of the offers are legitimate; others are not. It is important for you to be able to separate the two. When dealing with companies that sell products or services over the telephone (telemarketers), listen for the following tactics, which are frequently used by unethical telemarketers who want to trick you out of your money.

- **They know more about you than they should.** If your name and number came from a mailing list, the caller may know such personal information as your age, income, and occupation. Telephone callers may tailor their comments to what they know about you in an attempt to hold your interest and to gain your trust.
- **They will say anything.** They are always ready with an answer, no matter what you ask. Don't assume that every telephone salesperson is as honest as you are. Be skeptical.
- **They sound legitimate.** Good telephone swindlers (people who earn money by trickery or deceit) do not sound like telephone swindlers—that's what makes them good at what they do. If they sound believable it's probably because they have had a lot of practice at lying.
- **Their offer sounds too good to be true.** If the deal they are offering sounds almost too good to be true, it probably is too good to be true. Be very skeptical of these offers.
- **They will use high-pressure sales tactics.** Legitimate salespersons will respect your decision not to buy their products. Swindlers, on the other hand, will try to pressure you into making a decision. The harder they push, the more you should resist.
- **They insist that an immediate decision is necessary and in your best interest.** They might say "there are only a few left," or " this offer is only good today." Be wary of this tactic. It often means that the telemarketer wants to prevent you from researching the product or service he is trying to sell you.
- **They often advertise in recognized magazines and newspapers.** You may see an ad in a magazine and return a card asking for more information. Days later you receive a call. Do not assume that just because you requested information, based on an ad in a reputable publication, that the telemarketer works for a legitimate business.
- **They are unwilling to provide written information or references.** When you ask for written verification, swindlers will make excuses. This is a sure sign that something is wrong.
- **They will ask for your credit card number.** Be very careful about giving out a credit card number to a company that you are unsure of.
- **You are unlikely to get your money back.** Government agencies and better business groups will try to bring swindlers to justice, but once you give the dishonest telemarketers your money, you are unlikely to get it back.

Budgeting

A budget is an organized plan for spending and saving money. Creating a budget is not a cure-all for your money problems; it is simply an organized way of looking at your costs and goals and at what you are doing about them. Your budget records your efforts, successes, and failures, much as a thermometer records your body temperature.

What you do with the information in a budget is up to you. If you write out a budget and do not follow it successfully at first—if you do not save as much as you wanted to, perhaps—do not worry. Few people immediately succeed at following a budget. Like practicing good study habits, following a budget takes willpower. Only you can decide whether your goals are important enough for you to exercise the willpower necessary to achieve them. And, as a student of economics, you may have a better understanding than others that all of your decisions and actions mean trade-offs have been made and opportunity costs incurred.

Here is a five-step process for making a budget.

Step 1. Determine your income over the past year. You need to figure out dollar amounts for both your income and your expenditures over a year. To find your annual income, you may want to check your pay stubs.

Step 2. Determine your average monthly expenses. To figure out your expenses, you need to keep a list of what you spend for a month or two. An easy way to keep track of your spending is simply to ask for receipts for everything you buy and keep them in one place. Another way is to record your expenses in a journal each night. You might want to break your expenses down into four or five categories, such as

- School
- Clothes
- Entertainment, including movies, CD purchases, eating out, and so on
- Transportation
- Miscellaneous

Each day, register the dollar amount you spent in each category. After you have done this for a month or two, compute the dollar amounts you spent. Then ask yourself if these two months are typical. Take into account any unusual expenses. The point is to come up with your best estimate of your *average* monthly spending.

Step 3. Calculate your annual expenses. Once you have found your typical monthly cost in each category, multiply by 12 to find your yearly cost in each category.

Step 4. Decide how much you want to save. Refer back to the *Personal Economics* feature on page 22 to remind yourself of the value of saving. You want to carve out a spot in your budget for some savings. The only question is how much. You will need to make this decision based on your long-term goals. Obviously, if you have not already allowed for savings, you will need to take money from your other categories (school, clothes, etc.) to make up your savings.

Step 5. Write out a monthly budget. Exhibit PF-1 below shows the main elements of a monthly budget.

Column 1, which lists expense categories, can contain as many or as few categories as you want. Often, a person's stage of life determines the number of categories in this column. For example, a high school student may have fewer expense items than a woman in her thirties who is employed. The woman may have such expenses as health insurance and mortgage insurance that the high school student does not have.

EXHIBIT PF-1 Main Elements of a Monthly Budget

(1) Expense	(2) Budgeted	(3) Actual	(4) Difference
School	$10	$15	+$5
Clothing	$33	$37	+$4
Entertainment	$25	$30	+$5
Transportation	$60	$62	+$2
Savings	$37	$20	−$17
Miscellaneous	$12	$13	+$1
Total	**$177**	**$177**	**$0**

Column 2 lists the dollar amounts the person plans to spend in each category—the budgeted amounts.

Column 3 lists the actual dollar amounts the person ended up spending in each category.

Column 4 records the difference between the budgeted and actual expenses. To get this difference, subtract the dollar amount in column 2 from the dollar amount in column 3. A plus sign before the dollar amount means the person spent more in this category than planned. A minus sign means he or she spent less.

Buying and Financing a Car

If you are like most people, you will buy many cars in your lifetime. These purchases will probably be among your major expenses. And the costs don't end with the purchase of the car —you will then need to buy gasoline for the car, maintain it, and repair it from time to time—all factors that you should take into consideration when you buy the car. Here are some tips to keep in mind when buying a car, whether it be new or used.

1. **Know the type of car you want before you go shopping.** Think about the type of car you want before you set out to shop for one. Otherwise, a salesperson may sell you a car that does not really meet your needs—perhaps one that costs too much, is not fuel efficient, or does not have the safety features you want. If you like to "window-shop" for cars before you start talking to a salesperson, then tell the salesperson that you are only looking so you can walk around the lot viewing cars at your leisure.
2. **Do your homework.** Study the *Consumer Reports* articles before setting out to shop for a car. This magazine is full of information about such topics as safety, maintenance, and fuel economy for all the major makes and models. Some people take their *Consumer Reports* with them to car dealerships so the car salespersons will know that they have done their homework and are serious about getting a good car at a reasonable price. You can also find valuable information online at such Web sites as Edmunds.com.
3. **Investigate the competition.** Suppose you have decided that you want to buy a Ford. If there are two Ford dealerships in your town, visit both of them. The two dealerships then may compete for your business, perhaps by offering you a better price or more features on the car.
4. **Watch out for certain sales tactics.** Some car salespersons will use sales techniques that you should be aware of to avoid paying more than you need to. Here are a few of the more commmon techniques to watch out for.

   Lowballing is the practice of quoting an unusually low price to get you interested. Later, when you sit down to do business, the salesperson says she made a "mistake" and forgot to include some costs, or her managers won't let her sell the car for that price.

   Highballing is the practice of promising you an unusually high price for a trade-in (the used car you give to the dealer in partial payment for the car you are buying). Later, they say that the car has been checked out and is not really worth as much as they thought.

   Determining your income level, or the income level of your parents, is something many salespersons often try to find out. For example, a salesperson who learns that a customer is a physician may be less likely to bargain on price on the assumption that physicians are wealthy. If you are a teenager looking for a car, the salesperson might ask you what your parents do for a living.

Where you live can also affect the way that the salesperson deals with you. If you live nearby, they may be less likely to offer you a lower price than if you live farther away. The farther away you live, the less likely it is that you will return after shopping around.

Intimidation is another tactic you may encounter if you are a teenager seeking to buy a car. Salespersons may think they can take advantage of you because they are older and because this is the first time you have bought a car. Remember, though, that you are the customer, and you are in charge. The salesperson wants your business. Do not act intimidated (even if you feel that way), and do not be afraid to walk out of the car dealership at any time. There are other places you can buy a car.

5. **Your attitude matters.** If you act thrilled at seeing exactly the car you have always wanted, the salesperson is not very likely to lower the price. If you act as if you could take the car or leave it, you are in a better position. Do not give the impression that there is only one car in the world for you.

6. **Determine the value of the car.** If you're buying a new car, you need to know the wholesale price (dealer cost) of the car you want to buy. Some newsstands carry publications that list the wholesale price of most makes of cars. If you are buying a used car you can obtain estimates of the current market value of the car at several Web sites, such as Kelley Blue Book and Edmunds. You greatly increase your chances of getting the best price possible for the car you want if you know what the dealer paid for the car, or if you know what the "going rate" is for a used car.

7. **Know the value of your trade-in.** You may have an old car that you want to trade in when you buy your new car. To find out its value, look in the Kelley Blue Book Market Report, or go to Edmunds.com. Car dealerships have this information, but they will not give it to you. Banks, credit unions, and libraries usually carry the Blue Book and will let you see it.

8. **Drive the car.** Make sure you drive the car you are thinking about buying. Test-drive it without using the radio or air conditioner, which can sometimes mask car sounds of which you need to be aware. Salespersons often accompany you on a test-drive and talk to you while you're driving. If you want to drive in silence so you can hear the car, tell them so.

9. **Find out if there is a warranty; if there is, understand it.** New cars, as well as some used cars, come with warranties. A warranty is a guarantee or an assurance given by a seller stating that a product is in good working order. It may also state that the seller will provide certain types of service for a period of time. For example, a car seller may provide a warranty specifying that if anything goes wrong with the engine in the next five years, the seller will fix it free of charge. It is important to know what the warranty says, so make sure to ask about it and to read it carefully. Many dealers sell service contracts, or extended warranties, which frequently cost $1,500 to $2,000. Whether or not these contracts/warranties are good investments depends on the condition of the car and the reliability of the dealer. If you are buying a new car, be sure to distinguish between the new car's warranty and the extended warranty by asking the following questions:

   - What is the difference between the coverage under the warranty and the coverage under the service contract?
   - What repairs are covered?
   - Who pays for the labor? The parts?
   - Who performs the repairs?
   - How long does the service contract last?
   - What is the policy on cancellation and refund?

465

10. **Shop for the best rates when financing the purchase.** If you decide to borrow money to finance your car purchase, be sure to compare the interest rate the car dealership offers you with the rates offered by banks, credit unions, and savings and loan institutions. Interest rates on car loans vary, so shop around for the best rate.

11. **Be extra careful when buying a used car.** A new car loses about 25 percent of its value the first year. Therefore, used cars are much less expensive than new cars, and, if you get the right one, a much better value. Buying a used car always involves some risk, however. If you are buying the car from a dealer, you will probably not know who the previous owner was or why he sold or traded in the car. Obviously this is one advantage of buying a used car from the owner—you can ask questions and decide for yourself whether or not you think the owner has taken care of the car and is telling you the truth. Here are some additional points to keep in mind when buying a used car:

    - Do not buy a used car that is no longer in production. It will be hard to get parts for the car.
    - Do not buy a used car without taking it for a test-drive.
    - Watch out for used cars that are loaded with options, such as power windows, power seats, and so on. Such things need replacing as a car gets older.
    - Find out if the used car you want to buy has been recalled. A manufacturer will recall a car model if it finds out something is wrong with it. The owners of the cars are notified of the recall and asked to bring their cars in to be fixed (at no charge). Almost half the owners do not respond to a recall, however, so a used car you want to buy might have been recalled but never fixed. To learn about recalls and other safety information, call the Department of Transportation Auto Safety Hotline at 1-888-327-4236.
    - Have an auto mechanic inspect a used car you are thinking about buying. This inspection is particularly important, because a $50 inspection fee may save you hundreds of dollars and endless problems later on. In addition, it may put your mind at ease.
    - Look for the Buyer's Guide sticker on the window of the used car. The sticker, which is required by the Federal Trade Commission, gives you important information on the car, such as whether it comes with a warranty and what major problems may occur in any used car.
    - Be alert to those things on the car that you can check. For example, are the tires slick, with very little tread? Are there oil spots under the car?

Buying Insurance

Insurance is a gurarantee against loss. When you buy insurance from a company, you enter into a contract with that company. Your part of the contract says that you will make regular payments (called premiums) in exchange for the promise that the company will pay you for a certain kind of loss or damage should it occur. The type of insurance you are buying (car, life, health, personal property) and the amounts of money involved are spelled out in the contract.

Some people buy insurance and then, when they don't use it, say that they spent their money for nothing. The fact is, everyone buys insurance and hopes not to use it. No one buys car insurance hoping to have an accident; no one buys fire insurance hoping that his or her house will catch on fire; and no one buys health insurance hoping to get sick and go to the hospital. The best we can hope for is not to have to use the insurance we buy. But we do buy it because it usually gives us peace of mind. We buy it because we are not sure what the future holds.

Automobile Insurance

You should be aware, if you are not already, of your state's laws regarding automobile insurance. For example, if your state requires all drivers to have liability insurance, you can be assessed heavy fines and your license can be revoked if you drive without insurance. Know what you must have, then make the best decisions you can for the other types of coverages. For example, if you purchase an older model used car with lots of miles and some body damage, you might decide that collision coverage is not something you need.

Types of Coverage The following are brief descriptions of the different types of coverages.

Liability Insurance *Bodily injury* liability insurance pays for losses due to death or injury in a car accident that is the insured driver's fault. It covers people both inside and outside the car. Injured persons can make a claim against this coverage to pay for medical bills, lost wages, and damages due to pain and suffering. *Property damage* liability insurance covers damage done to another person's car, buildings, fences, and so on.

Medical Payments Insurance Medical payments insurance pays for medical expenses resulting from a car accident, no matter who is at fault. Some people do not purchase medical payments insurance because their health insurance pays for injuries sustained in an accident.

Uninsured Motorist Protection Insurance Some people drive their cars without having any automobile insurance. If one of them hits you with his or her car and you or your car suffers damages, you may not be able to collect any money from the person. To guard against this possibility, you may choose to purchase uninsured motorist coverage. This insurance would cover you if you were in an accident with an uninsured motorist or harmed by a hit-and-run driver.

Collision Insurance Collision insurance pays for the damage to your car if it is in an accident, no matter who is responsible for the accident. Your coverage is limited by the amount of the deductible, which usually ranges from $100 to $250. As always, the higher the deductible, the lower the premiums.

Comprehensive Insurance Comprehensive insurance is the companion of collision insurance. While collision insurance covers damage to your car if it is in an accident, comprehensive insurance covers just about everything else that can happen to a car. For example, it covers the damage if the car is stolen, is vandalized, or catches fire. As with collision insurance, the coverage is limited by the deductible.

Factors Determining Premiums An automobile insurance policy is a package of several types of coverage, each with its own premium. The sum of these premiums is what you pay for the policy. The following are some of the factors that determine how much you will pay.

- **Your Age** In most but not all states, a person's age affects his or her automobile insurance premium. Statistics show that drivers under the age of 25 have a higher accident rate than drivers between the ages of 25 and 35. For this reason, their premiums are higher. In many cases your premiums will be lower if you are listed on your parents' or gurardians' policy.
- **Where You Live** If you live in a densely populated area where vandalism and car theft are common, you will pay a higher premium than if you live in a sparsely populated area where these things are relatively uncommon.
- **Your Driving Record** If you have a history of car accidents and speeding tickets, your premium is likely to be higher than if you do not have such a history. This is why it is important for you to drive carefully and avoid accidents.

- **The Car You Drive** If you drive a new, expensive car that is difficult and costly to repair, you will pay a higher premium than if you drive an older car that is easy and inexpensive to repair.
- **How Much You Drive** If you drive only a few miles a week, you are likely to pay a lower premium than a person who drives many miles a week.
- **Whether or Not You Have Had a Driver Education Course** Many insurance companies will give you a discount on your premium if you have taken a driver education course. The discount is usually 5 to 10 percent.
- **Whether or Not You Have Air Bags in Your Car** Some insurance companies will give you a discount on the medical insurance part of your automobile insurance coverage if you have air bags in your car.
- **Whether or Not You Have Antitheft Devices in Your Car** Many insurance companies will discount the comprehensive part of your automobile insurance coverage if you have installed antitheft devices in your car.

What to Do in an Automobile Accident Here are the steps to take if you have a car accident.

1. **Check to see if anyone is injured.** Next, call the police. When you call the police, state where the accident occurred (the nearest cross streets). If someone has been injured, ask that an ambulance or rescue squad be sent immediately.
2. **Do not move injured persons.** If you move injured persons, you could harm them. Cover an injured person with a blanket or coat if one is handy.
3. **When police officers arrive, cooperate fully.** Be sure to answer police officers' questions honestly, but state only what you know to be the facts. It is natural to be shaken up after an accident, and some people in this condition quickly conclude that they must have been at fault. Remember to stay calm and state only the facts rather than guesses, assumptions, or beliefs.
4. **Ask a police officer where you can obtain a copy of the police report.** You may need a copy of the police report for insurance purposes or for a court case. Ask a police officer on the scene where you should go to obtain the report.
5. **Make sure you obtain the following information:** the names and addresses of all drivers and passengers in the accident; the license plate numbers, makes, and models of the cars involved; other drivers' license identification numbers; insurance identification numbers; the names, addresses, and telephone numbers of any witnesses to the accident; and the names of the police officers at the scene. This information may come in handy later, and your insurance agent may ask for it. Get into the habit of carrying a pencil or pen and paper in the glove compartment of your car so that you are always ready to write down the information you may need.
6. **If you have a camera in the car, take pictures of the accident scene.** Photograph the damage done to the cars; skid marks, if there are any; and so on. If you do not have a camera, make a sketch of the accident. You may need it later to refresh your memory.
7. **If you run into an unattended car, leave your name and telephone number on the car's windshield so that the owner can get in touch with you.** This response is simply the right thing to do.
8. **Get in touch with your insurance company as soon as possible.** Make sure you tell your insurance agent exactly what happened, and let the agent advise you as to what to

do next. The insurance company will probably want to have an insurance adjuster inspect your car before you get it repaired. It is a good idea to keep the name and telephone number of your insurance agent in the glove compartment of your car. That way, if you are out of town and have an accident, you can easily and quickly get in touch.

9. **Keep a record of your expenses.** Make sure to keep a record of all the expenses you incur as a result of an accident. This list might include lost wages, the cost of a rental car, and so on.
10. **Keep copies of all your paperwork.** There is a good chance that you will have to refer to certain papers later.

These are general guidelines. It is important to know the laws of your own state in dealing with motor vehicle accidents.

Health Insurance

Medical costs for major illnesses and injuries are often far beyond what the average family can pay. That is why most people feel the need to have health insurance. Because the premiums for health insurance are high, you, as a young adult, will want to be covered by your parents' or guardians' policy for as long as possible. Since many employers provide health insurance and pay a large portion of their employees' premiums, you will want to find a job that includes these benefits if at all possible.

If and when you need to purchase your own health insurance, you may want to explore local HMOs (Health Maintenance Organizations). These organizations offer members comprehensive medical care for a monthly or yearly fee. In exchange for the regular fee, members receive medical care from a selected group of doctors and hospitals. While many people prefer flexibility in choosing their medical providers, the HMO option is usually one of the more economical options for health insurance.

Life Insurance

At some point you will probably want to consider buying life insurance. Many people first consider purchasing life insurance when they begin a family. Life insurance guarantees payment to a specified person, the beneficiary, if the policyholder dies or reaches a certain age. People buy this type of insurance to financially protect loved ones in case of an unexpected, untimely death.

There are two major types of life insurance:

Term Life Insurance With term life insurance, you pay premiums to the insurance company, and in turn the beneficiaries you name are paid a certain sum of money if you die during a specific period. When the specific period ends, your coverage ends, and you receive no payments from the insurance company. When you buy term insurance, you are buying nothing but life insurance for the *term* of the policy. For this reason, term insurance is considerably cheaper than whole life insurance.

Whole Life Insurance As the name implies, whole life insurance covers a person for his or her whole life, until death. One important feature of whole life insurance is its cash value, the amount of money policyholders would receive if they decided to redeem, or cash in, their policy. Some people see the cash value that is accumulated in a whole life policy as a form of savings to be drawn on (borrowed) in later years. When policyholders make a withdrawal from the cash value in their insurance account, however, they give up insurance protection. Because of the cash values involved, whole life insurance is more expensive than term insurance.

469

Career Planning

If you haven't yet decided what you are going to do after you graduate from high school, the following information might be of assistance. Looking ahead, thinking about your future, and making some plans, even if you change them later, will increase your chances of leading a happy, fulfilling life.

Education

As you already know from reading this text, education and income are closely related, and education is becoming increasingly important in the era of globalization. You may want to review some of the features in the text that discuss the importance of education, such as

"Investing in Yourself" in Chapter 5
"Education—It's Like Multiplying Yourself" in Chapter 9
"Your Goal: Generic, Not Specific, Human Capital" in Chapter 12

Matching Your Abilities, Educational Interests, and Job

Ideally, we all would like to work at a job that is interesting, that we are able to do, and that pays relatively well. Protecting your future requires you to be aware of many things. When it comes to getting a job, you must consider what you are good at doing, what you are interested in, and what pays an income with which you can be comfortable. Talk to your school counselor about taking some interest and aptitude inventories to find out more about yourself.

How do you know if what you are interested in will be in demand and pay well when it is time for you to go job hunting? The U.S. Department of Labor attempts to predict the job and earnings outlook for the future. Two sources of information about jobs are the *Occupational Outlook Handbook* and *Occupational Projections and Training Data.* Additional information can be obtained from state job service centers, which can be found in the telephone book in the state government section.

Getting a Job

There's a good chance you have applied for, and got, part-time jobs while you have been in high school. So, you know something about finding and getting a job. As you look for full-time work, whether it be after high school or after college, the process will become more competitive and more important. Here are some tips to help you increase the chances of getting the job you want.

Application Forms When you apply for a job, you will have to fill out an application form. It is important that you do a good job filling out the form since often there are more applicants than open positions, and the form is used to decide who will be hired. It's not just the information you provide, but the neatness and accuracy (including spelling and grammar) of the forms that impact the employer's decsion about who to hire. Following are some things to consider when filling out an application form:

1. **Photocopy the form, if you can, before you start to fill it out.** Most people make mistakes when filling out application forms. When they erase the errors, scratch through them with pen, or type over them, the finished application comes out looking ragged and dirty. A neat, clean application is what you want. Therefore, fill out the photocopy of the application first, check it for mistakes, rewrite it where necessary, and then use it as a guide to fill out the actual application form that you will submit to the employer.

2. **Be neat.** Type the form, if possible. Suppose an employer reviews two application forms. One is neatly typed, and the other is filled in with pencil or pen, has a few scribbles and dark eraser marks, and generally looks shabby. The often-subtle message that an employer receives from a messy application form is that the applicant is untidy, impatient, and unlikely to take the time to do a job correctly.

3. **Be prepared.** Come to the interview prepared to fill in an application form when you visit the employer's premises. Suppose you visit a local company to ask if it is hiring. The personnel manager says yes and hands you an application form to fill out immediately. You need to be prepared with some information about yourself. For example, you may need (1) the names, addresses, and telephone numbers of former employers; (2) your Social Security number; and (3) previous home addresses. Keep this information with you when you visit prospective employers.

4. **Do not leave anything blank.** If something does not apply to you, simply write "n/a," which stands for "not applicable." If you leave some lines of an application form blank, the person reading the form will not know if you missed something.

The Résumé A résumé is a document you create that contains the following information: (1) your name, address, and telephone number; (2) the job you are seeking or your career goal; (3) your education; (4) your work experience; (5) honors you have received; and (6) any other information relevant to your ability to do the job you are seeking. A résumé should be well organized, easy to read, and no longer than two pages. Exhibit PF-2 on the next page of this handbook shows a standard way to organize a résumé.

The Interview The job interview is your best opportunity to present yourself in a favorable light to an employer. Keep in mind that you represent a risk to the employer, who does not know what type of employee you will be. Will you be consistently late to work, or on time? Will you be a good worker or not? Will you get along with others? To be equipped for an interview, keep these things in mind:

1. **Learn something about the company before the interview.** You will want to know things such as what the company produces, how long it has been in business, and how many employees it has. You want to be able to give a knowledgeable answer if an interviewer asks, "Do you know what it is we do here at our company?" You can usually obtain general information on a company at the local library or from persons who work for the company. You can also call the company before the interview and ask a few questions.

2. **Rehearse the interview.** One of the best ways to prepare for an interview is to rehearse it with a friend or two. Let your friend be the interviewer and you be the interviewee. Before you start the rehearsal, write down a list of questions the real interviewer is likely to ask you. Here is a possible list:

   - Why did you apply for this job?
   - What do you know about this job or company?
   - Why should I hire you?
   - What are your strengths and weaknesses?
   - What would you like to tell me about yourself?
   - What accomplishment has given you the greatest satisfaction?
   - What courses did you like best in school?
   - What courses did you like least in school?
   - Why did you leave your last job?
   - What do you hope to be doing in three to five years?
   - What are your hobbies?

471

EXHIBIT PF-2 Résumé

Alison Brandon
1976 Jackson Drive
San Marcos, CA 92069

(760) 555-7777

Job sought: Manager trainee at Vernon Building Supplies Company

Skills, education, and experience

Working with people: Both in high school and in my jobs, I have worked well with people. As treasurer of the senior class, and as vice president of the junior class, I worked on school projects that required me to argue my positions convincingly, listen to the arguments advanced by others, and find suitable compromise positions. I realize that I cannot always get my way, but I continue to state what I believe, accept that people may disagree with me, and move on to see if we can work together.

In my work experience I have enjoyed dealing with the public. I have learned to be patient, listen attentively, and recognize that if people get "hot under the collar," I should try to work things out in a cordial way.

Effective communication: In high school, I played a leadership role in my junior and senior classes. I learned that a part of good leadership is being able to communicate your views and opinions to others in a cordial way. I have developed this skill, which I believe will help me throughout my life.

Hard work and attention to detail: In my school courses, activities, and jobs, I have learned the need to work hard and attentively. I have learned that it is better to do something right the first time than have to re-do it.

	Chronology
September 2002 to June 2006	Attended Clarksville High School in San Marcos, California. I was treasurer of the senior class and vice president of the junior class, played on the tennis team for 3 years, worked as a member of the yearbook staff for 1 year, helped to raise $10,000 for the school library, and was on the honor roll for 5 semesters.
March 2006 to present	I worked as a salesperson in the women's clothing department at Dixon's Department Store in Carlsbad, California.
September 2005 to February 2006	I worked taking and filling orders at McDonald's in San Marcos, California.
May 2005 to August 2005	I was camp counselor at Fire Valley Girl's Summer Camp in Fire Valley, California. I was voted "Best Counselor for Summer 2005."

Recommendations available upon request

- What would you change about yourself?
- How do your education and work experience relate to this job?
- What salary do you expect?

3. **Arrive for the interview on time.** Arriving early or late makes a bad impression. When you arrive early, you may interrupt the person who expected you later. When you arrive late, you signal that you are not dependable.

4. **Do not brag, but do not ignore your strong points.** Sometime during the interview, tell the interviewer why you think you would be a good person to hire. The interviewer may give you this chance by simply asking, "Why do you think you are right for this job?" You have to be careful, however. It is one thing to state the truth and tell someone that you are a good person for the job; it is another thing to brag. No one wants to hire a bragger, but almost everyone wants to hire people who are confident about themselves and know how to tell others of their strengths in a positive, polite manner.

472

5. **Ask questions when you have a chance.** At the end of the interview, the interviewer will often ask if you have any questions. Here are some suggestions:
   - What would a day on this job be like?
   - To whom would I report?
   - Would I supervise anyone?
   - Why did the last person leave this job?
   - What is that person doing now?
   - What is the greatest challenge of this job?
   - Is this company growing?
6. **Listen carefully.** Many people get nervous in interviews. They wonder if they look right, if they are smiling enough, if they should not have said what they just said, or if the interviewer likes them. Feeling nervous is natural, but try your best to put such concerns aside and listen to what the interviewer is saying and asking. If you do not listen carefully—and if you do not respond directly and specifically—the interviewer may get the feeling that your mind is somewhere else and that perhaps you really do not want the job.
7. **Write a thank-you letter.** Soon after the interview, send a letter to the interviewer expressing your appreciation for the interview. If you need to follow up on something you said during the interview, do it in this letter.

Consumer Rights and Responsibilities

As a consumer, you have some rights and responsibilities. Here are some of the most fundamental rights and responsibilities.

Consumer Rights

In general, as a consumer, you have four basic rights: the right to be informed, the right to be safe, the right to choose, and the right to be heard.

The Right to Be Informed You have the right to the information you need to make a good consumer decision.

The Right to Be Safe Consumers have the right to a safe product—one that will not harm their health or lives.

The Right to Choose A consumer has the right to choose among a variety of products offered at competitive prices. Choice is not usually present if competition is prohibited, so firms cannot legally band together to prevent consumers from paying a lower price for a good.

The Right to Be Heard Consumers with complaints have the right to be heard. They can address complaints to various government and private agencies that deal with consumer affairs, or they can go to small-claims court.

Consumer Responsibilities

Just as you have rights as a consumer, you also have responsibilities.

The Responsibility to Obtain Information Yourself If you are going to buy a car, a pair of shoes, or anything else, you have to ask questions to get the information you need. You cannot simply wait for the seller to tell you everything there is to know about the subject. Also, when you are planning to make a purchase, especially a large one, it is your responsibility to

473

call the Better Business Bureau and ask whether it has received any complaints about the seller from whom you are planning to buy.

The Responsibility to Learn How to Assemble or Use the Products You Buy Some consumer goods come with instructions. In particular, most items that can be used incorrectly come with instructions telling you what to watch out for, how to use the product safely, and so on. Read the instructions carefully, and learn how to assemble or use the product.

The Responsibility to Make Fair Complaints and to Be Honest Consumers feel they have a right to expect honesty from sellers. In turn, sellers feel they have a right to expect honesty from consumers. You have a responsibility, when making consumer complaints, to provide the seller, or any government agency or court that gets involved, with the whole truth as you know it. This consumer responsibility should not be taken lightly.

The Responsibility to Act Courteously A consumer has the responsibility to be courteous. You have probably seen people in restaurants who treat servers rudely, order them about, and complain when their every request is not instantly fulfilled. Remember that a seller is simply there to sell you a product, not to be put down, to be argued with unnecessarily, or to do your full bidding.

The Responsibility to Seek Action Through Government Organizations If you have a complaint that you cannot settle with the seller, you have a responsibility to report this fact to the appropriate government agency. Do not hesitate to report a seller to a government agency if you feel that you have been wronged. Remember, as a consumer, you have the right to voice your complaints, and you also have a responsibility to exercise it.

Paying for College

If you plan to attend college but do not have the resources to pay for it, you may want to apply for financial aid. Following are brief descriptions of some of the best sources of aid and some tips on how to get more information.

Grants, Loans, and Work-Study Programs

The U.S. Department of Education offers the following major student financial aid programs. These six programs fall into three categories: grants, loans, and work-study programs. A grant is financial aid that you do not have to pay back. A loan is borrowed money that you must pay back with interest. A work-study program gives you the chance to work and earn money to help you pay for your college education.

If you need more information on the different kinds of grants, loans, and work-study programs than is given in this section, you can go to the U.S. Department of Education site on the World Wide Web (www.emcp.net/financialaid). Once there, click on "Student Financial Aid" and then "Funding."

Pell Grants A Pell Grant is an award to help first-time undergraduates pay for their education after high school. To obtain a Pell Grant, a person must show financial need and must be attending school at least half-time, which for most colleges means being registered for at least six semester hours. Applications for Pell Grants can be obtained from financial aid offices of colleges and universities and sometimes from high school guidance counselors' offices. The amount of a Pell Grant award depends on the degree of financial need and the cost of the school.

Federal Supplemental Educational Opportunity Grants A Federal Supplemental Educational Opportunity Grant (FSEOG) is an award to help first-time undergraduates with exceptional financial need, as determined by the school. Like a Pell Grant, an FSEOG does not have to be paid back.

Federal Work-Study The Federal Work-Study (FWS) program provides jobs for first-time undergraduates; it lets students earn money to help pay for their education. The student's job may be on or off campus, and the student receives at least the federal minimum wage. A student's work schedule and number of hours worked are determined by the school, not the student.

Federal Perkins Loans Federal Perkins Loans are low-interest loans for first-time undergraduates with exceptional financial need, as determined by the school. The student can borrow up to $4,000 per year for each year of undergraduate study. The student must repay this loan but may be allowed up to 10 years to do so.

Stafford Loans Stafford Loans are low-interest loans to students attending school at least half-time. These loans must be repaid.

PLUS Loans PLUS Loans (Parent Loans for Undergraduate Students) are for parents who want to borrow to help pay for their children's education. These loans must be repaid.

Getting Needed Information

The federal government has a toll-free number to call with questions about financial aid: 1-800-4-FED-AID. It is a good idea to call this number and inquire about the default rate of the college you are thinking about attending (the percentage of loans that are not repaid), because there may be restrictions on borrowing money to attend a college with a default rate of 30 percent or more. Other places to obtain information on financial aid are the financial aid office of the college you want to attend, the guidance counselor's office at your high school, and the Internet.

Renting an Apartment

Many young adults rent apartments. Here are some factors to consider if you are thinking of renting an apartment in the near future.

Location Most people consider it important to rent an apartment near their workplaces or schools. A convenient location cuts down on transportation costs.

Neighbors Know something about the people who will be your close neighbors before you move into an apartment. Simply asking the apartment manager to tell you about your neighbors may yield information. If quiet is particularly important to you, you should tell the apartment manager, who then may be more likely to rent you an apartment among some of the quieter tenants.

Safety Features Before you rent an apartment, make sure the apartment complex has fire escapes, smoke detectors, and safe stairs. Also important are such safety features as good lighting outside, good locks on the doors and windows, and no large shrubbery near windows where people can hide.

Crime in the Area You may want to know the amount and nature of crime in the area where an apartment is located. The local police department will usually provide this information.

Common Areas Most apartment complexes have common areas—areas that are shared by the tenants, such as a common television area, recreational facilities, or meeting rooms.

475

Check the condition of common areas. You may not want to live in an apartment complex that does not keep these areas in good repair.

Lease A lease is a contract that specifies the terms under which property is rented. The lease sets the rent for a period of time. The apartment owner or manager will ask you to sign a lease. Read it carefully—every word. Leases often contain formal language that you might find difficult to understand if you have not read many leases before. If you do not understand the terms of the lease, ask the apartment owner or manager to carefully explain them to you. If you do not believe that the apartment manager will correctly explain the lease, seek out a friend, relative, or attorney. Before you sign, be sure you know the conditions under which you can sublease the apartment and the conditions for renewing and ending the lease.

Condition of the Apartment Before you accept an apartment and begin paying rent, carefully inspect the premises with the owner or manager. If things need to be fixed (such as a shower rod or stove), urge the owner or manager to fix them promptly, and ask the manager to state in the lease that the repair will be made by a specified date. It is also a good idea to take a few pictures of the inside of the apartment before you move in (as well as after you move out). Get the pictures developed by a company that prints the date on photos. The photos can be important if, after you move out, you and the apartment owner or manager disagree on the state of the apartment when you moved in or out. Without photos, you may find that you get back less of your security deposit than you think you should.

Shopping for Food and Clothes

When you are first out on your own, much of your shopping will be for food and clothing. So, here is some basic information and a few tips to get you started toward getting the most for your money.

Food

Food buying involves many decisions and strategies. Let's look at where you can buy and the differences between those stores, and then some tips for buying food.

Where to Shop People buy food from three principal types of stores: supermarkets, discount warehouse food stores, and convenience stores. There are some basic differences that you should be aware of.

Supermarket Supermarkets in an area often differ in the prices they charge for specific items. A loaf of brand X bread may be $1.25 at one supermarket and $1.55 at the supermarket down the road. Therefore, it is a good idea to make a list of the food items you buy on a regular basis and check the prices at different supermarkets to find out which gives you the lowest weekly total for the same quality of service and convenience.

Discount Warehouse Food Store Discount warehouse food stores do not usually carry as large a variety of foods as supermarkets, but they do sell most items for less. Also, they tend to sell things in large quantities. For example, whereas you can buy a 1-pound jar of mayonnaise at a supermarket, you can buy a 5-pound jar of mayonnaise at a discount warehouse food store at a lower price per pound. Of course, the 5-pound jar may not be your best buy if you normally use only a small amount of mayonnaise.

Convenience Store Most convenience stores, such as 7-Eleven stores, are open 24 hours a day. They charge more than supermarkets, and they do not carry as large a selection. But for some people, what they lack in selection and price, they make up for in convenience. Do you need to pick up a few food items in a hurry? The nearest convenience store could be your best bet. But keep in mind—you will be paying more than you would in a supermarket for most items.

What to Consider While Shopping If you are like most people, you will do most of your grocery shopping at the supermarket. You should think about a number of things while you are shopping at the supermarket.

Have a list. Going food shopping without a written list of things to buy often leads to impulse buying (buying what you did not plan to buy). Writing out a list takes time and thought, but it can cut down on impulse buying and thus help you get some control over your food budget. A list can also help if you are trying to cut down on buying junk food, which you are more likely to buy when you do not make and follow a list.

Don't shop hungry. It is also a good idea to do your food shopping on a full stomach. If you are hungry, many foods will look good to you, and you may end up buying more than you should.

Know the unit price. To get the most for your money, you need to compare unit prices—the price per unit of measurement (such as ounces and pounds). Suppose your supermarket offers two sizes of the same laundry detergent, one small (40 ounces) and the other large (120 ounces). The small one is priced at $1.97, and the large one at $5.45. To compute the unit price—the price per ounce, in this case—you need to divide the price of each item by its weight.

In this case, the small size costs 4.9 cents per ounce, while the large size costs 4.5 cents per ounce. Many supermarkets list the unit price along with the total price for a product. If your supermarket does not, you may want to carry a calculator to compute unit prices.

Use coupons. Food coupons often appear in newspapers, magazines, and shopping circulars. Using them can lower your grocery bill. Keep in mind, though, that a time cost is involved in clipping the coupons out of the newspaper and gathering them before your shopping trip. You have to decide whether having a lower grocery bill is worth spending this time.

Try the private and generic brands. Products in food stores may carry national brand names, private brand names, or generic brand names. A national brand is a brand name owned by the maker of a product, such as Kellogg's and Coca-Cola. A private brand is a brand name often produced for a specific supermarket chain and includes the name of that chain. A generic brand is simply a brand name that identifies the product (for example, "Corn Flakes"). National brands are more expensive than private brands, and private brands are more expensive than generic brands.

Review your selections before checking out. It is a good idea to quickly look over the food selections in your cart before you enter the checkout line. Nutritionists say that to maintain a good diet we should regularly eat lots of grains, fruits, and vegetables. If you find that most of the items in your grocery cart are prepared foods and snacks, you may decide that for your health you should exchange potato chips for fresh fruit and the ice cream for yogurt.

Clothes

This section discusses some of the things you should keep in mind when you buy clothes.

Be aware of trade-offs. When you buy clothes, it is important to be aware of dollar price and durability. Durability refers to how long the clothing item will remain in good

477

condition. Usually the higher the quality, the more durable an item is, the higher its price. Low price does not necessarily mean better buy. You are not getting more for your money if you buy the cheaper, less durable item, but then have to return to the store to buy a replacement in the near future. In short, there are trade-offs to be considered.

Pick your spots to shop. We can buy clothes in a variety of places that differ in terms of selection, price, quality, and service. For example, consider both the upscale department store and the manufacturer's outlet. In the upscale department store, you will likely find high-quality clothing items at relatively high prices with good to excellent service. At the manufacturer's outlet you will find many items of the same quality at lower prices with little service. You have to be aware of the price you pay for the service and decide whether the service is worth this price.

Comparison shop, but not too long. An economist would never advise you to shop for clothes for as long as it takes to find exactly what you want at the lowest possible price. Some comparison shopping is good, but too much can be costly for you in terms of what else you could be doing.

Economic Skills Handbook

Learning and practicing some basic skills will help you better understand economic priniciples and apply them to real-world situations. Listed below are the skills covered in this handbook.

479

Illustrating Ideas with Graphs and Charts

A picture is worth a thousand words. It is with this familiar saying in mind that economists construct their graphs. With a few lines and some curves, much can be said. Make sure you know how to read and understand the graphs and charts most commonly used in economics. Before learning about specific kinds of graphs and charts, study the following list of general steps.

1. Read the title of the graph or chart to find out what information is being presented.
2. Find the labels for both the vertical and the horizontal axes to make sure you understand the two types of information being discussed.
3. Look for any legends that might be necessary for understanding the graph or chart.
4. Look at the graph or chart as a whole and try to state in your own words what the graph or chart "says."

Pie Charts

A pie chart is a convenient way to represent the parts of something that, added together, equal the whole. Suppose we consider a typical 24-hour weekday for Danny Chen. On a typical weekday, Danny spends 8 hours sleeping, 6 hours in school, 2 hours at football practice, 2 hours doing homework, 1 hour watching television, and 5 hours doing nothing (hanging out). It is easy to represent the breakdown of a typical weekday for Danny in pie chart form, as in Exhibit ES-1.

EXHIBIT ES-1 Pie Chart for Danny's Typical Day

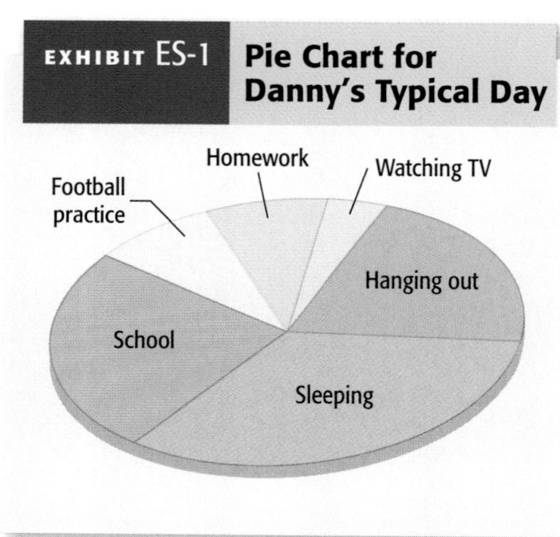

EXHIBIT ES-2 Federal Receipts, Selected Years

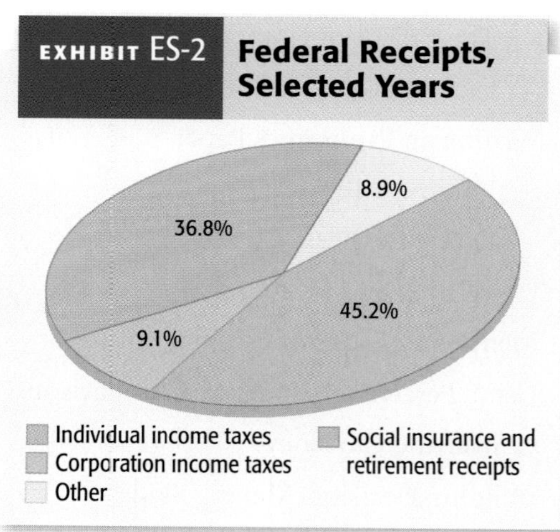

As you will notice, pie charts give you a quick visual message that shows rough percentage breakdowns and relative relationships. For example, in Exhibit ES-1 it is easy to see that Danny spends much of his time sleeping (the "sleeping" slice of the pie is the largest slice). He spends the same amount of time at football practice as doing his homework and twice as much time doing his homework as watching television.

Now look at ES-2 to see how an economist would use a pie chart to show how the total amount of money collected by the federal government is divided into four major categories.

Bar Graphs

The bar graph is another visual aid that economists use to convey relationships. Suppose we want to represent the U.S. unemployment rates over a 10-year period, as shown in ES-3. The bar graph helps you see at a glance how the rates fluctuate over this time period. You can also quickly identify the year with the highest rate and the year with the lowest rate.

480

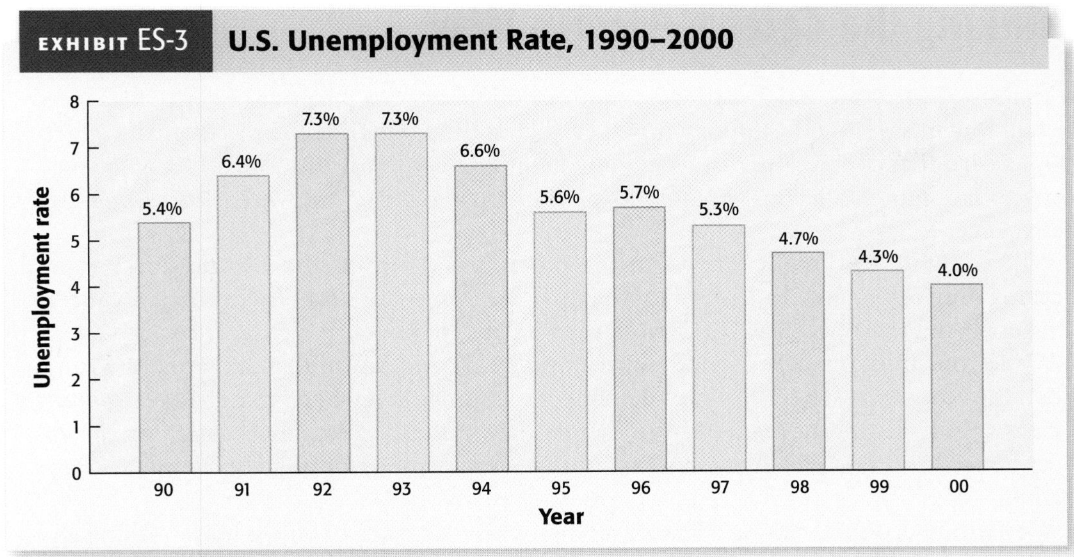

Line Graphs

Sometimes information is best and most easily displayed in a line graph. Line graphs are particularly useful to illustrate changes in a factor over some time period. Suppose we want to show the variations in the amount of money that people are saving. Follow the line in Exhibit ES-4 from left to right. What do you see happening? In which direction does the line tend to be going? Looking at the title of the graph you learn that the line represents the percentage of income that people are saving. Over the 30-year period shown in the graph, have people tended to save more or less money as a percentage of their income?

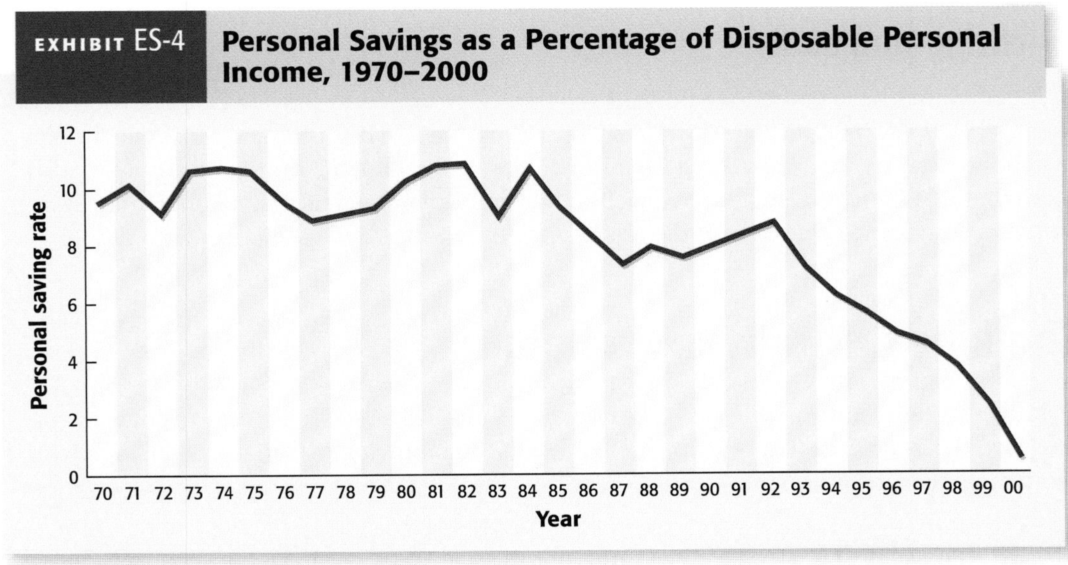

Practicing Your Skills

1. Does Danny spend more time at school or hanging out?
2. Which produces more federal tax revenue: corporate taxes or individual taxes?
3. Was the unemployment rate in the years from 1995 to 2000 trending up or down?
4. In which years during the period from 1970 to 2000 were people saving the greatest percentage of their income? What was the trend in the late 1990s?

481

Thinking the *Ceteris Paribus* Way

To illustrate the law of demand, an economist might say, "As the price of coffee falls, people will buy more coffee." Suppose, however, that at the same time the price of coffee falls, people learn that coffee causes cancer. Someone might say to the economist, "People aren't going to buy more coffee just because its price has fallen if they know that coffee can give them cancer."

Who is right? You might think that the economist is wrong and this person is right. It seems only reasonable to believe that people won't run out and buy more of a cancer-causing product just because it is cheaper than it used to be.

While your thinking here is good, the economist and the law of demand are not wrong. When the economist states the law of demand, he assumes that when price changes, *nothing else changes.* In Latin, the term used to denote that nothing else changes is *ceteris paribus* (pronounced "set eris pair ibus"). All economic laws assume nothing else changes, *ceteris paribus.*

Why would economists want to assume that when the price of coffee falls, nothing else changes? After all, other things change in the real world all the time. So why should we assume things that we know are not true?

Economists do not specify *ceteris paribus* because they want to say something false about the world. They specify it because they want to study what they believe is the real-world relationship between two variables, such as price and quantity demanded.

Suppose you were explaining the law of gravity to someone and you said, "If I drop a ball off the roof of a house, it will fall to the ground." Everyone would accept this as a true statement. But couldn't someone reach out and catch the ball before it hit the ground, thus making your statement false? Of course this could happen. But when you made your statement about the ball hitting the ground, you implied that nothing else would change—that nothing else would interfere with the ball falling. In this case you were thinking the *ceteris paribus* way.

Practicing Your Skills

A person has been eating one bowl of regular ice cream every day for 20 days. After the twentieth day, the person realizes she has put on 2 pounds. In her attempt to lose weight, she switches to low-fat ice cream. After 20 more days, she has gained 2 more pounds. Does this mean that low-fat ice cream adds as much weight as regular ice cream? Explain your answer, based on your knowledge of how the *ceteris paribus* assumption is used in economics.

Thinking Critically in Economics

There is a right and a wrong way to conduct economic analysis. To do it the right way, you must avoid certain fallacies, or errors in thinking. The following explanations will help you avoid making some of the more common critical thinking errors.

Cause and Effect

Suppose you are listening to your teacher explain the economic concept of scarcity. You look out the window and notice that it has started to rain. Three minutes later, your teacher says, "All right, that is enough about scarcity. Let's get out pencil and paper and take a pop quiz."

Two events occurred: (1) it started to rain and (2) your teacher announced a pop quiz. The two events occurred close together in time, so we could say that the two events are associated. But did the first event cause the second event? Did the rain the cause the quiz? Obviously not—it was just coincidence that they occurred a few minutes apart.

482

While this seems like a simple idea, it is an example of the kind of mistake many people make regarding cause and effect. The simple fact that two events are associated in some way does not make one event the cause of the other. In short, association is not causation.

The Fallacy of Composition

John is in the football stadium cheering on his team. Suddenly, John stands up so that he can see better. Does it follow that if everybody stood up, everybody could see better? No. The principle we learn from this observation is that what is good for the individual is not necessarily good for the group. The fallacy of composition is the erroneous view that what is good (or true) for the individual is necessarily good (or true) for the group.

Now suppose Mary moves to the suburbs because she dislikes the crowds in the city. Does it follow that if everyone moved from the city to the suburbs everyone would be better off? If your answer is yes, you have committed the fallacy of composition. If Mary moves to the suburbs because she dislikes crowds, she makes herself better off. But if everyone moved to the suburbs, not everyone would be better off, because the suburbs would become as crowded as the cities were.

Fact and Opinion

There is a difference between fact and opinion. A fact is something that is objectively true. It is a fact that you are reading this sentence at this moment. There is no room for doubt. An opinion, in contrast, is not necessarily objectively true. An opinion expresses a subjective, or personal, judgment, preference, or belief. For example, your friend may say that Thomas Jefferson was the most intelligent U.S. president. You may disagree with your friend's statement. The matter can never be proved, because you are both making subjective evaluations.

Practicing Your Skills

1. Explain what it means to say that association is not causation.
2. Give an original example that illustrates the fallacy of composition.
3. For each of the following, state whether it is a fact or an opinion:
   - **a.** The inflation rate in 1960 was 3.5 percent.
   - **b.** Alan Greenspan was the most successful Federal Reserve chairman ever.
   - **c.** High income tax rates are not good for the country.
   - **d.** During the Clinton administration, the federal deficit declined.

Writing an Economics Paper

Here are some guidelines to help you develop and write an effective economics paper.

Finding a Topic

Before you start to look for a topic, take a moment to think about the purpose of the essay and your intended audience. Is your assignment to report the factual information that you have learned about your topic or to express an opinion and develop an argument that will support your case? Who is going to read your essay? Your choice of topic might be very different if you were writing for a school newspaper than if you were writing for your teacher.

There are a number of ways to find a topic.You might make a list, as you read, of questions that you would like answered. Economics topics can be found in news and business magazines (such as *Time, Newsweek, Forbes,* and *Fortune*), newspapers, and encyclopedias. You might even discover an idea in a textbook. For example, you might want to go back to a topic that you found interesting in this text, and as you reread the pages, write down a question after every two or three paragraphs. Here are some questions that might come to mind as you read about business firms:

1. Why do some business firms earn higher profits than others do?
2. What determines where business firms will locate?
3. Do U.S. business firms face much competition from foreign business firms?
4. Do business firms do things differently today than, say, 20 years ago?

Keep in mind that it is important to find questions that you find interesting. You're the one who will be spending the time to research and write the essay. If you aren't interested in the topic of your essay, do you really think someone reading it will find it interesting?

At this stage, you should not be concerned with whether your questions make sense. You should simply write down the questions that come to mind. Ask anything you want. Then, once you have written down a few questions, go back to see if any of them contains a topic to write about. For example, look at question 3 above. This question contains a topic: "U.S. businesses and foreign competition." This phrase, then, could be the title of your economics paper.

Perhaps you have trouble coming up with questions as you read. If so, think about the fact that newspaper reporters often think in terms of the following questions:

- Who?
- What?
- Where?
- When?
- How?
- Why?

You might ask, "What is the world's largest business firm? What does it produce? Where is it located? How did it become so large?"

A common mistake of many students is to choose a topic that is too broad. For example, a student might consider writing about the topic "competition." That is an enormous topic about which many people have written entire books. You couldn't begin to address that topic within the scope of a brief paper, and any attempt would be very frustrating. Try to narrow the question down to one that you can realistically expect to answer.

Doing the Research

Let's assume that you have chosen "U.S. businesses and foreign competition" as your paper topic. The next step is to do your research.

Finding the Information The place to begin your research is the library, and a key person to speak with there is the librarian. You might tell the librarian, "I want to write a paper on U.S. businesses and foreign competition. Here are a few of the questions I would like to answer in my paper. Where would you suggest I begin my research?" Librarians are experts at finding information; they are some of the best investigators around.

Search the computerized library catalog using the subject index. To do this you need to identify a couple of key words that pertain to the topic—perhaps foreign competition, U.S. businesses, and foreign firms in the U.S. The librarian might be able to suggest other key words for your search.

Locate the books, and examine them to see if they have information relevant to your topic by checking the index at the back of the book. Look for the same key words you used to search the subject index of the card catalog.

You can also search for information in newspapers and magazines using a database, information in electronic form that can be accessed through a computer. If your library subscribes to a database service on newspapers, you can type in key words pertaining to your topic. The computer will then display a list of articles that contain information on your chosen subject from the newspapers in the database.

Other excellent sources of information are encyclopedias and dictionaries of economics, such as the *International Encyclopedia of the Social Sciences* and the *Fortune Encyclopedia of Economics*, edited by David R. Henderson.

Making Notecards As you conduct your research, it is important that you take clear and detailed notes. Each time you find some information that pertains to the topic, write down a summary of what you have found. Also note where you found your information. Keep detailed bibliographic references, including the name of the source, the author, the publisher, the city of publication, the date of publication, and the page where you found the information. This information will help you when it comes time to write the paper. If you copy passages from any source, be sure to note that they are quotations so that you can give proper credit in your paper. If you use someone else's words or ideas, you must let your reader know that you are doing so.

Working Hard Finally, keep in mind that research often requires a lot of tedious work. Often you will spend hours looking for a book that ends up being of little use to you when writing your paper. Research is not about finding the book or coming across the person who can give you all the answers. It is about making the best use of all the resources available to you.

Writing and Rewriting

Before you begin writing, you should prewrite, a process of generating and organizing ideas. One way to prewrite is to brainstorm, writing down everything that comes to mind about the topic. Once you have written down as many statements or ideas as you can, look at them to see if there is any theme that links them all.

Once you have identified that theme, it is now time to structure your paper. Structuring your paper involves figuring out the best way to tell your story. One useful way to organize your thoughts is to use index cards. Follow this procedure:

1. Write down each of the main points you want to make in your paper on a separate index card.
2. Organize the cards in the order in which you want to discuss each point.
3. Using your index cards, pretend you are giving an oral report. You may either say the words out loud or silently to yourself. The important point is to "hear" yourself "write" the paper.
4. Consider reordering your main points so your paper is better organized. This is where the use of index cards makes things easy. Now repeat step 3. Continue reordering your main points and orally presenting your paper until you have found the best way to present the information.
5. Using your sequenced index cards as your guide, write the paper. And remember, *writing* requires *thinking* and *preparation*—the free, unconstrained thinking used in prewriting and the focused thinking used in structuring.

If you remember only one thing about writing, let it be this: good writing is the result of rewriting. The process of rewriting begins with reading your paper sentence by sentence. After reading each sentence, ask yourself whether you have clearly communicated what you intended.

After reading each paragraph, try to identify its main message. Then ask yourself if you have communicated that message clearly.

Now go back and rewrite the sentences and paragraphs that need to be rewritten. Try to use as few words as possible to communicate your message. Much of rewriting is getting rid

485

of unnecessary words. Next, go through the paper again, sentence by sentence, correcting any grammatical and spelling errors.

Finally, read the paper from beginning to end without stopping. Then ask yourself whether a person picked at random would find it clear, organized, and interesting. If it fails this test, ask yourself why.

Practicing Your Skills

1. Skim the chapters of this text and find a topic that interests you. Then write three or four questions about that topic that you would like to answer. Remember, free up your mind to ask any question that is interesting to you. Now choose the most interesting question and turn it into a topic for a paper.
2. Visit your school library, city library, or both, and write a list of five sources that seem relevant to your topic. If any of your sources are books, identify the pages you think will be most useful. (Check the index.)
3. Make notes on your topic using the identified sources, filling at least 25 notecards. Arrange the notecards in an order that tells a story.
4. Write your paper using the notecards as a guide. Revise your paper as necessary.

Identifying Economic Trends

A trend is a general tendency in a particular direction. To illustrate, suppose Robert is currently graduating from high school. During his four years in high school, his grade point average, or GPA, looked like this:

Freshman year GPA = 2.45
Sophomore year GPA = 3.33
Junior year GPA = 3.45
Senior year GPA = 3.89

Robert's GPA has been rising during his time in high school. Here, then, is a trend—an upward trend in Robert's academic performance.

Consider another example. Suppose that this year, in a city in the Midwest, 2 feet of snow fell in the winter. Last year 3 feet of snow fell. Three years ago 4 feet of snow fell, and four years ago 5 feet of snow fell. There is a trend toward less snow.

Economists often try to identify trends in economic data. Four of the many variables for which they try to identify trends are

(1) the money supply,
(2) the average annual growth in the economy,
(3) the unemployment rate, and
(4) the inflation rate.

For example, the average annual growth rate in the money supply in the 1960s was 3.86 percent. It was higher in the 1970s, at 6.51 percent, and even higher in the 1980s, at 7.66 percent. Was there a trend in the average annual growth rate in the money supply? Yes, and the trend was upward.

When an economist identifies a trend in economic data that is going in the "wrong" direction, one of his or her jobs is to try to figure out how to reverse the trend. If a trend in a variable is going in the "right" direction, an economist will try to figure out what is causing this desirable trend. For example, the average annual inflation rate was relatively high in the 1970s, lower in the 1980s, and still lower in the 1990s. An economist is interested in knowing what happened to bring this desirable trend about.

EXHIBIT ES-5 National Debt, 1990–2001

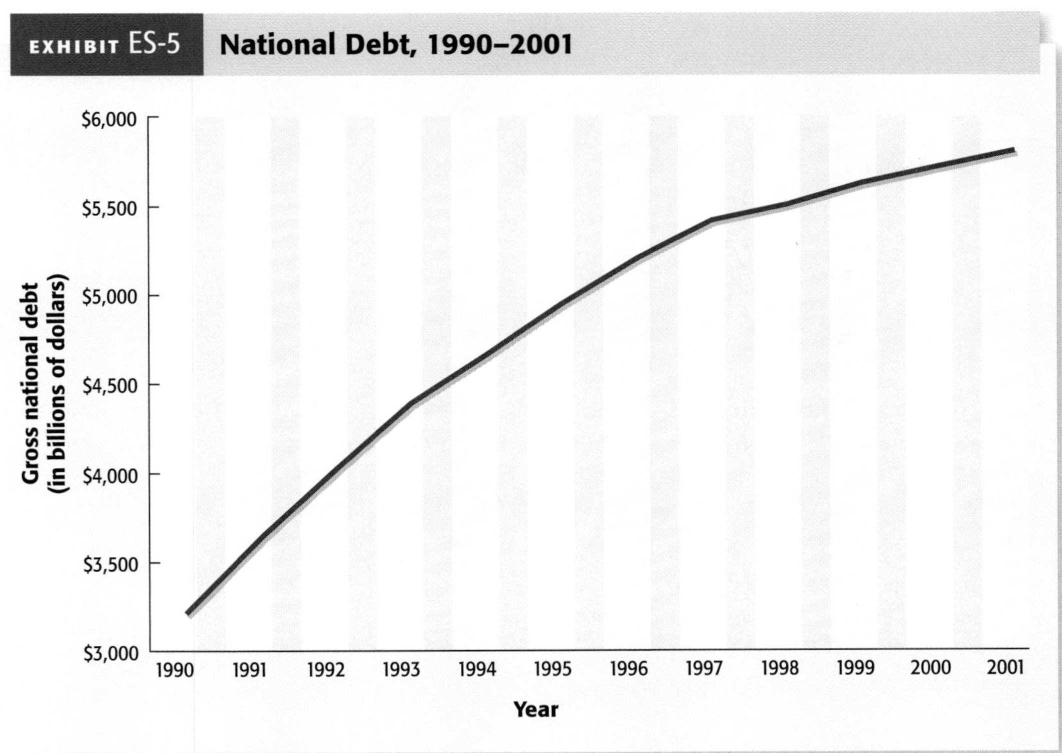

Practicing Your Skills

1. Global warming is defined as "an increase in the earth's average atmospheric temperature that causes corresponding changes in climate and that may result from the greenhouse effect." Is there anything in the definition of global warming that indicates a trend? If so, what?
2. Harry has promised himself that he will exercise three to four times each week. Today was his first day of exercising. Is this a trend? Explain your answer.
3. Look at Exhibit ES-5. Identify the trend.

Using Percentages to Make Comparisons

You have probably heard that you can't compare apples to oranges. For example, it probably wouldn't be meaningful to compare an increase in the price of aspirin from $3.50 a bottle to $3.89 to an increase in the price of steaks from $10.99 a pound to $11.99. On the other hand, we can say that medical care prices rose by 80 percent, while food prices increased by 39 percent. This type of comparison—comparing the percentage changes rather than the price changes—can be useful. This is why it is important to be able to work with and understand percentages—so you can compare apples to apples and organges to oranges.

Suppose you are a farmer. As a farmer, you produce certain food goods to sell. You also buy certain goods and services in your role as consumer. What might be of interest to you is the percentage change in the price of what you sell (food products) compared with the percentage change in the price of what you buy (all kinds of consumer goods and services).

To compute the change in the prices of what the farmer buys, we can look at the consumer price index (CPI) in different years. For example, in one year the CPI was 160.5, and in the next year it had risen to 163.0. Using the following formula , you can compute the percentage change in prices:

487

$$\text{Percentage change in CPI} = \frac{\text{CPI in later year} - \text{CPI in earlier year}}{\text{CPI in earlier year}} \times 100$$

$$= \frac{163.0 - 160.5}{160.5} \times 100$$

$$= \frac{2.5}{160.5} \times 100$$

$$= 1.56\%$$

In the first year the price index for food goods that farmers sell was 107, and in the next year it had fallen to 101. We use the formula that follows to compute the percentage change in prices:

$$\text{Percentage change in prices of food goods that farmers sell} = \frac{\text{Price index in later year} - \text{Price index in earlier year}}{\text{Price index in earlier year}} \times 100$$

$$= \frac{101 - 107}{107} \times 100$$

$$= \frac{-6}{107} \times 100$$

$$= -5.61\%$$

Having made our computations, we see that the prices of the goods farmers buy increased (1.56 percent) and the prices of the goods farmers sell fell (–5.61 percent) during the two-year period.

Practicing Your Skills

1. Valerie's objective is to cut back on buying clothes and entertainment in order to save money. Last month, she spent \$136 on clothes and \$98 on entertainment. This month, she has spent \$129 on clothes and \$79 on entertainment. Compute the percentage change in spending for each good, and then compare the changes. Is Valerie cutting back more in spending on clothes or entertainment?
2. Suppose the price index for the goods Juan sells is 132 in year 1 and 145 in year 2. The price index for the goods he buys is 124 in the first year and 135 in the second year. How much have prices increased between the two years for the goods he sells? For the goods he buys?

Converting Currency

Different nations, of course, have different currencies. In the United States, we have dollars. Mexico has pesos, most countries of the European Union have euros, Japan has yen, and so on. It is important to know how to convert from one currency to another.

Suppose you are in England and see that a sweater has a price tag of £20. How much does it cost in U.S. dollars? To answer this question, you need to know the exchange rate between dollars and pounds. You can get this information by looking at the business section of many newspapers or calling almost any bank.

Let's say the exchange rate is $2 for £1. To find out what the English sweater costs in U.S. dollars, simply use this formula:

Price of sweater in dollars = Price of sweater in foreign currency × Number of dollars needed to buy 1 unit of foreign currency

Let's find the price in dollars of the sweater costing £20, given an exchange rate of $2 for £1:

Price of sweater in dollars = £20 × $2 (per £1) = $40

The answer is $40.

Suppose you knew the price of the sweater in dollars and you wanted to find out its price in some other currency. You could use this formula:

Price of sweater in foreign currency = Price of sweater in dollars ÷ Number of dollars needed to buy 1 unit of foreign currency

Let's find the price in pounds of the $40 sweater, given an exchange rate of $2 for £1:

Price of sweater in foreign currency = $40 ÷ $2 (per £1) = £20

The answer is £20.

Practicing Your Skills

1. The price of an Indian shirt is 4,300 rupees and the exchange rate is 1 rupee = $0.02. What does the Indian shirt cost in dollars?
2. The price of a Swedish lamp is 500 kronor, and the exchange rate is 8 kronor = $1. What does the lamp cost in dollars?
3. Suppose you are working in Mexico, and you earn 2,000 pesos a week. The exchange rate is 1 peso = $0.25. What is your weekly pay in dollars?

Building Decision-Making Skills

As a consumer, citizen, and voter, you will make many economic decisions every day. One of the best ways to improve your decision-making skills is by learning and using a decision-making model.

The steps in the decision-making model are listed and described below using the hypothetical example of choosing a major for college.

Step 1. Define your need or want. The first step in the decision-making process is to define the need or want that requires a decision. When working through this step, it is important to be as specific as possible. Say you define your need or want as follows: I want to choose a major that I will enjoy and that will help me to fulfill my long-range goal of a happy, productive career.

Step 2. Analyze your resources. Your resources will vary according to the decision you have to make. In this case, your resources might include your parents and guidance counselors. For example, many guidance counselors can provide you with an interest inventory that can help you to determine your main areas of interest. You might also want to talk with college representatives or any friends or family members who are attending college.

489

Step 3. Identify your choices. The very fact that a decision needs to be made implies that choices exist. Brainstorm to come up with as many alternative choices as possible. Don't discard possible choices at this point. Regarding your major, you may feel that you are interested in art, art history, anthropology, sociology, and music.

Step 4. Compare the choices. At this point, you need to determine which choice is the best by using your available resources to gather information. Let's say that your guidance counselor tells you that you should look at the career opportunities that each major allows. Then you should try to imagine the outcome of each choice.

Step 5. Choose the best alternative. After you have compared your choices, it is time to choose the best one. This can be difficult if no one alternative stands out as the best. Suppose, for example, that all of the majors have basically the same appeal. You finally choose art history because it seems to combine your other interests and because it might lead to a career as a museum curator, which sounds exciting and rewarding.

Step 6. Make a plan to get started. You must make a plan of action. Your plan of action might include obtaining college catalogs, completing applications, and writing letters to art history departments for information about curricula.

Step 7. Evaluate your decision. Just because you have made a decision does not mean that you cannot change your mind. Look at the results of your decision. If the outcome is not what you had hoped it would be, perhaps it is time to start over with step 1. Continue to evaluate your decision as you learn more about your first choice.

Notice that the decision-making model contains words like *choices, wants,* and *resources.* As you have learned, scarcity exists and, as a result, choices have to be made. Decision making is part of economics, and using the decision-making model is a good example of thinking like an economist.

Practicing Your Skills

Identify a real-world situation in which you will need to make a decision in the near future. Use the seven-step process described above to make a decision for that situation. Compare the process used to your usual method of decision making. Do you think the seven-step process led you to a different decision than you would have made otherwise? Did the process lead to a better decision?

Databank

On the following pages you will find historical data for selected economic and economic-related topics, such as GDP, money supply, population, and personal income. The data will be of use as you study the principles of economics. Following is a list of the data included in this databank.

EXHIBIT R-1 U.S. Real GDP in Selected Years

Year	Real GDP (billions of 2000 dollars)	Year	Real GDP (billions of 2000 dollars)
1860	$ 72.9	1940	$ 1,034.1
1865	$ 88.1	1950	$ 1,777.3
1875	$125.2	1960	$ 2,501.8
1890	$267.7	1970	$ 3,771.9
1900	$355.8	1980	$ 5,161.7
1913	$ 531.1	1990	$ 7,112.5
1929	$865.2	2000	$ 9,817.0
1932	$643.7	2004	$10,755.7

Source: Bureau of Economic Analysis

EXHIBIT R-2 U.S. Real GDP, 1990–2005

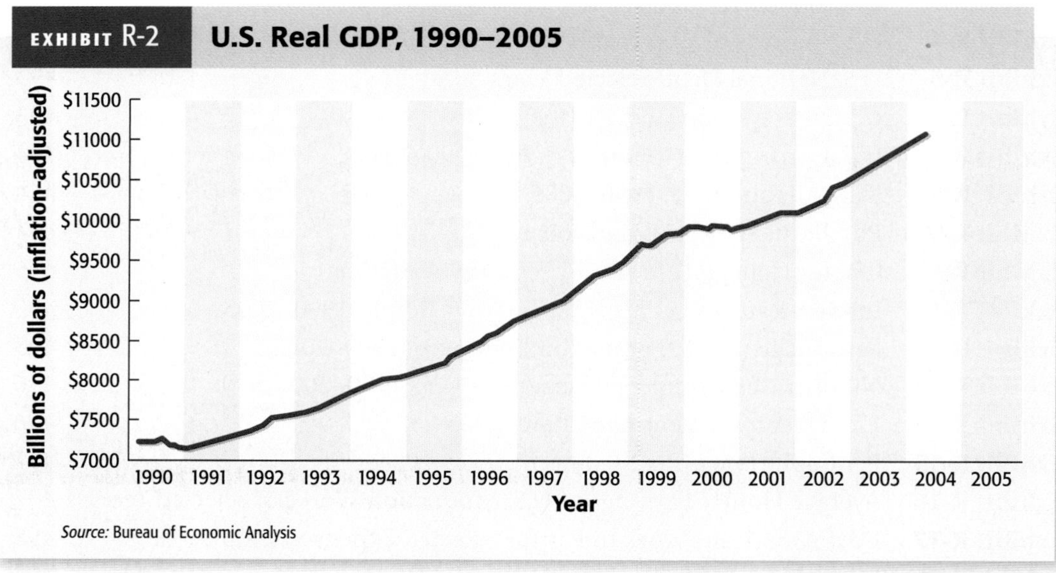

Source: Bureau of Economic Analysis

EXHIBIT R-3 U.S. Exports of Goods and Services, 1990–2004

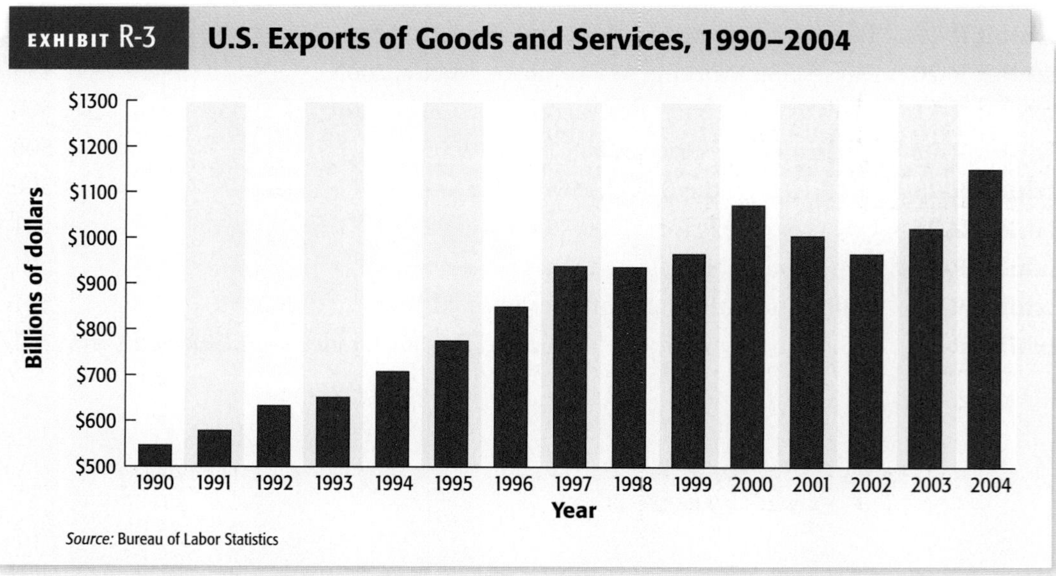

Source: Bureau of Labor Statistics

EXHIBIT R-4 **U.S. Imports of Goods and Services, 1990–2004**

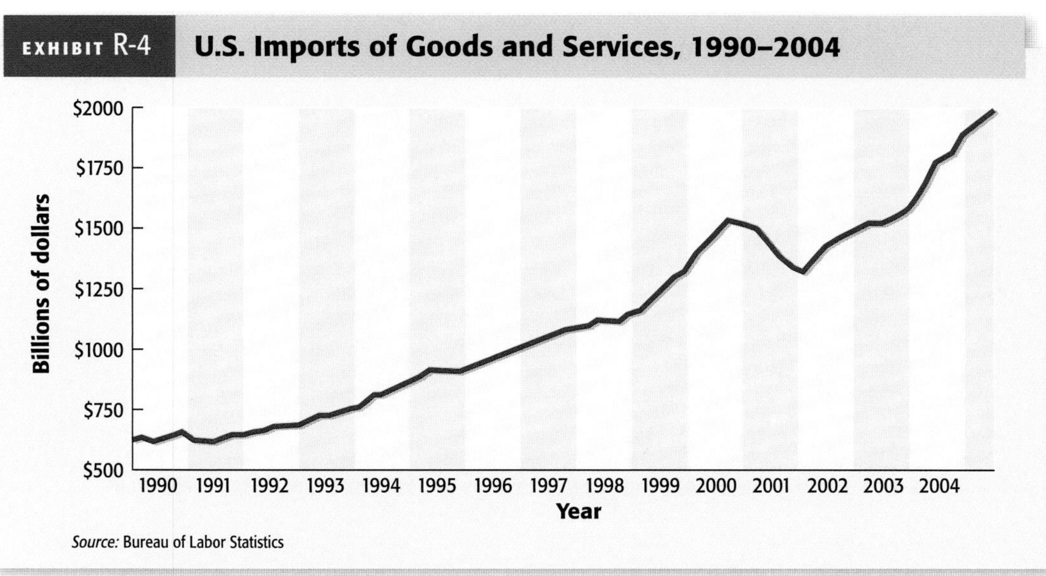

Source: Bureau of Labor Statistics

EXHIBIT R-5 **U.S. National Debt, Selected Years**

Year	National debt (trillions)
1990	$3.2
1995	$4.9
2000	$5.6
2001	$5.7
2002	$6.1
2003	$6.7
2004	$7.4
2005*	$7.9

*On October 13, 2005
Source: Economic Report of the President

Note: Exhibits R-3 and R-4 show exports and imports of goods *and services*. Exhibits 15-1 and 15-2 in Chapter 15 show exports and imports of goods only.

EXHIBIT R-6 **U.S. Money Supply (M1), 1990–2005**

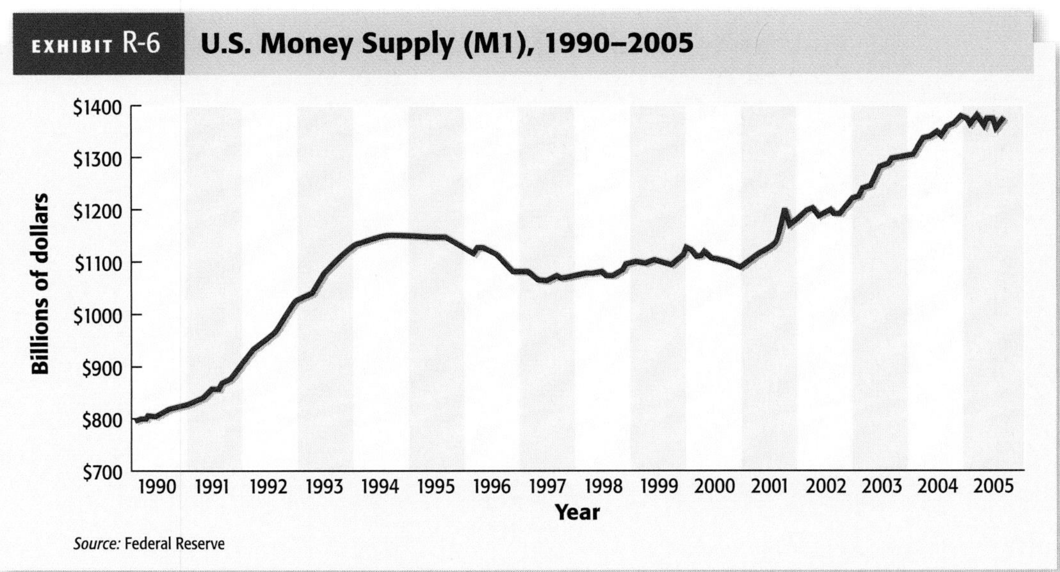

Source: Federal Reserve

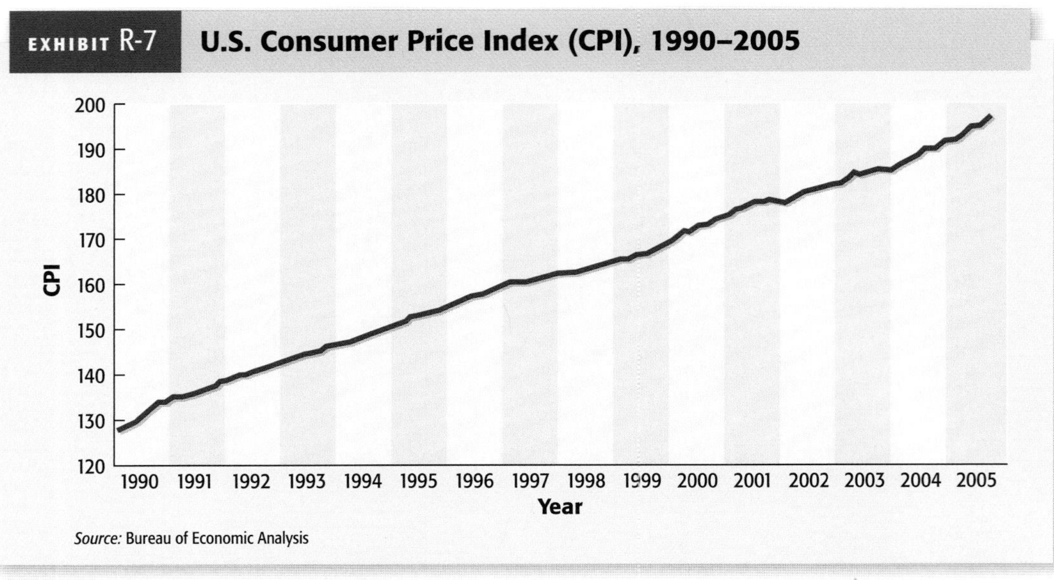

EXHIBIT R-7 **U.S. Consumer Price Index (CPI), 1990–2005**

Source: Bureau of Economic Analysis

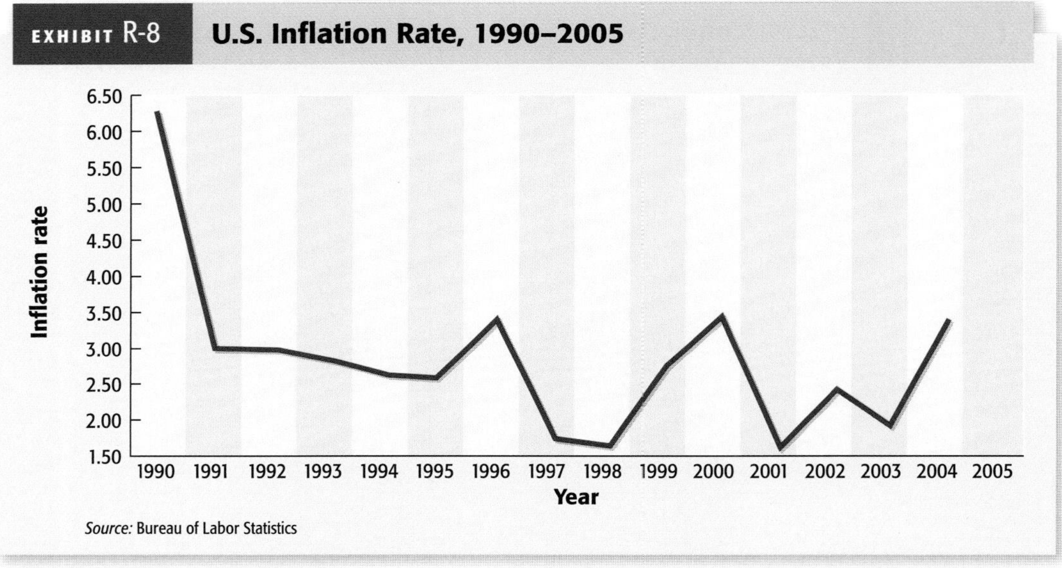

EXHIBIT R-8 **U.S. Inflation Rate, 1990–2005**

Source: Bureau of Labor Statistics

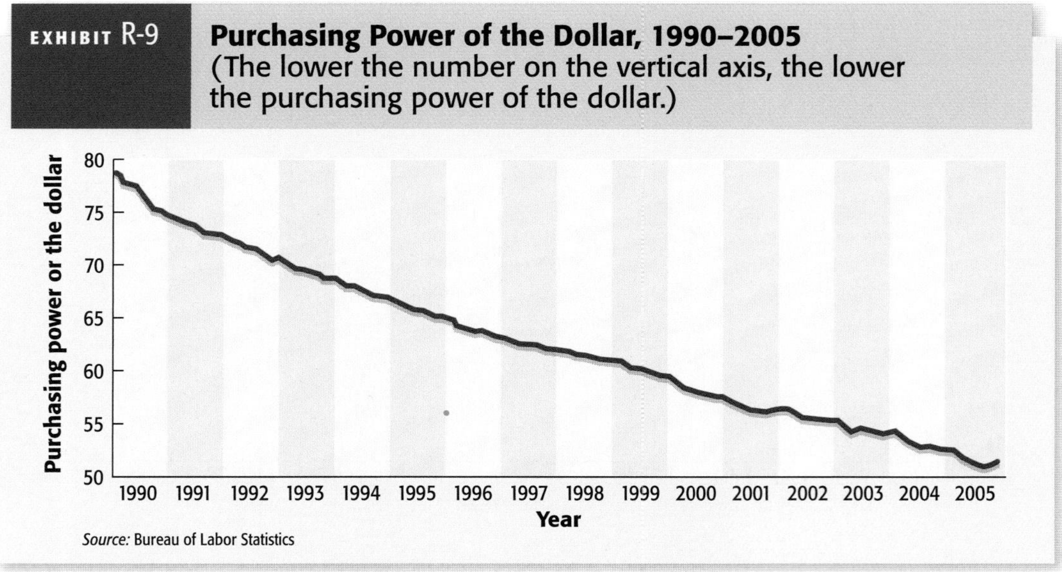

EXHIBIT R-9 **Purchasing Power of the Dollar, 1990–2005**
(The lower the number on the vertical axis, the lower the purchasing power of the dollar.)

Source: Bureau of Labor Statistics

EXHIBIT R-10 **CPI for College Tuition and Fees, 1990–2005**
(College tuition has risen steadily during the time period.)

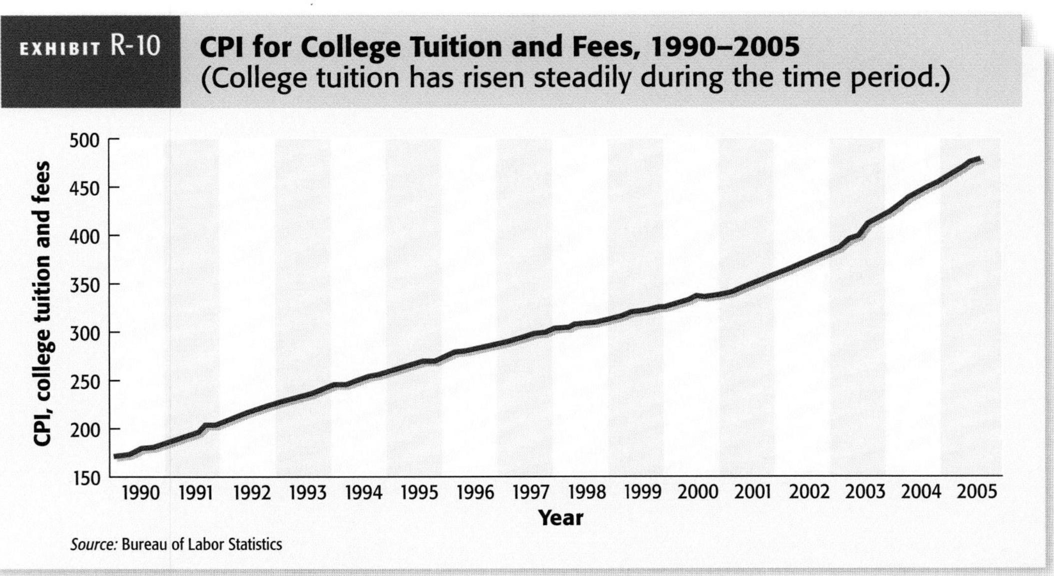

Source: Bureau of Labor Statistics

EXHIBIT R-11 **Interest Rate on 10-Year U.S. Treasury Bonds, 1990–2005**

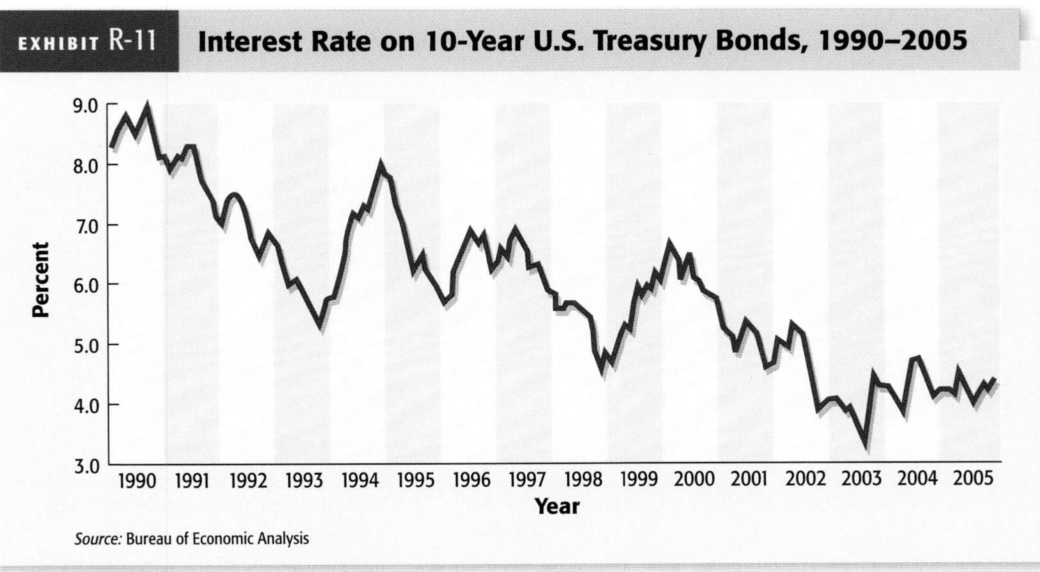

Source: Bureau of Economic Analysis

EXHIBIT R-12 **Percentage of U.S. Population Employed, 1990–2005**

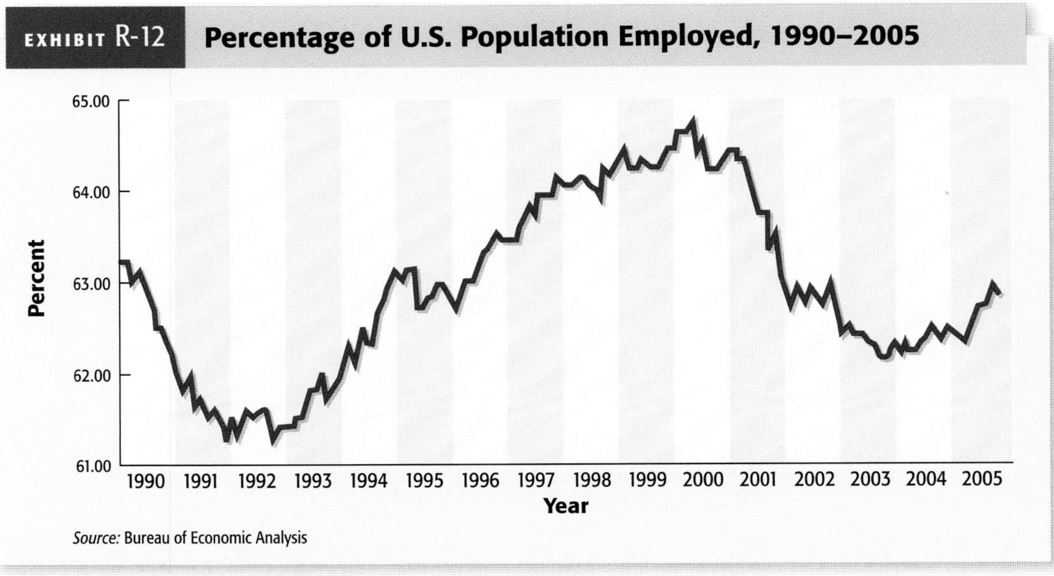

Source: Bureau of Economic Analysis

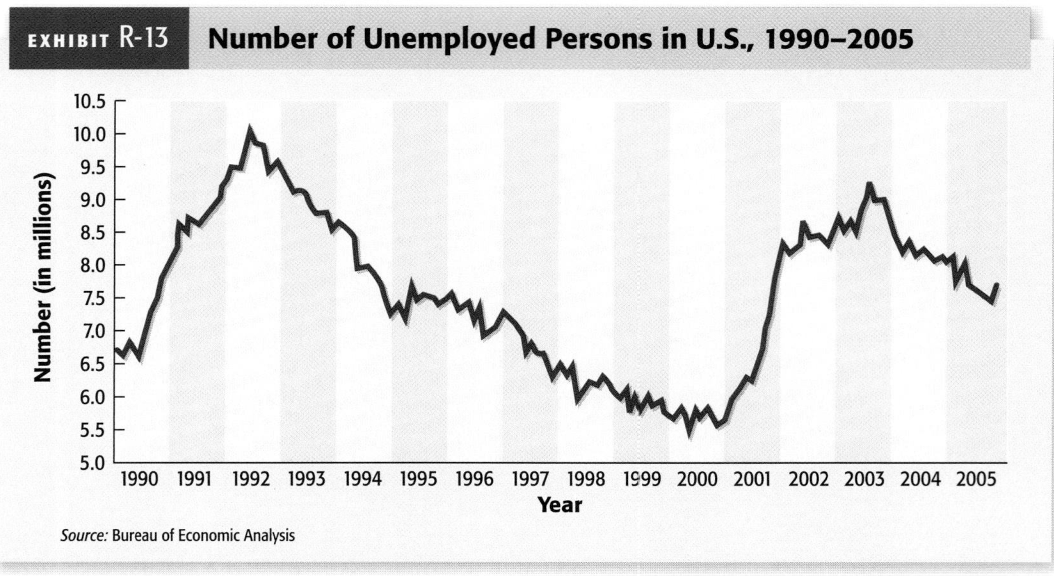

Source: Bureau of Economic Analysis

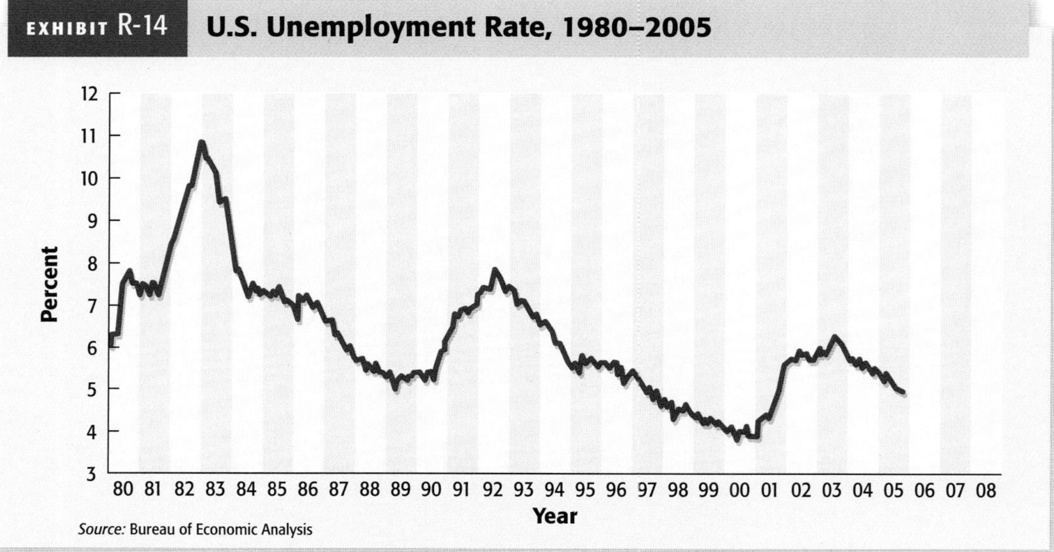

Source: Bureau of Economic Analysis

EXHIBIT R-15 Per Capita After-Tax Income, by State, 2004

State	Per capita after-tax income (dollars)
United States	$29,472
Alabama	$25,169
Alaska	$31,066
Arizona	$25,895
Arkansas	$23,432
California	$31,012
Colorado	$32,273
Connecticut	$38,790
Delaware	$31,445
District of Columbia	$45,442
Florida	$28,569
Georgia	$26,889
Hawaii	$29,174
Idaho	$24,414
Illinois	$30,931
Indiana	$27,070
Iowa	$28,164
Kansas	$27,949
Kentucky	$24,391
Louisiana	$24,932
Maine	$26,932
Maryland	$34,518
Massachusetts	$36,506
Michigan	$28,845
Minnesota	$31,904
Mississippi	$22,560
Missouri	$27,531
Montana	$25,123
Nebraska	$29,272
Nevada	$30,345
New Hampshire	$33,180
New Jersey	$36,421
New Mexico	$23,865
New York	$32,922
North Carolina	$26,246
North Dakota	$26,859
Ohio	$27,739
Oklahoma	$25,236
Oregon	$27,124
Pennsylvania	$29,656
Rhode Island	$30,420
South Carolina	$24,678
South Dakota	$28,507
Tennessee	$27,523
Texas	$28,176
Utah	$24,366
Vermont	$28,622
Virginia	$31,751
Washington	$31,860
West Virginia	$23,488
Wisconsin	$28,504
Wyoming	$31,022

Source: Bureau of Economic Analysis

EXHIBIT R-16 Average Hourly Earnings of U.S. Production Workers, Selected Years

Year	Hourly earnings
1995	$11.47
1997	$12.27
1999	$13.25
2001	$14.27
2003	$15.19
2005	$15.90

Source: Bureau of Labor Statistics

EXHIBIT R-17 Days Americans Work to Pay for Selected Expenses, 2005

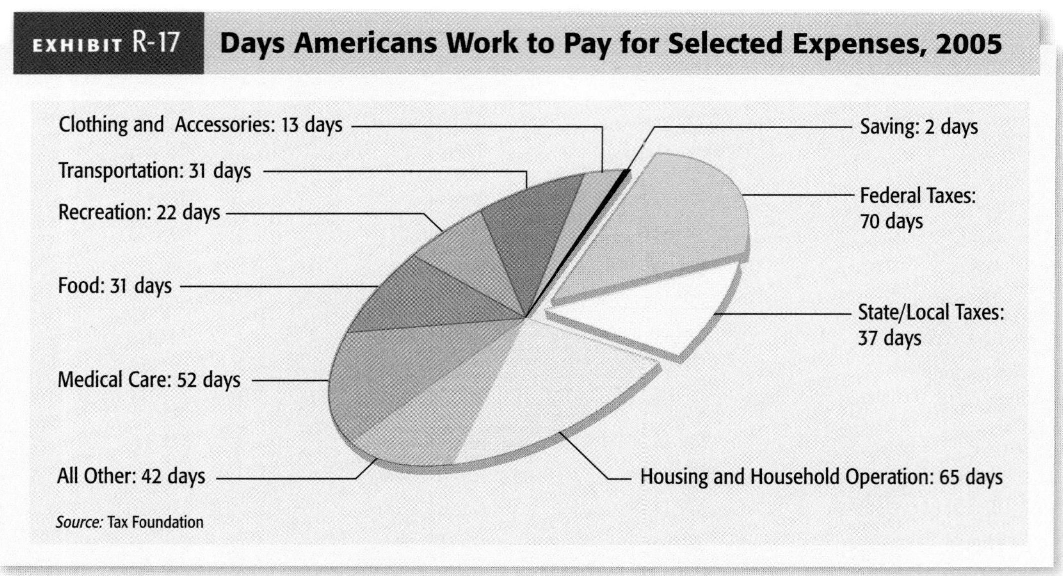

Source: Tax Foundation

EXHIBIT R-18 Percentage of U.S. Tax Filers Who Paid No Income Tax, 1950–2004

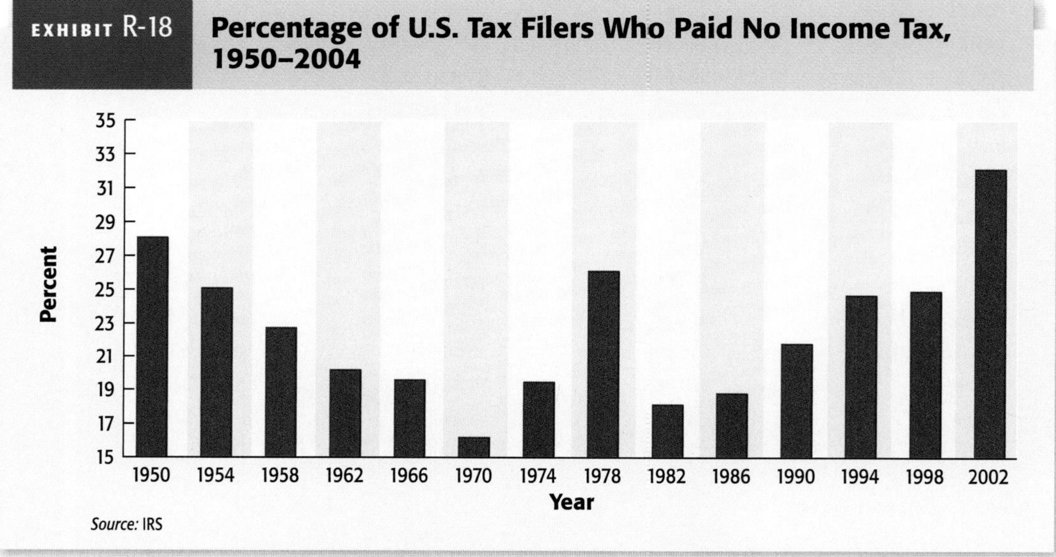

Source: IRS

EXHIBIT R-19 Taxes as a Percentage of Income, Selected Years

Year	Percentage of income	Year	Percentage of income
1990	5.9%	1980	30.3%
1910	5.0%	1990	30.5%
1920	11.6%	2000	33.6%
1930	11.2%	2001	32.6%
1940	17.6%	2002	29.8%
1950	24.6%	2003	28.9%
1960	27.4%	2004	28.6%
1970	29.4%	2005	29.1%

Source: IRS

EXHIBIT R-20 Days Spent Working to Pay Various Taxes, 2005

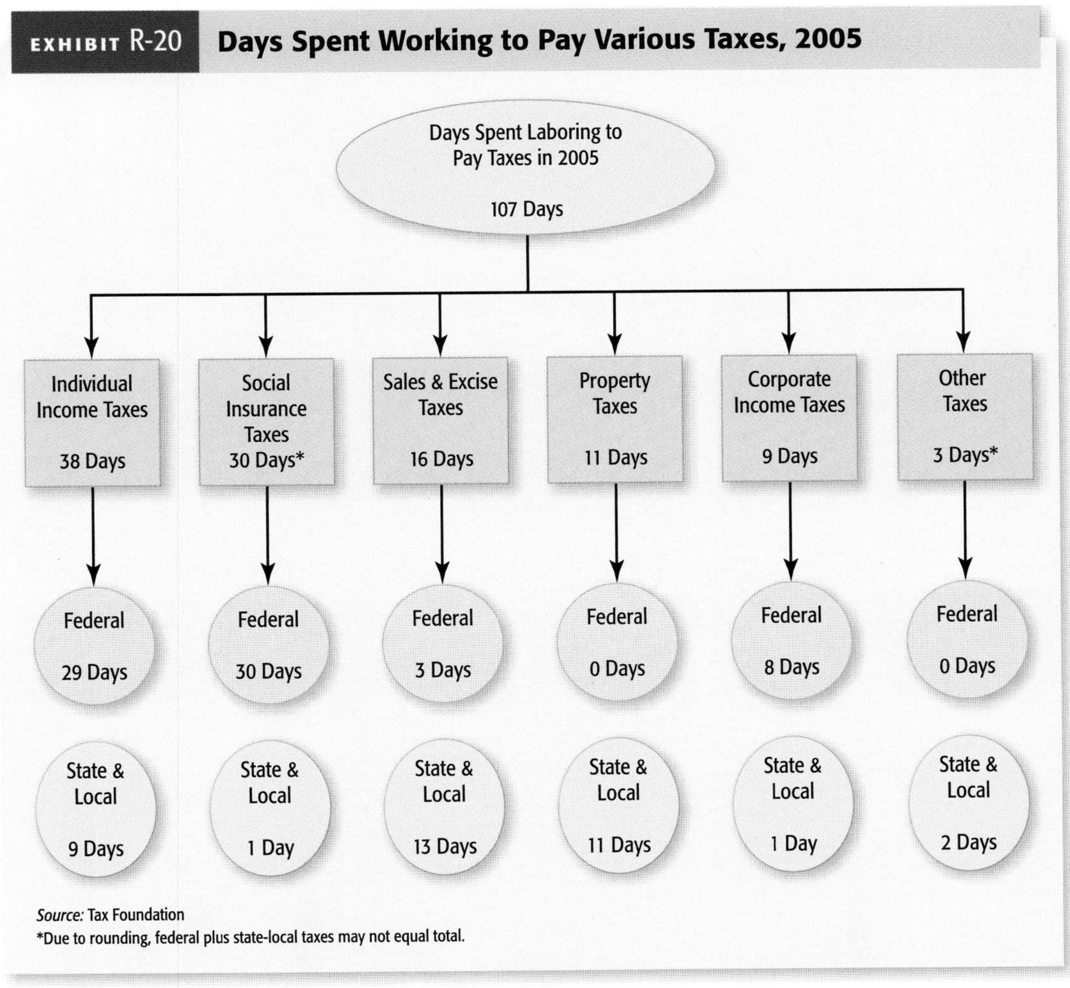

Source: Tax Foundation

*Due to rounding, federal plus state-local taxes may not equal total.

EXHIBIT R-21 Taxes as a Percentage of Income, Various Countries, 2003

Country	Percentage of income	Country	Percentage of income
1. Belgium	55.6%	13. Netherlands	42.3%
2. Hungary	52.6%	14. Slovakia	42.0%
3. Germany	50.7%	15. Spain	37.9%
4. Sweden	48.6%	16. Norway	37.0%
5. France	48.3%	17. Greece	36.0%
6. Italy	46.2%	18. Luxembourg	33.9%
7. Finland	45.9%	19. Portugal	32.5%
8. Austria	44.7%	20. Canada	30.2%
9. Denmark	44.2%	21. United States	30.0%
10. Turkey	43.2%	22. United Kingdom	29.7%
11. Czech Republic	43.0%	23. Switzerland	29.5%
12. Poland	42.9%	24. Ireland	25.8%
		25. Iceland	25.7%

Source: NationMaster

EXHIBIT R-22 Median House Price in U.S., 1990–2005

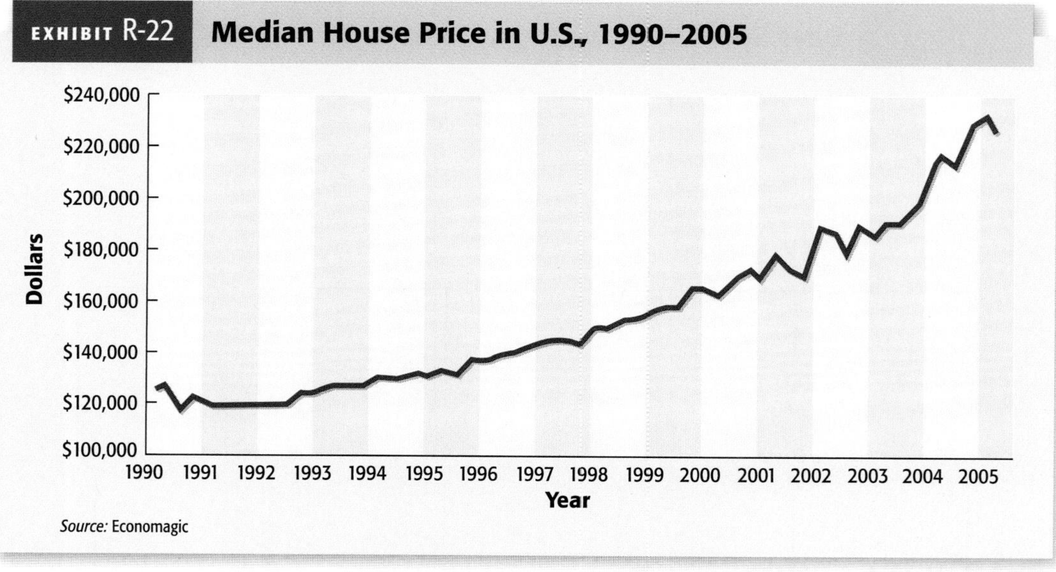

Source: Economagic

EXHIBIT R-23 Oil Prices, by the Barrel, 1990–2005

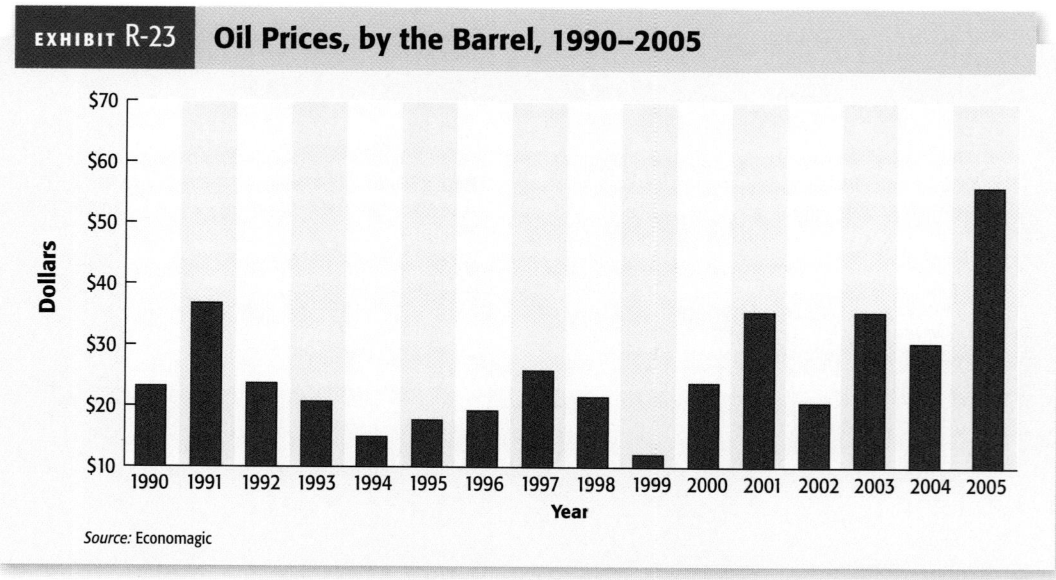

Source: Economagic

EXHIBIT R-24 U.S. Gasoline Prices, 2000–2005

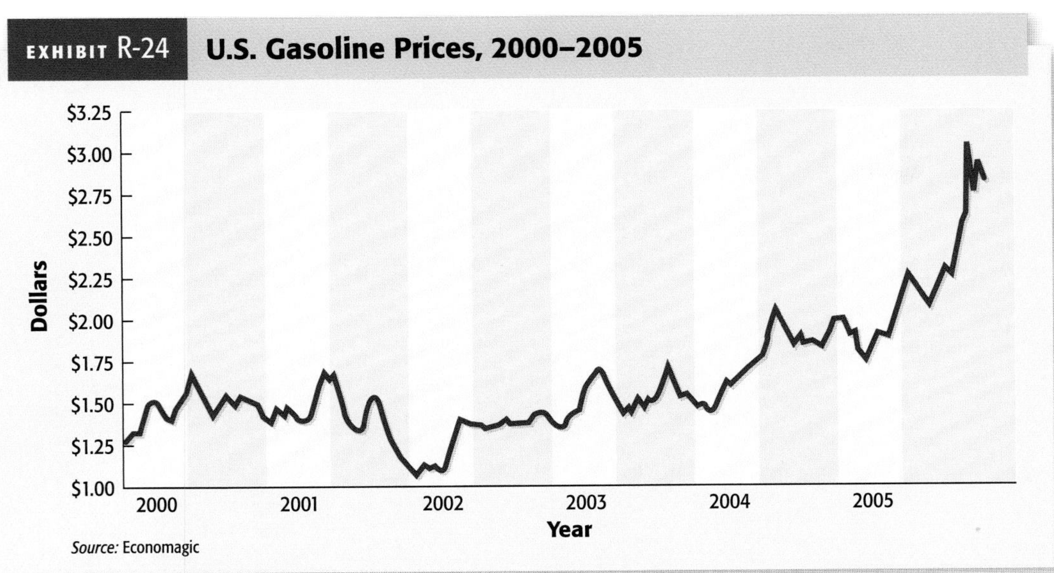

Source: Economagic

EXHIBIT R-25 U.S. Population, Selected Years

Year	Population
1960	180,671,000
1970	205,052,000
1980	227,726,000
1990	250,132,000
2000	282,388,000
2005*	297,411,000

* Population in October 2005
Source: Statistical Abstract of the United States

EXHIBIT R-26 Expectation of Length of Life, Selected Years

Year	Female (years)	Male (years)
1970	74.7	67.1
1980	77.4	70.0
1990	78.8	71.8
2001	79.8	74.4
2010*	81.4	75.6

* Projection
Source: Statistical Abstract of the United States

EXHIBIT R-27 U.S. School Enrollment, Public and Private, Grades 9–12, Selected Years

Year	Public (millions)	Private (millions)
1970	13.33	1.31
1980	13.23	1.33
1990	11.33	1.15
2000	13.51	1.28
2005*	14.77	1.43
2010*	14.65	1.45

* Projections
Source: Statistical Abstract of the United States

Glossary

absolute advantage The situation in which a country can produce more of a good than another country can produce with the same quantity of resources.

absolute real economic growth An increase in real GDP from one period to the next.

advancement in technology The ability to produce more output with a fixed amount of resources.

after-tax income The part of income that's left over after taxes are paid.

aggregate demand curve A curve that shows the quantity of goods and services that buyers are willing and able to buy at different price levels.

aggregate supply curve A curve that shows the quantity of goods and services that producers are willing and able to supply at different price levels.

antitrust law Legislation passed for the stated purpose of controlling monopoly power and preserving and promoting competition.

appreciation An increase in the value of one currency relative to other currencies.

asset Anything of value to which the firm has a legal claim.

average total cost The total cost divided by the quantity of output.

balance of trade The difference between the value of a country's exports and the value of its imports.

barrier to entry Anything that prohibits a firm from entering a market.

barter economy An economy in which trades are made in goods and services instead of in money.

base year In general, a benchmark year—a year chosen as a point of reference for comparison. When real GDP is computed, the outputs of different years are priced at base-year levels.

board of directors An important decision-making body in a corporation. It decides corporate policies and goals, among other things.

Board of Governors of the Federal Reserve System The governing body of the Federal Reserve System.

bond An IOU, or a promise to pay, issued by companies, governments, or government agencies for the purpose of borrowing money.

budget deficit The situation in which federal government expenditures are greater than federal government tax revenues.

budget surplus The situation in which federal government expenditures are less than federal government tax revenues.

business cycle Recurrent swings (up and down) in real GDP.

business firm An organization that uses resources to produce goods and services that are sold to consumers, other firms, or the government.

capital Produced goods that can be used as resources for further production. Such things as factories, machines, and farm tractors are capital.

cartel agreement An agreement that specifies how the firms that entered into the agreement will act in a coordinated way to reduce the competition among them.

circular flow of economic activity The economic relationships that exist between different economic groups in an economy.

closed shop An organization that hires only union members.

comparative advantage The situation in which a country can produce a good at lower opportunity cost than another country.

complement A good that is consumed jointly with another good. With complements, the price of one and the demand for the other move in opposite directions.

consumer price index (CPI) The most widely cited price index.

consumption Expenditures made by the household sector.

contract An agreement between two or more people to do something.

contractionary fiscal policy A decrease in government spending or an increase in taxes.

contractionary monetary policy A decrease in the money supply.

corporation A legal entity that can conduct business in its own name in the same way that an individual does.

coupon rate The percentage of the face value that the bondholder receives each year until the bond matures.

crowding in The situation in which decreases in government spending lead to increases in private spending.

crowding out The situation in which increases in government spending lead to reductions in private spending.

currency Coins issued by the U.S. Treasury and paper money (called Federal Reserve notes) issued by the Federal Reserve System.

deflation A decrease in the price level, or average level of prices.

demand The willingness and ability of buyers to purchase different quantities of a good at different prices during a specific time period.

demand curve The graphical representation of the law of demand.

demand deposit An account from which deposited funds can be withdrawn in currency or transferred by a check to a third party at the initiative of the owner.

demand schedule The numerical representation of the law of demand.

demand-side inflation An increase in the price level that originates on the demand side of the economy.

depreciation A decrease in the value of one currency relative to other currencies.

derived demand A demand that is the result of some other demand.

developed country A country with a relatively high per capita GDP.

direct relationship A relationship between two factors in which the factors move in the same direction. For example, as one factor rises, the other rises, too.

discount rate The interest rate the Fed charges a bank for a loan.

disutility The quality of bringing dissatisfaction or unhappiness.

dividend A share of the profits of a corporation distributed to stockholders.

double counting Counting a good more than once in computing GDP.

Dow Jones Industrial Average (DJIA) The most popular, widely cited indicator of day-to-day stock market activity. The DJIA is a weighted average of 30 widely traded stocks on the New York Stock Exchange.

dumping The sale of goods abroad at prices below their costs and below the price charged in domestic (home) markets.

economic plan A government program specifying economic activities, such as what goods are to be produced and what prices will be charged.

economic system The way in which a society decides what goods to produce, how to produce them, and for whom goods will be produced.

economics The science that studies the choices of people trying to satisfy their wants in a world of scarcity.

elastic demand The type of demand that exists when the percentage change in quantity demanded is greater than the percentage change in price.

elastic supply The kind of supply that exists when the percentage change in quantity supplied is greater than the percentage change in price.

elasticity of demand The relationship between the percentage change in quantity demanded and the percentage change in price.

elasticity of supply The relationship between the percentage change in quantity supplied and the percentage change in price.

employment rate The percentage of the noninstitutional adult civilian population that is employed.

entrepreneur A person who has a special talent for searching out and taking advantage of new business opportunities.

entrepreneurship The special talent that some people have for searching out and taking advantage of new business opportunities and for developing new products and new ways of doing things.

equilibrium In a market the point at which the quantity of a good that buyers are willing and able to buy is equal to the quantity that sellers are willing and able to produce and offer for sale (quantity demanded equals quantity supplied).

equilibrium price The price at which a good is bought and sold in a market that is in equilibrium.

equilibrium quantity The quantity of a good that is bought and sold in a market that is in equilibrium.

ethics The principles of conduct, such as right and wrong, morality and immorality, good and bad.

excess reserves Any reserves held beyond the required amount.

exchange rate The price of one country's currency in terms of another country's currency.

excludable public good A public good that individuals can be excluded (physically prohibited) from consuming.

expansionary fiscal policy An increase in government spending or a reduction in taxes.

expansionary monetary policy An increase in the money supply.

export spending The amount spent by the residents of other countries for goods produced in the United States.

exports Goods produced in the domestic country and sold to residents of a foreign country.

face value (par value) Dollar amount specified on a bond. The total amount the issuer of the bond will repay to the buyer of the bond.

federal funds rate The interest rate one bank charges another for a loan.

Federal Open Market Committee (FOMC) The 12-member policy-making group within the Fed. This committee has the authority to conduct open market operations.

Federal Reserve note Paper money issued by the Federal Reserve System.

Federal Reserve System (the Fed) The central bank of the United States.

fiscal policy Changes government makes in spending or taxation to achieve particular economic goals.

fixed cost A cost, or expense, that is the same no matter how many units of a good are produced.

fixed exchange rate system The system whereby currency exchange rates are fixed, or pegged, by countries' governments.

flexible exchange rate system The system whereby currency exchange rates are determined by the forces of supply and demand.

fractional reserve banking A banking arrangement in which banks hold only a fraction of their deposits and lend out the remainder.

franchise A contract by which a firm (usually a corporation) lets a person or group use its name and sell its goods in exchange for certain payments and requirements.

franchisee The person or group that buys a franchise.

franchiser The entity that offers a franchise.

free enterprise An economic system in which individuals (not government) own most, if not all, the resources and control their use. Government plays only a small part in the economy.

free rider A person who receives the benefits of a good without paying for it.

futures contract Agreement to buy or sell a specific amount of something (commodity,

505

currency, financial instrument) at a particular price on a stipulated future date.

globalization A phenomenon by which economic agents in any given part of the world are affected by events elsewhere in the world; the growing integration of the national economies of the world to the degree that we may be witnessing the emergence and operation of a single worldwide economy.

goods Anything that satisfies a person's wants or brings satisfaction; also, tangible products.

government purchases Expenditures made by the government sector. Government purchases do not include government transfer payments.

gross domestic product (GDP) The total market value of all final goods and services produced annually in a country.

hedge To try to avoid or lessen a loss by taking some counterbalancing action.

household An economic unit of one person or more that sells resources and buys goods and services.

human capital The knowledge and skill that people obtain from education, on-the-job training, and work experience and use in the production of goods and services; also includes honesty, creativity, and perseverance—traits that lend themselves to finding work.

import spending The amount spent by Americans for foreign-produced goods.

imports Goods produced in foreign countries and purchased by residents of the domestic country.

incentive Something that encourages or motivates a person to take action.

income distribution The way all the income earned in a country is divided among different groups of income earners.

index A portfolio of stocks, which represents a particular market or a portion of it, used to measure changes in a market or an economy.

inelastic demand The type of demand that exists when the percentage change in quantity demanded is less than the percentage change in price.

inelastic supply The kind of supply that exists when the percentage change in quantity supplied is less than the percentage change in price.

inferior good A good for which the demand falls as income rises and rises as income falls.

inflation An increase in the price level, or average level of prices.

initial public offering (IPO) A company's first offering of stock to the public.

intangible Not able to be felt by touch. For example, an economics lecture is intangible.

inventory The stock of goods that a business or store has on hand.

investment Expenditures made by the business sector.

investment bank Firm that acts as an intermediary between the company that issues the stock and the public that wishes to buy the stock.

labor The physical and mental talents that people contribute to the production of goods and services.

labor theory of value The belief that all value in produced goods is derived from labor.

labor union An organization that seeks to increase the wages and improve the working conditions of its members.

Laffer curve The curve, named after economist Arthur Laffer, that shows the relationship between tax rates and tax revenues. According to the Laffer curve, as tax rates rise from zero, tax revenues rise, reach a maximum at some point, and then fall with further increases in tax rates.

land All the natural resources found in nature. An acre of land, mineral deposits, and water in a stream are all considered land.

law of demand A law stating that as the price of a good increases, the quantity demanded of the good decreases, and that as the price of a good decreases, the quantity demanded of the good increases.

law of diminishing marginal returns A law that states that if additional units of a resource are added to another fixed resource, eventually the additional output will decrease.

law of diminishing marginal utility A law stating that as a person consumes additional units of a good, eventually the utility gained from each additional unit of the good decreases.

law of supply A law stating that as the price of a good increases, the quantity supplied of the good increases, and as the price of a good decreases, the quantity supplied of the good decreases.

less-developed country A country with a relatively low per capita GDP.

limited liability A condition in which an owner of a business firm can lose only the amount he or she has invested (in the firm).

loanable funds market The market for loans. There is a demand for loans (stemming from borrowers) and a supply of loans (stemming from lenders). It is in the loanable funds market where the interest rate is determined.

loss The amount of money by which total cost exceeds total revenue.

macroeconomics The branch of economics that deals with human behavior and choices as they relate to the entire economy.

marginal In economics, marginal means additional.

marginal cost The cost of producing an additional unit of a good; the change in total cost that results from producing an additional unit of output.

marginal revenue The revenue from selling an additional unit of a good; the change in total revenue that results from selling an additional unit of output.

market Any place where people come together to buy and sell goods or services.

market structure The setting in which a seller finds itself. Market structures are defined by their characteristics, such as the number of sellers in the market, the product that sellers produce and sell, and how easy or difficult it is for new firms to enter the market.

medium of exchange Anything that is generally acceptable in exchange for goods and services.

microeconomics The branch of economics that deals with human behavior and choices as they relate to relatively small units—an individual, a business firm, or a single market.

minimum wage law A federal law that specifies the lowest hourly wage rate that can be paid to workers.

mixed economy An economy that is neither purely capitalist nor purely socialist; an economy that has some elements of both capitalism and socialism. Most countries in the world have mixed economies.

monetary policy Changes the Fed makes in the money supply.

money A good that is widely accepted for purposes of exchange and in the repayment of debt.

money supply The total supply of money in circulation, composed of currency, checking accounts, and traveler's checks.

monopolistic competitive market A market structure characterized by (1) many buyers and many sellers, (2) the production and sale of slightly differentiated products, and (3) easy entry into and easy exit from the market.

monopolistic market A market structure characterized by (1) a single seller, (2) the sale of a product that has no close substitutes, and (3) extremely high barriers to entry.

national debt The sum total of what the federal government owes its creditors.

natural monopoly A firm with such a low average total cost (per-unit cost) that only it can survive in the market.

near-money Assets, such as nonchecking savings accounts, that can be easily and quickly turned into money.

negative externality An adverse side effect of an act that is felt by others.

neutral good A good for which the demand remains unchanged as income rises or falls.

nonexcludable public good A public good that individuals cannot be excluded (physically prohibited) from consuming.

normal good A good for which the demand rises as income rises and falls as income falls.

offshoring The term used to describe work done for a company by persons other than the original company's employees in a country other than the one in which the company is located.

oligopolistic market A market structure characterized by (1) few sellers, (2) the production and sale of either identical or slightly differentiated products, and (3) significant barriers to entry.

open market operations Buying and selling of government securities by the Fed.

opportunity cost The most highly valued opportunity or alternative forfeited when a choice is made.

option Contract that gives the owner the right, but not the obligation, to buy or sell shares of a good at a specified price on or before a specified date.

outsourcing The term used to describe work done for a company by another company or by people other than the original company's employees.

partnership A business owned by two or more co-owners, called partners, who share profits and are legally responsible for debts.

per capita real economic growth An increase from one period to the next in per capita real GDP, which is real GDP divided by population.

per-unit cost The average cost of a good. For example, if $400,000 is spent to produce 100 cars, the average, or per-unit, cost is $4,000.

perfectly competitive market A market structure characterized by (1) many buyers and many sellers, (2) all firms selling identical goods, (3) all relevant information about buying and selling activities is available to buyers and sellers, and (4) easy entry into and easy exit out of the market.

population growth rate The birthrate minus the death rate.

positive externality A beneficial side effect of an action that is felt by others.

price ceiling A legislated price—set lower than the equilibrium price—above which buyers and sellers cannot legally buy and sell a good.

price discrimination Practice by which a seller charges different prices (to different buyers) for the product it sells and the price differences do not reflect cost differences.

price floor A legislated price—set above the equilibrium price—below which buyers and sellers cannot legally buy and sell a good.

price index A measure of the price level, or the average level of prices.

price searcher A seller that can sell some of its output at various prices.

price taker A seller that can sell all its output at the equilibrium price but can sell none of its output at any other price.

private good A good of which one person's consumption takes away from another person's consumption.

private property Any good that is owned by an individual or a business.

production possibilities frontier A graphic representation of all possible combinations of two goods that an economy can produce.

profit The amount of money left over after all the costs of production have been paid. Profit exists whenever total revenue is greater than total cost.

progressive income tax An income tax whose rate increases as income level rises. Progressive income tax structures are usually capped at some rate.

proportional income tax An income tax that everyone pays at the same rate, whatever the income level.

public franchise A right granted to a firm by government that permits the firm to provide a particular good or service and excludes all others from doing so.

public good A good of which one person's consumption does not take away from another person's consumption.

public property Any good that is owned by the government.

quantity demanded The number of units of a good purchased at a specific price.

quantity supplied The number of units of a good produced and offered for sale at a specific price.

quota A legal limit on the number of units of a foreign-produced good (import) that can enter a country.

rationing device A means for deciding who gets what portion of the available resources and goods.

real GDP Gross domestic product (GDP) that has been adjusted for price changes; GDP measured in base-year, or constant, prices.

recession A slowdown in the economy marked by real GDP falling for two consecutive quarters.

regressive income tax An income tax whose rate decreases as income level rises.

required reserves The minimum amount of reserves a bank must hold against its deposits as mandated by the Fed.

reserve account A bank's checking account with its Federal Reserve district bank.

reserve requirement The regulation that requires a bank to keep a certain percentage of its deposits in its reserve account with the Fed or in its vault as vault cash.

resource Anything that is used to produce goods or services. For example, a person's labor may be used to produce computers, TV sets, and much more, and therefore a person's labor is a resource.

right-to-work law A state law that prohibits the practice of requiring employees to join a union in order to work.

savings account An interest-earning account.

scarcity The condition in which our wants are greater than the resources available to satisfy those wants.

services Tasks that people pay others to perform for them.

shirking The behavior of a worker who is putting forth less than the agreed-to effort.

shortage The condition in which the quantity demanded of a good is greater than the quantity supplied. Shortages occur only at prices *below* equilibrium price.

simple quantity theory of money A theory that predicts that changes in the price level will be strictly proportional to changes in the money supply.

socialism An economic system in which government controls and may own many of the resources.

sole proprietorship A business that is owned by one individual who makes all business decisions, receives all the profits or incurs all the losses of the firm, and is legally responsible for the debts of the firm.

specialize To do only one thing. For example, when a country specializes in the production of a good, it produces only that good.

stagflation The occurrence of inflation and high unemployment at the same time.

stockholder A person who owns shares of stock in a corporation.

stop-and-go, on-and-off monetary policy An erratic monetary policy.

store of value Something with the ability to hold value over time.

strike A work stoppage called by union members to put pressure on an employer.

subsidy A financial payment made by government for certain actions.

substitute A similar good. With substitutes, the price of one and the demand for the other move in the same direction.

supply The willingness and ability of sellers to produce and offer to sell different quantities of a good at different prices during a specific time period.

supply curve A graph that shows the amount of a good sellers are willing and able to sell at various prices.

supply schedule A numerical chart illustrating the law of supply.

supply-side inflation An increase in the price level that originates on the supply side of the economy.

surplus The condition in which the quantity supplied of a good is greater than the quantity demanded. Surpluses occur only at prices *above* equilibrium price.

509

surplus value The difference between the total value of production and the subsistence wages paid to workers.

Taft-Hartley Act An act, passed in 1947 by the U.S. Congress, which made the closed shop illegal and gave states the right to pass right-to-work laws. These right-to-work laws prohibit employers from establishing union membership as a condition of employment.

tangible Able to be felt by touch. For example, a book is tangible: you can touch and feel it.

tariff A tax on imports.

technology The body of skills and knowledge concerning the use of resources in production.

theory An explanation of how something works, designed to answer a question for which there is no obvious answer.

total cost The sum of fixed costs plus variable costs.

total reserves The sum of a bank's deposits in its reserve account at the Fed and its vault cash.

trade-off A situation in which more of one thing necessarily means less of something else.

traditional economy An economic system in which the answers to the three economic questions are based on customs, traditions, and cultural beliefs.

transaction costs The costs associated with the time and effort needed to search out, negotiate, and consummate an exchange.

unemployment rate The percentage of the civilian labor force that is unemployed.

union shop An organization that requires employees to join the union within a certain period after being hired.

unit-elastic demand The type of demand that exists when the percentage change in quantity demanded is the same as the percentage change in price.

unit of account A common measurement used to express values.

utility The quality of bringing satisfaction or happiness.

variable cost A cost, or expense, that changes with the number of units of a good produced.

velocity The average number of times a dollar is spent to buy final goods and services in a year.

vision A sense of how the world works.

wage rate The price of labor.

want A thing that we desire to have.

yield Equal to the annual coupon payment divided by the price paid for the bond.

Glosario

acciones Derecho sobre los activos de una sociedad; otorga al comprador parte de la propiedad.

accionista Persona que posee acciones de una sociedad.

activo Cualquier objeto de valor respecto del cual la empresa tiene un derecho legal.

acuerdo de cartel Acuerdo que especifica el modo en que las empresas que lo han suscripto actuarán en forma coordinada a fin de reducir la competencia entre ellas.

año base En general, un año de referencia, es decir, elegido como punto de referencia para realizar una comparación. Al calcular el PBI real, se asignan precios a las producciones de los distintos años al nivel del año base.

apreciación Aumento en el valor de una moneda en relación con otras.

arancel Impuesto a las importaciones.

avance tecnológico Capacidad de obtener una producción mayor con una cantidad fija de recursos.

balanza comercial Diferencia entre el valor de las exportaciones de un país y el valor de sus importaciones.

banco de inversión Empresa que actúa como intermediario entre la sociedad que emite acciones y el público que desea adquirirlas.

barrera de entrada Cualquier disposición que prohíba el ingreso de una empresa a un mercado.

beneficiario de la franquicia Persona o grupo que adquiere una franquicia.

bien inferior Bien cuya demanda disminuye a medida que las ganancias aumentan y se incrementa a medida que las ganancias disminuyen.

bien neutro Bien cuya demanda permanece invariable, independientemente de que las ganancias aumenten o disminuyan.

bien normal Bien cuya demanda aumenta a medida que aumentan las ganancias, y disminuye a medida que se reducen las ganancias.

bien privado Bien que al ser consumido por una persona no podrá ser consumido por otra.

bien público Bien cuyo consumo por parte de una persona no quita a otro la posibilidad de consumirlo.

bien público excluible Bien público de cuyo consumo puede excluirse (prohibirse físicamente) a los individuos.

bien público no excluible Bien público de cuyo consumo no puede excluirse (prohibirse físicamente) a ningún individuo.

bienes Toda cosa que satisfaga los deseos de una persona o le produzca satisfacción; también productos tangibles.

billete de la Reserva Federal Billete emitido por el Sistema de la Reserva Federal.

bono Vale o promesa de pago, emitida por empresas, gobiernos o agencias gubernamentales a fin de tomar dinero en préstamo.

buscador de precios Vendedor que puede vender parte de su producción a diversos precios.

caja de ahorro Cuenta que genera intereses.

cantidad de equilibrio Cantidad de un bien que se adquiere o vende en un mercado en equilibrio.

cantidad demandada Número de unidades de un bien adquiridas a un precio determinado.

cantidad ofrecida Número de unidades de un bien producidas y ofrecidas para la venta a un precio determinado.

capital Bienes producidos que pueden utilizarse como recursos para una nueva producción. Por ejemplo, las fábricas, máquinas y tractores agrícolas constituyen un capital.

capital humano Conocimientos y habilidades que los individuos obtienen de la educación, la capacitación en el trabajo y la experiencia laboral, y que utilizan en la producción de bienes y servicios. Comprende también la honestidad, la creatividad y la perseverancia, características adecuadas para obtener un empleo.

ciclo económico Fluctuación regular (de aumento y descenso) del PBI real.

ciencias económicas Ciencia que estudia las elecciones de las personas en un intento por satisfacer sus necesidades en un mundo de escasez.

cobertura ("*hedge*") Intento de evitar o disminuir una pérdida que resulte de medidas de contrarresto.

Comité para las Operaciones de Mercado Abierto de la Reserva Federal (FOMC) Grupo de 12 miembros a cargo del dictado de políticas dentro de la Junta de la Reserva Federal del Banco Central de los Estados Unidos. Este comité está autorizado a efectuar operaciones en el mercado abierto.

complemento Bien que se consume en forma conjunta con otro bien. En el caso de los complementos, el precio de uno y la demanda del otro se mueven en direcciones opuestas.

compras gubernamentales Gastos efectuados por el sector gubernamental. Las compras realizadas por el gobierno no incluyen pagos de transferencia del gobierno.

compromiso ("*trade-off*") Situación en la que más de una cosa significa necesariamente menos de otra.

concesionario de la franquicia Entidad que ofrece una franquicia.

consumo Gastos efectuados en el sector doméstico.

contrato Acuerdo entre dos o más personas de hacer algo.

contrato de futuros Contrato que establece la compra o venta de una cantidad determinada de un bien (productos primarios, divisas, instrumentos financieros) a un precio específico y en una fecha futura estipulada.

costo de oportunidad La oportunidad o alternativa de mayor valor perdida al realizar una elección.

costo fijo Costo o gasto que permanece invariable, independientemente de la cantidad de unidades de un determinado bien que se produzcan.

costo marginal Costo de producción de una unidad adicional de un bien; cambio que tiene lugar en el costo total como consecuencia de la generación de una unidad adicional de producción.

costo por unidad Costo promedio de un bien. Por ejemplo, si se gastan $400,000 para producir 100 automóviles, el costo promedio o costo por unidad es de $4,000.

costo total Suma de los costos fijos más los costos variables.

costo total promedio El costo total dividido por la cantidad de producción.

costo variable Costo o gasto que varía según el número de unidades de un bien producido.

costos de transacción Costos asociados con el tiempo y esfuerzo necesarios para buscar, negociar y llevar a cabo un intercambio.

crecimiento económico real absoluto Aumento del PBI real de un período a otro.

crecimiento económico real per cápita Incremento de un período a otro del PBI real per cápita, el cual consiste en el PBI real dividido entre la población.

cuasidinero Activos, tales como cajas de ahorro no corrientes, fácil y rápidamente convertibles en dinero.

cuenta de reserva Cuenta corriente de un banco en el banco del distrito de la Reserva Federal.

512

cuota Límite legal del número de unidades de un bien producido en el extranjero (importación) que pueden ingresar a un país.

curva de demanda Representación gráfica de la ley de la demanda.

curva de demanda total Curva que muestra la cantidad de bienes y servicios que los compradores desean y pueden adquirir a distintos niveles de precios.

curva de Laffer Curva así denominada en honor al economista Arthur Laffer, que muestra la relación entre las alícuotas y los ingresos fiscales. De acuerdo con esta curva, a medida que las alícuotas se incrementan desde cero, también se incrementan los ingresos fiscales, hasta llegar a un nivel máximo, luego del cual los ingresos disminuirán ante cualquier otro incremento de las alícuotas.

curva de oferta Gráfico que demuestra la cantidad de un bien que los vendedores desean y pueden vender a distintos precios.

curva de oferta total Curva que demuestra la cantidad de bienes y servicios que los productores desean y pueden ofrecer a distintos niveles de precios.

déficit presupuestario Situación en la que los gastos del gobierno federal son mayores que sus ingresos fiscales.

deflación Disminución del nivel de precios o del nivel promedio de precios.

demanda Voluntad y capacidad de los consumidores de adquirir diversas cantidades de un bien a distintos precios durante un período determinado.

demanda derivada Demanda que resulta de otra demanda.

demanda elástica Clase de demanda que existe cuando el cambio porcentual en la cantidad demandada es mayor que el cambio porcentual en el precio.

demanda elástica unitaria Clase de demanda que existe cuando el cambio porcentual de la cantidad demandada es igual al cambio porcentual del precio.

demanda inelástica Clase de demanda que existe cuando el cambio porcentual en la cantidad demandada es menor que el cambio porcentual del precio.

depósito a la vista Cuenta de la que se pueden retirar fondos depositados, ya sea en efectivo o por medio de una transferencia por cheque a un tercero, según lo disponga el propietario.

depreciación Disminución del valor de una moneda en relación con otras.

desabastecimiento Situación en la que la cantidad demandada de un bien es mayor que la cantidad ofertada. Dichos desabastecimientos sólo tienen lugar cuando se establecen precios *menores* al precio de equilibrio.

desutilidad La calidad de generar insatisfacción o infelicidad.

deuda nacional Suma total que el gobierno federal debe a sus acreedores.

diagrama de demanda Representación numérica de la ley de la demanda.

diagrama de oferta Cuadro numérico que ilustra la ley de la oferta.

dinero Bien ampliamente aceptado para fines de intercambio y amortización de la deuda.

directorio Importante órgano a cargo de la toma de decisiones en las sociedades anónimas. Establece las políticas y objetivos societarios, entre otras cosas.

discriminación de precio Práctica en virtud de la cual un vendedor establece distintos precios (para distintos compradores) respecto del producto que vende, y las diferencias de precio no reflejan las diferencias de costo.

distribución de las ganancias Modo en el que las ganancias obtenidas en un país se dividen entre los diversos grupos de generadores de ingresos.

dividendo Parte de las utilidades de una sociedad anónima que se distribuye entre sus accionistas.

doble contabilidad Contar un bien más de una vez para calcular el PBI.

dumping Venta de bienes en el extranjero a un precio inferior al de su costo y al que se cobra en el mercado interno.

economía de trueque Economía en la que el comercio se lleva a cabo mediante el intercambio de bienes y servicios en lugar de dinero.

economía mixta Economía que no es puramente capitalista ni absolutamente socialista; economía que posee tanto elementos del capitalismo como del socialismo. La mayoría de los países del mundo poseen economías mixtas.

economía tradicional Sistema económico en el que las respuestas a las tres preguntas económicas se basan en las costumbres, tradiciones y creencias culturales.

efecto atracción ("*crowding in*") Situación en la que la reducción del gasto público provoca un incremento del gasto privado.

efecto desplazamiento ("*crowding out*") Situación en la que el incremento del gasto público provoca una reducción del gasto privado.

elasticidad de la demanda Relación entre el cambio porcentual en la cantidad demandada y el cambio porcentual de precio.

elasticidad de la oferta Relación entre el cambio porcentual en la cantidad ofertada y el cambio porcentual de precio.

empresa comercial Organización que utiliza recursos para producir bienes y servicios que son vendidos a los consumidores, a otras empresas o al gobierno.

empresa de sindicalización obligatoria ("*closed shop*") Organización que sólo contrata a individuos afiliados a los sindicatos.

empresa de sindicalización obligatoria posterior a la contratación ("*union shop*") Organización que requiere a los empleados afiliarse al sindicato dentro de un período determinado luego de haber sido contratados.

empresa unipersonal Empresa que pertenece a un individuo, quien toma todas las decisiones comerciales, recibe la totalidad de las ganancias o afronta deudas en nombre de la empresa, y es legalmente responsable de las deudas de dicha empresa.

empresario Persona con un talento especial para buscar y aprovechar nuevas oportunidades comerciales.

equilibrio En un mercado, el punto en el que la cantidad de un bien que los compradores desean y pueden adquirir es igual a la cantidad que los vendedores desean y pueden producir y ofrecer para la venta (la cantidad demandada es igual a la cantidad ofertada).

escasez Situación en la que nuestras necesidades son mayores que los recursos necesarios para satisfacerlas.

especializarse Hacer sólo una cosa. Por ejemplo, cuando un país se especializa en la producción de un bien, produce sólo dicho bien.

estanflación La coexistencia de inflación y un alto desempleo.

estructura de mercado Marco dentro del cual se encuentra un vendedor. Las estructuras de mercado se definen según sus características, tales como el número de vendedores dentro del mercado, el producto que los vendedores producen y venden, y el grado de facilidad o dificultad con el que nuevas empresas pueden ingresar al mercado.

ética Principios de conducta, tales como lo correcto e incorrecto, lo moral e inmoral, y lo bueno y lo malo.

exportaciones Bienes producidos dentro del país y vendidos a residentes de otro país.

externalidad negativa Efecto colateral adverso de un acto que es experimentado por terceros.

externalidad positiva Efecto secundario positivo de una acción que beneficia a terceros.

flujo circular de la actividad económica Relaciones económicas que existen entre los distintos grupos económicos dentro de una misma economía.

franquicia Contrato por medio del cual una empresa (por lo general, una sociedad anónima) permite a una persona o a un grupo utilizar su nombre y vender sus productos a cambio de ciertos pagos y requisitos.

franquicia pública Derecho otorgado a una empresa por parte del gobierno, que permite a dicha empresa brindar un determinado bien o servicio, mientras que excluye a todos los demás de la provisión de dicho bien o servicio.

frontera de posibilidades de producción Representación gráfica de la totalidad de las combinaciones posibles de dos bienes que pueda producir una economía.

ganancia Suma de dinero que resta luego de que hayan sido pagados los costes de producción. Habrá una ganancia siempre que el ingreso total sea mayor que el costo total.

ganancias luego de la deducción de impuestos Parte remanente de las ganancias luego de abonarse los impuestos.

gastos en exportaciones Monto que gastan los residentes de otros países en la compra de bienes producidos en los Estados Unidos.

gastos en importación Monto que gastan los estadounidenses en la compra de bienes producidos en el extranjero.

globalización Fenómeno en virtud del cual los agentes económicos de cualquier parte del mundo se ven afectados por los hechos que tienen lugar en otro lugar del mundo; integración creciente de las economías nacionales del mundo hasta un grado tal que permite suponer que podamos estar siendo testigos del surgimiento y funcionamiento de una única economía mundial.

hogar Unidad económica de una o más personas que venden recursos y compran bienes y servicios.

holgazanear Conducta de un trabajador que trabaja con menor esfuerzo que el acordado.

huelga Suspensión del trabajo convocada por miembros de sindicatos a fin de ejercer presión sobre un empleador.

importaciones Bienes producidos en países extranjeros y adquiridos por residentes del país.

impuesto a las ganancias progresivo Impuesto a las ganancias cuya alícuota aumenta a medida que aumenta el nivel de ganancias. Las estructuras progresivas del impuesto a las ganancias tienen por lo general una alícuota máxima.

impuesto a las ganancias proporcional Impuesto a las ganancias en virtud del cual todos se encuentran sujetos a la misma alícuota, independientemente de sus ganancias.

impuesto a las ganancias regresivo Impuesto a las ganancias cuya alícuota disminuye a medida que las ganancias aumentan.

incentivo Algo que fomenta o motiva el actuar de una persona.

índice Cartera de acciones que representa un mercado en particular o una parte de él, utilizada para calcular los cambios registrados en un mercado o en una economía.

índice de precios Cálculo del nivel de precios o del nivel promedio de precios.

índice de precios al consumidor (IPC) El índice de precios más utilizado.

Índice promedio industrial Dow Jones (DJIA) El indicador más popular y utilizado de la actividad diaria bursátil. El DJIA es el promedio ponderado de 30 acciones de gran comercialización en la Bolsa de Comercio de Nueva York.

inflación Incremento en el nivel de precios o en el nivel promedio de precios.

inflación del lado de la demanda Incremento en el nivel de los precios, emergente del sector de la demanda dentro de la economía.

inflación del lado de la oferta Incremento en el nivel de precios que se origina en el lado de la oferta de la economía.

información asimétrica Información que una persona posee (en un intercambio) y que la otra persona no posee.

ingreso marginal Ingresos obtenidos de la venta de una unidad adicional de un bien; cambio que tiene lugar en los ingresos totales como consecuencia de la venta de una unidad adicional de producción.

iniciativa empresarial Talento especial que poseen ciertas personas para buscar y aprovechar nuevas oportunidades comerciales, así como también para desarrollar nuevos productos y formas de hacer las cosas.

intangible Que no puede sentirse mediante el tacto. Por ejemplo, una lección sobre economía es intangible.

inventario Existencias de bienes que un negocio o local tiene disponibles.

inversión Gastos efectuados por el sector empresarial.

Junta de Gobernadores del Sistema de la Reserva Federal Cuerpo directivo del Sistema de la Reserva Federal.

ley antimonopolio Legislación dictada para controlar el poder de los monopolios y preservar y promover la competencia.

ley contra la filiación sindical obligatoria Ley estatal que prohíbe requerir la afiliación de los empleados a un sindicato para poder trabajar.

ley de la demanda Ley que establece que a medida que el precio de un bien aumenta, disminuye la demanda de dicho bien, mientras que, a medida que el precio de un bien disminuye, aumenta la demanda de dicho bien.

ley de la oferta Ley que establece que, a medida que el precio de un bien aumenta, también aumenta la oferta de dicho bien, y que, a medida que el precio de un bien disminuye, también disminuye la oferta de dicho bien.

ley de la utilidad marginal decreciente Ley que establece que, a la medida que una persona consume unidades adicionales de un bien, la utilidad obtenida de cada unidad adicional de dicho bien disminuirá con el tiempo.

ley del rendimiento marginal decreciente Ley que establece que si se agregan unidades adicionales de un recurso a otro recurso fijo, la producción adicional obtenida disminuirá con el tiempo.

ley del salario mínimo Ley federal que establece el salario mínimo por hora que puede abonarse a los trabajadores.

ley Taft-Hartley Ley aprobada en 1947 por el Congreso de los Estados Unidos, la cual determinó la ilegalidad de las empresas de sindicalización obligatoria y otorgó a los estados el derecho de aprobar leyes contra la filiación sindical obligatoria. Dichas leyes prohíben a los empleadores requerir la pertenencia a un sindicato como condición para obtener un empleo.

libre empresa Sistema económico en el que los individuos (no el gobierno) son propietarios de la mayoría, si no de la totalidad, de los recursos y controlan su uso. El gobierno desempeña tan solo una función menor en la economía.

macroeconomía Rama de las ciencias económicas que estudia la conducta y las elecciones humanas en relación con la totalidad de la economía.

mano de obra Talento físico y mental que aportan los individuos a la producción de bienes y servicios.

marginal En economía, marginal significa adicional.

mecanismo de racionalización Medio para decidir quién recibe y qué parte recibe de los recursos y bienes disponibles.

medio de cambio Todo aquello que generalmente es aceptado a cambio de bienes y servicios.

mercado Todo lugar en el que los individuos se reúnen para comprar y vender bienes o servicios.

mercado competitivo monopólico Estructura de mercado caracterizada por (1) numerosos compradores y numerosos vendedores; (2) la producción y venta de productos apenas diferenciados; y (3) fácil ingreso y egreso del mercado.

mercado de fondos para préstamos Mercado para préstamos. Existe una demanda de préstamos (que se origina en los prestatarios) y una oferta de préstamos (que se origina en los prestamistas). Es en el mercado de fondos para préstamos donde se determina la tasa de interés.

mercado monopólico Estructura de mercado caracterizada por (1) un único vendedor; (2) la venta de un producto que no posee sustitutos cercanos; y (3) barreras extremadamente altas para el ingreso al mercado.

mercado oligopólico Estructura de mercado caracterizada por (1) pocos vendedores; (2) la producción y venta de productos idénticos o apenas diferenciados; y (3) barreras considerablemente altas para el ingreso al mercado.

mercado perfectamente competitivo Estructura de mercado caracterizada por (1) numerosos compradores y numerosos vendedores; (2) todas las empresas venden bienes idénticos; (3) toda información pertinente a las actividades de compraventa se encuentra disponible para los compradores y vendedores; y (4) un facuk ingreso y egreso del mercado.

microeconomía Rama de las ciencias económicas que estudia la conducta y las elecciones humanas en relación con unidades relativamente pequeñas, tales como un individuo, una empresa o un mercado único.

moneda Monedas emitidas por el Tesoro de los Estados Unidos y billetes (llamados billetes de la Reserva Federal) emitidos por el Sistema de la Reserva Federal.

monopolio natural Empresa con un costo total promedio tan bajo (costo por unidad) que sólo ella puede sobrevivir en el mercado.

necesidad Algo que deseamos tener.

oferta Voluntad y capacidad de los vendedores de producir y ofrecer a la venta diversas cantidades de un bien a distintos precios, durante un período determinado.

oferta elástica Clase de oferta que existe cuando el cambio porcentual en la cantidad ofertada es mayor que el cambio porcentual en el precio.

oferta inelástica Clase de oferta que existe cuando el cambio porcentual en la cantidad ofertada es menor que el cambio porcentual del precio.

oferta monetaria Oferta total de dinero en circulación, compuesto por divisas, cuentas corrientes y cheques de viajero.

oferta pública inicial (OPI) Primera oferta de acciones al público por parte de una sociedad.

opción Contrato que otorga al propietario el derecho, pero no la obligación, de comprar o vender acciones de un bien a un precio determinado, en una fecha determinada o con anterioridad a ella.

operaciones de mercado abierto Compraventa de títulos públicos por parte de la Junta de la Reserva Federal del Banco Central de los Estados Unidos.

oportunista ("*free rider*") Persona que recibe los beneficios de un bien sin pagar por él.

país desarrollado País con un PBI relativamente alto por persona.

país menos desarrollado País con un PBI per cápita relativamente menor.

PBI real Producto bruto interno (PBI) ajustado de acuerdo con los cambios de precios; PBI calculado sobre los precios de un año base o constantes.

pérdida Suma de dinero por la que los costos totales superan los ingresos totales.

plan económico Programa del gobierno que especifica las actividades económicas, tales como los bienes que deben producirse y los precios que se cobrarán.

plusvalía Diferencia entre el valor total de producción y los salarios de subsistencia abonados a los trabajadores.

política de expansión fiscal Incremento del gasto público o reducción de los impuestos.

política de expansión monetaria Incremento de la oferta monetaria.

política fiscal Cambios efectuados por el gobierno en los gastos o impuestos a fin de lograr determinados objetivos económicos.

política fiscal contraccionista Disminución en el gasto gubernamental o aumento de los impuestos.

política monetaria Cambios introducidos por el gobierno respecto de la oferta monetaria.

517

política monetaria contraccionista Disminución de la oferta monetaria.

precio de equilibrio Precio en el que se adquiere y vende un bien en un mercado en equilibrio.

precio máximo Precio establecido por ley— inferior al precio de equilibrio— por sobre el cual los compradores y vendedores no pueden comprar ni vender bienes de forma legal.

precio mínimo Precio establecido por ley— superior al precio de equilibrio— por debajo del cual los compradores y vendedores no pueden comprar ni vender bienes de forma legal.

producto bruto interno (PBI) Valor total de mercado de la totalidad de los bienes y servicios producidos anualmente en un país.

propiedad privada Todo bien que sea de propiedad de un individuo o negocio.

propiedad pública Todo bien de propiedad del gobierno.

recesión Desaceleración de la economía como consecuencia de la disminución del PBI real durante dos trimestres consecutivos.

recurso Todo aquello que se utilice para producir bienes o servicios. Por ejemplo, la mano de obra de un individuo puede utilizarse para producir computadoras, televisores y muchas otras cosas y, por lo tanto, la mano de obra constituye un recurso.

relación directa Relación entre dos factores en la que dichos factores se mueven en una misma dirección. Por ejemplo, al subir un factor, también sube el otro.

relocalización ("*offshoring*") Término utilizado para describir el trabajo efectuado para una compañía por personas distintas de los empleados originales de la compañía, en un país distinto de aquél en el que la compañía está localizada.

rendimiento Es igual al pago anual de un cupón, dividido por el precio abonado por dicho cupón.

requisito de reservas Disposición que establece que los bancos deben conservar un cierto porcentaje de los depósitos en su cuenta de reserva en la Junta de la Reserva Federal del Banco Central de los Estados Unidos, o en su bóveda, como efectivo de caja.

reserva del valor Aquello que tenga la capacidad de conservar el valor con el transcurso del tiempo.

reservas en exceso Toda reserva que supere la cantidad requerida.

reservas obligatorias Monto mínimo de reservas que debe poseer un banco respecto de sus depósitos, según lo determinado por la Junta de la Reserva Federal del Banco Central de los Estados Unidos.

reservas totales Sumas de los depósitos que los bancos conservan en sus cuentas de reserva en la Junta de la Reserva Federal del Banco Central de los Estados Unidos y el efectivo en caja.

responsabilidad limitada Condición en virtud de la cual el propietario de una empresa puede perder solamente el monto que ha invertido (en dicha empresa).

salario Precio de la mano de obra.

servicios Tareas cuya realización ciertos individuos encargan a otros a cambio de un pago.

sindicato Organización que procura incrementar los salarios y mejorar las condiciones de trabajo de sus afiliados.

sistema bancario de reserva fraccionaria Arreglo bancario en virtud del cual los bancos sólo conservan una fracción de los depósitos y otorgan el resto en préstamo.

Sistema de la Reserva Federal Banco central de los Estados Unidos.

sistema de tipo de cambio fijo Sistema en virtud del cual la tasa de cambio es determinada o fijada por el gobierno del país.

sistema de tipo de cambio flexible Sistema en virtud del cual la tasa de cambio es determinada por el juego de la oferta y la demanda.

sistema económico Modo en el que una sociedad decide qué bienes producir, cómo producirlos y para quién producirlos.

518

socialismo Sistema económico en el que el gobierno controla y puede poseer muchos de los recursos.

sociedad anónima Entidad legal que puede llevar a cabo una actividad comercial en su nombre, como si fuera un individuo.

sociedad de personas Sociedad que pertenece a dos o más copropietarios, llamados socios, quienes comparten las ganancias y son responsables por sus deudas ante la ley.

subsidio Pago financiero efectuado por el gobierno respecto de ciertas acciones.

substituto Bien similar. En el caso de los substitutos, el precio de uno y la demanda del otro se mueven en la misma dirección.

superávit Situación en la que la cantidad ofrecida de un bien es mayor que la cantidad demandada. El superávit sólo tiene lugar cuando existen precios *superiores* al precio de equilibrio.

superávit presupuestario Situación en la que los gastos del gobierno federal son menores que sus ingresos fiscales.

tangible Que puede sentirse o tocarse. Por ejemplo, un libro es algo tangible: puede tocarse y sentirse.

tasa de cambio Precio de la moneda de un país expresado en la moneda de otro país.

tasa de crecimiento de la población La tasa de nacimientos menos la tasa de defunciones.

tasa de descuento Tasa de interés que cobra la Junta de la Reserva Federal del Banco Central de los Estados Unidos a los bancos por el otorgamiento de préstamos.

tasa de desempleo Porcentaje de la fuerza laboral civil que está desempleada.

tasa de empleo Porcentaje de la población civil adulta no institucional que posee un empleo.

tasa de los fondos federales Tasa de interés que cobra un banco a otro por un préstamo.

tasa del cupón Porcentaje del valor nominal que el titular de un bono recibe por año hasta la fecha de vencimiento.

tecnología Cuerpo de técnicas y conocimientos vinculados con el uso de recursos para la producción.

teoría Explicación acerca del funcionamiento de algo, a fin de responder a una pregunta para la cual no existe una respuesta obvia.

teoría laboral del valor Creencia de que el valor total de los bienes producidos surge de la mano de obra.

teoría simple cuantitativa del dinero Teoría que predice que los cambios en el nivel de precios serán estrictamente proporcionales a los cambios en la oferta monetaria.

tercerización Término utilizado para describir el trabajo llevado a cabo para una compañía por otra compañía o por individuos distintos de los empleados originales de la compañía.

tierra Recursos naturales que se encuentran en la naturaleza. Tanto un acre de terreno como los depósitos de minerales y el agua de un arroyo se consideran tierra.

tomador de precios Vendedor que puede vender la totalidad de su producción al precio de equilibrio pero no a otro precio.

unidad de cuenta Medida común utilizada para expresar valores.

utilidad Calidad de proporcionar satisfacción o felicidad.

valor nominal (valor a la par) Monto en dólares consignado en un bono. Monto total que el emisor del bono debe abonar al comprador del bono.

velocidad Número promedio de veces en que se gasta un dólar para adquirir productos y servicios finales dentro de un año.

ventaja absoluta Situación en la que un país puede producir una mayor cantidad de un bien que lo que puede producir otro país con la misma cantidad de recursos.

ventaja comparativa Situación en las que un país puede producir un bien a un coste de oportunidad menor que el de otro país.

visión Sentido de cómo funciona el mundo.

519

Photo Credits

viii top left, Corbis, Gary D. Landsman
viii bottom left, Corbis, Royalty-Free
viii top right, Corbis, Royalty-Free
viii bottom right, Corbis, Peter Beck
ix left, Reuters/Corbis, Jonathan Evans
ix center, IndexStock, Dan Gair Photographic
ix right, Corbis, Royalty-Free
x top, Corbis, Larry Downing
x bottom left, Corbis,George Disario
x bottom center, Corbis, John Gress
x bottom right, Corbis, Peter Beck
xv istockphoto, Oleg Prikhodko
3 Corbis, Mike Zens
4 Hermera, Royalty-Free
4 Hermera, Royalty-Free
7 PhotoEdit, Richard Hutchings
9 Corbis, Matthew Mendelsohn
15 bottom left, istockphoto, Leah-Anne Thompson
15 bottom right, istockphoto, Kenneth O'Quinn
17 PhotoEdit, Daniel J. Shaefer
18 EMC database
20 Corbis, Kevin Lamarque
21 PhotoEdit, Tony Freeman
22 PhotoEdit, Bill Aron
23 istockphoto, Galina Barskaya
25 top left, istockphoto, Natalia Bratslavsky
25 top right, istockphoto, Willem Dijkstr
26 PhotoEdit, Ulrike Welsch
30 Corbis, Royalty-Free
30 Corbis, Royalty-Free
33 top left, PhotoEdit, David Young-Wolff
33 top center, istockphoto, Gautier Willaume
33 top right, istockphoto, Yvonne Chamberlain
33 bottom left, Corbis, Reuters/Raytheon
33 bottom center, istockphoto, Andy Hill
33 bottom right, istockphoto, Brandon Laufenberg
34 PhotoEdit, Leslye Borden
35 Corbis, Handout/Gerald Bourke
36 PhotoEdit, Mark Richards
38 PhotoEdit, Bill Bachmann
39 left, Library of Congress,
39 right, Library of Congress,
42 Corbis, Bernard Annebicque
43 Hermera,
44 Corbis, James Leynse
45 Corbis, Steve Raymer
47 PhotoEdit, Richard Lord
48 PhotoEdit, David Young-Wolff
50 PhotoEdit, Jeff Greenberg
51 Corbis, Belousov Vitaly
54 Corbis, Gary D. Landsman
54 Corbis, Gary D. Landsman
58 PhotoEdit, Robin Nelson
59 PhotoEdit, Davis Barber
63 top, Corbis, Chuck Savage
63 bottom, Corbis, Mario Anzuoni
64 Corbis, Painting by J.L.M. Ferris
67 PhotoEdit, Amy Etra
68 Corbis, Painting by Stearns
69 Corbis, Davis Factor
71 Corbis, A. Sneider
72 Corbis, Kim Kulish
75 top, PhotoEdit, John Neubauer
75 bottom, Corbis, Michael S. Yamashita
76 istockphoto, LeCajun
77 PhotoEdit, Michael Newman
79 istockphoto, Tony Tremblay
80 istockphoto, Jaimie D. Travis
81 Corbis, Joseph Sohm
84 left, istockphoto, Tomaz Levstek
84 top right, istockphoto, Ana Abejon
84 bottom right, istockphoto, Sharon Dominick
85 left, istockphoto, Jaimie D. Travis
85 istockphoto, Phil Date
86 Corbis, Royalty-Free
86 Corbis, Royalty-Free
87 Hespenheide Design, Hespenheide Design
91 Corbis, Sergei Karpukhin
92 Corbis, Lisa O'Connor
97 PhotoEdit, Dennis MacDonald
98 PhotoEdit, David Young-Wolff
100 left, istockphoto, Erik Seo
100 center, PhotoEdit, Cindy Charles
100 right, PhotoEdit, Tom McCarthy
101 istockphoto, Kevin Russ
106 Corbis, Ethan Miller
110 Reuters/Corbis, Jonathan Evans
110 Reuters/Corbis, Jonathan Evans
113 Corbis, Randy Faris
114 Corbis, Fred Prouser
118 Corbis, Kim Kulish
122 Corbis, Bob Rowan
128 Corbis, Peter Beck
128 Corbis, Peter Beck
133 istockphoto, Paige Foster
142 top left, istockphoto, Colin Stitt
142 top right, Hespenheide Design, Hespenheide Design
144 Corbis, Ron Kuntz
145 Corbis, Kevin Fleming
147 top left, istockphoto, Leigh Schindler
147 top center, istockphoto, Bonnie Jacobs
147 top right, istockphoto, Andrei Tchernov
148 PhotoEdit, Jeff Greenberg
149 PhotoEdit, David Young-Wolff
152 top left, istockphoto, Amanda Rohde
152 bottom center, istockphoto, Diane Diederich
153 left, istockphoto, Noraznen Azit
153 top, istockphoto, Kenneth C. Zirkel
153 bottom right, istockphoto, Gerville Hall
154 IndexStock, Dan Gair Photographic
154 IndexStock, Dan Gair Photographic
155 Corbis, Charles O'Rear
159 PhotoEdit, Billy E. Barnes
160 Corbis, Gary D. Landsman
161 Corbis, Sam Sharpe
162 PhotoEdit, Mark Richards
163 Corbis, Kim Kulish
167 PhotoEdit, Bonnie Kamin
168 PhotoEdit, Tony Freeman
169 PhotoEdit, Colin Young-Wolff
173 Corbis, James L. Amos
174 Corbis, McIntyre Photography, Inc.
177 PhotoEdit, David Young-Wolff
178 top left, istockphoto, Maurice van der Velden
178 top right, Hespenheide Design, Hespenheide Design
181 Corbis, Ralf-Finn Hestoft
182 istockphoto, Bobby Deal
186 Corbis, Peter Beck
186 Corbis, Peter Beck
189 PhotoEdit, Jeff Greenberg
190 Corbis, Royalty-free
191 PhotoEdit, Mark Richards
192 PhotoEdit, Spencer Grant
195 Corbis, Jeremy Horner
197 PhotoEdit, Tony Freeman
198 PhotoEdit, Park Street
199 PhotoEdit, A. Ramey
201 Corbis, Mike Theiler
202 istockphoto, Rene Mansi
203 Corbis, William Philpott
204 PhotoEdit, Tom McCarthy

521

205 Hespenheide Design, Hespenheide Design
207 PhotoEdit, Michael Newman
208 PhotoEdit, Cindy Charles
209 PhotoEdit, David Young-Wolff
210 PhotoEdit, David Young-Wolff
213 Corbis, Chuck Savage
214 Corbis, Heinz-Peter Bader
215 PhotoEdit, Michael Newman
216 Corbis, Gabe Palmer
217 PhotoEdit, David Young-Wolff
218 PhotoEdit, Cindy Charles
219 istockphoto, Scott Fichter
222 Corbis, Royalty-Free
222 Corbis, Royalty-Free
227 PhotoEdit, Jeff Greenberg
228 Corbis, Tim Tadder
230 PhotoEdit, Bill Aron
231 PhotoEdit, Bill Bachmann
232 Corbis, Mike Cassese
233 PhotoEdit, Jose Galvez
235 PhotoEdit, Michael Newman
236 bottom center, PhotoEdit, Felicia Martinez
236 bottom right, istockphoto, Jason Stitt
239 Corbis, David Butow
240 PhotoEdit, Jonathan Nourok
241 istockphoto, Lise Gagne
242 Corbis, Bettmann/Corbis
243 Corbis, Underwood & Underwood
245 left, Corbis, Royalty Free
245 right, istockphoto, Eric Dunetz
246 top center, Corbis, Toyota Motor Corp/Handout/Reuters/Corbis
246 bottom left, Corbis, Robert Landau
250 center, istockphoto, Brett Rabideau
250 bottom center, istockphoto, Kevin Russ
251 PhotoEdit, Jeff Greenberg
252 PhotoEdit, Dana White
252 PhotoEdit, Dana White
253 Corbis, Roger Ressmeyer
257 Corbis, Bettmann/Corbis
258 Corbis, Bettmann/Corbis
259 Corbis, David Bergman
260 PhotoEdit, Patrick Olear
262 Corbis, Bettmann/Corbis
265 PhotoEdit, Bill Aron
266 top, Corbis, Bettmann/Corbis
266 top center, istockphoto, Nathan Watkins
267 istockphoto, Michael Newman
268 PhotoEdit, Bill Aron
269 PhotoEdit, David Young-Wolff
271 PhotoEdit, Paul Conklin
277 PhotoEdit, David Young-Wolff
278 Corbis, H. Sitton
281 Corbis, Scott Olson
282 PhotoEdit, Don Smetzer
286 IndexStock, Jim McGuire
286 IndexStock, Jim McGuire
299 Corbis, Ronnie Kaufman
304 Corbis, Ted Streshinsky
306 Corbis, Bettmann/Corbis
310 IndexStock, Lawrence Sawyer
310 IndexStock, Lawrence Sawyer
317 Corbis, Royalty Free
318 istockphoto, peter chen
321 istockphoto, Andresr
322 PhotoEdit, Jeff Greenberg
325 Reprinted with permission of Universal Press Syndicate
326 Corbis, Kevin Wilton
327 Corbis, Bettmann/Corbis
328 Corbis, Robert Galbraith
330 istockphoto, Tomasz Resiak
332 Corbis, Louise Gubb
333 left, Hermera,
333 right, Hermera,
335 Corbis, Colin Garratt
336 Corbis, Royalty-Free
337 PhotoEdit, Spencer Grant
340 Corbis, Larry Downing
340 Corbis, Larry Downing
343 PhotoEdit, Mark Richards
344 istockphoto, Yvonne Chamberlain
345 Corbis, David James/Warner Bros
349 istockphoto, Lisa McDonald
352 Corbis, Emely/zefa
354 Corbis, John Springer
355 PhotoEdit, John Neubauer
358 PhotoEdit, David Young
359 PhotoEdit, Robert Brenner
361 Corbis, Joel Stettenheim
364 PhotoEdit, Richard Hutchings
364 PhotoEdit, Richard Hutchings
368 Corbis, Wally McNamee
371 left, Corbis, Mike Segar
371 right, Corbis, Dylan Martinez
374 PhotoEdit, Myrleen Ferguson Cate
377 Corbis, Poppy Berry
379 PhotoEdit, Mark Richards
381 right, istockphoto, Joachim Angeltun
381 left, istockphoto, Diane Diederich
382 left, Corbis, Jason Reed
383 left, PhotoEdit, Dennis MacDonald
383 right, PhotoEdit, Alan Oddie
385 istockphoto, Catherine dée Auvil/Ronnie Comeau
388 left, istockphoto, Mateusz Zagorski
388 right, istockphoto, Andrei Tchernov
389 top left, istockphoto, Nancy Louie
389 bottom, istockphoto, Jason Stitt
389 top right, istockphoto, Andrei Tchernov
390 Corbis, George Disario
390 Corbis, George Disario
391 Corbis, H. Prinz
396 PhotoEdit, Spencer Grant
397 Corbis, Louie Psihoyos
399 Corbis, Corbis-Royalty-Free
403 Corbis, Sherwin Crasto
404 Corbis, Pawel Kopcznski
405 Corbis, James Leynse
408 Corbis, Roger Ball
409 PhotoEdit, David Young-Wolff
410 istockphoto, Jim Jurica
412 PhotoEdit, David Young Wolff
413 Corbis, Michael S. Yamashita
414 Corbis, Vincent Kess
417 PhotoEdit, Jeff Greenberg
418 Corbis, Joson
420 left, PhotoEdit, Mark Richards
420 right, Corbis, Royalty-Free/Corbis
423 Corbis, Jayanta Shaw
424 Corbis, Ricki Rosen
428 Corbis, John Gress
428 Corbis, John Gress
431 left, Corbis, Premium Stock
431 right EMC
434 Corbis, Shaul Schwarz
435 Corbis, Bettmann
437 Corbis, Royalty-Free
438 Corbis, Alexander Benz
439 Corbis, Royalty-Free
443 istockphoto, Webking
444 istockphoto, Royalty-Free
445 Corbis, Ted Spiegel
446 Corbis, John Zich
447 Corbis, Jon Hicks
448 PhotoEdit, Spencer Grant
451 Corbis, Peter Beck
452 PhotoEdit, Robert Brenner
453 Corbis, Ethan Miller
454 Corbis, James Nelson
458 left, istockphoto, Bobby Deal
458 right, istockphoto, Kevin Russ
459 left, istockphoto, Galina Barskaya
459 istockphoto, Lisa McDonald

Index

523

C

526

F

G

527

H

I

529

M

532